| The 9 Competencies and 31 Component Behaviors (EPAS, 2015) | Chapter(s) Where Referenced |
|---|---|
| Competency 6—Engage with Individuals, Families, Groups, Organizations, and Communities: | 1, 2, 4 |
| a. Apply knowledge of human behavior and the social environment, person-in-environment, and other multidisciplinary theoretical frameworks to engage with clients and constituencies | 1, 5, 14 |
| b. Use empathy, reflection, and interpersonal skills to effectively engage diverse clients and constituencies | 1, 4, 5, 8, 12–14 |
| Competency 7—Assess Individuals, Families, Groups, Organizations, and Communities: | 1, 2, 4, 13, 14 |
| a. Collect and organize data, and apply critical thinking to interpret information from clients and constituencies | 1–6, 8–16 |
| b. Apply knowledge of human behavior and the social environment, person-in-environment, and other multidisciplinary theoretical frameworks in the analysis of assessment data from clients and constituencies | 1, 3–9, 13–16 |
| c. Develop mutually agreed-on intervention goals and objectives based on the critical assessment of strengths, needs, and challenges within clients and constituencies | 1, 3–5, 9–16 |
| d. Select appropriate intervention strategies based on the assessment, research knowledge, and values and preferences of clients and constituencies | 1, 3–5, 9–16 |
| Competency 8—Intervene with Individuals, Families, Groups, Organizations, and Communities: | 1, 2, 4, 13–15 |
| a. Critically choose and implement interventions to achieve practice goals and enhance capacities of clients and constituencies | 1–6, 8–16 |
| b. Apply knowledge of human behavior and the social environment, person-in-environment, and other multidisciplinary theoretical frameworks in interventions with clients and constituencies | 1, 3–5, 7–9, 13, 14, 16 |
| c. Use inter-professional collaboration as appropriate to achieve beneficial practice outcomes | 1, 2, 4, 5, 7–13, 15 |
| d. Negotiate, mediate, and advocate with and on behalf of diverse clients and constituencies | 1–13, 15, 16 |
| e. Facilitate effective transitions and endings that advance mutually agreed-on goals | 1, 4, 10, 12, 15, 16 |
| Competency 9—Evaluate Practice with Individuals, Families, Groups, Organizations, and Communities: | 1, 2, 4 |
| a. Select and use appropriate methods for evaluation of outcomes | 1, 4 |
| b. Apply knowledge of human behavior and the social environment, person-in-environment, and other multidisciplinary theoretical frameworks in the evaluation of outcomes | 1, 4, 5, 13 |
| c. Critically analyze, monitor, and evaluate intervention and program processes and outcomes | 1, 4, 13, 14, 16 |
| d. Apply evaluation findings to improve practice effectiveness at the micro, mezzo, and macro levels | 1, 4 |

# Introduction to Social Work & Social Welfare

## CRITICAL THINKING PERSPECTIVES

FIFTH EDITION

KAREN K. KIRST-ASHMAN
University of Wisconsin—Whitewater

 CENGAGE

Australia • Brazil • Mexico • Singapore • United Kingdom • United States

**CENGAGE**

---

***Introduction to Social Work and Social Welfare: Critical Thinking Perspectives,* Fifth Edition**
**Karen K. Kirst-Ashman**

Product Director: Jon-David Hague

Product Manager: Julie Martinez

Content and Media Developer:
Michelle Clark

Product Assistant: Stephen Lagos

Marketing Manager: Margaux Cameron

Art and Cover Direction, Production
Management, and Composition:
MPS Limited

Manufacturing Planner: Judy Inouye

Photo and Text Researcher:
Lumina Datamatics

Text and Cover Designer: MPS Limited

Cover Image: © Rawpixelz/
Shutterstock.com

For product information and technology assistance, contact us at
**Cengage Customer & Sales Support, 1-800-354-9706
or support.cengage.com.**

For permission to use material from this text or product, submit all requests online at **www.cengage.com/permissions**.

Library of Congress Control Number: 2015938966

Student Edition:
ISBN: 978-1-305-38839-0

Loose-leaf Edition:
ISBN: 978-1-305-85758-2

**Cengage**
20 Channel Street
Boston, MA 02210
USA

Cengage is a leading provider of customized learning solutions with employees residing in nearly 40 different countries and sales in more than 125 countries around the world. Find your local representative at: **www.cengage.com.**

Cengage products are represented in Canada by Nelson Education, Ltd.

To learn more about Cengage platforms and services, register or access your online learning solution, or purchase materials for your course, visit **www.cengage.com.**

Printed in Mexico
Print Number: 09      Print Year: 2020

To Nick, for his continuous encouragement, support, and assistance

# About the Author

*Karen K. Kirst-Ashman, BSW, MSSW, Ph.D.,* has been a full professor and was former chairperson in the Social Work Department at the University of Wisconsin—Whitewater, where she taught for 28 years. She is certified as a Licensed Clinical Social Worker in the state of Wisconsin. She earned her BSW degree in 1972 and MSSW in 1973 at the University of Wisconsin—Madison, and her Ph.D. in Social Work at the University of Illinois at Urbana—Champaign. She has worked as a practitioner and administrator in child welfare and mental health agencies. She received the University of Wisconsin—Whitewater's Excellence in Teaching Award in 1986 and the University Outstanding Teaching Award in 2007. She has been a member of the board of directors of the Council on Social Work Education (CSWE) in addition to being an accreditation site visitor. She is also a current member of CSWE, BPD, and NASW. She has served on the editorial board of *Affilia: Journal of Women and Social Work*, and as a consulting editor for many social work journals including the *Journal of Social Work Education.* She is the author of numerous publications, articles, and reviews concerning social work and women's issues. Other books she has authored or coauthored include *Understanding Human Behavior and the Social Environment* (10th ed.); *Understanding Generalist Practice* (7th ed.); *Human Behavior in the Macro Social Environment: An Empowerment Approach to Understanding Communities, Organization, and Groups* (4th ed.); *The Macro Skills Workbook* (2nd ed.); and *Generalist Practice with Organizations and Communities* (5th ed.).

# Brief Contents

# Contents

## PART III
## Social Welfare Policy

### CHAPTER 6

## An Overview of Social Welfare
## and Social Work History    177

# Preface

Given limited time and massive volumes of content, what vital information should be conveyed to students in an introductory course about social welfare and social work? What student learning outcomes should instructors strive to attain? This text focuses on the most significant elements of social work. Content complies with the new Council on Social Work Education's Educational Policy and Accreditation Standards (EPAS) (CSWE, 2015). The text's style is intended to be clear, readable, interesting, and engaging. The goal is to enhance students' ability to grasp the essence and spirit of generalist social work and the issues in social welfare that social workers address every day.

Themes integrated throughout the text include these:

- The advancement of human rights and social and economic justice.
- Client empowerment.
- Dimensions of human diversity ("age, class, color, culture, disability and ability, ethnicity, gender, gender identity and expression, immigration status, marital status, political ideology, race, religion/spirituality, sex, sexual orientation, and tribal sovereign status").[1]
- The significance of professional values and ethics.
- A generalist approach interrelating social work practice with individuals, families, groups, organizations, and communities.
- Numerous case examples dramatizing various aspects of social work.
- Various global and international perspectives.
- Identification of the relationship between the text's content and EPAS competencies and their component behaviors.

---

[1] These are the categories reflecting diversity as stated by the Educational Policy and Accreditation Standards passed by the Council on Social Work Education board of directors in 2015 (CSWE, 2015).

A key word describing this text is *integration:* These themes are infused throughout the book instead of being isolated in independent chapters. For example, values, ethics, aspects of diversity, and client empowerment are defined early on and then addressed throughout the text in various contexts including fields of practice. Boxed features appear regularly to emphasize important concepts and cases, to spark students' interest, and to stimulate critical thinking.

## The Fundamental Need for Critical Thinking

Critical thinking perspectives provide an underlying foundation for the text. They are stressed throughout by encouraging identification of values and evaluation of serious issues. Critical thinking involves three facets. First, it focuses on the questioning of beliefs, statements, assumptions, lines of reasoning, actions, and experiences. Second, it involves the assessment of the established facts and issues involved by seeking relevant information. This complies with the Council on Social Work Education's (CSWE) current emphasis on "research-informed practice" and "practice-informed research" (CSWE, 2015, Educational Policy [EP] 4). Third, it concerns asserting an opinion about the validity of the fact or process being considered.

Critical thinking is essential in social work because social workers address a vast range of issues and problems. New accreditation standards require that social workers demonstrate competency in applying critical thinking (or critical evaluation) to make informed, ethical judgments in practice and behavior (CSWE, 2015, EP 1, 4, 5, 7, 8, 9). Each chapter stresses the use of critical thinking by integrating a basic "Triple A" formula that students can readily comprehend and apply: (1) *ask* questions, (2) *assess* the established facts and issues involved, and (3) *assert* a concluding opinion. Issues addressed range from client rights to social policy to social work roles in a wide array of contexts. Case studies for critical thinking are presented at the end of each of the book's four main sections.

## Organization

The book is organized into four major parts: (1) the profession, (2) social work practice, (3) social welfare policy, and (4) client populations and contexts. A fifth section, the epilogue, focuses on personal values and consideration of a social work career. The intent is to give students a broad look at what social work is all about. Social welfare policy is stressed as the foundation of social welfare programs and social work practice. New accreditation standards require that students demonstrate competency in "policy practice," including being able to "analyze, formulate, and advocate for policies that advance human rights and social, economic, and environmental justice" (CSWE, 2015, EP 5c). Students are encouraged to explore issues based on theoretical orientations to social welfare policy development and the resulting program implementation.

Students are provided with thought-provoking information about social welfare and social work within a broad range of circumstances and fields of practice. Settings range from those focusing on child maltreatment, to health care, to work with older adults, to corrections. Social issues are raised in a way that encourages new insights and examination of personal values. This book stresses *what* social workers do, not *how* they do it. Abundant case examples give insights into who clients are and what issues they face in the macro social environment.

Concepts incorporated in the Council on Social Work Education Educational Policy and Accreditation Standards (EPAS), including the concepts of human rights; social, economic, and environmental justice; marginalization; alienation; research-informed practice; and policy practice, in addition to the newly articulated aspects of diversity—disability and ability, marital status, religion/spirituality, and tribal sovereign status—are discussed (CSWE, 2015). Macro aspects of generalist practice, in addition to micro and mezzo aspects, are frequently highlighted.

This book gives students contemplating a social work major a solid orientation to the profession. The text should help students determine whether

social work is really the field for them. For non-majors, the text is designed to provide a sound introduction to social welfare, social work, available services, social welfare policy development and implementation, and social workers' involvement in the helping process. The emphasis is on those issues and fields of practice in which social workers are most likely to be employed. For example, significant attention is given to child and family services, mental health, and health care.

Part 1, "The Profession of Social Work," includes three chapters. Chapter 1 introduces the new 2015 EPAS, defines social welfare and social work, discusses political values and views about social welfare, reviews content areas in the social work curriculum, introduces the various fields of practice, and reviews the social work career continuum. Critical thinking is defined, and its importance throughout the text is stressed. Chapter 2 focuses on the importance of social work values and ethics, thus providing a framework for remaining chapters. This chapter introduces the concept of ethical dilemmas, summarizes the NASW *Code of Ethics*, gives examples of practice applications, and helps students explore personal values. Chapter 3 defines and discusses various dimensions of human diversity, empowerment, resiliency, and cultural competence, paving the way for integration of this content throughout the book.

Part 2, "Social Work Practice," includes two chapters that focus on what social workers *do*. Chapter 4 defines generalist social work practice, introduces the wide range of social work roles, and describes the planned-change process. Emphases include the importance of client empowerment, appreciation of cultural differences, and intervention with macro systems. Chapter 5 focuses on the settings in which social workers practice, including rural and urban communities. It describes what micro, mezzo, and macro practice involve in terms of social workers' functions and practice settings. Finally, it explores social work licensure, employment, and salaries.

Part 3, "Social Welfare Policy," includes three chapters. Chapter 6 explains the historical development of social welfare and social work, thereby providing a context for the next chapter, which focuses on social welfare policy and policy practice. Chapter 7 defines policy, discusses its significance, and describes how it is developed and structured. The significance of social welfare policy as the basis upon which social programs are developed is stressed. Chapter 8 discusses the infrastructure of policies and programs designed to combat poverty and provide financial assistance to those in need. It also describes social insurance (including the Medicare Prescription Drug Program), public assistance programs, and current health care policy, and explores students' values about various aspects of social welfare.

Part 4, "Client Populations and Contexts," includes eight chapters that focus on specific social work settings. Chapter 9 introduces service provision for children and families. It describes supportive services for children and families, including those involving child maltreatment, intensive family preservation, and child day care. It stresses the importance of addressing macro issues. This chapter also reviews substitute services for children and families, including kinship care, foster family care, residential settings, and adoption.

Chapter 10 discusses social work with older adults. Issues include common problems facing older adults, critical thinking about Social Security, the global context for aging, contexts of social work practice with older adults, and empowerment for diverse populations of older adults.

Chapter 11 explores social work with people who have disabilities. Ethical implications for social work practice are discussed. Empowerment through policy practice and advocacy, legislative advocacy, and community support are stressed.

Chapter 12 explains social work roles in health care, health-care problems in the macro environment, issues involving health-care policy, managed care, and international perspectives on the global crisis of AIDS. Sensitivity to populations at risk and macro issues in practice are emphasized.

Chapter 13 addresses social work and mental health. Employment settings in mental health for social workers are identified, social work functions are explained, and clients' conditions are described. Managed care in mental health is critiqued, and cultural competence in the field is examined.

Chapter 14 explores alcohol and other drug abuse (AODA). It describes AODA terms, methods of ingestion, types of substances, the development and personal dynamics of abuse, the family dynamics

involved, the treatment process, treatment approaches, two treatment models, and available resources for treatment.

Chapter 15 focuses on social work with youths and in the schools. Positive social programming in macro practice, violence in the schools, bullying, and teenage sexual activity and pregnancy are examined. Social work roles with respect to each are discussed.

Chapter 16 explores social work and corrections. Questions requiring critical thinking are posed regarding the complexity of the crime rate, the issue of punishment versus empowerment, and health care for prisoners. Practice settings and gang membership are also discussed.

The epilogue, "Your Values and Your Future: Applying Critical Thinking Skills," serves as a capstone for the book. Students are urged to come to conclusions about various issues in social welfare policy and programming. Finally, they are encouraged to evaluate their personal characteristics and values and their potential for a career in social work, responding to many questions initiated in Chapter 1.

My sincere hope is that students will find this text interesting and informative and that instructors will find it an easy one from which to teach. The intent is to provide a sound foundation on which to build professional expertise and commitment.

## Relationship Between Content and the Educational Policy and Accreditation Standards (EPAS), and Professional Competencies

This book addresses accreditation standards established by the Council on Social Work Education (CSWE).[2] Our intent is to facilitate programs' ability to link content provided in this textbook with expectations for student learning and accomplishment. As is true in almost all learning, students must acquire knowledge before they are expected to apply it to practice situations.

CSWE has identified 31 component behaviors that operationalize 9 core competencies that are critical for professional practice (CSWE, 2015). For

[2]Please note that this content addresses standards posed in the EPAS. In no way does it claim to verify compliance with standards. Only the Council on Social Work Education Commission on Accreditation can make those determinations.

clarity, we have alphabetized in lowercase the component behaviors listed under each competency. **Multicolor icons** located within paragraphs clearly show the linkage between content in the textbook, and competencies and their component behaviors (see the multicolor image inserted in this paragraph).  Each icon is labeled with the specific behavior or competency that relates directly to the content conveyed in the paragraph. For example, an icon might be labeled EP [Educational Policy] 3b, which is the behavior, "engage in practices that advance social, economic, and environmental justice" (CSWE, 2015, EP 3b). Accredited social work programs are required to prove that students have mastered all component behaviors for competence as specified in the EPAS. (Please refer to http://www.cswe.org/File.aspx?id=79793 for the EPAS document.)

For all icons **"Competency Notes"** are provided at the end of each chapter. These Competency Notes explain the relationship between chapter content and CSWE's competencies and their component behaviors. They also list page numbers where icons are located and this content is discussed. A summary chart of the icons' locations in all chapters and their respective competency or practice behavior is placed in the inside front covers of the book.

## New to This Edition

This edition places a new emphasis on learning objectives and incorporates the 2015 EPAS throughout the entire book. In addition to updating subject matter throughout, other new and expanded content in this edition includes the following:

### Chapter 1
- Elaboration of competencies and their related behaviors inherent in the 2015 EPAS
- Environmental justice
- Introductory descriptions of quantitative and qualitative research
- Evaluation of practice and accountability

### Chapter 2
- Updated content on international social work organizations

### Chapter 3
- Incorporation of new content and concepts concerning human diversity recognized in the 2015 EPAS, including tribal sovereign status, (religion/)spirituality, (disability and) ability, and marital status as dimensions of diversity
- Updated information on racial demographics in the United States and other statistics
- New content on racial and cultural differences (including collectivism, the desire to keep problems within the family, and interpersonal harmony in Asian American families; and child-centeredness in African American families)
- The gender spectrum
- Updated statistics on the status of women

### Chapter 4
- Spokesperson, coordinator, and manager roles

### Chapter 5
- Expanded information concerning social work organizations
- Updated numbers of accredited social work programs
- Updated information on licensure, the Association of Social Work Boards, and NASW credentials
- New and updated data on social work practice settings and salaries including earning variations by geographical location

### Chapter 6
- Updated content on Charity Organization Societies
- Elaboration of trends during the progressive period
- Updated facts about the future of Social Security
- Updated content on the fringe economy and unsecured credit

### Chapter 7
- Using electronic media and supporting political candidates as approaches to policy practice and advocacy
- Updated content on social workers in politics

### Chapter 8
- Updated statistics on poverty
- New content on globalization

- Updated content on health care and the poor
- New and updated content on homelessness
- New content on OASDHI, Unemployment Insurance, Workers' Compensation, Medicare, TANF, SSI, Medicaid, CHIP, SNAP, and housing assistance

## Chapter 9
- Updated content on international legalized gay marriage
- New information on family life education
- New content on advocacy for resources at the macro level

## Chapter 10
- Updated demographic data and information on poverty concerning older adults
- Significantly expanded content on older adult abuse including incidence, types, assessment, and treatment
- New content on gay aging ("gayging")
- Assisted living facilities

## Chapter 11
- Updated citations on the NASW policy on people with disabilities
- Critical thinking about personal feelings and stereotypes concerning disabilities
- Update on the American with Disabilities Act including 2010 amendments

## Chapter 12
- New content on public health
- New content about Veterans Affairs (VA) health services and the social work role within the VA
- Updated content on the Affordable Care Act
- Updated statistics and content on HIV/AIDS concerning race and gender, treatment options, and international incidence

## Chapter 13
- Updated content regarding the 2013 Diagnostic and Statistical Manual of Mental Disorders (5th ed.) (DSM-5) including neurocognitive; depressive; paraphilic; disruptive, impulse-control, and conduct; and obsessive-compulsive and related disorders

- New content on managed care and mental health
- New content on cultural competence in mental health settings

## Chapter 14
- Updated statistics on the incidence of substance abuse
- Updated criteria on substance use disorders established by the DSM-5
- New recently appearing recreational drugs
- New content on engagement, assessment, and the importance of a continuing care plan during AODA treatment

## Chapter 15
- Updated and new content on gay, lesbian, and bisexual youth
- Updated content on youth violence including incidence in addition to risk and protective factors
- New content concerning bullying including the incidence, new case examples, and sexting
- Updated content on prenatal care for teenage mothers
- New content on teenage fatherhood

## Chapter 16
- Identity theft
- Social workers as Victim Specialists in FBI-operated specialized victims assistance programs
- Suggestions for preventing problematic behavior and emphasizing strengths in youths
- New content on gangs

## MindTap

MindTap for *Introduction to Social Work and Social Welfare* engages and empowers students to produce their best work—consistently. By seamlessly integrating course material with videos, activities, apps, and much more, MindTap creates a unique learning path that fosters increased comprehension and efficiency.

### For students:
- MindTap delivers real-world relevance with activities and assignments that help students build

critical thinking and analytic skills that will transfer to other courses and their professional lives.

- MindTap helps students stay organized and efficient with a single destination that reflects what's important to the instructor, along with the tools students need to master the content.
- MindTap empowers and motivates students with information that shows where they stand at all times—both individually and compared to the highest performers in class.

Additionally, for instructors, MindTap allows you to:

- Control what content students see and when they see it with a learning path that can be used as-is or matched to your syllabus exactly.
- Create a unique learning path of relevant readings and multimedia and activities that move students up the learning taxonomy from basic knowledge and comprehension to analysis, application, and critical thinking.
- Integrate your own content into the MindTap Reader using your own documents or pulling from sources like RSS feeds, YouTube videos, Websites, Googledocs, and more.
- Use powerful analytics and reports that provide a snapshot of class progress, time in course, engagement, and completion.

In addition to the benefits of the platform, MindTap for *Introduction to Social Work and Social Welfare* includes valuable resources to help students fully understand and master key social work concepts.

- The **Practice Behaviors Workbook** is now included online in MindTap. The experiential exercises provided here give students opportunities to develop the practice behaviors, facilitating their mastery over practical aspects of social work.
- Case Studies taken from **Careers in Social Work** provide students with examples and stories from social workers in the field highlighting real work application of concepts.
- Specially selected articles from **Questia,** an online database of professional journals and textbooks, give students further insight into social work concepts in practice. Students are asked to reflect on these articles so that they further understand and

apply what they have learned to their own lives and the real world.

- Newly selected videos from CNN and BBC bring to light important contemporary issues within society and provide critical thinking questions to assist students in thinking through issues that impact both social workers and those they serve.

## Supplements

### Online Instructor's Manual
The Instructor's Manual (IM) contains a variety of resources to aid instructors in preparing and presenting text material in a manner that meets their personal preferences and course needs. It presents chapter-by-chapter suggestions and resources to enhance and facilitate learning.

### Cengage Learning Testing powered by Cognero
Cognero is a flexible, online system that allows you to author, edit, and manage test bank content as well as create multiple test versions in an instant. You can deliver tests from your school's learning management system, your classroom, or wherever you want.

### Online PowerPoint®
These vibrant Microsoft® PowerPoint® lecture slides for each chapter assist you with your lecture by providing concept coverage using images, figures, and tables directly from the textbook.

## Acknowledgments
This book is possible due to the dedication and hard work of many people. I express my sincere appreciation to Michelle Clark, Senior Content Project Manager, for her conscientious and thorough oversight of the production process. I wish to express heartfelt thanks to Julie Martinez, Product Manager, and Gordon Lee, Product Manager, for their consistent enthusiastic encouragement and conscientious support. Many thanks to Stephen Lagos, Directors Assistant, for his efficient and diligent help.

Earnest appreciation is extended to Vicki Vogel who did an excellent job developing the index. Many thanks are extended to Jitendra Kumar, Senior Project Manager, who coordinated the day-to-day editing and production process and oversaw its progress. I also want to thank the following reviewers of this book for their help and input:

Sandra Alvarez—American International College

Patricia Coccoma—Florida Gulf Coast University

Heather Goltz—University of Houston-Downtown

Jill Gomez—UC Clermont College

Jennifer Hensley—Vincennes University

Rebecca Lasher—Western Carolina University

Melinda Pilkinton—Mississippi State University

Karen Sandell—UNC-Wilmington

Kimber Wickersham—Troy University

Christi Young—Southwestern Michigan College

Rochelle Zaranek—Macomb College

Sincere thanks go to Gary A. Kirst, MSW, for his support as a father and as a social worker. Many thanks to Gary S. Kirst for his input concerning the Turkana Tribe in Northern Kenya. Thankful recognition is also extended to my delightful nieces, nephews, and great nieces, who bring so much joy and inspiration to my life. Finally, I express my sincere gratitude and appreciation to Nick Ashman, who provided incredible support and encouragement throughout the 33-year process since this book's inception.

What is social work? How does it differ from sociology, psychology, or any other type of counseling? What types of people choose it as a career? This book answers these and many other questions you might have about what social workers do, what rules and policies they must follow, and whom they serve.

This book has four parts:

1. The Profession of Social Work
2. Social Work Practice
3. Social Welfare Policy
4. Client Populations and Contexts

Part 1 contains three chapters that emphasize key aspects of social work and provide a general introduction to the field. Chapter 1 defines social work and social welfare and discusses various theoretical perspectives you can use to think about how to help people. It introduces you to the concept of critical thinking, which will be emphasized throughout the book. It also describes the content areas in the social work curriculum.

Chapter 2 focuses on social work values and ethics. It summarizes social work's ethical principles and practitioners' ethical responsibilities to clients. It also challenges you to examine your own personal values and how they relate to social work values. Finally, it examines a range of ethical dilemmas that social workers potentially face.

Chapter 3 explores human diversity and the ways in which people might be empowered to enhance their well-being and reach their full potential. It stresses social work's quest for social and economic justice, especially for populations at risk of deprivation and oppression. Populations at risk include groups characterized by diverse aspects of "age, class, color, culture, disability and ability, ethnicity, gender, gender identity and expression, immigration status, marital status, political ideology, race, religion/spirituality, sex, sexual orientation, and tribal sovereign status" (Council on Social Work Education [CSWE], 2015).

I hope you will enjoy this book and gain a much better understanding of social work and social welfare. Let's begin.

# 1 Introduction to Social Work and Social Welfare

Kali9/iStockphoto.com

## Learning Objectives    This chapter will help prepare students to:

**LO 1**  Define social work and social welfare. **What Is Social Work?** (p. 5)

**LO 2**  Discuss various perspectives on social welfare (including residual, institutional, and developmental perspectives, as well as the concept of sustainability). **Perspectives for Viewing the Social Welfare System: Residual, Institutional, and Developmental** (p. 6)

**LO 3**  Explain critical thinking (including a framework for examining a wide range of concepts and issues). **Highlight 1.1** (p. 7)

**LO 4**  Explain the conservative–liberal continuum with respect to viewing the social welfare system. **The Conservative–Liberal Continuum** (p. 9)

**LO 5**  Examine your personal attitudes about some social welfare issues. **How Do You Fare on the Conservative–Liberal Continuum?** (p. 13)

**LO 6**  Explain social work's fields of practice. **Fields of Practice in Social Work** (p. 13)

**LO 7**  Explore the process of choosing a career. **The Continuum of Social Work Careers** (p. 15)

**LO 8**  Discuss the uniqueness of social work. **Social Work Builds on Many Disciplines** (p. 16)

**LO 9**  Identify relevant concepts in systems theories and the ecological perspective. **Highlight 1.3** (p. 22)

**LO 10**  Describe social work education's goals, curriculum, and competencies. **Accredited Social Work Programs** (p. 23)

*Case A: The couple is ecstatic. In their early 30s, they have been struggling with infertility for almost a decade and have been languishing on a waiting list to adopt a baby for almost five years. The moment has finally almost come: They will soon meet their new baby, Juliette. Alani, their social worker in the adoptions unit at a family services agency, is assisting them in completing the paperwork and helping them launch their new family life.*

*Case B: Cassius, a social worker at a community mental health center, is about to start the weekly support group session. His seven clients all are dealing with spouses who have Lou Gehrig's disease, which is characterized by deterioration of neurons in the brain stem and spinal cord. It involves loss of muscle function, paralysis, and finally death. The purpose of the group is to provide mutual emotional support and share information about coping with the disease. Cassius facilitates the group to keep things moving along and, when necessary, gives information about the disease. He notices that Erica, one of his clients, seems to be struggling to hold back a flood of tears. He knows that her husband, Tom, is deteriorating rapidly, so she must have had a rough week. This may be a difficult session.*

*Case C: Lolita is exhilarated. Several hundred people have shown up for and are eagerly participating in this "Take Back the Night" march against sexual assault. Lolita, a social worker at a rape crisis center, was one of the primary organizers of the event. The march's intent is to raise people's consciousness about this serious issue, promote education about sexual assault, and increase funding for crisis centers.*

*These vignettes portray brief moments in the actual lives of social workers. Some moments may be tremendously difficult, and others enormously satisfying.*

When you think of social work, what comes to mind? Helping people? Being on welfare? Facing bureaucratic red tape? Solving problems? Saving children? What do social workers actually do?

I once visited a quaint little crafts shop in Bar Harbor, Maine. It had little shadow boxes, about five inches square, filled with tacks. On these tacks, someone had painted little symbols to reflect the tools, tasks, and people involved in various professions. For example, one shadow box reflecting dentistry had tacks painted with tiny teeth, big toothy smiles, and toothbrushes (which is probably no surprise). I managed to find a box for social work. What do you think was painted on those tacks?

There were tiny images of the following: a Kleenex® box, a pencil, a compact car, a smiling face, a watch, and a heart. What do you think each of these is supposed to mean?

Here are some ideas. The Kleenex box reflects how social workers help people deal with tough, and frequently very sad, issues. Sometimes clients are hurting badly, and sometimes they cry. The pencil signifies record keeping and paperwork, a mainstay of what social workers do. It probably should have been a computer, but the artist most likely couldn't fit one on that little tack. The compact car symbolizes travel because social workers often must visit clients' homes and other agencies. The *smiling face signifies how social workers aim to help people solve their problems, to seek social justice on their behalf, and to make their lives a little bit better. (**Social justice** involves the concept that all citizens should be treated equally and have equal access to resources.) The watch reflects scheduling—there's always a lot to do and limited time in which to do it. Finally, the heart symbolizes caring about the welfare of others: That's the core of what the social work profession is all about.*

## What Is Social Work?   LO 1

The National Association of Social Work (NASW) defines **social work** as follows:

> *Social work is the professional activity of helping individuals, groups, or communities enhance or restore their capacity for social functioning and creating societal conditions favorable to this goal. Social work practice consists of the professional application of social work values, principles, and techniques to one or more of the following ends:*
>
> - *Helping people obtain tangible services (e.g., those involving provision of food, housing, or income).*
> - *Providing counseling and psychotherapy with individuals, families, and groups.*
> - *Helping communities or groups provide or improve social and health services.*
> - *Participating in relevant legislative processes.*
>
> *(NASW, 1973, pp. 4–5)*

What does this really mean? Imagine the vast range of human problems and issues. Because social workers can be in positions to help people deal with almost anything, it is difficult to define the field adequately in a few words. Highlighted here are some of the important concepts inherent in the definition just cited. Because of its breadth, the foundation of social work practice is referred to as *generalist practice*, described more thoroughly in Chapter 4.

Five themes permeate social work practice in virtually any setting (e.g., child welfare agencies, nursing homes, schools, or corrections facilities). First, social work concerns helping individuals, groups, or communities. Social workers provide counseling when necessary to help clients address problems. In addition to counseling an individual or family, much social work involves collaborating with organizations and communities to improve social and health

services. Second, social work entails a solid foundation of values and principles that guide what practitioners should and should not do. Third, a firm basis of techniques and skills provides directions for *how* social workers should provide treatment and accomplish goals. Fourth, social workers help people get the services they need by linking them to available resources. If the right resources are not available, social workers may advocate for service development on their clients' behalf. Fifth, social workers participate in legislative processes to promote positive social change. Such participation might include urging lawmakers to pass laws that improve social services and conditions. Social workers can also serve as expert witnesses to educate legislators about social issues and client needs, write or phone legislators to share socially responsible opinions, and run for elected office themselves.

NASW reports how Representative Bob Etheridge (D-N.C.) paid homage to social workers during Social Work Month (March 2001). He shared with the speaker of the U.S. House of Representatives the following remarks:

> *Social workers affect our lives in so many ways.... Their work touches all of us as individuals and as whole communities. They are educated, highly trained, and committed professionals. They work in family service and community mental health agencies, schools, hospitals, nursing homes, and many other private and public agencies.[1] They listen, they care. And, most importantly, they help those in need.*
>
> *(Vallianatos, 2001b, p. 1)*

---

[1] *Public agencies* are those run by a designated unit of government and are usually regulated by laws that directly affect policy. The county department of social services is a public agency. *Private agencies*, of course, are privately owned and run by people not employed by government. Chapter 5 describes social service agencies in greater detail.

## What Is Social Welfare?

What does the term *social welfare* mean? And exactly whose welfare are we talking about? Answers to these questions require critical thinking because, as a citizen and voter, your opinions are vital. You have the opportunity to help determine and shape how you and others are treated, how your own and their welfare is respected and nurtured.

A central theme of this book is encouraging you to think critically about problems, issues, and policies affecting people's lives and welfare. Highlight 1.1 defines critical thinking and provides a basic framework for analysis.

**Social welfare** is "a nation's system of programs, benefits, and services that help people meet those social, economic, educational, and health needs that are fundamental to the maintenance of society" (Barker, 2014, p. 402). Social welfare, then, is a broad concept related to the general well-being of all people in a society. Inherent in the definition are two basic dimensions: (1) what people get from society (in terms of programs, benefits, and services) and (2) how well their needs (including social, economic, educational, and health) are being met. Yet another way of portraying social welfare is the conception of an honorable, supportive society that offers its citizens the chance for adequate employment and the pursuit of happiness, affords an acceptably safe environment, advocates for justice and equality, and provides a context for financial security and growth (Reid, 1995).

How are social welfare and social work related? Simply put, **social work** serves to improve people's social and economic welfare. It does so in the many fields or settings discussed in this book, including health, mental health, and financial assistance, among many others. Populations served include older adults, children and families, people with disabilities, and people involved with the legal system.

Note that social work is not the only field concerned with people's social welfare. Others include those providing health, educational, recreational, and public safety services. Physicians, nurses, other health-care personnel, teachers, park recreational counselors, police, firefighters, and many others work to enhance people's well-being and quality of life.

Social welfare can be quite controversial on two counts. One involves individuals' responsibility to take care of themselves independently of government, which reflects the old saying "You get what you deserve." The other concerns society's responsibility to take care of all its members, especially those belonging to oppressed groups. There is constant political debate about what social services should and should not provide, and about who should receive them and who should not.

## Perspectives for Viewing the Social Welfare System: Residual, Institutional, and Developmental LO 2

The following section explores various perspectives that structure how you might think about social welfare. Each addresses the following questions: What should be the most important focus and goals of social welfare? Who should assume responsibility for people's social welfare? We can look at social welfare and the ways its programs

EP 7b*

---

*Note the multicolor icons next to designated content throughout the book. Accredited social work programs must demonstrate that they're teaching students to be proficient in nine core competencies that are operationalized by 31 component behaviors designated by the Council on Social Work Education's (CSWE) *Educational Policy and Accreditation Standards* (EPAS). Students require knowledge in order to develop skills and become competent. Our intent here is to specify what chapter content and knowledge coincides with the development of specific competencies and their component behaviors. (This ultimately is intended to assist in a social work program's accreditation process.)

Throughout each chapter, icons such as those located on this page call attention to the location of EPAS-related content. Each icon identifies what competency or its component behavior is relevant by specifying the designated Educational Policy (EP) reference number beneath it. Competency Notes are provided at the end of each chapter that describe how EPAS competencies and their component behaviors are related to content in the chapter.

EPAS competencies and their component behaviors are cited in the inside covers of this book. A summary chart indicating where icons are located throughout the book along with their component competencies and related behaviors is placed after the Table of Contents in the front of the book. Highlight 1.5 cites the competencies and their component behaviors directly.

The EPAS document lists component behaviors under each of the nine core competencies as bulleted items. To clarify the Competency Notes at the end of each chapter, the bulleted component behaviors have been alphabetized under each competency.

# HIGHLIGHT 1.1    WHAT IS CRITICAL THINKING?    **LO 3**

**Critical thinking** is (1) the careful scrutiny of what is stated as true or what appears to be true and the resulting expression of an opinion or conclusion based on that scrutiny, and (2) the creative formulation of an opinion or conclusion when presented with a question, problem, or issue. Critical thinking concentrates on "the process of reasoning" (Gambrill & Gibbs, 2009, p. 4). It stresses *how* individuals think about the truth inherent in a statement or *how* they analyze an issue to formulate their own conclusions. As Gambrill and Gibbs (2009) so aptly state, "Critical thinkers question what others take for granted" (p. 9).

Two dimensions in the definition of critical thinking are significant. First, critical thinking focuses on the questioning of beliefs, statements, assumptions, lines of reasoning, actions, and experiences.  Suppose you read a "fact" in a book or hear about it from a friend or an instructor. Critical thinking focuses on *not* taking this "fact" at face value. Rather, it entails the following "Triple-A" approach to examining and evaluating its validity:

**EP 4b, 5c, 7a, 8a**

1. *Ask* questions.
2. *Assess* the established facts and issues involved.
3. *Assert* a concluding opinion.

For example, a friend and fellow student might tell you, "It's impossible to get financial aid at our school." To what extent is this statement really true? To find out, you first *ask* questions about what the statement is really saying. What does "impossible" mean? Some people must be eligible for financial aid. What are the criteria for receiving aid? What experiences has your friend had to come to such a conclusion?

Second, you *assess* the established facts and issues involved by seeking relevant information. What does the financial aid policy state? To what extent does eligibility depend on students' and their parents' earnings? To what extent is a grade-point average or full-time student status involved? How many students are actually receiving aid at any given time? What percentage of the student population does this number reflect?

Third, you *assert* a concluding opinion. To what extent do you agree with your friend's statement? If you find out that only two people on your campus are receiving aid, then you might agree that such aid is almost impossible to get. However, if you find out that

about a third of the student population is receiving aid, then you might heartily conclude that your friend's statement is false.

Critical thinking can be applied to virtually any belief, statement, assumption, line of reasoning, action, or experience claimed as true. Consider the following statements of proposed "facts":

- Rich people are selfish.
- Taxes are unfair.
- A crocodile cannot stick its tongue out.
- Most lipstick contains fish scales.
- It is physically impossible for a person to lick his or her elbow.
- More than 75% of people who read this will try to lick their elbows.

These statements may seem silly (although some may also be true), but the point is that critical thinking can be applied to an infinite array of thoughts and ideas. For each statement, (1) what questions would you *ask*, (2) how would you *assess* the established facts and issues involved, and (3) what concluding opinion would you finally *assert*?

The second facet of the definition of critical thinking is the creative formulation of an opinion or conclusion when presented with a question, problem, or issue. Instead of being told a proposed "fact" to be scrutinized for its validity, you are asked your *opinion* about an issue, assumption, or action. Examples include the following:

- Should prisoners who commit violent crimes be ineligible for parole? (In other words, should they be required to serve their full sentences?)
- Should all interstate highways have toll booths to finance them and their repairs, so that only the people who use them pay for them (instead of general tax revenues paying for highway construction and repair)?
- What is the best way to eliminate poverty in this nation?

Consider answering the last question, which could be posed as a term paper or exam topic in one of your courses. First, what questions about it would you ask? What are the reasons for poverty in a rich industrialized country? What social welfare programs are currently available to address poverty? What innovative ideas

*(continued)*

**HIGHLIGHT 1.1 (continued)**

for programs might be tried? Where might funding for such programs be found? How much money would it take to eliminate poverty, and who would pay for this?

Second, what facts and issues would you seek to address and assess? You probably would first try to define poverty—what income level or lack of income makes a person or family "poor"? You then might research statistics, costs, and studies concerning the effectiveness of various programs intending to reduce poverty. You might also investigate innovative ideas. Perhaps there are proposals for programs that look promising. You might explore what various programs cost and how they are funded. Note that these suggestions only scratch the surface of how you might examine the issue.

Third, what opinion or conclusion would you assert? To what extent do you think it is possible to eliminate poverty? What kinds of resources and programs do you think it would take? What do you feel citizens and their government should do about poverty?

Critical thinking enhances self-awareness and the ability to detect various modes of distorted thinking that can trick people into assuming truth; critical thinking can help you do the following (Gambrill & Gibbs, 2009):

1. *Identify propaganda* ("ideas, facts, or allegations spread deliberately to further one's cause or to damage an opposing cause" [Mish, 2008, p. 996]). Propaganda may be true or untrue. It often sensationalizes a point of view by blowing it out of proportion. For example, a law firm with the slogan "Our Way Is the Only and Best Way" emphasizes its own prowess while demeaning the effectiveness of other firms. Critical thinking would prompt you to assess upon what basis this law firm is making its claim of superiority.

2. *Distinguish intentionally deceptive claims.* For instance, an advertiser might boast, "This miracle drug has been scientifically proven to make you lose a pound a day—without exercising or changing your eating habits!" when, in actuality, little or no meticulous research has been done. Critical thinking would lead you to question how the drug has been scientifically proven to be effective.

3. *Focus on and choose words carefully.* Critical thinking helps you focus your attention on the meaning of each word used to convey an idea or concept. For example, consider the statement "Schools produce a bunch of real losers these days." What does each word really mean or imply? Which schools produce "losers"? What is a "loser"? What does "a bunch" mean? To what are "these days" compared?

4. *Be wary of emotional ploys and appeals.* They play on your emotions and urge you to concur with their intent by using as little logical thinking as possible. For instance, a sales representative on a televised marketing program might urge you to "buy this genuine fake leather jacket now and we'll send a pair of matching gloves—and a pair of matching boots. This is the only time you'll get this additional value. Aren't they lovely? But you have to act now—we have only two jackets left!" The intent here is to pressure you to make a decision quickly based on desire rather than on logical thinking about what the jacket costs and how you will make the payments.

---

are developed from three different perspectives— residual and institutional (Blau, 2014; Chapin, 2014; Gilbert & Terrell, 2013; Segal, 2013), in addition to developmental (Dolgoff & Feldstein, 2013; Midgley & Livermore, 1997).

## The Residual Perspective

The **residual perspective** conceives of social welfare as focusing on problems and gaps. Social welfare benefits and services should be supplied only when people fail to provide adequately for themselves and problems arise. The implication is that it's people's own fault if they require outside help. Society, then, must aid them until they can once again assume responsibility for meeting their own needs. Gilbert and Terrell (2013) reflect:

*The traditional (i.e., residual) view is that social welfare itself is not a significant societal institution, but rather a supplemental activity necessary only when the "normal" helping channels fail to perform appropriately. Viewed as a temporary response to the failure of individuals and major institutions, social welfare is seen as a set of activities that, while necessary at times, is undesirable and expendable. (p. 12)*

Blaming women and children for being "on welfare," for example, reflects a residual view. The focus is on their supposed failures and faults; they are viewed in a demeaning and critical manner.

## The Institutional Perspective

The **institutional perspective** of social welfare, in contrast, views people's needs as a normal part of life. Society has a responsibility to support its members and provide needed benefits and services. It's not people's fault that they require such services, but rather it is an expected part of the human condition. People have a right to receive benefits and services on an ongoing basis. In many ways, this is a more humane and supportive approach to helping people. Public education available to all is an example of an institutional form of social welfare. Similarly, fire and police protection are available to all.

Prior to the Great Depression in the 1930s, the residual approach to social welfare dominated. Since then, however, both approaches have been apparent, depending on the program at issue. Temporary Assistance to Needy Families (TANF), described in a later chapter, is an example of a residually oriented program. Families in need receive temporary, limited financial assistance until they can get back on their feet.

## The Developmental Perspective

Another view on social welfare is the **developmental perspective**. This approach "seeks to identify social interventions that have a positive impact on economic development" (Midgley & Livermore, 1997, p. 574). It presumes that people living today in our complex world may require help and resources in order to function effectively and support themselves (Dolgoff & Feldstein, 2013). The developmental perspective originated after World War II in Third World countries seeking to design social welfare programs that would also enhance their economic development. This perspective gained impetus in the United States in the 1970s because "it justifies social programs in terms of economic efficiency criteria" (Lowe, 1995; Midgley & Livermore, 1997, p. 575).

There are three major ways that economic development can occur in a developmental context (Midgley & Livermore, 1997). First, "investments in [services to people such as] education, nutrition, and health care" can be evaluated so that people get the most for their money (p. 577). For example, investments in education may result in a more skilled labor force that, in turn, generates a stronger economy. Second, investment in physical facilities involving "the creation of economic and social infrastructure, such as roads, bridges, irrigation and drinking water systems, clinics, [and] schools … provide[s] the economic and social bases on which development efforts depend" (pp. 577–578). Workers must have a transportation system to get to work and a building in which to work to get anything done. Therefore, resources expended on developing such things are economically productive. Third, developing "programs that help needy people engage in productive employment and self-employment" is more economically viable than giving people public assistance payments over years and even decades (p. 578). It is an efficient economic investment to educate and train people in need so that they can get jobs and eventually support themselves.

The developmental perspective is relatively new and requires a more extensive grasp of social welfare issues and policies than can be described in an introductory book such as this. It involves both in-depth analysis of current social programs and the ability to creatively propose new ones. Therefore, it will not be a primary focus in this book.

What are your views about social welfare? Focus on Critical Thinking 1.1 poses some questions.

Highlight 1.2 explores a concept related to the developmental perspective on social welfare—the notion of sustainability on a global basis.

# The Conservative–Liberal Continuum    LO 4

**Political ideology** is the "relatively coherent system of ideas (beliefs, traditions, principles, and myths) about human nature, institutional arrangements, and social processes" that indicate how a government should be run and what principles that government should support (Abramovitz, 2007, p. 126). A person's political ideology will frame the way that

## FOCUS ON CRITICAL THINKING 1.1   WHAT ARE YOUR VIEWS ABOUT SOCIAL WELFARE?

We have established that a consistent theme in social work is the importance of thinking critically and formulating opinions about what is right and wrong. A key question here concerns your own views about social welfare. What ensuing questions might you ask? What facts would you need to seek out and assess? What opinions and conclusions would you finally assert?

A related question concerns the extent to which your opinions reflect residual or institutional views about social welfare programs, benefits, and services. What are your opinions about the following concerns posed? (The issues are more complicated than you might think.) Does your thinking lean more toward a residual or institutional perspective?

EP 1b

- Should single mothers of young children be required to work, or should they be entitled to public assistance while they care for their children at home?
- Should public housing be routinely provided to homeless people at public expense?
- Should homeless people who have mental illnesses be institutionalized, should they be allowed to roam at will in the community, or should adequate mental health services be provided on an outpatient basis regardless of the cost?
- Should children in families suspected of child abuse be placed elsewhere, or should treatment focus on strengthening the family so that children remain in their own homes?

## HIGHLIGHT 1.2   SUSTAINABILITY ON A GLOBAL LEVEL

The developmental perspective emphasizes the importance of economic development. Such progress can affect communities of any size, ranging from small local communities to nations as communities at the global level. The well-being of the global community has become a pressing concern. Consider that

[t]he world is changing. Our human activities are clearly becoming global in nature. Our understanding of nature—the infrastructure upon which all humankind rests—is changing as well.... We have reached a point in our understanding of systems at which social welfare must be considered part of a larger global imperative of planetary survival. There is a profound connection between the micro problems that individuals and families manifest (e.g., environmental pollution, the lack of sustaining and meaningful work, addiction, domestic violence) and the macro problems that local and global communities experience [e.g., rampant poverty, lack of educational infrastructure, widespread unemployment, inadequate food production, political unrest].

(Mary, 2008, p. 1)

A concept related to global and international development is the concept of sustainability. **Sustainability** involves "development that meets the current needs of the present generations without jeopardizing the ability of future generations to meet their needs" (Mary, 2008, p. 32; Pace, 2011). This concept encompasses much more than just economic development. In view of concerns about overpopulation and overcrowding, insufficient food and freshwater, global warming, and a host of other issues, sustainability involves the need for citizens of the earth to work together to save themselves and their world (Gamble & Weil, 2008; Healy, 2008; Mary, 2008).

An internationally supported document entitled the *Earth Charter* has been developed to define and stress the importance of sustainability on a global basis (Earth Charter Initiative, 2011). After many years of planning, cooperation, and compromise, socially concerned organizations around the world met to create a document with the following intent:

We must join together to bring forth a sustainable global society founded on respect for nature, universal human rights, economic justice, and a culture of peace. Towards this end, it is

*(continued)*

**HIGHLIGHT 1.2 *(continued)***

imperative that we, the peoples of Earth, declare our responsibility to one another, to the greater community of life, and to future generations.

*(Earth Charter Initiative, 2011)*

The charter emphasizes four categories of principles necessary to promote "a sustainable way of life by which the conduct of all individuals, organizations, businesses, governments, and transnational institutions is to be guided and assessed": "respect and care for the community of life [with all its diversity]," "ecological integrity," "social and economic justice, " and "democracy, nonviolence, and peace" (Earth Charter Initiative, 2011).

The charter calls for "a new sense of global interdependence and universal responsibility" where all the citizens of earth "imaginatively develop and apply the vision of a sustainable way of life locally, nationally, regionally, and globally" (Earth Charter Initiative, 2011). It has been endorsed by thousands of organizations around the globe and has significantly influenced the United Nations Educational, Scientific, and Cultural Organization (UNESCO) (Healy, 2008). It is "now increasingly recognized as a global consensus statement on the meaning of sustainability, the challenge and vision of sustainable development, and the principles by which sustainable development is to be achieved" (Earth Charter Initiative, 2011).

To achieve sustainability, Mary (2008) calls for major shifts in our economic system. For example, she suggests that some military spending could be shifted to the following earth-preserving goals:

Basic Social Goals

- Universal primary education
- Adult literacy
- School lunch programs for the world's forty-four poorest countries
- Assistance to preschool children and pregnant women in the world's forty-four poorest countries
- Universal basic health care
- Reproductive health and family planning
- Closing the condom gap

Earth Restoration Goals

- Reforesting the earth
- Protecting topsoil on cropland
- Restoring rangelands
- Stabilizing water tables
- Restoring fisheries
- Protecting biological diversity (pp. 188–189)

The application of sustainability to social work practice will be discussed further in Chapter 4.

person views the world. It affects what that person feels is valuable and what is not; it influences how an individual believes things should be and how they should not be.

Another way of thinking about how people should be served by social welfare programs involves political ideology and the conservative–liberal continuum (Blau, 2014; Dolgoff & Feldstein, 2013; Jansson, 2014). In some ways, this continuum reflects concepts similar to those of the residual and institutional perspectives of social welfare program development. However, the continuum focuses more on values related to social responsibility for human welfare.

Note that people are complex. It would be radically oversimplified to imply that each conservative individual has the identical views and ideas of each other conservative person; similarly, liberals also vary significantly in their views on various

issues (Dolgoff & Feldstein, 2013; Jansson, 2014). Regardless, various themes often characterizing conservatives and liberals are identified here.

## Conservatism

**Conservatism** is the philosophy that individuals are responsible for themselves, government should provide minimal interference in people's lives, and change does not necessarily mean improvement.

At least three concepts tend to characterize conservatives. First, conservatives often oppose change and thrive on tradition (Gilbert & Terrell, 2013; Page, 2014). "This defense of the status quo is underpinned by a belief that institutions and practices that have stood the test of time should not be readily abandoned for untested 'modern' alternatives" (Page, 2014, p. 144; Scruton, 2013). Conservatives generally feel that change results in more trouble than it's

JEWEL SAMAD/Getty Images

*Poverty is a social welfare issue. Depending on their political orientation, people view the causes of poverty and the potential solutions very differently.*

worth, so it's best to leave things the way they are. In other words, if it ain't broke, don't fix it.

Second, conservatives generally assume what they consider "a 'realistic' or 'common sense' view of human nature" (Page, 2014, p. 145). Page (2014) elaborates:

> While individuals are seen as having a propensity for rational action and selflessness, conservatives believe that these co-exist with baser impulses, which can give rise to selfish and anti-social forms of conduct. Given inherent human frailty, conservatives recognize that it is important to constrain undesirable conduct through the rule of law and the threat of punishment. (p. 145)

Therefore, conservatives feel that society has the responsibility of regulating people's behavior so that it's in compliance with the laws of God and society (Abramovitz, 2008; Blau, 2014).

Third, conservatives usually conceive of people as perfectly capable of taking care of themselves (Abramovitz, 2008). This implies that if people would work hard and take responsibility for their actions, they wouldn't need any help. Most people "on welfare" don't deserve such resources, but rather should make their own way. If people can get public assistance, they'll take it, and society is unwise for

giving it to a broad range of people. People have only themselves to blame if they don't succeed.

Government should provide minimal interference in people's lives and assistance only when it's absolutely necessary to help the very needy. Therefore, conservatives generally oppose "big government" and centralized federal control.

> *[C]onservatives are always alert to the possibility that governments can over-extend themselves and act in authoritarian ways that threaten ancient liberties.... In particular, they fear the prospect of a highly centralized socialist government that might exercise control in ways that threaten the free market ... [and] local autonomy.* (Page, 2014, p. 148)

## Liberalism

**Liberalism** is the philosophy that government should be involved in the social, political, and economic structure so that all people's rights and privileges are protected in the name of social justice.

At least three concepts tend to characterize liberals, more or less reflecting the opposite of a conservative perspective. First, liberals often seek change and tend to think there's always a better way to get things done (Dolgoff & Feldstein, 2013; Gilbert & Terrell, 2013; Jimenez, Pasztor, & Chambers, 2015). They are always looking for different approaches to improve policies and provide services. For example, liberals have tended to champion "efforts to assist persons of color, women, the disabled, and gay men and lesbians with regulations that curtail discrimination in employment and elsewhere" (Jansson, 2014, p. 49).

Second, liberals have a more positive perspective on human nature than conservatives (Abramovitz, 2008; Blau, 2014). They view people as rational beings fully capable of making their own choices and decisions about what is right and wrong. Each individual deserves the right to compete and be provided with equal opportunities to blossom and prosper.

Third, liberals view government as the best entity to provide a structure and an environment where adequate services and opportunities can be made available (Abramovitz, 2008; Blau, 2014; Gilbert & Terrell, 2013). Therefore, it is government's responsibility to make certain that citizens' needs are met, public participation is maximized, and people's equal rights are preserved in the context of social justice. Additionally, liberals assert that it's "the mission of government ... to balance market forces, to modify the power of elites in favor of the whole, and to ensure economic management for growth, employment, fair wages, and economic security" (Gilbert & Terrell, 2013, p. 18). Liberals also believe that it's the government's job to protect people from such impediments as racism, sexism, various other forms of discrimination, and poverty.

### Radicalism

A more extreme approach is **radicalism**, the philosophy that the social and political system as it stands is not structurally capable of truly providing social justice. Rather, drastic, fundamental changes are necessary in the basic social and political structure to achieve truly fair and equal treatment.

According to a radical philosophy, for example, "poverty results from exploitation by the ruling capitalist class"; such poverty exists for at least two reasons (Karger & Stoesz, 2014, p. 97). First, having a multitude of poor people as workers enables higher classes to keep wages low because of numerous replacement workers. If low-paid workers complain, they can simply be fired, with someone else eagerly waiting to take their place to avoid poverty. The working class thus serves to labor for the wealthy and keep them rich. Second, keeping a class of people in poverty enhances the "prestige" and status of the middle and upper classes. To remedy this state of affairs, an entirely new social structure would have to be developed.

A radical perspective requires the ability to propose a new social structure. It is far beyond the scope of this book to discuss how to plan new policies and promote broad social change. Therefore, from here on, when the term *radical* is used, it will be in the context of soliciting any *very general* ideas you might have about changing social welfare service provision.

### How Do You Fare on the Conservative–Liberal Continuum? **LO 5**

Return to Focus on Critical Thinking 1.1 and review the answers you gave to those questions. Do they lean toward a liberal or conservative point of view? Focus on Critical Thinking 1.2 contains a series of statements geared to assessing further your liberal or conservative views.

Note again that this discussion of conservatism and liberalism is overly simplified. Many people, and perhaps most, have a complex mixture of views depending on their perceptions and personal experiences. (That last sentence probably reflects a liberal perspective.)

## Social Work and Social Welfare History

Social work has been a developing field since the late 19th century. The profession is intimately intertwined with historical events and trends in social welfare. Social work emphasizes the importance of the social environment as it affects the quality of people's lives. Therefore, the way people are treated by laws that govern them and the services **EP 1** and resources provided to them are integral parts of the social work perspective.

Chapter 6 reviews the history of social welfare beginning in European medieval times, continuing throughout U.S. history, and culminating with today's programs and services. It elaborates on the effects of history on the social work profession's development. The chapter is placed immediately before Chapter 7 (which addresses policy, policy analysis, and policy advocacy) because today's programs, all based on current social welfare policies, are products of historical events concerning social welfare. Chapter 8 then discusses the policies and programs developed to combat poverty.

## Fields of Practice in Social Work **LO 6**

The remainder of the book focuses on **fields of practice** in social work. These are the various practice contexts that address certain types of populations and needs and require a special knowledge and skill base for effective work. Each field of practice involves a labyrinth of typical human problems and the services attempting to address them. Current fields of practice include children and families, aging, disabilities, health, mental health, substance abuse, schools, and corrections. Other contexts for practice are occupational social work (focusing on work in employee assistance programs or directed toward organizational change), rural social work

## FOCUS ON CRITICAL THINKING 1.2

# WHERE DO YOU STAND ON THE CONSERVATIVE–LIBERAL CONTINUUM?

Rate how much you agree with statements 1–6 by assigning a number for each. The scale is as follows:

| Strongly agree | Somewhat agree | Somewhat disagree | Strongly disagree |
|---|---|---|---|
| 1 | 2 | 3 | 4 |

1. I don't like change very much.
2. The old tried-and-true way of getting things done is usually the best way.
3. People will do whatever they can to get things for themselves.
4. If they're sure they can get away with it, students will inevitably cheat on exams.
5. People should be independent, take care of themselves, and not rely on the charity of others.
6. People who commit crimes should be punished with severity to match the severity of their crimes.

Now rate how much you agree with statements 7–12 by assigning a number for each. The scale is as follows:

| Strongly agree | Somewhat agree | Somewhat disagree | Strongly disagree |
|---|---|---|---|
| 4 | 3 | 2 | 1 |

7. I like to see and do new things because it makes life more interesting.
8. Trying some new way to get things done often results in a better, more effective approach.
9. People are generally good at heart.
10. It's often the bad things that happen to people that make them "go wrong."
11. With a little help and support, people who are less privileged than the rest can usually pull themselves together and do pretty well.
12. It's better to try to rehabilitate people who commit crimes than to throw them in jail.

Now add up your total score for all 12 items and divide by 12. A score of 1 means that you probably are quite conservative, a 2 that you're somewhat conservative, a 3 that you're somewhat liberal, and a 4 that you're quite liberal.

This exercise in no way defines your political orientation or labels you as a conservative or liberal for life. Its intent is to give you some food for thought about your own values.

Social work values tend to be more liberal than conservative, as is demonstrated by the NASW *Code of Ethics* and NASW's usual support of Democratic political candidates, who traditionally are more liberal than Republicans.

However, people's values and belief systems often are much more complex than that. For example, you may be conservative in that you don't want to pay a high percentage of taxes for social welfare programs. But you may also be liberal in that you believe in a woman's right to choice when it comes to having an abortion. Or you might feel just the opposite.

Social workers must continuously examine their personal values, on the one hand, and respect the values of their clients, on the other. They must constantly strive not to impose personal values on clients. It's a difficult but interesting task.

**EP 1b**

(addressing the unique problems of people living in rural areas), police social work (emphasizing work in police, courthouse, and jail settings with crime victims, alleged offenders, and their families), and forensic social work (dealing with the law, educating lawyers, and serving as expert witnesses) (Barker, 2014).

Social workers require information about people who need help in each area. They also must be knowledgeable about the services available to meet needs and the major issues related to each area. A social worker may be called on to work with a problem that clearly falls within one field of practice or a problem that involves several fields.

For example, the Wullbinkle family comes to a social worker's attention when a neighbor reports that Rocky, their 5-year-old son, is frequently seen with odd-looking bruises on his arms and legs. The neighbor suspects child abuse. Upon investigation, the social worker finds that the parents are indeed abusive. They often grab the child violently by a limb and throw him against the wall. This problem initially falls under the umbrella of family and children's services.

However, the social worker also finds a number of other problems operating within the family. The mother, Natasia, is seriously depressed and frequently suicidal, so she needs mental health services. And the father, Boris, is struggling with a drinking problem that is beginning to affect his performance at work. A program is available at his place of employment, where an occupational social worker helps employees deal with such problems. Thus occupational social work may also be involved. In addition, the maternal grandmother, Emma, is living with the Wullbinkle family. Emma's physical health is failing. Although her daughter dreads the idea of nursing home placement, the issue must be addressed. Emma, who is also overweight, finds it increasingly difficult to move around by herself. She is demanding more and more physical help and support from Natasia. Natasia, who has back problems, is finding it increasingly burdensome to help her mother. Finally, Vernite, Boris and Natasia's 12-year-old daughter, is falling behind in school, and truancy is becoming a problem. This last issue falls under the school's umbrella.

Most of the problems that social workers face are complex. They may involve a variety of practice fields all at one time. To understand clients' needs, social workers must know something about a wide range of problems and services.

# The Continuum of Social Work Careers `LO 7`

There are various ways to look at advancement through a social work career. Some workers progress through a series of levels, while others remain at an earlier point of entry. Degrees in social work include the baccalaureate, master's, and doctorate.

## Baccalaureate Social Workers (BSWs)

**Baccalaureate social workers** (BSWs) complete an accredited course of study, with required content described later in the chapter, to prepare for entry-level social work. They are also required to complete at least 400 hours of field experience supervised by a social work practitioner. Job settings involve many fields of practice and include child welfare agencies (e.g., those involving protective services, foster care, or adoption), residential treatment centers (e.g., serving adolescents with behavioral or emotional problems), services for people with various disabilities (including intellectual [mental retardation]), settings serving older adults, correctional institutions, public welfare agencies, schools, health centers and hospitals, substance abuse treatment centers, shelters for the homeless, shelters for domestic violence survivors, and family planning organizations.

At the preprofessional or paraprofessional level involving people who assist social workers in their practice are social service technicians and social service aides (Hopps & Lowe, 2008). **Social service technicians** typically hold an associate's degree (e.g., in human services) or a baccalaureate degree in a non–social work discipline and serve as a paraprofessional (a person trained to assist the social worker under the social worker's supervision in designated tasks such as conducting basic interviews, making referrals, and completing paperwork). **Social service aides** are people with a high school degree, often with relevant life experience or strong connections to the community, who perform clerical and scheduling tasks. Aides may or may not have an associate's degree.

## Master's Social Workers (MSWs)

**Master's social workers** (MSWs) receive more specialized training built on the same foundation as the BSW curriculum and integrated with field internships. Most master's programs require two years of study. However, many give *advanced standing* to BSWs (as opposed to people entering the program with non–social work undergraduate majors) where up to one year of study is waived because they've already completed the foundation curriculum.

Both BSWs and MSWs can find employment in a wide range of settings. However, there are some differences in the types of jobs for which each is qualified. MSWs are considered more specialized than BSWs. The implication is that MSWs are competent to address more difficult problems than BSWs and have the potential to assume greater responsibility. In reality, this distinction is not always so clear-cut. Performance expectations and job availability vary significantly depending on the area of the country and state.

The realm of psychotherapy is generally limited to MSWs instead of BSWs. **Psychotherapy**, sometimes referred to simply as **therapy**, is a skilled treatment process whereby a therapist works with an individual, couple, family, or group to address a mental disorder or alleviate other problems the clients) may be having in the social environment. Another difference between MSWs and BSWs is that higher-level supervisory and administrative positions in any field of practice often require an MSW or other master's-level degree. Such positions usually offer higher salaries. MSWs generally earn significantly more than BSWs, although years of experience enhance salaries for both groups.

Licensure or certification of some level of social work practice exists in all 50 states. Chapter 5 discusses this more thoroughly. Chapter 5 also discusses social work salaries and employment prospects at the BSW and MSW levels.

### Doctorates in Social Work

A small percentage of social workers hold doctorate degrees, either a Ph.D. (Doctor of Philosophy) or DSW (Doctor of Social Work). Either degree qualifies the holder to teach at the college level or conduct research. (Note that some social workers without a doctorate but with an MSW get jobs teaching at community colleges, in universities as part-time instructors, or, sometimes, in non–tenure-track faculty positions.) Some Ph.D.s or DSWs assume administrative positions or enter private practice in psychotherapy. These degrees involve advanced and specialized study, a focus on research, and completion of a dissertation.

This section has reviewed the continuum of social work careers according to the college and university degrees attained. Focus on Critical Thinking 1.3 suggests how you might start thinking about the career that's right for you in whatever field you choose.

## Social Work Builds on Many Disciplines   `LO 8`

The foundation of professional social work is a body of knowledge, skills, and values. Knowledge originates not only from social workers but also from a range of disciplines that focus on understanding people's needs and behavior. These include psychology, sociology, political science, economics, biology, psychiatry, counseling, and cultural anthropology. Figure 1.1 illustrates how social work knowledge builds on both other disciplines and its own firm and growing body of research. It summarizes the

primary focus and core concepts involved in each discipline. Social workers use knowledge drawn from each field, in conjunction with social work skills and values, to help individuals, families, groups, organizations, and communities solve problems and improve their quality of life.

## Social Work Is Unique

We have established that social work builds on the knowledge base of other professions in addition to its own. Other fields perform some of the same functions as social work. For instance, mental health clinicians in psychology, psychiatry, and counseling use interviewing skills, and some also use a planned-change approach. Figure 1.2 illustrates how social work overlaps, to some extent, with other helping professions. All, for example, have a common core of interviewing and counseling skills.

However, social work involves much more than simply sitting down with an individual, group, or family and solving some problem. (This is not to imply that this is all other helping professions do. Their own unique thrusts and emphases are beyond the scope of what can be included here.) Social work has at least five major dimensions that make it unique.

EP 6, 7, 8, 9

### Focus on Any Problem

First, social workers may focus on any problems or clusters of problems that are complex and difficult. Social workers don't refuse to work with clients or refer them elsewhere because those clients have unappealing characteristics. For instance, there may be a family in which sexual abuse is occurring, and that abuse must be stopped. Likewise, there may be a community in which the juvenile crime rate is skyrocketing, and something must be done.

Not every problem can be solved, but some can be—or at least alleviated. Social work practitioners are equipped with a repertoire of skills to help them identify and examine problems. They then make choices about where their efforts can be best directed.

### Targeting the Environment for Change

The second dimension that makes social work unique is that it often targets the environment

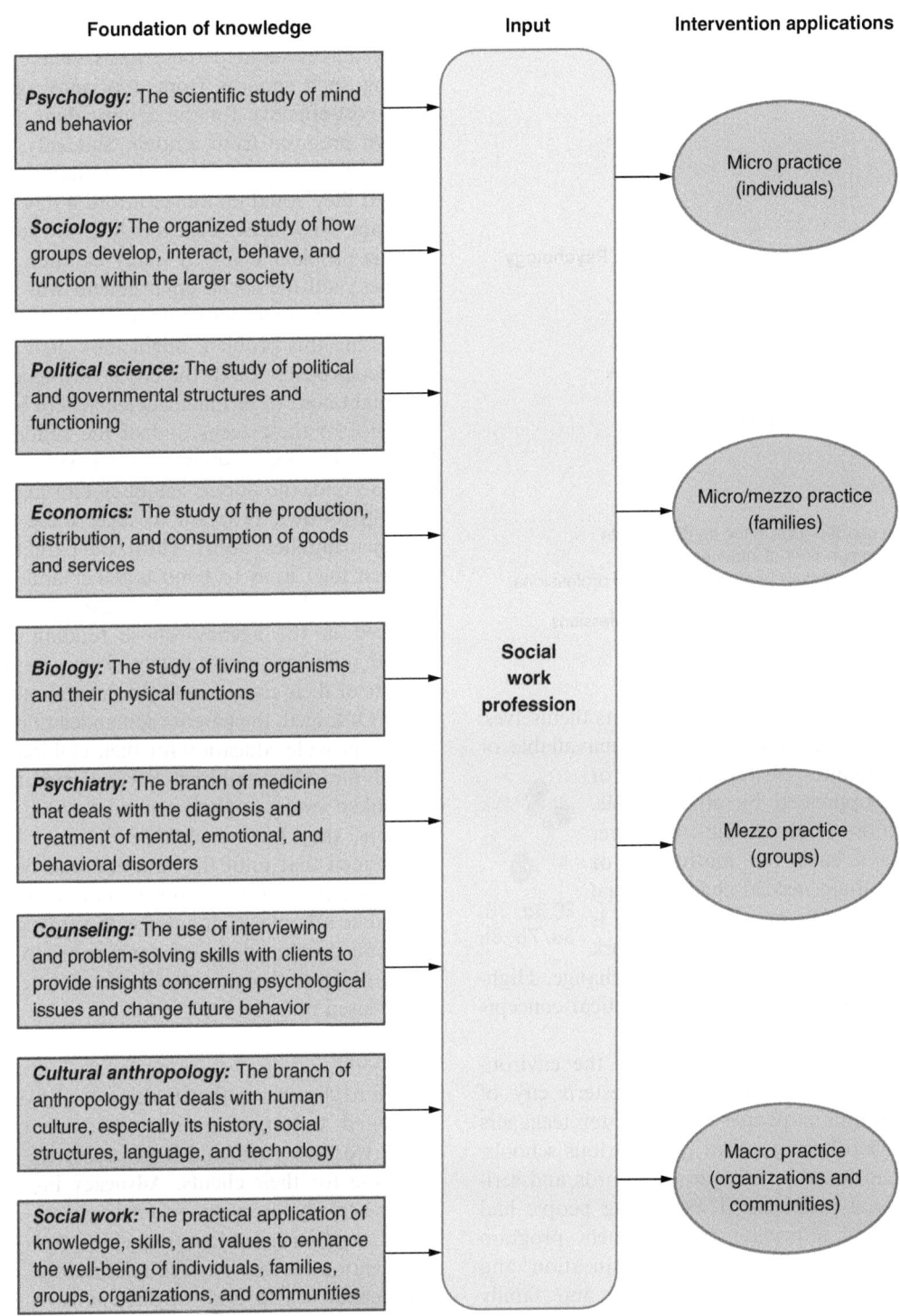

**FIG-1-1** The Social Work Knowledge Base

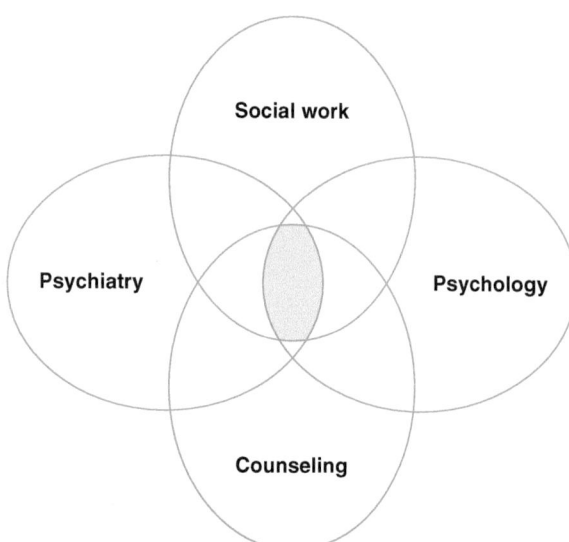

The shaded area in the center reflects a common core of interviewing and counseling skills used by the helping professions.

**FIG-1-2** Social Work and Other Helping Professions

encompassing clients, and not the clients themselves, for change. Sometimes services are unavailable or difficult to obtain, policies are unfair, or people are oppressed by other people. Administrators and people in power don't always have the motivation or insight to initiate needed change. Social workers must look at where change is essential outside the individual and work with the environment to effect that change. Highlight 1.3 discusses some of the theoretical concepts underlying social work practice.

EP 3a, 3b, 5a, 7b, 8b

Consider an example of targeting the environment for change involving a midwestern city of about half a million people. Several dozen teenagers in the city had been expelled from various schools. They all had lengthy delinquency records and serious emotional problems. These young people had been attending a private day treatment program that provided them with special education and counseling at the individual, group, and family levels. The day treatment approach allowed them to remain living at home in the community but still receive special treatment. The program had been paid for by public funds, with the county department of social services purchasing treatment services from

the private agency. The public schools had no special resources to help these teens. Therefore, purchasing such services from a private agency was more cost-effective for the county than developing its own program from scratch. Suddenly, however, money became scarce, and community leaders decided they could no longer afford a day treatment program. Now these teenagers had nowhere to go.

This problem involved many children and their families, and the social environment was no longer responding to their desperate needs. A social worker addressing this problem might look at it from several perspectives. First, the city's various communities might need to be made acutely aware both of the existence of these teens and of the sudden cuts in funding. The media may need to be contacted as well. Second, the public school system may need to develop its own program to meet these children's and their families' needs. Third, the parents of these children may need to band together and lobby for attention and services. In this case, social workers involved in the agency whose funding had been cut off mobilized immediately. They contacted the parents of their clients and told them about the situation. Outraged, the parents demanded that the community provide education for their children as it did for all the other children. Several parents became outspoken leaders of the group. Assisted by social workers, they filed a class-action suit. The court determined that until the situation had been evaluated, funding for services must continue. Eventually, the public school system (also with the help of social workers) developed its own programs to meet the needs of such teenagers, and the private program was phased out.

## Advocacy

The third dimension that makes social work unique is related to targeting the environment: namely, social workers often find it necessary to advocate for their clients. **Advocacy** involves actively intervening to help clients get what they need. Most frequently, this intervention focuses on "the relationship between the client and an unresponsive 'system'" (Epstein, 1981, p. 8). Clients have specified needs, and social agencies, organizations, or communities may not be meeting these needs. These unresponsive systems must be pressured to make changes so needs can be met.

EP 3a, 5c, 8d

# THINKING ABOUT YOUR CAREER

As a student, you may have some career goals clearly in mind. Or you may still be wondering what the best career path is. The following is a discussion of how you might think about determining a career course. You might be a student of traditional age or an older student returning to school. Note that not all career ideas and possibilities are mentioned because they are countless. Although this career consideration process is oriented toward social work, the purpose here is to stimulate your thinking, not to tell you what to do. Each person must decide for herself or himself how to spend time and life.

**EP 1b**

## 1. General orientation toward the future (conducting a self-assessment)

What values are important to you? Achieving personal satisfaction? Becoming famous? Earning money? Being respected? Building a family life? Finding security? Having adventures? Leading others? Finding excitement? Developing personal relationships? Having fun? Being loved? Helping others? Getting ahead? Being successful? Being happy? Being popular? Fitting into a work environment? Feeling important? Having free time? Traveling? Having a good reputation?

What work have you done or thought about doing in life?

What dimensions of work appeal to you most? Liking the people you work with? Communicating with others? Working alone? Working with others? Giving attention to detail? Solving problems creatively? Using specific skills? Being successful? Having flexibility? Having structured work expectations? Maintaining predictability? Helping others? Having opportunities to get ahead? Being productive? Making lots of money? Being a leader? Fitting in? Being challenged?

What jobs or careers come to mind? Which, if any, have you given any thought to?

Your answers may be vague or specific at this point, depending on where you are in your decision-making process. You may know more about what jobs you don't want (e.g., fast-food restaurant worker, waitress or waiter, pizza delivery person, factory worker, or cashier) because of prior experience in minimum-wage or close to minimum-wage jobs that you know you don't want to do for the rest of your working life.

Why are you taking the course that requires this book? Is it to fulfill some general education requirement? Is it because you're mildly interested in the topic? Or is it because you think this might be the major for you?

## 2. People-oriented versus non–people-oriented careers (exploring your options)

What types of things tend to interest you?

Do you enjoy being with others? Or do you prefer being by yourself?

Are you interested in human relationships, issues such as mental health, health, and women's concerns; and problems such as substance abuse, child maltreatment, and crime?

Do people tend to come to you to talk about their problems? Do you enjoy "helping" people?

If you say yes to these questions, then you might consider occupations that deal with people and continue the career consideration process addressed here. Non–people-oriented career courses might include those such as engineering, accounting, biology, chemistry, or computer science. Of course, it's not that you don't have to work with people in those jobs. Relating to and communicating with others in the work environment is always important. However, in non–people-oriented careers, the focus and goal are accomplishing specific tasks using specific skills, not interpersonal interaction and problem solving.

## 3. Ways of working with people

In what capacities do you think you'd like to work with people? Are you more interested in physical, business, legal, educational, spiritual, or psychosocial aspects?

Examples of hands-on work with people include being a medical doctor, nursing, **occupational therapy** (OT) (treatment that uses creative activity to improve psychological or physical rehabilitation), and **physical therapy** (PT) "the treatment of disease, injury, or deformity by physical methods such as massage, heat treatment, and exercise rather than by drugs or surgery" (Lindberg, 2007, p. 1034). These fields also have varying requirements in science, so you probably should have some interest in this area.

Many business careers also focus on developing relationships, but, of course, with the ultimate goal of

*(continued)*

**FOCUS ON CRITICAL THINKING 1.3 (continued)**

making a monetary profit instead of helping people improve their life conditions. To what extent is your ultimate goal to earn large amounts of money instead of having impacts on the human condition? This is a significant issue. One family comes to mind in which almost all members have various types of business degrees. They can't understand why I might be interested in how to address human problems such as child maltreatment, sexual assault, or mental illness. They cringe when I talk about watching movies about such issues. They think of these issues as someone else's problem and focus their energies on their own families, finances, and lives. Social work would not be their preferred field. Each of us must follow our own calling.

Law or teaching provides other career options. Law, of course, requires a serious interest in the legal process and more years of study beyond the bachelor's degree. In my school we see many students deciding between social work and teaching. They must determine whether they're more interested in helping children learn information and skills, or in working with clients and their families to help them deal with psychological, behavioral, and economic issues. Students more interested in pursuing a spiritual career such as rabbi, priest, or minister might seek education preparing them for such religious callings. One person comes to mind who, after receiving his master's degree in meteorology, decided that he really wanted to be a minister and attained a degree in divinity four years later.

If you're primarily interested in psychosocial aspects of human functioning and improving the human condition, continue reading the next section.

## 4. Selection of a major

To what extent do you understand the differences among fields addressing psychosocial issues such as social work, psychology, sociology, psychiatry, criminal justice, or counseling? How can you determine which field is for you?

If you decide you want to work with people concerning psychosocial issues, it's best to talk with advisers in the various majors available to you at your school. Think about what aspects of a major appeal to you most. Find out what kind of jobs its graduates tend to get. Explore what courses make up the curriculum, and determine the extent to which the major will give you the values, knowledge, and skills necessary for you to "hit the ground running" when you get your first job after graduating. Does it prepare you with skills such as interviewing, running groups and meetings, and working within organizations? Does the major provide a significant field internship to help prepare you for work with clients? To what extent does each major you're considering match your values, interests, and goals?

Understanding the primary focus of various majors can be confusing. Just a few alternatives will be mentioned here. Generally speaking, **psychology** emphasizes the study of behavior and cognitive processing (Barker, 2003). Work is often associated with treatment of mental disorders or testing people for intelligence or aptitude. A master's or Ph.D. degree is required to provide psychotherapy. **Sociology** is the study of human society, how various groups interact with each other, and how social institutions structure the social environment in which we live. **Social work** uses a significant amount of the knowledge produced both by sociology and psychology, and applies it to helping situations. Figure 1.1 illustrates the broad range of foundation knowledge contributing to social work practice. **Psychiatry** is the branch of medicine that specializes in the diagnosis and treatment of mental disorders. Psychiatrists must have advanced training beyond a medical degree and assume responsibility for diagnosing mental illness and prescribing psychotropic drugs. **Criminal justice** is the configuration of programs, policies, and agencies dealing with crime, incarceration, legal processes, and the rehabilitation of criminal offenders. Social workers can assume a wide range of positions in the criminal justice system. **Counseling** is a field overlapping various other fields, including social work, which focuses on problem solving and providing help to individuals, families, or groups. Often it involves additional education and expertise such as that in marriage and family therapy. Many social workers in clinical practice also are licensed marriage and family therapists. Generally, counseling focuses on providing some kind of psychotherapy, whereas social work also emphasizes the importance of the social environment concerning human behavior and advocacy to improve people's quality of life.

An issue related to choice of major involves the extent to which you're interested in attending graduate school. Some career paths require graduate education. Graduate school raises more questions. To what extent do you think you'll be tired of school by the time you graduate? So many seniors tell me they can't wait "to get out" and "work to make money" instead of doing schoolwork and spending money on tuition. To what

*(continued)*

**FOCUS ON CRITICAL THINKING 1.3** *(continued)*

extent is graduate school financially feasible? Do you have access to funding or loans? To what extent are you already financially burdened? What, if any, is your motivation to attend graduate school? Is your grade point average sufficient to be accepted?

If you decide to consider social work as a major or have already declared this major, the next section addresses some choices within the realm of social work.

## 5. Considering or choosing a social work major

Because social workers practice in so many different settings and work with so many kinds of people, it can be daunting trying to decide what field of practice is right for you. Such a struggle makes sense when you still know little about all the types of social work settings available. How can you make an informed choice without adequate information? Many students, even as they complete their major, have difficulty deciding what they prefer even as they enter a supervised field practicum within an agency setting. Usually, however, by that time students have narrowed their preferences considerably. It takes time to think things through as you acquire more information about the field and gain broader experiences.

The following list should at least give you an idea of the social work career options available. At this point, what interests you the most? What settings are most attractive to you? What client populations, problems, and issues concern you most? What are your reactions to considering work in the following settings, which are just a sampling of those available?

- Mental health settings such as inpatient hospitals, where people experience and seek treatment for various mental health problems.
- Health settings such as hospitals, where people need help understanding complex information and getting the appropriate resources.
- Settings aimed at enhancing the welfare of children, including protective services, adoption, foster care, school social work, and treatment for behavioral and emotional difficulties in outpatient, group home, or residential facilities.
- Settings for older adults, such as health-care facilities where older adults who require physical and medical support live, or supportive services aimed at keeping people in their own homes as long as possible.
- Agencies providing services to people with physical disabilities, including linking them to

appropriate services and advocating for services when necessary.
- Correctional settings for adults or juvenile delinquents, such as prisons where social workers help inmates by providing counseling and assisting in inmates' adjustment to the correctional environment or preparation for release, and probation or parole offices where they monitor the behavior of people released into the community.
- Domestic violence hotlines and programs addressing the needs of women who have been physically and emotionally abused.
- Counseling programs for alcohol and other substance abuse.
- Services for people with intellectual disabilities, such as those aimed at linking them to needed services, supervising noninstitutional living settings such as group homes, helping them gain employment, and advocating for resources that are unavailable.
- Crisis hotlines, where a wide range of crises, including threats of suicide or violence toward others, mental health and substance abuse, issues, or physical abuse are addressed and referrals to appropriate services made.
- Family planning agencies that help people make choices about contraception.
- Homeless shelters that provide temporary shelter, counseling, and training for people on the street.

Another facet of thinking about your career involves the types of responsibilities characterizing a work setting and the skills needed to practice effectively in it. What are your thoughts about undertaking the following?

- counseling
- running groups
- working with families
- linking people with needed resources
- coordinating service provision for people receiving multiple services through case management
- supervising staff or administering agencies
- supervising volunteers
- undertaking community organization
- running meetings
- writing grants
- developing policy
- promoting
- lobbying

There are lots of things to consider. Choosing a career is not easy.

# THEORETICAL WAYS OF VIEWING SOCIAL WORK: A FOCUS ON SYSTEMS IN THE ENVIRONMENT

Theoretical approaches provide ways of organizing information and looking at the world. For example, the **medical model** is a theoretical approach characterized by four major features (Barker, 2014). First, the focus of attention is the individual, who is seen as having something wrong, such as an illness. Therefore, treatment focuses on curing or helping the individual. Second, little attention is paid to factors outside the individual in his or her environment. The individual, not the environment, is the target of change. Third, the problem or illness is identified or diagnosed and categorized by placing a label on it. Fourth, the individual is the target of treatment that usually involves a series of clinical treatments.

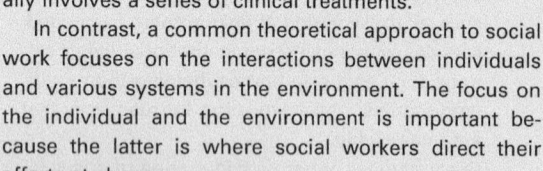

EP 1, 7a, 8a

In contrast, a common theoretical approach to social work focuses on the interactions between individuals and various systems in the environment. The focus on the individual and the environment is important because the latter is where social workers direct their efforts at change.

This system- and environment-oriented approach, called **ecosystems theory**, is particularly relevant to social work (Beckett & Johnson, 1995; McNutt, 2008). It combines some of the major concepts from two different theoretical perspectives: the ecological approach and systems theories.

## Important Concepts in Systems Theories

**Systems theories** focus on the dynamics among and interactions of people in their environment. A **system** is a set of elements that are orderly and interrelated to make a functional whole. Social work refers primarily to social systems composed of people (as opposed to, say, an industrial manufacturing system or an ant colony system). An individual, a family, a social services agency, and a neighborhood are all examples of systems.

Social workers work with and on the behalf of various sized systems. A **micro system** is an individual, and a **mezzo system** a group. Families, because of their intimate nature, arbitrarily lie somewhere between micro and mezzo systems. A **macro system** includes organizations and communities. Working with micro systems is considered **micro practice**, with mezzo systems **mezzo practice**, and with macro systems **macro practice**. This terminology is important because it's used throughout social work and this book.

## Target Systems and Client Systems

It's helpful to conceptualize social workers and clients in terms of systems. A **target system** or **target of change**

is the system that social workers need "to change or influence in order to accomplish [their] goals" (Pincus & Minahan, 1973, p. 58). Targets of change may be individual clients, families, formal groups, administrators, or policymakers. At the micro level, a 5-year-old child with behavioral problems might be the target of change, the goal being to improve behavior. At the mezzo level, a support group of people with eating disorders might be the target of change in an attempt to control their eating behavior.[2] Finally, at the macro level, an agency director might be the target of change when the social worker's aim is to improve some agency policy and the director is the primary decision maker capable of implementing that change.

Another system critical to the planned-change process is the **client system**—any individual, family, group, organization, or community that will ultimately benefit from social work intervention (Pincus & Minahan, 1973; Resnick, 1980a; Resnick, 1980b). For example, individual clients are client systems when the social worker's goal is to get them needed resources. Families are client systems when the practitioner is working on behalf of the entire family. Similarly, a community is the client system when a social worker is trying to help residents open a new community center to improve their quality of life.

## Important Ecological Concepts

Two important concepts taken from the ecological approach are the social environment and coping. The **social environment** includes the conditions, circumstances, and interactions that encompass human beings. Individuals must have effective interactions with their environment to survive and thrive. The social environment involves the type of home a person lives in, the type of work a person does, the amount of money that is available, and the laws and social rules people live by. The social environment also includes the individuals, groups, organizations, and systems with which a person comes into contact, such as family, friends, work groups, and governments.

**Coping** is the struggle to adjust to environmental conditions and overcome problems. This is significant because social workers often help people cope with problems in their environments.

---

[2]Eating disorders, extremely serious disturbances in eating patterns, are considered mental disorders by the American Psychiatric Association (APA) (APA, 2013). Examples include anorexia and bulimia.

## Professional Values

The fourth dimension that makes social work unique is its emphasis on and adherence to a core of professional values. The NASW *Code of Ethics* focuses on the right of the individual to make free choices and have a quality life (NASW, 2008). Social workers do not force people into specific ways of thinking or acting. Rather, they help people make their own decisions about how to think or act.

**EP 1, 1a**

## Partnership with Clients

The fifth dimension making social work unique is related to the core of social work values and how important it is for clients to make their own decisions. Social workers do not track people into specific ways of thinking or acting. Rather, they practice in a **partnership** with clients, making and implementing plans together. Most other professions emphasize the authority and expertise of the professional, on the one hand, and the subordinate status of the client as recipient of services, on the other.

**EP 7c, 8e**

# Accredited Social Work Programs

**LO 10**

One way of understanding social work is to review the content and expectations evident in the curricula of accredited social work programs. The Council on

Social Work Education (CSWE) is the organization that accredits social work programs throughout the United States. **Accreditation** is the official designation by an authorized body (in this case, CSWE) that an educational program meets specified standards. This is usually required in becoming licensed as a social worker (described more thoroughly in Chapter 5).

**EP 1**

To begin with, CSWE's Educational Policy and Accreditation Standards (EPAS) emphasize that social work programs must reflect certain values throughout their curricula. The EPAS states that social work's purpose "is to promote human and community well-being"; this purpose "is actualized through its quest for social and economic justice, the prevention of conditions that limit human rights, the elimination of poverty, and the enhancement of the quality of life for all persons, locally and globally" (CSWE, 2015, p. 1). The EPAS also specifies the nine areas in which graduates of social work programs must display competency. These are discussed in the following section. Subsequently, the core social work concepts of generalist practice, advanced practice, and field education will be introduced.

## Social Workers Demonstrate Competencies

**Competencies** are measurable behaviors that reflect social workers' acquisition of required knowledge, skills, and values so that they can demonstrate effective social work practice. Highlight 1.4 summarizes the nine required competencies for accredited social

---

| HIGHLIGHT 1.4 | SOCIAL WORKERS DEMONSTRATE COMPETENCIES |
|---|---|

CSWE (2015) requires that social work graduates demonstrate competency in the following nine major areas.

### Educational Policy Competencies

Social workers must:

1. Demonstrate ethical and professional behavior.
2. Engage diversity and difference in practice.
3. Advance human rights and social, economic, and environmental justice.
4. Engage in research-informed practice and practice-informed research.
5. Engage in policy practice.
6. Engage with individuals, families, groups, organizations, and communities.
7. Assess individuals, families, groups, organizations, and communities.
8. Intervene with individuals, families, groups, organizations, and communities.
9. Evaluate practice with individuals, families, groups, organizations, and communities. (pp. 3–9)

work programs. The subsequent sections summarize each competency. Highlight 1.5 at the end of the chapter cites parts of the EPAS directly.

### Competency 1: Demonstrate Ethical and Professional Behavior

Social workers should abide by the profession's ethical standards, use critical thinking skills in their practice, understand the profession's history and mission, comprehend the roles of other professions, and appreciate the significance of lifelong learning. They should identify personal values and not allow such values to interfere with professional practice. Practitioners should display a "professional demeanor" in behavior, appearance, and communication. They should be knowledgeable about developing technology and use it appropriately. Finally, they should seek help from supervisors and consultants when needed.

EP 1

### Competency 2: Engage Diversity and Difference in Practice

**Diversity** refers to the wide variety of differences characterizing people. People meriting special attention from the social work profession include, but are not limited to, groups distinguished by "age, class, color, culture, disability and ability, ethnicity, gender, gender identity and expression, immigration status, marital status, political ideology, race, religion/spirituality, sex, sexual orientation, and tribal sovereign status" (CSWE, 2015, p. 4). Any time a person can be identified as belonging to a group that differs in some respect from the majority of others in society, that person is subject to the effects of human diversity.

EP 2

Because social workers have a wide variety of clients, demonstrating almost every type of need and problem, they must be integrally familiar with the concept of human diversity. Three facets are especially significant. First, social workers must appreciate how diversity and various events mold life experiences at the personal, family, social, economic, and political levels. Second, practitioners should actively learn from their clients, who are most knowledgeable about their own lives. Third, social workers should strive to identify any personal preconceptions about people in a diverse group and regulate the influence of such values on their practice. Chapter 3

examines various aspects of human diversity in more depth.

### Competency 3: Advance Human Rights and Social, Economic, and Environmental Justice

The concepts of human rights in addition to social, economic, and environmental justice are related to the concept of human diversity. **Human rights** involve the premise that all people, regardless of race, culture, or national origin, are entitled to basic rights and treatment. **Social justice** is the idea that in a perfect world all citizens would have identical "rights, protection, opportunities, obligations, and social benefits" (Barker, 2014, p. 398). Similarly, **economic justice** involves the distribution of resources in a fair and equitable manner. **Environmental justice** is "the fair treatment and meaningful involvement of all people regardless of race, color, national origin, or income with respect to the development, implementation, and enforcement of environmental laws, regulations, and policies" (U.S. Environmental Protection Agency [EPA], 2015). In other words, everyone should be equally protected from exposure to risks in the environment that may endanger their health. Social work graduates must demonstrate competency in understanding these concepts and their theoretical frameworks; social workers must advocate on the behalf of these principles and incorporate the principles into their practice (CSWE, 2015, p. 5).

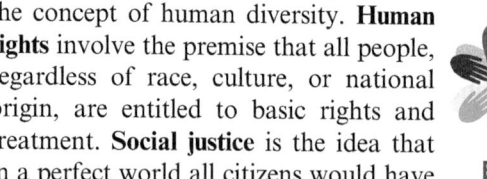

EP 3

Another important concept in social work is **populations at risk**, groups of people with some identified characteristics who are at greater risk of social and economic deprivation than those in the mainstream. Because social work practice involves getting people resources and helping them solve problems, social workers frequently work with populations at risk of such deprivations. It follows that social workers need information and insight concerning these people's special issues and needs. Therefore, social workers require both theoretical and practice content concerning the dynamics and results of differential, unfair treatment.

One especially important social work value is **empowerment**—the "process of increasing personal, interpersonal, or political power so that individuals can take action to improve their life situations" (Gutierrez, 2001, p. 210). Some groups of people suffer from stereotypes, discrimination, and oppression.

It is social work's task to empower clients in general and members of oppressed groups in particular.

### Competency 4: Engage in Practice-Informed Research and Research-Informed Practice

Social work students should be able to engage in **practice-informed research**. This means they should understand research techniques and be able to apply them in their own practice. When possible, they should participate in research where the goal is to enhance effective practice. This research, which closely involves the everyday work of practitioners, focuses on collecting data and providing results directly related to the processes of social work practice (Tripodi & Lalayants, 2008, p. 518).

**EP 4**

Research techniques include quantitative and qualitative techniques. "*Quantitative research methods* emphasize the production of precise and generalizable statistical findings" (Rubin & Babbie, 2014, p. 79). They include "experiments, survey research, and investigations that make use of numerical comparisons" (Barker, 2014, p. 350). "*Qualitative research methods* are more likely to tap the deeper meanings of particular human experiences and generate theoretically richer observations that are not easily reduced to numbers" (Rubin & Babbie, 2014, p. 79). Frequently used qualitative methods include "direct observation" and "intensive interviewing" (Rubin & Babbie, 2014, p. 669). One example of qualitative research is a field study where researchers go out into the field and conduct interviews to gather information or make other observations; another example is a "study and description of the behavior patterns of specific cultures or groups of people" (Barker, 2014, p. 147).

Social work programs have traditionally included a "Social Work Research" course or sequence of courses in their curricula that includes content on quantitative and qualitative research methods. Such a research course also includes content on evaluating a social worker's own practice. Note that throughout their careers, social workers should continue to monitor and learn new research methodology and approaches to effective practice. They should continuously evaluate their own ability to achieve their goals and initiate positive changes for clients.

Social work students must also demonstrate competency in **research-informed practice**. This means social workers should use the approaches and interventions in their practice that research has determined are effective. Social workers should employ critical thinking in using "research evidence to inform and improve practice, policy, and service delivery" (CSWE, 2015, p. 5).

**EP 4b**

Knowledge of social work research is important for two basic reasons. First, it can help social workers become more effective in their direct practice by choosing interventions that have been proven successful, thereby getting better and clearer results. Framing social work interventions so they can be evaluated through research provides information about which specific techniques work best with which problems. Evaluation of practice throughout the intervention process can help determine whether a worker is really helping a client.

Second, accumulated research helps build a foundation for planning effective interventions. Knowledge of what has worked best in the past provides guidelines for approaches and techniques to be used in the present and in the future. Research establishes the basis for the development of programs and policies that affect many people. Such knowledge can also be used to generate new theories and ideas to further enhance the effectiveness of social work practice.

*Evidence-Based Practice*    Another term frequently used in social work, which has a meaning similar to research-informed practice, is **evidence-based practice**. This is "the conscientious, explicit, and judicious use of current best evidence in making decisions about the care of clients" (Gambrill, 2000, p. 46; Gambrill & Gibbs, 2009; Race, 2008; Rubin & Babbie, 2014). Gambrill (2000) explains:

*It involves integrating individual practice expertise with the best available external evidence from systematic research as well as considering the values and expectations of clients. External research findings related to problems are drawn on if they are available and they apply to a particular client. Involving clients as informed participants in a collaborative helping relationship is a hallmark of evidence-based practice. Clients are fully informed about the risks and benefits of recommended services as well as alternatives (including the alternative of doing nothing) ... The term evidence-based practice is preferable to the term empirical practice. The latter term now seems to be applied to material that has been published, whether or not it is evidence-based. Such use represents an appeal to authority (not evidence). (pp. 46–47)*

*Content of Social Work Research* The content of social work research tends to fall within four major categories (Reid, 1995; Tripodi & Lalayants, 2008). First, many studies involve the behavior of individual clients and their interactions with others close to them, including families and small groups. Second, much research focuses on how services are provided to clients, what such services involve, and how successfully they accomplish their goals. Third, some studies address social workers' attitudes and educational backgrounds, in addition to major trends in the profession. Fourth, some research involves the study of larger systems such as organizations or communities, in addition to the social policies that affect them (Reid, 1995). This latter category emphasizes the importance of the more extensive social environment and its effects on clients' behavior and conditions.

## Competency 5: Engage in Policy Practice

Social workers must understand social welfare policies, their history, and how they affect work with clients. Policy, in its simplest form, can be thought of as **rules**. Our lives and those of social workers' clients are governed by rules—about how we drive our cars, when we go to school, how we talk or write sentences, and so on. (Note that  **EP 5** Chapter 6 explores the history of social welfare policy development.)

**Policies**, in essence, are rules that tell us which actions among a multitude of actions we may take and which we may not. Policies guide our work and our decisions. For the purpose of understanding social welfare and the provision of social welfare services, policy might be divided into two major categories: social welfare policy and agency policy. **Social welfare policies** are the laws and regulations that govern which social welfare programs exist, what categories of clients are served, and who qualifies for a given program. They also set standards regarding the type of services to be provided and the qualifications of the service provider.

In addition to the broader realm of social welfare policies, **agency policies** are standards adopted by individual organizations and programs that provide services (e.g., a family service agency, a department of human services, or a nursing home). Such standards may specify the agency's structure, the qualifications of supervisors and workers, the rules governing what workers can do, and the proper procedures for completing a family assessment.

Knowledge of policy and critical thinking about its effectiveness are vital for social workers. An organization's policy can dictate how much vacation an employee can have and how raises are earned. An adoption agency's policy can determine who is eligible to adopt a child. A social program's policies determine who gets needed services and resources.  **EP 5c**

Social workers must become actively involved in establishing and changing social welfare policies for the benefit of their clients; policies determine how money is budgeted and spent, and where resources are made available for clients. Practitioners must be competent in undertaking policy practice to enhance people's well-being and deliver effective social work services. **Policy practice** involves "efforts to change policies in legislative, agency, and community settings, whether by establishing new policies, improving existing ones, or defeating the policy initiatives of other people" (Jansson, 2014, p. 1).

Sometimes, for whatever reason, social welfare policies are unfair or oppressive to clients. Ironically, although such policies are intended to enhance people's welfare, sometimes they do not. A social worker may decide that a policy is ethically or morally intolerable and advocate on the behalf of clients to try to change it. Practitioners can work to change policy to advance social and economic justice and provide fair treatment to a wide range of people. Traditional social work curricula typically include a course or sequence of courses on "Social Welfare Policy and Services."

Social welfare policy sets the stage for what social workers can do in practice; Chapter 7 explores the topic more thoroughly. Other chapters discuss many types of social welfare policies that affect various client populations and social work practices.

## Competency 6: Engage with Individuals, Families, Groups, Organizations, and Communities

Social work students must demonstrate that they have the knowledge and skills to work with individuals, families, groups, organizations, and communities. Earlier we defined an individual as a micro system, a group as a mezzo system, a family as a micro or mezzo system, and organizations and communities as macro systems. Human relationships are essential when working with any of these systems and trying to get things done. Working with an individual or family, a social worker might serve as a counselor to solve problems or a broker to get resources. In mezzo practice, a practitioner **EP 6** might run various types of groups (e.g., support, therapy, educational).

In macro practice, social workers must work within organizational settings. They must abide by policies established by the agency and the government. They also must be able to work with agency personnel to change policies and practices when necessary. Social workers may also involve themselves in policy practice to change public policies at the local, state, and national levels. Finally, social workers work within the context of communities and often establish goals with residents to improve their quality of life (for example, increase service provision, establish a homeless shelter, or work together to improve neighborhoods by making them safer).

Another important concept in this competency is that social workers should be able to engage with any of these systems. **Engagement** is the initial period when practitioners orient themselves to the problem at hand and begin to establish communication and relationships with others also addressing the problem. You might look at social work as a planned change or problem-solving process. This process of social work practice can be structured into at least six steps (Chapter 4 discusses each in greater depth.):

1. engagement
2. assessment
3. planning
4. intervention
5. evaluation
6. termination

Traditional social work curricula typically incorporate a sequence of "Social Work Practice" courses that address these steps and teach the *doing* of social work. In the first stage of this process, engagement, students must learn to use "empathy, reflection, and [other] interpersonal skills to effectively engage diverse clients" (CSWE, 2015, p. 7).

In order to form relationships with clients and others, social workers must be knowledgeable about human behavior and how people function within their social environments. In order to empathize with clients and others, practitioners must be aware of how people's lives are shaped by their diverse situations and experiences. "Human Behavior and the Social Environment" is the basis for another course or sequence of courses traditionally included in the social work curriculum. HBSE focuses on various theoretical frameworks for understanding human development and behavior, explores issues often facing people throughout their life span, and examines social problems in the environment.

## Competency 7: Assess Individuals, Families, Groups, Organizations, and Communities

**Assessment** is the investigation and determination of variables affecting an identified problem including the client system's needs and strengths. It involves the "nature and extent of client needs and concerns, as well as critical information about client resources and supports and other environmental factors" so that a helping plan can be **EP 7** devised and implemented (Blythe & Reithoffer, 2000, p. 551).

In order to conduct assessments, social workers must be knowledgeable about human behavior and the social environment. People are constantly and dynamically involved in ongoing activity and communication with others in the environment. We have established that focusing on people's functioning within the environmental context is important in the engagement phase of social work practice. It is especially important during the assessment phase. Only after assessing and understanding people's ability to function can social workers proceed with an intervention plan.

Social work assessment seeks to discover what in any particular situation causes a problem to continue despite the client's expressed wish to change it. Focusing on the environment means more than looking at only the individuals themselves. It also involves exploring the client system's involvement with family members, neighbors, work colleagues, the political system, and agencies providing services within the community. This means that clients' problems are not viewed solely as their own fault. The forces surrounding the client frequently cause or contribute to problems, so social workers must focus their assessment on many levels. How the client and the problem fit into the larger scheme of things is critical. Poverty, discrimination, social pressures, and the effects of social welfare policies are all aspects of people's lives that can fall under scrutiny.

Focus on Critical Thinking 1.4 provides an example of how social workers might focus on the environmental context of a problem.

## FOCUSING ON THE ENVIRONMENTAL CONTEXT OF PROBLEMS

Trevor is a 15-year-old gang member in an inner city. The gang is involved in drug dealing, which, of course, is illegal. However, when assessing the situation and potential actions, a broader perspective is necessary. Looking at how the environment encourages and even supports the illegal activity is critical in understanding how to solve the problem. Trevor's father is no longer involved with Trevor's family. Now it's only Trevor, his mother, and three younger brothers. Trevor's mother works a six-day-per-week, nine-hour-per-day second-shift job at Harry's Hole, a local all-night diner, where she slings burgers. Although she loves her children dearly, she can barely make ends meet and has little time to supervise them.

All of the neighborhood kids belong to one gang or another. It gives them a sense of identity and importance, and it provides social support that often is lacking in their families. Easy access to drugs offers an opportunity to escape from impoverished, depressing, and apparently hopeless conditions. Finally, gang membership gives these young people a source of income. In fact, they can get relatively large amounts of money in a hurry.

**EP 7b, 8b**

The gang members' alternatives appear grim. There are few, if any, positive role models to show them other ways of existence. They don't see their peers or adults close to them becoming corporate lawyers, surgeons, or nuclear physicists. They don't even see anyone who is going or has gone to college. In fact, finishing high school is considered quite a feat. Neighborhood unemployment runs at more than 50%. A few part-time, minimum-wage jobs are available—cleaning washrooms at Bugger's Burger Bungalow or unloading freight at Shirley's Shop-Right. But these are unappealing alternatives to the immediate sources of gratification and income provided by gang membership and drug dealing. Even if another minimal source of income could be found, the other rewarding aspects of gang membership would be lost. Also, there's the all-consuming problem of having no positive future to look forward to, so the excitement of the present remains seductive.

This is not to say that it's right for people like Trevor to join vicious gangs and participate in illegal activities.

Nor does it mean that Trevor's plight is hopeless. Going beyond a focus on the individual to assess the many environmental impacts and interactions gives the social worker a better understanding of the whole situation. The answer might not be to send Trevor to the state juvenile correctional facility for a year or two and then return him to the same community with the same friends and same problems. Such a "remedy" focuses on the individual in a very limited manner.

A social work perspective views Trevor as a person who's acting as part of a family and a community. Trevor is affected, influenced, supported, and limited by his immediate environment. Continuing along this line of thought, other questions can be raised: How might Trevor's environment be changed? What other alternatives could be made available to him?

Many alternatives would involve major changes in the larger systems around him. Neighborhood youth centers with staff serving as positive role models could be developed as an alternative to gang membership. Trevor's school system could be evaluated. Does it have enough resources to give him a good education? Is there a teacher who could serve as his mentor and enthusiastic supporter? Can a mentorship system be established within the school? Are scholarships and loans available to offer him a viable alternative of college or trade school? Can positive role models demonstrate to Trevor and his peers that other ways of life may be open to them? Where might the resources for implementation of any of these ideas come from?

Concerning Trevor's family environment, can additional resources be provided? These might include food and housing assistance, quality day care for his younger brothers, and even educational opportunities for Trevor's mother so that she, too, could see a brighter future. Is there a Big Brother organization to provide support for Trevor and his siblings? Can the neighborhood be made a better place to live? Can crime be curbed and housing conditions improved?

There obviously are no easy answers. Scarcity of resources remains a fundamental problem. However, this illustration is intended to show how a social worker would look at a variety of options and targets of change, and not just at Trevor.

## Competency 8: Intervene with Individuals, Families, Groups, Organizations, and Communities

**Intervention** is the planning and implementation of a strategy to solve the problem and achieve goals. Social workers must be knowledgeable about what evidence-based practice approaches and techniques are most effective in specific situations. What is the most effective plan of action? They then must establish plans for the intervention that guide their work toward goal achievement. Practitioners must also work with other involved professionals because teamwork is typically necessary to achieve the most positive ends.

EP 8

Intervention requires knowledge about specifically *what* to do and *how* to do it. The social work knowledge base includes information about skills in addition to data concerning problems and services. A social worker must know what skills will be most effective in what situations.

Consider a family whose home suddenly burns to the ground. Its members need immediate shelter. The social worker decides it's necessary to use brokering skills—that is, skills for seeking out and linking people with the resources they need. In this situation, brokering skills take precedence over other skills. For instance, using less directive counseling techniques to explore the relationship between the spouses is inappropriate at this time because there is no current evidence of need. Such intervention may be necessary in the future, but only after the immediate crisis of a lack of shelter has been resolved.

Social workers can choose from a multitude of practice techniques and theories about these techniques. We have established that knowledge of the effectiveness of various techniques is critical to selecting those that can accomplish the most in a given situation and to implementing research-informed practice (Competency 4). Regardless of techniques chosen and used, emphasis is placed on client strengths and empowerment, ongoing client collaboration at all stages of the change process, and appreciation of diversity.

## Competency 9: Evaluate Practice with Individuals, Families, Groups, Organizations, and Communities

**Evaluation** is the process of determining the extent to which a given intervention was effective in achieving its goals. We have established that social workers must understand quantitative and qualitative research methodology and results so they might apply findings to enhance effective practice. Practitioners must also be able to evaluate the effectiveness of their own practice.

EP 9

Royse (2011) speaks directly to social workers about their need for **accountability** (a profession's responsibility to clients and the community that workers are effectively doing what they say they are going to do):

*Social workers are accountable for their interventions. As a professional, you must be able to determine whether the intervention you are using with a client is making any difference. Could you demonstrate that the client is improving? Or, at the very least, could you show that your intervention has not harmed the client? Even if you are not interested in conducting research on a large scale, you owe it to your clients and yourself to be able to evaluate your practice with them. (p. 7)*

We have already indicated that Highlight 1.5 at the end of the chapter cites the nine competencies and their component behaviors directly. The next section describes three other basic concepts underlying the social work curriculum.

## Other Basic Concepts Underlying the Social Work Curriculum

The EPAS also elaborates on the basic concepts underlying the social work curriculum. These include generalist practice, specialized practice, and field education (CSWE, 2015, pp. 10–11).

### Generalist Practice

Generalist practice incorporates all nine competencies and forms the heart of social work education and social work practice. It distinguishes social work from other professions. **Generalist practice** is the application of an eclectic[3] knowledge base, professional values, and a wide range of skills to target any size system for change within the context of four primary processes (Kirst-Ashman & Hull, 2015b). First, generalist practice emphasizes client empowerment. They "engage diversity in their practice and

---

[3]The term *eclectic* refers to "selecting what appears to be best in various doctrines, methods, or styles" (Mish, 2008, p. 394).

advocate for human rights and social and economic justice" (CSWE, 2015, p. 10). Second, it involves working effectively within an organizational structure and doing so under supervision. Third, it requires the assumption of a wide range of professional roles. Fourth, it involves the application of critical thinking skills to the planned-change (intervention) process. Chapter 4 elaborates further on generalist practice. Note that BSW programs prepare graduates for generalist practice by providing curricula that integrate all nine competencies (CSWE, 2015).

## Specialized Practice

Specialized practice, which characterizes MSW curricula, provides an advanced concentration that builds upon a generalist practice foundation. Therefore, "[m]aster's programs prepare students for both generalist practice and specialized practice" (CSWE, 2015, p. 10). For instance, concentrations might include a specialization in mental health, school social work, work with children and families, corrections, health, social services administration, or community organization.

## Field Education

Field education is considered the "signature pedagogy" of social work education by CSWE; signature pedagogy is the primary means of socializing professionals to become part of their discipline (CSWE, 2015, p. 11). Field education provides the opportunity for students to put their social work knowledge, skills, and values into practice. It helps students integrate their classroom experience in a real-world context. There they can practice their skills in a learning environment under supervision.

Field placement settings may vary. They include social service agencies, hospitals, schools, correctional facilities, organizational placements such as a state NASW branch office, policy-related placements such as legislative offices, or placements in community organizations. Any of these settings must provide appropriate social work supervision. BSW placements currently require a minimum of 400 hours and MSW placements a minimum of 900 hours. Many social work students find their field education to be the high point of their educational experience.

## HIGHLIGHT 1.5  KNOWLEDGE, SKILLS, AND VALUES NECESSARY FOR EFFECTIVE SOCIAL WORK PRACTICE

In the *Educational Policy and Accreditation Standards* (EPAS), the Council on Social Work Education (2015) identified knowledge, skills, and values that accredited baccalaureate and master's degree programs are mandated to convey to social work students. The EPAS is based on a competency approach. The following material is reprinted with permission (CSWE, 2015, pp. 2–9):

Social work competence is the ability to integrate and apply social work knowledge, values, and skills to practice situations in a purposeful, intentional, and professional manner to promote human and community well-being.... Overall professional competence is multi-dimensional and composed of interrelated competencies....

Competency-based education is an outcomes-oriented approach to curriculum design. The goal of the outcomes approach is to ensure that students are able to demonstrate the integration and application of the competencies in practice. In the EPAS, social work practice competence consists of nine interrelated competencies and component behaviors that are comprised of knowledge, values, skills, and cognitive and affective processes....

**Social Work Competencies**

The nine Social Work Competencies are listed below.... Each competency describes the knowledge, values, skills, and cognitive and affective processes that comprise the competency at the generalist level of practice, followed by a set of behaviors that integrate these components. These behaviors represent observable components of the competencies, while the preceding statements represent the underlying content and processes that inform the behaviors.

*(continued)*

**HIGHLIGHT 1.5 (continued)**

### Competency 1—Demonstrate Ethical and Professional Behavior

Social workers understand the value base of the profession and its ethical standards, as well as relevant laws and regulations that may impact practice at the micro, mezzo, and macro levels. Social workers understand frameworks of ethical decision-making and how to apply principles of critical thinking to those frameworks in

EP 1, 1a-e

practice, research, and policy arenas. Social workers recognize personal values and the distinction between personal and professional values. They also understand how their personal experiences and affective reactions influence their professional judgment and behavior. Social workers understand the profession's history, its mission, and the roles and responsibilities of the profession. Social Workers also understand the role of other professions when engaged in inter-professional teams. Social workers recognize the importance of lifelong learning and are committed to continually updating their skills to ensure they are relevant and effective. Social workers also understand emerging forms of technology and the ethical use of technology in social work practice. Social workers:

[1a]  make ethical decisions by applying the standards of the NASW Code of Ethics, relevant laws and regulations, models for ethical decision making, ethical conduct of research, and additional codes of ethics as appropriate to context;

[1b]  use reflection and self-regulation to manage personal values and maintain professionalism in practice situations;

[1c]  demonstrate professional demeanor in behavior; appearance; and oral, written, and electronic communication;

[1d]  use technology ethically and appropriately to facilitate practice outcomes; and

[1e]  use supervision and consultation to guide professional judgment and behavior.

### Competency 2—Engage Diversity and Difference in Practice

Social workers understand how diversity and difference characterize and shape the human experience and are critical to the formation of identity. The dimensions of diversity are understood as the intersectionality of multiple factors including but not limited to age, class, color, culture, disability and ability, ethnicity, gender, gender identity and expression, immigration status, marital status, political ideology, race, religion/spirituality, sex, sexual orientation, and tribal sovereign status.

EP 2, 2a-c

Social workers understand that, as a consequence of difference, a person's life experiences may include oppression, poverty, marginalization, and alienation as well as privilege, power, and acclaim. Social workers also understand the forms and mechanisms of oppression and discrimination and recognize the extent to which a culture's structures and values, including social, economic, political, and cultural exclusions, may oppress, marginalize, alienate, or create privilege and power. Social workers:

[2a]  apply and communicate understanding of the importance of diversity and difference in shaping life experiences in practice at the micro, mezzo, and macro levels;

[2b]  present themselves as learners and engage clients and constituencies as experts of their own experiences; and

[2c]  apply self-awareness and self-regulation to manage the influence of personal biases and values in working with diverse clients and constituencies.

### Competency 3—Advance Human Rights and Social, Economic, and Environmental Justice

Social workers understand that every person regardless of position in society has fundamental human rights such as freedom, safety, privacy, an adequate standard of living, health care, and education. Social workers understand the global interconnections of oppression and human rights violations, and are knowledgeable about

EP 3, 3a-b

theories of human need and social justice and strategies to promote social and economic justice and human rights. Social workers understand strategies designed to eliminate oppressive

*(continued)*

**HIGHLIGHT 1.5** *(continued)*

structural barriers to ensure that social goods, rights, and responsibilities are distributed equitably and that civil, political, environmental, economic, social, and cultural human rights are protected. Social workers:

[3a]   apply their understanding of social, economic, and environmental justice to advocate for human rights at the individual and system levels; and

[3b]   engage in practices that advance social, economic, and environmental justice.

### Competency 4—Engage in Practice-Informed Research and Research-Informed Practice

Social workers understand quantitative and qualitative research methods and their respective roles in advancing a science of social work and in evaluating their practice. Social workers know the principles of logic, scientific inquiry, and culturally informed and ethical approaches to building knowledge. 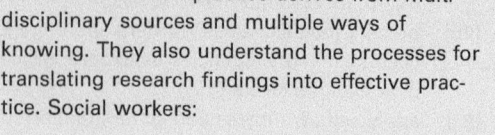 EP 4, 4a-c Social workers understand that evidence that informs practice derives from multidisciplinary sources and multiple ways of knowing. They also understand the processes for translating research findings into effective practice. Social workers:

[4a]   use practice experience and theory to inform scientific inquiry and research;

[4b]   apply critical thinking to engage in analysis of quantitative and qualitative research methods and research findings; and

[4c]   use and translate research evidence to inform and improve practice, policy, and service delivery.

### Competency 5—Engage in Policy Practice

Social workers understand that human rights and social justice, as well as social welfare and services, are mediated by policy and its implementation at the federal, state, and local levels. Social workers understand the history and current structures of social policies and services, the role of policy in service delivery, and the role of practice in policy development. Social workers understand

EP 5, 5a-c

their role in policy development and implementation within their practice settings at the micro, mezzo, and macro levels and they actively engage in policy practice to effect change within those settings. Social workers recognize and understand the historical, social, cultural, economic, organizational, environmental, and global influences that affect social policy. They are also knowledgeable about policy formulation, analysis, implementation, and evaluation. Social workers:

[5a]   Identify social policy at the local, state, and federal level that impacts well-being, service delivery, and access to social services;

[5b]   assess how social welfare and economic policies impact the delivery of and access to social services; and

[5c]   apply critical thinking to analyze, formulate, and advocate for policies that advance human rights and social, economic, and environmental justice.

### Competency 6—Engage with Individuals, Families, Groups, Organizations, and Communities

Social workers understand that engagement is an ongoing component of the dynamic and interactive process of social work practice with, and on behalf of, diverse individuals, families, groups, organizations, and communities. Social workers value the importance of human relationships. Social workers understand theories of human behavior and the social environment, and 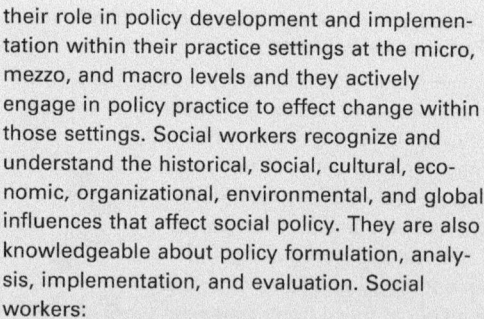 EP 6, 6a-b critically evaluate and apply this knowledge to facilitate engagement with clients and constituencies, including individuals, families, groups, organizations, and communities. Social workers understand strategies to engage diverse clients and constituencies to advance practice effectiveness. Social workers understand how their personal experiences and affective reactions may impact their ability to effectively engage with diverse clients and constituencies. Social workers value principles of relationship-building and interprofessional collaboration to facilitate engagement with clients, constituencies, and

*(continued)*

**HIGHLIGHT 1.5 *(continued)***

other professionals as appropriate. Social workers:

**[6a]**  apply knowledge of human behavior and the social environment, person-in-environment, and other multidisciplinary theoretical frameworks to engage with clients and constituencies; and

**[6b]**  use empathy, reflection, and interpersonal skills to effectively engage diverse clients and constituencies.

### *Competency 7—Assess Individuals, Families, Groups, Organizations, and Communities*

Social workers understand that assessment is an ongoing component of the dynamic and interactive process of social work practice with, and on behalf of, diverse individuals, families, groups, organizations, and communities. Social workers understand theories of human behavior and the social environment, and critically evaluate and apply this

**EP 7, 7a-d**

knowledge in the assessment of diverse clients and constituencies, including individuals, families, groups, organizations, and communities. Social workers understand methods of assessment with diverse clients and constituencies to advance practice effectiveness. Social workers recognize the implications of the larger practice context in the assessment process and value the importance of interprofessional collaboration in this process. Social workers understand how their personal experiences and affective reactions may affect their assessment and decision-making. Social workers:

**[7a]**  collect and organize data, and apply critical thinking to interpret information from clients and constituencies;

**[7b]**  apply knowledge of human behavior and the social environment, person-in-environment, and other multidisciplinary theoretical frameworks in the analysis of assessment data from clients and constituencies;

**[7c]**  develop mutually agreed-on intervention goals and objectives based on the critical assessment of strengths, needs, and challenges within clients and constituencies; and

**[7d]**  select appropriate intervention strategies based on the assessment, research knowledge, and values and preferences of clients and constituencies.

### *Competency 8—Intervene with Individuals, Families, Groups, Organizations, and Communities*

Social workers understand that intervention is an ongoing component of the dynamic and interactive process of social work practice with, and on behalf of, diverse individuals, families, groups, organizations, and communities. Social workers are knowledgeable about evidence-informed interventions to achieve the goals of clients and constituencies, including individuals, families, groups, organizations, and communities. Social workers understand theories of human behavior and the social environment, and critically evaluate and apply this knowledge to effectively intervene with clients and constituencies. Social workers understand methods of identifying, analyzing and implementing evidence-informed interventions to achieve client and constituency goals. Social workers value the importance of interprofessional teamwork and communication in interventions, recognizing that beneficial outcomes may require interdisciplinary, interprofessional, and interorganizational collaboration. Social workers:

**EP 8, 8a-e**

**[8a]**  critically choose and implement interventions to achieve practice goals and enhance capacities of clients and constituencies;

**[8b]**  apply knowledge of human behavior and the social environment, person-in-environment, and other multidisciplinary theoretical frameworks in interventions with clients and constituencies;

**[8c]**  use interprofessional collaboration as appropriate to achieve beneficial practice outcomes;

**[8d]**  negotiate, mediate, and advocate with and on behalf of diverse clients and constituencies; and

**[8e]**  facilitate effective transitions and endings that advance mutually agreed-on goals.

*(continued)*

**HIGHLIGHT 1.5** *(continued)*

*Competency 9—Evaluate Practice with Individuals, Families, Groups, Organizations, and Communities*
Social workers understand that evaluation is an ongoing component of the dynamic and interactive process of social work practice with, and on behalf of, diverse individuals, families, groups, organizations and communities. Social workers recognize the importance of evaluating processes and outcomes to advance practice, policy, and service delivery effectiveness. Social workers understand theories of human behavior and the social environment, and critically evaluate and apply this knowledge in evaluating outcomes. Social workers

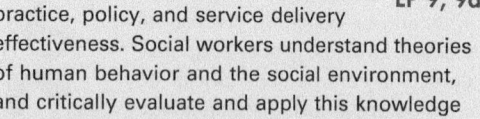

EP 9, 9a-d

understand qualitative and quantitative methods for evaluating outcomes and practice effectiveness. Social workers:

[9a]   select and use appropriate methods for evaluation of outcomes;

[9b]   apply knowledge of human behavior and the social environment, person-in-environment, and other multidisciplinary theoretical frameworks in the evaluation of outcomes;

[9c]   critically analyze, monitor, and evaluate intervention and program processes and outcomes; and

[9d]   apply evaluation findings to improve practice effectiveness at the micro, mezzo, and macro levels.

# Chapter Summary

The following summarizes this chapter's content as it relates to the learning objectives presented at the beginning of the chapter. Chapter content will help prepare students to:

## LO1 Define social work and social welfare.

Social work is the professional activity of helping individuals, groups, and communities enhance or restore their capacity for social functioning and creating societal conditions favorable to this goal. Social welfare is "a nation's system of programs, benefits, and services that help people meet those social, economic, educational, and health needs that are fundamental to the maintenance of society" (Barker, 2014, p. 402).

## LO2 Discuss various perspectives on social welfare (including residual, institutional, and developmental, as well as the concept of sustainability).

The residual perspective conceives of social welfare as focusing on problems and gaps. The institutional perspective of social welfare views people's needs as a normal part of life. Society has a responsibility to support its members and provide needed benefits and services. The developmental perspective "seeks to identify social interventions that have a positive impact on economic development" (Midgley &

Livermore, 1997, p. 574). Sustainability involves "development that meets the current needs of the present generations without jeopardizing the ability of future generations to meet their needs" (Mary, 2008, p. 32).

## LO3 Explain critical thinking (including a framework for examining a wide range of concepts and issues).

Critical thinking is (1) the careful scrutiny of what is stated as true or what appears to be true and the resulting expression of an opinion or conclusion based on that scrutiny, and (2) the creative formulation of an opinion or conclusion when presented with a question, problem, or issue. Examining and evaluating facts and issues involve three steps: (1) ask questions, (2) assess the established facts and issues involved, and (3) assert a concluding opinion.

## LO4 Explain the conservative–liberal continuum with respect to viewing the social welfare system.

Conservatism is the philosophy that individuals are responsible for themselves, government should provide minimal interference in people's lives, and change does not necessarily mean improvement. Liberalism is the philosophy that government should be involved in the social, political, and economic structure so that all people's rights and privileges are protected in the name of social justice. Radicalism is the philosophy that the social and political systems as they stand are not structurally capable of truly providing social justice, so fundamental changes in those systems are necessary.

### LO5 Examine your personal attitudes about some social welfare issues.

Responding to issues and questions regarding the importance of change and the responsibility of government can help an individual determine his or her personal stance on the conservative–liberal continuum.

### LO6 Explain social work's fields of practice.

Fields of practice in social work include children and families, aging, disabilities, health, mental health, substance abuse, schools, and corrections. Other contexts for practice are occupational social work, rural social work, police social work, and forensic social work.

### LO7 Explore the process of choosing a career.

The continuum of social work careers includes baccalaureate social workers (BSWs), master's social workers (MSWs), and social workers who have doctorates in social work (Ph.D. or DSW). When considering a career, it's important to think about your general orientation toward the future, the extent to which you are people-oriented versus non–people-oriented, the ways in which you would like to work with people, what majors are available, and, if appropriate, what type of social work you would like to practice.

### LO8 Discuss the uniqueness of social work.

Social work builds on many disciplines, including psychology, sociology, political science, economics, biology, psychiatry, counseling, and cultural anthropology. Social work is unique in that it focuses on people's most difficult problems, often targets the environment for change, stresses the need for advocacy on a client's behalf, stems from a core of professional values, and emphasizes the importance of working in a partnership with clients.

### LO9 Identify some relevant concepts in systems theories and the ecological perspective.

Important concepts in systems theories and the ecological perspective relevant to social work practice include system (micro, mezzo, and macro), client system, social environment, and coping.

### LO10 Describe social work education's goals, curriculum, and competencies.

The Council on Social Work Education's *Educational Policy and Accreditation Standards* require that accredited social work programs prove that students demonstrate nine competencies. These competencies along with their component behaviors are stated and explained. Courses offered in traditional social work curricula are identified. The core social work concepts of general practice, specialized practice, and field education are introduced.

## LOOKING AHEAD

This chapter introduced the basic concept of social welfare and the foundations of the social work profession. The next chapter focuses on social work values and ethics, a primary content area that underlies and guides the social work profession.

## COMPETENCY NOTES

This section relates chapter content to the Council on Social Work Education's (CSWE) Educational Policy and Accreditation Standards (EPAS) (CSWE, 2015). One major goal of social work education is to facilitate students' attainment of the EPAS-designated nine core competencies and their 31 related component behaviors so that students develop into competent practitioners.

Students require knowledge in order to develop skills and become competent. Our intent here is to specify what chapter content and knowledge coincides with the development of specific competencies and their component behaviors. (This ultimately is intended to assist in the accreditation process.) Therefore, the listing presented here first cites the various Educational Policy (EP) core competencies and their component behaviors that are relevant to chapter content. Note that the listing follows the order that competencies and their component behaviors are cited in the EPAS.

The EPAS document lists behaviors under each of the nine core competencies as bulleted items. To clarify the "Competency Notes" here, the bulleted component behaviors for each competency have been alphabetized under that competency. Competency component behaviors are alphabetized both under the icons placed throughout the book and in the "Competency Notes" cited at the end of each chapter.

You have observed that multicolor icons are dispersed throughout the chapter to indicate where relevant accompanying content is located. Page numbers noted below indicate where icons are placed in the chapter. Following the icon's page number is a brief explanation of how the content accompanying the icon relates to the specified competency or its component behavior.

The following identifies where Educational Policy (EP) competencies and their component behaviors are discussed in the chapter. To establish a clear relationship with icons throughout the chapter, Competency 1 will be referred to as EP 1, with its component behaviors as EP 1a, EP 1b, and so on. Similarly, Competency 2 will be referred to as EP 2, with its component behaviors as EP 2a, EP 2b, and so on.

**EP 1 (Competency 1)—Demonstrate Ethical and Professional Behavior.** *(p. 13):* Establishing a professional identity and demeanor includes having knowledge about the history of the social work profession and social welfare. *(p. 22):* Part of the demonstration of professional behavior involves using critical thinking to apply theoretical frameworks such as systems theory and ecological concepts to practice. *(p. 23):* Social workers adhere to a core of ethical principles that guide practice. *(p. 23):* Professional social workers must attain competency in the nine areas identified here. *(p. 24):* Competency 1 (EP1) is identified and described. *(p. 31):* EP 1 is cited.

**EP 1a Make ethical decisions by applying the standards of the NASW *Code of Ethics*, relevant laws and regulations, models for ethical decision-making, ethical conduct of research, and additional codes of ethics as appropriate to context.** *(p. 23):* Social workers should follow the NASW *Code of Ethics,* which emphasizes clients' self-determination, the right to make their own decisions. *(p. 31):* EP 1a is cited.

**EP 1b Use reflection and self-regulation to manage personal values and maintain professionalism in practice situations.** *(p. 10):* It's important for social workers to use personal reflection to understand their own views and values in order to practice objectively and not impose personal views of clients. *(p. 14):* Social workers should practice self-reflection regarding their own attitudes, views, and values so that personal views don't interfere with the development of professional values and ethics. *(p. 17):* It's important to practice personal reflection to determine one's most appropriate career path. *(p. 31):* EP 1b is cited.

**EP 1c Demonstrate professional demeanor in behavior; appearance; and oral, written, and electronic communication.** *(p. 31):* EP 1c is cited.

**EP 1d Use technology ethically and appropriately to facilitate practice outcomes.** *(p. 31):* EP 1d is cited.

**EP 1e Use supervision and consultation to guide professional judgment and behavior.** *(p. 31):* EP 1e is cited.

**EP 2 (Competency 2)—Engage Diversity and Difference in Practice.** *(p. 24):* Competency 2 (EP2) is identified and described. *(p. 31):* EP 2 is cited.

**EP 2a Apply and communicate understanding of the importance of diversity and difference in shaping life experiences in practice at the micro, mezzo, and macro levels.** *(p. 31):* EP 2b is cited.

**EP 2b Present themselves as learners and engage clients and constituencies as experts of their own experiences.** *(p. 31):* EP 2b is cited.

**EP 2c Apply self-awareness and self-regulation to manage the influence of personal biases and values in working with diverse clients and constituencies.** *(p. 31):* EP 2c is cited.

**EP 3 (Competency 3)—Advance Human Rights and Social, Economic, and Environmental Justice.** *(p. 24):* Competency 3 (EP3) is identified and described. *(p. 31):* EP 3 is cited.

**EP 3a Apply their understanding of social, economic, and environmental justice to advocate for human rights at the individual and system levels.** *(p. 21):* Social work is unique in that practitioners are charged with changing policies and the environment on people's behalf.

*(p. 21):* Advocacy for human rights is a major focus of social work and a dimension of it that makes it unique. *(p. 31):* EP 3a is cited.

**EP 3b Engage in practices that advance social, economic, and environmental justice.** *(p. 21):* Social workers should seek changes in the environment that enhance social, economic, and environmental justice. *(p. 31):* EP 3b is cited.

**EP 4 (Competency 4 )—Engage in Practice-Informed Research and Research-Informed Practice.** *(p. 25):* Competency 4 (EP4) is identified and described. *(p. 32):* EP 4 is cited.

**EP 4a   Use practice experience and theory to inform scientific inquiry and research.** *(p. 32):* EP 4a is cited.

**EP 4b Apply critical thinking to engage in analysis of quantitative and qualitative research methods and research findings.** *(p. 7):* Critical thinking can be used to analyze quantitative and qualitative research methods and findings. *(p. 25):* Social workers must use critical thinking to understand research methodology and integrate positive findings about practice into their own work. *(p. 32):* EP 4b is cited.

**EP 4c Use and translate research evidence to inform and improve practice, policy, and service delivery.** *(p. 32):* EP 4c is cited.

**EP 5 (Competency 5)—Engage in Policy Practice.** *(p. 26):* Competency 5 (EP5) is identified and described. *(p. 32):* EP 5 is cited.

**EP 5a   Identify social policy at the local, state, and federal level that impacts well-being, service delivery, and access to social services.** *(p. 21):* Social workers must seek to identify social policies where change is necessary in order to meet people's needs. *(p. 32):* EP 5a is cited.

**EP 5b Assess how social welfare and economic policies impact the delivery of and access to social services.** *(p. 32):* EP 5b is cited.

**EP 5c Apply critical thinking to analyze, formulate, and advocate for policies that advance human rights and social, economic, and environmental justice.** *(p. 7):* Critical thinking can be used to analyze, formulate, and advocate for

beneficial policies. *(p. 21):* Social workers must use critical thinking about policy both to understand how it affects practice and to advocate for improved policies for clients. *(p. 26):* Practitioners should advocate for improved social policies on clients behalf. *(p. 32):* EP 5c is cited.

**EP 6 (Competency 6)—Engage with Individuals, Families, Groups, Organizations, and Communities.** *(p. 16):* Social work is unique in that practitioners work with individuals, families, groups, organizations, and communities on a wide range of problems and issues. *(p. 27):* Competency 6 (EP6) is identified and described. *(p. 32):* EP 6 is cited.

**EP 6a Apply knowledge of human behavior and the social environment, person-in-environment, and other multidisciplinary theoretical frameworks to engage with clients and constituencies.** *(p. 32):* EP 6a is cited.

**EP 6b Use empathy, reflection, and interpersonal skills to effectively engage diverse clients and constituencies.** *(p. 32):* EP 6b is cited.

**EP 7 (Competency 7)—Assess Individuals, Families, Groups, Organizations, and Communities.** *(p. 16):* Social work is unique in that practitioners work with individuals, families, groups, organizations, and communities on a wide range of problems and issues. *(p. 27):* Competency 7 (EP7) is identified and described. *(p. 33):* EP 7 is cited.

**EP 7a Collect and organize data, and apply critical thinking to interpret information from clients and constituencies.** *(p. 7):* Critical thinking can be used to interpret information from clients. *(p. 22):* Systems theories and ecological concepts provide useful conceptual frameworks to guide social work assessment. *(p. 33):* EP 7a is cited.

**EP 7b Apply knowledge of human behavior and the social environment, person-in-environment, and other multidisciplinary theoretical frameworks in the analysis of assessment data from clients and constituencies.** *(p. 6):* Residual, institutional, and developmental perspectives can provide frameworks for analyzing social welfare and human behavior. *(p. 21):* Social workers must apply knowledge of human behavior and the social environment to assess what services people need.

*(p. 28):* Assessment in this case example requires the application of a wide range of knowledge about human behavior and the social environment. *(p. 33):* EP 7b is cited.

**EP 7c  Develop mutually agreed-on intervention goals and objectives based on the critical assessment of strengths, needs, and challenges within clients and constituencies.** *(p. 23):* The social work profession stresses the importance of working together with clients to develop mutually agreed-on goals. *(p. 33):* EP 7c is cited.

**EP 7d Select appropriate intervention strategies based on the assessment, research knowledge, and values and preferences of clients and constituencies.** *(p. 33):* EP 7d is cited.

**EP 8 (Competency 8)—Intervene with Individuals, Families, Groups, Organizations, and Communities.** *(p. 16):* Social work is unique in that practitioners work with individuals, families, groups, organizations, and communities on a wide range of problems and issues. *(p. 29):* Competency 8 (EP8) is identified and described. *(p. 33):* EP 8 is cited.

**EP 8a Critically choose and implement interventions to achieve practice goals and enhance capacities of clients and constituencies.** *(p. 7):* Critical thinking should be used to choose and implement interventions. *(p. 22):* Systems theories and ecological concepts provide useful conceptual frameworks to guide social work intervention. *(p. 33):* EP 8a is cited.

**EP 8b Apply knowledge of human behavior and the social environment, person-in-environment, and other multidisciplinary theoretical frameworks in interventions with clients and constituencies.** *(p. 21):* Social workers should apply knowledge of human behavior and the social environment to intervene with macro systems, and to improve policy and service delivery on their clients' behalf. *(p. 28):* Intervention in this case example requires the application of a wide range of knowledge

about human behavior and the social environment. *(p. 33):* EP 8b is cited.

**EP 8c Use inter-professional collaboration as appropriate to achieve beneficial practice outcomes.** *(p. 33):* EP 8c is cited.

**EP 8d Negotiate, mediate, and advocate with and on behalf of diverse clients and constituencies.** *(p. 21):* Social workers should advocate on their clients' behalf, including those clients who reflect a dimension of diversity. *(p. 33):* EP 8d is cited.

**EP 8e Facilitate effective transitions and endings that advance mutually agreed-on goals.** *(p. 23):* The social work profession stresses the importance of working together with clients to attain mutually agreed-on goals. *(p. 33):* EP 8e is cited.

**EP 9 (Competency 9)—Evaluate Practice with Individuals, Families, Groups, Organizations, and Communities.** *(p. 16):* Social work is unique in that practitioners work with individuals, families, groups, organizations, and communities on a wide range of problems and issues. *(p. 29):* Competency 9 (EP9) is identified and described. *(p. 34):* EP 9 is cited.

**EP 9a Select and use appropriate methods for evaluation of outcomes.** *(p. 34):* EP 9a is cited.

**EP 9b Apply knowledge of human behavior and the social environment, person-in-environment, and other multidisciplinary theoretical frameworks in the evaluation of outcomes.** *(p. 34):* EP 9b is cited.

**EP 9c Critically analyze, monitor, and evaluate intervention and program processes and outcomes.** *(p. 34):* EP 9c is cited.

**EP 9d Apply evaluation findings to improve practice effectiveness at the micro, mezzo, and macro levels.** *(p. 34):* EP 9d is cited.

# 2 Social Work Values and Ethics

Laura Duplain/Getty Images

## Learning Objectives    This chapter will help prepare students to:

**LO 1** Review the NASW *Code of Ethics* (including self-determination, privacy and confidentiality, conflict of interest and dual relationships, sexual relationships, respect for colleagues, and referral for services). **The NASW *Code of Ethics*** (p. 41)

**LO 2** Introduce critical thinking about ethical dilemmas. **Focus on Critical Thinking 2.1** (p. 42)

**LO 3** Provide case examples concerning ethical issues. **Social Workers' Ethical Responsibilities to Clients** (p. 43)

**LO 4** Discuss ethical issues concerning the Internet. **Highlight 2.2** (p. 45)

**LO 5** Examine ethical conflicts faced by military social workers during combat. **Highlight 2.3** (p. 51)

**LO 6** Introduce the importance of social welfare in a global context. **International Social Welfare in a Global Context** (p. 53)

**LO 7** Recognize ethical obligations at the macro level. **Highlight 2.4** (p. 55)

**LO 8** Define and discuss human rights (including the human rights violation of human trafficking). **Global Human Rights** (p. 55)

**LO 9** Examine international social work (including international social work organizations). **International Social Work** (p. 58)

**LO 10** Differentiate between personal and professional values. **Personal and Professional Values** (p. 60)

*How might you answer these questions?*

- *How do you determine what is right and what is wrong?*
- *Have you ever run into situations in which it's difficult to decide what is the right thing to do? If so, what were the circumstances?*
- *What personal values do you have about controversial issues such as the death penalty? Abortion? School prayer? Gun control? Affirmative action? Assisted suicide?*

*Social work is a values-based profession; that is, everything social workers do must be with professional values in mind.* **Values** *involve what you do and do not consider important and worthwhile. They also involve judgments and decisions about relative worth—that is, about what is more valuable and what is less valuable.*

*The Council on Social Work Education (CSWE), the organization that accredits social work programs throughout the United States, establishes standards guiding social work education. CSWE (2015) cites social work's purpose, which is based on its professional values:*

> The purpose of the social work profession is to promote human and community well-being. Guided by a person and environment framework, a global perspective, respect for human diversity, and knowledge based on scientific inquiry, the purpose of social work is actualized through its quest for social and economic justice, the prevention of conditions that limit human rights, the elimination of poverty, and the enhancement of the quality of life for all persons, locally and globally. (p. 1)

**Ethics** *involve principles that specify what is good and what is bad. They clarify what should and should not be done. The National Association of Social Workers (NASW* Code of Ethics *is based on professional values (NASW, 2008). CSWE requires that social work programs educate students to achieve competence in applying "frameworks of ethical decision-making" to "practice, research, and policy arenas" (CSWE, 2015, p. 3).*

*Dolgoff, Harrington, and Loewenberg (2012) explain, "Ethics are deduced from values and must be in consonance with them. The difference between them is that values are concerned with what is* good *and* desirable, *while ethics deal with what is* right *and* correct" *(p. 25). Values determine what beliefs are appropriate. Ethics address what to* do *with or how to* apply *those beliefs to do the "right" thing. Cournoyer (2014) clearly summarizes the importance of social work ethics:*

> We must consider every aspect of practice, every decision, every assessment, every intervention, and virtually every action we undertake as social workers from the perspective of your professional ethics and obligations. This dimension supersedes all others. Ethical responsibilities take precedence over theoretical knowledge, research findings, practice wisdom, agency policies, and, of course, our own personal values, preferences, and beliefs. (p. 144)

*Professional judgments may seem to be a simple matter of common sense. However, in real-life decisions, values and ethical principles conflict constantly. This can result in* ethical dilemmas—*problematic situations in which one must make a difficult choice among two or more alternatives. A dilemma occurs when no one answer can conform to all the ethical principles involved.*

*For example, a client might inform her social worker that she plans to murder her mother-in-law because she can't take the condescending nagging anymore. On the one hand, is the social worker required to report to the authorities that this client has threatened to harm another person? On the other, how can this worker maintain confidentiality and report the threats at the same time?* Confidentiality *is the ethical principle that workers should not share information provided by or about a client unless that worker has the client's explicit permission to do so.*

*Social workers have established guidelines to ethical decision making that can help them get through the difficult decision-making process when solving an ethical dilemma (Kirst-Ashman & Hull, 2015b; Dolgoff et al., 2012; Reamer, 1998). The* NASW Code of Ethics *offers a good starting point for discussing professional values and ethics. It highlights some of the field's primary values and provides suggestions for working in an ethical manner. However, it's only a beginning. The potential value conflicts and ethical dilemmas social workers may face are infinite.*

*It should be clear to you by now that the social work profession has a strong set of values. Some of you reading this are embracing these values and deciding whether to become a social worker. Others take this course out of some level of interest in people's welfare or simply for the credits. You may have personal opinions strongly opposed to some of the value stances. Regardless, the content of this book will provide some provocative food for thought. It seeks to challenge some of your views about the world and enhance your understanding of people and their environments, and ways they can work together to improve the welfare of all.*

## The NASW *Code of Ethics*   **LO 1**

We have established the importance of ethics in guiding professional behavior. Because of its significance, we will examine various aspects of the NASW *Code of Ethics* (2008), which has four primary facets. First, the preamble summarizes social work's general goals or mission and identifies its core values. The mission "is to enhance human well-being and help meet the basic human needs of all people, with particular attention to the needs and empowerment of people who are vulnerable,

**EP 1, 1a**

oppressed, and living in poverty" (NASW, 2008). The six core values include these:

1. *Service:* Providing help, resources, and benefits so people can achieve their maximum potential.
2. *Social justice:* Upholding the condition that in a perfect world all citizens would have identical "rights, protection, opportunities, obligations, and social benefits," regardless of their backgrounds and membership in diverse groups (Barker, 2014, p. 398).
3. *Dignity and worth of the person:* Holding in high esteem and appreciating individual value.

4. *Importance of human relationships:* Valuing the dynamic reciprocal interactions between social workers and clients, including how they communicate, think and feel about each other, and behave toward each other.
5. *Integrity:* Maintaining trustworthiness and sound adherence to moral ideals.
6. *Competence:* Having the necessary skills and abilities to work effectively with clients.

The second major facet in the *Code*, "Purpose of the NASW Code of Ethics," identifies its six major aims:

1. Identifying primary social work values.
2. Summarizing broad ethical principles as guidelines for practice.

3. Helping determine relevant considerations when addressing an ethical dilemma.
4. Providing broad ethical standards to which the public in general may hold the profession accountable.
5. Socializing new practitioners to the mission, goals, and ethics inherent in the profession.
6. Articulating specific standards that the profession may use to judge its members' conduct.

Of particular note is the *Code's* emphasis on the complexity of ethical dilemmas. The *Code* provides no simple formula for resolution; rather, it stresses that ethical dilemmas may be viewed from a range of perspectives. Therefore, social workers must use critical thinking to resolve ethical issues with the *Code* as a springboard. Focus on Critical Thinking 2.1

---

## FOCUS ON CRITICAL THINKING 2.1 — WHAT SHOULD A SOCIAL WORKER DO? **LO 2**

The following are examples of ethical dilemmas confronting social workers. Answers are difficult because there are no perfect solutions. What would you do if you were a social worker in each of the following situations?

**EP 7a, 8a**

### Scenario A[1]

Evita was a hospital social worker called in to talk with parents who had just brought their 6-week-old infant Eric, the youngest of their three children, to the emergency room. Eric, whose skin had turned blue and who was not breathing, was placed on a respirator in intensive care for three days. After that time, the medical staff determined that he was brain dead, and the parents, Bill and Brenda, sorrowfully gave their permission to "pull the plug."

Evita had the opportunity to speak with Bill and Brenda as they waited steadfastly by Eric's bedside hoping he would revive. She discovered that Bill had been babysitting Eric while Brenda ran some errands. Eric had been sleeping on the bed when Bill lay down to take a nap next to him. Apparently Bill had fallen asleep and rolled over on Eric, accidentally smothering him. Evita thought it was odd that Bill had not awakened when Eric, an active baby who was large for his age, must have been struggling desperately for breath. Bill admitted that he had had a couple of beers prior to his nap but insisted that he was not drunk.

Tests revealed that Eric displayed no sign of injuries or other suspicious symptoms. The physician in charge

of Eric was unaware of the story's details. Therefore, she determined that Eric must have died of *sudden infant death syndrome* (SIDS), which she planned to cite as the cause of death. *SIDS* is "the death of a seemingly healthy baby in its sleep, due to an apparent spontaneous cessation of breathing" (Lindberg, 2007, p. 1370).

Evita knew Eric's death was not due to SIDS. Yet informing the overseeing physician about what really happened would probably do little good. Bill and Brenda were filled with sorrow and blamed themselves for the tragedy.

### Critical Thinking Questions

What good would it do to raise suspicions about the cause of death and parental competence? Might it only put the parents through an agonizing investigation and potentially cause removal of the other two children? If you were Evita, what would you do?

### Scenario B

Harry is a county Department of Social Services worker whose clients consist primarily of poor, female-headed families receiving public assistance. During one of his meetings with Dora, a single mother of three small children, she happily reveals that she is babysitting for several neighborhood children. She is thrilled to earn the extra income and is proud to share her news with Harry. Regulations state that people receiving public assistance must report any additional income, with benefits then

*(continued)*

**FOCUS ON CRITICAL THINKING 2.1** *(continued)*

decreased proportionately. But reporting her extra income would probably undermine Dora's trust and destroy Harry's relationship with her. And Dora would probably stop babysitting because it would no longer get her ahead. She is barely making ends meet as it is with her meager public assistance payments. Dora already is participating in a compulsory job-training program, preparing her for full-time employment.

### Critical Thinking Questions

What good would it do to report this scanty income despite the fact that regulations require such reporting? Dora likely will get a full-time job soon, at which time public assistance payments will no longer be an issue. What should Harry do?

### Scenario C

Ping is a social worker at a mental health center that provides individual and group counseling for a wide range of problems and issues. One of Ping's clients is Cheyenne, age 14, who is depressed and potentially suicidal. During one of their individual counseling sessions, Cheyenne tells Ping that she is sexually active. She states that if she gets pregnant with her current boyfriend she will surely kill herself. Cheyenne asks Ping to help her get some form of contraception, possibly from Planned Parenthood. Cheyenne indicates that her boyfriend refuses to use condoms because he says

he doesn't like to feel restricted. Ping knows Cheyenne's parents are very religious and are fervently against premarital sex. They would never consent to Cheyenne using contraception and would vehemently oppose Ping's interference in this matter.

### Critical Thinking Questions

What about Cheyenne's life and well-being? What should Ping do?

### Commentary

When confronting an ethical dilemma, it's important to use ethical reasoning to determine the right thing to do. By definition a dilemma has no perfect answer or it wouldn't be a dilemma. There would simply be a more obvious solution. Strom-Gottfried (2007) proposes a strategy of asking and answering six questions to help make such a decision:  **EP 1**

- Who will be helpful?
- What are my choices?
- When have I faced a similar dilemma?
- Where do ethical and clinical guidelines lead me?
- Why am I selecting a particular course of action?
- How should I enact my decision? (p. 27)

[1]This case is based on one presented in Robison and Reeser (2000, pp. 2–3).

provides examples of ethical dilemmas social workers may experience.

The *Code's* third facet, "Ethical Principles," is based on the six core values described previously and sets forth standards to which all practitioners should strive. For example, the ethical principle relating to the value *of social justice* states that "social workers challenge social injustice." Likewise, the principle based on *integrity* states that "social workers [should] behave in a trustworthy manner."

The final facet of the *Code*, the "Ethical Standards," is by far the most extensive. It encompasses 155 specific principles clustered under six major categories. These include social workers' ethical responsibilities to clients, to colleagues, in practice settings, as professionals, to the social work profession, and to the broader society. Highlight 2.1 lists the concepts involved in each, and subsequent sections discuss the major categories, providing some specific examples for each.

## Social Workers' Ethical Responsibilities to Clients   **LO 3**

The first category of ethical standards addresses how practitioners should behave with respect to clients and what aspects of worker–client interaction are most significant within an ethical context. It is beyond the scope of this book to cover all 16 areas within this category, so we will focus on only a few arbitrarily selected ones. These are self-determination, privacy and confidentiality, conflict of interest and dual relationships, and sexual relationships with clients. After each, examples of compliance and of violation are provided.

### Self-Determination

Practitioners should nurture and support client **self-determination**—each individual's right to make his or her own decisions. Applied to social work, this means that practitioners are responsible for

## HIGHLIGHT 2.1 ETHICAL STANDARDS IN THE NASW *CODE OF ETHICS*

1. Social Workers' Ethical Responsibilities to Clients
   1.01 Commitment to Clients
   1.02 Self-Determination
   1.03 Informed Consent
   1.04 Competence
   1.05 Cultural Competence and Social Diversity
   1.06 Conflicts of Interest
   1.07 Privacy and Confidentiality
   1.08 Access to Records
   1.09 Sexual Relationships
   1.10 Physical Contact
   1.11 Sexual Harassment
   1.12 Derogatory Language
   1.13 Payment for Services
   1.14 Clients Who Lack Decision-Making Capacity
   1.15 Interruption of Services
   1.16 Termination of Services

2. Social Workers' Ethical Responsibilities to Colleagues
   2.01 Respect
   2.02 Confidentiality
   2.03 Interdisciplinary Collaboration
   2.04 Disputes Involving Colleagues
   2.05 Consultation
   2.06 Referral for Services
   2.07 Sexual Relationships
   2.08 Sexual Harassment
   2.09 Impairment of Colleagues
   2.10 Incompetence of Colleagues
   2.11 Unethical Conduct of Colleagues

EP 1a

3. Social Workers' Ethical Responsibilities in Practice Settings
   3.01 Supervision and Consultation
   3.02 Education and Training
   3.03 Performance Evaluation
   3.04 Client Records
   3.05 Billing
   3.06 Client Transfer
   3.07 Administration
   3.08 Continuing Education and Staff Development
   3.09 Commitments to Employers
   3.10 Labor-Management Disputes

4. Social Workers' Ethical Responsibilities as Professionals
   4.01 Competence
   4.02 Discrimination
   4.03 Private Conduct
   4.04 Dishonesty, Fraud, and Deception
   4.05 Impairment
   4.06 Misrepresentation
   4.07 Solicitations
   4.08 Acknowledging Credit

5. Social Workers' Ethical Responsibilities to the Social Work Profession
   5.01 Integrity of the Profession
   5.02 Evaluation and Research

6. Social Workers' Ethical Responsibilities to the Broader Society
   6.01 Social Welfare
   6.02 Public Participation
   6.03 Public Emergencies
   6.04 Social and Political Action

(1) informing clients about available resources, (2) helping them define and articulate their alternatives, and (3) assisting them in evaluating the consequences of each option. The goal is to assist clients in making the best, most informed choices possible.

*Example of Compliance* Gilda is a social worker in a protective services unit for older adults in a large urban county's Department of Social Services. Her job is to visit older adults who may be at risk of some harm (e.g., being unable to care for themselves or

suffering physical abuse by others), assess the situation, and help them in whatever ways possible. Sometimes Gilda connects clients with appropriate resources like Meals on Wheels, an agency that delivers daily hot meals to older adults' homes for minimal cost. Other times, Gilda helps place older adults in more structured settings, such as nursing homes, to meet their increasingly dependent needs.

One of Gilda's clients, Desiree, age 89, tripped on a crack in the sidewalk outside her home and severely sprained her ankle. Desiree is adamant that she will not leave her home, no matter what. She feels that would destroy her independence and effectively be the first step into the grave. However, Desiree is having a terrible time getting around in her own home. She can barely walk and usually has to crawl to the bathroom when no one is around to help her.

Gilda thinks Desiree would probably be better off in a more structured setting where she could get the help she needs. However, Gilda respects Desiree's right to self-determination. So she works out a plan with Desiree that's satisfactory to the client. Desiree will temporarily reside in a nearby health-care facility for older adults until she can once again put pressure on her ankle and walk. Gilda makes arrangements with the facility for Desiree to stay there. Gilda also helps Desiree arrange for someone to watch her home and forward her mail to her temporarily.

*Example of a Violation*    Jorge is a job coach for a county social services department. His job involves evaluating people's strengths, skills, and interests: linking them with appropriate employment; and helping them adjust to their work environments. Daisy, age 19, is one of Jorge's clients. Daisy emphasizes that she would like to get a job as a secretary or administrative assistant. Daisy says that she's generally shy with people and would like a job in which she could work in a more solitary manner. She also says that she has always been good at typing. Jorge knows that Daisy never graduated from high school, and he

doesn't believe that her typing or writing skills are anywhere near adequate for such a position. Therefore, he decides not to inform Daisy about available clerical positions. Rather, he steers her to think about becoming a sales clerk.

## Privacy and Confidentiality

Social workers must uphold client privacy and confidentiality. **Privacy** is the condition of being free from unauthorized observation or intrusion. We have established that **confidentiality** is the ethical principle that workers should not share information provided by a client or about a client unless they have the client's explicit permission to do so.

There is more to confidentiality than may be immediately apparent. Confidentiality means more than not revealing information about clients to others. It also involves not asking for more information than is necessary, as well as informing clients about the limitations of confidentiality within the agency setting. For example, will supervisors, researchers, or students have access to private information? Must statistics and other data about clients' personal lives be submitted to public regulatory agencies or funding sources for **accountability**? (Accountability was defined in Chapter 1 as a profession's responsibility to clients and the community that workers are effectively doing what they say they are going to do.) Highlight 2.2 explores some issues involving confidentiality and the Internet.

---

## HIGHLIGHT 2.2    SOCIAL WORK, CONFIDENTIALITY, AND THE INTERNET

**LO 4**

The Internet has become a primary and essential means for communicating information among social work professionals. Internet etiquette (or "netiquette") in some ways corresponds with ethics in person-to-person or "hard-copy" situations, but in other ways it does not (Guffey & Loewy, 2013, p. 113). "Cyberspace remains a new culture and has unique social forces and social sanctions that have no functional equivalent in the real world" (Marson, 2000, p. 20). For example, client confidentiality is important in virtually all situations, yet the means of maintaining it electronically are unique. At least three issues are significant (Marson, 2000).

**EP 1c, 1d**

First, social workers and their agencies must be well versed in any Internet functions they undertake. It must be clear who has access to client information and how. In the real world, workers lock their offices and, sometimes, their filing cabinets when they go home. They must know how to do the same thing in the electronic environment if that's where client communications and records are kept. Some simple rules apply:

1. Keep passwords confidential.
2. Avoid calling up a password on the screen when others are in the room (this is akin to talking loudly about clients in a crowded lunchroom).

*(continued)*

**HIGHLIGHT 2.2** *(continued)*

3. Avoid writing the password down or making it readily available on some database.
4. Alter passwords every few months.

Second, any language used should be professional and socially appropriate. Many people seem to feel more comfortable using derogatory language on the Internet. Perhaps it's the anonymity or lack of physical interpersonal contact that makes people using the Internet feel more informal and, possibly, freer. It might be tempting to "send sensitive, confidential, inflammatory, or potentially embarrassing messages" (Guffey, 2010, p. 110). Guffey and Loewy (2013) reflect:

> **Don't send anything you wouldn't want published.** E-mail creates a permanent record that does not go away even when deleted. Every message is a ... communication that can be used against you or your employer. Don't write anything that you wouldn't want your boss, your family, or a judge to read. (p. 113)

Professional ethics can provide guidelines for proper behavior. The NASW *Code of Ethics* states that "[s]ocial workers should not use derogatory language in their written or verbal communications to or about clients" (NASW, 2008, 1.12).

A third issue involving confidentiality concerns the ease with which information can be shared with large numbers of people such as those on a *listserv*, "a computerized system by which subscribers are able to communicate to all other subscribers by sending a transmission to one address" (Marson, 1998, p. 21). It is easy to reply to all listserv members, instead of only the person who initiated a contact or raised a question. Information conveyed in chatroom conversations (in which a number of people can communicate concurrently at a Website) should also be carefully monitored.

Social workers use the Internet for many reasons, including the following (Marson, 1998):

- *Networking.* This involves the establishment of communication and interpersonal interaction among people to provide support, exchange information, or achieve some designated goal. For example, social workers in one state network with each other to share information about pending social legislation and advocate for positive changes.
- *Sharing resource material to improve practice and agency service.* However, note that not all resource material is of equal value or even of any value. For example, one brief Internet search revealed Websites entitled Captain Ozone, Cheesy-wotsits, Evil Fluffy Bunnies of Doom, and Puppet Terrors. It's important to evaluate the validity of any Website concerning its currency, the reliability of who developed or sponsors the site, the content's purpose and intended audience, and accuracy (Guffey, 2008).
- *Identifying referral services for specific client needs.* Marson (1998) cites a case in which

  > an anonymous social worker had a client who was suffering from terminal lung cancer and was receiving hospice services at her home. [A **hospice** is a place of rest or a system of services providing care for people who are terminally ill. The idea is to make people as comfortable as possible in the little time they have before they die.] The client's physical isolation made a dreadful situation worse. In an effort to assist with her last months, the social worker linked the client to UseNet's cancer support group [on the Internet], which provided her with the support vital for her morale. (p. 24)

- *Seeking out or conducting research.* It's easy to consult with colleagues and to exchange documents regarding effective practice techniques and research projects.
- *Communicating efficiently.* Sometimes it's difficult to reach people, especially when they're busy and unavailable. When information must be conveyed quickly, e-mail provides a good alternative.

*Example of Compliance* Mackenzie is a school social worker who is just beginning a support group for sixth-grade children coping with their parents' recent divorces. Early in the first session, she explains to the children the limits of confidentiality. For example, if they share anything about wanting to hurt someone or themselves, committing a crime, or participating in sexual activity, it's her responsibility to report it. This way, group members know where they stand. If they share this kind of information, they know Mackenzie has no choice but to report it.

*Example of a Violation*  Peter and Piper are social work counselors at a group home for adolescent boys with emotional and behavioral problems. They and their significant others occasionally have dinner with a mutual friend, Jack, a county social services worker, along with his significant other. The three social workers regularly compare "battle stories" about their most difficult cases. This occurs despite the fact that they have very different caseloads and their significant others are present to hear their discussion. Sometimes, after a few cocktails, voices elevate, and other diners can overhear.

## Conflict of Interest and Dual Relationships

The *Code of Ethics* warns practitioners to be acutely aware and steer clear of any possible conflicts of interest that might obstruct professional judgment. In the social work context, a **conflict of interest** is a clash between the responsibilities of the professional role and the potential for personal gain. An example is a hospital social worker who encourages clients to purchase health insurance policies from her spouse, who is an insurance salesperson. To what extent might this practice not be in the clients' best interest? To what extent will this worker be biased to experience personal income gain? Another example involves a practitioner running for office who pressures clients to vote for her. To what extent does this interfere with her ability to work with and help these clients? What if the clients don't agree with the worker's political views? How will this alter the clients' perception of the worker–client relationship? "Similarly, a practitioner who invests money in a client's business is embedded in a conflict of interest; the professional's financial interests may clash with her duty to the client (for example, if the professional's relationship with the client becomes strained because they disagree about some aspect of their shared business venture)" (Reamer, 2001, p. 5).

A client who is a used car salesman may even "offer to sell ... [a worker] a car at a discount"; Dolgoff, Lewenberg, and Harrington (2005) emphasize to workers, "Don't accept his offer, no matter how good it is!" (p. 142). Such a scenario may result in the client expecting something from the worker in return, such as special treatment or personal closeness.

The *Code* emphasizes that clients' best interests must be protected to the maximum extent possible. If these interests are jeopardized, termination of the worker–client relationship and appropriate referral elsewhere may be necessary.

One type of conflict of interest involves dual or multiple relationships. Corey, Corey, Corey, and Callanan (2015) explain:

> *[**Dual** or] **multiple relationships** occur when professionals assume two or more roles at the same time or sequentially with a client. This may involve assuming more than one professional role (such as instructor and [counselor] ... ) or blending a professional and nonprofessional relationship (such as counselor and friend or counselor and business partner). Multiple relationships also include providing [counseling] ... to a relative or a friend's relative, socializing with clients, becoming emotionally or sexually involved with a client or former client, combining the roles of supervisor and [counselor,] ... having a business relationship with a client, borrowing money from a client, or loaning money to a client. (p. 254)*

The *Code of Ethics* states that "[s]ocial workers should not engage in dual or multiple relationships with clients or former clients" where such people have any risk of being harmed (NASW, 2008, 1.06c). As in other potential conflicts of interest, social workers should always give top priority to clients' best interests. Dolgoff and his colleagues (2012) reflect:

> *Must dual-role relationships necessarily interfere with professional relationships? Do they always result in conflict? In modern society where everyone fills multiple roles, there are many situations where social workers and clients participate in dual or multiple relationships. Both may be members of the same political party, church, mosque, or synagogue, or their children may attend the same school or be classmates. There is no reason for a social worker to withdraw from these activities simply because the client also engages in them. The issue is to separate the professional relationship from other relationships [in order to avoid ethical dilemmas]. (p. 126)*

However, it remains important for the worker to remember that

> *there is always the potential for a conflict of interest and of exploitation of the person seeking help. This makes it critical that whenever there is a possibility of a dual relationship the ... [practitioner],*

*who is the person who knows the difficulties that could arise in such relationships, must think about and perhaps discuss with a supervisor the potential conflicts of interest and exploitation before entering into such a relationship.*

*(Syme, 2003, p. 8)*

**Example of Compliance[2]**   Javon is a social worker at a substance abuse counseling center. He has just received a referral of a client, Laura Hedgehog, whose name is not familiar to him. When she arrives at his office, he is surprised to find out he knows her. He used to work with her at another social services agency several years ago and had even formed a mild friendship with her. She apparently had since married and changed her last name. Laura greets Javon enthusiastically and emphasizes how happy she is that he will be her counselor. She stresses how much she trusts his competence and knows he can help her. Javon feels uncomfortable about this dual relationship, knowing Laura both as a client and a former colleague. Javon gently thanks her for her confidence and then explains how he feels such a dual relationship would create a serious ethical dilemma for him. He feels he cannot be objective and offer her the best help possible. He refers her to one of his colleagues, whom he candidly describes as an excellent counselor.

**Example of a Violation**   Huda is a protective services worker whose primary job is to investigate alleged cases of child maltreatment and make recommendations for treatment, sometimes involving children's removal from the home. Huda attends the first session of a yoga class where she is startled to see that the instructor, Hope, is the mother in one of the families with whom Huda is currently working. Huda participates in the whole class, after which Hope approaches her. Hope enthusiastically welcomes her and says she'd be happy to give Huda a discount in registration fees. Huda thinks to herself, "What would it hurt? I'm pretty strapped for cash this month. It certainly won't influence my decision about her family or anything like that." *Will it?*

## Sexual Relationships

Another type of dual relationship involves sexual relationships, which the *Code* emphasizes by addressing it as a separate topic. Simply put, social workers

should not have sexual relationships with current clients, clients' relatives, or others personally involved with clients. The *Code of Ethics* also discourages social workers from having sexual relationships with former clients. If a social worker pursues this under "extraordinary circumstances, it is social workers—not their clients—who assume the full burden of demonstrating that the former client has not been exploited, coerced, or manipulated, intentionally or unintentionally" (NASW, 2008, 1.09c). Additionally, social workers should not provide clinical services to clients with whom they were formerly sexual partners.

The *Code* uses powerful language to emphasize that workers should not have sex with clients under any circumstances. Parsons (2001) explains that the "inappropriateness of [a] sexual relationship between helper and client rests in the fact that the helping relationship is unbalanced in power…. Thus, the reciprocal nature characteristic of a healthy intimate relationship is not possible" (p. 146). Corey and his colleagues (2015) indicate that harmful effects can range "from mistrust of opposite sex relationships to hospitalization and, in some cases, suicide. Other effects of sexual intimacies on clients' emotional, social, and sexual adjustment" include "negative feelings about the experience, a negative impact on their personality, and a deterioration of their sexual relationship with their primary partner" (p. 290).

**Example of Compliance**   Tyrone is a social worker with a caseload of families, mostly young women, receiving public assistance. Diana, one of his clients, has worked quite hard to get through a job-training program and find stable employment. They had hit it off since the beginning and respected each other's efforts. One day, Diana casually asks Tyrone if he'd be interested in dinner and a movie the following weekend. He politely declines. They continue working together until Diana gets back on her feet and leaves Tyrone's program.

**Example of a Violation**   Alyssa, age 24, is a counselor at a community-based halfway house for men on parole who are also substance abusers. **Halfway houses** are transitional dwellings that provide structure, support, and guidance for persons unable to function independently in the community. They are transitional because they provide a middle ground between a full-time residential setting (e.g., an institution or prison) and the relative freedom of living in

---

[2]This example is loosely based on one presented in *Ethical Decisions for Social Work Practice* (7th ed.) by Dolgoff et al. (2005, p. 247).

the community.[3] *Parole* is the "conditional release of a prisoner serving an indeterminate or unexpired sentence," usually for good behavior or the promise of good behavior, under the supervision of a designated parole officer (Mish, 2008, p. 902).

Most of the clients residing in the halfway house are in their 20s and early 30s. Alyssa finds herself physically attracted to Butch, a good-looking, charming 26-year-old parolee who resides in the house. She fights her feelings but finally gives in. When he asks her for a date, she assents and begins an intimate relationship with Butch "on the sly." Agency policy clearly forbids any such relationships with current clients or anyone who has been a client within the past six months.

## Social Workers' Ethical Responsibilities to Colleagues

The NASW *Code of Ethics* specifies 11 areas in which practitioners have ethical responsibilities to colleagues. The focus is on maintaining respect for colleagues even when differences of opinion arise and on working cooperatively for clients' benefit. Social workers should make referrals to professionals with other areas of expertise when necessary. In addition, they should address situations in which colleagues are functioning ineffectively due to personal problems or unethical conduct. They should either approach the colleague directly or go through appropriate channels (such as in the agency or through professional associations) to help alleviate the problem. Arbitrarily, two areas involving social workers' ethical responsibilities to colleagues are discussed here—respect and referral for services.

### Respect

Social workers should respect and work cooperatively with colleagues. They should avoid unfounded criticism of colleagues, including that directed at personal characteristics unrelated to professional performance.

*Example of Compliance* Bo, a social worker at a diagnostic and treatment center for children with multiple disabilities, has a different professional orientation than many of her colleagues in the other

disciplines there. For example, she feels that the family environment is important and so often works with families to discuss issues and link them with needed services. She sees the entire family as the client system. However, Darwin, the agency's psychologist, does not see such family work as important. Rather, he views the child as the client and focuses on changing the child's behavior by using structured behavior modification techniques. He primarily does individual therapy with children and offers consultation to other therapists (including speech, occupational therapy,[4] and physical therapy[5]) regarding how to control and improve children's behavior.

Bo respects Darwin and strives to work together with him in a cooperative effort. Although she does not always agree with his treatment focus, she appreciates how they both bring their professional strengths to the process.

*Example of a Violation* Simon, a foster care worker, intensely dislikes his colleague Joellen, a worker in the same unit. He feels that she is lazy, knows little, and fails to take her job seriously. Simon takes every opportunity to criticize Joellen behind her back to other workers by focusing on the fact that she has a high-pitched, screechy voice and a grating, cackling laugh.

### Referral for Services

Social workers should refer clients to other professionals when these others have the knowledge and skills necessary for making progress with clients. Practitioners should make such referrals as smoothly as possible, conveying vital information to the new service provider. Workers should receive no personal payment or gain from such referrals.

*Example of Compliance* Jacob is a housing worker for a county social services department who helps "disadvantaged populations who need assistance in obtaining quality and affordable housing in the housing market" (Gibelman, 1995, pp. 298–299). One of Jacob's clients, Kendra, has significant physical

---

[3]Clients using halfway houses may also include people with histories of mental illness.

[4]*Occupational therapy* is "therapy for those recuperating from illness that encourages rehabilitation by performing the activities of daily life" (Lindberg, 2007, p. 949).

[5]*Physical therapy* is "the treatment of disease, injury, or deformity by physical methods such as massage, heat treatment, and exercise rather than by drugs or surgery" (Lindberg, 2007, p. 1034).

disabilities, including advancing arthritis and declining eyesight. Jacob determines that housing is only one of Kendra's needs. Her health requirements are also critical. Jacob acknowledges that he knows little about the health services that Kendra needs and so refers her to another agency worker with expertise in that area. Meanwhile, Jacob continues working to fulfill her housing needs.

*Example of a Violation*  Olivia is a case manager for people with intellectual disabilities (formerly referred to as mental retardation). Tyler, age 20, has just begun living in a group home for people with intellectual disabilities and working in **sheltered employment**, a program involving work in a safe, closely supervised environment for people who have trouble functioning more independently. Clients usually receive at most minimum and usually significantly less than minimum wage. Because of his relatively high level of functioning, Olivia thinks Tyler could actually do well in regular employment (e.g., doing maintenance work or stocking shelves at a grocery store). He has good job skills, such as readily complying with supervisors' instructions, being punctual, and taking his work seriously.

The problem is that Olivia has a large caseload of clients and can barely keep up with her most critical work. Referring Tyler to a job specialist, filling out all the required paperwork, and arranging whatever transportation is necessary would take a huge amount of time. On the one hand, referring Tyler would help him better live up to his potential, enhance his self-esteem because he could hold a regular job, and, frankly, earn him more money. On the other, it's not really hurting him to remain where he is, despite the fact that it's not the best work setting for him. Olivia decides that Tyler will stay working in sheltered employment. Her time is too valuable, and she simply doesn't have enough of it.

## Social Workers' Ethical Responsibilities in Practice Settings

This section of the *Code of Ethics* focuses on appropriate behavior in practice settings. Social workers who supervise others should be competent and evaluate supervisees fairly. Supervision should be used "to guide professional judgment and behavior" (CSWE, 2015, p. 4). Any information or data social workers record should be

**EP 1e**

accurate. They should advocate for increased funding both inside and outside their agencies when resources are needed for clients. They also should "act to prevent and eliminate discrimination in the employing organization's work assignments and in its employment policies and practices" (NASW, 2008, 3.9e). Finally, practitioners should make sure their employers are aware of unethical practices. The following is an example of a dilemma faced by a social worker in an agency setting. Highlight 2.3 discusses some of the special ethical conflicts experienced by social workers serving in the military practice setting during active combat.

## Case Example

Lakeisha got a job as a social worker at a nursing home three weeks ago. She is just beginning to feel comfortable there and is gradually learning the agency's policies and practices. Unfortunately, twice she's observed a disturbing scenario. Papers such as wills or insurance statements must be signed by witnesses. On two occasions, Lakeisha saw the nursing supervisor, who is really quite powerful within the agency, ask a resident with Alzheimer's disease[6] to sign the paper for another patient with the same disease. Witnesses who sign legal papers are supposed to be of sound mind, and these residents obviously were not. No one was safeguarding either of the patients' best interests. Lakeisha was new at the agency and did not want to come across as a troublemaker, yet this signing practice was clearly wrong. The *Code of Ethics* instructs social workers to "act on behalf of clients who lack the capacity to make informed decisions" and to "take reasonable steps to safeguard the interests and rights of those clients" (NASW, 2008, 1.14). Lakeisha was also responsible for making sure the agency was aware of unethical practices (NASW, 2008, 3.09c). What should Lakeisha do?

*Example of Compliance*  Lakeisha decides that she cannot overlook this unethical practice despite the fact that speaking up might endanger her job. She has more than five months of probation to go. She resolves to speak with the nursing supervisor. If that doesn't work, she will go over the nursing

---

[6]*Alzheimer's disease* is a common brain disease of unknown origin that is characterized by mental decline and numerous cognitive problems.

| HIGHLIGHT 2.3 | ETHICAL CONFLICTS FOR MILITARY SOCIAL WORKERS DURING COMBAT | LO 5 |

Practitioners who serve as professional social workers in the military experience exceptional ethical dilemmas. Military social workers now participate in virtually all levels of practice and assume a wide range of positions, including program manager, consultant to military leaders, researcher, client advocate, officer, and direct service provider; their arenas of involvement include "military family policy, child welfare, health care, substance abuse, mental health, hostage repatriation, combat stress, and humanitarian relief" (Harris & Pehrson, 2008, p. 270).

**EP 4a, 4b, 4c**

Simmons and Rycraft (2010) conducted an in-depth *qualitative* study "of the ethical challenges faced by 24 military social workers who were deployed during Operation Iraqi Freedom, and Operation Enduring Freedom (combat operations in Afghanistan)" (p. 9). (As introduced in Chapter 1, **qualitative research methods** are those "that emphasize depth of understanding and the deeper meanings of human experience, and that aim to generate theoretically richer, albeit more tentative, observations"; frequently used qualitative methods include "direct observation" and "intensive interviewing" [Rubin & Babbie, 2014, p. 669].)

"*Qualitative research methods* are more likely to tap the deeper meanings of particular human experiences and generate theoretically richer observations that are not easily reduced to numbers" (Rubin & Babbie, 2014, p. 79).

All participants in the study had a master's degree in social work and a clinical license. (The latter is described more thoroughly in Chapter 5.) Simmons and Rycraft (2010) maintain that "the ethical challenges faced in combat areas by social workers serving as active duty components of the military can teach all social workers about dealing with challenges in extremely stressful environments" (p. 11). Although military social workers do not take part in the actual fighting, they are often deployed in combat areas where fighting is taking place. There they provide "mental health prevention and treatment services" to service men and women who are fighting the war (pp. 9–10).

Issues military social workers face include "serving during controversial wars, meeting the needs of the individual client while simultaneously meeting the needs of the military unit, the military's particular expectations regarding confidentiality, and personal fears inherent to the specific deployment" (Simmons & Rycraft, 2010,

p. 10). A key concern for these social workers in their practice is the basic ethical concept of self-determination on the part of individual soldiers versus the needs of fellow soldiers and the military operation itself.

The study focused on the answers to two primary questions. The first question asked participants, "How do you deal with situations where a patient/client with mild trauma symptoms wants to go home (needs of the client) and his/her unit needs them to continue fighting (needs of the unit)?" (p. 12). Social workers' answers came together to cluster in three areas. First, military social workers "would analytically work through a problem before taking action" (p. 12). This required careful assessment of the client, the client's strengths and weaknesses, and the client's ability to handle the trauma.

The second cluster of answers involved "problem-focused intervention" (p. 13). Practitioners "would work with the clients, focusing on the problem, helping them to deal with their concerns" while keeping them in the combat context (p. 13). Some social workers indicated that keeping clients on the job was better for their mental health in the long run. It would prevent them from experiencing failure, long-term regret, and even potential suicide.

The third cluster of the social workers' answers were "mission oriented" (p. 13). Here workers indicated that they "would focus on the mission, reminding clients that they voluntarily signed up for military service" (pp. 13–14). Practitioners might also emphasize how important the client was to the military and the mission, and discuss the client's "good prognosis for recovery" (p. 14).

The second major question posed in the study was, "While deployed, what other ethical dilemmas did you face? How did you deal with them?" (p. 14). Four clusters of social workers' answers merit discussion. The first cluster involved "confidentiality and privacy" (p. 14). Military social workers indicated that maintaining these values was very difficult while being in such close contact and having very little privacy in any aspect of combat-zone life.

A second cluster of answers concerned "conflicts with commanders" (p. 14). Issues included military leaders ignoring social work recommendations and some leaders having little regard for the importance and relevance of mental health problems. (Mental health is discussed more thoroughly in Chapter 13.)

A third cluster of answers focused on "relationships and boundaries" (p. 15). Social workers found it quite

*(continued)*

**HIGHLIGHT 2.3** *(continued)*

difficult to keep distinct boundaries between themselves and their clients while living in such close quarters. "A military social worker on deployment eats, sleeps, [and] showers with people they will see professionally as well" (p. 15).

Finally, a fourth cluster of answers involved "diagnosis and treatment" (p. 15). At times it was hard to determine what really was in a client's best interest. Who was just pretending to have a problem and who was in real agony? In such instances, when possible, it was good to seek out a second opinion.

Simmons and Rycraft (2010) reflect that the ethical issues identified here are not so far removed from those faced by social workers in other contexts. Granted, the military environment is more extreme in terms of structure, rigidity, and purpose.

Answers to the first question posed by the study involved the needs of the individual (self-determination) versus the requirements of the military unit and mission. The researchers determined that the military social workers participating in the study based decisions primarily on clinical criteria and judgments, rather than on what might be right or wrong.

Answers to the second question concerning other ethical dilemmas focused on confidentiality and privacy, conflicts with commanders, relationships and boundaries, and diagnosis and treatment. How different are these (although much more intense in the military) from those dilemmas faced by practitioners in other fields of social work practice? The answer is that they reflect similar issues. For example, many a social worker has approached his or her supervisor or agency director with "an amazingly brilliant idea," only to be turned down or ignored. That's simply part of working life.

Simmons and Rycraft (2010) conclude that we should respectfully hold military social workers and their work in high regard. "[F]urther analysis and dialogue about the ethical and practical concerns of military social workers is important"; only then can we aim to ensure "that the integrity of the social work profession and the care provided to those individuals served by military social workers is optimal" (p. 17).

supervisor's head and speak with the home's director, who is also her immediate supervisor.[7] If worst comes to worst, she'll report this to the state agency that licenses and regulates nursing homes. She knows that will make almost everyone at the home angry because it will make the entire agency and all its employees look bad to the outside world.

*Example of a Violation* Lakeisha determines that she doesn't want to make waves. After all, she thinks to herself, the practice really isn't hurting anybody, is it? The papers being signed aren't all that important anyway. She decides to forget that she ever saw the signings happen and look the other way if she ever sees it again.

---

[7]When a worker has a complaint, it's often most useful to go directly to the people the complaint involves and give them feedback. Subsequently, if that doesn't work, it's usually best to go to a supervisor and, as needed, gradually go up the chain of command. Going over supervisors' and administrators' heads without first approaching them with complaints generally makes them angry. It implies that they can't handle the problem at their level and may make them look incompetent to those above them in the agency's power structure.

## Social Workers' Ethical Responsibilities as Professionals

Social workers' ethical responsibilities as professionals include eight broad dimensions by which they should judge their behavior and responsibility. First and foremost, they should be competent to do their jobs. If they are not, they should either seek education and learn the skills they need to become competent or find another line of work. Next, they should not "practice, condone, facilitate, or collaborate with any form of discrimination on the basis of race, ethnicity, national origin, color, sex, sexual orientation, age, marital status, political belief, religion, or mental or physical disability" (NASW, 2008. 4.02). "Social workers should not permit their private conduct to interfere with their ability to fulfill their professional responsibilities" (NASW, 2008, 4.03). Some types of conduct interfere with a practitioner's ability to function. For instance, one agency administrator actively supported a racist candidate running for public office (Reamer, 2006). As a result, several agency staff resigned in protest, and the administrator's supervisor and other personnel were "concerned that the social worker's private conduct was harming the hospital's reputation and interfering with her ability to perform her duties" (Reamer, 2006, p. 199).

Social workers should also be honest, avoid fraud, and seek help when personal problems begin to interfere with their professional effectiveness. They should represent themselves and their qualifications accurately. They should never take credit for someone else's work.

Finally, social workers should never solicit clients for personal gain. Reamer (2006) provides an example:

> A social worker at a public child welfare agency provided [social] … services to families whose children had been placed in foster care after allegations of abuse and neglect. She also maintained a small private practice [where she billed clients for counseling on a private basis]. The social worker told a couple she worked with at the child welfare agency that they would need to obtain long-term counseling if they hoped to regain custody of their child. She mentioned that she had a private practice outside the agency, gave the couple her business card, and said, "It might be in your best interest to see me regularly for counseling." The couple felt coerced but nonetheless agreed to see the social worker privately to increase their chances of regaining custody of their child. (pp. 208–209)

## Social Workers' Ethical Responsibilities to the Social Work Profession

Ethical responsibilities to the social work profession focus on two dimensions—integrity, and evaluation and research. **Integrity** refers to social workers' promotion of high practice standards. Social workers should strive to maintain and enhance professional knowledge, values, and ethics. They should  participate in activities aimed at professional contributions such as "teaching, research, consultation, service, legislative testimony, presentations in the community, and participation in their professional organizations" (NASW, 2008, 5.01c). In addition, they should contribute to the social work knowledge base.

**EP 4a, 4c**

Similarly, social workers should encourage research and evaluation of practice effectiveness, monitor practice policies and interventions to ensure effectiveness, and maintain current knowledge of evaluation

approaches. Research should be done in an ethical manner. Social workers should be honest with all involved regarding what they plan to do while conducting the research, who will have access to any information and findings gained, and who deserves credit for any findings obtained.

## Social Workers' Ethical Responsibilities to the Broader Society

Ethical responsibilities to the broader society include four areas that reflect the core of social work—namely, to advocate and work for people's general welfare. Social workers should promote people's general welfare on all levels, from the local to the global. They should become actively involved in the formulation of public policy and flock to provide help during emergencies (e.g., floods, tornadoes, or earthquakes).

**EP 3a, 3b, 6, 7, 8, 9**

As part of their professional responsibilities, social workers should pursue social and political action to ensure fair and equal access to resources and opportunities. They should actively support policies to improve the human condition and promote social justice for all. They should especially work to enhance opportunities for "vulnerable, disadvantaged, oppressed, and exploited people and groups" (NASW, 2008, 6.04b). They should support conditions and policies that respect cultural diversity. Similarly, they should work to prevent and eliminate conditions and policies discriminating against or exploiting people, especially vulnerable populations. Highlight 2.4 presents two situations in which social workers are ethically responsible for helping people and go beyond their job of providing direct services to clients.

# International Social Welfare in a Global Context   `LO 6`

Even beyond a macro focus at the national level, international issues are of concern to social workers. **Globalization** is the "process of global integration in which diverse peoples, economies, cultures, and political processes are increasingly subjected to international influences" (Khinduka, 2008; Midgley, 1997, p. xi). The world is indeed getting smaller. I recently traveled to Southeast Asia, including Ho Chi Minh City in Vietnam. As we motored along a main roadway after dusk, it was amazing to see

Jim West/Alamy

*Social workers have the ethical responsibility to promote people's general welfare. One issue involves an adequate minimum wage. Here Detroit workers rally on the behalf of a wage increase.*

family members huddled around 12-inch television sets in tiny home after tiny home. I thought of the millions of American homes in which essentially the same thing was happening, although the television sets and homes were much bigger.

We also stayed in a huge new hotel in the cosmopolitan, modern city–state of Singapore. My roommate was going to a grocery store in a shopping center next door to pick up deli items for an informal supper in our room. I jokingly told her to pick up some Merkt's cheese spread, a brand found all over the Midwest, including Wisconsin, where we live. When she returned and showed me her bounty, she held up a plastic container of Kaukauna cheese spread, amazingly made in Wisconsin only a few miles from my home. I was astonished. We were on the other side of the world.

The world is also getting more interdependent. In a global economy, what social and economic forces impact one nation may well result in repercussions in many other nations. Hokenstad and Midgley (1997) explain:

*Social work is one of many players in the response to these realities of global interdependence. The scope of global poverty and the intensity of ethnic conflict require first political and economic responses by nations and international organizations. Global challenges require action on many levels by many actors. Nevertheless, these are problems that are directly related to social work commitment and expertise. Social workers at the local level are directly involved with the implications of international realities by working with refugees or helping displaced workers. At the national level in many countries, the profession is active in promoting economic and social justice policy. Internationally, social work organizations are increasingly active in combating human rights violations. Thus, it is essential for social workers to have an international perspective and understanding to be effective practitioners in today's world. (pp. 3–4)*

Note that the distinction will be made between the terms *international* and *global*. **International** concerns relationships and issues between two or more

| HIGHLIGHT 2.4 | SOCIAL WORKERS' ETHICAL OBLIGATIONS TO HELP PEOPLE AT THE MACRO LEVEL LO 7 |

The following two scenarios reflect situations in which social workers might confront an ethical dilemma that goes beyond their own practice with individuals, families, and groups.

EP 2a, 3a, 3b

### Scenario A

The private social service agency Jack works for does not have a formalized affirmative action policy for hiring personnel. He has overheard the agency director make several crude racial remarks and jokes about people of color. He cannot believe that a person with such authority has gotten away with that. The agency has no people of color on staff despite having numerous clients who are. Jack feels that recruiting staff members who are people of color is essential to the agency's ability to perform the way it's supposed to. He also believes that current staff members, including the agency director, need feedback to work on changing their prejudicial and discriminatory behaviors.

Jack determines that he must confront this ethical issue despite possible negative consequences, including being fired. He decides to talk with his colleagues to see if he can muster more support. He knows that often a cohesive group can have a greater impact on making changes in organizations and communities than can one person alone. He finds out that several other agency workers feel the same way he does.

Together, they develop a plan to talk to the agency director and provide some suggestions.

### Scenario B

L'Toya is a worker at a rural county social services agency. She, her colleagues, and agency administrators have identified a significant lesbian and gay population within the area. She and the other professionals would like to implement a new program providing support groups for lesbians and gay men dealing with several issues, including single parenthood and legal difficulties such as housing discrimination. Two relatively powerful members of the county board get wind of the idea and react in an angry, negative fashion. They consider people with a sexual orientation other than heterosexuality sinful. They also contend that there are no gay or lesbian people in the area—they surely would know about it if there were.

L'Toya works with the other interested professionals to devise a plan. First, these two board members need to be educated regarding the issues and needs of lesbians and gay men. Perhaps other board members are more knowledgeable and enlightened, and would be more supportive. Maybe some advocates of a gay rights organization in another part of the state can help; perhaps they can assess the needs of gay men and lesbians by conducting some research in the area. L'Toya and the others are on their way to developing a plan.

---

nations. **Global** involves relationships and issues concerning all nations around the globe.

## Global Human Rights  LO 8

In response to the atrocities of World War II, the General Assembly of the United Nations adopted a Universal Declaration of Human Rights (UDHR) in December 1948 (United Nations, 1948). **Human rights** involve the premise that all people, regardless of national origin, are entitled to basic rights and treatment. Mapp (2008) elaborates:

EP 3a, 3b, 5

*Within the [UDHR], there are three areas of rights: [1] political and civil rights, [2] social, economic, and cultural rights, and [3] collective rights. Political and civil rights are often referred to as "negative freedoms" as they require a government to refrain from an overuse of its power*

*against individuals. Included in this are rights such as freedom of speech and the right to a fair trial. The second groups of rights—social, economic, and cultural rights—are referred to as "positive freedoms" as they require a government to take action for them to be realized for individuals. They include such rights as medical care, the right to an education, and the right to a fair wage. The last group, collective rights, are rights for groups of people and include the rights to religion, peace, and development. (pp. 17–18)*

### A Global Human Rights Violation: Human Trafficking

An atrocious violation of human rights is human trafficking. **Human trafficking** is the transfer of people across international boundaries to enslave them in some way, usually involving forced labor or sexual exploitation; human trafficking may also include infants and children who are purchased for adoption on the black market (Potocky, 2008). Another aspect of human trafficking concerns the harvesting of human organs (Childress, 2006: Hodge, 2008). It is estimated that about 11.4 million women and girls and 9.5 million men and boys people around the world (a total of almost 21 million people) are victims of human trafficking at any given time (International Labor Organization, 2014).

Three conditions commonly characterize trafficking (Mapp, 2008). The first involves movement of the victim from one place to another. Internationally, victims are usually targeted in countries experiencing economic hardship or serious political unrest and sent to "wealthy, industrialized nations" (Hodge, 2008, p. 145; Mapp, 2008). Second,

> *deception or coercion is involved. Although the migration might be voluntary, the person is not truly aware of what lies ahead. Many people migrate willingly for better-paying work, but it may become trafficking when they arrive at their destination and realize the work is not what they were promised. They may have been promised a good wage for domestic labor but find that they are imprisoned in a house and paid nothing. They may have signed a contract for factory labor only to arrive and find they have been sold into prostitution.*
>
> *(Mapp, 2008, p. 32)*

The third element of trafficking involves being forced into some form of physical labor or sexual activity against the victim's will.

## A Case Example of Human Trafficking

People targeted as victims are often exceptionally vulnerable, poor, or socially isolated. Consider, for example, Safah, a 14-year-old Iraqi girl who was placed in an orphanage after her father's death (Bennett, 2006). There she was befriended by a seemingly kind nurse who said she wanted to adopt Safah. Because the nurse indicated the formal adoption process would take too long, she developed a plan to get Safah out of the orphanage. The nurse instructed Safah to pretend she had appendicitis and scream out in pain so that Safah would be taken to the hospital. Once there "the nurse whisked Safah into a waiting car. The next three weeks were the worst in Safah's life. 'I was tortured and beaten and insulted a lot in that house,' Safah says. She

wouldn't provide many details about what happened in the whiskey-soaked den" of a house in a middle-class district of Baghdad; she became "desperate" when she understood she was to be sold to Sa'ad, a man in Dubai, for $10,000 (Bennett, 2006). Safah confided her situation to a neighborhood boy who reported the situation to the police. Both Safah and the nurse were placed in the same prison for the next six months until bureaucratic red tape could be untangled and Safah sent back to the orphanage.

## The Extent of Human Trafficking

Although it is difficult to obtain accurate numbers because of the secrecy and shame involved, it is estimated that 600,000 to 800,000 people are trafficked annually across international borders (Hodge, 2008). These numbers include people transported to the United States, which is, after Italy, and followed by Germany and the Netherlands, the most common destination for victims (Monzini, 2004). In the United States most "victims in FBI [Federal Bureau of Investigation] human trafficking cases are women and young girls from Central American and Asian countries"; however, increasing numbers of young males and American citizens (e.g., teenage runaways) are also becoming victims (Federal Bureau of Investigation, 2008). It is estimated that "[t]here are 100,000 people in the [United States] under age 18 who are in the commercial sex industry," many of whom may be victims of human trafficking (Malai, 2014, p. 8). The problem continues to escalate (de Silva, 2007).

## Controlling Victims

A number of factors are used to keep victims under control once they have been seized (Fred, 2004a). First, they may be coerced into labor to pay back the "debt" they accrued by being transported into the new country. Second, captors may threaten to physically injure the victims or report them to immigration authorities for deportation if they don't obey. Third, captors may threaten to harm the victims' families at home or inform their families about the victims' status to shame them. Fourth, captors may disorient victims by moving them frequently from one location to another (e.g., brothels).

## Consequences for Victims

Consequences of trafficking for victims are very serious.

> *Many trafficking victims will have permanent physical damage from being brutally beaten or*

*raped by their traffickers. Those who've been used as prostitutes may have sexually transmitted [infections] ..., while those who've slaved as laborers may have back problems, hearing loss, and respiratory or cardiovascular diseases. A number of victims, especially children, also show signs of malnourishment.*

(*Fred, 2004a, p. 4*)

### The NASW Policy Statement on Human Rights

The National Association of Social Workers (NASW) Policy Statement on human rights indicates that social workers must:

- advocate for the rights of vulnerable people;
- be especially vigilant about human rights violations related to children's rights and exploitation such as child labor, child prostitution, and other crimes of abuse and ... take leadership in developing public and professional awareness regarding these issues;

  **EP 1a, 2, 3a, 3b, 5b, 5c**

- work in collaboration with nongovernmental organizations and community groups when entitlements are nonexistent or inadequately implemented and ... become a leading force for the health and welfare of all people, including the world's most vulnerable;
- Maintain the "struggle for human rights as "a vital priority for the social work profession in the 21st century." (NASW, 2012, pp. 206–207)

### Social Workers' Responsibility to Empower Victims

What can social workers do about this critical global human rights issue? There are a number of suggestions:

1. Social workers should "look below the surface" when working with clients and seek to identify victims of human trafficking so that they can be helped (Fred, 2004a, p. 4).

   **EP 2, 3a, 3b, 5b, 5c, 8a, 8c, 8d**

2. Social workers should advocate for the development of programs and provision of services to help victims of human trafficking to escape bondage and get what they need. Such services may include "legal assistance, financial assistance, and help with food and housing" (Mapp, 2008, p. 46). Social workers can also link victims to existing resources.

3. Social workers can strive to formulate and implement "policies that punish those who exploit others into forced labor. In addition, these efforts can be focused on those who commit their crimes within our borders, as well as extraditing citizens who commit crimes in other countries" (Mapp, 2008, p. 46). For example, social workers can encourage state and national legislators "to pass [strong] anti-trafficking legislation" (Mapp, 2008, p. 48).

   They can also support the passage and implementation of legislation helping victims, such as the federal

   *Victims Trafficking and Violence Protection Act of 2000 (P.L. 106-386), which was amended in 2003 by the Trafficking Victims Protection Reauthorization Act (P.L. 108-193). This statute explicitly recognizes that existing laws often fail to protect victims of trafficking and, paradoxically, often punish victims more severely than they do traffickers. Accordingly, the law stipulates that victims of severe trafficking should not be inappropriately penalized for unlawful acts committed as a result of being trafficked, such as using false documents, entering the country without documentation, or working without documentation (P.L. 106-386). This provision, at least in principle, removes one of the key threats that traffickers use to coerce young women and children into the sex industry [i.e., deportation or incarceration].*

   (*Hodge, 2008, p. 148*)

   Additionally, this legislation created a unique type of visa for people who experience extreme forms of trafficking, including forced sexual acts, and for victims younger than age 18 (Hodge, 2008). The visa allows victims to remain in the United States while they help in the prosecution of perpetrators. It also allows victims to receive a range of services, including those provided by the federal witness protection program. "After three years, permanent residency may be granted (Aronowitz, 2004)" (Hodge, 2008, p. 148).

4. Social workers can educate others about the issue and what might be done to address it (Mapp, 2008).

5. On a global level, social workers can work together with other practitioners, groups, and international organizations in this and other countries to address the core variables that allow for and encourage human trafficking. Goals may include community development to tackle such issues as "poverty and gender discrimination" (Healy, 2008; Mapp, 2008, p. 46).

**Community development** is "a planned approach to improving the standard of living and general well-being of people" (Butterfield & Chisanga, 2008, p. 381). It emphasizes identification, enhancement, and linkage of communities' strengths to generate "self-reliant, self-sustaining communities that mobilize resources for the benefit of their members" (Homan, 2011, p. 61). Mapp (2008) explains:

> *An example of empowering oppressed people, thus reducing their vulnerability to forced labor, can be found in the case of the Self Employed Women's Association (SEWA) of India.... Its goal is to assist self-employed women in South and Southeast Asia who face personal barriers such as high rates of illiteracy, having to care for multiple children, and living in slum conditions, as well as macro barriers such as exploitation by moneylenders and harassment by employers and officials. Today, SEWA is the largest single union in India and has founded a bank with 70,000 accounts in order to provide micro-finance loans to its members. The bank also provides insurance for its members, while the union assists with child care and legal aid. Through methods such as these, the women are able to provide for themselves and their families without resorting to forced labor. (pp. 47–48)*

EP 1, 2, 2b, 3a, 3b, 5c, 7a, 8c, 8d

# International Social Work   **LO 9**

**International social work** is "international professional action and the capacity for international action by the social work profession and its members. International action has four dimensions: internationally related domestic practice and advocacy, professional exchange, international practice, and international policy development and advocacy" (Healy, 2008, p. 10). An important concept inherent in this definition is *action*, namely, planning and getting things done. Social workers work together on an international basis to establish goals to enhance human well-being.

The first dimension in international action concerns *internationally related domestic practice and advocacy*. Healy (2008) explains:

> *Social workers are increasingly called on to deal with problems that have an international dimension, meaning that two or more countries are involved in some way in the case or policy issue. There are many examples of internationally related domestic practice problems, including refugee resettlement, work with other international populations, international adoption work, and social work in border areas. (p. 10)*

"Domestic" responsibilities for social workers include, on the one hand, knowledge about people of other national origins in order to conduct culturally competent, effective practice with these people. Learning about various cultures from the people they work with is an ongoing, career-long process. Link, Ramanathan, and Asamoah (1999) assert that an international perspective allows social workers to have expanded "insights about the human condition and more adequately understand, analyze, and predict human behavior" (p. 31). They provide an example of "the 18th Street Gang members in Los Angeles," whose families originated in El Salvador and who maintain an ongoing cultural connection with that country. An international perspective helps social workers

> *recognize how artificial it is to see national borders as separations between micro or macro systems.... These disenfranchised young people are frequently rounded up and deported to El Salvador, where they pick up with another branch of their gang so that their interactions are seamless despite the structural efforts of immigration and law enforcement to disband or break them.*

> (DeCesare, 1993; Link, et al., 1999, p. 31)

Another aspect of internationally related "domestic" responsibility involves the support of legislation both nationally and internationally that provides fair and humane treatment to people. An example is immigration legislation. "It is logical that as part of accepted advocacy responsibilities of the profession, social workers have an obligation to monitor such legislation as it is being proposed, to follow impending votes at the [United Nations] and foreign policy directives and to ensure that social work's voice is heard on relevant issues" (Healy, 2008, pp. 11–12).

Healy (2008) continues:

*The second dimension in the definition of international action is the capacity to exchange social work information and experiences [professional exchange] internationally and to use the knowledge and experience to improve social work practice and social welfare policy at home. This includes a range of actions, such as reading foreign periodicals and books in one's field, corresponding with professionals in other countries or hosting visitors, participating in professional interchange at international meetings, and identifying and adapting social welfare innovations in other countries to one's own setting. Increasingly, professional exchange is facilitated by technological advances in computer-assisted communications and teleconferencing....*

*The third dimension of international action is the preparation of some professional social workers to contribute directly to international development work [international practice] through employment or volunteer work in international [community] development agencies. (pp. 12–15)*

The fourth dimension of international action is "the capacity of the social work profession as a worldwide movement" to publicly support values and legislation concerning "important social issues" (Healy, 2008, p. 15). International social work organizations such as those described in the next section provide mechanisms to accomplish this.

## International Social Work Organizations

International social work organizations that actively engage social workers around the globe include the International Federation of Social Workers (IFSW) and the International Association of Schools of Social Work (IASSW). Initially founded in 1928 at the first International Conference on Social Work, IFSW "is a global organization striving for social justice, human rights, and social development through the promotion of social work, best practice models [practice approaches that

**EP 8c**

have proven to be most effective] and the facilitation of international cooperation" (including that between social workers and their professional organizations); its membership includes 750,000 professional social workers in 90 countries around the world (International Federation of Social Workers, 2014). IFSW "promotes social change, problem solving in human relationships and the empowerment and liberation of people to enhance well-being" (IFSW, 2014). It is especially involved in "protesting human rights violations" (Hokenstad & Midgley, 1997, pp. 4–5). (IFSW's home Website is http://www.ifsw.org/.)

IASSW is

*an international association of institutions of social work education, organizations supporting social work education and social work educators. Its mission is:*

*To develop and promote excellence in social work education, research, and scholarship globally in order to enhance human well being.*

a. *To create and maintain a dynamic community of social work educators and the [programs].*

b. *To support and facilitate participation in mutual exchanges of information and expertise.*

c. *To represent social work education at the international level.*

*(IFSW, 2014)*

IASSW stresses the importance of social development and the quest for social justice on the behalf of oppressed populations. It also has served as a consultant to the United Nations. (IASSW's home Website is http://www.iassw.aiets.org/.)

### International Social Work: Codes of Ethics

Although the NASW *Code of Ethics* is the primary code followed by social workers in the United States, note that other ethical codes also are available in other nations and on an international basis. Consider, for example, the Canadian Association of Social Workers (CASW) Code of Ethics, accessible at its home Website (http://www.casw-acts.ca/) (CASW, 2014).

**EP 1a**

IFSW and IASSW have developed an *Ethics in Social Work, Statement of Principles* that may be applied when addressing *international* (involving two or more nations) or *global* (involving the entire world) ethical issues. Often, these issues concern human rights. The document, concurrently supported by both organizations, consists of the following five parts:

1. Preface
2. Definition of social work
3. International conventions [that refer to various organizations' specific statements of human rights]
4. Principles
5. Professional conduct. (International Association of Schools of Social Work, 2014; IFSW, 2014)

The "principles" in the *Ethics in Social Work, Statement of Principles* include "human rights and human dignity" and "social justice." The former indicates how "social work is based on respect for the inherent worth and dignity of all people, and the rights that follow from this. Social Workers should uphold and defend each person's physical, psychological, emotional, and spiritual integrity and well-being." It continues that "social workers have a responsibility to promote social justice, in relation to society generally, and in relation to the people with whom they work"; this involves "challenging negative discrimination," "recognizing diversity," "distributing resources equitably," "challenging unjust policies and practices," and "working in solidarity" (i.e., social workers as a group have the responsibility to confront social injustice).

## Personal and Professional Values

**LO 10**

We have established that values involve what is considered important and what is not. They concern making judgments about right and wrong. We all have the right to our personal values; we all have our own ideas about how things should be. It's a wonderful thing to be able to enjoy our own opinions and have the freedom to express them. An ongoing task for social workers is to identify their own values and distinguish between those and their professional values. As you now know, clients' right to self-determination is a key principle in social work. Therefore, social workers must be careful not to impose their personal values on clients. How difficult do you think this might be?

For example, consider a social worker who strongly supports women's rights. She may work

**EP 1b, 2c**

### FOCUS ON CRITICAL THINKING 2.2 — IDENTIFYING PERSONAL VALUES

Social workers must identify their own personal values so that they are careful not to impose them on clients. What are your personal values and opinions concerning the following issues? How easy or difficult would it be for you to work with people having the opposite opinions?

**EP 1b, 2c, 5c**

- Should there be a death penalty for extreme crimes? If so, for what types of crimes (e.g., terrorism, murder, or armed robbery)?
- Should women be allowed the freedom of choice regarding abortion? If not, are there any circumstances under which an abortion could be performed (e.g., rape, incest, or a threat to the life of the mother)?
- Should women change their names to those of their spouses when they marry? Why or why not?

- Should people who are critically ill and in intense pain be able to "pull their own plug"—that is, put themselves to death?
- Should teachers in elementary and secondary school be able to use corporal punishment (i.e., inflicting punishment by causing physical pain)?
- Should prayers be allowed in public schools? What if there are children of various faiths involved (e.g., Buddhist, Muslim, Roman Catholic, Methodist, Unitarian, Hindu, or atheists)?
- Should schools provide sex education to children? If so, what should be taught?
- Should oil companies be allowed to develop untouched lands in the Arctic to keep domestic gas prices down? Or should lumber companies be allowed to cut down old-growth trees such as the giant redwoods in California?

with a Hispanic family that rigidly adheres to patriarchal values. In this family, the wife and daughters are expected to be obedient and follow the rules imposed by the father. Female family members are given much less respect, are allowed less input, and generally have significantly less power than male members. In this case the social worker must work hard to respect the family's values, but she must also focus on the right of self-determination for the family's females. It is the worker's responsibility to help such women articulate their feelings and identify their alternatives as they see them within their own cultural frame of reference. Clients must evaluate the potential positive and negative consequences for each alternative within their own cultural environment. The worker must do all this and still keep her own values in check throughout the intervention process.

Another example concerns a social worker whose adult client has a life-threatening disease and desperately needs surgery to ensure survival. However, the client refuses such medical help because it conflicts with his strong religious beliefs. The social worker personally feels that this perspective is ridiculous, yet he still must respect the client's right to make his own decisions. Focus on Critical Thinking 2.2 identifies a number of potentially controversial issues involving personal values.

# Chapter Summary

The following summarizes this chapter's content as it relates to the learning objectives presented at the beginning of the chapter. Chapter content will help prepare students to:

## LO1 Review the NASW Code of Ethics.

The six core values of the NASW *Code of Ethics* are service, social justice, dignity and worth of the person, the importance of human relationships, integrity, and competence. Social workers have ethical responsibilities to clients, to colleagues, in practice settings, as professionals, to the social work profession, and to the broader society.

## LO2 Introduce critical thinking about ethical dilemmas.

Case examples were provided and critical thinking questions posed concerning issues in a hospital setting, a county Department of Social Services, and a mental health center.

## LO3 Provide case examples concerning ethical issues.

Ethical issues were introduced. Examples of both compliance and a violation were provided for cases concerning self-determination, privacy and confidentiality, conflict of interest and dual relationships, sexual relationships, respect for colleagues, and referral for services.

## LO4 Discuss ethical issues concerning the Internet.

Suggestions for maintaining electronic confidentiality should be followed. Language used should be professional. Various reasons exist for social workers to use the Internet.

## LO5 Examine ethical conflicts faced by military social workers during combat.

Ethical conflicts faced by military social workers during combat often focus on self-determination on the part of the individual versus the needs of the military operation. Other ethical conflicts include confidentiality and privacy, conflicts with commanders, relationships and boundaries, and diagnosis and treatment.

## LO6 Introduce the importance of social welfare in a global context.

The world is becoming more interdependent among nations. Social workers should be concerned about human well-being on a global level and about human rights violations.

## LO7 Recognize ethical obligations at the macro level.

Macro examples were provided concerning establishing a formalized affirmative action policy in an agency and initiating a program serving lesbians and gay men.

### LO8 Define and discuss human rights.

Human rights involve the premise that all people regardless of race, culture, or national origin are entitled to basic rights and treatment. Human trafficking is a major human rights issue. It involves the transfer of people across international boundaries to enslave them in some way, usually involving forced labor or sexual exploitation. Social workers have the responsibility to help human trafficking victims and advocate on their behalf.

### LO9 Examine international social work.

International social work is "international professional action and the capacity for international action by the social work profession and its members" (Healy, 2008, p. 10). International social work organizations include the International Federation of Social Workers (IFSW) and the International Association of Schools of Social Work (IASSW). IFSW and IASSW have developed an *Ethics in Social Work, Statement of Principles.*

### LO10 Differentiate between personal and professional values.

Social workers should distinguish between their personal and professional values. They should never impose personal values on clients.

## LOOKING AHEAD

This chapter established the significance of social work values in all aspects of practice. Primary values include an appreciation of human diversity and respect for people's rights to self-determination, optimal health, and enhanced well-being. The next chapter will focus on these and related value issues in the context of human diversity.

## COMPETENCY NOTES

The following identifies where Educational Policy (EP) competencies and their component behaviors are discussed in the chapter.

**EP 1 (Competency 1)—Demonstrate Ethical and Professional Behavior.** *(p. 41):* Social workers should demonstrate ethical behavior. *(p. 43):* Ethical questions raised provide a strategy for ethical decision making. *(p. 58):* Assuming an international

perspective and learning about other cultures is an ongoing, career-long process.

**EP 1a Make ethical decisions by applying the standards of the NASW *Code of Ethics*, relevant laws and regulations, models for ethical decision-making, ethical conduct of research, and additional codes of ethics as appropriate to context.** *(p. 41):* Social workers should use the NASW *Code of Ethics* as a guide or ethical practice. Subsequent sections explore various principles championed by the *Code.* *(p. 44):* This highlight summarizes ethical standards identified by the NASW *Code of Ethics.* *(p. 57):* The NASW Policy Statement on human rights reflects the application of NASW ethical standards. *(p. 59):* The IFSW/IASSW *Ethics in Social Work, Statement of Principles* is described.

**EP 1b Use reflection and self-regulation to manage personal values and maintain professionalism in practice situations.** *(pp. 60, 60):* Social workers must practice personal reflection about their personal values to make certain that these don't conflict with professional values and ethical practice.

**EP 1c Demonstrate professional demeanor in behavior; appearance; and oral, written, and electronic communication.** *(p. 45):* Social workers should be careful to communicate professionally and ethically when using the Internet.

**EP 1d Use technology ethically and appropriately to facilitate practice outcomes.** *(p. 45):* Social workers should use technology ethically in their communications in their practice.

**EP 1e Use supervision and consultation to guide professional judgment and behavior.** *(p. 50):* Supervision is an important process in guiding professional practice.

**EP 2 (Competency 2)—Engage Diversity and Difference in Practice.** *(p. 57):* Social workers should be especially vigilant about the oppression involved in human rights violations against various diverse populations. *(p. 57):* Social workers have the responsibility to empower oppressed populations, who are often members of diverse groups. *(p. 58):* Practitioners should recognize the extent to which a culture's structures and values affect people.

**EP 2a Apply and communicate understanding of the importance of diversity and difference in shaping life experiences in practice at the micro, mezzo, and macro levels.** *(p. 55):* Social workers should be aware of their ethical responsibilities to fight oppression and discrimination affecting diverse groups.

**EP 2b Present themselves as learners and engage clients and constituencies as experts of their own experiences.** *(p. 58):* Social workers should view themselves as learners and engage the people from various cultures with whom they work as important sources of information.

**EP 2c Apply self-awareness and self-regulation to manage the influence of personal biases and values in working with diverse clients and constituencies.** *(pp. 60, 60):* Practitioners must strive to identify any personal values and biases concerning diverse groups and prevent them from interfering from effective ethical practice.

**EP 3 (Competency 3)—Advance Human Rights and Social, Economic, and Environmental Justice.**

**EP 3a Apply their understanding of social, economic, and environmental justice to advocate for human rights at the individual and system levels.** *(p. 53):* As their ethical responsibility to society, practitioners should seek understanding of social, economic, and environmental issues and advocate for enhanced well-being. *(p. 55):* Social workers should advocate for human rights and social and economic justice. *(p. 55):* Practitioners should strive to understand any oppressive circumstances imposed on people globally. Human trafficking poses a major example of oppression. *(p. 57):* Social workers have a responsibility to advocate for human rights. *(p. 57):* Practitioners should be especially vigilant about human rights violations and advocate to stop them. *(p. 58):* Advocacy for human rights and justice is a major goal of international social work.

**EP 3b Engage in practices that advance social, economic, and environmental justice.** *(p. 53):* As their ethical responsibility to society, social workers should promote people's welfare on all levels. *(p. 55):* Practitioners should choose intervention approaches that advance social justice on

the behalf of diverse groups. *(p. 55):* Social workers should advocate for human rights on a global basis. *(p. 57):* Social workers should engage in practices that advance social and economic justice such as advocating for human rights. *(p. 57):* Practitioners should engage in practices that advance social and economic justice for victims of human trafficking. *(p. 58):* International social work involves engaging in practices that advance social, economic, and environmental justice.

**EP 4 (Competency 4)—Engage in Practice-Informed Research and Research-Informed Practice.**

**EP 4a Use practice experience and theory to inform scientific inquiry and research.** *(p. 51):* The research discussed here is based on practice experience. *(p. 53):* Social workers should contribute to social work research through their practice experience whenever possible.

**EP 4b Apply critical thinking to engage in analysis of quantitative and qualitative research methods and research findings.** *(p. 51):* Critical thinking is required to structure the research paradigm described in this scenario and to analyze and apply research findings.

**EP 4c Use and translate research evidence to inform and improve practice, policy, and service delivery.** *(p. 51):* The research discussed here can be used to inform and improve practice, policy, and service delivery. *(p. 53):* Social workers should use research evidence to guide their practice.

**EP 5 (Competency 5)—Engage in Policy Practice.** *(p. 55):* It's important for social workers to understand the global interconnections of oppression and the significance of global human rights.

**EP 5b Assess how social welfare and economic policies impact the delivery of and access to social services.** *(p. 57):* Social workers should seek understanding about how social welfare and economic policies affect human rights and people's access to the services they need. *(p. 57):* Practitioners should actively seek out clues that human trafficking is occurring and analyze policies that allow it to occur.

**EP 5c Apply critical thinking to analyze, formulate, and advocate for policies that advance human rights and social, economic, and environmental justice.** *(p. 57):* Social workers should apply critical thinking skills to understand and advocate for policies that advance human rights. *(p. 57):* Practitioners should apply critical thinking skills to analyze policies that affect human trafficking and advocate for policies to stop it. *(p. 58):* An international social work perspective maintains that practitioners should advocate for policies and services that advance social well-being for people from various cultures both domestically and internationally. *(p. 60):* Social workers should scrutinize personal values and how they relate to professional values when thinking critically about policy issues.

**EP 6 (Competency 6)—Engage with Individuals, Families, Groups, Organizations, and Communities.** *(p. 53):* Social workers practice by working with systems of all sizes, including macro systems.

**EP 7 (Competency 7)—Assess Individuals, Families, Groups, Organizations, and Communities.** *(p. 53):* Social workers practice by working with systems of all sizes, including macro systems.

**EP 7a Collect and organize data and apply critical thinking to interpret information from clients and constituencies.** *(p. 42):* Social workers must use critical thinking when assessing clients and their situations. *(p. 58):* Practitioners must understand and apply knowledge about various cultures to understand the human behavior of people from these cultures both domestically and abroad.

**EP 8 (Competency 8)—Intervene with Individuals, Families, Groups, Organizations, and Communities.** *(p. 53):* Social workers practice by working with systems of all sizes, including macro systems.

**EP 8a Critically choose and implement interventions to achieve practice goals and enhance capacities of clients and constituencies.** *(p. 42):* Social workers must use critical thinking when undertaking interventions with clients. *(p. 57):* Practitioners should seek interventions that stop human trafficking and support human rights.

**EP 8c Use interprofessional collaboration as appropriate to achieve beneficial practice outcomes.** *(p. 57):* Practitioners should work together with colleagues and organizations on a global basis to address the variables that encourage human trafficking. They should work together for community development to empower oppressed people. *(p. 58):* A core dimension of international social work involves professional exchange and working together. *(p. 59):* International organizations such as IFSW and IASSW emphasize collaboration with colleagues.

**EP 8d Negotiate, mediate, and advocate with and on behalf of diverse clients and constituencies.** *(p. 57):* Social workers should strive to establish strong anti-trafficking laws and support the passage of legislation to help victims. *(p. 58):* Practitioners should advocate for positive legislation and services at the domestic and international levels.

**EP 9 (Competency 9)—Evaluate Practice with Individuals, Families, Groups, Organizations, and Communities.** *(p. 53):* Social workers practice by working with systems of all sizes, including macro systems.

# 3 Empowerment and Human Diversity

George Rose/Getty Images

## Learning Objectives    This chapter will help prepare students to:

**LO 1** Discuss human diversity and differences in status (including discrimination, oppression, marginalization, alienation, power, privilege, acclaim, stereotypes, prejudice, populations at risk, and social and economic justice). **Human Diversity and Differential Treatment** (p. 66)

**LO 2** Employ critical thinking skills to appraise self-awareness (including that concerning racial self-awareness, cultural self-awareness, the treatment of intersex people and people with various forms of gender expression, and the feminist perspective). **Focus on Critical Thinking 3.1** (p. 68)

**LO 3** Explore empowerment and related concepts (including the strengths perspective and resiliency). **Empowerment and a Strengths Perspective** (p. 68)

**LO 4** Examine empowerment for women in groups. **Highlight 3.1** (p. 69)

**LO 5** Recognize various aspects of human diversity (including age, class, color, culture, disability and ability, ethnicity, gender, gender identity and expression, immigration status, marital status, political ideology, race [together with values characterizing various racial groups], religion/spirituality [in addition to the basic tenets of Islam and discrimination against Muslim people], sex, sexual orientation, and tribal sovereign status). **Facets of Human Diversity** (p. 72)

**LO 6** Define cultural competence and apply it to social work. **Focus on Critical Thinking 3.2** (p. 75)

**LO 7** Examine the social construction of gender. **Focus on Critical Thinking 3.3** (p. 90)

*How many of the following sound familiar to you?*

Stereotype: *White males are second-rate basketball players.*
Stereotype: *Women are too emotional to make good supervisors.*
Stereotype: *All Hispanic people speak Spanish as their primary language.*
Stereotype: *Elderly people can't think well.*
Stereotype: *Gay and lesbian people really want to be the opposite gender.*
Stereotype: *People with physical disabilities are unemployable.*

*Do you have stereotypes about people from other ethnic groups, races, religions, or age groups? How about people of the other gender or those with disabilities? If so, what are these stereotypes? To what extent do you think that they really characterize every person belonging to that group?*

*Some people are short, and others are tall. Some are pinkish white, others ebony black, and still others various shades of golden brown. Some have astonishing IQs, and others struggle to make it through early elementary grades. Some are very young, and others are very old. Some are agile athletes; others can barely hit a volleyball over a net let alone get a basketball through a hoop; and still others can't walk at all. Our society is a vast, surging concoction of many types of diversity.*

*This chapter explores various aspects of human diversity, with a focus on the importance of equality, justice, and empowerment, especially for people at risk of discrimination and oppression.*

## Human Diversity and Differential Treatment  **LO 1**

To explore and begin to understand the depth involved in human diversity, it's important to understand the concepts involved. These include discrimination, oppression, marginalization, alienation, stereotypes, prejudice, populations at risk, and social and economic justice.

### Discrimination, Oppression, Marginalization, and Alienation

A major social work value involves the importance of people being treated fairly and equally. Unjust treatment impairs people's ability to determine their own life paths and achieve their optimal well-being. Membership in groups that differ from the mainstream can place people at increased risk of inequitable treatment in the

**EP 2, 2a**

forms of discrimination, oppression, marginalization, alienation, economic deprivation, and poverty. **Discrimination** is the act of treating people differently based on the fact that they belong to some group rather than on merit. **Oppression** involves putting extreme limitations and constraints on some person, group, or larger system. **Marginalization** is the condition of having less power and being viewed as less important than others in the society because of belonging to some group or having some characteristic (e.g., racial, economic, ethnic, or political) (Barker, 2014). *Alienation*, related to marginalization, is the feeling that you don't fit in or aren't treated as well as others in the mainstream of society (Barker, 2014).

**Economic deprivation** is the condition of having inadequate or unjust access to financial resources. The latter can result from a number of circumstances, including unemployment, job discrimination, insufficient work benefits, and unsatisfactory public fiscal policies (e.g., unfair tax rates or eligibility standards for financial benefits and services that make them inaccessible to those in need). Related to economic deprivation is poverty, a concept that has been defined in many ways. One definition of **poverty** is the condition "of not having enough money to buy things that are considered necessary and desirable" (Kornblum & Julian, 2012, p. 196). One way of looking at this involves not having enough resources to exist. Another view concerns having enough to live but significantly less than what others around you possess.

It is social workers' responsibility to appreciate diversity and recognize that differences significantly affect people's ability to function and have access to life experiences. Differences may expose people to "oppression, poverty, marginalization, and alienation as well as privilege, power, and acclaim" (CSWE, 2015, p. 4). People with many resources have advantages. They may have *power*, the ability to move people on a chosen course to produce an effect or achieve some goal (Homan, 2011). Related to power are privilege and acclaim. **Privilege** entails special rights or benefits enjoyed because of elevated social, political, or economic status. **Acclaim** is "enthusiastic and public praise" (Lindberg, 2007, p. 7).

### Stereotypes and Prejudice

Stereotypes often contribute to discrimination, oppression, marginalization, alienation, economic deprivation, and poverty. A **stereotype** is a fixed mental picture of a member of some specified group based on some attribute or attributes that reflect an overly simplified view of that group, without consideration or appreciation of individual differences. Stereotypes are  **EP 1b, 2b, 2c** related to **prejudice**—a negative opinion or prejudgment about an individual, group, or issue that is not based on fact.

Stereotypes and prejudice can involve preconceived ideas based on a person's skin color, gender, age, ethnic heritage, or external appearance. What mental images and assumed expectations come to mind when you picture a 77-year-old woman, a person using a wheelchair, or a gay man? To what extent do these images reflect stereotypes instead of unique characteristics and strengths?

It's easy to envision a number of scenarios concerning potential discrimination and oppression based on stereotypes. For instance, think of an African American family moving into a small, virtually all-White Midwestern town. Picture a 58-year-old woman applying for a job in a software production center where all the employees are under age 30. Or consider a gay couple expressing affection in a primarily heterosexual bar.

Membership in any diverse group provides a different set of environmental circumstances. A wealthy, middle-aged Asian American man who just immigrated to Los Angeles from Tokyo experiences a very different world from an older adult woman of Scandinavian heritage living in Michigan's economically depressed Upper Peninsula.

Becoming aware of any stereotypes and prejudices they hold is an ongoing, career-long process for social workers. They must not allow such personal feelings to interfere with fair, effective practice that is guided by professional values and ethics.

What stereotypes do you harbor about various groups? Focus on Critical Thinking 3.1 provides a self-awareness exercise that might give you some insights.

### Populations at Risk and Social and Economic Justice

"**Diversity** emphasizes the similarity and dissimilarity between numerous groups in society that have distinguishing characteristics" (Lum, 2011, p. 129). We have established that factors involved in diversity shape life experiences and may result in oppression or privilege. **Populations at risk** are people at greater risk of deprivation and unfair treatment because they share some identifiable characteristic that places them in a diverse group. Multiple factors characterize diversity, including "age, class, color, culture, disability and ability, ethnicity, gender, gender identity and expression, immigration status, marital status, political ideology, race, religion/spirituality, sex, sexual orientation, and tribal sovereign status" (CSWE, 2015, p. 4).  **EP 2, 3a, 3b**

To reemphasize, a major responsibility of social work practitioners is to pursue social and economic justice for populations at risk and people in need. Recall from Chapter 1 that **social justice** involves the idea that in a perfect world all citizens would have identical "rights, protection, opportunities, obligations, and social benefits," regardless of their backgrounds and membership in diverse groups (Barker, 2014, p. 398). Similarly, **economic justice**

**FOCUS ON CRITICAL THINKING 3.1**  RACIAL SELF-AWARENESS  **LO 2**

Self-awareness is a key quality for people entering social work and other helping professions. To assess your own level of self-awareness, ask yourself these critical thinking questions:

**EP 1b, 2c, 7a, 8a**

- What adjectives and concepts automatically come to mind when you think of Hispanics? Native Americans? American Indians? African Americans? Asian Americans? Caucasians?
- Do all of the adjectives for each group apply to every single person in that group?
- In what group or groups do you include yourself? Do all the adjectives and concepts you identified for that group characterize you accurately?

- When did you first become aware of your race? Did you think of yourself as being different from people of other races? If so, in what ways?
- In what ways, if any, have you noticed people of different races being treated differently? What do you think are the reasons for such treatment?
- What experiences have you had with people of races different from your own? To what extent were they positive or negative, and why?
- While you were growing up, was your school integrated with people from other racial backgrounds? How about your neighborhood?
- Did you or your parents have friends of different races? Why or why not?
- Did you ever question why all our presidents have been males? (Schram & Mandell, 2000)

concerns the distribution of resources in a fair and equitable manner.

In real life, social and economic justice are hard goals to attain. Rarely are rights and resources fairly and equitably distributed. Even the definitions *of fair* and *equitable* are widely debated. Do they mean that all people should receive the same income regardless of what work they do, or even whether they have jobs? As you now know, social workers must constantly be on the lookout for injustice because it is their ethical responsibility to combat it whenever necessary and possible to do so.

## Empowerment and a Strengths Perspective  **LO 3**

Simply put, social workers help people solve problems. However, to do this, practitioners must focus on clients' strengths. Concentrating on the problem at hand tells workers what is wrong but not what to do about it. Focusing on clients' strengths provides social workers with clues about how to proceed by building on these strengths. Practitioners should view themselves as learners and consider their clients as important providers of information.

One example of emphasizing client strengths concerns Michael, a middle-aged man who has moderate

intellectual (cognitive) disabilities (Saleebey, 2006b, p. 85). A social work student working with Michael visited him in his apartment one day. Michael was capable of living alone if he had some supportive supervision, including help with getting groceries, paying bills, and organizing other necessary activities. The student noticed that

**EP 2b, 7c**

Michael's walls were covered with intricately drawn maps of his town, state, and country, and was awestruck at the careful detail and attractive colors. Taking the initiative, the student worked with Michael to make the local newspaper and museum aware of his talent and his output. The paper published articles about Michael, and a local museum exhibited his work. Subsequently, a greeting card company with national distribution approached Michael and other amateur artists with intellectual or physical disabilities about initiating a whole new card line.

We have established that *empowerment* is the "process of increasing personal, interpersonal, or political power so that individuals can take action to improve their life situations" (Gutierrez, 2001, p. 210). Empowerment means increasing, emphasizing, developing, and nurturing strengths and positive attributes. It aims at enhancing individuals', groups', families', and communities' power and control over their destinies.

Cowger (1994) maintains that social work historically has focused on dysfunction, pathology, and "individual inadequacies" (p. 262). He states that "if assessment focuses on deficits, it is likely that deficits will remain the focus of both the worker and the client during remaining contacts. Concentrating on deficits or strengths can lead to self-fulfilling prophecies" (p. 264). He continues that a strengths perspective can provide "structure and content for an examination of realizable alternatives, for the mobilization of competencies that can make things different, and for the building of self-confidence that stimulates hope" (p. 265).

Saleebey articulates a **strengths perspective** that is essentially based on empowerment. He cites at least five primary underlying principles (2013, pp. 17–20):

1. "Every individual, group, family and community has strengths."

2. "Trauma and abuse, illness and struggle may be injurious but they may also be sources of challenge and opportunity."

3. Social workers should assume that they "do not know the upper limits of the capacity to grow and change and take individual, group, and community aspirations seriously."

4. Social workers "best serve clients by collaborating with them."

5. "Every environment is full of resources." (Some capitalized letters converted to lowercase.)

As noted previously, empowerment implies that people lack power and thereby need it increased. Several designated groups of people suffer from stereotypes, discrimination, and oppression. It is social work's task to empower clients in general and members of oppressed groups in particular. Highlight 3.1 discusses some research concerning effective empowerment approaches with women.

---

## HIGHLIGHT 3.1    EMPOWERMENT FOR WOMEN IN GROUPS    LO 4

Parsons (2001) conducted a qualitative study of effective empowerment strategies for women. There is substantial support for the use of consciousness-raising as a strategy to empower women (GlenMaye, 1998). **Consciousness-raising** is the process of facilitating people's understanding of a social issue, with personal implications when there was little grasp of that issue before. Women often  **EP 7d, 8d** don't realize the relationship between their troubles and the world around them, thereby unjustly assuming all the blame themselves (Barnett, Miller-Perrin, & Perrin, 2011). For example, women in relationships in which they are regularly battered frequently blame themselves, not their abusers, for their problems. A woman might think that she shouldn't have yelled back at him because that was only asking to be punched. Or she might think that she should have ironed his collar the correct way and then he wouldn't have had to hit her in retribution.

Parsons (2001) studied two women's groups and evaluated the conditions conducive to women's empowerment. The Domestic Violence Survivors (DVS) was made up of women coping with battery who were trying to regain control of their lives. The All Families Deserve a Chance group was made up of women receiving public assistance who wished to advocate for improved policies and conditions for themselves and other women receiving aid. The two groups were chosen because they reflected two very different objectives. One involved improving the lives of individuals by gaining personal control, a *micro* goal. The other concentrated on advocating for change in social policy, a *macro* goal.

The following themes emerged as providing successful conditions for women's empowerment within a group setting.

- *Safety:* Knowing nothing horrible will happen makes group members feel more comfortable about participating and having control.
- *Mutual interaction:* Having the ability to interact and communicate with other group members without feeling threatened is reassuring.
- *Commonality:* Finding out that they are not the only ones having these problems is empowering.
- *Acceptance:* Feeling that they belong, regardless of their problems, self-criticism, or mistakes, gives group members increased self-confidence and a sense of power.

*(continued)*

**HIGHLIGHT 3.1 *(continued)***

- *Validation:* Having what they say about their experiences be "confirmed" and "heard" by others helps them learn "that they [are] ... not crazy" (Parsons, 2001, p. 168).
- *Interdependence:* Feeling that they can rely on each other for help and support bolsters their confidence and ability to take action.

Strategies used by the social workers running the groups were also found to enhance feelings of empowerment. First, social workers provided support by encouraging group members to speak, listening to what they had to say, and believing them. Group members thus felt they had the right to be listened to and to think through their issues. One group member explained:

[The group leader] is like a mentor. She challenges you. She won't let me get away with being afraid. She isn't going to let me get in the way of me. Her instincts for people have made me aware of my own feelings. She taught me that even though I am not always strong, I am not a weak person. I have high expectations, push myself. She says you are doing a good job even though you are not doing everything you want to be doing. She has more faith in me than I do in myself sometimes. I say, if she has this kind of faith in me, why can't I have it myself?

*(Parsons, 2001, p. 170)*

Providing support for survivors of violence is vital (Barnett et al., 2011). Breton and Nosko (1997) cite an interaction demonstrating worker support that occurred in another group for women who had suffered domestic violence:

*Woman:* I have no self-esteem.
*Worker:* What does self-esteem mean to you?
*Woman:* I don't know, really.
*Worker:* Well, then, maybe you have some. (p. 137)

A second effective social work strategy for empowerment involved educating group members about relevant issues (Barnett et al., 2011). For the DVS, such education entailed talking about the cycle of violence (i.e., building up of tension, explosive battering incident, making up)—how difficult it is to break it and how perpetrators do all they can to maintain their control through violence. For All Families Deserve a Chance, the social worker taught women the steps for advocacy. Group members learned how to clarify their position, formulate recommendations for changing public assistance policy, and effectively communicate with decision makers.

Third, the social workers actively advocated on the group members' behalf. Workers demonstrated that they were ardently on their clients' side by encouraging them, spurring them on, and readily bestowing positive feedback for their achievements.

Fourth, the social workers helped group members learn how to express, deal with, and resolve conflict without anger or violence. Fifth, the social workers encouraged the women to take risks by trusting others and allowing themselves to hope that things could actually get better. Sixth, the social workers provided a role model for group members, thereby affording guidance for more effective communication and appropriate assertiveness in addition to conflict management. Finally, group members learned that taking small steps could enhance empowerment. Small successes slowly led to increased confidence and achievement of bigger goals.

## Resiliency: Seeking Strength amid Adversity

A concept related to the strengths perspective and empowerment is **resiliency**: the ability of an individual, family, group, community, or organization to recover from adversity and resume functioning even when suffering serious trouble, confusion, or hardship (CSWE, 2015, p. 10; Greene, 2012). For example, Norman (2000) provides an illustration of this notion:

*When a pitched baseball hits a window, the glass usually shatters. When that same ball meets a baseball bat, the bat is rarely damaged. When a hammer strikes a ceramic vase, it too usually shatters. But when that same hammer hits a rubber automobile tire, the tire quickly returns to its original shape. The baseball bat and the automobile tire both demonstrate resiliency, (p. 3)*

Resiliency involves at least two dimensions—*risk factors* and *protective factors* (Greene & Conrad, 2012, pp. 32, 34; Norman, 2000, p. 3). In this context, **risk factors** involve "stressful life events or adverse environmental conditions that increase the **vulnerability** [defenselessness or helplessness] of individuals" or other systems (Norman, 2000, p. 3). **Protective factors**, on the other hand, "buffer, moderate, and protect against those vulnerabilities" (p. 3).

For example, Watkins (2002) studied six urban girls between ages 11 and 14 who were at risk of negative influences including poverty, "poor parental education, tenuous family structure, … history of abuse or neglect, and the influence of negative home environments" (p. 117). The study investigated how these girls were able to survive and even thrive in the midst of adversity, demonstrating their capacity for resiliency. Two of the girls are described as follows (Watkins, 2002):

*Shatika: This 12-year-old African American girl was tall and thin. She described herself as "I'm what you call light-skinned." Adolescent acne (which she called "skin bumps") was noticeable on her forehead, nose, and cheeks. Shatika's brown hair with red highlights was pulled behind her ears with a rubber band. She explained that her hair "needed to be done," but her mother was unable to afford the cost of a permanent. Shatika was very soft-spoken and hesitatingly made eye contact as the interview process was explained….*

*Daisy: This 13-year-old Caucasian girl was petite with symmetrical fullness of hips and breasts. Her heavily permed dark blond hair was shoulder length and she wore a ribbon to keep her hair out of her small and closely set gray eyes. Daisy was dressed in "daisy dukes"—short shorts with matching gingham shirt. As she spoke in soft, hushed tones, Daisy made it clear that she was willing to help with the project only if she could be assured that no one would "find out my secrets." She said, "I ain't never got to talk about me before and it could help me. It's good to talk with someone sometimes to hear yourself." (p. 119)*

The study found that these girls exhibited resiliency when they actively sought means to enhance their own well-being and protect them from harm in at least two ways (Watkins, 2002). First, the girls used their own positive relationship-building skills to seek positive, close connections with people who were or became central in their lives. Such people might include a parent or parents, members of their extended family (several girls mentioned their close relationships with their aunts), other adults such as "youth workers, coaches, clergy, neighbors, [or] teachers," and peers with whom they were "sharing activities, hanging out together, keeping secrets, and 'keeping … out of trouble'" (Watkins, 2002, pp. 121–122).

A second way these girls used resiliency was in developing strategies to protect themselves in an unsafe urban environment. "The girls would deliberately prearrange travel companions when walking to the corner store. To avoid danger, they would map out the route they would take through the streets. They developed other physical resistance strategies, such as personal safety plans or not 'hanging on the streets'" (Watkins, 2002, p. 125).

Resiliency can also characterize larger systems. An example at the organizational level is a public university experiencing budget cuts of several million dollars. That university is resilient to the extent that it responds to the risk of loss, protects its most important functions, makes plans to adapt to the shortfall of resources, and continues providing students with a quality education. Resiliency involves focusing on the university's strengths to maintain basic functioning.

Resiliency may also be demonstrated at the community level (Queiro-Tajalli & Campbell, 2012). One illustration involves a group of urban neighborhoods that addresses an increasing crime and drug use problem. These troubles put the community at risk of disorganization and destruction. Community strengths include availability of organizations that provide resources; residents' expectations for appropriate, positive behavior; and opportunities for "neighborhood youths to constructively participate in the community" (Greene & Livingston, 2012, p. 79). A resilient community might use its concerned citizens to form neighborhood organizations that oversee community conditions and upkeep, work with public services to improve conditions, and advocate for increased resources (Homan, 2011). Neighborhood Watch programs may be formed, where neighborhood residents volunteer to carefully watch each other's premises to prevent and combat crime. Community residents might work with local police and schools to establish drug education and prevention programs for young people. They might also advocate for more police to increase surveillance and apprehension of drug dealers. Many communities have successfully driven out drug vendors, reclaiming and securing their neighborhoods and parks so children can feel safe in these places. A resilient community uses its strengths to address the risks threatening it and protect its residents.

# Facets of Human Diversity   **LO 5**

We have established that human diversity is the vast range of differences among groups, including those related to "age, class, color, culture, disability and ability, ethnicity, gender, gender identity and expression, immigration status, marital status, political ideology, race, religion/ spirituality, sex, sexual orientation, and tribal sovereign status" (CSWE, 2015,

EP 1, 1b, 2, 2a, 2b, 7c

p. 4). Highlight 3.2 provides summary definitions for these concepts.

Social workers must understand human diversity for two reasons. First, many members of diverse groups are populations at risk of discrimination, oppression, marginalization, and alienation. Second, it's necessary to recognize the values and issues of diverse groups to appreciate differences and build on strengths.

Social work by nature addresses virtually any type of problem posed by any type of person

---

## HIGHLIGHT 3.2    DIMENSIONS OF DIVERSITY

**Age:** Some period of time during a person's life span. Age is often considered an important aspect of human diversity for older adults as they experience *ageism,* discrimination based on preconceived notions about older people, regardless of their individual qualities and capabilities.

**Class** (or **Social Class**): People's status or ranking in society with respect to such standards as "relative wealth, power, prestige, educational level, or family background" (Barker, 2014, p. 396).

**Culture:** "A way of life including widespread values (about what is good and bad), beliefs (about what is true), and behavior (what people do every day)" (italics deleted) (Macionis, 2013, p. 5).

**Disability (and Ability):** "Any physical or mental im-pairment [or ongoing health or mental health condi-tion] that substantially limits one or more major life activities"; these activities include "seeing, hearing, speaking, walking, breathing, performing manual tasks, learning, caring for oneself, and working" (Equal Employment Opportunity Commission, 1997, p. 1). **Ability** is the capacity to perform and get things done in various activities.

**Ethnicity:** The affiliation with a large group of people who have "common racial, national, tribal, religious, linguis-tic, or cultural origin or background" (Mish, 2008, p. 429).

**Gender:** "The social and psychological characteristics associated with being female or male" (McCammon & Knox, 2007, p. 112).

**Gender Expression:** The manner in which we express ourselves to others in ways related to gender that include both behavior and personality.

**Gender Identity:** A person's internal psychological self-concept of being either a male or a female, or, possi-bly, some combination of both (Gilbert, 2008).

**Immigration Status:** A person's position in terms of legal rights and residency when entering and residing in a country that is not that person's legal country of origin.

**Marital Status:** The state of being legally married or legally unmarried.

**People of Color:** "A collective term that refers to the major groups of African, Latino and Asian Americans, and First Nations Peoples [Native Americans] who have been distinguished from the dominant society by color" (Lum, 2011, p. 129).

**Political Ideology:** The "relatively coherent system of ideas (beliefs, traditions, principles, and myths) about human nature, institutional arrangements, and social processes" that indicate how a government should be run and what principles that government should sup-port (Abramovitz, 2010, p. 131).

**Race:** The category of people who share a common descent and genetic origin that may be distinguished by "certain physical traits," or "interests, habits, or characteristics" (Mish, 2008, p. 1024).

**Religion/Spirituality:** People's spiritual beliefs concern-ing the origin, character, and reason for being, usually based on the existence of some higher power or powers, that often involves designated rituals and pro-vides direction for what is considered moral or right.

**Sex:** "The biological distinction between being female and being male, usually categorized on the basis of the reproductive organs and genetic makeup" (McCammon & Knox, 2007, p. 606).

**Sexual Orientation:** Sexual and romantic attraction to persons of one or both genders.

**Tribal Sovereign Status:** The right of federally recog-nized American Indian tribes to govern themselves, identify their members, oversee their lands, and con-duct tribal operations.

from any type of background. To help people, practitioners must be open-minded, nonjudgmental, knowledgeable, and skilled. Because the range of human diversity is endless, learning about it is a continuous process.

## Intersectionality of Diverse Factors

The concept of **intersectionality** involves the idea that people are complex and can belong to multiple, overlapping diverse groups. "The intersectional perspective acknowledges the breadth of human experiences, instead of conceptualizing social relations and identities separately in terms of either race *or* class *or* gender *or* age *or* sexual orientation"; rather, an intersectional approach focuses on the "interactional affects" of belonging to multiple groups (Murphy, Hunt, Zajicek, Norris, & Hamilton, 2009, p. 2). People may experience injustice from a combination of reasons. The concept of intersectionality

EP 2

> *underscores the complex nature of cultural and personal identities and human experiences that cannot be defined simply by one dimension of inequality or difference—either race or gender or sexual orientation or ability. The social worker, who is involved in working with individuals, families, groups, and communities belonging to diverse groups, must develop the cultural competence to work with people at the intersections of the multiple dimensions of diversity.*
>
> *(Murphy et al., 2009, p. 42)*

Murphy and her colleagues (2009) provide the following case example demonstrating the complexity of intersectionality:

> *The Vue family emigrated from Laos six months ago. They were happy to find a small apartment that is convenient to a grocery store and meatpacking plant where Mr. Vue works long hours. They have three daughters, aged five years, four years, and six months. Shortly after they moved in, a neighbor called the local Department of Human Services (DHS). The neighbor, Mrs. Smith, had spotted one of the girls sitting alone in front of the apartment door one afternoon. Mrs. Smith was surprised to see the front door open, the younger girl on the couch, and the infant sleeping. The police arrived on the scene about the same time Mrs. Vue returned*

> *home, carrying grocery bags. She was taken aback to see the police in her apartment. Mrs. Vue said she had left the children for thirty minutes to buy milk. The children were taken into DHS custody, and Mr. and Mrs. Vue were told that they would have to appear in court three days later.*
>
> *The Vue family will be assigned a case worker who is responsible for understanding how race, ethnicity, and class affect this family. Moving from a small village in Laos, could this family have understood the new dangers and expectations that come with parenting in the United States? How does their economic position affect their ability to find appropriate child care? What other factors affect their needs as a family? (p. 42)*

## Race and Ethnicity

Race and ethnicity are related concepts that reflect primary dimensions of human diversity. **Race** refers to the category of people who share a common descent and genetic origin that may be distinguished by "certain physical traits" or "interests, habits, or characteristics" (Mish, 2008, p. 1024). **Ethnicity** refers to the affiliation with a large group of people who have "common racial, national, tribal, religious, linguistic, or cultural origin or background" (Mish, 2008, p. 429). Race implies a greater genetic determinant, whereas ethnicity often relates to cultural or national heritage.

EP 2

Other terms often used are *minorities* and *people of color*. The collective term *people of color* "refers to the major groups of African, Latino, and Asian Americans, and First Nations Peoples [Native Americans] who have been distinguished from the dominant society by color" (Lum, 2011, p. 129).[1] **Minorities** are members of "a group of people who, because of physical or cultural characteristics, are singled out from the others in the society in which they live for differential and unequal treatment, and who therefore regard themselves as objects of collective discrimination" (Lum, 2011; Sue et al., 1998, p. 11; Wirth, 1945, p. 347). It is interesting that in the past many minorities did indeed make up a

---

[1]Note that not all Hispanic people are people of color. Consider, for example, a White woman born in Argentina who speaks Spanish, the national language, and whose ancestors originated in Spain.

smaller proportion of the total population than did **Anglos** (i.e., U.S. citizens of European heritage, also referred to as *Caucasians* or *Whites*). However, some minority populations such as Latinos, Latinas, or Hispanics are making substantial gains and within several decades may surpass Anglos in actual numbers. Highlight 3.3 discusses the terms used to describe the Latino, Latina, and Hispanic population in the United States.

## Culture

**Culture**, another dimension of diversity, is "a way of life including widespread values (about what is good and bad), beliefs (about what is true), and behavior (what people do every day)" (italics deleted) (Macionis, 2013, p. 5). Culture involves "the sum total of life patterns passed on from generation to generation within a group of people  and includes institutions, language, religious ideals, habits of thinking, artistic expressions, and patterns of social and interpersonal relationships" (Hodge, Struckmann, & Trost, 1975; Lum, 2007, p. 4). Aspects of culture are often related to people's

**EP 2**

ethnic, racial, and spiritual heritage. Focus on Critical Thinking 3.2 discusses cultural competence and stresses how important it is for social workers to be aware of their clients' values, traditions, and customs.

### Ethnic and Cultural Differences in Various Racial Groups

We've established that understanding and appreciating diversity are essential for social workers to practice effectively with clients. Because families provide a primary arena for conveying values, much of the following discussion will focus on them.

Three points are helpful when we think about multicultural diversity. The first is that certain values tend to characterize each major racial and ethnic group. However, the second point concerns how critical it is not to overly generalize. Various individuals may embrace such cultural values to different degrees. The third point involves the importance of respect for and appreciation of the differences within large groups. For example, American Indians have been referred to as "Indians" only for the past 500 years (Harjo, 1999). In reality,

---

| HIGHLIGHT 3.3 | TERMS USED TO DESCRIBE LATINOS, LATINAS, AND HISPANIC PEOPLE |
|---|---|

The federal Office of Management and Budget originally coined the term *Hispanic* in 1980 for use in the census (Guzman & Carrasco, 2011). According to the original definition, a Hispanic was "a person of Mexican, Puerto Rican, Cuban, Central or South American or other Spanish culture or origin, regardless of race" (Green, 1999, p. 256). However, the concept is much more complex than this.  For example, does this umbrella term include Brazilians who speak Portuguese, South American Indians whose original language is not Spanish, Filipinos who speak Spanish, or immigrants from Spain (Green, 1999)?

**EP 1c**

Alternative terms are **Latino** and **Latina**, which make reference both to the Latin American languages, including Spanish, and to Latin America itself. However, this term omits South Americans who speak English, such as those from Belize or the Guyanas, and "people whose family roots extend to Italy, Germany,

and some areas of the Mediterranean" (Green, 1999, p. 256).

Still other terms often used are **Chicano** and **Chicana**, both of which refer to U.S. citizens with a Mexican heritage. The obvious disadvantage of these terms is that they focus only on Mexico and exclude people with origins in other countries, including those that are primarily Spanish speaking.

Longres and Aisenberg (2008, p. 31) summarize several points. Some people prefer not to refer to themselves as Hispanic because it's not rooted in Spanish but "imposed by American society." The terms *Latino* and *Latina* are probably the most widely accepted. Additionally, these terms allow users to distinguish between men and women, giving women greater "visibility." In general, it's best to use whatever terms people and communities prefer. This book will use the terms *Hispanic* and *Latino* or *Latina* interchangeably unless a specific group (e.g., Puerto Rican Americans or Chicanos or Chicanas [Mexican Americans]) is discussed.

## FOCUS ON CRITICAL THINKING 3.2 — CULTURAL COMPETENCE   LO 6

Social workers need to attain **cultural competence**—"mastery of a particular set of knowledge, skills, policies, and programs used by the social worker that address the cultural needs of individuals, families, groups, and communities" (Lum, 2005, p. 4). Cultural competence, strongly supported by the NASW *Code of Ethics,* involves the following six tasks for social workers (Arredondo et al., 1996; Lum, 2011; NASW, 2008, 1.05; Neukrug, 2013):

EP 2a, 7a, 7b, 7c, 8a, 8b

1. Develop an awareness of personal values, assumptions, and biases.
2. Establish an appreciation of other cultures and nurture attitudes that respect differences.
3. Understand how one's own cultural heritage and belief system differ from and may influence interaction with clients who have a different cultural background.
4. Recognize the existence of stereotypes about, discrimination against, and oppression of various diverse groups.
5. Commit to learning about clients' cultures.
6. Acquire effective skills for working with people from other cultures.

### Cultural Issues to Address

Therefore, an important aspect of cultural competence involves understanding various cultural issues. Consider the population breakdown. The *Statistical Abstract of the United States* (ProQuest, 2014) indicates that almost 63% of the total U.S. population of 313,914 million is non-Hispanic White; more than 12.3% is African American; less than 0.75% is American Indian and Alaskan Native; 5.7% is Asian; and more than 0.3% is Native Hawaiian and other Pacific Islander. Almost 2.4% reported being a member of more than one race. Almost 17% are Hispanic, who may be of any race. Two facts stand out from these figures: (1) There is significant diversity in the population, and (2) a person's race is not always clear-cut. A person's family line and genetic heritage may be quite complex.

The racial mix of the United States is rapidly changing. Currently, more than one-third of U.S. residents are people of color, and it's predicted that "nondominant groups are expected to become the majority by the year 2042" (Neukrug, 2013, p. 226). Given such a

diverse world, social workers and other helping professionals must be prepared to work with people having cultural backgrounds quite different from their own.

Social workers and other helping professionals must address at least four issues to work effectively with multicultural clients. First, they should rebuff the **melting pot myth**, which implies that we're all blended together into one big pot of creamed soup, that we all become essentially the same (Neukrug, 2013, p. 201). In reality, we're more like a salad bowl filled with various types of vegetables and croutons. Although we're all in there together, we maintain our individual and cultural distinctiveness.

The second issue that social workers must address is how people from various cultures have different ideas and expectations about what should happen during the intervention process (Neukrug, 2013). For example, an approach rooted in "Western values stresses the expression of feelings, self-disclosure, cause-and-effect thinking, 'open-mindedness,'" and personal self-control (Neukrug, 2013, p. 202). However, people from other cultures may assume very different perspectives. For example, a Hispanic man might emphasize the importance of family over what's best for himself as an individual. Similarly, he may find the blatant expression of emotions inappropriate and distasteful.

The third issue concerns **worldviews**—one's perception of how the world functions (in terms of relationships with other people, social and economic activity, spirituality, values, and nature) in addition to how one fits into that context. With an **ethnocentric worldview**, people perceive their own race, ethnic background, or cultural values as being better than that of others (Neukrug, 2013). Essentially, it's similar to the view "My way is not only the best way, it's the only way."

Consider the following interesting example:

A white female elementary school teacher in the United States posed a math problem to her class one day. "Suppose there are four blackbirds sitting in a tree. You take a slingshot and shoot one of them. How many are left?" A white student answered quickly, "That's easy. One subtracted from four is three." An African immigrant youth then answered with equal confidence, "Zero." The teacher chuckled at the latter response and stated that the first student was right and that, perhaps, the second student should study more math. From

*(continued)*

**FOCUS ON CRITICAL THINKING 3.2 (continued)**

that day forth, the African student seemed to withdraw from class activities and seldom spoke to other students or the teacher.

*(Sue, 1992, pp. 7–8, cited in Neukrug, 2013, p. 229)*

What the teacher didn't know was that the African boy viewed the problem from an entirely different perspective. He looked at the whole picture of what shooting a bird with a slingshot meant. If the teacher had sought clarification of his answer instead of making fun of him, she might have better understood. The student's answer made perfect sense to him: If you shoot a slingshot at four birds sitting in a tree and hit one, the other three will fly away immediately, of course, and none will be left. Nigerian educators frequently use this anecdote to portray how differently people in the United States and Africa view the world. The African perspective takes into account how all the parts involved in a problem work together. In contrast, an Anglo perspective tends to focus on individuals searching for isolated, specific, technical aspects of a problem to determine the one correct answer.

The fourth issue concerns the importance of family. Anglos tend to focus on the **nuclear family**—the immediate family group composed of parent[s] and children—and give less credence to the **extended family**—relatives beyond the nuclear family, including at least grandparents, aunts, uncles, and cousins (Richmond & Guindon, 2013). A related concept is *kinship*, which refers to the state of being related through a common ancestry.

For example, I once worked as a social worker at a day treatment center for children and adolescents with emotional and behavioral problems. They attended the center during the day to receive special education and therapy, and then returned to their homes in the

community at night and on weekends. A number of African American clients seemed to be staying at a different relative's home each week. This was a problem because clients were bused in from all over the city, so scheduling the bus route was a nightmare. The treatment center's administrators, all of whom were Anglos, identified multiple residences as a problem. However, it really was a strength and should have been viewed as such. These adolescents had a strong kinship system with their extended families. Many relatives were ready and willing to take care of these children when their nuclear family (in this case, their mothers) did not always have the resources and capabilities to do so.

Another example of the strengths demonstrated by extended families involves Navajo who live on a reservation stretching from the south central Colorado plateau to parts of Arizona, New Mexico, and Utah. The tribe opened and ran its own nursing home for tribal members (Mercer, 1996). The home's staff had to be very sensitive to the fact that residents had numerous visitors from their extended family, many of whom were quite distant from the nuclear family and some of whom would travel great distances at significant cost. This was in stark contrast to many Anglo nursing homes, in which staff are accustomed to receiving few visitors for residents, and often only immediate family. Staff there frequently view visits as cumbersome and unmanageable. Chapter 10 elaborates further on the Navajo's empowering treatment of older adult family members.

## Critical Thinking Questions

How would you describe your racial and cultural background? How would you explain your worldview? How would you describe the dynamics, closeness, and strengths of your own nuclear and extended families?

they make up more than 560 individual nations identified by the U.S. federal government within its borders (Weaver, 2013). Nations include Tsististas, Lakota, Dine, Muscogee, and Ojibway (Harjo, 1999). They are strikingly "diverse in terms of language, cultures, social systems, forms of government, and spiritual belief systems" (Weaver, 2013, p. 171).

The following section discusses some of the values, beliefs, and perspectives assumed by several cultural groups in our society: Hispanics, Native Americans, African Americans, and Asian Americans. Figure 3.1 summarizes the primary concepts.

### Hispanics

We have established that the terms *Hispanic*, *Latino*, and *Latina* have generally been used to refer to people originating in countries in which Spanish is spoken. However, we have also established that the terms refer to people originating in a wide range of places. Essentially, no one term is acceptable to all groups of people. Primary Hispanic groups in the United States in terms of size are Mexican Americans (more than 65% of Hispanics), Puerto Ricans (more than 9%), Central American (more than 8%), and South American (approaching 6%) (ProQuest, 2014). Cuban Americans make up about 3.5% of

| Hispanics | Native Americans | African Americans | Asian Americans |
|---|---|---|---|
| • Common language<br>• Extended family<br>• Respect for older adults<br>• Spirituality<br>• Division of gender roles | • Extended family and respect for older adults<br>• Noninterference<br>• Harmony with nature<br>• Less formal and rigid concept of time<br>• Spirituality<br>• Differences due to acculturation<br>• Tribal sovereign status | • Extended family<br>• Child centeredness<br>• Respect for older adults<br>• Gender-role flexibility<br>• Strong religious beliefs | • Family vs. individual as primary unit<br>• Family interdependence and collectivism<br>• Filial piety<br>• Patriarchal hierarchy<br>• Internal family resolution of personal problems<br>• Interpersonal harmony |

**FIG-3-1** Common Cultural Values for Four Diverse Groups

Hispanics (U.S. Census Bureau, 2011). However, for any particular family, Goldenberg and Goldenberg (2002) caution, "Socioeconomic, regional, and demographic characteristics vary among Hispanic American groups, making cultural generalizations risky" (p. 326).

Santiago-Rivera, Arredondo, and Gallardo-Cooper (2002) reflect:

*Perhaps no other ethnic group in the United States is as heterogeneous in its ethnicity, physical appearance, cultural practices and traditions, and Spanish language dialects as the Latino population. Latinos in the United States are a diverse group of multigenerational [people] … from different Spanish-speaking countries as well as long-term residents in the southwest United States. All have unique social, economic, and political histories. Latino groups vary in their ancestry, blending indigenous [people originating in an area] (e.g., Aztec and Mayan) and Spanish cultural traditions and, for some Latino groups, African traditions. (p. 56)*

It's important not to make stereotyped assumptions about such a diverse group. Santiago-Rivera and her colleagues (2002) continue:

*Although it is not often reported, Latinos may also be of Asian heritage. The Philippine islands, conquered by Spain, were populated by people of Asian heritage. Whereas the native language of the island is Tagalog, Spanish surnames are commonplace, and in the United States, Filipinos may claim either Asian or Latino heritage. In South America and*

*Mexico, there are settlements of Chinese families as well. Peru is one such example. (p. 23)*

Keeping in mind that more specific variations exist within the many subgroups, we will discuss some cultural themes important to Hispanic families in general. Hispanic heritage is rich and diverse, but the groups tend to share similarities in terms of values, beliefs, attitudes, culture, and self-perception. These include the significance of a common language and culture; the importance of family relationships, including extended family and other support systems; spirituality; and the traditional strictness of gender roles.

*The Significance of a Common Language and Cultural Pride*  The first theme important in understanding the environment for children growing up in Hispanic families is the significance of a common language (Delgado-Romero, Nevels, Capielo, Galvan, & Torres, 2013). Almost 60% of Latinos and Latinas indicate they speak English only or speak it fluently; however, almost 80% of Latinos and Latinas indicate they speak Spanish fluently (Longres & Aisenberg, 2008). Therefore, social workers should "know that there is a growing population of bilingual Latinos who have varying degrees of language proficiencies in English and Spanish" (Santiago-Rivera et al., 2002, p. 121). For instance, recent immigrants may use little if any English, whereas people whose families have been here for centuries may be bilingual or lack any knowledge of Spanish. One strong implication of such diversity is the need for social workers to assess Latino clients' language history and use on an individual basis.

Another important note is the fact that so many cultural activities and aspects of cultural pride are associated with Spanish. Consider the events and holidays (e.g., Cinco de Mayo for Mexican Americans, which refers to the glorious day a small Mexican army defeated a French army battalion), culture, history, and foods, all associated with Spanish origins, that are so meaningful in daily cultural life (Guzman & Carrasco, 2011).

*The Importance of Family and Extended Family* A second theme reflecting a major strength in many Hispanic families is the significance placed on relationships with nuclear and extended family, including "aunts, uncles, cousins, and grandparents, as well as close friends," referred to as **familismo** (Brammer, 2012; Delgado-Romero et al., 2013; Diller, 2015; Santiago-Rivera et al., 2002, pp. 42–43).

> *Latino families are typically large, intergenerational, and interdependent, and offer an important source of support to their members.... Extended family ties are highly valued and serve as a source of pride and security.... This emphasis on respect and responsibility to family members often leads to [older] ... adults both being cared for and taking on caregiving responsibilities within the family.... [Older adults] are often cared for within the family rather than through formal social services. When nursing homes are used, family members often continue to fulfill supportive caregiving responsibilities.*
>
> *(Kolb, 1999; Weaver, 2005, p. 148)*

Another important related concept reflecting a cultural strength is *compadrazco* (godparentage). **Compadres** (godparents) often serve as "substitute parents" who "may be prominent leaders or older people who hold some position of authority and respect within the Latino community. Such individuals play an important role in the Latino family's life and are included in all traditional celebrations. The practice of godparentage formalizes relationships between the child's parents and the *compadres* and promotes a sense of community" (Gonzalez & Acevedo, 2013; Santiago-Rivera et al., 2002, p. 44).

*Spirituality and Religion* A third theme characterizing many Hispanic families is the importance of spirituality and religion (Gonzalez & Acevedo, 2013; Longres & Aisenberg, 2008).

> *Spirituality has a fundamental shaping influence on the lives of many Latinos. Catholicism is a defining force of family and gender roles for Latino people.... Latino Catholicism revolves around the concepts of life and death. This fatalistic belief system emphasizes that God will provide. There is a pervading sense that much of what happens is beyond an individual's personal control. Most Latinos are Roman Catholic, but many espouse beliefs and practices influenced by indigenous and African belief systems.*
>
> *(Santiago-Rivera et al., 2002; Weaver, 2005, p. 147)*

Examples of such folk beliefs are the following (Negroni-Rodriguez & Morales, 2001, p. 135; Santiago-Rivera et al., 2002; Weaver, 2005):

***Espiritismo (among Puerto Ricans):*** "[T]he belief in spirits. Everyone is believed to have spirits of protection, and these can be increased by performing good deeds and decreasing evil. Latinos who ascribe to *espiritismo* believe that loved ones can be around in spirit after death and can lead one's life in times of difficulties. *Espiritistas* (spiritist healers) communicate with spirits and can be incarnated by them. Healing can take place with prescribed folk healing treatment."

***Curanderismo (among Mexican Americans and other Central and South Americans):*** The practice of curing "physical, emotional, and folk illnesses. *Curanderoslas* are healers who use a range of treatments, such as herbal remedies, inhalation, sweating, massage, incantations, and *limpieza* (a ritual cleansing)."

***Santeria (among Cuban Americans):*** Practices that combine "African deities with Catholic saints. The [**santeros** and **santeras**] are priests who function as healers, diviners, and directors of rituals."

*Division of Gender Roles* A fourth theme often characterizing Hispanic families involves a strict division of gender roles (Delgado-Romero et al., 2013; Diller, 2015; Longres & Aisenberg, 2008). This is reflected in two major concepts (Gonzalez & Acevedo, 2014; Weaver, 2005). **Machismo** is the idea of male "superiority" that "defines the man as provider, protector, and head of the household"; **marianismo**, on the other hand, is the idea that, "after the Virgin

Mary," females are valued for their "female spiritual sensitivity and self-sacrifice for the good of husband and children.... The mother and wife roles offer power to exercise authority in the home. However, women are also expected to be dependent on men" (Negroni-Rodriguez & Morales, 2001, p. 135).

Santiago-Rivera and her colleagues (2002) note that these beliefs may give mothers an important yet challenging role in the family. If a woman is self-effacing and giving at all times, she may appear to outsiders to be more like a submissive doormat. However, those who know Latinas, especially mothers, often note that women are the silent power in the family.

Weaver (2005) indicates that "[a]lthough distinct gender roles exist, it is important to recognize that not all Latinas fit these roles to the same extent. For example, Latinas are often stereotyped as passive and submissive, but many changes have taken place in marriages and families in the last decade. Many Latinas now work outside the home and may wield decision-making power about family finances. It is important to understand evolving gender roles within Latino families" (p. 146). Today 56.5% of Hispanic women are in the workforce compared to 59.9% of African American women and 58.5% of White women (ProQuest, 2014). From a strengths perspective, Hispanic women function as socializers, educators, and promoters of values and beliefs within family systems. Hispanic couples vary widely in terms of who assumes decision-making power and responsibility for family support, as do couples in any other ethnic or racial group. Other factors to consider that influence gender roles include educational level, income, location, history in this country, verbal communication, and family structure (Santiago-Rivera et al., 2002).

### American Indians, Native Americans, or First Nations Peoples

We have stressed that there are more than 560 separate American Indian nations with distinctive dialects, beliefs, and customs (Bureau of Indian Affairs, 2014; Weaver, 2013). Weaver (2013) comments on the terms used to refer to these indigenous peoples (that is, people who originally populated these geographic areas):

*While these diverse groups are often referred to by general labels such as Native American or*

*American Indian, many indigenous people prefer to be referred to as a member of a specific tribal nation such as Comanche or Arapaho. Some indigenous people find the use of labels that include the term American (i.e., Native American, American Indian) to be offensive since indigenous people predate the founding of the United States and the labeling of this continent. The terms indigenous and First Nations are preferred by some Native people. While there is no consensus on on acceptable term, usage of some terms is more common in certain geographical areas. Additionally, individuals often have strong preferences about terminology. (p. 171)*

Some people feel that the term *First Nations Peoples* emphasizes the true status of these population groups as the first inhabitants of North America who populated intact nations before Europeans arrived. Additionally, the term *Native American* is "a broader designation" than that referring to North American peoples because it may include Hawaiians and Samoans (American Psychological Association, 2010, p. 75). This book will arbitrarily use the terms *American Indian* and *First Nations Peoples* interchangeably when referring to these population groups. When quoting other sources, sometimes the term *Native American* is used.

Whenever possible, it's best to identify the participants' specific group (American Psychological Association, 2010; Brave Heart & Chase, 2005). Although some nations consist of fewer than 100 people (Weaver, 2007), others including the Cherokee, Chippewa, Choctaw, Navajo, and Sioux have well over 100,000 members (ProQuest, 2014). Weaver (2011) further describes the picture:

*Extensive diversity also exists among people within Native nations in terms of their cultural identity. Some people are very knowledgeable about and grounded in their indigenous culture, while others are not. Sometimes this is based on choices an individual has made; however, it is more often the result of decades of damaging U.S. policies that tried to assimilate Native people. These policies were deliberate in their attempts to eradicate indigenous cultures. Many people lost their ability to speak their language and lost touch with their cultural traditions when they were forcibly taken away from their community and sent to government or church-run boarding schools. This sort of cultural loss impaired their ability to pass on cultural traditions to their children, and left many Native people with limited knowledge of their indigenous heritage. (p. 224)*

Sensitivity to differences among American Indian nations and to individuals within nations, along with appreciation of these differences, is vital to effective social work practice. However, as with Hispanic people, several themes characterize many First Nations Peoples. These include the importance of family ties and extended family, noninterference, harmony with nature, the concept of time, and spirituality. Tribal sovereign status is another significant concept.

*The Importance of Family and Extended Family* As with Hispanic people, *family ties* including those with extended family are especially important (Bearse, 2008; Brammer, 2012; Ho, 1987; Paniagua, 2014). The sense of self is secondary compared to that of the family and the tribe (Paniagua, 2014). Diller (2015) explains:

*Family ties define existence, and the very definition of being a Navajo or a Sioux resides not within the individual's personality but rather in the intricacies of family and tribal responsibilities. When strangers meet, they identify themselves not by occupation or residence but by who their relatives are. Individual family members feel a close and binding connection with a broad network of relatives (often including some who are not related by blood) that can extend as far as second cousins. The very naming of relationships, in fact, reflects the unusual closeness that exists between relatives.... [For instance,] the concept of "in-law" has no meaning with Native culture because after entry in to the family system, no distinctions are made between natural and inducted individuals. (p. 270)*

Edwards and Edwards (2002) continue:

*It is sometimes confusing to accurately identify family members, as cousins may be affectionately referred to as brothers and sisters, and respected aunts and uncles (sometimes several times removed) may be addressed as mothers, fathers, and grandparents are. Elders are often referred to as "Grandmother" or "Grandfather" when there are no kinship ties to these people. (p. 247)*

Elders typically are turned to for advice and consultation on important matters (Garrett & Portman, 2011). Paniagua (2014) explains:

*American Indians emphasize the "administration" of the family by the father and older relatives. Thus, mutual respect between wife and husband, between parents and children, between immediate family members and other relatives, and between family members and the tribe is highly valued.... An important part of the American Indian cultural value of familism [the well-being of the family is most important and the interests of the individual secondary] is the tradition of consulting tribal leaders, elders, and medicine men or women when marital conflicts emerge. (p. 160)*

Children receive supervision and instruction not only from their parents but also from relatives of several generations; thus biological parents have "greater opportunity to engage in more fun-oriented activities with their children" and often are able to establish relationships with their children that are "less pressured and more egalitarian than that of the dominant culture" (Brammer, 2012; Ho, 1992, p. 76).

*Noninterference* A second significant concept in American Indian culture involves the emphasis on **noninterference** (Diller, 2015; Sue, 2006; Sue & Sue, 2008). Garrett and Portman (2011) elaborate:

*Respecting another person's natural right to self-determination means not interfering with that person's ability to choose, even when it is to keep that person from doing something foolish or dangerous. In Native American tradition, noninterference means caring in a very respectful way. Interfering with the activity of others, by way of aggression, for example, is neither encouraged nor tolerated. Above all, respect for others in this way ultimately shows respect for oneself and one's community. (p. 51)*

Although First Nations life emphasizes collective work and common goals, it also stresses the individual's right to have opinions (Paniagua, 2014). Therefore, "American Indians rarely tell their children what to do and often encourage them to make their own decisions" (Paniagua, 2014, p. 160). Locke (1998) explains:

*Many Native American Indians use noncoercive parenting styles that encourage the child's self-determination.... Child-rearing practices are characterized by early training in self-sufficiency, and psychological development is in harmony with knowledge gained from the natural world.... [American] Indian parents are generally quite permissive in their training, and children have no fixed schedules for eating or sleeping. (pp. 68–69)*

Another facet of noninterference involves how fathers or older male adults in a family do not control families. Rather, they administer or organize the family so that it may arrive at a decision regarding how to proceed (Paniagua, 2014).

*Harmony with Nature*   A third conceptual theme that characterizes American Indian culture is that of **harmony with nature** (Baruth & Manning, 1999; Dhooper & Moore, 2001; Diller, 2015; Ho, 1987). Ho (1987) reflects:

*American Indians hold nature as extremely important for they realize that they are but one part of a greater whole. There are many rituals and ceremonies among the tribes that express both their reverence for nature's forces and their observance of the balance that must be maintained between them and all other living and nonliving things. (p. 71)*

*A Less Rigid Concept of Time*   A fourth concept basic to First Nations life and related to harmony with nature is the *concept of time* (Bearse, 2008; Diller, 2015; Paniagua, 2014; Sue & Sue, 2008; Weaver, 2005). Time is considered an aspect of nature. Time flows along with life. It is not something that should take precedence over how you relate to others in your life. Therefore, time should not control or dictate how you live and spend your time. Hence other aspects of life, including interaction with other people, become more important than punctuality.

*Spirituality*   One other theme reflecting the perspective of many First Nations Peoples is that of *spirituality* (Bearse, 2008; Brammer, 2012; Garrett et al., 2013; Weaver, 2005). Dhooper and Moore (2001) explain:

*It was not until the passage of the American Indians Religious Freedom Act of 1978 that Native Americans were permitted religious freedom in the United States. Prior to that time, they were considered heathens and were often arrested and*

*imprisoned for practicing their religion. Religion is a universal concept among Native Americans. When they refer to the universe they include the world, god, the self, and others. Their religion embraces many gods or spirits, but there is usually one great god or Great Spirit to whom reference is made. Faith, an outgrowth of their religiosity, is a harmonizing force that gives purpose and significance to their culture, life, and land (Kasee, 1995). They believe in the reincarnation and infinite existences of their spirits and consider the elements and forces of nature such as the rain, sun, lightning, water, and fire as objects of worship. They believe that the natural world is controlled by the supernatural through spirits. From their perspective, every sphere of life is governed by religion. God and nature are inseparable, and being in disharmony with God will cause disharmony with nature, which will have a negative impact upon the self. (pp. 178–179)*

*Differences Due to Acculturation*   Note that the extent to which these five themes characterize any individual Native American person or family varies tremendously (Bearse, 2008). Sue and Sue (2008) reflect:

*Although some of the value differences between [American] Indians and non-[American] Indians have been presented, many Indians are acculturated and hold the values of the larger society. [Acculturation is "the adaptation of language, identity, behavior patterns, and preferences to those of the host/majority society" (Lum, 2004, p. 229).]... Five cultural orientation types were formulated by M. T. Garrett and Pichette (2000):*

1. *Traditional. The individual may speak little English, thinks in the native language, and practices traditional tribal customs and methods of worship.*
2. *Marginal. The individual may speak both languages but has lost touch with his or her cultural heritage and is not fully accepted in mainstream society.*
3. *Bicultural. The person is conversant with both sets of values and can communicate in a variety of contexts.*
4. *Assimilated. The individual embraces only the mainstream culture's values, behavior, and expectations.*

5. *Pantraditional.* *Although the individual has only been exposed to or adopted mainstream values, he or she has made a conscious effort to return to the "old ways." (p. 353)*

*Tribal Sovereign Status* One other important concept related to the identity and pride of American Indians involves tribal sovereign status. **Tribal sovereignty** is the right of federally recognized American Indian tribes to govern themselves, identify their members, oversee their lands, and conduct tribal operations (The Leadership Conference, 2014). American Indian nations "possess a nationhood status and retain inherent powers of self-government" (Bureau of Indian Affairs [BIA], 2014). The BIA (2014) further explains:

EP 2

*A federally recognized tribe is an American Indian or Alaska Native tribal entity that is recognized as having a government-to-government relationship with the United States, with the responsibilities, powers, limitations, and obligations attached to that designation, and is eligible for funding and services [e.g., for building schools, health care centers, or roads] from the Bureau of Indian Affairs.*

*Furthermore, federally recognized tribes ... are entitled to receive certain federal benefits, services, and protections because of their special relationship with the United States.... Tribes, therefore, possess the right to form their own governments; to make and enforce laws, both civil and criminal; to tax; to establish and determine members (i.e., tribal citizenship); to license and regulate activities within their jurisdiction; to zone; and to exclude persons from tribal lands.*

Tribal members retain the right to vote, to hold public office, to serve in the Armed Forces, and to pay taxes (the latter with some limitations). Additionally, they "are generally subject to local laws.... Most tribes now maintain tribal court systems and facilities to detain tribal members convicted of certain offenses within the boundaries of the reservation" (BIA, 2014).

### African Americans

There are 41.2 million African Americans in the United States (ProQuest, 2014). Fifty-five percent live in the South, 18.1% in the Midwest, 17.6% in

the Northeast, and 9.4% in the West (McRoy & Lombe, 2011). Consider the following facts (ProQuest, 2014):

- Of African Americans 25 and older, 84.3% of males and 85.5% of females have at least a high school degree. Almost 23% of African American women and 19.2% of African American men have at least a bachelor's degree.
- African Americans are more likely to live in poverty. In the African American population, 27.3% are poor compared with 12.8% of Whites.
- The highest poverty rates are evident among families headed by women. Thirty-nine percent of African American families and 28% of White families headed by women with no spouse present live in poverty.
- The poverty rate of African Americans aged 65 or older is 17.3%, which is more than twice the rate of White older adults (of whom 7.7% live in poverty).
- African American unemployment rates are 11.4%, almost twice that of Whites (6.1%).
- The median[2] income for African American households is $32,229 versus $52,214 for Whites. This is less than 62% of White median income.

McRoy and Lombe (2011) reflect:

*Despite income gains, the racial-wealth gap has widened considerably during the last 20 years.... The average net worth for Blacks is $6,166 compared with $67,000 for Whites.... The root of the wealth inequality lies in a past in which African Americans were denied opportunities to accumulate assets. The discrepancies in wealth mean that many African Americans do not benefit from the cushion that assets provide in poverty reduction and social mobility across generations. (p. 280)*

African Americans, like other racial, cultural, and ethnic groups, reflect great diversity. "The term *African American* subsumes a diverse array of peoples including African Americans born in this country, Africans, and individuals from the West Indies and Central and South America" (Diller, 2015, p. 284).

---

[2]A *median* is a value in the exact middle of an ordered listing of values where half of the values fall above and half of the values fall below it.

Despite this diversity, however, four dynamics have "shaped African American experience and culture" (Black, 1996; cited in Diller, 2015, p. 285):

- *African legacy—rich in culture, custom, and achievement.*
- *History of slavery and deliberate attempt to destroy the core and soul of the people.*
- *Racism and discrimination and ongoing efforts to continue the psychological and economic subjugation started during slavery.*
- *Victim system and process by which individuals and communities are denied access to the instruments of development and advancement.*

*(Black, 1996, p. 59)*

Devore (2001) cautions that, on the one hand, we should "begin with the understanding that African American families are not homogeneous. One cannot point to the [typical] African American family. No composite exists. Therefore, social workers must understand that African American [families] will differ in style and composition, but will experience persistent racism" (p. 34).

On the other hand, Solomon (2002) maintains that although many groups have been effectively integrated into the dominant culture (e.g., "Dutch, German, Scandinavian, and Irish"), this has not been the case with African Americans (p. 299). She continues that "the result has been the maintenance of a distinctive culture that possesses elements of the dominant culture, elements of other subcultural groups who have been oppressed, and elements that are a consequence of the unique African American experience. This cultural distinctiveness may be observed" in a variety of ways (Solomon, 2002, p. 299). These include three general commonalities that tend to characterize African American families.

*The Importance of Extended Family and "Child-Centeredness"* First, extended family ties are very important for African American families (Diller, 2015; Moore, 2008; Sue & Sue, 2008). West-Olatunji and Conwill (2011) elaborate:

*One of the important values among African American families is the idea of child-centeredness. This means that the purpose of an African American family is the rearing of children. The importance of a child-centered family is reflected in the number of participants in child development in African*

*American communities. Parke (2004) reiterated the importance of the role of grandmothers and other extended family members. The family in African American culture can include members of the nuclear family, the extended family, friends, neighbors, fictive kin [those who are treated as kin, but are not actually related], and church members. This sense of community is part of the socialization process whereby children become aware of the values in their culture and are helped to understand these beliefs.... These parental and community relations are key to the development of the African American child because they incorporate other values like collectivism and sensitivity to other peoples' needs. (p. 29)*

These values reflect a significant strength in that children often receive nurturance and support from multiple caring family members and others, who also provide each other with mutual aid.

*Gender-Role Flexibility* A second, related dimension characterizing African American families is role flexibility (Diller, 2015; Moore, 2008; Weaver, 2005). Winkelman (1999) explains that traditional gender roles

*tend to be less rigid, with few uniquely male or female characteristics.... Both male and female African American children are taught to be assertive and nurturing. The emphasis on interdependence, cooperation, flexibility, adaptation, and mutual respect has required an abandonment of traditional definitions of sex roles. (p. 297)*

Paniagua (2014) continues:

*Sometimes the mother plays the role of the father, and thus functions as the head of the family, and older children sometimes function as parents, caring for younger children (Boyd-Franklin, 2003). In fact, it is not uncommon for older African American children to drop out from schools so that they can go to work and help their younger siblings secure a good education. (p. 51)*

*Spirituality and Religion* A third theme in African American life involves strong religious beliefs and a close relationship with the church, especially an African American church (Diller, 2015; Moore, 2008; Paniagua, 2014). Many African American families consider the church to be a part of the extended family, providing similar nurturance and support (Paniagua, 2005). Dhooper and Moore (2001) explain:

> The African American church continues to address not only the religious and spiritual needs of the individual, family, and community, but also their social needs. It serves as a coping and survival mechanism against the effects of racial discrimination and oppression and as a place where African Americans are able to experience unconditional positive regard. (p. 101)

Frame (2003) reflects that for many African Americans,

> [spirituality] and identity are inseparable. Religion is not compartmentalized into a set of beliefs, doctrine, or dogma. Instead, it is in the life and breath of most African Americans, whether or not they are involved in organized religion.... Some African Americans believe that spirit may be found in everything. Religion and spirituality are considered major strengths for African Americans, which contributed to their resilience, their survival of slavery, and their ability to overcome present struggles. For many African Americans, spirituality dominates their thinking and is integrally related to their sense of security, adjustment, identity development, behavior, and problem-solving ability.... When they find themselves in a crisis or particularly stressed, many African Americans seek solace and strength in their religious and spiritual practices....
>
> The focus of worship in most African American churches is on God, who through Jesus Christ, enters into a personal relationship with believers, reconciles, liberates, heals, and guides.... There is an emphasis on God's "healing presence in life despite suffering and pain" (Wimberly, 1991, p. 16). Worship in African American churches is spirited, emotional, expressive. It often includes "involuntary acts of praise" (Mitchell & Mitchell, 1989, p. 105). In addition, clapping, dancing, and shouting are common in African American worship, which results in spiritual uplifting and an indwelling sense of hope in the worshiper.... There is the expectation that upon leaving a worship service, participants are empowered to manage the demands of daily life. (pp. 132–133)

## Asian Americans

Asian Americans are composed of three basic groups that, in turn, consist of numerous subgroups. These include, but are not limited to, "East Asians (Asian Indians, Chinese, Japanese, Koreans, Filipinos), Southeast Asian refugees (Vietnamese, Cambodians, and Laotians), and Asian Pacific Islanders (Hawaiians, Samoans, and Guamanians)" (Paniagua, 2014, pp. 113–114). Obviously, there is huge variation among these groups despite the fact that they are clustered under the umbrella term *Asian Americans.*

Diller (2015) explains that "unlike African Americans, [Latinos and Latinas], and Native Americans, Asian Americans have been quite successful economically and educationally, even in comparison with the White population"; this includes median income levels, rate of small business ownership, and attainment of educational degrees (p. 301). However, he maintains that this provides an overly simplistic view and urges us to consider the following facts:

> High median income does not take into consideration the number of wage earners, the level of poverty among certain Asian subgroups, or the discrepancy between education and income for Asian workers. Education in the Asian community is bimodal; that is, there are both highly educated and uneducated subpopulations. Asian towns in large urban areas represent ghettos with high unemployment, poverty, and widespread social problems. Underutilization of services does not necessarily mean a lack of problems, but may in fact have alternative explanations such as face-saving, shame, or the family's cultural tendency to keep personal information hidden from the outside world. In short, the belief in Asian success does not mean that there is any less racism or discrimination directed toward Asian Americans or that there are not serious problems within crowded urban enclaves.
>
> (Diller, 2015, p. 302; Sue & Sue, 2008)

Discussed here are six themes that tend to characterize many Asian American families. These include the significance of family, interdependence and collectivism, filial piety, patriarchal hierarchy, the desire to keep problems within the family, and the maintenance of interpersonal harmony.

*The Significance of Family*   First, like Hispanics, Asian Americans tend to consider the family as the primary unit and individual family members as secondary in importance (Balgopal, 2008; Diller, 2015; Slattery, 2004). Kim (2011) reflects:

> *Individual family members feel a strong sense of obligation to the family as a whole and a commitment to maintaining family well-being.... Honor and duty to one's family are very important, more important than one's own fame and power; personal accomplishment is interpreted as family achievement. In fact, individual family members are expected to make sacrifices for the family. Individual members are also expected to follow the role expectations set by their family as a whole. (p. 51)*

*Interdependence and Collectivism*   A second theme, also related to the significance of the family, that is common among Asian American families involves interdependence and collectivism (Green, 1999; Kim, 2011; Kim & Park, 2013; Sandhu & Madathil, 2013; Sue & Sue, 2008). The concepts of interdependence and collectivism are related. **Family interdependence** means that all family members have a stake in and should take responsibility for the entire family's welfare. **Collectivism** involves how "[i]ndividuals should feel a strong sense of attachment to the group to which they belong and should think about the welfare of the group before their own welfare. Group interests and goals should be promoted over individual interests and goals" (Kim & Park, 2013, p. 166). For example, Chinese culture emphasizes "kinship from birth to death, and it is expected that the family will serve as a major resource in providing stability, a sense of self-esteem, and satisfaction" (Goldenberg & Goldenberg, 2002, p. 341).

*Filial Piety*   A third theme concerns **filial piety**—"a devotion to and compliance with parental and familial authority, to the point of sacrificing individual desires and ambitions" (Brammer, 2012; Kim & Park, 2013; Kirst-Ashman & Hull, 2012b, p. 459; Sandhu & Madathil, 2013). For example, "[a]dult children are expected to take care of their aging parents, especially when the parents are unable to take care of themselves. Children should not place their parents in retirement or nursing homes" (Kim, 2011, p. 51). Sandhu and Madathil (2013) elaborate that

filial piety "means taking care of one's parents; not being rebellious; showing love, respect, and support. It also includes accepting the advice of one's parents, concealing their mistakes, displaying sorrow for their sickness and death, and carrying out sacrifices in their names after their death. The shortcomings of parents are overlooked" (p. 321).

*Patriarchal Hierarchy*   A fourth related theme distinguishing many Asian American families involves their patriarchal hierarchy (Diller, 2015; Goldenberg & Goldenberg, 2002; Sandhu & Madathil, 2013). Balgopal (2008) explains:

> *Asian families are generally patriarchal, and in traditional Asian families, age, sex, and generational status determine the roles that members play. The father is the head of the family, and his authority is unquestioned; he is the main disciplinarian and is usually less approachable and more distant than the mother; the mother is the nurturer and caretaker. (p. 156)*

*The Desire to Keep Problems Within the Family*   A fifth theme often characterizing Asian American families is the desire to keep problems within the family (Diller, 2015; Kim, 2011; Paniagua, 2014; Sandhu & Madathil, 2013). Individuals are expected to "use one's inner resources and willpower" to solve personal problems (Kim, 2011, p. 50). The other choice is "to defer to the authority figure in the family ... to make final decisions" and resolve issues (an alternative related both to filial piety and patriarchal hierarchy) (Sandhu & Madathil, 2011, p. 321). Taking one's problems outside of the family often results in loss of face and shame for the person violating this family expectation (Diller, 2015; Paniagua, 2014; Sandhu & Madathil, 2013).

*Interpersonal Harmony*   Finally, a sixth premise often reflected in the values of Asian American families is "the maintenance of interpersonal harmony" (Kim, 2011, p. 51; Kim & Park, 2013, p. 166). **Interpersonal harmony** involves accommodating to other's needs and avoiding confrontation or being offensive, Kim (2011) explains:

> *In a disagreement, one should overlook differences in an effort to maintain harmony. One should always try to be accommodating and conciliatory and never directly confrontational. Non-verbal communication plays an important part in maintaining*

*interpersonal harmony. An individual should never express his or her feelings at the expense of maintaining harmony. One should not say things that may offend another person or that would cause the other person to lose face. In fact, one should always provide a dignified way for the other person to save face [or avoid embarrassment]. (p. 51)*

## A Note on Difference

Of course, any discussion of these general cultural themes of values and behaviors is just that—general. Actual practices vary dramatically from one ethnic group to another and from one family to another. It's important not to make mistaken assumptions about an individual's values and expectations simply because that person is a member of some group.

## National Origin and Immigration Status

**National origin**, another dimension of diversity, involves the country of birth of individuals, their parents, or their ancestors. National origin often is an important factor in people's cultural values and expectations. How individuals are raised, what they're taught, and how they learn to perceive the world around them vary dramatically from one corner of the world to another. Understanding values and customs derived from national origin helps social workers better understand their clients' perspectives and needs.

EP 2

An important related concept to national origin is immigration status. **Immigration** involves the permanent movement from one country to another. **Immigration status** is a person's position in terms of legal rights and residency when entering and residing in a country that is not that person's legal country of origin. Social workers are often called upon to work with immigrants, so it's important to understand the terms and issues involved. Potocky-Tripodi (2002) defines many of the important concepts:

*The fundamental distinction between immigrants and refugees is that* immigrants *leave their countries voluntarily (usually in search of better economic opportunities) whereas* refugees *are forced out of their countries because of human rights violations against them. Therefore, immigrants are*

*also sometimes referred to as* voluntary migrants *or* economic migrants, *and refugees may be referred to as* involuntary migrants *or* forced migrants. *Refugees are also sometimes referred to, or refer to themselves, as* exiles *or* émigrés....

*Legally, anyone who is not a citizen of the United States is termed an* alien. *Aliens are further classified as immigrants and nonimmigrants, and as documented or undocumented (Loue, 1998). In this classification, an* immigrant *is a person who has been legally admitted into the United States and granted the privilege to be a permanent resident (a "green card" holder). A* nonimmigrant *is a foreign-born person who is in the United States temporarily, such as a tourist, a student or a journalist. Nonimmigrants also include temporary, or seasonal, workers, who come to the United States to work during certain periods of the year and return to their countries during the rest of the year. This typically refers to agricultural laborers.*

*A* documented alien *is one who has been granted a legal right to be in the United States. This legal right is determined by admissions policy. The admissions policy details many categories of people who are eligible to be legally admitted. It also specifies how many people from each country may be legally admitted into the U.S. each year....*

*An* undocumented alien *is one who does not have a legal right to be in the United States. These people are also sometimes referred to as* illegal immigrants. *They are also referred to as* deportable aliens, *because if discovered by immigration authorities, they are subject to deportation, or forcible return to their countries of origin. There are two ways in which people become undocumented aliens. One is by entering the U.S. illegally. This means that the person has not received authorization to enter the United States. For example, people who cross the border from Mexico without going through the immigration authorities are undocumented aliens. The second way that people become undocumented aliens is by entering the U.S. legally, but then violating the terms of the visa (the authorization to stay in the U.S.). For example, a tourist may be granted a visa to stay in the United States for a limited period of time. If the person stays after that time period has expired, then that person becomes an undocumented alien. (pp. 4–5)*

Many people from other countries may receive or need social services. Immigrants represent an important portion of the U.S. population. In 2011 almost 4.4 million people, 13% of the total population, were foreign-born (ProQuest, 2014). Segal (2010) reports:

*Individuals and families from around the globe form a continuous stream of immigrants to the United States. The backlog of visa applications and waiting lists to enter the nation stretches to several years. Undocumented immigrants, both those who arrive without legal papers and those who overstay their visits, abound. Record numbers of refugees and asylees are admitted from countries in political turmoil. Disproportionately large numbers of entrants into the United States in recent years have been people of color from Asia, Africa, and Central and South America, and despite encountering a series of barriers, an overwhelming majority remains applying for permanent residence. (p. 29)*

People with different national origins often find it difficult to integrate themselves into the mainstream culture, especially when language barriers exist (Garcia, 2009; Gushue & Sciarra, 1995). Finding employment and adequate housing and "fitting into" the social fabric of neighborhoods and communities can be difficult. Kamya (1999) cites "social isolation, cultural shock, cultural change, and goal-striving stress as four significant experiences" newcomers often face (p. 607). They may have difficulties understanding new behavioral expectations imposed on them, interacting effectively with others in the new culture, and achieving the goals they had hoped for. Highlight 3.4 identifies some of the differences between cultural expectations in the United States and those adopted by the Turkana tribe in northern Kenya.

## HIGHLIGHT 3.4 APPRECIATING CULTURAL DIFFERENCES IN NATIONAL ORIGIN

Imagine a family of the Turkana tribe in northern Kenya immigrating to the United States.[3] What difficulties would members face in terms of cultural differences and expectations? Primarily nomadic goatherds, these people are not accustomed to handling currency, as their subsistence is based on *bartering* (exchanging goods for other goods). Even if they enter a store, have currency, and want to make a purchase, it is unthinkable to pay the asking price without trying to negotiate a lower cost.

**EP 2a, 2b**

Another difference is the common practice of polygamy. The number of a man's wives reflects his wealth, with each wife being purchased with some negotiated number of goats. A wealthy man is one with many wives and many goats.

The Turkana tribe's conception of time reflects yet another difference. Many tribal members have never seen watches. Their time is not split into precise units such as minutes and hours. Rather, they depend on the position of the sun in the sky to determine what should be done at that time of day. They value relationships and mutual respect more than rigorous scheduling and strict punctuality. For example, the person providing this information was two days late for a meeting due to international and internal transportation difficulties. Instead of being angry, tribal members were unconcerned about the lateness and cheerfully welcomed their visitor when he finally arrived. A two-day delay most likely would not be accepted so tranquilly in the United States.

One aspect of U.S. culture Turkana tribe members would probably appreciate is the ready access to public education, as education is highly valued there. Four years of primary school and another four years of secondary are available to children, but it still costs each family an additional $100 for elementary and $300 for secondary school per year. In the United States, this may not seem like much, but in northern Kenya, a professional person holding an exceptionally good job might earn $1,000 in an entire year.

The point of this is not to make judgments about which cultural values are better or worse, but rather to emphasize that significant differences do exist based on ethnicity and national origin. Social workers, then, must listen carefully to such clients regarding their needs, work with them as they adjust to new conditions, and provide the best services possible to meet their needs.

[3]This information was gathered from a personal communication with Gary S. Kirst, who had visited the Turkana tribe recently as well as several times in the past.

Increasing cultural competence is helpful in working with a population having a different national origin. Consider the following example. Thanh, a counselor at a homeless shelter, is seeing an increasing number of Haitian immigrants enter the shelter. He determines that he must enhance his knowledge of their cultural values to work with them more effectively. As he does this, he begins to understand that the predicament of Haitian immigrants is significant due to its complexity in the context of economic and political oppression (Allen, 1995). Thanh discovers that a local organization exists primarily to assist immigrants of Caribbean origin socially, economically, and politically. The organization's goals include enhancing the community's well-being through assisting the development of new and existing businesses, advocating for necessary housing, and helping immigrants get jobs (Allen, 1995). Obtaining this information about Haitian immigrants enhances both Thanh's understanding of their culture and his ability to communicate with his clients. It also makes him aware of a whole new set of resources potentially available to clients.

Note that when we speak about any racial, ethnic, or cultural group, it is important not to overgeneralize. Persons with other national origins may embrace traditional cultural norms to various degrees. They may also experience **acculturation**, already defined as "the adaptation of language, identity, behavior patterns, and preferences to those of the [host or majority] society" (Lum, 2004, p. 229). In other words, people from another country may gradually blend into the larger society and adopt its values and customs. Therefore, for a given racial, ethnic, or cultural group, it is important that social workers not assume that all members comply with all cultural values or conform to the same extent. Being of German ethnic heritage does not automatically mean a person loves sauerkraut, liver sausage, and raw ground beef with onions on rye bread simply because these are traditional ethnic foods.

The following addresses the difference in acculturation between first-generation and later-generation immigrants:

*As family members differentiate according to ability levels of the language of the dominant culture, distinct forms and levels of acculturation begin to emerge. Children, having gained a knowledge of the language and wanting to be accepted by their* *peers, take on the ways of the dominant culture. Parents, more isolated because of language and perhaps suspicious of the ways of the dominant culture, enter into conflict with their children. Issues of racial/cultural identity also emerge because children and parents feel differently about their cultural heritage. (Gushue & Sciarra, 1995, p. 597)*

## Class

**Class** or **social class**, another aspect of diversity, refers to people's status or ranking in society with respect to such standards as, "relative wealth, power, prestige, educational level, or family background" (Barker, 2014, p. 396).

**EP 2, 2c**

What comes to mind when you think of social class? Whom do you picture when you think of people in higher classes? In lower classes? How would you characterize yourself in terms of class membership? How do you relate to people of other classes?

Social workers must carefully scrutinize their own answers to these questions. They must strive to avoid imposing stereotypes and prejudgments. Rather, they must continue to expand their knowledge base about the environmental circumstances characterizing people's lives in other social classes.

## Political Ideology

Political ideology is another aspect of diversity. **Political ideology** is the "relatively coherent system of ideas (beliefs, traditions, principles, and myths) about human nature, institutional arrangements, and social processes" that indicates how a government should be run and what principles that government should support (Abramovitz, 2010,

**EP 2**

p. 131). Chapter 1 introduced the "standard" political ideologies concerning social welfare and government policies to address it—conservatism, liberalism, and radicalism (Abramovitz, 2008, p. 368). Your political ideology forms your views on how the government should be run, what responsibilities the government should assume, and what laws and policies should be established and implemented. Abramovitz (2010) explains:

*The debate on the proper role of government often centers on which of three sites for resource distribution—the family, the market, or the government—should bear the heaviest burden in ensuring the well-being of people. We don't usually think of it this way, but all three systems play this role. The family distributes resources to its members by supporting those who do not work or otherwise cannot care for themselves. The breadwinners supply the wages needed to buy the food, clothing, shelter, medical care, and a host of other goods and services needed by family members. In exchange, adult women and other unpaid family members shop, cook, clean, care for children, and maintain the household. Conservatives believe the families can and should be self-sustaining. Liberals argue that from the start many families, especially those with limited income, have needed some kind of outside help to sustain themselves. Radicals hold that because low wages and high unemployment can raise profits, the operation of the system of production deprives families of resources needed for successful family maintenance. (pp. 147–148)*

## Gender, Gender Identity, and Gender Expression

Gender is another aspect of diversity that is really much more complex than it may initially seem. "**Gender** refers to the social and psychological characteristics associated with being female or male. Characteristics typically [and historically] associated with the female gender include being gentle, emotional, and cooperative: characteristics  typically [and historically] associated with the male gender include being aggressive, rational, and competitive" (McCammon & Knox, 2007, p. 112). Focus on Critical Thinking 3.3 explores the concept of gender more thoroughly.

EP 2, 2a

Other important concepts related to gender are gender identity, gender expression, gender roles, and gender-role socialization. **Gender identity** is a person's internal psychological self-concept of being either a male or a female, or, possibly, some combination of both. *Gender expression* concerns how we express ourselves to others in ways related to gender that include both behavior and personality. **Gender roles** are the "attitudes, behaviors, rights, and responsibilities that particular cultural groups associate" with being male or female (Yarber & Sayad, 2013, p. 127). **Gender-role socialization** is the

process of conveying what is considered appropriate behavior and perspectives for males and females in a particular culture.

We will differentiate the concepts of gender and sex. **Sex** "refers to whether one is biologically female or male, based on genetic and anatomical sex. **Genetic sex** refers to one's chromosomal and hormonal sex characteristics.... **Anatomical sex** refers to physical sex: gonads, uterus, vulva, vagina, penis, and so on" (emphasis added) (Yarber & Sayad, 2013, p. 127). Gender, then, emphasizes social and psychological aspects of femaleness or maleness; sex, on the other hand, focuses on the biological qualities of being male or female.

### Women as Victims of Oppression

Despite the fact that a wide range of gender expression exists, the mainstream culture is primarily segregated by gender in terms of women and men. As racial, ethnic, and cultural backgrounds affect you, so does your gender affect how you are treated and what worldview you assume. Women experience many issues, expectations, and life situations that men do not, and they perceive the world in a different way.

EP 2

Some disturbing facts reflect the different life contexts of women and men in this country. Consider the following:

- Approximately 57.7 percent of all women work outside of the home (ProQuest, 2014). About 62.5 percent of single mothers and 59.6 percent of married mothers are employed outside of the home (ProQuest, 2014).
- On the average, women's full-time, year-round median weekly earnings are approximately 79.9 percent of men's (ProQuest, 2014).
- For all races, women earn significantly less than men do at every educational level (Kirk & Okazawa-Rey, 2013; Renzetti, Curran, & Maier, 2012; ProQuest, 2014).
- "More women than men make up the working poor, and women of color are more than twice as likely to be poor than [White] women" (Kirk & Okazawa-Rey, 2013, p. 316).
- "Even with a college education ... and equivalent work experience and skills, professional women are far less likely than men to get to the top of their professions or corporations. They are halted

# FOCUS ON CRITICAL THINKING 3.3

## WHAT DOES GENDER REALLY MEAN?    LO 7

In an overly simplistic, naive view of the world, one might think, "You're either a male or you're a female. Period." However, in reality, neither gender nor sexual orientation are such simple concepts.

Historically, Money (1987) proposed eight factors of gender that portray some of its complexity. The first six are physical variables that include (1) chromosomal predisposition to gender; (2) the presence of either ovaries or testes; (3) exposure to male or female hormones prior to birth and brain differentiation resulting from hormones prior to birth; (4) the presence of female or male internal reproductive organs; (5) exterior genital appearance; and (6) the production of either male or female hormones during puberty. The remaining two are psychological variables: (7) the gender assigned at birth ("It's a boy" or "It's a girl") and (8) a person's *gender identity* (the perception of oneself as being either "female" or "male").

**EP 2, 3b, 7a**

However, now we realize that gender is even more complex. Carroll (2013a) explains:

> In Western culture, when babies are born, the genital anatomy is used to determine biological sex. If there is a penis, the child is a boy; if there is no penis, the child is a girl. Today we know that gender is much more complicated than that. Our biology, gender identity, and gender expression all intersect, creating a multidimensional **gender spectrum**. One person can be born female ([with] XX [chromosomes]), identify as a woman, act feminine, and have sex with a man, whereas another can be born female (XX), identify as a woman, act masculine, and have sex with both men and women. (p. 79)

It is estimated that 1 out of every 2,000 babies born has some combination of physical characteristics demonstrated by both sexes (Crooks & Baur, 2014; Intersex Society of North America, 2008a). Reasons include having "an atypical combination of sex chromosomes or as a result of prenatal hormonal irregularities" (Crooks & Baur, 2014, p. 120). For example, Klinefelter's syndrome is a sex-chromosome disorder in which males are born with an extra X chromosome, resulting in an XXY designation; "the Y chromosome triggers the development of male genitalia, but the extra X prevents them from developing fully" (Carroll, 2013b, p. 86). Results include a feminized body appearance, low testosterone levels, small testicles, and possibly infertility (Lee, Cheng, Ahmed, Shaw, & Hughes, 2007). Treatment may involve testosterone therapy.

Another example of contradiction in physical gender is a genetic female who as a fetus is exposed to excessive androgens (a class of male hormones); as a result she develops external genitals that resemble a male's (Crooks & Baur, 2014). Her clitoris is enlarged enough to resemble a penis, and the labia (folds of tissue around the vaginal entrance) may converge and resemble a scrotum (the pouch that holds the male testes). When diagnosed at birth, cosmetic surgery can often be performed to "feminize" the person's genitalia.

There are many other examples of people who have some mixture of male and female predisposition and configuration of reproductive structures. Such a person is referred to as **pseudohermaphrodite** or **intersex**. A true **hermaphrodite** is a person "born with fully formed ovaries and fully formed testes, which is exceptionally rare" (Carroll, 2013b, p. 86).

Many times parents and medical staff members make the arbitrary decision to surgically alter infants with ambiguous sexual characteristics soon after birth to make them conform more closely to one gender or another. The Intersex Society of North America (ISNA) (2008c) raises serious questions regarding the right of parents and physicians to physically alter a child without that child's knowledge and consent. Such procedures apparently are undertaken theoretically in the best interests of the child, possibly without parental consent (ISNA, 2008b). The ISNA (2008c) makes several recommendations regarding how intersex children and their families should be treated. First, these children and their parents should be treated with respect; physicians and medical staff members should address the condition and issues openly and honestly without shame. Second, families with intersex children should be referred to social workers or other mental health professionals to address issues and potential decisions. Third, these families should also be connected with other families who have intersex children for peer support and deeper insight into the issues involved. Fourth, after careful consideration, an intersex child should be assigned a gender "as boy or girl, depending on which of those genders the child is more likely to feel as she or he grows up." Such gender assignment should not involve surgery because surgery may destroy tissue that the child may want later on in life. Fifth, the child

*(continued)*

**FOCUS ON CRITICAL THINKING 3.3 *(continued)***

should receive medical treatment "to sustain physical health" (e.g., "surgery to provide a urinary drainage opening when a child is born without one"). Sixth, surgeries to make the child "look 'more normal'" should be avoided until the child is old enough to decide for him- or herself.

## Critical Thinking Questions

When infants are born with an ambiguous or unclear gender, should they be assigned to one gender or the other? At that time, should they be physically altered to more closely resemble the assigned gender? If so, who should be responsible for making this decision? To what extent might children with ambiguous genitals (even after being given an assigned gender as the ISNA suggests) fit in with their peers and be able to function well socially? Would it be better to wait until children reach adulthood to determine gender or to do any relevant surgery? Why or why not? Should society become more open-minded and expand its views of sex and gender to include more variations of male and female (a proposal that the ISNA does not support)?

## Other Forms of Gender Expression

Another variation in the expression of gender involves **transgenderism,** including "people whose appearance and/or behaviors do not conform to traditional gender roles" (Crooks & Baur, 2014, p. 129). Among these people are **transsexuals**, people who feel they are imprisoned in the physical body of the wrong gender. Because their gender identity and sense of self are at odds with their biological inclination, they often seek to adjust their physical appearance to that of their gender identity through surgery and hormonal treatment. Many transsexual people prefer to be referred to as *transgender* people. The word *transsexual* emphasizes *sexual,* whereas *transgender* emphasizes *gender,* which they say is the real issue.

Several other groups of people are also often included under the transgender umbrella. *Transvestites* are people who derive sexual gratification from dressing in the clothing of the opposite gender. In our society, most transvestites are heterosexual males (Rathus, Nevid, & Fichner-Rathus, 2014; Wheeler, Newring, & Draper, 2008). This might be due to the fact that women experience much greater freedom and flexibility in how they dress. **Drag queens** are gay men who dress up as women. Lesbians who dress up in traditionally masculine clothing may be referred to as **drag kings. Female impersonators** are men who dress up as women, usually for the purpose of providing entertainment. They may be heterosexual or gay. A common performance involves mimicking the dress and style of famous female performers, often lip-synching (moving their lips to a song and music without producing any sound) their greatest hits.

## The Social Construction of Gender

Considering these diversities of gender expression, the concept of gender doesn't appear to be quite so clear. One theoretical approach to understanding how we view and interpret gender as a society refers to the social construction of gender. **Social construction** refers to the perspective where the social world is considered

**EP 7b, 8b**

a social creation, originating and evolving through our everyday thoughts and actions. Most of the time, we assume and act as though the world is a given, objectively predetermined outside of our existence. However, ... we also apply subjective meanings to our existence and experience. In other words, our experiences don't just happen to us. Good, bad, positive, or negative—we also attach meanings to our reality.

*(Leon-Guerrero, 2014, p. 9)*

The **social construction of gender** "looks at the structure of the gendered social order as a whole and at the processes that construct and maintain it" (Lorber, 2010, p. 244). It assumes that traditional gender expectations are not facts carved in stone, but rather perceptions and expectations that can be changed. Lorber (2010) reflects:

Gender and sexuality are performances, and ... individuals modify their displays of masculinity and femininity to suit their own purposes. Males can masquerade as women, and females can pass for men.... [One might argue] that, like clothing, sexuality and gender can be put on, taken off, and transformed. Transgendered people especially display the fluidities of gender and sexuality, challenging normals to prove that they aren't also creating their gendered identities through their appearance and behavior.... [A] focus of gay, lesbian, and transgender studies ... turns the [two categories of male and female] ... sex, sexuality, and gender inside out with "third terms"—inter-sexuality, bisexuality, transgendering [and many others]. (p. 195)

## Critical Thinking Questions

To what extent do you think people should be given freedom in gender expression? Which aspects of gender expression do you find acceptable? What could society do to make such practices more acceptable and appreciated?

by unseen structural barriers, such as men's negative attitudes to senior women and perceptions of their leadership abilities and styles, their motivation, training, and skills" (Hyde & Else-Quest, 2013; Kirk & Okazawa-Rey, 2013, p. 316). Even in social work, where the majority of people are women, "women continue to experience inequity" (Pace, 2014, p. 11).

- Women are clustered in low-paying supportive occupations, such as clerical workers, teachers, and service workers, while men tend to assume higher-paying occupations such as high-level managers, professionals, and construction workers (ProQuest, 2014; Shaw & Lee, 2012; U.S. Census Bureau, 2011).

- More than 68% of single women and 62.3% of married women with children under age 6 work outside the home (ProQuest, 2014).

- "Most women employed outside the home still carry major responsibility for housework and raising children" (Kirk & Okazawa-Rey, 2013, p. 313).

- In a recent year, "nearly ten million adult children over age 50 provided basic care for an aging parent: … 28 percent of women [compared to 17% of men in this group].… This included help with dressing, feeding, bathing, and other personal care, as well as grocery shopping, driving parents to appointments, and helping them with financial matters" (Kirk & Okazawa-Rey, 2013, p. 223).

- A "sexual assault [including rape] occurs about every two minutes" (Shaw & Lee, 2012, p. 504).

- Only a small percentage of all rapes is ever reported (Carroll, 2013b; Crooks & Baur, 2014; Shaw & Lee, 2012).

- According to various studies, women have between a 15% and 25% chance of being raped sometime in their lives (Hyde & Else-Quest, 2013). It is "estimated that one in four U.S. college women was a victim of rape or attempted rape" (Kirk & Okazawa-Rey, 2013, p. 264).

- "Nearly one in four women in the United States reported experiencing violence by a current or former spouse or boyfriend at some point in her life, and U.S. women experience some two million injuries from intimate partner violence each year. Abuse-related injuries include bruises, cuts, burns and scalds, concussion, broken bones, penetrating injuries from knives, miscarriages, permanent injuries such as damage to joints, partial

loss of hearing or vision, and physical disfigurement" (Kirk & Okazawa-Rey, 2013, p. 262).

Women, therefore, often are victims of oppression manifested in many ways. They generally earn less than men and are more likely than men to be poor. They are also more likely to be primary caregivers for children and older adults. They are victimized by specific kinds of violence, including sexual assault and domestic violence, infrequently experienced by men.

Important concepts related to these issues are sexism and sex discrimination. *Sexism* is "prejudice or discrimination based on sex, especially discrimination against women" that involves "behavior, conditions, or attitudes that foster stereotypes of social roles based on sex" (Mish, 2008, p. 1141). **Sex discrimination** is the differential and potentially unfair treatment of people based solely on their gender. Examples include paying males more than females for the same or comparable jobs and hiring only one gender for certain jobs.

Many people are initially turned off by the concepts of sexism and sex discrimination. They find it difficult consciously to recognize and accept the possibility that this is an imperfect, sexist world. They think that things are supposed to be fair and that they shouldn't have to waste their time and energy battling such problems as sexism. For many women, it's easier to adopt an "out of sight, out of mind" philosophy. In other words, if one doesn't think about a problem, then it doesn't really exist. Why dwell on problems that are nonexistent or insignificant?

To what extent do you think sexism and sex discrimination exist today? How much do they account for the discrepancies between women and men in terms of their life circumstances and treatment? How might you begin to think about these concerns so that you could figure out the reasons for their existence? What theoretical perspective might help you organize information and your view of the world to increase your understanding?

One such theoretical framework is the *feminist perspective* described as follows:

> *A feminist perspective is one in which women's experiences, ideas, and needs are valued in their own right. Put another way … [the perspective that views] man as the norm ceases to be the only recognized frame of reference for human beings.*

*Women's experiences are seen as constituting a different view of "reality"—an entirely different ... way of making sense of the world.*

*(Cummerton, 1986, p. 85)*

Focus on Critical Thinking 3.4 explores the meaning of feminism for women and men and raises some provocative questions.

## FOCUS ON CRITICAL THINKING 3.4

## WHAT IS FEMINISM?

How do you respond to these questions?

- What words and images come to mind when you hear the word *feminism*?
- What does feminism represent and suggest to you?
- How would you define feminism?
- To what extent do you feel the concept is significant or meaningless in your life?

EP 3a, 7b, 8b

Some people have extremely negative reactions simply to the word *feminism.* The emotional barriers they forge and the resulting resistance they foster make it difficult even to think about the concept. Others consider feminism a radical ideology that emphasizes separatism and fanaticism. In other words, they think feminism involves the philosophy adopted by women who spurn men, resent past inequities, and strive violently to overthrow male supremacists. Still others think of feminism in terms of an outmoded tradition of women seeking equality with men. They feel it is neither relevant in contemporary times nor merits their attention.

### What Is a Feminist?

Both men and women can be feminists. The definition of feminism proposed here is designed to relate to basic concepts involving the daily lives of people like you. It entails readily understandable concepts. Many people have failed to develop a sensitivity to the sexist barriers surrounding them. For one thing, it's painful to acknowledge such unfairness. For another, it's easy to assume "that's the way things are" simply because people haven't thought about other, better ways of doing things.

For our purposes, **feminism** is the philosophy of equality between women and men that involves both beliefs and actions, that infiltrates virtually all aspects of life, that often necessitates providing education and advocacy on behalf of women, and that appreciates the existence of individual differences and personal accomplishments regardless of gender (Kirst-Ashman, 1992). Five major components within this definition relate directly to the values and goals of professional social work.

First, *equality* is the core of feminism. Equality does not mean identicalness or sameness. It does not mean that women are trying to shed their female identities and become clones of men. Nor does it mean that women should seek to adopt behaviors that are typically "masculine." Feminism does promote equal or identical rights to opportunities and choices. It relates to women's and men's rights not to be discriminated against and not to be denied opportunities and choices on the basis of gender.

The second major component inherent in feminism is the fact that it embodies *both beliefs and actions.* Beliefs concern how we look at the world and perceive other people; actions reflect expression of the beliefs. Feminism espouses a belief system that views other people objectively and fairly. It means avoiding both stereotypes and assumptions about people on the basis of gender. A person who fails to behave in accordance with expressed feminist beliefs is not a true feminist, according to our definition. For example, one of your instructors might say he supports feminist principles yet frequently emphasizes how women are too emotional and make sexist jokes that fixate on breast size. Feminism involves acting on one's beliefs on behalf of gender equality and fair, respectful treatment.

The third critical aspect in the definition of feminism is the idea that *all aspects of life* are involved. The concept of equality does not apply only to an equal chance of getting a specific job or promotion. It also involves having the rights to hold personal opinions about political issues and to make decisions within personal relationships. It entails a woman's right to make a decision about what to do on a Friday night date or whether to have a sexual encounter. Essentially, this aspect includes the acknowledgment that our social, legal, and political structure is oriented toward men, not women.

The fourth important aspect of feminism is the frequent necessity of providing *education and advocacy* on the behalf of women, a dimension coinciding with major social work roles. This might involve giving feedback to a person behaving in a sexist fashion or speaking out on the behalf of others being treated unfairly.

*(continued)*

## FOCUS ON CRITICAL THINKING 3.4 *(continued)*

For example, I once went to a travel agency for vacation information. While the lone travel agent worked with another customer, I waited patiently for about 15 minutes. At that point, two men in business suits walked in. As soon as the agent was finished with her customer, she looked directly at the men—as if I were invisible—and asked them if she could help them. If I had behaved more compatibly with feminist principles, I might have assertively stated that I had been waiting for quite a while and that men should not be given precedence simply because of gender. As it was, I was furious and stomped out. I missed an opportunity to educate the agent regarding her sexist behavior so that she might treat women more equitably in the future.

The fifth major concept involved in the definition of feminism is the *appreciation of individual differences*. The feminist perspective lauds the concept of empowering women by emphasizing individual strengths and qualities. Feminism stresses freedom and the right to make choices about one's own life. Note that this concept applies to both women and men.

A feminist perspective refutes and challenges the idea that the potential of women and men is limited by their gender. Rather, it proposes that women should be empowered to develop their abilities and pursue activities to achieve optimal well-being.

In many ways a feminist perspective conforms with the core of traditional social work practice in terms of principles and values; both emphasize the significance of being concerned with "human dignity and the rights of self-determination" (Van Den Bergh & Cooper, 1986, p. 3). Both stress the importance of individuals' interactions with their environments and communities.

### Critical Thinking Questions

In light of the preceding discussion, do you think that you are a feminist? Your answers to the following questions can help you reach a conclusion:

- Do you believe that women and men should have the same rights?
- Do you believe that women and men should have the same access to jobs and social status?
- Do you believe that women and men should not be discriminated against or denied opportunities and choices on the basis of their gender?
- Do you think that employers should treat women and men equally in work settings?
- Do you believe that ideally people's attitudes and behavior should reflect the equal treatment of women and men?
- Do you think that many people need to become more educated about women's issues?
- Would you be willing to advocate on behalf of women (e.g., for poor women or women who have been raped)?
- Do you believe that both women and men have the right to their own individual differences (of course, differences that don't harm other people)?
- Do you think that our society is generally structured legally, socially, and economically by and for men instead of women? (This last question is probably the most difficult, and perhaps the most painful, to answer.)

If you answered "yes" to all or most of these questions, according to our definition, there's a good chance that you are a feminist.

---

### The Special Issues and Needs of Men

We've discussed how women are a population-at-risk that experiences disadvantages and discrimination based on gender. Men, however, also have disadvantages based on their gender that should be addressed. Kosberg and Adams (2008) cite the following special issues experienced by men:

EP 2, 2a, 7c

1. *Society attempts to socialize men to conform to male gender-role stereotypes. Men should be tough, strong, vital, definitive, and unemotional.*

*They should be as unfeminine as possible. These demands place great pressure on men to refrain from expressing emotion. This, in turn, negatively affects their ability to gain insight into their emotions and behavior. It also hampers their ability to communicate freely even in their most intimate and important relationships. Such pressures may prevent them from seeking the human support and love they need.*

2. *Men risk greater health problems than women. They don't live as long. In the United States, the average life expectancy for men is 74.1 years and for women 79.45 years (ProQuest,*

*2014). They are more likely than females to be murdered, to successfully complete suicide attempts, to be homeless, to die in car accidents, to abuse mind-altering substances, and to experience injuries related to their work.*

3. *Men who experience major disturbances or losses in their lives such as divorce or death of a loved one may have difficulty turning to others for emotional support and help. They may experience difficulties in undertaking domestic tasks for which they've never learned the skills. Inability to cope may have harmful effects on their self-concepts. Providing care to children or aging partners may be exceptionally difficult when they were not socialized into those roles.*

4. *Men of color experience even greater difficulty. They are more likely to be poor, uneducated, and incarcerated. They are also more likely to experience health problems and die earlier than White men.*

5. *Men are more likely to use detrimental coping mechanisms such as turning to substance abuse and denial. Because of the pressures on them to be strong and independent, they often underuse community services, especially those involving mental health.*

Blundo (2008) makes a number of recommendations regarding social work practice with men. Note that the majority of social workers are women. First, practitioners should strive to be aware of any gender-role stereotypes and expectations they harbor toward men just as with any other diverse group. Biases might affect practitioners' objectivity and effective practice. Second, it's important to be aware of the wide range of diversity among men. It's essential to understand how gender-role stereotypes and expectations affect men's behavior and emotions in order to develop appropriate goals when working with men. It's also crucial to be aware of and attend to the special issues faced by men of color. Third, traditional treatment has focused on repairing the deficits inherent in masculinity (e.g., helping a man to become better at expressing emotion and seeking help when needed), so it's important to focus on strengths. The extent to which a man is an active problem solver and doer should be used to his advantage instead of disadvantage.

## Sexual Orientation

**Sexual orientation**, another significant aspect of diversity, involves sexual and romantic attraction to persons of one or both genders. People having a sexual orientation toward the same gender are generally referred to as **gay** if they are male and **lesbian** if they are female. However, many people use the term *gay* to refer to both lesbians and gay men. The older term referring to same-gender sexual orientation is **homosexual**. People having a sexual orientation toward persons of the opposite gender are **heterosexual** or **straight**. People sexually oriented toward both genders are referred to as **bisexual**. Because lesbian, gay, and bisexual people face some of the same problems, when referring to them as a group, we will use the term **LGB** (i.e., lesbian, gay, or bisexual). Note that sometimes the term **LGBT** (i.e., lesbian, gay, bisexual, and transgender [as described in Focus on Critical Thinking 3.3]) is used to describe this population when addressing issues experienced by all of the groups included.

**EP 2**

A newer acronym being employed to refer to people whose sexual orientation is not strictly toward the opposite biological gender is LGBTQ. Here "Q" stands for "queer" or "questioning" (Carroll, 2013b, p. 270; Rosenthal, 2013, p. 234). Other terms used are LGBTI (lesbian, gay, bisexual, transgender, and intersex) (Alderson, 2013) and LGBTQI (lesbian, gay, bisexual, transgender, questioning, and intersex).

However, Alderson (2013) cautions:

*Terminology is often challenging when writing or talking about groups who have been historically oppressed and disenfranchised. Postmodern writers have become very sensitive to the labels used to describe individuals....*

*Identities [labels used to refer to some group of people] describe one aspect of a person. A lesbian woman, for example, is more than just her nonheterosexual identity—she is also someone's daughter, someone's neighbor, and someone's friend. She is a lover, a worker, and an inhabitor of earth. Similarly, referring to a transsexual individual as a "transsexual" diminishes this person's existence to this one aspect of self....*

*Identity labels—when chosen at all—are picked by individuals themselves to describe some aspect that defines their sense of self. Consequently, they can be transient labels, inaccurate labels, or over-simplified labels. Such is also the case with some LGBTI [or LGBTQI] individuals—our sexuality and gender is so much more than the label we give it. (pp. 2–4)*

## Numbers of LGB People

It's difficult, if not impossible, to state exactly how many people are LGBTQI. As has been discussed, the issue remains complex.

"[H]omosexuality is stigmatized. Gay men, lesbian women, and bisexual individuals are often reluctant to reveal their identities in research surveys for reasons of personal hesitancy as well as conceptual problems surrounding what constitutes sexual orientation" (Yarber & Sayad, 2013, p. 193). Such stigmatization also affects transsexual, questioning, and intersex people.

"Estimates for homosexuality range from 2 to 4% to greater than 10% in males and 1 to 3% in females …, whereas estimates for bisexuality are approximately 3%" (Carroll, 2013b, p. 272). Based on Alfred Kinsey's work in the 1940s and 1950s, many people have arbitrarily used 10% as the proportion of males who are gay. Additionally, many lesbian and gay organizations maintain that they make up 10% of the population. One major lesbian and gay organization is called "The Ten Percent Society." The controversy regarding the actual number of lesbian, gay, and bisexual people continues. Regardless of whether lesbian, gay, and bisexual people make up 1% or 10% of the population, they are a sizable minority group.

Focus on Critical Thinking 3.3 explored the complexity of sexual orientation and gender.

## Homophobia

A major problem LGBTQI people face is **homophobia**—an extreme and irrational fear of LGBTQI people simply because of their non-traditional (or nonheterosexual) sexual orientation. LGBTQI people are some of the primary groups at risk of discrimination and oppression. Highlight 3.5 reflects the feelings of one person who faces homophobia every day.

EP 2, 2a

Although not all LGB people suffer every day from homophobia in all its forms, all LGB people endure some forms at some times (Tully, 2001). To help LGB people cope with the results of homophobia, social workers must understand their life situations and environmental issues. Note that, although the following discussion focuses on LGB people, it may certainly apply to LGBTQI people.

LGB people may suffer from the effects of homophobia in at least three ways, one of which is *overt victimization*. Dworkin (2000) remarks,

*Anti-LGB violence is more common than most people realize.... All the symptoms commonly*

---

### HIGHLIGHT 3.5   REFLECTIONS ABOUT BEING A LESBIAN IN A HOMOPHOBIC SOCIETY

Jackquelyn is a doctoral student in a counseling program at a prestigious Eastern university. She reflects on what it's like to live as a lesbian in a homophobic world:

I am a European American upper-middle-class student.... I am thoroughly embedded in a Euro-centric, achievement-oriented, individualistic way of life that I am finding to be increasingly maladaptive.... I seek to unify various parts of me. I am female, lesbian-identified, White, athletic, academic, emotional, and other things that my culture insists be compartmentalized from one another, from other people, and from myself

as a whole person.... Politically, I am a lesbian, but I am also a White person who confronts racism and ethnocentrism. My labels do not describe me fully, of course; the word lesbian does not account for my full range of emotional, behavioral, and cognitive ways of being.... I have been told overtly and covertly that I don't belong. Professors, supervisors, and peers ... [treat me like an object] in offices, ... [make offensive gestures] in the hallways, [and] use sexualized language in professional conversations with me.

*(Lowe & Mascher, 2001, pp. 773–774)*

*associated with posttraumatic stress[4] are likely to follow a physical or verbal attack, in varying degrees of intensity, depending on the circumstances of the attack and the vulnerability of the victim. In a four-year study of hate crimes against LGB people, Herek et al. [1997] found that stress, depression, and anger lingered for as long as five years after the attack. In addition to posttraumatic symptoms, an LGB client can experience anxiety about his or her sexual identification.... Often there is regression to earlier stages of the coming out process. (p. 170)*

A second way LGB people encounter homophobia involves *covert victimization*—discrimination that is not obvious. For instance, Jay, a 21-year-old gay man and college student, applies for a part-time job at Hilda's Humongous Hamburgers, a local fast-food restaurant. Daryl, the manager, somehow finds out that Jay is gay. He then hires another applicant who is heterosexual (or so Daryl thinks) because that applicant is more "appropriate."

A third way LGB people suffer from homophobia involves *internalizing* it (Dworkin, 2000; Miller, 2008; Tully, 2001). If the majority of those around LGB people are homophobic, making fun of and severely criticizing them, it's fairly easy for LGB people to start believing it themselves. Results may include "low self-esteem, depression, suicidal ideation, substance abuse, isolation, self-loathing, ... or acting out" (Tully, 2001, p. 610).

## Marital Status

We've established that marital status is the state of being legally married or legally unmarried. However, as you know, relationships are extremely complex. There are many degrees of intensity, communication, and caring or lack of caring in a person's relationship with a significant other. This is so whether the couple is legally  **EP 2** married or not. People who are legally married may actually live apart. People who are not married may live together and have an intensively intimate

AP Images/Eric Risberg

*Sexual orientation is an important facet of human diversity. Here two partners marry at City Hall in San Francisco on Tuesday, June 17, 2008, the first full day same-sex marriages had been legalized throughout California.*

relationship. Perhaps a better term for describing people's living condition is *relationship status.* Life circumstances and opportunities may be very different depending on their relationship status.

## Age

At each age in life people have different needs and require different services to optimize their well-being. This book introduces social work with people of various ages. There are chapters on children and youth, and content on families with members who represent a range of ages. Because more than 13.7% of the U.S. population is age 65 or older, it is important for social  **EP 2** workers to understand the strengths, needs, and issues of this group (ProQuest, 2014). This will be even more evident as the baby boomer population reaches retirement age. As people age, they are more likely to experience increasing health problems and to require more

---

[4]*Posttraumatic stress disorder* is a condition in which a person continues to reexperience some traumatic event like a bloody battle or a sexual assault.

health and other support services. Kropf and Hutch-inson (2000) explain:

> *Social workers are serving more [older adult] …*
> *clients than ever before. [Older] … adults are a*
> *diverse population, presenting a wide range of*
> *practice needs and social issues. Social workers*
> *encounter two general types of [older adult] …*
> *clients. One group, older people with developmen-*
> *tal disabilities, have used social services at earlier*
> *life stages and continue to use services into their*
> *later life. The second type of [older adult] …*
> *client seeks a practitioner's help for conditions*
> *associated with the aging process. An example is*
> *the older person who requires assistance with*
> *household maintenance because of physical disabil-*
> *ities associated with aging. Both types of clients*
> *have similarities to younger clients. However, the*
> *unique aspects of aging must be understood if*
> *social work practice with older clients is to be*
> *effective. (p. 3)*

Chapter 10 explores in much greater depth the misconceptions about older adults, their needs, resources available to them, and the social work services involved.

## Disability and Ability

A **disability** is "[a]ny physical or mental impairment [or ongoing health or mental health condition] that substantially limits one or more major life activities"; these activities include "seeing, hearing, speaking, walking, breathing, performing manual tasks, learning, caring for oneself, and work-ing" (Equal Employment Opportunity  **EP 2** Commission, 1997, p. 1). It is estimated that 600 million people in the world today live with some kind of disability, another aspect of diversity (Mack-elprang, 2008). More than 22.3 million people in the United States have disabilities (ProQuest, 2014). Disabilities differ dramatically concerning how they affect people as they may involve cognitive, physi-cal, and psychiatric conditions (Clute, 2008; Patch-ner & DeWeaver, 2008; Sullivan, 2008).

Note that we have defined **ability** as the capacity to perform and get things done in various activities. Ability may involve competence and the use of skills. Of course, people vary dramatically in ability

level across a wide variety of tasks, behaviors, talents, and functions.

Many mistaken beliefs and misunderstandings exist concerning the abilities and prospects of people who have various types of disabilities, often minimiz-ing these people's potential. Myths include, for exam-ple, that people with paraplegia (paralysis of both legs due to a spinal cord injury or disease) or intellectual (cognitive) disabilities are unable to work. Because people with disabilities have unique strengths and needs, social workers can provide a range of services to help them improve their quality of life. Chapter 11 addresses types of disabilities, special needs, the issues involved, an emphasis on people's strengths, and social workers' involvement in service provision. Chapter 13 explores social work in mental health.

## Religion and Spirituality

Religion and spirituality reflect yet another aspect of human diversity. **Religion** involves people's spiritual beliefs concerning the origin, character, and reason for being, usually based on the existence of some higher power or powers, that often involves designated rituals and provides direction for what is considered moral or right. **Spiritual-**  **EP 2** **ity**, a related concept, "includes one's values, beliefs, mission, awareness, subjectivity, experience, sense of purpose and direction, and a kind of striving toward something greater than oneself. It may or may not include a deity" (Frame, 2003, p. 3). Religion implies membership in a spiritual organization with customs, traditions, and structure. Spirituality may involve religion, or it may reflect a personal, internalized view of existence.

Social workers help people cope with many diffi-cult issues. Consider the following:

> *An [older adult] … hospice patient spends his last*
> *days overwhelmed by depression. A young woman,*
> *estranged from family and friends, numbs her lone-*
> *liness with one-night stands and alcohol. A grieving*
> *couple drift apart after the death of their child.*
>
> *(Miller, 2001, p. A12)*

Gotterer (2001) maintains that spirituality can be "a bastion of strength" for clients, offering "emo-tional consolation, inspiration, guidance, structure and security. It can foster personal responsibility, identity, respect for ethical codes, meaningful ritual, and community building" (p. 188). Gotterer (2001) suggests that

> social workers, typically involved with vulnerable people in situations of pain or crisis, need a greater awareness of spiritual and religious issues. Tragedies such as the untimely death of a loved one force a person to confront the inexplicable. People Hearing death often wonder whether there is an afterlife. Trying times may cause a person to question the meaning and purpose of life. Those subjected to serious disease or long-term oppression need some way to make sense of their experience. Spiritual concerns such as hope, meaning, inner strength, and doubt are relevant in many clients' lives. (p. 187)

O'Neill (1999) warns, however, that the social work community concurs that

> one overriding principle is that of self-determination: social workers should never try to impose their own beliefs on clients. "There are many people who really do need faith and we need to honor it," said [Leona] Furman [associate professor at the University of North Dakota, who undertook the first major national survey of social workers' spirituality]. "We also need to honor those who don't have" the need to seek spiritual help and guidance. (p. 3)

As already indicated, spirituality can also be expressed in ways other than those determined by formal religions. Highlight 3.6 describes Kwanzaa, which "emphasizes spiritual grounding" for many African Americans (Karenga, 2000, p. 62).

### Islam and Muslims: A Population at Risk of Prejudice and Discrimination

Alavi (2001) cites the following scenario:

> During an annual meeting for the Catholic Archdiocese of Cincinnati, a primary agenda item concerned anti-Muslim furor in the United States during the 1979 Iranian hostage crisis. Particular attention went to a young boy in Wilmington, Ohio, a small, closely knit farming community that was proud of its Quaker college, considered a beacon of tolerance and intellectualism. The fifth-grade boy on the meeting's agenda had an American mother and an Iranian father working at the college.

> Being the lone child in town with an Iranian connection made him the only target of abuse in the entire school system. The first sign of trouble, a large rock, flew through his bedroom window, shattering glass on him and landing in the crib of his baby sister. By the end of the week, things were so bad that school administrators decided to dismiss the boy 15 minutes early every day. This would enable him to run home and lock the door before the other children caught up with him and beat him up, as they had done from the beginning of the hostage crisis.

> That child was my son, Jason. Although he had always been a confident and popular boy, he was never again able to fit into the social scene of his school. He carried the stigma of being "Iran Man" until graduation, and as an adult he feels little desire to see any of his school colleagues again. (p. 344)

Similar pictures exist today after the September 11, 2001 (9/11), terrorist attacks. Ahluwalia and Zaman (2010) reflect that since 9/11:

> There has been an increase in attention to and awareness of the experiences of Muslims ... in America. Less favorable public opinion ... and media portrayal ... of Muslims in America have contributed to an increasingly hostile sociopolitical climate. The media have consistently and repeatedly displayed images of suspected terrorists—people with "Islamic-sounding names," those who "appear" Muslim, and men who wear turbans.... Alongside this growing interest, the post-9/11 era has witnessed a dramatic backlash against U.S. Muslims ... with a sharp increase in and record high rates of discrimination, hate crimes, and religious profiling.... As a result, Muslim ... Americans are currently in a precarious situation, left vulnerable to poor physical and psychological outcomes resulting from increased stress and challenges. (p. 467)

An estimated 1.9 million to 3 million Muslims live in the United States; two-thirds of them were born here (Schaefer, 2011). This is a population-at-risk of prejudice and discrimination (Nassar-McMillan, 2011). Because of the fear, the unfair condemnation, and the misperceived relationship between Muslims and the terrorist extremists, it is critically important for social workers to develop an understanding of Muslim religion and culture. Highlight 3.7 explains some of the terms often used in association with the word *Muslim*.

## HIGHLIGHT 3.6  KWANZAA: A SPIRITUAL CELEBRATION OF LIFE, CULTURE, AND HISTORY

**Kwanzaa**, meaning "first fruits of the harvest" in Swahili, is a week-long celebration of life, culture, and history for many African Americans (Woodward & Johnson, 1995, p. 88). Developed by African American Maulana Karenga in 1966, it is celebrated annually from December 26 through January 1. It was created as a means of reaffirming community and heritage, strengthening the bonds among "African people both nationally and internationally" (Canda & Furman, 2010; Karenga, 2000, p. 57). Karenga explains:

It was conceived as a cultural project, as a way to speak a special African truth to the world by recovering lost models and memory, reviving suppressed principles and practices of African culture, and putting them in the service of the struggle for liberation and ever higher levels of human life.

Kwanzaa is based on the following seven principles called the Nguzo Saba (Canda & Furman, 2010; Karenga, 2000, pp. 58–59; Official Kwanzaa Web Site, 2013; Woodward & Johnson, 1995, p. 88). They each focus on concepts in Swahili because that is the most extensively spoken language in Africa.

1. *Unity (Umoja):* African Americans strive for harmony and a feeling of community in their families, neighborhoods, and nations.
2. *Self-determination (Kujichagulia):* African Americans "define" themselves, "name" themselves, "create" for themselves, and "speak for" themselves "instead of being defined, named for, and spoken for by others" (Karenga, 2000, p. 58).
3. *Collective work and responsibility (Ujima):* African Americans work together in their communities and help each other solve their problems.
4. *Cooperative economics (Ujamaa):* African Americans work together to establish their own economic base, taking responsibility for each other, developing businesses, and sharing wealth.
5. *Purpose (Nia):* African Americans adopt a guiding principle that they will build a world community restoring them "to their historical greatness" (Karenga, 2000, p. 58).
6. *Creativity (Kuumba):* African Americans do as much as possible to make their communities "more beautiful and beneficial" than before they inherited them (Karenga, 2000, p. 58).
7. *Faith (Imani):* African Americans believe strongly in themselves, focus on their strengths, and have faith that in the future they will blossom and stand out as a "free, proud, and productive people" (Karenga, 2000, p. 59).

Kwanzaa is a time when African Americans gather together to celebrate their culture, reach out to old friends, and forge commitments to a bright future. Each day, family members light a candle and focus on one of the Nguzo Saba's seven principles. At the end of the celebration, they exchange gifts usually having cultural significance (Woodward & Johnson, 1995). Kwanzaa is a celebration of African heritage and culture that serves as an avenue of empowerment for African American communities.

---

The following describes the foundation of Islam:

*Islam embraces the monotheism [the belief in one god] of Christianity and Judaism, accepts the Hebrew Bible, and ... [reveres] Jesus as a prophet. It is centered on the Koran—the Islamic scriptures [or Quran], which Muslims believe were revealed to the prophet Muhammad—which command five basic devotional duties, called the "Five Pillars."*

(Sheler, 2001, p. 50)

Ahluwalia and Zaman (2010) further explain that these pillars include:

1. *Shahadah (Declaration of faith):* "There is no deity, but God, and Muhammad is his messenger."
2. *Salat: the performance of prayer five times daily.*
3. *Zakat: the annual distributing of 2.5% of one's accumulated wealth to the poor.*
4. *Sawm: fasting from sunrise to sunset during the holy month of Ramadan.*
5. *Hajj: the pilgrimage to the holy city Mecca [an Arabian city near the Red Sea that is the birthplace of Muhammad] at least once in a lifetime, if physically and financially capable (Abdul Rauf, 2004). (p. 408)*

Frame (2003) explains that

*Muslims believe that they are called by God (Allah) to be grateful for their blessings and to choose to serve God. For Muslims, both faith and*

## HIGHLIGHT 3.7 TERMS OFTEN ASSOCIATED WITH MUSLIMS

The first thing to understand is the meaning of the terms often involved when referring to people who are Muslims. Many of the associations are erroneous (Schaefer, 2011).

**Islam** is a term "derived from the Arabic word meaning peace, the inference being that one who willingly submits to the will of God is a person who has found peace" (Alavi, 2001). **Muslims** are followers of Islam (Pickett, 2002).

The term **Arab American** is a relatively new term. It refers to a diverse group of people who are descendants of people from 22 Arab-speaking nations in North Africa and West Asia (Ajrouch, 2008; Schaefer, 2011). Religious affiliations include Muslim and Christian (Ajrouch, 2008).

"Arabs are an ethnic group and Muslims are a religious group" (Schaefer, 2011, p. 263).

Schaefer (2011) explains the term **Middle Eastern**:

Further complicating the use of collective terms of identity such as Arab and Muslim is evoking the term Middle Eastern (Middle Eastern American). Although it is also frequently used, the Middle East is an ambiguous geographic designation that includes large numbers of people who are neither Muslim nor Arab (such as Israeli Jews). Collectively, ... Middle Easterners are lumped together and ... subjected to prejudice and discrimination but are not eligible for supportive efforts such as affirmative action. (p. 264)

---

*good works are required, but faith is also considered a gift from God.... Muslims believe that people are essentially created good. Although they may make poor choices, persons can be forgiven if they repent and follow their repentance with ethical living. (pp. 68–69)*

Many people have leapt to the conclusion that Islam encourages terrorist attacks. Alavi (2001) stresses that Muslims worldwide have reviled the 9/11 assault and that Islam forbids murdering innocent people. "In fact, American Muslim and Arab-American organizations and leaders were among the first to react in an organized fashion to condemn the terrorist attacks on that very same day, long before it became clear that individuals calling themselves Muslims were involved in the attacks" (Abdelkarim, 2002).

Robert S. Mueller III, former director of the Federal Bureau of Investigation (FBI), reported that numerous American Muslim

*leaders have generously sent educational materials to our [FBI] field offices and to our headquarters. They have taken the time to talk with our agents and support professionals to help them better understand Muslim perspectives and Muslim beliefs. Muslim Americans have cooperated with our interviews and supported our investigations.... The active work of many in the American Muslim community in cities nationwide has merited public*

*thanks and praise. But perhaps the greatest act of support has been the way Muslim and Arab Americans have responded to our urgent need for translators. Six days after September 11, I announced that the FBI was seeking Arabic and Farsi language experts. The response was extraordinary. Within hours, our switchboard was overwhelmed with calls. Those who came forward included doctors, lawyers, engineers, academics—Muslim and Arab Americans from all walks of life who were willing to quit their jobs, come to work for the FBI, and give something back to their country in the fight against terrorism.*

*(Mueller, 2002)*

It is estimated that there are 1.3 billion Muslims worldwide, and, as we've established, 1.9 million to 3 million in the United States (Schaefer, 2011). It is also estimated that Muslim Americans are members of the following ethnic and racial groups:

- *20–42 percent African American,*
- *24–33 percent South Asian (Afghan, Bangladeshi, Indian, and Pakistani),*
- *12–32 percent Arab, and*
- *15–22 percent "other" (Bosnian, Iranian, Turk, and White and Hispanic converts).*

*(Schaefer, 2011, p. 266)*

The degree to which individuals practice Muslim beliefs and traditions also varies radically from "traditional—strongly practicing" to "assimilated [into the mainstream culture]—marginally practicing" or "nonpracticing" (Nadir & Dziegielewski, 2001, p. 159).

Although there is great diversity, several values tend to characterize the life of Muslims; these include conception of family, selection of marriage partners, diet, and dress (Nadir & Dziegielewski, 2001). Note that traditional values often conflict with current practices and expectations in the United States. "Family is considered to be the cornerstone of Muslim society, and parents are expected to raise children who will work for social justice. Obedience to parents is a divinely ordained value" (p. 152). Muslims face the dilemma of raising children in a non-Muslim environment. For example, "Muslim children in the public schools, in general, receive negative messages about Islam from their textbooks and their teachers" (p. 154).

Western-style dating (i.e., spending time alone together doing various activities in the process of getting to know each other) is prohibited to avoid risking sexual relationships prior to marriage. Instead,

> arranged, not forced, marriage is the tradition in Islam. Chaperoned courtship provides opportunities to meet one's future spouse and discuss concerns and plans for the future. As individuals become more identified with mainstream U.S. culture and less religious, traditional practices meet with resistance from young people, who participate in mixed-gender activities and live in isolated communities far from other Muslims.
>
> (Nadir & Dziegielewski, 2001, pp. 152–153)

Diet restrictions include being forbidden to eat pork and pork by-products. Islam also prohibits the consumption of alcohol or other mind-altering substances. "During the month of Ramadan in which the receipt of the Koran is celebrated, Muslims may not eat, drink, smoke, or have sexual intercourse between sunup and sundown" (Frame, 2003, p. 69).

Islam provides guidelines for both men's and women's dress, emphasizing modesty.

> Traditionally, Muslim women show nothing but their face, hands, and feet when they are in the company of those not part of their **mahram** (close family members, those who are not eligible to marry the woman, including her father, grandfather, brothers, sons, uncles, nephews, sons-in-law, and father-in-law). The women's clothing is opaque, loose-fitting, long-sleeved, and ankle-length.
>
> (Nadir & Dziegielewski, 2001, p. 151)

They also wear a veil, a **khimar**, over their head, neck, and breasts, although dress requirements become less formal when women are with close family.

Nadir and Dziegielewski (2001) reflect:

> Because of media stereotypes and sensationalism, many non-Muslims perceive Islam as oppressive to women. Many Muslim women, however, do not agree, as they see Islam as a way of life that provides them with a sense of purpose, peace, and freedom not common in Western society.… It is important to recognize that many of the inequities Muslim women face are the result of cultural or political traditions that have nothing to do with and are not sanctioned by the teachings of Islam. (p. 154)
>
> Muslim men must also adhere to a dress code. They are required to cover from their navel to their knees. Their garments must be loose-fitting. Traditionally Muslim men wear a shirt, which covers their private area, and loose-fitting slacks.… [In addition, they] are forbidden to wear gold or silk. (p 152)

# Chapter Summary

The following summarizes this chapter's content as it relates to the learning objectives presented at the beginning of the chapter. Chapter content will help prepare students to:

**LO1 Discuss human diversity and differences in status (including discrimination, oppression,** *marginalization, alienation, power, privilege, acclaim, stereotypes, prejudice, populations at risk, and social and economic justice).*

Discrimination is the act of treating people differently based on the fact that they belong to some group rather than on merit. Oppression involves putting extreme limitations and constraints on some person, group, or larger system. Marginalization is the condition of having less power and being viewed as less important than others in society because of belonging to some group or having some characteristic (e.g., racial, economic, ethnic, or political). Alienation, related to marginalization, is the feeling that you don't fit in or aren't treated as well as others in the mainstream of society. Power is the ability to move people on a chosen course to produce an effect or achieve some goal. Privilege entails special rights or benefits enjoyed because of elevated social, political, or economic status. Acclaim is "enthusiastic and public praise" (Lindberg, 2007, p. 7).

A stereotype is a fixed mental picture of a member of some specified group based on some attribute or attributes that reflect an overly simplified view of that group, without consideration or appreciation of individual differences. Prejudice is a negative opinion or prejudgment about an individual, group, or issue that is not based on fact. Social workers must address these issues with diverse populations.

Populations at risk are people at greater risk of deprivation and unfair treatment because they share some identifiable characteristic that places them in a diverse group. Dimensions of diversity include age, class, color, culture, disability and ability, ethnicity, gender, gender identity and expression, immigration status, marital status, political ideology, race, religion or spirituality, sex, sexual orientation, and tribal sovereignty. Social justice involves the idea that in a perfect world all citizens would have identical "rights, protection, opportunities, obligations, and social benefits" regardless of their backgrounds and membership in diverse groups (Barker, 2014, p. 398). Economic justice concerns the distribution of resources in a fair and equitable manner. Being a member of various diverse groups places people at risk of unfair and unequal treatment.

## LO2 *Employ critical thinking skills to appraise self-awareness (including that concerning racial self-awareness, cultural self-awareness, the treatment of intersex people and people with various forms of gender expression, and the feminist perspective).*

Questions were posed concerning personal attitudes about race, culture, worldview, family structure, treatment of intersex people, freedom of gender expression, the meaning of gender, fair treatment on the basis of gender, and the feminist perspective.

## LO3 *Explore empowerment and related concepts (including the strengths perspective and resiliency).*

Empowerment is the "process of increasing personal, interpersonal, or political power so that individuals can take action to improve their life situations" (Gutierrez, 2001, p. 210). The strengths perspective emphasizes people's strengths in order to pursue their empowerment.

Resiliency is the ability of an individual, family, group, community, or organization to recover from adversity and resume functioning even when suffering serious trouble, confusion, or hardship. Resiliency can characterize individuals and larger systems.

## LO4 *Examine empowerment for women in groups.*

Themes emerging as providing successful conditions for women's empowerment within a group setting include safety, mutual interaction, commonality, acceptance, validation, and interdependence.

## LO5 *Recognize various aspects of human diversity (including age, class, color, culture, disability and ability, ethnicity, gender, gender identity and expression, immigration status, marital status, political ideology, race [together with values characterizing various racial groups], religion/spirituality [in addition to the basic tenets of Islam and discrimination against Muslim people], sex, sexual orientation, and tribal sovereignty).*

The concept of intersectionality involves the idea that people are complex and can belong to multiple, overlapping diverse groups. Race refers to a category of people who share a common descent and genetic origin that may be distinguished by "certain physical traits" or "interests, habits, or characteristics" (Mish, 2008, p. 1024). Ethnicity refers to the affiliation with a large group of people who have "common racial, national, tribal, religious, linguistic, or cultural origin or background" (Mish, 2008, p. 429). Race implies a greater genetic determinant, whereas ethnicity often relates to cultural or national heritage. Other terms such as minorities and people of color are also commonly used to refer to people of different racial and ethnic heritage. People of color "is a collective term that refers to the major groups of African, Latino, and Asian Americans, and First Nations Peoples [Native Americans] who have been distinguished from the dominant society by color" (Lum, 2011, p. 129).

Culture, another dimension of diversity, is "a way of life including widespread values (about what is good and bad), beliefs (about what is true), and behavior (what people do every day)" (italics deleted) (Macionis, 2013, p. 5). Aspects of culture are often related to people's ethnic, racial, and spiritual heritage.

Ethnic and cultural differences are discussed concerning Hispanics; American Indians, Native Americans, or First Nations Peoples; African Americans; and Asian Americans. Themes characterizing Hispanic families include the significance of a common language and cultural pride, the importance of family and extended family, spirituality and religion, and division of gender roles. Values reflected in Native American families include the importance of family ties and extended family, noninterference, harmony with nature, a less rigid concept of time, and spirituality. Themes evident in many African American families include the importance of extended family and child centeredness, gender-role flexibility, spirituality and religion. Values characterizing Asian American families include the significance of family, interdependence and collectivism, filial piety, a patriarchal hierarchy, the desire to keep problems within the family, and interpersonal harmony.

National origin means the country of birth of individuals, their parents, or their ancestors. Immigration concerns the permanent movement from one country to another. Immigration status is a person's position in terms of legal rights and residency when entering and residing in a country that is not that person's legal country of origin. People may have legal or illegal immigration status.

Class refers to people's status or ranking in society with respect to such standards as "relative wealth, power, prestige, educational level, or family background" (Barker, 2014, p. 396). Political ideology is the "relatively coherent system of ideas (beliefs, traditions, principles, and myths) about human nature, institutional arrangements, and social processes" that indicate how a government should be run and what principles that government should support (Abramovitz, 2010, p. 131).

Sex "refers to whether one is biologically female or male, based on genetic and anatomical sex" (Yarber & Sayad, 2013, p. 127). Gender "refers to the social and psychological characteristics associated with being female or male" (McCammon & Knox, 2007, p. 112). Gender identity is a person's internal psychological self-concept of being either a male or a female, or, possibly, some combination of both. Gender expression concerns how we express ourselves to others in ways related to gender that include both behavior and personality. Gender roles are the "attitudes, behaviors, rights, and responsibilities that particular cultural groups associate" with being male or female (Yarber & Sayad, 2013, p. 127). Women are often victims of oppression on the basis of gender. Feminism is defined. Men address special issues and have special needs due to their gender. Sexual orientation involves the sexual and romantic attraction to persons of one or both genders. LGBTQI people are often victims of homophobia.

At each age, people have different needs and require different services to optimize their well-being. Because there is a growing percentage of people in the U.S. population age 65 or older, it is important for social workers to understand the strengths, needs, and issues of this group.

Disabilities affect millions of people globally. Disabilities vary dramatically and include cognitive, physical, and psychiatric conditions. Ability is the capacity to perform and get things done in various activities.

Religion involves people's spiritual beliefs concerning the origin, character, and reason for being, usually based on the existence of some higher power or powers, that often involves designated rituals and provides direction for what is considered moral or right. Spirituality concerns "one's values, beliefs, mission, awareness, subjectivity, experience, sense of purpose and direction, and a king of striving toward something greater than oneself. It may or may not include a deity" (Frame, 2003, p. 3). Religion implies membership in a spiritual organization with customs, traditions, and structure. Spirituality may involve religion, or it may reflect a personal, internalized view of existence. Kwanzaa is a week-long celebration of life, culture, and history for many African Americans

Islam involves a belief in one god and is centered on the Koran, the Islamic scriptures. Values characterizing Muslim life include conception of family, selection of marriage partners, diet, and dress. Because of the fear, the unfair condemnation, and the misperceived relationship between Muslims and terrorist extremists, it is important for social workers to develop understanding of the Muslim religion and culture.

### LO6 Define cultural competence and apply it to social work.

Social workers need to attain cultural competence—that is, the "mastery of a particular set of knowledge, skills, policies, and programs used by the social worker that address the cultural needs of individuals, families, groups, and communities" (Lum, 2005, p. 4). NASW identifies six tasks necessary to achieve cultural competence. Cultural issues important to address include the melting pot myth, cultural expectations about intervention, worldviews, and values concerning nuclear and extended families.

### LO7 Examine the social construction of gender.

There are many types of gender expression on a gender spectrum. Concepts include intersex, transgenderism, transsexuals, and transvestites. The notion of gender is socially constructed according to social values and beliefs.

## LOOKING AHEAD

This chapter described various aspects of human diversity and emphasized the importance of social workers being knowledgeable about these dimensions. The significance ascribed to diversity is based on the social work values discussed in Chapter 2. Part 1 of this book has established a foundation for understanding social welfare and social work. The two chapters in Part 2 will explain the process of and settings for generalist social work practice.

## COMPETENCY NOTES

The following identifies where Educational Policy (EP) competencies and their component behaviors are discussed in the chapter.

**EP 1 (Competency 1)—Demonstrate Ethical and Professional Behavior.** *(p. 72):* Learning about diverse groups is an ongoing, career-long process.

**EP 1b Use reflection and self-regulation to manage personal values and maintain professionalism in practice situations.** *(p. 67):* Practitioners must practice personal reflection and self-regulation about any prejudices or stereotypes they harbor to prevent these biases from interfering with effective, ethical practice. *(p. 68):* Social workers should practice reflection and self-regulation as part of racial self-awareness. *(p. 72):* Social workers should strive to remain open minded and nonjudgmental.

**EP 1c Demonstrate professional demeanor in behavior; appearance; and oral, written, and electronic communication.** *(p. 74):* Social workers should be knowledgeable about and use sensitivity when communicating with and about various racial, ethnic, and cultural groups. *(p. 110):* Questions are posed to encourage the articulation and communication of practice decisions.

**EP 2 (Competency 2)—Engage Diversity and Difference in Practice.** *(p. 66):* Differences in life experiences may result in oppression, discrimination, marginalization, alienation, privilege, power, and acclaim. *(p. 67):* Dimensions of diversity are identified here. *(p. 72):* Subsequent sections explore each aspect of diversity. *(p. 73):* The significance of the intersectionality of multiple factors involved in diversity is discussed. *(p. 73):* Ethnicity and race are dimensions of diversity. *(p. 74):* Culture is a dimension of diversity. *(p. 82):* Tribal sovereign status is an aspect of diversity. *(p. 86):* Immigration status is an aspect of diversity. *(p. 88):* Class is a dimension of diversity. Social workers should strive to understand the mechanisms of oppression imposed by social class. *(p. 88):* Political ideology is a dimension of diversity. *(p. 89):* Gender, gender identity, and gender expression are dimensions of diversity. *(p. 89):* Various aspects of gender expression and sex, both facets of human diversity, are explored. *(p. 90):* Women are discussed as victims of oppression. *(p. 94):* Men experience disadvantages based on their gender. *(p. 95):* Sexual orientation is a dimension of diversity. *(p. 96):* Cultural values involving homophobia negatively affect LBG people and often expose them to discrimination. *(p. 97):* Marital status is an aspect of diversity. *(p. 97):* Age is a facet of diversity. *(p. 98):* Disability and ability are aspects of diversity. *(p. 98):* Religion and spirituality are facets of diversity.

**EP 2a Apply and communicate understanding of the importance of diversity and difference in shaping life experiences in practice at the micro, mezzo, and macro levels.** *(p. 66):* Diversity and difference significantly shape life experiences. *(p. 72):* Practitioners should recognize the extent to which aspects of diversity shape life experiences. *(p. 75):* Social workers should recognize how cultural values and expectations shape life experiences. *(p. 87):* The lack of resources available to the Turkana tribe shapes its members' life experiences. *(p. 89):* Gender is an important factor in shaping life experiences. *(p. 94):* Gender is one facet that shape's men's life experiences. *(p. 96):* Having a sexual orientation that is not heterosexual shapes life experiences.

**EP 2b Present themselves as learners and engage clients and constituencies as experts of their own experiences.** *(p. 67):* Exploring personal prejudices and stereotypes is a lifelong process. *(p. 68):* Social workers should view themselves as learners and their clients as informants concerning client strengths. *(p. 72):* Learning about human diversity from clients is an ongoing process for social workers. *(p. 87):* Social workers should learn from their clients about their needs and conditions.

**EP 2c Apply self-awareness and self-regulation to manage the influence of personal biases and values in working with diverse clients and constituencies.** *(p. 67):* Social workers should strive to become aware of any stereotypes and prejudices they harbor so that such ideas do not interfere with adherence to professional values to guide practice. *(p. 68):* Practitioners must work hard at developing self-awareness regarding any prejudices and stereotypes they may harbor toward any diverse group. *(p. 88):* Social workers must gain sufficient self-awareness to avoid imposing stereotypes and prejudgments on people about social class.

**EP 3 (Competency 3)—Advance Human Rights and Social, Economic, and Environmental Justice.**

**EP 3a Apply their understanding of social, economic, and environmental justice to advocate for human rights at the individual and system levels.** *(p. 67):* Social workers should advocate for social and economic justice. *(p. 93):* A feminist perspective advocates for human rights and social and economic justice.

**EP 3b Engage in practices that advance social, economic, and environmental justice.** *(p. 67):* Social workers should engage in practices that advance for social and economic justice. *(p. 90):* Recommendations are made for advancing social justice for intersex children.

**EP 7 (Competency 7)—Assess Individuals, Families, Groups, Organizations, and Communities.**

**EP 7a Collect and organize data and apply critical thinking to interpret information from clients and constituencies.** *(p. 68):* When assessing any client situation, practitioners should think critically about their personal perceptions of racial differences so that these perceptions don't interfere with ethical practice. *(p. 75):* Social workers should apply critical thinking when assessing cultural issues. *(p. 90):* Data regarding gender and gender expression should be collected and interpreted. *(p. 110):* Critical thinking questions are posed to collect, organize, and interpret client data.

**EP 7b Apply knowledge of human behavior and the social environment, person-in-environment, and other multidisciplinary theoretical frameworks in the analysis of assessment data from clients and constituencies.** *(p. 75):* Social workers must understand and apply knowledge about cultural issues to understand and assess people's functioning in their environments. *(p. 91):* Social workers may use the theoretical framework of the social construction of gender to understand gender expression. This may help guide the process of assessment. *(p. 93):* Practitioners can use theoretical frameworks such as the feminist perspective to help guide their practice.

**EP 7c Develop mutually agreed-on intervention goals and objectives based on the critical assessment of strengths, needs, and challenges within clients and constituencies.** *(p. 68):* Practitioners should asses clients' strengths. *(p. 72):* Social workers should assess their clients' strengths in order to build on these strengths. *(p. 75):* Practitioners should assess and emphasize the strengths involved in various cultures.

*(p. 94):* Social workers should understand the special issues, strengths, needs, and challenges of men.

**EP 7d Select appropriate intervention strategies based on the assessment, research knowledge, and values and preferences of clients and constituencies.** *(p. 69):* Social workers should select the appropriate intervention strategies when working with domestic violence survivors in groups. Counseling approaches are described.

**EP 8 (Competency 8)—Intervene with Individuals, Families, Groups, Organizations, and Communities.**

**EP 8a Critically choose and implement interventions to achieve practice goals and enhance capacities of clients and constituencies.** *(p. 68):* When practicing intervention in any client situation, practitioners should think critically about their personal perceptions of racial differences so that these perceptions don't interfere with ethical practice. *(p. 75):* Social workers should apply critical thinking about cultural issues during

intervention. *(p. 110):* Critical thinking questions are posed to encourage thinking about effective interventions.

**EP 8b Apply knowledge of human behavior and the social environment, person-in-environment, and other multidisciplinary theoretical frameworks in interventions with clients and constituencies.** *(p. 75):* Social workers must understand and apply knowledge about cultural issues to intervene effectively with clients as they function within their environments. *(p. 91):* Social workers may use the theoretical framework of the social construction of gender to understand gender expression. This may help guide the process of intervention. *(p. 93):* Practitioners can use theoretical frameworks such as the feminist perspective to help guide their practice.

**EP 8d Negotiate, mediate, and advocate with and on behalf of diverse clients and constituencies.** *(p. 69):* One strategy for working with domestic violence survivors in groups is to advocate on their behalf.

CASE STUDY FOR CRITICAL THINKING

# An Agency Providing Foster Family Care

Consider the following ethical dilemma involving an agency providing foster family care for children (Robison & Reeser, 2000). (*Foster family care* is the provision of substitute care with a family for a planned temporary or extended period when parents or legal guardians are unable to care for a child.) This case study illustrates how the social work profession must continuously address the issue of quality of care versus cost of care. The more intensive and extensive the services provided, the greater the cost. Similarly, social workers must frequently struggle with the issue of providing quality service to clients at minimal cost. The case study also shows how important the agency context is for how social workers can provide services.

*Case Study:* Jose directs an agency that places children in foster family care. The state mandates that no more than six children may be placed with any one family. The intent is to make certain that the family's ability to care for the children is not overextended.

Jose's agency must make enough money to cover its own costs and pay its workers' salaries. Any "money the agency makes from the placement that is not used for the placement itself or for training the foster parents is used to support other agency activities," such as various programs serving poor people. The state pays an annual administrative fee of $8,933 per child placed in a foster home by the agency (Robison & Reeser, 2000, p. 238).

Being a foster parent is not always easy. Sometimes, when needed, the agency's social workers provide training in such skills as effective parenting, communication, behavior management, and anger control:

> *The problems that the foster parents face with the children can be remedied if they are the result of lack of proper training, and in the worst cases, children are taken from the home. But there are always going to be marginal cases, "gray areas" [where training won't help].... The agency has solved the problem of what to do with cases that fall into the "gray areas" through "benign neglect," preferring to assume that the problems are not serious enough for the child to be taken out of the home.*
>
> (Robison & Reeser, 2000, p. 238)

A problem is that the agency is receiving for placement increasingly difficult children who have more extreme problems. Workers report that provision of training for the foster parents is not working because the children's behavioral and emotional problems are so extreme. All the workers can do is tell foster parents they must "deal with" the problems "somehow" (p. 238).

Jose decides to cut down the number of children placed in a foster home from six to four. This would alleviate some of the stress placed on the parents and allow them to give each child more time and attention. However, this means that both the agency and the foster parents (who are also paid by the state) make significantly less money. In fact, Jose's agency is starting to lose money instead of making it. If that doesn't stop, the agency will have to close.

**Critical Thinking:** How would you use the three-step Triple-A critical thinking process to establish what might be done in this case?

First, *ask* questions like these:

EP 1c, 7a, 8a[5]

- What options are possible other than the one Jose chose?
- Can children somehow be screened to determine which ones are the most difficult to handle?
- Could these more difficult children be placed in special homes run by the most effective foster parents, with less difficult children placed in homes having six foster children?
- Does decreasing the number of foster children from six to four really make sense? Will this actually solve the problem of better managing difficult behavior? (Workers feel that training still will not help.)
- How possible and effective might it be to decrease the number of children per foster home to five instead of four? Would this be more financially feasible?
- Could other areas of the agency's budget be cut to make up for the decreased number of children in each home?
- What other questions could you ask when thinking about possible solutions in this case?

Second, *assess* the established facts and issues involved. How would you seek answers to the questions just posed and to others you might think up? What information do you need? Where might you find this information? Who could help you get it?

Third, *assert* a concluding opinion. The case poses a difficult problem. After carefully considering the facts, what final conclusion might you reach?

---

[5]Competency Notes explaining this icon are located at the end of Chapter 3.

# SOCIAL WORK PRACTICE

Part 2 includes two chapters that introduce you to the *doing* of social work practice. Chapter 4 discusses the process of social work practice. It defines generalist practice and explains the various roles social workers can assume. It also examines the planned-change process social workers follow as they work with clients.

Chapter 5 describes the various practice settings in which social workers do their work. It explains how practitioners work with individuals, families, groups, organizations, and communities. It also introduces you to the professional organizations in social work and discusses career options.

# The Process of Generalist Practice

Barros & Barros/The Image Bank/Getty Images

## Learning Objectives    This chapter will help prepare students to:

**LO 1**  Define generalist practice.  **A Definition of Generalist Practice** (p. 115)

**LO 2**  Discuss professional identity. **Highlight 4.2** (p. 119)

**LO 3**  Describe the planned-change process.  **Steps Involved in Planned Change** (p. 121)

**LO 4**  Apply critical thinking skills.  **Focus on Critical Thinking 4.1** (p. 122)

**LO 5**  Discuss cross-cultural variations in communication.  **Highlight 4.3** (p. 128)

**LO 6**  Emphasize strengths during the assessment process.  **Highlight 4.4** (p. 129)

**LO 7**  Describe examples of intervention with macro systems.  **Highlight 4.5** (p. 132)

**LO 8**  Relate sustainability to social work. **Highlight 4.6** (p. 134)

*Working with individuals (micro systems), a social worker can:*

● *Help a homeless person get medical help from a community clinic and find a place to stay at a local shelter.*
● *Counsel a young woman regarding what type of contraception is best for her.*
● *Assist an older adult in a hospice in making his end-of-life decisions and help him rest as comfortably as possible during his final days.*

*Working with families (micro/mezzo systems), a social worker can*

● *Help strengthen families and teach parenting skills to stop or prevent child abuse.*
● *Link homeless families with needed resources.*
● *Teach conflict resolution strategies to families besieged with contention.*

*Working with groups (mezzo systems), a social worker can*

● *Run a social skills group for adolescents with intellectual (cognitive) disabilities.*
● *Lead a support group for parents of children diagnosed with cancer.*
● *Be in charge of an agency meeting in which various agency staff discuss a client's progress.*

*Working with organizations and communities (macro systems), a social worker can*

● *Initiate cooperation among social service agencies to sponsor a holiday gift collection program for needy families.*
● *Contact legislators and advocate for increased funding for low-income housing for poor people.*
● *Work with residents in a neighborhood with a high crime rate to start a Neighborhood Watch program in which neighbors, working together, watch each other's homes and report suspicious behavior to reduce crime.*

*These scenarios provide examples of what generalist social workers can do at various levels of practice. There are many ways to describe what social workers do. We have established that they work with individuals, families, groups, organizations, and communities to enhance people's well-being. They are prepared to help individuals with highly personal issues and with broad problems that affect whole communities. Social workers identify problems, even difficult ones, and try to help people solve them.*

*The foundation of social work practice is* generalist practice *(CSWE, 2015, p. 10). There are many specific definitions of generalist practice. However, all of these definitions appear to involve some common ideas; these include "the concepts of systems, multiple methods, problem solving, and partnership with client. The definitions emphasize the purpose and values of social work, the various roles or capacities in which social workers serve, and the use of the planned change process to address social problems and restore social functioning" (Hernandez, 2008, p. 264).*

*Some dimensions are exceptionally important in conceptualizing the definition of generalist social work practice (Association of Baccalaureate Program Directors,*

2008). First, the importance of multiple-level interventions (including those with individuals, families, groups, organizations, and communities) should be emphasized. Intervention *is the process of planning and implementing steps to make positive changes and attain goals that solve clients' problems or improve clients' quality of life. Second, generalist practice should emphasize evaluation of practice effectiveness. Interventions should be chosen based on a history of successful application for specific situations, referred to as* evidence-based practice. *Third, generalist practice should focus both on issues concerning individuals, families, and groups, and those concerning social justice and human rights. Generalist social workers, then, must have infinite flexibility, a solid knowledge base about many things, and a wide range of skills at their disposal.*

**Micro practice** *is intervention involving an individual client (a micro system).* **Mezzo practice** *involves work with small groups (mezzo systems). Social work with families combines micro and mezzo practice because it involves a small group (i.e., the family) but one with intimate ties.* **Macro practice** *is intervention involving organizations and communities (macro systems).*

*Integral links exist among micro, mezzo, and macro practice. Generalist practice skills build on each other in a progression from micro to mezzo to macro levels. Relating to individuals in groups (mezzo practice) requires basic micro skills. Likewise, macro practice requires mastery of both micro and mezzo skills for relating to and working with individuals and groups in organizational and community (macro) settings.*

*Note that throughout this book the terms* social worker, generalist social worker, *and* generalist practitioner *are used interchangeably. Specialized aspects of social work practice, usually referring to social workers with master's degrees, will be specified as such.*

## A Definition of Generalist Practice

LO 1

Generalist social work practice may involve almost any helping situation you can think of. A generalist practitioner may be called on to help a homeless family, a child unable to get along with peers, a pregnant teenager, a sick older adult unable to care for herself any longer, an alcoholic parent, a community that's trying to address its drug abuse problem, or a public assistance agency struggling to amend its policies to conform to new federal regulations. Therefore, as has been established, generalist practitioners must be well prepared to address many kinds of difficult situations.

The social work profession has struggled with the concept of generalist practice for many years. In the past, new practitioners were educated in only one skill area (e.g., work with individuals, groups, or communities) or one area of practice (e.g., children and families, or policy and administration). A generalist practitioner needs competence in a wide variety of areas instead of being limited to a single track.

For our purposes, we will define *generalist practice*[1] as the application of an eclectic knowledge base,[2] professional values, and a wide range of skills to target individual, family, group, organizational, or community systems for change within the context

---

[1]Most of the concepts involved in the definition are taken directly from or based on those required by the Educational Policy and Accreditation Standards (CSWE, 2015).

[2]The term *eclectic* refers to "selecting what appears to be best in various doctrines, methods, or styles" (Mish, 2008, p. 394).

## HIGHLIGHT 4.1   CONCEPTS IN THE DEFINITION OF GENERALIST PRACTICE

1. Acquiring an eclectic knowledge base
   A. Systems theory
   B. Ecological perspective
   C. Curriculum content areas
      (1) Values and ethics
      (2) Diversity
      (3) Populations at risk and social and economic justice
      (4) Human behavior and the social environment
      (5) Social welfare policy and services
      (6) Social work practice
      (7) Research
      (8) Field education
   D. Fields of practice
2. Emphasizing client empowerment
3. Using professional values
   A. National Association of Social Workers (NASW) *Code of Ethics* and, as applicable, the International Federation of Social Workers (IFSW)/International Association of Schools of Social Work (IASSW) *Ethics in Social Work, Statement of Principles.*
   B. Recognition and management of personal values

   C. Application of professional values and strategies of ethical reasoning to make ethical decisions and solve ethical dilemmas.
4. Applying a wide range of skills
   A. Micro
   B. Mezzo
   C. Macro
5. Targeting systems at any size
   A. Individual
   B. Family
   C. Group
   D. Organization
   E. Community
6. Working in an organizational structure
7. Using supervision appropriately
8. Assuming a wide range of professional roles
9. Following the principles of evidence-based practice
10. Employing critical thinking skills
11. Using a planned-change process
    A. Engagement
    B. Assessment
    C. Planning
    D. Implementation
    E. Evaluation
    F. Termination

of five primary processes. First, generalist practice emphasizes client empowerment. Second, it involves working effectively within an organizational structure and doing so under supervision. Third, it requires the assumption of a wide range of professional roles. Fourth, it concerns following the principles of evidence-based practice (choosing intervention plans based on evidence of past effectiveness and evaluating the outcomes of intervention to improve future service provision). Fifth, it involves the application of critical thinking skills to the planned-change process. Highlight 4.1 outlines the basic concepts involved in this definition.

Figure 4.1 illustrates how the various concepts involved in the definition of generalist practice fit together. The large square in the top half of the figure portrays the organizational structure. An organization (or agency) employs social workers and provides the context for them to do their jobs. *Organizational*

*structure* involves how lines of authority and communication operate within an agency, how the administration runs the organization, and what the agency environment is like. Social workers practice within this environment with all its constraints, requirements, and rules, similar to any other place of employment. Thus, in Figure 4.1, a social worker is represented as a smaller rectangle within this large square.

That same rectangle contains the terms *knowledge, skills*, and *values*. These illustrate how social workers bring to their job a broad knowledge base, professional values, and a wide range of skills so they can do their work effectively. Also in the large upper square is another rectangle representing supervision. A downward-pointing arrow links the supervision rectangle to the social worker rectangle, indicating that part of working as a generalist practitioner involves receiving and using supervisory input appropriately.

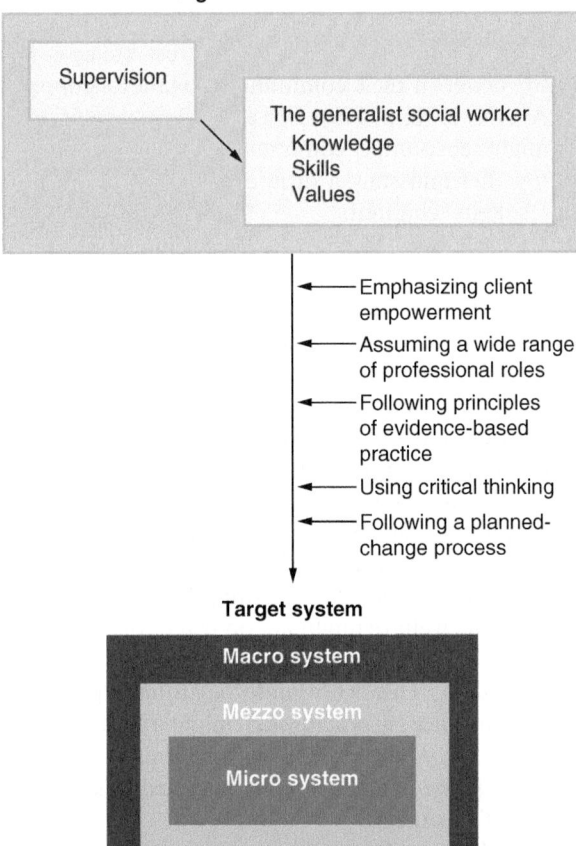

**FIG-4-1** A Pictorial View of Generalist Practice

Chapter 1 discussed the eclectic knowledge base supporting social work; Chapter 2, social work values and ethics; and Chapter 3, client empowerment. The following sections review the other concepts involved in the definition of generalist practice.

## Working in an Organizational Structure Under Supervision

Social workers most likely work within an organizational structure (or agency context) under supervision. As mentioned previously, **organizational structure** is the formal and informal manner in which tasks and responsibilities, lines of authority, channels of communication, and dimensions of power are established and coordinated within an organization. Understanding the organizational structure involves knowing how decisions are made, what chain of command is followed, what procedures regulate service provision to clients, and how the social work job expectations fit into the larger scheme of things.

EP 1e

**Supervision** is the process by which a designated supervisor watches over a worker's performance, directs activities, and provides feedback. A good supervisor can be valuable in helping social workers perform effectively within an agency setting.

The next section introduces another important aspect of professional agency life within an organizational structure—consultation.

## The Use of Consultation

**Consultation** is the act of seeking help from someone with expertise in a subject to devise a plan or solve a problem. It usually involves a colleague, administrator, expert, or other who has the appropriate competence or experience.

Consultation differs from supervision. Supervision is generally an ongoing process within an organization. It is undertaken by someone designated as a supervisor who has responsibility for overseeing a supervisee's work. Consultation, on the other hand, is sought out when needed from someone who has specific experience or expertise. It is usually a time-limited process and is oriented toward some specific issue (Harkness, 2008). Consultation may be provided informally among colleagues when help

The large square at the bottom of Figure 4.1 illustrates social workers' potential target system. We have established that generalist practitioners may choose to work with a micro, mezzo, or macro system as the target of their change efforts. These three systems are arbitrarily portrayed in concentric squares to reflect their respective sizes.

An arrow flows from the organizational structure square down to the target system square. This depicts how social workers apply their knowledge, skills, and values to help change a micro, mezzo, or macro system. Likewise, five smaller arrows lead from concepts listed to the right of the application arrow into the application process. This depicts how social workers use client empowerment, a wide range of professional roles, evidence-based practice, critical thinking, and the planned-change process to solve a problem or help a system improve its functioning.

is needed and sought out. It may also be imparted on a formal contractual basis when one party seeks out the established expertise of another. Consultation can occur internally within an agency or expert help can be sought outside of the agency, depending on the assistance needed. It is a generalist practitioner's professional responsibility to use both supervision and consultation appropriately.

## A Wide Range of Roles

Assuming a wide range of professional roles is a key concept in the definition of generalist practice. We have emphasized that generalist practitioners can tackle a wide range of problems using many different methods; that is, they assume many roles. We have established that a professional role consists of the behaviors and activities involved in **EP 8d** performing some designated function. Roles characterizing generalist practitioners include the following (Kirst-Ashman & Hull, 2015b, pp. 30–31):

- *Counselor:* One who provides guidance to clients and assists them in a planned-change or problem-solving process. For example, a worker might help a troubled teenager make decisions about friendships and sexual activity by identifying alternatives and evaluating their potential consequences.
- *Educator:* One who gives information and teaches skills to others (Yessian & Broskowski, 1983). For instance, a practitioner might teach child management skills to parents.
- *Broker:* One who links client systems to needed resources (Connaway & Gentry, 1988). For example, a worker might refer a client to a substance abuse treatment center for inpatient treatment.
- *Case manager (or case coordinator):* A practitioner who, on the behalf of a specific client, coordinates needed services provided by any number of agencies, organizations, or facilities. For instance, a worker might coordinate the many services needed by a cerebral palsy[3] patient living in a group home.

- *Mobilizer:* One who identifies and convenes community members and resources to identify "unmet community needs" and "effect changes for the better in their community" (Halley, Kopp, & Austin, 1998, p. 179). For example, a practitioner might encourage community residents to band together and start a drug education program for residents' children.
- *Mediator:* One who resolves arguments or disagreements among individual, family, group, organizational, or community systems in conflict (Yessian & Broskowski, 1983). For instance, a worker might serve as a go-between to reach an agreement between an agency that wants to start a group home for people with intellectual disabilities and neighborhood residents who oppose having the facility in their neighborhood.
- *Negotiator:* One who serves as an intermediary to settle disputes, but clearly takes the side of one of the parties involved. For example, a social worker in public welfare might act on behalf of her clients to negotiate for better benefits for them.
- *Facilitator:* One who guides a group experience. For instance, a practitioner might run a support group for young women with bulimia.[4]
- *Spokesperson:* One who is authorized to speak on behalf of others.
- *Coordinator:* One who coordinates people by bringing them together and organizing their performance.
- *Manager:* One who assumes some level of administrative responsibility for a social services agency or other organizational system.
- *Advocate:* One who speaks out on behalf of clients to promote fair and equitable treatment or gain needed resources. For example, a worker might meet with an administrator on behalf of a client to change an agency policy to benefit the client.

Regardless of the role assumed by a practitioner, a social worker should identify as a professional social worker and conduct himself or herself accordingly (CSWE, 2008b, EP 2.1.1). Highlight 4.2 addresses several aspects of professional identity.

---

[3]*Cerebral palsy* is a disability involving problems in muscular control and coordination resulting from damage to the brain before it has matured—that is, before or during birth.

[4]*Bulimia* is an eating disorder occurring primarily in females and characterized by uncontrolled overeating followed by purging activities such as self-initiated vomiting and the use of diuretics, as well as excessive guilt and shame over the compulsive behavior.

## HIGHLIGHT **4.2**   PROFESSIONAL IDENTITY AND CONDUCT   LO 2

Social workers should identify with the profession. It is an honorable, meaningful field, which seeks at its core to improve people's lives and pursue social and economic justice. Social workers' practice and behavior should represent the field's mission and primary values (the latter of which were discussed in Chapter 2). Workers should manifest a commitment both to the development and growth of the profession and to their own professional growth. There are many sides to "professional behavior." Three aspects of professionalism are described here, which include personal reflection, lifelong learning, and professional demeanor (CSWE, 2015).

EP 1, 1b, 1c, 1e, 6b, 9a

First, social workers should "use reflection and self-regulation to manage personal values and maintain professionalism in practice situations" (CSWE, 2015, p. 4). Evaluation of your perceptions means taking time to look deeply at your attitudes, values, and opinions. One theme inherent in this book is the importance of evaluating and critically thinking about any stereotypes and prejudgments you harbor. Such assumptions can conflict with professional values and interfere with objective, effective, and professional practice. It's a continual process of reflecting about such assumptions and self-regulating (correcting) them.

Second, professional practitioners should "recognize the importance of lifelong learning" and be "committed to continually updating their skills to ensure they are relevant and effective" (CSWE, 2015, p. 4). Learning about new research results, intervention approaches, cultural differences, aspects of oppression, and the dynamically changing social environment is an ongoing process. When I was very young and had just zipped through school to get my MSW degree, I thought I had worked hard enough and could stop learning. Boy, was I wrong. Learning had just begun. If anything, it accelerates exponentially over a career.

There are many ways to enhance learning. Listen to and learn from your clients. Consult with supervisors and colleagues. Ask questions. Creatively think about what practice alternatives might be available to you and your clients. Watch what's going on around you in agency life—everything from treatment techniques to

how management treats you and your clients. Seek out knowledge from professional books, journals, and newspapers. Attend professional training sessions; these can address virtually any area of practice ranging from cognitive-behavioral treatment approaches to legislative advocacy to running task groups. Join professional organizations and be an active member. This is a way to network, keep in touch, and simply learn about what's up in the field.

Third, social workers should "demonstrate professional demeanor in behaviour; appearance; and oral, written, and electronic communication" (CSWE, 2015, p. 4). Part of professional demeanor entails using empathy and other interpersonal skills. Another aspect is following ethical principles. Communication should be straightforward, relevant, purposeful, and clear. I always say that anything you write should be good and appropriate enough to place before a judge in court.

Professional demeanor also involves personal appearance. Sheafor and Horejsi (2008) talk about developing a personal "style." They reflect:

[Social workers'] uniqueness is expressed in their clothing, hairstyle, posture, speech, and in a hundred other choices and behaviors that send out messages about who they are and what they believe about themselves and others.

One's professional style must be appropriate to the situation, the clients served, and the agency setting. For example, a social worker dressed in a three-piece suit will surely have difficulty establishing rapport with a group of street people yet may be highly effective in persuading a city council to create needed services for people living on the street. Similarly, a worker might dress casually when working with children and families but should dress more formally when making a court appearance in their behalf.

"Know thyself" is an important admonition for the social worker.... It is helpful for the social worker to step back periodically and examine how others perceive his or her style. Clues from clients, family, friends, colleagues, and supervisors are helpful in making these assessments. (p. 41)

### Social Workers as Supervisors and Managers

Note that many social workers advance in the hierarchy of organizations to become supervisors or

managers. Even when primary job responsibilities involve administrative capacities instead of direct work with clients, it's imperative that social workers maintain a generalist perspective. This means that they should continue to focus on the potential for targeting positive change at any level of practice—including work with individuals, families, groups, organizations, and communities (Gibelman, 2005). Additionally, social work concerns providing ongoing advocacy for client systems, whether these systems are individuals, families, or large groups of clients.

A social work *supervisor* is "a licensed social worker to whom authority is delegated to direct, coordinate, enhance, and evaluate the on-the-job performance of the supervisees for whose work he or she is held accountable" (Kadushin & Harkness, 2014, p. 11). The supervisor is then held accountable for the employees' work. Gibelman and Furman (2008) elaborate upon the supervisory role:

> The supervisor is expected to be qualified for this role by virtue of experience and education. Relevant skills include the ability to motivate employees, coordinate work and workload, set goals and limits, provide corrective feedback, monitor and improve work processes, and educate and consult with employees (Kurland & Salmon, 1992; Menefee, 2000; Rautkis & Koeske, 1994; Walsh, 1990). Typically, a social worker assumes the role of supervisor after working in the field for several years (Gibelman & Schervish, 1997). Ideally, specialized training is provided before the supervisor assumes this position. Supervisors may, and often do, maintain a small active caseload as well. (p. 90)

*Managers* generally assume greater responsibility for more aspects of agency functioning than supervisors. Typically, they still provide supervision for designated employees below them in the agency's power structure who, in turn, supervise employees below them, and so on. The terms "manager" and "administrator" are usually used interchangeably (Gibelman, 2005, p. 13). Kirst-Ashman and Hull (2015a) describe the role of manager in generalist practice:

> A manager *in social work is one who assumes some level of administrative responsibility for a social services agency or other organizational system ([Brody, 2005;] Yessian & Broskowsky, 1983).*
>
> *Administrators utilize three levels of skills— technical, people, and conceptual (Lewis, Lewis, Packard, & Souflee, 2001, p. 8).* Technical skills *include those used to direct an agency's basic activities such*

*as overseeing counseling techniques, developing programs, or evaluating the agency's effectiveness.* People skills *concern "interpersonal effectiveness such as oral communication, listening, conflict management, leading, and motivating" (p. 8).* Conceptual skills *are those oriented toward assessing and understanding the overall operation of the agency and how it fits into its larger macro environment. These also concern being able to solve complex problems and develop creative solutions. The term* management *refers to all "the tasks and activities involved in directing an organization or one of its units: planning, organizing, leading, and controlling" (Hellriegel, Jackson, & Slocum, 2002, p. 7). (p. 22)*

Social workers may assume a wide range of administrative roles. These include lower-level management positions with administrative responsibility for a small agency unit or department. They also may include "upper-level managers," including the chief executive officer (CEO) or executive director who has the primary responsibility for running a large social services organization (Gibelman, 2005, p. 13; Gibelman & Furman, 2008).

## Evidence-Based Practice (EBP)

Chapter 1 introduced the importance of social work research and the increasing focus on evidence-based practice. Rubin and Babbie (2014) explain:

**EP 4b, 4c**

> Evidence-based practice (EBP) is a process in which practitioners make practice decisions in light of the best research evidence available. But rather than rigidly constrict practitioner options, the EBP model encourages practitioners to integrate scientific evidence with their practice expertise and knowledge of the idiosyncratic circumstances bearing on specific practice decisions....
>
> EBP also involves evaluating the outcomes of practice decisions. Although EBP is most commonly discussed in regard to decisions about what interventions to provide clients, it also applies to decisions about how best to assess the practice problems and decisions practitioners make at other levels of practice—such as decisions about social policies, communities, and so on.
>
> For example, a clinical practitioner following the EBP model with a newly referred client will

*attempt to find and use the most scientifically validated diagnostic tools in assessing client problems and treatment needs.... [The social worker will] then develop a treatment plan in light of the best research evidence available as to what interventions are most likely to be effective.... At the level of social policy, evidence-based practitioners will attempt to formulate and advocate policies that the best research available suggests are most likely to achieve their desired aims. Likewise, evidence-based practitioners working at the community level will make practice decisions at that level in light of community-level practice research. Moreover, evidence-based practitioners at each level will utilize research methods to evaluate the outcomes of their practice decisions to see if the chosen course of action is achieving its desired aim. If it is not, then the evidence-based practitioner will choose an alternative course of action—again in light of the best research evidence available and again evaluating its outcome. (p. 28)*

### Critical Thinking Skills

Chapter 1 defined **critical thinking** as (1) the careful scrutiny of what is stated as true or what appears to be true and the resulting expression of an opinion or conclusion based on that scrutiny, and (2) the creative formulation of an opinion or conclusion when presented with a question, problem, or issue. The process of critical thinking involves asking questions, assessing facts, and asserting a conclusion (the Triple-A approach).

**EP 4b, 5c, 7a, 8a**

Social workers must have the ability to think critically as they work with clients to achieve goals. Critical thinking in social work practice usually involves four dimensions (Gibbs et al., 1994). First, practitioners should be predisposed to ask questions about how their clients are served and treated. Second, they should investigate how interventions are supposed to work and whether they are really effective. Third, they should carefully examine any assertions presented as facts by evaluating arguments on both sides of an issue. Fourth, they should use "scientific reasoning" to analyze arguments, keeping their eyes open for inconsistencies and deviations from the truth.

In other words, don't believe everything you hear. Rather, critically evaluate for yourself whether it's true. Focus on Critical Thinking 4.1 identifies some common fallacies to watch out for.

## Steps Involved in Planned Change

**LO 3**

**Planned change** involves the development and implementation of a strategy for improving or altering "some specified condition, pattern of behavior, or set of circumstances in an effort to improve a client's social functioning or well-being" (Sheafor & Horejsi, 2012, p. 88). Planned change is a process whereby social workers engage a client, assess issues, identify strengths and problems, establish a plan of action, implement the plan, evaluate its effects, and finally terminate the process.

**EP 6, 7, 8, 9**

Another term often used to describe what generalist practitioners do is **problem solving** (finding a solution to some difficulty or the answer to some question), initially introduced by social work pioneer Helen Harris Perlman in 1957. Essentially, problem solving refers to the same process as planned change, although many debate the nuances of difference. Social work's more recent emphasis on client strengths may be at odds with the more negative connotations of the word *problem*. The term *change* may have more positive implications despite the fact that most social work intervention deals with problem situations. Thus, the term *planned change* will arbitrarily be used here.

Social workers help people deal with problems ranging from personal relationships to lack of resources to blatant discrimination. For instance, a social worker may need to address the problem of a battered woman who is economically and emotionally dependent on her abusive husband and who also has three children to protect. Another social worker might have an adolescent client who has committed a number of serious crimes and who is heavily involved with drugs. Still another social worker may need to advocate for change in a public assistance policy that discriminates against people who don't speak English well and are unable to follow an intricate, exasperating application process to receive benefits. Regardless of the problem being addressed, the planned-change effort follows the same course of action, described shortly.

# USING CRITICAL THINKING TO AVOID THE FALLACY TRAP

**LO 4**

A number of fallacies can trick people into false beliefs (Gambrill, 2005; Gambrill & Gibbs, 2009, pp. 107–119). A **fallacy** is a false or erroneous idea, often hidden behind what appears to be a sound argument or presentation. A fallacy or mistaken assumption can trick you into believing what is not true. Fallacies often appear to be true, but really are not. They include the following.

## Relying on Case Examples

Just because something worked for one person doesn't mean it will work for everyone. It's important to identify what other variables might have been operating.

### Example in everyday life

Ernestine lost 20 pounds in two weeks on the baked bean diet. That baked bean diet is the best thing and it really works. I think I'll try it.

### Critical Thinking Questions

What proof is there that this baked bean diet really works? How nutritious is it? Does it endanger a person's health if practiced for long? Can other people readily maintain the same willpower as Ernestine, or is she exceptional? How many baked beans can other people really tolerate over that same time? What else was going on in Ernestine's life (e.g., excessive exercise) that could have contributed to her weight loss?

### Example in social work practice

Harvey stopped drinking completely after seeing an alcohol and drug abuse counselor for six weeks who used guilt therapy. If you have a drinking problem, you should go to a counselor who uses guilt therapy. It's great.

### Critical Thinking Questions

What is guilt therapy anyway? Did the therapy really help Harvey stop drinking, or was it something else (e.g., his wife threatened to leave him, or he joined Alcoholics Anonymous)? How long will Harvey stay "on the wagon"?

## Relying on Testimonials

This is similar to relying on case examples. However, here a person swears that something is effective based on personal experience.

### Example in everyday life

Gambrill and Gibbs (2009) provide an interesting example:

> After taking so many other medicines without being helped, you can imagine how happy and surprised I felt when I discovered that Natex was doing me a lot of good. Natex seemed to go right to the root of my trouble, helped my appetite and put an end to the indigestion, gas, and shortness of breath. ("Local Lady Took Natex Year Ago— Had Good Health Ever Since," 1935, May 27, p. 7)

This woman's testimonial appeared on the same page of a newspaper as her obituary (p. 109).

### Critical Thinking Questions

What proof is there that Natex helped? What else might have affected this woman's condition? What caused her death?

### Example in social work practice

Georgia, an agency worker, insists that the most effective child management technique is to bonk the misbehaving child on the nose with a flyswatter. She swears it immediately and permanently curbs obnoxious behaviors such as swearing, hitting other children, and sticking fingers into various facial orifices.

### Critical Thinking Questions

What are the theoretical underpinnings of the flyswatter approach to behavior management? How has it been proved effective, with whom, and under what conditions? What are some potential negative consequences of this technique? To what extent can it cause children physical injury?

## Being Vague

Making a generalized, imprecise statement about occurrences or conditions may give false impressions. Vagueness can lead to inaccuracies and potentially bogus assumptions.

### Example in everyday life

Life in Salt Lake City is better.

### Critical Thinking Questions

Does this mean life there is good or bad? Does "better" refer to housing conditions, social life, employment

*(continued)*

## FOCUS ON CRITICAL THINKING 4.1 *(continued)*

opportunities, quality of restaurants, climate, or access to the mountains for good skiing?

### Example in social work practice
Working with the neighborhood group improved community conditions.

### Critical Thinking Questions
What conditions? Specifically, how were they improved? What proof exists that the neighborhood group, and not some other factors, "improved" conditions?

### Being Biased or Unobjective
When a person is so committed to one side of an issue that the other side hardly seems to exist, beware. One sidedness works against objective evaluation of an idea, practice, or issue. As Gambrill and Gibbs (2009) observe, one sidedness reflects this attitude: "In matters controversial, my perception's rather fine. I always see both points of view: the one that's wrong and mine" (p. 111).

### Example in everyday life
All politicians are crooks. They don't know anything, and all they do is steal your money.

### Critical Thinking Questions
How many politicians do I know? What has led me to believe they're all crooks? What exactly is a political crook? Don't politicians differ regarding their stands on issues? How logical is it to clump them all into one bunch? How do they get away with stealing your money? Aren't most politicians monitored by the public? If there weren't any politicians, who would run the government, and how? If I don't like politicians, why don't I run for office myself and fix the system?

### Example in social work practice
The social services agency I work for is the only one in the state that's any good.

### Critical Thinking Questions
To what extent am I biased in claiming that my organization's the best one? What proof do I have that mine is better than the others? How do I know that other agencies don't have similar strengths? How many agencies am I familiar with anyway?

### Believing That If It's Written Down It Must Be Right
Stating something as a fact in a book, article, newspaper, or other medium such as radio or television doesn't mean it's accurate or true.

### Example in everyday life
The book said that there have been thousands of alien sightings and abductions, so it must be true. There are even some photos of flying saucers in there.

### Critical Thinking Questions
What concrete evidence is there that flying saucers have been here? Who has said they've been abducted, and what do they say about it? Are those really saucers in the pictures or some doctored-up hoax?

### Example in social work practice
This textbook says that critical thinking is a necessity in social work practice.

### Critical Thinking Questions
What does critical thinking mean? Does it make sense to scrutinize so carefully the things you're told? Is your ability to think as good as that of the people who write textbooks? What have you agreed with and disagreed with so far in this book? Do you tend to agree with everything you read or hear on television or the Internet?

### In Conclusion
The point is that critical thinking concerns not necessarily accepting situations or stories at face value. Rather, it entails using your own judgment to seriously consider their worth and relevance.

*Case Example* We have established that a key feature of a generalist social work approach is that virtually any problem may be analyzed and addressed from multiple levels of intervention (i.e., involving individual, family, group, organizational, or community level). An example of the application of a generalist approach involves DeRon, a school social worker in a large, urban community that serves primarily a low-income population. In his role he may be called upon to work with students with behavioral problems, "to help collect data on the students' behaviors, to recommend behavioral intervention strategies, to teach social skills and

**EP 6b, 7a, 7c, 7d, 8d**

Romilly Lockyer/Stone/Getty Images

*Planned change includes micro-, mezzo-, and macro-level practice. Social workers often work with other agency and community members in groups to solve problems and achieve positive change.*

strategies to the student, and/or to provide support for the student as part of the behavior intervention plan" (Atkins-Burnett, 2010, p. 180). He participates with other professionals (e.g., speech therapists, psychologists, teachers) on multidisciplinary teams to determine treatment and educational plans. Often, he serves as a case manager who coordinates the treatment efforts. The school is legally responsible for providing supportive and remedial services to students who experience difficulties in their learning environment.

DeRon receives a new case referral, Peyton, a 5-year-old boy who has severe speech and behavioral problems. He stutters and has difficulty enunciating words and formulating sentences. He frequently refuses to obey his parents at home, often lashing out in violent temper tantrums. At school he has poor communication and relationship-building skills with his peers. He is unable to play with peers without acting out aggressively, such as hitting them in the stomach or poking them in the eye. Such

behavior causes serious problems for him with his kindergarten teacher.

As a generalist practitioner, DeRon can assess the situation and proceed with this case at the individual, family, group, organizational, and community levels. First, on an individual level, Peyton requires speech and behavioral assessments to determine a treatment plan. To what extent are his speech difficulties physiologically based? What speech therapy goals might be established? How do Peyton's speech problems affect his ability to interact with others? Peyton is having difficulty interacting with family members, peers, and other adults. How are his parents and other family members reacting to and handling his speech and behavior problems? DeRon may assess Peyton's behavior and work with parents, teachers, and Peyton to improve his behavior and interpersonal relationships.

On the level targeting family intervention, Peyton's parents may require family counseling and education about behavior management techniques. Before DeRon gives the family any help he must first use empathy and other interpersonal skills to engage family members in the planned-change process. DeRon may provide some short-term help, but his job is to focus on Peyton's school performance. Therefore, he may want to help link Peyton's parents with resources and services outside the school, which would involve other organizations in the community.

Intervention at the group level may address Peyton's peer relationships. His teacher may need consultation regarding behavioral control in the classroom. Peyton might benefit from membership in a treatment group with other children experiencing similar difficulties. Group involvement might include discussing feelings and behavior, providing role models for improved behavior, and encouraging positive interaction among group members.

In the school's organizational setting, DeRon may serve as Peyton's case manager, leading multidisciplinary teams and coordinating the involved staff's treatment and educational approaches. As already noted, he may serve as a consultant to teachers and other school staff about how to deal with Peyton's behavior. DeRon might also organize and "lead parent education and informational groups" within the school context for Peyton's parents and other parents whose children demonstrate similar behavioral difficulties (Atkins-Burnett, 2010, p. 187). Also as noted, DeRon may refer Peyton's family to services and resources provided by other organizations in the community as needed.

Intervention at the community level attends to and promotes changes in the broader macro environment. A school social worker may:

> facilitate the development of relationships that link the services of the school with those found in the community.… [T]o function in the public school … a social worker must stay informed about legislation and litigation that affect the school and other service providers' responsibility to this group as well as their roles and those of others. Social workers will need to be advocates for many of the children and their families.

> (Atkins-Burnett, 2010, pp. 187–188)

Thus, for example, if needed services are not provided in the community, DeRon may advocate for their development on the behalf of Peyton's family and other families with similar needs. DeRon may also advocate for policies and legislation that enhance resource provision and availability.

Note that intervention involving the various levels of practice (individual, family, group, organizational, and community) is often not clearly delineated. For example, DeRon may assess and work with Peyton on an individual level, but at the same time work with family and school staff to address the same issues. The important point is that generalist practitioners may involve systems of various sizes in the planned-change process.

Figure 4.2 illustrates the generalist approach to assessing this situation and planning intervention at the individual, family, group, organizational, and community levels.

Figure 4.3 illustrates the six primary steps involved in planned change: engagement, assessment, planning, implementation, evaluation, and termination.

### Step 1: Engagement

**Engagement** is the initial period when practitioners orient themselves to the problem at hand and begin to establish communication and a relationship with others also addressing the problem. Regardless of whether workers pursue change with individuals, families, groups, organizations, or communities, they must establish rapport with clients and target systems in order to communicate and get things done. Engagement is based on the acquisition of a range of micro skills. Both the words social workers speak (verbal communication) and their coinciding actions and expressions (nonverbal communication) can engage others in the helping process.

EP 6b

**Nonverbal communication** is body language and sounds that convey information about how a person feels without saying so in words. It includes body positions, facial expressions, vocal tone and expression (e.g., raising your voice or speaking very quietly and meekly), and vocal noises other than words (e.g., grunts, snorts, chortles, hums). Patterson and Welfel (2000) explain:

> You have been with people whose body language invites communication, and you have been with others whose body language indicates disinterest and perhaps even anxiety about communicating.

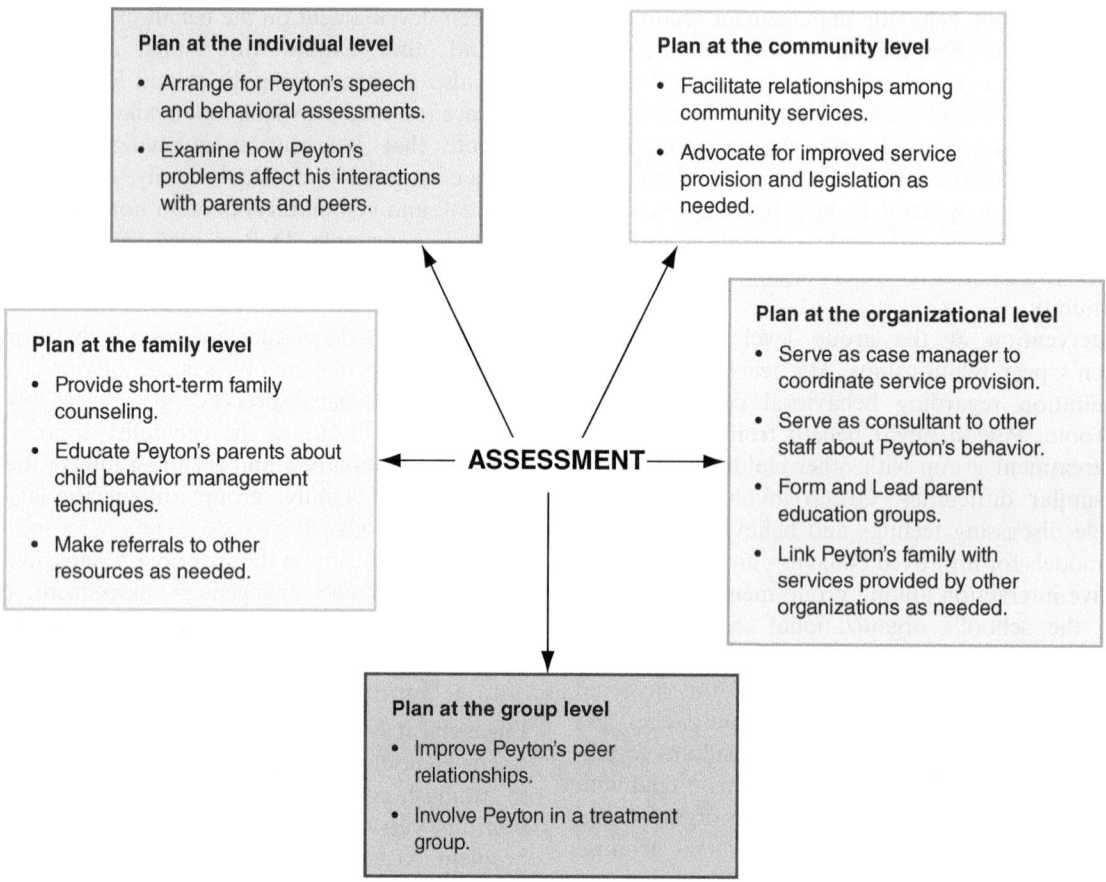

**FIG-4-2** Initiating Micro-, Mezzo-, or Macro-level Change During Assessment

*The active, interested listener faces and leans toward the speaker in a posture of interest and even excitement. Eyes are focused in the general direction of the person's face. Arms are in an open mode in relation to the trunk, as if to say, "I am very interested in receiving, with all my sensory processes, what it is you want to say to me." The attentive listener maintains an interested facial expression and makes encouraging gestures (nods, smiles, hand gestures, and so forth). (pp. 41–42)*

Social workers also need to pay attention to cultural variations in people's nonverbal and verbal behavior. Highlight 4.3 discusses some of the differences among cultures.

Many other dimensions are involved in engagement. Social workers' overall demeanor—including their ability to convey warmth, empathy, and genuineness, concepts related to nonverbal behavior—can enhance engagement. Conveying *warmth* involves

enhancing workers' positive feelings toward another person by promoting a sense of comfort and well-being in that person. *Empathy* involves not only being in tune with how clients feel but also conveying to them in a sincere and open manner that workers understand how they feel. *Genuineness* simply means that workers continue to be themselves while working to accomplish goals in their professional role.

Likewise, how social workers introduce themselves and arrange an initial meeting's setting affects the engagement process. Other engagement skills include alleviating initial client anxiety and introducing the worker's purpose and role.

## Step 2: Assessment

According to Hepworth, Rooney, Rooney, and Strom-Gottfried (2013), **assessment** is "a process occurring between practitioner and client, in which information is gathered, analyzed, and synthesized

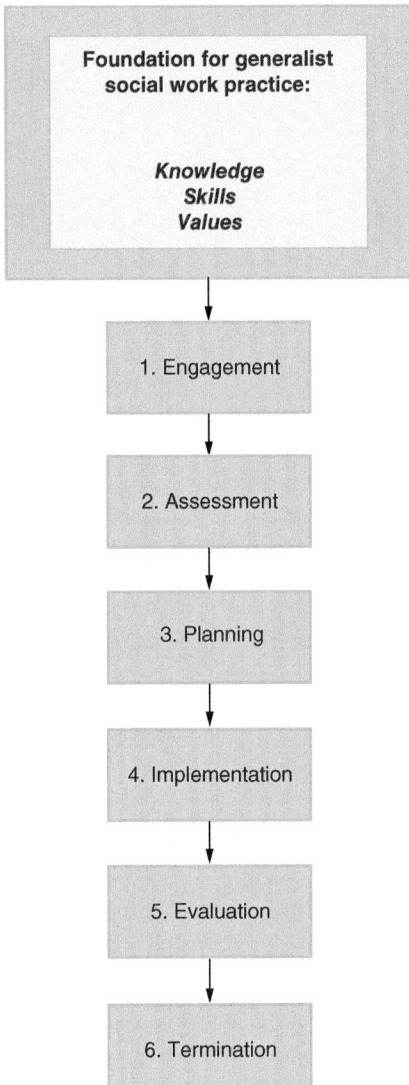

Foundation for generalist
social work practice:

*Knowledge*
*Skills*
*Values*

1. Engagement

2. Assessment

3. Planning

4. Implementation

5. Evaluation

6. Termination

**FIG-4-3** Planned-Change Steps in Generalist Social Work Practice

to provide a concise picture of the client and his or her needs and strengths" (p. 186). Meyer (1995) defines *assessment* simply as "knowing, understanding, evaluating, individualizing, or figuring out" (p. 260). For our purposes, *assessment* is the investigation and determination of variables affecting an identified problem or issue as viewed from micro, mezzo, or macro perspectives. It refers to gathering relevant information about a problem so decisions can be made about

**EP 7a, 7b, 7c**

potential solutions. It's also important to work with the client to develop a mutually agreed-on focus of work and desired outcomes.

The crucial task of generalist practice is to look beyond the individual and examine other impinging factors within the client's environment. In a given case, the emphases on different assessment categories may vary. However, each category must still be reviewed and considered for its potential contribution to the problem.

For instance, a couple may come to a social worker for help in their marital relationship. Thus assessment of the mezzo aspects, or relationship issues of the situation, would be emphasized. However, a generalist practitioner would also consider both the micro aspects, such as the strengths, needs, and issues of each partner, and the macro aspects impinging upon their situation. Macro aspects might involve the fact that both spouses have been laid off from their jobs at the local bowling pin manufacturing plant. They had both held these jobs for more than 10 years. The layoffs were probably due to a serious economic downturn and a decrease in the growth of recreational facilities such as bowling alleys. The social worker might not be able to do much about the economy's current condition. However, the economic impact on the couple is vital to the assessment of the couple's current conflictual situation.

In addition to limitations, the social worker also must assess the client's strengths. Highlight 4.4 discusses how a social worker assesses an individual's mental health problems and needs by emphasizing strengths. Chapter 13 elaborates on mental health issues and practice.

### *Human Diversity and Assessment*
Social workers must also take aspects of diversity into consideration when conducting assessments. Chapter 3 discussed various facets of human diversity including "age, class, color, culture, disability and ability, ethnicity, gender, gender identity and expression, immigration status, marital status, political ideology, race, religion/spirituality, sex, sexual orientation, and tribal sovereign status" (CSWE, 2015, p. 4). For each case, social workers should ask themselves whether any aspects of diversity may be significant.

 **EP 2**

# CULTURAL DIFFERENCES IN NONVERBAL AND VERBAL COMMUNICATION

**LO 5**

Cultural expectations for nonverbal communication vary widely. Anglos may stress the importance of making direct eye contact, leaning forward to express interest, and shaking hands upon meeting. However, people from other cultures do not necessarily feel the same way. For example, Corey and Corey (2011) explain some of the differences in eye contact:

EP 1c, 2

> In American middle-class culture, direct eye contact is usually considered a sign of interest and presence, and a lack thereof is interpreted as being evasive. It is common for individuals to maintain more eye contact while listening and less while talking. Some research indicates that African Americans may reverse this pattern by looking more when talking and slightly less when listening. Among some Native American and Latino groups, eye contact by the young is a sign of disrespect. Some cultural groups generally avoid eye contact when talking about serious subjects. (p. 198)

> In Chinese culture, when two people "talk to one another," they "use much less eye contact, especially when it is with the opposite sex"; this implies, for instance, that a male social worker's extended gaze at a female Chinese client could "be considered rude or seductive" (Zhang, 2010, p. 76).

Other expectations regarding facial expressions, including smiling, also differ. The following provides an example:

> In general, the value that is placed on control of emotional expressions contributes to a demeanor among selected Asian groups that is often interpreted by Eurocentric individuals as "flat," "stoic," "enigmatic," or even "inscrutable." Koreans, for example, in keeping with the national character of the "Land of the Morning Calm," may present with a demeanor referred to as my-po-jung (lack of facial expression). Casual smiling and direct eye contact when greeting or interacting with strangers is considered inappropriate.
>
> *(Chan & Lee, 2004, p. 273; cited in Murphy & Dillon, 2011, p. 105)*

A difference between Japanese people and Anglos involves how Anglos typically nod their heads to indicate that they concur with what the speaker is saying. Japanese people, on the other hand, may nod their heads to indicate they are paying close attention to what's being said. However, this behavior has nothing to do with agreement (Lum, 2004, p. 175).

An additional aspect of nonverbal behavior involves the amount of space people allow among themselves as they interact. Ivey, Ivey, and Zalaquett (2010) explain:

> A comfortable conversational distance for many North Americans is slightly more than arm's length, and the English prefer even greater distances. Many Latin people often prefer half that distance, and those from the Middle East may talk practically eyeball to eyeball. As a result, the slightly forward leaning we recommend for attending behavior is not going to be appropriate all the time. A natural, relaxed body style that is your own is most likely to be effective, but be prepared to adapt and flex according to the individual with whom you are talking. (p. 75)

The way clients from various cultural backgrounds respond verbally also differs considerably. "Many cultures of the world do not place as much premium on talking as do the cultures in the Western Hemisphere." Consider the following case example cited by a counselor about his client (Berg-Cross, Craig, & Wessel, 2001):

> Ms. B. was an undergraduate student from Asia. She had failed in one of her clinical rotations in an allied health field. Her failure was attributed not to her knowledge or her ability in her field but to poor judgment in her interpersonal relations. She came to see me in total frustration. One of her negative evaluations by her field supervisor had to do with her insufficient verbal participation in case conferences. Essentially her supervisors were saying that she didn't talk much and interpreted that as a lack of interest and involvement. When this ... [counselor] explored further her lack of participation in classroom and group discussions, the client uttered in frustration, "I only speak if I have anything to say. In this country people talk even if they have nothing to say." She told me she just doesn't engage in superficial conversation. (p. 862)

How things are said also varies from culture to culture (Brave Heart & Chase, 2005):

> First Nations clients may manifest a more indirect communication style, and the social worker must listen closely for disguised requests. Content is often veiled in stories and ... [symbolic comparisons]. First Nations clients often respond indirectly to questions, and the worker must listen closely; the response may initially appear unrelated, but the answer is usually given in a disguised manner, in a story or through recounting a personal experience or that of another individual. (p. 39)

| HIGHLIGHT **4.4** | ASSESSMENT: EMPHASIZING STRENGTHS AND EMPOWERMENT | **LO 6** |

## Traditional Versus Strengths-Based Assessments

A traditional social work assessment model for an individual seeking mental health services involves seven dimensions: (1) presenting problem, (2) problem history, (3) personal history, (4) substance abuse history, (5) family history, (6) employment and education, and (7) summary and treatment recommendations (Graybeal, 2001, p. 235). The traditional medical model described in Chapter 1 focuses on identifying what's wrong with the individual and then trying to fix it. Each dimension emphasizes the negative because the eventual goal is to cure the problem. A strengths-based perspective maintains that "individuals will do better in the long run when they are helped to identify, recognize, and use the strengths and resources available in themselves and their environment" (Graybeal, 2001, p. 234).

**EP 7a, 7c**

Graybeal (2001, p. 238) emphasizes the importance of identifying and using a client's strengths in addition to focusing on problems. For example, when assessing the presenting problem (i.e., the stated reason the client seeks treatment), traditional information solicited includes "detailed descriptions of problem(s)" and a "list of symptoms" (p. 238). A strengths-based assessment also explores personal strengths and available resources, and emphasizes potential solutions to the problem.

Similarly, the problem, personal, substance abuse, and family histories focus on more than all the bad things that have occurred. In addition, the social worker conducting a strengths-based assessment seeks information about what happened during the good times when the problem was not evident. What variables kept the client functioning well and staying healthy? What coping strategies were used? Who provided needed support during crises?

Traditional assessment of employment and education focuses on the facts concerning what occurred and on identification of gaps and problems. Strengths-based assessment of problems emphasizes the individual's skills, interests, and connections with other people in the community, including "spiritual and church involvement."

Finally, the traditional assessment summary and treatment recommendations focus on making a diagnosis and recommending a treatment plan.

A strengths-based assessment downplays labeling the problem and instead stresses a summary of "resources, options, possibilities, exceptions, and solutions" (p. 240).

Graybeal (2001) indicates that significant differences exist between a traditional problem oriented and a strengths-based assessment in cases concerning depression and suicidal thoughts. Consider Sara, who seeks help for her depression.

### Traditional Assessment

*Presenting problem:* Sara, age 24, looking tired, haggard, and older than her years, reports a history of lethargy, depression, lack of self-confidence, low self-esteem, feelings of disheartenment, and thoughts of suicide. She also reports significant weight loss and difficulty sleeping.

*Problem history:* Sara indicates that these feelings of depression originated at age 16 when she was in a serious car accident in which some of her facial bones were crushed. She experienced 10 difficult and painful plastic surgeries that restored her face nearly to its original condition. She indicates that she has been helped by therapy and medication twice beginning at the time of the accident, although she has not been involved with a therapist for more than a year.

### Strengths-Based Assessment

*Presenting problem:* Sara, age 24, reports feelings of depression, uselessness, and loneliness. She also reports significant weight loss and difficulty sleeping. She indicates that these feelings began when her sister moved two states away. Although she has had thoughts of suicide, she is not seriously considering that now. She states that she feels best when at work and when telephoned by her sister.

*Problem history:* Sara indicates that her depression began at age 16 when she was in a serious car accident resulting in a series of painful facial surgeries. She indicates that members of her family and friends were very supportive of her throughout her physical and emotional trauma. She reports that her depression lifted when she first started this job but gradually crept back over the past few months. She has been involved in therapy twice in the past that she found very helpful. She is hopeful that therapy will result in improving her

*(continued)*

**HIGHLIGHT 4.4** *(continued)*

mood, energy level, and social life. Eventually, she hopes to have friends instead of a therapist provide her with the support she needs.

### Differences Between Traditional and Strengths-Based Approaches in Sara's Assessment

Note that the traditional assessment of the presenting problem stresses the bad things about Sara's problem— how she looks, feels, and experiences difficulties. The strengths-based assessment identifies the problems but also recognizes strengths. Sara has a strong support system in her sister; although her sister has moved away, they still maintain phone contact. It's also a strength that Sara is currently not considering suicide, although she has in the past.

The traditional problem history assessment goes into more detail about Sara's car accident at age 16. It also states that Sara has not been involved in therapy for a year. In contrast, the strengths-based assessment notes the supportiveness of relatives, a significant strength, during Sara's years of surgery and recovery. It also reports that Sara's mood lifted when she first started her job, so there were some positive variables involved there. The strengths-based approach indicates that Sara has found therapy helpful in the past, that she

is hopeful it will be helpful again, and that eventually she hopes to develop a social support system so she will no longer need therapy. In summary, focusing on strengths provides some clues for how to proceed in helping Sara fight her depression.

### Aspects of Assessment Focusing on Families, Groups, Organizations, and Communities

When scrutinizing a problem, generalist social workers also look at potential aspects of assessment involving families and groups. When assessing Sara's personal, substance abuse, and family histories, the social worker works with her to examine her relationships with family members and others. Might she need to resolve some issues with her family members? Should they be involved in treatment? Might a support group be appropriate in which she could talk with others also suffering from depression? Or might a socialization group be useful in which members strive to improve their interpersonal behavior and social skills? This may be fitting because Sara has expressed a desire to improve her social life.

Aspects of assessment focusing on organizations and communities might involve how accessible treatment is to Sara. Does agency policy allow her to receive affordable treatment? If she can't afford it, is advocacy to change policy needed on her behalf?

---

*Case Example*   Consider Andrew, a hospital social worker whose client, Florence, age 78, was temporarily hospitalized for complications from diabetes.[5] Andrew is now helping Florence arrange to stay with relatives until she is well enough to return home. In the process of helping Florence, Andrew must identify aspects of diversity that might affect the assessment process or Florence's treatment.

Andrew discovers that Florence is of Italian heritage, a relevant aspect of ethnic and cultural diversity. Florence also feels strongly about her membership in a local Roman Catholic church that many other older adults of similar heritage also attend. For several reasons, Florence's church involvement is very important to her. Therefore, Andrew must take this into consideration when developing Florence's treatment

plan with her. She needs a means of maintaining contact with her church.

Another aspect of diversity to consider is Florence's age. Is Florence being treated differently or in a discriminatory manner because of ageism? *Ageism* refers to discrimination based on preconceived notions about older people, regardless of their individual qualities and capabilities. Andrew closely evaluates his own attitudes here. For instance, is he tempted to make assumptions about Florence's mental capability because of the stereotype that older people don't think as well as when they were younger?

Likewise, Andrew must be aware of any sexist biases he might harbor. *Sexism* refers to any preconceived notions about a person based solely on gender. For instance, does Andrew feel that Florence is a dependent person who needs to be taken care of simply because she's a woman? Such a bias fails to take into account the client as a unique individual with her own strengths and weaknesses.

---

[5]*Diabetes* is a disease of the pancreas in which the body doesn't manufacture enough insulin to process sugars adequately.

## Step 3: Planning

Assessment sets the stage for the intervention by identifying problems and strengths. **Planning** specifies what should be done. The following aspects of planning are important:

EP 4c, 7c, 7d

- The social worker should work *with* the client, not dictate *to* the client, to create the treatment plan.
- The social worker, together with the client, should prioritize the problems so that the most critical ones are addressed first.
- The social worker should identify the client's strengths to provide some guidance for the planned-change process.
- The social worker should identify alternative interventions. Should individual, family, group, organizational, or community systems be targets of change?
- Any course of action considered should be evidence-based. That is, it should be included among those established as the most effective interventions for that particular practice scenario based on scientific research.
- The social worker should help the client evaluate the pros and cons of each course of action to choose the best approach. Figure 4.4 depicts this process.
- With the client, the social worker should develop *goals*—the results that the client and worker seek to accomplish.
- The social worker should establish a *contract* with the client—that is, an agreement between a client and worker about the goals, time frames, and responsibilities of people involved in the intervention process.

## Step 4: Implementation

**Implementation** is the process whereby client and worker follow their plan to achieve their goals. It is the actual *doing* of the plan. As you know, social work intervention can involve virtually any size system. Highlight 4.5 describes a series of potential social work interventions involving macro client systems.

EP 8a

## Step 5: Evaluation

**Evaluation** is the process of determining the extent to which a given intervention was effective in achieving

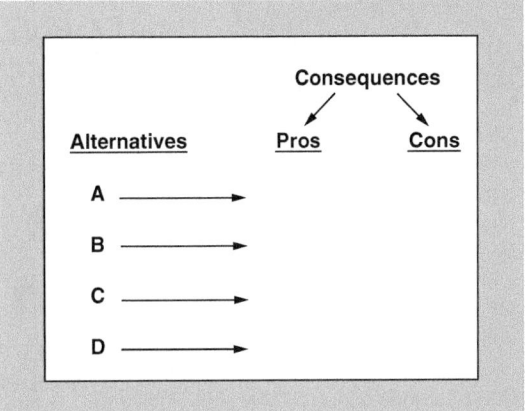

**FIG-4-4** Social Workers Help Clients Identify Alternatives and Evaluate the Pros and Cons of Each

its goals. After engagement and assessment, a social worker makes a plan with the client, implements the plan, and then evaluates the extent to which the plan was successful. It boils down to the social worker asking, "Does it work?" and "How do we know that it works?" Social workers need to be accountable; that is, they must prove that their interventions have been effective. Each goal must be evaluated in terms of the extent to which it has been achieved.

EP 9a, 9b, 9c, 9d

For example, consider Yvonne, a parole[6] officer for adults. George had been imprisoned for six years for armed robbery. He had been drunk when he committed the offenses. As a result, George's goals include attending biweekly Alcoholics Anonymous meetings, avoiding drinking altogether, seeking work from at least four sources weekly, checking in to the halfway house[7] where he resides by 8:00 pm every evening, and faithfully attending his weekly meetings with Yvonne on time. If George goes out drinking and gets a ticket for driving under the influence, he and Yvonne must evaluate the extent to which his rehabilitation plan is working. Does

---

[6]*Parole* is "the conditional release of a person from prison prior to the end of the sentence imposed" (Nichols, 1999, p. 961).

[7]*Halfway houses* are transitional dwellings that provide structure, support, and guidance for persons unable to function independently in the community. They are transitional because they provide a middle ground between a full-time residential setting (e.g., an institution or prison) and the relative freedom of living in the community. Persons requiring halfway houses include those on probation, substance abusers, and those with a history of mental illness.

## HIGHLIGHT 4.5

# IMPLEMENTATION WITH MACRO CLIENT SYSTEMS

LO 7

"A **client system** is any individual, family, group, organization, or community that will ultimately benefit from generalist social work intervention. A **macro client system** involves larger numbers of clients, families, or groups of clients with similar characteristics or qualifications for receiving resources or services, or an agency or community that will be the beneficiary of the macro intervention process" (Kirst-Ashman & Hull, 2015a, p. 9). The concept of macro intervention concerns agency or social change that affects larger numbers of people than an individual, family, or small group. The following are examples of interventions involving communities and organizations on the behalf of macro client systems. Social workers might initiate any of these for the benefit of their clientele, community, or organization.

EP 3a, 5b, 5c, 8c, 8d

### Fundraisers

Social workers can initiate, advocate for, help organize, and implement fundraising events for a wide range of purposes. Fundraising might involve a door-to-door campaign. It might also entail sponsoring special events and charging fees for admission to activities such as bingo nights, turkey dinners, or community dances. Similarly, it might involve selling donated things such as baked goods, crafts, or rummage items to finance some event or activity. Sponsored activities might include a bus trip to Washington, D.C., to march in favor of gay and lesbian rights, a Thanksgiving dinner for the local homeless, or renovations for a community recreational center.

### Advocacy for Agency Policy Changes

Social workers can advocate to change internal agency policies when they're inefficient, ineffective, or discriminatory. Although an agency's administration is supposed to institute such changes, it often doesn't. Sometimes administrators are too far removed in the administrative structure from direct service provision to clients to know what's really going on. Other times, they are resistant to change because it requires greater effort or more money.

You may not have any experience in social work, but think of the jobs you've had. Were supervisors always aware of and sensitive to the issues you faced daily? Were the employers' rules and requirements always

sensible and fair? Were employees and customers always treated in the most effective, efficient, and considerate way possible? Were you never disgusted with or angry at how you or others were treated? If you can answer "yes" to these four questions, you're lucky. In some ways, agencies, businesses, and other organizations can have similar problems. For whatever reason, agency social workers might be in the position of having to advocate with their own agency on the behalf of clients.

For instance, one worker advocated to initiate a policy to reserve the agency's best parking spaces for clients. Historically, staff would park in the best spots in the parking lot each morning because they always got there first. Clients thus regularly got the very worst parking spots—if there were any spots left at all.

Social workers can also advocate for change when an agency policy gets in the way of their doing their jobs. The policy might state that social workers should visit their clients' homes only when absolutely necessary to hold down transportation costs. The workers might strongly feel that it's essential to visit clients in their home environments to assess accurately what's going on in the family. Therefore, it's their responsibility to advocate for positive policy change and try to negotiate results.

### A Volunteer Dental Program

Social workers can initiate and help organize programs for dentists to volunteer to help people with chronic illnesses, developmental disabilities, or other problems prohibiting them from working and having dental insurance. The program can also be made available to people working in low-paying jobs that don't provide dental insurance. Social workers can contact potential volunteers, help coordinate efforts, work with social service agencies to publicize the service, and link clients with the resource when they need dental help.

For instance, Harry, age 60, has severe heart disease and serious, painful gum disease. Because of numerous health expenses, he is financially strapped. He did have upper dentures made several years earlier. His coverage as a veteran at a Veteran's hospital helped as it allowed him to have his lower teeth removed, but prohibited coverage for any further work. Harry's mouth was in appalling shape, and he had extreme difficulty eating and talking. A social worker helped initiate and

*(continued)*

**HIGHLIGHT 4.5 (continued)**

organize a Tri-County Troubled Teeth Treatment program in which dentists were systematically recruited to volunteer some of their time. One dentist in the program worked carefully with Harry during a half dozen appointments. At the end of the process, Harry couldn't believe he had brand-new porcelain lower dentures. He beamed at the dentist in appreciation.

### Murals

Large pictures painted or drawn on walls or ceilings, known as murals, can provide an important means of self-expression and cultural pride. For example, concerning Chicanos and their pride in their history, Treguer (1992) comments about murals:

> Pre-Columbian themes, intended to remind Chicanos of their noble origins, are common. There are motifs from the [ancient] Aztec [manuscripts, ] … gods from the Aztec [temples, ] … allusions to the Spanish conquest and images of the Virgin of Guadalupe, a cherished Mexican icon. (p. 23)

Additionally, such murals can reflect religious and spiritual symbols, and issues related to social justice. Delgado and Barton (1999) remark,

> In some Latino communities, scenes of police brutality, arson, alcohol and other drug abuse, prison, U.S. imperialism (particularly related to government sponsored terrorism in the Caribbean and Latin America), and infant mortality are commonplace.… In essence, mural scenes are based on historical events and are a daily reminder of the trials and tribulations of being Latino in this country and of the search for social justice. (p. 233)

Delgado and Barton (1999) describe a case in Holyoke, Massachusetts, where a large Puerto Rican population lives. They note how "El Arco Iris (the Rainbow), an after school program" under the auspices of "a local community based organization, received funds to create a mural" (p. 241). Having obtained authorization from the owner of a deserted building, 20 Puerto Rican young people painted a mural of a nature panorama on one of the building's large, blank walls. The youths incorporated the U.S. and Puerto Rican flags into the landscape. They positioned the Puerto Rican flag above the U.S. flag, with the latter depicted upside down. Although the youths' intent was to demonstrate the harmony between the two countries, several other community residents were offended by the upside-down U.S. flag. The incident caused serious debate among community residents with different cultural heritages. On the positive side, it stimulated discussion and consciousness raising among groups throughout the community. It also brought together Puerto Rican community members, including adults and young people, "to fight for their beliefs and to strengthen their voice within the community" (Delgado & Barton, 1999, p. 241). Eventually, the Puerto Rican youths decided to end the controversy by enlarging the Puerto Rican flag to cover the U.S. flag.

Delgado and Barton (1999) conclude,

> Social workers can play an instrumental role in helping communities negotiate with government authorities and private parties for the painting of murals using their spaces. Murals in prime locations can serve to empower communities to organize to seek services and other resources to help them develop their capacities to help themselves. (p. 236)

---

George require more intensive inpatient treatment instead? Is his parole unsuccessful, and so he should return to prison? What appropriate research-based knowledge is available for Yvonne and George to reconsider these goals and develop alternative ones?

Note that evaluation is also essential in mezzo and macro practice. For example, social workers must determine whether intervention involving agency functioning and service provision is successful. *Program evaluation* is the systematic examination of the success, effectiveness, and efficiency of an ongoing program (i.e., a structured plan and procedures for providing designated services to a sizable number of clients or a community).

### Step 6: Termination

**Termination** is "the end of the professional social worker–client relationship" (Kirst-Ashman & Hull, 2015b, p. 315). The worker–client relationship eventually must come to an end. It is not a good ending for a worker to get up one day and, out of the blue, say, "Well, good-bye." Termination in generalist practice involves specific skills and techniques, regardless of the level of intervention.

EP 8e

Appropriate timing of the termination is important. At least three basic types of termination exist

## HIGHLIGHT 4.6

# THE CONCEPT OF SUSTAINABILITY AND THE PROCESS OF SOCIAL WORK

**LO 8**

Chapter 1 established that **sustainability** involves "development that meets the current needs of the present generations without jeopardizing the ability of future generations to meet their needs" (Mary, 2008, p. 32). It refers to establishing policies, practices, and behaviors that will sustain the environment and people's quality of life instead of harming it. How does all this apply to social workers and their practice? At the level of working directly with clients, Healy (2008) emphasizes the importance of adopting helping strategies that are more self-supporting and likely to continue after the immediate intervention. For instance, social workers should consider the extent to which clients would continue to use any skills taught on an ongoing basis in view of their "time, financial resources, energy, literacy, and cultural acceptability" (p. 366). One illustration is a

**EP 3b, 5a, 8b, 8c, 8e**

> program for teen mothers in May Pen, Jamaica, [that] teaches teen mothers how to use educational toys with their children and how to make the toys from scraps—milk carton blocks decorated with cut-outs from old magazines, for example; these homemade and resource-efficient toys are used in the program, although its grant would pay for expensive developmental toys from abroad. Through this simple strategy, the likelihood of sustainability is increased.
>
> *(Healy, 2008, p. 366)*

When the grant runs out and external funding dries up, the mothers are more likely to continue the practices they learned because they have simple resources readily available.

On a macro level, social workers can advocate for policies supporting sustainability and serve as leaders in implementing them (Gamble & Weil, 2008). Examples of movements promoting sustainability include those emphasizing environmental, green, antiwar, women's, and human rights issues (Gamble & Weil, 2008). Running for office provides one avenue of doing so. Mary (2008) stresses that becoming involved in politics and influencing politicians is critical; she suggests "writing to or meeting with local representatives around fiscal priorities and restructuring tax systems, and educating ourselves on the issues to present them in our own professional, civic, and personal arenas of power" (p. 189).

Also on a macro level, when social programs are developed to help communities, the communities' potential to continue them on an ongoing basis should be considered. "In planning and administering social programs, social workers can also use the concept of sustainability to assess program dependence on material and human resources, including available leadership talent and human energy. Many programs do not survive past the term of outside grants, as they fail to consider availability of ongoing resources" (Healy, 2008, p. 366).

---

(Hellenbrand, 1987, p. 765). First, some terminations are predictably expected. That is, goals have been achieved, and it is time for clients to take what they have learned and go out on their own. Other terminations are "forced." For example, a worker might leave the agency, or a client might leave an institution for some reason or lose eligibility to receive services. Finally, there are "unplanned" terminations. Perhaps the client simply fails to come back, or the family moves, or the client is no longer motivated to return. Or maybe other aspects of the client's life take precedence over the problem he or she originally came to the social worker to help solve.

The most effective terminations follow a thoughtful, planned process so that clients are prepared for the relationship to end. Social workers need to

acknowledge that endings are near before they abruptly occur. They need to encourage clients to share feelings about the termination and, in turn, to share their own. Additionally, practitioners need to identify clearly whatever progress has been made. This increases the chance that the client will use what has been learned during this intervention to help solve other problems in the future.

The client may be an individual, group, or large agency. Regardless, each needs help in the transition from depending on the worker for support or guidance to making decisions and functioning independently.

Highlight 4.6 discusses how the concept of sustainability (introduced in Chapter 1) might be applied to the process and practice of social work on both micro and macro levels.

# Chapter Summary

The following summarizes this chapter's content as it relates to the learning objectives presented at the beginning of the chapter. Chapter content will help prepare students to:

### LO1 Define generalist practice.

Generalist practice is the application of an eclectic knowledge base, professional values, and a wide range of skills to target individual, family, group, organizational, or community systems for change within the context of five primary processes. First, generalist practice emphasizes client empowerment. Second, it involves working effectively within an organizational structure and doing so under supervision. Third, it requires the assumption of a wide range of professional roles. Fourth, it concerns following the principles of evidence-based practice. Fifth, it involves the application of critical thinking skills to the planned-change process.

### LO2 Discuss professional identity.

Social workers should identify with the profession. Some aspects of such identification include continual personal reflection and professional development, career-long learning, professional demeanor, and advocacy for client access to social work services.

### LO3 Describe the planned-change process.

The planned-change process involves engagement, assessment, planning, implementation, evaluation, and termination. Each step is defined and discussed.

### LO4 Apply critical thinking skills.

Critical thinking questions are posed to address the common fallacies of relying on case examples, relying on testimonials, being vague, being biased or unobjective, and believing that if it's written down it must be right.

### LO5 Discuss cross-cultural variations in communication.

Cross-cultural differences in nonverbal and verbal communication include amount of eye contact, emotional expression, personal space, verbal responses implying agreement, and the value of talk.

### LO6 Emphasize strengths during the assessment process.

Traditional assessment approaches emphasize the negative because the eventual goal is to cure the problem. A strengths-based assessment emphasizes identifying and using a client's strengths in addition to focusing on the problem. Strengths can be used to identify resources to solve problems.

### LO7 Describe examples of intervention with macro systems.

Examples of intervention work with macro systems include fundraisers, advocacy for agency policy changes, volunteer dental programs, and community murals.

### LO8 Relate sustainability to social work.

Sustainability involves "development that meets the current needs of the present generations without jeopardizing the ability of future generations to meet their needs" (Mary, 2008, p. 32). It is important to initiate and build on social work strategies and programs that are more self-supporting and likely to continue after the initial intervention or startup.

## LOOKING AHEAD

This chapter discussed the process of generalist social work practice. The next chapter will explain the various practice settings in which this process is implemented.

## COMPETENCY NOTES

The following identifies where Educational Policy (EP) competencies and their component behaviors are discussed in the chapter.

**EP 1 (Competency 1)—Demonstrate Ethical and Professional Behavior.** *(p. 119):* Professional social workers should participate in lifelong learning and skill development.

**EP 1b Use reflection and self-regulation to manage personal values and maintain professionalism in practice situations.** *(p. 119):* Professional social workers should practice reflection and self-regulation.

**EP 1c Demonstrate professional demeanor in behavior; appearance; and oral, written, and electronic communication.** *(p. 119):* Professional social workers should demonstrate professional demeanor. *(p. 128):* Social workers should attend to cultural differences in verbal and nonverbal communication so that they might communicate effectively with people from other cultures.

**EP 1e Use supervision and consultation to guide professional judgment and behavior.** *(p. 117):* Working under supervision in an organizational setting and using consultation are discussed as important aspects of generalist practice. *(p. 119):* Professional social workers should use supervision and consultation to enhance practice effectiveness.

**EP 2 (Competency 2)—Engage Diversity and Difference in Practice.** *(p. 127):* Practitioners should be sensitive to cultural differences in nonverbal and verbal communication. *(p. 128):* It's vital for social workers to be concerned about aspects of diversity during assessment. Practitioners should investigate how aspects of diversity may expose clients to oppression. The following case example includes consideration of ageism and sexism, both forms of oppression.

**EP 3 EP (Competency 3)—Advance Human Rights and Social, Economic, and Environmental Justice.**

**EP 3a Apply their understanding of social, economic, and environmental justice to advocate for human rights at the individual and system levels.** *(p. 132):* Social workers should advocate for human rights and services at the macro level.

**EP 3b Engage in practices that advance social, economic, and environmental justice.** *(p. 134):* Establishment of sustainable services and resources can advance social, economic, and environmental justice.

**EP 4 (Competency 4)—Engage in Practice-Informed Research and Research-Informed Practice.**

**EP 4b Apply critical thinking to engage in analysis of quantitative and qualitative research methods and research findings.** *(p. 120):* Practitioners should apply critical thinking to understand and use research findings. *(p. 121):* Social workers should understand and use critical thinking in their analysis of research findings.

**EP 4c Use and translate research evidence to inform and improve practice, policy, and service delivery.** *(p. 120):* Social workers should undertake evidence-based practice, which emphasizes using approaches research has shown to be most effective in specific practice situations. *(p. 131):* When planning, social workers and their clients should choose from among evidence-based interventions.

**EP 5 (Competency 5)—Engage in Policy Practice.**

**EP 5a Identify social policy at the local, state, and federal level that impacts well-being, service delivery, and access to social services.** *(p. 134):* Sustainability involves considering what policies and services can be maintained over time to enhance the capacities of clients and communities.

**EP 5b Assess how social welfare and economic policies impact the delivery of and access to social services.** *(p. 132):* Social workers should assess how policies impact access to services and advocate for change when necessary.

**EP 5c Apply critical thinking to analyze, formulate, and advocate for policies that advance human rights and social, economic, and environmental justice.** *(p. 121):* Practitioners should apply critical thinking to analyze, formulate, and advocate for policies that enhance people's well-being. *(p. 132):* Social workers should analyze, formulate, and advocate for policies that advance social well-being on the behalf of macro client systems.

**EP 6 (Competency 6)—Engage with Individuals, Families, Groups, Organizations, and Communities.** *(p. 121):* The planned-change process includes engagement with systems of all sizes.

**EP 6b Use empathy, reflection, and interpersonal skills to effectively engage diverse clients and constituencies.** *(p. 119):* Professional social workers should use effective interpersonal skills. *(p. 123):* Engagement involves using empathy and other positive interpersonal skills. *(p. 125):* Engagement involves using empathy and other interpersonal skills.

**EP 7 (Competency 7)—Assess Individuals, Families, Groups, Organizations, and Communities.** *(p. 121):* The planned-change process includes the assessment of systems of all sizes.

**EP 7a Collect and organize data, and apply critical thinking to interpret information from clients and constituencies.** *(p. 121):* Practitioners should apply critical thinking during the assessment process. *(p. 123):* Social workers must collect, organize, and interpret client data to undertake the planned-change process. *(p. 127):* Assessment involves the collection, organization, and interpretation of client data. *(p. 129):* Assessment emphasizing strengths involves collecting, organizing, and interpreting client data.

**EP 7b Apply knowledge of human behavior and the social environment, person-in-environment, and other multidisciplinary theoretical frameworks in the analysis of assessment data from clients and constituencies.** *(p. 127):* Assessment involves looking beyond the individual and examining other impinging factors within the client's environment.

**EP 7c Develop mutually agreed-on intervention goals and objectives based on the critical assessment of strengths, needs, and challenges within clients and constituencies.** *(p. 123):* The school social worker in this case example assesses his client's behavioral limitations. *(p. 127):* Social workers should assess client strengths and limitations. *(p. 129):* This highlight and case example stress how workers should focus on clients' strengths. *(p. 131):* A social worker should identify and assess client strengths to incorporate them in the planned-change process. It's vital that social workers develop mutually agreed-on intervention goals and objectives with clients.

**EP 7d Select appropriate intervention strategies based on the assessment, research knowledge, and values and preferences of clients and constituencies.** *(p. 123):* This case example involves selecting appropriate intervention strategies that target systems of various sizes. *(p. 131):* Practitioners should work with the client system to plan the most appropriate intervention strategies.

**EP 8 (Competency 8)—Intervene with Individuals, Families, Groups, Organizations, and Communities.** *(p. 121):* The planned-change process includes intervention with systems of all sizes.

**EP 8a Critically choose and implement interventions to achieve practice goals and enhance capacities of clients and constituencies.** *(p. 121):* Practitioners should apply critical thinking during the intervention process. *(p. 131):* Implementation is the step in the planned-change process where the plan is followed to achieve goals.

**EP 8b Apply knowledge of human behavior and the social environment, person-in-environment, and other multidisciplinary theoretical frameworks in interventions with clients and constituencies.** *(p. 134):* Knowledge of human behavior and the social environment is necessary to establish sustainable services and resources.

**EP 8c Use inter-professional collaboration as appropriate to achieve beneficial practice outcomes.** *(p. 132):* Several projects are discussed where social workers collaborate with colleagues and clients for effective policy action. *(p. 134):* Sustainability by necessity involves cooperation with other entities that will assume responsibility for service provision.

**EP 8d Negotiate, mediate, and advocate with and on behalf of diverse clients and constituencies.** *(p. 118):* Mediator, negotiator, and advocate roles are defined and examples of each provided. *(p. 123):* The school social worker in this case example may advocate to improve resource provision and legislation when necessary. *(p. 132):* Social workers should advocate for services at the macro level when such services are needed.

**EP 8e Facilitate effective transitions and endings that advance mutually agreed-on goals.** *(p. 133):* Termination in the planned-change process involves a thoughtful and effective ending or transition in the worker/client relationship. *(p. 134):* To establish sustainable changes, careful forethought must be given concerning transitions and endings.

**EP 9 (Competency 9)—Evaluate Practice with Individuals, Families, Groups, Organizations, and Communities.** *(p. 121):* The planned-change process includes evaluation of interventions with systems of all sizes.

**EP 9a Select and use appropriate methods for evaluation of outcomes.** *(p. 119):* Professional social workers should select effective intervention plans. *(p. 131):* Social workers must use appropriate methods to evaluate interventions.

**EP 9b Apply knowledge of human behavior and the social environment, person-in-environment, and other multidisciplinary theoretical frameworks in the evaluation of outcomes.** *(p. 131):* In order to conduct effective evaluations, social workers must apply knowledge of human behavior and the social environment.

**EP 9c Critically analyze, monitor, and evaluate intervention and program processes and outcomes.** *(p. 131):* Effective evaluation is necessary to determine to what extent goals have been achieved.

**EP 9d Apply evaluation findings to improve practice effectiveness at the micro, mezzo, and macro levels.** *(p. 131):* Evaluation findings should be applied to improve practice effectiveness at all levels.

# 5 Practice Settings

Digitalskillet/iStockphoto.com

## Learning Objectives   This chapter will help prepare students to:

**LO 1**   Identify the context of social work practice today (in organizations and communities, including rural and urban communities). **Social Work Practice Today in Organizations and Communities** (p. 140)

**LO 2**   Explain the core intervention approaches in practice (with individuals, families, groups, organizations, and communities). **Social Work Practice with Systems of All Sizes** (p. 145)

**LO 3**   Propose questions to stimulate critical thinking about involvement in various systems. **Focus on Critical Thinking 5.1** (p. 147)

**LO 4**   Identify some professional associations in social work. **Professional Organizations and Associations in Social Work** (p. 158)

**LO 5**   Describe social work licensure. **Highlight 5.5** (p. 159)

**LO 6**   Discuss social work careers, employment settings, and salaries. **Careers in Social Work** (p. 161)

*Consider these questions:*

- *Why are social welfare programs the way they are today?*
- *What social welfare problems and issues do we foresee in the future?*
- *What kinds of treatment groups do social workers run?*
- *What fields of practice do most social workers go into?*

*This chapter addresses these and many other questions and issues concerning social welfare and social work in the past, present, and future. Chapter 4 discussed generalist social work practice. This chapter focuses on the contexts in which social work has been, is, and will be practiced.*

## Social Work Practice Today in Organizations and Communities **LO 1**

Chapter 4 discussed the process of generalist social work practice. The following sections continue the exploration of the current context of practice, including social work's organizational and community settings; primary treatment approaches used in practice with individuals, families, groups, organizations and communities; key professional social work organizations; and social workers' most common employment settings according to fields of practice.

### Settings in Social Work Practice: Organizations and Communities

Social work practice generally takes place within the context of organizations and communities. *Organizations* are entities made up of people that have rules and structure to achieve specified goals. Social workers practice under the auspices of organizations providing social services.

### Social Services in the Context of Social Agencies

*Social services* include the tasks that social work practitioners and other helping professionals perform with the goal of improving people's health, enhancing their quality of life, increasing autonomy and independence, supporting families, and helping people and larger systems improve their functioning in the social

EP 6a, 7b, 8b, 9b

environment (Barker, 2014). That is quite a mouthful. In essence, social services include the wide range of activities that social workers perform to help people solve problems and improve their personal well-being.

A **social agency** or **social services agency** is an organization providing social services that typically employs a range of helping professionals including social workers in addition to office staff, paraprofessionals (persons trained to assist professionals), and sometimes volunteers (Barker, 2014). Social agencies generally serve some designated client population experiencing some defined need. Services are provided according to a prescribed set of policies regarding how the agency staff should accomplish their service provision goals.

Social agencies come in many forms. For example, they can be either public or private. ***Public* social agencies** are run by some designated unit of government and are usually regulated by laws impacting policy. For instance, a county board committee oversees a public welfare department and is responsible for establishing its major policies. (Of course, such a committee must function in accordance with the wishes of the state or federal governments that often provide at least some of the money for the agency's programs.)

***Private* social agencies**, in contrast, are privately owned and run by people not employed by government. The services they provide include individual and group counseling, family planning, and other services for children and older adults (Barker, 2014). Note that services sometimes resemble those furnished by public social agencies such as corrections, protective services for children, and job preparation and training for public assistance recipients.

Private social agencies may be either nonprofit or proprietary. **Nonprofit** social agencies seek to accomplish some service provision goal, not to make a profit for private owners. Sources of funding for services can include taxes, private donations, grants, and service fees. A board of directors presides over a private nonprofit agency, formulating policy and making certain that agency staff run the agency appropriately.

**Proprietary** or **for-profit** private social agencies also provide some designated social services, often quite similar to those provided by nonprofit private social agencies. However, a primary purpose for the existence of a proprietary social agency is to earn a profit for its owners.

Sometimes public agencies buy services from private agencies through a **purchase-of-service contract** or agreement. In a typical scenario, a public agency needs specialized services that it does not normally provide. It may be more cost-effective for the public agency to purchase the service from a private agency. The private agency then assumes responsibility for developing and overseeing service provision.

## Social Work Practice in the Context of Communities

A **community** is "a number of people who have something in common with one another that connects them in some way and that distinguishes them from others" (Homan, 2011, p. 8). A key feature of a community is the fact that participants share some mutual characteristic, such as "common location, interest, identification, or some combination of these characteristics" (Fellin, 2001, p. 1).  EP 6a, 7b, 8b, 9b

Thus communities can be of two primary types—those based on geographic proximity and those based on common ideas, interests, loyalty, and a feeling of membership (Martinez-Brawley, 1995). Locality-based communities include smaller towns such as Crouch, Idaho; Eggemoggin, Maine; and Necessity, Louisiana. Larger communities include mammoth urban environments such as the greater Los Angeles Metropolitan Area or New York City. Still other locality-based communities include smaller portions of larger cities such as a struggling inner-city ghetto or a posh suburban neighborhood.

Nongeographic communities are based on some commonality other than location. For example, African Americans might form a community based on racial identification and a shared history and culture. Similarly, a community of professional social workers shares common values, beliefs, and generalist practice skills. Additionally, gay communities and military communities exist that have distinct compositions, configurations, and purposes. Members of such communities exhibit many common values, expectations, and beliefs. Even scuba divers make up a community based on common interests, activities, and experiences.

In the social work perspective, communities are entities in which citizens can organize or be organized to address mutual concerns and improve their overall quality of life. Social workers have the responsibility to examine the community environment in which their clients reside. Although social workers are surely focused on how specific clients function as individuals, they are also concerned about the environment in which clients live and whether adequate resources are available.

The following sections discuss the special circumstances concerning social work practice in rural and urban communities and those involved in urban and rural social work.

### The Special Circumstances of Social Work Practice in Rural Communities

Social work practice in rural communities merits special attention. What do you picture when you think of a rural environment? A farmer wearing a straw hat and chewing on a blade of grass? Cows grazing? Endless, lonesome prairie? Barren desert? Some things you probably *don't* think of are skyscrapers, chaotic traffic jams, and  EP 2a, 2b thousands of people swarming on crowded streets.

Defining the concept of a rural community is not an easy task. An increasing population, spreading suburban sprawl, and decreasing numbers of farmers complicate the issue of what *rural* means. Yet you may have a sense that life in rural America is quite different than that in urban enclaves.

The U.S. Census Bureau (2011) defines a **rural community** as one that is not an "urbanized area" (a "densely settled territory that contains 50,000 or more people") or an "urban cluster" (a "densely settled territory with at least 2,500 people but fewer than 50,000 people") (pp. 3–4). But this definition allows for vast discrepancies in economic and social status. Consider the difference between a well-to-do bedroom community 35 miles outside of Chicago where corporate commuters reside in huge mansions versus a farming community in South Dakota where farmers are just managing to get by (Davenport & Davenport, 2008).

One definition of a rural community involves three major facets—having a low population density (i.e., number of residents per square mile), being located a significant distance from large urban hubs, and concentrating its activity in some specialized area like lumbering, farming, ranching, or mining (Davenport & Davenport, 2008). Some definitions indicate that to be "rural," a community must be unincorporated and have fewer than 2,500 inhabitants (Carlton-LaNey, Edwards, & Reid, 1999).

Rural communities experience special problems:

*Rural communities experience many of the same social problems as their urban counterparts. Nevertheless, some problems are specific to rural communities. Although the problems themselves may not differ greatly from those in urban centers, they are magnified by the rural communities' inability to target the needed resources in ways that alleviate suffering and ultimately eliminate the problems.*

*The list of problems with which rural and small town residents must cope includes poverty, lack of transportation, inadequate child care, unemployment, substandard housing, and insufficient health care. Problems of access and adequacy, for example, remain critical issues that must be addressed in rural social work practice. Krout (1994) noted that access problems add time and expense to service delivery efforts, ultimately discouraging both the development of new services and the expansion of existing services into rural areas. For example, rural homebound individuals who could benefit from home-delivered meals and thereby maintain independence are denied this service because it is too expensive. The cost of delivering meals to remote areas can significantly limit the amount of money available for the service itself.*

*Health care is another significant problem. Rural areas, particularly low-income areas, are under-served because of a lack of physicians and other health care providers. The South especially suffers from a maldistribution of health care professionals and facilities.*

(Carlton-LaNey et al., 1999, p. 7; Daley & Avant, 2014)

Social workers practicing in rural communities must address at least four special issues. First, they must be true generalists who are prepared to work with individuals, families, groups, local organizations, and the community, using a wide range of skills to meet clients' diverse needs (Daley & Avant, 2014; Davenport & Davenport, 2008; Lohmann, 2005). Urban areas with large populations and a larger tax base can better afford to specialize in service provision. For example, public and private social service agencies might provide specific services such as substance abuse counseling, older adult protective services, services for people with intellectual disabilities, crisis counseling for victims of sexual assault, shelter for victims of domestic violence, and so on. A rural community, on the other hand, probably does not have the resources or enough population to support such specific services (Daley & Avant, 2014; Davenport & Davenport, 2008). Therefore, rural practitioners typically must be more flexible and willing to address a broader range of people with a varied assortment of problems.

A second special issue involves interagency cooperation (Carlton-LeNay et al., 1999, p. 10). Because fewer, more general services are usually provided by public agencies, it's critical for agencies and their staffs to work more closely together than in many urban communities. It's common for practitioners and agency administrations "to know each other and to reach out to each other regularly" to meet clients' diverse needs (Carlton-LeNay et al., 1999, p. 10). In urban areas with hundreds of available services, this may not be the case.

A third issue involving rural social work is the importance placed on understanding the community, knowing its values, and developing relationships with rural residents (Daley & Avant, 2014). People living in rural communities have different life experiences than those living in bustling cities. Because there are fewer people, social interactions and relationships tend to be much more informal. Rural social workers and their family members might attend the same church or school, participate in the same civic clubs and organizations, and shop at the same grocery store as clients. Therefore, a rural practitioner must be careful to portray an

| HIGHLIGHT **5.1** | CASE EXAMPLE OF A DUAL RELATIONSHIP IN A RURAL COMMUNITY |
|---|---|

Corey and his colleagues (2015) relate the following example of a dual relationship in a small rural community setting:

Millie, a [social work] therapist in a small community, experienced heart pain one day. The fire department was called, and the medic on the team turned out to be her client, Andres. To administer proper medical care, Andres had to remove Millie's upper clothing. During subsequent sessions, neither Andres nor Millie discussed the incident, but both exhibited a degree of discomfort with each other. After a few more sessions, Andres discontinued his therapy with Millie.

**EP 1a**

- Can this case be considered an unavoidable dual relationship? Why or why not?
- What might Millie have done to prevent this outcome?
- Should Millie have discussed her discomfort in the therapy session following the incident? Why or why not?
- If you were in Millie's situation, what would you have done?

*Commentary:* This case illustrates how some roles can shift and how some multiple relationships are unavoidable, especially in small communities. In small communities, therapists must anticipate frequent, and sometimes uncomfortable, boundary crossings with clients. In our view, Millie should have discussed with Andres how he would like to handle chance encounters in the community during the informed consent process. [Very early in the worker–client relationship, the worker should provide the client with information about the parameters of their relationship. For example, this may include limits of confidentiality and the worker's responsibility to report any criminal behavior to the authorities. In small communities this may also include how informal meetings should be handled because they are so likely to occur.] Even so, we doubt that Millie could have predicted this awkward boundary crossing with Andres. Clinically, Millie might have salvaged the therapy relationship by processing [that is, talking about and dealing with] her own discomfort with a colleague, and then processing the event with Andres. By allowing the discomfort to remain hidden, Millie failed to practice with the best interests of her client in mind. In this instance, neither Millie's nor Andres's needs were being met in the therapeutic relationship. (pp. 268–269)

image that reflects positively on his or her agency (Daley & Avant, 2004). Private lives might be more public—some say it's like "life in a goldfish bowl" (Davenport & Davenport, 2008, p. 538). For example, it would not be impressive for a social worker counseling a client with an alcohol problem to be cited in the local newspaper for driving under the influence (DUI).

Because of the close interpersonal nature of rural communities, there is a strong likelihood that dual relationships exist (Daley & Hickman, 2011). As described in Chapter 2, dual or "multiple relationships occur when professionals assume two or more roles at the same time or sequentially with a client" (e.g., both social worker and neighbor or member of the same church, temple, mosque, or synagogue) (Corey, Corey, Corey, & Callanan, 2015, p. 254). Especially in rural communities, dual and multiple relationships may be unavoidable. Watkins (2004) suggests that rural social workers in such situations

"above all, do no harm; practice only with competence; do not exploit; treat people with respect for their dignity as human beings; protect confidentiality; act, except in the more extreme instances, only after obtaining informal consent; [and] practice, insofar as possible, within the framework of social equity and justice" (p. 70).

Highlight 5.1 provides an example of a dual relationship occurring in a small community.

The fourth issue important for rural social work practice involves emphasizing the strengths inherent in rural communities (Tice, 2005; Daley & Avant, 2014). Because of the informal nature of relationships, rural clients are often integrally involved with informal social support systems of other people willing to help them out—sometimes referred to as **natural helping networks** (Alleman & Holly, 2014; Tracy, 2002; Watkins, 2004). Such networks can include family members, neighbors, coworkers, fellow church members, community benefactors, and others not providing formal agency services who are willing to volunteer assistance. (Social support systems are discussed in more detail later in the chapter with respect to working with families.)

## Urban Social Work

**Urban social work** is practice within the context of large cities, with their vast array of social problems, exceptional diversity, and potential range of resources (Delgado & Staples, 2008). Phillips and Straussner (2002) stress how urban social workers "need to be sensitive to the situations commonly found in the cities and to be  **EP 2a, 2b** knowledgeable about the nature of urban life and the range of impact that the urban environment can have on people" (p. 20). Practitioners need to learn from their clients about their issues and needs. Work in the urban context is important in view of how both the national and global population has been shifting from rural to urban settings. People often flock to cities in search of new opportunities, higher-paying jobs, and greater access to activities and services. Many times, although hopes are high, actual opportunities are scarce or nonexistent, which results in a "disproportionate number of the poor" in the "country's largest cities" (p. 107).

Urban areas are characterized by a number of conditions (Marsella, 1998). First, population is denser and often contains diverse population subgroups (for example, ethnic, racial, cultural, age, sexual orientation). Second, urban economic conditions involve a range of industries, businesses, rent levels, and transportation availability and costs. Third, the urban environment is often a bustling tangle of concrete, traffic, noise, and questions about air quality—in sharp contrast to the more natural rural environment. Fourth, an urban lifestyle entails more condensed interaction and contact with many people. Fifth, the political situation may be intense with many layers of bureaucracy and numerous people in "the system" who have various amounts of power. Sometimes crime, corruption, and social injustice are evident. Conditions in urban environments are often very different than those addressed by rural social workers.

Watkins (2004) explains:

*Urbanization brought dramatic changes in the way people interacted with each other. Individuals moved away from extended family and other primary relationships to cities where primary relationships were replaced by more role-based interactions [for example, employee, renter, customer, student]. Population density and crowding were accompanied by emotional distancing to preserve a sense of privacy and individuality. In low-income neighborhoods, needs overwhelmed the resources of neighbors. Many persons in need were new to the cities and had no support networks. Formalized or institutionalized social services were a rational response to the peculiar social patterns and needs of these urban residents.... However, when federal, state, and local governments increased their role in providing services, the programs were no longer tailored to a specific community. In efforts to increase efficiency and fairness, services became more bureaucratic and standardized. The new model of service delivery that developed preferred secondary, "professional" relationships and interactions that were rule- and role-based rather than more personal. Needy individuals were depersonalized into "clients."... Personal relationships between client and social workers were not only unlikely in the urban environment, they were actively discouraged. (p. 67)*

At least five problems tend to characterize urban areas more than rural areas (Phillips & Straussner, 2002). For one thing, "problems such as poverty, discrimination, overcrowded housing, crime and violence, homelessness, high rates of school dropouts, substance abuse, and HIV/AIDS exist in communities of all sizes. However, they occur with greater frequency and therefore are more visible in the cities" (p. 25).

A second problem is the widespread occurrence of discriminatory behavior because of the wide variety of ethnic, racial, religious, and cultural groups living in cities. Groups may be in conflict and fighting for power and resources. Often public schools are disadvantaged because of inadequate funding, resulting in poorer buildings, libraries, laboratory equipment, and technology, as well as underpaid staff.

Migration of people ill-equipped for the pressures and demands of urban living is a third problem characterizing cities. Phillips and Straussner (2002) explain:

*With their promise of freedom and opportunity, the cities have always been magnets for both the adventurous and the desperate. Most people move to urban areas in search of better opportunities for work or for education, either for themselves or their families, and for many, the cities have served and continue to serve as gateways to success.*

*However, some who migrate to urban areas, whether from other parts of the United States or from other countries, are faced with unemployment, underemployment, discrimination, poor housing, and language barriers. Those without families or social supports to help them make the transition to the new culture and to city life are at greater risk for poverty, social isolation, and personal and family problems. (p. 27)*

Financial shortfalls or unavailability of resources make up a fourth problem characterizing urban areas. "Some cities do not have the financial resources to provide services that would assist people in maximizing their potential, while other cities may have the resources, but do not choose to provide services, particularly for the poor. Consequently, there may be a lack of affordable, good-quality housing, or a lack of adequate police protection, schools, or recreational facilities. For example, pre-school children and their parents are underserved in many urban communities" (Phillips & Straussner, 2002, p. 28). Because of cities' dense population, service gaps can affect huge numbers of people.

The fifth problem characterizing cities involves greater amounts of psychological stress. Stressors including "noise, dirty streets," "abandoned buildings," overcrowded housing, lack of geographic mobility, and substance abuse can impose psychological pressure and increase general anxieties (Phillips & Straussner, 2002, p. 29).

As in other types of social work, urban social workers use micro-practice skills in their work with clients, including establishing and working toward goals, using effective communication and interviewing techniques, respecting client values and perspectives, emphasizing strengths, expressing empathy, and "developing self-awareness" to combat biases and effectively understand clients' perspectives (Phillips & Straussner, 2002, p. 201).

Highlight 5.2 discusses skills urban social workers must develop and use. Focus on Critical Thinking 5.1 raises questions to help you think about and understand your home community regardless of whether it's urban, rural, or something that's not quite either.

# Social Work Practice with Systems of All Sizes  `LO 2`

Social workers require skills to work with virtually any system, regardless of its size. These include individuals, families, groups, and organizations, and communities. The following sections will explore social work practice with each type of system.

## Social Work Practice with Individuals

Social work practice with individuals involves many dimensions of communication, interaction, sensitivity, and decision making as the practitioner follows the planned-change process. Two important aspects arbitrarily selected for discussion here are interviewing skills and professional roles.

### Interviewing Skills in Practice with Individuals

One essential aspect of social work practice with an individual (a micro system) involves interviewing skills. Hepworth, Rooney, Rooney, and Strom-Gottfried (2013) explain:

**EP 6b**

*Interviews in social work have a purpose, structure, direction, and focus. The purpose is to exchange information systematically with a view toward illuminating and solving problems, promoting growth, or planning strategies or actions aimed at improving the quality of life for people. The structure of interviews varies somewhat from setting to setting, from client to client, and from one phase of the helping process to another. Indeed, skillful interviewers adapt flexibly both to different contexts and to the ebb and flow of each individual session. (p. 47)*

Ivey, Ivey, and Zalaquett (2014) state that several facets are important in the development of interviewing and other micro-practice skills; one is *"attending behavior,"* the use of "individually and culturally appropriate verbal following, visuals [eye contact], vocal quality, and body language" (p. 64). They explain further:

1. Visual/eye contact. *Look at people when you speak to them. [But as discussed in an earlier chapter, be very sensitive to cultural differences concerning what kind of eye contact and when is considered appropriate.]*

## HIGHLIGHT 5.2   SKILLS NECESSARY FOR URBAN SOCIAL WORK

Urban social workers must focus on using skills in at least four major arenas (Phillips & Straussner, 2002):

1. *Paying close attention to human diversity:* Because urban environments more likely have a wider variety of ethnic, racial, and religious backgrounds, urban social workers must be sensitive to the wide range of cultural differences,  **EP 1, 5c, 8a, 8d** become knowledgeable about their various clients' cultures, and focus on the identification and use of clients' respective cultural and personal strengths. Urban practitioners must also be attuned to the potential discrimination experienced by people "based on race, ethnicity, culture, age, gender, religion, sexual orientation, disability, poverty, or language spoken. While historically various immigrant groups such as the Irish, the Jews, the Italians, the Chinese, and the Japanese have experienced discrimination in the United States, the most persistent discrimination today is experienced by Native Americans; blacks, including African Americans, people from the Caribbean, and people from Africa; Latinos; Asians; and people of Middle Eastern backgrounds" (Phillips & Straussner, 2002, p. 26).

2. *Understanding their agency environment:* Urban agencies may be large and complex, or may serve large client populations. Urban workers must understand the intricacy of their agency's power structure, who has decision-making power about what they can and can't do, and where resources are located. Large bureaucracies are often highly impersonal. They tend to emphasize the following rules and regulations to coordinate their complex maze of service provision. Often workers are called on to work with other personnel they don't know. Workers must then be sensitive to other staff members' roles and use good communication skills to

work effectively in collaboration with other service providers. Even smaller agencies in urban settings must work within a complex interplay of numerous organizations also addressing client needs. Urban social workers must understand the functioning of other agencies serving the same clients and work carefully with other staff to coordinate service provision.

3. *Seeking resources in the external urban environment:* Urban social workers often function in a complex labyrinth of many public and private agencies, each providing specialized services in one of a broad range of areas (for example, mental health counseling, administration of public assistance, domestic violence shelter, sexual assault hotline, or adolescent pregnancy prevention). This differs from rural agencies that often provide a broader range of services to a smaller population; in other words, they are less likely to specialize to the degree that urban agencies can. In their broker role, urban social workers must often seek resources in a confusing tangle of red tape and available services.

4. *Using advocacy:* Note that just because urban areas tend to have larger and more services, this does not mean that there are no significant gaps in service due to limited or lacking resources. Such gaps may involve massive numbers of people. At the agency level, an urban practitioner may need to develop a coalition with colleagues and approach decision-making administrators with suggestions for positive changes. On another level, public policy may not serve clients' best interests. Therefore, strategies to change legislation may include the use of letter-writing or e-mail campaigns to lawmakers, lobbying (seeking direct contact with legislators to influence their opinions), or using the mass media to publicize clients' needs and issues to gain public support for positive change.

2. Vocal qualities. *Communicate warmth and interest with your voice. Think of how many ways you can say "I am really interested in what you have to say," just by altering your vocal tone and speech rate....*

3. Verbal tracking. *Track the client's story. Don't change the subject; stick with the client's topic.*

4. Body language: *Be yourself—authenticity is essential to building trust. To show interest, face clients squarely, lean slightly forward with an*

## FOCUS ON CRITICAL THINKING 5.1  YOUR COMMUNITY  LO 3

Your own community environment has served an important function in shaping your personal development and belief system. Thinking about and understanding your community can help you understand yourself and others in that community.

### Critical Thinking Questions

EP 7a

- Is your community in a rural or urban setting, or somewhere in between?
- How would you describe your community?

- What are the strengths of the community to which you belong?
- What are the weaknesses inherent in that community?
- What is the ethnic/racial/cultural composition of the community?
- What is the history of the community?
- What beliefs, attitudes, and values do you think tend to characterize that community?
- How has membership in that community affected your life and value system?

---

*expressive face, and use encouraging gestures. Especially critical, smile to show warmth and interest in the client. (p. 66)*

A second aspect basic to the development of interviewing skills involves the use of open and closed questions. Ivey, Ivey, and Zalaquett (2012) describe the concepts:

*__Open questions__ are those that can't be answered in a few words. They tend to facilitate deeper exploration of client issues. They encourage others to talk and provide you with maximum information. Typically, open questions begin with* what, how, why, *or* could*: For example, "Could you tell me what brings you here today?"*

*__Closed questions__ enable you to obtain important specifics and can usually be answered in very few words. They may provide important information, but the burden of guiding the talk remains on the interviewer. Closed questions often begin with* is, are, *or* do*: For example, "Are you living with your family?" (p. 77)*

A third facet important in interviewing is the use of client observation skills; Ivey and his colleagues (2012) reflect:

*Jiggling legs, making complete body shifts, or suddenly closing one's arms most often indicates discomfort. Hand and arm gestures may give you an indication of how you and the client are organizing things. Random, discrepant gestures may indicate confusion, whereas a person seeking to control or organize things may move hands and arms in straight*

*lines and point fingers authoritatively. Smooth, flowing gestures … may suggest openness. (p. 68)*

### Professional Roles in Practice with Individuals

Another dimension important in practice with individuals involves the professional roles a worker can assume. Micro-practice roles include counseling, educating, brokering, and case management, all roles described in Chapter 4. In a *counselor* role, social workers follow the planned-change process described in Chapter 4 and help clients develop solutions to problems. For example, a social worker in corrections might work out with a client on parole a plan for finding housing and employment. Or a social worker who does alcohol abuse counseling might explore with a client her reasons for using alcohol and establish plans to maintain sobriety.

In an *educator* role, a social worker might teach an abusive parent effective child management techniques. Similarly, a hospital social worker might inform a person receiving kidney dialysis about the disease's progression and the dialysis process. (*Kidney dialysis* is a process by which a machine removes uric acid and urea from the blood, thereby substituting for the function of normal kidneys.)

Social workers in the *broker* role link clients to needed resources and services. For instance, a social worker might refer a homeless person to a shelter and to agencies providing financial assistance and job training. Social workers performing *case management* functions coordinate services provided by a number of agencies or services on a client's behalf. For example, a client with quadriplegia (i.e., paralysis of all four limbs due to spinal cord injury or disease) might be receiving resources from a variety of agencies including housing, transportation, financial assistance, personal care, and job training. A *case manager* or *case coordinator* synchronizes and oversees services to make sure the client gets what he or she needs.

Note that frequently a social worker may assume a range of roles with the same clients. For example, consider a family including two parents and children ages 2, 4, and 7 that has been referred to a Protective Services worker to assess possible child maltreatment and develop a service plan if necessary. After conducting the assessment, the worker may serve as counselor to help the parents learn to control their anger and behavior more effectively. The educator role might include teaching them child behavior management skills. The worker might serve as broker in linking the family to resources where they receive resources such as rental vouchers (that subsidize rent for eligible families) to ease their economic stress. The practitioner might also take on the facilitator role if these parents participate in a group she's leading of parents that have maltreated their children. Finally, the worker might become an advocate for the family to receive needed services that are not readily available.

## Social Work Practice with Families

As noted previously, social work with families combines micro and mezzo practice because it involves a small group (i.e., the family) linked by ties of an intimate nature. Working with families is a very important aspect of social work as later chapters will emphasize (Rasheed & Rasheed, 2008). The major goal of family social work is to improve a family's ability to  **EP 6a, 7b, 7d, 8b, 9b** function. It might involve teaching parenting skills, helping the family address a crisis, or linking the family with needed resources. Collins, Jordan, and Coleman (2013) explain:

> *A family social worker has many ways to provide on-the-spot and concrete assistance. For example, when a teenager and a parent become involved in a conflict, the family social worker can work with the conflict to identify the problem and intervene in "teachable moments." A family social worker can help the parent and child to discover what led up to the argument by identifying problematic and repetitive interactions that solidify into ongoing*

> *dysfunctional patterns. The family social worker does not view arguments and crises as paralyzing; rather, they are gifts that generate rich opportunities for change at a time when the family is most vulnerable and open to working on issues. The family social worker can assist the parent and teenager to replace problem behavior with healthier and more satisfying interactions. When a young child throws a temper tantrum, the family social worker can teach the parent more effective methods of dealing with problematic behavior in the moment. (p. 3)*

Maluccio, Pine, and Tracy (2002) stress that when working with families, social workers should:

- *Be responsive to the styles and values of families from communities of color, immigrants, and other special populations [e.g., lean-ing forward toward the client and maintaining eye contact to demon-strate attentiveness are considered rude and intrusive by many First Nations Peoples].*  **EP 6b**
- *Break complex tasks into smaller specific steps [e.g., how to look for housing; how to talk with your child's teacher].*
- *Assess the key skills needed for less stressful family interactions [e.g., accepting "no," giving direct commands, handling anger].*
- *Explain and model appropriate skills, using techniques such as role play, modeling, or videotaped practice.*
- *Assess individual learning styles and ways to teach adults and children [e.g., children learn differently as they age with increasing ability for complex thought; an adult may learn more effectively by observing a modeled behavior than being given verbal instructions or vice versa].*
- *Establish homework and other means of ensuring generalization of skills from one setting to another [e.g., asking family members to practice new communication techniques when in their own home setting].*
- *Promote and reward skill acquisition [e.g., praise family members when they follow through on homework or reach goals].*
- *Emphasize strategies that help develop the strengths of family members [e.g., high motiva-tion to improve or exceptional aptitude at coping with family crises].*

● *Motivate the family to stay involved even when faced with challenges and setbacks [e.g., an alcoholic family member falls off the wagon or a teenager runs away]. (pp. 149–150)*

Social workers can also help families deal with crises and problems they encounter in the external environment. For example, if a breadwinner is laid off, a social worker can help the family cope with these new conditions, link the family with available resources, and assist in the search for new employment. Sometimes it's necessary to advocate for resources that aren't readily available or to change social policies that are not in families' best interests.

### The Importance of Social Support Systems for Families

Social workers can help families get connected with social support systems that provide four types of support (Ragg, 2006, p. 382). First, **emotional support** involves people "who can listen to the client, understand his situation, provide encouragement, and celebrate his successes." Second, **instrumental support** includes others "who can offer concrete types of help, such as money, rides, shelter, and so forth." Third, **informational support** embraces people "who can provide important information to the client so that she can make the right connections and actions." Fourth, **appraisal support** involves those "who can give honest feedback to the client on how he is performing and acting."

Maluccio and his colleagues (2002) explain:

*Social support [including emotional, informational, and concrete] can occur spontaneously, as in one neighbor bringing meals to another, or it can occur in professionally arranged helping networks, such as Meals on Wheels. Formal social services staffed by paid human service professionals ... often provide social support as either the sole or partial focus of their service; for example, a social worker facilitating a parent education group may provide information, resource referrals, skills training, and emotional support for the participants. Informal support ... can be delivered by kinship networks, volunteers, or local community groups.... In many cases social workers can be the catalysts that mobilize and enhance various forms of informal helping to benefit individual clients, family members, and communities. (p. 175)*

A social worker can identify potential participants in a social support system that might be available to provide various types of support to a family, link the family with participants in the social support system, and facilitate how the system can help the family. For example, a worker could link a family with needed child care resources, including relatives, friends, neighbors, or a day care center. Another example of enhancing social support involves more formal family support programs that "address family self-sufficiency by offering services such as job training, English as a second language, and literacy classes" (Maluccio et al., 2002, p. 151). Still another example concerns "support groups for children experiencing life transitions or losses as in children of divorce, teenage parents, or children of battered women" (Maluccio et al., 2002, p. 184). Community programs such as neighborhood or cultural centers can also provide programming (e.g., recreational or educational) to help once struggling families prosper.

An example of how social support systems can serve a family involves Gene, age 13, who lived with his mother and younger brother Perry, age 8, in a federal low-income housing project for people whose family incomes are not high enough to pay for regular housing (adapted from Maluccio et al., 2002). Gene, a husky young 5'5" young man with bright red hair, already had a long history of truancy and delinquent behavior including illegal drug use and petty shoplifting. His problematic behavior and connections with delinquent peers were linked to inadequate parental support and supervision.

The family's social worker, Olivia, helped Gene's mother, Emily, identify more effective means of addressing Gene's behavior. One idea involved having Gene, who was athletically inclined, join the school's football team. Gene, a relatively popular student, already had some mildly positive relationships with other team players who were doing well in school and had no problems with the law. Emily agreed that joining the team might be a good idea, so she encouraged this plan of action, to which Gene agreed. Meanwhile, Olivia linked Gene with the football coach, who became part of Gene's supportive social network. Olivia and Emily contacted Gene's uncle, who lived only a few blocks from her family, and asked whether he would transport Gene home from practice. The uncle, Emily's brother, readily agreed because he had been quite concerned about Gene's downward spiral into trouble. Olivia and Emily then asked her church to contribute funding needed for required team equipment and transportation costs, which it did.

*Working with families is a very important aspect of social work.*

Another concern was what Gene would do on days when there was no practice. With Emily's approval, Olivia worked with Gene to involve him in a number of other after-school activities in which he expressed some interest. Olivia also arranged for a tutor to help him in subjects with which he was having difficulty.

In addition, Olivia worked with Emily to link both herself and Gene's younger brother Perry to a broader social support system. Emily joined a group for Parents Without Partners (who meet to provide support, discuss mutual concerns about raising children, and offer opportunities for social interaction) and became more actively involved in her church. She signed Perry up both for recreational activities at the local YMCA[1] and as a participant in a Big Brothers program so Perry could have the

opportunity to form a special relationship with a supportive adult role model.

In this case, Gene's football team involvement, his linkage with the coach, the uncle's help with transportation, the church's funding contribution, other after-school activities, tutoring, Emily's Parents Without Partners group, her church activities, and Perry's YMCA and Big Brothers program involvement all helped to expand and strengthen this family's social support system.

Thus, there is a wide range of social support systems in which people and their families can be involved. Focus on Critical Thinking 5.2 raises questions regarding your own social support systems.

## Social Work Practice with Groups

As with other levels of treatment, social work practice with groups can involve any number of problems, goals, and types of people. The two primary types of groups in social work practice are treatment and task.

EP 7b

---

[1]The YMCA (Young Men's Christian Association) is a global group of organizations that serves to enhance young men's and others' physical, mental, emotional, and interpersonal well-being, and offers a range of recreational and other services (Barker, 2014).

YOU, YOUR FAMILY, AND
SOCIAL SUPPORT SYSTEMS

We have established that social support
systems are very important for individuals and families.

EP 7a

Critical Thinking Questions

With what social support systems have you and your
family been involved during your lifetime? What kinds
of support were provided? In what ways did they help
you and your family?

*Treatment Groups*

**Treatment groups** help individuals solve personal
problems, change unwanted behaviors, cope with
stress, and improve quality of life.
Efforts focus on clients solving their
personal problems, enhancing personal
qualities, or providing each other with
support. Highlight 5.3 identifies and
defines five primary types of treatment
groups—therapy, support, educational,
growth, and socialization—and pro-
vides examples of each (Toseland & Horton, 2008;
Toseland & Rivas, 2012, p. 20). Corey (2012) provides an overview of many treatment groups:

EP 6b, 7c,
7d

*Group counseling has preventive as well as reme-
dial aims. Generally, the [treatment] … group has
a specific focus, which may be educational, career,
social, or personal. Group work emphasizes interpersonal communication of conscious thoughts,
feelings, and behavior within a here-and-now time
frame. [Treatment] … groups are often problem
oriented, and the members largely determine their
content and aims…. Group counseling tends to
be growth oriented in that the emphasis is on discovering internal resources of strength. The participants may be facing situational crises and
temporary conflicts, struggling with personal or
interpersonal problems of living, experiencing difficulties with life transitions, or trying to change
self-defeating behaviors. The group provides the
empathy and support necessary to create the atmosphere of trust that leads to sharing and exploring
these concerns. Group members are assisted in developing their existing skills in dealing with interpersonal problems so that they will be better able
to handle future problems of a similar nature.*

*The group [leader] … uses verbal and nonver-
bal techniques as well as structured exercises.
Basically, the role of the group [leader] … is to
facilitate interaction among the members, help
them learn from one another, assist them in establishing personal goals, and encourage them to
translate their insights into concrete plans that involve taking action outside of the group…. Group
[leaders] … perform their role largely by teaching
members to focus on the here-and-now and to identify the concerns they wish to explore in the group.
(p. 4)*

Corey (2012) continues by identifying potential
goals sought by treatment group members, including
the following:

- *To increase awareness and self-knowledge; to
  develop a sense of one's unique identity*
- *To recognize the commonality of members'
  needs and problems and to develop a sense of
  connectedness*
- *To help members learn how to establish meaningful and intimate relationships*
- *To assist members in discovering resources
  within their extended family and community as
  ways of addressing their concerns*
- *To increase self-acceptance, self-confidence,
  self-respect, and to achieve a new view of oneself and others*
- *To learn how to express one's emotions in a
  healthy way*
- *To develop concern and compassion for the
  needs and feelings of others*
- *To find alternative ways of dealing with …
  conflicts*
- *To become aware of one's choices and to make
  choices wisely*

# HIGHLIGHT 5.3 TREATMENT GROUPS IN SOCIAL WORK

There are five major types of treatment groups in social work practice.

1. *Therapy:* Groups that help members with serious psychological and emotional problems change their behavior. Corey (2012) explains:

> Some therapy groups are primarily designed to correct emotional and behavioral disorders that impede one's functioning or to remediate in-depth psychological problems. The goal may be either a minor or a major transformation of personality structure.... The people who make up the group may be suffering from severe emotional problems, deep personal conflict, effects of trauma, or psychotic states. Many of these individuals are in need of remedial treatment rather than developmental and preventive work. (p. 7)

   *Examples:* Groups formed to treat "depression, sexual difficulties, anxiety, and psychosomatic disorders"[2] (Corey, Corey, & Corey, 2010, p. 16).

2. *Support:* Groups whose members share common issues or problems and meet on an ongoing basis to cope with stress, give each other suggestions, provide encouragement, convey information, and furnish emotional support (Jacobs, Masson, & Harvill, 2009; Kurtz, 2004). "Strong emotional bonds often develop quickly in support groups because of members' shared experiences. Emotional bonding may also occur because members are stigmatized by the larger community and find comfort and power in their association with each other. Frequently, there is a high level of self-disclosure of emotionally charged material in support groups" (Toseland & Rivas, 2012, p. 23). Note that support groups differ from therapy groups in two main ways. First, support groups place greater emphasis on members supporting and helping each other—in contrast to therapy groups, in which the focus is on the leader assisting members in solving serious personal problems. Second, support groups differ from therapy groups in stressing ongoing coping and support instead of alleviating psychological difficulties.

   *Examples:* A group of persons living with AIDS, recovering alcoholics, adult survivors of sexual abuse, and veterans experiencing post-traumatic stress disorder.[3]

3. *Educational:* Groups that provide some type of information to participants. "Educational groups are used in a variety of settings, including treatment agencies, schools, nursing homes, correctional institutions, and hospitals.... All educational groups are aimed at increasing members' information or skills. Most groups routinely involve presentation of information and knowledge by experts. They also often include opportunities for group discussion to foster learning" (Toseland & Rivas, 2012, pp. 23–24).

   *Examples:* A group of parents learning child behavior management techniques, teens receiving sex education, a group of older adults interested in finding jobs, and a group of older adults in a nursing home requesting information about their prescribed drugs.

4. *Growth:* Groups aimed at expanding self-awareness, increasing potential, and maximizing health and well-being, "especially through improved relationships with others. They provide a supportive atmosphere in which individuals can gain insights, experiment with new behaviors, get feedback, and grow as human beings. The bond in growth groups stems from members' commitment to help one another develop and maximize their potential" (Toseland & Rivas, 2012, p. 24).

   *Examples:* A group of heterosexual singles exploring their attitudes about the opposite gender, "a values clarification group for adolescents," and a group of gay men focusing on gay pride issues (Toseland & Rivas, 2012, p. 24).

5. *Socialization:* Groups that help participants improve interpersonal behavior, communication, and social skills so they might better fit into their social environment. "The personal needs of members and the goals of the group are often met through program activities rather than exclusively through group discussion. Thus, socialization groups feature a learning-through-doing approach in which members improve their interpersonal skills by participating in program activities" (Toseland & Rivas, 2012, p. 26).

   *Examples:* An urban neighborhood's youth activities group, a school-based group of shy teens working to improve interpersonal skills, and a Parents Without Partners group sponsoring various social activities such as parties and outings (Toseland & Rivas, 2012).

*(continued)*

**HIGHLIGHT 5.3 (continued)**

### Commentary

Sometimes it's difficult to put a particular group in a specific category. What transpires in treatment groups is as complex as the people who make them up. For instance, consider an exceptionally creative treatment group program with adolescent residents from several group homes developed by Susan Ciardiello, a clinical social worker (Fiske, 2002b). (*Clinical social workers* "diagnose and treat mental, behavioral, and emotional disorders, including anxiety and depression. They provide individual, group, family, and couples therapy" and "work with clients to develop strategies to change behavior or cope with difficult situations" [Bureau of Labor Statistics, 2014].) Adolescents typically are placed in residential treatment (including group homes and larger institutions) because of behavioral and emotional problems (discussed more thoroughly in later chapters). For many reasons ranging from their normal quest for independence to having had severely negative experiences with the adults in their lives, it's difficult for these young people to trust adults. "Adolescents in groups can provide an environment where they learn from each other and benefit from the wisdom and experience of those traveling the same path" (p. 16).

Ciardiello first surveyed the adolescents to determine their primary interests—not surprisingly, "hip-hop music and basketball" (p. 17). She then pursued a three-faceted group treatment program. First, she divided participants into two co-ed basketball teams that played each other twice a week. However, instead of just playing neighborhood ball, the difference was that she "arranged it so that the players would get points when they demonstrated teamwork and self-control" (p. 17).

The program's second facet involved a biweekly disc jockey program, for which Ciardiello sought funds from a major recording company and purchased equipment. The program consisted of two parts. During the first hour, the group listened to various carefully chosen hip-hop songs that addressed issues significant in the teens' lives such as drugs, poverty, child abuse, romantic relationship concerns, hope for the future, and racial pride. Participants then discussed how the lyrics

affected them and related the songs to their own lives. It allowed them to share stories, empathize with each other, provide support, suggest means of coping, and develop trust. During the second hour, participants were rewarded by taking turns being the DJ and even making their own music.

The program achieved such success that a third empowering facet was added. The group members started their own magazine titled *The Real Deal: Kids Keeping It Real*. Through it they could express themselves and their opinions and talk about things that interested them. Ciardiello indicated that this three-pronged approach to a treatment group incorporating sports, music, and writing "decreased unexcused absences from the [group] homes and improved relations among residents" (p. 18).

What type of treatment group would you label this? *Therapeutically*, throughout the three facets of the program, participants worked on identifying feelings and controlling angry outbursts. One potential result was to help them better understand themselves, improve self-esteem, and make more effective decisions to control behavior that caused them problems. Group members also provided *support* to each other by listening to each other's opinions and making suggestions about coping. *Educationally*, participants learned how to be a DJ, a potentially viable job skill, and worked on writing skills through the magazine. As a *growth* group, they worked on expanding awareness of social issues and interpersonal dynamics. Finally, the entire process involved *socialization*, through which they learned how to get along better with their peers. Hence this treatment group appears to be a combination of approaches. It provides a good illustration of how social workers can be ingeniously resourceful and imaginative in their interventions.

[2]*Psychosomatic disorders* are physical symptoms (e.g., stomachaches, numbness, pain) caused by emotional problems.

[3]*Posttraumatic stress disorder* is the psychological and emotional reaction to an extremely stressful and disturbing experience such as a battle, rape, fire, or earthquake.

- *To make specific plans for changing certain behaviors*
- *To learn more effective social skills*
- *To learn how to challenge others with care, concern, honesty, and directness*
- *To clarify one's values and decide whether and how to modify them. (pp. 4–5)*

### Task Groups

*Task* or *work groups* are those applying the principles of group dynamics to solve problems, develop ideas, formulate plans, make decision, and achieve goals. Task groups in the macro social environment are formed to meet the needs of individuals, families, groups, organizations, or communities. For example, an agency task group might focus on developing treatment strategies to meet the needs of Eastern European immigrants seeking agency resources. This targets both individuals and families. Another task group might include social services personnel and representatives from community groups coordinating a neighborhood watch program aimed at preventing crime. This task group works on behalf of various neighborhood groups and the entire community. Still another organizational task group might consist of representatives from various departments to review the agency's policy manual and recommend changes. This task group serves the organization.

The main difference between task and treatment groups is that the task group's aim is to achieve a desired goal or to implement a change in the group's external environment. In contrast, a treatment group's purpose is to alter group members' behaviors or attitudes in the internal group environment (Toseland & Horton, 2008). Highlight 5.4 discusses task groups, which fall into three categories, those meeting client, organizational, and community needs (Toseland & Rivas, 2012).

Focus on Critical Thinking 5.3 urges you to consider the types of groups with which you've been involved. They may include task or treatment groups.

---

## HIGHLIGHT 5.4    TASK GROUPS IN SOCIAL WORK

Task groups are often found in organizations and communities. They serve the needs of clients, organizations, or communities. Toseland and Rivas (2012) identify the various types:

> Task groups with the primary purpose of serving client needs include teams, treatment conferences, and staff development groups. Task groups with the primary purpose of serving organizational needs include committees, cabinets, and boards of directors. Task groups with a primary purpose of serving community needs include social action groups, coalitions, and delegate councils. (p. 29)

### Task Groups Serving Client Needs

1. *Team:* A group of two or more people gathered together to work collaboratively and interdependently to achieve a designated purpose (Daft, 2012; Toseland & Rivas, 2012).

   *Example:* A team of social workers in a Veterans Health Administration (VHA) hospital[4] where social workers assigned to the temporary housing unit for homeless vets, a substance abuse counseling unit, and the hospital surgical unit work together on behalf of a homeless vet who is an alcoholic and has serious kidney malfunctioning.

2. *Treatment conference:* A group that meets to establish, monitor, and coordinate service plans on behalf of a client system (Fatout & Rose, 1995; Toseland & Rivas, 2012).

   *Example:* A group of professionals (including a social worker, psychologist, psychiatrist, physician, teacher, and unit counselor) at a residential treatment center[5] for children with severe behavioral and emotional problems meeting to discuss the progress of a client residing there and to make recommendations for future treatment.

3. *Staff-development groups:* A group that comes together "to improve services to clients by developing, updating, and refreshing workers' skills. Staff development groups provide workers with an opportunity to learn about new treatment approaches, resources, and community services; to practice new skills; and to review and learn from their previous work with clients" (Toseland & Rivas, 2012, p. 34).

   *Example:* A group of social workers and other counseling professionals who work at a mental health clinic attend a series of seminars about the use and effects of various psychotropic drugs (drugs that affect the mind and behavior).

### Task Groups Serving Organizational Needs

4. *Committee:* A group of persons "delegated to consider, investigate, take action on, or report on some matter" (Daft, 2012; Mish, 2008, p. 250).

   *Example:* A group of staff representatives appointed to investigate, assess, and make

*(continued)*

## HIGHLIGHT 5.4 (continued)

recommendations about the quality of food served in a nursing home.

5. *Cabinet:* A group formed "to provide advice and expertise about policy issues to chief executive officers or other high-level administrators. Policies, procedures, and practices that affect the entire organization are discussed, developed, or modified in cabinets before being announced by a senior administrative officer" (Toseland & Rivas, 2012, pp. 36–37).

    *Example:* "A weekly meeting of supervisory social work staff and the director of social services in a large municipal hospital" (Toseland & Rivas, 2012, p. 37).

6. *Board of directors:* "A group of people authorized to formulate the organization's mission, objectives, and policies, in addition to overseeing the organization's ongoing activities. A board of directors also has ultimate control over the agency's higher administration, including its executive director or chief executive officer" (Kirst-Ashman, 2014, p. 145).

    *Example:* "Members of the governing board of a family service agency" (Toseland & Rivas, 2012, p. 37).

### Task Groups Serving Community Needs

7. *Social action group:* A group formed to engage in some planned-change effort to modify or improve aspects of their macro social or physical environment (Staples, 2004; Toseland & Rivas, 2012).

    *Example:* A group of agency workers and clients who join forces to conduct a letter-writing campaign to legislators to place stoplights at a dangerous intersection.

8. *Coalition:* An alliance "of individuals, groups, and organizations with similar goals that become more influential and powerful when united" (Kirst-

Ashman, 2014, p. 173). "Coalition members agree to pursue common goals, which they believe cannot be achieved by any of the members acting alone" (Toseland & Rivas, 2012, p. 40).

    *Example:* "A group of family planning and community health-care clinics who have formed a pro-choice coalition to influence state and federal legislation on abortion" (Toseland & Rivas, 2012, p. 40).

9. *Delegate council:* A group of representatives from a series of agencies or units within a single agency that meet to discuss issues of mutual concern. Representatives may be elected by their constituencies or appointed by agency decision makers; goals may include "facilitating interagency communication and cooperation, studying communitywide social issues or social problems, engaging in collective social action, and governing large organizations" (Toseland & Rivas, 2012, p. 41).

    *Example:* A group of professionals working in rape crisis centers throughout a state, with each agency designating a representative to meet in the council to discuss education and treatment issues.

[4]The Veterans Health Administration offers veterans an extensive array of health and mental health services. These include inpatient hospital care; outpatient health care; in-home care; nursing home care; medication; reproductive health care for women; and inpatient and outpatient (intensive or regular) mental health counseling to meet many needs including readjustment after return from active duty, mental disorders, substance use disorders, and suicide prevention (U.S. Department of Veterans Affairs, 2011b).

[5]Discussed more thoroughly in a later chapter, a *residential treatment center* is an agency that provides children with serious emotional and behavioral problems with residential round-the-clock care; education (often with an emphasis on special education); interpersonal skills training; and individual, group, and sometimes family therapy.

## Social Work Practice with Organizations and Communities

**Macro practice** is intervention involving organizations and communities (macro systems). Historically, **community organization** has been the term used to refer to macro practice in social work that is a specific area of practice in its own right. The methods and directions of social work practice have changed and evolved, just as the economic and social realities of the times have drastically changed. However, reviewing the historical perspective on community practice will help us to understand the significance of community assessment and work today.

EP 5c, 7b, 7d, 8c

## PARTICIPATION IN GROUPS

Think of a task or treatment group in which you've participated and consider the following.

### Critical Thinking Questions

What kind of group was it? What was the group's purpose? To what extent

**EP 7a**

was the group effective (i.e., did it achieve its goals)? Why or why not? How would you describe the group's functioning? Who led the group and how well was it directed? How could the group's functioning have been improved?

Traditional methods of community organization engaged in by social workers included social action, social planning, and locality development (Rothman, 2001). **Social action** is coordinated effort to advocate for change in a social institution to benefit a specific population (e.g., homeless people), solve a social problem, correct unfairness (e.g., racism),[6] or enhance people's well-being. Social action applies macro-practice skills to advocate for people in local, state, national, and global communities. Frequently social action can be used to remedy imbalances of power.

**Social planning** involves "a technical process of problem-solving regarding substantive social problems, such as delinquency, housing, and mental health" (Rothman, 2001, p. 31). Experts or consultants work, usually with designated community leaders, to solve specific problems. People in the general community have little, if any, participation in or input into the problem-solving process. For example, a city might call in an urban renewal expert to recommend what should be done with a deteriorating area in the community.

**Locality development** emphasizes "community change ... pursued through broad participation by a wide spectrum of people at the local community level in determining goals and taking civic action" (Rothman, 2001, p. 29). The idea is to involve as many people as possible within the community in a democratic manner to define their goals and help themselves. Locality development fits extremely well

with social work values because individual dignity, participation, and free choice are emphasized.

### Macro Practice Today

Today macro practice remains a major thrust of generalist social work. The basic concept of community is just as important as ever. However, Rothman (2007) proposes a new outlook more appropriate to current macro practice that calls for "multi modes of intervention" (p. 11). Two new ideas predominate.

**EP 3a, 3b, 5c, 8d**

One major initiative is that the traditional three community organization methods should be updated to reflect a modification in focus. First, "social advocacy" should replace social action (Rothman, 2007, p. 12). "**Social advocacy** deems the application of pressure as the best course of action to take against people or institutions that may have [brought about] ... the problem or that stand in the way of its solution—which frequently involves promoting equity or social justice. When interests clash in this way, conflict is a given" (p. 12). Advocacy becomes the focus of attention.

"Planning and policy practice" then replace the traditional social planning approach (Rothman. 2007, p. 12). Planning continues to involve "proposing and enacting particular solutions" (p. 12). **Policy practice** entails "efforts to change policies in legislative, agency, and community settings, whether by establishing new policies, improving existing ones, or defeating the policy initiatives of other people" (Jansson, 2011, p. 15). Establishing policy becomes the objective.

"Community capacity development" is substituted for community development (Rothman, 2007, p. 12).

---

[6]*Racism* is "a belief that race is the primary determinant of human traits and capacities and that racial differences produce an inherent superiority of a particular race," most often resulting in prejudice or discrimination (Mish, 2008, p. 1024).

*Community capacity development* assumes that change is best accomplished when the people affected by problems are empowered with the knowledge and skills needed to understand their problems, and then work cooperatively together to overcome them. *Thus there is a premium on consensus as a tactic and on social solidarity [unity including diverse community groups that is based on mutual interests, support, and goals] as [a means] … and outcome. (p. 12)*

Here **community capacity** (the potential use of the community's inherent strengths, resources, citizen participation, and leadership) is stressed.

The second primary initiative posed for contemporary macro practice involves the flexibility of mixing various aspects of these three approaches to get things done. Rothman (2007) reflects that macro practice is often a complex process that requires emphasizing various aspects of these three approaches depending on the situation. For example, planning and policy practice may require varying degrees of social advocacy. **Advocacy**, of course, involves stepping forward on the behalf of the client system in order to promote fair and equitable treatment or gain needed resources. **Policy advocacy** is "policy practice that aims to help powerless groups, such as women, children, poor people, persons of color, gay men and lesbians, and people with disabilities to improve their resources and opportunities" (Jansson, 2011, p. 15).

Rothman (2007) provides several examples of people undertaking policy advocacy to improve policies that affect groups at risk of harm; these policy advocates include:

*Dr. David Kessler, who as head of the Federal Drug Administration clashed with the pharmaceutical companies on behalf of safe and affordable medications for patients; Dr. C. Everettt Koop, who as Surgeon General, stood up to the cigarette companies in the first major effort to warn the public about the serious health dangers in smoking; and Peter Edelman, who faced off with the Clinton administration over sizable service cuts affecting welfare recipients. (p. 21)*

Another example of a more flexible combination of methods involves community capacity development with an emphasis on planning. Rothman (2007) explains:

*Classic [community] capacity development typically has the practitioner starting with a blank page and encouraging residents to decide what situations within their community bother them the most and then what changes they want to initiate.…*

*Community economic [capacity] development [that emphasizes planning], on the other hand, starts with a concrete agenda and organizing mechanisms. It believes that what distressed communities need most is an upgrade of economic conditions. Residents are called on to mount programs and actions that will accomplish that. According to Soifer (2002), this means concentrating on housing development, land development, job creation, and setting up more relevant financial institutions—primarily banks. (p. 25)*

### Skills in Macro Practice

Necessary macro skills involve at least three facets. First, agency or public social policies may require change. For example, social workers may advocate to change a policy that requires all persons receiving public assistance to undergo mandatory drug testing—a practice that is expensive, condescending, and invasive.

A second important macro skill entails initiating and conducting projects within agency or community contexts. An example of a project is fundraising for homeless families in need of food and clothing. Another is initiating an in-service training program to teach agency staff a new treatment technique. (**In-service training programs** are educational sessions provided by an agency for its staff to develop their skills or improve their effectiveness.)

A third significant macro skill concerns planning and implementing new social service programs within an agency or community. An example is development of a program to educate students on a college campus about date rape. Another is developing a new recreation and field trip program for residents in a nursing home.

### Generalist Practice: A Multi-Level Process

The point of generalist social work practice is to seek change at all levels of practice, depending on what the client system needs. Many times, a social worker will simultaneously pursue a combination of goals involving change at the individual, family, group, organizational, or community level.

**EP 7d**

For example, a teacher refers Ralph, age 8, to Juanita, the school social worker. The teacher reports that Ralph is consistently mounting fellow students on the playground in a manner resembling sexual intercourse (more vulgarly referred to as "humping"). Ralph also makes frequent sexual comments and uses sexual language quite inappropriate for his age. Juanita suspects the possibility of sexual abuse. (A later chapter on child welfare discusses child sexual abuse in more depth.)

At the individual (micro) level, Juanita talks with Ralph about what's occurring in his life at home. She informs the school principal, Adolf, that she intends to report the situation to Child Protective Services, which would initiate a more thorough investigation. Adolf forbids Juanita to make the referral on the basis that there is not enough evidence. Why cause trouble when you don't have to? But in her state, Juanita is required to report any *suspected* child abuse (which includes sexual abuse). Juanita knows that it is her ethical responsibility to report Ralph's behavior.

At the organizational and community (macro) levels, Juanita must address the issue with Adolf and possibly the School Board, which supervises Adolf. The school (a macro system) must change so that it becomes responsive to instances of possible abuse instead of simply ignoring them. In the event that Ralph's victimization is proved, family counseling may be called for at the micro/mezzo level and possibly group therapy for Ralph at the mezzo level.

# Professional Organizations and Associations in Social Work LO 4

There are many professional organizations within social work. They may involve social work practitioners or social work educators. We will describe two of the largest social work organizations here— the National Association of Social Workers (NASW) and the Council on Social Work Education (WCSWE). Subsequently, some of the other social work organizations will be identified.

## The National Association of Social Workers

The National Association of Social Workers (NASW) has already been mentioned several times, especially with respect to its *Code of Ethics*.

Established in 1955, NASW is the major social work organization with the largest and broadest membership in the profession. Persons holding bachelor's or master's degrees in social work and students in accredited social work programs can join.

NASW fulfills at least five purposes. First, membership in a professional organization lends credibility. Most, if not all, established professions have an organization to which members can belong. Such membership bolsters members' professional identity, helps them identify with other members, and enhances the visibility of a profession.

EP 1c, 5c, 8c

NASW's second purpose is to provide opportunities for networking. State, regional, and national conferences and meetings enable members to talk with each other and share news and ideas. Such meetings also provide a means for finding out about new career and job opportunities.

NASW's third purpose is to provide membership services. These include *Social Work,* a quarterly journal that addresses various aspects of practice: *NASW News,* a national newspaper published almost monthly that focuses on relevant research, social welfare policy and service issues, and social workers' accomplishments around the country and the world: and newsletters published by some state chapters.

NASW's fourth purpose is to sponsor organized efforts for lobbying on behalf of socially responsible social welfare policies and services. NASW exerts influence in support of causes and political agendas concurrent with professional social work values. It has also helped states establish licensing regulations for social workers. Highlight 5.5 discusses the importance of licensing for social workers and identifies the common levels of licensure.

NASW's fifth purpose is to publish policy statements on various issues (e.g., youth suicide, health care, people with disabilities, affirmative action, and environmental policy) to help guide members in their practice (NASW, 2012).

## The Council on Social Work Education

The Council on Social Work Education (CSWE) is the body that accredits bachelor's and master's programs in social work education. A doctorate of social work and doctorate of philosophy in social

| HIGHLIGHT **5.5** | SOCIAL WORK LICENSURE AND CATEGORIES OF SOCIAL WORK PRACTICE | **LO 5** |

Every state, the District of Columbia, Puerto Rico, the Virgin Islands, and every Canadian province have laws that define and regulate social work practice, involving some form of licensure or certification (Association of Social Work Boards [ASWB], 2008). Social work licensure means that one has fulfilled designated requirements to practice social work in a particular state. Certification is used instead of licensure in a number of states. Some feel that *licensure* is a stronger word, implying more advanced skills than *certification.* For example, a social worker with a bachelor's degree might be certified, and one with a master's degree licensed.

EP 1

Many states have several levels of licensure; they may require a designated level of educational attainment, an examination, and possibly some work experience (at least for higher levels) to qualify for each level (SocialWork Licensure.org, 2014). A fee is charged to take the exam.

Typically, there are five categories of practice that jurisdictions may legally regulate (ASWB, 2014).

1. *Associate:* Associate degree (Note that this category involves use of the same examination used for the Bachelors level, but requires a lower score for passing. Few jurisdictions offer the Associate option [ASWB, 2014]).
2. *Bachelors:* Baccalaureate social work (BSW) degree upon graduation.
3. *Masters:* Master's degree in social work (MSW) with no post-degree experience.
4. *Advanced Generalist:* MSW with two years of postmaster's supervised experience.
5. *Clinical:* MSW with two years of post-master's direct clinical social work experience.

The Association of Social Work Boards (ASWB), initiated in 1979, established and sustains licensing examinations for social workers in all 50 states (SocialWork Licensure.org, 2014); the ASWB also maintains licensing examinations in the District of Columbia, the U.S. Virgin Islands, and all ten Canadian provinces (ASWB, 2013).[7] Although some states offer licenses or certification for only one level of practice, most offer such validation at two or more levels of practice.

Nationally, the following are true about social work licensure (SocialWorkLicensure.org, 2014):

- All states require clinical social workers to be licensed.

- Most states require social workers with master's degrees to be licensed, regardless of whether they perform clinical work.
- Many states require baccalaureate social workers to be licensed.
- Titles for various levels of licensure may vary from state to state. For example, a "Clinical Social Worker" in one state might be called a "Licensed Social Worker," a "Licensed Clinical Social Worker," or an "Independent Social Worker" in other states.

The structure of examinations and specific requirements for each level vary from state to state, so people interested in becoming a social worker should explore the regulations in their own state, province, or jurisdiction. ASWB examinations for each level include 170 multiple-choice questions that are administered electronically and provide four hours for test completion (ASWB, 2014).

Because of the differences in requirements from one jurisdiction to another, licensure does not automatically transfer from one locale to another (ASWB, 2011). Social workers with licensure in one state who want similar recognition in some other state must complete the application process in that other state. A major purpose of licensing is to protect clients from unqualified service providers and maintain the legitimacy of the profession (ASWB, 2013). Ginsberg (2001) comments on the significance of a social work degree with respect to licensing and getting jobs:

Although there are many professions engaged in human services work, it is becoming the law in most states that persons may not refer to themselves as social workers or hold a position designated as a social work job unless they have a social work degree. State licensing and regulation laws ... provide legal protection for the title of social worker. But even without legal regulation, many social work employers want employees with social work preparation because they understand the social services system and have developed some of the skills needed to practice social work. (p. 44)

### Additional Credentials

Whereas licensing represents minimal standards to protect clients as consumers of services at the state level,

*(continued)*

**HIGHLIGHT 5.5 *(continued)***

the National Association of Social Workers (NASW) credentials represent an "added badge of accomplishment" (SocialWorkLicensure.org, 2014). After receiving an educational degree and earning a professional license, "credentials (in the form of professional certifications)" are voluntary; they "denote professional commitment and achievement and represent a 'license plus' feature of certifying knowledge and experience that meets or exceeds excellence in social work" (NASW, 2014b). The advanced practice specialty certifications reflect an expanded depth of knowledge and skills in some specialized domain of practice.[8] Advanced NASW credentials include the following (Note that each credential is followed by "MSW" or "BSW and MSW" to denote the applicable educational level or levels) (NASW, 2014b):

- Academy of Certified Social Workers (ACSW), instituted in 1960, "the most widely recognized and respected social work credential," designating social workers who earn it as "qualified providers of social services." (MSW)
- Diplomate in Clinical Social Work (DCSW), demonstrating "the highest level of expertise and excellence for clinical social workers" and representing "leaders in the area of clinical social work." (MSW)
- Advanced practice specialty credentials are available in the following nine areas:
  - Addictions (MSW)

- Case Management (BSW and MSW)
- Clinical (MSW)
- Education (School Social Work) (MSW)
- Gerontology (BSW and MSW)
- Health Care (MSW)
- Hospice and Palliative (BSW and MSW)
- Military (Military Service Members, Veterans, and Their Families) (BSW and MSW)
- Youth and Family (BSW and MSW)

- Advanced practice specialty credentials may include several categories. For example, within the Gerontology specialty area, MSWs may apply for a Clinical Social Worker in Gerontology (CSW-G) or an Advanced Social Worker in Gerontology (ASW-G), whereas BSWs may seek a Social Worker in Gerontology (SW-G) designation. Each category for each advanced practice specialty credential has its own criteria for eligibility. Such criteria include a specified social work degree and NASW membership; additional criteria may consist of practice experience with a specific client population, post-graduate continuing education hours, and a state license.

[7]More information can be obtained at http://www.aswb.org and http://www.socialworklicensure.org/articles/aswb-exam.html.

[8]For more information on specific requirements for advanced credentials, see http://www.naswdc.org/credentials/default.asp.

work are also available, but CSWE has determined that they need not be accredited. CSWE's membership is composed primarily of social work educators but also includes practitioners. CSWE develops guidelines for the social work curriculum as explained in Chapter 1. In social work, **accreditation** is the official confirmation that a school, college, or program fulfills the necessary requirements in curricular development, program structure, resources, and academic achievement to assume that status.

It is important to make sure a social work program is accredited. To be eligible for licensure or certification, many states require graduation from an accredited program. As of March 2015, the United States had 504 accredited baccalaureate (BSW) programs with 16 more in candidacy for accreditation, and 235 master's (MSW) programs with 19 more in candidacy (CSWE, 2014). There were 98 doctoral (Ph.D. or DSW) programs in the United States as of June 2014 (GradSchools.com, 2014).

## Numerous Other Social Work Organizations

Numerous other organizations reflect more specific facets or subsets of social work. They can focus on client populations, areas of expertise or interest, or membership in special groups. Examples include the Association for Community Organization and Social Administration, the Association of VA Social Workers, the Latino Social Workers Organization, the Rural Social Work Caucus, and the School Social Work Association of America. Forty-one social work organizations and how to access them are identified on the Social Work Portal, sponsored by NASW, at http://www.naswdc.org/swportal/.

# Careers in Social Work    LO 6

Because social workers are employed in such varied areas of human life, it is difficult to gather accurate data on what members of the entire profession are doing. The Bureau of Labor Statistics predicts that between 2012 and 2022 the number of social workers will increase by 19%, "which is faster than the average for all occupations" (U.S. Department of Labor, 2014).

Highlight 5.6 summarizes the findings of two surveys addressing the fields of practice in which social workers are employed. Ongoing research by a group of social work educators and researchers called the Social Work Educational Assessment Project (SWEAP, formerly called the Baccalaureate Education Assessment Project [BEAP]) regularly collects information about BSW graduates. Some of the data gathered reflects BSW employment both at graduation and two years thereafter (hereafter referred to as *alumni*) (Hull, 2004; Buchan, Hull, Rogers, Rodenhiser, & Smith, 2004). Another survey, sponsored by the National Association of Social Workers (NASW), reviews the major fields of practice in which MSWs (full-time) tend to be employed (O'Neill, 2003). Respondents in this study were all NASW members, the vast majority of whom have MSWs (versus BSWs as their highest degree or degrees in other fields). Note that dashes in the chart reflect lack of data due to different data-gathering techniques.

| HIGHLIGHT **5.6** | EMPLOYMENT SETTINGS FOR SOCIAL WORKERS BY FIELDS OF PRACTICE | | |
|---|---|---|---|
| | BSWs (Employment at Graduation) (%) | BSWs (2 Years Postgraduation) (%) | MSWs (%) |
| Corrections/criminal justice | 34.5 | 3.0 | — |
| Child welfare/child protective services | 12.6 | 18.7 | — |
| Child welfare/family | — | — | 7 |
| Youth services | 7.1 | — | — |
| Mental/behavioral health | 6.1 | 14.9 | 37 |
| Aging/geriatrics | 5.4 | 11.1 | 4 |
| Family services | 5.3 | 7.9 | — |
| Mental retardation/developmental disabilities | 5.0 | 6.0 | — |
| Alcohol, drug, or substance abuse | 4.4 | 3.9 | 3 |
| Crisis intervention | 2.9 | 4.3 | — |
| School social work | 2.6 | 5.5 | 5 |
| Health/medical care | 2.5 | 7.3 | 8 |
| Violence/victim services | 2.2 | 2.0 | 1 |
| Education/training | 1.7 | 2.1 | — |
| Housing | 1.2 | 1.3 | — |
| Public assistance/public welfare | 1.0 | 1.5 | — |
| Adult protective services | 0.7 | 0.7 | — |
| Community planning | 0.7 | 1.5 | <1 |
| Group services | 0.6 | 0.9 | — |
| Rehabilitation | 0.5 | 1.0 | — |
| Grief/bereavement | 0.3 | 0.7 | — |
| Income maintenance | 0.2 | 0.3 | — |
| Occupational/EAP[9] | 0.1 | 0.4 | 1 |
| Adolescents | — | — | 3 |
| Disabilities | — | — | 1 |

[9]EAP stands for employee assistance program; these are services provided by organizations that focus on the prevention and treatment of workers' mental health and adjustment problems that interfere with their work performance. Chapter 13 describes them more fully.

Be cautious when interpreting this information, however, because a major difference between the two surveys involves social workers' years of experience. For example, BSW respondents have only 2 years of experience at the time of the survey, whereas MSWs have a median of 16 years ("Survey Data," 2004). (The *median* is the midpoint of a range of figures where half the values fall above the median and half fall below.) There's no way to tell how results might differ if both groups had identical lengths of experience.

Note that the two surveys reflect some different categories because data were not gathered in identical ways. The categories listed here for MSWs reflect only those in which the most social workers were employed. Because of this and because some responses didn't fit clearly into defined categories, none of the columns add up to 100%.

It's interesting to note that few social workers (of BSWs, 1.2% at graduation and 1.8% two years after) are employed in public welfare and income maintenance. This refutes the stereotype of a social worker sitting in a drab office reviewing applications for welfare checks. Rather, the BSW survey reflects the wide range of practice contexts where social workers find employment.

Let's focus for a moment on the differences in employment settings experienced by BSWs who have jobs at graduation and what they're doing as alumni two years later. Figure 5.1 highlights the differences in practice areas where most BSWs find jobs. Whereas more than a third of people at graduation find jobs in corrections, for two-year alumni this drops to only 3%. What are the implications? Might it be that it's relatively easy to find jobs in corrections, but most people discover they don't like it and leave quickly?

The second most common job placement for BSWs at graduation is child welfare and protective services: 12.6% of BSWs start out there. Two years later this figure jumps to 18.7% of BSWs surveyed. BSW alumni also shift in greater numbers to the fields of mental health, aging, and health care. Smaller increases occur in family services, school social work, developmental disabilities, and crisis intervention.

Figure 5.2 compares BSW alumni with MSWs concerning their fields of practice. Three major trends immediately surface. First, the largest proportion of MSWs (37%) work in mental health. Second, most BSWs work in the child welfare and family

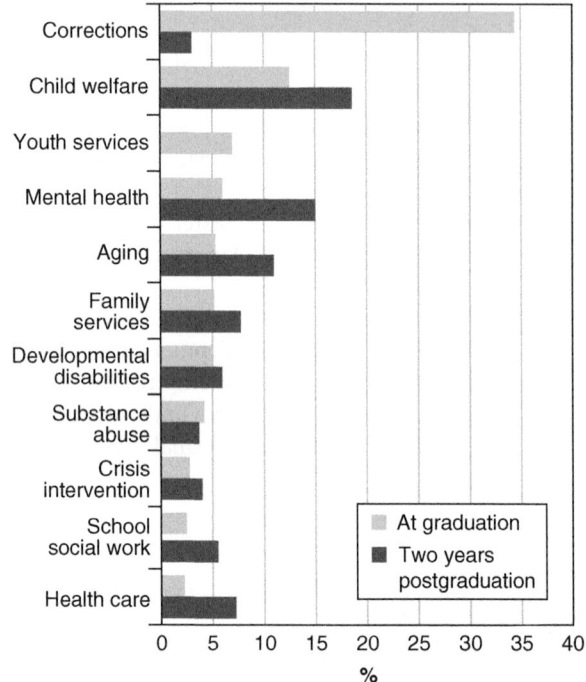

**FIG-5-1** Employment of BSW Graduates

arena (26.6%).[10] Third, BSWs are also somewhat more likely to work in the areas of aging and disabilities than their MSW counterparts.[11] Note that although fewer than 1% of MSWs cited "community development" as their major practice field, 4% indicated that they were engaged in this area to some extent.

An alternative approach to examining where social workers are employed involves the structure and funding sources of the agency. An earlier part of this chapter discussed public and private organizational settings. Figure 5.3 depicts where BSWs (at their first social work job) and MSWs are employed in the public and private sectors (Hull, 2004; O'Neill, 2003). This can provide clues regarding where to seek jobs.

Most social workers at both the BSW and MSW level are employed in private social service agencies, with the rest (more than a third) working in public

---

[10]Note that the categories in the BSW study of *child welfare/ protective services* and *family services* were combined to reflect this result. The intent is to compare this figure with the MSW study's category of *child welfare/family*.

[11]Note that the BSW study uses the term *mental retardation/ developmental disabilities*, whereas the MSW study simply uses the word *disabilities*.

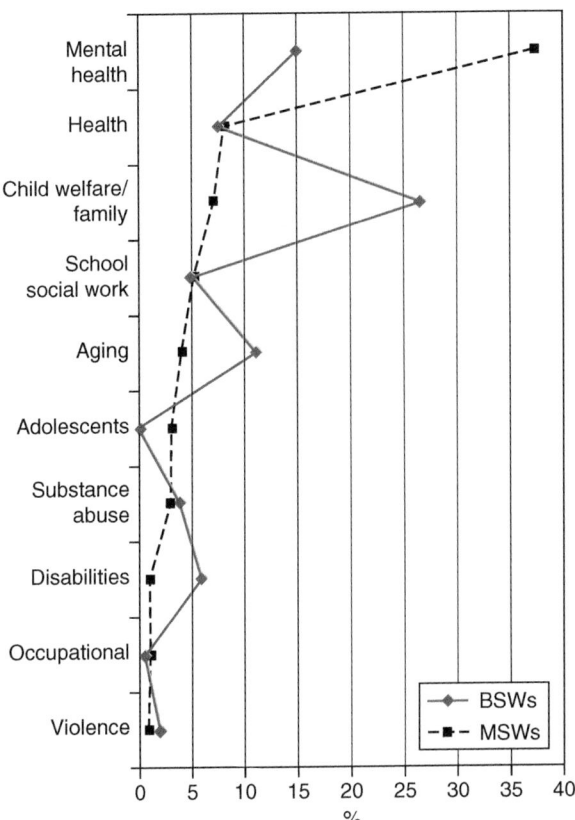

**FIG-5-2** BSW and MSW Fields of Practice

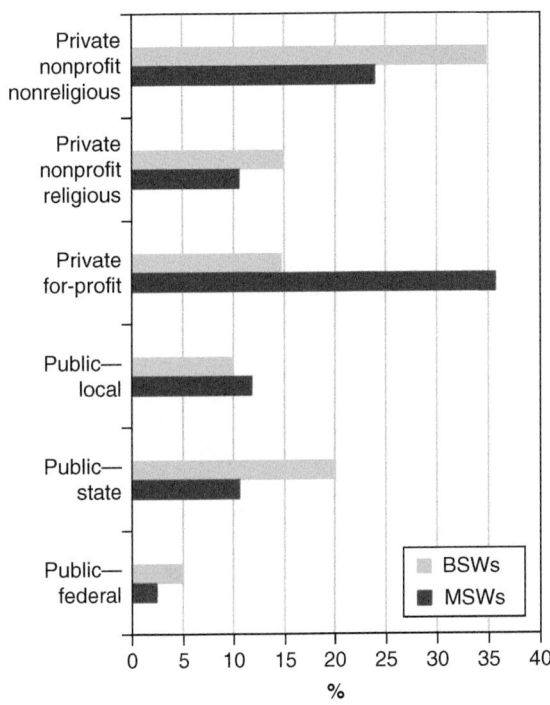

**FIG-5-3** Public- and Private-sector Employment

agencies. More than one-third of BSWs get their first social work job in private *nonprofit* nonreligious settings (e.g., family service agencies, Planned Parenthood, United Way). In contrast, more than one-third of MSWs work in private *for-profit* agencies. This probably reflects the significant number of MSWs providing private therapy in agencies where a major goal is to make a profit. Note that BSWs are also more likely than MSWs to work in public *state* agencies. The smaller percentages of practitioners working for the federal government include both military and nonmilitary jobs, with military jobs being less common.

Services provided to clients by BSWs and MSWs also vary somewhat, as illustrated in Figures 5.4 and Figures 5.5, respectively. Data were gathered differently in the two surveys, so the charts use different formats to illustrate results. BSW alumni were asked to cite their four prioritized major roles; Figure 5.4 summarizes what they felt their first major role was

(Hull, 2004). More than 38% identified case management (the coordination of needed services provided by any number of agencies, organizations, or facilities) as their primary role. Advocacy (speaking out on behalf of clients to promote fair and equitable treatment or gain needed resources) was cited by more than one-quarter of respondents. Other roles mentioned were counseling, identified by almost 12%; administration, almost 8%; coordination, almost 5%; brokering (linking client systems to needed resources), almost 2%; and providing education and training, almost 2%. Other roles (consultant, mediator, facilitator, and so on) were identified by fewer than 1% each.

The NASW survey asked MSWs what services they typically provided to their clients without prioritizing them ("Survey Data," 2004). As Figure 5.5 illustrates, 81% identified counseling, 23% information and referral, 22% screening and assessment, 20% case management, 14% crisis management, and 7% medication adherence assistance services. It's notable that "social workers in organizational settings provided more information/referral, screening/ assessment, case management, and crisis interventions than those in private practice settings" (p. 8).

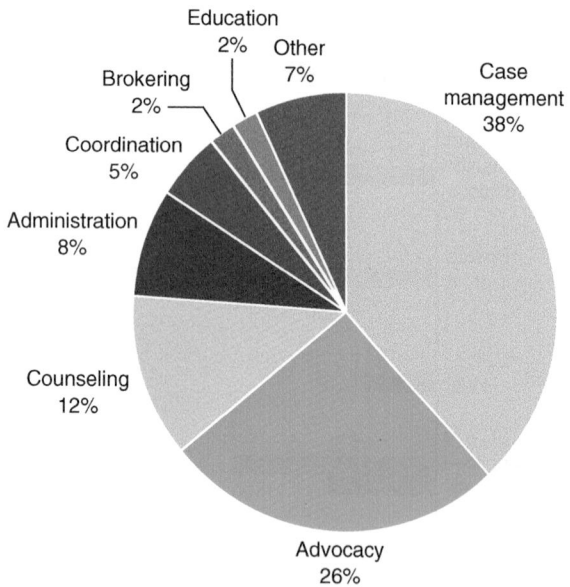

**FIG-5-4** BSWs' Major Roles

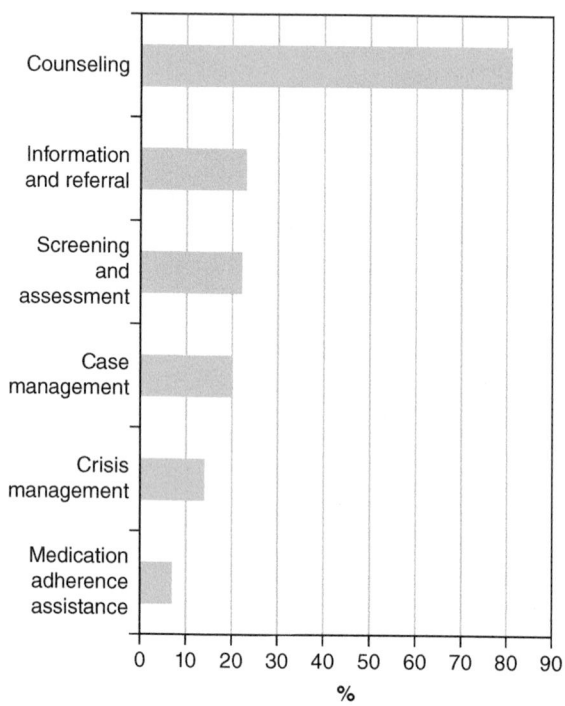

**FIG-5-5** MSW Services to Clients

Private practice focuses on providing some type of counseling or therapy, usually within an office context, to address some psychological issue or problem for a specified fee. Twenty-three percent of MSWs surveyed work only in private practice, 18% work both in private practice and organizational settings, and 45% work only in organizational settings ("Survey Data," 2004, p. 8).

When we compare Figures 5.4 and 5.5, at least two implications are evident. Both BSWs and MSWs provide counseling and case management.

However, BSWs are much more likely to view case management as a major role, whereas MSWs tend to focus on counseling. Second, more than one-quarter of BSWs identify advocacy as a major function, which we have established as a critical basis of the profession.

## Social Work Salaries

When looking at salary data, remember that there is tremendous variation in salary from one geographic location, field of practice, and type of job (e.g., direct service versus administration) to another. Standards of living (including rent, utilities, and taxes) vary dramatically between parts of the country. Take this into consideration when reading the salary data discussed here. The idea is to give you

a general picture of what to expect as a BSW entering the field and as a seasoned MSW who has been in the field many years.

It makes sense that more education usually provides greater opportunities and potentially higher salaries. BSWs tend to work at the foundation level of practice with skills that apply to social work fields of practice across the board, whereas MSWs tend to specialize. People with MSW degrees earn significantly more than those with BSWs (O'Neill, 2003; NASW, 2010; Pace, 2010).

The Bureau of Labor Statistics[12] cites annual earning information for social workers (U.S. Department of Labor, 2014). However, please note that it does not distinguish between BSWs and MSWs. It also divides the fields of practice differently than the other surveys, structuring information within four major categories of social workers. These include: (1) child, family, and school, (2) health care, (3) mental health and substance abuse, and (4) social

---

[12]For further information, you may access the Bureau of Labor Statistics Website at http://www.bls.gov/ooh/community-and-social-service/social-workers.htm.

workers in other positions (U.S. Department of Labor, 2014):

1. *"Child, family, and school social workers"* (47% of the total) "protect vulnerable children and help families in need of assistance. They help parents find services, such as child care, or apply for benefits, such as food stamps. They intervene when children are in danger of neglect or abuse. Some help arrange adoptions, locate foster families, or work to get families back together." Clinical social workers provide mental health counseling and therapy to children and families to help these clients deal with life crises, adjustment problems, and changes. School social workers "work with teachers, parents, and school administrators to develop plans and strategies to improve students' academic performance and social development." School social workers often "deal with problems such as aggressive behavior, bullying, or frequent absences from school."

2. *"Health-care social workers"* (24% of the total) "help patients understand their diagnosis and make the necessary adjustments to their lifestyle, housing, or health care." For example, a social worker might help a client adjust to a change in living conditions due to health-related issues and resulting health-care needs. This might involve moving from a hospital back to the home environment. These social workers also may provide information about available services and make needed referrals. Additionally, they may offer services such as support groups for clients striving to cope with health-care issues. Finally, practice in this category might involve working with other medical staff to help them understand how health issues affect clients' psychological state, coping ability, and overall adjustment. Three specialties within the health-care category are notable. First, *geriatric social workers* work with older adults and their families such as helping clients and their families adjust to nursing home placement. Second, *hospice and palliative care social workers* help clients "adjust to serious, chronic, or terminal illnesses. *Palliative care* focuses on relieving or preventing pain and other symptoms associated with serious illness. *Hospice* is a type of palliative care for people who are dying." Third, *medical social workers*

"in hospitals help patients and their families by linking patients with resources in the hospital and in their own community." They may assist in developing discharge plans, refer clients to agencies providing needed services, run support groups, and do follow-up with clients to determine their post-discharge condition.

3. *"Mental health and substance abuse social workers"* (almost 19% of the total) "help clients with mental illnesses or addictions." They may link clients with services such as support groups. Clinical social workers may provide individual, family, or group therapy.

4. *Other social workers* (10%) have positions that do not fall neatly into the aforementioned three categories. These jobs might include other social work positions in local government, state government, and individual and family services.

The median annual pay for all social workers, including BSWs and MSWs, is $44,200 ($21.25 per hour) (Bureau of Labor Statistics, 2014). Figures 5.6 through 5.8 report the median annual earnings for: child, family, and school social workers; health-care social workers; and mental health and substance abuse social workers, respectively. The graphs reflect those areas of practice within each of the three major categories that employ the largest number of social workers in that category. Bars denote areas of practice and are ordered in terms of the number of social workers employed, from greatest to least. For example, in Figure 5.6 the first bar represents "Individual and family services," which employs the greatest number of social workers in the "Child, family, and school social workers" category. "State government" employs the second greatest number, "Local government" the third greatest number, and so on.

Figure 5.9 compares median annual earnings in all three categories reflected in Figures 5.6 through 5.8, in addition to the 10% of social workers not fitting in any of these categories (Bureau of Labor Statistics, 2014). Social workers who work in mental health and substance abuse had median annual earnings of $39,980. Child, family, and school social workers had median annual earnings of $41,530. Health-care social workers had median annual earnings of $49,830. Social workers not falling into any of these categories had median annual incomes of $54,560.

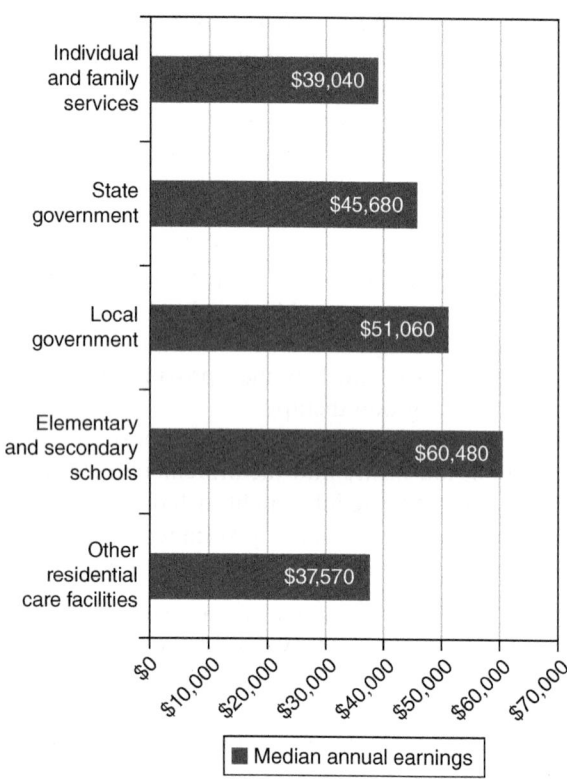

**FIG-5-6** Median Annual Earnings for Child, Family, and School Social Workers, May 2013
*SOURCE:* Bureau of Labor Statistics. (2014). Occupational outlook handbook, May 2013: Child, family, and school social workers. Retrieved from http://www.bls.gov/oes/current/oes211021.htm (Note that more detailed information about this category is available on this Website.)

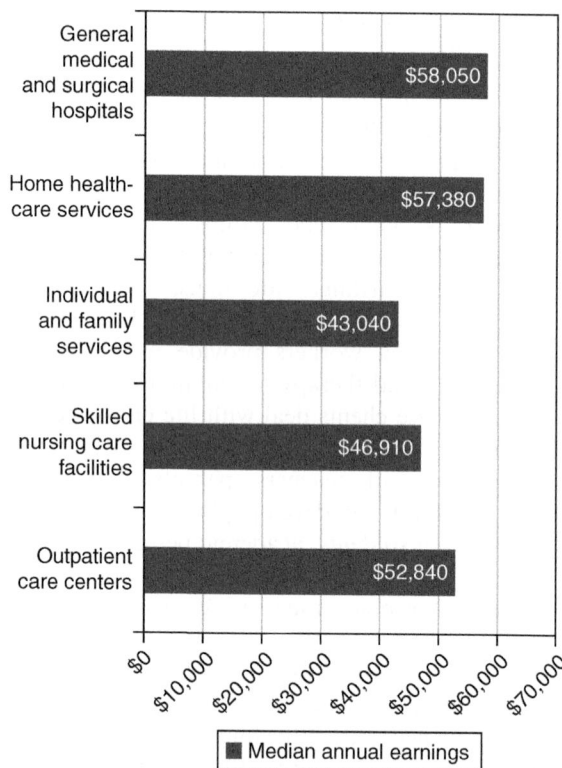

**FIG-5-7** Median Annual Earnings for Health-Care Social Workers, May 2013
*SOURCE:* Bureau of Labor Statistics. (2014). Occupational outlook handbook, May 2013: Healthcare workers. Retrieved from http://www.bls.gov/oes/current/oes211022.htm (Note that more detailed information about this category is available on this Website.)

It's important to remember that salaries fluctuate dramatically by region and state. Variation in cost of living is one major factor. One source relates huge differences in average annual salary by state, based on its reported data from the Bureau of Labor Statistics (Social Work License Map, 2014). The highest average annual salary for mental health and substance abuse social workers was $59,000 ($28.36 per hour) in New Jersey. The lowest for this group was $28,830 ($13.86 per hour) in South Carolina. For child, family, and school social workers, the highest average annual salary was $61,690 ($29.66 per hour) in Connecticut. The lowest for this group was $29,390 ($14.13 per hour) in West Virginia. Health-care social workers earned the most in Washington, D.C., at $66,270 ($31.86 per hour) and the least in Mississippi

at $35,800 ($17.21 per hour). All other social workers not fitting into these three categories earned the most in South Dakota at $65,170 ($31.33 per hour) and the least in New Mexico at $38,360 ($18.44 per hour).

Prior research has established a number of other facts about salary trends ("Practitioners Surveyed," 2003; "Survey Data," 2004). Social workers in private practice (which requires an MSW) earn higher salaries than workers in other organizational contexts. Practicing for longer periods of time as a social worker also is related to higher earnings. Level of degree is yet another variable. Social workers with an MSW degree will generally earn $15,000 more annually than social workers with a BSW degree (NASW, 2010). An additional influential variable

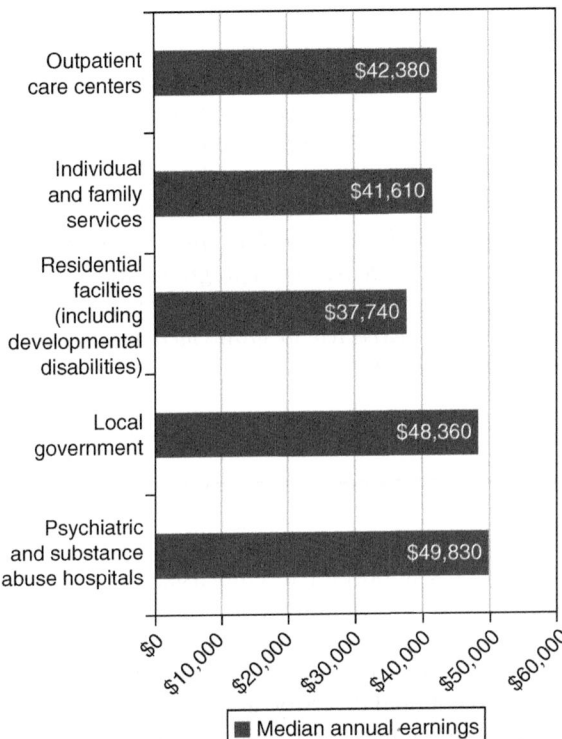

**FIG-5-8** Median Annual Earnings for Mental Health and Substance Abuse Social Workers, May 2013
*Source:* Bureau of Labor Statistics. (2014). Occupational outlook handbook, May 2013: Mental health and substance abuse social workers. Retrieved from http://www.bls.gov/oes/current/oes211023.htm (Note that more detailed information about this category is available on this Website.)

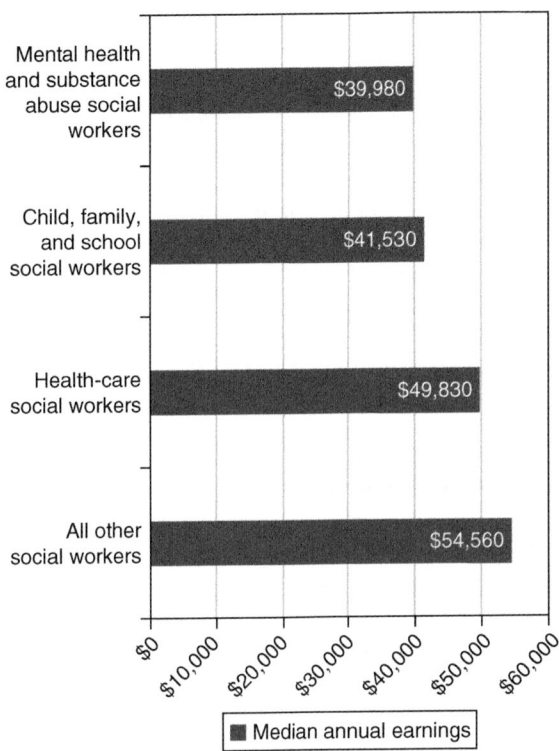

**FIG-5-9** Median Annual Earnings for Social Workers in the Four Major Categories of Practice, May 2012
*Source:* Bureau of Labor Statistics. (2014). Occupational outlook handbook: Social workers. Retrieved from http://www.bls.gov/ooh/community-and-social-service/social-workers.htm (Note that more detailed information about this category is available on this Website.)

concerning salary level involves gender (Brandwein, 2008; Pace, 2010). Employment in professions characterized by a majority of women, such as social work, pays less than occupations where men prevail (Brandwein, 2008). In 2004, male social workers earned 14% more than their female counterparts, even when other variables such as educational level, field of practice, and practice experience were controlled (Brandwein, 2008). The 2009 NASW survey indicated that male social workers' salaries surpassed females' by more than 17% (Pace, 2010). Male social workers' salaries notably exceed the salaries of female social workers in virtually every field of practice and organizational setting; this difference is reflected both in public and private agencies, and among university faculty (NASW Center for Workforce Studies, 2011).

# The Future Employment Outlook for Social Work

According to the Bureau of Labor Statistics (2014):

*[We have established that the] [o]verall employment of social workers is projected to grow 19 percent from 2012 to 2022, faster than the average for all occupations. Employment growth will be driven by increased demand for health care and social services, but will vary by specialty.*

*Employment of child, family, and school social workers is projected to grow 15 percent from 2012 to 2022, faster than the average for all occupations. Child and family social workers will be needed to work with families to strengthen parenting skills, prevent child abuse, and identify alternative homes for children who are unable to live with their biological families. In schools, more social workers will be needed due to rising student enrollments.*

*However, growth of this specialty may be limited by budget constraints at all levels of government. Specifically, the availability of federal, state, and local funding will be a major factor in determining the employment growth in schools.*

*Employment of health-care social workers is projected to grow 27 percent from 2012 to 2022, much faster than the average for all occupations. As baby boomers age, they and their families will require help* *from social workers to find care, increasing the need for health-care social workers.*

*Employment of mental health and substance abuse social workers is projected to grow 23 percent from 2012 to 2022, much faster than the average for all occupations. Employment will grow as more people seek treatment for mental illness and substance use disorders. In addition, drug offenders are increasingly being sent to treatment programs rather than to jail. As a result, use of substance abuse treatment programs is expected to grow, increasing demand for these specialists.*

## Chapter Summary

The following summarizes this chapter's content as it relates to the learning objectives presented at the beginning of the chapter. Chapter content will help prepare students to:

### LO1 Identify the context of social work practice today (in organizations and communities, including rural and urban communities).

Social services include the tasks that social work practitioners and other helping professionals perform with the goal of improving people's health, enhancing their quality of life, increasing autonomy and independence, supporting families, and helping people and larger systems improve their functioning in the social environment. A community is "a number of people who have something in common with one another that connects them in some way and that distinguishes them from others" (Homan, 2011, p. 8). From a social work perspective, communities are entities in which citizens can organize or be organized to address mutual concerns and improve their overall quality of life.

Rural communities involve those having low population density, being located far from urban hubs, and concentrating activities in some specialized area such as farming or lumbering. Social workers practicing in rural communities must be true generalists, providing a wide range of services. They must work in close cooperation with other agencies. They must strive to understand the community and its values, developing relationships with community residents.

Dual or multiple relationships must be addressed carefully. It's important to emphasize the strengths inherent in a rural community.

Urban social work is practiced within the context of large cities, with their vast array of social problems, exceptional diversity, and potential resources. Urban communities are characterized by their own special conditions. Problems characterizing urban communities include multiple problems resulting from dense population, widespread occurrence of discriminatory behavior, migration of people unprepared for the stress of urban living, financial shortfalls or unavailability of resources for a large population, and higher stress levels. Urban social workers should pay close attention to human diversity, understand their agency environment, seek resources in the external urban environment, and use advocacy when necessary.

### LO2 Explain the core intervention approaches in practice (with individuals, families, groups, organizations, and communities).

Micro practice is intervention involving an individual client (a micro system). Working with families combines micro and mezzo practice because it involves a small group (i.e., the family) linked by ties of an intimate nature. Social support systems can provide various types of support to family members.

Mezzo practice is social work intervention with groups. Treatment groups include therapy, support, educational, growth, and socialization groups. Task groups include teams, treatment conferences, staff-development groups, committees, cabinets, boards of directors, social action groups, coalitions, and delegate councils.

Macro practice is intervention involving organizations and communities (macro systems). Traditional macro practice or community organization may involve three approaches—social planning, locality development, and social action. Contemporary macro-practice approaches include "social advocacy," "policy practice," and "community capacity development" (Rothman, 2007, p. 12). Macro practice can address agency or public policy change, project initiation, and program development.

The point of generalist social work practice is to seek change at any level of practice, depending on what the client system needs.

### LO3 *Propose questions to stimulate critical thinking about involvement in various systems.*

Critical thinking questions addressed community involvement, support from social support systems, and group participation.

### LO4 *Identify some professional associations in social work.*

Professional organizations in social work include the National Association of Social Workers and the Council on Social Work Education. Numerous other organizations reflect more specific facets or subsets of social work. They can focus on client populations, areas of expertise or interest, or membership in special groups.

### LO5 *Describe social work licensure.*

All states have laws that define and regulate social work practice, involving some form of licensure or certification. Typical categories of licensure include bachelors, masters, advanced generalist, and clinical. NASW provides a wide range of advanced and advanced practice specialty credentials.

### LO6 *Discuss social work careers, employment settings, and salaries.*

There is a wide range of fields of practice in social work. Many students earning a bachelor's degree in social work are most likely to get jobs in corrections and, secondly, in child welfare. Two years after graduation, BSWs are most likely to work in child welfare, mental health, aging, family services, and

health care, in descending order. The largest proportion of MSWs work in mental health. When identifying practice roles, BSWs tended to identify case management, advocacy, and counseling, in that order. Most MSWs identify counseling as a major role, then information and referral, screening and assessment, and case management.

Median annual earnings differ across fields of practice. The lowest annual median earnings are in mental health and substance abuse, with increasing median earnings first by child, family, and school social workers, and then by health-care social workers. Salaries vary dramatically by region and state. MSWs tend to earn appreciably more than BSWs. Working in private practice and practicing for longer periods of time are related to higher salaries. Male social workers earn notably more than female social workers in all fields of practice.

## LOOKING AHEAD

Building on the process of social work practice discussed in the last chapter, this chapter described various settings in which social work takes place. Part 3 of this book includes three chapters focusing on social welfare policy. Policy establishes the parameters for what social workers can do, including how they practice and in what contexts. The next chapter lays the groundwork for understanding policy by reviewing the history of social welfare and social work.

## COMPETENCY NOTES

The following identifies where Educational Policy (EP) competencies and their component behaviors are discussed in the chapter.

**EP 1 (Competency 1)—Demonstrate Ethical and Professional Behavior.** *(p. 146):* Keeping abreast of the issues involved in urban social work and the skills needed is part of a career-long learning process. *(p. 159):* Obtaining social work licensure and professional credentials is part of establishing a professional identity. Social work licensure and other credentials help to define professional practice and roles.

**EP 1a Make ethical decisions by applying the standards of the NASW Code of Ethics,**

relevant laws and regulations, models for ethical decision-making, ethical conduct of research, and additional codes of ethics as appropriate to context. *(p. 143):* Social workers often struggle with ethical dilemmas when they strive to make ethical decisions. This case example involves a dual relationship in a rural setting.

**EP 1c Demonstrate professional demeanor in behavior; appearance; and oral, written, and electronic communication.** *(p. 158):* NASW is a professional organization that promotes professional demeanor.

**EP 2 (Competency 2)—Engage Diversity and Difference in Practice.** *(p. 173):* Questions are posed to assess potential ageism and sexism on the part of the client in this case example.

**EP 2a Apply and communicate understanding of the importance of diversity and difference in shaping life experiences in practice at the micro, mezzo, and macro levels.** *(p. 141):* Social workers should understand that living in a rural environment shapes life experiences. *(p. 144):* Social workers should understand that living in an urban environment shapes life experiences. *(p. 173):* Questions are posed to help assess the extent to which aspects of diversity shape the client's life experiences.

**EP 2b Present themselves as learners and engage clients and constituencies as experts of their own experiences.** *(p. 141):* Attending to changing rural issues and conditions requires listening to clients about their issues and needs. *(p. 144):* Attending to changing urban issues and conditions requires career-long learning. Practitioners should listen to their urban clients about their issues and needs.

**EP 3 (Competency 3)—Advance Human Rights and Social, Economic, and Environmental Justice.**

**EP 3a Apply their understanding of social, economic, and environmental justice to advocate for human rights at the individual and system levels.** *(p. 156):* Macro practice involves understanding social, economic, and environmental justice issues in order to advocate for human rights and necessary services.

**EP 3b Engage in practices that advance social, economic, and environmental justice.** *(p. 156):* Macro practice involves engaging in practice that advances social, economic, and environmental justice.

**EP 5 (Competency 5)—Engage in Policy Practice.**

**EP 5c Apply critical thinking to analyze, formulate, and advocate for policies that advance human rights and social, economic, and environmental justice.** *(p. 146):* Social workers should strive to establish policies and programs that meet the needs of urban clients and improve their quality of life. *(p. 155):* Social work with and within organizations and communities includes analyzing policies and advocating for improvements. *(p. 156):* Social workers should engage in practices that advance social and economic justice through policy practice and policy advocacy for oppressed groups. *(p. 158):* NASW advocates for policies that meet clients' needs.

**EP 6 (Competency 6)—Engage with Individuals, Families, Groups, Organizations, and Communities.**

**EP 6a Apply knowledge of human behavior and the social environment, person-in-environment, and other multidisciplinary theoretical frameworks to engage with clients and constituencies.** *(p. 140):* Practitioners must understand social services and social agencies in order to engage clients within the context of their environment. *(p. 141):* Practitioners must understand communities in order to engage clients and other macro systems in the process of service provision. *(p. 148):* For engaging clients and others, social workers must be knowledgeable about systems of all sizes, including families.

**EP 6b Use empathy, reflection, and interpersonal skills to effectively engage diverse clients and constituencies.** *(p. 145):* Interpersonal skills involved in interviewing are discussed. *(p. 148):* Social workers should use empathy and other interpersonal skills to work effectively with families. *(p. 151):* The treatment group leader uses empathy and other interpersonal skills with group members and models such skills for them.

**EP 7 (Competency 7)—Assess Individuals, Families, Groups, Organizations, and Communities.**

**EP 7a Collect and organize data, and apply critical thinking to interpret information from clients and constituencies.** *(p. 147):* Critical thinking about your own community helps prepare you for community assessment in practice. *(p. 151):* Critical thinking about your own family and social networks can help you better understand other families as you assess them. *(p. 156):* Critical thinking about your own participation in groups helps prepare you to assess groups. *(p. 173):* Critical thinking questions are posed to help collect, organize, and interpret client data.

**EP 7b Apply knowledge of human behavior and the social environment, person-in-environment, and other multidisciplinary theoretical frameworks in the analysis of assessment data from clients and constituencies.** *(p. 140):* Practitioners must understand social services and social agencies in order to assess how clients function within their environment and help clients get necessary services. *(p. 141):* Practitioners must understand communities in order to assess how clients function within their environment and help clients get necessary services. *(p. 148):* For accurate assessment, social workers must be knowledgeable about systems of all sizes, including families. *(p. 150):* For accurate assessment, practitioners should be knowledgeable about the range of systems in the social environment in which people participate, including groups. *(p. 155):* In order to practice effectively, social workers should understand how people function in organizations and communities. Theoretical frameworks for undertaking practice with and within organizations and communities are discussed.

**EP 7c Develop mutually agreed-on intervention goals and objectives based on the critical assessment of strengths, needs, and challenges within clients and constituencies.** *(p. 151):* The treatment group leader helps group members develop a mutually agreed-on focus of work and desired outcomes.

**EP 7d Select appropriate intervention strategies based on the assessment, research**

knowledge, and values and preferences of clients and constituencies.** *(p. 148):* Social workers should select intervention strategies for families that are effective. *(p. 151):* The treatment group leader should use the appropriate intervention strategies, including those discussed here. *(p. 155):* Practitioners should choose the appropriate strategy for working in and with organizations and communities. *(p. 157):* Social workers can choose from a range of intervention strategies when working with individuals, families, groups, organizations, and communities.

**EP 8 (Competency 8)—Intervene with Individuals, Families, Groups, Organizations, and Communities.**

**EP 8a Critically choose and implement interventions to achieve practice goals and enhance capacities of clients and constituencies.** *(p. 146):* Social workers should strive to establish policies, programs, and resources that meet the needs of urban clients.

**EP 8b Apply knowledge of human behavior and the social environment, person-in-environment, and other multidisciplinary theoretical frameworks in interventions with clients and constituencies.** *(p. 140):* For effective intervention, social workers must understand human behavior and practice within the context of social agencies. *(p. 141):* Practitioners must understand communities in order to intervene with clients and help them get necessary services. *(p. 148):* For effective intervention, social workers must be knowledgeable about systems of all sizes, including families.

**EP 8c Use inter-professional collaboration as appropriate to achieve beneficial practice outcomes.** *(p. 155):* Social workers can collaborate with colleagues and clients to improve policies, conditions, and service provision in organizations and communities. *(p. 158):* NASW membership provides a mechanism for collaborating with colleagues to undertake effective policy action.

**EP 8d Negotiate, mediate, and advocate with and on behalf of diverse clients and constituencies.** *(p. 146):* Social workers should advocate for the services and resources that urban clients need. *(p. 156):* Macro practice involves advocacy on the behalf of clients.

**EP 9 Evaluate Practice with Individuals, Families, Groups, Organizations, and Communities.**

**EP 9b Apply knowledge of human behavior and the social environment, person-in-environment, and other multidisciplinary theoretical frameworks in the evaluation of outcomes.** *(p. 140):* Practitioners must understand social services and social agencies in order to evaluate the effectiveness of such services. *(p. 141):* Practitioners must understand communities in order to evaluate the effectiveness of social services. *(p. 148):* For evaluation of practice, social workers must be knowledgeable about systems of all sizes, including families.

CASE STUDY FOR CRITICAL THINKING

# An Older Adult Woman with Multiple Needs

The case presented here involves an older adult woman facing various problems. Critical thinking for this case focuses on the assessment phase of the planned-change process in social work. Chapter 4 discussed how assessment in generalist practice stresses understanding the many aspects of a problem. Information is needed about the client and about those aspects of the client's environment that the worker feels are useful. The social worker might help this client by focusing on the individual (micro), family (micro/mezzo), group (mezzo), and community and organizational (macro) levels of practice. Aspects of human diversity are also important to explore.

EP 2, 2a, 7a[13]

**Case Study:** A social services worker in a rural county receives a call about Georgia from Georgia's neighbor. Georgia, age 84, lives in an old farmhouse where she has lived for most of her life. Georgia's health is deteriorating. She is falling more and more frequently, and her eyesight is failing. The neighbor worries that Georgia may fall, break something, and lie helpless for days.

The worker visits Georgia to assess her and her situation. The worker needs information to make decisions about what he and Georgia can do. Georgia may need some supportive services or even health-care-center placement.

The information needed falls into four major categories. These include micro, mezzo, and macro levels of assessment in addition to consideration of elements of human diversity. In each category, problems must be defined and strengths identified.

**Critical Thinking:** How would you use the three-step Triple-A critical thinking process to establish what might be done in this case? First, *ask* questions. On the individual level, you might ask

- What are Georgia's most critical problems?
- What things about Georgia contribute to her problems?
- What are Georgia's primary strengths upon which a treatment plan might be built?
- How does Georgia feel about herself and her situation?

On the family level, you might ask

- Does Georgia have any relatives in the immediate vicinity?
- Does she have children who are available to help out?
- What are her relationships with relatives who might be accessible?

---

[13]Competency Notes explaining this icon are located at the end of Chapter 5.

On the group level, you might ask

- Does Georgia have friends she can talk to?
- Do people visit her? If so, how often?
- Does she have opportunities to get out of the house at all?

On the organizational and community levels, you might ask

- What services might be available to help Georgia with her identified problems?
- Is there a Meals-on-Wheels program available (through which daily hot meals are delivered to older adults at minimal cost)?
- Is there a Visiting Friends program through which paraprofessionals (people with specialized training who perform a limited range of professional tasks under the professional's supervision) regularly visit older adult residents in their homes and help them with shopping, paying bills, making medical appointments, and so on?
- If needed services are not available for Georgia and other needy older adult residents, should you seek to get some developed?

Concerning aspects of diversity, you might ask

- Are there any significant aspects of diversity characterizing Georgia and her situation?
- What is her ethnic and racial heritage? How does this affect her life circumstances?
- Is Georgia being treated differently or in a discriminatory manner because of her age (and people's unfair, preconceived notions about older people and their abilities)?
- Is Georgia suffering any negative consequences because she is a woman and is being treated in a sexist manner?

The second step in critical thinking involves *assessing* the established facts and issues involved. Did you get as much information from Georgia as possible? Are there any other potential sources of information you can think of?

The third step in critical thinking is *asserting* a concluding opinion. What might be your final recommendations for providing Georgia with the resources and services needed to enhance her quality of life?

# SOCIAL WELFARE POLICY

Part 3 of this book includes three chapters that introduce social welfare policy as the groundwork for social service provision. Policy dictates how social welfare programs may be implemented. It also structures the context in which practitioners can do their work.

Chapter 6 provides a brief overview of social welfare and social work history. History provides the necessary background to understand how people think about social welfare and develop social welfare policy.

Chapter 7 describes social welfare policy development and the structural components of policy. Because policy drives what programs can do, it must be clearly understood. The chapter explores value perspectives on social responsibility and social welfare program development. Additionally, it formulates an approach to policy analysis to evaluate how social welfare policy affects and serves clients. Finally, it defines policy practice and policy advocacy as basic responsibilities of generalist practitioners.

Chapter 8 describes the policies and programs that are designed to combat poverty in the United States. The concept of poverty is defined, and explanations for its existence are discussed. Social insurance and public assistance are defined and discussed, along with specific programs under the umbrella of each.

# 6 An Overview of Social Welfare and Social Work History

AP Images/Khampha Bouaphanh

## Learning Objectives    This chapter will help prepare students to:

**LO 1** Describe historical views about social welfare. **Early European Approaches to Social Welfare** (p. 178)

**LO 2** Review the history of social welfare in the United States (focusing on major social welfare issues, diverse groups, and policy changes). **U.S. Social Welfare History: Early Colonization to the Mid-1800s** (p. 181)

**LO 3** Propose questions to stimulate critical thinking about historical trends and events. **Focus on Critical Thinking 6.1** (p. 192)

**LO 4** Discuss the foremost events in the history of the social work profession. **The Development of the Social Work Profession** (p. 209)

*You might feel that history is boring and irrelevant in view of alarming contemporary issues, rapidly accelerating technological advances, and global political, economic, and social concerns. However, events in history have shaped our current ways of thinking. To comprehend how and why social welfare programs are the way they are today, it is critical to understand social welfare history. Current social welfare policy and programs didn't simply appear out of nowhere. Rather, a long history of ideas, values, and events has shaped the present—and paves the way for the future. Figure 6.1, which introduces this chapter, identifies major events in the history of social work.*

EP 1

*The profession's history is intertwined with the history of social welfare. Social work grew and matured in response to significant social trends, events, and needs as they occurred over time. What social workers could do in the past and what they can do now are governed by social welfare policies and programs. It is beyond the scope of this book to provide a detailed history of social welfare and social work.[1] Therefore, our focus will be on the key trends, events, and figures. The time line depicted in Figure 6.3 at the end of this chapter summarizes some of these events.*

*Note that when we talk about ideas, trends, and social movements over time, it is impossible to quantify them as abruptly halting one year and being replaced by something else the next year. Ideas and concepts change gradually, and transitions between them are indistinct. Therefore, this chapter will periodically reflect some overlap from one section or historical period to another.*

*Because Europe, especially England, provided the primary model for the development of current social welfare strategies in North America, we will initially focus on what occurred there. We will then concentrate on events and developments in the United States from the early years to the present.*

## Early European Approaches to Social Welfare   `LO 1`

Some of our current basic ideas about how people should or should not be treated can be traced back a millennium to medieval times. Until the mid-1300s, **feudalism** reigned in Europe as the principal type of political organization. In this system,

wealthy landed gentry oversaw the labor of landless serfs who made a living by working their overseer's lands. In return, serfs received general protection and care during sickness and old age.

EP 2

Other sources of aid included medieval hospitals that provided refuge and care for older adults, the

---

[1]Many thorough books have been written about social welfare and social work history. This chapter can provide only a brief overview of and introduction to major concepts. For further, more extensive information, you might refer to *From Poor Law to Welfare State* by W. I. Trattner (New York: Free Press, 1999); *A New History of Social Welfare* by P. J. Day and J. Schiele (Boston: Allyn & Bacon, 2013); *The Faces of Social Policy: A Strengths Perspective* by C. J. Tice and K. Perkins (Pacific Grove, CA: Brooks/Cole, 2002); *Social Welfare: A History of the American Response to Need* by M. J. Stern and J. Axinn (Boston: Allyn & Bacon, 2012); *Milestones* by R. L. Barker (Washington, DC: NASW Press, 1999), or to topics such as "Social Welfare History," "Social Welfare Policy," "Social Work Profession: History," "National Association of Social Workers," and "Council on Social Work Education" in T. Mizrahi & L. E. Davis (Editors-in-Chief), *Encyclopedia of Social Work* (New York: Oxford, 2008).

## A Time Line of Major Events in Social Work

| | |
|---|---|
| 1898 | First training course offered for "charity workers" by New York Charity Association |
| 1918 | Formation of American Association of Medical Social Workers |
| 1919 | Formation of Association of Training Schools for Professional Social Work (later becoming the American Association of Schools of Social Work [AASSW]) |
| | Formation of National Association of School Social Workers |
| 1920 | Formation of American Association of Social Workers |
| 1926 | Formation of American Association of Psychiatric Social Workers |
| 1927 | AASSW development of educational requirements for its membership that quickly evolved into accreditation standards for MSW programs |
| 1929 | Beginning of Great Depression that opened doors for social workers in the public sector |
| 1936 | Formation of American Association of Group Workers |
| 1942 | Formation of National Association of Schools of Social Administration (NASSA) |
| 1943 | Recognition of NASSA as official accrediting body for baccalaureate programs |
| 1946 | Formation of National Council on Social Worker Education (NCSWE) to coordinate AASSW and NASSA activities |
| | Formation of Association for Study of Community Organization |
| 1949 | Formation of Social Worker Research Group |
| 1952 | Formation of Council on Social Work Accreditation (CSWE) reflecting the merger of AASSW and NASSA |
| | Writing of first CSWE Curriculum Policy Statement and Accreditation Standards |
| 1955 | Formation of National Association of Social Workers (NASW) |
| | Formation of National Association of Puerto Rican Hispanic Social Workers |
| 1956 | Publication of profession's primary journal, *Social Work* |
| 1960 | NASW approval of *Code of Ethics* |
| 1960s | War on Poverty that focused attention on social change versus individual pathology |
| 1962 | CSWE development of criteria for accrediting BSW programs |
| 1968 | Formation of National Association of Black Social Workers (NABSW) |
| | Formation of National Association of Puerto Rican Social Service Workers (NAPRSSW) |
| 1969 | Formation of Association of American Indian Social Workers (later called National Indian Social Workers Association) |
| | Formation of Asian American Social Workers organization |
| 1974 | CSWE accreditation of BSW programs |
| 1976 | NASW establishes Political Action for Candidate Election (PACE) |
| 1977 | Formation of Group for Advancement of Doctoral Education in social work (GADE) |
| 1979 | Incorporation of American Association of State Social Work Boards (AASSWB) to synchronize state licensing procedures |
| 1982 | Formation of Association for Advancement of Social Work with Groups (AASWG) |
| 1984 | CSWE declares common generalist practice foundation for both BSW and MSW programs |
| 1987 | NASW initiates Center for Social Policy and Practice to disseminate information about social welfare policy |
| 1991 | Formation of Academy of Certified Baccalaureate Social Workers (ACBSW) |
| 1996 | NASW approval of revisions of *Code of Ethics* |
| 1998 | U.S. social workers commemorate more than 100 years of social work |

**FIG-6-1** Major Events in the History of the Social Work Profession in the United States impoverished, orphans, and people with serious ill-nesses and disabilities, as well as charitable help from the church. These times reflected a rigid social structure with little mobility, free choice, or potential for personal growth and change. Grounded in Judeo-Christian thought, a common theme was that those who were better off should provide help to those who were poor. That some people were poor and others were rich was perceived as an unalterable fact of life. The church played a primary role in redistributing resources from the rich to the poor. It emphasized "good deeds, love of one's enemies, and entry into heaven through mercy and charity" (Trattner, 1999, p. 3).

## England After Feudalism's Demise

As time passed, trade increased, technology bloomed, and the feudal system with its rigid hierarchy of power and social expectations underwent a gradual demise. With the development of urban factories, rural people were drawn to the cities looking for work and, they hoped, better wages. Centralized government became stronger, and the church lost both political and financial power. With these changes, people gained mobility and independence but lost much of the safety and security the old feudal system had provided. Many wandered in search of work, with pain, suffering, and poverty the norm.

Political leaders decided that something must be done to control the mobile population and provide some relief for the poor. In 1348 the Black Death (bubonic plague) began its destruction of almost a third of the English population, causing a serious labor shortage. As people migrated in search of competitive wages, political leaders passed legislation to regain social control. For example, the Statute of Laborers, passed in 1349, restricted the unemployed from moving about and established maximum wages allowable. The intent was to make people stay put and take whatever work was available there instead of seeking better options.

In 1531 another statute was passed forbidding able-bodied people from begging, with violations punishable by bloody public whippings while naked. However, this legislation also provided for designated government figures to help people unable to work (referred to as the "impotent poor") by assigning them legitimate areas where they could beg. Subsequent laws addressed who should receive aid, from

whom, and under what conditions, as well as what punishments should befall those who did not obey the rules.

## The English Elizabethan Poor Law of 1601

The 1601 Elizabethan Poor Law is often considered the first piece of legislation establishing coherent, consistent public support for needy people through local taxes. It also was the first to establish categories of eligible recipients by identifying the following three:

1. **Dependent children** without relatives capable of supporting them were placed in service under whatever citizen placed the lowest bid for public reimbursement to provide the child's care. Boys served as apprentices, theoretically being taught a trade, until their 24th birthday, and girls provided domestic help until they were either 21 or married.
2. The **impotent poor** included those who were physically or mentally unable to work. They were given either "indoor relief" (i.e., placed *inside* institutions providing food and shelter called **almshouses** or **poorhouses**) or "outdoor relief" (i.e., offered the opportunity to live *outside* of the institution but receive material help in the form of food, clothing, and fuel).
3. The **able-bodied poor** (impoverished people who were physically capable of working) were provided any substandard employment available and forced to work or suffer jail or other punishment, even death. Some people were forced into **workhouses**, special facilities in which poor people were forced to work and live. Unlike the impotent poor, these people were considered undeserving of help because they should be able to take care of themselves.

One later change in the poor laws, the 1662 Law of Settlement, established a notable new principle of social welfare service provision, the **residency requirement**. Potential aid recipients were required to establish that they had dwelled in some location for some designated time before they could receive assistance or benefits from the political body governing that location. People who had moved and needed help were required to return to their former parish (a portion of a county coinciding with the original religious parish and serving as a unit of local government) to receive help.

## The Speenhamland System

In 1795 what became known as the *Speenhamland system* (because it was developed in Speenhamland. England) reflected a new approach to the problems of working poor people. Bread had become so expensive that many poor people could not afford it. Speenhamland government leaders responded by initiating the policy of supplementing the income of all poor people so that everyone would have what was deemed the minimum income necessary for survival. Unfortunately, the result was an unexpected flop for two reasons (Garvin & Tropman, 1998; Reid, 1995). First, wages fell. Why would employers pay higher wages when the government would supplement workers' wages to the minimum necessary for survival? Why shouldn't employers let the government pay the difference to have wages reach the minimum level, rather than taking it out of their own pockets? Second, unemployment soared because people didn't have to work. They would get the same amount whether they worked or not. And even if they did work, they had little chance of getting ahead. In other words, there were no *work incentives*—logical rewards or benefits that encourage people to work.

## The English Poor Law Reforms of 1834

As time passed, people began to resent the Speenhamland system for two reasons (Garvin & Tropman, 1998): (1) It cost a fortune to support *everyone,* and (2) people felt it created a dependent population of people who would never get out of poverty. The Poor Law Reforms of 1834 significantly reduced all outdoor relief and brought back workhouses as the only place where able-bodied people could receive benefits.

Three important ideological trends resulted from these reforms (Garvin & Tropman, 1998). First, public attitudes toward the poor became hostile and resentful. Second, the public came to blame the poor for their poverty. Why couldn't those people pull themselves up by their bootstraps and make it on their own? Today we would refer to this as a form of **blaming the victim**—that is, ascribing fault to the people who are hurt, have problems beyond their control, have few resources, or have been victimized by some crime or unexpected circumstance. This reflects the attitude that if only poor people would expend a little more effort and put in a full day's work every day, they wouldn't be poor (Barker, 2014). The third result of these reforms was the concept of being *less eligible* (Garvin & Tropman, 1998; Reid, 1995). This is the idea that benefits should be lower than what the poorest working people could earn. People who received public assistance, then, would always be poorer than the poorest people who worked.

# U.S. Social Welfare History: Early Colonization to the Mid-1800s   LO 2

Early poor laws in the American colonies closely resembled, and in some cases were identical to, those in England, although each colony remained unique in its specific legislation. The colonists maintained a strong sense of individualism and commitment to personal freedom; however, they also expressed concern for the well-being of others and respect for a sense of community (Reid, 1995). The result was an interesting and uneven blend of programs and services, such that the beneficiaries of some programs received substantial help and others received very little.

The colonists viewed the poor as a natural part of the social order and the community. In many ways, this reflected an *institutional* view of social welfare—namely, it is simply society's ongoing responsibility to provide its citizens with needed benefits and resources.

Services often reflected a mix of public and private collaboration, with services being provided in a relatively informal manner (Reid, 1995). Local government units assumed the responsibility of administering aid but often called upon local churches for help (Dolgoff & Feldstein, 2009).

Early residency requirements for assistance were established. Communities tended to provide aid for their own residents, shunning strangers. Communities also made decisions about who was worthy to receive benefits and who was not. This demonstrated the concept of the **worthy poor** versus the **unworthy poor**, the former deserved help and the latter did not (the implication being that the unworthy poor were doing something wrong).

The worthy poor were pitied, and the community found ways to care for them. One of the easiest was for families to take turns housing the poor during the year. A second way to help the poor was to reduce their taxes. Still another way involved providing free medical attention to them, with physicians either

donating such care or receiving inducements such as tax breaks.

Dependent children were frequently placed in apprenticeships. This was viewed positively for a number of reasons (Trattner, 1999). First, apprenticeships afforded them some connection with a family and the related stability. Second, it provided a context in which they might be disciplined and taught to become good citizens. Third, it saved the community the cost of caring for children. Finally, it trained children to develop a useful skill and become productive community members. Because labor was scarce in colonial America, people who had learned trades were highly valued. Highlight 6.1 discusses some of the early philosophical views about children.

By the 1820s and 1830s, ideas were changing, and people were beginning to view poverty as a "social problem" and "a potential source of crime, social unrest, and long-term dependence" (Reid, 1995, p. 2209). Therefore, interest began to turn to reform. People now believed that outdoor relief had spoiled poor people and that it resulted only in dependence. Therefore, great almshouses were built in which the poor could be housed and converted into industrious, functional citizens.

## Focus on Mental Health and Mental Illness

In colonial America, people who had mental illness, often referred to as "lunatics," typically were cared for by their own families or boarded out to other families, with communities paying these families to provide care (Dembling, 1995; Fellin, 1996, p. 56). As time passed, people with mental illness increasingly were placed in almshouses, clustered together with the poor and people with other disabilities.

By the early 19th century, the **moral treatment movement**, the first of three focusing on mental health policy, had been initiated by Philippe Pinel, a French physician who worked in a Parisian hospital for the "insane." The idea was that people with mental illness "should be treated with humane, sympathetic, and personal care in a hospital or asylum setting" (Fellin, 1996, p. 57; Lin, 1995; U.S. Department of Health and Human Services [USDHHS], 1999). (Figure 6.2 summarizes the three major mental health movements occurring in the United States during the 19th

| Movement | Time Frame | Emphasis |
|---|---|---|
| Moral treatment | 1770s–1900 | Humane treatment in structured institutional settings |
| Mental hygiene | 1900–1945 | Specialized psychiatric units and psychotherapy |
| Deinstitutionalization | Early 1950s to present | Provision of care in people's own communities |

**FIG-6-2** Major Mental Health Movements in the United States

## HIGHLIGHT 6.2      DOROTHEA DIX: MENTAL HEALTH ADVOCATE

A notable early advocate during the 1840s for people with mental illness was Dorothea Dix (Barker, 2014; Fellin, 1996; Trattner, 1999). A volunteer Sunday school teacher in a Massachusetts women's prison, she was appalled by the treatment of people with mental illness who were placed there. She waged a dynamic publicity campaign condemning the deplorable conditions in which these people were forced to live.

EP 3a, 5c, 8d

Trattner (1999) explains how Dix "described vividly how many of the unfortunate crazed were impounded in cabins, cages, closets, stalls, and other pens of one kind of another, often chained and then abandoned to

filth and neglect, or else brutally beaten—a horrifying picture" (p. 65).

Beginning in Massachusetts and then focusing on other states, she insisted that it was the public's responsibility to establish hospitals providing more humane treatment and medical care for persons with mental illness.

As a result of Dix's and her followers' efforts, more than 30 state mental hospitals were established (Fellin, 1996). Unfortunately, "although well intentioned, her selling and marketing of state-run institutions were based on two dubious premises: first, that such asylums were the most cost-effective means of treatment, and second, that insanity was a highly curable phenomenon" (Gomory, 1997, p. 165).

and 20th centuries. The last two will be described in greater detail later in the chapter.)

In the United States, the movement assumed "more of a moralistic flavor related to the idea that bad habits lead to tendencies toward mental disorders" (Fellin, 1996, p. 57; Rochefort, 1993). Structured, "corrective" settings providing a remedial environment were thought to help cure mental illness (Lin, 1995, p. 1705). Highlight 6.2 focuses on Dorothea Dix, an early advocate for the humane treatment of people with mental illness.

### Focus on American Indian (First Nations Peoples) History: Treaties and Federal Control[2]

Most of social welfare history in the United States, including that discussed thus far, is written from a very White perspective (Lewis, 1995). In reality, American history did not begin in 1492 when Columbus "discovered" America. Rather, North America had been populated for 25,000 years or more (Day & Schiele, 2013; Lewis, 1995). During initial European colonization, there were hundreds of different nations with

EP 2

a wide range of well-developed, self-sufficient societies (Weaver, 2003, 2008).

Residents of a conquered society generally remain on their own land and at least retain hope of regaining control. European victory over American Indian nations, however, usually resulted in their permanent removal from their lands, pressures to surrender their values and culture, and imposed submission to external laws and regulations.

### Treaties

As Whites pushed westward in exploding numbers and with an insatiable desire for land, the United States, newly formed and in its infancy, decided to deal with First Nations Peoples by developing treaties. The United States viewed **treaties** as formal means of delineating the legal and political relationships between the federal government and various indigenous nations. The first treaty to be established (of more than 600 over the next century) was with the Delaware nation in 1778. Congress finally ceased making treaties with nations in 1981 when other type of agreements and legislation formally replaced the treaty process (Lewis, 1995).

### Other Early Policies

A significant early piece of legislation was the 1781 Articles of Confederation. This was related to treaties because it gave the federal government singular and complete authority over Indian affairs,

---

[2]For greater detail and good introductory content on American Indians, see Lewis (1995, pp. 216–231), which provides an excellent beginning source for understanding some of the crucial issues experienced by First Nations Peoples.

reinforcing the government's right to make treaties in any way it saw fit (Lewis, 1995). Thus the federal government could develop treaties regardless of First Nations Peoples' locations in North America. The implication is that, as the government broke treaties, First Nations Peoples could be moved from place to place, usually further west.

Other significant pieces of legislation, the Trade and Intercourse Acts passed between 1770 and 1834, reinforced two more ideas (Canby, 1981; Lewis, 1995). One was that American Indians and non-American Indians should be separated. The other was that the federal government should control all relations between American Indians and Whites. The federal Bureau of Indian Affairs, established in 1824, reflected an attempt to address issues with American Indians.

The theme during this period was the conviction that American Indians had an inferior culture and that the federal government was responsible for civilizing them and making them Christians (Lewis, 1995). White people believed that the federal government should interfere not only in political matters but also in social, economic, religious, and cultural practices.

### Removal Policy

Tensions continued to mount as Whites pushed westward into American Indian territory. The Indian Removal Act, passed in 1830, resulted in thousands of American Indians being removed from their own lands and placed on distant **reservations**. Such areas of relocation were generally smaller than their homelands and had clearly defined boundaries. There they experienced the spread of disease and numerous restrictions such as being forbidden to participate in spiritual ceremonies.

The Cherokee Nation poses a heartrending example of the cruel removal practice. By the early 1800s, the Cherokee had called western Georgia home for almost 1,000 years (Cherokee Messenger, 1995). By this time the nation had adopted many European customs, including women wearing gowns, and had developed a system of "roads, schools, and churches" (Cherokee Messenger, 1995). Their literacy rate in their own tongue was 90%, they published a bilingual newspaper and a range of textbooks, and they established a written constitution as an independent nation (Lewis, 1995). Most of them worked as farmers and ranchers (Golden Ink, 1997).

After gold was discovered in Georgia in 1828, the tension increased between the Cherokee and their non-Native counterparts. Although the Cherokee challenged the legality of the 1830 Indian Removal Act in the Supreme Court and at first appeared to be successful, it was determined that they could be removed if they signed a treaty to that effect (Golden Ink, 1997). Against the majority's will, in 1835 a small faction (less than 3%) of the Cherokee Nation signed such a treaty relinquishing all land east of the Mississippi in return for promised new western lands, cash, equipment, and supplies (Cherokee Messenger, 1995; Golden Ink, 1997). Three years later, 17,000 Cherokee men, women, and children were torn from their land and made to endure squalid conditions on a 1,200-mile trip to Indian Territory in the West (Cherokee Messenger, 1995). On that journey 4,000 perished "from hunger, exposure, and disease" (Cherokee Messenger, 1995). This infamous journey is aptly and sadly called "The Trail of Tears."

In all, during the 1830s between 70,000 and 100,000 American Indians were uprooted from their homes and herded to Oklahoma (Lewis, 1995).

### Focus on Chicano and Chicana History: The Treaty of Guadalupe Hidalgo

The history of the Southwest and its early inhabitants merits attention, especially in view of the large and growing U.S. Chicano and Chicana population. Beginning in the early 1500s the Spanish conquistadors, along with their Native allies, conquered the Aztec Empire in Central Mexico; from there expansion took place in all directions,  **EP 2** overtaking areas including Arizona, New Mexico, Texas, and California (Englekirk & Marin, n.d.; Sanchez, n.d.). Colonization of these regions continued, with many of the residents having a mixed heritage including Spanish and Native American ancestry.

In view of a growing population, increasing infiltration by Anglos (Whites), and budding trade with other areas, the struggle for control of land escalated. Texas declared itself an independent republic in 1836 but continued grappling with Mexico over its southern boundary (Library of Congress, 2004). When the United States decided to annex Texas in 1845, the boundary struggle with Mexico continued.

Conflict intensified and war was declared in 1846, initiating the Mexican-American War. Subsequently, the United States attacked Mexico on numerous fronts, eventually capturing Mexico City in mid-1847 (Library of Congress, 2004). The result was the February 2, 1848, signing of the Treaty of Guadalupe Hidalgo, in which Mexico ceded more than half of its territory to the United States, including contemporary Arizona, New Mexico, and upper California, in addition to portions of Colorado, Nevada, and Utah in exchange for $15 million; additionally, Mexico recognized U.S. retention of Texas with its southern boundary at the Rio Grande (U.S. National Archives and Records Administration, n.d.). (The remaining portions of present-day states were ceded under the 1853 Gadsden Purchase [Curiel, 1995].)

The Treaty of Guadalupe Hidalgo did address the rights of Mexicans living in the ceded regions. It provided the options of retaining their land and becoming U.S. citizens, which the vast majority chose, or moving south into Mexico (Curiel, 1995). Although the treaty guaranteed land, personal, and religious rights, Anglos generally opted to ignore these guarantees (Day & Schiele, 2013). Many Anglos took Chicano landowners to court over land rights, usually winning because many Chicanos had lost proof of land titles during the conflict and could not afford to hire attorneys to defend themselves adequately (Day & Schiele, 2013). As a result, Chicanos were generally disenfranchised from their property and their rights, becoming strangers in their own land (Curiel, 1995). Many were forced into hard agricultural labor that Anglos preferred not to do. Anglos commonly viewed Chicanos as a "minority" group with its own culture; although Chicanos outnumbered Anglos and were living in their own homelands, they were marginalized, discriminated against, and commonly treated as second-class citizens (Curiel, 1995). This set the stage for the discrimination and many of the issues Chicanos must deal with today.

# The Civil War Era

The Civil War (1861–1865) had a huge impact on the social structure of the United States. Day and Schiele (2013) explain that it "affirmed federal responsibility over states' rights and laid the groundwork for the United States to become a welfare state" (p. 191).

Jansson (2015) describes how, despite the fact that the main conflict concerned "the legal status of slaves," President Abraham Lincoln (whose administration lasted from 1861 until his 1865 assassination) did not initially propose an immediate end to slavery (p. 134). Although his decisions were apparently made in the context of political concerns, such an omission might raise questions regarding the strength of Lincoln's opposition to slavery.[3] It was not until 1863 that he issued the Emancipation Proclamation, declaring freedom for all slaves in Confederate states at war with the Union. Note that this sidestepped the issue of freedom for slaves in border slave states, including Delaware, Kentucky, Maryland, Missouri, and West Virginia (Tice & Perkins, 2002).

## Focus on African Americans: The Freedmen's Bureau

A major problem during this era involved the newly freed, dislocated former slaves, who had no property and few resources. Although charity groups in the North sent supplies and volunteers to help displaced people, this only scratched the surface in terms of meeting people's needs. National concern about the issues and needs resulted

**EP 2**

in Congress establishing the Bureau of Refugees, Freedmen, and Abandoned Land (more commonly known as the Freedmen's Bureau) in 1865. (Note that its formal name emphasizes how legislators sought to avoid giving African Americans preferential treatment [Jansson, 2015].) This bureau, the "first federal welfare agency" (Reid, 1995, p. 2210), established "a precedent for federal participation in social welfare during emergency periods" (Stern & Axinn, 2012, p. 91).

The Freedmen's Bureau was placed under the auspices of the War Department. This emphasized its temporary, crisis-related (postwar) purpose, as opposed to status as an institutional program designed to meet ongoing needs. Eligibility for resources was based purely on need. In its initial three years, the bureau distributed rations to 18.3 million people, more than 28% of whom were White (Day & Schiele, 2013;

---

[3]Possible reasons for Lincoln's hesitation in eradicating slavery include having as a top priority keeping the Union together, believing that the Constitution gave him no authority to free slaves, being concerned that the Confederacy would only "fight harder" and the war would last longer if slaves were freed, and fearing alienation of the border slave states (Tice & Perkins, 2002, p. 74).

Tice & Perkins, 2002). Additionally, it provided transportation home for refugees, distributed medical supplies, built 46 hospitals, and established more than 4,300 schools for African American children (Stern & Axinn, 2012). The Freedmen's Bureau was disbanded in 1872.

One of the Freedmen's Bureau's initial goals was to distribute 40 acres of abandoned or confiscated land to each male refugee. This could be accomplished only if the government took possession of such property and legally distributed it. The results of this program were modest: Only a little more than 1% of eligible African Americans were allocated property (Jansson, 2015). President Andrew Johnson (whose administration lasted from 1865 to 1869) subsequently proclaimed that the African Americans had no legal right to these properties and forced recipients to return lands to their former owners (Jansson, 2015).

# The 1870s to 1900

Economic growth skyrocketed between the Civil War and the early 20th century (Stern & Axinn, 2012). Three broad trends emerged in the United States both economically and socially (Garvin & Cox, 1995). The first was **industrialization**. Mammoth growth in manufacturing and technology brought with it numerous social problems. These included poor working conditions, long hours, safety concerns, and the use of child labor (Garvin & Cox, 1995; Jansson, 2015).

The second trend was **urbanization**. Concurrent with the centralization of industry within urban settings was the tremendous growth of urban populations. Masses of people moved from rural to urban areas in search of work and prosperity. Unfortunately, most were forced to move into the oldest, most crowded, and least sanitary portions of the cities.

The third trend was explosive **immigration**, the movement of people from their nation of origin to settle permanently in some other country. In this case, people, primarily from northwestern Europe, came to the United States. Immigrants brought with them their own problems. Many came from poor rural environments and had little to start their lives with in this country, and many became ill during the immigration process. Immigrants usually were forced to live in some of the worst conditions and accept whatever work they could find.

## Focus on Children: Early Policies

The 1870s saw the origins of child welfare policy as it has evolved today (Karger & Stoesz, 2014). Prior to this time, abandoned, unwanted, or orphaned children had been placed in almshouses along with adults suffering from poverty and disabilities. By this time, however, people were beginning to view children as special beings requiring treatment qualitatively different from that provided adults and people with disabilities. Orphanages intended solely for children began to multiply, replacing almshouses as places to house children. This practice was, however, still institutional placement.

The Reverend Charles Loring Brace, founder of New York's Children's Aid Society, became the first proponent of placing children in homes other than their own instead of in institutions. Brace gathered up thousands of juvenile paupers from the New York City streets and sent them to live with farm families in the Midwest. He believed that farmers were the ideal citizens and that farming was the ideal occupation. A staunch believer in the importance of the environment, as stressed by Social Darwinism, Brace felt that placing children in such positive environments would make them better, more productive citizens.

By the early 20th century, most large cities had their own children's aid societies that placed or "farmed out" children to families instead of putting them in institutions. This movement reflected the beginnings of foster care and adoption in the United States. Highlight 6.3 discusses the early development of protective services.

## Settlement Houses, Charity Organization Societies, and Generalist Social Work

In response to the rapidly growing social problems, two social and ideological movements became the foundation for social work practice in the 1880s and continued into the early 1900s (Lewis & Suarez, 1995). They were the settlement house movement and charity organization societies.

### Settlement Houses

**Settlement houses** were neighborhood-based centers where humanitarians, interested students, and others "settled" (hence the name) to help people living in poverty improve their communities and their lives: goals included meeting residents' needs, such as

## THE EARLY DEVELOPMENT OF PROTECTIVE SERVICES

The concept of protective services was born under some unusual circumstances in 1874. Etta Wheeler, a New York City relief worker for the poor, discovered that Mary Ellen Wilson, age 9, who had been an indentured servant since age 18 months, "was being tied to a bed, whipped, and stabbed with scissors" (Karger & Stoesz, 2014, p. 319). It was subsequently determined that Mary Ellen was the illegitimate child of her tormentor, Mary Connelly's first husband.

Wheeler "sought help from the police, benevolent societies, and charitable gentlemen," but to no avail (Watkins, 1990, p. 501). Finally, in desperation, she appealed to the president of the New York Society for the Prevention of Cruelty to Animals. Interested in the case, he helped Wheeler get "a special warrant" from a New York Supreme Court judge to remove Mary Ellen from the abusive home (Watkins, 1990, p. 502).

Historical and current myths often imply that children living in the 1870s had to be categorized as animals before they could receive legal protection (Watkins, 1990). In reality, the court never treated Mary Ellen as if the same laws applied to her as to animals. However, the case received extensive publicity focusing on how Mary Ellen had been treated worse than what was legally allowed for animals. It brought to people's attention how children were sometimes in need of protective treatment.

What happened to Mary Ellen? Wheeler's own mother, and later her sister, took Mary Ellen in; Mary Ellen "was married at age 24 and had two daughters" (Watkins, 1990, p. 502). "As a punishment to herself, but more as a warning to others," Mary Connelly was sentenced to "one year in the Penitentiary at hard labor," the maximum sentence possible ("Mary Ellen Wilson," 1874, p. 8; Watkins, 1990, p. 502). As a result of Mary Ellen's case, societies for the prevention of cruelty to children were established all over the country in the late 1800s and early 1900s.

providing education and training, and advocating for human rights and improved community conditions (Day & Schiele, 2013).

Day and Schiele (2013) elaborate:

*Settlement houses were run in part by client groups, and they emphasized social reform rather than relief or assistance. Three-fourths of settlement workers were women, and most were well-educated and dedicated to working on problems of urban poverty. Early sources of funding were wealthy individuals or clubs such as the Junior League, and at first their founders tried to provide "culture" to members, such as art, music, and lectures. When they found a need, they added new features such as playgrounds, day care, kindergartens, baths, and classes in English literacy. Other services included art exhibits, lectures, and classes in homemaking, cooking, sewing, and shopping, especially for immigrant women who were not used to the facilities available in the United States such as grocery stores and the products they offered (fresh bread, milk, and canned goods). Settlement workers tried to improve housing conditions, organized protests, offered job training and labor searches, supported organized labor, worked against child labor, and fought*
*against corrupt politicians. Over time settlement houses became centers of social reform, and clubs, societies, and political groups such as the Socialist party used them as bases of operation. (p. 213)*

Settlement houses formed a strong foundation for generalist social work practice within communities in at least three ways (Smith, 1995). First, the settlement house approach addressed the problems of people in an environmental context instead of focusing on individual pathology. Environmental problems created difficulties for individuals, who were not viewed as the targets of blame, punishment, and change. Settlement houses thus focused on addressing social issues and improving living conditions, especially for the poorest and least fortunate people.

Second, an environmental focus led naturally to an emphasis on advocacy and social reform. (We have established that **advocacy** is the act of standing up for and defending the cause of another.) This is appropriate when the macro social environment requires change to meet people's needs.

Third, settlement houses emphasized the empowerment of people. At its most basic level, *empowerment* involves providing people with authority or power.

According to the settlement house perspective, people had strengths and capabilities to effect their own change. Families and neighborhoods were seen as potential vehicles for positive change. The concepts of community organization and group work (both described in Chapter 5) developed within the settlement house context. Jane Addams and Ellen Gates Starr opened perhaps the most famous settlement house, Hull House, in Chicago in 1889. Highlight 6.4 focuses on Jane Addams, an immensely important figure in the development of social work and advocacy for social change.

---

## HIGHLIGHT 6.4   JANE ADDAMS

Jane Addams "built her reputation as the country's most prominent woman through her writing, her settlement work, and her international efforts for world peace" (Jane Addams Hull House Museum, 1997). She attained "worldwide recognition in the first third of the 20th century as a pioneer social worker in America, as a feminist, and as an internationalist" (Haberman, 1972).

EP 1

Born in Cedarville, Illinois, on September 6, 1860, Jane was the youngest of six children in a well-to-do family. Her mother died when Jane was 2. Six years later, her father remarried and she gained two stepbrothers. Jane deeply respected her father, John Addams, a miller, who was "a shrewd and careful investor" and one of Cedarville's "leading citizens" (Stroup, 1986, p. 2). John "was a local political leader who served for 16 years as a state senator and fought as an officer in the Civil War; he was a friend of Abraham Lincoln, whose letters to him began 'My Dear Double D-'ed Addams'" (Haberman, 1972).

"Because of a congenital spinal defect, Jane was not physically vigorous when young nor truly robust even later in life," although the defect was corrected later by surgery (Haberman, 1972).

After graduating from the local school, Jane sought a college education at the Rockford Lemale Seminary (later called Rockford College) and graduated in 1881 as class valedictorian. Shortly afterward, her father died, which distressed her greatly as "she lost one of the most powerful influences in her life" (Stroup, 1986, p. 6).

Jane subsequently pursued further study in the field of medicine. "For seven months she worked at her medical studies with considerable zeal and secured high marks for her efforts. But the strain was too much, and her health broke down, forcing her to return to Cedarville" (Stroup, 1986, p. 6). Over the next few years, Jane "was hospitalized intermittently, traveled and studied in Europe for 21 months, and then spent almost two years in reading and writing and in considering what her future objectives should be" (Haberman, 1972). Jane "wanted more in life" than marriage; if "her brothers could have careers in medicine and science, why couldn't she? Besides, she disliked household duties and the prospect of raising children held no appeal" (Women in History, 2005).

Stroup (1986) describes Jane's initial thoughts about the settlement house movement:

[In the spring of 1887 at age 27], Jane went to Madrid along with four friends [including Ellen Starr]. Their tour included a bullfight, and when her friends left the arena because of the brutality, Jane stayed to see five bulls killed. She was drawn to the activity because of its callousness and at the same time repelled because of her idealism. This seems to have been a significant experience in her life because the very next morning she approached Ellen Starr with the idea of establishing a "big house" right in the middle of "horrid little houses" as a means of bringing help to the poor. Ellen was enthusiastic about the idea, and from this experience, Hull House was conceived. Its birth had to wait until Jane and Ellen discovered the work of Cannon Samuel Barnett in the East Side of London.

Toynbee Hall had come into existence only four years prior to Jane Addams's visit. Barnett was its first warden, or "head resident," and it was the first settlement house. Its staff was composed of university men, mainly from Oxford, who lived in the slums of London ... to learn conditions firsthand and to contribute to the improvement of life there with their own personal and financial resources.... It was this idea of the settlement house that Jane Addams also finally used. She believed that what Barnett had been able to do for the poor people of London she might attempt for the poor people of Chicago. She had found her mission, the purpose that she had struggled to find for so many years. (p. 9)

*(continued)*

**HIGHLIGHT 6.4 (continued)**

In 1889 with Ellen Gates Starr, an art teacher, Jane rented a house from "Charles J. Hull, an early resident of Chicago" who "had built his house when the neighborhood was young. It was a two-story brick house, set back from the street, and it seemed perfect as a settlement house" (Stroup, 1986, p. 10). A wide range of programs were developed at Hull House that served as models for other settlement houses around the country. These included nurseries, children's clubs, a gymnasium, a library, an art gallery, a music school, an auditorium, a cafeteria, an employment bureau, a cooperative residence for women who worked, and a curriculum offering a range of classes including music, art, language, and mathematics (Johnson, 2005; Quam, 1995). Jane and other Hull House staff fought for improved conditions involving workplaces, housing, and sanitation; they advocated for improved policies concerning child labor laws, workplace safety, compulsory education, and women's rights (Johnson, 2005). Jane herself was appointed a neighborhood sanitation inspector to improve conditions and get more resources for people who needed them (Quam, 1995).

> Hull House was a refuge for individuals who had no other place to turn in time of trouble. One child, for example, was lodged at the House until he could return to live with his parents. His mother didn't want him because he had been born with a cleft palate. On another occasion, a new bride took shelter in Hull House because her husband beat her during the first week of marriage.
>
> *(Stroup, 1986, p. 12)*

Jane "directed her efforts at the root causes of poverty" and continued living and working at Hull House until her death (Women in History, 2005). However, she was also actively involved in many other organizations and causes. She and her colleagues "forged a powerful reform movement" that initiated projects including "the Immigrants' Protective League, the Juvenile Protective Association, the first juvenile court in the nation, and a Juvenile Psychopathic Clinic (later called the Institute for Juvenile Research)" (Jane Addams Hull House Museum, 1997). Hull House workers advocated for and helped pass laws involving child labor and mandatory education, which eventually spread to the national level. "They worked for legislation to protect immigrants from exploitation, limit the working hours of women, ... recognize labor unions, and provide for industrial safety" (Women in History, 2005).

Jane, an exceptional speaker, often spoke publicly on the behalf of human welfare. She also wrote 11 books and published many articles. Her national efforts involving advocacy to improve social conditions included being the first female president of the National Conference of Charities and Corrections (an organization of social welfare agencies that changed its name to the National Conference of Social Work in 1917). Jane was involved in establishing the Chicago Federation of Settlements in 1894, and later helped found the National Federation of Settlements and Neighborhood Centers in 1911. Additionally, she was a member of national associations and committees too numerous to name here that were aimed at improving a wide range of social conditions and policies. She was a robust supporter of women's right to vote.

Jane was also a strong advocate for international peace. She initially helped form and later became president of the Women's Peace Party in 1915. She served as a delegate for a wide range of peace conferences around the world. Against opposition, she advocated for the United States to denounce war and join with other countries to form global organizations striving for international harmony. Because of her efforts, she was awarded the Nobel Peace Prize in 1931. Jane died in 1935 "three days after an operation revealed unsuspected cancer" (Haberman, 1972). She is remembered and revered as one of the most important advocates for human rights and well-being ever living in this country.

## Charity Organization Societies

The settlement perspective contrasted strikingly with **charity organization societies**. These were agencies that emphasized cooperation among organizations providing assistance, promotion of efficiency, and elimination of fraud. Stern and Axinn (2012) explain that charity organization society movement emphasized "a scientific approach to poverty." The approach stressed

> *the need for a new economy in which the fittest would become the richest. It feared that social welfare measures that supported dependency and misfits would end in the weakening of mankind. The belief in the possibility of an evolution toward a*

*more affluent society, combined with belief in the openness of that society to individual achievement, made the acquisition of personal wealth not only a sign of fitness, but a condition of moral superiority as well. (pp. 95–96)*

Teaching people morality in addition to providing minimal aid would allow people to take care of themselves (Lewis & Suarez, 1995). Initially, the societies used "friendly visitors" who tried to help people figure out how to solve their problems.

As time passed, charity organization societies sought to establish a base of scientific knowledge and apply it to the helping process. The scientific emphasis in fields such as medicine and engineering inspired this orientation. The societies "wanted to

## HIGHLIGHT 6.5    MARY RICHMOND

Born on August 5, 1861, in Belleville, Illinois, Mary Ellen Richmond, "a frail woman who spent most of her life overcoming chronic invalidism in order to help others" (Trattner, 1999, p. 255), "was the only surviving child of Henry and Lavinia Richmond" (Webster.edu, 2005). Tragedy struck Mary at the age of 3 when her mother became sick and died. She was then sent "to live with her grandmother and two aunts in Baltimore" (Webster.edu, 2005). "Frequently ill, she spent a lonely, unhappy childhood in Baltimore" (Trattner, 1999, p. 255). There she attended high school, graduating in 1878. At that time one of her aunts became ill, so Mary assumed responsibility for her care until the aunt died 10 years later. Soon after her aunt's death Mary began working for the Baltimore Charity Organization as an assistant treasurer in 1989, becoming its general secretary two years later.

EP 7a

As early as 1897, Mary began to advocate for the development of professional schools of social casework (which emphasizes helping individuals and families) and structured social work education programming. In 1899 she wrote the first book that provided a thorough description of practical techniques used in doing charitable work with poor people called Friendly Visiting Among the Poor. Topics included suggestions for exploring health, child care, religious involvement, and financial management (Webster.edu, 2005). Her basic belief was that the poor could be helped and reformed by using structured, planned methods.

In 1900 Mary became general secretary of the Philadelphia Society for Organizing Charity, where she stressed the use of volunteers (Longres, 1995). In 1909 she became the director of the Charity Organizational Department of the Russell Sage Foundation, where she conducted major social work research. The New York School of Philanthropy provided another setting where she taught and conducted research over the following years. One of Mary's major achievements was the

development and wide dissemination of educational materials training workers in the process and techniques of social casework.

Mary "wrote Social Diagnosis, the first book to address professional social work practice, in 1917. A guide for the beginning caseworker, the book outlined ways to diagnose and assess need, and it greatly influenced the new profession" (Segal, Gerdes, & Steiner, 2004, p. 50). Mary focused on defining typical tasks performed by early charity workers, especially those related to assessing the causes of families' poverty and dependence (Popple & Leighninger, 2005). She steadfastly investigated the process used by charity organization workers and established a process involving "diagnosis, prognosis, and treatment as entities in a chainlike series; the treatment of individuals, then, was an extended, logical process, the techniques of which could be ordered, described, analyzed, and transmitted from one generation of social workers to another" (Trattner, 1999, p. 255). Mary's work established social casework as a cornerstone of social work by emphasizing individual functioning within the person's and family's environment. Although her primary focus was the individual and family, she did not disapprove of social reform involving larger systems; she simply felt that such reform efforts were generally unsuccessful and that work with individuals would always be necessary (Trattner, 1999). In essence, Mary provided the first articulate formulation of social work theories and techniques upon which the profession could be based.

Mary was a self-taught woman with no college background who read extensively and applied her knowledge in various avenues of social work research. It is interesting that despite her lack of formal training, she strongly advocated for professional social work education and the formal provision of necessary knowledge and techniques. Mary died in 1928 after a flourishing career in which she served as one of the founders of professional social work.

study the problem of dependence, gather data, test theories, systematize administration, and develop techniques that would lead to a cure" (Popple, 1995, p. 2283). The impetus to obtain social work professionalism began when the societies recognized the fact that friendly visitors needed more education and training to perform their tasks effectively (Brieland, 1995; Popple, 1995).

Charity organization societies focused on curing individuals, not on empowering communities. Traditional social casework developed from the former approach. Additionally, because expert knowledge was emphasized, the significance of administration and supervised practice was incorporated in the casework concept. This emphasis on expertise contrasted sharply with the settlement approach, which stressed the empowerment and self-sufficiency of all. Highlight 6.5 focuses on the life and contributions of Mary Richmond, a primary proponent of the charity organization movement and a significant force in the early definition of social work.

### Focus on American Indians: Attempts at Assimilation

Earlier we discussed how treaty formulation and tribal relocation characterized the early treatment of American Indians. From the 1870s to 1900, a new trend, *assimilation*, emerged, perhaps because the federal government was "developing a conscience" (Lewis, 1995, p. 219). In this context, **assimilation** is the process of incorporating another culture into the mainstream culture. The assimilated culture (i.e., that of First Nations Peoples) was thus expected to assume the dominant culture's values and practices while relinquishing its own. The most destructive legislation relating to American Indians in the United States was the Indian General Allotment Act of 1887 (also known as the Dawes Act) (Lewis, 1995). Its intent was to assimilate American Indians by giving them land and potential citizenship in return for turning their backs on their culture and becoming "productive" citizens (Lewis, 1995, p. 219).

One problem was that the European orientation of White Americans emphasized the importance of individuals owning their own property. The concept of sharing communal land, so integral to American Indians, was neither understood nor respected. Over the ensuing 35 years, the Dawes Act resulted in the

EP 2

loss of 75% of all American Indian lands, much of it being sold to non-American Indians or reverting back to federal control (Lewis, 1995).

At least three other thrusts were involved in assimilation (Lewis, 1995). First, the Bureau of Indian Affairs assumed responsibility for American Indian children's education, forcing them to abandon their own language, religion, and customs and to dress, speak, and act like Whites. Second, government officials ignored the authority of tribal leaders when addressing legal and political issues. Third, missionaries were sent to reservations to "civilize" American Indians and purge them of their traditional spiritual beliefs and practices (Lewis, 1995, p. 220).

Assimilation attempts were finally mildly obstructed in 1934 with the Indian Reorganization Act. This legislation banned the practice of allocating tribal lands to individuals, established a credit fund to provide tribes with loans, and gave American Indians preference for being hired in the Bureau of Indian Affairs (Lewis, 1995).

Even this restructuring met with resistance from many First Nations Peoples. As was typical, the act did not include any American Indian notions about how leadership should be structured or people governed (Lewis, 1995). Focus on Critical Thinking 6.1 raises some questions regarding the effects national policy can have on people's self-determination and human rights.

## The Progressive Period: 1900 to the 1920s

The years from 1900 to the 1920s were characterized by the Progressive movement (Karger & Stoesz, 2014; Stern & Axinn, 2012), although settlement houses and charity organization societies continued to characterize the early 20th century. Historical overlap and gradual transitions among trends occur as people's ideas change slowly over time.

The Progressive period was an era when socially mindful and religious people pursued "a unique blend of social reform" (Karger & Stoecz, 2014, p. 42). This period emphasized a government that would assume active responsibility for the welfare of its citizens. Trends during this era included:

- *anti-big business attitudes,*
- *a belief that government should regulate the public good,*

- *a strong emphasis on ethics in business and personal life,*
- *a commitment to social justice,*
- *a concern for the "common man," and*
- *a strong sense of paternalism.*

*(Karger & Stoecz, 2014, p. 42)*

Regulations were established that addressed political corruption and business practices (Reid, 1995). Many people tackled major issues such as child labor, women's working hours, women's suffrage, income security, and family welfare (Stern & Axinn, 2012).

The following are some of the major events characterizing the Progressive era:

- The National Association for the Advancement of Colored People (NAACP), "the largest and oldest of the U.S. civil rights organizations," was created in 1909 (Barker, 2014, p. 282). Initially formed in outrage over the lynching of African Americans, and currently having more than 1,500 chapters in all 50 states, the NAACP protects the rights of African Americans through legal proceedings, enforcement of civil rights laws, and provision of information to the public (Barker, 2014).
- The National Urban League was established in 1911 to help African Americans, especially those moving to New York City from the rural South, to find suitable employment and adjust to urban life; the organization soon expanded its influence to other cities (Nittle, 2011).
- Between 1911 and 1919, most states initiated pension programs that provided assistance to single mothers (Jansson, 2015). These were the first

financial assistance programs for mothers with dependent children.

- A major step forward in the development of protective services was the first White House Conference on Dependent Children in 1909. The "resulting strong recommendation in favor of family care strengthened the movement for home rather than institutional care for dependent and delinquent children" (Trattner, 1999, p. 216). Seven conferences were held at the White House from 1909 to 1970 (Child Welfare League of America [CWLA], n.d.). Another important result of the initial conference was the formation of the U.S. Children's Bureau in 1912. One of its purposes was to collect systematic information on children. This marked the first time that children's welfare had been considered significant enough to spur creation of a permanent federal agency to oversee it (Trattner, 1999).
- In 1920 the 19th Amendment to the U.S. Constitution granted women the right to vote.

### Focus on Mental Health Policy

Mental health policy in the beginning of the 20th century reflected the **mental hygiene movement**, replacing the earlier focus on moral treatment. The mental hygiene movement, which lasted from about 1900 to about 1945, was an initiative that focused on the improvement of mental health. It was characterized by three main ideas (Fellin, 1996; Lin, 1995; USDHHS, 1999). First, people were becoming disillusioned with mental hospitals and the substandard conditions in many. Second, although institutionalization was not abandoned, alternative types of care such as specialized psychiatric units in hospitals were being developed. This paved the way for the next *mental health movement (community mental health)*, an initiative that focused on treatment within the community context. Finally, the concept of "mental illness" began to replace "insanity," and psychotherapy as a treatment method gained in popularity. Chapter 13 discusses psychotherapy and mental health issues generally in greater detail.

## Focus on Asian Immigration

The "Progressive period" label notwithstanding, this era was not so progressive for Asians and Hispanics trying to enter the United States. The first Asian people to immigrate to the United States during the mid-19th century were Chinese, who came to the United States like many others seeking a better life (Jansson, 2015). They often performed "manual labor for farmers, manufacturers, miners, and the railroads" (Jansson, 2015, p. 128). Chinese immigrants were easy to exploit. "They could be paid minimal wages (coercive tactics were used when they threatened to strike for higher wages) and used to depress the wages of White workers, and they did not constitute a political threat because as 'aliens' and people of color they were denied legal rights. (The California Supreme Court ruled in 1854 that Chinese people could not testify in court against Whites, even if one of their number had been murdered by a White citizen.) They were disallowed from owning mines by tax levies, could not become citizens, were required to attend segregated schools, and could not vote" (Jansson, 2015, p. 128). Blatant racism and apprehension that Chinese immigrants were stealing jobs away from their White counterparts resulted in the Chinese Exclusion Act of 1882, which denied the Chinese further access to the country (Jansson, 2015; Lu, 2008).

Japanese immigrants soon began to replace the Chinese in the U.S. labor market (Jansson, 2015). Like the Chinese, they were the victims of stereotypes and discrimination; for example, their children, too, attended segregated schools, they were prohibited from marrying interracially, laws banned the ownership of land, unions pro-  **EP 2** hibited their entry into certain skilled trades, and instead they were diverted into manual labor jobs less appealing to White employees (Murase, 1995).

Japanese immigration soon began to be politically discouraged, and finally the Immigration Act of 1924 halted Asian immigration almost altogether, a state of affairs lasting until 1968 (Day & Schiele, 2013). This act limited the number of immigrants allowed from any particular nationality to 2% of that nationality's population living in the United States in 1890. The effect was a greater percentage of people of Northern European heritage being admitted because a greater percentage already lived in the United States; because few Japanese lived in the United States during 1890, few were subsequently allowed admission (Jansson, 2015).

## Focus on Chicano and Chicana and Puerto Rican Immigration

Initiated by the Mexican Revolution of 1910, large numbers of Chicano and Chicana professionals and businessmen in addition to laborers entered the United States as refugees (Curiel, 1995). As many as 1 million Chicanos and Chicanas migrated to the United States between 1910 and 1930 (Curiel, 1995; Meier, 1990). Substantial  **EP 2** immigration continued across a 2,000-mile, relatively open boundary until 1924 when the U.S. Border Patrol was born; even then people continued to cross over to work on farms, orchards, and ranches and in food-processing plants (Jansson, 2015). White farmers and businessmen promoted Chicano and Chicana immigration. Hiring migrant labor was much cheaper than employing other citizens at minimum wage. No legal consequences existed for employers who hired people without documentation even if these employers were fully aware of their status. Employers did not concern themselves with the workers' conditions and could readily discourage protests.

When the Great Depression (described next) shook the economy in the 1930s, many Americans, including Chicanos, lost their jobs and found themselves desperately competing for survival (Curiel, 1995). To decrease the economic pressure, entire Chicano families were abruptly deported; shockingly, it is estimated that half of the deportees were U.S. citizens (Curiel, 1995).

Puerto Ricans migrated to the United States throughout the 20th century. (Highlight 6.6 provides a brief history of Puerto Rico.) Upon obtaining U.S. citizenship in 1917, Puerto Ricans gained the ability to readily travel back and forth without constraints.

## HIGHLIGHT 6.6   A BRIEF HISTORY OF PUERTO RICO

Campos (1995) presents a thumbnail sketch of Puerto Rico's history. The Taino Indians were the original inhabitants of Puerto Rico, which became a Spanish possession after Christopher Columbus "discovered" it in 1493. (Note how condescending the word *discovered* is when the island had probably been occupied for many centuries.) The Spanish conquerors believed that gold was plentiful on the island and coerced the Indians into working the mines. Poor treatment resulted in many Indian deaths, while others escaped the island entirely. When the available gold supply was exhausted, the Spaniards turned to agriculture, bringing in African slaves to work in the fields. Slavery was finally abolished in 1875.

The 19th century saw increased immigration to Puerto Rico from China, Spain, and other European countries, which together with the existing Spanish, Indian, and African residents resulted in a significantly diverse population (Campos, 1995). In 1898, after the Spanish-American War ended, Spain gave Puerto Rico to the United States under the Treaty of Paris of 1899.

No Puerto Rican representatives were allowed to participate in this process or to influence what was to happen to their country. Puerto Rico then came under U.S. military rule until the U.S. president appointed an American governor two years later.

Many Puerto Ricans, who attained U.S. citizenship in 1917 under the Jones Act, expressed ambivalence about that new status. One faction felt it was an asset, while another preferred that Puerto Rico pursue independence. It wasn't until 1950 that Puerto Ricans were allowed to write their own constitution; in 1952 they could first elect their own governor and legislature.

Currently, a close relationship exists between Puerto Rico and the United States where both are committed to a common citizenship, legal tender, protection, and the value of democracy. Practically speaking, the United States retains control over specified arenas including federal and military operations and foreign affairs (e.g., the U.S. Post Office) (Campos, 1995). Puerto Rico has primary control over its educational system, budget, governing laws, and correctional system. There is an ongoing internal debate among Puerto Rican citizens whether to maintain their current political status, amend that status (e.g., become an independent nation), or become a U.S. state (Gonzalez, 2013).

# The Great Depression and the 1930s

The Great Depression was initiated by the shocking stock market crash of 1929. The general trend over the next decade was an increasing reliance on the federal government to control and provide social services (Leiby, 1987). The Great Depression of the 1930s had a global impact, obliterating the idea that individuals control their own destiny. It became clear that the world contained various macro systems that worked together to profoundly affect individual lives. The United States was plagued by huge decreases in manufacturing productivity and wages, on the one hand, and skyrocketing unemployment, on the other. Banks closed, farmers lost everything, and urban poverty spread (Garvin & Tropman, 1998). Highlight 6.7 focuses on more of the Depression's consequences.

President Franklin Delano Roosevelt (holding office from 1933 to 1945) aggressively addressed the crisis. In 1933 he initiated the New Deal, a vigorous plan that created a wide range of social programs and significantly extended federal control in social welfare matters. Reid (1995) contends that the New Deal established a new perspective on how a welfare state operates that still is in effect today.

## Early Initiatives of the New Deal

In view of the social and economic crisis, Roosevelt initiated a range of programs to address people's dire needs. Initially, the New Deal emphasized "increased spending for the unemployed and more public works," in addition to significant cuts in federal spending (Stern & Axinn, 2012, p. 168). Roosevelt pursued a three-pronged approach involving "cash relief, short-term work relief, and the expansion of employment" by hiring unemployed workers to undertake public works (Stern & Axinn, 2012, p. 180). Eventually, it was determined that more was needed to address the ominous economic conditions imposed by the Great Depression. The programs developed provide

---

HIGHLIGHT **6.7**     HUMAN CONDITIONS DURING
THE GREAT DEPRESSION

Jansson (2015) lists some of the immediate consequences of the Depression:

- *People from all levels of socioeconomic status were affected.*
- *Some families were forced to leave their homes and live in tents, and some had to share a small apartment with at least two other families.*
- *Single women clustered together in a single residence and often were compelled to depend on a single wage earner for sustenance.*
- *People raised crops in home gardens when they couldn't afford to buy food.*

- *Teenagers were booted from their homes to fend for themselves when families couldn't afford to support them.*
- *Middle-class citizens "feared foreclosure or evictions" and "had to pawn family possessions" to keep afloat.*
- *Starvation and malnutrition were rampant.*
- *Health care was often unavailable because people were denied care when they couldn't pay for it.*
- *Serious disturbances in family life and suicides were common occurrences. (p. 208)*

---

examples of what a government can do for its citizens during a national economic emergency.

### The Federal Emergency Relief Act

In 1933 Roosevelt signed the Federal Emergency Relief Act (FERA), which provided federal grants to the states that would be administered by government units at the state and local levels to people in need. Although FERA's intent was to aid the unemployed, many working poor who could not earn enough to support their families also received aid. Additionally, it established camps for displaced persons, provided loans to college students, and purchased and sold 4 million acres of land to tenant farmers.

### The Civilian Works Administration

Shortly after FERA was signed into law, Roosevelt assumed his presidential prerogative and created the Civilian Works Administration (CWA) in 1933. The CWA channeled funds to finance various public works such as building roads, cataloging resources in libraries, digging drainage ditches, and renovating parks. The intent, of course, was to create jobs.

### The Civilian Conservation Corps

Another program developed as part of the New Deal was the Civilian Conservation Corps (CCC), also created in 1933. This program initially recruited males between 18 and 25 who were receiving public assistance, and transported them to revitalize parks

in the West and participate in reforestation, flood prevention, and fire control projects. Once again, the intent was to provide employment to a population that had an exceptionally high unemployment rate. Similarly, the National Youth Administration (NYA) provided part-time work for high school and college students to encourage them to remain in school.

### The Public Works Administration

In 1935 Roosevelt established the Public Works Administration (PWA). The PWA's intent was to encourage economic growth and help struggling industries; this was done by contracting with private businesses to build public facilities, thereby increasing the number of available jobs (Barker, 2014). Projects tended to be extensive and complex, such as "bridges, airports, dams, and school buildings" (Jansson, 2015, p. 220).

### The Works Progress Administration

Similarly, in 1935 Roosevelt established the Works Progress Administration (WPA) (renamed the Works Projects Administration in 1939). This was yet another program designed to provide work for unemployed people with various skills. One thrust was to support the "work of artists, musicians, writers, and scholars" (Barker, 2014, p. 458). WPA also provided jobs in a wide range of activities, from "heavy construction [of dams, bridges, parks, roads, and airports] to the painting of murals in local libraries and orchestral performances in the schools" (Stern & Axinn, 2012, p. 182; Jansson, 2015).

### An End to the Programs

FERA, along with CWA, was terminated when the Social Security Act of 1935 was passed; CCC, NYA, PWA, and WPA saw their demise in the early 1940s at the beginning of World War II. Much of the legislation passed during the Depression was not intended to be permanent; rather, its purpose was to provide temporary jobs so people could support themselves during those hard times instead of being forced to accept charity.

### The Social Security Act of 1935

The most notable piece of legislation shaping social welfare policy during this period was the Social Security Act of 1935. Consisting of 11 titles (or major parts, each of which addresses a specified issue and program), this legislation totally reconfigured the social welfare system and placed the burden on the federal government to provide a coordinated system of resources. It established a structure of benefits in three major categories: (1) social insurance, (2) public assistance, and (3) health services ("federal monies for state and local public health works") (Tice & Perkins, 2002, p. 156). (Note that, because of their significance, Chapter 8 elaborates upon current policies and programs in greater detail. Although the Social Security Act of 1935 forms the basis for current policies and programs, numerous modifications and additions to the social welfare system have been made since that time.)

Federal legislation affects service provision in two basic ways. First, it provides federal funding to states to help them pay for programs and services. Without federal help, states often wouldn't have the money for many resources and services. Second, federal legislation imposes rules on the states that receive funding. If a state wants federal money, it must abide by the rules or forfeit the funding. All states want money. Therefore, federal legislation has set the stage for the types of programs that states must provide by making rules and establishing requirements to receive funding.

### Social Insurance

Social insurance and public assistance both provide **financial benefits**—benefits in the form of cash or coupons that can be used in place of cash. **Social insurance** is a government program providing benefits related to certain designated risks working people assume; these include "old age, disability, death of a breadwinner, unemployment, and work-related injury and sickness" (Barker, 2014, p. 398). It's a type of insurance because workers and their employers pay premiums while they're working. They then receive benefits when encountering the specified conditions permitting benefits. The idea is that benefits are people's *right*: They worked and paid the premiums, and so deserve the benefits.

The Social Security Act established old age insurance (pensions) for older adults, in addition to unemployment insurance and worker's compensation for the unemployed (Tice & Perkins, 2002). **Unemployment insurance** provides cash benefits to employees who lose their jobs. **Workers' compensation** gives cash benefits to employees who suffer work-related injuries or illness.

### Public Assistance

In contrast to social insurance, **public assistance** programs are based on *need*. Public assistance is a government program providing financial resources to people who can't support themselves. The Social Security Act established public assistance for older adults (Old Age Assistance), dependent children in single-parent families and children with disabilities (Aid to Dependent Children), and people who are blind (Aid to the Blind) (Tice & Perkins, 2002).

Often there is much greater stigma attached to people receiving public assistance than to those receiving social insurance. Many feel that it's their own fault that they're needy and that they should do something about it. Unlike people receiving social insurance, the argument goes, they never paid premiums for public assistance and so don't really deserve benefits. (Note that people receiving public assistance may also be eligible for social insurance benefits, depending on their work history and status.)

In reality, though no fault of their own, many people are in serious need of help—including many children. Highlight 6.8 focuses on public assistance for children and families.

## War and Wealth: The 1940s

The U.S. involvement in World War II (1941–1945) brought an end to the Depression as unemployment plummeted and incomes rose significantly (Stern & Axinn, 2012). Many people felt optimistic about the

## HIGHLIGHT 6.8 — PUBLIC ASSISTANCE FOR CHILDREN AND FAMILIES

The Social Security Act of 1935 expanded the government's responsibility for the well-being of children and their families. Title IV, Aid to Dependent Children (ADC) (later changed to Aid to Families with Dependent Children [AFDC] in 1962 to emphasize the importance of the family), "provided public relief to needy children through cash grants to their families"; another provision, Title V, broadened the role of the Children's Bureau to provide greater protection for children at risk of poverty, maltreatment, or delinquency (Karger & Stoesz, 2014, p. 320). The current public assistance program, which replaced AFDC in 1996, is Temporary Assistance for Needy Families (TANF), discussed further along with other public assistance programs in Chapter 8.

future and believed that the Social Security Act had adequately solved most of the problems related to poverty.

A significant piece of 1940s legislation was the Serviceman's Readjustment Act of 1944, commonly referred to as the G.I. Bill. Its purpose was to give veterans opportunities for "education and training, home and business loans, and employment services" to help them return to civilian life (Segal & Brzuzy, 1998, p. 33).

It is beyond the scope of this chapter to discuss the intricacies of World War II. However, the history of social welfare includes not only policies providing services that enhance people's welfare but also those depriving people of resources and even causing them harm. Unfair, racist treatment is of special concern to social workers. Highlight 6.9 addresses the atrocious and unjust treatment of Japanese Americans during World War II.

## Peace and Complacency: The 1950s

During the 1950s, the population exploded, resulting in the current huge bloc of aging baby boomers. (Chapter 10 addresses issues related to older adults more thoroughly.) Many people think of the 1950s as a period of domestic complacency and relative conservatism. Criticisms of social welfare policy at the time focused on restricting eligibility for benefits and making it difficult to continue getting them (Stern & Axinn, 2012).

## HIGHLIGHT 6.9 — JAPANESE AMERICAN INTERNMENT DURING WORLD WAR II

On December 7, 1941, Japanese aircraft bombed Pearl Harbor, and the United States entered the war the following day. Within days, Japanese Americans were placed under close and hostile public scrutiny. A few weeks later, California declared that Japanese Americans could no longer assume any civil service positions, including holding public office. Japanese American citizens were fired from their jobs, forced to close their businesses, unlawfully confined, and even viciously assaulted (Day, 2009).

EP 2

Although Roosevelt declared that all German, Italian, and Japanese aliens should leave the West Coast, only Japanese Americans were pressured to remain away more permanently (Day & Schiele, 2013). Japanese American soldiers were identified and discharged or assigned menial labor such as kitchen work.

By the fall of 1942, permanent detention (concentration) camps called "relocation centers" were established throughout the West, especially in California. With no trial or due process, more than 112,000 Japanese Americans, two-thirds of whom were citizens, were forced to leave their homes and live in guarded camps until their release in 1944.

The secretary of the treasury charged the Federal Reserve Bank of San Francisco to look after Japanese American property, and the Farm Security Administration was supposed to do the same for Japanese farms and equipment. However, little, if anything, was done. The detainees lost $400 million worth of property, of which less than 10% was ever returned (Day & Schiele, 2013).

## FOCUS ON CRITICAL THINKING 6.2 — PERSONAL RIGHTS OF ASSISTANCE RECIPIENTS

Critical thinking involves the three-step, Triple-A process: (1) ask questions, (2) assess facts, and (3) assert a conclusion. How would you answer the following questions?

### Critical Thinking Questions

- To what extent should the government be allowed to intervene in the personal lives of people who receive financial assistance?
- To what extent should the government be allowed to intervene in the personal lives of its employees?

- To what extent should the government be allowed to intervene in your personal life?
- How should governmental intervention differ, if at all, concerning its involvement in the lives of people receiving assistance or people it employs, or in your own life?
- To what extent is the assumption true that a man romantically involved with a mother should be expected to provide her and her family financial support? To what extent, if any, does this reflect a sexist approach?

**EP 2, 5c**

For example, one social worker employed in a county public assistance program during those years reflects on how policies urged workers to literally look under beds and in closets to determine if "there was a man in the house." Two somewhat conflicting assumptions were at work (Stern & Axinn, 2012). First, it was assumed that a legally unattached man living in the home of a family receiving benefits made the home morally unsuitable for raising children. Second, such a man should be able to provide support for the family so it would no longer require benefits. (Focus on Critical Thinking 6.2 poses some questions regarding the appropriateness of these policies.) A California Supreme Court decision in 1967 effectively ended such policies when the court determined that workers could not be fired for failing to comply with such rules (Stern & Axinn, 2012; *Parrish v. Civil Service Commission,* 1967). Later court decisions eliminated man-in-the-house rules altogether (*King v. King,* 1968; *Shapiro v. Thompson,* 1969).

## Amendments to the Social Security Act

A major 1950 piece of social welfare legislation involved amendments to the Social Security Act. Public assistance coverage was broadened to include people who had temporary and permanent disabilities through a program entitled Aid to the Disabled (later called Aid to the Permanently and Totally Disabled) (Tice & Perkins, 2002). Additionally, the ADC program was expanded to provide benefits to

primary caregivers of dependent children (Stern & Axinn, 2012).

## The End of School Segregation

In a landmark ruling in 1954 in *Brown v. Board of Education,* the Supreme Court overturned the "separate but equal" doctrine and declared that racial segregation in public schools was unconstitutional—even when separate schools provided the same quality of education. Although this decision paved the way for stopping blatant racial discrimination in various other public settings such as train and bus stations, restaurants, and recreational facilities, it took many years of struggle to effectively put this principle into practice (Pollard, 1995).

## Focus on Mental Health: The Deinstitutionalization Movement

After World War II, the third mental health movement of the last century gained momentum, and it continues to characterize mental health service provision to this day (Fellin, 1996). The **deinstitutionalization movement** (following the mental hygiene movement) is an initiative that focuses on providing services and care for people within their own communities rather than in institutional settings (Fellin, 1996; Lin, 1995; USDHHS, 1999). It stresses placing people back in the community and providing mental health treatment and services to them there. The deinstitutionalization movement resulted from the increasing belief that, with outpatient psychotherapeutic treatment and psychotropic drugs (i.e., drugs intended to affect mental or emotional functioning), people with mental illness could function in the community environment (Fellin, 1996; USDHHS, 1999). This effort has also been referred to as the *community mental health movement.*

# The 1960s and the War on Poverty

Any sense of optimism or complacency in the 1950s began to weaken as the 1960s began and poverty remained a large problem. Three dynamics shaped this view (Stern & Axinn, 2012). First, large pockets of poverty characterized various regions of the country, and attention was focused on what could be done to ameliorate this poverty. For example, "if the people of Appalachia suffered from the decrease of jobs in coal mining, then the expansion of factory employment seemed appropriate" (Stern & Axinn, 2012, p. 234). Questions might be raised regarding what could be done to stimulate employment and industrial growth in that area.

A second dynamic shaping the nation's perspective on poverty involved the fact that the risk of poverty for people of color was significantly greater than that for Whites. People of color clearly experienced regular discrimination in employment throughout the country.

The third dynamic concerning poverty involved the fact that public assistance rolls were escalating even as unemployment decreased. Prior to the 1960s, the two had a correlated relationship. That is, when unemployment was low, public assistance rolls declined because more people were working. But now this was no longer the case. Public assistance rolls were escalating regardless of whether employment was available.

## The Public Welfare Amendments of 1962

Under the administration of President John F. Kennedy (serving from 1961 until his assassination in 1963), significant new amendments to the Social Security Act were passed. The Public Welfare Amendments of 1962 were rooted in the idea that supportive social services would enhance welfare recipients' ability to get back on their feet and eventually become self-supporting. Services included job training, job placement, and counseling, among others (Trattner, 1999).

The act directed the federal government to assume 75% of the cost of providing social services to people receiving public assistance. This was a tremendous incentive for states to provide services because they had to assume only 25% of the financial burden for doing so. The idea was to reduce welfare rolls. Unfortunately, this did not work, and welfare rolls continued to escalate.

## The "Great Society"

During the 1960s, President Lyndon B. Johnson (whose administration lasted from 1963 to 1969) initiated the "War on Poverty" in an effort to fashion a "Great Society." The intent was to eliminate poverty and provide a high quality of life for all. The War on Poverty was founded on the idea that what poor families really needed was encouragement and training to acquire needed job skills, allowing them to achieve economic independence (Leiby, 1987). However, the poor faced not only economic hardship, but also psychological and sociological barriers (e.g., prejudice and discrimination) to living effective, successful lives (Leiby, 1987). Some theorists referred to the poor as living in a **culture of poverty**—the pattern of values, norms, and expectations conveyed from one generation to another that limits people to a life of poverty and discourages them from taking advantage of economic and social opportunities (Barker, 2014; Karger & Stoesz, 2014). The War on Poverty intended for poor families to be offered and have greater access to the resources and services they needed to pursue economic independence and a better quality of life.

As a result, numerous new programs were developed at the federal level, as the War on Poverty was entirely a federal initiative (Leiby, 1987). The Economic Opportunity Act of 1964 established a range of programs, including Volunteers in Service to America and Operation Head Start, among many others.

Highlight 6.10 describes some of these programs. Primary efforts were concentrated on fighting poverty in poor neighborhoods and communities by increasing jobs, resources, and opportunities for residents (Karger & Stoesz, 2014). Such programs encouraged citizen participation. This was a time of activism for professional social workers on behalf of various populations in need, reflecting a renewed optimism that poverty could be eliminated and a good quality of life enjoyed by all.

Many other initiatives were undertaken during the War on Poverty. For instance, the Food Stamp

## HIGHLIGHT 6.10    THE ECONOMIC OPPORTUNITY ACT OF 1964

The following programs were established when the Economic Opportunity Act, also referred to as the "antipoverty bill," was passed in 1964 (Trattner, 1999, p. 322):

- Volunteers in Service to America (VISTA): A program designed to recruit volunteers to work in urban and rural neighborhoods experiencing economic and cultural problems, and to assist residents in enhancing their communities.
- Job Corps: A program that recruited impoverished youths ages 16–24 from disadvantaged urban and rural communities, and provided them with "residential training, employment, and work skills" (Barker, 2003, p. 232).

- Upward Bound: A program targeting school-age children and presenting them with special educational resources and incentives to prevent them from dropping out of school.
- Neighborhood Youth Corps: A program employing teenagers in local organizations.
- Operation Head Start: A program giving preschoolers resources designed to meet educational, health, and recreational needs throughout the year.
- Community Action Program (CAP): A program that developed and coordinated efforts by neighborhood organizations to fight poverty and improve social and economic conditions for community residents. (Operation Head Start was initially funded and coordinated under CAP.)

---

Act of 1964 initiated a program in which eligible needy families could receive coupons that could be exchanged for food. Another initiative involved greatly expanded coverage by the Social Security Act in 1965 to include **Medicare** (a social insurance program of health care for older adults) and **Medicaid** (a public assistance program of health care for needy children and families). The Housing and Urban Development (HUD) Act of 1968 provided new low-income housing opportunities for eligible families. Chapter 8 describes all four of these programs in greater detail.

Amendments to the Social Security Act in 1967 reorganized resource and service distribution. These changes

*divorced income maintenance functions from social services functions and split public welfare departments into two sections: social services, whose workers provide counseling services and services to neglected, abused, or dependent children and older people; and assistance payments, whose workers determine eligibility and set amounts of grants based on state levels of need, number in family, and their own discretion.*

*(Day & Schiele, 2013, p. 321)*

The driving force behind this change was the idea that "services to the poor should not be connected to

whether they receive financial aid" (Day & Schiele, 2013, p. 321).

### Focus on Mental Health: The Community Mental Health Centers Act

In 1963 the Community Mental Health Centers Act was passed, providing federal funding for community mental health centers, education for mental health staff, and opportunities for outpatient treatment (Trattner, 1999). This, of course, was a manifestation of the deinstitutionalization movement. However, problems arose for three reasons (Lin, 1995). First, treating people in the community was much more complicated and difficult than anticipated. Second, many professionals preferred not to work with this population with its long-term problems. Third, communities either did not have or would not commit the resources necessary to sustain community care. As a result, many people with mental illness ended up on the streets or in jail, for lack of better placement and services. These problems continue to this day.

Note that during the 1960s a trend toward legal advocacy developed (Lin, 1995). As a consequence of the civil rights movement, it focused on emphasizing and clarifying the rights of mental patients. Two court cases are particularly significant (Lin, 1995). In *Wyatt v. Stickney* (1971), a federal court ruled that mental patients should not be exposed to extreme or possibly damaging types of treatment. In *O'Connor v. Donaldson* (1975), the Supreme Court determined that mental illness and treatment needs are insufficient grounds for confining a person involuntarily (Lin, 1995).

### Focus on Older Adults: The Older Americans Act of 1965

Unlike the Social Security Act, the Older Americans Act (OAA) of 1965 is not a policy to provide programming and resources directly to people. Rather, it establishes an "administrative structure" for the coordination and delivery of social services to older people (Barusch, 2015, p. 424). The OAA created an Administration on Aging (AOA) under the auspices of the Department of Health, Education, and Welfare to oversee state and area offices throughout the country.

**3a, 5a, 8a**

Benefits coordinated by AOA offices include transportation; provision of hot meals delivered to people's homes or provided at senior centers ("focus points" where seniors can gather for a variety of purposes); preventive health care such as inoculations or health education; recreation; home care (in which various services involving health, daily living support, or other social services are provided in people's own homes); information; and resource referral (Barusch, 2015; Dobelstein, 2003, p. 258). Anyone age 60 or older is eligible for services, regardless of their economic status. Because the focus is on coordination of services, not prescriptions about what should be provided, services vary dramatically from one location to the next (Dobelstein, 2003). Chapter 10 discusses service provision to older adults in detail.

## Civil Rights in the 1960s

The concept of **civil rights** "refers primarily to claims by African Americans and other … [people] of color, women, and people of different sexual orientations to be free to do the same kinds of things and have the same kinds of civil entitlements that everyone else in the society enjoyed" (Garvin & Tropman, 1998, p. 255).

**EP 2, 3a, 5a, 5c**

During the early 1960s, "poverty was widespread in America, and nonwhite people were systematically discriminated against in all facets of American life" (Day & Schiele, 2013, p. 308). It might be said that the civil rights movement actually began in 1955 when organizers selected a young African American minister named Martin Luther King, Jr., to spearhead a bus boycott in Montgomery, Alabama (Jansson, 2015). The protesters refused to comply with the public policy whereby African Americans were relegated to the backs of buses while Whites got to sit in the front. After a long period of controversy and conflict, including violent acts of retribution against African Americans, the policy was withdrawn.

The Civil Rights Act of 1964 was the most important piece of civil rights legislation since the Civil War. Chapin (2014) describes it as a "landmark law [that] attempted to decrease discrimination by:

- barring unequal application of voter registration requirements;
- outlawing segregation in hotels, restaurants, theaters, and other public accommodations;
- encouraging school desegregation and authorizing the U.S. attorney general to file lawsuits against schools that resisted integration;
- empowering federal agencies to withhold funds from programs that practiced segregation; and,
- creating the Equal Employment Opportunity Commission (EEOC) to oversee antidiscrimination efforts in employment." (p. 281)

Jimenez, Pasztor, and Chambers (2015) report on what happened after the act passed:

*A movement of college students from across the country known as Freedom Summer sponsored a voter registration drive in the South. Three students working in the effort, two Whites and one African American, were murdered, and almost 100 others were beaten by Southerners who objected to their efforts to register African Americans to vote. Congress responded by passing the Voting Rights Act of 1965, which put federal registrars in districts where local officials were obstructing registration of African American voters. Within months, approximately 250,000 African Americans had become registered voters, and the number of Black elected officials increased from 1,000 in 1969 to more than 7,200 in 1989. The southern states' voter registration numbers doubled within four years of the law's enactment. (p. 241)*

FOCUS ON CRITICAL
THINKING 6.3

CIVIL RIGHTS

Consider the following questions:

Critical Thinking Questions
- Why did it take so long to establish equal rights for people of color?

EP 1b, 2, 5c, 8a

- If you were denied certain rights held by others on the basis of some personal characteristic, how would you feel?
- If you were forced to sit in the back of a bus because of some personal characteristic, how would you feel?
- How might you react to such circumstances?

Focus on Critical Thinking 6.3 raises some key questions concerning these acts and the issues they address.

## Focus on Mexican Americans: The Chicano and Chicana Movement

No clearly defined dates exist for the "Chicano movement" (Curiel, 1995). During the 1960s, various Chicano and Chicana groups came together to address their social and economic plight. Common goals included celebration of their ethnic and cultural identity and traditions, in addition to enhanced socioeconomic status (Curiel, 1995). A key how Chicano and Chicana income levels issue involved continued to lag significantly behind those of their White counterparts.

EP 2, 2a, 3a

Because Chicano and Chicana agricultural laborers were prevented from joining labor unions, they lacked power and were deprived of economic opportunities to get ahead (Day & Schiele, 2013). A leading political figure and vigorous advocate for the rights of farm workers was Cesar E. Chavez. Born in 1927 in Yuma, Arizona, on a farm homesteaded by his grandfather in the 1880s, he was to become one of the most famous activists of the 20th century.

Chavez's family became migrant agricultural workers when they lost their farm during the Great Depression. At age 25, Chavez was picking apricots on a farm near San Jose, California, when a community organizer for a Hispanic-based self-help group, the Community Service Organization, recruited him to work for the grassroots (i.e., sponsored directly by citizens) organization. He began working part-time,

went on to work full-time, and eventually became the organization's director.

In 1962, when the Community Service Organization ignored his pleas to advocate more intensively on the behalf of farm workers, Chavez quit and founded the National Farm Workers Association (NFWA). He then traveled from farm to farm and camp to camp, recruiting members and urging workers to strive for fair wages and improved health conditions. In addition to better wages, issues included providing rest breaks, making clean drinking water available, prohibiting dangerous pesticide use, and providing protection from agricultural hazards. In 1965 the NFWA initiated a successful five-year strike and boycott against grape growers. In 1966 it became affiliated with the American Federation of Labor–Congress of Industrial Organizations (AFL-CIO), the oldest and most extensive labor union in the United States.

Chavez continued leading vital advocacy efforts on the behalf of farm workers until his death in 1993 at the age of 66. Jimenez and colleagues (2015) reflect:

*Coming from a humble background, Cesar Chavez rose to a position of leadership because of his determination in the face of major opposition, his courage to keep fighting for the rights of workers, and his unwavering belief that social justice should be extended to everyone. His legacy of courage and leadership improved the lives of generations of farm workers, and he will be particularly remembered for his efforts on behalf of the millions of people who quietly toil in the agricultural fields of California. (p. 248)*

## Focus on American Indians: Striving for Self-Determination

As with other population groups, the 1960s reflected the beginning of a more progressive era for Native Americans in their quest for self-determination. Despite the fact that policies enacted in the 1950s aimed at *terminating* the special status of and benefits for certain tribes, and even breaking up reservations, these were eventually abandoned during the 1960s. The 1960s began a period  **EP 2, 2a** of activism in which "Native American protest groups formed to assert their rights" (Tice & Perkins, 2002, p. 212).

According to Tice and Perkins (2002),

*[t]he most famous of these groups, the American Indian Movement (AIM), staged protests at Alcatraz in 1969, by then an unoccupied prison island, and in 1973 at Wounded Knee on Pine Ridge Reservation. In the former instance, AIM was trying to exercise its claimed treaty rights to unused federal lands. The protesters were removed in 1971. At Wounded Knee, they were armed and protesting the domination of the tribal government by Whites. This action ended in violence as federal civilian and military forces took control of the reservation. Two Native Americans were killed and two federal officials wounded. (p. 212)*

The struggle for self-determination continues today (Lewis, 1995). At least two critical social policy issues emerge (Weaver, 2008). First, American Indians must have rights to govern themselves and make their own decisions instead of being the victims of coercion by the federal government. Second, ongoing economic development must be pursued.

## A Return to Conservatism in the 1970s

As the 1960s ended, so did the War on Poverty. The public was sick of the seemingly endless spending and questionable results. Johnson also had been battered by intense opposition to the Vietnam War and was increasingly unpopular in the polls. As a result, he withdrew from the presidential race, which was then won by Richard M. Nixon (who served from 1969 until his resignation in 1974). Nixon and subsequent presidents Gerald Ford (serving from 1974 to 1977)

Historically, First Nations Peoples were often discouraged from practicing their customs. Here, women celebrate their culture by performing traditional dances in Gallup, New Mexico.

Chuck Place/Alamy

and Jimmy Carter (serving from 1977 to 1981) "were relatively conservative presidents who had little outward interest in major social reforms. Yet, social spending rose dramatically during this ... [supposedly] conservative period" (Jansson, 2015, p. 306).

## Old Age, Survivors, Disability, and Health Insurance

One notable change in social welfare benefit provision occurred in 1971 when it was proposed that the public assistance programs Old Age Assistance, Aid to the Blind, and Aid to the Permanently and Totally Disabled became social insurance programs. In 1972 these programs were replaced by the Supplementary Security Income (SSI) program. Because social insurance programs provide benefits to workers and their families based on their *right* to them rather than their *need,* recipient rolls soared. The changes obviously reflected a shift in public opinion regarding who was considered needy and who had the right to receive benefits without question. Older adults and people with disabilities automatically received benefits without having to prove they were poor enough to need such resources.

### Focus on Social Welfare Policies Concerning Child and Family Welfare

Despite conservative times, one emerging concern involved child abuse and neglect. LeVine and Sallee (1999) describe conditions from the 1950s to 1970s: "The majority of services to children were financial in nature and not treatment oriented. Furthermore, what services and counseling children received were inconsistent and unorganized. Thus child abuse and neglect were 'rediscovered' in the late 1960s and early 1970s" (p. 31).

In 1974 the Child Abuse Prevention and Treatment Act was passed in response to increasing public concern about child maltreatment. To receive funding, states must establish a centralized reporting agency, collect systematic data about child maltreatment, and pass laws to protect children under age 18 from maltreatment (Liederman, 1995).

In 1975 Title XX of the Social Security Act was passed (Liederman, 1995). It "make[s] grants available to states to provide social services to welfare recipients as well as to people above the poverty line" (Chapin, 2014, p. 89). One of its major goals was to prevent institutionalization of children (Barker, 2003; LeVine & Sallee, 1999).

The Indian Child Welfare Act of 1978 addressed the importance of maintaining children's racial and cultural identity. It reflected a response to concerns that American Indian children were being removed from their homes and placed in non-American Indian foster family and adoptive homes. The concern was that the linkage with their heritage, customs, and cultural identity was being severed. The act thus required that American Indian children be placed in homes that nurture the distinctive values, customs, and heritage of American Indian culture (Liederman, 1995).

The 1980 Adoption Assistance and Child Welfare Act had an impact on programs for children and families in two significant ways (Liederman, 1995). First, federal funding helped states assess, treat, and prevent child maltreatment. Second, funding was made available to states to help them pay for out-of-home care for children when necessary. This legislation also stressed the importance of *permanency planning* for children—that is, finding them a permanent home as soon as possible when return to their birth parents is not viable.

## Conservative Extremes in the 1980s and Early 1990s

President Ronald Reagan (serving from 1981 to 1989) launched an overt return to conservative social welfare policies. Reagan "discounted the importance of racism and discrimination" (Jansson, 2015, p. 346). He asserted that individuals could attain success if they worked hard enough and he emphasized "self-sufficiency"; he maintained that the government's role in economic issues and in people's lives should be minimal (Jansson, 2015, p. 346). Reagan's primary accomplishments were (1) reducing taxes, (2) significantly increasing the defense budget, and (3) slashing social welfare spending (Haynes, 1991; Jansson, 2015). Reagan's frugal social welfare policies continued during President George H. W. Bush's term (from 1989 to 1993). Results included significant increases in the numbers of people living in poverty, in homelessness, in the oppression of vulnerable populations, and in racial tension leading to various confrontations (Day & Schiele, 2013; Jansson, 2015; Karger & Stoesz, 2006).

### Focus on People with Disabilities: 1990s Legislation

Two positive pieces of legislation passed in the 1990s are of special significance for people with developmental or other disabilities in terms of improving access to resources (De-Weaver, 1995). The Americans with Disabilities Act (ADA) of 1990 requires that public buildings, areas, and workplaces provide ready access to people with physical or mental disabilities. The intent is to let them actively involve themselves in everyday life as readily as possible.

EP 5a

The second important piece of legislation is the Developmental Disabilities Assistance and Bill of Rights Act of 1990. This law accomplishes several things—including establishing grant programs for, promoting advocacy on behalf of, and requiring adequate services for people with developmental disabilities (DeWeaver, 1995). Chapter 11 discusses both pieces of legislation more thoroughly.

## Welfare Reform in the Clinton Era

When Bill Clinton was elected president in 1992 (his service ending in 2001), liberals hoped for positive changes in social welfare policy. However, he faced a Senate and House of Representatives dominated by Republicans as early as 1994, so most of his proposals were squelched. Clinton should be recognized, however, for decreasing some proposed reductions in spending on social programs and reducing proposed tax cuts, in addition to ending annual budget deficits; note that had surpluses been applied to strengthening Social Security and Medicare, the nation might not now be in such dire financial straits in terms of its deficit and future support of these programs (Jansson, 2012).

A major conservative policy established during his presidency is the Personal Responsibility and Work Opportunities Act (PR WO A) of 1996, which affects public assistance, SSI, immigrants' ability to receive benefits, child care, and nutritional and food programs. One of its facets, Temporary Assistance for Needy Families (TANF), described more thoroughly in Chapter 8, greatly restricts benefits compared to the program preceding it (Aid to Families with Dependent Children [AFDC]). TANF essentially changed "welfare as we know it" by placing time limits on benefits, allowing states great discretion in benefit distribution, and establishing stringent work requirements.

Additional significant pieces of legislation implemented during the Clinton era were the Family and Medical Leave Act of 1993 and the Crime Bill of 1994 (Jansson, 2015; Marx, 2004; Stern & Axinn, 2012). The Family and Medical Leave Act requires that both public and private employers with 50 or more employees provide each employee up to 12 weeks of unpaid annual leave after a birth or child adoption, while caring for an ill family member (parent, spouse, or child), or during recuperation from illness (Stern & Axinn, 2012). Although health benefits must continue, the fact that the time is unpaid discourages many people from using this option. The 1994 Crime Bill increased funding for hiring more police officers and building more prisons, in addition to enacting federal penalties and developing social services to decrease domestic violence.

## The Conservatism of George W. Bush

The election of George W. Bush in 2000 and his reelection in 2004 mark an era of what he terms "compassionate conservatism." This is the philosophy that although government should not interfere directly with people's lives, it should help people to help themselves. The compassionate part involves the fact that people should be helped. The conservative part concerns the idea that people should be responsible for their own actions and lives. Bush's presidency was characterized by at least three major themes (Blau & Abramovitz, 2010; Jansson, 2012).

First was the emphasis on homeland security. Domestic and foreign policy were critically intertwined during his terms because of the costs involved. With a finite amount of money available, spending in one area limits funding available to finance other areas. After two airplanes slammed into the World Trade Center towers on September 11, 2001, Bush initiated a "war on terrorism" and established a Homeland Security Agency. Despite no solid evidence, Bush maintained that Iraqi leaders were concealing weapons of mass destruction and that there were relationships between Iraq and the Afghanistan terrorist organization Al Qaeda (which took responsibility for the September 11 attack) (Jansson, 2015). Bush demanded information about the alleged weapons, failed to get enough for his satisfaction, and declared war on Iraq in spring 2003, despite little international support. Although Bush declared victory on May 1 of that year, the costs involved to maintain control and to rebuild the social and political infrastructures skyrocketed far beyond initial projections (Jansson, 2012). Money spent on the war and security issues takes potential funding away from many social programs in addition to escalating the national debt. Bush initiated huge increases in defense spending while concurrently slashing spending on domestic programs (Jansson, 2012). Many questions have also been raised regarding "the administration's policy of monitoring of communications in this country without a court order" (Blau & Abramovitz, 2010, p. 121).

A second theme characterizing Bush's presidency was the push to trim the federal government and give more decision-making capabilities to the states. Critics of this trend caution that this may result in inconsistent access to resources and programs, in addition to greater inequities between the "haves" and "have nots."

A third theme involved shifting service provision from the public to the private sector. Bush maintained that private organizations and businesses are generally more efficient than government agencies and give people a wider range of choices (Jansson, 2015). Bush also supported "faith-based initiatives" in which public funding would go to religious organizations, a plan that Congress did not support (Jansson, 2012). Although many religious organizations have a long history of providing effective social services, those receiving public funding have always carefully separated service provision from religious activities (Jansson, 2012). Bush proposed allowing such organizations greater freedom in terms of how they spend funding and combine these two facets. Critics of this view question the validity of using public funds to sponsor religious activities and wonder how such activities could be monitored for fairness and objectivity. A problem with financing religious

activities with public funding involves a basic right to religious freedom. Which religious services should be supported? Those sponsored by Christians, Muslims, Roman Catholics, Jews, Buddhists, Unitarians? To what extent should public taxes finance religious doctrines and projects in which not everyone believes?

When Bush first took office he initiated and succeeded in getting a huge tax cut. The rationale was that giving money back to people would stimulate the economy because they would spend that money, which would in turn benefit business and the economy. However, critics maintained that the cut would have little effect on the economy because it primarily benefited the wealthy, who wouldn't spend the money anyway; in reality, 1% of the population received 40% of the tax benefits (Jansson, 2012). Giving money to the rich and taking programs and benefits away from the poor increases inequity and the chasm between the rich and the poor.

Focus on Critical Thinking 6.4 raises some issues to consider for the future of social welfare.

---

# FOCUS ON CRITICAL THINKING 6.4    WHAT ARE FUTURE ISSUES IN SOCIAL WELFARE?

Since the September 11, 2001, destruction of the World Trade Center, attention has been focused on the "war on terrorism," the aftermath of the war in Iraq, and the significant American military presence in many Middle Eastern nations. Many resources are being diverted to national and international security and to supporting troops. What effects will this have on domestic social welfare programs? Specific issues include the following.

EP 5b, 5c

## Critical Thinking Questions

- Consider the following facts about Social Security (Social Security Administration, 2014d). Ninety percent of people age 65 and older receive Social Security benefits. Such benefits make up 38 percent of all income for older adults. Today there are 2.8 workers for each person receiving Social Security; by 2033, there will be only 2.1 workers for each beneficiary. "[C]ongressional projections show Social Security running deficits every year until its trust funds are eventually drained in

about 2037" (CBSNews.com, 2011). What do you think should be done about Social Security? For example, should the minimum age to receive benefits be raised? Should benefits be reduced? Should worker contributions be raised?

- What is the future of Medicare in view of the increasing proportion of older adults compared with working people, who support Medicare through taxes? What will happen when more people receive benefits from a much smaller contributing pool?

- To what extent should we continue to build new prisons to house an ever-increasing number of inmates at enormous public expense instead of focusing on treatment and rehabilitation?

- What should be done about the scarcity of low-cost housing and the large population of homeless people roaming the streets?

- Where should spending priorities be placed? On the "war on terrorism"? Supporting troops on an international level? Cutting the national deficit? Expanding social programs?

# The Great Recession

A severe recession, often referred to as "the Great Recession," began in December of 2007 and by the spring of 2009 was pronounced as the most devastating one since the Great Depression (Jansson, 2015, p. 477). A **recession** is an economic downturn where businesses make less money, unemployment mounts, people's access to usable capital plummets, and their capacity to make purchases shrinks (Barker, 2014). The Great Recession characterized the end of the Bush administration and the beginning of the Obama presidency.

Jansson (2015) describes the progression of the crisis. The calamity was initially triggered beginning in the 1980s by the elimination of federal regulations governing banking lending (originally instituted during the Great Depression). Some of the abolished regulations had required banks to hold significant funds in reserve in the event that large numbers of loans and mortgages went delinquent, a common occurrence during recessions. Other eliminated regulations required that people who purchased homes submit significant down payments. This, in effect, would hold down monthly interest payments on the house and keep people from overextending themselves financially.

However, large American banks went on a "speculative spree," lending to people with low incomes who would not have qualified financially for loans in the past; as a result banks were making escalating profits (Jansson, 2015, p. 477). People who were required to make very low or no down payments on mortgages thought they could afford such purchases because house prices were skyrocketing at unrivaled levels. These people felt that if they had trouble making house payments, they could always sell their real estate at a great profit. They failed to realize that this was a "housing bubble" that was unsustainable and unrealistic. So, when the price of housing took a nose-dive, many people were left owing much more on the mortgage for their house than the house was worth. Because these people had put little or no money down on the house in the first place, it was to their advantage simply to walk away. Foreclosures were the result. Because of the avalanche of foreclosures, banks began to fail. Government assistance kept many of them solvent.

Double-digit unemployment did not help the situation. When people are unemployed, they have little money to pour into the economy. Unemployment is common during recessions. Shrinking profits and resources result in layoffs and business closures.

## The "Fringe Economy"

Another facet contributing to economic problems involves people living in poverty and their problems with credit. Karger and Stoesz (2014) discuss the "fringe economy" and the credit options that maintain it (p. 113). The **fringe economy** is a configuration of financial resources that parallels how resources are attained in the main economy. It involves "pawnshops, check cashers, and payday lenders" in addition to services provided by mainstream banks; such services include "high-interest credit cards and expensive check overdraft protection, high-interest home financing and refinancing loans, and deferred interest retail payments" (p. 113). It serves people who have no or almost no resources, must live day to day and paycheck to paycheck (if they have a paycheck), and are desperate to survive.

 **EP 4a**

"Credit is a bridge between real household earnings and consumption decisions, offering relief during periods of economic distress and uncertainty" (Karger & Stoesz, 2014, p. 113). People with "good" credit can borrow and pay back with no collateral required. However, people with "questionable" or "compromised" credit must usually provide some collateral before receiving credit in addition to paying exorbitant interest rates. Limited credit cards, pawnshops, and payday loans are among credit options for people who are poor.

Limited or "unsecured" credit cards are for people considered greater credit risks after assessing the cardholders's potential to pay the card back and that individual's credit card history (Karger & Stoesz, 2014, p. 113). Most often, the amount of credit available is quite limited and the interest rates are excessive. Borrowers must often provide collateral such as funds in an established bank account or a car title (Karger & Stoecz, 2014). There may be monthly participation fees in addition to fees for cash advances. Rates skyrocket with missed payments.

Pawnshops provide fixed-term loans in return for holding collateral. "The customer is given a pawn ticket that includes his or her name and address, a description of the pledged good, the amount lent, the maturity date, and the amount that must be repaid to reclaim the property" (Karger & Stoesz, 2014, p. 132). At or before the date of maturity, the customer may repay the loan and regain his or her property. If the customer does not repay the loan on time, the pawnshop retains whatever the item is that served as collateral. Many pawnshops have an established maximum that they will loan regardless of the collateral's value. For instance, if the pawnshop's loan limit is $1,000, that is all it will loan even if an item is worth $3,000. Some pawnshops allow customers to borrow indefinitely to maintain access to the collateral, but usually at excessive interest rates (e.g., 15% per *month*).

To use payday loan outlets, customers must have a valid checking account to qualify to cover the loan's interest and the loan itself. Loans usually are for a maximum of $300 and are borrowed for 14 to 18 days. Interest usually is about 20% for the loan period, but can be as high as 37%. After paying the interest, the customer may extend the loan for a few additional periods, but must pay the interest for each extension period. Whereas pawnshops have collateral they keep upon loan default, payday loan outlets can be more aggressive. They can ruin your credit rating or press criminal charges for writing a bad check.

# The Presidency of Barack Obama

Jansson (2015) reflects on the candidacy of Barack Obama, the nation's first multiracial president:

> *Relatively progressive voters saw Obama as an agent for change. He voiced liberal concerns. He spoke about positive functions of government. He lauded free markets, but wanted regulations to protect citizens from their excesses, such as higher minimum wages, reversal of some anti-union regulations, and crackdowns on private health insurance companies that often withdrew coverage when enrollees became ill. Independents and moderates often viewed him as a prudent reformer. He appealed to non-partisan voters who had tired of gridlocked government. (p. 477)*

## The Stimulus Plan

As indicated earlier, Obama entered the national scene in the midst of the Great Recession. One of the first things he did as president was enact a Stimulus Plan to address the dire economic situation. Jansson (2015) calls it a *"disguised* social welfare" plan because it outwardly emphasized economic growth, but actually included such a wide range of social programs (p. 480). Goals included:

- Protecting and generating jobs to encourage economic revitalization.

- Helping people most devastated by the recession.
- Investing in technology in health and science to enhance economic viability and growth.
- Supporting projects aimed at long-term benefits such as improving transportation systems, protecting the environment, and strengthening infrastructure.
- Stabilizing budgets at the state and local levels to prevent cutbacks in vital services and arbitrary increases in state and local taxes. (Jansson, 2015)

By September 2009, more than $12.5 trillion had been spent to help the economy; spending focused on saving banks and mortgage companies, battling against foreclosures to help mortgage holders, bailing out the floundering General Motors and Chrysler Corporation, and funding other aspects of the Stimulus Plan; this comprised the largest amount ever expended over such a short time period in American history (Jansson, 2015).

## Health-Care Reform

Obama's health-care reform plan entitled the Patient Protection and Affordable Care Act (ACA) of 2010 was passed as amended by Congress. The plan's intent is to "hold insurance companies accountable, lower health-care costs, guarantee more choice, and enhance the quality of care for all Americans" (WhiteHouse.gov, 2011b).

Jansson (2015) explains:

> *The legislation proposed that in 2014 states establish "insurance exchanges" to allow uninsured consumers, as well as businesses, to purchase insurance coverage that provided basic coverage. (Individuals and businesses would be mandated to insure themselves and their employees—or they would have to pay penalties to states that would use the funds to insure them.) (p. 491)*

Several advantages of the ACA are emphasized (Jimenez et al., 2015). First, insurance companies are prohibited from denying coverage for preexisting conditions. Second, the ACA eliminates the lifetime annual limitation on benefits imposed by insurance companies. Third, young adults may remain on their parents' insurance plan until age 26 instead of about age 19 (except, in some instances, for full-time students).

The law remains controversial. There have been delays in some aspects of implementation. Questions have been raised about cost and effectiveness. Jansson (2015) maintains that "[d]espite its flaws, the ACA promised to give most Americans health insurance" (p. 525).

## Foreign Policy

Obama's foreign policy has concentrated on a number of issues. These include refocusing on the al Qaeda threat in Afghanistan and Pakistan, ending the war in Iraq, keeping nuclear weapons out of terrorists' possession, and opposing the Islamic State of Syria and Iraq (ISIS) (also referred to as the Islamic State of Syria and the Levant [ISIL]) (The White House, 2014; WhiteHouse.gov, 2011a).

# The Development of the Social Work Profession  `LO 4`

Despite the different paths taken by the Settlement house and charity organization movements, social work pioneers were always dedicated to helping people victimized by the worst depths of poverty and oppression (Hernandez, 2008). Social work education actually began in 1898 when the New York Charity Organization Society **EP 1c** offered a summer course to train charity workers (Beless, 1995). In the early 20th century, social workers continued to seek a professional identity regarding what social work practice involved. The emphasis on scientific advances and the enticing new therapeutic approaches introduced during the first half of the century (e.g., psychodynamic and social learning theories) strengthened the profession's commitment to social casework (Landon, 1995). Social casework stressed therapeutically helping individuals and families solve their problems. Thus the target of change was the individual or family.

The divergence between the settlement orientation, emphasizing group and community work, and the individually oriented charity organization approach remained strong. Therefore, three method tracks—casework, group work, and community organization—characterized social work through the 1950s. Casework was further fortified by developing fields of practice or specializations that were generally incorporated under its umbrella. These included medical social work, psychiatric social work, child welfare, and school social work (Brieland, 1995).

## Early Development of Social Work Education

Beless (1995) describes the initial development of formal social work education in the United States. In 1919, 17 U.S. and Canadian schools of social work joined together to form the Association of Training Schools for Professional Social Work. This organization soon changed its name to the American Association of Schools of Social Work (AASSW) and by 1927 had established membership requirements based on education. The AASSW also began developing criteria for what was considered adequate preparation for professional social work practice. These formed the foundation for the initial accreditation standards for master's degrees in social work education (Stuart, 2008).

**Accreditation** is the recognition and confirmation that an organization such as nursing home, mental health center, university, or other social service provider meets specific standards developed to make certain that the services provided are appropriate and effective. Accreditation with respect to social work education means that accredited programs must comply with a range of standards. These address curricular content and structure, staffing, adherence to nondiscrimination policies, adequate financial support from the college or university, and other variables.

## Social Work During the Great Depression

During the Great Depression, the Social Security Act switched many aspects of service provision from the private to the public sector. Thus the type of social work jobs available and the characteristics of people getting them shifted (Popple, 1995). Prior to the Depression, social work was close to becoming a profession of graduate degrees only. The field was oriented to providing casework with a theoretical foundation in psychotherapy. Many clients were not poor but suffered from other problems such as mental health issues. Efforts to change communities and social policies were most often overlooked.

The Depression changed all this, however. The Social Security Act spurred a massive increase in the number of social work jobs, the majority of which involved problems for stable people caused by unemployment (Popple, 1995). Essentially, these jobs

## HIGHLIGHT 6.11   SOCIAL WORK ACCREDITATION AT THE BACCALAUREATE AND MASTER'S LEVELS

By 1942 several undergraduate social work programs had formed their own separate organization, the National Association of Schools of Social Administration (NASSA). By 1943 NASSA was officially acknowledged as the accrediting organization for baccalaureate programs that developed and oversaw their curricular and program standards (Beless, 1995).

Having two accrediting bodies for social work education was awkward and confusing. Therefore, in 1946 a coordinating body, the National Council on Social Work Education (NCSWE), was created to research the situation and make suggestions for achieving better coordination and consistency. The subsequent report and recommendations resulted in the birth of the Council on Social Work Education (CSWE) in 1952, representing the merger of the American Association

of Schools of Social Work (AASSW) and NASSA (Beless, 1995; Hoffman, 2008; Watkins & Holmes, 2008). At this time, the first Curriculum Policy Statement and Accreditation Standards were issued that reflected new guidelines for master's education concerning curricular content and structure (Brieland, 1995). Additionally, students were required to develop a philosophical approach to practice that emphasized human dignity (Brieland, 1995). Such a broad goal inferred that social work should be more than merely casework. Rather, social work should seek to benefit society in general and oppressed populations in particular. Although CSWE's objective was to oversee social work education, at this time it viewed undergraduate education as "preprofessional" and declined to offer these programs accreditation.

required different skills than the ability to perform therapy, as many master's degree social workers (MSWs) were doing. The need became evident for practitioners to work in the public sector assisting people in solving their problems, meeting their needs, and obtaining necessary resources—tasks unrelated to providing "therapy." Thus numerous bachelor's degree social workers (BSWs) were being employed in these jobs. However, MSWs refused to accept BSWs as professional colleagues, and AASSW would not acknowledge baccalaureate social work programs (Stuart, 2008). Highlight 6.11 explores how accreditation for social work programs was established.

## Social Work in the 1950s

We have established that the economy grew rapidly during and after World War II with the increased demand for production of goods. Despite CSWE's call for social work to assume a broader role in seeking social justice (via its Curriculum Policy Statement and Accreditation Standards), the relative affluence of the 1950s once again encouraged social workers to turn to psychotherapy and casework (Popple, 1995). During this decade, 85% of social work students selected casework as their orientation of choice (Popple, 1995). MSWs dominated the scene, and BSW programs were not yet being accredited.

## Formation of the National Association of Social Workers

In 1955 seven separate professional organizations came together to form the National Association of Social Workers (NASW) (Brieland, 1995; Clark, 2008). The intent was to provide a unified force to move the profession ahead and pursue broad goals far beyond what any more limited specialty organization might accomplish (Brieland, 1995). The following organizations participated in the merger (Brieland, 1995; Goldstein & Beebe, 1995):

- The American Association of Group Workers (founded in 1936)
- The American Association of Medical Social Workers (founded in 1918)
- The American Association of Psychiatric Social Workers (founded in 1926)
- The American Association of Social Workers (founded in 1921)
- The Association for the Study of Community Organization (founded in 1946)
- The National Association of School Social Workers (founded in 1919)
- The Social Work Research Group (founded in 1949)

The need for a unifying generalist approach was inherent in this merger. Many social work leaders and educators became increasingly concerned about the profession's commitment to rectifying social injustice and advocating on behalf of positive social change.

## Social Work in the 1960s to the Early 1980s

The 1960s and the War on Poverty produced a new focus on social change versus individual pathology. Many came to realize that poverty and other vast social problems still existed in the United States. A series of federal administrations began implementing antipoverty programs. At first, these programs generally disregarded social workers because the intent was to empower the poor themselves (Popple, 1995). However, it soon became clear that expertise was needed in a range of fields, including community organization, administration, and direct practice, for programs to run effectively (Popple, 1995). As a result, most social work schools added social policy, social planning, and administration areas of specialization to their curricula (Stuart, 2008). This probably reflected the growing awareness of the importance of working with and within organizations as a major facet of generalist practice.

At this point, the social work profession faced a serious problem—namely, fewer than a quarter of all people holding social work jobs were identified as professional social workers because only they had MSW degrees (Popple, 1995). Needless to say, it did not enhance the profession's reputation or accountability that the vast majority of the people doing social work were not considered social workers. Thus a logical move was to emphasize the BSW as the viable entry-level qualification to the social work profession—people performing social work jobs should be social workers. CSWE began developing criteria for accrediting BSW programs in 1962 and finally offered accreditation to programs in 1974.

The prolific development of BSW programs in the late 1960s and early 1970s emphasized the need for a generalist foundation in social work practice (Landon, 1995). Many social work leaders began calling for a unified foundation for all social work practice (Bartlett, 1970; Boehm, 1959) and referring to social work practice as occurring among various-sized systems (Pincus & Minahan, 1973; Schwartz, 1961; Siporin, 1975). Social workers needed a broad base of skills to

work with individuals, families, groups, organizations, and communities. Baccalaureate and master's programs required differentiation regarding purpose. The fact that CSWE made accreditation available to BSW programs in 1974 and required a generalist practice foundation for the BSW level of practice was a big forward step. Another important step occurred in 1984 when CSWE affirmed that the foundation for both undergraduate and graduate educational levels should include the knowledge, skills, and values inherent in generalist practice (Landon, 1995).

Other important developments, including the first NASW *Code of Ethics* in 1960, the establishment of Political Action for Candidate Election (PACE) in 1976, and increasing attention to BSW professionalism, are illustrated by the time line introducing this chapter.

## Social Work Today

Currently, the social work professional assumes the stance that the foundation level of social work is generalist practice. "Baccalaureate programs prepare students for generalist practice. Master's programs prepare students for generalist practice and specialized practice" (Council on Social Work Education, 2015, p. 10). Therefore, the BSW with its foundation of generalist practice may be considered the entry level into the profession, with the MSW reflecting both a foundation of generalist practice and an advanced specialization. The curriculum in an accredited program is structured to facilitate students' achievement of the specified competencies. These competencies reflect the generalist practice foundation. Examples of specializations in MSW programs include administration, mental health, families and children, school social work, medical social work, gerontology, substance abuse, and a wide range of others.

As later chapters will explain, BSWs can provide many services, such as crisis intervention, case management, community organization, and the linking of clients with services, while working with a wide range of populations. MSWs usually fulfill more specialized functions, such as providing psychotherapy, working in supervision and administration, or assuming higher levels of decision-making responsibility.

# Chapter Summary

The following summarizes this chapter's content as it relates to the learning objectives presented at the beginning of the chapter. Chapter content will help prepare students to:

## LO1 Describe historical views about social welfare.

The 1601 English Elizabethan Poor Law is considered the first piece of legislation establishing coherent, consistent public support for needy people through taxes. The Speenhamland system initiated a policy of supplementing the income of all poor people so that everyone would have the necessary minimum income. The English Poor Law Reforms of 1834 significantly reduced all outdoor relief and brought back workhouses as the only place where able-bodied people could receive benefits.

## LO2 Review the history of social welfare in the United States (focusing on major social welfare issues, diverse groups, and policy changes).

Early poor laws in the American colonies closely resembled, and in some cases were identical to, those in England, although each colony remained unique in its specific legislation. The poor were viewed as part of the natural social order in communities. Services often reflected a mix of public and private collaboration, frequently provided informally. Early residency requirements for assistance were established.

Economic growth skyrocketed between the Civil War and the early 20th century. In the early 1900s settlement houses and charity organization societies were founded. Settlement houses were neighborhood-based centers where humanitarians, interested students, and others "settled" to help people living in poverty improve their communities and their lives; goals included meeting residents' needs, such as providing education and training, and advocating for human rights and improved community conditions. Jane Addams, along with Ellen Gates Starr, started the first settlement house, Hull House, in Chicago. Charity organization societies used expert knowledge to support people in caring for themselves through the use of "friendly visitors." Mary Richmond was an early advocate for the development of professional schools of social casework.

During the Progressive period from 1900 to the 1920s, people felt that government was responsible for people's welfare. Many issues were tackled, including child labor, women's working hours, women's suffrage, income security, and family welfare. Many advocacy groups were established, and steps were taken toward meeting human needs.

The Great Depression was initiated by the stock market crash of 1929. The general trend over the next decade was an increasing reliance on the federal government to control and provide social services.

President Franklin Delano Roosevelt initiated a range of programs, referred to as the New Deal, to address people's dire needs. Programs included the Federal Emergency Relief Act, the Civilian Works Administration, the Civilian Conservation Corps, the Public Works Administration, and the Works Progress Administration.

The Social Security Act of 1935 established current programs for social insurance, public assistance, and health services. A significant piece of 1940s legislation was the Serviceman's Readjustment Act of 1944, commonly referred to as the G.I. Bill.

The 1950s marked a time of relative peace and complacency. During this period the population exploded, resulting in the current large bloc of aging baby boomers. Aid to the Permanently and Totally Disabled became a later amendment to the Social Security Act. The year 1954 marked the end to school segregation in *Brown v. Board of Education.*

The 1960s was characterized by the War on Poverty in an effort to fashion a "Great Society." Poverty became a primary focus of public attention, and numerous new social welfare programs were developed. The Economic Opportunity Act of 1964 established programs including Volunteers in Service to America (VISTA) and Operation Head Start among many others.

The 1970s marked a return to conservatism, followed by increasing conservatism during the 1980s and early 1990s. The Clinton era from 1992 to 2001 was characterized by the squelching of most of his proposals by the Republican Senate and House. Clinton did manage to diminish cuts in social programs and decrease tax cuts. The Personal Responsibility and Work Opportunities Act of 1996 was passed that replaced AFDC for public assistance for needy families.

George W. Bush's conservative regime in the first decade of the 21st century emphasized homeland security, transferring more decision-making power from the federal government to the states, and increased provision of services from the private sector, including faith-based organizations.

Barack Obama, the first multiracial president, ran on a platform that emphasized change. Entering his administration during the Great Recession, he focused on a Stimulus Plan, health-care reform, and improving international relations, especially by combating terrorism.

Numerous policies depicted the treatment of diverse groups throughout U.S. history. People affected included American Indians, Latinos and Latinas, African Americans, and Asian Americans.

The U.S. government established treaties with American Indians that removed them from their native lands and relocated them on distant reservations. Anglos considered American Indians as culturally inferior. The federal government liberally interfered with Native American social, economic, religious, and cultural practices. The story of the Cherokee and their Trail of Tears is especially sad. From the 1870s to 1900 the federal government pursued the assimilation (the process of incorporating another culture into the mainstream culture) of First Nations Peoples. Native Americans' struggle for self-determination escalated during the 1960s.

In 1845 the United States annexed Texas, continuing to struggle over its boundary with Mexico, a situation greatly affecting Hispanics in the Southwest. In the 1848 Treaty of Guadalupe Hidalgo, Mexico ceded more than half of its territory to the United States, becoming the U.S. Southwest. Although Hispanics were often in the majority and were living in their native territory, Anglos often treated them as a "minority." After the Mexican Revolution of 1910, numerous Chicanos and Chicanas fled to the United States as refugees to find work. After the Great Depression when work was scarce, many, including U.S. citizens, were deported. Puerto Ricans obtained U.S. citizenship in 1917 and can travel to and from the mainland United States at will. During the 1960s the Chicano movement advocated for the appreciation of Chicano culture and improved socioeconomic status for Chicanos and Chicanas, especially agricultural laborers.

Lincoln issued the Emancipation Proclamation freeing the slaves in 1863. After the Civil War, the federal government established the Freedmen's Bureau to distribute rations and land to African Americans in need. Very few actually received any land, and those who did were forced to return it later.

The first Asian people to immigrate to the United States during the mid-19th century were Chinese. They experienced blatant racism and limited rights. After the Chinese Exclusion Act of 1882, Japanese immigrants soon began to replace the Chinese. They, too, experienced limited rights. The Immigration Act of 1924 halted Asian immigration almost altogether.

Advocacy for civil rights for people of color characterized the 1960s. The Civil Rights Act of 1964 strengthened civil rights and established the Equal Employment Opportunity Commission.

American history also is characterized by policies affecting other people in special groups or who are experiencing special issues. These individuals included people with mental health concerns, children (child welfare matters), older adults, and people with disabilities.

In colonial times, people who had mental illness, often referred to as lunatics, were typically cared for by their own families or boarded out to other families, with communities paying these families to provide care. During the Progressive period in the early 20th century, mental health policy reflected the mental hygiene movement. This emphasized, among other things, alternative types of care to institutionalization. The deinstitutionalization movement characterized the period following World War II. It stressed the provision of mental health care in the community instead of in institutions. The 1963 Community Mental Health Centers Act provided funding for a range of community mental health programs.

The 1870s saw the origins of child welfare policy as it has evolved today. Charles Loring Brace became the first proponent of placing children in homes other than their own instead of in institutions. The concept of Protective Services was born in 1874 with the case of Mary Ellen Wilson. The 1974 Child Abuse Prevention and Treatment Act established a centralized reporting agency and required states to pass laws protecting children under age 18. The Indian Child Welfare Act of 1978 addressed the importance of maintaining children's racial and cultural identity.

The Social Security Act of 1935 is a social insurance program that provided benefits to older adults and people with disabilities. It also established Title IV, Aid to Dependent Children (ADC), providing public assistance for children in need. In 1962 the name was changed to Aid to Families with Dependent Children (AFDC). The Personal Responsibility and Work Opportunities Act (PR WO A) of 1996 replaced AFDC and placed a range of limitations on public assistance benefits.

The Older Americans Act (OAA) of 1965 established an administrative structure for the coordination and delivery of social services to older people. OAA provides numerous benefits to people age 60 or older regardless of income. In 1972, Supplemental Security Income (SSI), a social insurance program, replaced earlier public assistance programs based on need.

Major legislation for people with disabilities includes the Americans with Disabilities Act of 1990 and the Developmental Disabilities Assistance and Bill of Rights Act of 1990.

### LO3  *Propose questions to stimulate critical thinking about historical trends and events.*

To encourage critical thinking, questions were posed concerning government policy and the self-determination for First Nations Peoples, personal rights of public assistance recipients, civil rights, and future issues in social welfare.

### LO4  *Discuss foremost events in the history of the social work profession.*

Early social work was based in the settlement house and charity organization movements. As a result, casework, group work, and community organization were the three tracts characterizing social work through the 1950s. In 1919, the Association of Training Schools for Professional Social Work was formed by U.S. and Canadian schools of social work. The name was soon changed to the American Association of Schools of Social Work (AASSW). AASSW formed the foundation for initial accreditation standards for master's social work education.

During the Great Depression, social work switched many aspects of service provision from the private to the public sector. By 1942, different organizations formed to address BSW and MSW accreditation. In 1946 the National Council on Social Work Education (NCSWE) was formed to coordinate accreditation at both levels. NCSWE's findings resulted in the birth of the Council on Social Work Education (CSWE), the current body that accredits both BSW and MSW programs.

The relative affluence of the 1950s encouraged social workers to focus on psychotherapy and casework instead of social justice issues. In 1955 seven social work organizations joined to form the National Association of Social Work (NASW).

The 1960s and the War on Poverty produced a new concentration on social change versus individual pathology. There was some debate regarding whether BSW programs should be accredited, but CSWE finally began accrediting them in 1974 along with MSW programs. The prolific development of BSW programs in the late 1960s and early 1970s emphasized the need for a generalist foundation for social work practice. Today, generalist practice, which characterizes the BSW foundation, has been established as the foundation of social work practice upon which specializations can be built (CSWE, 2015).

## LOOKING AHEAD

This chapter discussed the history of social welfare and social welfare policy in the United States. It provides a foundation for understanding current social welfare policy, programs, and policy development. The time line in Figure 6.3 highlights some of the major events in social welfare history as discussed in this chapter. The next chapter will discuss policy development and the structural components of policies. It will also focus on theoretical perspectives regarding personal values and social welfare policy and program development, thereby setting the stage for policy and program analysis in various practice contexts.

**English History**

| | |
|---|---|
| 1300s | Feudalistic societies in Europe |
| 1348 | Europe devastated by Black Death |
| 1349 | Statute of Laborers |
| 1531 | Able-bodied people forbidden from begging |
| 1601 | Elizabethan Poor Law |
| 1662 | Law of Settlement |
| 1795 | Establishment of Speenhamland system |
| 1834 | Poor Law Reforms |

**U.S. History**

| | |
|---|---|
| 1770s | Beginning of moral treatment movement in mental health |
| 1778 | First treaty between federal government and Native American Delaware tribe |
| 1824 | Establishment of Bureau of Indian Affairs |
| 1830 | Indian Removal Act |
| 1838–1839 | Trail of Tears |
| 1840s | Dorothea Dix advocates for people with mental illness |
| 1846 | Beginning of the Mexican-American War |
| 1848 | The Treaty of Guadalupe Hidalgo (where Mexico ceded more than half of its territory to the United States) |
| 1861–1865 | Civil War |
| 1865 | Establishment of Freedmen's Bureau |
| 1874 | Etta Wheeler initiates child protective services |
| 1882 | Chinese Exclusion Act of 1882 |
| 1880s | Growth of settlement houses and charity organization societies |
| 1870s | Federal attempts at assimilation for Native Americans |
| 1899 | Treaty of Paris of 1899 (where Spain ceded Puerto Rico to the United States) |
| 1900s | Beginning of mental hygiene movement in mental health |
| 1909 | Establishment of National Association for the Advancement of Colored People (NAACP) |
| | First White House Conference on Dependent Children |
| 1910 | Establishment of National Urban League |
| | First major wave of Mexican immigration in response to the Mexican Revolution of 1910 |
| 1911 | States begin to establish mothers' pensions |
| 1917 | Jones Act granting U.S. citizenship to all people born in Puerto Rico from then on |
| 1924 | Immigration Act of 1924 (which imposed stringent requirements on immigrants entering the United States, especially from Asia) |
| 1929 | Stock market crash initiates the Great Depression |
| 1933 | Federal Emergency Relief Act (FERA) |
| | Establishment of Civilian Works Administration (CSW) |
| | Establishment of Civilian Conservation Corps (CCC) |
| 1935 | Establishment of Public Works Administration (PWA) |
| | Establishment of Works Progress Administration (WPA) |
| | Social Security Act of 1935 |
| 1941 | U.S. enters World War II |
| | Japanese American internment in response to bombing of Pearl Harbor |
| 1942 | Permanent relocation centers for Japanese American internment |
| 1944 | Serviceman's Readjustment Act of 1944 (G.I. Bill) |
| 1945 | World War II ends |
| 1950 | Amendments to Social Security Act adding Aid to Disabled |

**FIG-6-3** Major Events in the History of Social Welfare

| Early 1950s | Beginning of deinstitutionalization movement in mental health |
| 1954 | *Brown v. Board of Education* ending school segregation |
| 1962 | Public Welfare Amendments of 1962 |
| Early 1960s | Initiation of War on Poverty and Great Society |
| 1962 | Formation of National Farm Workers Association (NFWA) led by Cesar Chavez |
| 1963 | Community Mental Health Centers Act |
| 1964 | Economic Opportunity Act of 1964 |
| | Food Stamp Act of 1964 |
| | Civil Rights Act of 1964 |
| 1965 | Older Americans Act of 1965 |
| 1967 | Amendments to Social Security Act |
| 1969 | American Indian movement protests at Alcatraz |
| 1971 | *Wyatt v. Stickney* |
| | American Indian movement protests at Wounded Knee |
| | Establishment of Supplementary Security Income (SSI) |
| 1974 | Child Abuse Prevention and Treatment Act |
| 1975 | Passage of Title XX of Social Security Act |
| | *O'Connor v. Donaldson* |
| 1978 | Passage of Indian Child Welfare Act of 1978 |
| 1980 | Passage of Adoption Assistance and Child Welfare Act |
| 1990 | Passage of Americans with Disabilities Act of 1990 |
| | Passage of Developmental Disabilities Assistance and Bill of Rights Act of 1990 |
| 1993 | Family and Medical Leave Act of 1993 |
| 1994 | Crime Bill of 1994 |
| 1996 | Personal Responsibility and Work Opportunities Act of 1996 (including Temporary Assistance for Needy Families [TANF]) |
| 2001 | Terrorist attacks on the World Trade Center |
| 2003 | War on Iraq |
| | The Medicare Modernization Act of 2003 |
| Late 2007 | Beginning of "the Great Recession" |
| 2009 | The Obama Stimulus Plan |
| 2010 | Passage of the 2010 Patient Protection and Affordable Care Act (ACA) |

**FIG-6-3** *(continued)*

## COMPETENCY NOTES

The following identifies where Educational Policy (EP) competencies and their component behaviors are discussed in the chapter.

**EP 1 (Competency 1)—Demonstrate Ethical and Professional Behavior.** *(p. 178):* As professionals, social workers should understand the profession's history and its mission. *(p. 188):* Jane Addams is an important figure in the history of social work. Being a professional social work includes understanding the profession's history.

**EP 1b Use reflection and self-regulation to manage personal values and maintain professionalism in practice situations.** *(p. 202):*

Critical thinking questions encourage personal reflection about discrimination.

**EP 1c Demonstrate professional demeanor in behavior; appearance; and oral, written, and electronic communication.** *(p. 209):* Understanding the history of the profession contributes to an identity as a professional social worker and to professional demeanor.

**EP 2 (Competency 2)—Engage Diversity and Difference in Practice.** *(p. 178):* This and subsequent sections of this chapter review how culture's structures and values changing over time serve to oppress, marginalize, alienate, or create or enhance privilege and power. *(p. 183):* The forms and mechanisms of oppression against First Nations People are discussed from a historical perspective. *(p. 184):* The forms and mechanisms of oppression against Latinos and Latinas are discussed from a historical perspective. *(p. 185):* The forms and mechanisms of oppression against African Americans are discussed from a historical perspective. *(p. 191):* The forms and mechanisms of oppression against American Indians from the 1870s to 1900 are discussed. *(p. 192):* Critical thinking questions are posed that relate to the oppression of First Nations Peoples. *(p. 193):* The oppression of and discrimination against Asian people in terms of immigration are discussed. *(p. 193):* The oppression of and discrimination against Chicanos and Chicanas in terms of immigration are discussed. *(p. 197):* The oppression of and discrimination against Japanese Americans during World War II is discussed. *(p. 198):* Critical thinking questions are raised to examine the extent to which public assistance policy might oppress recipients. *(p. 201):* The oppression of and discrimination against people of color during the early 1960s is discussed. *(p. 202):* Critical thinking questions encourage exploration of the reasons for historical oppression, the lack of civil rights, and the dynamics involved. *(p. 202):* The oppression of Chicanos and Chicanas is discussed). *(p. 203):* The oppression of American Indians is discussed.

**EP 2a Apply and communicate understanding of the importance of diversity and difference in shaping life experiences in practice at the micro, mezzo, and macro levels.** *(p. 202):* Race and ethnicity, both dimensions of diversity, can significantly shape life experiences for Chicanos and Chicanas. *(p. 203):* Race and ethnicity, both dimensions of diversity, can significantly shape life experiences for American Indians.

**EP 3 (Competency 3)—Advance Human Rights and Social, Economic, and Environmental Justice.**

**EP 3a Apply their understanding of social, economic, and environmental justice to advocate for human rights at the individual and system levels.** *(p. 183):* Dorothea Dix provides an excellent example of an advocate for human rights. *(p. 201):* The Older Americans Act of 1965 provides for the coordination of resources that advance the social well-being of older adults.

*(p. 201):* Civil rights legislation that advocated for social and economic justice is discussed. *(p. 202):* Cesar Chavez provides an excellent example of one who advocates for human rights, and social and economic justice.

**EP 4 (Competency 4)—Engage in Practice-Informed Research and Research-Informed Practice.**

**EP 4a Use practice experience and theory to inform scientific inquiry and research.** *(p. 207):* Being members of a lower socioeconomic class can result in economic oppression with respect to receiving financial credit.

**EP 5 (Competency 5)—Engage in Policy Practice.**

**EP 5a Identify social policy at the local, state, and federal level that impacts well-being, service delivery, and access to social services.** *(p. 201):* The Older Americans Act of 1965 provides an example of a policy that advances human rights for older adults. *(p. 201):* The Civil Rights Act of 1964 provides an example of a policy that impacts the well-being and access to services for people of color. *(p. 204):* Legislation is discussed that advocates for the rights of people with disabilities.

**EP 5b Assess how social welfare and economic policies impact the delivery of and access to social services.** *(p. 206):* Critical thinking questions are raising that encourage thought about how social welfare and economic policies impact service delivery.

**EP 5c Apply critical thinking to analyze, formulate, and advocate for policies that advance human rights and social, economic, and environmental justice.** *(p. 183):* Dorothea Dix provides an excellent example of an advocate for policies that advance human rights, and social and economic justice. *(p. 192):* Critical thinking questions are raised regarding the government's treatment of American Indians from a historical perspective. *(p. 198):* Critical thinking questions are raised regarding public assistance policy. *(p. 201):* The Civil Rights Act of 1964 advocated for social and economic justice. *(p. 202):* Critical thinking questions are raised regarding civil rights. *(p. 206):* Critical thinking questions are asked that encourage analysis of policies' impact on human rights, and social and economic justice.

**EP 7 (Competency 7)—Assess Individuals, Families, Groups, Organizations, and Communities.**

**EP 7a Collect and organize data, and apply critical thinking to interpret information from clients and constituencies.** *(p. 190):* Mary Richmond stressed the importance of collecting, organizing, and interpreting client data.

**EP 7b Apply knowledge of human behavior and the social environment, person-in-environment, and other multidisciplinary theoretical frameworks in the analysis of assessment data from clients and constituencies.** *(p. 182):* Theoretical frameworks for assessing child development are reviewed. Such knowledge is useful for assessing clients in their social environment.

**EP 8 (Competency 8)—Intervene with Individuals, Families, Groups, Organizations, and Communities.**

**EP 8a Critically choose and implement interventions to achieve practice goals and enhance capacities of clients and constituencies.** *(p. 201):* The Older Americans Act of 1965 provides an example of a policy that enhances the capacities of older adults. *(p. 202):* Critical thinking questions encourage consideration of policies that advance civil rights and, in effect, enhance the capacities of clients.

**EP 8d Negotiate, mediate, and advocate with and on behalf of diverse clients and constituencies.** *(p. 183):* Dorothea Dix provides an excellent example as an advocate for people with mental disorders.

Policy, Policy Analysis, Policy
Practice, and Policy Advocacy:
Foundations for Service Provision

Janine Wiedel Photolibrary/Alamy

## Learning Objectives   This chapter will help prepare students to:

**LO 1**   Define social welfare policy and agency
policy. **Social Welfare Policy** (p. 222)

**LO 2**   Explore the process of policy
development. **Social Welfare Policy
Development** (p. 224)

**LO 3**   Identify how social welfare programs are
structured. **Structural Components of Social
Welfare Programs** (p. 227)

**LO 4**   Engage in critical thinking about policy
formulation. **Focus on Critical
Thinking 7.1** (p. 229)

**LO 5**   Explore values and how they affect policy
development. **Value Perspectives and

**Political Ideology: Effects on Social
Responsibility and Social Welfare Program
Development** (p. 230)

**LO 6**   Propose a model for analyzing a policy's
appropriateness and adequacy. **Policy
Analysis** (p. 233)

**LO 7**   Describe policy practice and policy
advocacy. **What Are Policy Practice and
Policy Advocacy?** (p. 236)

**LO 8**   Identify methods social workers can use in
policy practice (including involvement in
politics). **Approaches to Policy Practice and
Policy Advocacy** (p. 238)

*Policies have huge effects on citizens—including you. The following newspaper headlines focus on controversial policies and their ramifications[1]:*

*"State Legislature May Slash Budget Across the Board: Local Officials Furious"*

*"County Executives Can Retire as Millionaires—A Retirement Policy Fluke?"*

*"Fetuses May Qualify for Federal Aid"[2]*

EP 5a, 5c

*The* first headline *concerns a northern state legislature's serious consideration not to share state tax revenues with communities (cities, towns, and villages). The intent is to address a huge state budget crunch resulting from a lagging economy. This decision will result in a 10% decrease in one small community's total budget— hence the headline. Elected community officials are irate because such decisions by the state have a direct impact on local service provision such as garbage pickup, health care services, fire and rescue emergency services, and law enforcement. They indicate that such a slash focused on one budget item could wipe out the entire roads department budget (including road repair and snow removal) or the whole fire department budget and half of the rescue squad budget.*

*Critical thinking about policy: Policy—in this case, state public policy—has a direct effect on people's quality of life. How would you like it if you had to take your own garbage to the dump every Saturday because there was no pickup? What if your defective electric toaster started a fire in your kitchen, and no fire department was available to respond to your emergency? What if an older relative suddenly collapsed from a heart attack, and there was no rescue squad to call for help?*

*The* second headline *concerns a county board (the elected group that oversees county responsibilities and staff) that has approved a change in retirement policy that was not well publicized to the voting public. The policy's alleged intent is to retain good employees (including the board members themselves) by providing generous retirement benefits, thus rewarding long-term employees for staying with the county. However, an investigation by the local media reveals that the new policy actually will grant well over a million dollars in retirement benefits to some highly paid, high-level, long-term county employees if they choose to receive their benefits in one lump sum. The retirement formula is based on long-term employment and salary level. Therefore, only those in high-level positions who receive high salaries will be eligible for these extraordinary benefits.*

*Critical thinking about policy: Amazingly, potential recipients include the board chair, other long-term board members, and additional county government leaders. Most board members claim that they had no idea of the ramifications of this policy*

---

[1]Note that the ideas for the first two headlines were based on real events, but details in the ensuing discussion have been altered significantly.

[2]This headline was taken from the *Milwaukee Journal Sentinel*, Feb. 1, 2002, page A1, from an article by M. Johnson.

*because they had not done the requisite calculations. Much of the public feels that the board tried to "pull a fast one" but got caught. A citizen group is collecting signatures on a petition calling for a recall election in which they can vote current board members out. County government is in turmoil. Such huge retirement allocations will hike up county taxes, and citizens will be forced to bear the burden. This retirement policy has direct implications for the county's citizens who are financially responsible.*

*Another negative implication involves the impact on other county employees' morale and reputation. The policy is not their fault; they had no input into the decision to enact it. Yet the public is scrutinizing all county employees as if they are to blame for the problem. County employees say they work long, hard hours and are committed to contributing to a strong community that fosters residents' health and well-being.*

*The vast majority of them will receive adequate, but certainly not exceptional, retirement benefits. It has already been established that the controversial retirement formula requires a high salary for the extraordinary benefits to kick in.*

*This example shows how policy—in this case, on the local level—has a major impact on various groups of citizens. Effects include county citizens' financial responsibility for huge outlays of cash, board members' potential receipt of large sums of money, and innocent county workers' diminished morale and reputation.*

*The* third headline *reflects a presidential policy decision "that developing human fetuses could be classified by states as unborn children so more low-income women would have access to prenatal care paid by the government" (Johnson, 2002, p. A1). The result is that states could choose to provide health care to the fetuses via their mothers in programs designed to provide health care to children, not women.*

***Critical thinking about policy:*** *This policy decision resulted in a heated debate between right-to-choose and anti-abortion proponents. People supporting the right to choose maintain that pregnant women have the right to decide what happens to their own bodies, including the right to have an abortion. People backing the anti-abortion perspective feel that abortions are wrong and so should be illegal.*

*Right-to-choose advocates "immediately labeled the move a blatant attempt to establish a fetus as a living person. They believe it lays the foundation ... to make abortion a crime" (p. A1). Rather, these proponents recommended extending "health care coverage to more women than designating a fetus an unborn child" (p. A12). But anti-abortion advocates praised the decision, calling it a "compassionate" move to provide health care to pregnant women by expanding their access to prenatal care.*

*This policy has important potential implications for pregnant women. It paves the way for states to decide whether to pay for health care for unborn children—in essence, health care for pregnant women who were not eligible for services under child health care programs. It may also have implications for future judicial decisions concerning women's right to choose whether to have an abortion.*

*Regardless of where you stand on issues like these, the point is that policies significantly affect people. Sometimes they primarily affect only some category of people or segment of the population, such as pregnant women. Other times they may affect virtually everyone to one extent or another. For example, policy changes may result in cutbacks of essential community services or skyrocketing taxes for all citizens.*

*If you do not have any experience as a recipient of a social welfare program, you may not understand how important such programs can be to people who depend on their benefits. The examples given here illustrate how policies implemented through public services and programs can directly impact someone like you or those close to you. Policies regulate a wide range of social programs to provide many types of services for various groups of people (e.g., children, older adults, people with disabilities, and those with health or mental health needs). Social welfare policies provide the basis for social welfare program implementation—what programs can and cannot do.*

## Social Welfare Policy   `LO 1`

In a very broad sense, we have defined **policy** as rules that govern people's lives and dictate expectations for behavior. Policy determines how governments, communities, and organizations run in a predictable, coordinated fashion. We have also defined **social welfare policy** as the laws and regulations that govern which social welfare programs exist, what categories of clients are served, and who qualifies for a given program. Social welfare policy involves "decisions of various levels of the government, especially the federal government, as expressed in budgetary expenditures, congressional appropriations, and approved programs" (Morris, 1987, p. 664). For example, social welfare policy determines who is eligible for public assistance. In addition, social welfare policy sets standards regarding the types of services to be provided and the qualifications of service providers. For instance, social welfare policy specifies what social workers can do for physically abused children, in addition to what qualifications they must have to work in this practice area.

Note that throughout the rest of this book, for brevity's sake, when we use the term *policy* we will be referring to social welfare policy. Obviously this is the policy arena most relevant to a book about social work and social welfare.

EP 5

Social workers must be well versed in social welfare policies. They must know what is available for a client and how to get it. For example, Enrique, a social worker for a county social services department, has a young female client, Daniela, with three small children, who has just been evicted from her apartment. Although the rent was relatively low and the apartment small (one bedroom), Daniela had been unable to pay the rent for the past three months. All her money had gone to clothing and feeding her children.

Enrique needs to know what other resources, if any, are available for Daniela and whether she is eligible to receive these resources. Policies determine the answers to a variety of questions: Does Daniela qualify for some temporary additional public assistance to help her relocate? Is there a local shelter for the homeless available whose policies allow Daniela and her children admission? If so, what is the shelter's policy for how long she can stay? Is there any low-rent housing available? If so, what does its policy designate as the criteria and procedure for admittance? Such questions may continue endlessly.

**Social welfare programs** are simply the implementation (i.e., the putting into action) of social welfare policy. Sometimes the distinction between a social welfare policy and program is unclear. Some policies inherently provide detailed directions for how they should be implemented. In other words, they essentially *are* the program. Other policies are quite vague

## HOW POLICIES STRUCTURE AND COORDINATE LIFE

Policies serve to synchronize three primary arenas of life: "(1) the government; (2) the economy; and (3) private life" (Einbinder, 1995, p. 1850). All three are integrally intertwined. For example, consider the first headline cited at the beginning of the chapter, concerning a state slashing its budget. First, the national economy suffers a decline. As a result, unemployment increases, people reduce their spending, and less money circulates in the economy. Thus the state government gets less money in taxes (e.g., from personal earnings and sales) and must cut its spending. The economy affects government.

EP 3a, 3b, 5b, 5c, 8d

Government also affects the economy. Various governmental units make decisions about economic policy. For instance, a state might decide to decrease taxes levied on businesses within the state to encourage more firms to relocate there. The intent is for more companies to employ more people, who, in turn, pay more taxes. Additionally, because a larger number of businesses are contributing to the tax pool, the pool should be larger as well, even with a lower tax rate.

People's private lives are directly affected by both the government and the economy. What tax rates does the government levy on their earnings? Is the economy healthy enough for them to keep their jobs? As a result of these and other factors, do they have sufficient resources to purchase bare necessities or luxuries? Within this complicated system of policies and controls, are they able to maintain a good quality of life?

All citizens should be aware of what policies exist because of policies' direct effects on many aspects of life. They should also be alert to *changes* in policies for similar reasons.

Social workers must pay special attention to social welfare policies for two reasons. First, these policies dictate how programs are administered and how services are provided. Second, some policies are unfair, ineffective, or inefficient, and social workers must advocate for them to be changed.

---

and require substantial elaboration regarding how they should be put into operation. In these instances, the social welfare program becomes more extensive than the policy on which it is based.

Consider the following fictitious policy: All publicly funded social service agencies have to provide child care for their employees. This policy simply mandates that agencies must provide this service; it does not elaborate upon details. A program must be developed that responds to the following questions, among others: Where will child care be provided (e.g., in the agency or in a separate day care center)? How will child care be funded? Who will run the child care center? What kind of environment will be available to the children (e.g., a stimulating, activity centered milieu or basic overseeing with little interaction)?

Highlight 7.1 expands on how policies structure and coordinate people's lives.

### Agency Policy

Chapter 1 established that a second type of policy directly affecting social workers' ability to practice

is *agency policy.* This entails standards adopted by organizations and programs that provide services (e.g., a treatment center for troubled youths, a department of social services, or a sheltered workshop[3] for people with cognitive disabilities).

The terms *social services agency, human services agency,* and *social welfare agency* can be used interchangeably to refer to an agency or organization that provides social welfare services. Similarly, for our purposes, the words *agency* and *organization* mean the same thing. A **social services agency** is a coordinated system of staff units and processes providing social services. Such agencies typically employ social workers, other professionals providing various social services, paraprofessionals (people with specific knowledge and skills who, under close supervision, carry out various duties previously undertaken only by professionals), clerical staff, and sometimes volunteers. Services are provided

---

[3]A *sheltered workshop* is an organization that provides testing, counseling, social skills training, job training, sheltered employment, and job placement services for people with various disabilities or needs for rehabilitation (Barker, 2014).

according to a prescribed set of social welfare and agency policies.

Agency policy may specify the agency's structure, the qualifications of supervisors and workers, the rules governing what workers may or may not do, and the proper procedures to follow for completing an assessment.

Agency policy may address in greater detail how agencies can implement social welfare policy. It can iron out the wrinkles and specify rules regarding how agency staff should work within their individual agency setting. Agency policy can also address questions about how the agency runs on a daily basis. What hours do staff work? How are staff members evaluated for job performance and raises? Who is responsible for supervising whom throughout the organizational structure? This involves everyone from the director or chief executive officer (CEO) running the entire agency down to practitioners working directly with clients.

# Social Welfare Policy
# Development   **LO 2**

EP 1c, 7b, 8b

How social welfare policies develop in government agencies is an extremely complex process due to the many opinions, people, and formal processes involved. However, to facilitate your basic understanding and emphasize the importance of policy for social work practice, Figure 7.1 depicts a basic six-phase process of how policy is developed and implemented. The process proposed here is quite simplistic, but it gives a general idea of how policies come into being.

An example that illustrates the policy development process is the development of and change in policy governing the provision of financial aid to needy children and families (Macarov, 1995). The value assumption upon which the policy was initially based was that it is most desirable for children to remain in their own homes, cared for by their own parents, rather than being institutionalized. Implications concern helping to keep a family together even when parents are poor and have trouble supporting children. This value is reflected in Aid to Families with Dependent Children (AFDC), a primary program that provided financial assistance to poor families with children until 1996, when new legislation was passed. (The next chapter discusses this and newer legislation more thoroughly.)

## Phase 1

The *first phase* involves recognizing society's values about what is considered important or worthwhile. Absolute values are hard to pin down because of the tremendous number of people we're talking about.

*Case Example*   For illustration, we will start with the value that children are generally best cared for within their own families. The task of identifying society's values becomes more complex because values also change over time. For instance, the value that children should remain in their own homes might be superseded by the value that all parents should work to support their families.

## Phase 2

The *second phase* of the policy process concerns identifying problems and needs that require attention.

**FIG-7-1** Social Welfare Policy
Development

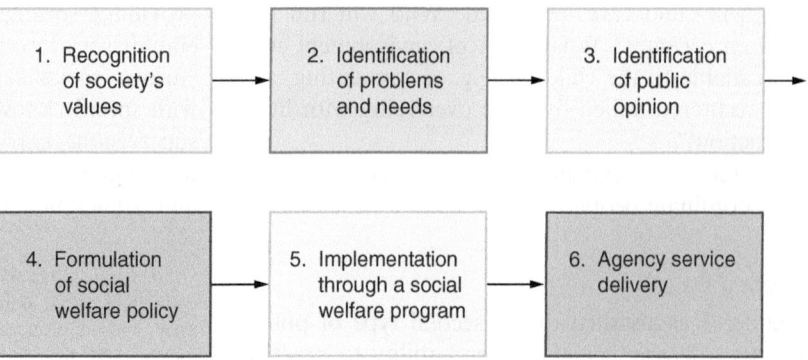

*Case Example*   The problem related to our example is poverty and poor people's inability to provide adequate care for their families. Although the societal value is that children should remain in their own homes, a significant number of parents, mostly single mothers who are primary caregivers for children, lack resources to provide their children with adequate care. What should be done to address this problem?

## Phase 3

The *third phase* of the policy process involves the identification of public opinion about an identified problem and people's related needs. Society's current values tend to guide public opinion concerning what should be done. Public opinion reflects values but involves more specific recommendations about what should be *done* to put these values into action. Values held by the majority sway public opinion in that direction. Such a prevailing public view might be perceived as the norm or expected standard. Highlight 7.2 discusses how the relationship between

public opinion and policy development is often unclear.

*Case Example*   For several decades prior to 1996, general public opinion maintained that poor families should be given minimal assistance to keep children in their own homes.

## Phase 4

In the *fourth phase* of the social policy process, legislators confronted with a problem or need and swamped with public opinion undertake the complicated formulation of social welfare policy to address the issue. It is beyond the scope of this text to elaborate on all the political processes involved. The following issues complicate the formulation of social policy (Barusch, 2015; Chapin 2014; DiNitto, 2011; Meenaghan, Kilty, & McNutt, 2004):

- It is difficult to obtain a problem consensus because of the multiple perspectives and opinions involved. True public opinion is hard to pin down.

## HIGHLIGHT **7.2**   PUBLIC OPINION AND POLICY DEVELOPMENT

Identification of public opinion is the third phase of the policy development process. Note, however, that the process may be more complicated than this. For one thing, majority public opinion is not always the deciding factor regarding what policy will be developed. Politicians usually pay attention to public opinion. Voters formulate public opinion, and they also vote politicians into or out of office. Thus it is usually in politicians' best interests to keep voters happy and to promote policies supported by voters.

However, many times such controversy exists over a policy issue that it is virtually impossible to satisfy the majority—or even to identify the majority. Sometimes many people will be dissatisfied no matter which side of the issue a politician supports. Consider the strong opposing opinions people hold over the death penalty or the right of women to get abortions.

Other times, it's difficult for legislators to get accurate information about public opinion on a particular issue. National Gallup polls aren't regularly done for every policy issue. Politicians must act on the basis of the information that is available. Sometimes this is

biased because a small minority feels very strongly about an issue and regularly contacts politicians to voice their opinion. Consider people who have very strong feelings about the right to own guns. Hearing only from people supporting that side of the issue might leave legislators with the impression that most people hate gun control, when this may or may not be true.

Finally, even if legislators who formulate and vote on policy have fairly accurate data on public opinion, they may not pay much attention. Because the legislative decision-making process is so complex (as described in the fourth phase of the policy formulation process), public opinion about one issue may get lost. A politician may need to compromise significantly to get anything passed at all. Sometimes politicians will bargain by withdrawing support for one policy in order to pass another policy that is more important to them. Finally, politicians may receive extreme pressure from other party members or powerful leaders to support or not support a policy despite their own personal feelings to the contrary.

- Legislators' perceptions of the problem depend on the information and pressure they receive. Various factions and interest groups have varying degrees of access to legislators and wield varying degrees of influence.
- Because policy is formulated in such a political environment, the actual policy can change dramatically in focus while it is being debated. The policymaking process is characterized by an ongoing struggle of give and take, conflict resolution, and compromise.

Consider a loosely analogous theoretical situation regarding how difficult it can be to come to a satisfactory consensus. Suppose during the first meeting of one of your classes your instructor indicates that it is the class's responsibility to determine how students will be graded. The only criterion given is that some configuration of exams and assignments must be specified and that they must not be too easy. Imagine the wide range of opinions students would probably voice. Some would want objective exams, and others would prefer essays. Some would want two exams, others four, and still others none. Some would prefer term papers, and others would opt for experiential assignments such as visits to relevant organizations or interviews with relevant people. Some would advocate for group projects, and others would express hatred for group projects and desire individual ones instead. It is difficult to establish a consensus: Controversy and differences of opinion tend to characterize decision making even in a relatively small group. Imagine magnifying this many times over in the complex legislative process.

*Case Example* After much legislative debate and struggle, Aid to Dependent Children (ADC), renamed AFDC in 1962, was initially formulated as part of the Social Security Act of 1935.

## Phase 5

Following the initial formulation of social policy, the *fifth phase* of the social welfare policy process

*Policy development is a complex legislative process. Here, congressional leaders discuss international issues and conflicts.*

White House Photo/Alamy

is implementation through a social welfare program. Consider the following:

> *Once a bill becomes law, policy practitioners may think that their task is done; it is only the beginning, however, because the law is then sent to the appropriate executive branch agency for interpretation and implementation into a program. Legislative policies are often broad and general in their language; it is then up to the various departments to interpret the broad language and make it specific enough so that programs can be created and implemented. Monitoring this implementation is extremely important and is the next target where intervention can occur.*

**EP 1c, 8c**

*(Rocha, 2007, p. 151)*

Social workers may be called upon to work with administrators and agency staff to figure out what words mean when translated into actual behavior. People may cling to old beliefs and behaviors and resist change. Worker input and communication may be necessary to help people who will actually be implementing the policy understand *how* they can implement it. This might involve lots of e-mails, reports, conversation, and time.

*Case Example*   The ensuing implementation process of ADC required substantial effort and specification of detail to make the program clear and functional.

## Phase 6

In the *sixth phase* of social welfare policy development and implementation, social services are delivered by social workers and other staff in the context of social service agencies.

*Case Example*   Social service agency staff work directly with clients who apply for and receive benefits. Highlight 7.3 explores how the six-phase process of policy development applies to this case example when society's values change.

# Structural Components of Social Welfare Programs    **LO 3**

Understanding a social welfare policy means investigating exactly what it says and what it does. There are five broad components to explore in order to understand any policy: (1) what people's needs and

the program's goals are, (2) what kinds of benefits are provided, (3) what the eligibility criteria are to receive benefits, (4) how the program is financed, and (5) how the program is administered and run (Chapin, 2014, p. 186; Dolgoff & Feldstein, 2013, p. 133).

## What Are People's Needs and Program Goals?

We have established that social welfare programs are the implementation of policies that are, in turn, the results of public values and opinion and the political process. Programs exist to meet certain goals related to addressing problems, fulfilling needs, or improving people's lives (Dolgoff & Feldstein, 2013, p. 129; Gilbert & Terrell, 2013). Social welfare program goals address a wide range of problems including child maltreatment, "teen pregnancy, homelessness, and substance abuse." They attend to needs such as "economic security, child care, and health care." They improve people's quality of life "through such means as education, socialization, and recreation" (p. 129).

Goals may be formal and clearly stated or implicit and unspoken. Consider the Supplemental Nutrition Assistance Program (SNAP, also referred to as food stamps) as an example. It "has a stated objective to alleviate hunger and malnutrition by enabling low-income households to purchase a nutritionally adequate diet"; another stated goal is to enhance the market for food grown and distributed internally within the country (Dolgoff & Feldstein, 2013, p. 129). Low-income families using food stamps to "purchase" food results in profits for growers, producers, and distributors, thereby enhancing the economy. "But food stamps may not be used for the purchase of alcoholic beverages and tobacco, pet food, and cleaning and paper products, including toilet paper. Implicit in a portion of these restrictions is a moral objective to control the behavior of recipients" by regulating what they can and cannot buy (Dolgoff & Feldstein, 2013, p. 129).

## What Kinds of Benefits Are Provided?

What does a particular social welfare program provide to recipients? Cash? Food? Housing? Counseling? In this context, a *benefit* is anything a client receives through a social welfare program. Because different programs serve people with different needs, the types of benefit also vary.

## HIGHLIGHT 7.3   WHEN VALUES CHANGE

Society's values—namely, that it is most desirable for children to remain in their own homes and be cared for by their parents (primarily the mother) rather than being institutionalized—have gradually changed. New values stress how parents, including mothers, should work to support their families. In light of more and more mothers working outside the home, it's important to think critically about how values affect policy. The following explains how newer societal values came to characterize child care:

EP 5a, 5b, 5c

"As programs that require ... parents [receiving financial assistance] to work became more popular, extensive child care facilities were needed. The desire of many mothers to take jobs outside the home also made such facilities a growth industry. As a result, providing child care outside the home has become not only accepted but prestigious. This social change led to a value change according to which contact with other children, even as early as age 2 or younger, is healthy, and professionally trained personnel provide better care than "amateur" mothers. This has reached the point to where working mothers are now postulated by some as more caring, and more capable of child care, than nonworking mothers."

(Macarov, 1995, p. 140)

This change in society's values led to a change in social policy, as illustrated by the following simplified process:

*Phase 1—Recognition of society's (changing) values:* Society's values changed from viewing parental child care as the optimum choice to viewing day care outside of the home as equally or even more valuable. (Note that you may or may not agree with the interpretation of how societal values have

changed regarding this issue. That's not the point. The point is to provide an example of how policies can change in response to modifications in values.)

*Phase 2—Identification of problems and needs:* The problem remains generally the same: A significant number of parents, primarily single mothers who are primary caregivers for children, lack resources to provide their children with adequate care.

*Phase 3—Recognition of public opinion:* Society's new values were reflected in public opinion regarding this issue. Public opinion stressed the importance of parents, including single mothers, working to support themselves and their families. Requiring single parents, including mothers, to work outside the home means that someone must be responsible for caring for young children.

*Phase 4—Development of social welfare policy:* The Temporary Assistance to Needy Families (TANF) program was enacted in 1996 as part of significant legislation restructuring financial assistance eligibility and requirements. (Chapter 8 discusses this legislation more thoroughly.) This newer legislation requires parents to receive job training and get jobs. It also places a five-year lifetime limit on recipients' ability to receive TANF payments; there had been no time limitation for the earlier AFDC.

*Phase 5—Implementation through social welfare programs:* The TANF program is being implemented throughout the United States. Because national policy gives states significant discretion in how to distribute benefits, each state has developed and is evaluating its own program.

*Phase 6—Service provision by workers in agency settings:* Social workers and other agency staff provide resources and services directly to clients according to the national policy and to state and local programs.

Benefits might be divided into two basic categories—cash and in-kind. **Cash benefits** obviously involve providing eligible clients with prescribed amounts of money based on what the policies governing the program allow. **In-kind benefits** include virtually any benefit other than cash. Examples are food products (e.g., those available from agricultural

surpluses), food stamps that can be exchanged for food, free school lunches, low-income housing, rent subsidies (e.g., whereby programs pay partial rent), day care, and personal social services.

**Personal social services** are those intended to enhance people's quality of life by improving their ability to function within their environment. Such

## FOCUS ON CRITICAL THINKING 7.1

## WHICH BENEFITS ARE MOST BENEFICIAL TO PEOPLE LIVING IN POVERTY?   `LO 4`

The next chapter discusses poverty and the programs implementing policies to help people who are poor. Some programs provide minimum cash benefits and allow people to determine for themselves how to budget the money and spend it. Other programs provide in-kind benefits, and the recipients have no choice in what they get.

**EP 5b, 5c**

Dobelstein (2003) questions the value of in-kind benefits versus cash. He indicates that "total federal government spending for all social programs, including cash and in-kind programs [including medical care], when added together is more than enough to raise the poor above the present poverty" line (p. 124). (The **poverty line** is the minimum amount of money the government believes a person needs to achieve the lowest acceptable standard of living [Orshansky, 1965].)

In other words, Dobelstein maintains that, if the government would divert the money it spends on in-kind benefits to providing cash directly, it would spend no more and possibly spend less. He continues that "the share of cash expenditures as a portion of all income-maintenance expenditures has been decreasing over the past 25 years, while the share of in-kind benefits has been increasing" (p. 125). (**Income maintenance programs** are all those that provide people with enough money, goods, and services to achieve an adequate standard of living and quality of life.)

Do you think it is better to provide people living in poverty with all cash, all in-kind, or some combination of both benefits? What are the pros and cons of each choice? Consider the following questions.

### Critical Thinking Questions

- To what extent does provision of cash benefits allow for personal choice, thereby respecting an individual's right to self-determination and human dignity?
- To what extent does the provision of in-kind benefits ensure that individuals get their basic needs met?
- To what extent does the provision of in-kind benefits restrict individuals? For instance, people eligible for low-income housing (by having incomes under a designated level) must live in the housing provided; they have no choice about where to live. Similarly, people receiving food stamps must use them for food. Although such coupons allow people some choice in the food they obtain, recipients cannot choose to pay the electric or heating bill or to purchase toilet paper with them.
- What are the advantages and disadvantages of some mixture of cash and in-kind benefits?
- Where do your answers stand on the conservative-liberal continuum, and why?

services (e.g., counseling) usually target specific groups (e.g., children or older adults) or particular problems (e.g., family planning or counseling). Subsequent chapters will describe programs implementing policies designed to provide various benefits to a range of populations in a variety of contexts. Focus on Critical Thinking 7.1 raises some key issues related to cash versus in-kind benefits.

### What Are the Eligibility Criteria for the Program?

**Eligibility** is the condition whereby people meet the designated criteria or requirements to receive benefits. For example, to be eligible for a particular

public assistance program, an individual must fulfill the required criteria. **Public assistance** is provision by the government of minimum monetary support to people who are unable to provide for themselves.

A common criterion used to determine eligibility is a **means test**—the evaluation of all the resources clients have at their disposal to determine if they have the *means* to pay for services or buy things for themselves. A means test might include assessment of people's "income, assets, debts and other obligations, number of dependents, and health factors" (Barker, 2014, p. 263). If people fail the means test, they are ineligible to receive benefits. Eligibility is an extremely important concept because it is the key to whether a person can obtain benefits.

## Who Pays for the Program?

How the program is financed entails the fourth structural component for understanding a social welfare policy. There are several ways to finance social welfare programs (Dolgoff & Feldstein, 2013). National, state, and local taxes provide a primary avenue for getting funds. Sometimes funding is diverted from the general tax pool (referred to as **general revenues**); other times funding involves **earmarked taxes**, that is, taxes designated to finance specific programs and services. For example, a county might increase its sales tax to help pay for a new stadium. Or funds from a state lottery might be earmarked to subsidize (partially pay for) citizens' property taxes. Finally, taxes might be collected specifically from employers and their employees to provide some benefit. Social Security, described more thoroughly in later chapters, is an example of such a program.

Sometimes benefits are not provided directly by government agencies. Rather, funds are collected by such agencies through taxes, and then specific services are purchased from another social service provider. Recall from Chapter 5 that this process is referred to as a **purchase-of-service agreement**. The purchasing agency and the provider agency agree in advance what types of services will be provided, for how long, and at what cost.

People who receive some benefit may also pay for it directly. Of course, many social welfare programs provide benefits to people with few resources. Therefore, a **sliding fee scale** might be used, with the amount paid based on the recipient's ability to pay rather than on fixed fees. The more income the person has, the more he or she is required to pay. Planned Parenthood, an agency providing family planning services and reproductive health care, including contraception, is an example of an agency that uses a sliding fee scale. Such family planning clinics are especially beneficial resources for teens and women with low incomes.

Finally, some programs are financed in a combination of ways. For example, a private agency providing mental health counseling may receive funding from various sources. This includes some funding through sliding-scale fees from clients, some through purchase of service by the state and county for clients unable to pay for the service themselves, some through grants furnished by private foundations, and some through charitable contributions from local citizens.

## How Is the Program Administered and Run?

The fifth structural component involved in understanding a social welfare program is the level of government that actually oversees and runs the program. Is it national, state, or local? Many times this involves a combination. For example, consider Medicaid, a program that pays for medical and hospital services for eligible people in need. (Medicaid is discussed more thoroughly in the next chapter.) It is administered by state government but overseen at the federal level.

Another example involves TANF, mentioned earlier, a primary program providing financial assistance to needy families. (The next chapter also describes TANF in greater detail.) TANF policy dictates that the federal government grant sums of money to states. States then have much discretion regarding how to administer the program and spend the money. They may channel more into cash benefits or provide more in-kind benefits such as child care or nutritional programs for children.

A food bank located in a large city is an example of a locally administered program. **Food banks** are organizations that distribute food items such as canned goods and staples such as flour and rice to eligible people living in poverty. This food bank may be financed by the city and county governments and by charitable contributions from private citizens.

There are other ways to look at how programs are administered and run. For example, you can explore program administration and service provision at the individual agency level. Chapter 5 reviewed the types of social agencies that implement social welfare programs, including public, private, nonprofit, for-profit, and proprietary.

# Value Perspectives and Political Ideology: Effects on Social Responsibility and Social Welfare Program Development   LO 5

Chapter 1 introduced some basic value differences about whether social welfare is the primary responsibility of individuals or of society in general. It also discussed some related perspectives concerning how social welfare policy and programs should be developed. The concepts will be reviewed here, and some questions posed for assessing the values that characterize a range of specific social welfare programs discussed in later chapters. An additional issue to be addressed is whether social welfare benefits should be available to everyone or to only a select few.

Note that the following discussion simplifies highly complex and controversial concepts. The purpose is not to provide an absolute decree for how to think about these issues, but rather to offer a foundation for thinking about how values affect social welfare policy and program development.

## The Conservative-Liberal Continuum

**Conservatism** is the philosophy that individuals are responsible for themselves, that government should provide minimal interference in people's lives, and that change does not necessarily mean improvement (Blau & Abramovitz, 2014; Dolgoff & Feldstein, 2013; Jansson, 2014). It involves the idea that if people fail or have problems, except in extreme circumstances, it is generally their own fault. Conservatism also reflects "a 'realistic' or 'common sense' view of human nature" (Page, 2014, p. 144). It assumes that "[i]ndividuals are largely self-interested (motivated by personal gain) and inherently competitive (more interested in their own good than that of others)" (Blau & Abramovitz, 2014, p. 141). If people have access to free benefits, they will readily take them and "milk" the system. Similarly, if people don't have to work, they probably won't. Therefore, government should not interfere in people's lives unless it is absolutely necessary (e.g., for people who are extremely "worthy" poor, as described in Chapter 6, or who need help in an emergency like a flood or hurricane). Government does have the responsibility, however, of enforcing laws because of people's inherent self-interest. Thus, these primary principles are involved in conservatism:

- It is each individual's responsibility to work and succeed.
- Failure to succeed is generally the individual's fault.
- The government should not interfere unless absolutely necessary, except for enforcing laws to

control people's behavior (which is inherently self-centered).

**Liberalism**, in contrast, is the philosophy that supports government involvement in the social, political, and economic structure so that all people's rights and privileges are protected in the name of social justice (Jansson, 2014). Social welfare is the collective responsibility of society. It is society's obligation to assist people in adjusting to the turbulent and demanding contemporary environment. People will prosper only if given the chance to. Thus these major principles are involved in liberalism:

- It is society's responsibility to care for and support its members.
- Failure to succeed generally is due to complex, unfair stresses and problems in the environment.
- It is government's responsibility to support its citizens and help them cope with the stresses and problems in their environment.

See Figure 7.2, the top portion of which contrasts some of the basic principles of conservatism and liberalism. These include the view of responsibility, the conception of where problems and needs lie, and the divergent perspectives on government's responsibility.

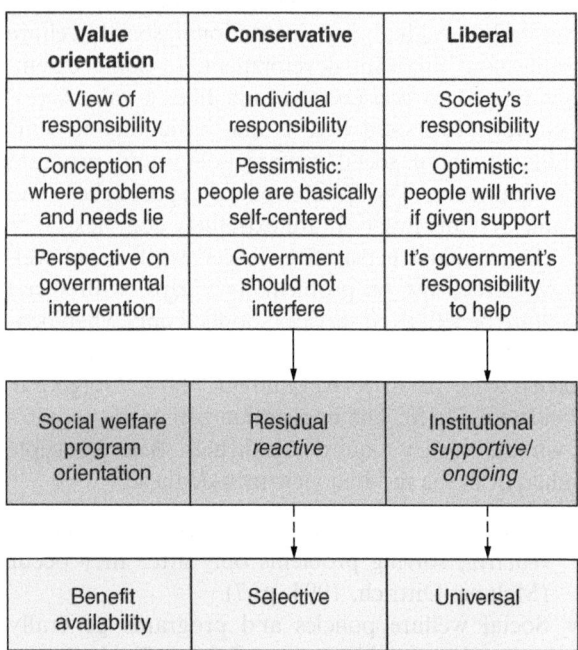

| Value orientation | Conservative | Liberal |
|---|---|---|
| View of responsibility | Individual responsibility | Society's responsibility |
| Conception of where problems and needs lie | Pessimistic: people are basically self-centered | Optimistic: people will thrive if given support |
| Perspective on governmental intervention | Government should not interfere | It's government's responsibility to help |
| Social welfare program orientation | Residual *reactive* | Institutional *supportive/ ongoing* |
| Benefit availability | Selective | Universal |

**FIG-7-2** Conservative versus Liberal Value Orientations

## Radicalism

**Radicalism** is the philosophy that the social and political system as it stands is not structurally capable of truly pursuing social justice (Marx, 2004). Rather, drastic, fundamental changes are necessary in the system to achieve true fair and equal treatment.

Radicalism involves extremes. It can reflect extreme conservatism or extreme liberalism. Essentially, the primary principle involved in radicalism is that the system requires a major overhaul to achieve more appropriate goals. Two questions may be asked:

- What goals should the system pursue?
- How should the system pursue these goals?

Chapter 1 established that a radical perspective requires the ability to propose a new social structure. It is beyond the scope of this introductory book to teach you how to plan new policies and promote major social changes. Therefore, critical thinking about social welfare policy in the remaining chapters will focus on the conservative-liberal continuum.

## Residual and Institutional Perspectives on Social Welfare Policy and Program Development

We have established how policies and program implementation initially flow from society's values. Similarly, residual and institutional social welfare policy and program development, to some extent, are related to conservative and liberal values, respectively. Proposed here is one basic way to start thinking about social welfare policy and program development. The philosophical approaches and value systems involved are extremely complex.

The **residual perspective** conceives of social welfare as focusing on problems and gaps, with social welfare benefits and services supplied only when people fail to provide adequately for themselves and problems arise (Blau & Abramovitz, 2014; Dolgoff & Feldstein, 2013). The implication is that it's people's own fault if they require outside help. Basic concepts inherent in the residual view include these:

- Social welfare policies and programs should be *reactive*, solving problems only after they occur (McInnis-Dittrich, 1994, p. 7).
- Social welfare policies and programs generally respond to problems caused by individual personal failure.

The **institutional perspective** of social welfare, in contrast, views people's needs as a normal part of life (Blau & Abramovitz, 2014; Dolgoff & Feldstein, 2013). It is society's ongoing responsibility to support its members and provide needed benefits and services. It is not people's fault that they require such services, but rather an expected part of the human condition. Basic concepts inherent in the institutional view include these:

- Social welfare policies and programs should provide ongoing support to all people in need.
- Social welfare policies and programs relieve existing tensions and help solve problems distressing people in their environment.

The central portion of Figure 7.2 reflects how the residual perspective relates somewhat to the conservative value orientation and the institutional perspective to the liberal value orientation.

## Universal Versus Selective Service Provision

One other perspective on social welfare policy and programming involves the concepts of universal versus selective benefits. **Universality** is the idea that social welfare benefits should be equally available to anyone regardless of their financial status (Dolgoff & Feldstein, 2013; Segal, 2013). Public education through high school is a universal social welfare benefit available to all citizens regardless of status, class, or income level. This is despite the fact that the quality of education varies dramatically from one locale to another. Social Security is another universal program because it is available to all people who work (Blau & Abramovitz, 2014; Dolgoff & Feldstein, 2013).

Universality contrasts sharply with *selectivity*—the idea that social welfare benefits should be "restricted to those who can demonstrate need through established eligibility criteria" (Segal, 2013, p. 8). Any public assistance program requiring a means test that limits benefits to "the needy" reflects selective service provision. To some extent, the concept of universality coincides with the institutional perspective on social welfare, and the concept of selectivity with the residual (Dolgoff & Feldstein, 2013). Focus on Critical Thinking 7.2 raises some questions regarding the pros and cons of universal versus selective service provision.

## UNIVERSAL VERSUS SELECTIVE SERVICE PROVISION

Popple and Leighninger (2015) reflect:

"There are many arguments for and against each type of approach. The universal basis of allocation carries relatively little stigma and fits with democratic notions of equal treatment for all. Recipients can be seen as citizens or consumers. Proponents of selectivity herald its cost effectiveness; instead of resources being spread over a vast population, money or services can be used where they are most needed. This can help fill in the gaps between needy and non-needy groups. Debates over the future shape of Social Security in our society involve these issues, with some observers suggesting that we should stop paying Social Security to those who don't need it and instead target more money to the less-well-off [older adults] ...

Critics of selectivity argue, however, that it may be more cost effective to provide social

**EP 5b, 5c**

welfare benefits across the board rather than to spend time and money sorting out those who are "truly disadvantaged." These critics add that selectivity leads to a two-track system; benefits for low-income groups don't seem as important to society as benefits for the majority and are thus allowed to be a lesser quality. This was one argument in the recent health care reform debate; the system people can afford to pay for (on their own or through insurance) is often superior to publicly financed health care for everyone." (p. 41)

When thinking about any social welfare policy, you might, then, ask two questions concerning the universality-selectivity issue.

### Critical Thinking Questions

- Should benefits be available to everyone or only to a select group?
- What would be the relative costs for each option?

Note that the bottom of Figure 7.2 shows how selective benefit availability coincides to some extent with a conservative value orientation and a residual perspective on social welfare policy and programming. Similarly, the figure shows how universal benefit availability corresponds somewhat with a liberal value orientation and an institutional perspective toward social welfare.

This connection, however, is not perfect. Therefore, the arrows leading from the residual and institutional social welfare program orientations to selective and universal benefit availability, respectively, are broken instead of solid lines. Actual policies may reflect a combination of selective, universal, residual, and institutional aspects. For example, student loans are universally available in that anyone can apply for them (Dolgoff & Feldstein, 2013). However, they are selective in that students must meet a financial needs test to actually receive them.

Another example of the complex and intertwining nature of these concepts involves disaster relief after the horrifying earthquake and tsunami that

devastated a large area in northern Japan on March 3, 2011. Relief initially was residual: Its main goal was to fulfill temporary needs in reaction to the catastrophe (although the earthquake causing the tsunami, of course, was no one's fault). However, institutional relief is also needed over a longer term to help rebuild Japan's economic infrastructures.

People who lost virtually everything require years of help in rebuilding their homes, work, communities, and lives. Disaster relief was also universal in that its availability was intended for everyone in need regardless of income level or social status. Universality was imperfect, however, because equitable distribution was initially difficult or impossible. Many areas were impenetrable because of destroyed roads, bridges, docks, and airstrips.

## Policy Analysis                                      **LO 6**

We have discussed different value perspectives that shape social welfare policy. Examining a policy from a values perspective is one way of understanding it.

Another approach involves evaluating the appropriateness and effectiveness of a social welfare policy, a form of policy analysis. However, *policy analysis* is a broad term that can have many specific meanings. Some analyses are filled with complex flowcharts, graphs, and cost figures. Others are narratives that resemble a short story. Others reveal some combination of approaches.

EP 3a, 3b, 5c, 7b, 8b, 8d

Policy analysis can target how well a stated policy attains its goals, who should most likely benefit from the policy, whether the benefit type is appropriate, how efficiently the program that implements the policy is financed, or how the policy compares with alternative policies (Gilbert & Terrell, 2013; Haynes & Mickelson, 2010; Jansson, 2014). Policy analysis is conducted by specialists who carefully scrutinize policies and make recommendations to legislators for future policy changes. Policy analysis is undertaken by social workers who evaluate a policy's effectiveness with respect to clients. Finally, policy analysis can and should be undertaken by all citizens who are affected by a range of policies and who, as voters, are responsible to provide input into policymaking.

For our purposes, **policy analysis** is a systematic evaluation of how effectively a policy addresses the targeted problem or issue, meets people's needs, and achieves its goals. Most of the remaining chapters in this book focus on programs that implement social welfare policy. The model of policy analysis proposed here provides one framework from which you can evaluate for yourself how appropriate a policy is and how well its program implementation works.

## The Five-E Approach to Policy Analysis

The proposed Five-E model of basic policy analysis for social welfare policy is as follows:

- How *effective* is the policy?
- How *efficient* is the policy?
- Is the policy *ethically* sound?
- What does *evaluation* of potential alternative policies reveal?
- What recommendations can be *established* for positive changes?

Figure 7.3 summarizes the Five-E approach. Policy analysis involves scrutiny of both the policy and the program implementation resulting from the policy.

Effectiveness

Efficiency

Ethical considerations

Evaluation of alternatives

Establishment of recommendations for positive change

**FIG-7-3** The Five-E Approach to Policy Analysis for Social Welfare Policy

## How Effective Is the Policy?

*Effectiveness* involves the extent to which a policy accomplishes its goals. What are the outcomes of the policy? How well does the policy's program implementation achieve its stated goals?

It is important to use critical thinking and ask questions to seek information. What are the program's strengths, on the one hand, and weaknesses, on the other? What empirical data are available to support program effectiveness? What do benefit recipients say about the policy and program implementation? Do workers administering the program support its effectiveness?

*Case Example*   Popple and Leighninger (2011) describe and analyze a policy concerning mandatory drug testing (e.g., a urine test) for people receiving public assistance.[4] The basic idea is that people receiving public money should not be wasting it on illegal drugs but should spend it on nurturing and supporting their children. An assumption is that people receiving assistance are likely to be irresponsible and do "bad" things such as use drugs. Note that

*as of June 2012, 19 states had policies to require either applicants or recipients to undergo a drug test.... Among those 19 states, only Florida and Georgia require all applicants to undergo a drug test. Several other states ... require that applicants be screened for substance abuse and subsequently tested if that screening indicates that the person is at risk for substance abuse.... Several additional*

[4]The case example, the arguments posed, and many of the questions raised are adopted from a policy analysis of the issue discussed on pp. 230–231 from P. R. Popple and L. Leighninger, *The Policy-Based Profession: An Introduction to Social Welfare Policy Analysis for Social Workers*, 5th ed. (Boston: Allyn & Bacon, 2011).

*states … require drug testing of applicants and/ or recipients who had previously been convicted of a drug felony.*

(McCarty, Aussenberg, Falk, & Carpenter, 2013, p. 8).

Our target of policy analysis involves Maryland, the first state to propose such testing for all public assistance applicants (Popple & Leighninger, 2011). A state legislative committee approved a policy whereby anyone refusing the test would get no financial benefits. People testing positive for drug use would be forced to enter an expensive drug rehabilitation program. And failure to cooperate fully in the program would result in decreased benefits to the recipient's family.

How effective is the policy? What does *effectiveness* in this context mean? (**Policy effectiveness** is the extent to which a policy accomplishes what it is intended to accomplish.) Does testing reduce drug use? Do welfare recipients who test positive and enter treatment stop using drugs? No clear evidence exists regarding the results of testing recipients for drugs.

Popple and Leighninger (2011) discuss drug testing in the general workplace:

*It is estimated that around [3%] of the workforce uses illicit drugs before coming to work or on the job. In an effort to maintain worker efficiency and productivity and to prevent safety hazards, public and private employers have set up a number of forms of drug testing for employees. These generally involve urine tests for traces of drugs in the body. They can be voluntary or required (usually the latter) and can be carried out at varying time intervals. In some cases, positive tests can lead to punitive measures such as firing the employee. In other cases, employers may use the results of the test to refer employees for drug counseling and other treatment. (p. 230)*

Proponents of drug testing for welfare recipients argue that forcing abusers to get treatment improves their ability to be productive citizens, as well as enhancing their own and their family's well-being. Critics counter that such drug testing violates recipients' privacy and forces them to endure a humiliating experience. Estimates of recipients who abuse drugs range from 10% to 16%, depending on the source (Popple & Leighninger, 2011). However, a study in Louisiana, a state that also initiated drug

testing for recipients, found that only 2% tested positive. Therefore, no hard evidence exists that most welfare recipients abuse drugs.

## How Efficient Is the Policy?

**Policy efficiency** is the extent to which a policy and its implementation through a program are economical. To what extent does the policy address the problem or issue it intends to with the least expenditure of time, effort, and money?

*Case Example* Drug testing is very expensive, especially when conducted on a large population such as people receiving public assistance. Maryland determined that testing welfare recipients for drugs for one year would cost at least $1.2 million. Additionally, the state would have to pour significant additional funds into providing treatment for recipients who tested positive. Needless to say, the Maryland legislature determined that the policy was too expensive and dropped it after two months. (Note that currently the Affordable Care Act [ACA] requires Marketplace insurance companies to cover substance abuse treatment. However, the specific benefits provided depend on the plan selected and the state in which the recipient lives [Healthcare.gov, n.d.]).

## Is the Policy Ethically Sound?

To what extent do the policy and the program implementing it respect people's rights to dignity, confidentiality, and self-determination? Is the policy honest and straightforward in its stated intent?

Do people who might be affected by the policy clearly understand it and its implications? Does it concur with current legal requirements?

**EP 1a**

*Case Example* We have already raised numerous ethical concerns, including violating individual rights and forcing innocent people to subject themselves to the demeaning process of drug testing. Additionally, some questions have been raised regarding whether drug testing in this context is legal and constitutional. How would you like it if drug testing was required for you to go to school?

## What Does Evaluation of Potential Alternative Policies Reveal?

To what extent does the policy under examination propose the best way to address the issue or solve the problem? Are there other more effective, efficient, and ethical policy approaches?

*Case Example*   What other alternative policy approaches to the problem of possible drug abuse by public assistance recipients might be proposed? One alternative is to limit the focus on the potential drug abuse of welfare recipients and to concentrate on drug abuse prevention with respect to the general population. Anti-drug programs could be conducted on a large-scale basis in the schools. Two other alternatives also involve the general population (Burke, 2008). First, legislative policies should emphasize the availability and use of evidence-based treatment approaches (in other words, treatment that really works). Second, insurance companies could be required to pay for substance abuse treatment to the same extent that they cover other chronic health problems such as diabetes or hypertension.

**EP 4c**

Burke (2008) raises questions concerning the prominent trend of spending money for enforcement, that is, reducing the supply of available drugs and arresting offenders. She indicates that there is no proof that supply has been reduced despite increased expenditures toward that end. She also explains that the 2005 cost to incarcerate a dealer or abuser for one year was approximately $22,000. She suggests that diverting money from incarceration to prevention and treatment might be more effective. The active debate on how to approach the drug problem continues to rage.

## What Recommendations Can Be Established for Positive Changes?

How can the policy be amended so that it becomes more effective, efficient, and ethically sound? Or should this policy be eradicated and a new one developed to take its place?

*Case Example*   We established that Maryland legislators withdrew their policy on drug testing. Instead, they decided to require all public assistance applicants to undergo an extensive interview process by trained substance abuse counselors in order to discover ongoing drug addiction. Apparently, the legislators felt that this was a positive change. However, this policy approach still is founded on the degrading assumption that people receiving public assistance should somehow be subjected to scrutiny for drug abuse.

# What Are Policy Practice and Policy Advocacy?

**LO 7**

It is the responsibility of social workers not only to analyze social welfare policies but also to strive to make changes when clients are inadequately served, treated unfairly, or could be served more effectively. **Advocacy** is active intervention on the behalf of a client system to help clients get what they need. Hepworth, Rooney, Rooney, and Strom-Gottfried (2013) elaborate a bit by defining *advocacy* as

**EP 1, 1c, 3a, 8d**

> *a process of affecting or initiating change either with or on behalf of client groups to:*
> - *obtain services or resources that would not otherwise be provided*
> - *modify or influence policies or practices that adversely affect groups or communities*
> - *promote legislation or policies that will result in the provision of requisite resources or services. (p. 452)*

Social workers advocate on their clients' behalf to obtain or improve service provision. This may or may not involve changing a policy. Rather, advocacy is an umbrella concept that includes a wide range of scenarios. Advocacy might involve assisting a client in urging a landlord to make needed rental unit repairs. It can entail providing an argument to an agency administrator to make an exception to some rule on a client's behalf. It also might mean advocating to improve a public assistance policy to provide adequate benefits to clients or to expunge a policy that requires humiliating drug testing to receive benefits.

## Advocacy Used in Policy Practice

Advocacy in the policy arena, thus, is a more specific subset of advocacy. Jansson (2011) defines **policy practice** as "efforts to change policies in legislative, agency, and community settings, whether by establishing new policies, improving existing ones,

## HIGHLIGHT 7.4    FIGURES PURSUING POLICY PRACTICE AND ADVOCACY IN A HISTORICAL CONTEXT

Three cases reveal how social workers and other community advocates conducted policy practice and advocacy to improve social conditions and service provision. In 1966, George Wiley led various social workers, clients receiving public assistance, civil rights workers, and assorted other welfare rights groups to take a stand against unfairness and inequity in public assistance policy and program implementation. Together, in 1967 they formed the National Welfare Rights Organization (NWRO), which planned and executed major welfare rights demonstrations (Day & Schiele, 2013). Under Wiley's leadership, "the NWRO became an advocate for the poor in court, where it challenged welfare laws. The NWRO also appeared on behalf of the poor before congressional committees, again to promote welfare reform. The NWRO's efforts were augmented by the volunteered legal services of lawyers who shared the organization's convictions and supported the welfare reform movement. Many cases were argued and won before the Supreme Court, resulting in the expansion of the rights of those on welfare" (Jansson, 2015, p. 333). The organization "demanded publicity about welfare rights and benefits, information heretofore kept classified, and after extended struggles prepared and distributed handbooks on client rights to welfare mothers" (Day & Schiele, 2013, p. 325).

EP 8c

Marian Wright Edelman provides another excellent example of policy practice and advocacy. She gave up other career aspirations to become a much-needed civil rights lawyer in the 1960s. She handled many civil rights cases, especially helping students get "out of jail" after involvement in civil rights efforts (Jansson, 2015, p. 316). Driven by her strong beliefs in positive change and hard work, she endured many hardships including being intimidated by dogs and even being thrown in jail herself. One of her greatest accomplishments was the establishment of the Children's Defense Fund (CDF) in 1973. This advocacy organization's purpose was "to provide systematic and long-term assistance to children and adolescents and to ensure that their needs are an important matter of public policy" (Jansson, 2015, p. 316). Work involved grant solicitation from a range of sources and lobbying legislators for positive change. Issues included teen pregnancy, mental health, family support, and child care. This paved the way for further attention to the necessity of providing adequate child care for the nation's children. In May 1996, over 3,000 organizations, along with the Children's Defense Fund, sponsored a "Stand for Children Rally" in Washington, D.C. Then, in 1997, President Bill Clinton and his wife, Hillary, sponsored another major event, the White House Conference on Child Care (Trattner, 1999, p. 133).

A final example of policy practice and advocacy involves the establishment of the Political Action Committee for Candidate Election (PACE) by the National Association of Social Workers (NASW) in 1976. PACE solicits information from political candidates to establish their positions on social welfare issues and determine the extent to which their stances comply with social work values and goals. It organizes NASW members throughout the country to support appropriate candidates, encourage social workers to run for office, solicits funds, and provides significant campaign donations (Myers & Granstaff, 2008; NASW, 2014c).

or defeating the policy initiatives of other people" (p. 15). Policy practice may also involve advocacy on behalf of "relatively powerless groups, such as women, children, poor people, African Americans, Asian Americans, Latinos, Native Americans, gay men and lesbians, and people with disabilities, [to] improve their resources and opportunities" (Jansson, 2011, p. 15). This is also referred to as **policy advocacy**. Highlight 7.4 profiles several people who pursued advocacy through policy practice at various times in history.

### Social Workers, Policy Practice, and Policy Advocacy

There are many ways that social workers and others can pursue policy practice and advocacy. It's important to stress that:

*policy practice is within the reach of all social workers. It can be as basic as registering to vote and voting, or as involved as running a political campaign or even running for office. The most important policy practice role is to become involved in one's community. Active participation in community affairs can open the way for involvement in local policy decision making, which may in turn lead to a national role. When greater numbers of social workers and social service agency clients become involved in the policymaking process, social welfare policies will become more responsive to people's needs.*

(Segal & Brzuzy, 1998, p. 261)

Cummins, Byers, and Pedrick (2011) depict a rather creative means by which one social work faculty member has undertaken policy advocacy:

*Ruth White describes herself as a "ranter." "I am always ranting about something," she says. She teaches social policy courses at Seattle University's BSW program. She already had several venues for her advocacy efforts, including a column in a parenting magazine and frequent commentaries in the Seattle papers with her op-ed pieces [citing opinions]. She had always wanted to have a radio talk show, particularly when she heard others on the radio expressing their views. She expressed the thought out loud and was overheard by the manager of the student radio station at Seattle University, KSUB, Seattle. The manager agreed it was a good idea and asked Dr. White to e-mail her ideas for the show. Before she had a chance to do so, the manager e-mailed her, stating the management team had discussed the idea and wanted her to proceed. And so she was off and running with her own radio show, Policy Brief, airing on Wednesdays at 9:00 A.M. Pacific Time, online at www.ksubseattle.org or FM96.*

*Ruth White's goal in hosting a radio show on social policy was to engage more young people in policy practice issues and get them involved. She structured the show around current policy issues, the first one being organized around the Farm Bill pending in Congress and issues of hunger. Another program was on the challenge of AIDS. She invited a panel for each hour-long show to address the particular issue from a variety of perspectives: service provider, client or consumer, activist, and policymaker. She always tried to include a student on each panel who was involved in the issue in some way, to help make the connections with her student audience. Her time slot saw an increase in the number of listeners despite the limitation of being available online only for some time.*

*Ruth's other goal was to educate the public in general about social policy issues and how they can help change policy and get involved in the policy-making process. (p. 138)*

# Approaches to Policy Practice and Policy Advocacy   LO 8

Advocating for policy or program implementation change—whether at the national, state, local, or agency level—can involve a number of approaches. At least 12 methods exist that social workers can use to conduct policy practice and advocacy (Hepworth et al., 2013; Kirst-Ashman & Hull, 2015a, 2015b):

1. *Persuade:* In the policy practice context, **persuasion** is the process of attempting to influence decision makers by presenting an argument or rationale for another point of view. What information might a worker give decision makers so that they might view the issue or problem from a different perspective that coincides more with social work values?

2. *Use **grievance** (or **complaint**) processes:* These are "administrative procedures designed to ensure that clients or client groups who have been denied benefits or rights to which they are entitled get equitable treatment" (Kirst-Ashman & Hull, 2015a, p. 237). Usually this involves an outside objective person or group making a decision regarding whether rights or policies have been violated. Initiating a complaint or grievance process draws attention to an issue and forces an agency or governmental unit to publicly make a determination regarding the complaint's validity.

3. *Initiate legal action:* This involves filing a lawsuit. As with following a formal complaint or grievance process, pursuing this alternative brings an issue to public attention and forces a decision to be made. A downside of legal action, however, is that it's expensive.

4. *Form coalitions with other social workers and agencies:* A **coalition** is a temporary alliance of various individuals or groups who come together to pursue the same goal or goals. These can enhance political pressure. Greater numbers working together can wield greater political clout.

**EP 8c**

5. *Provide expert testimony in formal settings:* Doing this in courtrooms or community forums or before a legislature can help persuade decision makers. Social workers can significantly influence the development of policies and services by advocating forcefully on their clients' behalf.

6. *Gather information and supportive data to bolster claims about issues and recommendations for change:* Conducting surveys and researching facts can provide persuasive information.

7. *Educate pertinent community groups:* This can be helpful in initiating policy change. Various forms

---

## HIGHLIGHT 7.5   FOCUS ON ANOTHER POLICY PRACTICE ROLE: SOCIAL WORKERS IN POLITICS

Note that some social workers have also assumed political roles. In 2014, two social workers were members of the U.S. Senate and another seven were members of the U.S. House of Representatives (Congressional Research Institute for Social Work and Policy [CRISP], 2013; NASW, 2013).

Former NASW Government Relations Manager Dave Dempsey indicated that such people "have not forgotten their roots as social workers"; he continued that "social workers who become politicians can bring their principles, values, ethics, knowledge, and skills to bear on social problems in a larger context than individual practice.... Virtually all the social worker politicians that I've had a chance to talk to personally have made the point that social work skills fit the political process and environment beautifully" (Fred, 2004b, p. 11). Social workers have skills that are readily adoptable to work in public office. These include "interpersonal skills, like active listening and conflict management and resolution and technical skills, such as program development and grant writing. Social workers also have knowledge in group dynamics, social systems and social policy, as well as possessing analytical and interactional skills" (Stoesen, 2007, p. 4).

Sen. Barbara Mikulski (D-Md.) provides an excellent example of a social worker who became a successful politician. First elected as a U.S. senator in 1986, she "is one of the highest-ranking social workers in the country's political system" (CRISP, 2013; Stoesen, 2007b, p. 4). She has served as a long-term advocate for older adults, women, and people living in poverty; she has composed legislation protecting older adult couples from bankruptcy when one spouse has to enter a nursing home, pressed for "a prescription drug benefit under Medicare," written legislation requiring national "standards for mammograms," and advocated for "legislation that gives uninsured women access to screenings and treatment for breast and cervical cancer" (Fred, 2004b, p. 11). She is the former Chair of the Senate Appropriations Committee and of subcommittees of the Health, Education, Labor, and Pensions

Committee (HELP); she has served on numerous other Senate committees and has been the recipient of numerous honors and awards (Maryland Manual On-Line, 2014). In March 2012, the U.S. Senate honored her for being the "longest-serving woman" in the U.S. Congress (Maryland Manual On-Line, 2014).

Rep. Susan Davis (D-Ca.), first elected in 2001, provides another example of how a social worker can strive to affect national policy. She has "fought to regulate the dietary supplement industry and pushed for legislation requiring that health plans provide coverage for second medical opinions" (Fred, 2004b, p. 11). She has been a strong advocate for veterans regarding access to loans and "expanded education benefits," and for military families concerning "increases in pay and benefits, improved housing," and better health care; additionally, she has been influential in supporting provisions of the Affordable Care Act concerning access to quality health care for low-income women and others (Congresswoman Susan Davis, 2014).

Nancy Humphreys, founding Director of the Nancy A. Humphreys Institute for Political Social Work at the University of Connecticut School of Social Work, emphasizes that social workers can play a wide range of political roles; these include "observer, advocate, voter, lobbyist, campaigner, trainer, as well as elected official" (Lewis, 2014; Stoesen, 2007b, p. 4). One doesn't necessarily have to start off by running for national office or the presidency. Political involvement can take many forms, although Humphreys emphasizes that social workers should keep their social work identity with its inherent value base (Stoesen, 2007b). Policy practice and political advocacy does not necessarily mean devoting oneself to a new career. We have noted that even e-mailing or writing legislators or newspapers about important issues can help change or implement policy. There's also potential for involvement at local levels such as running for the local school board, city council, or town board. We have also indicated that actively supporting political candidates is still another avenue of political involvement.

of media can be used to disseminate information and gain public support. These include newspapers, television, public presentations, and panel discussions at professional conferences and public events. Relevant groups can also be educated by letter-writing and e-mail campaigns concerning issues.

8. *Provide decision makers with relevant information:* Sometimes collecting signatures on a petition can emphasize that substantial numbers of people feel as you do.

9. *Organize groups of clients affected by the policy:* This can help to convey to decision makers the strength of a policy change appeal.

10. *Practice legislative advocacy:* This is the process of influencing legislators to benefit some category of clients. Some of the approaches mentioned here (e.g., writing letters and working with other agencies and client groups) can be used to address issues in the political arena. The more people come together to raise issues and suggest policy changes, the greater the potential impact on politicians. NASW's PACE, described in Highlight 7.4, is an example of how an organization might undertake legislative advocacy. Lobbying—that is, hiring individuals (called lobbyists) who attempt to influence legislators' decisions and votes through direct communication—is another means of conducting legislative advocacy.

11. *Use electronic communication to promote positive change. Segal (2013) explains:*

*"Email is just one aspect of using the Internet and electronic communication to influence the political process. The exponential use of social communication sites such as Facebook and MySpace, as well as professional sites such as LinkedIn, has the potential for connecting millions of people in direct and immediate communication. The potential for using these electronic linkages as a way to promote political action or educate people about pressing issues is still evolving. Anecdotal accounts have surfaced of email alerts and YouTube broadcasts helping to bring people together for social action, such as the gatherings at the state capitol in Madison, Wisconsin, of protesters fighting the governor's efforts to scale back pay and benefits to union employees. As the use of all forms of electronic communication grows, so too will the possibilities of fusing these media as a policy practice tool for organizing and advocating for social change." (p. 377)*

The National Association of Social Workers (NASW) at both national and state levels and other social work organizations can use the Internet to alert their members about critical issues and provide suggestions for action. For example, in Wisconsin, NASW-WI typically informs members about current legislation that involves social work and social issues significant for social workers. Members are thus encouraged to contact and exert influence upon their legislators regarding how these legislators should vote on such legislation based on social work values and ethics.

12. *Support political candidates:* Social workers should become educated regarding political candidates' views on a range of social issues. They can not only vote for candidates who support favorable actions and causes, but also participate in campaigns helping to get these candidates elected. Highlight 7.5 introduces one other potential policy practice role for social workers—becoming politicians themselves.

# Chapter Summary

The following summarizes this chapter's content as it relates to the learning objectives presented at the beginning of the chapter. Chapter content will help prepare students to:

## LO1 *Define social welfare policy and agency policy.*

Social welfare concerns the laws and regulations that govern which social welfare programs exist, what categories of clients are served, and who qualifies for a given program. Social welfare programs are the implementation of social welfare policy. Agency policy involves standards adopted by organizations and programs that provide services and guide the provision of service.

## LO2 *Explore the process of policy development.*

Phases of policy development include recognition of society's values about what is considered important, identification of problems and needs that require attention, identification of public opinion about an identified problem and people's related needs, formulation of a policy by legislators, implementation of the policy through a social welfare program, and delivery of social services by social workers and other staff in the context of social service agencies.

### LO3  Identify how social welfare programs are structured.

The five broad components to explore in order to understand any policy are (1) what people's needs and the program's goals are; (2) what kinds of benefits are provided; (3) what the eligibility criteria are to receive benefits; (4) how the program is financed; and (5) how the program is administered and run.

### LO4  Engage in critical thinking about policy formulation.

Critical thinking questions were posed concerning whether cash or in-kind benefits are most beneficial to people living in poverty, and the value of universal versus selective service provision.

### LO5  Explore values and how they affect policy development.

Conservatism is the philosophy that individuals are responsible for themselves, that government should provide minimal interference in people's lives, and that change does not necessarily mean improvement. Liberalism, in contrast, is the philosophy that supports government involvement in the social, political, and economic structure so that all people's rights and privileges are protected in the name of social justice. Radicalism is the philosophy that the social and political system as it stands is not structurally capable of truly pursuing social justice. Each value philosophy shapes how policies are developed in terms of individual responsibility to take care of oneself versus governmental responsibility to oversee the population's overall well-being.

The residual perspective, related to conservative values, conceives of social welfare as focusing on problems and gaps, with social welfare benefits and services supplied only when people fail to provide adequately for themselves and problems arise. This is also related to the concept of selectivity, the idea that social welfare benefits should be to anyone regardless of their financial status. The institutional perspective of social welfare, related to liberal

values, in contrast, views people's needs as a normal part of life. This is also related to the concept of universality, the idea that social welfare benefits should be equally available "to all members of society, regardless of their income or means" (Segal, 2013, p. 8). Social policies, then, would be developed and services provided according to the value stance adopted.

### LO6  Propose a model for analyzing a policy's appropriateness and adequacy.

The Five-E approach to policy analysis is proposed involving the following questions: (1) How *effective* is the policy? (2) How *efficient* is the policy? (3) Is the policy *ethically* sound? (4) What does *evaluation* of potential alternative policies reveal? (5) What recommendations can be *established* for positive changes?

### LO7  Describe policy practice and policy advocacy.

Policy practice involves the "efforts to change policies in legislative, agency, and community settings, whether by establishing new policies, improving existing ones, or defeating the policy initiatives of other people" (Jansson, 2011, p. 15). Policy advocacy concerns the practice of advocating for improved "resources and opportunities" on the behalf of "relatively powerless groups, such as women, children, poor people, African Americans, Asian Americans, Latinos, Native Americans, gay men and lesbians, and people with disabilities" (Jansson, 2011, p. 15).

### LO8  Identify methods social workers can use in policy practice (including involvement in politics).

Social workers can develop and join advocacy organizations such as the Social Work Advocacy Group (through NASW) or Children's Defense Fund. They can join political action committees such as NASW's Political Action Committee for Candidate Election (PACE). Additionally, social workers can use persuasion with decision makers, use grievance processes, initiate legal action, form coalitions with others, provide expert testimony in formal settings, gather information to support their causes, educate pertinent community groups, provide decision makers with relevant information, organize groups of clients affected by the targeted policy, practice legislative advocacy, use electronic communication for positive change, support political candidates, or run for political office themselves.

## LOOKING AHEAD

This chapter provided a basic perspective on social welfare policy and the ways in which programs are implemented based on their policy foundation. The next chapter will discuss policies regulating the primary financial programs in the United States. Subsequent chapters will discuss various contexts in which workers practice, the populations with whom they work, and the policies and programs that govern what they do.

## COMPETENCY NOTES

The following identifies where Educational Policy (EP) competencies and their component behaviors are discussed in the chapter.

**EP 1 (Competency 1)—Demonstrate Ethical and Professional Behavior.** *(p. 236):* Policy practice and advocacy are among important professional roles.

**EP 1a Make ethical decisions by applying the standards of the NASW Code of Ethics, relevant laws and regulations, models for ethical decision-making, ethical conduct of research, and additional codes of ethics as appropriate to context.** *(p. 235):* Social workers should evaluate the extent to which a policy reflects professional ethics.

**EP 1c Demonstrate professional demeanor in behavior; appearance; and oral, written, and electronic communication.** *(p. 224):* Policy development requires clear oral and written articulation of the features involved. *(p. 227):* When working with legislators, administrators, and others in the process of policy development, professional demeanor must be demonstrated through various types of communication and other behavior. Initial formulation of policy requires clear, effective oral and written communication. *(p. 236):* Part of professional demeanor involves effective communication. Policy practice and policy advocacy require clear articulation of needs and recommendations.

**EP 3 (Competency 3)—Advance Human Rights and Social, Economic, and Environmental Justice.**

**EP 3a Apply their understanding of social, economic, and environmental justice to advocate for human rights at the individual and system levels.** *(p. 223):* Social work practitioners should advocate for policies that are socially and economically just. *(p. 234):* Social workers should apply their understanding of social, economic, and environmental justice to advocate for policies that advance human rights. *(p. 236):* Policy advocacy involves advocating for human rights and social and economic justice.

**EP 3b Engage in practices that advance social, economic, and environmental justice.** *(p. 223):* Social workers must understand the importance of policy and policy development before they can become involved in policy practice. *(p. 234):* Social workers should engage in policy practice that advances social, economic, and environmental justice.

**EP 4 (Competency 4)—Engage in Practice-Informed Research and Research-Informed Practice.**

**EP 4c Use and translate research evidence to inform and improve practice, policy, and service delivery.** *(p. 236):* Social workers should utilize research to determine the effectiveness of alternative policy approaches.

**EP 5 (Competency 5)—Engage in Policy Practice.** *(p. 222):* Policy and related concepts are defined and discussed.

**EP 5a Identify social policy at the local, state, and federal level that impacts well-being, service delivery, and access to social services.** *(p. 220):* Policies are identified that impact people's well-being. *(p. 228):* Social policy regarding child care and how it changes with changing social values is discussed.

**EP 5b Assess how social welfare and economic policies impact the delivery of and access to social services.** *(p. 223):* The importance of assessing the impacts of social welfare and economic policies is stressed. *(p. 228):* Changing values and how they affect child care policy is discussed. *(p. 229):* It's important to assess how social welfare and economic policies affect people living in poverty. *(p. 233):* Social workers should assess the impacts of universal versus selective service provision policies.

**EP 5c Apply critical thinking to analyze, formulate, and advocate for policies that advance human rights and social, economic, and environmental justice.** *(p. 220):* Critical thinking is used to assess different policies. *(p. 223):* Social workers should analyze policies and advocate for policies that advance social and economic justice. *(p. 228):* Critical thinking is necessary for analyzing, formulating, and advocating for policies that improve the well-being of children and families involved in child care. *(p. 229):* Critical thinking questions are posed to explore which benefits are most beneficial to people living in poverty. *(p. 233):* Practitioners should critically appraise the extent to which social welfare policies concerning service provision should be universally or selectively applied. *(p. 234):* Social workers should apply critical thinking to analyze, formulate, and advocate for policies that advance social, economic, and environmental justice.

**EP 7 (Competency 7)—Assess Individuals, Families, Groups, Organizations, and Communities.**

**EP 7b Apply knowledge of human behavior and the social environment, person-in-environment, and other multidisciplinary theoretical frameworks in the analysis of assessment data from clients and constituencies.** *(p. 224):* A theoretical framework is provided to assess policy needs and assist in policy development. *(p. 234):* Social workers can use the Five-E theoretical framework for policy analysis to assess how policies affect people's well-being.

**EP 8 (Competency 8)—Intervene with Individuals, Families, Groups, Organizations, and Communities.**

**EP 8b Apply knowledge of human behavior and the social environment, person-in-environment, and other multidisciplinary theoretical frameworks in interventions with clients and constituencies.** *(p. 224):* A theoretical framework is provided to assess policy needs and assist in policy development. *(p. 234):* Social workers can use the Five-E theoretical framework for policy practice and analysis to assess how policies affect people's well-being, and, in effect their ability to intervene with clients.

**EP 8c Use inter-professional collaboration as appropriate to achieve beneficial practice outcomes.** *(p. 227):* Collaboration with colleagues and others is necessary for undertaking policy practice and formulating effective social policy. *(p. 237):* Examples are provided of how social workers and other community advocates work together for effective policy action. *(p. 238):* Forming coalitions and collaborating with colleagues is an important part of policy practice and policy advocacy.

**EP 8d Negotiate, mediate, and advocate with and on behalf of diverse clients and constituencies.** *(p. 223):* Social workers should advocate for policies that improve people's quality of life. *(p. 234):* Social workers can advocate for policies that enhance human well-being by using the Five-E policy analysis framework. *(p. 236):* Policy advocacy is an important part of social work practice.

# 8 Policies and Programs to Combat Poverty

Bruce Ayres/Stone/Getty Images

## Learning Objectives   This chapter will help prepare students to:

**LO 1**   Recognize poverty as a global and national problem.   **Highlight 8.1** (p. 247)

**LO 2**   Address variables related to poverty in the United States (including gender and the feminization of poverty, single parenthood, race, and social class) and explore steps to empower women.   **Poverty in the United States** (p. 247)

**LO 3**   Investigate proposed explanations for poverty.   **Reasons People Are Living in Poverty** (p. 251)

**LO 4**   Engage in critical thinking about poverty (including its conditions, its dynamics, and programs developed to address it).   **Focus on Critical Thinking 8.1** (p. 254)

**LO 5**   Explore the consequences of poverty.   **Poverty Has Consequences** (p. 254)

**LO 6**   Examine the dynamics of homelessness.   **Highlight 8.2** (p. 256)

**LO 7**   Describe major social programs that address poverty.   **Social Welfare Policies and Programs** (p. 257)

*Think about these questions:*

- *Do you know people who live in poverty?*
- *What does poverty mean to you?*
- *Where would you place yourself on the continuum ranging from poor to middle class to wealthy?*
- *Who is to blame for people living in poverty? Is it their own fault, or are they victims of unfair social conditions?*

*Now consider the following facts:*

- *In the United States, 12.8% of Whites, 27.6% of African Americans, 12.3% of Asian and Pacific Islanders, 11.8% of Asian Americans, and 25.3% of Hispanics live in households with incomes below the poverty line; 15% of the total population or more than 46.2 million people are poor (ProQuest, 2014). (The poverty line [or poverty level] is the annual cash income level, according to family size, that the federal government determines is necessary to maintain each individual or family at a minimal subsistence level.)*
- *21.4% of all U.S. children under age 18 and 8.7% of people age 65 or older are poor (ProQuest, 2014).*
- *When considering race as a factor, 38.6% of African American children and 33.7% of Hispanic children under age 18 live in poverty, whereas 18.1% of White children do (ProQuest, 2014).*
- *The quality of living for the majority of Americans has been decreasing in recent years (Kornblum & Julian, 2012).*
- *The median (midpoint) household income in the United States is $50,054; 25.1% of all households have incomes of less than $25,000, and 21% have incomes of $100,000 or more (ProQuest, 2014).*
- *The median income for African American households is 61.7% and for Hispanic households almost 74% of the median income for White households (ProQuest, 2014).*
- *About 1% of all households in the United States have more than one-third of the wealth (Kornblum & Julian, 2012).*

*A huge and widening chasm exists between the wealthy and the impoverished, the "haves" and the "have-nots" (Kornblum & Julian, 2012, p. 189). This is true not only in the United States but also around the world, as Highlight 8.1 explains. This chapter explores the policies and programs designed to combat poverty in the United States.*

*Interestingly, although this chapter addresses policies formulating programs to combat poverty, there are many questions about their effectiveness. Do they really combat poverty, or do they simply alleviate some of people's most desperate needs?*

## HIGHLIGHT 8.1   INTERNATIONAL PERSPECTIVES: POVERTY IS A GLOBAL PROBLEM   LO1

The gap between rich and poor is dramatically increasing not only in the United States but also all over the world. Kornblum and Julian (2012) report that 1.2 billion of the 6.4 billion people on Earth are so poverty-stricken that they must survive on $1 per day or less. They continue:

EP 3, 5b, 5c

> One-fifth of the world's people live in the richest nations (including the United States), and their average incomes are 15 times higher than those of the one-fifth who live in the poorest nations. In the world today there are about 160 billionaires and about 2 million millionaires, but there are approximately 100 million homeless people. (p. 188)

Individual nations are no longer isolated and able to function independently from each other. **Globalization** involves the increasing interdependence and interconnectedness among nations around the world. People are more mobile than ever before. They can readily communicate with each other due to advances in technology. Nations are economically dependent on each other. Eitzen and Zinn (2012) explain:

> [G]lobalization is not a thing or a product, but rather a process. It involves such activities as immigration, transnational travel, using e-mail and the Internet, marketing products in one nation that are made elsewhere, moving jobs to low-wage economies, transnational investments, satellite broadcasts, the pricing of oil, coffee, wheat, and other commodities, and finding a McDonald's and drinking a Coke or Pepsi in virtually every major city in the world.... [I]t follows

that globalization is not simply a matter of economics, but also has far reaching political, social, and cultural implications.... [G]lobalization refers to changes that are increasingly remolding the lives of people worldwide. Globalization is not just "something out there," but is intimately connected to the everyday activities of institutions, families, and individuals within societies. (p. 1)

Because of their growing interdependence, U.S. citizens can no longer remain isolated and "safe" from global crises. For example, when corporations move their operations to other nations where labor is cheaper, jobs are lost for U.S. citizens. "With an international perspective, it becomes clear that the well-being, income distribution, and social security of people in one region are intimately related to worldwide economic, environmental, political, health, and other forces" (Bibus & Link, 1999, p. 98).

In view of the social injustices that exist in the world, it is important for social workers to pursue economic survival and social justice from an international perspective. Social justice, which involves equal treatment for all, is related to economic justice—the distribution of resources in a fair and equitable manner. Social work has historically been committed to seeking social justice and helping oppressed populations including ethnic minorities and people living in poverty. Holscher (2012) reflects that social workers should "be concerned with their collective responsibilities as global citizens toward changing those institutions and social, economic, and political processes that create, perpetuate, and deepen the injustices and hardships that are often at the root of Third World poverty, conflict, and cross-border migrations" (p. 49).

## Poverty in the United States   LO2

People living in poverty obviously have less access to resources and, therefore, greater need. We have proposed that **poverty** is the condition of having inadequate "money to buy things that are considered necessary and desirable" (Kornblum & Julian, 2012, p. 196). This concept is more complex than might be immediately apparent.

EP 2

What is considered "necessary and desirable" in Vietnam, Jamaica, or Morocco may be very different from what fulfills these criteria in the United States. Some people also expand the definition of poverty to include a **culture of poverty**, a condition characterized not only by lack of economic resources but also by deprivation, low expectations for what life can give, lack of hope for the future, and despair (Macionis, 2013, p. 45).

When the U.S. government refers to *poverty*, it uses a designated formula focusing on the number of persons living in a family or household and the amount of income that family receives. Note the difference between income and wealth. *Income* is the amount of money earned by family members in a year. **Wealth** is the accumulated amount of money and other assets that makes up a person's total worth; this includes cars, property, stocks, and anything else of value the individual or family owns. The U.S. government gauges poverty by focusing on income because total wealth is too difficult to measure. It has established a **poverty line** (or **poverty level**) that refers to the annual cash income level, according to family size, that the federal government determines is necessary to maintain each individual or family at a minimal subsistence level.

According to this measure, more than 46.2 million people live in poverty in the United States (ProQuest, 2014). White people, who have proportionately greater numbers, make up most of the impoverished population in the United States. However, as the data presented earlier suggest, people of color are much more likely to be poor.

## Gender, Family Structure, and Race

More than 57.7% of all women work outside the home (ProQuest, 2014). In general, women working full-time earn 79.9% of what men earn (ProQuest, 2014). Chapter 3 established a number of facts. For one thing, discrepancies between men's and women's incomes exist regardless of occupation. Women tend to be clustered in low-paying, supportive occupations such as clerical workers, teachers, and service workers, whereas men tend to be found in higher-paying occupations such as managers, skilled blue-collar workers, construction workers, and engineers. Men also dominate in occupations involving math and science. Women are less likely than men to become doctors, dentists, or lawyers. They are also less likely to reach the top of their professions, a barrier that has been labeled the **glass ceiling**.

**EP 2a**

Consider the following facts regarding family structure (ProQuest, 2014). Twenty-seven percent of households with children under age 18 are headed by single women. The median income of female-headed families is about 45% of the median for families with two parents present. More than 68% of single women with children under age 6 and 77% of single women with children aged 6 to 17 work outside the home.

Race is another factor involved in poverty, which is reflected in the following statistics (ProQuest, 2014). Among individuals, 12.8% of all White people are below the poverty line compared to 27.6% of African Americans, 25.3% of Hispanics, 16.3% of Native Hawaiians and other Pacific Islanders, and 10.5% of Asian Americans and Pacific Islanders. (More than 24% of American Indians and Alaskan Natives live in poverty [U.S. Census Bureau, 2010]). We have already established that the median income for all African American households is 61.7% and for Hispanic families almost 74% of the median income for all White families. African American (29.4%) and Hispanic (27.7%) females are significantly more likely to be poor than White females (14%). Similarly, 38.6% of all African American and 33.7% of all Hispanic children are poor compared to 18.1% of White children. Twenty-eight percent of White female-headed families are poor, and more than 39% of African American and 41% of Hispanic female-headed households live below the poverty line. As a result, children living in single-parent families headed by women, especially women of color, are at greater risk of poverty. All three of these variables—race, single parenthood, and female family head—increase risk.

Is this disturbing news for you? What do you think are the reasons for such discrepancies?

## The Feminization of Poverty

An important concept, the **feminization of poverty** refers to the fact that women as a group are more likely to be poor than are men (Brandwein, 2008; Burn, 2005; Figueira-McDonough, 2008; Hyde & Else-Quest, 2013).

*Case Example*  Ginny, a divorced single mother of three, isn't making it. She doesn't earn enough at her waitress job, even with Saturday night tips, to pay the rent and put enough food on her table. Her babysitter has quit, and her sister-in-law says she can't help out anymore. Now what? Ginny surely has no money to pay a new babysitter even if she could find one. Ginny is frantic. Where will she go? What will she do?

Consider how the feminization of poverty may be involved here. We have established that women in general earn less than men, even with equivalent education and experience in the same field, although women tend to enter fields with lower pay. Additionally, single women with children are at increased risk of lower incomes and poverty. If Ginny is a non-Asian woman of color, her risk is even greater.

In what ways might Ginny be the victim of oppression? What aspects of her situation decrease her potential to maintain an adequate standard of living and provide for her family? What opportunities are unavailable to her? What support systems are lacking?

In addition to having a greater likelihood of being poor, women are more likely to be primary caregivers for children and older adults than men, which can detract from their focus on career and making money. And they are victimized by specific kinds of violence, including sexual assault and domestic violence, rarely experienced by men.

As with other populations at risk and oppressed groups, social workers assess women's problems and issues within the context of their macro environments. Often problems are identified and goals defined with empowerment in mind. Sometimes planned changes focus on the individual; other times the focus is on the macro environment. Gutierrez and Lewis (1998) identify at least three approaches that assist in this assessment process: (1) using "a gender lens," (2) using "empowerment through consciousness-raising, " and (3) thinking about a "grassroots, bottom-up approach" to changing communities (pp. 100–101). These principles help guide social workers' analysis of women's position within the macro social environment and provide clues for their empowerment.

### A Gender Lens

Using a gender lens to view the plight of women in the macro social environment assumes that sexism is relevant to the experiences of many women and is the basis for many of women's difficulties. Such a gender lens emphasizes that women not only are part of the larger community but themselves make up a community of women within that larger community. In essence, this establishes a new way of looking at the world, with women and their issues becoming the focus (Hyde, 2008).

### Empowerment Through Consciousness-Raising and Critical Thinking

**Consciousness-raising** is the process of facilitating people's understanding of a social issue with personal implications when there was little grasp of that issue before. (Chapter 3 discussed consciousness-raising as a means of empowerment for women in groups.) In

this case, it involves a serious examination by women of themselves and their feelings about a range of issues involving women. Using this approach, social workers can help women become aware of the issues engulfing them in their environment before these women take steps to address them.

One basic approach for consciousness-raising entails helping women ask themselves a series of questions and think about potential answers. Such questions involve critical thinking and might include these:

*"Who am I?" What are my needs, my desires, my visions of a life that is safe, healthy, and fulfilling?*

*"Who says?" What is the source of my self-definition and that of my reality? Does it conform to my experience of self and the world?*

*"Who benefits from this definition?" Does it conform to my needs, my "truths"? Is it possible for me to live by these definitions? If not, …*

*"What must change, and how?"*

(Bricker-Jenkins & Lockett, 1995, p. 2535)

A social worker can help a woman answer these questions by focusing on and helping her define her self-worth, her values, and her treatment by the world. If she determines that her treatment is unfair or inadequate because she is a woman, how can she make changes in her macro environment to receive better or fairer treatment? Consciousness-raising thus can become a foundation of empowerment. First, a woman explores herself. Next, she examines issues and appraises her status. Finally, she proposes plans to improve her life and her environment.

*Case Example*  Jazlyn is a single mother of two children, ages 2½ and 4. For the past few months, she's been receiving public assistance through Temporary Assistance to Needy Families (TANF). She is about to begin a job training program in food services. One of her problems is finding adequate and flexible day care. Another problem is the high rent on her tiny apartment, given the shortage of adequate affordable housing. Still other problems are lack of a social life and difficulties in obtaining credit to buy a sorely needed new car. Her "ex" ruined her credit rating while they were married.

Alone, Jazlyn feels stuck. She views her problems as personal and individual. She tends to blame herself after the fact for making the "wrong decisions." Jazlyn's social worker, Rochelle, in a *counselor* role, can help Jazlyn think through these issues, identify alternatives, evaluate their pros and cons, and develop a plan of action. Part of Jazlyn's consciousness-raising concerns her growing awareness that she is not alone, but rather shares the same plight with many other women. She can come to realize that many things in her world are not her fault, but rather result from basic social conditions working against her. As an *educator,* Rochelle can provide information about resources, services, and tactics for macro change.

### Empowerment Through a Grassroots, Bottom-Up Approach

The final facet of empowerment involves proposing and working toward positive changes in the macro environment. A **grassroots, bottom-up approach** means that people at the bottom of the formal power structure, such as ordinary citizens, band together to establish a power base and pursue macro changes. Often the focus is on helping individual community residents strengthen relationships among themselves, develop shared goals, and establish coordinated plans to achieve these goals. The focus of change is usually an issue that directly affects the community residents involved.

The common theme of women's grassroots efforts is that women work together to initiate and implement change. Examples of established grassroots organizations include the National Organization for Women, the National Women's Political Caucus, the Women's Action Alliance, and the Older Women's League.

Another phrase often used for this approach is "the personal is political" (Gutierrez & Lewis, 1998, p. 101; Hyde, 2008). In other words, some problems and issues that tend to affect women on the basis of their gender go beyond the personal or the individual. Rather, such problems are structurally based, affecting many women. The implication, then, is the need for macro-level social change to improve conditions and provide services. Consider Jazlyn's plight discussed in the case example. Think about the ways in which a social worker like Rochelle might help women directly affected by circumstances and a lack of resources pursue macro changes. As a *mobilizer,* Rochelle can discuss with Jazlyn and other clients having similar concerns how to join together and confront community leaders and politicians about their various problems. Together they can raise issues and try to identify a plan of action to address them. Specific questions to ask involve critical thinking and include the following:

- Should they form a social action group?
- Can community funds be directed to help subsidize child care centers? Can Jazlyn and other local women establish their own center, pooling resources to pay for staff and volunteering their free time to help cut costs?

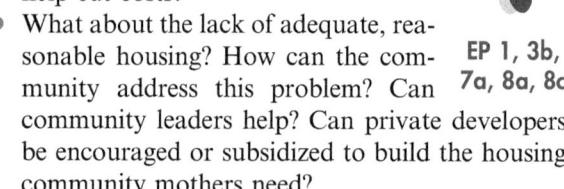

- What about the lack of adequate, reasonable housing? How can the community address this problem? Can community leaders help? Can private developers be encouraged or subsidized to build the housing community mothers need?

EP 1, 3b, 7a, 8a, 8c

- Might community events be organized to fulfill the social needs of single mothers and decrease their isolation? Can interested women form clubs or socialization groups to help them "get out" regularly? In a *facilitator* role, could Rochelle assist in establishing and coordinating such a group?
- How can Jazlyn and other community women work together to find ways to establish credit? As a group, might they approach local banks and businesses to discuss the issue? Can processes be established to determine when credit problems are not their fault, but rather the fault of ex-spouses?

### Poverty and Social Class

Sociologists, who study how societies are structured, tend to divide the population into categories of social position based on the extent to which people have access to the goods and services the society values. Another term for this categorization is **social stratification**. The population, then, is divided into **social classes**—"categories of people who have similar access to resources and opportunities" (Kendall, 2015; Macionis, 2013, p. 31). People in the same social class share things in common such as educational and employment opportunities, access to health care, and ability to acquire material possessions.

EP 2, 7b, 8b

Nineteenth-century philosophers did much to shape the way we think about people and social class. Karl Marx, for example, viewed social class primarily as an economic phenomenon related to a person's wealth. Max Weber expanded on this idea, claiming that a person's social class is determined by status and power in addition to wealth. **Status** is one's social standing and prestige in comparison to others. Chapter 3 introduced the related concepts of power, privilege, and acclaim. **Power** is the ability to move people on a chosen course to produce an effect or achieve some goal (Homan, 2011). Status and power are related to privilege and acclaim (CSWE, 2015). **Privilege** entails special rights or benefits enjoyed because of elevated social, political, or economic status. **Acclaim** is "enthusiastic and public praise" (Lindberg, 2007, p. 7). People who experience acclaim such as high-level politicians, well-known professionals, and famous entertainers maintain broad influence over what other people think. Subsequently, people with much privilege and acclaim have greater power to influence and control their destinies and those of others.

As you know, people live in very different circumstances and experience dramatically diverse levels of status and power. Consider, for instance, a homeless man who has a mental illness and who lives under the basement-level steps in a six-story parking garage (that is, when police or custodial staff don't chase him away). His status, power, and life are radically different from those of a physician who is also the administrator of a large, prestigious research hospital next door and who parks his Mercedes-Benz CL65 AMG in that same parking garage.

We might think of our society as having several basic classes (Kendall, 2015). *Upper-class* people include "investors, heirs, and executives" who have extensive wealth, power, and status; this includes the billionaire creators of a computer company, powerful politicians from wealthy families, "sports or entertainment celebrities," chief executive officers (CEOs) of big corporations, and "top-level professionals" earning millions of dollars a year (Kendall, 2013, p. 32).

**Upper-middle-class** people include "professionals (for example, physicians and attorneys), business analysts, owners of small businesses, stockbrokers, and corporate managers. These individuals generally do not own the means of production but have substantial control over production and other workers" (Kendall, 2013, p. 32).

**Middle-class** people include "white-collar office workers, middle-management personnel, teachers, and people in support positions (for example, medical technologists, nurses, and legal and medical secretaries), semiprofessionals, and nonretail salesworkers, such as insurance salespeople and real estate agents" (Kendall, 2013, p. 32).

**Working-class** people include blue-collar workers who perform manual and semiskilled jobs in industrial settings or occupy lower-level service positions (for example, "day care workers, checkout clerks, cashiers, and counter help in fast-food restaurants") (Kendall, 2013, p. 32). On the whole, they receive less prestige and have less access to resources than the classes above them.

The **working poor** are those who assume unskilled positions that might be seasonal, such as migrant agricultural workers, or work in jobs that receive the lowest pay (such as "hotel cleaning staff" or "lawn maintenance workers"); despite the fact that they're employed, they often live paycheck to paycheck, just barely getting by (Kendall, 2013, p. 33). The working poor often labor "in jobs that have unpleasant or dangerous working conditions and offer no benefits" (Kendall, 2013, p. 33).

Finally, the **chronically poor** or **underclass**, are impoverished "seldom employed, and caught in long-term deprivation that results from low levels of education and income and high rates of unemployment. Some are unable to work because of age or disability; others experience discrimination based on race/ethnicity. Single mothers are overrepresented in this class because of the lack of jobs, lack of affordable child care, and many other impediments to the mother's future and that of her children. People without a 'living wage' often must rely on public or private assistance programs for their survival" (emphasis omitted) (Kendall, 2015, pp. 231–232).

# Reasons People Are Living in Poverty  `LO3`

At least two major explanations have been proposed to explain the existence of poverty. They include "structural forces" operating in the economic and political systems, and individual factors (Rank, 2008).

## Structural Causes of Poverty

One explanation for the existence of poverty involves structural factors in society. These concern how the social structure, shaped by economics and politics, fails to provide viable opportunities for everyone to find work. Three structural aspects are involved. These include economic and political factors, in addition to discrimination based on race and gender.  **EP 2, 7b, 8b**

Economic explanations for poverty focus on the structure of the economy (Coleman & Kerbo, 2009; Eitzen, Zinn, & Smith, 2014). Poverty occurs when wages are too low and not enough adequately paying jobs exist for people to earn what they need to survive. Another structural concern related to poverty involves the escalating number of technical jobs requiring specialized training. People without such training can be left behind. Still another factor contributing to poverty is the increasing trend for industries to move from North America to other parts of the world where production costs are cheaper because people are willing to work for less. The result, of course, is decreased availability of jobs here. The plight of many U.S. farmers poses yet an additional structural worry. If farming costs soar here and imported food is cheaper, farmers are put out of business because they can't compete. Where, then, do they turn to make a living?

Political explanations for poverty emphasize that politicians shape social policies that, in turn, structure the existence of poverty. Such policies can decrease, maintain, or increase poverty (Coleman & Kerbo, 2009; Eitzen et al., 2014). For example, decreasing levels of financial assistance, resources, and services available to poor people will likely increase the number of poor and the depths of their poverty. Similarly, increasing the tax rate for people in the working and lower classes, while decreasing the rate for people in the middle and upper classes, will also increase the likelihood that people in lower classes will be poor.

The third structural feature that encourages poverty involves racial and gender discrimination. Considerable research has established that our society reflects significant "economic, social, and political discrimination" based on variables of gender and race, especially for the African American and Hispanic populations (Rank, 2008, p. 391). Racial segregation in communities often results in the concentration of people of color in poor urban environments with few resources (Rank, 2008).

One idea proposes that the wealthy find that having a social class of poor people is useful (Gans, 1971). First, poor people can do the "dirty work" for rich people that the latter don't want to do. Poor people are more willing to take service jobs, jobs requiring hard labor, or those posing danger than their richer counterparts. Second, having a poor social class emphasizes that the wealthy are higher in the social structure. It reinforces their higher status and allows them to look down on classes below them.

## Individual Factors Causing Poverty

As earlier chapters pointed out, there has been a historical tendency of blaming the victim when talking about poverty (Rank, 2008). In other words, it's the idea that if a person is poor, it's his or her own fault. This line of thinking blames poor people. It implies that they must have the wrong attitude about work, must not be motivated, and must not be trying hard enough. Substantial research indicates that this is not true; poor people express attitudes, ideas, and motivation very similar to those of middle-class people (Rank, 2008). So, why are they poor? One major difference involves their background and available opportunities from the day they're born. **Human capital**, the "skills, education, and credentials" people bring with themselves as they seek employment has critical consequences for their ability to get a job and for their economic success (Rank, 2008, p. 391).

Several variables contribute to having more or less human capital (ProQuest, 2014; Rank, 2008; U.S. Census Bureau, 2011). First, the families of poor people simply have less money than the families of rich people. Therefore, the playing field is not equal. Poor people start out behind. Fewer resources means decreased access to quality education and more lucrative opportunities. A second variable affecting human capital involves how poor people are more likely to originate in a single-parent family. Single-parent families have fewer resources and generally earn less than families where both parents are present. Third, poor people's families are more likely to have greater numbers of children than richer families. This means that whatever resources are available must be spread around more thinly. Fourth, poor people are more likely to have some disability that affects their ability to work.

Regardless of the cause, when a person starts out with disadvantages including a poverty-stricken environment, it's tough "to get ahead." Financial resources, strong familial support, and positive role models all improve a person's chances to succeed in work and maintain a good quality of life.

When thinking about impoverished children, several home visits come to mind. At the time, I was working as a social work counselor in a day treatment center for children and adolescents experiencing emotional, behavioral, and academic problems. The center provided counseling and special education for young people requiring special treatment but living in their own homes or with some other family in the community. The following are three case examples of children ensnared in poverty.

*Case Example*   The first case involved a home visit with a 16-year-old client, Danielle, at the two-room apartment where she, her mother, and her little brother lived. I knocked, and Danielle invited me in. I noticed that the door into the apartment from the dark, dingy hallway didn't quite shut tightly. The walls inside the tiny apartment looked grimy, with peeling yellowed wallpaper. I stood there for a moment until Danielle asked me if I'd like to sit down. This was perplexing because the only furniture in the room was a shabby table and a twin bed. For lack of other options, I sat down on the bed, as did Danielle. There we discussed the business for which I had come, involving Danielle's progress and future plans. I noticed the only other items in the two rooms were an old 18-inch television on the table, two mattresses on the floor with some bedding on top in the other room, and eight brown paper bags filled with what looked like clothes or rags. They apparently shared a bathroom down the hall with some other tenants. Her mother and brother were nowhere to be seen; in fact, her mother, a cocaine addict, was rarely around.

Danielle had a dream of marrying one of the many men 10 to 20 years her senior with whom she was having sex. Her vision included living in a neatly painted white house surrounded by a white picket fence in a well-to-do neighborhood and living happily ever after. She balked when I gently questioned how realistic that picture was. I presented to her other potential alternatives such as finishing school and getting a job. (A higher level of education is clearly related to higher income later in life.) But Danielle was several years behind her grade in school and was not much motivated to achieve in that area. She didn't understand what purpose academic achievement had. No one in her family, or her neighborhood for that matter, had ever thought much of school. It hadn't seemed to do any of them any good. Instead, she was hoping to find some Prince Charming to save her and care for her. The adult boyfriends she described didn't sound much like Prince Charming to me.

It was much more difficult for Danielle to climb out of poverty than it had been for the students I had known in my middle-class high school to survive and prosper. That school boasted a strong academic

program and active parental involvement. There, the majority of students simply assumed they would go to college. The main concern for many was whether they would get into one of the exclusive eastern private schools.

*Case Example*   Another young person living in poverty was Mike, an exceptionally bright 14-year-old who attended the day treatment center. Mike found life depressing and tried to escape through drugs. He simply withdrew, caused virtually no problems—(except failure to perform in school), and hoped that those around him would forget he was there. Like Danielle, he lived with his mother, a single parent who busied herself with her own life and relationships, and so was rarely home. Mike treasured an old broken camera he said his father had given him long ago. Mike's dream was to travel from his Midwestern home to Utah, where he thought his father lived with a new family. However, he had not had any contact with his father for more than seven years.

Mike grasped ideas quickly and had a perceptive sensitivity concerning others' feelings. I felt that Mike was clearly "college material." When I approached him about the possibility, he chuckled and then quickly apologized because he didn't want to offend me. He explained, "Are you kidding? Me? Go to college? How could I ever go to college? I'm so far behind. Who would ever pay for it?" I couldn't respond because I didn't know the answer. What options were realistically open to Mike? What real chances did he have to "get ahead"?

*Case Example*   One other example, from the same treatment center, was Rosalie, age 13 going on 23. Rosalie looked like an attractive grown woman. She wore lots of makeup and expensive clothes. Although she supposedly lived with her mother, who had an intellectual disability, she usually resided with other people. Rosalie's attendance at the treatment center was spotty at best. She was too busy at night in her job as a prostitute. At that she made very good money and could afford many more things than her peers. She returned one Monday with a noticeable increase in bust size. She said one of her friends had taken her to a special clinic for implants, but it probably was her pimp. Eventually, Rosalie quit the center and disappeared. The perceptions of the future her teachers and social workers offered her could not compete with the concrete rewards she was getting from her life on the streets.

## FOCUS ON CRITICAL THINKING 8.1

## WHAT IS IT LIKE TO LIVE IN POVERTY?   L04

What kind of background do you come from? How would you[1] describe it in terms of having adequate resources to grow, develop, and thrive? Do you come from a middle- or upper-class family in which resources were plentiful and you had lots of "stuff"? Or did your family have difficulty scraping by and paying essential bills on time? Poor people must make hard choices regarding what things they can possess or what activities they can pursue. There's little room for luxury.

EP 1b, 2c, 6b, 7a, 8a

### Critical Thinking Questions

Of the following items, which do you feel are absolute necessities for your daily life? Which could you live without? How would you prioritize them in order of importance? What would it be like to be poor and forced to make hard choices? What would it be like to have to live without?

A home that you or your family own
A room of your own
A home or apartment that your family rents
A single room where you and your family can stay
A working kitchen along with a range of utensils

A plug-in electric frying pan
Electricity
Heat
Air conditioning
Three meals a day that are nutritionally well balanced
Three meals a day of macaroni and artificial cheese
A private shower with hot water
Running water
Access to a communal water supply
A washer and dryer
A good job that pays adequately or well
A minimum-wage job
Health insurance
Dental insurance
Nice clothes
Two changes of old clothes
A cell phone
A brand-new car
An old broken-down car
An 85" flat screen TV
An Apple iPad
A used desktop

[1]The idea for this is derived from Burger and Youkeles (2000, p. 313).

### The Importance of Empowerment

One way of looking at poverty involves understanding how difficult it can be for people with few resources and little support to break through into a higher social class. Few or no role models may exist. People who experience frequent failure and deprivation may quit trying to achieve in the system. Why try if there's no hope? This is the reason the concept of empowerment is so critical. People in poverty must be empowered to see that change is possible. They must be provided viable options and credible hope.

Focus on Critical Thinking 8.1 explores what it might be like to be poor.

## Poverty Has Consequences   L05

The impacts of poverty are devastating and far-reaching, affecting virtually all areas of life. Among them are health care, education and jobs, housing,

and criminal justice issues (Henslin, 2011; Kornblum & Julian, 2012).

### Health Care

Historically, many people living in poverty experienced health problems and poor access to health care. It is no newsflash that health care is expensive. Kornblum and Julian (2012) explain:

EP 2, 2a

*By almost every standard, the poor are less healthy than the rest of the population. For example, the mortality rates for poor infants are far higher than those for infants in more affluent families, and poor women are much more likely to die in childbirth. Poor women are also far more likely to give birth to their children in a municipal hospital. Inadequately housed, fed, and clothed, the poor can expect to be ill more often and to receive less adequate treatment. (p. 207)*

The Patient Protection and Affordable Care Act (ACA) (also referred to as Obamacare), introduced in Chapter 6, was passed in 2010 and will be implemented over the subsequent 10 years; the most significant reforms were to be implemented in 2014 (Jimenez et al., 2015). The intent is to provide access to quality health care for most Americans. The ultimate effects of the law in terms of health-care provision to people living in poverty are yet to be determined (Jimenez et al., 2015). Positive provisions of the law include the following:

- Insurance companies can no longer deny coverage for pre-existing conditions or place lifetime limits on insurance coverage;
- The requirement that Americans (with some exceptions) who are not currently covered by other health insurance policies purchase health-care coverage or pay mounting penalties;
- An expansion of mental health services;
- Allowance of parents to include children in their health policies until age 26;
- An expansion of the Medicaid program (a form of public assistance based on need that is described later in the chapter) (Jimenez et al., 2015).

Subsides were also built into the law for poor and some middle-class people, based on income; these vary depending on the state of residence and the plan selected (Obamacare Facts, 2014). Jimenez and his colleagues (2015) reflect:

*While the act did not guarantee access for everyone, it was a significant step toward that goal. Such protections prompted a great deal of public controversy and political bickering.... In the end, the new framework for providing health care will have some gaps and unexpected glitches in the future. (p. 396)*

One noticeable health issue often affecting people living in poverty involves dental health. People who can't afford health insurance that may involve life or death issues surely can't afford dental insurance or expensive uninsured trips to the dentist to maintain their teeth and gums.

### Education and Jobs

"In every respect, poor children get less education than those born into more affluent families" (Kornblum & Julian, 2012, p. 285). Henslin (2011) indicates:

*Although public schools hold the idea of giving all children an equal opportunity to succeed, the poor are at a disadvantage. Because our schools are supported by property taxes, and property in poorer areas produces fewer taxes, the schools that the poor attend have smaller budgets. This translates into outdated textbooks, inexperienced teachers, and lower test scores (Kozol, 1999). Lower test scores, in turn, affect students' chances of going to college. (p. 198)*

Other facts regarding education that characterize poor people produce lifelong effects on their quality of life. Poor people are more likely to drop out and not graduate from high school (Macionis, 2013). They are also then much less likely to attend college. Less-educated people get lower paying jobs, experience less job security, receive fewer employment benefits, and find it much more difficult to become economically successful (Kornblum & Julian, 2012; Macionis, 2013). Henslin (2011) elaborates:

*Unlike the career paths that are open to the children of the middle class and the rich, the low-paying jobs of the working poor lead to fewer opportunities. Because workers are often laid off from these dead-end jobs, their incomes, already low, are erratic. During unemployment, they have to cope with the complex bureaucracies of unemployment insurance, welfare, and other social programs. Such experiences add to the stresses already knitted into their daily lives. (p. 198)*

### Housing

Poor people experience poor housing conditions. Henslin (2011) explains:

*Most of the poor live in substandard housing. Many rent from landlords who neglect their buildings. The plumbing may not work. The heating system may break down in winter. Roaches and rats may run riot. And, unlike mortgage payments, the monthly rent does not build up equity in a home. (p. 197)*

Note that poor people also don't have the buffer of money necessary to get into good housing. Renting attractive housing not only requires a high monthly rental price but also one or more months' rent in advance for a security deposit.

Many people can't afford rent at all. Highlight 8.2 explores homelessness in the United States.

# HIGHLIGHT 8.2    HOMELESSNESS IN THE UNITED STATES    LO6

A **homeless person** is defined as one who "lacks a fixed, regular, and adequate nighttime residence," or who sleeps in a temporary shelter for people without adequate residence or in a place (e.g., an abandoned building) not intended for the purpose of sleep (U.S. Department of Housing and Urban Development, 2011).  EP 2, 2a

In other words, homeless people are those who must live mainly on the streets (or in temporary shelters). Because many homeless are transient or, sometimes, temporarily homeless, it's difficult to determine the exact number of homeless people at any given point in time. It is simply difficult to keep track of them. However, it is estimated that between 9% and 15% of the U.S. population becomes homeless at some time during their lives (Mooney, Knox, & Schacht, 2015).

## Who Are the Homeless?

Homeless people are "the poorest of the poor" (Karger & Stoesz, 2014, p. 434). The National Alliance to End Homelessness (2014) describes the homeless population. On any day, 610,042 people are homeless in the United States according to a January 2013 count. (Note that other sources estimate the number of homeless as being much higher [Karger & Stoecz, 2014]). Almost 63% of the homeless are male and more than 37% female. Women are much more likely to be homeless and accompanied by their family (more than 79%) than are men (almost 21%). More than 22% of people in the homeless population are children. Almost 38% of all adults with a disability are homeless. About 9% of all veterans are homeless. About 18% of all homeless people are considered "chronically homeless" (i.e., experiencing long-term homelessness, usually involving a mental or physical disability).

## What Causes Homelessness?

A major reason for homelessness is lack of affordable housing; housing is regarded as affordable when no more than 30% of a household income is needed to pay for it (Mooney et al., 2015). Many people lost their homes during the 2007–2008 housing crisis when home values plummeted. They found they owed more on their mortgage than their property was worth. Many could no longer afford their homes or their rent. All homelessness is related in some way to poverty (Karger & Stoecz, 2014).

The National Alliance to End Homelessness (2014) identifies still other causes of homelessness. Families may become homeless due to some financial catastrophe such as a severe illness or the death of a provider. Young people may become homeless as they run away from tragic, abusive, neglectful, or tumultuous home situations. Homelessness may result for veterans due to disabilities experienced in the military such as post-traumatic stress disorder (PTSD).

Because homeless people are poor, some of the causes of homelessness are related to the causes of poverty. *Structural* causes of homelessness include unavailability of adequate low-rent housing, increased numbers of single-parent families, increased unemployment and inadequate numbers of jobs, decreased salary levels as industries move overseas and low-paying service jobs increase in number, and inadequate care of people with mental illness who have been released from institutions into the community (Mental illness is discussed further in Chapter 13.) (Wong, 2008). *Individual* factors that increase the likelihood of homelessness include mental illness and alcohol and other substance addictions (Macionis, 2013).

## Solving the Homelessness Problem

How can we solve the homelessness problem? The 1987 McKinney-Vento Homeless Assistance Act at least began to address the problem by creating more than 20 programs to address the issue. These included programs providing grants to establish emergency shelters, incentives to develop transitional housing and single-room occupancy (SRO) dwellings, and other supportive services. A 1990 amendment mandated that homeless children be able to attend school even when prior educational records and verification of residency are unavailable. However, considering the fact that homelessness is still an extensive problem, this legislation has not been enough.  EP 5c, 8d

Solving the problem would require major structural changes in addition to addressing individual needs. Affordable rental housing should be increased; housing development takes money at the outset, but research indicates that expansion of such resources is cost-effective in the long run (Wong, 2008). Other recommendations include refurbishing abandoned housing in urban settings to provide low-cost housing, conserving SRO lodging, legally requiring local governments to

*(continued)*

**HIGHLIGHT 8.2 (continued)**

provide shelter for their homeless populations, and establishing viable community alternatives for people suffering from mental illness (Hartman, 1987). Issues of homeless people should also be addressed at the individual level by providing services people need to function independently. Services might include outreach to homeless people in the community, provision of brokers and case managers to link them with the services they need, and assistance in finding jobs (Wong, 2008). Funding needs to be diverted to help people get back on their feet, or keep from slipping in the first place.

Karger and Stoesz (2014) conclude:

Homelessness cannot be eradicated without basic changes in federal housing, income support, social services, health care, education, and employment policies. Benefit levels for these programs must be made adequate; the erosion of welfare benefits

must be stopped; residency and other requirements that exclude homeless persons must be changed; and programs (including outreach) must be made freely available to the homeless and the potentially homeless. Moreover, a real solution to the homeless problem must involve the provision of permanent housing for those who are currently or potentially homeless. Federal programs and legislation should be coordinated and expanded to provide decent, affordable housing, coupled with needed services, for all poor families. Finally, both the states and the federal government should intervene directly in the housing market by controlling rents, increasing the overall housing stock, limiting speculation [e.g., converting SRO hotels into condos for wealthy urban residents], and providing income supports. (p. 357)

## Criminal Justice Issues

Poverty also is related to criminal justice issues (Macionis, 2013; Mooney et al., 2015). Henslin (2011) explains the differential treatment experienced by people who are poor in the criminal justice system:

*The life experiences of the poor also make them more likely to commit robberies and assaults, crimes that are especially visible and for which offenders are punished severely. Those most likely to be the victims of these crimes are other people in poverty. White-collar crime may be more pervasive and costly to society, but it is less visible and carries milder punishments.... [W]hen the poor are arrested, they lack the resources to hire good lawyers to defend themselves. Often, they cannot even post bail, and they remain in jail for months while they await trial. (p. 198)*

Focus on Critical Thinking 8.2 addresses residual versus institutional perspectives on poverty and its related issues. It urges you to explore which views you hold.

# Social Welfare Policies and Programs

LO7

Chapter 6 established that the Social Security Act of 1935 was one of the most significant pieces of legislation shaping social welfare policy during the last

century. It established programs in three major categories:

1. *Health and welfare services:* Services provided to people including "child welfare services, vocational rehabilitation, activities for ... [older adults], maternal and child health services, maternity and infant care projects, comprehensive health services, and a variety of public health activities" and a range of other public programs (U.S. Census Bureau, 2011, p. 349).

EP 1, 5c, 8d

2. *Social insurance:* Financial benefits provided to people to "provide protection against wage loss resulting from retirement, prolonged disability, death, or unemployment, and protection against the cost of medical care during old age and disability" (U.S. Census Bureau, 2011, p. 347).
3. *Public assistance:* Financial benefits and in-kind benefits (services or goods versus cash) provided to people who can't support themselves.

Chapter 6 also introduced divergent principles governing social insurance and public assistance, the two categories of programs discussed in this chapter. (The third category, health and welfare services, will be covered in subsequent chapters that address various fields of social work practice.) Social insurance is considered people's *right* because workers and their employers pay premiums while they

## RESIDUAL VERSUS INSTITUTIONAL PERSPECTIVES ON POVERTY

Earlier chapters established that the **residual perspective** on social welfare maintains that individuals are ultimately responsible for securing their own personal well-being. It's people's own fault if they're poor. Society should only step in to provide resources when major problems arise. Then such provision should only be temporary until individuals get themselves back on their feet and can take care of themselves.

EP 6b, 7b, 8b

The **institutional perspective** on social welfare, on the other hand, views people's needs as an ongoing part of life. Society has the responsibility to support its members and provide needed benefits and services. It's not people's fault that they require such services but rather an expected part of the human condition. In other words, people have the right to receive benefits and services on a continuous basis. It's society's responsibility to address the problems of poverty and take care of poor people living in poverty.

### Critical Thinking Questions

- What do you think are the reasons for poverty in the United States?
- To what extent do you feel it is the government's responsibility to alleviate poverty?
- To what extent do you feel that it is the fault of poor people that they are poor?
- What resources and services do you feel the government should provide citizens? Under what circumstances should they be offered? Explain.
- Do your views coincide more with the residual or institutional perspective on social welfare and poverty? Explain.

work. Insurance protects people in the event of harm or loss. For example, you buy car insurance so that if you crash your car the insurance pays for repairs and any legal costs. Like other types of insurance, social insurance covers risks assumed while working, such as unemployment, injury, or illness, and inevitable conditions such as old age or death. Financial benefits are provided when such conditions occur. People receiving social insurance benefits work and pay premiums, so the benefits for them and their families are considered their right.

Public assistance, in contrast, is based on *need*. When people are unable to support themselves, the government provides financial benefits to help them do so. People receiving public assistance benefits never paid premiums, as did people collecting social insurance benefits. Therefore, many people believe that public assistance is not people's right and resent the fact that people need and get it. Public assistance is often derogatorily referred to as "welfare"—for example, TANF, which replaced Aid to Families with Dependent Children (AFDC) in 1996.

Note that terms can be confusing because they are used in different ways. Chapter 1 defined *social welfare* broadly as the general well-being of all people in a society. This is quite different from what most people mean when they refer to people "on welfare." Common negative conceptions about public assistance and its recipients are examined later in the chapter.

Both social insurance and public assistance are considered **income maintenance** programs, that is, programs that provide income. Such programs theoretically provide people with enough money, goods, and services to preserve an adequate standard of living and quality of life.

Figure 8.1 identifies some of the social programs under the U.S. social welfare system's social insurance and public assistance umbrellas. These reflect only a few examples of the many programs in the huge social welfare system.

## Social Work Roles

Social workers may or may not work in social service agencies implementing the programs this chapter discusses. However, they will most likely work with clients who are concerned about financial matters and who receive benefits from these programs. Therefore, brief overviews of major social insurance and public assistance

EP 1

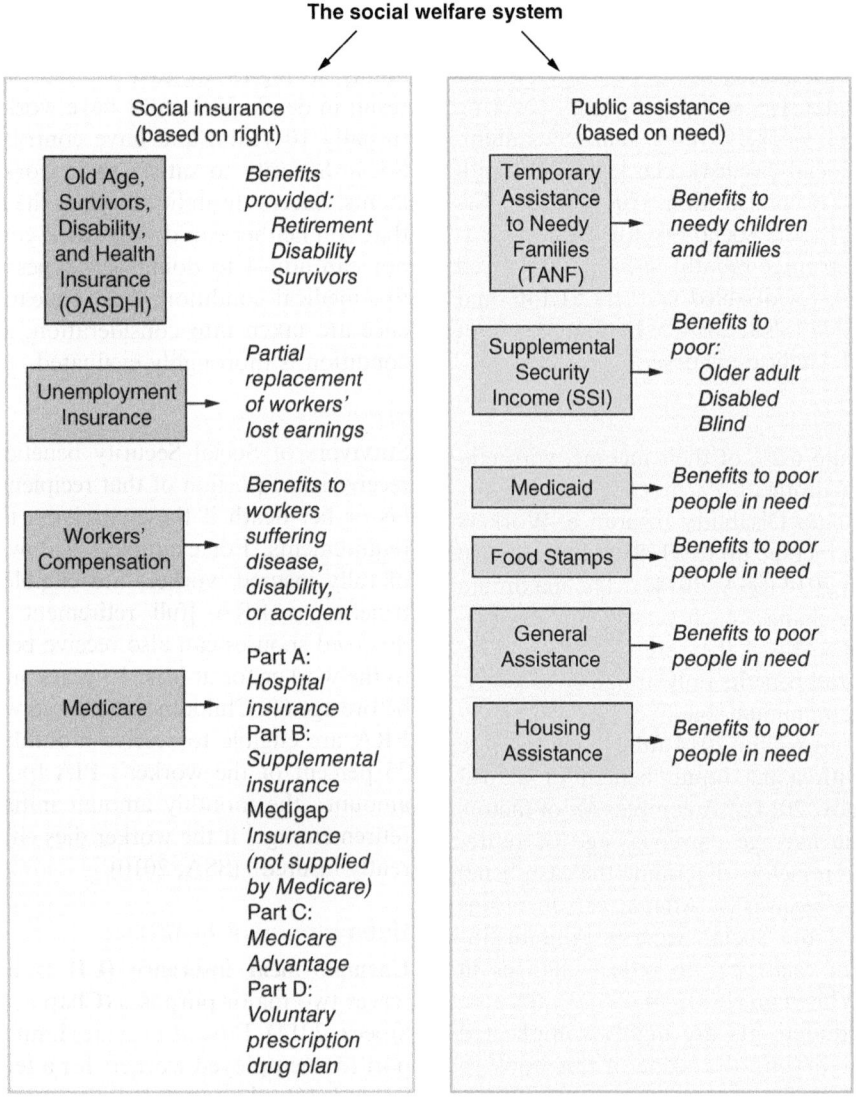

**FIG-8-1** Social Insurance and Public Assistance

programs are provided. Note that it's also important for you as an individual to understand these systems because, on a personal level, sooner or later they will probably impact you, your parents, and other older relatives.

## Social Insurance Policy

The primary social insurance programs in the United States include Old Age, Survivors, Disability, and Health Insurance (OASDHI); unemployment insurance; workers' compensation; and Medicare.

## Old Age, Survivors, Disability, and Health Insurance (OASDHI)

The term **Social Security**, commonly used in the United States, is the program that provides financial benefits to workers who are retired or have a disability, their spouses or dependent children, and designated survivors of workers upon their death. Social Security includes the financial benefits provided by Old Age, Survivors, Disability, and Health Insurance (OASDHI) and Medicare. Because these programs are types of social insurance, people are eligible to receive benefits only if they contributed an adequate part of their earnings according to established financial formulas. OASDHI, initially created by the Social Security Act of 1935, is the nation's most extensive social program, covering about 90% of all workers; more than 59 million people receive Social Security checks each month (Social Security Administration, 2014d). Benefits are administered by the Social Security Administration (SSA). The average monthly benefit for retired workers is $1,294, for disabled workers $1,146, and for survivors $1,244 (SSA, 2014d). Each major facet of OASDHI and Medicare is described briefly.

### Retirement Benefits

Workers contribute 6.2% of their income, with employers matching another 6.2%, to Old Age and Survivors Insurance and Disability Insurance. Workers pay these fees on income up to $118,500 in 2015, up from $117,000 in 2014 (SSA, 2014a). The maximum ceiling of income changes each year. People are eligible to receive benefits if they are 62 or older, but they can receive full benefits only at age 66 or older. In the future, the minimum age to receive full benefits will increase to 67. In 2014 full retirement age was 66 years with a maximum benefit of $2,642 (Answers.USA.gov, 2014). "A complex set of factors including lifetime average earnings, age of retirement, and inflation factors determine the cash benefits that a person receives.... After a person begins receiving benefits, the Social Security Administration adjusts them each year to reflect changes in cost of living" (Whiteman, 2001, pp. 22–23). Because the eligibility requirements are highly complicated and complex, it's beyond the scope of this book to describe them in detail.

There has been much debate in recent years regarding the future of Social Security, especially with respect to retirement. Chapter 10 will review some of the issues as a major area of concern for people as they age.

Note that family members of retired or disabled Social Security beneficiaries may also receive benefits if they satisfy designated conditions. For example, a spouse or child may each receive some amount of benefits if they fulfill the required criteria (Derochie, 2012).

### Disability Benefits

The following are conditions for receiving OASDI disability benefits (SSA, 2014c). Workers are eligible for disability benefits five months after they apply for benefits. The medical condition must involve disability lasting for at least one year or be expected to result in death. You must have worked long enough (usually 10 years) and have contributed enough to Social Security to satisfy their work credit requirements. Severe disability is when the SSA determines that you neither can do the work you previously did nor can adjust to doing new types of work due to this medical condition. Age, education, and experience are taken into consideration, and the medical condition is thoroughly evaluated.

### Survivors Benefits

Survivors of Social Security beneficiaries may also receive some portion of that recipient's benefits after his or her death if these survivors fulfill designated requirements. For example, "widows and widowers of fully insured workers are eligible for unreduced benefits at FRA [full retirement age]. Surviving divorced spouses can also receive benefits if married to the worker for at least 10 years and not remarried before age 60. Children of deceased workers ... under FRA are eligible to receive monthly benefits up to 75 percent of the worker's PIA [primary insurance amount—the monthly amount initially paid at full retirement age] if the worker dies either fully or currently insured" (SSA, 2010).

### Unemployment Insurance

**Unemployment insurance (UI)** is a program that serves two major purposes (Chapin, 2014; Karger & Stoecz, 2014). First, it provides limited financial support to unemployed workers for a temporary period. Second, UI allows unemployed workers to continue purchasing goods and services, which, in effect, stabilizes the economy during economic downturns. To receive UI, workers have to be unemployed after being employed a designated amount of time and be actively seeking new employment. Eligibility criteria emphasize that workers may not receive unemployment insurance if they've lost their job through any fault of their own; the focus is on job loss due to economic reasons such as industrial cutbacks or layoffs (Karger & Stoecz, 2014).

Overseen by the U.S. Department of Labor, states can determine "the amount of benefits, eligibility, and length of benefit time" (Karger & Stoecz, 2014, p. 206). This results in discrepancies among states in terms of what and how benefits are received.

Note that many unemployed people are not eligible for UI. These include "part-time, temporary, and self-employed workers" in addition to those who work in occupations not covered by UI and those whose UI benefits have already run out (Chapin, 2014, p. 317).

## Workers' Compensation

**Workers' Compensation (WC)** is "a state-mandated insurance program that provides compensation to employees … who suffer job-related injuries and illnesses"; benefits may include medical care, rehabilitation services, disability benefits to compensate for lost wages, and death benefits to survivors (NOLO, 2014). The emphasis is on covering almost all job-related illnesses and injuries, regardless of who was at fault, although some exceptions exist (NOLO, 2014). For instance, an injured employee cannot receive WC if the injury occurred while being intoxicated, the injury was self-inflicted (e.g., the injured person initiated a fight and was subsequently injured), or the injured person was in the act of committing a serious crime. WC is not always available in every job (NOLO, 2014). For example, states may determine that a minimum number of employees is necessary or that certain types of work don't qualify. All states exclude workers such as "farm workers, domestic employees, and seasonal or casual workers" (NOLO, 2014). Because states have wide discretion in how WC is structured, funding, administration of the program, and benefit levels differ significantly from one state to another (Karger & Stoecz, 2014; NOLO, 2014).

Social workers have little to do with either WC or UI, which concentrate on providing some minimum income and ignore all other social, emotional, and physical needs. In any case, both programs are inadequate to meet actual needs, and their eligibility standards place strict limitations on whom they cover (Jones, 1995; Nackerud, 2008; Terrell, 2008).

## Medicare

The Health Insurance for the Aged Act, passed in 1965, created Medicare and Medicaid (the latter will be discussed later as a public assistance program). **Medicare** is a form of social insurance financed by both employer and employee contributions based on earnings and other federal tax revenues. People who are eligible for Medicare include those who are 65 or older, have specified disabilities, or have kidney disease.

Medicare comprises four main facets—Parts A, B, C, and D. Part A, Hospital Insurance, pays for four basic types of services. First, it covers services provided in and by hospitals (which is probably pretty obvious from the title). Second, it pays for limited stays in skilled nursing facilities such as nursing homes. Third, it covers some services (e.g., nursing care and speech, physical, and occupational therapy[2]) for people under a physician's care who are confined to their homes. Fourth, it provides **hospice care**, care that involves health, homemaker, and other social services provided either at home or in a supportive, homelike facility for people suffering from a terminal illness. The idea is to make people as comfortable as possible during their final hours.

Note that all these services have designated time limits. Benefits are restricted based on certain criteria and also are limited in duration. People first must meet the requirements to receive treatment. Then treatment is administered according to complicated rules. Like OASDHI, the program is complex. Social workers accustomed to the programs and rules governing them often can help people navigate through the miles of red tape required to establish eligibility for benefits.

Medicare's Part B, Supplementary Medical Insurance, is designed to do just as its name implies—supplement benefits provided by Part A. It is "a voluntary component that covers physician services, outpatient hospital services, certain home health-care service, and durable medical equipment" (e.g., wheelchairs, hospital beds, or prosthetic devices) (DiNitto & Johnson, 2012, p. 172).

However, there are many things it does not cover, including dental and vision care, routine physical examinations, and long-term nursing care; Medicare does provide some time-limited nursing home coverage (DiNitto & Johnson, 2012).

Medicare Part B also is not free. Beneficiaries can enroll only during designated periods, have initial **deductibles** (the amount you must pay out of your

---

[2]*Physical therapy* is "the treatment or management of physical disability, malfunction, or pain by physical techniques, as exercise, massage, hydrotherapy, etc." (Nichols, 1999, p. 996). *Occupational therapy* is "therapy that utilizes useful and creative activities to facilitate psychological or physical rehabilitation" (Nichols, 1999, p. 914).

| Participants Pay | Of Total Paid for Drugs | Total Amount Potentially Paid by Participants |
|---|---|---|
| 100% Up to | $0–$310 | $310 |
| Copayments | $310–$2,840 | Copayments |
| 50–93% | $2,840–$4,550 | $4,550 |
| Small copayments | $4,550+ | Small copayments |

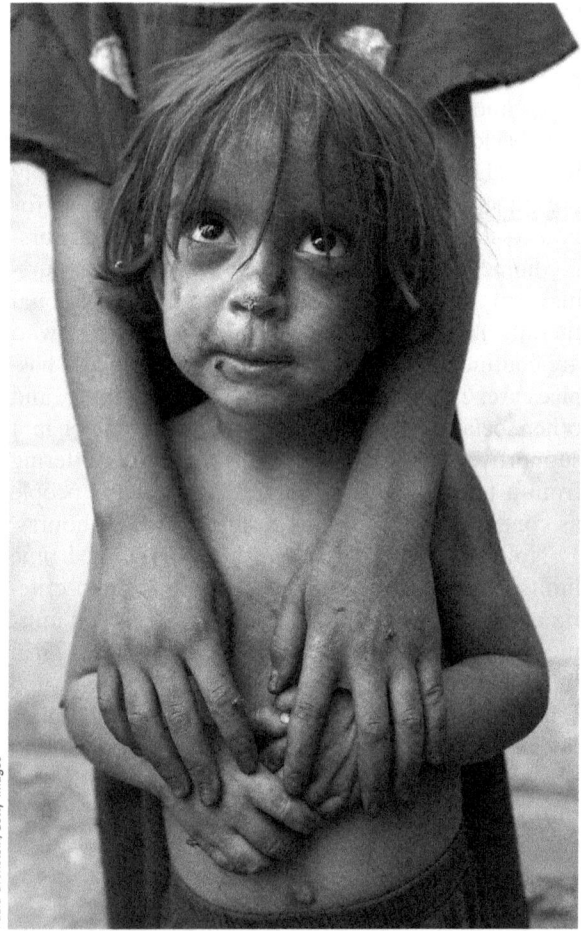

Paula Bronstein/Getty Images

*Too many children live in poverty (ProQuest, 2014); 21.4% of all children under age 18 in the United States live in poverty. When considering race as a factor, 38.6% of African American children and 33.7% of Hispanic children live in poverty here.*

own pocket before the plan will pay the rest), and pay a monthly fee.

Medicare Part C, now called Medicare Advantage, allows beneficiaries to "enroll in a private health plan, such as a health maintenance organization (HMO) or preferred provider organization (PPO), and receive all Medicare-covered Part A and Part B benefits and typically Part D benefits" (Kaiser Family Foundation [KFF], 2014c). Medicare must approve all organizations offering Medicare Advantage. Participation in Medicare Advantage plans has increased over time: in 2014, there were 16 million Medicare Advantage beneficiaries, which involved 30% of all Medicare beneficiaries (KFF, 2014c).

Costs for Medicare Advantage depend on the plan chosen. Variables affecting cost include a monthly premium (in addition to the monthly Part B premium), required deductibles for specified services, copayments (amounts paid for each office visit or service received), and following of the plan's rules (such as seeing only providers included in the plan's network) (Centers for Medicare and Medicaid Services [CMS], 2014b).

Medicare recipients may also opt to purchase what has been called **Medigap insurance**. Sold by private companies, these plans may cover services and treatment (gaps) not covered by other parts of Medicare such as "copayments, coinsurance, and deductibles" (CMS, 2014b, p. 91). Like most other types of insurance, the amount and type of coverage vary according to how much people are willing to pay for it.

Medicare Part C and Medigap insurance do not cover all the health care and services a person may need. For example, "coverage for the costs of long-term care in nursing homes, adult family homes, assisted living, and adult day care must be covered by private means [such as additional personal insurance policies] or by welfare [public assistance] programs" (DiNitto, 2011; Whiteman, 2001, p. 36).

Medicare Part D involves a voluntary prescription drug plan initiated in 2006 in which more than 37 million Medicare beneficiaries have enrolled in 2014 (Hoadley, Summer, Hargrave, Cubanski, & Neuman, 2014). Costs of the plan vary depending on the plan chosen. Variables affecting cost include monthly premiums, annual deductible, and required copayments (CMS, 2014b). Persons with higher incomes ($85,000 for individuals or $170,000 for married couples filing jointly) may have to pay more for their prescription drugs (CMS, 2014b). Most drug plans have a gap in coverage referred to as the "donut hole"; it may begin when you have paid a specified total amount and continue until you reach

## POLICY ISSUES IN SOCIAL INSURANCE

Two as yet unanswered issues exist concerning problems in the U.S. social insurance system as it now stands. First, people eligible for benefits are those who have had "substantial recent employment in the regular employment sector" (Meyer, 2001, p. 40). The problem is this does not cover people who have been able to get only part-time or temporary work on a sporadic basis.  **EP 5c** Many people, especially those with low skill levels, are primary family breadwinners yet can't find adequate employment to qualify them for social insurance. Meyer (2001) asks, "How should the social insurance system be adapted to fit this new economy and integrated with other benefits for children?" (p. 41).

The second issue concerns how supplementary benefits (including "sick leave, pensions, and 'family-friendly' policies like on-site child care and flexible hours") are rarely offered for workers in minimum-wage, low-paying, part-time, temporary, or seasonal jobs (p. 41). For these workers, many of whom have low skill levels, any crisis such as illness can result in devastation because, without sick leave, income can abruptly cease.

### Critical Thinking Question

What programs or policies do you think can or should be developed to remedy this situation?

---

a significantly higher coverage amount (CMS, 2014b). While in this donut hole, beneficiaries are required to "pay 45% of the plan's cost for covered brand-name drugs and 65% of the plan's cost for covered generic drugs until you reach the end of the coverage gap. Not everyone will enter the coverage gap because their drug costs won't be high enough" (CMS, 2014b, p. 101).

Focus on Critical Thinking 8.3 raises some key unresolved policy issues concerning social insurance in general.

## Public Assistance Policy

We have established that public assistance provides resources for people in *need* and that social insurance is based on people's *right* to receive benefits. Financing comes from general tax revenues—that is, taxes collected by federal, state, and local entities on personal income and property. Primary categories of public assistance include  **EP 3a, 5a, 5c, 8d** Temporary Assistance to Needy Families (TANF); Supplemental Security Income (SSI), which includes Old Age Assistance (OAA), Aid to the Blind (AB), and Aid to the Permanently and Totally Disabled (APTD); Medicaid; food stamps; general assistance; and housing assistance.

### Historical Perspectives on Public Assistance to Families

Prior to August 1996, a primary program providing minimal financial assistance to individuals and families in the United States was Aid to Families with Dependent Children (AFDC). It was originally established as Aid to Dependent Children (ADC) by the Social Security Act of 1935. AFDC was a program providing payments funded by federal and state governments to children deprived of parental support because a parent was absent from the home, had died, or was incapable of managing the household for physical or mental reasons (Barker, 2014). Most families receiving benefits were single mothers whose partners were not in the home.

AFDC established eligibility standards based on the number and age of children in the family, the family's income, the applicant's motivation and readiness to work, and the applicant's willingness to work together with the welfare department to establish paternity and seek child support (Abramovitz, 1995, p. 184). Eligible families passed an **income test** (or **means test**)—that is, an eligibility guideline that established the maximum amount of income a family could earn without losing benefits. Those who made too much money were ineligible for benefits.

Eligible families could potentially receive financial assistance for many years in addition to Medicaid (provision of health care for qualified recipients), food stamps (coupons used like cash to purchase food) (the program is now officially called the Supplemental Nutrition Assistance Program [SNAP]), and partial financial support for housing; however, some states subtracted the monetary value of food stamps and housing allowances from AFDC payments (Abramovitz, 1995). (Medicaid and food stamps are described later in the chapter.)

## Temporary Assistance to Needy Families (TANF)

In 1996 Congress passed the Personal Responsibility and Work Opportunity Reconciliation Act (PRWORA) that set up a new grant program, Temporary Assistance to Needy Families (TANF). This placed a limit on federal funding given to states and allowed states much greater discretion in benefit distribution.

As noted previously, TANF supplanted AFDC. Instead of providing cash payments directly to eligible poor families as AFDC did, TANF gives funds to states. These funds take the form of **block grants**—sums of money provided by the federal government that allow significant discretion in how the money should be spent. (This contrasts with **categorical grants** whereby specific amounts of funding are earmarked for specific objectives in designated programs.) Under AFDC states were required to provide resources to everyone who was legally eligible according to prescribed criteria. In other words, eligible people were *entitled* to help. Under TANF, on the other hand, the concept of entitlement is gone. No one is entitled to assistance (Karger & Stoecz, 2014). This also marks the first time that the federal government placed a limit on federal money provided to states for public assistance (Abramovitz, 1997).

TANF's stated goals are as follows:

1. *Provide assistance to needy families so that children can be cared for in their own homes.*
2. *Reduce the dependency of needy parents [on government benefits] by promoting job preparation, work, and marriage.*
3. *Prevent and reduce the incidence of out-of-wedlock pregnancies.*
4. *Encourage the formation and maintenance of two-parent families.*

*(Administration for Children and Families [ACF], 2014)*

Note that among these there is no stated goal to decrease poverty (Chapin, 2014; Jimenez et al., 2015). Should not a major goal be to reduce poverty instead of to decrease welfare roles? TANF participation rates have decreased significantly more than poverty has decreased, resulting in more people including children who live in poverty (Chapin, 2014; Jimenez et al., 2015). Of those who left the roles, 50% to 60% found employment in jobs paying just above the minimum wage (Karger & Stoesz, 2014). Of course, a central theme endorsed by TANF is promotion of work. However, looking more carefully at what happens to the people involved raises serious concerns. Research has established that most parents who left TANF "are likely to work in short-term, low-wage jobs with minimal benefits and have limited chances for increased earnings or wages" over time (Jimenez et al., 2015, p. 273). Pavetti, Finch, and Schott (2013) reflect:

*One measure of the extent to which TANF provides a safety net for poor families in need is the TANF-to-poverty ratio, or the ratio of the number of families receiving TANF for every 100 families with children in poverty; the lower the ratio, the more limited is TANF's reach in helping families in poverty.... Between 2006/2007 and 2010/2011 (... two–year averages improve their reliability), the TANF-to-poverty ratio fell in almost three-quarters of the states. In many cases the decline was moderate to substantial.... [T]he national TANF-to-poverty ratio declined from 68 families receiving TANF for every 100 families in poverty in 1996 [the year in which TANF was enacted] to 32 out of 100 in 2006 and 27 out of 100 in 2011.*

Floyd and Schott (2013) indicate that the TANF-to-poverty level dropped even further in 2012, as just 25 families received TANF benefits for every 100 poor families.

Chapin (2014) affirms:

*TANF did not change the reality of the social context that shapes these families. Affordable high-quality daycare for mothers on TANF continues to be in short supply, and when one person is working full-time and also doing all of the home chores, time for parental involvement is greatly reduced. These pressures have only been ratcheted up in the current economic downturn, as working mothers receiving TANF compete in the low-wage labor market with growing numbers of newly unemployed individuals, and as states and localities cut back further on necessary supports.*

*We know that poverty is a powerful predictor of all sorts of negative outcomes for children, from dropping out of school to teenage pregnancy to juvenile crime. Children in families receiving TANF are still living in poverty. (pp. 323–324)*

Schott and Pavetti (2011) note that:

*In 2011, states implemented some of the harshest cuts in recent history for many of the nation's most vulnerable families with children who are receiving [TANF] assistance.... The cuts affect 700,000 low-income families that include 1.3 million children; these families represent more than one-third of all low-income families receiving TANF nationwide.*

*A number of states have cut cash assistance deeply for families that already live far below the poverty line, ended it entirely for many other families with physical or mental health issues or other challenges, or cut child care or other work-related assistance that make it harder for many poor parents fortunate enough to have jobs to keep them.*

Issues concerning TANF include: time limits; work, child care, and transportation; equitable treatment by states; impositions on family structure; education and training for better jobs; and job quality and the effectiveness of TANF.

### Time Limits

TANF establishes time limits for how long recipients may receive benefits (ACF, 2014). Clients must find work within two years of beginning the program (or sooner if the state so chooses) and can receive no more than five years of benefits in their lifetime. Barusch (2015) explains:

*Under federal law, families that have received 60 months of TANF cash assistance are not eligible for further federally funded cash assistance. States may elect a shorter limit. They may also give "hardship extensions" to up to 20 percent of their TANF caseload from the limit. Recipients who have been on TANF for longer than 60 months may be supported with state funds. (p. 159)*

TANF time limits reflect a huge change from AFDC where people who met the guidelines could receive

assistance as long as they needed it (Abramovitz, 1997).

A problem with time limits involves people with multiple hardships that makes it difficult, if not impossible, for them to maintain adequate ongoing employment. Acs and Loprest (2007) explain:

*Numerous studies have documented the prevalence of barriers to work among welfare recipients, both before and after welfare reform. Some of the barriers measured include physical health, mental health, domestic violence, substance abuse, criminal history, education levels, and work history. (p. 55)*

### Work, Child Care, and Transportation

Work, child care, and transportation are interconnected issues for many TANF recipients. Parents who work need to have someone care for their children and they need some means of transportation to get to work.

*Work Requirements*    TANF significantly increases the strictness of work requirements to make people eligible for financial assistance compared to AFDC. "All states require recipients to be involved in work activities, which can include limited training and education activities directly related to work, within two years after they begin to receive assistance; many states impose immediate work requirements" (Chapin, 2014, pp. 325–326). For families participating in TANF, states must achieve a 50% employment rate for single-parent families and a 90% employment rate for two-parent families (Karger & Stoecz, 2014). With some exceptions, TANF recipients who refuse to work may experience reduced benefits or termination of assistance (SSA, 2014b).

Questions concern how parents will cope with child care needs, work stress, homemaking responsibilities, and parenting. TANF will not allow mothers with children age 6 or older to cite lack of adequate child care as their rationale for not working outside the home (SSA, 2014b).

*Child Care*    AFDC required states to provide child care, but TANF does not (DiNitto, 2011). States can provide child care if they so choose. Jimenez and his colleagues (2015) discuss TANF and child care:

*Child care funds for TANF recipients are paid for out of block grants given to states for this purpose, as well as from a separate federal fund known as the*

*Child Care and Development Fund. States have a great deal of flexibility as to how to meet child-care needs for TANF recipients. [This flexibility includes determination of eligibility requirements for receipt of child-care assistance, payment rates to child-care providers, and copayments TANF recipients must make (Hagen & Lawrence, 2008).] The funds are provided in the form of vouchers designed to meet 75% of child care costs in local communities, but the demand for child care has far outstripped the supply, both in terms of federal funding and in the availability of child care facilities. Many low-income families, including those on TANF, receive no help with child care, and the costs of licensed child care are often prohibitive. These families must settle for substandard child care arrangements, even though research suggests that good child care can have positive long-term consequences for children's cognitive, emotional, and social well-being. Child care support generally ends as soon as the TANF grants end or shortly thereafter. (p. 271)*

**Transportation**  Another issue involves how child care may not be readily available where the TANF recipient lives (Lens, 2002). Still another concern involves how many TANF recipients get service jobs where they must work odd shifts. Child care may not be available during these "off" times. Consider that

*many recipients need such specialized child care because they work in the services industry, which requires night and weekend hours. Still others need sick-child care or special needs care for children with disabilities. The need for such daycare varies, but in all instances the demand outstrips the supply of suitable facilities.*

*(Lens, 2002, p. 284)*

States may choose to divert some TANF money to help finance transportation. States are not required to spend TANF funding on transportation: however, "almost every state does, in one way or another, because the lack of transportation continues to be documented as one of the leading barriers to employment participation, especially among otherwise-unemployed single mothers" (National Resource Center, 2010). A big problem is that most TANF recipients live in urban or rural areas, whereas many jobs are in the suburbs. Public transportation is often sorely lacking. Cars, car insurance, and gas are exorbitantly expensive (as we so well know). States could choose to use TANF resources to finance "a variety of transportation services, from paying for recipients' car repairs, to using volunteers to drive recipients to work, to organizing county-run van pools" (Lens, 2002, p. 285).

Focus on Critical Thinking 8.4 poses a number of questions regarding potential problems and issues affecting mothers receiving TANF benefits.

---

**FOCUS ON CRITICAL THINKING 8.4**

## WORKING MOTHERS, CHILD CARE, AND THE QUALITY OF FAMILY LIFE

Many questions can be raised concerning potential effects of TANF's restrictions.

### Critical Thinking Questions

- Who will provide all the additional child care services for newly working mothers?

EP 5c

- Will funding be adequate in view of the potential influx of children requiring care?
- What if no adequate day care is available?
- Will centers accept infants or toddlers who are not yet toilet trained—children many current child care facilities reject?

- How will these services be monitored for adequacy, safety, and quality?
- Is it fair to force women into assuming responsibility for both household caregiving and outside work when the same pressures do not generally apply to men?
- How will mothers adjust to separation from their children?
- How will children be affected by limited access to their single parent?
- How does this policy affect children's welfare?

### Equitability Among States

TANF "eliminated the federal income test that previously determined eligibility for AFDC" (Abramovitz, 1997, p. 312). Instead, TANF lets states establish their own eligibility rules. However, with budget pressures, states could establish eligibility levels so low that only the very poorest of the poor would receive benefits.

Additionally, benefit levels vary appreciably from state to state, which raises questions regarding the program's fairness. DiNitto (2011) explains:

*Most states have maintained cash benefits at the 1996 level. Some have increased TANF benefits, but six states and the District of Columbia actually reduced benefits below their 1996 level. In most states, the real value of cash TANF benefits has continued to decline. (p. 257)*

Falk (2015) elaborates on the huge variation in benefit levels among states:

*Most states base TANF cash benefit amounts on family size, paying larger cash benefits to larger families on the presumption that they have greater financial needs. The maximum monthly cash benefit is usually paid to a family that receives no other income (e.g., no earned or unearned income) and complies with program rules. Families with income other than TANF often are paid a reduced benefit. Moreover, some families are financially sanctioned for failure to meet a program requirement (e.g., a work requirement), and are also paid a lower benefit.... For a family of three, the maximum TANF benefit paid in July 2013 varied from $170 per month in Mississippi to $923 per month in Alaska. In all states, the maximum TANF cash assistance amount for this sized family [three people including a single parent and two children] was less than 50% of poverty-level income. (p. 11)*

### Impositions on Family Structure

One of TANF's intents is to control family structure. Chapin (2014) indicates that "one stated goal of TANF is to reduce the number of out-of-wedlock pregnancies and births by promoting marriage (Office of Family Assistance, 2009). In 2005, TANF was reauthorized with a renewed focus on work and on strengthening families through the promotion of responsible fatherhood and healthy marriages. The TANF legislation gave states more flexibility to provide assistance to two-parent families" (p. 325). This, in effect, discourages the provision of resources for single-parent families.

Blau and Abramovitz (2014) comment on people's reality:

*For the Bush administration, marriage combined with work points the way out of poverty. In some respects, this position makes sense, because two married people can combine their incomes and share housing costs. Yet for poor women, the reality does not quite match the theory. Poor women are less likely to meet men who earn enough to raise the family out of poverty. They have little incentive to marry an adult for whom they are going to have to care, and no reason to do so if as up to 30 percent of women on welfare report, that adult is abusive. (p. 317)*

TANF also encourages limiting family size. States usually calculate benefit amounts according to the number of children present. TANF allows states to establish "a family cap that denies assistance to children born into families already receiving public assistance" (Karger & Stoesz, 2014, p. 230). To date at least 17 states have such a family cap policy; additionally, two states have a flat-rate maximum benefit where a set maximum amount is granted to recipients regardless of family size (Falk, 2014). "Additionally, some states do not increase benefits—or provide a smaller than usual increase in benefits—for a family already on the rolls when a new baby is born" (Falk, 2014, p. 13).

### Education and Training for Better Jobs

States spend comparatively small amounts on providing education and training for participants; "less than 2% ($407 million) was used to 'enhance skills' in 2006" (DiNitto, 2011, p. 262). "In 2006, only 7 percent of TANF work participants were involved in educational activities" (DiNitto & Johnson, 2012, p. 160). How can former  **EP 8a** TANF recipients seek better jobs and experience upward mobility with little or no education and training? In contrast, pregnancy prevention programs received more than a sevenfold increase from 2000 ($102 million) to 2006 ($723 million), amounting to 2.5% of the total TANF budget (DiNitto, 2011).

### Job Quality and the Effectiveness of TANF

A foundation principle of TANF focuses on work (Chapin, 2014; Gilbert & Terrell, 2013). DiNitto and Johnson (2012) reflect:

*Studies of recipients who left TANF shortly after its passage show that about 75 percent worked at some point during the year after leaving, and between 30 and 40 percent worked in all four quarters the year following exit. About one-half to two-thirds of "welfare leavers" were still working one to two years after exiting TANF.*

*These studies do not reflect the economic crisis that hit especially hard beginning in the fall of 2008. The real indictment of welfare reform is that, even in better economic times, many families who left TANF remained poor and experienced hardships because of low earnings. Most TANF leavers work in the low-wage service sector. About 41 percent of TANF leavers had incomes below the poverty threshold even when the value of [other benefits and incentives] ... were added to earnings.*

*The problems that led families to welfare— illness, mental illness, substance abuse, and other disabilities; lack of education and skills; childcare and transportation problems—remain barriers to TANF recipients obtaining and retaining jobs.... Questions arise as to the point of work-focused welfare given little empirical support for its effectiveness. (pp. 164–165)*

Focus on Critical Thinking 8.5 asks some questions concerning your views about public assistance and where current policy stands on the conservative–liberal continuum.

---

## FOCUS ON CRITICAL THINKING 8.5 — THE CURRENT STATE OF PUBLIC ASSISTANCE

### Where Do You Stand on the Conservative–Liberal Continuum?

Remember that **conservatism** generally reflects the view that individuals should be responsible for themselves, that people will take advantage of the system if allowed to, and that government should not interfere in people's lives. Thus government should react and provide benefits only when it absolutely has to. **Liberalism**, in contrast, generally espouses the view that it is society's responsibility to care for its people and that people will rise to the occasion and care for themselves if provided the support they need. Thus the government should be integrally involved in improving people's lives.

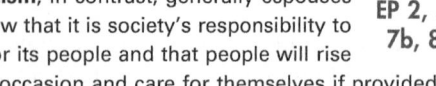

EP 2, 5c, 7b, 8b

### Critical Thinking Questions

- Where do you stand on the conservative–liberal continuum with respect to what benefits should or should not be provided to needy families?
- Whose responsibility is it to provide for poor families and their young children—the responsibility of individual parents or society in general?

- Do you feel that people are basically lazy and are likely to abuse the system if they can? Or do you feel that people will function much better if they receive adequate resources?
- To what extent do you feel that government should involve itself in caring for people in need? Or should people be given the responsibility to care completely for themselves and their families?

### Residual Versus Institutional Social Welfare Programming

Do you believe that financial assistance programs to families in need should be *residual* in nature, reacting only to problems and serious needs? Or should programs provide ongoing *institutional* support to them?

### Where Does TANF Policy Stand on the Conservative–Liberal Continuum?

To what extent does TANF policy reflect a conservative or liberal perspective concerning consistency in benefit provision from one state to another? Time limits for receiving benefits? Requirements that single parents (primarily mothers) work outside the home? Provision of child care and transportation?

## Supplemental Security Income (SSI)

**Supplemental Security Income (SSI)** is a federal public assistance program that provides a minimum income to poor people who are older adults, have a disability, or are blind. Most of it is administered by the federal government through the Social Security Administration. However, it is funded by general tax revenues, not employer and employee contributions as with social insurance. Older adults' eligibility is determined by a means test and proof of fitting into one of the three categories. Older adults must be at least 65, and people who are blind or disabled must have medical established proof of their disability. Children under age 18 must have "severe functional limitations," which may result in death, and are expected to continuously affect the child for at least one year.

The Social Security Administration provides the following facts (2014e). The Federal maximum SSI benefit is adjusted annually. Due to an increase in the Consumer Price Index, SSI benefits increased in 2014. As of January 1, 2014, the maximum Federal SSI benefit for individuals was $721 and for a couple $1,082. Some states provide higher benefits as they supplement these base figures. Eligibility for SSI is determined by income and some other designated resources (e.g., bank accounts or land owned), extent of disability, living arrangement, and other factors. Limitations on acceptable resources are extremely strict. Individuals must have no more than $2,000 and couples no more than $3,000.

Blau and Abramovitz (2014) cite some additional issues. Assessment of eligibility is very strict. Rules for assessment are complex. As a result, only 55–60% of people eligible for SSI in fact receive it. Initially intended for people with physical disabilities, those with mental disabilities have more difficulty becoming eligible. People with a mental illness who can work periodically or part-time are ineligible for SSI.

## Medicaid

**Medicaid** is a public assistance program funded by federal and state governments that pays for medical and hospital services for eligible people who are unable to pay for these services themselves and are determined to be in need. It was established in 1965 along with Medicare by the Health Insurance for the Aged Act.

The federal government disburses 57% of Medicaid payments, with the states paying the remaining 43% (DiNitto, 2011). Under federal guidelines, states administer the Medicaid program. A state agency must oversee Medicaid administration. Usually this is the state Department of Health and Social Services, a designated state health agency, or some other state human services unit. The designated agency may process health claims itself or contract with other agencies such as health insuring organizations (e.g., a health maintenance organization [HMO]). Payments for services are made directly to health-care providers.

States vary widely in terms of their eligibility criteria, the amount of benefits provided, how long benefits are offered, the range of benefits, and how the program is administered (Barusch, 2015; Karger & Stoecz, 2014; Stern, 2015). Criteria for Medicaid recipients include income and resources, age, pregnancy, disability, blindness, and immigration status (CMS, 2011). (Many immigrants who have been legally admitted to the country are ineligible [DiNitto, 2011].) Widely ranging health and medical services are covered, "including inpatient hospital services, outpatient hospital services, rural health clinic services, laboratory and X-ray services, skilled nursing facility (nursing home) services, and physician services" (Barusch, 2015, p. 156).

In 2014, more than 67.9 million people were recipients of Medicaid or the Children's Protection Insurance Fund (CHIP) (CMS, 2014a). (CHIP, discussed in the next section, "provides health coverage" to "children in families with incomes too high to qualify for Medicaid, but can't afford private coverage" [Medicaid.gov, 2014].) Total Medicaid spending in the United States for 2012 was more than $415 billion (KFF, 2012b). It is estimated that costs will escalate over the next several years (USDHHS, 2010). The Affordable Care Act significantly expands benefits and recipients (Blau & Abramovitz, 2014).

Note that Medicaid is a major player in financing long-term nursing home care for older adults; 64% of the 1.8 million people living in nursing homes residents rely at least partially on Medicaid to cover their care costs, which make up 31% of the total Medicaid budget (Blau & Abramovitz, 2014). Medicaid covers some of the many gaps in Medicare for older adults in poverty. Chapter 10 further addresses issues affecting and services for older adults.

Medicaid is an extremely significant and vital health-care program in the United States. Major questions are being raised across the country concerning where the money will come from to finance future health-care costs in general and Medicaid costs in particular.

## The Children's Health Insurance Program (CHIP)

In 1997 Congress passed the State Children's Health Insurance Program (SCHIP) that extended health-care coverage to children whose families were living under 200% of the poverty line (Jimenez et al., 2015). This helped to alleviate the major problem of children living in low-income families without insurance. Targeted families were not poor enough to receive Medicaid, but were still too poor to purchase health insurance. In 2009 President Obama signed into law the **Children's Health Insurance Program (CHIP)** Reauthorization Act (CHIPRA); CHIP (formerly SCHIP) expanded coverage to children in families earning up to 300% of the poverty line (Chapin, 2014). SCHIP served almost 8 million children in 2013 (Jimenez et al., 2015; Medicaid.gov, 2014). "Like Medicaid, CHIP is a state-federal partnership. All states have a CHIP program, and they have considerable freedom in how they design their programs. They can be simple expansions of the Medicaid coverage already available to children in the state, an entirely separate program, or some combination of these. States' programs vary on a wide range of elements, including eligibility levels, whether or not to charge cost-sharing or premiums, and how the enrollment process works" (Families USA, 2011). Services provided "include doctors' visits, hospitalizations, emergency room visits, immunizations, and dental care" (Chapin, 2014, p. 434).

CHIP is a "block grant, which means it has a pre-determined, fixed annual [federal] funding level"; this differs from Medicaid, where "federal funding increases automatically to compensate for increases in health care costs" (Jimenez et al., 2015, pp. 422–423). The Affordable Care Act affects and effectively supports CHIP (Chapin, 2014).

## Supplemental Nutrition Assistant Program (SNAP)/Food Stamps

The Food Stamp Program involves vouchers distributed through a federal program to be used like cash by needy families to purchase food. "Benefits may not be used for alcoholic beverages, tobacco, paper products, diapers, personal care products, or ready-to-eat foods" (Segal, 2013, p. 190). The program's intent is to fight hunger. It was renamed the **Supplemental Nutrition and Assistance Program (SNAP)** in 2008 to better reflect its intent of *supplementing* nutrition instead of providing all the food a family requires (Segal, 2010). Originally created in 1964, the Food Stamp Program, now SNAP, is administered through the U.S. Department of Agriculture and is paid for completely by the federal government, except for administrative costs, which are shared with the states (Barusch, 2015).

Blau and Abramovitz (2014) further explain the current situation. Although originally benefits were distributed in the form of coupons, now states have replaced this system with an electronic benefit transfer, in essence, debit cards. Each card's maximum monthly benefit in 2012 was $526 for a household of three people and $688 for a household of four. However, the actual amount allocated to a household is likely much less than these figures, due to a calculation method based on income. To be eligible in the first place, people must satisfy a means test. People who receive TANF, SSI, or general assistance (described next) routinely receive benefits.

After falling to a low in 2001 and 2002, participation has recently increased "as a result of the Great Recession, restoration of benefits for 'legal non-citizens,' and some modifications in eligibility determination" (Barusch, 2015, p. 158). The program has consistently "suffer[ed]," however, "from charges of fraud and abuse, the stigmatization of participants, and an intimidating and needlessly complex application process" (Blau & Abramovitz, 2014, p. 435).

## General Assistance

**General assistance (GA)** includes programs run by state and local agencies that provide basic cash and in-kind benefits to people who satisfy whatever means test has been established and are ineligible for other types of public assistance. It's usually the last resort for people who are desperately in need but are not eligible for benefits provided by other programs. GA recipients are often childless or under age 65. Hence they're ineligible for TANF or SSI, respectively. Some

GA recipients suffer from a disability but haven't had it long enough to qualify for SSI benefits.

GA is the only public assistance program that is financed completely by state, county, or local governments. Guidelines for who can receive GA vary from location to location and from state to state. Most states restrict benefits to those who are extremely poor, living far below the poverty level: states usually require able-bodied recipients to work if they want to receive benefits (Blau & Abramovitz, 2014). Many states and localities have severely cut back on GA benefits in recent years, and the number of GA programs is decreasing (Blau & Abramovitz, 2014).

### Housing Assistance

Adequate housing is a problem for vast numbers of Americans. Many find it to be the single most expensive item in their monthly budget. There's often little left over for food and clothing, let alone luxury items, after the rent is paid. And it must be paid, or families will be out on the street.

One of the problems is a serious lack of affordable, low-income housing. One reason is the recent extensive renovation of downtown urban areas into higher-rent districts, so that poor people can no longer afford to live in their old neighborhoods. Another reason is the mass abandonment of other dilapidated, aging, urban properties. Building owners and landlords often find such buildings too expensive to keep up. Unable to find anyone who wants to buy the properties, they simply abandon them.

Some housing assistance is available, primarily from the U.S. Department of Housing and Urban Development (HUD). Dolgoff and Feldstein (2013) explain:

*The primary purpose of housing assistance is to reduce housing costs and improve housing quality for low-income households by providing decent and safe rental housing for eligible low-income families, [older adults,] ... and persons with disabilities. Other goals include promoting residential construction, expanding housing opportunities for disadvantaged groups and groups with special needs, promoting neighborhood preservation and revitalization, increasing home ownership, and empowering [people living in poverty] ... to become self-sufficient. Approximately 1.2 million households receive housing assistance. (p. 245)*

HUD has pursued several goals in recent years to improve low-income housing (Department of Housing and Urban Development [HUD], 2014). First, it has established a "capital fund ... for the development, financing, and modernization of public housing developments and for management improvements." Second, it has instituted administrative procedures for demolishing or disposing of old, dilapidated housing developments. Third, it has established a program for selling all or portions of housing developments to residents or resident organizations. Fourth, it has pursued "revitalization [of public housing] in three general areas: physical improvements, management improvements, and social and community services to address resident needs." Fifth, HUD can provide "choice vouchers" to "[a]llow very-low-income families to choose and lease or purchase safe, decent, and affordable privately-owned rental housing."

Means tests are used to determine eligibility. However, housing assistance has been cut back significantly in recent years and is not automatically available to everyone in need. Usually people must apply for rent subsidies, low-rent housing, or other assistance. Because demand greatly exceeds supply, they often remain on long waiting lists until benefits or residences become available, sometimes years later.

## Chapter Summary

The following summarizes this chapter's content as it relates to the learning objectives presented at the beginning of the chapter. Chapter content will help prepare students to:

### LO1 Recognize poverty as a global and national problem.

Poverty is the condition of having inadequate "money to buy things that are considered necessary and desirable" (Kornblum & Julian, 2012, p. 196).

Economic data indicate that global poverty and economic inequality are significant problems. Globalization involves the increasing interdependence and interconnectedness among nations around the world. More than 46.2 million people live in poverty in the United States.

## LO2 Address variables related to poverty in the United States (including gender and the feminization of poverty, single parenthood, race, and social class) and explore steps to empower women.

Variables related to an increased potential for poverty include being female, living in a female-headed family, and being a person of color. The feminization of poverty refers to the fact that women as a group are more likely to be poor than are men.

The empowerment of women involves several approaches. Using a gender lens to view the plight of women in the macro social environment assumes that sexism is relevant to the experiences of many women and is the basis for many women's difficulties. Consciousness-raising is the process of facilitating people's understanding of a social issue with personal implications when there was little grasp of that issue before. A grassroots approach means that people at the bottom of the formal power structure, such as ordinary citizens, band together to establish a power base and pursue macro changes, in this case, on the behalf of women.

Poverty is related to social class. Society can be viewed as having a range of classes with varying degrees of economic resources and access to opportunity. Poverty is related to social class.

## LO3 Investigate proposed explanations for poverty.

Structural causes of poverty include economic and political factors, in addition to discrimination based on race and gender. Individual factors increasing the potential for poverty include having little human capital, originating in a single-parent family or a family with more children, and having a disability.

## LO4 Engage in critical thinking about poverty (including its conditions, its dynamics, and programs developed to address it).

Critical thinking questions were raised concerning what it's like to be poor, residual versus institutional

perspectives on poverty, potential practice goals when using a grass roots approach, the limitations of social insurance, TANF restrictions for working mothers, and liberal versus conservative perspectives on public assistance.

## LO5 Explore the consequences of poverty.

The impacts of poverty are devastating and far-reaching, affecting virtually all areas of life. Consequences of poverty include poorer health care, lower levels of education, lower paying jobs, poorer housing, and negative consequences in the criminal justice system.

## LO6 Examine the dynamics of homelessness.

A homeless person is defined as one who "lacks a fixed, regular, and adequate nighttime residence" or who sleeps in a temporary shelter for people without adequate residence or in a place not intended for the purpose of sleep (U.S. Department of Housing and Urban Development, 2011). It is estimated that hundreds of thousands of people are homeless in the United States. Homeless people are the poorest people. Homelessness is often related to losing a job, failure to pay rent, or some other catastrophic event. Solutions to homelessness involve provision of adequate housing and helping individuals get services and jobs.

## LO7 Describe major social programs that address poverty.

Social insurance involves financial benefits provided to people to "provide protection against wage loss resulting from retirement, prolonged disability, death, or unemployment, and protection against the cost of medical care during old age and disability" (U.S. Census Bureau, 2011, p. 347). Social insurance programs include Old Age, Survivors, Disability, and Health Insurance (OASDHI); Unemployment Insurance; Workers' Compensation; and Medicare.

Public assistance includes financial benefits and in-kind benefits (services or goods versus cash) provided to people who can't support themselves. Public assistance programs include Temporary Assistance to Needy Families (TANF), Supplemental Security Income (SSI), Medicaid, the Children's Health Insurance Program (CHIP), Supplemental Nutrition Assistance Program (SNAP) (food stamps), general assistance, and housing assistance. Policy issues include adequacy of services and who should be responsible for financing services.

Several concerns are raised about TANF. They include issues regarding time limits; work, child care, and transportation; equitability among states; impositions on family structure; education and training for better jobs; and job quality and the effectiveness of TANF.

## LOOKING AHEAD

This chapter addressed the problem of poverty and discussed programs implementing policies to help poor families and children. Families obviously need adequate financial resources to provide a protective, nurturing environment for their children. In addition to financial resources, many families need other *supportive services* to remain intact and thrive. Sometimes, for many reasons, children must be removed from their homes of origin, either temporarily or permanently, and be provided with *substitute care.* The next chapter explores a number of such supportive and substitute services. Chapter 9 is the first of several chapters in Part 4 of this book that address various client populations and the contexts in which services are provided.

## COMPETENCY NOTES

The following identifies where Educational Policy (EP) competencies and their component behaviors are discussed in the chapter.

**EP 1 (Competency 1)—Demonstrate Ethical and Professional Behavior.** *(p. 250):* Working on the behalf of clients and making ethical decisions about how to proceed reflects ethical and professional behavior. *(pp. 257, 258):* Social programs are examined because it's part of the professional social work role to make referrals to the appropriate services.

**EP 1b Use reflection and self-regulation to manage personal values and maintain professionalism in practice situations.** *(p. 254):* Practitioners should practice personal reflection concerning their feelings about poverty and people who are poor in order to better understand their clients who are poor.

**EP 2 (Competency 2)—Engage Diversity and Difference in Practice.** *(p. 247):* Social workers should understand that people living in poverty are oppressed, marginalized and alienated. *(p. 250):* Social class is a dimension of diversity. *(p. 251):* Practitioners should understand how the structural causes of poverty result in oppression and discrimination. *(p. 254):* People living in poverty are oppressed, marginalized, and alienated. *(p. 256):* People who are homeless are marginalized and alienated. *(p. 268):* Critical thinking questions encourage the examination of conservative, liberal, residual, and institutional perspectives toward public assistance and what perspectives might result in oppression.

**EP 2a Apply and communicate understanding of the importance of diversity and difference in shaping life experiences in practice at the micro, mezzo, and macro levels.** *(p. 248):* Gender, race, single parenthood, and having a female family head are factors shaping life experiences and increasing the risk of poverty. *(p. 254):* Living in poverty shapes people's life experiences. *(p. 256):* Homelessness shapes life experiences.

**EP 2c Apply self-awareness and self-regulation to manage the influence of personal biases and values in working with diverse clients and constituencies.** *(p. 254):* Practitioners must work hard at gaining self-awareness regarding any personal biases they might harbor concerning people living in poverty.

**EP 3 (Competency 3)—Advance Human Rights and Social, Economic, and Environmental Justice.** *(p. 247):* Social workers should recognize the importance of human rights, and social, economic, and environmental justice at the global level.

**EP 3a Apply their understanding of social, economic, and environmental justice to advocate for human rights at the individual and system levels.** *(p. 263):* Practitioners should advocate on the behalf of people who need public assistance and promote programs that effectively meet their needs.

**EP 3b Engage in practices that advance social, economic, and environmental justice.** *(p. 250):* Potential practices that advance social and economic justice for women are suggested.

**EP 4 (Competency 4)—Engage in Practice-Informed Research and Research-Informed Practice.**

**EP 4c Use and translate research evidence to inform and improve practice, policy, and service delivery.** *(p. 277):* Critical thinking questions encourage the assessment of research evidence to assert an opinion involving WIC policy and policy practice.

**EP 5 (Competency 5)—Engage in Policy Practice.**

**EP 5a Identify social policy at the local, state, and federal level that impacts well-being, service delivery, and access to social services.** *(p. 263):* Practitioners should advocate on the behalf of people who need public assistance and promote programs that effectively meet their needs.

**EP 5b Assess how social welfare and economic policies impact the delivery of and access to social services.** *(p. 247):* Social workers should recognize how social welfare and economic policies impact poverty and access to services at the global level.

**EP 5c Apply critical thinking to analyze, formulate, and advocate for policies that advance human rights and social, economic, and environmental justice.** *(p. 247):* Social workers should analyze policies that affect poverty and human rights at the global level. *(p. 256):* Practitioners should advocate for policies and services that advance social well-being for people who are homeless or potentially homeless. *(p. 257):* Social workers analyze policies that address poverty and advocate for policies that advance social well-being. *(p. 263):* A critical thinking question is introduced and raised concerning policy issues in social insurance and the enhancement of human rights and well-being. *(p. 263):* Social workers analyze policies that address poverty and advocate for policies that advance social well-being. *(p. 266):* Critical thinking questions are raised concerning TANF policy, the needs of TANF recipients, and how well these needs are being met. *(p. 268):* Critical thinking questions encourage the examination of conservative, liberal, residual, and institutional perspectives toward public assistance and what perspectives might advance human rights and social and economic justice. *(p. 277):* Critical

thinking questions are posed to analyze the effectiveness of the WIC program.

**EP 6 (Competency 6)—Engage with Individuals, Families, Groups, Organizations, and Communities.**

**EP 6b Use empathy, reflection, and interpersonal skills to effectively engage diverse clients and constituencies.** *(pp. 254, 258):* Critical thinking questions are posed to help develop empathy toward clients living in poverty.

**EP 7 (Competency 7)—Assess Individuals, Families, Groups, Organizations, and Communities.**

**EP 7a Collect and organize data, and apply critical thinking to interpret information from clients and constituencies.** *(p. 250):* Critical thinking questions are posed concerning assessment of a case situation. *(p. 254):* Critical thinking questions are raised concerning what it's like to be poor. This should enhance students' ability to assess client situations.

**EP 7b Apply knowledge of human behavior and the social environment, person-in-environment, and other multidisciplinary theoretical frameworks in the analysis of assessment data from clients and constituencies.** *(p. 250):* As practitioners assess client situations, they must understand and apply knowledge about people's socioeconomic conditions to understand how they can function in their environments. *(p. 251):* As they assess practice situations, practitioners must understand and apply knowledge about people's socioeconomic conditions to understand how they can function in their environments. *(p. 258):* The residual versus institutional theoretical frameworks on poverty can help social workers understand poverty and propose possible solutions. *(p. 268):* Critical thinking questions encourage the examination of conservative, liberal, residual, and institutional theoretical frameworks toward public assistance. This should enhance students' ability to assess client situations that involve public assistance. *(p. 277):* The Five-E theoretical framework is used to assess policy within the context of policy practice.

**EP 8 (Competency 8)—Intervene with Individuals, Families, Groups, Organizations, and Communities.**

**EP 8a Critically choose and implement interventions to achieve practice goals and enhance capacities of clients and constituencies.** *(p. 250):* Critical thinking questions are posed regarding how to proceed with intervention. *(p. 254):* Critical thinking questions are raised concerning what it's like to be poor. This should enhance students' ability to intervene with clients. *(p. 267):* Provision of education and training can enhance client capacities and their ability to get better jobs.

**EP 8b Apply knowledge of human behavior and the social environment, person-in-environment, and other multidisciplinary theoretical frameworks in interventions with clients and constituencies.** *(p. 250):* In preparation for intervention, practitioners must understand and apply knowledge about people's socioeconomic conditions to understand how they can function in their environments. *(p. 251):* As they prepare for intervention in practice, practitioners must understand and apply knowledge about people's socioeconomic conditions to understand how they can function in their environments. *(p. 258):* The residual versus institutional theoretical frameworks on poverty can help social workers understand poverty and propose potential

solutions. *(p. 268):* Critical thinking questions encourage the examination of conservative, liberal, residual, and institutional theoretical frameworks toward public assistance. This should enhance students' ability to undertake social work intervention with clients receiving public assistance. *(p. 277):* The Five-E theoretical framework is used to assess policy within the context of intervention involving policy practice.

**EP 8c Use interprofessional collaboration as appropriate to achieve beneficial practice outcomes.** *(p. 250):* Questions are posed that suggest working with colleagues and clients to achieve improved policies and services for women.

**EP 8d Negotiate, mediate, and advocate with and on behalf of diverse clients and constituencies.** *(p. 256):* Practitioners should advocate for policies and services that advance social well-being for people who are homeless or potentially homeless. *(p. 257):* Social workers advocate for policies that address poverty and advance social well-being. *(p. 263):* Social workers advocate for policies that advance social well-being for people in need.

## CASE STUDY FOR CRITICAL THINKING

# The WIC Program

The case presented here is an example of a social welfare policy, the Special Supplemental Food Program for Women, Infants, and Children (WIC).

***Case Study:*** WIC is a nutritional program designed to supplement the diets of low-income women and their young children up to age 5 who are determined by a health professional to be at nutritional risk according to federal guidelines (Food and Nutrition Service [FNS], 2011). Participants receive either food items or, more typically, coupons that can be exchanged for specific food that is high in important nutrients, including infant cereal, iron-fortified adult cereal, vitamin C-rich fruit or vegetable juice, eggs, milk, cheese, peanut butter, canned beans/peas, canned fish, "[s]oy-based beverages, tofu, fruits and vegetables, baby foods, whole-wheat bread, and other whole-grain options" (FNS, 2011). Physicians may also prescribe special infant formulas or medical foods when needed. Additionally, eligible women receive nutritional counseling to educate them about their own and their children's nutritional needs.

EP 4c, 5c, 7b, 8b[3]

WIC is administered through the U.S. Department of Agriculture, with state agencies (e.g., a state health department) distributing benefits. Eligibility includes (1) being a pregnant woman, new mother, infant, or child up to age 5; (2) having an income level at or less than 185% of the poverty level (in November 2009, $40,793 for a family of four in the 48 continuous states, Washington, D.C., Guam, and Territories; $51,005 in Alaska; and $46,916 in Hawaii); (3) fulfilling state residency requirements; and (4) having been determined to be "at risk" by a health-care professional (FNS, 2011). A person in a family participating in "certain other benefit programs, such as the Supplemental Nutrition Assistance Program, Medicaid, or Temporary Assistance for Needy Families, automatically meets the income eligibility requirement" (FNS, 2011). "Nutrition risk" factors involve medical conditions such as having anemia or being underweight, having a history of problem pregnancies, or inadequate diet and nutrition (FNS, 2011). Approximately 8.7 million people, the majority of whom are children, receive WIC benefits each month (FNS, 2011). Note that eligibility requirements are more lenient than those of TANF and other public assistance programs (Karger & Stoesz, 2010). The total WIC federal budget for 2010 was $7,252 billion (FNS, 2011).

***Critical Thinking:*** You can apply critical thinking to evaluate the usefulness of this program by following the Five-E approach to policy analysis.

1. First, *ask* questions.

    a. How *effective* is the policy?
    b. How *efficient* is the policy?

---

[3]Competency Notes for this case study are located at the end of Chapter 8.

    c. Is the policy *ethically* sound?

    d. What does *evaluation* of potential alternative policies reveal?

    e. What recommendations can be *established* for positive changes?

2. Second, *assess* the established facts and issues involved.

    a. How *effective* is the WIC policy and its resulting program implementation? WIC advocates cite research that program participation results in improved conditions at birth, including higher birth weights and reductions in preterm births (Devaney, 2007; DiNitto, 2005; FNS, 2009). There also appear to be fewer infant deaths (FNS, 2009). Additionally, infants and young children generally prosper from good nutrition, which enhances normal development. More specifically, adequate iron in the diet has been found to reduce iron-deficiency anemia—a condition involving decreased hemoglobin levels in red blood cells that results in fatigue and lack of vitality (Devaney, 2007; DiNitto, 2005; FNS, 2009). Some research indicates that children involved with WIC demonstrate improved growth in weight and height (Devaney, 2007). Other research showed that such children experience improved cognitive development (FNS, 2009). Additional benefits not directly related to the program's stated goals include improved prenatal care and better immunization records (Devaney, 2007; DiNitto, 2005; FNS, 2009).

       Critics caution that although results sound good superficially, it is difficult to find comparable groups to establish that WIC is really the cause of positive results (DiNitto, 2005).

       Others have raised questions regarding the effectiveness of nutritional counseling (DiNitto, 2005). What does such counseling involve? Is it really useful and worth the expense? Would providing information about other topics such as cooking be more effective?

       From this discussion, how effective do you feel the WIC policy and program are? What other information would help make your decision easier?

    b. How *efficient* are the WIC policy and program? Participation in WIC is associated with significantly decreased Medicaid costs for newborns and new mothers during the first 60 days after birth; for every dollar spent on prenatal care, it is estimated that $1.77 to $3.13 is saved in Medicaid costs (Dolgoff & Feldstein, 2009; FNS, 2009). This implies that mothers and infants are generally healthier due to the WIC program, so they don't have to seek as much help from Medicaid.

       Critics of the program, including the Institute of Medicine, report that because there really is no valid classification system for "risk," conducting expensive assessments is a waste of time and money (Food and Nutrition Board, 2002). If anything, the entire population of low-income mothers and young children is at risk of nutritional deprivation. Money could better be spent providing more food or getting it to more people.

       It is estimated that 90% of people eligible to receive WIC benefits do actually receive them (DiNitto, 2005). However, that is not 100%. Additionally, due to funding limitations, people may be placed on prioritized waiting lists (Dolgoff & Feldstein, 2009). Besides those who didn't apply to begin with, many women, infants, and children did not receive benefits because of funding limitations (Dolgoff & Feldstein, 2009).

       What does this mean to you in terms of efficiency? Do you think it's efficient because it saves public spending on Medicaid? Or do you think it's inefficient because it fails to reach a significant number of people who are eligible and sometimes makes potential recipients endure waiting lists?

c. To what extent is the policy *ethically* sound? We just established that some people who are eligible for WIC do not receive benefits. Is this fair? Or should nutritional support be provided to all pregnant women, new mothers, infants, and small children? What are our society's ethical values concerning the importance of healthy pregnancies, mothers, and children? What is society's responsibility for their care?

d. How does the *evaluation* of potential alternative policies compare with WIC? WIC's goals are to improve the nutritional intake of eligible mothers and children at risk of poor nutrition and to educate mothers about nutrition to prevent problems related to a poor diet. What other policies might be developed to achieve the same goals? Would they be able to better meet the established goals? Are there more efficient, less expensive ways to meet these goals?

e. What recommendations can be *established* for positive changes? How could the program be improved? How could benefits reach more eligible mothers? Would increased federal and state funding help? What changes in policy could facilitate program implementation?

3. The third step in critical thinking is to *assert* a concluding opinion. In summary, what do you think about WIC? Should it be continued, expanded, reduced, or discarded?

# PART FOUR

# CLIENT POPULATIONS AND CONTEXTS

Part 4 includes eight chapters that focus on various fields of practice in social work, the client populations served, the social welfare policies governing that service, and the context in which benefits are provided. They include social work and services:

1. For children and families.
2. For older adults.
3. For persons with disabilities.

281

4. In health care.
5. In mental health.
6. In substance use, abuse, and dependence.
7. In the schools.
8. In the criminal justice system.

# 9 Social Work and Services for Children and Families

Steve Skjold/Alamy

## Learning Objectives   This chapter will help prepare students to:

**LO 1**  Emphasize the wide diversity in families and their structure.  **The Diversity of Families** (p. 285)

**LO 2**  Describe child welfare and its continuum of services.  **Major Thrusts of Services for Children and Families** (p. 288)

**LO 3**  Examine supportive services in child welfare (including child maltreatment and child protective services, family preservation, child day care, family life education, and respite care).  **Supportive Services** (p. 289)

**LO 4**  Engage in critical thinking (about advocacy to combat child maltreatment and controversial issues in adoption).  **Focus on Critical Thinking 9.1** (p. 298)

**LO 5**  Address the need to advocate for resources (for children and families).  **An Ongoing Macro Issue: Advocacy for Resources** (p. 303)

**LO 6**  Describe substitute placements for children.  **Substitute Services** (p. 304)

**LO 7**  Discuss adoption.  **Adoption** (p. 313)

*Consider the following cases involving children and their families.*

*Case A: Burgundy, age 23, is a single mother desperately seeking day care for her children Sean and Shane, ages 1½ and 3. She has just found a clerical job at a law office not far from her home. Her sister can baby-sit for her in the mornings but has her own job to go to in the afternoons. Some of the available day care costs as much as she will make in her new job. Other day care centers won't take children who aren't toilet trained, which Sean definitely is not. Burgundy is at her wit's end!*

*Case B: Clark and Lois aren't doing well. They have three children to support, and not nearly enough money is coming in to pay the rent and buy groceries. Clark was laid off eight months ago from his job at the airplane factory. The economy's depressed, and he's been unable to find anything else. And then there are medical bills for Lois's breast cancer. She's had surgery and is only now finishing up radiation and chemotherapy treatments. Clark feels as if he's losing his grip on things.*

*The least bit of aggravation makes him blow his stack. He finds himself more frequently slapping the kids around when they don't behave. The other day, he caught himself right before he hit one of them with a baseball bat.*

*Case C: Corazon is exhausted. Her daughter Juanita, age 9, is bedridden with a rare skin disease that makes any movement difficult and painful. Juanita requires almost constant care and attention. Corazon, a single parent, has no relatives or friends in the area willing to give her a break and help out even for a few hours by caring for Juanita. Corazon feels as if she's going crazy.*

*Case D: Tom, 15, is clinically depressed. He attends a school that focuses on fulfilling special education needs, addressing school behavior problems, and providing family counseling. He had been in five foster homes since his parents were killed in a car accident. The multiple placements were not Tom's fault but were simple results of fate. Two foster families moved out of the state when breadwinners got better jobs. One foster mother became pregnant and decided that having a foster child in addition to her own was simply too much. One foster father had a heart attack and died. The other foster family began having problems with their own teenage children, and so Tom was removed from the home. Tom and his older brother and sister have been separated for the past 10 years. For various reasons, "the system" has been unable to keep the three siblings together. Tom is doing poorly in school partly due to multiple school changes and partly due to his despair at the misfortune and loneliness that has characterized his life.*

*Case E: Ginny, age 18 months, has a severe intellectual disability (previously referred to as mental retardation) and so can do little more than lie in a prone position, suck on a bottle, and cry. She was removed from her home because her mother, a crack addict, did not provide adequate care. Shortly after Ginny arrived at her foster home, Ginny's foster mother took her to a diagnostic and treatment center for children with multiple disabilities. During a physical examination, the physician noticed that Ginny had odd-looking bruises around her vaginal area. They wondered what and who had caused them.*

Commentary: *Cases A through C depict families that need supportive help to stay intact. For whatever reasons, families can become stressed or weakened and have trouble making it on their own. Causes may be economic, health related, or emotional. Sometimes a family is hit with an unexpected crisis such as job loss or serious illness; other times, long-term problems wear a family down and undermine its ability to keep itself afloat.*

*Cases D and E portray children who can no longer stay with their families in their own homes. When families have such serious needs and problems that they can't care for their children, substitute services are necessary.*

*Because the family is the core of most people's lives, this chapter explores issues relevant to families. People who receive other types of social services (e.g., those concerning health, mental health, disabilities, or aging) are also members of families. Because of the complexity of people's needs and the services developed to meet them, the same individual or family may receive services or use resources from various fields of practice. Therefore, a thorough understanding of services for children and families is basic to understanding social welfare and social work.*

## The Diversity of Families    `LO1`

Before talking about the wide range of programs and services geared to helping children and families, it's important to emphasize the enormous diversity of families and their configurations or structure. A **family** is "a primary group whose members assume certain obligations for each other and generally share common residences" (emphasis omitted) (Barker, 2014, p. 155). This definition shows how flexible the notion of family has become. First, a family is a **primary group**—that is, "people who are intimate and have frequent face-to-face contact with one another, have norms [that is, expectations regarding how members in the group should behave] in common, and share mutually enduring and extensive influences" (Barker, 2014, p. 335). Thus family members have significant influence on each other. The second concept in the definition of family involves having

obligations for each other, which means a sense of mutual commitment to and responsibility for other family members. The third concept in the definition is common residences, such that, to some extent, family members live together.

**Family structure** is "the nuclear family as well as those nontraditional alternatives to nuclear family [that] are adopted by persons in committed relationships and the people they consider to be 'family'" (CSWE, 2002). The traditional family structure in the United States consisted of two married parents who had never been divorced living together in one household with their own birth children. Today, however, typical family structures are much more varied. A **single-parent family** is a family unit in which only one of the parents, usually the mother, is present in the household. A **stepfamily** is a family structure in which one or both members of a married couple bring a child or children from a prior marriage or relationship to the family unit. Children may be biologically a combination of his or hers from past relationships, and possibly theirs together. "A **blended family** is any nontraditional configuration of people who live together, are committed to each other, and perform functions traditionally assumed by families. Such relationships may not involve biological or legal linkages. The important thing is that such groups *function* as families" (Zastrow & Kirst-Ashman, 2013, p. 168). Stepfamilies are a type of blended family. An **intergenerational family** is one in which family members include persons spanning at least three generations (e.g., grandparents living under the same roof and caring for grandchildren while the parents work).

Social workers must be sensitive to the various configurations families may take and appreciate this aspect of diversity. Open-mindedness is essential when we assess the strengths of any family group, regardless of its structure. Workers should not make assumptions about how families *should be* but should work with the family group that *is*. Highlight 9.1 examines the special situation of gay, lesbian, and bisexual families.

---

## HIGHLIGHT 9.1    GAY AND LESBIAN FAMILIES: A POPULATION AT RISK

At special risk of discrimination are families with lesbian, gay, or bisexual (LGB) parents. Marsiglia and Kulis (2015) explain that "lesbians and gays in many parts of the country continue to be denied the fundamental right to ... bring up or adopt children. Many people believe that members of these groups are unable to raise children without causing them irreparable damage" (p. 244). Patterson (2014) continues:  EP 1b, 2, 2a, 2c, 3a, 5c, 8d

Like families headed by heterosexual parents, lesbian and gay parents and their children are a diverse group.... Unlike heterosexual parents and their children, however, lesbian and gay parents and their children are often subject to prejudice because of their sexual orientation that can turn judges, legislators, professionals, and the public against them, sometimes resulting in negative outcomes, such as loss of physical custody, restrictions on visitation, and prohibitions against adoption.... Negative attitudes about lesbian and gay parenting may be held in the population at large ... as well as by psychologists.... As with beliefs about other socially stigmatized groups, the beliefs held generally in society about lesbians and gay men are often not based in personal experience, but are frequently culturally transmitted.

### Children Growing Up in Gay and Lesbian Families

Despite these additional stressors, children growing up in lesbian or gay homes do just as well as those raised in heterosexual homes (American Association of Marriage and Family Therapy [AAMFT], 2014; Marsiglia & Kulis, 2015; Patterson, 2014; Petrocelli, 2012). (It is estimated that in the United States from 1 to 9 million children have one or both parents who are gay or lesbian [AAMFT, 2014].) Most children in LGB families "want people to understand that there's lots of love in their household ... it's the pressure from society that makes things hard for them.... Their lives are as traditional and boring as anyone else's" (Carton, 1994, p. 45). Their parents do what parents do—help with homework and school projects, drive them to soccer games, save up for college, and scold them for being naughty (Morales, 1995).

Patterson (2014) asserts:

Results of research to date suggest that children of lesbian and gay parents have positive relationships with peers and that their relationships with adults of both sexes are also satisfactory. The picture of lesbian mothers' children that emerges is one of general engagement in social life with peers, with fathers, with grandparents, and with mothers' adult friends—both male and female, both heterosexual and homosexual.

*(continued)*

**HIGHLIGHT 9.1 (continued)**

Fears about children of lesbians and gay men being sexually abused by adults, ostracized by peers, or isolated in single-sex lesbian or gay communities have received no support from the results of existing research.

Sometimes research results have favored same-sex parents over heterosexual parents (AAMFT, 2014). For example, some research indicated that adolescents with same-sex parents felt "more connected at school. Another study reported that children in gay and lesbian households are more likely to talk about emotionally difficult topics, and they are often more resilient, compassionate and tolerant."

## Marital Status

An issue that has directly affected many LGB people and their families is the issue of same-sex marriage. The option of marriage provides many potential consequences for people. Historically, for heterosexual couples it has involved access to health insurance benefits, social insurance benefits, property rights, child custody rights, and many other legal advantages.

The right of lesbian and gay people to marry legally in the United States has been and remains a hotly debated issue. However, in June 2015 the U.S. Supreme Court ruled that all states must legalize gay marriage.

A May 2015 Gallup poll found that 60% of Americans now support same-sex marriage (Gallup, 2015). However, that means that 37% still do not support it (with 3% expressing no opinion) (Gallup, 2015). Nevertheless, this reflects a radical change since 1996 when 68% of Americans opposed same-sex marriage (Gallup, 2015).

## Same-Sex Marriage at the International Level

From an international perspective, the following 20 nations have legalized same-sex marriage (as of August 2015); each is followed by the year of legalization:

- The Netherlands (2000)
- Belgium (2003)
- Spain (2005)
- Canada (2005)
- South Africa (2006)
- Norway (2008)

- Sweden (2009)
- Portugal (2010)
- Iceland (2010)
- Argentina (2010)
- Denmark (2012)
- Brazil (2013)
- France (2013)
- Uruguay (2013)
- New Zealand (2013)
- The United Kingdom (2014)
- Luxembourg (2014)
- Finland (2015)
- Ireland (2015)
- The United States (2015) (Freedom to Marry, 2015)

## What Do You Think About Same-Sex Marriage?

This controversy over whether same-sex marriage is right or wrong continues throughout the United States. The core of the dispute focuses on a person's constitutional right to find happiness in an intimate relationship with another person versus the religious approach about the sanctity of marriage between a man and a woman. What are your opinions regarding this issue? Do you feel LGB people have the right to marry? Why or why not?

## Special Issues Gay and Lesbian Families May Face

Gay and lesbian families may have to address at least four issues that don't affect heterosexual families (AAMFT, 2014). First, courts may discriminate against them in custody and visitation disputes. Second, discrimination against gay men and lesbians may occur that involve co-parenting and blended family decisions and plans. Heterosexual parents may resent their lesbian and gay counterparts. Third, extended family may not be as welcoming to gay and lesbian family configurations as they are to heterosexual families. Fourth, difficulties may arise in communicating about family relationships with school teachers and administrators, physicians and other medical staff, and children's peers and their parents. Many people have a heterosexual mindset with expectations about how families *should* be structured, namely in a heterosexual fashion.

EP 2

# Major Thrusts of Services for Children and Families   `L02`

One way of classifying services for children and families is to place them on a continuum, as shown in Figure 9.1. At one end of the continuum, families require basic financial and material resources to survive. Some families require additional supportive help (e.g., counseling) to continue functioning and remain intact. Some families need very little help to enhance their functioning and thrive. Others require comprehensive services and resources to solve problems and function as independent, healthy entities. The three middle boxes in Figure 9.1 reflect the continuum of need ranging from limited to moderate to extensive. Finally, at the other end of the continuum, some families are unable to function regardless of the resources and help they receive. In these cases, children must be removed from the home and substitute services provided.

Note that in the past, treatment and services involving children were referred to as "child welfare." The next section describes this field and the current status of practice with children and families.

## Child Welfare: A Historical Social Work Field of Practice

**Child welfare** is the traditional term for the network of policies and programs designed to empower families, promote a healthy environment, protect children, and meet children's needs. Basic goals of child welfare include:

EP 1

- Meeting vulnerable children's unmet emotional, behavioral, and health needs. Providing adequate resources to address external conditions such as poverty and inadequate health care so children can develop and thrive in a healthy, nurturing social environment. Empowering families by building on strengths so parents can effectively provide for and protect their children.
- Improving internal family conditions involving interpersonal dynamics, communication, substance abuse, and conflict.
- Safeguarding children from various forms of neglect and abuse.
- When necessary, making permanent family living conditions available through adoption or transfer of guardianship.

Child welfare has always focused on children and families, with services traditionally provided by public agencies. Pecora, Whittaker, Maluccio, Barth, and DePanfilis (2010) comment:

*Historical areas of service [include] foster care and adoptions, in-home family-centered services, child protective services, and residential services— where social work has a legitimate, long-standing, and important mission and role.... Readers also should be conscious of the many other fields of practice in which child and family services are provided or that involve substantial numbers of social work programs, such as services to adolescent parents, child mental health, health, education, special education, and juvenile justice agencies. (p. vii)*

In recent years the emphasis concerning children and families has shifted from a focus on the child to one on the family and social environment. Children are now viewed in the context of their families and other people around them. The idea is that this environment must be strengthened to provide a nurturant, supportive setting in which children can grow

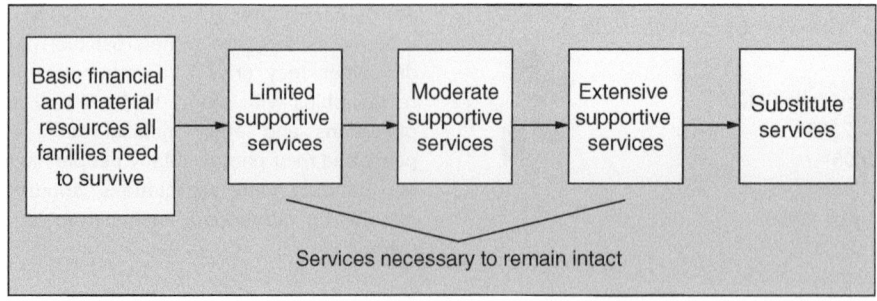

**FIG-9-1** Continuum of Need for Families' Survival

and thrive. The next sections describe an array of services ranging from those supporting families to those providing options for substitute care outside of families.

# Supportive Services   L03

**Supportive services** are those that "support, reinforce, and strengthen the ability of parents and children to meet the responsibilities of their respective statuses" (Kadushin & Martin, 1988, p. 83; Kemp, Burke, Allen-Eckard, Becker, & Ackroyd, 2014). The intent is simply to provide external support to enhance family functioning while children remain in the home. Services include basic financial and other resource assistance (discussed in Chapter 8); various types of mental health treatment such as family therapy, individual counseling, and group therapy (discussed more thoroughly in Chapter 13, which focuses on social work and mental health); child protective services; intensive family preservation services; day care; family life education; and respite care.

*Case Example*  An example of supportive services involves Billy, a 13-year-old boy with moderate intellectual disabilities (Kadushin & Martin, 1988; Koch, 1979).[1] His parents, Norm and Norma Needing, had increasing difficulty controlling his behavior as he grew older and bigger. Billy was picking on his younger brother Benny and acting out **EP 7d** uncontrollably in public settings such as grocery stores and restaurants. The Needings were at their wits' end and were considering placing Billy in an institutional setting.

Billy was referred by his school social worker to FACT (Family and Child Training), a program providing a range of services to persons with intellectual disabilities and their families. FACT assigned the case to Earl E. Riser, a social worker serving both as case coordinator and treatment provider. The first order of business was to assess the situation and develop a treatment plan. After spending substantial time observing Billy and his interactions both at school and at home, Earl worked with the Needings

to develop goals and specify a plan for how to proceed.

Goals included improving Billy's interactions with peers and with Benny through supervised recreational activities, his ability to respond positively to parental guidance and directives, and his behavior in public places. The Needings attended parenting classes provided by FACT. Earl met weekly with the Needings to discuss what they had learned and help them apply the skills at home. Billy was enrolled in recreational activity groups sponsored and supervised by FACT staff. Initially, Billy was accompanied by a child care worker who modeled appropriate behavior for Billy and implemented the behavior modification program. Billy gradually learned how to relate much more positively with Benny, his peers, and his parents. Billy enjoyed his new levels of interaction and acceptance, so his overall quality of life was significantly enhanced. Because family life had stabilized, the Needings no longer considered residential placement.

Further along the continuum of family needs are **substitute services** (described later in greater depth), whereby another family or environment is substituted for the child's own family. Here "someone else takes over all aspects of the parental role on a temporary or permanent basis" (Kadushin & Martin, 1988, p. 344). Substitute services include foster care; residential placement in a group home, treatment center, or institution; independent living; and adoption.

An example of substitute care in an institutional setting could have involved the Needing family. For instance, suppose the family had not been referred to FACT or FACT had failed to help the family improve its functioning. The Needings might then have pursued Billy's placement in a residential institution.

## Child Maltreatment and Child Protective Services

Jaron, age 3, and Tomas, age 2, attended a day-care center while their mother, Joyita, worked during the day. Laura, the day-care center social worker, and Sonja, Jaron's and Tomas's teacher, became increasingly concerned about the boys' health and hygiene. Their clothes were smeared with dirt, and their hair was filthy. They had an exceptionally strong, unappealing odor, apparently due to very infrequent

---

[1]This case example is loosely based on one provided in the sources cited. Various situational variables such as referral source have been changed.

bathing. Their teeth were dark with tartar. And they were ravenously hungry when they arrived at the center each day. The situation screamed neglect. Laura had the choice of sitting down with Joyita and talking with her about the problems or referring the case to child protective services.

Consider another case. Peter, age 6, had been placed in foster care with Becca for the past year. Peter's mother, Mary, had visitation rights every Saturday afternoon. During their lives, Peter and his four siblings had periodically been removed from the home because of neglect and placed in foster care. Mary had a long history of drug use and abuse. She had started treatment programs on numerous occasions but was never able to complete them. After one of the Saturday visits with Mary, Becca noticed that Peter had a series of small circular burns on his left arm that looked as if they might be from a lighted cigarette. Was Peter actually being tortured on Saturday afternoons? Becca called Peter's social worker.

Another case involved Juanita, age 13, who was referred to Cheung, the school social worker, by Agate, Juanita's English teacher. Agate had given Juanita and the rest of her class an assignment to write a poem on any subject they wished. Juanita had written 18 poems. (How many times have you done 18 times the work a teacher assigned you?) Each of Juanita's poems involved explicitly sexual language and imagery. Juanita lived with her mother, sisters, and a stepfather. There was some concern about potential sexual abuse by the latter. Upon further investigation after referral to child protective services, it was determined that a maternal uncle, not the stepfather, was guilty of sexual abuse.

These four children are victims of various types of child maltreatment. Before we discuss the types of supportive services and treatment provided for this grave family problem, it's important to understand some of the reasons why it occurs and the ways it affects children.

## What Are Child Maltreatment, Abuse, and Neglect?

**Child maltreatment** is the umbrella term for physical abuse, sexual abuse, psychological abuse, neglect, and psychological maltreatment. Each term will be defined and discussed here. However, note that child maltreatment can be complex, with each case

being unique in its own way. Therefore, sometimes terms will overlap, depending on the individual situation.

**Physical abuse** occurs when

*a child younger than 18 years of age has experienced an injury ... or risk of an injury ... as a result of having been hit with a hand or other object or having been kicked, shaken, thrown, burned, stabbed, or choked by a parent or parent-surrogate.*

*(Kolko, 2002, p. 22)*

Physical indicators include bruises, lacerations, fractures, burns, head injuries, and internal injuries. Often the injuries don't make sense. For example, they might occur in odd patterns or places. A doughnut-shaped burn will appear on the buttocks if a child has been immersed in very hot water, or she may have bruises on the soles of her feet from being hit there with a stick. Explanations for injuries may not be logical. Consider a child who says he broke his leg when he tripped on a crack in the sidewalk, but there are no sidewalks in his neighborhood. Still another clue involves frequent or multiple injuries that are hard to explain.

Physically abused children can also exhibit behavioral indicators such as extreme passivity and submissiveness in order to avoid provoking an abusive parent or other caregiver. Other children will express themselves with marked aggression and hostility, modeling the behavior of a violent parent.

*Sexual abuse is any sexual activity with a child where consent is not or cannot be given.... This includes sexual contact that is accomplished by force or threat of force, regardless of the age of the participants, and all sexual contact between an adult and a child, regardless of whether there is deception or the child understands the sexual nature of the activity. Sexual contact between an older and a younger child also can be abusive if there is a significant disparity in age, development, or size, rendering the younger child incapable of giving informed consent. The sexually abusive acts may include sexual penetration, sexual touching, or non-contact sexual acts such as exposure or voyeurism. (Emphasis added.)*

*(Berliner & Elliott, 2002, p. 55)*

**Incest**, a form of sexual abuse, is "sexual intercourse between people too closely related to legally marry (usually interpreted to mean father-daughter, mother-son, or brother-sister combinations)" (Yar-ber & Sayad, 2013, p. 587). Physical symptoms of sexual abuse include physical damage to or bleeding in the genital or anal areas. Emotional indicators are depression, low self-esteem, and thoughts of suicide. Other clues include compulsive masturbation and sexual behavior or knowledge inappropriate to a child's age.

**Child neglect** is "the failure of a parent, guardian, or other caregiver to provide for a child's basic needs. Neglect may be:

- Physical (e.g., failure to provide necessary food or shelter, or lack of appropriate supervision)
- Medical (e.g., failure to provide necessary medical or mental health treatment)
- Educational (e.g., failure to educate a child or attend to special education needs)
- Emotional (e.g., inattention to a child's emotional needs, failure to provide psychological care, or permitting the child to use alcohol or other drugs)" (Child Welfare Information Gateway, 2008).

For example, a child might lack appropriate winter clothing in a cold climate and, as a result, suffer frequent illness. Or a 6-year-old child might be left alone in charge of her two younger siblings. Constant hunger is yet another symptom.

**Psychological maltreatment** involves "a repeated pattern of behavior that conveys to a child that he or she is unwanted, worthless, valued only to the extent that he or she can meet others' needs, or is threatened with physical or psychological attack" (Downs, Moore, & McFadden, 2009, p. 213). Such maltreatment can involve withdrawal of support, attention, and encouragement. It may also entail active criticism, disapproval, and censure of children and their feelings and behavior.

The following categories reflect types of psychological maltreatment (Crosson-Tower, 2014; Downs et al., 2009; Hart & Brassard, 1991, 2001; Hart, Brassard, & Karlson, 1996; Hart, Brassard, Davidson, Rivelis, Diaz, & Binggeli, 2011; Miller-Perrin & Perrin, 2013):[2]

**EP 7a**

1. *Spurning* includes "belittling, degrading, shaming, ridiculing; singling out one child to do most of the household chores or to criticize and punish; and publicly humiliating" (Downs et al., 2009, p. 219). For example, "Jose's dad publicly humiliated him by coming to soccer games and screaming at him whenever he would fail to get in the correct position, fail to hold on to the ball, fail to kick it accurately to a fellow player, etc. 'You clumsy jerk! You poor excuse for a son! Can't you even pass!' he would bellow" (Hart et al., 2011, p. 128). Another example of spurning is refusing to help a child who asks for or needs help (Miller-Perrin & Perrin, 2013).

2. *Terrorizing* occurs when the caregiver "verbally assaults the child, creates a climate of fear, bullies and frightens the child, and makes the child believe that the world is hostile and unsafe" (Crosson-Tower, 2014, p. 197). Such actions cause "extreme fear and/or anxiety in a child" (Miller-Perrin & Perrin, 2013, p. 192). For instance, "Lamar's mother knew her son was in the apartment when she fired a shot through the front door in an attempt to kill his father" (Hart et al., 2011, p. 129). Other examples of terrorizing include threatening to harm the child him- or herself or threatening to commit suicide (Miller-Perrin & Perrin, 2013).

3. *Isolating* occurs when the caregiver cuts the child off from "normal social experiences, prevents the child from forming friendships, and makes the child believe that he or she is alone in the world" (Crosson-Tower, 2014, p. 197). For example, "Detian's family homeschooled her and would not allow her to play with neighborhood children. She could only leave the house with her parents or older sister, and she was strictly forbidden to converse with any adults or children who were not family members. She was told that other people didn't share the family's beliefs and were of the devil" (Hart et al., 2011, p. 129). Another example of isolating involves strapping a baby in a portable car seat all day to keep her from being underfoot (Hart et al., 2011). Still another illustration involves "locking a child in a closet or room" (Miller-Perrin & Perrin, 2013, p. 192).

4. *Exploiting* or *corrupting* includes "modeling, permitting, or encouraging such antisocial

---

[2]These categories of psychological maltreatment are based on the "1995 Guidelines for Psychosocial Evolution of Suspected Psychological Maltreatment of Children and Adolescents, published by the American Professional Society on the Abuse of Children (APSAC)" (Hart et al., 2011, p. 126).

behavior as prostitution, performance in pornography, criminal activity, or substance abuse; [and] encouraging developmentally inappropriate behavior such as parentification [expecting the child to act like a parent] or infantilization [treating an older child like an infant]" (Downs et al., 2009, p. 213). For instance, "after Seth's father lost his job and the family home was lost to foreclosure, Seth's parents began a downhill slide into meth-amphetamine addiction. To help his parents obtain drugs, and to provide income for the family, Seth began selling drugs" (Hart et al., 2011, p. 129).

5. *Denying emotional responsiveness* includes "being detached and uninvolved, interacting only when absolutely necessary, and failing to express love and affection to the child" (Downs et al., 2009, p. 213). For example, "baby Jose was fed and changed on a regular schedule, but his parents rarely interacted with him. When they did, they changed him or bathed him but without any expression of affection. There was no cuddling, little talking, and no eye contact" (Hart et al., 2011, p. 129).

Downs and her colleagues (2009) explain the complexity of psychological maltreatment:

*Psychological maltreatment is related to other forms of maltreatment; it is the psychological dimension of abuse, neglect, and sexual abuse. Terrorizing may be embedded in physical abuse; denying emotional responsiveness may be the psychological aspect of physical neglect. However, psychological maltreatment may also exist by itself, without other forms of maltreatment. (p. 214)*

We have established that child maltreatment in general is a complex issue. What's important is not that a particular case fits neatly into a clearly defined category, but rather that children are protected and their needs addressed. Highlight 9.2 provides an international perspective on child abuse—small children being sold as slaves in West Africa.

---

HIGHLIGHT 9.2 INTERNATIONAL PERSPECTIVES: THE CHILD SLAVE TRADE IN WEST AFRICA

Juliette Zinwue was thrilled! Although she lived in a small village in Benin, West Africa, she was actually going to travel somewhere in a car; some men said they would take her to work in Abidjan, a city in the Ivory Coast, and paid her parents to do so (Robinson & Palus, 2001). However, the journey soon turned into a horror story. Placed in a wealthy woman's home located in active, crowded Abidjan, Juliette "now rises at 6 AM to sweep the house and courtyard, wash dishes and clean out the garbage cans. She spends the rest of the day at a local market selling trinkets and hair accessories at her boss's stall" (Robinson & Palus, 2001, p. 40). She started three years ago. Today she's 10.

EP 2, 3

Chapter 2 established that human trafficking including the enslaving of children for the sex trade is a major global issue today (de Silva, 2007; Dixon, 2009). It is estimated that 200,000 West and Central African children are sold into slavery each year (Dixon, 2009). Robinson and Palus (2001) report on these children's experiences. The root of the problem is poverty. In the poorest countries, including Benin, where up to three-quarters of the population survives on less than SI a day, children have no schools to attend and little hope for viable future employment. They are often sold, sometimes for the meager fee of $15, because impoverished parents feel the children might be better off in a richer country— even as slaves. Most girls find themselves working as domestic help or prostitutes. Boys end up as field hands on plantations or as workers on fishing boats. Generally, "Africa has the highest rate of child labor in the world: 41% of 5- to 14-year-olds work" (p. 40).

The practice is bolstered by tradition. Historically, young children resided with wealthier urban extended family members or were hired out as servants to newly married couples. However, the current practice of selling them to strangers in other countries is purely a matter of business. Somebody is making money in the process, and it surely is not the children. Although West African nations are attempting to halt the slavery process, it is difficult. Borders between nations are easily crossed, and police have few resources for enforcement.

Juliette resolutely states, "I don't care that I have not been to school ... but I would like to go to church" (p. 41). She can't though, because she doesn't get Sundays off.

## How Many Children Are Maltreated?

The actual number of child maltreatment cases is difficult to determine. Specific definitions for who is included in specific categories vary dramatically from one state or locale to another. One thing, however, is certain—any figures that are reported reflect a minimal number of actual cases. All indications are that vast numbers of cases go unreported.

In 2008 there were almost 2 million reported and investigated acts of child maltreatment in the United States, almost 774,000 of which were substantiated (U.S. Census Bureau, 2010). This, of course, doesn't reflect other cases not reported or investigated. "Recent findings suggest that the incidence of child maltreatment is increasing dramatically"; one study found that the incidence had doubled over a decade (Petr, 2004, p. 20). Of substantiated cases, 71% involved neglect, 16.3% physical abuse, 9.2% sexual abuse, 7.1% emotional maltreatment, and 2.2% medical neglect (U.S. Census Bureau, 2010).

## What Causes Child Maltreatment?

People who physically abuse children tend to have the following needs (Crosson-Tower, 2014; Runyon & Urquiza, 2011):

- A need for personal support and nurturance.
- A need to overcome isolation and establish social contacts.
- A need to learn appropriate parenting skills.
- A need to improve self-esteem.

**EP 7a**

Crosson-Tower (2014) elaborates:

*It is generally agreed that parents who abuse their children usually have a dearth of coping mechanisms. They may not have achieved the degree of social competence of nonabusive parents and lack their problem-solving abilities. Some authors see these parents as less flexible and more easily overwhelmed.... Although some studies do not find a history of abuse or dysfunctional childhoods, others suggest that they might be in evidence.... This may lead them to less appropriate disciplinary standards.... A number of abusive parents are inconsistent and approach child rearing with negativity.... Their attitude leads them to feel less effective and overwhelmed, and as a result, they tend toward more aggressive models of discipline. (p. 92)*

Parents who neglect their children appear to have characteristics similar to physically abusive parents, although poverty may add to the stresses that result in neglect (Crosson-Tower, 2014; Erickson & Egeland, 2011). Erickson and Egeland (2011) explain that neglectful parents tend to exhibit a number of characteristics. They display "a lack of understanding of the emotional complexity of human relationships, especially the parent-child relationship" and "have difficulty seeing things from the child's perspective" (p. 115). Such parents "often have unresolved issues of trust, dependency, and autonomy (reflecting their own childhood history) and may seek to meet their own needs through the parent-child relationship" (p. 115). There is evidence that they are more likely to be depressed or have other mood disturbances. Other primary "risk factors include violence in the marital relationship, parental unemployment, other stressful life events, and the absence of a helpful, supportive social network" (p. 116). Neglectful parents may not have had their own needs met in their own childhoods.

Parents who physically abuse their children are actively lashing out. In contrast, neglectful parents are withdrawing and failing to provide adequately for their children.

Crooks and Baur (2014) describe people who sexually abuse children: No clear-cut description characterizes perpetrators of sexual abuse

*other than that most [offenders] are male and are known to the victim.... Child molesters cover the spectrum of social class, educational achievement, intelligence, occupation, religion, and ethnicity. Evidence suggests that many ... offenders, especially those who are prosecuted, are shy, lonely, poorly informed about sexuality, and moralistic or religious.... Many are likely to have poor interpersonal and sexual relations with other adults, and may feel socially inadequate and inferior.... However, it is not uncommon to encounter [offenders] ... outside the legal system who are well educated, socially adept, civic-minded, and financially successful. (pp. 525–526)*

Other possible characteristics include "alcoholism, severe marital problems, sexual difficulties, poor emotional adjustment, and various brain disorders" (Crooks & Baur, 2014, p. 526).

Crosson-Tower (2014) adds that sexuality for a perpetrator "provides not only tension release but also enhances self-esteem and makes the individual feel more personally effective. Pornography may feed into this to normalize a distorted view of sexual relations. Sexuality and aggression also become fused in his mind" (p. 131).

Miller-Perrin and Perrin (2013) describe some of the characteristics of parents who emotionally maltreat their children:

> *Such parents, compared with nonabusive parents, appear to exhibit more difficulties with interpersonal and social interactions, problem solving, and psychiatric adjustment.... Emotionally abusive parents had more difficulty building relationships, exhibited poor coping skills, and displayed deficits in child management techniques. In addition, emotionally abusive mothers demonstrated a lack of support networks (both personal and community) as well as greater levels of perceived stress, marital discord, and alcohol and drug use. (p. 201)*

### Child Protective Services and the Social Work Role

**Child protective services (CPS)** are interventions aimed at protecting children at risk of maltreatment. CPS social workers are usually employed by state or county public agencies whose designated task is to protect children from harm. Miller-Perrin and Perrin (2013) describe agency functioning:

EP 1, 7d

*CPS agencies carry out their responsibility of protecting children in four ways: (a) by investigating reports of maltreatment, (b) by providing treatment services, (c) by coordinating the services offered by other agencies in the community to child victims and their families, and (d) by implementing preventive services.... Ideally, the goal of CPS in all cases is to prevent child abuse and neglect in children's own homes through the provision of various services. (p. 264)*

Interventions in child maltreatment cases follow the same sequential steps used in other areas of social work intervention. These include receipt of the initial referral; gathering information about the case through a social study; assessment of the situation; case planning including goal setting; provision of treatment; evaluation of the effects of treatment; and termination of the case (DePanfilis, 2011; Pecora et al., 2010). Note that a protective services agency may provide treatment directly to the family, but more frequently the family is referred to another agency for treatment; a protective services worker usually assumes "a case management role" (Crosson-Tower, 2014, p. 290). (Chapter 4 established that *a case manager* is a practitioner who, on the behalf of a specific client system, coordinates needed services provided by any number of agencies, organizations, or facilities.) Highlight 9.3 focuses on the importance of risk assessment in cases of child maltreatment.

---

HIGHLIGHT **9.3**

## THE ASSESSMENT OF RISK AND RESILIENCY IN CHILD MALTREATMENT CASES

A key word in the assessment of child maltreatment is *risk* (DePanfilis, 2011; Shlonsky & Gambrill, 2005). After a case involving suspected maltreatment is reported, it's the social worker's job to *assess* the extent to which children are at risk of maltreatment. It is also vital that the family's strengths and resiliency be assessed (Crosson-Tower, 2014). Family strengths provide the basis for treatment planning to protect children from maltreatment and keep the family safely together if at all

EP 7a, 7b, 7c, 8b

possible. Crosson-Tower (2014) urges that the following questions be answered during the assessment process:

1. "Is the child at risk from abuse or neglect and to what degree?
2. What is causing the problem?
3. Could services be offered to alleviate the problem?
4. Is the home a safe environment or must the child be placed elsewhere?" (p. 216)

*(continued)*

**HIGHLIGHT 9.3** *(continued)*

Assessment focuses on many of the dynamics contributing to maltreatment discussed earlier. A numerous variables have been found to affect a worker's decision that a case assumes a high level of risk and merits intensive agency intervention (Crosson-Tower, 2014; Kadushin & Martin, 1988; Myers, 2002). These include:

- Clearly visible proof of abuse or environmental characteristics that obviously endanger a child
- The degree of the child's helplessness and vulnerability (e.g., a child with a physical disability or an infant being extremely vulnerable)
- Self-destructive behavior on the part of the child. A history of severe abuse
- Abusers who show no or little regret for their child's abuse and have difficulty accepting responsibility
- Abusers who openly reject the child or blame the child for the problem
- Serious emotional disturbances on the part of parents
- Lack of cooperation by the parents
- Families that are exposed to numerous and severe psychological and social pressures
- Isolation of the family and lack of social support systems.

Protective elements potentially demonstrating *resiliency* (the ability to recover from adversity and resume functioning) should also be assessed. These elements may relate to the child or children, the parents and family in general, and to the encompassing environment (Crosson-Tower, 2014). Factors associated with the child include the following:

- "Child is in good health and result of a normal pregnancy and birth *or*
- Mother receives and accepts support around any current or past problems with child
- Child has above-average intelligence
- Child has easy temperament, is well bonded with caretakers, and feels secure

- Child has healthy self-esteem, is able to problem solve (age appropriate), and shows age-appropriate degree of autonomy
- Child has good peer relationships
- Child has experienced relatively healthy development free from trauma
- Child has hobbies and interests" (Crosson-Tower, 2014, p. 219).

Protective elements associated with the parents or the family in general include the following:

- "Positive parent-child relationship with secure attachment
- Appropriate structure/family rules with fair, non-physical discipline
- Parents model healthy self-esteem and good problem-solving abilities
- Presence of concerned and caring extended family
- Higher parental educational level
- Family expects prosocial behavior" (Crosson-Tower, 2014, p. 219).

Protective elements related to the family's relationship with its environment include the following:

- Access to health and educational resources
- Consistent parental employment
- Adequate housing
- Mid to high socioeconomic status
- Family is affiliated with religious faith community
- Presence of other positive and influential adult models. (Crosson-Tower, 2014, p. 220)

Assessment interviews involve both adults and children. Questions focus on the parents' history and current functioning; the way parents perceive their children; the way the family system functions as a whole; the condition of the home environment; the external support (e.g., friends or relatives) available to the family; and the children's condition, level of development, and overall functioning (Crosson-Tower, 2014).

Following assessment, a treatment *plan* is developed providing direction for how to proceed. Treatment goals for maltreatment victims can "include increasing self-esteem, decreasing feelings of hopelessness and helplessness, decreasing aggressive behaviors, and decreasing negative behaviors such as

lying, suicide attempts, running away, promiscuity, and drug or alcohol abuse" (Winton & Mara, 2001, p. 165). These can be achieved through individual counseling, group therapy, or family therapy.

Of course, basic aspects of treatment for physically abused children involve meeting their medical needs and keeping them safe. Sometimes removal from a dangerous situation is necessary, at least temporarily.

Treatment goals for parents focus on strengthening their "coping skills, parenting skills, and child management techniques" (Winton & Mara, 2001, p. 171). Intervention may involve individual counseling or family therapy. Many believe that group therapy, including self-help groups such as Parents Anonymous, is often the most effective (Parents Anonymous, 2014; Winton & Mara, 2001). Through such groups, parents learn that they are not alone and can discover how others are experiencing stress and frustration. They can share coping ideas with each other, suggest new child management techniques, provide mutual support, and improve their communication skills.

Treatment for families experiencing abuse or neglect varies radically depending on the resources and services available, the level of risk to the children's well-being, the family dynamics, and motivation of the abusive or neglectful caregivers. An intensive family preservation approach (described in detail later in the chapter) involves a social worker spending concentrated time with a family, identifying specific treatment goals, emphasizing family strengths, and teaching other skills as needed.

## Working with and Referring to Other Agencies

During the intervention process, CPS staff often work with the courts to declare that children require protection and to determine appropriate safe placement for them. CPS workers are frequently called on to testify in court to report assessment information and make recommendations (DePanfilis, 2011). In the event that family problems  **EP 1, 8c** cannot be resolved, CPS workers may work with the courts to develop alternative long-term or permanent placements.

Additionally, social workers may make referrals to a number of social services (Alexander, 2004). **Respite care** is the temporary provision of care for those requiring such care (in this case children) so that the regular caregivers (in this case parents) have some time away from caregiving responsibilities (Murphy, 2004). This can ease stress and allow

parents to take a break. **Day care** is the regular provision of care for children or others dependent on help when regular caregivers must work or be away from the home. This is another way of providing alternative child care for children so parents can attend to their own needs, go to work, and practice newly learned skills. **Support services** involve a wide range of programs providing assistance in helping parents undertake their daily tasks and assume their responsibilities; examples include "parent educational services, employment counseling and training services, budget management, legal services, homemaker services, … referrals to food banks, and transportation" (Alexander, 2004, p. 419). **Parental aides** are trained paraprofessionals, sometimes volunteers, who go into the home, serve as positive role models for behavior management and parent-child relationships, and provide someone for the parents to talk to. In effect, this is another way of taking the pressure off. Finally, **Big Brother/Big Sister** or **adopted grandparent programs** are programs where volunteers are paired with a child and, under supervision, offer that child guidance and friendship. Such a program can let a child form a special relationship with a supportive adult role model or mentor.

Referral opportunities are endless. It's up to the social worker to accurately assess family members' needs and creatively link them to available services.

*Case Example* Cynthia, age 7, came to school one day with odd-looking bruises on her arm. Her teacher, Kara Lot, noticed them immediately and asked her where she got them. Cynthia, an aggressive, boisterous child who loved to get attention from her teachers, told Kara that she had tripped, fallen down the stairs, and hit her arm on some toys at the bottom. Kara thought that this seemed a bit peculiar but accepted Cynthia's answer and forgot about the incident.

Three days later, Kara again noticed some odd bruises on Cynthia's arm. She also observed that Cynthia was having difficulty writing, as if her fingers were sprained. Again she asked Cynthia what was wrong. The child answered that she had probably bumped her hand on something. But this time Kara did not leave the matter at that. That same day she talked to the school social worker, who, in turn, referred the matter to a protective services worker at the local social services agency.

The protective services worker assigned to the case, Brian Bornthumper, immediately began a case assessment. He interviewed both Cynthia and her parents. He focused on the elements indicating that abuse was taking place and on the probable risk that Cynthia would come to further harm. He also examined the needs of the family as a whole and of its individual members.

Brian assumed as nonthreatening an approach as possible and maintained a focus on the family's and the child's welfare. He discovered that Cynthia's family had moved to the area from another state only a year before. Cynthia's mother, Amelia, was a shy, withdrawn woman who found it difficult to make new friends. She had no relatives in the area. Additionally, Cynthia's baby sister, Julie, had been born only three months after the move. Julie was a colicky baby who rarely slept more than two hours at a time and cried almost incessantly. Cynthia's father, George, was a mop salesman who was frequently out of town. And when he was home, he spent his time watching football and other sports on television or sleeping.

Amelia obviously was under severe stress. She felt lonely, isolated, and worthless. Even Julie didn't seem to love her. All the baby did was cry. George was hardly ever home, and when he was, he ignored the family. Amelia felt that her marital relationship was deteriorating. As a result of all these stresses, she found herself violently exploding at Cynthia. Whenever Cynthia did something the least bit wrong, Amelia found herself screaming at the girl and often physically assaulting her.

In fact, Amelia's relationship with her own family was quite poor. Her childhood memories were filled with her father beating her with little provocation.

Cynthia's family exemplified the types of needs that are common in abusive families. Loneliness, isolation, lack of emotional support, marital problems, life crises, and lack of effective parenting skills were all apparent. Brian conducted an assessment by gathering relevant information regarding family relationships, history, emotional status, and stress levels; child management approaches; and available support systems. As a CPS worker, he sought to strengthen the family and enhance family members' interactions among themselves and with others in their environment.

Brian initially made several referrals to the appropriate services, after which he served as case manager, coordinating efforts and monitoring progress. He met with the family regularly to accomplish this. For instance, Brian referred Amelia to a Parents Anonymous group, in which she could experience mutual support, vent her frustrations, develop relationships, improve communication skills, and learn new coping methods. He referred both George and Amelia to a parent effectiveness training group to improve their ability to cope with and control their children's behavior. He also referred them to a local family services agency for marital counseling. The intent was to work on improving communication within the marriage and to address possible ways for George to spend more time with Amelia, provide her with greater support, and become more involved with the family.

In addition, Brian referred Cynthia to the family services agency for individual counseling. He also

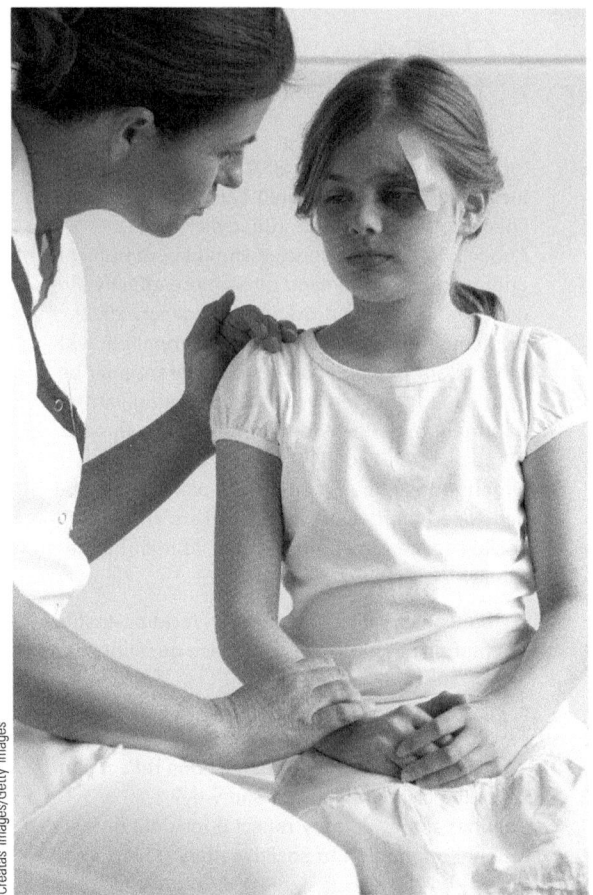

Creatas Images/Getty Images

*Social workers work with abused children and their families.*

worked with her school social worker to involve her in a volleyball team and local Girl Scout troop.

Brian suggested that Amelia join a recreational group so she could develop some friendships and have some time to herself. Amelia decided to become a member of a bowling team and started attending an aerobics class. Finally, Brian helped Amelia find a day-care center that would care for her children while she attended these activities.

In effect, Brian worked with this family to develop its members' strengths, improve communication and mutual support, utilize more effective behavior management techniques, stop abuse, maintain safety, and improve overall family functioning.

Sometimes it's necessary for social workers to do more than simply make referrals, as Brian's work with Cynthia and her family illustrates. Focus on Critical Thinking 9.1 addresses advocacy and child maltreatment in the macro arena.

## Intensive Family Preservation: One Treatment Approach

**Family preservation services** are "short-term, family-based services designed to assist families in crisis by improving parenting and family functioning while keeping children safe" (ACF, n.d.). Family preservation is based on the idea that children can be protected safely in their own homes when families are strengthened. This is done by giving parents the resources and services they need to function effectively. Family preservation stresses that it is in children's best interests to help them remain in their own homes. Removing them can traumatize them and result in permanent harmful consequences. The concept of family preservation has become a major thrust in agencies throughout the country. It involves doing everything possible to keep the child in the home

EP 8a

---

An ongoing part of the social worker's role is to evaluate the effectiveness of policy at the macro level and advocate for positive change where needed. Macro improvements are called for in at least five areas:

EP 3a, 5a, 5b, 5c, 8d

- More funding should be tunneled to the *prevention* of child maltreatment (Chadwick, 2002; Daro & Donnelly, 2002; Miller-Perrin & Perrin, 2013). Until now "services and interventions have developed as *responses* to the problems of abuse as the problems have been recognized" (Chadwick, 2002, p. 509). Preventing children from suffering from maltreatment in the first place is certainly much better for them than reacting after it has already occurred (Wells, 2008).
- A more supportive system geared toward improving resources and services for families in general is essential to maintain family strengths. Families need tangible resources, including adequate shelter, food, clothing, and other necessities, to thrive (Alexander, 2004; Wells, 2008).
- More community and neighborhood supports should be initiated and developed. Current availability of resources and services is significantly

inconsistent (Chadwick, 2002). For example, families in rural settings should have better access to child protective services (Chadwick, 2002).
- Public and private agencies should communicate and cooperate with each other more effectively concerning service provision (Chadwick, 2002). Sometimes "interventions are incompatible with others"; for example, an abusive parent may be imprisoned for a long period, conflicting with a treatment plan developed to reunite the family (Chadwick, 2002, p. 517).
- Organized continuing education plans should be developed to educate social workers and other social service providers about child maltreatment (Chadwick, 2002).

With the conservative–liberal and residual–institutional orientations in mind, answer these questions.

## Critical Thinking Questions

- To what extent do these suggestions reflect conservative or liberal values, and why?
- To what extent do they reflect a residual or institutional orientation to social welfare policy, and why?

and provide treatment for the family. Family preservation services are also referred to as family-based services, "home-based services, or in-home treatment" (Alexander, 2004; Berg, 1994, p. 4).

Six goals of family preservation services are "(1) to protect children, (2) to maintain and strengthen family bonds, (3) to stabilize the crisis situation, (4) to increase the family's skills and competencies, (5) to facilitate the family's use of a variety of formal and informal helping resources, and (6) to prevent unnecessary out-of-home placement of children" (Berry, 2005; Downs et al., 2009; Piccola & Tracy 2008; Tracy, 1995; Tracy, Haapala, Kinney, & Pecora, 1991, p. 1).

In past decades, working with families usually involved focusing on protecting the child. This, in turn, often meant removing the child from the home. Services were then provided in a segmented manner by a variety of workers. For example, consider an alleged case of child abuse. One protective services intake worker would gather the intake data when the child was initially referred. Another outreach protective services worker would provide services to the family. Still another would work with the foster family if the child was placed there. And so it went.

Family preservation, in contrast, emphasizes service provision to the family unit in a more coordinated fashion. For instance, one worker might do the majority of the engagement, assessment, planning, intervention, evaluation, and termination. The child is likely to remain in the home during the entire process. All services are provided or coordinated by a designated worker with the intent of helping the intact family solve its range of problems. Service can be "provided by a treatment team" proceeding with a coordinated and unified effort, with the team "often made up of case manager, worker/therapist, and such support staff as the parent educator, homemaker, and so on" (Berg, 1994, p. 5).

### Key Themes in Family Preservation

At least 11 themes tend to characterize family preservation programs (Berry, 2005; Crosson-Tower, 2013; Downs et al., 2009; Maluccio, 1990, pp. 23–25; Piccola & Tracy, 2008). They include:

1. *Crisis orientation:* Family preservation is based on intervention when a crisis is taking place

within the home. Workers can then take advantage of the family's motivation to alleviate the stress it's experiencing.

2. *Focus on family:* The family is all-important; it is considered the optimum place for children to remain. All intervention emphasis is directed toward keeping the family together and strengthening its members.

3. *Home-based services:* Services are provided in the home whenever possible. The ongoing thrust is improving the home environment.

4. *Time limits:* Because family preservation workers intervene during times of crisis, they work quickly. The intervention process in most models ranges from 4 to 12 weeks, although some extend longer than that. Setting time limits helps workers and their clients evaluate progress regularly.

5. *Limited, focused objectives:* All intervention objectives are clearly specified. The primary goal is to alleviate the crisis situation and strengthen the family unit so that a crisis is less likely to erupt again.

6. *Intensive, comprehensive services:* Workers' time and attention are concentrated on the families and their progress. Workers may spend as much as 20–25 hours each week arranging for resources and providing services (e.g., problem solving, counseling, and parenting skills education).

7. *Emphasis on education and skill building:* The family preservation approach is a positive one. It assumes that people are capable of learning and can improve if they are given appropriate information and support.

8. *Coordination:* Because intervention is intensive and numerous resources may be involved, coordination is very important. Sometimes other service providers and specialists are involved with a case, requiring coordination of treatment efforts.

9. *Flexibility:* Each family is different, having varying problems and needs. Flexibility enables practitioners to match a wide range of services and resources with the individual family's needs.

10. *Accessibility:* Workers in family preservation must be readily accessible to families in crisis. Their work is intensive and time-limited. Workers' caseloads typically are small so they can concentrate their efforts.

11. *Accountability:* Accountability is the obligation of justifying one's work by accomplishing identified goals. The emphasis on focused objectives and time-limited interventions enhances workers' ability to evaluate their effectiveness.

The family preservation approach is expensive because workers have small caseloads; therefore, the ratio of worker salary to number of cases is high. For example, consider a worker being paid $36,000 per year who works with 12 families over the entire year. The cost of her salary is about $3,000 per family. Another worker serving in a more traditional child welfare capacity might have 90 cases in a year. The cost of her salary per case is only about $400. This is a bit oversimplified, but you probably get the idea.

*Case Example* The following case illustrates how the themes just described might be employed in practice. (They are noted in italics.) Mary Jo, age 24, is the mother of three children—Ralphie, Sherry, and Jenna, ages 6, 4, and 3, respectively. Mary Jo has had a long, traumatic history of drug abuse and involvement with violent men. At her lowest point, high on crack, she was beaten bloody by her latest boyfriend and taken to the hospital emergency room. Her children, who had been removed from the home several times because of her neglect related to substance abuse, were taken from the home again. Mary Jo was told that unless she successfully underwent substance abuse treatment, she was not getting her children back.

It was a rough year, but she made it. She successfully completed a tough inpatient program and remained off crack. At the end of the year, she was desperate to get her children back. She was identified as a good potential recipient of family preservation services due to the *crisis* of trying to get her kids back and learning the skills she needed to do so. Edria was assigned as her social worker.

With a small caseload of two families, Edria was able to *focus on the family* and provide Mary Jo and her children with *intensive, comprehensive services.* Primary problems involved Mary Jo's homemaking abilities, child management skills, budgeting capability, and anger management. All three children were unruly and difficult to control, but only Ralphie was dangerous. He had set a number of fires and had threatened Mary Jo with a knife on three occasions.

Edria provided *home-based services* because she needed to help Mary Jo work out problems immediately when they occurred in her home environment. She also had to be *flexible* because of Mary Jo's unique set of needs. Edria focused on *education and skill building.* She helped Mary Jo work out a child behavior management program that identified negative behaviors requiring change and specified new, more appropriate behaviors to be established. Edria also worked with Mary Jo to teach her more effective responses to the children's behavior to enable her to regain control. One facet of this involved anger control, whereby Mary Jo developed a new awareness of her previously uncontrolled emotions and new, more appropriate responses to the children's behavior. For example, she replaced erratic physical punishment with a more methodical system involving positive and negative consequences. Edria also helped Mary Jo develop better household management and budgeting skills.

Edria established *limited, focused objectives* with Mary Jo concerning each area of skill development. The relatively high cost of treatment emphasized that Edria must be *accountable* for achieving these objectives. Because her time with Mary Jo was intensive, she also had to establish *time limits* within which objectives would be achieved. Edria's time was expensive, and she couldn't work with Mary Jo forever. But while she was working with Mary Jo, Edria had to be readily *accessible.* If a behavioral crisis occurred at 9:30 PM on a Saturday night, Edria needed to be available to help.

One other aspect of Edria's work with Mary Jo involved *coordination.* Remember that Ralphie had exhibited some fairly serious behavioral problems.

In addition to the child behavior management program being implemented at home, he was also receiving individual therapy provided by another social worker specializing in child counseling. Edria needed to coordinate objectives and progress between this therapist and the home program.

This turned out to be a successful intervention. Mary Jo regained substantial control over her children's behavior, although they never became perfect angels. Ralphie no longer threatened her or exhibited dangerous behavior. Mary Jo had immensely improved control of her temper. Finally, Mary Jo was running the household more effectively, including paying her bills and balancing her checkbook. She still hated to dust and hoped to win the lottery, but she was maintaining a status quo. The family was together and relatively happy. Edria went on to another case. That was a hard part of the job—leaving a family after becoming so involved. However, she wished Mary Jo the best and knew that tomorrow would be just as action packed when she started out with a new family preservation case.

## Child Day Care

**Child day care** is an agency or program that provides supervision and care for children while parents or guardians are at work or otherwise unavailable. It is critical for many families because the majority of women work outside the home (ProQuest, 2014; U.S. Census Bureau, 2011). Consider that 62.5% of all single women and 59.6% of all married women are employed; of women with children under age 6, 68.1% of single mothers and 62.3% of married mothers work outside the home (ProQuest, 2014).

Although not all day-care centers employ social workers, practitioners often work with clients requiring day care and must help them with referrals. This is especially true because Temporary Assistance for Needy Families (TANF) requires that parents receiving public assistance get training and find work. (TANF, described in Chapter 8, is the program replacing Aid to Families with Dependent Children that "provides cash assistance based on need, income, resources, and family sizes" [Dolgoff & Feldstein, 2009, p. 216].) Social workers may also have to help parents find high-quality day care.

Many types of day care are available. Downs and her colleagues (2009) describe the various forms of day care that are most common and the advantages and disadvantages of each. In about 67% of all working families with preschoolers, family members provide day care. Each parent takes turns caring for children while the other is working outside the home, or relatives such as grandparents or siblings provide supervision.

Outside the family, day care is provided in three basic ways. First, parents can hire someone such as a baby-sitter or a nanny to come into their home and provide care, which about 5% of working families with preschoolers do. Although most parents prefer this option, it's too expensive to be practical for many families. Second, parents can take their children to the care providers' homes for supervision. This is referred to as **family day care** and is used

by 11% of families with preschoolers. Third, larger, organized day-care centers in addition to preschool and Head Start programs can provide care. More than a third of all families use these larger settings. (Note that all of these numbers add up to more than 100% because many families use multiple sources of day care.)

Almost two-thirds of preschoolers and almost 70% of school-aged children are in some type of day-care arrangement; school-aged children are in care including that provided "by relatives, day-care homes, enrichment activities, and school-based programs" (Downs et al., 2009, p. 55). Downs and her colleagues (2009) elaborate:

> *The type of arrangement parents make varies with the age of the child.... Preschoolers are more apt to be cared for by relatives than nonrelatives. About a quarter of all preschoolers are cared for in day-care centers, with smaller percentages cared for in day-care homes or at home by babysitters. Preschool-aged children of working mothers spend long hours in day care, with an average of 32 hours per week.*
>
> *Once children reach school-age, the time spent in school accounts for much of their time while their parent is working. However, grade school-aged children also need supplementary care.... As children get older, self-care during nonschool hours becomes more likely. (p. 55)*

Advantages of family day care include a small caregiver-to-child ratio, proximity to the home, and opportunities to develop a closer relationship with the caregiver.

A chief disadvantage of family day care is that the vast majority of such care is unregulated and the caregiver unsupervised; another disadvantage is that the caregiver probably lacks formal training in how to provide educational opportunities for children.

**Day-care centers** are agencies that can care for from 15 to 300 children, although they average about 60. Advantages include being licensed under state supervision, usually having staff trained in child supervision and early education, and being able to provide a wider range of opportunities and activities than what's available in family day care. Disadvantages may include increased impersonality due to size, lack of parental knowledge of their children's individual caregivers, strict and inflexible

## HIGHLIGHT 9.4 — WHAT MAKES FOR HIGH-QUALITY DAY CARE?

The quality of day care varies dramatically among day-care providers; the following variables are associated with high-quality day care (Downs et al., 2009; Papalia & Feldman, 2012; Santrock, 2009); policy can require changes to improve day care:

EP 3a, 5a, 5b, 5c, 8d

- Well-trained caregivers who can provide educational experiences to enhance social, emotional, and intellectual development.
- A well-structured program that provides multiple growth opportunities unavailable at home.
- A low caregiver-to-child ratio that allows for greater interaction and attention.
- A safe, positively oriented environment where well-trained caregivers display positive characteristics "such as warmth, sensitivity, and responsiveness" and provide "stimulating interactions," which are so "crucial to early cognitive,

linguistic, and psychosocial development" (Papalia & Feldman, 2012, p. 203).
- Sufficient chances to interact positively with other children.
- A physical environment that's interesting and thought-provoking.

In contrast, the worst day care provides no more than custodial care that gives children only the bare necessities of supervision and physical care. Crosson-Tower (2009) indicates that characteristics of good day care such as low caregiver-to-child ratios and stimulating environments have higher costs. She warns that "a two-tier system" may be developing, one for the middle-class and rich, and another for the poor (Crosson-Tower, 2009, p. 139; Scarr, 1998, p. 105). The implication is that "more public support" should be provided "for child care so that quality services can be made available to any working family" (Crosson-Tower, 2009, p. 139).

---

hours, inconvenient locations, and restrictions regarding care for infants or sick children. Highlight 9.4 discusses variables involved generally in the quality of day care.

### Other Supportive Services

Many other supportive services are clustered under the child welfare umbrella. They are not necessarily jobs assumed by social workers. However, because the broker role in social work is so important, practitioners must be aware of and knowledgeable about these services to be able to provide clients with appropriate referrals. Examples of other supportive services include family life education and respite care.

### Family Life Education

**Family life education (FLE)** involves group or classroom learning experiences for the purpose of increasing people's knowledge, developing skills, or enhancing self-awareness concerning issues and crises relevant at some point during the life span (Harris, 2008; National Council on Family Relations [NCFR], 2014; Riley, 1995). Several aspects of this definition are important. First, FLE is a learning experience. It can involve a classroom

setting or the distribution of educational information (NCFR, 2014). FLE can also occur in a group context. Such groups usually involve a social worker or other professional providing information for 6 to 12 group members; weekly meetings last from one and a half to two hours and are held over a one- to eight-week period (Barker, 20014).

A second aspect of the definition involves the purpose of FLE meetings. Because they may address either normal developmental or specific crisis issues, they may be appropriate for almost anyone, depending on people's learning needs. They may focus on at least the following six categories of educational development (NCFR, 2014):

1. How families fit into the social and cultural environment. Topics may include relationships with government agencies, religious organizations, or the educational system, in addition to the general social milieu in which families live. Specific topics might involve understanding people in the social environment who have different cultural backgrounds and outlooks, health care, demographic profiles of the population, community history, and working with public and private agencies.

2. "Internal dynamics of families." This may include: parenting issues and behavioral control of children; interpersonal relationships and communication; managing conflict; making rational decisions; coping with crises such as divorce, death, or substance abuse; and any other topic relevant to family life (such as economic struggles or the adjustment of blended families).
3. Normal development throughout the lifespan. Topics might focus on prenatal care, infancy, childhood, adolescence, and the various phases of adulthood (Zastrow & Kirst-Ashman, 2013).
4. "Human sexuality." Subjects can include reproduction, contraception, family planning, and virtually any aspect of sexual relationships and interaction (such as any physical or emotional aspects of sexual behavior).
5. Management of economic resources. Issues addressed might involve budgeting, saving for college or retirement, and establishing financial priorities.
6. Legal issues relevant to families. Topics might include family law concerning marriage or divorce, determining the custody of children, paying taxes, or contributing to or receiving benefits from Social Security.

Examples of FLE within the group context include groups focusing on (1) normal development, (2) crisis, (3) personal growth, and (4) life adjustment (Riley, 1995).

*Normal development groups* provide information about various normal life stages. Examples include sexuality, premarital and marital education, and parenting education programs (Harris, 2008).

*Crisis groups* are oriented toward people facing a serious life turning point or upheaval. Often these people are unprepared for the crisis and require information and help to cope. Examples of such crises are serious illness, divorce, recent death of a loved one, and loss of a job. Group leaders usually must give members emotional support in addition to information.

*Personal growth groups* help people develop specified social skills. They are unlike crisis groups because there's no sudden upheaval involved, and they differ from life adjustment groups because members are not striving to cope with a chronic problem. Rather, group members have in common the interest of improving themselves in some way. Examples are

groups focusing on assertiveness training, time management, and communication skills.

*Life adjustment groups* help people who are dealing with some ongoing problematic issue. Most often, group members are coping with a crisis of their own or of someone close to them. This differs from a crisis group because it focuses on long-term issues instead of temporary crises. Examples are parents of children with a chronic illness or developmental disability, caregivers for older adults with Alzheimer's disease, and adults with Parkinson's disease.[3]

### Respite Care

We've established that *respite care* is supervision of a child by another caregiver, allowing the parent an interval of relief from the responsibilities of child care. In essence, it gives the individual a break, a brief time during which the caregiver is free from stressful responsibilities. It allows an opportunity for parents to run errands or simply to relax. Some agencies use volunteers to provide respite care; others have programs in which parents can drop children off and have them be supervised for a few hours (Mather, Lager, & Harris, 2007). One of this chapter's opening vignettes, involving Corazon and Juanita, provides an example of a situation in which respite care would be appropriate.

Note that respite care can apply not only to parents but also to other caregivers with primary responsibility for a dependent. For example, respite care might be provided to a person caring for a spouse dying of a rapidly debilitating disease. It might also apply to an adult child caring for an aging parent who has limited mobility.

# An Ongoing Macro Issue: Advocacy for Resources   `LO5`

Hoefer (2012) stresses the importance of advocacy in social work:

*One of the defining elements of social work practice is that social workers are trained to see the*

---

[3]Parkinson's disease is a neurological illness causing deterioration of brain cells and characterized by "tremors, especially of the fingers and hands, muscle rigidity, and a shuffling gait" (Nichols, 1999, p. 961).

*connections between problems happening to individuals and problems occurring to larger numbers of people due to organizational or governmental policies that impose costs, monetary or otherwise, or deny services to people in need.*

EP 3a, 8d

*Examples of the types of costs that people in need must pay as a result of organizational or governmental policies include spending time waiting for assistance in a first-come, first-served line to apply for financial assistance; paying higher prices at local markets in low-income areas because public transportation is not available to other shopping areas; paying high fees to cash checks because banks are not located nearby; and having higher levels of cancer and other diseases because low-income housing is located near industrial dumping zones or other sources of considerable pollution.*

*Often people in need are denied services because organizations and governments change the definition of eligibility (such as when a person with a savings account with more than $500, rather than $1,000, is no longer eligible for a program). Service is also denied when eligibility levels are shifted downward, leading to more people not qualifying because they earn too much; and when the benefits available are restricted, for example, when an organization does not pay for mental health services.*

*Advocacy is a core concern of social workers. Social workers are not content with only understanding current policy, the forces that shaped it, and what its effects are. Such analysis and understanding is but a first step in assisting clients with their situation. Indeed, because policy shapes what social workers can do to assist their clients and how they can practice social work, the importance of understanding and being able to conduct effective advocacy is vital to all social workers.* *(pp. 1–2)*

## Advocacy for Children

Social workers live and struggle with many issues in providing supportive services to children and families. This book reflects only the tip of the iceberg. Children are indeed a population at risk, and social workers have a responsibility to advocate on their behalf. *Advocacy*, of course, involves taking an active, directive role on behalf of a client or client group in need of help. One important aspect of child advocacy is the acknowledgment and support of the basic rights of children. The concern for children's rights can be considered on a universal level; that is, every child should have certain specific rights such as the right to adequate food, clothing, shelter, and a decent home environment.

In an era of shrinking and competitive resources, ongoing advocacy is necessary for the following:

- Quality, accessible day care for children of working parents.
- Improved maternal and child health care in view of the high proportion of low-birth-weight babies (March of Dimes, 2015).
- Better prevention and treatment programs to address child maltreatment.
- Welfare reform to raise families' income levels above the poverty line.

# Substitute Services    `LO6`

Earlier we established that substitute services are those replacing

*another family for the child's own family, so that someone else takes over all aspects of the parental role on a temporary or permanent basis. Such a change is necessary when the home presents deficiencies so serious that even intensive home-based preventive services cannot assist the family in providing the child with minimally adequate social, emotional, or physical care.*

*(Kadushin & Martin, 1988, p. 344)*

When the best attempts at providing supportive services to maintain children in a healthy family environment do not work, alternative living arrangements for the children become necessary. These substitute family environments then give children the supervision, shelter, food, and clothing required to meet their daily needs. Figure 9.1 portrayed the continuum of care from supportive to substitute services.

Children are removed from their parents' care for a number of reasons. Parents may be unable to care for children because of their own serious illness, physical disability, emotional immaturity, intellectual disability, or substance abuse. They may neglect, abandon, or abuse their children. Children may have such serious developmental, emotional, or physical disabilities that parents are incapable of caring for them. Finally, there may not be sufficient community resources to provide the necessary supportive services to keep children in their own homes.

Length of removal depends on the severity of problems in the home environment and the extent to which it can be strengthened to allow the children's safe return. Changing a child's living environment often involves a change in **legal custody**—formal assumption of caregiving responsibilities for a child, including meeting that child's daily needs.[4]

A guiding principle is to keep children in the *least restrictive* setting in which they can function with the greatest amount of independence. The overriding goal is to have children return to a normal family and community environment if at all possible.

Substitute care services can be placed on a continuum reflecting their intensity of supervision and restrictiveness. This continuum of care for children and adolescents ranges from supportive services for families with children remaining in their own homes to removal from the home and placement in a formal treatment setting. Pecora and his colleagues (2010) reflect:

**EP 7d**

*It is useful to conceptualize child welfare as a comprehensive continuum of services with a strong preventive component. Each child welfare service tries to prevent the use of a more intensive and intrusive service, and child welfare services in the aggregate endeavor to prevent the transition of children into more restrictive services like juvenile justice. (p. 68)*

Children's placement can be ranked from the least restrictive (a ranking of 1) to most restrictive (a tanking of 9) as follows (Proch & Taber, 1987) (see Figure 9.2):

- Home of parent (rank 1).
- Home of relative (2).
- Foster family home (3).

- Specialized foster family home (4).
- Group home (5).
- Private child welfare institution (6).
- Shelter (7).
- Mental health facility (8).
- Correctional facility (9). (pp. 9–10)

A theme characterizing substitute services is **permanency planning**—"a comprehensive care planning process directed toward the goal of a permanent, stable home for a child [placed in substitute care]" (Barker, 2014; Rycus, Hughes, & Ginther, 1988, p. 45). Children need a stable, healthy home environment. Being bounced from temporary home to temporary home does not contribute to emotional stability. Therefore, an ultimate goal of substitute care is to give children permanent homes.

Types of substitute services discussed here include kinship care, foster family care, residential placements, and adoption.

### Kinship Care

One type of out-of-home placement involves relatives or part of the child's family's supportive network, in what is referred to as kinship care. **Kinship care** is the placement of children in the home of "a relative, close family friend, godparents, or tribe or clan member when the children's parents are unable to provide care" (Crosson-Tower, 2013, p. 286). There are positive reasons for placing children with people who are already close to them:

*Family strengths often include a kinship network that functions as a support system. The kinship support system may be composed of nuclear family, extended family, blended family, foster family, or adoptive family members or members of tribes or clans. The involvement of kin may stabilize family situations, ensure the protection of children, and prevent the need to separate children from their families and place them in the formal child welfare system.*

(*Child Welfare League of America, 1994, p. 1*)

**Informal kinship care** is a situation where a family takes children in without intervention by social service agencies. **Formal kinship care**, on the other hand, is a situation where a social services agency gains legal custody of a child and places that child in a kinship home, which it licenses. The agency

---

[4]Note that legal custody may also involve granting responsibility to a caregiver for persons who are not children but who cannot function independently. Examples include people with severe intellectual disabilities and older adults with serious mental incapacities.

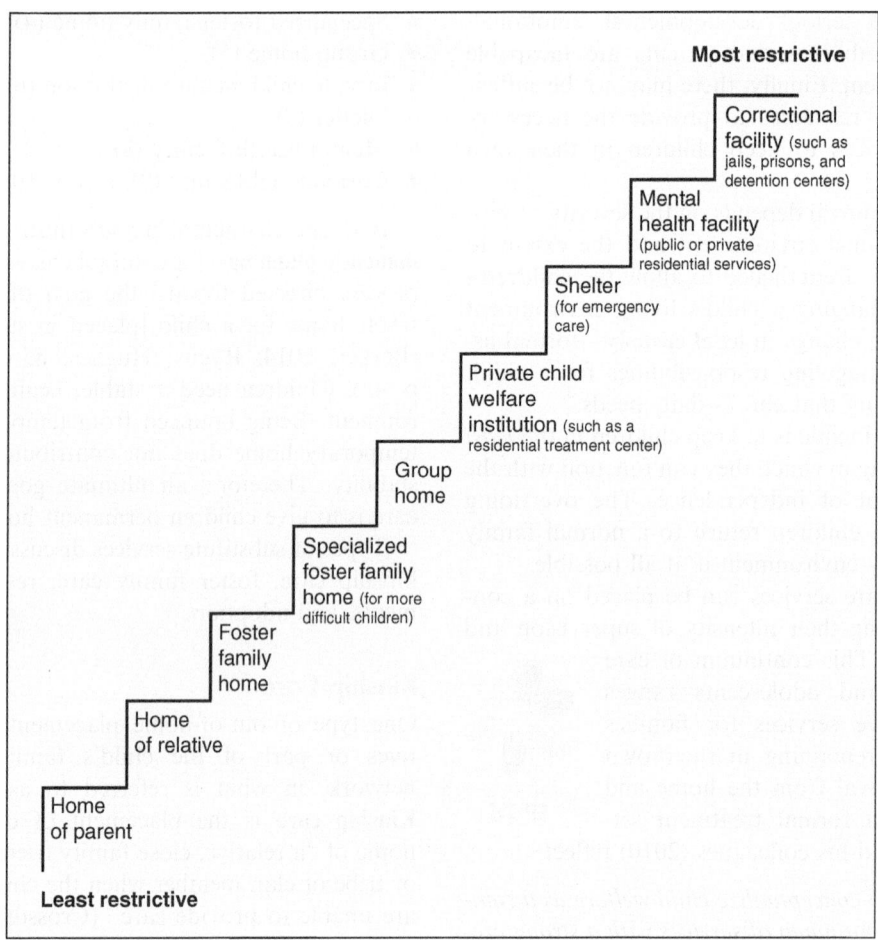

**FIG-9-2** Continuum of Care: Restrictiveness of Setting

pays the caregivers and is expected to monitor the home's compliance with standards to oversee the child's well-being.

## Foster Family Care

**Foster family care** is the provision of substitute care with a family for a planned temporary or extended period when parents or legal guardians are unable to care for a child. Foster care involves a serious placement decision when a family is in such crisis that adequate care for children in their own home is impossible.

At least four basic principles underlie foster care (Crosson-Tower, 2013; Downs et al., 2009; Everett, 2008; Pecora et al., 2010). First, the child's own family is important to the child, so that home environment should be maintained if at all possible. Therefore, supportive services should be provided to keep the child in the home. If the child still must

be removed from the home, efforts should be made to maintain communication between children and parents to support and maintain the parent-child relationship. Second, when the child must be removed from the home, the foster care placement should provide a healthy, nurturing environment until the child is placed in a permanent family setting. Third, the child's own family should be viewed as the client system, with the child's return to a safe, healthy family environment a primary goal. In the event that a return to the family of origin is not viable, a plan for permanent placement should be developed either through adoption by a foster family or for independent living if the child is old enough (Everett, 2008). Fourth, foster parents or child care staff in group homes are viewed as an important part of the treatment team working together toward the goal of permanent placement. Highlight 9.5 discusses some reasons children require foster family care.

## HIGHLIGHT 9.5   REASONS FOR FOSTER FAMILY CARE

Children need foster family care for various reasons (Crosson-Tower, 2013). The family might have an emergency such as a sudden illness or accident. Parents might be under such stress that they cannot care for their children adequately and desperately require relief. They may need time to address their problems and issues such as homelessness or substance abuse. Children may have to be temporarily removed from the home for their own safety because of abuse or neglect. Foster care may reflect a temporary placement to provide residence for the child before more permanent placement in an institution or adoption. The following are examples of reasons for placing children in foster care (Crosson-Tower, 2009):[5]

*Example A:* Cindy, a mother of five children, had heart disease. Although her physician told her to stop, she continued to have children because her religious beliefs prohibited her from using contraception. She had five more but died of a heart attack during the birth of her 10th child. Devin, her husband, was overwhelmed at being left alone with 10 children and began to drink. As an alcoholic, he relinquished his children to foster care but refused to give them up permanently for adoption.

*Example B:* Felicia, age 15, was a serious student who wanted to go to college. Unfortunately, her mother,

Mystique, who was quite unstable and into drugs, was vacillating emotionally between two men—her current boyfriend and her ex-husband. As a result, Mystique moved from one man to the other every six months or so, dragging Felicia with her. Because this forced Felicia to keep switching schools and school districts, her grades began to fall. Seriously depressed, she longed for some stability. Finally, at her wit's end, she slit her wrists in the girls' locker room at school. Her school social worker called protective services, and Felicia was placed in a foster home. Much relieved, Felicia was happy in her new environment, finished school, and applied to college. She still maintained regular contact with Mystique.

*Example C:* Mariko, a single mother, was shocked to find out she had colon cancer. The prognosis was fair to good if she had surgery immediately and underwent the subsequent radiation and chemotherapy. But what would she do with her two children April, age 2, and Mac, age 4, during recovery? Mariko's family lived in a different state, and she had no friends able to care for her children. She decided to place them in foster care until she recovered.

[5]These examples are loosely based on those provided by Crosson-Tower (2009). Details and facts concerning the cases have been changed.

### Types of Foster Family Homes

Depending on their circumstances, children should be placed in the type of foster family care that best serves their needs. At least four types of foster family care reflect special circumstances for children needing more specific types of care—shelter homes, long-term foster homes, specialized foster homes, and treatment foster care (Downs et al., 2009, pp. 299–300). **Shelter homes** provide a transitory haven for children during assessment and placement. **Long-term foster homes** offer an ongoing residence for children unable to return to their parents' home and unadoptable for various reasons. One is that parents refuse to give up guardianship, as in Devin's case in Highlight 9.5. (**Guardianship** is the legal responsibility to care for another person and oversee that person's affairs. A child's guardian assumes decision-making responsibilities, such as giving consent for major surgery. This differs from custody,

whereby the custodian is responsible only for daily care.) Other children aren't adopted because they have serious disabilities or health problems that adoptive parents couldn't afford. Additionally, there is often a shortage of people seeking to adopt children who are not infants.

**Specialized foster homes** serve children with special needs, such as intellectual disabilities or conditions such as fetal alcohol syndrome[6] or being infected with HIV. Other specialized homes prepare older children for living independently. Finally, **treatment foster care** provides specialized treatment for children with serious behavioral and emotional problems. The idea here is that a family setting

[6]Fetal alcohol syndrome (FAS) is "a condition in a fetus characterized by abnormal growth, neurological damage, and facial distortion caused by the mother's heavy alcohol consumption" (Kelly, 2001, p. 567).

offers a less restrictive environment than a group home or institution for children requiring more structured behavioral management. Parents in such homes need specialized training to provide children with a therapeutic experience.

## Social Work Roles in Foster Family Care

Social workers in foster care fulfill various functions. Before foster home placement, a worker must first carefully assess the risk in the child's own family to determine the necessity of removal from the home. The worker must conclude that supportive services will be unable to sustain the children and their family in the home environment.

EP 1

Second, when a foster care placement is necessary, the worker must select the best available foster home. This should be "the least restrictive, most homelike environment possible," one that best meets the child's "particular physical, emotional and social needs" (Rycus et al., 1988, p. 55). For example, it's best to place children closer to their own homes to encourage involvement of the natural parents. Also, the fewer changes (e.g., a different school or lifestyle) the child is forced to experience, the better. The social worker also must assess the child's needs and "anticipated behavior problems" to place the child with a foster family that can best meet those needs (p. 55).

Throughout the foster care pre-placement, placement, and post-placement process, the social worker fulfills a third function: case management (Crosson-Tower, 2013). Coordinating services might require home visits, contacting schools regarding the child's performance, and dealing with crises such as children running away or natural and foster parents arguing.

The fourth function for foster care workers involves counseling and helping the children, natural parents, and foster parents prepare for changes, adjust to new circumstances, and work toward the children's return to the natural home (Crosson-Tower, 2013). The worker should convey clear information about what's happening to all of them and encourage them to ask questions. The worker should also strive to develop "a supportive relationship" with children to help them deal with changes (Rycus et al., 1988, p. 58).

Children often are frightened of the unknown and worry about what will happen to them. They naturally experience a torrent of emotions including rejection, self-blame, anger, despair, depression, and apprehension. The worker may need to help a child verbalize such feelings to deal with them. For instance, a worker might say, "You look like you're about ready to cry. You probably feel really sad right now, and that's OK. You can cry if you like. I have lots of tissues," or, "I know how mad you are about having to move. It's a hard time, and it's OK to feel mad" (Rycus et al., 1988, p. 65). Regardless of how their parents treated them or what mistakes their parents made, children usually continue to care about their parents.

For example, one worker, Jannah, explained how difficult it was for her to work with Angel, a 9-year-old child in foster care (Crosson-Tower, 2009).[7] Before each of her mother's scheduled visits, Jannah would prepare Angel for her mother's visit by talking about how Angel felt toward her mother and what Angel might realistically expect during the visit. As the meeting time approached, Angel would eagerly await her mother by sitting at the front window, watching for her mother's car to pull in the driveway. Sometimes her mother would show up, but more frequently she wouldn't. Then Jannah had to watch Angel bite her lower lip and try to keep from crying in disappointment. Watching Angel's intense pain would infuriate Jannah. However, Jannah forced herself to remember that Angel deeply loved her mother and that their relationship was one of the most important things in Angel's life.

Foster care workers also counsel the birth parents. Sometimes goals involve teaching effective parenting skills and decreasing or controlling stressful life issues (e.g., poverty, substance abuse, social isolation, interpersonal conflict, mental illness). Other times, workers focus on maintaining the parent-child relationship, for several reasons (Crosson-Tower, 2013). It has been found that children adjust better to foster care when they maintain contact with their birth parents. They experience less trauma upon the initial separation. Ongoing involvement with their children may be part of the treatment process for the birth parents. Watching foster parents effectively interact with children may teach birth parents

---

[7]This example is loosely based on one provided by Crosson-Tower (2009). Details and facts concerning the case have been changed.

improved parenting and child management skills. Last, such ongoing contact may facilitate the transition of children returning home in the event that reunion occurs. When children do return home, foster care workers can provide counseling and careful supervision to the birth parents.

Additionally, foster care workers counsel foster parents. This might involve preparing foster parents for a new foster child by providing information or helping foster parents integrate the child into their own family system. Foster care workers help foster parents develop effective ways of handling foster children and attending to their individual needs. These workers also must help foster parents deal with the grief they experience when foster children to whom they're especially attached return home. Finally, foster care workers can act as mediators between birth parents and foster parents.

*Case Example* Jamie, age 13, had lived with his foster parents, Millie and Mert Muffin, since he was 6 months old. The Muffins, who had two other adult children of their own, dearly loved Jamie and considered him an integral member of their family. He also had an ongoing relationship with his birth parents, Jack and Jill Smith, whom he visited every other Sunday. The Smiths had five other children, all older than Jamie.

During his first few months of life, Jamie suffered from a condition called *failure to thrive,* a condition where an infant remains "below the third percentile for weight for a period of time" or demonstrates a significant decrease in the "rate of gaining weight from the time of birth" (Bukatko & Daehler, 2012, p. 181). Despite intensive medical attention, Jamie didn't improve. The Smiths had been involved with their county social services before because of neglect concerning their other children. After a child protective services assessment, the court placed Jamie in foster care with the Muffins.

Jack Smith, who had a 10th-grade education, was a janitor at a local grade school; Jill didn't work outside the home. Along with her twin sister, she had been institutionalized throughout her childhood in a setting for persons with intellectual disabilities or mental illness. She had attended some high school classes but didn't graduate.

Over the years, the Smiths maintained an involvement with the social services system. All of their

children had been in foster care at one time or another. Jamie's siblings all experienced difficulties in school, truancy, or skirmishes with the law. Because of the Smiths' limited ability to cope with raising their five other children, on the one hand, and the stability provided Jamie by the Muffins, on the other, Jamie remained in foster care. A pleasant, cooperative boy who loved both his families, Jamie had an intellectual disability, some congenital orthopedic problems, and poor coordination. He had always attended special education classes.

An ongoing problem was the huge discrepancy in lifestyle and values between the Smiths and the Muffins. Bill, Jamie's foster care worker, was constantly struggling to establish compromises that both families could live with. For example, Jack Smith and Millie Muffin could barely stand being in the same room with each other. Jack felt that Millie "mollycoddled" Jamie to the point of making him a "sissy." Millie thought Jack was a "macho man" who pushed Jamie into inappropriate, dangerous activities such as skateboarding and trampoline jumping—both difficult and dangerous for Jamie with his coordination problems.

Bill worked with the families to help them come to mutual agreements. One was that Jamie join a track team and a bowling league for children with intellectual disabilities. In the past, Millie wouldn't allow him to do so because she feared he'd hurt himself. Furthermore, she would not permit him to attend any activities with other children by himself, but rather stayed there with him. Reluctantly, she agreed to let him attend events alone. For his part, Jack agreed to stop encouraging Jamie to ride a skateboard and play on the trampoline. Instead, Jamie could play baseball or soccer with other children in the Smiths' neighborhood when he visited.

Another problem between the Smiths and the Muffins involved religious differences. The Muffins were Methodist, and the Smiths Roman Catholic. Each couple wanted Jamie to adopt their own faith. Bill helped both couples understand that constant bickering would do neither Jamie nor themselves any good. The reality was that, when Jamie was visiting the Smiths, he would attend the Catholic church with them regardless of what the Muffins requested.

Similarly, when he was with the Muffins, he would attend the Methodist church with them regardless of what the Smiths said. Bill helped the couples agree that this arrangement should continue, given that it was what they would do anyway. When Jamie grew older, he could choose his own faith.

The Smiths and the Muffins would never be best friends. However, Bill helped them realize that both families had Jamie's best interests at heart, despite their radical differences. Bill stressed this as a strength. He also worked with both families to help them focus on Jamie's future. As Jamie entered adolescence, he needed to realize his own capabilities and make his own decisions to the fullest extent possible. Bill discussed with both families the value of vocational aptitude testing—another means of emphasizing Jamie's strengths to best prepare him for his future.

### Important Trends in Foster Care: Permanency Planning and Family Preservation

Crosson-Tower (2009) comments on ongoing trends in foster care that focus on permanency planning.

*At one time the only apparent options for permanency for a child were family reunification or adoption. Today alternatives are considered. For example, there is now extensive exploration of the child's extended family as a potential placement alternative. Kinship care ... is a viable plan for children whose parents cannot care for them but who can find a home with relatives, godparents, or close family friends. This trend may have gained strength from minority families who are connected with their own culture and extended families and who, in the past, have solved child care problems within their own familial circle. However, as increased stressors are placed on these families and they begin to look to the dominant culture to solve more of their problems, formalized kinship agreements may become more effective.*

*The nature of adoption has also changed. In contrast to the closed adoptions of the past, adoptions may now be arranged according to the child's needs. Open adoption, in which the child maintains contact with the birth parents and/or the foster parents, provides children with more consistency while still offering permanence. Subsidized adoptions [where additional funds are provided to adoptive parents for children who have special needs or characteristics that make it difficult for them to be adopted] by adoptive or foster parents help*

*fund stable homes for children whose medical or emotional needs, and the financial obligation inherent in meeting these needs, may have formerly [interfered with or prohibited] ... their ability to be adopted.*

*Finally, permanent foster homes or guardianship arrangements make it possible for many children to have more consistency in their lives. Such arrangement might not have been sanctioned in the past, but today there is greater emphasis on children's needs. (pp. 331–332)*

## Residential Settings: Group Homes, Treatment Centers, and Independent Living Arrangements

**Residential care** is treatment provided by child welfare agencies that reflects greater intensity and restrictiveness on the substitute care continuum than foster family care. They can be more beneficial for some troubled children than their own family environment in several ways. According to the Child Welfare League of America (2005):

*Residential care's primary purpose is to address the unique needs of children and youth who require more intensive services than a family setting can provide. Either on-site or through links with community programs, residential services provide educational, medical, psychiatric, and clinical/mental health services, as well as case management and recreation.... Within residential settings, children and their families are offered a variety of services, such as therapy, counseling, education, recreation, health, nutrition, daily living skills, pre-independent living skills, reunification services, aftercare, and advocacy. (p. 1)*

Residential facilities may demonstrate advantages for some children in a number of ways (Crosson-Tower, 2013; Downs et al., 2009). First, they can provide a treatment **milieu** (an all-encompassing environmental setting), in which rules for how to behave are more clearly specified than in most families, thus providing greater structure. This, in turn, allows for more consistency and predictability in the children's living environment. Many residents feel safer in this more controlled setting.

Second, in most settings children interact with multiple caregivers instead of one or two parents.

This allows children to experience less intensive interactions in a less concentrated emotional and interpersonal environment.

Third, the treatment milieu provides a "group living experience, where children and youths learn to develop responsibility to the group and to develop and improve relational skills and behavior and where peer pressure can have a positive impact" (Cohen, 1992, p. 59).

Fourth, children in residential settings often come with unique histories reflecting wide ranges of behavior. Consider that such children

*come with histories of lying, stealing, fighting, truancy, breaking things, hurting people, and running away. They come with tales of sexual abuse by parents, stepparents, relatives, and live-ins. They come with tales of beatings and confinements in closets and being tied up. They come from parents who yell at them constantly but never discipline them, from homes in which they could do no wrong, and from homes in which they were barely noticed.*

*There are those who fight the program every step of the way, those who have to be pushed or dragged through the program, and those who are*

*so proud of their accomplishments you think they're going to burst. There are those who seem to do everything right, but you wonder what's really going on in their heads.*

*(Stein, 1995, p. 17)*

The residential milieu is oriented to addressing a wide range of emotional and behavioral issues. Therefore, it is designed to tolerate and deal with a wider range of negative behaviors, individualize treatment plans, and attend to children's diverse needs. Conversely, in families, similar rules and expectations often apply to everyone, and more extreme forms of troublesome behavior are unacceptable.

Highlight 9.6 describes scenarios in which children require placement in a residential setting.

Residential settings discussed here include group homes, residential treatment centers, and independent living services. Because most group homes and residential treatment centers are oriented toward mental health, their therapeutic aspects will be discussed in Chapter 13. Correctional facilities for youths that involve incarceration are, of course, the most restrictive on the service continuum. Chapter 16 discusses these further.

## HIGHLIGHT 9.6  WHO IS PLACED IN RESIDENTIAL SETTINGS?

Three examples reflect the types of behavior typically leading to placement in a residential setting.

*Example A:* Robert, age 13, already has a long record of criminal offenses, including theft, assault, and drug possession. He also has flunked several courses at school, having been truant most of the time. Robert lives with his parents, who are alcoholics and have a history of physically abusing him. Because he tends to fly into vicious rages at the least provocation, foster care is not a viable option. The juvenile court has ordered that Robert be placed in a residential facility.

*Example B:* Bree, age 15, constantly fights with her parents. She refuses to go to school, screaming that she hates it. When her parents try to force her to go by driving her there themselves, she leaves school anyway and runs away for several days. She smokes marijuana regularly and has started using crack cocaine. She likes to date men in their 20s and has been sexually active since

age 12. Her parents are at a loss as to what to do. The school social worker suggests residential placement.

*Example C:* Jaron, age 9, stabbed his 6-year-old sister to death. He has a long history of torturing and killing small animals. He has also set several fires in the home that, fortunately, were discovered before major damage was done. He frequently threatens to kill his parents and schoolmates. People around him including his parents fear that he means it. He is referred to a residential treatment center for young children with serious emotional disturbance and behavioral problems.

Each child is unique, so each placement decision must be made based on the problems and needs involved in that particular case. On one hand, children should be placed in the least restrictive setting. On the other, children require placement that can respond to the severity of their problems and the intensity of the supervision required.

## Group Homes

Group homes provide greater structure and more intensive therapeutic care than that found in foster family homes. A **group home** is a setting that provides a substitute living situation and family environment for a group of children originating in different families. A small-group context allows residents to benefit from the group experience, yet still receive enough individual attention and treatment. The actual physical structure of a group home is usually a sizable single-family dwelling that blends into a residential neighborhood. Depending on the residents' needs, it can be staffed either by a live-in married couple or by counselors who work various shifts. Such shifts include those that are overnight where staff remain awake in order to provide supervision when necessary.

Group homes provide more structure than foster family homes but less than residential treatment centers. Thus they allow more "space" for adolescents seeking independence than for those living with their parents while providing consistent expectations and rules. Residents are expected to attend school, do assigned chores, and participate in counseling as specified in their treatment plans.

## Residential Treatment Centers

**Residential treatment centers** are bigger agencies that are more structured and therefore more restrictive than smaller group home settings. They typically consist of either larger dormitory settings or a series of smaller units or cottages forming one center. Each has its own supervising staff and assigns juvenile residents according to such variables as age and type

---

## HIGHLIGHT 9.7 WHO WORKS IN RESIDENTIAL TREATMENT CENTERS?

Residential treatment centers have various responsibilities concerning residents' care and treatment (Crosson-Tower, 2013; Stein, 1995). Basic needs such as food and shelter must, of course, be met, so staff are employed to prepare food and to maintain the building and grounds. Supervisors and administrators oversee service provision, making certain that children are treated appropriately and that treatment plans are carried out. Designated medical staff must be available (although usually not on-site) to meet health and dental needs.

Residential staff attend to the children's daily care and supervise them when they're not in school. Sometimes referred to as counselors or child care workers, residential staff oversee daily living activities, implement treatment plans, and monitor behavior.

Residents' educational needs must also be met. Most children in residential treatment centers are lagging academically. Either their problems have consumed their energy, leaving little or none for academics, or they have long histories of truancy. And once they fall behind in school, there is little incentive to work hard because, compared with their peers, they look and feel like academic failures. Although some residents may attend public school, many remain on-site for their education. The center's educational staff assess children's abilities and develop individualized

educational plans designed to maximize each student's ability to succeed.

Treatment staff attend to the children's emotional and behavioral needs. Consider that

the behavior of children is a major concern in residential treatment and likely to consume considerable time and effort, regardless of the philosophical or treatment orientation of the program. No matter what their other problems may be, it is problems with their behavior that most often bring children into residential treatment.

(Stein, 1995, p. 107)

Social workers, psychologists, and other therapists assess problems and strengths, develop treatment plans, provide individual and group counseling, and work with the other staff components to coordinate services and monitor children's progress. They may also make home visits and do family counseling. Group treatment is very important in residential treatment centers because peer pressure is so significant for children and adolescents. Additionally, most treatment plans involve improving interpersonal relationships. Groups can focus on managing anger, eliminating substance abuse, improving communication and social relationships, or dealing with issues resulting from victimization.

of problem. Structured expectations usually revolve around a behavior management system based on behavior modification approaches. Highlight 9.7 describes the staff working in residential treatment centers.

### Independent Living Services

An alternative available to older adolescents fast approaching adulthood is **independent living services**. These are settings that serve as a transitional residence between out-of-home placement and entrance into adulthood with its onerous responsibilities. Independent living services aim to prepare young people to function independently in society. Services focus on helping them develop skills they can use in their personal and work worlds. These include decision-making, budgeting, and planning skills to organize their lives: educational, vocational, and job search skills to establish a career; and interpersonal skills to develop and maintain relationships.

# Adoption   `L07`

**Adoption** is the legal act of taking in a child born to other parents and formally making that child a full member of the family. Adoptive parents take on all the rights and responsibilities given to birth parents or other former legal guardians, who relinquish all rights concerning that child.

### Types of Adoption

Adoptions are undertaken either by people related to a child by blood or by unrelated adoptive parents. Examples of **blood-related adoptions** include a stepparent married to a birth parent adopting the birth parent's child, grandparents adopting their daughter's child, and other relatives adopting a child born into some branch of their own family.

Unrelated adoptions occur when the adoptive parents have no prior blood link to the child being adopted. **Agency** (or **relinquishment**) **adoptions** are conducted through a public or private social service organization, with the agency contracting with the adoptive parents, providing counseling, assessing the placement, and overseeing the entire adoption process. **Independent adoptions**, in contrast, are

initiated and conducted independently by the adoptive and birth parents, without agency involvement. **International** (or **intercountry**) **adoptions** are those in which parents adopt children from other countries. Federal regulations that require the evaluation and acceptability of the adoptive home and proof of being orphaned govern these adoptions (Barth, 2008, p. 35). **Special needs adoptions** involve children who have traditionally been more difficult to place in adoptive homes. These include children who have special characteristics or circumstances, including physical, intellectual, developmental, or emotional disabilities, racial background, or older age than is usually preferred, such that adoption is difficult without providing medical or other assistance (Barth 2008). Sometimes such adoptions involving financial assistance are referred to as **subsidized adoptions**. Finally, **transracial adoptions** are those by parents of a different race than that of the child. For example, White parents might adopt an African American or Asian child. Highlight 9.8 stresses the importance of cultural competence for social workers in the adoption field or involved in any other aspect of practice with children and families.

### The Adoption Process

Several steps are involved in the adoption process. In step 1, a child is identified as being in need of adoption. For example, children may have been removed from an extremely abusive environment, or the parents may have abandoned them or died.

In step 2, the child must be legally freed so that adoption can take place. Assistance should be given to children to ease the trauma of separation from birth parents or guardians. Similarly, they may require help in adjusting and becoming attached to the new adoptive parents. Guardianship rights of the birth parents must be formally terminated.

In step 3, adoptive parents are selected. Here the social worker conducts a home study in which potential adoptive parents are evaluated on a number of variables. These include "motivation," "stability of the relationship," "age," "physical and emotional health," and "financial stability" (Crosson-Tower, 2013, p. 333).

## HIGHLIGHT 9.8 CULTURAL COMPETENCE ISSUES

Children and adolescents of color are rapidly growing segments of the U.S. population (ProQuest, 2014; U.S. Census Bureau, 2011). Learning about clients' cultures and values is an ongoing process that social workers must continuously pursue. Henderson and Thompson (2011) explain (although they use the term "counselor," their points apply equally well to social workers):

EP 1, 1b, 2, 2a, 2b, 2c

> Counselors [and social workers] will always have opportunities to work with children who have cultural practices and beliefs that the [social workers and] counselors do not know. Baruth and Manning (2007) list the challenges counselors may face in those situations. Counselors may have communication difficulties and may misunderstand the culture and the impact of the culture on the process of counseling [and intervention]. Mental health professionals may hold mistaken assumptions about cultural assimilation [the incorporation of people from another culture into the mainstream culture] and acculturation [adapting the cultural values and expectations of the mainstream society]. The counselor and the client may have different social class values and orientations, and the counselor may be working from stereotypical generalizations. Counselors may make an assumption of cultural bias and may not be able to understand the [client's] world-view [a person's perceptions about how the world should function]. (p. 43)

Henderson and Thompson (2011) continue:

> Children's lives reflect the culture in which they are raised. The rich, varied landscape of the United States includes a constellation of kinship systems, parenting practices, spiritual traditions, and many other ways of being in the world that influence child rearing. When young people enter school, they encounter other children who have family structures, housing arrangements, and other lifestyle differences. Sometimes as the awareness of these disparities increase[s], tension builds as children struggle to reconcile life at home with life at school.

> Children who have ethnic or social class backgrounds different from those of the mainstream population may face challenges related to not being accepted, receiving unfair treatment, being ridiculed, and being subjected to lower expectations. The socio-economic status of a family contributes sometimes favorably and sometimes unfavorably to the activities, friends, education attainment, lifestyle, occupational aspirations, and social roles of the family members. (p. 53)

Social workers must strive to learn about other cultures from their clients in order to understand their clients' life circumstances. Only then will practitioners be able to help these clients effectively. The following are questions social workers might ask to investigate the cultural perspectives of children and their families:

1. "What is the country of origin and cultural identity of the child and his or her family?
2. Which generation of family emigrated [from another country to the United States]?
3. What languages are spoken? Where are the languages spoken [e.g., at home or in the neighborhood]?
4. What English knowledge do the parents have? Can they understand the written word? Spoken word? How adequately can they express themselves in English?
5. What are the sleeping and eating patterns at home?
6. What are the expectations for children in the culture?
7. What is the level of acculturation?
8. Which holidays, celebrations, and cultural responsibilities are important?
9. What is the attitude of the family about play?
10. Who are the playmates of the child at home and in the community?
11. With what materials does the child play? What are the child's play activities?
12. What are the family members' attitudes toward discipline?
13. What are the patterns of discipline?
14. What responsibilities and expectations does the child have at home?" (Fascoli, 1999; Henderson & Thompson, 2011, p. 53; Kottman, 2001)

Evaluation regarding motivation concerns the reasons why applicants want to adopt. Is it because they can't have their own children? Have they looked into the possibility of infertility treatment? Have they lost a child and are trying to replace it? Is it that they want to help some child have his or her own family? If so, to what extent will they be able to deal with this child's "baggage" in terms of the child's past problems? Investigation of the stability of the applicants' relationship is obviously important. Placing a child with people whose attachment and communication are deteriorating certainly is not in the child's best interest. The age variable concerns how "agencies usually consider applicants who are within normal child-rearing ages" (p. 333). However, the child's age is also an important aspect. For example, older children might be placed with older applicants. Because placement should be in the child's best interest, applicants should be healthy and capable of physically and emotionally caring for that child. Physical examinations are required. Additionally, "social workers should look for applicants who appear emotionally stable, are mature, have a good self-concept, and are able to meet a child's emotional needs" (p. 333). Applicants must also be financially stable in order to fulfill an adopted child's physical, educational, social, and other needs. "Despite these requirements [for applicants], agencies often find that they must be flexible, respectful of cultural diversity and increasingly different family values and lifestyles" (Crosson-Tower, 2013, p. 334).

In step 4, after the potential adoptive parents have been approved, the agency places the child with them. The agency social worker helps the adoptive family integrate the child into the family system.

Step 5 involves the family reconfiguring itself and its intra-family relationships to accommodate the new child. Here "adoptive families undergo stresses and adjustments unique to the adoptive experience and lasting throughout the family life cycle whether the child is adopted in infancy or later" (Smith & Howard, 1999, p. 8). At least four types of agency services may be provided after placement. First, education on such issues as child behavior management can be helpful. Second, therapy may be necessary to deal with concerns such as the child's grief at the loss of his or her family of origin or readjustment issues experienced by the entire adoptive family. Third, ongoing support groups may help both parents and adopted children handle emotional and relationship issues. Fourth, adoptive families may need help linking up with necessary resources (e.g., programs offering financial assistance, special education services, and therapy for children requiring special help).

Finally, in step 6, the adoption is formally legalized, and the birth parents' legal rights are terminated.

## Social Work Roles in Adoption

Social workers assume various roles with respect to adoption. They always have the professional responsibility of advocating for children and serving children's best interests. They may help women with unwanted pregnancies evaluate their alternatives and determine the best course of action. Social workers may assess the readiness of a child for adoptive placement, especially if that child is older and has conflicting feelings about permanently leaving birth parents. Social workers may be in the position of helping children cope with their grief at bidding a final farewell to their birth family. One study revealed that adopted children often express strong

**EP 1**

> *feelings of loss and abandonment.... One 6-year-old boy expressed his fear that someone would come and take him away, and talked about his nightmares, which reflected both strong anxiety and grief.... Although some children feared being kidnapped or abandoned again, others voiced their desire, expectation, or hope for a reunion with their birth family.*
>
> *(Smith & Howard, 1999, p. 48)*

One moving incident involved a practitioner who recollected working with "two preschool age brothers who clung together and sobbed over a picture of their mother, trying to stroke her long hair in the photograph" (Downs et al., 1996, p. 331).

Social workers conduct extensive home studies of the appropriateness of potential adoptive families. Finally, social workers may help birth parents, adopted children, and adoptive parents evaluate their situations and choices realistically, make decisions, and cope with issues.

Several other issues characterize adoptive families that social workers can help these families address (Crosson-Tower, 2013):

● *Lack of control:* Adoptive parents may experience feelings of inadequacy and lack of control because of their infertility. They may have been at the agency's mercy for years, patiently waiting for a child to become available. The integration of the child into the family system may be more difficult than they had anticipated.

For example, one adoptive family, the Humperdinks, consisted of two parents, two teenage sons, and a 20-year-old daughter. The Humperdinks wanted to provide a needy child with a good home. The mother was a special education teacher, and the father a newspaper reporter. They adopted Katrine, age 11, whose parents had been killed in a car accident. She was a pleasant child with no history of problematic behavior, so they were totally taken aback by a problem they had never anticipated. The Humperdinks were a family of readers. Typically, one would find all five of them reading various newspapers and magazines and an endless assortment of novels. Katrine, in contrast, was an average student who simply did not enjoy reading. She read only when she had to. The family required fairly extensive counseling to work on such goals as appreciating each family member's unique strengths, including Katrine's, and identifying activities other than reading they could all do together.

● *Something wrong with the kid:* Adoptive family members may worry that the adopted child has negative genetic traits or behavioral problems related to past treatment.

● *Strains on the adoptive mother and marriage:* Adopted children may manifest extreme needs that place pressure on the adoptive mother and, consequently, on the adoptive parents' marriage. Consider that

*the mother is typically the primary focus of the child's anger, extreme dependence, or rejection. Mothers are more likely to be in the child's presence, to discipline the child, and to represent the family to school, neighbors, and others in the community. Mothers are subjected to more of the talking back, noncompliance, and control struggles than fathers.... One mother reported her frustration*

*with her child's unfillable need for reassurance. This child, adopted at age 5, had experienced significant neglect. The child experienced panic when the mother was out of sight, even in the next room. When the mother would use the bathroom, the child would curl up against the door begging her to let him in. Consistent and very frequent reassurance and affection did nothing to alleviate his neediness His incessant need to be near her, and her alone, left the mother feeling trapped and smothered.... The demanding child known by the mother is not the child known by the father. His wife's need to catalog the child's sins, her need for his sympathy, and her frustration and anger often appear exaggerated to the father. He sees a child pretty much being a child. She describes a monster. Tension in the marital pair emerges or is intensified by this very different understanding of the child.*

*(Smith & Howard, 1999, pp. 61–62)*

● *Quest for identity:* Adoptive children often ask themselves who they really are. Born to one set of parents and living with another, what does that make them? How should they think of themselves? How can they be positive about themselves and confident? Counseling is often needed to help them address these concerns.

● *Behavioral acting out* (Downs et al., 2009): It's logical that children who have been uprooted from their birth families experience various degrees of insecurity, apprehension about the future, and pressure to establish their own identities. As a result, as many other children do, some adopted children act out. They may be seeking to establish some control over their lives. They may find that acting out gets them the attention they crave. Or they may use negative actions as a means of keeping themselves emotionally isolated from other people because they're terrified of getting close. They may believe that maintaining emotional distance keeps them from being vulnerable to rejection. Acting-out behaviors may include lying, stealing, committing acts of vandalism, engaging in sexual activity, wetting or soiling, and stockpiling food (Downs et al., 2009; Smith & Howard, 1999).

Focus on Critical Thinking 9.2 addresses several other controversial issues in adoption.

Numerous controversial issues characterize adoption today. First, in recent decades, the number of children available for adoption has *decreased*. Reasons for this include increased use of contraception, the possibility of abortion, and social acceptance of single-parent families. The greatest demand is for healthy, very young, White children, who are in the least supply; children of color, older children, and those with special needs are in the greatest supply.

EP 5c

This leads us to a second issue—*transracial adoption*.

## Critical Thinking Questions

- To what extent is it appropriate for parents of one race to adopt children from another?
- On one hand, adoptive parents are needed for children of color. On the other, to what extent is it in a child of color's best interests to be placed with, for example, White parents?
- To what extent will these children be deprived of the rich fabric of cultural heritage manifested by their own race?
- How can they develop a strong, confident identity as a person of color in a White environment?
- To what extent will that child experience prejudice and discrimination in a social environment dominated by another race?

A third issue concerns *special needs adoption*. Unquestionably, children who have special needs are more difficult and often more expensive to care for.

## Critical Thinking Questions

- To what extent is it fair for agencies to encourage such adoptions when it's difficult for adoptive parents to fully comprehend the responsibilities involved in caring for a child with special needs?
- To what extent should financial burdens fall on such parents? To what degree should financial and medical assistance be provided to such adoptive parents?

A fourth issue involves *open adoption. Openness* is the extent to which, first, information about all parties involved (adopted child, adoptive parents, birth parents) is available, and second, the adoptive child and birth parents maintain contact with each other (Pecora et al., 2010).

## Critical Thinking Questions

- What can the adoptive parents know about the birth parents, and vice versa? What can the adopted child find out about the birth parents?

In the past, many people feared that openness concerning adoption might place children and parents in difficult or confusing positions. However, Grotevant and McRoy (1998) report that this really is not the case. In actuality, openness does not cause children to feel pulled between their family of origin and their adoptive family, or confused about which family is responsible for providing guidance and support.

Many other questions can be raised about openness.

## Critical Thinking Questions

- Should children have ready access to their medical records and birth family history to identify hereditary diseases to which they might be prone?
- To what extent might adoptive parents feel threatened if their adopted children could readily contact the birth parents?
- Who should be allowed to make the decision about whether adoption records should be open? How open should they be—fully or only under some conditions and circumstances? This is a complex issue.

This is a complex issue.

A fifth topic generating controversy involves independent versus agency adoptions. Although the independent adoption process may proceed more quickly than that in agency adoptions, Crosson-Tower (2013) raises three major concerns about independent adoptions. First, there is no guaranteed protection of the child's rights.

No extensive home study is conducted, and no evaluation of the appropriateness of the adoptive family is done. Second, once the child is placed, no follow-up is performed. No one monitors the extent to which the child is integrated into the family or whether the child is thriving. Third, there are no guarantees of confidentiality as there are in agency adoptions.

One other question about independent adoption involves the potential of black market adoptions, in which babies can be sold (Mather et al., 2007).

## Critical Thinking Question

- To what extent does the flexibility inherent in independent adoption make black market adoption possible?

# Chapter Summary

The following summarizes this chapter's content as it relates to the learning objectives presented at the beginning of the chapter. Chapter content will help prepare students to:

## LO1 Emphasize the wide diversity in families and their structures.

Families involve primary groups, mutual obligations, and common habitation. Family structure is "the nuclear family as well as those nontraditional alternatives to nuclear family which are adopted by persons in committed relationships and the people they consider to be 'family'" (CSWE, 2002). Variations in family structures include single-parent families, stepfamilies, blended families, and intergenerational families. Lesbian, gay, and bisexual families experience a special risk of discrimination.

## LO2 Describe child welfare and its continuum of services.

*Child welfare* is the traditional term for the network of policies and programs designed to empower families, promote a healthy environment, protect children, and meet children's needs. Child welfare services respond to a continuum of need ranging from limited to moderate to extensive.

## LO3 Examine supportive services in child welfare (including child maltreatment and child protective services, family preservation, child day care, family life education, and respite care).

Supportive services involve the provision of external support to enhance family functioning while children remain in the home. They include basic financial assistance, mental health treatment, child protective services, intensive family preservation services, day care, family life education, and respite care.

Child maltreatment is the umbrella term for physical abuse, sexual abuse, and neglect, and psychological abuse. Physical abuse involves injury and results in physical and behavioral symptoms. Sexual abuse entails sexual activity with children. Incest involves sexual intercourse between family members. Child neglect concerns failure to provide for a child's needs. Psychological abuse entails

belittlement, humiliation, and causing damage to self-esteem. Almost 2 million cases of child maltreatment are reported and investigated in the United States annually. Child protective services are interventions aimed at protecting children at risk of maltreatment. The assessment of risk and protective factors is an important aspect of treatment planning.

Family preservation services are concentrated services provided to families in crisis in order to strengthen the family and prevent children's out-of-home placement. Child day care is an agency or program that provides supervision and care for children while parents or guardians are at work or otherwise unavailable. Family life education involves learning experiences for the purpose of increasing people's knowledge, developing skills, or enhancing self-awareness concerning issues relevant at some point during the life span. Respite care is supervision of a child by another caregiver, allowing the parent an interval of relief from the responsibilities of child care.

## LO4 Engage in critical thinking (about advocacy to combat child maltreatment and controversial issues in adoption).

Critical thinking questions regarding child maltreatment involve the conservative–liberal and residual–institutional orientations to addressing the issue. Questions concerning adoption include those examining transracial adoption, special needs adoption, openness about information, and independent adoptions.

## LO5 Address the need to advocate for resources (for children and families).

Advocacy is a major responsibility for social workers. Ongoing advocacy is needed to increase quality, accessible day care; improve maternal and child health; prevent and address child maltreatment; and help families get out of poverty.

## LO6 Describe substitute placements for children.

Substitute services assume all aspects of parental responsibilities on a temporary or permanent basis. Kinship care involves informal or formal placement with a relative or part of the child's family's supportive network. Foster family care is the provision of substitute care with a family for a planned temporary or extended period when parents or legal guardians are unable to care for a child. Permanency planning is currently an important theme in foster care. A group home provides a substitute setting and family environment for a group of children originating from different families. Residential treatment centers are bigger agencies that are more structured and provide daily care, meet educational needs, and address emotional and behavioral issues. Independent living services provide out-of-home placement for youths approaching adulthood during their transition to adulthood.

*LO7 Discuss adoption.*

Adoption is the legal act of taking in a child born to other parents and formally making that child a full member of the family. Types of adoptions include blood-related, unrelated, agency, independent, international, special needs (often subsidized), and trans-racial adoptions. Social workers can help adoptive families address issues involving lack of control, concerns about the adopted child, pressures on adoptive parents, and psychological and behavioral issues of the child.

## LOOKING AHEAD

This chapter addressed the needs of families by focusing on children. Chapter 10 will shift the focus to the other end of the life span by talking about older adults—their needs and the policies and programs that serve them.

## COMPETENCY NOTES

The following identifies where Educational Policy (EP) competencies and their component behaviors are discussed in the chapter.

**EP 1 (Competency 1)—Demonstrate Ethical and Professional Behavior.** *(p. 288):* Professional social workers should be knowledgeable about the history of the profession; child welfare reflects an important facet of that history. *(p. 294):* Professional roles in child protective services are discussed. *(p. 296):* Professional roles include the broker and case management roles, as the case example illustrates. *(p. 308):* Professional social work roles involve ethical decision-making and effective treatment planning in the context of foster family care. *(p. 314):* As a professional social worker, learning about clients' cultures and values is a life-long process. *(p. 315):* Professional social work roles and behavior involve ethical decision-making and effective treatment planning in the context of work in adoption.

**EP 1b Use reflection and self-regulation to manage personal values and maintain professionalism in practice situations.** *(p. 286):* Social workers should use reflection and self-regulation to manage personal values and not let them negatively affect practice with nonheterosexual clients. *(p. 314):* Social workers should use reflection and self-regulation to manage personal values and prevent them from interfering with culturally sensitive practice.

**EP 2 (Competency 2)—Engage Diversity and Difference in Practice.** *(p. 286):* Sexual orientation is a dimension of diversity. Social workers should recognize the extent to which gay and lesbian people are oppressed and alienated. Information is provided and questions are posed to assess the oppression and discrimination experienced by people with nonheterosexual orientations. *(p. 287):* Social workers should be knowledgeable about human rights issues such as gay rights and gay marriage from a global perspective. *(p. 292):* Social workers should recognize the global interconnections of oppression, in this case, regarding the child slave trade. *(p. 314):* People with cultural values and customs that differ from the mainstream ones may be oppressed and marginalized.

**EP 2a Apply and communicate understanding of the importance of diversity and difference in shaping life experiences in practice at the micro, mezzo, and macro levels.** *(p. 286):* Social workers must recognize how sexual orientation shapes life experiences. *(p. 314):* Practitioners should recognize the extent to which cultural values and customs shape life experiences.

**EP 2b Present themselves as learners and engage clients and constituencies as experts of their own experiences.** *(p. 314):* Social workers should view themselves as learners and seek knowledge about cultural values and customs from their clients.

**EP 2c Apply self-awareness and self-regulation to manage the influence of personal biases and values in working with diverse clients and constituencies.** *(p. 286):* Social workers must work hard at gaining self-awareness regarding any prejudices and stereotypes they may harbor toward people with nonheterosexual orientations. *(p. 314):* Social workers should strive to develop self-awareness concerning their own cultural values and biases in order to work effectively with people from diverse groups.

**EP 3 (Competency 3)—Advance Human Rights and Social, Economic, and Environmental Justice.** *(p. 292):* Social workers should understand the oppression experienced by African children who are victims of the slave trade.

**EP 3a Apply their understanding of social, economic, and environmental justice to advocate for human rights at the individual and system levels.** *(p. 286):* Social workers should advocate for human rights on the behalf of people with nonheterosexual orientations. *(p. 298):* Practitioners should advocate for children's human rights by supporting policies that stop and prevent child maltreatment. *(p. 302):* Social workers should advocate for policies and resources that make high-quality day care available to everyone who needs it, regardless of socioeconomic status. *(p. 304):* Social workers should advocate for policies that advance the social well-being of children.

**EP 5 (Competency 5)—Engage in Policy Practice.**

**EP 5a Identify social policy at the local, state, and federal level that impacts well-being, service delivery, and access to social services.** *(p. 298):* Potential policy changes are discussed that would improve access to services to combat child maltreatment. *(p. 302):* Potential policy requirements are discussed that would improve policy governing day-care provision.

**EP 5b Assess how social welfare and economic policies impact the delivery of and access to social services.** *(p. 298):* Potential policy changes are discussed and questions posed to discuss how policy changes could improve the delivery of and access to social services concerning child

maltreatment. *(p. 302):* Potential policy requirements are discussed that would improve the delivery of social services involving day-care provision.

**EP 5c Apply critical thinking to analyze, formulate, and advocate for policies that advance human rights and social, economic, and environmental justice.** *(p. 286):* Social workers should strive to establish policies and programs that advance the social well-being of people with nonheterosexual orientations. *(p. 298):* Critical thinking questions are posed concerning the conservative–liberal and residual–institutional orientations in terms of policies to address child maltreatment. *(p. 302):* Social workers should advocate for policies and resources that make high-quality day care available to everyone who needs it, regardless of socioeconomic status. *(p. 317):* Critical thinking questions are raised concerning controversial issues and policies in adoption.

**EP 7 (Competency 7)—Assess Individuals, Families, Groups, Organizations, and Communities.**

**EP 7a Collect and organize data, and apply critical thinking to interpret information from clients and constituencies.** *(p. 291):* Categories of assessment concerning psychological maltreatment are identified to prepare workers for appropriately collecting, organizing, and interpreting client data. *(p. 293):* Causes of child maltreatment are discussed to prepare social workers for the assessment process. *(p. 294):* Social workers must collect and organize the appropriate data during assessment to develop effective treatment plans.

**EP 7b Apply knowledge of human behavior and the social environment, person-in-environment, and other multidisciplinary theoretical frameworks in the analysis of assessment data from clients and constituencies.** *(p. 294):* Social workers can use the theoretical framework of risk and resiliency assessment to determine how to proceed in child maltreatment cases.

**EP 7c Develop mutually agreed-on intervention goals and objectives based on the critical assessment of strengths, needs, and challenges within clients and constituencies.**

*(p. 294):* Needs and challenges in the form of risk factors in addition to strengths potentially demonstrating resiliency should be assessed in child maltreatment cases.

**EP 7d Select appropriate intervention strategies based on the assessment, research knowledge, and values and preferences of clients and constituencies.** *(p. 289):* This case example discusses the selection of appropriate intervention strategies when providing supportive services. *(p. 294):* Child protective services implement interventions that seek to prevent future child maltreatment. *(p. 305):* Intervention strategies for the treatment of children, when appropriate, should involve placement in the least restrictive setting.

**EP 8 (Competency 8)—Intervene with Individuals, Families, Groups, Organizations, and Communities.**

**EP 8a Critically choose and implement interventions to achieve practice goals and enhance capacities of clients and constituencies.** *(p. 298):* Treatment approaches that emphasize family preservation seek to prevent the removal of children from their own homes.

**EP 8b Apply knowledge of human behavior and the social environment, person-in-environment, and other multidisciplinary theoretical frameworks in interventions with clients and constituencies.** *(p. 294):* Social workers can use the theoretical framework of risk and resiliency assessment to determine how to intervene in child maltreatment cases.

**EP 8c Use inter-professional collaboration as appropriate to achieve beneficial practice outcomes.** *(p. 296):* Working in protective services often requires inter-professional collaboration with other agencies for effective treatment.

**EP 8d Negotiate, mediate, and advocate with and on behalf of diverse clients and constituencies.** *(p. 286):* Social workers should advocate for people with nonheterosexual orientations. *(p. 298):* Practitioners should advocate for policies and services that advance children's well-being by stopping and preventing child maltreatment. *(p. 302):* Social workers should advocate for policies and resources that make high-quality day care available to everyone who needs it, regardless of socioeconomic status. *(p. 304):* Social workers should advocate for policies that advance the social well-being of children.

# 10 Social Work and Services for Older Adults

David Grossman/Alamy

## Learning Objectives   This chapter will help prepare students to:

**LO 1**   Describe the issue of "global graying." **Highlight 10.1** (p. 325)

**LO 2**   Demonstrate empowerment when working with older adults (that incorporates values and goals, and provide case examples of active aging). **An Empowerment Perspective** (p. 326)

**LO 3**   Discuss issues older adults commonly face (including ageism, discrimination in employment, poverty, retirement, health-care issues, abuse, living conditions and family variables, and transitional issues). **Common Issues Facing Older Adults** (p. 328)

**LO 4**   Engage in critical thinking (about confronting myths about older adults, financing Social Security, determining whether Social Security discriminates against women, and proposing

how older adults might be empowered through macro practice). **Focus on Critical Thinking 10.1** (p. 330)

**LO 5**   Explain the concept of "gayging." **Highlight 10.2** (p. 337)

**LO 6**   Examine contexts for social work practice with older adults (including home-and community-based services, discharge planning in hospital settings, and service provision in nursing homes). **Contexts for Social Work Practice with Older Adults** (p. 338)

**LO 7**   Explore empowerment strategies for diverse older adult populations (including African American grandparents who are primary caregivers for grandchildren and the culturally competent treatment of older Navajo people residing in a nursing home). **Empowerment for Diverse Populations of Older Adults** (p. 343)

*Consider the following facts:*

- *In 2012, more than 13.7% of U.S. residents were 65 or older (ProQuest, 2014).*
- *It is estimated that in 2050 that figure will increase to 20.9% (ProQuest, 2014).*
- *It is predicted that the percentage of people in the United States age 65 and older will be 14.8% in 2015 and will increase to 20.9% in 2050 (ProQuest, 2014).*
- *"The great advances in health and well-being of the 20th century will lead to significant increases in the average life span in the 21st century" (White House, 2005b). For example, it is projected that people born in 2010 will live almost eight years longer than those born in 1970 (ProQuest, 2014).*

*People in the United States generally live longer than people in many other countries because of better nutrition and living conditions and significant advances in medicine and technology. On one hand, a higher proportion of older people means more people who are either retired or unable to work due to health reasons.*

*On the other, it means a smaller proportion of younger workers who pay taxes on current earnings and support social programs. Lower birth rates have also contributed to fewer people entering the workforce. This ratio of workers (paying taxes into Social Security) to recipients (of Social Security benefits) is referred to as the **dependency ratio**. It compares the number of people age 65 and older to 100 people of traditional working age; the U.S. Census Bureau predicts that the dependency ratio will increase from 21 in 2010 to 28 in 2020 to 35 in 2030 with respect to older adults (Ortman, Velkoff, & Hogan, 2014). The Social Security Administration (2014a) indicates that today there are 2.8 workers to support every older adult; it predicts that by 2033 there will be only 2.1 workers for every older adult. The increase in the older adult population reflects the retirement of baby boomers (people born between 1946 and 1964 when birth rates skyrocketed after World War II).*

*Older adults who receive benefits depend on workers to keep Social Security afloat. Potential issues resulting from this trend include an increasing burden on future workers to support older generations (the higher the dependency ratio, the greater the burden), significantly less money collected from taxes on earnings for social services and programs, deteriorating pension programs because of inadequate support, and struggles among members of different age groups for shrinking resources (Mooney, Knox, & Schacht, 2015). For whatever reason, most people think of 65 as the general retirement age (although, as we will discuss, the age for receiving full Social Security benefits is gradually creeping up).*

*Of course, this does not mean that all people work until age 65, their hair turns gray, and they abruptly retire. In reality, some people retire at age 65, others at 40, and still others at 80 or older. Consider the famous comedian and actor George Burns, who continued to tell stories and crack amazingly clever jokes until two years before his death at age 100. My own Aunt Mabel worked as a maid at a motel until age 82, when she no longer had the strength to drag the heavy service carts up the outside stairways in the summer heat and winter snow. There were no elevators available. (She was still active and driving at age 94.)*

*In view of this changing world, the increasing numbers of older adults, and dwindling resources, there are various implications for social work and social workers. (Note that Highlight 10.1 addresses a similar scenario on a global basis.) First, social workers will be called on to serve increasing numbers of older adults; indeed, social work with this population is a rapidly growing field. Second, social workers will be primary proponents of emphasizing and building on the strengths of older adults to maximize their self-determination and quality of life. Third, developing policies and services to meet future needs is an important priority in social welfare. Fourth, advocacy on behalf of older adults for essential resources and services will surely be necessary.*

## HIGHLIGHT 10.1

## INTERNATIONAL PERSPECTIVES: "GLOBAL GRAYING" AND EMPOWERMENT OF OLDER ADULTS

**LO 1**

EP 3

"Global graying" is an international "phenomenon that affects the smallest Pacific islands as well as the most developed welfare states" (George, 1997, p. 57). Consider that throughout history, people age 65 or older never made up more than 2–3% of the total population; today they make up "14% of the population in developed nations," which is expected to rise to 18% in 2023 and to as high as 25% of the total population in 30 years (Kornblum & Julian, 2012, p. 293).

Older adults are treated very differently depending on their culture. Mooney and colleagues (2009) provide the following facts:

- Some tribal societies simply let older adults die or actually kill them when these people are no longer "useful" and, instead, require care.
- Scandinavian nations pay for home care services for older adults who remain in their homes but require assistance in daily tasks such as food preparation and cleaning.
- "Eastern cultures such as Japan revere [older adults,] ... in part, because of their presumed proximity to honored ancestors" (p. 482).

It is anticipated that the world will face at least three key issues as greater numbers of people age (George, 1997). First, "it is expected that graying will bring greater dependence as a result of greater longevity accompanied by chronic ill health" (p. 59). Second, "there will be an inadequate supply of caregivers because of smaller family sizes (for example, China's one-child policy and a resulting family structure of four grandparents, two

parents, and one child), [and] women's increasing participation in paid employment outside the home" (p. 60). Third, "state finances will be inadequate to support the increasing dependence of older people" (p. 60).

What can social workers do about this from a global perspective? Social workers bring with them at least three strengths as they address the issues involved in aging (George, 1997). First, they emphasize self-determination and the achievement of maximum autonomy. Second, they focus on changing not only the individual but also the environments encompassing the individual including the political milieu. Third, they build plans that stress existing strengths.

Social workers can advocate on behalf of older adults around the world to establish policies and services that meet their vital needs for "health and autonomy" (George, 1997, p. 68). Initiatives can include:

- Educating the public to see older adults as a "resource" instead of as a burden (Torres-Gil & Puccinelli, 1995, p. 164).
- Expanding community-based care to maintain people in their own homes as long as possible.
- Providing supportive measures (e.g., financial assistance, tax incentives, respite care) to family members who care for aging relatives.
- Emphasizing the significance of older adults as having sufficient numbers to wield political clout and become important participants in the political process.
- Educating upcoming generations to prepare to care for an increasing proportion of older adults, on the one hand, and for themselves as they age, on the other.

# An Empowerment Perspective

**LO 2**

An empowerment approach for working with older adults stresses at least five basic values (KPMG Consulting, 2002, p. 12). First, older adults should be treated with "dignity"; they should be "treated with respect regardless of the situation." Their self-esteem is essential. Second, older adults should be "in control" of their own

**EP 7c**

lives, making their own choices and doing as much for themselves as possible. Third, active "participation" in family and community life and activities is vital. Older adults' views regarding social policies and practices should be encouraged and appreciated. Fourth, they should be treated fairly and have their rights treated equally with those of other citizens. Fifth, older adults have the right to "security" that includes "adequate income" and "access to a safe and supportive living environment." The conceptual model for healthy aging in Alberta, Canada, included four major goals to pursue on the behalf of older adults (KPMG Consulting, 2002):

- Promoting health and preventing disease and injury—*enabling people to increase control over and improve their health. Health promotion focuses on enhancing the capabilities and capacities of individuals, families and communities to make healthy choices and develop healthy and supportive environments.*
- Optimizing mental and physical function—*enabling people to remain as independent as possible in carrying out the routines of daily living.*
- Managing chronic conditions—*enabling people to effectively manage conditions caused by injuries or diseases, by facilitating self-care and independence and using collaborative approaches with professionals and caregivers.*
- Engaging with life—*enabling people to have meaningful relationships with others and be involved in activities that are satisfying and purposeful. (p. 1)*

Rizzo and Seidman (2009) reflect:

*This conceptual model incorporates the different levels of society and encompasses macro, mezzo, and micro perspectives. It focuses on the health of the population, the health-care systems, and the availability of partnerships that are capable of developing health strategies. Furthermore, it connects with the individual by incorporating some of social work's core values, including dignity, autonomy, participation, fairness, security, and recognizing and building on strengths and capacities (KPMG, 2002). The strategic framework … takes into account health determinants, health strategies, and partnerships.… [F]ive crucial methods of promoting health [include]: developing policy, building supportive environments, enriching community action, expanding individual skills, and enhancing awareness of the framework among health services (KPMG, 2002). (p. 6)*

Generally speaking, an empowerment perspective for older adults involves giving them respect, appreciating difference, valuing their choices, and promoting health. This is so when interacting at the individual level. It is also so in terms of how older adults are treated in their communities and by social policies.

## Active Aging

Rizzo and Seidman (2009) discuss the concept of *active aging:*

*The [World Health Organization] (2002) coined the term active aging based on the concept of healthy aging. However, active aging conveys a more inclusive definition that goes beyond the principles of health care to include the human rights of older adults and the United Nations' principles of independence, participation, dignity, care, and self-fulfillment. The term "active" represents one's participation in social, economic, cultural, spiritual, and civic affairs throughout life. The WHO (2002) conceptualization of active aging is based on three concepts: participation in life, meaning the family and community; health, meaning health promotion and activities to maintain an optimal health status; and security, including financial, community, and family security. (p. 4)*

Hillier and Barrow (2011) provide a number of examples of older adults who are actively involved in life:

- *Playing music can bring great joy to people of any age ("Making Music," 2005). Music can decrease stress and lower blood pressure. It provides an excellent hobby for people who used to play and are now retired with more time to spend doing what they want. Joyce Gast, who lives in Miami, picked up her French horn after a lull of 15 years and joined a band in the community: one of her fellow band members is 90 years old ("Making Music," 2005). Playing music even can be enjoyed by those who never played before. "For instance, Judy Murray of Winchester, Massachusetts, took up violin at age 51"; she laughs at how she is struggling to learn, but says she enjoys it each time she plays ("Making Music," 2005).*

- *Frances Woofenden, 84, is a "competitive trick water skier who also bikes 10 miles a day" (Smith, 2009). She's proud of her strong and flexible knees on which she can elegantly maneuver "like a dancer"; she also takes pride in her appearance and prefers wearing "cotton-candy colored lipstick" (Smith, 2009). Woofenden has gained national attention and has starred in television commercials and magazine adds sponsoring V8 that stress a healthy lifestyle.*

- *Gloria Cox hasn't been able to walk for a long time without the assistance of a walker, but more recently has acquired a new skill (Karas, 2009, cited in Hillier & Barrow, 2011, pp. 227–228). Cox has arthritis, but used to love to bowl. Teen volunteers taught her how to play electronically on a Wii bowling video game. She says it's not quite the same, but she swings her arm using the same motion as she did when she was trying to knock down real bowling pins. However, now she can remain contentedly in her chair. She's having fun.*

- *Lorraine, 92, and Roland, 93, reunited and married after many decades of separation (Garvey & Houde, 2009). After going their own ways early on in their youth, both married others,* had children, and subsequently lost their spouses when they died. Loraine's and Roland's siblings, who had kept in touch, eventually helped Loraine and Roland reconnect. "The look in their eyes just before they kissed for the first time as husband and wife echoed the innocent gazes in the picture on the altar"; the photo of them had been taken in the 1920s with Roland wearing old coveralls and Lorraine having bobbed hair and wearing a simple frock (Garvey & Houde, 2009).

- *Former President Jimmy Carter provides a superb example of active aging and the pursuit of civic duty. After leaving presidential office following his 1980 defeat, Jimmy Carter faced "'an altogether new, unwanted, and potentially empty life' at the age of 56" (American Experience, 2010). Instead, in 1982 he used his determination and energy to open the Carter Center and become extensively involved in humanitarian efforts. The Center "has developed dozens of programs to alleviate suffering and improve lives around the world. Its efforts fall broadly under two categories, 'Waging Peace' and 'Fighting Disease.' The Carters' peace work includes conflict resolution, election monitoring, and the promotion of human rights and democracy. Health programs include agricultural initiatives to eliminate hunger in Africa, Rosalynn Carter's mental health task force, and programs to control or eradicate preventable diseases afflicting the world's poorest people" (American Experience, 2010). In addition, Jimmy Carter has also established a poignant role as an older adult statesperson; he has undertaken diplomatic missions under each president following Ronald Reagan, including peace missions to Ethiopia, North Korea, Haiti, and the former Yugoslavia (American Experience, 2010). "In May 2002 he became the highest American official to visit Cuba since Fidel Castro came to power, receiving front-page coverage which showed he had not exactly retired from the world stage, even at the age of 77" (American Experience, 2010).*

The important thing for social workers is to focus on the strengths of older adults. Yes, increasing age does bring with it some developing problems over time. However, emphasizing the interests, talents, and assets of older adults focuses on the positives instead of dwelling on the negatives. Practitioners should establish a mind-set of listening well to their older adult clients, encouraging them to fulfill their dreams, and helping them accomplish their goals.

Because social workers are helpers, they typically have contact with older adult clients who are dealing with issues and problems. Therefore, much of this chapter focuses on common concerns and difficulties faced by older adults within the context of empowering them.

## Demographic Characteristics of Older Adults: Race, Gender, and Social Class

Three important variables in discussing the older adult population are race, gender, and social class. People of color represent about 20% of older adults in the United States (Macionis, 2013; U.S. Census Bureau, 2011). Projections suggest this will increase to 25% in 2035; the population of older adults of color is expected to grow at a rate almost 2 1/2 times that of the White older adults between 2004 and 2030 (Mooney, Knox, & Schacht, 2009). This is partially due to higher fertility rates and increased immigration, especially on the part of Hispanics; note, however, that the gap in fertility rates among racial groups in the United States has been dwindling (Mather, 2015; University of Nebraska Omaha, 2015). The fact that people of color tend to experience higher rates of heart disease, diabetes, and arthritis than Whites has direct implications for social workers and other professionals working in health care (Mooney et al., 2009; Newman, 2000).

EP 2

Although the overall U.S. population is approximately 49% male and 51% female, the population of people age 65 and older is about 43.6% male and 56.4% female (ProQuest, 2014). The average life expectancy for women is age 81, and for men 78.7 (ProQuest, 2014). People age 65 and older are most likely to die from heart disease, cancer, chronic lower respiratory diseases, and stroke in that order (ProQuest, 2014). Note, however, that women are more likely than men to suffer from "disabling diseases

such as arthritis, Alzheimer's, diabetes, deafness, cataracts, broken bones, digestive conditions, and osteoporosis" (Kirk & Okazawa-Rey, 2010, p. 220).

In previous chapters we established how women are more likely to be poor and to earn less than men, even for comparable work. Living longer means savings must be stretched out further, which means women are more likely to run out of money toward the end of their lives. In addition, earning less or not working outside the home means they are likely to receive lower Social Security benefits. "In 2011, 3.6 million [older adults] … (or 8.7%) were living in poverty in the United States"; women are more likely to be poor (10.7%) than men (6.6%) (Leon-Guerrero, 2014, p. 149). The social welfare system and social workers must, therefore, be prepared to address this population's needs.

Social class is the third important variable affecting older adults. People populating the lower social classes tend to have shorter life expectancies, to experience more severe incapacitating illnesses, and generally to have a lower quality of life (Mooney et al., 2009). One study revealed that 26% of people age 65 or older who have annual incomes of at least $35,000 label their health as "excellent"; in contrast, only 10% of older adults with incomes less than $10,000 could say the same thing (Mooney et al., 2009; Seeman & Adler, 1998). People of lower social classes generally are "chronically unemployed, underemployed, dependent on welfare, or working for a subsistence wage" (Longres, 2000, p. 239). Many barely survive, let alone have enough resources to save for old age.

## Common Issues Facing Older Adults

**LO 3**

I just told my father, age 73, who is a retired MSW social worker, that at this moment I'm writing about problems experienced by older adults. (He happens to be at my home planting daffodil bulbs for next spring.) He replied, "Older adults don't have problems. Why are you writing about that?" The point is that it's easy to focus on all the negatives about growing older instead of the positives.

This chapter emphasizes how social work with older adults is founded on clients' strengths and seeks to maximize their well-being. However, older people are more likely to experience some types of problems than are those who are younger. As people age, they eventually become weaker and more vulnerable to certain illnesses and diseases. **Primary aging** refers to the fact that physiological variables involving such decline will inevitably occur. However, there are huge variations among people concerning how fast this progresses. **Secondary aging**, then, concerns how the primary aging process can either be hastened or slowed by lifestyle and behavior. Factors that can slow aging include physical exercise, healthful diet, stress management, and ready access to adequate resources and medical treatment (McInnis-Dittrich, 2014; Quadagno, 2005; Seeman & Adler, 1998).

The following section addresses some of the problematic issues affecting older adults. The intent is to establish the context for how social workers strive to focus on their strengths and meet their needs. Such matters include ageism, discrimination in employment, poverty, retirement, health care, older adult abuse, living conditions, and transitional issues.

## Ageism

**Ageism** involves harboring negative images of and attitudes toward people simply because they are older. Ageism is similar to sexism or racism in that it involves prejudice toward and discrimination against people who fit into a certain category. Ageism, like sexism and racism, also fails to identify individual strengths as means  **EP 2** of empowerment. Focus on Critical Thinking 10.1 reviews some of the typical myths and stereotypes about older people that are grounded in ageism.

One example of ageism involves how the media typically emphasize the importance of youth, beauty, strength, and physical prowess. For example, advertisers pitch expensive facial creams that minimize wrinkles and bring back youthful glow to aging skin. Still other reflections of ageism are discussed in the following sections.

## Discrimination in Employment

One survey of 1,400 workers revealed that younger and older workers view the employment status of older workers quite differently. More than half of the workers age 50 and older felt that people in their age group were valued by employers; however, only 25% of workers in younger age groups felt people age 50 and older were valued employees (Porter & Walsh, 2005). It's true that people in general will eventually experience increased weakness and slowness as they age. However, this occurs at vastly different rates depending on the individual. Additionally, the younger old—those closer to age 65—are much more likely to enjoy good health than the older old—those age 85 and older.

Congress passed the Age Discrimination in Employment Act (ADEA) in 1967 that prohibited discrimination against people age 40–65. This means that employers can no longer do things like advertise for employees "who are under 30." However, employers can still state that a job is "entry level" or requires "2–3 years' experience," and then reject older people on the basis of being "overqualified" (Mooney et al., 2009, p. 502).

The ADEA also did little to help people age 65 and older. As the next section explains, many older adults require additional income to keep afloat, and many want to work.

## Poverty

Whereas until the early part of the 20th century older adults were very likely poor, Social Security currently supports a large proportion of older people. Of the older adults living in the United States, almost half would fall below the poverty line if they were not receiving Social Security benefits (Karger & Stoesz, 2014). These benefits do not make people rich. In January 2015, average monthly benefits for retired workers were $1,328 (SSA, 2014a). However, lumped together with personal savings, other assets, and occasionally pensions, these benefits allow many people to make it.

Poverty rates for older adults vary widely depending on age, gender, and race. Barusch (2015) explains:

*The very old have lower incomes, primarily because at higher ages we see a disproportionately high number of single women.... Similarly, the very old are also more likely to live on incomes below poverty. Americans 80 years or older had a poverty rate of 11.5 percent in 2008, and 29.6 percent lived on incomes at or below 125 percent of the poverty level (U.S. Census Bureau, 2009).*

# CONFRONTING MYTHS ABOUT OLDER ADULTS

**LO 4**

One dimension of critical thinking involves evaluating assumptions made by many people. Numerous stereotypes about older adults are cited here (Greene, 2000; Harrigan & Farmer, 2000; Hillier & Barrow, 2011). Confronting stereotypes involves *asking* questions, *assessing* facts, and *asserting* a conclusion.

## Critical Thinking Questions

**EP 1b, 2, 2c, 7a**

What are your conclusions about each of the following myths?

*Myth A:* All older adults are burdened with multiple physical complaints and are riddled with disease.

*Fact:* Older adults do experience increasing weakness and illness as they age. Of people age 65 or older, 80% experience at least one form of chronic illness, such as arthritis, heart disease, or diabetes (Coleman & Kerbo, 2009). However, as with the younger population, huge variation exists concerning individual health status. Regardless of age, some people are simply healthier and stronger than others, for many reasons. A healthful lifestyle in terms of diet and exercise correlates with better health. Newman and Newman (2015) report:

> The level of independent functioning among adults 80 years and older is high.... The area of greatest limitation is walking. The percentage of adults needing assistance is small for those ages 65 to 74, increases slightly for those 75 to 84, and increases markedly for those 85 and older. However, even among this oldest group, fewer than half require help with walking, and fewer than 25% need help with other basic tasks of self-care [bathing, showering, dressing, eating, getting in and out of bed or a chair, walking, and using the toilet] (Administration on Aging, 2012). (p. 578)

*Myth B:* Old people are unattractive, have no teeth, and can barely see or hear.

*Fact:* Older adults, like their younger cohorts, pay varying degrees of attention to their personal appearance, hygiene, and conformity to current, popular styles. Many older people take great pride in their appearance and their strong social skills. They actively strive to put forth a pleasant, attractive persona. Physical changes such as the

tendency of skin to wrinkle and body fat to redistribute do occur. However, these are facts of life having little to do with a person's overall appearance and personality.

Older adults lacking "access to a lifetime of preventative dental care or fluorinated water" experience greater risk of losing their teeth as they age (McInnis-Dittrich, 2014, p. 34). The most common reason for tooth loss involves inflammation of the gums and bones surrounding the teeth, "usually caused by dental plaque, which can be removed with regular brushing and routine cleaning" (McInnis-Dittrich, 2014, p. 34). Think about what times were like when many older adults were young. There was no preventive dental care or fluoride in the water supply (to combat cavities). They lived in an era in which they *expected* to lose their teeth and wear dentures. Everyone else did. My grandmother, born in 1890, told the story of how she never could stand pain very well. Whenever she got a toothache, she would get someone to pull the tooth out with the equivalent of pliers. Eventually she had no teeth left.

Sight and hearing tend to deteriorate with advancing age. However, having access to advanced medical services and techniques can slow the decline and even improve conditions. Hearing aids are now much more usable than in the past. Vision can be enhanced by glasses, contacts, laser surgery, and other new surgical techniques. One professor required cataract surgery at the relatively young age of 48. She had been nearsighted since her early teens and could barely find her glasses when she put them down somewhere. As the cataracts developed, her vision became increasingly cloudy, and she viewed the world as if through a dense fog. Reading and driving became almost impossible. Cataract surgery involves removing the natural lens in your eye and replacing it with an artificial one. After the 15-minute outpatient surgery, her distance vision was better than it had been at age 14. She marveled at medical advances as she recalled the effects of her own grandmother's cataract surgery years before. At that time, the natural lens could be removed but not replaced internally. Her grandmother had to wear glasses almost three-quarters of an inch thick to replace the lenses she lost in order to restore only a portion of her vision.

*(continued)*

**FOCUS ON CRITICAL THINKING 10.1** *(continued)*

*Myth C:* "Old people sleep all the time" (Harrigan & Farmer, 2000, p. 33).

*Fact:* Older people don't necessarily sleep less than younger people, but their sleeping patterns are somewhat different. "Older adults need about the same amount of sleep as young adults—7 to 9 hours each night. But seniors tend to go to sleep earlier and get up earlier than when they were younger. Older people may nap more during the day, which can sometimes make it hard to fall asleep at night.... As people get older, they spend less time in deep sleep, which may be why older people are often light sleepers" (National Institute on Aging, 2009).

*Myth D:* You can't teach an old dog new tricks; "old people are set in their ways" (Harrigan & Farmer, 2000, p. 35).

*Fact:* Greene (2000) reflects:

Life span and life course theorists reject the view that growth ends with adulthood. They point out that, while there may be growth limits for attributes such as height, other qualities such as creativity and abstract reasoning do not fit this model. In this context, growth refers to differentiation,

increased complexity, and greater organization, and can occur at every age. (p. 29)

Harrigan and Farmer (2000) add that

this growth and change vary from person to person and within each individual and are related to an individual's personality.... For example, a woman who is assertive, confident, and positive as she approaches new experiences will probably view old age as one more new and exciting adventure. Someone who approaches life from a pessimistic, complaining viewpoint no doubt will behave similarly as an aged person. (p. 36)

*Myth E:* All old people are senile.

*Fact:* Most older adults do not have dementia, and it is certainly not inevitable (Plassman et al., 2007). **Dementia** is a condition that involves various cognitive problems, such as impaired memory, poor judgment, and inability to control emotions. However, the likelihood of dementia does increase with advancing age; only 5% of people in their 70s, have dementia, 24% in their 80s, and 37.4% in their 90s, and older (Plassman et al., 2007).

---

*Older women have a higher risk of poverty than older men. In 2009, older women over 65 had nearly twice the poverty rate of men in the same age bracket. The rate for women that year was 10.7 percent; for men, 6.6 percent. At the intersection of age, gender, and race, older women of color experience high rates of poverty in the United States....*

*[P]eople of color experience higher rates of poverty in their later years. African American and Hispanic [older adults] ... have the highest rates of poverty. In 2009, the poverty rate for African American women was 21.8 percent, while the rate for Hispanic women was 21.3 percent. By 2010, the overall rate for both groups was 18.0 percent, compared with 9.0 percent for older Whites (Administration on Aging, 2011).*

*Likewise, older women living alone in the United States are consistently the poorest group among the poorest of the aged, faring worse than*

*older couples. The highest risk of poverty among the aged was experienced by Hispanic women who lived alone, among whom nearly half (40.8 percent) had incomes below the poverty threshold (Administration on Aging, 2011). African American women who lived alone also experienced an elevated risk of poverty, with an overall poverty rate of 30.7 percent. Clearly, those who are most risk of poverty are most likely to benefit from anti-poverty programs. (pp. 419–421)*

## Saving Social Security

We have established that Social Security is a primary means of keeping older adults out of poverty. There has been much concern about the adequacy and ongoing solvency of the Social Security system. As Chapters 6 and 8 explained, workers automatically pay into Social Security, a type of social insurance, based on their earnings up to a specified annual maximum. It is tempting to think of Social Security as a savings account that automatically receives a percentage of each paycheck and lies there waiting for you to collect interest once you retire. But this is not the case. In reality, the money that workers contribute today is being spent to pay benefits to retired and other workers, as well as other government expenses. Tomorrow's beneficiaries—including you—must depend on tomorrow's workers.

The problem introduced at the beginning of the chapter is that the number of workers paying into the Social Security system is falling compared to the number of retirees and other beneficiaries receiving payments from it. As noted, this worker-to-beneficiary ratio is referred to as the **dependency ratio**. Whereas there were almost nine working people for every older adult in 1950, it is predicted there will be fewer than three after 2030 (Ortman, Velkoff, & Hogan, 2014). So the disturbing question is, "Who's going to pay for your Social Security when you retire?"

It is predicted that Social Security will start going into the red as early as 2015, when baby boomers are retiring and the dependency ratio changes (Karger & Stoesz, 2014). At that point, workers' contributions will be less than the benefits that must be paid out, and any benefits paid must come from reserves. By 2037, without changes the fund's reserves will be depleted; however, OASDI taxes should be enough to pay 75% of anticipated benefits until 2084 (Karger & Stoesz, 2014). Many indicate that it's much better to plan far ahead "so that individuals and families have time to adjust their retirement plans, and so that changes can be phased in slowly over time" (White House, 2005a).

Some indicate that fixing and saving the system will require cutting benefits and/or increasing payroll taxes. Benefits can be decreased in several ways, including

- Providing them at older ages (which has already been done to a limited degree).
- Decreasing the actual amount of benefits paid out to individuals.
- Increasing the maximum amount of income that can be taxed. In 2014, income was taxed up to a maximum of $117,000 and in 2015 the maximum is $118,500 (SSA, 2014a). The maximum will likely increase annually.

- Cutting the increases in benefits regularly made to adjust for cost-of-living increases.
- More controversially, providing benefits only to those whose income or assets fall under some arbitrary line. This, of course, is quite radical because it violates the idea that all who pay into a social insurance system should benefit from returns.

Focus on Critical Thinking 10.2 urges you to think about how this problem should be solved.

Another controversial issue is whether Social Security discriminates against women. Focus on Critical Thinking 10.3 raises some key questions.

## Retirement

Previously we established the concept of age 65 as the magic number for retirement. A hundred years ago, the notion of retirement was essentially unknown. Most people didn't live that long. Few had enough savings to support them without working. No programs such as Social Security or pension plans existed to pick up the slack when their work careers ended. As we know, the Social Security Act of 1935 established 65 as the age when people stop working and begin receiving maximum benefits. Current policy indicates that by 2022, people won't be able to receive Social Security benefits until age 67 (Mooney et al., 2015).

One survey of nonretired workers indicated that the average age of planned retirement was 64; 15% planned on retirement before age 60, 22% between ages 60 and 64, 25% at age 65, and 31% after that (Carroll, 2008). Retirement might sound good to many, but it often requires quite an adjustment. Retirees must cope with a new way of life. How does a retiree respond when someone asks, "And what do you do?" Many people's careers or jobs become a substantial part of their personal identities. What happens when they give up that significant part of their lives? How might the loss affect their self-concept and self-respect?

Another potential problem in retirement involves reduced income. How much adjustment is involved when retirees can no longer spend money and buy things as they used to? Still another aspect of retirement concerns losing daily work routines. Retirees must discover new ways to spend their time.

## FOCUS ON CRITICAL THINKING 10.2

# HOW WOULD YOU FIX SOCIAL SECURITY?

What are your own thoughts and values concerning the Social Security crisis? How would you answer the following questions?

### Critical Thinking Questions (concerning raising the retirement age)

EP 3a, 5a, 5b, 5c, 8d

- Because people tend to live longer, should the retirement age be raised?
- If so, to what age?
- When would you like to be able to retire? If you haven't thought much about this, when would your parents (or grandparents) like to retire?

### Critical Thinking Questions (concerning decreasing benefits)

- Should benefits be decreased?
- If so, for whom—current recipients? Note that Social Security is a major source of income for most retired Americans. "Social Security comprises at least 90 percent of the income of 20 percent of older married couple beneficiaries and 41 percent for single beneficiaries. It comprises at least 50 percent of the income of 52 percent of older married couples and 72 percent of single beneficiaries" (DiNitto, 2011, p. 163).
- Should benefits for future recipients be reduced? If so, when should this start? How much should they be reduced?
- Do you want reduced benefits?
- Would your parents and grandparents want reduced benefits?

### Critical Thinking Questions (concerning increasing the maximum amount of income that can be taxed)

- Should the maximum amount of income that can be taxed be increased more than it regularly is now?

- If so, by how much?
- Should all income regardless of the amount be taxed?
- Should people who pay significantly more into the fund receive proportionally more benefits?
- To what extent is it fair to pay significantly more into a social insurance program and get the same benefits as those paying significantly less?
- Should richer people help support poorer people by sharing their wealth through the Social Security system?
- What is fair?

### Critical Thinking Questions (concerning cutting increases in benefits)

- Should cost-of-living increases in benefits be decreased?
- If so, by how much?
- How would a decreasing standard of living affect the many people depending on Social Security?
- How severe would these effects be on recipients living 20 years after first receiving Social Security benefits in terms of their quality of life?

### Critical Thinking Questions (concerning offering Social Security benefits only to those less well off)

- Should benefits be given only to retirees who are less well off?
- If so, how well off?
- To what extent is this fair to workers who paid significant taxes into the fund for decades and then don't qualify for benefits?
- To what extent would this transform a social insurance system into a public assistance system? To what extent is this right or wrong?

### Health Care

Medicare, established in 1966, is not the total answer to health care for older adults. Although it helps pay for medical expenses for an estimated 54 million people (Kaiser Family Foundation [KFF], 2014c), it pays only half for a visit to a physician and nothing for long-term care, hearing aids, glasses, or dental work. Chapter 8 discussed the partial

## DOES SOCIAL SECURITY DISCRIMINATE AGAINST WOMEN?

One ongoing criticism of Social Security is that it discriminates against women. When a woman turns age 66, she is eligible to receive benefits equal to one-half of the benefits her husband receives. This is true whether she has ever worked outside the home or not. However, if she has worked outside the home, she may choose to take her own benefits instead. She cannot receive both.

EP 2, 5c

How is this discriminatory? First, women who have been homemakers their entire lives are entitled to only half of what their husbands receive. Does this imply that their share of the marital partnership is worth only half of the husbands'? The system provides them with no way of making contributions based on their own labor within the home.

Many women work outside the home for years, build up their own benefits, but end up taking half of their husbands' anyway. Why? The husbands' benefits are worth more than twice as much as theirs, so they're better off taking half of the husbands'. We've established that men tend to enter higher-paid professions, earn significantly more than women in the same professions, and spend less time out of the workforce raising children and caring for a home. Thus women's contributions, as structured by the current system, are often significantly less than their husbands'. Barusch (2000) explains:

Wives in dual-worker couples face a choice. They can receive benefits based on their earnings, or they can receive benefits as dependents. They cannot do both. Those who left the labor force to raise children or care for the sick, and those whose wages were lower than their spouses' receive more as dependents than on the basis of their own work histories. So they receive no benefit for the payroll taxes withheld from every one of their paychecks. (p. 570)

Note that a few positive changes have been made in the system.

For example, many divorced spouses may begin collecting Social Security benefits at age 62 if their former spouses are eligible even if the former spouse has not yet claimed benefits. In addition, payments to disabled widows and widowers aged 50–59 were increased.

*(DiNitto, 2011, p. 160)*

### Critical Thinking Questions

Should the system be further reformed to make it more equitable? If so, how should the contributions of homemakers be measured? What about those who take time off to bear and raise children?

---

supplementary coverage available in Medicare Part B, Medigap insurance (to fill in Medicare's gaps), and the Medicare Modernization Act's prescription drug benefit. However, these also cost older adults more. And good coverage costs much more.

The older people get, the more likely they are to have long-term illnesses and to take more time to recuperate. Older adults spend two times as much on health care as younger population groups (Mooney et al., 2009).

### Abuse of Older Adults

Physical and emotional abuse of older adults is receiving increasing public attention. **Older adult abuse** is "the violation of an [older adult's] … human and civil rights by any other person or persons"; such abuse may involve a lone incident or multiple,

recurring acts (Gisby & Butler, 2012, p. 210). Such abuse includes not only inflicting physical or emotional harm but also taking advantage of older adults financially or neglecting them (e.g., ignoring the fact that medical treatment is needed) (Hooyman & Kiyak, 1999). Coleman and Kerbo (2009) report shocking incidents of abuse involving family caregivers. One involved a man who sexually assaulted his 74-year-old mother-in-law. The victim's daughter refused to make a big deal of it or to allow her mother to report the incident to authorities. Another incident entailed an angry son chasing his 75-year-old father around with a hatchet.

In private homes, perpetrators of older adult abuse often are people who live with the victim, such as a spouse or adult child; frequently alcohol abuse is involved (McInnis-Dittrich, 2014). Older adults are also subject to abuse when living in residential settings. Abuse is more likely to occur when residents are isolated from family and friends who otherwise might look out for them.

It's difficult to determine the exact percentage of older adults who are abused. An estimated 1.5 million cases of physical abuse of older adults occur in the United States each year (Kornblum & Julian, 2012). A review of a wide range of research studies focusing on older adult abuse found that about 6% of all older adults suffered abuse (Cooper, Selwood, & Livingston, 2008; Gisby & Butler, 2012; Payne, 2012). Because it's so difficult to assess and monitor, older adult abuse may actually be 7% or higher (Gisby & Butler, 2012).

## Types of Abuse

Inherent in the description of older adult abuse are seven categories of maltreatment (Gisby & Butler, 2012, pp. 210–211). These include the following:

1. *"Physical abuse*
   *This includes hitting, pinching, slapping, misuse of medication, restraint or inappropriate sanctions."* A practitioner should look for vague, inadequate, or illogical explanations concerning problems. A physical problem or injury may be identified. The explanation provided may not be good enough. It's then important to find out what really caused this problem or injury?

2. *"Sexual abuse*
   *This includes hitting, pinching, slapping, misuse of medication, restraint or inappropriate sanctions. "It may include being forced to watch pornography or talked to or touched in a sexual way. Indicators might include social withdrawal, or the abused person using explicit or untypical sexual language or behavior. There may be physical evidence, e.g. torn, stained or bloody clothing, trauma to the rectum or genitals, or presence of unexplained sexually transmitted"* infections.

3. *"Psychological or emotional abuse*
   *This includes threats of harm or abandonment, intimidation, coercion, verbal abuse, [or] isolation/withdrawal from services or support networks."* Psychological abuse often occurs in conjunction with other types of abuse. The older adult being victimized may become *"emotionally withdrawn" or "depressed" as a result of other forms of abuse.*

4. *"Neglect and acts of omission*
   *This may include ignoring medical or physical care needs and failure to provide access to appropriate services."* Examples may involve deprivation of medication, food, heating, air conditioning, or medical treatment. Neglect or acts of omission may be purposeful or unintended. Aging makes people more vulnerable to health issues and deprivations. Older adults require the provision of adequate care.

5. *"Financial abuse*
   *This can be complex and diverse in nature; it is often perpetrated by individuals considered trustworthy by virtue of position, for example [,] family or [caregivers].... Financial abuse includes theft, fraud, [financial] exploitation, undue pressure over wills, property, inheritance or financial transactions; or the misuse or misappropriation of property, possessions or benefits."* Older adults, especially those suffering from dementia, can be manipulated or deceived regarding what is in their best financial interest.

6. *"Discriminatory abuse*
   *This includes forms of harassment, slurs, inappropriate language or threats focused on the victim's sex, race, age, religion, sexuality or disability and leads to individuals receiving unequal treatment in, or being excluded from, opportunities such as health care, justice and protections from others."* As mobility becomes more difficult, contacts with others in support networks become harder to maintain, and health issues accelerate, it becomes easier to be victimized by deprivation or unequal treatment.

7. *"Institutional abuse"*
   *Older adults who reside in caregiving facilities (including nursing homes and medical settings such as hospitals) may not receive adequate and effective care. Adherence to institutional rules, regulations, and requirements may take precedence over resident or patient care. Older adults may not receive the individualized, responsive care they need. Food may be inadequate. Toileting needs may not be addressed properly. Individual health needs or cleanliness may be ignored.*

## Assessment and Treatment of Older Adult Abuse

Assessment of older adult abuse involves at least three aspects (McInnis-Dittrich, 2014). First, the practitioner should closely observe the older adult's appearance, behavior, and living situation. Second, the worker should conduct a careful appraisal of the older adults' strengths and ability to function. Third, the practitioner should conduct interviews with the older adult to solicit specific information.

Interviewing requires use of good communication skills (Gisby & Butler, 2012). "Listening nonjudgmentally is important ... as is valuing and respecting opinions expressed" (p. 216). The older adult should be treated with "dignity" and "respect" (p. 216). The practitioner should not place blame on the older adult, but rather discover the dynamics of the situation and what could be done to improve it.

Note that the older adult should be interviewed alone as he or she may experience fear or hesitation if the abuser or others are present (McInnis-Dittrich, 2014). Fear may result from dread of retaliation by the abuser, or even concern that the abuser or others may no longer provide care.

If there is satisfactory evidence that abuse has occurred, the practitioner should contact Adult Protective Services (APS). Subsequent counseling might focus on the following matters:

- "Educating victims about resources and options
- Breaking through denial and shame
- Safety planning [determining what actions to take if abuse takes place] ...
- Building support networks ...
- Traumatic or post traumatic stress [distressing physical and emotional effects after experiencing a traumatic event]
- Family counseling [to address intra-family relationships, resolve differences, and alleviate stress that may result in abuse]" (National Committee for the Prevention of Elder Abuse [NCPEA], 2008)

When abuse is related to stress experienced by caregivers, provision of supportive services can relieve some of the stress (NCPEA, 2008). Such services can help out and give caregivers a break. Services include support groups where caregivers can empathize with each other, provide a means to vent tensions, and discuss suggestions for coping and care

provision. Delivering meals to the home (e.g., Meals on Wheels) can ease the caregiving burden. Periodic telephone contacts can check up on how things are going and provide older adults with a means to communicate their concerns. Other services include respite programs and adult day care (both discussed later in the chapter).

## Living Conditions and Family Variables

Another issue facing many older adults concerns their living conditions. Many older adults prefer to live on their own or with other family members. However, many older people's homes are located in older, deteriorating, inner-city neighborhoods with high crime rates. This puts them at greater risk of harm and also makes it increasingly difficult to maintain their homes.

Relatively few older adults need the around-the-clock nursing and maintenance care of a nursing home. People are more likely to need this care when they suffer from debilitating chronic illnesses. Nursing homes vary markedly in cost and quality of service. Wealthy people can pay for private homes that have excellent facilities and attentive staff. People with fewer resources must often be satisfied with whatever care they can get.

## Transitional Issues

As people get older, they are more likely to experience serious losses with which they must learn to cope. One issue already discussed concerns retirement and the accompanying drastic changes in productivity and routine. Other issues involve adjusting to more structured living situations. One spouse may die, leaving the other to adjust to a much more isolated life. Health may decline, requiring an older adult to accept and adjust to increasing levels of assistance and dependence. Losses in ability such as sight, hearing, and mobility may also require the application of coping skills. There are many areas in which social workers can provide important assistance with respect to older adults' adjustment.

Note that lesbian, gay, and bisexual (LGB) people not only face the same issues and transitions that heterosexual people do but also continue to suffer the consequences of homophobia. Highlight 10.2 describes one dimension of homophobia—invisibility.

HIGHLIGHT **10.2**   "GAYGING" AND INVISIBILITY **LO 5**

Older adults can experience *invisibility*—the condition that others fail to acknowledge, attend to, or even notice their existence (Hooyman, 2008; Hooyman & Kiyak, 1999; Petrocelli, 2012; Tully, 2000). The myths discussed in Focus on Critical Thinking 10.1 tend to reinforce the views often held by younger people that older adults are inadequate, of lesser or little value, and unworthy of notice. Hence older adults become invisible. Obviously such unfair, discriminatory attitudes and treatment fail to uphold human dignity and appreciate human diversity.

EP 1b, 1c, 2, 2a, 2b, 2c

Lesbian, gay, and bisexual (LGB) people experience an additional dimension of invisibility. **Gayging** (gay aging) results in additional stresses and scenarios not experienced by heterosexuals (Petrocelli, 2012; Tully, 2000, p. 197). Petrocelli (2012) explains:

"Older adult gay men and lesbians are all too familiar with gay bashing; religious bigotry; degradation; and the hate spewed from the mouths of family, friends, the media, teachers, classmates, police, clergy, and strangers. Older adult gay men and lesbians know what it means to be victims of housing, military, and employment discrimination, police brutality, and medical maltreatment. Older adult gay men and lesbians understand the feeling of loss due to abandonment. They can speak volumes on the experiences of isolation and having no family or children to support their emotional, spiritual, and medical health needs.

Nursing homes and senior-citizen centers consist mainly of heterosexual older adults and a small percentage of closeted gay men and lesbians. A percentage of older adult residents and medical staff are heterosexist [having prejudicial attitudes about and practicing discriminatory behavior toward people who are not heterosexual, with the underlying belief that heterosexuality is the only normal way of being] and homophobic, leaving no room or incentive for gay and lesbian older adults to come out and find true camaraderie, understanding, services, treatment, and comfort at the end of life. While heterosexuals have paths laid out that guide and help fulfill their lives and needs and passions, gay

men and lesbians need to create their own paths to find fulfillment. Otherwise, if gay men and lesbians follow heterosexual paths, they will surely find discomfort, discrimination, and lack of understanding and protection. Heterosexuals travel paths of comfort knowing that their sexual identity is supported, reinforced, and protected. Gay men and lesbians trying to travel the same path as heterosexuals are sure to be denounced and isolated. Therefore, older adult gay men and lesbians forge on with less energy to cope with years of discrimination that just keeps on coming.

Senior housing is built on a foundation of the "don't ask, don't tell" policy. The policy is not blatantly written anywhere to say that older adult gay men and lesbians are not welcome. It need not be. Discrimination against gay older adults runs rampant throughout many housing complexes without any rules or policies to protect them or prevent the discrimination. Simultaneously, antigay sentiment proliferates everywhere, both privately and publicly and by many, which only increases the oppressive life of gay older adults.

Picture if you will an older adult lesbian relating her life story to her straight, heterosexist, nursing-home-facility roommate. Can you picture what the straight older neighbor's reaction would be if her own history includes being conservative, right wing, Mormon, and antigay? Can you imagine the older adult lesbian's difficulties while conversing with the straight neighbor? Looking at this scenario, it is not hard to understand what helps to reinforce and maintain gay and lesbian depression and isolation." (pp. 17–18)

LGB older adults of color are at risk of experiencing discrimination because of race in addition to risks associated with age and sexual orientation. Social workers are trained to be sensitive to all these factors in empowering clients and providing help. Think about the following example:

Consider the older African-American gay man who, because of a stroke, has been confined to the hospital's intensive care unit. The hospital, long known for its racist practices, began treating African Americans in the 1970s and has few

*(continued)*

**HIGHLIGHT 10.2 (continued)**

doctors or nurses who are minorities of color. Most of the hospital support staff are Hispanic or African American. The patient's Puerto Rican lover, a 70-year-old retired artist, is kept from visiting because he is not considered a family member. Because he believes the true nature of the relationship to be a private matter, he remains quiet. The hospital social worker, being sensitive to the perceived needs of the patient and his friend, arranges for visitation. There are times when empowering individuals requires institutional flexibility.

*(Tully, 2000, p. 217)*

The following provides still another example of how a social worker must be sensitive to sexual orientation to empower a client:

Cecilia, a 54-year-old lesbian who was the guardian of her 90-year-old hospitalized terminally ill mother, was referred to the hospital social worker to assess the mother's pending death and the impact it might have on Cecilia. Her sexual orientation was not germane to the immediate problem, but it would be important to know that Cecilia's partner of 30 years was the

primary caretaker of Cecilia's mother and more likely to need the services.

*(Tully, 2001, pp. 608–609)*

There are several ways social workers can address the issue of LGB people's invisibility for all clients including those who are older adults (Tully, 2001). First, practitioners can make their offices more "homosocial" or welcoming to people regardless of sexual orientation (p. 609). Including magazines and other reading material oriented to gay issues and interests can help. Second, using admissions or intake forms that feature more inclusive terms than *spouse* or *marital status* is constructive. When soliciting information, phrasing questions by using terms such as *significant other, partner, mate,* and *special friend* reflects more flexibility toward and acceptance of nonheterosexual orientations (p. 609). Note that although same-sex marriage is now legal, many older LGB people may have long-term partners where marriage had not been an option. Third, careful listening can provide clues to sexual orientation. For example, clients who mention involvement in lesbian/gay activities or events may, in fact, be lesbian or gay. However, they also may not be, so social workers must be careful not to succumb to stereotypes or jump to conclusions.

# Contexts for Social Work Practice with Older Adults   `LO 6`

As in services for children and families, there exists a continuum of care for older adults ranging from supplemental services for people in their own homes to intensive residential care. A primary value stressed when working with older adults is *autonomy*. Social workers strive to keep older adults as independent and autonomous as possible for as long as possible. Assessing and emphasizing strengths and capacities are essential to maximize autonomy.

EP 7c, 7d, 8e

Because older adults may have many needs, social workers practice in a wide range of agencies and settings. Three broader contexts for service provision are long-term care through home health and community services, discharge planning in hospitals, and service provision in nursing homes.

## Long-Term Care Through Home-Based and Community Health Services

**Long-term care** is the provision of health, social, and personal services over an extended period of time to people who are unable to care for themselves in some, most, or almost all ways. The intent is to promote people's socio-emotional and physical well-being in the least restrictive environment possible. Long-term care implies that recipients need either ongoing or periodic help over an extended period. Nursing homes, discussed more thoroughly later, provide one type of long-term care. A second type includes services provided to people living in their own homes. Finally, a third kind of long-term care includes services made readily available to people in their community.

### Home-Based Services

As you know, social workers in the broker role link clients to services and in the case manager role oversee and coordinate service provision. **Home-based services** or **home care** are types of assistance provided to people in their own homes (Kaye, 2008; McInnis-Dittrich, 2014). They may involve either assistance to family members caring for an older adult relative or provision of services by formal social service agencies.

An **informal support network** is a system of individuals who provide emotional, social, and economic support to a person in need. The family is a major informal support network. Informal support networks also include friends, neighbors, and fellow worshipers. For example, members of an informal support network might periodically chauffeur an older adult who no longer can drive herself to the grocery store. Similarly, an older adult with vision problems might need help paying bills and balancing his checkbook. Investigating the adequacy of an older adult's informal support network is an important aspect of social work assessment.

Social workers have an exceptional skill set for working with people in informal support networks. Workers have knowledge about human development and family dynamics. They have communication and intervention skills. They have learned how to work with individuals, families, groups, organizations, and community. They know how to identify community resources and make referrals to them. For example, a social worker might help a family arrange for respite care while family members do other things such as going to work, getting groceries, or simply participating in recreational activities. **Respite care** is temporary care for an older adult or other person in need, giving the primary caregivers (often family members) some time free of responsibility. (Note that Chapter 9 introduced the concept of respite care with respect to child care.) Another example involves a social worker arranging for telephone reassurance services (i.e., calling older adults daily or periodically to make sure they're all right) when primary caregivers are unavailable.

In contrast, **formal support networks** include public and private agencies and their staffs, which provide services, including health care (e.g., nursing), social services, and housekeeping help, to older adults in need. Home-based services provided by formal support networks may be necessary for two reasons. First, they address needs directly involving the home itself, such as cleaning or repair. Second, they more efficiently serve recipients who have difficulty transporting themselves outside the home to receive services elsewhere. Home-based services include any provided to people directly in their homes and those intended to facilitate people's ability to remain in their homes. They include homemaker and chore services (to assist in daily living tasks such as cooking, cleaning, home maintenance, and laundry), home health care (e.g., physical *therapy*[1] or a visiting nurse), transportation, Meals on Wheels,[2] and respite care.

### Community-Based Services

**Community-based services**—those provided outside the home in the community—form another dimension of the formal support network (Kaye, 2008; McInnis-Dittrich, 2014). They can fulfill a wide range of functions, from providing health care to meeting psychological and social needs. The following are examples of community-based services (Kropf, 2000):

- *Adult day care:* This service provides supervision outside the home for older adults who live at home but whose primary caregivers are unavailable during the day, usually because they must work. It differs from respite care in that it is provided on a regular schedule and is generally provided in a daycare center outside the home (respite care can be provided either inside or outside the home). Adult day-care centers may also offer older adults a range of therapeutic services and provide opportunities for socializing and participation in activities (NCPEA, 2008).

- *Hospices:* A **hospice** is a homelike residence, emphasizing residents' comfort and peace, where a person can reside and interact with loved ones in the days or weeks preceding death. These programs provide compassionate end-of-life care to terminally ill people. "Patients are admitted to a hospice program when medical science can offer no cure to them and, in all likelihood, they are

---

[1]Physical therapy is "the treatment of disease, injury, or deformity by physical methods such as massage, heat treatment, and exercise" (Lindberg, 2007, p. 1034).

[2]Meals on Wheels is a program in which meals are delivered directly to the homes of people who need them. This service can be sponsored or cosponsored by public agencies such as human service departments or private organizations such as senior centers.

expected to die within six months. The patient is aware of the prognosis at admission and agrees to a program of palliative care aimed toward comfort rather than cure" (Reese, 2013, p. 7). The intent is to make people as comfortable as possible during their final days. Services may be provided either in a comfortable setting outside the home or in the individual's home.

- *Senior centers:* Here seniors can gather for social, recreational, and educational reasons. Senior centers often offer a wide range of services and activities. These include meals, provision of information, "health, fitness, and wellness programs," "transportation," volunteer opportunities, "recreational activities," and "educational and arts programs" (National Council on Aging [NCOA], 2015.

- *Congregate Meal Program:* Initially instituted by the 1973 Older Americans Act, this program provides hot meals for seniors at a variety of community locations. It offers seniors a source of good nutrition and an opportunity to socialize with their peers.
- *Senior home repair and maintenance programs:* These provide physical help in home upkeep. They may involve a handyperson service whereby volunteers make home repairs such as fixing pipes or repairing roofs as needed. They may also include seasonal services such as lawn mowing or snow removal.

Focus on Critical Thinking 10.4 gives you a framework to organize your thoughts as they relate to care for older adults.

## FOCUS ON CRITICAL THINKING 10.4
## MACRO PRACTICE EMPOWERMENT FOR OLDER ADULTS

Social workers have the responsibility to become politically involved, and to "analyze, formulate, and advocate for policies that advance human rights and social, economic, and environmental justice" on the behalf of older adults (CSWE, 2015, EP 5c). Huber, Nelson, Netting, and Borders (2008) explain that such advocacy involves:

> vigilant efforts by, with, or on behalf of older persons to influence decision makers in structures of imbalanced power and to promote justice in providing for, assisting with, or allowing needs to be met. Vigilant efforts implies a constant monitoring and attention devoted to the situation because it is too easy for people to fall through the cracks, particularly if they are highly vulnerable. By, with, or on behalf of older persons means that every effort will be made to empower older persons themselves to do what needs to be done, but sometimes it takes people working together to get things done. (pp. 4–5)

Keeping a careful eye on proposed legislation addressing older people's health-care and social service needs is critical. For example, increasing the age at which older people can first begin receiving Social

Security benefits significantly and negatively impacts older adults' financial standing. Likewise, monitoring the availability of adequate health care for older adults is paramount. Legislative advocacy involves efforts to change legislation to benefit some category of clients—in this case, older adults. It includes such actions as contacting elected officials about some issue or policy under debate. It might also entail communicating with other professionals and clients, encouraging them to contact officials concerning their views and recommendations. Public officials usually listen to their constituents when they want to get reelected.

EP 3a, 5c, 8a, 8c, 8d

Working to improve and develop community services for older adults raises other important macropractice possibilities (Greene, Cohen, Galamboss, & Kropf, 2007). For example, community-based adult day-care services can be expanded. Day-care programs can provide a wide range of "medical and social services … ; to older adults who commute from home" to attend the program; services include "medical and psychiatric treatment," recreational and social opportunities, meals, transportation, and personal care (Hillier &

*(continued)*

**FOCUS ON CRITICAL THINKING 10.4** *(continued)*

Barrow, 2011, p. 274). Hillier and Barrow (2011) describe one example:

> The On Lok Health Center in San Francisco ... provides day-care services to elders in China-town. A van with hydraulic lift transports [older adults] ... to the center, where each day begins with exercise and reality orientation. People are introduced to one another in both English and Chinese. On Lok assumes responsibility for pro-viding all services needed by the functionally dependent. If not for On Lok, the participants would need institutional care. (p. 275)

Another example of a community-based program is one directed at educating local clergy to enhance linkages "between organized and informal support systems" (Biegel, Shore, & Gordon, 1984, p. 99). A university school of social welfare provided training with the following goals: "to impart a foundation of knowledge of the aging process, to examine the specific needs and contributions of aged individuals, to impart knowledge of community resources available for the aged individuals, and to increase participants' awareness of creative ways to min-ister to the aged" (Biegel et al., 1984, p. 99).

With all this in mind, think about the following.

## Critical Thinking Questions

- To what extent do the preceding suggestions for empowerment reflect *residual* versus *institutional*

policies and programming? (Recall that residual policies focus on reactions to problems, gener-ally providing as few benefits as possible. Insti-tutional policies view social services as people's right, providing ongoing benefits to enhance people's lives and well-being.)
- To what extent does current service provision for older adults demonstrate *conservative* versus *liberal* values?

Now consider the three basic, divergent principles involved that relate to the following.

## Critical Thinking Questions

- Who should assume responsibility? Should older adults be expected to provide for and take care of themselves? Or is it society's responsibility to help them when they need it?
- Who is to blame for older adults' problems and needs? To what extent will older adults take advantage of social welfare benefits when they really don't need them? Will providing ongoing services and benefits significantly enhance their health, welfare, and comfort?
- To what extent should the government interfere in people's lives? Is it the government's respon-sibility to improve older people's health and functioning?

## Discharge Planning in Hospital Settings

More than one-third of people entering hospitals for care are 65 or older (McInnis-Dittrich, 2014). Many hospital discharges result in nursing home placement. Social workers are integrally involved as leaders in interdisciplinary treatment planning[3] and in linking patients with necessary services. A common primary function of hospital social work-ers is **discharge planning**. This is the comprehen-sive assessment of a patient's abilities and needs, the development of a plan to facilitate that patient's transition out of the hospital and back into a

community or agency setting, and the implementa-tion of that plan. Discharge planning also involves identifying the appropriate resources available to meet needs and working closely with the patient, family members, and other health-care providers to implement the plan as effectively as possible. Advo-cacy on the patient's behalf to make certain needs are met is frequently required.

Social workers must be prepared to deal with multiple potential problems when conducting dis-charge planning (Naleppa & Reid, 2003). The pa-tient may be confused, difficult to work with, or suffering from an unstable physical condition. Fam-ily members may be unavailable or may disagree with plans proposed by the patient or treatment team. Adequate financial resources for an appropri-ate placement or access to the placement itself may be unavailable.

---

[3]*Interdisciplinary treatment* involves teams composed of profes-sionals from various disciplines, such as doctors, nurses, social workers, psychologists, physical therapists, and occupational therapists who, in collaboration, share findings, make recommen-dations, and implement treatment plans.

*Case Example*[4]  Esra Tratnor, age 81, was admitted to the hospital after his two daughters, Vicki and Karen, suddenly noticed that he was having "spells" during which he would speak garbled nonsense or babble incessantly. This was quite unlike Esra, who was a quiet, withdrawn man of few words. Esra remained coherent the rest of the time.

The diagnosis was an inoperable brain tumor the size of a lemon. Upon hearing this, Esra insisted on returning to his farmhouse—the same house in which he was born. He wanted to live out his remaining days watching the birds and deer. He had been living alone since his wife of 53 years died 6 years ago.

Except for a liquid supplement, doctors prescribed no treatment except to make Esra as comfortable as possible. They anticipated ongoing mental and physical deterioration in the 6–12 months he had to live.

Esra gave Aiko, the hospital social worker, consent to contact Vicki and Karen regarding discharge plans. One or the other of them had visited him every day of his hospital stay. Aiko reviewed options with them. Although they were very concerned about their father, both were adamant about being unable to take him into their own homes. Both had full-time jobs, husbands, and children, and no available room. Thus the only two alternatives for Esra were to return home and be provided with supportive home-based services or to enter a nursing home.

Aiko requested a psychiatric evaluation to assess Esra's mental competence. The psychiatrist's conclusion was that, although Esra manifested moderate depression, he was capable of making his own decisions. The psychiatrist prescribed an antidepressant.

Aiko consulted the hospital's attorney, who indicated that Esra had the right to return home because he had been pronounced mentally competent. Esra accepted Meals-on-Wheels (he confessed to being a pretty bad cook) but refused other home-based services, including a visiting nurse and homemaker help. He insisted on remaining independent. Aiko asked Esra if he could afford the prescribed antidepressants and nutritional supplements. Esra replied that although he had no medical insurance to cover them, Vicki and Karen would help him out. In reality, he had no intention of taking expensive drugs or of seeking financial help from his daughters.

Three weeks after his hospital discharge, Esra was readmitted with a broken hip. Apparently he had been climbing a stepladder to trim the branches of a tree in his front yard and had fallen. Luckily, neighbors noticed immediately and called an ambulance.

This time Esra was noticeably disoriented and confused. A psychiatric evaluation determined that he was mentally incompetent. Healing and rehabilitation for his hip would require extensive physical care for a long time, perhaps until his death. Vicki and Karen discussed with Aiko what they should do. Vicki couldn't bear the thought of placing her beloved dad in a nursing home, so she relented and said he could stay with her. Her own children would have to double up in a room. She would take an extended leave of absence from work to care for him. The court appointed Vicki legal guardian, and Esra moved in.

Two months later, Vicki called Aiko in desperation, saying that she just couldn't take it anymore. The friction between her and her husband over Esra's residence in their home was escalating precipitously, financial pressure from her loss of income was contributing to the tension between them, and her 17-year-old son had been busted for dealing drugs. Aiko provided Vicki with information about potential nursing home or hospice placement.

## Assisted Living Facilities

**Assisted living** facilities provide a combination of lodging, support services and health care, as needed (NIHSeniorHealth.gov, 2015). You might look at assisted living as a long-term care option somewhere on a continuum ranging from completely independent living on the one hand, and the nursing home environment, which provides more intensive care, on the other. When people find it difficult to fulfill all the tasks and responsibilities inherent in living independently, they may choose to enter assisted living. Assisted living *assists* or helps people with their daily living requirements.

Assisted living includes independent residences or apartments in a facility that also has shared common areas for such things as dining and recreation. Individual units vary widely in size and cost.

Services usually provided in assisted living include "up to three meals a day; assistance with personal care; help with medications, housekeeping, and laundry"; 24/7 security and on-site staff availability; and "social and recreational activities" (NIHSenior Health.gov, 2015). People generally may choose

---

[4]Vicki Vogel creatively developed the idea and substance for this case example.

which services they want. People requiring more help with self-care (such as eating, bathing, dressing, walking, toileting, and managing finances) may also be provided those services. Some residents may have some degree of cognitive difficulty or dementia. Note that higher levels of care cost more. Each resident has an individualized plan that changes with the resident's changing needs.

### Service Provision in Nursing Homes

**Nursing homes** or **skilled care facilities** are residential centers that "provide nursing care and rehabilitation for people who have severe functional limitations as a result of acute illness, surgery, or advanced dementia" (Newman & Newman, 2015, p. 586). Nursing home care is more intensive than that provided in assisted living because residents have greater needs.

Most of older adults do not reside in nursing homes. However, a person's likelihood of spending time in a nursing home is fairly good (U.S. Department of Agriculture, 2013). About 70% of people age 65 and older will need some type of long-term care services in their lives. Although many of these people will receive home care, more than 40% will enter a nursing home at some point. About 10% of all nursing home residents will reside there for 5 years or longer. Approximately 1.3 million people age 65 and older reside in nursing homes (Newman & Newman, 2015).

The older you are, the more likely you are to have health problems that require extensive attention and help. You also become more likely to spend time in a structured environment that attends to such needs. About .9% of people ages 65 to 74 live in nursing homes, but 25% of people age 95 and older do (Newman & Newman, 2015).

About two-thirds (66.4%) of nursing home residents are women (ProQuest, 2014). Because women generally live longer, they face a 50% greater chance of entering a nursing home than men (U.S. Department of Agriculture, 2013).

In terms of staffing, nursing homes consist of six categories (Stahlman & Kisor, 2000):

1. Dietary departments plan menus and focus on nutrition.
2. Activities departments plan and operate a range of activities for residents, such as outings, crafts, games, and celebrations.
3. Nursing services attend to the ongoing daily care of residents and oversee their health-care needs.

4. Social services address the social and emotional needs of residents, work with their families, assist in financial planning, and link residents with services when necessary.
5. Housekeeping and laundry staff perform basic daily maintenance tasks.
6. Other medical staff, including a medical director and various medical specialists (e.g., physical therapists, dermatologists), attend to residents' varying special needs.

Highlight 10.3 focuses on the roles of social workers in nursing homes.

# Empowerment for Diverse Populations of Older Adults  L07

Practice with older adults is "complex and demanding, given the range of needs of this population, the various subgroups of at-risk [older adults,] ... and

*Regular physical activity and social interaction provide a means of empowerment for older adults.*

Rolf Bruderer/Getty Images

## HIGHLIGHT 10.3  A FOCUS ON PRACTICE: SOCIAL WORKERS' ROLES IN NURSING HOMES

Social workers help nursing home residents in many ways. First, they assess a resident's strengths and needs to develop and implement an appropriate treatment plan.

Second, they counsel residents when needed, helping them cope with illnesses and deteriorating functioning, deal with emotional problems, enhance social skills, and make decisions.

**EP 1, 7c, 7d, 8d**

Third, social workers address issues concerning the residents' families. Sometimes communication difficulties must be ironed out. Other times social workers educate residents and their families about complicated medical conditions and treatments. Social workers also may assist residents and their families in making financial decisions such as applying for public assistance or a pension, contacting lawyers, or discussing end-of-life issues such as funeral arrangements.

Fourth, social workers link residents with outside services when needed. Perhaps a resident needs access to library holdings or wheelchair-capable transportation, or requires new glasses, a hearing aid, or a wheelchair.

Fifth, social workers assist other nursing home staff in understanding residents' needs and respecting their dignity. They can help residents maximize their autonomy by making their own choices whenever possible. This might involve how their room is decorated, what they wear, or what they can choose to eat. Because nursing homes are structured settings that provide such extensive care, maintaining residents' autonomy is an ongoing goal.

Finally, social workers advocate for clients. Sometimes they advocate for improved quality of care or individualized attention within the nursing home setting. Other times they advocate for agency or social policies that provide more resources or better services for clients.

Sahlins (2010) provides a case example where a nursing home social worker's plans, which were developed in conjunction with her client Millie Goldstein, are explained. Note that Millie's strengths, supports, and interests are emphasized:

The social worker will meet with Mrs. Goldstein to provide support and to encourage her to attend her care-plan meetings, discuss her medical condition with her doctor, and express her feelings about adjustment to her recent stroke and her progress toward her rehabilitation goal or returning to the community.

The social worker will assist Millie in contacting her local rabbi because she wishes him to visit.

The dietary department [after the social worker's advocacy efforts] will honor Millie's preference not to eat pork or shellfish.

The social worker will provide outreach to family and support ... concerning major life changes in the family's situation due to the patient's illness and ... encourage positive visits with the patient as they all adjust to their new family roles.

The social worker will encourage family members to bring in photo albums and will arrange brief visits with grandchildren. The daughter plans to arrange to bring the cat for a visit and has obtained a picture of the cat for the resident to put on her bulletin board, along with several pictures of her family and grandchildren.

The social worker will encourage Millie to maintain contact with her friends through phone calls.

The social worker will introduce the resident to several [other] ... women living in the facility who play [the card game] canasta. (p. 138)

---

the multiple roles social workers must undertake to address their needs" (Zuniga, 1995, p. 173). Demographic trends indicate that practitioners will be working with increasing numbers of older people.

An empowerment orientation to practice "can assist older people to utilize their strengths, abilities, and competencies in order to mobilize their resources toward problem solving and ultimately toward empowerment"; empowerment rests on principles such as involving clients integrally in the problem definition and planned-change process, emphasizing and using clients' strengths, teaching needed skills, using support networks and collective action, and linking clients with necessary resources (Cox & Parsons, 1994, p. 19).

Older adults often must deal with decreased power on several levels. First, physical health tends to decline as people age, so older adults must rely increasingly on supportive help to survive. Second, although older adults generally maintain good mental health, the incidence of dementia increases with age (McInnis-Dittrich, 2014). Third, they often experience loss of support systems as their peers' health declines. Fourth, we have established that retirement may require adaptation on the part of older adults, requiring them to learn new ways to occupy their time. They may also experience feelings of uselessness when no longer employed. Fifth, older adults may encounter age discrimination by younger people based on prejudicial stereotypes, such as emphasis on physical, mental, and economic weakness.

## Concepts and Strategies in Empowerment

Four concepts are essential in empowering older adults—adaptation, competence, relatedness, and autonomy (Zuniga, 1995). First, social workers should focus on **adaptation**, the ability to adjust to new experiences, issues, and even losses. An empowering approach emphasizes how people use their strengths to survive, adapt to **EP 7c, 7d** new experiences, and learn to appreciate the positive aspects of these new experiences. A second concept is **competence**, the ability to think about, make plans for, and carry out actions and goals. Social workers can help older adults focus on and emphasize what they *can do* instead of what they *can't* do; each individual should appreciate her or his own level of competence. **Relatedness**, the third concept, is the capability of experiencing a sense of belonging with others and relating to other people. Hence, practitioners should work to strengthen older adults' relationships with others, including friends, family members, and professional caregivers (e.g., visiting nurses, physical therapists). Support, activity, and educational groups are other mezzo options. Finally, **autonomy** is the ability to function by oneself with little or no help to the extent that this is possible. Autonomy involves helping people live as independently as possible. McInnis-Dittrich (2014) comments:

> *One of the most frequently stated goals older adults voice is their desire to maintain their independence as long as possible. This desire coincides with the social work profession's commitment to*

> *promote self-determination and preserve the dignity of the individual. On the surface, there appears to be no conflict. In reality, as older adults require more and more support services and experience increasing difficulties in maintaining independent living, tensions between older adults' desires and families' and social workers' perceptions of need are inevitable. A worker can appreciate the desperate efforts on the part of an older adult to stay in his or her own home. Yet when struggling with stairs or a deteriorating neighborhood, and difficulties in completing the simple activities of daily living challenge the feasibility of that effort, professional and personal dilemmas abound. Who ultimately must make a decision about an older adult's ability to stay in his or her own home? Who decides that an older adult is showing poor judgment about financial decisions? When does Protective Services step in to remove an older adult from a family member's home due to neglect or abuse despite the older adult's objections? When do the wishes of the family supersede the wishes of the older adult? These are difficult questions for which there are no simple answers. (pp. 19–20)*

Social workers may employ five strategies to increase their sensitivity to older adults and thus enhance their effectiveness (Toseland, 1995):

1. *Identify and face any preconceived notions and stereotypes about older adults.* These must be identified before they can be eliminated or changed.

2. *Appreciate the different life situations experienced by people from different age groups within the older adult population.* For example, women seeking work in the 1930s will have experienced very different conditions from those employed in the 1940s (Toseland, 1995). Women in the 1930s probably had a very difficult time finding jobs during the Great Depression when unemployment was skyrocketing. However, women in the 1940s likely had a pick of many jobs when men were off fighting World War II and industry was begging women to come to work.

3. *Understand that older adults are individuals with unique characteristics, experiences, and personalities, just like anybody else.* Highlight 10.4 contrasts the personalities and life

**EP 1b, 2, 2a, 2b, 2c**

## HIGHLIGHT 10.4 DIVERSITY AND INDIVIDUAL DIFFERENCES AMONG OLDER ADULTS

Just like younger people, older people are unique individuals. Consider one woman, Myrtle, age 84, whose life was filled with difficulties, including a decade of tuberculosis, the abrupt death from a heart attack of her husband at age 51 as he slept beside her, her caregiving responsibilities for her own aging and mentally ill mother for 15 years, and the need to pinch pennies her entire life. Nonetheless, Myrtle remained cheerful, optimistic, and interested in the world around her throughout her life. One of her nieces took her to China, Disney World, New Orleans, and Europe after she turned 78 (not all in one trip, of course).

Contrast Myrtle with Paula, also age 84, Myrtle's maid of honor 65 years earlier. Paula had a long, good life with a husband who adored her. He cooked and cleaned for her in addition to holding a lucrative

engineering job. He died when she was 78. At that time, Paula remained financially well off. Paula began experiencing health problems, including hearing loss and diabetes, at age 80. Complications from the diabetes forced her to enter a nursing home at age 83. Paula had always been persnickety. She demanded that she get her own way, and usually she did, thanks to her devoted spouse. She was never interested in the world around her, despite the many innovations developed during her lifetime (e.g., television, jetliners, computers, the Internet). She was always a complainer; everything was always wrong.

Myrtle visited Paula faithfully every Sunday for years and endured her endless whining and complaining. There could hardly be two more different people.

---

approaches of two women who were friends for many decades.

4. *Learn about how both gender and cultural background influence the aging experience.* Both older adult women and older adult people of color are much more likely to experience poor health, poverty, substandard housing conditions, and social isolation. Long-term experiences with discrimination can affect attitudes and expectations. Worker sensitivity to cultural differences in terms of communication, family relationships, and gender roles is critical. (Chapter 12 discusses a range of cultural and ethnic differences more thoroughly.)

5. *Understand the developmental aspects of later life, including people's physical, mental, living, and socioeconomic conditions.*

There are at least six specific empowerment strategies for micro practice with older adults (Cox & Parsons, 1994). First, social workers can listen carefully to what clients are saying and work to understand what they mean. "Engaging and drawing out the emotions of [older adult] … clients and helping them frame their situations in view of past experiences and events are effective listening techniques" (Cox & Parsons, 1994, p. 112).

Second, social workers can help clients identify their coping skills and their abilities to implement

planned change. Encouraging clients to talk about what's important to them, including their significant life experiences, is helpful. Exploring how they've coped with their difficulties in the past can also be valuable.

Third, social workers can show clients recordings of other older adults talking about how they've learned to cope with similar issues. As with support group involvement, this may help clients understand that they aren't isolated and alone in their concerns.

Fourth, workers can share newspaper articles, stories, and other informative materials with clients, especially those about older adults who have initiated service activities and political action. The Gray Panthers, an advocacy organization for the rights and socioeconomic needs of older adults, provides a good example of how people can work together for legislative and political change.

Fifth, practitioners can connect clients with other older people by forming support and educational groups. "Group interventions are an efficient, effective way to address residents' psychosocial and life-stage-related concerns, and they also effectively decrease depression, loneliness, and isolation" (Sahlins, 2010, pp. 37–38). Groups can focus on virtually any topic of interest to clients, including retirement issues, discussion about books or news, or specific health or mental health issues.

Sixth, social workers can encourage clients to help others. For example, one social services agency organized a number of older adult clients and helped them assess their special competencies. They were then organized as volunteers to help each other. Those who could drive chauffeured others who couldn't for grocery shopping and medical appointments. People with good eyesight read to those who could not see as well. People with exceptional organizational skills organized and oversaw the volunteer activities. Many people put their strengths to use and became productive members of the community.

### Empowerment for People Facing Death

The prior section addressed empowering older adults by maximizing their social support, involvement in activities, and quality of life. Another important issue facing older adults, especially as they advance in age, is the idea of preparing for and coping with their eventual death. Social workers help people during their most difficult crises. Dealing with death—be it their own or that of a loved one—is certainly one of those times. It's hard because addressing death makes you face your own mortality. Yet, helping people get through their most trying times may be the most useful and rewarding service practitioners can offer. Social workers can empower clients by playing important roles that include counseling, offering emotional support, providing information, and assisting clients or their loved ones as they cope with ensuing death.

EP 1, 8e

#### Phases of Emotion

Kubler-Ross (1969) developed a five-stage model of emotions that appear to be involved when people face death or extreme loss (James, 2008; Kanel, 2015). These stages include the following:

1. *Denial and isolation.* An initial response to bad news is refusal to believe the news is true. "That just can't be!" "There must be some mistake." "The case records were confused." "The test results must have been flawed."
2. *Anger.* Another emotional response is anger that "it had to happen to me!" "It's not fair." "It isn't right." "Why me?!!!"
3. *Bargaining.* Still another emotional response involves bargaining, trying to make deals to get a

better outcome. "Maybe there's something I can do to make the problem stop or go away." "I'll pray really hard." "I'll take the right vitamins and go through all the experimental treatments. I'll do anything to make it go away."
4. *Depression.* Depression involves feelings of extreme sadness, fatigue, and hopelessness. "It's no use. It's over anyway." "Nothing will improve." "Poor me." "I might as well lie down and die right now."
5. *Acceptance.* A final stage involves accepting the inevitable and more objectively looking at the end. Acceptance involves people who "are in the process of disengaging from this life if they are dying or disengaging from a loved one if that person is dying or has died" (Kanel, 2012, p. 146; Kubler-Ross, 1969, pp. 35–77).

A significant aspect of Kubler-Ross's phases is that they focus on how normal it is to express strong emotions when you find out you're dying or that someone close to you is dying. Note that not all of these stages occur for everyone, however, nor do they occur in the same order they're presented here. Many people vacillate back and forth among emotional stages. Hopefully, these people finally experience acceptance.

McInnis-Dittrich (2014) describes the potential emotional turmoil involved when addressing death:

*It is not uncommon for a relative of a dying person to become extremely angry at the dying person, blaming him or her for not seeking medical treatment earlier or for persisting in self-destructive behavior, such as heavy smoking or drinking. This intense anger may seem incongruous with the sadness and deep affection a family member really feels for a dying older adult. Older adults may also lash out at family caregivers, which may seem alarmingly ungrateful. The emotional roller coaster that accompanies the dying process is unpredictable and disconcerting to both an older adult and the family support system. (p. 289)*

#### Empowerment of a Person Who Is Dying

There are several suggestions for empowering and helping a person who is dying cope with his or her own impending death. First, encourage the client to talk about his or her feelings, even the negative ones. People must let their feelings out before they can deal with them. Convey that you are willing to talk about even difficult matters. Don't discourage crying. This is just another means of coping with sadness. Sometimes, when talking about feelings and establishing a perspective, it's helpful to examine one's life. A life review of both positive and negative events can help a person find acceptance and set his or her mind at peace.

EP 7d, 8e

A second suggestion for helping a client who is dying involves focusing on spirituality, if that client has religious or spiritual beliefs. "The social worker's responsibility is to be especially responsive to and respectful of the client's unique religious and spiritual traditions"; such beliefs may help the client "prepare to leave this life and enter the transformation of death" (Derezotes, 2006, p. 252).

A third suggestion for empowering a dying person involves providing assistance in making any necessary decisions that may be of concern to the client. Does the client have opinions about his or her funeral or other treatment near or after death? Are there certain items that the person would like to give to loved ones? If so, encourage the client to indicate what they are and who should receive them. You might also provide the client with needed information such as that about medications, treatments, or pain relievers. Some clients might benefit from information about hospice care as a possible choice for them. We have established that a **hospice** is a homelike residence, emphasizing residents' comfort and peace, where a person can reside and interact with loved ones in the days or weeks preceding death.

Social workers can also help older adults complete documents to make decisions about their future in the event they lose mental competence. **Advance directives** are "written instructions by the individual [who is mentally competent] to healthcare providers and family members about end-of-life decisions" (McInnis-Dittrich, 2014, p. 292). Two types of advance directives include living wills and Durable Power of Attorney for Health Care (McInnis-Dittrich, 2014). "A **living will** is a written document that states what the patient does or does not want in medical treatment should he or she become incapacitated" (McInnis-Dittrich, 2014, p. 293). For instance, a living will could indicate whether or not an individual chooses to live on life support when brain functioning has ceased. The **Durable Power of Attorney for Health Care** "is a legal document that designates another person to make decisions about

health care when a patient becomes incapacitated" (McInnis-Dittrich, 2014, p. 293).

## Helping Loved Ones Cope

Kanel (2015) provides eight suggestions for helping survivors of a loved one after that person has died. This is another task of social workers who work in nursing homes and other settings such as hospitals where death is often experienced.

1. "Help survivors actualize the loss. Talk about the loss. What happened? Ask.
2. Help them identify and express feelings. If they are dealing with anger, be indirect (what do you miss the most/least?). Four common difficult emotions are anger, guilt, anxiety, and helplessness.
3. Help survivors in living without the deceased. The problem-solving approach works well for this. Discourage major life changes for a while.
4. Facilitate emotional withdrawal from the deceased. Encourage survivors to go on.
5. Provide time to grieve. Crucial times include 3 months and 1 year after the death, anniversaries of the death, and holidays. Help clients prepare in advance for these.
6. Educate clients about customary grieving reactions of other individuals to help normalize the experience.
7. Allow for individual differences [including cross-cultural differences]. Be sensitive to individual styles.
8. Provide for continuing support. Encourage clients to join support groups." (p. 140)

## Empowerment of African American Grandparents Who Become Primary Child Caregivers

Multiple examples exist of how social workers and social welfare programs can empower older adults. Various facets of the older adult population can be targeted and assisted in many creative ways.

Okazawa-Rey (1998) describes one approach to empowerment for African American grandparents who have become primary caregivers for their grandchildren. This reflects one type of programming social workers can initiate, develop, and provide. The problem addressed is one well established at the community and national levels. Many people have become

EP 2

addicted to crack cocaine or methamphetamine and are ignoring their responsibilities as parents and productive citizens to pursue drug use. "Grandparents have always played major roles in the lives of their grandchildren, but in recent years this role has magnified in intensity, as more and more grandparents have become the primary caregivers of grandchildren" (Cox, 2005, p. 128). Newman and Newman (2015) reflect

*African Americans value strong kinship bonds and a supportive extended family system. Caregiving responsibilities are shared among kin and non-kin as needed. Grandparents tend to support working parents by providing care to young children and are cared for in return. Their active role in the family often contributes a strong moral and religious strength and provides emotional support to the parent generation that reduces stress in the household. (p. 544)*

An example of a program responding to the needs of grandparents who become primary caregivers to grandchildren is the Grandparents Who Care Support Network of San Francisco. Most members were "poor and working class, middle-aged and [older adult] ... African-American women" (Okazawa-Rey, 1998, p. 54). They had gained custody of their grandchildren because of their own children's neglect. This is due to drug abuse, incarceration because of drug convictions, and an unwillingness to relinquish their grandchildren to strangers in the public foster care system (McAdoo, 2007).

These grandparents found themselves in the strange and unusual circumstance of suddenly having responsibility for small children at a stage in life when they thought they were done with all that. This situation was compounded by the health problems many of these children suffered due to poor prenatal care, parental drug use during pregnancy, and child neglect. These grandparents "desperately need[ed] day care, special education services, transportation, respite care, and money" (Okazawa-Rey, 1998, p. 54). To get services, they found themselves trying to negotiate the confusing maze of bureaucracies governing service provision.

Two health-care workers, Doriane Miller and Sue Trupin, identified the problems and needs and established Grandparents Who Care (Okazawa-Rey, 1998). The program was based on four principles. First, individual health problems transcend any assignment of individual blame; rather, they are related to problems in the environment. Second, cultural, legal, and organizational barriers often hinder access to needed services. Third, even if people can obtain needed services, these may be inadequate to meet their needs. Fourth, empowerment at the micro, mezzo, and macro levels is necessary for maintaining optimal health and well-being. The grandparents require not only support as individuals (a facet of micro practice) but also the development of an organization (an aspect of macro practice) to provide support group services (a dimension of mezzo practice).

## Mezzo-Practice Perspectives: Establishing Support Groups

Grandparents Who Care established a series of support groups to provide information, emotional support, and practical advice. "Support groups can play important roles in combating the isolation that is frequently experienced by grandparent caregivers" (Cox, 2005, p. 133). Groups consisted of 2 to 25 grandparents, were co-led by professional health-care personnel, including social workers and nurses, and met weekly for 90 minutes. Grandparents Who Care had a board of directors made up of grandparents, citizens, and concerned health-care professionals who advise the organization.

Group members supported each other in addressing a range of issues. For example, "When one woman faces a particular problem with her grandchild in the school system, another one will describe her dealings with this system and offer suggestions concerning the most effective ways to intercede" (Okazawa-Rey, 1998, p. 58). In this way, members could share their experiences and work through issues. The professional co-leaders could assist the group by providing technical information about service availability, eligibility, and accessibility.

## Macro-Practice Perspectives: Expanding Influence

Grandparents Who Care expanded its work in several macro dimensions to further empower its members. First, grandparents were trained as group leaders to go out and form new groups, thereby extending support to grandparents elsewhere in the community.

Second, Grandparents Who Care undertook political advocacy and lobbying on its members' behalf. One problem that advocates addressed involved the legal difficulties grandparents experienced in receiving foster care payments. As relatives, they did not technically qualify as foster parents. Other financial support available to them was not nearly as good as that provided to unrelated foster parents. Grandparents Who Care advocates lobbied with a state legislator to pass a bill allowing grandparents to receive increased benefits.

## Appreciation of Spirituality and Empowerment for Navajo Older Adults in a Nursing Home

The Navajo community traditionally has maintained a rich fabric of cultural traditions, values, and spiritual beliefs. It is a nongeographical community because of its intricate interpersonal relationships, sense of identity, and recognition of members' belongingness, regardless of where they reside. Members are tied to each other by much more than simple location. Of course, many Navajos live on the Navajo reservation, a large geographical community located in the south central Colorado Plateau, which includes parts of Arizona, New Mexico, and Utah. (*Geographical communities* have geographical boundaries and occupy a designated space.)

An ongoing theme in social work practice is the importance of responding to diverse ethnic and cultural values and needs. The following account portrays how the Navajo community and a nursing home it sponsors have responded to meet the needs of aging members in ways differing from commonly held Euro-American traditions.

### A Focus on Traditional Navajo Values

Traditional Navajo older adults, referred to here as "Grandparents," adhere to cultural values that differ from Euro-American traditions. For one thing, Mercer (1996) explains that

> *traditional Navajo religion deals with controlling the many supernatural powers in the Navajo world. Earth Surface People (living and dead humans) and Holy People (supernatural beings) interact.... Navajos abide by prescriptions and proscriptions (taboos) given by the Holy People to maintain harmony with others, nature, and supernatural forces.... The goal of traditional Navajo life is to live in harmony and die of old age. If one indulges in excesses, has improper contacts with dangerous powers, or deliberately or accidentally breaks other rules, then disharmony, conflict,*

> *evil, sickness of body and mind, misfortune, and disaster result. (pp. 182–183)[5]*

Thus, when an imbalance occurs, a person may become sick, which can be attributed to "infection by animals, natural phenomena, or evil spirits such as ghosts (**chindi**) and witches" (p. 183). Preventive ceremonies can address the root of the illness, involve the appropriate Holy People, seek to restore harmony, and forestall ill fortune. "As major social and religious events involving entire communities, ceremonies are a major investment of time and resources for the afflicted person, extended family, and clan" (p. 183).

Another primary traditional value in Navajo life is the importance placed on the extended family. Referred to as a **clan**, such families include a much more extensive membership than that of grandparents, parents, and children. The Navajo community has "more than 60 clan-based kinship groups" (p. 183). A related concept is the importance of the **hogan**, or home, as the center of Navajo family life.

### Culturally Competent Treatment of Older Adult Navajo People

Mercer (1996) explored the treatment of older adult Navajo people, the Grandparents, who resided in the Chinle Nursing Home, a nonprofit agency whose board of directors was composed solely of Navajos. She investigated how treatment for Grandparents in Chinle differed from typical treatment provided outside the reservation. She found that, essentially, Chinle emphasized the importance of **cultural care**—"the learned and transmitted values and beliefs that enable people to maintain their well-being and health and to deal with illness, disability, and death" (Bearse, 2008; Leininger, 1990, 1992; Mercer, 1996, p. 186).

**EP 1c, 8e**

Mercer (1996) found that culturally competent care was applied in at least six major areas (pp. 186–188):

1. *Communication:* Few Navajo Grandparents were fluent in English, so translators were used. Such translation was done with great sensitivity,

---

[5]This case example is taken from S. O. Mercer (1996, March). Navajo elderly people in a reservation nursing home: Admission predictors and culture care practices. *Social Work, 41*(2), 181–189. Copyright 1996, National Association of Social Workers, Inc., Social Work. Reprinted with permission.

because the Navajo language often has no word that means exactly what an English word does. Additionally, sensitivity was important while listening because interrupting a speaker is considered extremely rude.

2. *Clan associations and social structure:* Clan associations are very important to Navajo people. Upon introduction, Navajos traditionally announce their clan membership. Nursing home staff were sensitive to the fact that Grandparents often had many visitors from their clan who had traveled great distances at significant cost.

3. *Personal space, modesty, privacy, and cleanliness:* Grandparents valued personal space. They often found it difficult and uncomfortable to sleep in the high nursing home beds, having been accustomed to mattresses or sheep skins on the floor. Staff complied with Grandparents' wishes to sleep where they wanted and usually found that Grandparents eventually adjusted to sleeping in beds.

Grandparents also valued modesty and privacy. Therefore, communal showering was a problem. Rather, Grandparents often preferred sweat baths, which they felt cleansed them both physically and spiritually. The nursing home provided saunas to simulate these sweat baths and offered showers to residents twice each week.

Finally, Grandparents often preferred sleeping in their daytime clothes rather than changing into nightgowns or pajamas. Staff allowed Grandparents to sleep in whatever they wanted. In time most chose night clothes.

4. *Traditional food:* Grandparents preferred "grilled mutton [meat of a mature sheep], mutton stew, fry bread, corn, fried potatoes, and coffee" (p. 187). In response, nursing home staff served lamb three times a month and usually baked fresh bread. Staff also encouraged family members to bring foods Grandparents preferred, as long as these complied with health-related dietary constraints.

5. *Dying and death:* "Traditional Navajo people have many restrictions regarding contact with the dead. They do not talk about death, believing that discussing death may 'bring it to you'" (p. 187). Navajo families will usually move a dying person to a nearby brush shelter to avoid having death occur in the hogan. In the event of a home death, that hogan is usually deserted and even demolished.

Traditionally, people touching a dead body followed specific rituals to avoid taboos. Similarly, most Grandparents and staff sought to avoid touching a dead person or his or her clothing. Usually a dying Grandparent was transferred to a hospital so that death would not occur in the nursing home. If a death did occur there, cleansing rituals were performed before other residents inhabited the room.

Because of their aversion to talking about death, no Grandparents would discuss such issues as living wills or power of attorney. Staff respected this value and did not pressure residents to do so.

6. *Cultural rituals:* To hold cultural rituals, a hogan was constructed near Chinle and was made available for ceremonies and prayers that remain important aspects of Grandparents' lives.

Examples of how diverse communities and social agencies may respond to members' values and needs are countless. The important thing for social workers is to respect and appreciate cultural differences and strive to help social services meet diverse members' needs.

# Chapter Summary

The following summarizes this chapter's content as it relates to the learning objectives presented at the beginning of the chapter. Chapter content will help prepare students to:

*LO1 Describe the issue of "global graying."*
Global graying is an international phenomenon where the proportion of older adults is increasing globally. When addressing this issue, social workers should emphasize self-determination, enhancement of the environment and political milieu on the behalf of older adults, and existing strengths of the older adult population.

*LO2 Demonstrate empowerment when working with older adults (that incorporates values and goals, and provide case examples of active aging).*

An empowerment perspective for working with older adults stresses values and goals involving respect, appreciating difference, valuing choice, and promoting health. Active aging emphasizes "participation in life," "health," and "security" (Rizzo & Seidman, 2009). Various examples of active aging are provided.

### LO3 Discuss issues older adults commonly face (including ageism, discrimination in employment, poverty, retirement, health-care issues, abuse, living conditions and family variables, and transitional issues).

Ageism involves harboring negative images of and attitudes toward people simply because they are older. Older adults experience discrimination in employment. Almost half of the older adults living in the United States would fall below the poverty line if they were not receiving Social Security benefits. Current debate focuses on a variety of ways to save Social Security. Suggestions include changing benefit amounts, worker contribution amounts, time lines, and criteria for recipients.

Factors that increase the potential for poverty include advanced age, female gender, and being a person of color. The average age of planned retirement is 64. The older people get, the more likely they are to experience health problems.

An estimated 1.5 million older adults are victims of physical or emotional abuse. Older adult abuse is "the violation of an [older adult's] ... human and civil rights by any other person or persons"; such abuse may involve a lone incident or multiple, recurring acts (Gisby & Butler, 2012, p. 210). In addition to physical and emotional, types of abuse include sexual, financial, discriminatory, and institutional abuse in addition to neglect. Suggestions for assessment and treatment are provided.

Many older adults prefer to live on their own or with other family members. Transitional issues as people age include coping with health problems and increasing dependence.

### LO4 Engage in critical thinking (about confronting myths about older adults, financing Social Security, determining whether Social Security discriminates against women, and proposing

*how older adults might be empowered through macro practice).*

Critical thinking questions are posed concerning untrue myths about older adults, including that they are riddled with disease, are unattractive, sleep all the time, can't learn new things, and are senile. Questions raised about Social Security concern raising the retirement age, decreasing benefits, increasing the maximum amount of income that can be taxed, cutting increases in benefits, and offering benefits only to those who are less well off (establishing a means test). Questions also concern whether Social Security is fair to women and, if so, whether it should be reformed. Finally, critical thinking questions are raised about how older adults might be treated, resources provided, and services developed from residual versus institutional and conservative versus liberal perspectives.

### LO5 Explain the concept of "gayging."

"Gayging" is the invisibility, lack of attention, and unfair treatment many LGB people experience as they get older (Tully, 2000). Social workers must be sensitive to their needs and their increased risk of discrimination.

### LO6 Examine contexts for social work practice with older adults (including home- and community-based services, discharge planning in hospital settings, and service provision in nursing homes).

Home-based services are types of assistance provided to people in their own homes, either formally or informally by informal support networks. Community-based services are those provided to meet psychological and social needs outside the home in the community. Discharge planning is the comprehensive assessment of a patient's abilities and needs, the development of a plan to facilitate that patient's transition out of the hospital and back into the community or agency setting, and the implementation of that plan. *Assisted living* facilities provide a combination of lodging, support services and health care, as needed. It represents a less intensive caregiving alternative to nursing home placement. Nursing homes or skilled care facilities are residential centers that "provide nursing care and rehabilitation for people who have severe functional limitations as a result of acute illness, surgery, or advanced dementia" (Newman & Newman, 2015, p. 586).

*LO7 Explore empowerment strategies for diverse older adult populations (including African American grandparents who are primary caregivers for grandchildren and the culturally competent treatment of older Navajo people residing in a nursing home).*

In nursing homes, social workers can empower residents by developing plans based on strengths, helping residents make decisions, addressing issues of concern raised by family members, linking residents with outside services, assisting other staff in understanding residents' needs, and advocating for residents' rights. Empowerment strategies should focus on adaptation, competence, relatedness, and autonomy (Zuniga, 1995). Increasing sensitivity to older adults and their issues can enhance effective work with this population.

Empowerment of people facing death includes understanding the emotional stages they may undergo, encouraging the expression of feelings, focusing on spirituality, and helping the individual make decisions including those involving legal documents. Suggestions for helping loved ones cope with grief are provided.

Grandparents Who Care is an example of a program that stresses empowerment. It provided support for African American grandparents who were the primary caregivers of their grandchildren. Support groups and political advocacy were emphasized.

The Chinle nursing home in the central Colorado Plateau offers another example of empowerment by providing culturally sensitive care to older adult Navajo residents. Its programming emphasized traditional values including: culturally sensitive communication; clan associations and social structure; respect for personal space, modesty, privacy, and cleanliness; traditional food; rituals concerning dying and death; and other cultural rituals.

## LOOKING AHEAD

This chapter addressed the needs of older adults, a population at risk in terms of poverty, discrimination, and other problems associated with aging,

such as declines in health. It discussed service provision to older adults and approaches to empowerment. Chapter 18 focuses on another population at risk that has special needs for policies and services—people with disabilities.

## COMPETENCY NOTES

The following identifies where Educational Policy (EP) competencies and their component behaviors are discussed in the chapter.

**EP 1 (Competency 1)—Demonstrate Ethical and Professional Behavior.** *(p. 344):* This Highlight discusses social workers' professional roles in nursing homes. *(p. 347):* One of social workers' most important roles involves helping people deal with crises, including those who are facing death.

**EP 1b Use reflection and self-regulation to manage personal values and maintain professionalism in practice situations.** *(p. 330):* Stereotypes and biased personal values that practitioners have about older adults should be confronted and managed. *(p. 337):* Social workers must practice personal reflection and and self-regulation to manage personal values and biases they might harbor about LGB older adults. *(p. 345):* Social workers must work hard to use self-reflection concerning their personal values and address any prejudices and stereotypes they may harbor toward older adults.

**EP 1c Demonstrate professional demeanor in behavior; appearance; and oral, written, and electronic communication.** *(p. 337):* Social workers should use language that is respectful of and sensitive to LGB relationships and situations. *(p. 350):* Communication with Navajo grandparents should be culturally sensitive.

**EP 2 (Competency 2)—Engage Diversity and Difference in Practice.** *(p. 328):* Social workers should understand the variables related to race, gender, and social class that affect and oppress segments of the older adult population. *(p. 329):* Social workers should recognize the extent to which older adults can be oppressed, marginalized, and alienated because of negative false stereotypes. Practitioners should understand that ageism and other forces such as job discrimination and poverty (described in subsequent sections) serve as mechanisms of oppression and discrimination. *(p. 330):* Stereotypes about older adults serve to oppress, marginalize, and alienate them. *(p. 334):* Critical thinking questions stimulate thought about Social Security and discrimination against women. *(p. 337):* Sexual orientation and aging are aspects of diversity. *(p. 345):* Practitioners must understand how society potentially oppresses and alienates older adults. *(p. 348):* Race and culture, both aspects of diversity, are discussed in this and the next section concerning African Americans and Navajo people, respectively.

**EP 2a Apply and communicate understanding of the importance of diversity and difference in shaping life experiences in practice at the micro, mezzo, and macro levels.** *(p. 337):* Social workers should recognize how sexual orientation and aging shapes life experiences for LGB older adults. *(p. 345):* Practitioners should recognize the extent to which their age shapes life experiences for older adults.

**EP 2b Present themselves as learners and engage clients and constituencies as experts of their own experiences.** *(p. 337):* Social workers should view themselves as learners and engage LGB older adults as informants. *(p. 345):* Social workers should view themselves as learners and consider older adults experts of their own experiences.

**EP 2c Apply self-awareness and self-regulation to manage the influence of personal biases and values in working with diverse clients and constituencies.** *(p. 330):* Stereotypes and biased personal values that practitioners have about older adults should be confronted and addressed. *(p. 337):* Social workers must strive for self-awareness and and self-regulation to manage personal values and biases they might harbor about LGB older adults. *(p. 345):* Social workers must work hard to develop self-awareness and not allow any personal biases they may harbor toward older adults to affect their practice.

**EP 3 (Competency 3)—Advance Human Rights and Social, Economic, and Environmental Justice.** *(p. 325):* It's important for social workers to understand the global ramifications for older adults as a population at risk.

**EP 3a Apply their understanding of social, economic, and environmental justice to** advocate for human rights at the individual and system levels. *(p. 333):* Critical thinking questions encourage thought about how social and economic justice might be achieved through Social Security. *(p. 340):* Critical thinking questions encourage thought about advocating for older adults' human rights and about society's responsibility to respect and care for these people.

**EP 5 (Competency 5)—Engage in Policy Practice.**

**EP 5a Identify social policy at the local, state, and federal level that impacts well-being, service delivery, and access to social services.** *(p. 333):* Social Security policy impacts people's well-being and access to resources.

**EP 5b Assess how social welfare and economic policies impact the delivery of and access to social services.** *(p. 333):* Critical thinking questions are raised concerning the impact of Social Security on people's access to resources.

**EP 5c Apply critical thinking to analyze, formulate, and advocate for policies that advance human rights and social, economic, and environmental justice.** *(p. 333):* Critical thinking questions encourage thought about how social and economic justice might be achieved through Social Security policy. *(p. 334):* Critical thinking questions encourage thought about the extent to which Social Security policies advance the social well-being of women. *(p. 340):* Critical thinking questions address the relationship between political orientation and policies that empower older adults.

**EP 7 (Competency 7)—Assess Individuals, Families, Groups, Organizations, and Communities.**

**EP 7a Collect and organize data, and apply critical thinking to interpret information from clients and constituencies.** *(p. 330):* During assessment, stereotypes about older adults should be confronted and questioned.

**EP 7c Develop mutually agreed-on intervention goals and objectives based on the critical assessment of strengths, needs, and challenges within clients and constituencies.** *(p. 326):* Social workers should assess and emphasize older adult clients' strengths to help them maintain the most autonomy possible in the least restrictive environment. *(p. 338):* Social workers should assess and emphasize strengths in addition to assessing limitations when working together with older adults. *(p. 344):* The case example illustrates how a nursing home social worker developed mutually agreed-upon goals with the client. *(p. 345):* An empowerment perspective emphasizes the assessment and appreciation of older adult clients' strengths.

**EP 7d Select appropriate intervention strategies based on the assessment, research knowledge, and values and preferences of clients and constituencies.** *(p. 338):* Appropriate intervention strategies for working with older adults are discussed. *(p. 344):* This case example demonstrates how the social worker developed appropriate intervention strategies. *(p. 345):* Appropriate intervention strategies for working with older adults are described. *(p. 348):* Appropriate interventions are suggested for helping clients and their loved ones deal with death.

**EP 8 (Competency 8)—Intervene with Individuals, Families, Groups, Organizations, and Communities.**

**EP 8a Critically choose and implement interventions to achieve practice goals and enhance capacities of clients and constituencies.** *(p. 340):* Critical thinking questions are raised about implementing macro interventions and pursuing policy practice to enhance the capacities of older adults.

**EP 8c Use inter-professional collaboration as appropriate to achieve beneficial practice outcomes.** *(p. 340):* Political advocacy involves collaboration with colleagues, clients, and other macro systems.

**EP 8d Negotiate, mediate, and advocate with and on behalf of diverse clients and constituencies.** *(p. 333):* Social workers should advocate for just and adequate Social Security benefits. *(p. 340):* Social workers should advocate at the macro level for policies and services that enhance the lives of older adults. *(p. 344):* Advocating for clients is part of the nursing home social worker's role.

**EP 8e Facilitate effective transitions and endings that advance mutually agreed-on goals.** *(p. 338):* Social workers should facilitate effective transitions in living settings for older adults. *(p. 347):* Social workers can help clients and their families prepare for and cope with death. *(p. 348):* Specific suggestions are proposed for helping clients and their families cope with death. *(p. 350):* Culturally sensitive communication and behavior should be used when addressing the concept of death in Navajo families.

# 11 Social Work and Services for People with Disabilities

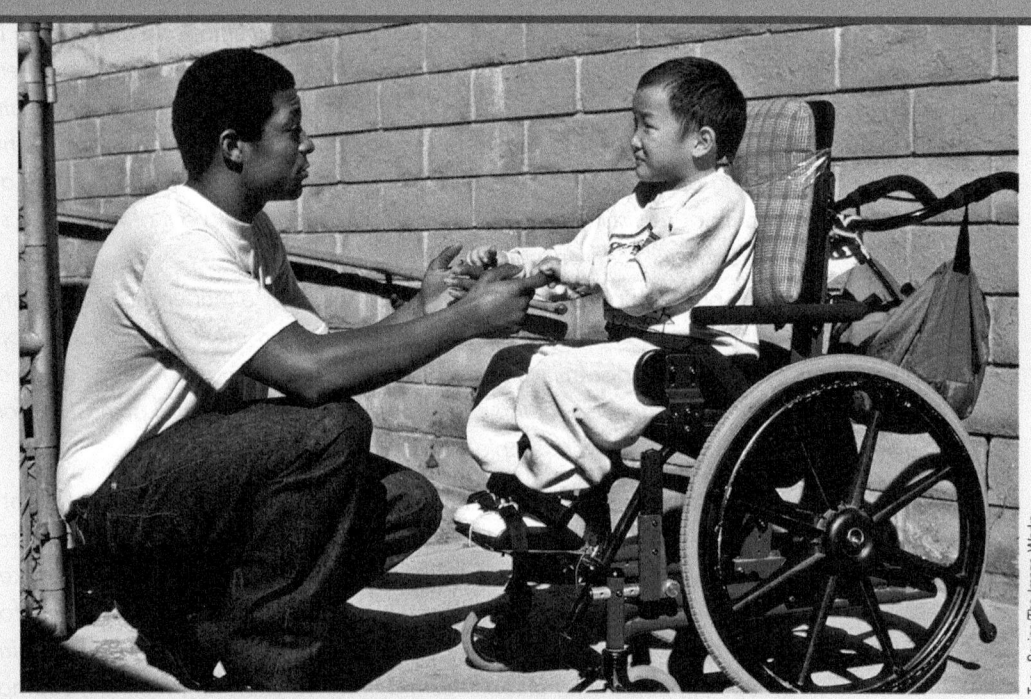

Tony Savino/The Image Works

## Learning Objectives    This chapter will help prepare students to:

**LO 1** Define mobility disabilities (and identify a range of specific disabilities clustered under its umbrella). **People with Mobility Disabilities** (p. 360)

**LO 2** Investigate the importance of self-determination (for people with disabilities as an ethical aspect of social work practice). **Ethical Implications for Social Work Practice: The Importance of Self-Determination** (p. 360)

**LO 3** Engage in critical thinking (about personal feelings and stereotypes concerning disability, residual versus institutional approaches to service provision for people with disabilities, empowerment through language, deinstitutionalization, and the Americans with Disabilities Act). **Focus on Critical Thinking 11.1** (p. 362)

**LO 4** Define developmental disabilities (and identify a range of specific disabilities clustered under its umbrella). **What Are Developmental Disabilities?** (p. 364)

**LO 5** Examine historical perspectives concerning developmental disabilities. **Treatment over Time of People with Developmental Disabilities: The Quest for Social and Economic Justice** (p. 368)

**LO 6** Describe generalist social work practice with people who have developmental disabilities. **Generalist Social Work and People Who Have Developmental Disabilities** (p. 372)

**LO 7** Discuss avenues of empowerment (legislative and community empowerment). **Empowerment Through Legislation: Seeking Social and Economic Justice** (p. 373)

*Jane, age 20, was on a motorcycle outing with her fiancé, age 21, when he crashed head-on into a tree while trying to evade an oncoming car.*[1] *He was killed instantly. Jane's leg was so mangled she ultimately had to have it removed. "One year later she was seen by a social worker during her rehabilitation of the amputation. She was demonstrating signs of complicated grief and traumatic stress: continuing to live in her fiancé's room, refusing to let anyone remove his possessions from the room, delaying rehabilitation of her severed limb, and developing increasing fears and phobias. With the social worker she began to confront her anger toward her fiancé for losing control of the bike and causing her amputation, an emotion that seemed unacceptable to her since she had survived and he had not. Expressing and working through these feelings empowered her to become active in making more realistic plans for her life, including moving out of her fiancé's room"* (Christ, Sormanti, & Francoeur, 2001, p. 126).

*Jane provides an example of a person who has experienced a disability resulting from an accident happening when she was an adult. Of course, people can also be born with disabilities or gradually acquire them as a result of chronic debilitating illness. Regardless of the cause, social workers can fulfill at least the following roles when working with people who have disabilities:*

- *As counselors, social workers help people explore their feelings, confront issues, and make life plans. They can work with individuals, families, or groups to address various aspects of life with disability. For example, social workers may help families of people with disabilities discuss interpersonal issues, focus on strengths, cope with difficulties, and address needs. Similarly, working with groups of people with disabilities may involve exploring feelings, coping mechanisms, and potential resources in addition to providing mutual support.*
- *As educators, social workers provide information about disabilities and related issues.*
- *As brokers, social workers link people who have disabilities and their families with needed services.*
- *As rehabilitative team members, social workers consult with occupational therapists, physical therapists, speech therapists, psychologists, nurses, and other medical personnel to develop coordinated treatment plans for people with disabilities.*
- *As case coordinators, social workers synchronize and oversee service provision for people with disabilities who have multiple needs.*
- *As advocates, social workers seek to improve the treatment of people with disabilities through legislation and agency provision of service.*

*More than 37 million people in the United States, or almost 12% of the population age 5 or older, have some type of disability; more than 20.4 million people*

---

[1]This vignette was cited in "Chronic Physical Illness and Disability," by G. H. Christ, M. Sormanti, and R. B. Francoeur in A. Gitterman (Ed.), *Handbook of Social Work Practice with Vulnerable and Resilient Populations* (2nd ed., pp. 124–162), 2001, New York: Columbia University Press.

EP 2

*age 16 and older have some condition that prevents them from work-
ing or limits the amount of work they can do (ProQuest, 2014). Who
are people with disabilities? They are anyone who has a permanent
"physical or mental impairment [or ongoing health or mental health
condition] that substantially limits one or more major life activities";
these activities include "seeing, hearing, speaking, walking, breathing, performing manual tasks, learning, caring for oneself, and working" (Equal
Employment Opportunity Commission, 1997, p. 1). Disabilities, which vary widely
in severity and the extent to which they affect daily functioning, can commence at
any point in life, from birth to old age.*

*To some extent, disabilities are related to socioeconomic status. Socioeconomic
status is usually determined by taking "education, income and occupation" into
account; people with disabilities are more likely to face barriers to education and
to be poor (American Psychological Association, 2014). They have more difficulty
finding jobs and tend to have high medical expenses.*

*How various people including experts categorize disabilities varies markedly,
depending on what aspects of the disability they emphasize (Patchner & DeWeaver,
2008). For example, developmental disabilities involve early onset and a lifelong
time span. This umbrella concept can include difficulties in cognitive ability, such as
intellectual disability (formerly mental retardation), and physical disabilities, such as
orthopedic problems affecting bones and joints, and hearing problems.*

*Mobility disabilities, in contrast, can occur at any time. Mobility disabilities
reflect a lack of physical ability to get around and conduct life tasks.*

*However, different categories of disability may overlap. Some mobility disabil-
ities can also be considered developmental. For instance, a person with cerebral
palsy (a type of developmental disability involving problems in muscular control)
who cannot walk without crutches also has a mobility disability.*

*Mobility disabilities are also a type of physical disability because they involve
physical bodily performance, as opposed to cognitive or emotional functioning.
Many developmental disabilities such as hearing loss or visual impairment are
also physical disabilities because of their physical rather than mental nature. The
matter is further complicated because many people have multiple disabilities.*

*The point of this discussion is not to confuse you but to clarify this chapter's
overall approach to the wide range of disabilities. Arbitrary distinctions are made
regarding how disabilities are sorted and discussed. It is far beyond the scope of
this chapter to cover all disabilities. Thus the intent is to provide a general introduction to what disabilities might involve and how social work practitioners help
empower people who have them.*

*On one hand, social workers practice directly with people who have disabilities
and their families on the micro and mezzo levels. On the other, social workers have
a responsibility to advocate on behalf of people with disabilities to make sure they
get the resources and services they need.*

*A primary goal of social work education is to teach students "to promote human and community well-being…. [T]he purpose of social work is actualized through its quest for social and economic justice, the prevention of conditions that limit human rights, the elimination of poverty, and the enhancement of the quality of life for all persons, locally and globally" (CSWE, 2015, p. 1). Social workers strive to enhance people's living conditions in their social environment to make them as comfortable and supportive as possible. One way to accomplish this is to "analyze, formulate, and advocate for policies that advance human rights and social, economic, and environmental justice" (CSWE, 2015, EP 5c).*

## People with Mobility Disabilities

**LO 1**

People who have **mobility disabilities** "are those whose physical differences require them to achieve physical activities in a variety of alternate ways" (Mackelprang & Salsgiver, 2009, p. 177). For example, a person with a spinal cord injury may require a wheelchair to move from place to place and achieve the mobility needed to conduct the business of life. Mobility disorders may be **congenital**—that is, "acquired before, during, or immediately after birth"— or they may be **acquired** at some time later in life (Mackelprang & Salsgiver, 2009, p. 178). Many congenital mobility disabilities are also considered developmental disabilities (e.g., cerebral palsy, orthopedic problems) and will be discussed later in the chapter. A number of acquired mobility problems are described in Highlight 11.1.

## Ethical Implications for Social Work Practice: The Importance of Self-Determination

**LO 2**

It's easy to make false assumptions about people who have mobility and other physical disabilities. Myths people may have about disabilities include the following:

*Myth:* The more severe a physical disability is, the less intelligent the person.

EP 1b, 2, 2c

*Fact:* A person may have a severe physical disability and yet have a brilliant mind.

*Myth:* People with physical disabilities are unable to function normally in society.

*Fact:* People with physical disabilities can live productive, fruitful, happy lives when they receive the support they need.

*Myth:* People with one kind of disability also have other disabilities.

*Fact:* One disability may have nothing to do with other disabilities. A person with one disability can function as well as anyone else in other areas. This myth sometimes is referred to as the **spread of disability**.

For example, Steve, age 19, has quadriplegia— the paralysis of all four limbs. He broke his neck in a swimming accident three years ago. He tells the story of how he went out to eat with his parents at a local family restaurant several months after the accident. The waitress approached the table and began to take orders. When it was Steve's turn to order, the waitress turned to his father and asked, "What would he like to order?"

Steve's father replied, "I don't know. Why don't you ask him?"

The waitress turned to Steve and shouted verrrrrry slowly, "WHAT … WOULD … YOU … LIKE … TO … ORDER?"

Steve, whose hearing was just fine, shouted back verrrrrry slowly, "A … QUARTER POUND … CHEESEBURGER … AND … FRIES … PLEASE!"

The waitress had made the assumption that because Steve couldn't walk and had limited use of his arms, he couldn't hear, either. She also took for granted that there was something

EP 1a, 2a, 3b

| HIGHLIGHT **11.1** | **ACQUIRED MOBILITY DISABILITIES** |

The following are examples of *acquired* mobility disabilities (Mackelprang & Salsgiver, 1999). All may require the use of supportive equipment depending on the severity.

**Stroke**: "A blockage or hemorrhage of a blood vessel leading to the brain, causing an inadequate oxygen supply and often long-term impairment of sensation, movement, or functioning" (Nichols, 1999, p. 1295). Brain cells die when they don't receive adequate oxygen, causing damage to the nervous system. Strokes can result in a wide range of symptoms including partial or total paralysis, memory loss, speech or language deficits, and inability to think clearly.

**Muscular dystrophy**: "Any of a group of hereditary diseases characterized by a progressive wasting of the muscles" (Mish, 2008, p. 818). Some forms progress so quickly that people require the use of wheelchairs by the time they reach adolescence. Symptoms include increasingly weakened muscles, an awkward gait, and increasing lack of coordination.

**Rheumatoid arthritis (RA)**: A chronic condition in which a person's immune system attacks the joints, causing pain, inflammation, stiffness, swelling, and deterioration. Joints tend to experience progressive deformity, often resulting in the need for increased support through devices such as canes, crutches, or

wheelchairs. About 1% of the adult population in the United States has this disease, three-quarters of whom are women (Mackelprang & Salsgiver, 1999).

**Multiple sclerosis (MS)**: A disease of the brain tissue in which the myelin sheath—the fatty material wrapped around and insulating the parts of nerve cells that conduct nerve impulses in the brain to other nerve cells—deteriorates, thereby causing varying degrees of muscular dysfunction, paralysis, and muscle tremors.

**Myasthenia gravis (MG)**: A disease affecting voluntary muscles (those controlled by one's will) in which nerve impulses are impaired, resulting in fatigue, weakness, and difficulties controlling muscles. Virtually any muscles can be affected, and symptoms range from weakness in the arms and legs to difficulties in swallowing, controlling eye movements, or breathing.

**Spinal cord injury**: Damage to the spinal cord, often due to accidents or incidents of violence, resulting in the loss of muscular control and inability to experience sensation. Paraplegia is paralysis of the lower part of the body; quadriplegia is paralysis from the neck down. The severity of effects depends on the location and extent of damage to the spinal cord.

wrong with his brain. She made the mistake of assuming a spread of disability—namely, that a person with one disability automatically has others. People with disabilities have

*the right to participate fully and equitably in society. This participation includes the freedom, to the fullest extent possible, to live independently, to exercise self-determination, to make decisions about their living conditions and treatment plans, to obtain an education, to be employed, and to participate as citizens.*

(*NASW, 2015b, p. 232*)

The concept of self-determination has special ethical implications for adults with mobility and other physical disabilities. "Client **self-determination** is each individual's right to make his or her own decisions. The notion of self-determination is closely linked with the concept of **autonomy**"—a person's ability to function independently (Major, 2000, p. 9)

(emphasis added). Related to the type and degree of their disabilities, people with physical disabilities often experience greater difficulties maintaining autonomy than able-bodied people. For example, a person with a serious visual impairment may have great difficulty getting around in an unfamiliar neighborhood without assistance.

Gilson, Bricout, and Baskind (1998) interviewed six people with physical disabilities who felt that social workers tended to focus more on their health status and limitations than on themselves as unique individuals. Ethical concerns included stereotyping people based on the disability label and clearly visible disabilities, ignoring strengths, accessing personal information without receiving client permission, and not consulting with clients as expert resources for information about their disabilities and issues. Despite the small sample size, this study, with its implications of paternalism by practitioners, raises serious ethical questions regarding social workers' efforts to maximize self-determination. Apparently it is easy for social workers to make assumptions about people with disabilities that emphasize weakness instead of strength.

Social workers should follow three recommendations to maximize service provision and client self-determination. These include adopting a consumer-centered approach, learning about services and resources, and advocating for clients with disabilities whenever possible.

## Adopting a Consumer-Oriented Approach

First, social workers should adopt a **consumer-centered approach** (Tower, 1994, p. 191). Treating people as consumers means accepting that they know their own needs and can make intelligent decisions about services. The term *consumer* implies greater power and choice than does the term *client.* This approach contrasts sharply with that of making decisions about what's best for clients without their input, recommendations, and consent. Adopting

EP 1b, 1c, 2b, 7c

a consumer-centered approach, of course, is important in working with any client. However, because of stereotypes and misconceptions about disability, social workers must be particularly vigilant about this when working with clients who have disabilities.

Four facets of a consumer-centered approach are especially important. First, social workers must listen carefully to what the client is saying instead of jumping to conclusions based on the disability label. Second, they must ask questions and seek clarification whenever they do not understand something. Third, they must scrutinize any possible assumptions they may be making about their client and his or her disability. In essence, they must use introspection to confront their stereotypes and work to get rid of them. Focus on Critical Thinking 11.1 addresses the issue of stereotypes and poses questions to help explore them. Fourth, workers should obtain clients' *informed consent.* This is the condition in which clients grant permission for a social worker to undertake the intervention process after the worker clearly informs clients of all the facts, risks, and alternatives involved (NASW, 2008, 1.03).

---

## FOCUS ON CRITICAL THINKING 11.1 — HOW DO I REALLY FEEL ABOUT PEOPLE WITH DISABILITIES?

**LO 3**

Mackelprang (2012) stresses:

> An essential element of competent social work practice is practitioner self-awareness and understanding. Awareness of one's beliefs and attitudes are especially important when working with people and groups different from oneself. This self-reflection can prevent or alter ethnic, sexist, heterosexist and other stereotypes [including those about disability]. (p. 558)

The following questions may help you explore how you really feel about disabilities.

### Critical Thinking Questions

1. *"What are the prevalent attitudes I carry about disability as a group and people with disabilities? These attitudes are often reflected in the language one uses to describe disability. For example, many people think of someone who uses a wheelchair for mobility as confined or wheelchair bound. Put downs ... such as 'That's so retarded' and 'She was crippled by fear', often*

have negative disability connotations" (Mackelprang, 2012, p. 558).

2. *When I think about disabilities, what thoughts and images come to mind? Are there any that frighten me or make me feel uncomfortable? If so, what are the reasons for these feelings? How can I address them?*

3. *"To what degree are my beliefs stereotypical ... [or do they involve pity]?"* (Mackelprang, 2012, p. 558) *How might I reframe my thinking to combat stereotypes or condescending ideas, emphasizing strengths and competence instead?*

4. *"When necessary, what can I do to educate myself, challenge [my attitudes involving pity,] ... and work effectively with people with disabilities? This involves learning about and acknowledging people's potentials and strengths.... Working with people with disabilities includes multiple roles beyond clients or patients, and includes ... colleagues and peers [with disabilities], as well as mentors and supervisors"* (Mackelprang, 2012, p. 559).

*Case Example*   Kachina is a case manager for people with severe physical disabilities. Earlier chapters established that case managers are practitioners who, on behalf of a specific client, assess needs; coordinate required services provided by any number of agencies, organizations, or facilities; and monitor service provision. Usually one individual is designated case manager for specific cases and coordinates a range of services, often provided by a variety of workers from different agencies. The intent is to make total service provision as effective and efficient as possible.

Kachina often coordinates services of group homes, in-home support services, Meals-on-Wheels, medical centers, physical therapists, speech therapists, occupational therapists, and others depending on individual client needs. Kachina always makes it a point to work the service plan out with individual clients, obtaining their permission to proceed. She reviews with clients the pros and cons of each prescribed service. She works hard to make certain clients understand what each service involves and what expectations they must fulfill. For example, physical therapy might involve a designated number of weekly sessions, physical work, and possible pain. Positive results may include significantly increased agility, flexibility, strength, and speed. Clients then can make informed decisions about whether to proceed with that service.

## Learning About Services and Resources

A second way social workers can maximize service provision and self-determination for people with disabilities is to learn about services and resources. People with physical disabilities have the same needs and wants as able-bodied people. They simply have more obstacles getting in the way of what they need. Services include those associated with rehabilitation, employment, health, place of residence, recreation, and personal care. Financial resources include various sources of public funding such as disability insurance, workers' compensation, Supplemental Security Income (SSI), and other forms of public assistance.

### The Self-Determination Movement: Recommendations for Policy Change

Social workers should familiarize themselves with various advocacy and resource groups (Major, 2000). For example, the Self-Determination Movement maintains that people with disabilities have the same right to make decisions about themselves and direct their own lives as people who don't have disabilities; this includes their right to seek and choose services (The Arc, 2011; Major, 2000). People supporting this movement provide an information network, advocacy, and a range of supportive services. Additionally, supporters encourage public policy changes that incorporate self-determination initiatives.

The Self-Determination Movement is founded on four primary principles (National Program Office on Self-Determination [NPOSD], 1998). First, *freedom* concerns people with disabilities having the same rights as other citizens. They should be able to choose where they want to live and how to spend their time just like anybody else.

The second principle, *authority*, involves people with disabilities having control over their own finances, prioritizing how their money should be spent, and developing their own budgets. Consider the following example:

> *A married couple who had been previously receiving supports and services from two different agencies "frequently sought psychiatric hospitalizations to be together" (NPOSD, 1998). After implementing a self-determination program, the couple now lives together and is served by one agency. Because the couple can supply each other with many of the supports they need, they are much more comfortable and content with their situation. What is equally important to note here is that the overall cost of providing their services has decreased significantly.*

*(Major, 2000, p. 12)*

*Support*, the third foundation principle for the Self-Determination Movement, involves having people with disabilities make decisions about where their support comes from. Instead of being given "supervision," people with disabilities should be able to seek their own support systems for companionship. Similarly, they should be able to determine what specific tasks necessitate formal assistance from paid staff and others.

The final principle, *responsibility*, involves the wise disbursement of public funding. Resources used by people with disabilities should be considered as investments in their quality of life, and not simply as lists specifying purchase of specific services. Just as all citizens should be responsible for the efficient and effective use of resources, so should they.

## FOCUS ON CRITICAL THINKING 11.2

# RESIDUAL VERSUS INSTITUTIONAL APPROACHES TO SERVICE PROVISION FOR PEOPLE WITH DISABILITIES

### Critical Thinking Questions

- To what extent do the suggestions for empowerment through promoting self-determination for people with disabilities reflect *residual* versus *institutional* policies and programming? (Recall that residual policies focus on reactions to problems, generally providing as few benefits as possible. Institutional policies view social services as people's right and provide ongoing benefits to enhance people's lives and well-being.)

**EP 5c, 7a**

- To what extent does service provision for people with disabilities demonstrate *conservative* versus *liberal* values?

Now consider the three basic principles involved that relate to the following questions (these are similar to the questions posed concerning value orientations to service provision to older adults):

### Critical Thinking Questions

- Who should assume responsibility? Should people with disabilities be expected to provide for and take care of themselves? Or is it society's responsibility to help them when they need it?
- Who is to blame for the problems and needs of people with disabilities? To what extent will people with disabilities take advantage of social welfare benefits when they really don't need them? Will providing ongoing services and benefits significantly enhance their health, welfare, and comfort?
- To what extent should the government interfere in people's lives? Is it the government's responsibility to improve the health and functioning of people with disabilities?

---

Similarly, people with disabilities should be able to contribute to their communities' well-being in meaningful ways (e.g., volunteering, voting, running for public office).

The National Association of Social Workers' (2015b) issue statement on people with disabilities stresses the importance of self-determination:

*This approach encompasses a continuum that ranges from involving the client in the decision making about the treatment plan to having people with disabilities define the goals of such a plan. People with disabilities may define program objectives in organizations where they are themselves employed as decision makers…. People with disabilities may become … experts, assisting others as well. (p. 232)*

### Advocating for Clients with Disabilities Whenever Possible

A third suggestion for social workers to maximize service provision and client self-determination involves advocating for clients with disabilities when necessary in collaboration with them (NASW, 2015b). Clients may need expanded services or additional resources. Social work practitioners work with their clients to determine their needs. Workers also strive to change agency policy and laws governing resources to benefit people with physical disabilities. Subsequent sections of the chapter discuss advocacy in more detail.

Sometimes political advocacy is necessary. The Americans with Disabilities Act of 1990 (ADA), discussed more thoroughly later in the chapter, is a good example of positive legislation on behalf of people with disabilities. Focus on Critical Thinking 11.2 raises questions concerning value orientations to working with people who have disabilities and to social welfare policy perspectives.

## What Are Developmental Disabilities?

**LO 4**

Five attributes characterize people with **developmental disabilities** (Centers for Disease Control and Prevention [CDC], 2011; Patchner & DeWeaver, 2008; Developmental Disabilities Assistance and Bill of Rights Act of 1990, Pub. L. No. 101-496). First, the disability is both severe and chronic, resulting from some mental or physical impairment. Second, the disability occurs before age 22. Third, the conditions are likely to be permanent. Fourth, the disability "results in substantial functional limitations in three or more of the following areas of major life activity: (i) self-care, (ii) receptive and expressive language, (iii) learning, (iv) mobility, (v) self-direction, (vi) capacity for independent living, and (vii) economic self-sufficiency" (Developmental Disabilities Assistance and Bill of Rights Act of 1990). Fifth, a developmental disability demonstrates the need for lifelong supplementary help and services.

Examples of developmental disabilities are intellectual disabilities, cerebral palsy, epilepsy, orthopedic problems, hearing impairment or deafness, visual impairment or blindness, and autism (Barker, 2003; CDC, 2008, 2013; DeWeaver, 1995). Each has serious implications for living in the macro social environment.

## Intellectual Disabilities

**Intellectual disabilities** (also referred to as **mental retardation** and, sometimes, **cognitive disabilities**) involve a condition manifested before age 18 such that an individual scores significantly below average on standard intelligence tests and has deficits in adaptive functioning (i.e., the ability to conduct daily living tasks) (American Psychiatric Association, 2013; Friend, 2011; Smith & Tyler, 2010). Although it's impossible to identify a precise number, it appears that about 4 million Americans have developmental disabilities (Administration for Community Living [ACL], 2015). One study found that 1 in 6 children had a developmental disability (Centers for Disease Control [CDC], 2015c).

*Mental retardation* (not *intellectual disabilities*) has been the term traditionally used in federal legislation governing the provision of special education. However, in fall 2010 President Barack Obama signed into law a bill that would change the term *mental retardation* to *intellectual disability* in many aspects of federal policy; in order to avert costs, the changes in specific pieces of legislation will occur over the next several years as they are periodically reviewed and revised (Diament, 2010). Focus on Critical Thinking 11.3 examines the language used to refer to people with such disabilities.

## Cerebral Palsy

**Cerebral palsy** is a disability involving problems in muscular control and coordination resulting from

---

## FOCUS ON CRITICAL THINKING 11.3  EMPOWERMENT THROUGH LANGUAGE: PEOPLE WITH INTELLECTUAL DISABILITIES

### Critical Thinking Questions

How do the words you use to describe people affect your opinions about them and the way you view them? To what extent can labels place people in a negative—or positive—light?

The following brief discussion focuses on the significance of words with respect to people who have intellectual disabilities. After reading it, think about what terms might be best to use when talking about this population. Terms used to discuss these people have changed over time (Mackelprang, 2008; Mackelprang & Salsgiver, 2009). In the past, derogatory terms included *crippled, handicapped, retarded,* and *disabled,* among others. Using such terms to define people with the disability stated first (e.g., handicapped person) placed emphasis on the disability, not the fact that you are referring to a unique individual. Current terminology emphasizes placing the person

**EP 1c**

first, and hence using terms like "person with a disability."

The term *mental retardation* clearly has negative connotations. One of the nastiest things children call other children when they're angry or making fun of others is "Retard!" or "Mental!" Social workers and others working with people who have this type of disability are trying to use less negative terms.

Friend (2011) reflects that other terms (e.g., *cognitive disability, cognitive impairment, mental impairment, mental disability,* and *mental handicap*) may still be used in various contexts. Much apparently depends on tradition and the terminology used in current legislation. The new change in federal law from using *mental retardation* to *intellectual disability* should gradually influence state legislation. This book will use the term *people with intellectual disabilities* because it is more positive and thus most empowering, in addition to being the new legal term.

damage to the brain before it has matured—that is, before or during birth. Problems include lack of balance, difficulty walking, weakness, and uncontrolled or restricted movements, depending on where in the brain the damage occurred. It should be emphasized that these people may experience only motor impairment, with intellectual ability being unaffected.

## Epilepsy

**Epilepsy** (commonly referred to as **seizure disorder**) is an abrupt change in an individual's conscious state that may involve unconsciousness, convulsive motor activity, or sensory distortions. Seizures are caused by sudden bursts of electrical activity in some brain cells causing reactions in other brain cells. Epilepsy can result from virtually any type of injury to or condition in the brain including high fevers, chemical imbalances, infections, and physical damage; in up to 70% of all cases, the specific cause remains unidentified (Friend, 2011).

## Orthopedic Problems

**Orthopedic problems** are "defects or diseases of the muscles and bones" (Hallahan, Kauffman, & Pullen, 2012, p. 405). Although there is no neurological impairment, orthopedic problems result in an inability to move about normally. Usually difficulties involve "the legs, arms, joints, or spine, making it difficult or impossible for the child to walk, stand, sit, or use his or her hands" (Hallahan et al., 2012, p. 405). These problems can have genetic origins or can result from injury, disease, accidents, or other developmental disorders (Hallahan et al., 2012).

## Deafness and Hardness of Hearing

"The deaf and hard of hearing community is diverse. There are variations in the cause and degree of hearing loss, age at the onset, educational background, communication methods, and how individuals feel about their hearing loss" (National Association of the Deaf [NAD], 2011). Two opposing perceptions of people who are deaf exist, one based on the medical model and one a cultural model (Sheridan & White, 2008). The medical model views deafness as a medical problem and focuses on alleviating a person's "deficits" such as improvement of hearing, if possible, and use of spoken language. The cultural perspective views **the Deaf** (a capitalized term) as a community with its own culture, a vibrant, expressive use of sign language, and a strong emphasis on its members' strengths.

It's very important for social workers to respect how people identify and feel about themselves (NAD, 2011; Sheridan & White, 2008). Prioritizing needs and referrals to services and support systems clearly depends on clients' values and reference group. Social workers who work with people who are deaf should be culturally competent and preferably fluent in the use of sign language (Sheridan & White, 2008).

The degree to which people are unable to hear varies dramatically. The term **hardness of hearing** refers to people with mild to moderate hearing loss. People who are **deaf** experience a moderate to severe hearing loss that may include no hearing ability. Any of these people may or may not identify themselves with the Deaf community. Those who identify with the Deaf feel they are an integral part of the community with all its culture and customs and appreciate the richness of their sign language. On the other hand, people who are hard of hearing or deaf may have little contact with other Deaf people who use sign language and do not feel they are part of the Deaf community. One factor that may be involved is the time of life when the hearing loss occurs and how strongly group identification has already been established. Note that identification may change over the life span. "Individuals can choose an audiological or cultural [lifestyle] perspective. It's all about choices, comfort level, mode of communication, and acceptance [of hearing loss]" (NAD, 2011).

Note that the National Association of the Deaf (NAD) and the World Federation of the Deaf (WFD) strongly recommend the use of the terms *deaf* and *hard of hearing* over *hearing impaired* (NAD, 2011). NAD (2011) indicates that hearing people are comfortable with "hearing impaired" and feel that it's "politically correct." On the other hand, people who are deaf and hard of hearing feel that the terms "deaf" and "hard of hearing" are "not negative in any way at all" (NAD, 2011). They feel the term *hearing impaired* is negative for them because it sets up a standard of "hearing" that implies there's something wrong with them when there is not.

## Visual Impairment

**Visual impairment** is difficulty in perception compared to the norm that is experienced through sight. Many people have a mild visual impairment correctable by glasses or contact lenses. People of special concern here are those whose vision cannot be corrected and so experience significant functional limitations. Rothman (2003) explains:

> *We are all familiar with the expression "20/20 vision." Having 20/20 vision means that one can see, at a distance of 20 feet, what a "normal" eye can see. As visual acuity decreases, the standard 20 that represent "20 feet" remains the same, but the second number changes. The higher the second number, the greater the visual impairment. To be legally blind [emphasis added] a person's vision must be 20/200, meaning that he or she can see at 20 feet what the "normal" eye can see at 200 feet. A measure of 20/80 in the best eye, with corrections, indicates a visual impairment. Using this model, there are about 500,000 people in the United States who are legally blind (Mackelprang & Salsgiver, 1999, p. 125) and a much larger number who are visually impaired. (p. 131)*

## Autism Spectrum Disorders

**Autism spectrum disorders (ASD)** are conditions "that share similar characteristics in the areas of (a) social interaction, (b) verbal or nonverbal communication, and (c) repetitive behaviors or interests. Unusual responses to sensory stimuli are also often present. The key word in the term *ASD* is *spectrum,* which implies similar characteristics but great variance in the actual behavioral patterns exhibited" (American Psychiatric Association, 2013; Smith & Tyler, 2010, p. 406). Autism spectrum disorders involve three syndromes, although significant differences in characteristics and behavior exist within each syndrome. These syndromes, ranging from most severe to mildest on the spectrum, are: autism, Asperger syndrome, and pervasive developmental disorder—not otherwise specified (Smith & Tyler, 2010, p. 406).

**Autism** is an all-encompassing condition often characterized by the following six characteristics (Hallahan et al., 2012):

1. People with autism have an intense inner-directedness and problems such as inability to participate in "normal" social interaction and relationships.
2. They tend to experience communication difficulties. They might have difficulties acquiring language in the first place, effectively expressing their thoughts and feelings, or accurately reading the meaning of nonverbal behavior and facial expressions.

3. People with autism often demonstrate repetitive self-stimulating movements such as waving a hand in front of their eyes for a long time.
4. They may experience an intense obsession with objects, a limited range of interests that can capture their attention, and a compulsive need for predictability and sameness (e.g., they won't tolerate a piece of furniture being moved).
5. Autism is characterized by demonstration of "cognitive deficits similar to those of people with intellectual disabilities," but with some aspects "peculiar to autism" (Hallahan et al., 2012, p. 244). For example, people with autism may have difficulty organizing and understanding information. They might easily remember a series of words but have absolutely no idea about what the words mean (Friend, 2011).
6. People with autism often experience difficulties with sensory perception, being either overly sensitive to or extremely unresponsive to types of sensory stimulation. They might not respond to sounds as if they were deaf, or they might be unresponsive to some sounds (e.g., a school bell signaling the beginning and end of classes), but very responsive to other sounds (e.g., whispering by peers). Examples of being hypersensitive include the inability to tolerate fluorescent lights or the touch of another person.

**Asperger syndrome (AS)** involves abnormalities including the same characteristics displayed in autism, but in a much milder form (Hallahan et al., 2012). For example, a person with AS might do reasonably well in school and be fairly adept at communication. However, that person might also find it difficult to establish "normal" interpersonal relationships and might feel the compulsive need to control his or her environment. Hallahan and his colleagues (2012) elaborate:

> *Many of the social interaction difficulties of those with Asperger syndrome are due to their inability to think about situations in a nuanced way. They are often overly literal in how they 'read' the behavior and language of others. And they often interpret situations using logic to the exclusion of emotion or sentiment. Stephen Shore (2003) provides an example of his struggles with being overly literal:*
>
> > *A friend of mine & said he felt "like a pizza." "What do you mean—"feel like a pizza?" And it wasn't until college that I realized, "Oh, he meant*

*he felt like EATING a pizza." At this time, idioms [unusual expressions in a language that mean something different from the precise individual words involved] usually go zipping past me but I am often able to "pull them back" for further examination before I say something ridiculous. But it takes some additional thinking on my part, to figure out "Well, what's the meaning? How do I interpret this?" (pp. 245–246)*

The third disorder in the autistic spectrum is **pervasive developmental disorder—not otherwise specified (PDD-NOS)**. In this condition, not all "ASD characteristics (problems in communication, social interaction, and repetitive or manneristic behaviors) are present or they are mild" (Smith & Tyler, 2010, p. 413). "The PDD part of the diagnosis signifies characteristics very similar to those of autism and Asperger syndrome, but the characteristics are not as clearly expressed. The NOS part refers to [not having] other specified disorders or syndromes" (Smith & Tyler, 2010, p. 413).

## Multiple Disabilities

Any individual may experience several disabilities at the same time. For instance, a person with intellectual disabilities may also have an orthopedic problem or epilepsy. A developmental disability may originate in some genetic disorder or from a problem occurring before, during, or after birth. It may also result from problems derived from some combination of these conditions.

# Treatment over Time of People with Developmental Disabilities: The Quest for Social and Economic Justice LO 5

Because of the difficulties experienced by people with developmental disabilities, community support systems and available agency resources are extremely important. How community residents and macro-level decision makers view people with developmental disabilities has tremendous implications for the latter's quality of life. To more fully understand the macro social

EP 2

environment's impacts, Mary (1998) describes how community attitudes and resulting social policies have changed in recent decades.

## Prior to the Late 1960s: Individual Pathology

Until the late 1960s, community treatment and public policy emphasized individual pathology. The medical model formed the basis for conceptualizing developmental disabilities. People were considered "patients," with caregivers focusing on individual diagnoses and the resulting problems (Mary, 1998, p. 249; NASW, 2009). This traditional approach focused on what was wrong with a person, what that person could not do, and how that individual couldn't function very well independently, if at all. Many people with developmental disabilities were placed in large state or regional institutions, where they received custodial care and were kept clean and safe. These times obviously did not foster the current strong professional values of client self-determination and empowerment.

## The 1970s and 1980s: A Community-Based Approach

The 1970s and early 1980s saw significant changes in how people with developmental disabilities were viewed. Principles becoming important, especially for people with intellectual disabilities, were "normalization," deinstitutionalization, "individual program planning," and "the developmental model" (Mary, 1998, p. 249).

### Normalization

**Normalization** is the belief that every person, even those with the most severe disabilities, should have life conditions and behavioral patterns that are as close as possible to those ordinarily experienced by others in the social and physical environment. Previously, people with developmental disabilities had been placed "out of sight and mind" in obscurely located institutions. During the 1970s and 1980s, however, communities and organizations started viewing such people as clients who had a right to live as normally as possible. This approach "shifted much of the problem from the individual to the environment" (Mary, 1998, p. 250). Instead of focusing on people's negative diagnoses, emphasis was placed on the importance of the social environment for an individual's quality of life.

## FOCUS ON CRITICAL THINKING 11.4

## DEINSTITUTIONALIZATION: AN ATTEMPT AT EMPOWERMENT

Think about people with intellectual disabilities who need some degree of support and care.

### Critical Thinking Questions

Is it better to shelter and coddle them, to ensure that they're protected from life's perils—and many of its pleasures? Or is it worth the effort to encourage as much independence as possible? Consider the following issues concerning deinstitutionaliza-tion. Although the proponents of dein-stitutionalization had good intentions and many successes, there were also  EP 8a significant problems. For one thing, simply placing clients in the community did not necessarily mean integration or acceptance in that community (Mary, 1998). It did not mean automatic attitude readjust-ments on the part of community residents to alter their old stereotypes and unfounded fears about people with developmental disabilities.

Another problem with deinstitutionalization con-cerned inadequate community resources and services.

Institutions were expensive, but so were community-based services. People could get lost and be severed from service provision altogether. Frequently commu-nity-based services were furnished by a complicated mixture of state, local, public, and private agencies pro-viding an unevenly distributed conglomeration of ser-vices. Service provision could be confusing to clients and their families because some services were available to the general public and others only to those with spe-cific disabilities. (Try calling the Social Security Office to get some specific information about a case. See how well you understand what's going on—and you're in college, at that.) Other criticisms of deinstitutionalization included people being discharged too quickly and sometimes inappropriately (e.g., without adequate plan-ning for continued community service provision).

### Critical Thinking Questions

To what extent do you think the concept of deinstitu-tionalization is good or bad? What are your reasons? Under what circumstances might it be more likely to work?

### Deinstitutionalization

A parallel concept to normalization is **deinstitutional-ization**—the practice of moving people who require supportive care for physical or mental conditions from institutional settings into the community (Segal, 2008; Mary, 1998; Mish, 2008). Community facilities vary in size and complexity, and include larger transitional settings, group homes, family homes, and individual residences. Placement depends on client needs and facility availability. Sometimes these facilities are referred to as **community-based residential facilities (CBRFs)**. As explained earlier, deinstitutionalization assumes that the more people with developmental disabilities can be assimilated into the community and lead "normal" lives, the better their quality of life will be. Focus on Critical Thinking 11.4 addresses some of the problems with this approach.

### Individual Program Planning

Social workers, often functioning as case managers, developed *individual programs*, a third principle

espoused in the 1970s and 1980s. Such programs emphasized people's environments and intervention results that would enhance their functioning within those environments. With intervention, the focus was on helping people with disabilities maximize independence and self-determination in the least re-strictive environment possible (Garvin & Tropman, 1998; Mackelprang, 2008; Mary, 1998). The concept of *least restrictive environment* (discussed in Chapter 9) concerns the encouragement of clients to enjoy as much freedom and to make as many decisions for themselves as they can. This concept is related to normalization and deinstitutionalization. That is, people living in the community are more likely to lead normal lives and make their own decisions than those living under institutional care. Evaluating the effectiveness of entire programs was also stressed.

### The Developmental Model

The fourth important concept during the 1970s and 1980s was that treatment should be guided by a *developmental model* based on a continuum of service. People received services depending on the type and intensity of their needs. People with developmental disabilities were *clients* whom professionals assessed in terms of their needs. These professionals then determined necessary services depending on where the clients fell on the developmental continuum of service. You might picture a ruler. If a client was assessed as functioning at the 6¼-inch point, then that client would receive the services appropriate for that exact point. Likewise, a client at the 10-inch point would receive services designated for that level of assessment. Emphasis was placed not on the individual as a unique personality but rather on the assessed level of need and the designated services available to address that need.

Often clients' needs change over time. One assumption was that many clients made progress toward greater independence in a step-by-step process. A client had to master one skill first before attempting a more difficult one. For example, a young woman with mild intellectual disabilities might start out living in a group home where she could learn basic housekeeping, cooking, and self-care skills including shopping and paying bills. She might then move to an apartment complex or boarding house for people with intellectual disabilities. House parents or residential caregivers would not be living with her, but would be available in another apartment to help her with problems or questions. Eventually the woman might achieve enough self-care mastery to live on her own or with a roommate.

Another assumption was that clients' needs changed over time, but they required increasing levels of help and assistance. A person with a deteriorating orthopedic problem involving his knees might require increasingly more intensive help as he lost mobility. Depending on his assessed state of need at any time, in the 1970s and 1980s he would have received a designated level of service.

## The 1990s and Beyond: Consumer Empowerment

The 1990s brought with them a significantly greater emphasis on individual choice and personalized planning for people with developmental disabilities (DePoy & Gilson, 2004; Freedman, 1995; Mary, 1998). Previously, people with developmental disabilities had been viewed as clients whom

professionals assessed and provided services to based on their level of functioning. There was relatively little variation of service provision at the assessed level. Today's perspective reflects four new important concepts—individualization, choices, innovation, and family support.

### Individualization

Today practitioners should assume a much more *individualized* approach wherein that "services are driven by client needs, and clients are viewed as consumers with choices" (Mackelprang, 2012; Mary, 1998, p. 253). We have established that the term *consumer* implies greater power and choice than does the term *client.* Each client has a unique set of needs. As consumers, clients should be able to choose their purchases or resource providers within a competitive market rather than having someone else do so for them.

### Emphasis on Choice

A key word here is *choice.* The ruler concept explained earlier as characterizing the 1970s and 1980s no longer applies. Rather, clients are encouraged to make choices and decide what supports they want and what goals they wish to pursue. Earlier we discussed the importance of self-determination for people with disabilities.

Consider Dimitri, 44, a quadriplegic whose condition is the result of a congenital spinal cord malformation. Instead of professionals assessing his capabilities and designating where it is best for him to live, he can make those decisions himself. With practitioners and other caregiving professionals' input regarding what resources and services are available,  EP 3b, 7c, 7d
Dimitri can determine the environment that will give him what he perceives as the highest quality of life. Of course, his choices are influenced by his own capabilities and the resources available. It is impossible for Dimitri to live in an apartment alone with no supportive help. His viable choices might include living in a nursing home or in a group home for people with severe physical disabilities, staying in an apartment with the necessary supportive attendants, or living with his family whose members would serve as primary caregivers (assuming, of course, that they were willing to do so).

## HIGHLIGHT 11.2   A WORD OF CAUTION ABOUT CHOICE

Mackelprang and Salsgiver (1996) caution that practitioners "not be too quick to assume that consumers already have knowledge and abilities rather than recognizing that they may need assistance to develop their strengths" (p. 12). They present an example involving Jim, age 28, who had suffered traumatic brain injury. Although technically not a developmental disability because the injury occurred after age 22, it still illustrates concepts commonly addressed when working with people who have developmental disabilities.

While residing in an independent living center, Jim initially sought help with financial planning. As his counselor, an MSW student, helped him with budgeting issues, it became apparent that Jim was also experiencing difficulty in his marriage. However, because Jim did not specifically seek help concerning his marriage, the student decided not to interfere with those issues. Because of his head injury, Jim lacked insight into the depths of his relationship problems. By the time he began to understand how far his marital situation had deteriorated, his wife had divorced him, retaining custody of their adolescent daughter.

As Mackelprang and Salsgiver (1996) suggest,

[this] case illustrates the conflict between absolute self-determination and the need to sometimes impose professional intervention. Although some would argue against any change in Jim's intervention, a social work approach would have allowed for broader intervention and ultimately may have been more empowering to Jim and his family. (p. 13)

---

Another example is Juanita, who has cerebral palsy resulting in major difficulties controlling her arm movements. With professional help and practice, she has learned to dress herself if her clothes have zippers and no buttons. However, it takes her more than an hour each time and leaves her physically exhausted. A personal care attendant can do the job in about four minutes. Juanita might choose to have the attendant help her dress even though this option reflects less independence. This choice might be in her best interest to save herself substantial time and energy (Renz-Beaulaurier, 1998).

The concept of choice is important. However, social workers must also carefully evaluate a client's ability to make choices, as Highlight 11.2 explains.

### Innovation

A key concept in today's approach toward working with people with developmental disabilities is **innovation**—the initiation, development, and application of new ideas. Innovative service provision may involve a unique combination of services depending on what an individual wishes to accomplish. In other words, "consumers define their own vision of the future—where they want to live, learn, work, and recreate—in a community that they define" (Mackelprang, 2012; Mary, 1998, p. 253).

For example, Larisa, age 7, has spina bifida, a condition in which the spinal column has not fused shut and so some nerves remain exposed. Although she had surgery immediately after birth to close her spinal column, damage to the unprotected nerves resulted in paralysis and difficulties with bladder and bowel control. Larisa has an individualized service plan designed to meet her unique needs. She can live at home with an innovative combination of supports. A motorized wheelchair maximizes her mobility. Family counseling gives her parents information and help in responding to her special needs. A wheelchair-accessible van transports her to and from school. A teacher's aid assists her as needed in completing school assignments. Designated medical staff help Larisa and her family meet her special health and surgical needs.

### Family Support

One other important concept in current service provision for people with developmental disabilities is *family support*. Families often need special resources and help to respond to the extraordinary needs of members with developmental disabilities. For example, parents with a young child who has a developmental disability may experience a range of stresses, including avoidance by others, exhaustion from the long-term burden of caregiving, lack of adequate information about the condition, and child behavior management problems.

## HIGHLIGHT 11.3  DISCRIMINATION AGAINST PEOPLE WITH DEVELOPMENTAL DISABILITIES

People with developmental disabilities historically have suffered from and continue to experience discrimination. Consider the example of Sandra, a 35-year-old woman with Down syndrome who was denied a heart-lung transplant even though insurance covered the $250,000 necessary for the operation (Shapiro, 1995). Down syndrome is a congenital type of intellectual disability "characterized by moderate to severe mental retardation, slanting eyes, a broad short skull, broad hands with short fingers, and trisomy of the human chromosome numbered 21" (Mish, 2008, p. 376). The two hospitals granted approval to conduct this type of surgery "made issue of her intelligence and rejected her" (Shapiro, 1995, p. 59). One hospital administrator

EP 2

allegedly said, "We do not feel that patients with Down syndrome are appropriate candidates for heart-lung transplantation" (Shapiro, 1995, p. 59). Others at the hospitals indicated that they doubted she could maintain the rigorous medical requirements involved in taking medication and monitoring her health after the operations.

Sandra and her doctor strongly disagreed with these allegations. Sandra had bused tables in a public cafeteria, lived in her own apartment, and "testified eloquently before committees" on the behalf of people with developmental disabilities (Shapiro, 1995, p. 59). Sandra already had assumed responsibility for taking various medications and monitoring her blood pressure every day. Publicity compelled the hospitals to reconsider her plea. Without the surgery, Sandra had only a few years to live.

---

Family members' strengths must be identified and fortified. Examples of strengths include good communication skills, sincere caring and consideration for each other, effective organizational and planning skills, a strong support network of friends and relatives, spiritual involvement with clergy and religious groups, and adequate financial resources.

Social workers and other professionals working with people who have developmental disabilities continuously strive to individualize plans, emphasize choice, initiate innovative treatment approaches, and maximize family support. Nonetheless, discrimination against them persists, as Highlight 11.3 shows.

## Generalist Social Work and People Who Have Developmental Disabilities  LO 6

Social workers often must use brokering, case management, and advocacy skills to provide effective services. We've established that **brokering** is the linkage of clients (consumers) to needed resources. **Case management** is the process of organizing, coordinating, and maintaining "a network of formal and informal supports and activities designed to optimize the

EP 1, 3a, 3b, 7c, 8d

functioning and well-being of people with multiple needs" (Moxley, 1989, p. 21). Obviously, many people with developmental disabilities require an innovative range of services to maximize self-determination and pursue an optimal quality of life. The key here is coordinating and monitoring services so clients with ongoing or changing needs get these needs met.

**Advocacy** is the "process of affecting or initiating change either with and/or on behalf [of clients or] client groups to: [1] obtain services or resources for clients that would not otherwise be provided, [2] modify or influence policies, procedures, or practices that adversely affect [individuals, families,] groups or communities, [or] [3] promote new legislation or policies that will result in the provision of [much-needed] & resources or services" (Hepworth et al., 2013, p. 452). There is usually no problem when adequate resources and services are available. However, in reality, this is often not the case. When clients are not getting their needs met, the practitioner is obliged to advocate on their behalf. Resources may require redistribution. Policies may require change and improvement. New services may need development.

*Case Example* One facet of advocacy is helping clients advocate for themselves when they can instead of doing it for them (Mackelprang & Salsgiver, 2009). This is another form of client empowerment. For example, it might be easy for Gamal, a social worker, to advocate for his client RyAnne, age 38, who has muscular dystrophy. We have established that this condition is "any of a group of hereditary diseases characterized by a progressive wasting of the muscles" (Mish, 2008, p. 818).

RyAnne was diagnosed with the disease at age 12. Although RyAnne can take a few steps by herself, it is difficult for her, and she usually uses a motorized wheelchair. Balance is difficult because she has lost eight of her toes to the disease. She has little strength in her arms and hands, and so accomplishes tasks such as writing and eating very slowly. As her muscles deteriorate, her voice is weakening, so she tries to do most of her necessary talking earlier in the day when she is stronger. RyAnne is a strong-willed, independent-minded person who prides herself in accomplishing her goals. For example, she has earned a bachelor's degree in accounting and is able to work part-time at her own pace.

RyAnne lives with other people who have physical disabilities in a group home where Gamal is the social worker. RyAnne has several issues to address, such as some funding glitches and the need for some new medical equipment, including a new wheelchair. Gamal talks to RyAnne about these needs and volunteers to make the calls, write the letters, and advocate on her behalf. He is taken aback when RyAnne responds with a dour look on her face and then avoids eye contact with him. He asks her what's wrong. She hesitantly responds that she would rather do it herself, although she admits she will probably need help negotiating the complicated bureaucratic maze. Gamal suddenly grasps the issue. He backs off and volunteers to help find out whom she needs to contact and what information she needs to present. Although it will be much slower for her to advocate for herself than for him to do it, the process will empower her. Gamal realizes that it's best to support her in her advocacy efforts instead of performing the primary advocacy role himself.

# Empowerment Through Legislation: Seeking Social and Economic Justice  `LO 7`

At least three positive pieces of legislation passed in the recent decades are of special significance for people with developmental or other disabilities in terms of improving access to resources in the macro social environment (DeWeaver, 1995; Mackelprang, 2008; U.S. Department of Justice, 2014).

**EP 3b, 5a, 5b, 8d**

## The Americans with Disabilities Act of 1990

The Americans with Disabilities Act of 1990 (ADA) (Pub. L. No. 101-336) intends to provide the millions of American people who have physical or mental disabilities with access to public facilities and equal employment opportunities (U.S. Department of Justice, 2014.). It aims to wipe out discrimination against people with disabilities and instead offer them inclusion into the mainstream of community life. The ADA defines people with disabilities as those who have substantial physical or mental difficulties that significantly hinder at least one primary life activity, who have an established record of such hindrances, or who are regarded by other people as demonstrating such difficulties (ADA.gov, 2014). "Major life activities include, but are not limited to, caring for oneself, performing manual tasks, seeing, hearing, eating, sleeping, walking, standing, lifting, bending, speaking, breathing, learning, reading, concentrating, thinking, communicating, and working" (ADA.gov, 2014).

The ADA reflects one attempt by a national macro system to affect and improve the lives of a population at risk and provide greater social and economic justice. The ADA consists of five major provisions. Title I forbids job and employment discrimination against people with disabilities. This includes discrimination concerning "job application procedures, hiring, advancement, compensation, job training, and other conditions and privileges of employment *simply because they have disabilities*" (Kopels, 1995, p. 399; emphasis added). Title II forbids public facilities, organizations, and transportation providers to discriminate against people with disabilities. Title III "prohibits discrimination in public accommodations and services operated by private entities" (Kopels, 1995, p. 338). Title IV requires that state and national telecommunication relay services accommodate people who are hard of hearing and allow them communication access. Finally, Title V includes a number of miscellaneous provisions relating to more specific aspects of service provision and access. In essence, the law requires "universal access to public buildings, transit systems, and communications networks" (Friend, 2011; Smo-lowe, 1995, p. 54).

In response to a range of Supreme Court deci-sions addressing some of the more nebulous con-cepts inherent in the ADA, the 2008 Amendments to the Americans with Disabilities Act were signed into law. Taking effect in January 2009, the Amend-ments attempted to clarify who is protected by the law and revised "the definition of 'disability' to en-compass more broadly what impairments substan-tially limit a major life activity" (ADA Amendments Act of 2008). Clarification of terms and who is in-cluded appears to be an ongoing process.

In 2010 new directives for implementing the ADA were issued by the Department of Justice (U.S. Department of Justice, 2011, 2014). These reg-ulations determine more specific criteria for accessi-bility in a wide variety of contexts. Some directives concern better access to voting at polling places and easier admittance to various businesses includ-ing stores, malls, hotels, and doctors' offices (U.S. Department of Justice, 2014). Other regulations tar-get access to recreational settings "such as swimming pools, play areas, marinas, or golf facilities" (U.S. Department of Justice, 2011). Directives also involve better access for people using mobility devices such as wheelchairs, enhanced ability to employ service animals, better access to ticket sales for recreational or other events, and improved use of communication technology for people with vision, hearing, or speech disabilities (U.S. Department of Justice, 2014).

The ADA "has legitimized the idea that the fundamental problems facing people are less medi-cal than social and structural" (Renz-Beaulaurier, 1998, p. 81). It redefines problems as belonging to the *community,* and not to people with disabilities living in the community. For example, "the problem of how to get up the steps (problem within the indi-vidual) changes to how to get a ramp installed (prob-lem outside the individual)" (Renz-Beaulaurier, 1998, p. 80). Thus, significant improvements clearly have been made in terms of accessibility for and inclusion of people with disabilities. However, Focus on Criti-cal Thinking 11.5 poses some questions regarding the overall effectiveness of the ADA.

## The Developmental Disabilities Assistance and Bill of Rights Act of 1990

The second major piece of 1990s legislation is the Developmental Disabilities Assistance and Bill of

Rights Act of 1990 (Pub. L. No. 106-402), which ac-complished several things (DeWeaver, 1995). First, it renewed funding for four major grant programs on behalf of people with developmental disabilities. Second, it increased the total estimated number of people with developmental disabilities, thereby ac-knowledging that more resources are necessary. Third, it called for advocacy on behalf of people with developmental disabilities. It requires provision of adequate services so people can attain their opti-mum potential, quality of life, and independence as integral members of the community.

## Individuals with Disabilities Education Improvement Act of 2004 (IDEA)

Major legislation has positively affected educational programming for children with learning and other disabilities in the past few decades (Lightfoot, 2009; Mackelprang, 2008). Mackelprang and Sals-giver (2009) explain:

*The All Handicapped Children Act of 1975 is one of the few pieces of legislation known to profes-sionals in human services and education by its original number, Pub. L. No. 94-142. The All Handicapped Children Act of 1975 went through several levels of evolution and was renamed the Individuals with Disabilities Education Act (IDEA) in 1990, and most recently the Individuals with Disabilities Education Improvement Act [of 2004] [Pub. L. No. 108-446].... Individuals from birth up through the age of twenty-one years are covered under this historic act. IDEA stipulates that "free appropriate public education" be pro-vided at public expense to all children, including children with disabilities from age three through twenty-one years. The education of children with dis-abilities should be provided in the most open and "normal" environment possible (the least restrictive environment). When children need to be diagnosed, be evaluated, and receive prescriptions, the diagno-sis, evaluation, and prescription should not produce stigmatization and discrimination. Parents and the child need to be primary players in any remedial or pedagogical plan established for the child's educa-tion (Albrecht, 1992; Altschuler, 2007)....*

*It is important ... to understand some of the unique qualities of IDEA as a disability law. First, it covers ... youths [with disabilities] through age twenty-one or until high school graduation, which-ever comes first. Second, it mandates public support*

# FOCUS ON CRITICAL THINKING 11.5

## DOES THE AMERICANS WITH DISABILITIES ACT (ADA) ACTUALLY HELP PEOPLE WITH DISABILITIES ATTAIN SOCIAL AND ECONOMIC JUSTICE?

Although the ADA has helped people with disabilities in some areas, questions must be raised about its effectiveness in others. The courts continue to address complaints filed concerning the ADA to clarify terms with various degrees of ambiguity (U.S. Department of Justice, 2014). For example, employers and public agencies must make only "reasonable accommodation" for people with disabilities. What does the term *reasonable accommodation* mean? What kind of accommodation is reasonable and what is unreasonable? Another unclear term involves *discriminatory practices* (U.S. Department of Justice, 2014). When does a *practice* (which is somewhat vague in itself) become *discriminatory*? How can discrimination against capable people with intellectual or other developmental disabilities be prohibited? How can the law be enforced?

**EP 5a, 5b, 5c**

The unemployment rate of people with disabilities significantly exceeds that of able-bodied people (ProQuest, 2014; U.S. Census Bureau, 2011). The incomes of people with disabilities are far less than those of their able-bodied counterparts (Mackelprang, 2008). Of people with a disability, 20.6% are employed; this contrasts with a 69.4% employment rate for people without a disability (ProQuest, 2014). More people with a disability, about one-third, were employed in 1990 before the ADA was passed (Smolowe, 1995).

Therefore, the battle for equal access and opportunity for people with disabilities has not been won. Much of the public attention to the act has focused on people with physical disabilities, many of whom require wheelchairs for transportation. In what ways do people with intellectual and other developmental disabilities fit in? Kopels (1995) states that the ADA "will be successful only to the extent that these individuals [with disabilities] and those who advocate on their behalf learn about the ADA and use it as a means to ensure employment opportunities" (p. 345). Mackelprang and Salsgiver (1996) call for the social work profession to ally itself with the movement to enhance access for people with either physical or mental disabilities. They encourage social workers to "become more involved in disability advocacy work in agencies with activist philosophies" and to work with the disability movement to "better empower oppressed and devalued groups, and understand the needs of people with disabilities" (p. 134).

### Critical Thinking Questions

To what extent do you think the ADA has been effective? What might be done to improve its effectiveness?

---

*of substantial services placing financial and service responsibility on states and schools. Third, it mandates substantial involvement of both … individuals [with disabilities] and their families. Fourth, IDEA is entitling legislation: not only are people eligible for services, but schools and states are responsible for providing services. (pp. 144–145)*

# Social Work and Community Empowerment for People with Disabilities

Social workers are concerned with how organizations, communities, and the government can offer resources and supports to people with disabilities. This is possible in at least two ways. First, federal and state legislation can make programs available to community residents with disabilities. (Note that we just reviewed three pieces of federal legislation passed on behalf of this population.) Second, social workers can work with community residents to establish their own resources within the community.

**EP 5c, 8c, 8d**

Some examples of how to make progress through legislation, direct community support, and social work advocacy are presented next. The populations at risk addressed include people with visual impairment and those with intellectual disabilities.

## Legislative Empowerment for People with Visual Impairment

The Rehabilitation Act of 1973 (Pub. L. No. 93-112) and its 1992 amendments (Pub. L. No. 102-569) mandated reimbursement for some services provided by agencies specifically designated to help people with visual impairment (Asch & Mudrick, 2008). Another example of supportive legislation is the 1936 Randolph-Sheppard Act (Pub. L. No. 74-734) that gave people who are blind "preference in getting jobs running vending operations on federal land" (Asch & Mudrik, 2008).

Additionally, people who are legally blind, who are unemployed, and who have assets falling below prescribed levels may receive Supplemental Security Income (SSI). We have established that SSI is a federal program that offers uniform assistance to people who are blind, are older adults, or have a disability. Maximum monthly federal payments to SSI recipients in 2015 were $713 for an individual and $1,100 for a couple (Social Security Administration, 2015). Benefits are provided on the basis of need instead of work history.

Several pieces of legislation make reading materials more accessible for people with visual impairment. For example, the 1931 Pratt-Smoot Act (Pub. L. No. 71-787) established a Library of Congress program that later formed the foundation for regional centers providing Braille and recorded materials to people with visual impairment.

Highlight 11.4 suggests how social workers can work with communities to further empower people with visual impairment.

## Community Empowerment for People with Intellectual Disabilities

Considerable time will be spent here discussing people with intellectual disabilities for three reasons. First, they constitute a large proportion of people with developmental disabilities. Second, they are likely to use services provided by state agencies. Third, social workers are an integral part of service provision to this population.

As for people with visual impairment, legislation provides support and programs for some people with intellectual disabilities. Funding for people with intellectual disabilities comes from a range of sources depending on whether individuals fulfill eligibility criteria, which often are related to their income level. For example, SSI may be available to people with intellectual disabilities who satisfy a means test (i.e., as Chapter 8 explained, a person

---

## HIGHLIGHT 11.4   SOCIAL WORK AND COMMUNITY EMPOWERMENT FOR PEOPLE WITH VISUAL IMPAIRMENT

Laws and mandated programs make some resources available to people with visual impairment. However, social workers can serve as important advocates in their communities and agencies for additional needed services. One goal might be to disseminate information concerning the issues addressed by and strengths inherent in people with visual impairment. These people and their families require precise, relevant information about what services are available, what their legal rights are, and what alternative approaches can be used to undertake activities of daily living (Asch, 1995; Asch & Mudrick, 2008). For example, social workers can help people realize that the long cane ("a mobility aid used by individuals with visual impairment who sweep it in a wide arc in front of them"), guide dogs, human guides,

EP 7d

recorded information, adapted computers, and other technological devices (e.g., reading machines that convert print into spoken words) can help people organize home, work, and social lives in an effective and efficient, although different, manner (Asch, 1995; Hallahan et al., 2012, p. 460).

Another goal social workers might pursue with communities is sponsorship of self-help groups in which people with visual impairment can discuss issues, suggest ideas to each other, and offer mutual support. A third goal might be to work with schools that have students with visual impairment to educate parents about services, resources, and aids. Schools can encourage students with visual impairment to participate in sports, recreation, and other extracurricular and educational activities just as children with normal vision do.

or family must have an income less than a designated amount to be eligible for benefits).

Social workers can help communities and social service organizations develop resources and programs to integrate people with intellectual disabilities and enhance their quality of life. For instance, one state has a Community Options Program (COP), funded at the state level, that "provides assessments, case plans, and community services as an alternative to nursing home placements" (The Arc Milwaukee, n.d., b, p. 2).

**EP 7d**

### The Arc and Related Resources

One excellent example of how a community can use a support system for people with intellectual and other developmental disabilities is an organization called The Arc. Historically known as the ARC (Association for Retarded Citizens of the United States), the organization is now called The Arc of the United States, or more commonly The Arc (The Arc, 2014). The name "was changed to reflect a broader mission, a new direction, and a change in the terminology used in the disability field" (The Arc Racine County, n.d.). The Arc currently has established chapters in communities nationwide. The following discussion focuses specifically on The Arc organizations. However, the types of services The Arc offers can certainly be sponsored by other organizations and community groups.

Typically funded through a variety of sources including donations by private citizens, corporations, local service clubs, and foundations, as well as government service contracts, The Arc chapters provide a wide range of services that reflect a creative meld of public services, private contributions, and community resources. Nationally The Arc takes pride in being the country's leading advocate for people with intellectual and developmental disabilities (The Arc, 2014). Social workers are often integrally involved with the provision of The Arc chapters' services, which may include information and referral services, help lines, noninstitutional residential facilities, vocational and employment programs, support services, intervention advocacy, volunteer programs, and recreational activities.

### Information and Referral Services and Help Lines

An **information and referral service** provides information about what services and resources are available in a community and assists people in accessing them. A **help line** is an information and referral system based on telephone contact. Persons requiring information about services, laws, or issues related to a specific problem or population—in this case, intellectual or other developmental disabilities—call a trained professional (often a social worker), who connects them with the appropriate resource or gives them necessary information. Many of The Arc chapters develop an extensive computerized system that can quickly identify relevant linkages between questions, needs, information, and resources.

### Noninstitutional Living Facilities

One type of resource that can help people with a disability maintain maximum independence and self-determination is a noninstitutional living facility. As discussed earlier in the context of deinstitutionalization, the intent is to place people in the least restrictive setting possible. Social workers often oversee or work in such settings. These include adult family care homes, where clients reside in the home of caregivers who supervise and care for them. Another setting is a group home or community-based residential facility (CBRF). Residents often are selected on the basis of having similar needs such as required levels of supervision and support. For example, one CBRF might have residents capable of taking care of personal needs and being employed.

Other, even more independent, supported living options include living with a roommate or by oneself in an apartment. Some limited supervision and assistance, such as help with paying bills or arranging transportation to work, is usually needed in these cases.

### Vocational and Employment Programs

The Arc chapters are also quite creative regarding vocational and employment opportunities. They can help clients gain employment by preparing them for the expectations of the workplace, assisting in placement, helping employers restructure jobs to maximize clients' ability to complete job tasks, and providing job coaching in basic work skills (e.g., getting to work on time or following a supervisor's instructions).

### Other Support Services

Social workers and other human service professionals offer multifaceted support services. Organizations

## HIGHLIGHT 11.5    EMPOWERMENT OF OLDER ADULT CAREGIVERS

Family services can support older adult caregivers who find it increasingly difficult to maintain the same level of care as in the past. For example, because of decreasing strength, an aging caregiver might find it much more difficult to assist a person with a severe disability in dressing himself. Family services for older adult caregivers can help during crises such as a caregiver experiencing her own acute health problems. They can also assist caregivers in long-term planning for and with the person who has the disability. A common concern of aging caregivers is what will happen to the individual with a disability when the caregiver can no longer assume that function.

can provide outreach support services to clients in their own homes that involve instruction in daily living skills, budgeting and financial management, transportation, parenting skills, and personal issues such as interpersonal interaction, leisure activities, self-esteem, and assertiveness.

People who are unable to function in more demanding settings may receive "day services"; these aim to "maximize an individual's independent functional level in self-care, physical and emotional growth, mobility and community transportation, socialization, recreation, leisure time, and educational and prevocational skills" (The Arc Milwaukee, n.d., a, p. 2).

Respite care programs help parents and other caregivers for persons with intellectual disabilities, giving them a break from their responsibilities. Highlight 11.5 focuses on the special needs of aging caregivers.

Support groups can focus on many different issues. For instance, parent support groups "provide parents with an opportunity to get together and share stories, concerns, and achievements with other parents who are experiencing similar circumstances" (The Arc, n.d., a, p. 2). Support groups for seniors with disabilities give them opportunities to share concerns, discuss suggestions for prospering, and talk about how to maximize their quality of life.

### Advocacy

Intervention advocacy "is designed to respond to the needs of persons with disabilities and their families when serious problems arise affecting legal rights, safety and health, financial security, or access to community resources" (The Arc, n.d., c, p. 2). The service system is complicated, and clients and their families may find it difficult to negotiate. As emphasized previously, social work advocacy is often necessary to get clients the resources and services they need.

### Community Volunteers

Volunteers can help Arc programming in many ways. These include performing clerical duties and answering phones; caring for small children while parents attend support groups; serving as matched "friends" with persons who have disabilities to provide support and encouragement; giving support via telephone to persons needing intermittent help; participating  EP 3a, 3b, 8d in fund-raising activities; assisting in supervision at events such as group outings; and helping with household upkeep and maintenance (The Arc, n.d., c). Social workers often seek out, organize, and oversee volunteers performing such functions.

### Recreational Activities

Recreational activities and functions represent still another means of enhancing the quality of life for people with disabilities. Examples include athletic programs, Special Olympics, and summer camps at which groups of clients of any age can interact socially, work on crafts, play games, learn appreciation for nature, increase leisure skills, and gain confidence in expressing themselves (The Arc, n.d., c).

The past few sections have suggested means by which social workers and communities can empower people with intellectual disabilities. The following case example examines various dimensions of how a community both pursues and falls short of empowerment for one of its citizens.

*Case Example*   Consider Frank and how his community both succeeds and fails in supporting him. Frank, age 58, lives in a midwestern town of about 8,000 people in a rural farming community. Frank has mild intellectual disabilities. He graduated from high school, but only because in those days students like him were passed on whether they could perform the work or not. He is very proud of the high school ring he purchased at graduation. However, his community, especially the school system, did not serve him well. Instead of receiving special services and training that might now be available, the system basically ignored him and passed him on through.

A major problem for Frank is his speech. He has difficulty forming words and takes considerable time to structure his sentences. His comprehension of verbal communication is good, and he has an excellent sense of humor. His speech often fools people who don't know him well into thinking he is much less competent than he really is. Speech therapy might have helped if it had been available when he was young.

Frank works at a Center for People with Developmental Disabilities (that provides sheltered employment along with opportunities for socialization and other activities) in addition to working six hours per week as a janitor at Hilda's Happy Hot Dog Haven. Frank has a solid work history. For almost 20 years he worked at a local tanning factory hauling deer hides from one area to another as they proceeded through the leather making process. It was gruesome, backbreaking work, and when Frank got home, he was exhausted. At the time, he was living with his father, who cooked for him, did his laundry, and helped him with other daily living tasks.

Work at the tanning factory was not without problems. Frank told his relatives about another "guy at work" who liked to pick on him. Frank had lots of experience being picked on. The guy would draw a knife and tease Frank, pretending to cut him and

*Special Olympics provide an excellent means of empowerment for people with intellectual disabilities. Begun in 1968 when Eunice Kennedy Shriver organized the first sports competition at Soldier Field in Chicago, Special Olympics is now an international program that provides year-round opportunities for sports participation. Here, a Special Olympics athlete competes in a race in California at UCLA.*

actually slitting his right hand one time. Frank also told how, one night after work, he slit all "the guy's tires." The guy, who was fired shortly thereafter, never did find out who did it.

Frank was a saver. He would wear the same pair of polyester pants for years until the threads in the hem seams gave way. Although Frank made little more than minimum wage, he put almost all of it in savings while he lived with his dad. When the plant closed and he was laid off, he had accumulated more than $40,000. Investing with the help of his brother Sharif and a slick financial planner brought his assets to almost $200,000 by the time he turned 61. Unfortunately, this prevented him from receiving public assistance and resources because he did not meet various programs' means tests.

When his father died, Frank was able, with Sharif's help, to live in and pay rent for his own apartment. He preferred living alone to living with a roommate. One of Frank's strengths was his strong relationship with Sharif and his family, even though they lived 185 miles away. Frank didn't see his family as often as he liked since busing was deregulated and federal regulations no longer required companies to sponsor less popular runs. Sharif and his wife were periodically forced to endure a deadly dull four-hour trip through flat farmland to pick Frank up and spend another four hours to drive him home.

A major strength in Frank's life was his involvement with the local Center for People with Developmental Disabilities, an agency that did not have a means test. In its sheltered employment program, Frank felt productive and established many social contacts. As one of the highest-functioning clients, he achieved significant social status. At the center's periodic social dances, he was quite accomplished and admired. Frank also had a knack for taking pictures and videos, which he did regularly at the center's events. The center sponsored or cosponsored numerous events including Special Olympics, bowling tournaments, picnics, and outings to movies. Frank was extremely proud of a Volunteer's Award plaque he received from the center for all of the time he spent photographing and videotaping events.

At the center, he was assigned a social work case manager, Mandze, who helped to coordinate services and activities. To evaluate his daily living skills, she linked him with a trainer who tried to teach him how to cook. However, Frank didn't like to cook, so he ended up subsisting mostly on frozen dinners. (It

might be noted that Sharif, who had superior intelligence, could barely boil water; he didn't like to cook, either.) Mandze also helped coordinate any other supportive services Frank might need with Sharif and his family.

Although Mandze and Sharif tried to encourage Frank to manage his own finances and checkbook, this was too difficult for him. Frank didn't like doing computations or writing checks because he was afraid of making mistakes. When mail-ordering gifts for family members, he would always send cash despite the risk of losing it. Sharif finally gave up and determined that it was easier simply to keep track of Frank's finances himself than to keep after Frank.

Another major community strength was the spiritual and emotional support Frank received from his church. He attended services regularly and was involved in a group called the Sunday Evening Club, consisting of adult church members who met every other Sunday for a potluck dinner and a chance to socialize or hear speakers.

Frank's work at Hilda's was helpful in terms of making him feel useful and conserving his savings. However, the six-hour weekly work allocation was minimal. The management could have given him many more hours if they had not viewed him as an inadequate, "retarded" person. And the town provided no public transportation, so Frank had to walk to get anywhere, including two miles to work.

In summary, community strengths for Frank include the Center for People with Developmental Disabilities, its sheltered employment program, his social worker Mandze, public recognition via the Volunteer's Award, his spiritual involvement at church, his job at Hilda's, and strong connections with his family. Community weaknesses for Frank include the history of inattention to his special needs, local residents who made fun of him in a demeaning manner whenever they had the chance, inadequate involvement in his paid work environment, and lack of public transportation. Thus, in some ways, Frank's community environment supported and integrated him, thereby enhancing his quality of life. In other ways, the lack of community support hindered his ability to live the most useful, productive, and happiest life possible.

Highlight 11.6 reviews three other examples of how social workers might help people with intellectual disabilities become more integrally involved in community life.

| HIGHLIGHT 11.6 | EMPOWERMENT FOR PEOPLE WITH INTELLECTUAL DISABILITIES: CREATING LINKAGES WITH COMMUNITY LIFE |

Kretzmann and McKnight (1993) cite a number of situations in which adults with intellectual disabilities can be mainstreamed[2] and integrated as part of a large community. These are the types of scenarios social workers can actively seek out on their clients' behalf. The following three are adapted from Kretzmann and McKnight's ideas.

*Example A:* Reggie, age 28, thrives at playing games, so Reggie's social worker linked him with the local Boys Club. He now volunteers there regularly, teaching children games and supervising their activities.

*Example B:* Gina, age 22, spent most weekdays at a day program with other people who have intellectual disabilities. She passed much of her time coloring and watching other residents. She is an exceptionally warm person who lights up with a dazzling smile when spoken to or given any attention. Her social worker at the day program introduced her to a local day-care center to see if she could help out there.

At first, her social worker or other day program staff always accompanied her to the day-care center and provided some supervision. Now she goes to the center by herself several times a week. The children love her and the attention she pays to them. She always has time to listen to what they have to say and bestow affection when needed. They realize she's different from their other teachers because sometimes they have to help her out in completing activities, but they don't care. They love her anyway.

*Example C:* Hugh, age 68, lives in a group home. He loves to bowl. Danyelle, his group home social worker, found out that a local church had a Thursday night bowling league. She talked to the team members and asked if they would consider including Hugh on their team. They were a bit hesitant because they take bowling very seriously and play to win. They were even more hesitant when they discovered that Hugh was not a very good bowler. However, Hugh obviously was ecstatic about being on the team. Team members worked out a rotation system whereby Hugh could periodically bowl but his score was omitted from the final total. Hugh beamed proudly as he wore his Beaver's Bowling Buddies T-shirt.

[2]Mainstreaming is the incorporation of people with a disability or some other special attribute into the general population, thus providing them access to the experiences and opportunities that other people normally have. Examples of such special groups include people with intellectual and other developmental disabilities.

# Chapter Summary

The following summarizes this chapter's content as it relates to the learning objectives presented at the beginning of the chapter. Chapter content will help prepare students to:

*LO1 Define mobility disabilities (and identify a range of specific disabilities clustered under its umbrella).*

People with mobility disabilities "are those whose physical differences require them to achieve physical activities in a variety of alternate ways" (Mackelprang & Salsgiver, 2009, p. 177). Acquired mobility disabilities include stroke, muscular dystrophy, rheumatoid arthritis, multiple sclerosis, myasthenia gravis, and spinal cord injury.

*LO2 Investigate the importance of self-determination (for people with disabilities as an ethical aspect of social work practice).*

To maximize self-determination, social workers should adopt three approaches. First, they should assume a consumer-centered approach, accepting people as knowing their own needs and as being capable of making intelligent decisions about services. Second, social workers should learn about services and resources so that they may convey this information to clients. Third, they should advocate for people with disabilities whenever possible.

*LO3 Engage in critical thinking (about personal feelings and stereotypes concerning disability, residual versus institutional approaches to service provision for people with disabilities, empowerment through language, deinstitutionalization, and the Americans with Disabilities Act).*

Critical thinking questions were posed concerning personal biases about disability, who should be responsible for funding and providing services to people with disabilities, how words can affect how people with intellectual disabilities are viewed, the pros and cons of deinstitutionalization, and the extent to which the ADA is effective.

## LO4 Define developmental disabilities (and identify a range of specific disabilities clustered under its umbrella).

Developmental disabilities are severe and chronic, occur before age 22, are likely to be permanent, and result in substantial functional limitations. Developmental disabilities include intellectual disabilities, cerebral palsy, epilepsy, orthopedic problems, deafness and hardness of hearing, visual impairment, and autistic spectrum disorders. Some people have multiple disabilities.

## LO5 Examine historical perspectives concerning developmental disabilities.

Prior to the late 1960s, community treatment and legislation focused on individual pathology. During the 1970s and 1980s, people assumed a more community-based approach. Important concepts included normalization, deinstitutionalization, individual program planning, and the developmental model. During the 1990s and beyond, consumer empowerment has been emphasized. Major concepts include individualization, emphasis on choice, innovation, and family support.

## LO6 Describe generalist social work practice with people who have developmental disabilities.

Case management and advocacy are important when working with people who have developmental disabilities. Case management is the process of organizing, coordinating, and maintaining "a network of formal and informal supports and activities designed to optimize the functioning and well-being of people with multiple needs" (Moxley, 1989, p. 21).

Advocacy is "the process of affecting or initiating change either with and/or on behalf [of clients or] client groups to: [1] obtain services or resources for clients that would not otherwise be provided, [2] modify or influence policies, procedures, or practices that adversely affect [individuals, families,] groups or communities, [or] [3] promote new legislation or policies that will result in the provision of [much-needed] ... resources or services" (Hepworth, Rooney, Rooney, Strom-Gottfried, & Larsen 2010, p. 430).

## LO7 Discuss avenues of empowerment (legislative and community empowerment).

Legislation that has empowered people with disabilities includes the Americans with Disabilities Act (ADA) of 1990 that forbids discrimination and requires public accommodations in many circumstances. Another example of legislation is the Developmental Disabilities Assistance and Bill of Rights Act of 1990 that renewed grant programs and acknowledged that more resources were needed for people with disabilities. The Individuals with Disabilities Education Improvement Act of 2004 requires that a free appropriate public education be provided to all children (including children with disabilities) from ages 3 to 21 in the least restrictive environment possible. Ways social workers can work toward empowerment include advocating for federal and state legislation to make resources available to clients and working with community residents to establish resources.

Legislation empowering people with visual impairment includes the Rehabilitation Act of 1973, the Randolph-Sheppard Act, and the 1931 Pratt-Smoot Act. SSI can provide benefits to people who are legally blind. Social workers can advocate for services, link people with needed resources, establish self-help groups, and work with schools to empower children with visual impairment.

Communities can empower people with intellectual disabilities by establishing and using The Arc chapters, providing information and referral services and help lines, providing noninstitutional living facilities, offering vocational and employment programs, developing other support services, advocating for equal rights, soliciting community volunteers to help The Arc programming, providing recreational activities, and initiating various creative linkages with community life.

## LOOKING AHEAD

Many people with disabilities require special health services. Another field of practice in which social practitioners serve clients is health care. Chapter 12 will explore social work roles, health-care policy problems in the macro environment, and AIDS in an international context.

## COMPETENCY NOTES

The following identifies where Educational Policy (EP) competencies and their component behaviors are discussed in the chapter.

**EP 1 (Competency 1)—Demonstrate Ethical and Professional Behavior.** *(p. 372):* Professional social work roles including broker, case manager, and advocate are discussed in the context of people who have developmental disabilities.

**EP 1a Make ethical decisions by applying the standards of the NASW Code of Ethics, relevant laws and regulations, models for ethical decision-making, ethical conduct of research, and additional codes of ethics as appropriate to context.** *(p. 360):* Self-determination is a major principle espoused by the NASW *Code of Ethics.*

**EP 1b Use reflection and self-regulation to manage personal values and maintain professionalism in practice situations.** *(p. 360):* Social workers should practice self-reflection so that they might recognize and manage personal values and presumptions they harbor regarding people with disabilities. *(p. 362):* Social workers must be especially vigilant regarding stereotypes they and others might harbor when working with people who have disabilities.

**EP 1c Demonstrate professional demeanor in behavior; appearance; and oral, written, and electronic communication.** *(p. 362):* A consumer-oriented approach emphasizes the importance of demonstrating a professional demeanor. *(p. 365):* Professional demeanor includes communicating appropriately and using the correct terminology.

**EP 2 (Competency 2)—Engage Diversity and Difference in Practice.** *(p. 359):* Disability is a dimension of diversity. *(p. 360):* Social workers should recognize the ways in which society oppresses people with disabilities. *(p. 368):* People with developmental disabilities have historically experienced oppression, marginalization, and discrimination. *(p. 372):* An example of discrimination against a person with disabilities is presented.

**EP 2a Apply and communicate understanding of the importance of diversity and difference in shaping life experiences in practice at the micro, mezzo, and macro levels.** *(p. 360):* Social workers should recognize and communicate their understanding of how disability shapes life experiences.

**EP 2b Present themselves as learners and engage clients and constituencies as experts of their own experiences.** *(p. 362):* A consumer-oriented approach emphasizes the importance of social workers as learners who look to clients as experts concerning their own experiences.

**EP 2c Apply self-awareness and self-regulation to manage the influence of personal biases and values in working with diverse clients and constituencies.** *(p. 360):* Social workers should develop self-awareness regarding their personal biases about people with mobility disabilities.

**EP 3 (Competency 3)—Advance Human Rights and Social, Economic, and Environmental Justice.**

**EP 3a Apply their understanding of social, economic, and environmental justice to advocate for human rights at the individual and system levels.** *(p. 372):* Social workers should apply their understanding of social, economic, and environmental justice to advocate on the behalf of people who have developmental disabilities. *(p. 378):* Social workers should apply their understanding of social and economic justice to advocate for community empowerment for people with disabilities.

**EP 3b Engage in practices that advance social, economic, and environmental justice.** *(p. 360):* Social workers should engage in practices and interventions that advance self-determination and social and economic justice for people with mobility disabilities. *(p. 370):* Practitioners should emphasize clients' right to self-determination, a practice that advances social justice. *(p. 372):* Social workers should advocate on the behalf of people who have developmental disabilities to advance social, economic, and environmental justice for them. *(p. 373)*: Legislation that advocates on the behalf of people with disabilities is discussed. *(p. 378)*: Social workers should engage in practices that advance social, economic, and environmental justice for people with disabilities through community empowerment.

**EP 5 (Competency 5)—Engage in Policy Practice.**

**EP 5a Identify social policy at the local, state, and federal level that impacts well-being, service delivery, and access to social services.** *(p. 373)*: Legislation that impacts service delivery to people with with disabilities is discussed. *(p. 375)*: The ADA and its impacts for people with disabilities are discussed.

**EP 5b Assess how social welfare and economic policies impact the delivery of and access to social services.** *(p. 373)*: The effects of social welfare and economic policies upon people with disabilities is discussed. *(p. 375)*: The ADA and its impacts on the delivery and access to social services for people with disabilities are discussed.

**EP 5c Apply critical thinking to analyze, formulate, and advocate for policies that advance human rights and social, economic, and environmental justice.** *(p. 364)*: Critical thinking questions are posed to encourage thought about residual versus institutional approaches to service provision for people with disabilities; respecting their rights and seeking social, economic, and environmental justice is emphasized. *(p. 375)*: Discussion and ensuing critical thinking questions focus on analysis of the ADA and its effectiveness. *(p. 375)*: Social workers should advocate for policies that advance the social well-being of people with disabilities.

**EP 7 (Competency 7)—Assess Individuals, Families, Groups, Organizations, and Communities.**

**EP 7a Collect and organize data, and apply critical thinking to interpret information from clients and constituencies.** *(p. 364)*: Critical thinking questions are posed to encourage thought about policies that advance social well-being.

**EP 7c Develop mutually agreed-on intervention goals and objectives based on the** critical assessment of strengths, needs, and challenges within clients and constituencies. *(p. 362)*: A consumer-orientated approach stresses working with clients on mutually agreed-on goals. *(p. 370)*: Social workers should emphasize client self-determination and develop with clients mutually agreed-on intervention goals. *(p. 372)*: A case example illustrates how a social worker develops mutually agreed-on intervention goals and objectives as a client engages in self-advocacy.

**EP 7d Select appropriate intervention strategies based on the assessment, research knowledge, and values and preferences of clients and constituencies.** *(p. 370)*: Social workers should work in conjunction with clients to select appropriate intervention strategies. *(p. 376)*: Some intervention strategies for working with people who have visual impairment are discussed. *(p. 377)*: Subsequent sections address appropriate intervention strategies at the community and organizational levels on the behalf of people with disabilities.

**EP 8 (Competency 8)—Intervene with Individuals, Families, Groups, Organizations, and Communities.**

**EP 8a Critically choose and implement interventions to achieve practice goals and enhance capacities of clients and constituencies.** *(p. 369)*: Critical thinking questions address the effectiveness of institutionalization as an approach to intervention.

**EP 8c Use inter-professional collaboration as appropriate to achieve beneficial practice outcomes.** *(p. 375)*: Social workers can collaborate with colleagues and client to develop policies that provide resources to people with disabilities.

**EP 8d Negotiate, mediate, and advocate with and on behalf of diverse clients and constituencies.** *(p. 372)*: Social workers should advocate on the behalf of people who have developmental disabilities. *(p. 373)*: Practitioners should advocate on the behalf of people with disabilities. *(p. 375)*: Legislation that advocates on the behalf of people with disabilities is discussed. *(p. 378)*: Social workers should advocate for community empowerment for people with disabilities.

# 12 Social Work and Services in Health Care

© Photographee.eu/Shutterstock.com

## Learning Objectives    This chapter will help prepare students to:

**LO 1**  Identify major types of health problems. **Health Problems** (p. 387)

**LO 2**  Describe social work roles (in health-care provision). **Social Work Roles in Health Care** (p. 387)

**LO 3**  Review the current status of health care in the United States. **Health Care in the United States Today** (p. 391)

**LO 4**  Engage in critical thinking (about health-care coverage, overgeneralizations regarding various racial and ethnic groups, and ways to address the HIV/AIDS problem in sub-Saharan Africa). **Focus on Critical Thinking 12.1** (p. 393)

**LO 5**  Explore value discrepancies between cultural values (those of Asians and Pacific Islanders [API] and health-care provision (in the United States). **Cultural Competence and the U.S. Health-Care System** (p. 397)

**LO 6**  Describe HIV and AIDS (including its essence, its treatment, empowerment for people living with AIDS, and social work roles). **The Health Crisis of HIV and AIDS in the United States** (p. 401)

**LO 7**  Examine AIDS as an international problem (particularly in sub-Saharan Africa). **Global Perspectives: HIV and AIDS** (p. 407)

*Consider the following questions:*

- *Do you have health insurance?*
- *If so, how much does it cost you each month?*
- *Can you readily afford your monthly premiums for health insurance?*
- *Have you attempted to obtain health insurance on the exchanges under the Affordable Care Act (ACA) (to be explained later in the chapter)?*
- *Are you eligible for a subsidy (a grant from the government based on your income to help pay for health insurance) under the ACA?*
- *What is your deductible (the amount you must pay for health care before your insurance kicks in)?*
- *In the event of illness, could you afford your deductible?*
- *Do you have any concerns about health insurance?*
- *Do you have any worries about your future health issues?*
- *Do any members of your family have concerns and issues concerning their health insurance and care?*
- *Why is health care in the United States so expensive?*

*These questions address issues and concerns in the current health-care environment. This environment is characterized by legislative change, questions about costs and benefits, and uncertainty regarding the future.*

*The World Health Organization (WHO) defines* **health** *as "a state of complete physical, mental, and social well-being and not merely the absence of disease and infirmity" (WHO, 2014a). This definition goes beyond the conception of health as simply the lack of illness. Rather, it stresses the importance of strengthening and maximizing health, and not merely curing what's wrong.*

*Good health and health care involve every one of us. No one is immune to all the health problems encountered in life. People suffer maladies ranging from influenza, to chronic back pain, to cancer. Consider that more than 35 million people were discharged from U.S. hospitals in one recent year (ProQuest, 2014).*

*Social workers can play an important role in helping people live healthful lifestyles and seek the health services and resources they need. Practitioners can empower people by facilitating their pursuit of physical, mental, and social well-being.*

*Many social workers also practice in the arena of mental health. Note that sometimes health care is also used as an umbrella term to include mental health care. Although some of the issues involved in both mental health and physical health care are similar, this chapter will focus on the provision of physical health care and services. Chapter 13 will explore assessment issues and mental health services in greater detail.*

# Health Problems

LO 1

Health problems include virtually any physical malfunction, injury, or disease you can imagine. They can affect anyone in the population, from an infant born two and half months prematurely, to a 97-year-old suffering from arthritis and heart disease, to a young adult badly burned during a devastating fire in his apartment building.

At least five key factors cause or contribute to health problems (Coleman & Kerbo, 2009). First, people who pursue unhealthful lifestyles are more likely to experience health problems and die at a younger age. These include:

- Lack of regular exercise.
- An unhealthful diet high in fat and cholesterol.
- Cigarette smoking.
- Being overweight.
- High levels of stress over long periods.

A second factor related to health problems is physical injuries. Sometimes these are related to mortality (i.e., death). For example, in 2010, of young people age 15–24 in the United States who died, almost 42% did so as a result of accidents, including motor vehicle accidents, almost 16% from homicide, and more than 15.5% from suicide (ProQuest, 2014).

A third factor contributing to health problems involves environmental factors. Air pollution is a serious threat, especially in larger cities such as Los Angeles, Beijing, Bangkok, and Mexico City. During the 1990s, simply breathing the air in Mexico City during one day was the equivalent of smoking two packs of cigarettes (Weiner, 2001). Other environmental dangers include water pollution, use of pesticides, and exposure to buried nuclear and other industrial wastes.

Poverty is the fourth variable related to health problems. It is associated with malnutrition, poor indoor air quality, higher death rates, lack of access to medical care, unsafe water, and poor sanitation conditions (Mooney et al., 2015).

Contagious disease poses the fifth serious health concern. On a global level, such diseases as cholera and typhoid still plague people in nonindustrialized nations; the industrialized countries have virtually eliminated them with improved sanitation. However, respiratory and intestinal diseases still afflict people in the United States regularly. Sexually transmitted infections of various types also continue to infect millions of people annually (Yarber & Sayad, 2013). Human immunodeficiency virus (HIV), which causes acquired immune deficiency syndrome (AIDS), poses another major problem, one that will be discussed later in the chapter.

# Social Work Roles in Health Care

LO 2

Social workers who work in the health-care field are often referred to as **medical social workers**. Social workers serve in both direct-practice (e.g., hospitals, medical clinics, diagnostic and treatment centers, public health departments, Veterans Affairs health facilities, and managed care settings) and macro-practice capacities concerning health care.

EP 1

## Social Work Roles in Direct Health-Care Practice

Dhooper (2012) explains social work's involvement in health-care practice:

> *Social work has been a part of the health care scene for more than 100 years. It has an impressive history of significant contributions to the field of health care in such settings as hospitals, clinics, rehabilitation centers, nursing homes, health departments, hospices, and home health agencies. Social workers have been involved in health care at all levels: preventive care, primary care [ongoing care for patients prior to the onset of disease symptoms or care for those experiencing early symptoms], secondary care [treatment of full blown illness], tertiary care [treatment of illness seriously endangering a person's health], restorative care [help during recovery from illness], and continuing care. Depending on the major purposes and functions of each health care setting, their roles have varied, requiring differential professional skills. (p. 1)*

Health-care settings in which social workers practice include hospitals, medical clinics, diagnostic and treatment centers,[1] public health settings, and managed care companies.

## Hospitals, Medical Clinics, and Diagnostic and Treatment Centers

Social workers can fulfill many functions in hospitals, medical clinics, and diagnostic and treatment centers, including the following:

EP 6b, 7d, 8e

1. *Help patients understand and interpret technical medical jargon.* Physicians often receive little training in interpersonal and communication skills. Social workers can help define technical terms, explain physical and health implications of illnesses and injuries, and communicate with patients to make certain they understand what's happening to them.
2. *Offer emotional support.* Receiving a medical diagnosis can be a scary thing. Most patients are not experts on most illnesses, injuries, and health issues. Social workers can help patients look more objectively at health conditions and understand realistic potential consequences of various treatments.
3. *Help terminally ill people deal with their feelings and make end-of life plans.* (This is discussed more thoroughly later in the chapter.) Social workers can also help people requiring more intensive care than that provided at home make the transition to a more supportive setting, such as a group home, nursing home, or hospice.
4. *Help patients adjust their lives and lifestyles to accommodate to new conditions when they return home after medical treatment.* For example, persons diagnosed with heart disease or asthma, or those adjusting to an amputation or to blindness, may require help in adapting their behavior and habits to make life as healthy and efficient as possible.
5. *Help parents of children who have serious illnesses or disabilities cope with these conditions and respond to children's needs.*

6. *Serve as brokers who link patients with necessary supportive resources and services after leaving the medical facility. Discharge planning,* introduced in Chapter 10, is often involved. This is the comprehensive assessment of a patient's abilities and needs, the development of a plan to facilitate that patient's transition out of the hospital and back into a community or agency setting, and the implementation of that plan. Discharge planning focuses on the client's ability to function after a hospital or institutional stay. Placement is required that provides enough support, on the one hand, and allows for as much independence as possible, on the other. For example, a person recuperating from severe injuries suffered during a car accident might require a rehabilitative setting where time allows for rest, the appropriate therapy, and recovery. The discharge plan may also include ongoing medication, involvement with medical specialists, or significant supportive services.
7. *Help patients make financial arrangements to pay hospital and other medical bills.* Social workers often assist patients in contacting insurance companies or applying for financial assistance, guiding them through the complex maze of rules and policies.
8. *Provide health education aimed at establishing a healthful lifestyle and preventing illness.*

*Case Example* Donald, age 73, and Gerri, age 71, have been married for 50 years. At Donald's most recent annual physical examination, he was diagnosed with prostate cancer. (The *prostate* is "a gland surrounding the neck of the bladder" in men that releases "a fluid component of semen" [Lindberg, 2007, p. 1096]). It is the second most common form of cancer in men, the first being lung cancer (Hyde & DeLamater, 2014). Prostate cancer is usually slow to spread and, when caught and treated early, generally has a good prognosis. Donald and Gerri, both retired, are avid health advocates who work out at their local health club four times a week and vigilantly eat food high in fiber and low in fat. They visibly tremble at the thought of not rinsing dishes thoroughly after washing because of the possibility of ingesting soap residue. When Donald and Gerri found out about the cancer they were terrified. They wouldn't even tell any of their friends, whom they thought would immediately start discussing Donald's imminent death.

---

[1]Diagnostic and treatment centers are facilities to which persons such as children with diagnosis of various conditions, treatment multiple disabilities are brought for assessment, planning, and specialized treatment by a range of therapists (e.g., speech, occupational, or physical therapists).

Bethany, the hospital social worker involved, sat down with them and discussed realistic expectations for and consequences of treatment. Donald's physician had recommended chemotherapy and radiation treatments instead of surgically removing the prostate gland. Bethany encouraged Donald and Gerri to express their feelings and fears. She provided them with statistics about the high success rates of treatment and facts about its effects. Donald and Gerri's terror subsided, and they began to develop a more realistic view of what lay ahead. Bethany encouraged them to turn to their three children and their families for support, which they did.

It's interesting to note that prior to this experience, neither Donald nor Gerri had a positive word to say about social work and social workers. They had run a successful hardware store business that Donald had inherited from his father. They had believed that people who turned to social workers or other such helpers were weak and lazy and didn't have the wherewithal to make it on their own. Now they changed their minds. They had developed sincere respect for Bethany, who helped them through an emotionally turbulent time.

## Public Health Departments and Other Health-Care Contexts

**Public health** is the complex system of health-care programs and policies that focus on "the health of the community as a whole" (MedicineNet.com, 2014). Public health initiatives include encouraging lifestyles that contribute to good health, conducting research about factors affecting health such as diseases and injuries, and identifying and managing infectious diseases (CDC Foundation, 2014). General public health goals include (MedicineNet.com, 2014; WHO, 2014b):

1. The *appraisal* of community health to recognize problems and prioritize solutions.
2. The articulation of public health *policies* to address community health problems and seek solutions.
3. The assertion that health care is available to the *entire community* population "including health promotion and disease prevention."

Such broad goals relating to such a wide range of issues result in multiple facets of service provision. Facilities providing public health services include local, state, and federal health departments and agencies; private foundations and agencies focusing on specific health issues (e.g., the American Cancer Society, the March of Dimes); social service organizations; community health and mental health centers; family planning clinics; and virtually any other public agency providing services and benefits related to healthy living.

Specific services include any aiming to enhance health and mental health or prevent disease. These include crisis intervention, substance abuse treatment, health services for pregnant women, services to prevent and stop child maltreatment, health education, stress management training, and mental health counseling.

The breadth of public health can be revealed by identifying some of its successful campaigns; these include vaccinations in response to the spread of infectious diseases, motor-vehicle safety, workplace safety, stopping smoking, food safety, and reduction of deaths due to coronary heart disease (MedicineNet.com, 2014; WHO, 2014b).

### Veteran's Affairs Hospitals

The U.S. Department of Veterans Affairs (VA) manages the biggest health-care operation in the country, serving 8.3 million veterans at 150 major medical centers (hospitals and health-care systems) and other service-provision locations totaling more than 1,700 sites; these other services include the following (U.S. Department of Veterans Affairs [VA], 2014a):

- *Community-based outpatient clinics:* Medical clinics located in the community that provide primarily outpatient services. Such clinics usually offer better access for clients in terms of location and help clients avoid the much larger, multifaceted medical complex.
- *Community living centers:* Skilled nursing facilities (nursing homes) for clients who can no longer care for themselves independently.
- *Domiciliaries:* "Safe, home-like environment[s]" that provide various types of care including "medical, psychiatric, vocational, educational," or help with personal problems.
- *Vet Centers:* Agencies that provide "readjustment counseling and outreach services" to veterans returning from combat zones and to their family members as needed. Treatment generally relates to clients' military involvement (e.g., posttraumatic stress disorder).

The VA offers a full range of medical benefits and treatments in addition to mental health services

(VA, 2014d). Medical benefits include preventive care such as regular medical exams, health education, immunizations, and counseling regarding the inheritance of genetically related conditions. Inpatient benefits include surgical procedures, kidney dialysis, acute care, intensive care, transplant services, treatment in centers specializing in spinal cord injury or traumatic brain injury, and ongoing treatment in "polytrauma" centers that provide a continuum of ongoing care (from initial assessment and rehabilitation to supportive care in a long-term placement).

The VA provides a wide range of other services and programs for veterans, including blind rehabilitation services, cancer programs, centers for women veterans, diabetes programs, and homeless programs, among many others (VA, 2014d). It also provides education (through the GI bill), life insurance, vocational rehabilitation, pensions, and burial benefits in VA cemeteries, among a range of other services (VA, 2014d).

*Social Work Practice at the VA* The VA requires that social workers function at the licensed independent practice level (Manske, 2008). It employs 11,000 social workers (VA, 2014c). VA social workers provide help to clients concerning a wide range of issues. The VA explains that

*VA social workers can advise Veterans, their family members, Caregivers and friends about getting help from the VA or from community agencies to enable them to continue to live in their own home, or help with programs such as Meals on Wheels.*

*VA social workers are responsible for ensuring continuity of care[2] through the admission, evaluation, treatment, and follow-up processes. This includes coordinating discharge planning and providing case management services based on the patients' clinical and community health and social services resources. VA social workers develop and implement treatment approaches [that] address individual [personal] and social problems.*

*(VA, 2014c)*

Social workers serve many roles in the VA setting. Specific tasks include: linking veterans with financial, housing, or other community assistance;

helping veterans make the transition to new living conditions (e.g., a skilled nursing facility), assisting with the application process for benefits; arranging for respite care for caregivers of veterans; providing counseling for relationship or mental health problems; helping veterans who are dealing with grief and loss; addressing substance abuse issues; and assisting with child-care and child behavior management matters, on the one hand, or ailing parents, on the other (VA, 2014c). Highlight 12.1 portrays how one social worker describes his work at the VA.

Social workers also help veterans make the oftentimes difficult transition from combat to "normal" living. Chapter 13 discusses how social workers can help veterans deal with posttraumatic stress disorder.

### Managed Care Settings

Increasing numbers of social workers are also practicing in various facets of managed care. Kornblum and Julian (2009) define **managed care** as

*a wide range of health plans and practices that depart from the traditional model of private health insurance provided by one's employer. In the traditional model, insured patients chose their physician; physicians treated patients with absolute clinical autonomy; insurers generally paid physicians whatever they billed on a fee-for-service basis; and employers paid premiums for their workers to private insurers, regardless of the cost. Managed care has altered all these arrangements by setting limits on individual medical visits or treatments—that is, by managing care. (p. 61)*

Social workers hold management positions in managed care. They also participate in assessment to determine whether patients are eligible for benefits and which are most appropriate. Managed care, discussed more thoroughly later in the chapter, involves work in health insurance companies, hospitals, and *health maintenance organizations* (HMOs). HMOs are organizations that provide a wide range of health-care services for participants and employers, who typically pay an established monthly fee for services. These services generally must be provided by facilities and practitioners designated by the HMO.

### Macro Practice in Health Care: Seeking Empowerment

As administrators and members of administrative committees in health-care facilities, social workers

---

[2]*Continuity of care* refers to the efficient ongoing provision of services by different or the same agencies to meet clients' needs as their circumstances and needs change.

## HIGHLIGHT **12.1**     A VA SOCIAL WORKER TELLS HIS STORY

A social worker talks about what it's like to work at the VA (Kolb, 2007):

I work as a social worker in an outpatient primary care clinic with over 4,000 people assigned to it. I engage in a brief therapy model. Brief therapy is treatment of limited duration that emphasizes specific goals to solve clearly designated problems. I also serve as a referral source and provide resources within the agency and community. The visits to the social worker can be as simple as completing an advance directive (an advance directive is a witnessed, written document that explains ahead of time what should be done or not done medically when a person is no longer competent to make life and death decisions about his or her own health care), or as complex as assisting a client to find the next level of care if the client is not functioning adequately in the current living environment.

Many of our clients come to the clinic over a period of several years. Over time, a level of trust and rapport are developed [that] promotes a better ability to assess a client's changing needs during different life stages.

I do have scheduled appointments when appropriate, but much of my time is unscheduled to accommodate walk-in clients and for issues that arise during appointments with [staff from] different disciplines. It is very common for clients to bring up psychosocial concerns (for example, family conflict or not getting needed resources) during other appointments that are then referred to and addressed by the social worker on the same day.

Case Example:

I received a phone call from a client who stated he was going to kill himself. The caller further stated that he had a loaded handgun sitting next to him and he stated he intended to use the gun. This client would not divulge his identity or location to me. I was able to attract the attention of another clinic employee and quickly wrote a note stating that the client was suicidal and we needed assistance immediately. That employee contacted the authorities while I continued to converse with the client.

I engaged the client in open-ended conversation to make the client feel comfortable. Over time I was able to ask the patient identifying questions like, "When did a provider last see you in the clinic?" "When did you last get medication refills?" "Who is your health-care provider?" With this information I was able to utilize computerized medical record programs to identify the caller and obtain his address. I then provided that information to the local police who went to the client's residence and placed him under emergency detention due to his threats to himself and others. It was reported that there was indeed a loaded gun found in the client's residence.

I have spoken to the client since this event. He stated that he appreciated being listened to. He stressed how much he valued my concern for his well-being and my efforts to keep him on the phone to establish his identity. He sincerely appreciated my commitment to get him the help he needed and wanted. (pp. 11–12)

work to develop agency policies that promote effective health care available to people who need it. Additionally, social workers can advocate for more comprehensive health coverage. Social workers and the National Association of Social Workers have historically served as significant forces in advocating for improved health-care legislation, policies, and resources.

EP 1, 3a, 3b, 5c, 8d

# Health Care in the United States Today

LO 3

The provision of health care today in the United States is expensive and complex. The next sections will review the Patient Protection and Affordable Care Act of 2010, the context of managed care, and problems in health-care provision (including the effects of poverty, social class, and race, in addition to escalating health-care costs).

## Patient Protection and Affordable Care Act of 2010 (ACA)

For more than a century, U.S. politicians have been debating the issue of **national health insurance**—a publicly funded program that would expand the current system of health-care provision to give some level of coverage to everyone, regardless of their ability to pay. Prior to 2010 all industrialized countries except for the United States had established some kind of national system so that all citizens would have access to some type of health-care coverage (Coleman & Kerbo, 2009).

After a long and bitter debate, Congress passed the Patient Protection and Affordable Care Act of 2010 (ACA) (introduced in earlier chapters), also often referred to as Obamacare. Henslin (2011) reports:

> The intention of this law is to reduce the inequalities in health care by requiring all U.S. citizens and legal residents to have medical insurance. Those who cannot afford health insurance will be provided it by raising taxes on those who have higher incomes....
>
> Only as the years pass will we see what impact this law has on inequalities in health care. In advance, however, we can be certain that the law will not eliminate the inequalities. These are built into our social structure. People with higher incomes will always be able to afford higher-quality medical care. And ... **EP 2** unless there is fundamental change—which there will not be—[people living in poverty] ... will continue to be exposed to more harmful conditions at work. In the absence of such fundamental change, they will also continue to eat less healthy food, exercise less, and have a higher rate of obesity. The end result is that they will continue to suffer from more health problems and to die at a younger age. (p 327)

According to the Obama administration, the ACA promotes a wide range of health-care advantages involved in improving quality while lowering costs (Healthcare.gov, 2011). The plan's intent is to "hold insurance companies accountable, lower health-care costs, guarantee more choice, and enhance the quality of care for all Americans" (WhiteHouse.gov, 2011b).

Jansson (2015) explains:

> The legislation proposed that in 2014 states establish "insurance exchanges" to allow uninsured consumers, as well as businesses, to purchase insurance coverage that provided basic coverage. (Individuals and businesses would be mandated to insure themselves and their employees—or they would have to pay penalties to states that would use the funds to insure them.) (p. 491)

**Subsidies** (grants from the government based on an individual's income to help pay for health insurance) were also built into the law for poor and some middle class people, based on income; these vary depending on the state of residence and the plan selected (Obamacare Facts, 2014). Folger (2013) explains the choice of plans available on the exchanges. People may choose among bronze, silver, gold, and platinum health-care plans. All plans offer the same benefits, but costs vary. The higher the plan level, the more the plan will pay toward a person's health care. However, the lower the plan level, the more a person must pay out-of-pocket. This generally involves higher **premiums** (the monthly cost for the insurance), higher **deductibles** (the amount an individual must pay for health care before the insurance kicks in), higher **copayments** (specified amounts the individual is responsible for paying when receiving a health-care service), and higher levels of **coinsurance** (the individual's specified share of payment for a health-care service) (p. 2).

The Obama administration indicates that the act achieves a number of positive accomplishments (Healthcare.gov, 2011a; U.S. Department of Health and Human Services [USDHHS], 2014). The ACA:

1. Allows states to cover more people on Medicaid.
2. Encourages access to preventive services without cost.
3. Permits young adults under age 26 to remain on their parents' health insurance policy.
4. Provides tax credits to help more Americans pay for insurance even if they lose or change jobs or in the event that they become ill.
5. Offers consumer protection by closer monitoring of insurance companies and their practices.
6. Ends lifetime maximums and most annual maximums imposed by insurance companies.
7. Cracks down on insurance fraud.

**8.** Extends health insurance coverage to people with pre-existing health conditions.

**9.** Provides a 50% discount on brand-name pre-scription drugs for older adults on Medicare who enter the "donut-hole" where their drugs are not covered (described in Chapter 8).

**10.** Offers tax credits to small businesses for providing health insurance to their employees.

Adversaries of the ACA vehemently say that it is not possible to provide better service to more people without incurring more costs. Initial court challenges by states focused on whether the law was constitutional in that it required citizens to purchase insurance from private companies; however, in 2012 the U.S. Supreme court ruled that it was really a tax, which Congress could legally impose (Mooney et al., 2015). The law requires "virtually all Americans to purchase health insurance or pay a fine" (Danner, 2010). Many small business owners maintain they can't afford health insurance for all employees and that the Act involves "an onslaught of new taxes and burdensome paperwork"; it may be much more economical for them to forego the tax credit rather than purchase expensive insurance (Danner, 2010).

At any rate, people are polarized concerning the pros and cons of the ACT. There have been delays in some aspects of implementation. Questions have been raised about cost and effectiveness. Questions also involve people purchasing health insurance plans on the ACA exchanges. Cheaper plans in terms of monthly costs have higher out-of-pocket payments for health care. What happens when someone insured with a lower level plan that has lower monthly premiums, but also higher deductibles, copayments, and coinsurance, gets really sick and needs really expensive medical treatment? How much can that person afford to pay?

Although the ACA has inevitable hurdles and snags, it has the potential of providing health care to many more Americans (Jansson, 2015; Jimenez et al., 2015). Health care is vital for everyone, including clients.

This discussion has addressed only a few of the issues involved in the ACA and health-care provision. It is essential for social workers to keep abreast of developments and changing conditions regarding health care as part of a career-long learning process. Focus on Critical Thinking 12.1 focuses on the issue of cost versus choice.

## FOCUS ON CRITICAL THINKING 12.1    HEALTH-CARE COSTS AND POLICY    LO 4

Much of the debate in the United States about establishing a national system has historically focused on two issues—cost and freedom of choice. Health insurance and health care is expensive. Questions involve what types of coverage should be included and how coverage should be funded. The freedom-of-choice debate also concerns the extent to which each citizen could choose his or her own health-care provider. The United States has a strongly ingrained commitment to freedom of choice. The ACA exchanges are limited to those insurance companies that choose to participate. Plan participants generally must choose from physicians connected in the plan's network.

**EP 5c**

### Critical Thinking Questions

- How do you think health care should be handled in the United States? Should coverage be universal, that is, available to all? To what extent does the Affordable Care Act (ACA) accomplish this? To

what extent should individuals have a choice in terms of selecting benefits and health providers?
- To what extent is the ACA plan selection (bronze, silver, gold, and platinum) fair and just?
- Do your views reflect a *conservative* or *liberal* perspective regarding this issue?

These value orientations involve the following variables:

- Is it individuals' responsibility to take care of themselves and their families with minimal governmental interference? Or is it the government's responsibility to provide health-care services because they are so critically important to survival?
- Because health care is increasingly expensive, who should bear the burden of paying for it? Workers? Employers? All citizens through increased taxes and subsequent government funding? People who are rich?

## Managed Care

Managed care is "the country's major approach to improving access, controlling cost, and ensuring quality of health care" (Dhooper, 2012, p. 281). This is true for virtually all health insurance companies including those participating in the ACA exchanges. We've established that *managed care* is "a wide range of health plans and practices that depart from the traditional model of private health insurance provided by one's employer" (Kornblum & Julian, 2009, p. 61). It is a health-care system where the "managed care provider is expected to provide all elements of health care covered in the enrollee's contract in return for a fixed monthly or annual payment per person enrolled" (Chapin, 2014, p. 415). Managed care is a primary context in which social workers practice. Even social workers who are not employed in health-care or nursing home settings will still work with clients for whom health care is a major concern.

Although there are various definitions of managed care, a major concept characterizing any form of it is **capitation** or **cost containment** (Vandiver, 2008, p. 145).

Capitation *is a term used to indicate a specified amount paid periodically to the provider for a group of specified services, regardless of quantity rendered. With capitation, a reimbursement system involves paying providers a fixed amount to service a client/consumer over a given period.*

(*Chambers & Wedel, 2005, p. 201*)

In other words, a rate is established that the managed care organization is given for each insured patient. An identified group or range of health and mental health-care providers contracts with the managed care organization to provide health care at a negotiated rate. Instead of paying for each visit or treatment received on a **fee-for-service** basis, the contracted health-care providers are supposed to provide whatever services the insured patients (in individual insurance plans) in addition to their families (in family insurance plans) require.

One intent of capitation is to control medical costs (Vandiver, 2008). Providers are paid one sum per patient regardless of how many services providers supply. However, medical costs have continued to escalate. It has been difficult to establish whether managed care is less expensive than the old approach

that was based on fee-for-services because of the complexity of the managed care environment and other variables that are difficult to control and measure (Vandiver, 2008).

Another potential goal of managed care is to improve health-care outcomes. That is, health and mental health services should be of high quality and readily accessible to clients. Yet they should also be cost-effective. However, research has indicated that improved quality of care has not necessarily been achieved in a range of areas (Vandiver, 2008). Managed care "fundamentally transformed" traditional relationships between clients and workers (Lohmann, 1997, p. 201). Historically, social workers in agency settings established treatment plans in conjunction with clients, in addition to stressing informed consent and confidentiality to comply with ethical standards. Managed care takes these decisions out of workers' and clients' hands and puts them into the hands of third-party decision makers. A managed care representative, often a utilization reviewer or case manager, then reviews documentation and regulates "the services that clients receive, especially what specific services will be provided and at what cost" (Corcoran, 1997, p. 194). To some, managed care "represents the complete (and seemingly sudden) triumph of financial management concerns over virtually all other professional considerations" (Lohmann, 1997, p. 202).

### *Ethical Dilemmas in Managed Care*

Think about the positive potential of managed care:

*Done right, managed care is not just a cheap imitation of fee-for-service medicine. It can work better. Its simplest contribution is to link hospitals, doctors and specialists so that they can administer care more efficiently. Besides saving money, shared electronic records and preset treatment protocols can improve the care that individual patients receive.*

**EP 1a**

(*Spragins, 1998, p. 62*)

However, cost cutting and inappropriate decisions often hamper this potential effectiveness. The following are sad occurrences involving managed care that illustrate some of its potential problems:

- "A Medicare HMO threatened to take a 94-year-old's wheelchair" (Vallianatos, 2001a, p. 7).

- A woman experiencing a "life-threatening asthma attack" was taken to a more distant HMO-sponsored hospital instead of being rushed to the nearest medical facility (Vallianatos, 2001a, January, p. 7).
- "A person with AIDS was denied approval by his managed care organization … of medications he had previously been on" (Vallianatos, 2001a, January, p. 7).
- A man "suffered a stroke … after his HMO failed to treat his blood disorder. Clots have since cost him both legs. 'They treated my stroke like the flu,' he says" (Spragins, 1998, p. 62).
- A 62-year-old woman "lost a kidney after her primary care doctor … [working under the auspices of a managed care system] refused her repeated requests to see a specialist for her constant abdominal pain." She noted that he prescribed "range-of-motion exercises" when she really "had an infected kidney" (Spragins, 1998).

Social workers must work within their agency settings. However, they are also responsible for maintaining ethical practices and for making sure clients' needs are met. Several ethical issues may be raised concerning managed care.

The first involves the potential conflict between "the gatekeeping role of some managed care organizations and client self-determination" (Corcoran, 1997, p. 196). With managed care, clients often no longer have the right to the service provider of their choice. Rather, clients are offered a limited range of providers or the managed care utilization reviewer makes this determination.

Similarly, managed care may conflict with the ethical principle of informed consent. Consider that:

*informed consent requires that the client know in advance the clinical procedures, the risk of those procedures, and the available alternative procedures. Managed care may destroy informed consent by restricting the available procedures to a limited number. For example, a managed care company may determine the preferred practice and the preferred providers, with little consideration or disclosure of alternative procedures.*

*(Corcoran, 1997, p. 196)*

Managed care also has the potential to violate client confidentiality (Dhooper, 2012). Social workers are bound by the National Association of Social Workers (NASW) *Code of Ethics*, which emphasizes how "social workers should respect clients' right to privacy" and "protect the confidentiality of all information obtained in the course of professional service" (NASW, 2008, 1.07a, 1.07c). (Chapter 2 reviewed major tenets of the NASW *Code*.) Additionally, it specifies that social workers "may disclose confidential information when appropriate with valid consent from a client" (NASW, 2008, 1.07b). However, the *Code* also provides an exception. It indicates that social workers should maintain confidentiality "except for compelling reasons. The general expectation that social workers will keep information confidential does not apply when disclosure is necessary to prevent serious, foreseeable, and imminent harm to a client or other identifiable person" (NASW, 2008, 1.07c). If a managed care organization demands information before providing services, what should the worker do? What if the worker does not agree with the organization's expressed need for information and believes that the regulations violate clients' right to privacy? Workers may be required to report confidential information whether or not they feel it's ethical in order for clients to receive necessary health care. Highlight 12.2 suggests what social workers can do to address some of these issues.

### Problems Plaguing U.S. Health Care

The health-care environment in the United States historically has been weighed down by a number of problems. These include the effects of poverty, social class, and race, in addition to escalating health-care costs.

### *The Effects of Poverty, Social Class, Race*

People living in poverty historically have been more likely to have poorer health (Kornblum & Julian, 2012). In 2011, although more than 21.7 million people below the poverty level were enrolled in the Medicaid program, 29.6% of people living in poverty, or almost 13.7 million of them, had no insurance of any kind during that year **EP 2** (ProQuest, 2014). For example, one study found that people with private insurance were twice as likely to get the surgery they needed as people receiving Medicaid (Coleman & Kerbo, 2009). Economic variables inevitably affect health; generally

## HIGHLIGHT 12.2

## RESPONDING TO ETHICAL DILEMMAS: IMPROVING HEALTH-CARE PROVISION ON THE MACRO LEVEL

Managed care is here whether we like it or not. Social workers must respond to any ethical dilemmas it poses. There are at least five suggestions for how social workers might shape the future managed care environment (Barusch, 2015; Dhooper, 2012; Vandiver, 2008). First, social workers can participate in the formation and scrutiny of contracts with health providers to make sure they're fair. Second, practitioners can advocate for managed care organizations to pay attention and respond to consumers' rights and needs. Third, social workers can stand up and speak out on the behalf of

EP 3a, 5c, 8c, 8d

Medicaid recipients to make sure these clients are receiving the effective services they need. Fourth, workers can encourage Medicaid participants' greater participation in the planning and implementation of managed care programs. For example, social workers can initiate surveys evaluating recipients' opinions of treatment and treatment effectiveness, make certain that grievance procedures are in place and used when appropriate, and advocate for recipient representation on advisory groups to maximize consumer input. Fifth, social workers can also lobby legislators for improvements in the effectiveness of health-care provision.

speaking, "the poorer people are, the sicker they are" (Henslin, 2011, p. 326).

Social class is another variable related to poorer health; Leon-Guerrero (2014) explains:

*Although no factor has been singled out as the primary link between socioeconomic position and health, scholars have offered many factors— standard of living, work conditions, housing conditions, access to better quality food, leisure activities, and the social and psychological connection with others at work, at home, or in the community—to explain the relationship....*

*The type of work available to poorly educated people can cause illness or death by exposing them to hazardous conditions. Poor and middle-class individuals who live in poor neighborhoods are exposed to air, noise, water, and chemical pollution that can increase rates of morbidity and mortality. Inadequate and unsafe housing contributes to infectious and chronic diseases, injuries, and illnesses, including lead poisoning when children eat peeling paint. The diet of [people living in lower socioeconomic classes] ... increases the risk of illness. [People with few resources] ... have little time or opportunity to practice healthy activities such as exercise, and because of life stresses, they may also be encouraged to adopt behaviors that might further endanger their health. Finally, poverty limits individual access to preventative and therapeutic health care. (pp. 262–263)*

People of color, who are more likely to live in poverty, also are more likely to lack adequate health care (Coleman & Kerbo, 2009; Kornblum & Julian, 2012). African American men are one-third less likely to undergo heart bypass surgery than their White counterparts (Coleman & Kerbo, 2009; Kornblum & Julian, 2009). Whites are twice as likely to get a kidney transplant as African Americans (Coleman & Kerbo, 2009). The life expectancy for White males is 4.7 years greater than that for African American males, and it is 3.3 years greater for White than African American females (ProQuest, 2014). Historically, the American people have experienced unequal access to health care related to poverty, social class, and race. In 2011, more than 48.6 million, or more than 15.7%, of Americans (including people at all income levels) lacked any health insurance (ProQuest, 2014), and millions more had strikingly insufficient coverage (Macionis, 2010). It is yet to be determined how the ACA will address and hopefully improve this situation.

### The Escalating Cost of Health Care

The U.S. health-care system costs significantly more per capita than the health-care system in any other industrialized nation (Mooney et al., 2015). In 2009, the United States spent 17.6% of its gross domestic product on health care (Kaiser Family Foundation [KFF], 2011). The expenditure for health care amounted to $8,402 per person in 2010 (KFF,

2012a). Mooney and her colleagues (2015) argue that health-care costs are soaring for at least five reasons:

1. *The rapid acceleration of technological advances has increased the types of services, drugs, and testing available.*
2. *The rate of obesity is very high.* About one-third of Americans are obese (Squires, 2012). Obesity is related to a range of physical conditions that require medical treatment and such treatment is expensive.
3. *Administrative overhead for running health-care organizations is huge.* Administrative expenses for health care are six times higher than in Western European countries (Mooney et al., 2015). Reinhardt (2008) indicates that much of this expense is excess spending used for "product design, underwriting, and marketing."
4. *The price of prescription drugs is skyrocketing.* Americans pay 50% more for their prescription drugs than people pay for them in other developed nations (Brill, 2013).
5. *Costs of public and private health insurance continue to rise.* In 1990 the national health expenditure per person was $2,660 (ProQuest, 2014). We've already indicated that in 2010 it was $8,402 (KFF, 2012a).

Some also feel health costs are rising because the overall population is aging. Because of better medical treatment, more people are living longer. The older people are, the more likely they are to suffer from more health problems that require more expensive treatment. However, the percentage of older adults in the United States is less than in other rich nations where health-care spending is significantly less (Mooney et al., 2015).

# Cultural Competence and the U.S. Health-Care System    **LO 5**

Another important issue involves the U.S. health-care system's responsiveness to the needs and values of the nation's various racial, ethnic, and cultural groups. Social workers have the ethical responsibility to examine, attend to, and advocate for positive change concerning these groups' health and welfare. It is beyond the scope

**EP 1c, 2, 2a, 7d**

of this book to examine the treatment of every cultural group, so we will explore one case example—the U.S. health-care system's treatment of Americans with Asian and Pacific Islander roots in the context of their cultural values. The U.S. health-care system is a huge bureaucracy, with many of the characteristics of traditional bureaucracies. Although management approaches vary within its many organizational structures, strict regulations and decision-making hierarchies for health-care provision tend to dominate. A problem commonly faced by such bureaucracies is the lack of cultural sensitivity. Rigid rules do not provide flexibility for adapting to culturally diverse values and needs. A major goal in social work is to enhance service provision for clients. Lack of responsiveness to clients' cultural values and belief systems can represent a major barrier to the provision of effective services.

The following discussion describes six general dimensions important in understanding Asian and Pacific Islander (API) cultures with respect to involvement in the health-care system. (Note, however, that we should not overgeneralize. For example, we should not assume that all members of API groups adhere to traditional API values to the same extent. Focus on Critical Thinking 12.2 addresses this issue.) Subsequent content addresses five topics concerning in U.S. health-care policy—informed consent, advance directives, decisions about nursing home placement, disclosure of terminal illness, and making end-of-life decisions—and examines implications for improved health-care provision

## Value Dimensions in API Cultures Relating to Health-Care Provision

At least five concepts inherent in API cultures relate directly to U.S. health-care provision. These include filial piety, collective versus individual decision making, emphasis on harmony versus conflict, nonverbal communication, fatalism, and a sense of shame at asking for help.

### Filial Piety

An important value dimension in API cultures is **filial piety**—"the expression of respect for and showing affection toward parents, as well as sacrificing for them in times of need" (Baskin, 2012, p. 172; Kim, 2011). For example, "*Oya-KoKo*, a Japanese version of filial piety to parents, requires a child's

# THE HAZARDS OF OVERGENERALIZING

Note that when we speak about any racial, ethnic, or cultural group, it is important not to overgeneralize. Here we talk about general value dimensions evident in API cultures. However, individuals or families from any ethnic or racial group may embrace traditional cultural norms to various degrees. They may also experience **acculturation**, which we have established as "the adaptation of language, identity, behavior patterns, and preferences to those of the host/majority society" (Lum, 2004, p. 229). In other words, members of a diverse group may gradually blend into the larger society and adopt its values and customs.

EP 7a

Braun and Browne (2000) comment on other influential dynamics:

Some of the factors, besides timing of immigration, that influence culturally linked health behaviors include socioeconomic status, language spoken at home, extent to which the community (and family) is ethnically homogeneous, educational attainment, and expectations about returning to one's ancestral home. (p. 186)

Therefore, when we think about a racial, ethnic, or cultural group, it's important not to assume that all members comply with all cultural values or conform to the same extent. Being of Chinese ethnic heritage does not automatically mean a person loves pan-fried dumplings, Szechuan shrimp, roast pork lo mein, kung pao chicken, or mushroom egg foo young simply because these might be traditional ethnic foods. The trick is to view each person as a unique personality, yet be sensitive to the possible cultural values and beliefs that person may hold.

Another word of caution concerns differences among the many cultures included under the API umbrella. For example, a common theme in many API cultures is the importance of extended family and the subordination of individual family members. However, in Cambodian culture, the family group is not necessarily more significant than any individual; if anything, the relationship of a couple is the significant facet in a family's structure (DuongTran & Matsuoka, 1995). Another example concerns the Filipino culture. Whereas many API cultures are patriarchal, "[a]mong Filipinos, sex roles are egalitarian rather than patriarchal. Filipinos place a high value on family, but they are also encouraged to be independent and competitive" (Weaver, 2005, p. 170).

Consider the following questions regarding your own ethnic and cultural heritage.

## Critical Thinking Questions

- What traditions and values characterize your heritage?
- To what extent do your own values comply with traditional ideas?
- What are the reasons for these discrepancies?

sensitivity, obligation, and unquestionable loyalty to lineage and parents" (Ho, 1992, p. 37). Especially significant is the obligation of younger people to care for parents as they age.

### Collective Versus Individual Decision Making

In contrast to the individualist orientation emphasized in U.S. health care, API values center on reliance on the family or larger group to make ultimate decisions about any individual member's care (Kim, 2011; Mokuau, 2008; Sue & Sue, 2008; Yeo & Hikoyeda, 2000; Vakalahi & Godinet, 2014). In the U.S. health-care system the focus is on individuals making decisions about their own medical care.

### Emphasis on Harmony Versus Conflict

API cultures emphasize the importance of members getting along and not causing trouble for the family, a concept that characterizes collectivist societies (Kim, 2011; Martin, Paglinawan, & Paglinawan, 2014). The implication, then, is that individuals must "endure hardship and pain," especially if addressing issues that might disturb or cause discomfort for other family or group members (McLaughlin & Braun, 1999, p. 325). For example, in Vietnamese culture, getting along harmoniously is done through civility, gracious politeness, and courtesy; at times this occurs at the expense of being honest and direct (DuongTran & Matsuoka, 1995).

Many values in Hawaiian culture reflect the importance of harmony and affiliation, including sharing resources, being congenial, fulfilling promises, and using one's intellect (Martin, et al., 2014; Mokuau, 1995, 2008).

There also tends to be respect for clearly defined family structures and hierarchies of authority, which clarifies expectations and encourages predictability of behavior. For instance, Samoan culture stresses "hierarchical systems with clearly defined roles. The highly structured organization of the family defines an individual's roles and responsibilities and guides the individual in interactions with others" (Ewalt & Mokuau, 1996, p. 261).

### Nonverbal Communication

A fourth value inherent in API cultures involves silent or nonverbal communication. Yamashiro and Matsuoka (1997) explain that "in Asian and Pacific [Islander] cultures, language may not accommodate all that individuals think and feel—especially for those who are not socialized to use language as a primary means for expressing feelings" (Fong, 2008; Leong, Lee, & Chang, 2008; Paniagua, 2014; Yamashiro & Matsuoka, 1997, p. 180). Diller (2015) remarks:

**EP 1c**

> *Asians also tend to have a very different nonverbal communication system. Providers need to be aware of this, because unlike the Western therapeutic focus on speaking, much of the communication in Asian cultures is nonverbal. The meanings of facial expressions, gestures, eye contact, and various cultural symbols or metaphors are usually completely different from Western ones. Research has found Asians to have a "low-contact" culture—[where people are] … more comfortable with little physical contact and larger interpersonal distances. (p. 313)*

Much can be learned by carefully observing people's silent responses and subtle nonverbal gestures. For example, it is "improper" for children "to discuss issues of death and dying with parents, yet concern by either party may be expressed by nonverbal cues such as bowing of the head or eye contact" (McLaughlin & Braun, 1999, p. 324).

API cultures value both self-control and inconspicuousness, both of which discourage the sharing of information, especially about personal issues (Kitano & Maki, 1996). For example, conventional

Japanese tradition stresses the value of personal self-control and discourages the expression of annoyance, dissatisfaction, or distress (Murase, 1995). Laotian culture emphasizes the avoidance of embarrassment by exhibiting concentrated emotional control; direct criticism of another's mistakes is considered rude and degrading (DuongTran & Matsuoka, 1995).

### Shame at Asking for Help

API values include an emphasis on family, cooperation, and harmony, and an aversion to causing trouble. All these contribute to avoidance of the U.S. health-care system. For Asian Americans and Pacific Islanders, "there is stigma about and shame in experiencing mental and emotional distress" (Balgopal, 1995, p. 236; Fong, 2008; Kim, 2011; Leong et al., 2008). Thus family and group members strongly prefer to deal with issues and illnesses within the family, rather than expose problems to outsiders. For example, Chinese Americans generally feel that revealing family problems outside of the family dishonors the family name; even issues such as intellectual disability, losing a job, inferior performance at school, or tangling with the law are considered shameful and kept within the family (Lum, 1995).

When it becomes obvious to family members that the family is incapable of resolving health problems, they hesitantly turn to health-care providers as a last resort. For example, Japanese Americans will seek mental health help only when faced with an extremely severe and unmanageable problem (Murase, 1995).

For physical illness, API families tend to pursue external health-care services "only if emergency care is needed" (McLaughlin & Braun, 1999, p. 325). Once that step is taken, health-care professionals are expected to make collectivist decisions—that is, those "in the best interest of the greatest number of people involved with the patient" (McLaughlin & Braun, 1999, p. 325).

### Conflicts Between API Cultural Values and the U.S. Health-Care System

Conflicts between API cultures and U.S. health-care system policies and practice revolve around at least five areas: informed consent, advance directives, decisions about nursing home placement (McLaughlin & Braun, 1999), disclosure of terminal illness, and end-of-life decisions (Yeo & Hikoyeda, 2000).

Given these conflicts, the U.S. health-care system can either detract from the health and well-being of Asian Americans and Pacific Islanders or empower them.

## Informed Consent

In the U.S. health-care system, individual patients are subject to **informed consent**, which involves a person's right to receive adequate information about "the consequences and risks of a medical procedure" or treatment process, evaluate alternatives, and give permission for a procedure before it's begun (Pietsch & Braun, 2000, p. 38). In many API cultures, this presumed right does not comply with prevailing values and norms (McLaughlin & Braun, 1999). For instance, "unlike the custom among White people, for whom the individual patient is the decision maker, many Japanese and Chinese families assign decision-making duties to the eldest son. In Pacific Islander families, it may be less obvious who the decision maker is" (McLaughlin & Braun, 1999, pp. 323–324). The entire family may share duties and assume designated responsibilities such as getting food. Because of the collective nature of decision making in API cultures, it is customary for "all family members" to "receive the same level of detail about the patient's diagnosis, prognosis, and treatment options" (Braun, Mokuau, & Tsark, 1997; McLaughlin & Braun, 1999, p. 324).

Three problematic issues relate to informed consent (Kim, 2011; McLaughlin & Braun, 1999). First, consider Asian Americans' and Pacific Islanders' emphasis on harmony and conformity to group wishes. Given the API cultural orientation toward cooperation, patients may feel obligated to sign consent papers presented to them when they don't really want to. Second, cultural norms emphasizing silence and inconspicuousness may prevent patients from voicing contrary opinions, asking questions about illnesses, and declining to sign papers. Third, health-care personnel are often unaware of how API cultural values can affect the consent process and interfere with its integrity.

## Advance Directives

A second problematic issue concerning API cultures and the health-care system involves **advance directives**. Introduced in Chapter 10, these are written, witnessed, signed instructions regarding what individuals wish to have done in the event that they are unable to make decisions (McLaughlin & Braun, 1999; Yeo & Hikoyeda, 2000). They can either describe what should be done under certain medical circumstances or identify some other individual to make these decisions. For example, what should be done for a person who is brain-dead and living on a respirator? Should that person be kept alive as long as possible, or should someone "pull the plug"?

Two issues tend to surface here with respect to API cultures (McLaughlin & Braun, 1999). First, health-care practitioners are legally required to "approach patients for copies of advance directives" (McLaughlin & Braun, 1999, p. 331). However, in Chinese, Japanese, and Hawaiian cultures, people avoid discussing death for fear of inviting it or suffering negative consequences (Corr, Nabe, & Corr, 2009). Second, it is pointless for Asian Americans and Pacific Islanders to discuss such issues because of their collectivist approach. They assume that family members will address those issues when the appropriate time comes.

## Decisions About Nursing Home Placement

Many Asian Americans and Pacific Islanders embrace the concept of filial piety and believe that children should care for aging parents (Balgopal, 1995; DuongTran & Matsuoka, 1995; Lum, 1995; McLaughlin & Braun, 1999; Murase, 1995; Paniagua, 2014). For them, nursing home placements are to be avoided at all costs. Thus API families tend to wait until situations reach crisis proportions before investigating possible nursing home placement (McLaughlin & Braun, 1999; Murase, 1995). Stress may escalate due to pressure to maintain two incomes, care for both children and aging parents, and deal with the physical and cognitive health problems experienced by aging parents.

Interestingly, in contrast to Western culture, "many traditional API cultures expect death to occur at home and have mourning traditions that involve keeping the body at home for a number of days before burial" (McLaughlin & Braun, 1999, p. 331; Nichols & Braun, 1996). Thus imminent death may not spur API families to remove the dying member to a nursing or hospital facility.

## Disclosure of Terminal Illness

Although physicians generally tell family members about a terminal illness, informing the patient about ensuing death is taboo in many API cultures

(Yeo & Hikoyeda, 2000). It may be "that the family does not want the patient to become disheartened and give up on living, that the family feels it is disrespectful to speak of such things to an elder, or that talking about death is 'polluting' or will cause bad luck" (McLaughlin & Braun, 1999, p. 330). People in Japan, for example, believe that "a patient should not be informed of a terminal illness because he or she would lose the strength and hope needed to cope with the illness" (Yeo & Hikoyeda, 2000, p. 114).

**EP 8e**

Health-care personnel thus face an ethical dilemma. Policy and professional ethics may require that a patient be informed of a terminal diagnosis so that practitioner and patient can discuss and weigh treatment options. However, culturally, the patient may not want to know and may well choose ignorance if given that option.

### End-of-Life Decisions

A related issue to disclosure of terminal illness is whether to continue life support for individuals who cannot make decisions and have no hope of recovery (e.g., those who are brain-dead) (Yeo & Hikoyeda, 2000). We have established that traditional API cultures tend to rebuff advance directives. Yeo and Hikoyeda (2000) explain:

> Cultural values might emphasize longevity over quality of life, especially for one's parent. Some families do not want to make decisions that would preclude the possibility of a miracle from either God or the American medical system, of which they might have unrealistically high expectations. (p. 104)

Highlight 12.3 proposes five recommendations to address the five value conflicts discussed here—informed consent, advance directives, placement decisions, disclosure of terminal illness, and end-of-life decisions.

## The Health Crisis of HIV and AIDS in the United States  `LO 6`

In 2014, 1.2 million people died from AIDS around the globe, and there were 2 million new HIV infections (or 5,600 each day) (KFF, 2015). A total of 36.9 million people in the world are living with HIV today (KFF, 2015).

In the United States, it is estimated that 1.1 million people are HIV infected (KFF, 2014b). There are approximately 50,000 new cases each year (CDC, 2014).

Race and gender are variables involved in HIV transmission in the United States. Consider the following facts (KFF, 2014b):

- African Americans and "Latinos account for a disproportionate share of new HIV infections, relative to their size in the U.S. population."
- African Americans have a new infection rate for HIV that is higher than any other racial group. This rate is eight times that of Whites. Latinos have three times the infection rate of Whites.
- 506,000 African Americans (or 2% of their entire population) are living with HIV, the highest rate for all racial groups.
- Almost half (48%) of all the people who die from HIV/AIDS are African Americans.
- African Americans have a lower survival rate from HIV/AIDS than most other racial groups. Additionally, their deaths tend to occur at younger ages than in other racial groups.

"More than 275,000 women are living with HIV in the [United States] today" (KFF, 2014b). In 2010, women accounted for 20% (9,500) of new transmissions in the United States; this reflected the first annual decrease after a decade of increasing rates (KFF, 2014b). In 2010, African American women accounted for 64% or almost two-thirds of new HIV infections among women (KFF, 2014b). Latinas accounted for 15% of new HIV infections (KFF, 2014b).

Because of its significance on a national and global level, this section will devote considerable attention to AIDS and health care.

### What Are HIV and AIDS?

**Acquired immune deficiency syndrome (AIDS)**, caused by the human immunodeficiency virus (HIV), is a disease that destroys the body's immune system. Infected people thus gradually become increasingly vulnerable to **opportunistic diseases**—conditions and infections that themselves are usually not life threatening but that take advantage of a weakened immune system and use this opportunity to invade it.

HIV is a type of virus called a *retrovirus*. A *virus* is a submicroscopic, infectious parcel of genetic

## HIGHLIGHT 12.3

## RECOMMENDATIONS FOR A MORE CULTURALLY COMPETENT HEALTH-CARE SYSTEM

Large service provision systems are never perfect. There are always quirks and problems because such broadly ranging people are involved. Bureaucracies have established rules to assist in their functioning. A large health-care system cannot adapt itself perfectly to all its beneficiaries' needs. However, an ongoing concern for social workers is the need to assess large systems' functioning, recommend improvements, and work to achieve positive changes. This is especially true in view of the U.S. population's cultural diversity.

EP 5c, 7d, 8c, 8d

How can the U.S. health-care system become more sensitive to API (and other) cultures? And how can social workers address this issue? Five recommendations are proposed here:

1. Provide training for health-care personnel that sensitizes them to API cultural values and issues. Staff should be taught to carefully observe periods of silence, nonverbal behavior, and family or group interaction for clues to understanding such behavior. They should pay careful attention to "the language used to discuss the patient's disease, ... whether decisions are made by the patient or by the larger family unit, ... the relevance of religious beliefs, ... [and] the patient's and family's degree of fatalism versus an active desire for control of events" (Braun & Browne, 2000, p. 186).

2. Encourage personnel in the health-care system to "begin addressing end-of-life planning issues with whole families (not just individual patients) earlier in the life course (rather than waiting until the end) and in nonhospital venues"

(McLaughlin & Braun, 1999, p. 333). Agency policy should encourage staff to tune in to cultural values regarding collectivist versus individual perspectives on decision making and to work with families accordingly.

3. Urge the health-care system to begin investigating the adoption of family-centered rather than individual-centered decision making models for virtually all health-related decisions (Fong, 2008; McLaughlin & Braun, 1999; Mokuau, 1995; Paniagua, 2014). Health-care personnel should seek to understand individuals' and families' values and to work within those value systems to the greatest extent possible. The health-care system should respect both the individual's and the family's right to self-determination.

4. Establish "parallel services" whereby attention and treatment are tailored to meet the cultural needs and expectations of API people. For example, some "successful programs in San Francisco and Los Angeles" use "language, signs, food and drinks, and [service] providers" representing "the culture being served" (Braun & Browne, 2000, p. 186). The downside of this approach, of course, is that it's expensive to duplicate services. In the event that it's financially unfeasible to develop parallel services, programs could at least employ bilingual staff to assist in the assessment and treatment process (Braun & Browne, 2000).

5. Encourage social workers to advocate for policy and practice changes in the health-care system. The system should respect and appreciate cultural diversity and self-determination, not pretend they don't exist.

material, resembling in some ways a tiny living organism and in other ways inert (lifeless) material, that can grow and multiply only within the living cells of bacteria, plants, and animals. There is no cure for a virus. Note that viruses also cause the common cold and influenza; available medications may alleviate symptoms but will not cure the virus.

A **retrovirus** is a special kind of virus that invades normal cells and causes them to reproduce more of the virus rather than reproduce themselves like other normal cells. HIV attacks normal white blood cells

(called *T-cells*) that fight off diseases invading the body (Yarber & Sayad, 2013). The specific type of T-cell that's vulnerable has *CD4 molecules* on its surface that help coordinate the body's resistance "to certain microorganisms such as viruses" (About.com, 2011). Hereafter, we will refer to these cells as *CD4 T-cells.*

After invading the CD4 T-cell, HIV immediately begins destroying this host cell and injecting its own genetic material into the cell. The transformed CD4 T-cell then begins producing more HIV instead of reproducing its former self. As the invaded CD4 T-cells produce more of the virus and fewer disease attacking white blood cells, the body's immune system deteriorates. As a result, the body is left defenseless and becomes easy prey to other diseases that eventually may cause death. HIV is a frightening agent that has continued to mutate into various strains, making it difficult to find a cure.

People may have contracted HIV and be HIV-positive but not yet be diagnosed with AIDS. HIV gradually destroys the immune system, so it may take a while to develop the serious conditions characterizing AIDS. According to the CDC, full-blown AIDS diagnosis applies when a person has a positive HIV blood test and has a CD4 T-cell count of less than 200 (normal people have between 500 and 1600) or has any of a number of "life-threatening opportunistic infections" (CDC, 2014; Hyde & DeLamater, 2014, pp. 463–464). Among the numerous illnesses that may develop as the immune system plummets are ***Pneumocystis carinii* pneumonia** (a rare form of pneumonia from which people with normal immune systems are protected); **Kaposi's sarcoma** (a rare skin cancer); Cytomegalovirus ("an infection that usually affects the eyes"); ***Candida*** ("a fungal infection that can cause thrush [a white film in your mouth] or infections in your throat or vagina"; "serious weight loss"; brain tumors" [AIDS InfoNet.org, 2014]); and an array of other diseases and health problems including "tuberculosis"[3] or "invasive cervical cancer" (Hyde & DeLamater, 2014, p. 462).

HIV affects each individual differently. Some people go for years before experiencing negative effects; others exhibit symptoms much earlier. Initial indications include a dry cough, abdominal discomfort, headaches, oral thrush, loss of appetite, fever, night sweats, weight loss, diarrhea, skin rashes, fatigue, swollen lymph nodes, and lack of resistance to infection. Unfortunately, other illnesses have similar symptoms, so it's easy for people to overlook the possibility that they are HIV-positive. As AIDS progresses, the immune system becomes less capable of fighting off opportunistic diseases mentioned earlier. AIDS is one of the most deadly global health problems (KFF, 2014a,

2015). Highlight 12.4 reviews methods of HIV transmission.

### Measurement of the CD4 T-Cell Count

Several tests have been developed to determine if a person has been exposed to the AIDS virus. The CDC (2014) describes several tests that are currently available:

> The most common HIV test is the **antibody screening test (immunoassay)**, which tests for the antibodies that your body makes again HIV. The immunoassay may be conducted in a lab or as a rapid test at the testing site. It may be performed on blood or oral fluid.... Because the level of antibody in oral fluid is lower than it is in blood, blood tests tend to find infection sooner after exposure than do oral fluid tests. In addition, most blood-based lab tests find infection sooner after exposure than rapid HIV tests.

Several other tests can also be used (CDC, 2014). Some detect "both antibodies and antigen (part of the virus itself)." These tests may be used as early as three weeks after exposure to HIV. "The *rapid test* is an immunoassay used for screening" that generates results "in 30 minutes or less." Because of the potential of getting a false-negative result, a follow-up test should always be administered. In the event that any of these tests produce positive results, a follow-up diagnostic test should be performed to verify the accuracy of the positive diagnosis.

"**RNA tests** detect the virus directly (instead of the antibodies to HIV) and thus can detect HIV at about 10 days after infection—as soon as it appears in the bloodstream, before antibodies develop." However, RNA tests are more expensive than antibody tests, so are usually used only to verify a positive antibody test, "or as part of a clinical workup."

Two home tests are also available (CDC, 2014). The Home Access HIV-1 Test System involves sending a blood sample to a lab for assessment. The OraQuick In-Home HIV Test examines oral fluid and is tested at home. However, it is more likely to produce false-negative results.

### Treatment for AIDS

No cure exists for HIV or AIDS. However, treatment can significantly delay the progress of the disease. A major breakthrough was the discovery of antiviral drugs (e.g., azidothymidine or AZT) that

---

[3]Tuberculosis is a disease usually affecting the lungs that is characterized by the development of tubercules ("small, firm, rounded nodule[s] or swelling[s]") (Nichols, 1999, p. 1402).

## HIGHLIGHT 12.4     HOW IS HIV TRANSMITTED?

Transmission of HIV has been clearly documented through the exchange of bodily fluids from one person to another. "Semen, blood, and vaginal secretions are the fluids most often implicated in transmission of HIV" (Kelly, 2008, p. 499).

Kelly (2008) describes various means of transmitting HIV:

Several routes of HIV infection have been clearly documented:

1. Anal or vaginal intercourse.
2. Oral-genital activity.
3. Contact with semen or vaginal fluids from an infected person.
4. Organs transplanted from infected persons.
5. Contact with infected blood, through use of contaminated needles and syringes shared by drug users or used for tattooing, ear piercing, or injection of steroids.
6. Transfer from mother to child [during pregnancy or birth]....

Sharing anal intercourse is especially risky behavior, because the virus from the semen enters the bloodstream through the many small tears in the colon. [The colon is not lined with a mucus membrane like the vagina, so it is much more likely to experience tears]....

The risks associated with oral-genital sex have been difficult to quantify, partly because this behavior usually is practiced in conjunction with other sexual activities that may be highly risky. However, there have been cases in which HIV was transmitted from a man's semen during fellatio (oral sex performed on a male). [For example, any cuts or sores in the mouth might allow for tainted semen to enter the bloodstream.]

Although ordinary kissing appears to pose only a minor threat, the CDC [Centers for Disease Control] has reported a case of HIV transmission through kissing. Both parties had gum disease, confirming the earlier suspicion that viruses carried in saliva could enter the body through tiny breaks or sores within the mouth or enter the lymphatic cells in the tonsils. Experts therefore continue to caution against prolonged, wet deep kissing (French kissing)....

Casual contacts with infected persons—even in crowded households, social settings, schools, or the workplace—are not dangerous. There are no documented cases of HIV being transmitted through food, water, toilets, swimming pools or hot tubs, shared drinking or eating utensils, telephones, or used clothing. Several research studies have demonstrated that the virus is not transmitted by insects. (pp. 499–500)

One group with a high likelihood of HIV transmission includes IV drug users who share needles, as this may involve direct injection of minute quantities of HIV infected blood. People, heterosexual and gay, who engage in unprotected anal intercourse increase risk of transmission. Of course, many types of sexual interaction that includes unprotected transmission of bodily fluids enhance the risk of contracting HIV.

Yarber and Sayad (2013) explain transmission during pregnancy and birth:

About one quarter to one third of all untreated pregnancy women infected with HIV will pass the infection to their babies. HIV can also be transmitted to babies through the breast milk of mothers infected with the virus. If an HIV-infected woman is treated with certain drugs during pregnancy, she can greatly reduce the chances that her baby will get infected with HIV. If she is treated and her baby is delivered by cesarean section, the chances of the baby being infected can be reduced to a rate of 1%. HIV infection of newborns has been almost eradicated in the United States because of voluntary prenatal HIV testing and medical treatment, yet 100 to 200 infants are still infected with HIV annually. Many of these infections involve women who were not tested early enough in pregnancy or who did not receive prevention services. (p. 533)

"can stop the virus from multiplying"; however, such drugs "cannot repair the person's damaged immune system" (Hyde & DeLamater, 2014, p. 463). Another step forward was the discovery of protease inhibitors that "attack the viral enzyme protease, which is necessary for HIV to make copies of itself and multiply" (Hyde & DeLamater, 2014, p. 463).

Today most treatment involves **highly active antiretroviral therapy (HAART)**. Carroll (2013b) explains:

> *HAART is the combination of three or more HIV drugs, often referred to as "drug cocktails" [or "cocktail drugs"]. This development, in conjunction with the development of HIV RNA testing (which allows health-care providers to monitor the amount of virus in the bloodstream), has allowed for better control of HIV and has slowed the disease progression. (p. 425)*

There are some downsides to HAART. People taking the drugs should be tested every 3 to 6 months to ascertain that the drugs remain effective (Carroll, 2013b). The drugs simply stop being effective for some people. Unfortunately, HIV can also mutate and become resistant to drugs (Hyde & DeLamater, 2014). Some long-term HAART users experience negative side effects "such as diabetes-like problems, brittle bones, and heart disease, which means the patient must stop the treatment or switch to another" (Hyde & DeLamater, 2014, p. 463). Finally, HAART treatment can be quite expensive (Greenberg, Bruess, & Oswalt, 2014).

HAART has cut the death rate from conditions resulting from HIV/AIDS by 75% since the 1990s; however, 10,000 people in the United States still die from HIV/AIDS-related causes annually (Rathus, Nevid, & Fichner-Rathus, 2014).

Various types of clinical research are currently being conducted to combat HIV, although clinical trials take years to complete; for example, some researchers are trying to develop a vaccine to prevent transmission of HIV (Hyde & DeLamater, 2014).

### Empowerment for People Living with AIDS

Empowerment is a key concept for social workers helping persons with AIDS. Empowerment involves feeling good about ourselves and feeling that we have some control and direction over our lives. Empowerment is clearly related to hope.

Because of the prevalence of AIDS in the United States, social workers will likely work directly or indirectly with persons having the disease. The essence of social work practice with people who are HIV-positive involves providing support, focusing on strengths, and seeking empowerment. People need to develop positive feelings  **EP 1c, 7c**

about themselves and maximize the control they have over their lives. Social workers can help HIV-positive people seriously consider alternatives and make their best choices. It's important to remain as active in normal life activities as possible.

With the advent of cocktail drugs and significantly longer life expectancies for people with AIDS, the concept of empowerment becomes especially important. Persons with AIDS should never be referred to as *victims*. Rather, they should be referred to as *people living with AIDS*, with an emphasis on *living*. The word *victim* implies helplessness, powerlessness, and lack of control. People living with AIDS need to be viewed as individuals capable of empowerment, not as helpless victims. Hope should be maintained because many people living with AIDS have years of fruitful living ahead of them. Much research and effort are being directed at combating the disease. Highlight 12.5 explores the importance of critically evaluating both the positive and negative sides of life experiences.

### *Social Work Roles and Empowerment for People Living with AIDS*

Social workers assume many roles when working with people living with AIDS. First, a social worker can provide counseling, in which a client's issues are addressed, feelings and emotions are expressed and discussed, and plans are made. A social worker may help a client work out issues and objectively evaluate life situations. The  **EP 1, 3a, 8d** worker may also assist the client in focusing on positives, even when the client is coping with the negative aspects of HIV/AIDS.

Social workers may help HIV-positive people deal with feelings of fear, guilt, anger, depression, hopelessness, abandonment, and any other emotions they may experience. Regardless of how clients feel, it is crucial to bring these feelings out in the open so clients can deal with them. Emotional repression and isolation should be avoided. If health significantly deteriorates, social workers may also help people with AIDS cope with disfigurement and loss of function. Highlight 12.6 discusses the importance of dealing with all life issues, including death.

As an educator, a social worker can provide information about the progression of the disease, drug treatments, stress management, positive lifestyle choices, and safe sex practices. Social workers

## HIGHLIGHT 12.5 — EVALUATING THE CONSEQUENCES OF LIFE EXPERIENCES

Maintaining a meaningful quality of life involves focusing on the positive instead of the negative aspects of life. Each moment of each day, we can choose how to look at the exact same situation in either a positive or a negative light. For example, many of us dream of winning the lottery. When one man won $21 million, he was thrilled. He had spent many happy hours over the years with his pals at a local bar, watching the televised announcements of lottery winners and hoping that he would be one of them. Finally, it happened. Ecstatic, he said he would "take care of" all of his bar buddies. Although envious, they were also happy that he had won and were enthusiastically looking forward to their "cut."

EP 7c

However, the story does not have the happiest of endings. It seems the man forgot to give his friends the share they felt they had coming. Hard feelings emerged as former friends bandied about threats of lawsuits for unfair treatment. The winning man found that he no longer had friends at the bar. For that matter, he no longer had friends in his neighborhood, so he decided to move to a "better" neighborhood where he knew no one. He had lost most of his friends.

Additionally, he had to get an unlisted telephone number because he and his wife couldn't stand the barrage of solicitations. The man was approached by almost everyone he knew, including relatives. They either not so subtly hinted that they could use a few extra bucks or asked him point-blank for loans they felt they would never have to repay. Taxes eradicated a third of his winnings almost immediately. Still wealthy, he bought a red Porsche. But the man's life had

changed. He no longer experienced the same sense of belongingness, peace, and happiness that he had in his poorer days.

There are numerous other examples of positive and negative sides to any event. The birth of a long awaited baby may mark a couple's most joyous occasion. However, the hospital and other medical costs not covered by insurance may place a heavy financial burden on them. Finding reasonable yet high-quality day care so that the mother can return to work may be difficult. A colicky baby may keep them both up much of the night, making the thought of getting up the next day a nightmare.

The moral of this story is the importance of focusing on the positive aspects of any particular situation. People with AIDS need to work hard at identifying, concentrating on, and enjoying the positive elements in their daily lives.

One person living with AIDS emphasizes that positives can come from any negative experience. Working through difficulties makes people stronger and wiser. He cites some of the positives that he has experienced since contracting AIDS, which include

> learning to accept [my] limitations; learning to cope by getting in touch with [my] strengths; experiencing a clarity of purpose; learning to live one day at a time; learning to focus on the good in [my] life here and now; and the incredibly moving experience of having complete support from [my] family, friends, lover, people [I] hardly know, and sometimes even complete strangers.

*(Haney, 1988, p. 252)*

## HIGHLIGHT 12.6 — EMPOWERMENT BY DEALING WITH LIFE AND DEATH

It is important for people with AIDS to deal not only with life but also with death. Social workers can help people with AIDS address any spiritual issues that may concern them. Helping people with AIDS discuss plans for what will happen after their death can be useful. In a way, this may help them gain greater control. They may need to write a will or make funeral arrangements.

EP 8e

They may want to finish unsettled business or resolve disputes with significant others. A useful concept in working with people who are facing their own death is the idea of making them "the star of their own death." In other words, instead of avoiding issues concerning death because this can make people feel uncomfortable, emphasize that people approaching death have the right to make decisions and settle their affairs.

may also provide *crisis intervention*, a brief and time-limited therapeutic intervention through which a social worker helps a client learn to cope with or adjust to extreme external pressures. Examples of crises experienced by people with AIDS include sudden bouts of illness, job loss due to illness, and escalating expenses for medical treatments.

Empowerment can come from interpersonal reconnections. Having AIDS often makes people feel isolated from family, friends, and others, and disconnected from their old lives. Social workers can help people with AIDS reconnect with other people. Support systems are essential and can include family members, friends, intimate others, and coworkers. Lines of communication need to be maintained. Significant others must also express and face their feelings in order to deal with them and support people living with AIDS. Otherwise they might shun negative feelings by avoiding and withdrawing from people with AIDS.

Social workers may also provide *family counseling,* in which they help the person with AIDS discuss issues with other family members. Just as clients themselves must learn to cope, so must significant others and family members. Their feelings and fears must also be elicited so that they can be addressed.

Social workers, as brokers, may help link clients to needed resources and services. People with AIDS may need services concerning health, income maintenance, housing, mental health care, and legal assistance.

Social workers may refer clients with AIDS to support groups, in which they can talk with others who also have AIDS and are experiencing similar problems and issues. HIV-positive people need not feel isolated and alone. They can see that there are other people who understand their issues and feelings. Additionally, such groups provide excellent channels for gaining information on how others have worked out similar problems. Social workers can also facilitate support or educational groups by serving as leader and keeping the group on track.

In addition, social workers can provide case management services to people living with AIDS. Earlier chapters established that case management involves assessing a client's needs, developing plans to meet these needs, linking the client with the appropriate services, monitoring service delivery, and advocating for the client when necessary (Taylor-Brown, 1995).

Note that part of case management involves *advocacy*—the act of stepping forward and speaking out on the behalf of clients to promote fair and equitable treatment or gain needed resources. Social workers may advocate for clients with AIDS whether those workers are case managers or not.

Advocacy may be necessary for several reasons. Advocacy can target unfair treatment when HIV-positive people are discriminated against, denied services, fired from jobs, or evicted from housing. Advocacy can also be used to seek necessary resources such as health care or financial assistance when it's not readily available.

# Global Perspectives: HIV and AIDS  `LO 7`

Consider these international scenarios. In China, AIDS has become an "epidemic that races across the country" following a "route [from Burma] of drug smugglers, of truck drivers, of migrant workers and the prostitutes that wait for them." Consider this picture:

**EP 3**

*Chen Ah-Yan usually gets up after midnight. She lounges on an L-shaped couch with three other girls in a tiny room open to the sticky air of the street, watching music videos half-heartedly and calling out to passers-by. Occasionally … [she] catches the attention of a man in one of the fancy cars with blackened windows cruising the streets—"drug smuggler," she comments casually—and brings him upstairs to the makeshift room not much larger than a twin mattress. The slim 18-year-old wearing dark-red lipstick … came to this town [from the country] a few months ago [seeking excitement]…. "Sure, we know about AIDS," Chen giggles. "But we're just here to have fun."*

*(Fang, 2001, pp. 22–23)*

The following are prevalence rates for all adults in other regions (KFF, 2015): the Caribbean, 1.1% of all adults; Eastern Europe and Central Asia, 0.9%; Latin America, 0.4%; Western and Central Europe, and North American, 0.3%; and Asia and the Pacific, 0.2%.

In sub-Saharan Africa, 4.8% of all adults are HIV-positive (KFF, 2015). We've already indicated that worldwide there are 36.9 million people who were HIV positive in 2014, 1.2 million deaths from AIDS-related conditions, and an estimated 2 million new infections annually (KFF, 2015). "Unscrupulous entrepreneurs" are "hustling for corpses" as thousands die from AIDS and funeral parlors are swamped with bodies; picture this scene:

> *So fast are AIDS victims piling up that ... morgues and cemeteries are out of space. A lively black market has grown up in stolen burial equipment. Crooked morgue workers sell corpses to favored undertakers, or to the highest bidder, sometimes even before bereaved families arrive to claim a body—leaving the relatives no choice but to pay the undertaker who collected the remains.*

> *(Masland, 2001, p. 45)*

## HIV and AIDS in Sub-Saharan Africa: An International Crisis

Countries with the highest rates of HIV infection are in sub-Saharan Africa, which represents 68% of all cases around the world (Macionis, 2013). We've established that 25 million people are HIV-positive there. Women are hardest hit, as they account for 59% of adults living with HIV/AIDS in the region (AVERT, 2014). Young people age 15 to 24, especially young women, are at exceptional risk of contracting the virus (KFF, 2015). "The social and economic consequences of the AIDS epidemic are widely felt, not only in the health sector but also in education, industry, agriculture, transport, human resources and the economy in general. The AIDS epidemic in sub-Saharan Africa continues to devastate communities, rolling back decades of development progress" (AVERT, 2011).

Although HIV/AIDS is a major problem throughout the region, percentages of infection vary from one country to another. Consider the following facts:

> *Almost all of the region's nations have generalized HIV epidemics—that is, their national HIV prevalence rate is greater than 1%. In [nine] countries, 10% or more of adults are estimated to be HIV-positive. South Africa has the highest number of people living with HIV in the world (6.8 million). Swaziland has the highest prevalence rate in the world*

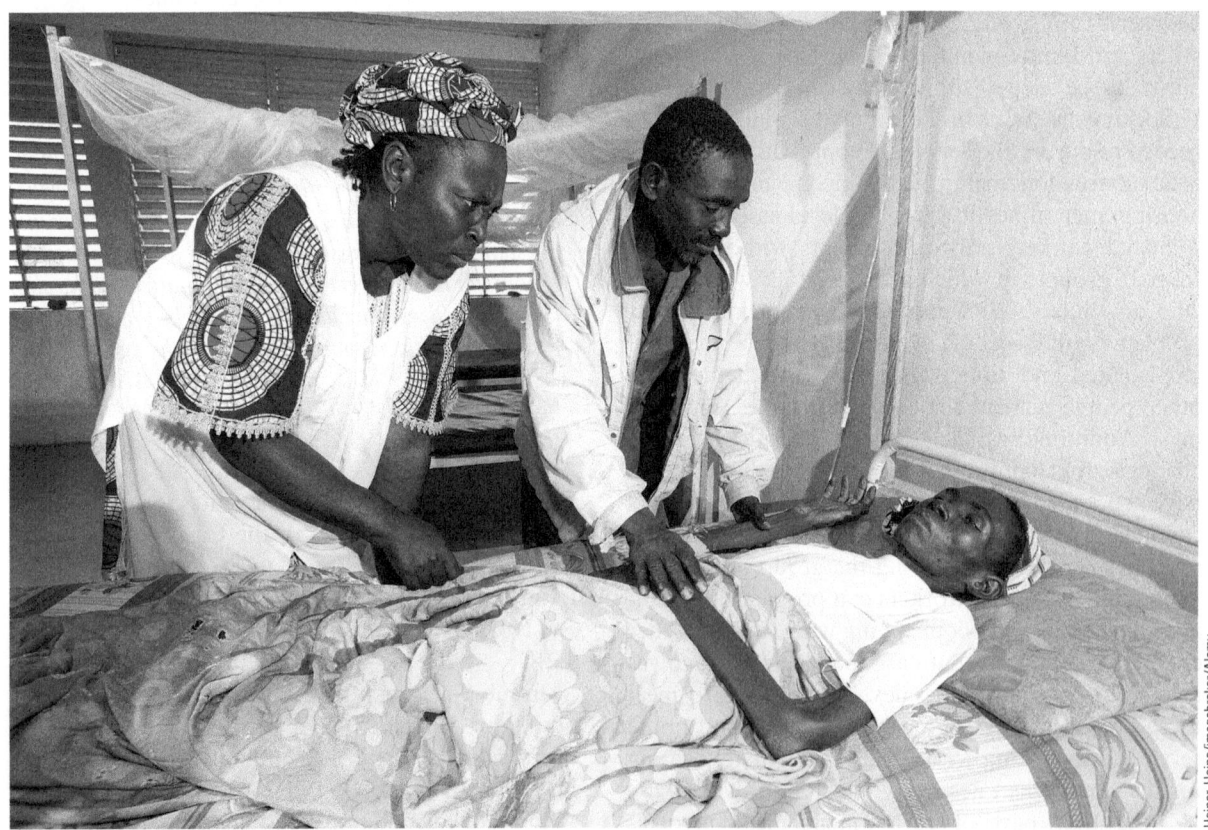

*A person with HIV/AIDS rests in a hospital bed in Garoua, Cameroon, Africa.*

Heiner Heine/imagebroker/Alamy

| HIGHLIGHT **12.7** | **WHAT WOULD YOUR LIFE BE LIKE IF YOU HAD AIDS AND LIVED IN SUB-SAHARAN AFRICA?** |
|---|---|

What might your life would be like if you lived in sub-Saharan Africa. Consider the following scenarios (McGeary, 2001):

*Scenario A:* Fundisi Khumao, age 22, has AIDS and tuberculosis (TB). He knows he has TB but does not acknowledge that he has AIDS. AIDS is something not to be talked about. Breathing is tremendously **EP 6b** difficult for him and often characterized by violent coughing spasms. He lives in abject poverty. He is cold and alone. Vomiting, constipation, and extreme weakness are common occurrences. Before he got sick, he worked as a hairdresser in a large city. There he had several girlfriends, from one of whom he likely caught HIV. When he couldn't work anymore, he retreated to his rural village. No medicine is available for AIDS, and he has no money anyway. Fundisi won't go to a hospital because he feels people go there only to die.

*Scenario B:* Laetitia Hambahlane, age 51, has AIDS and admits it. She worked as a domestic servant for wealthy people in a large city before she became too sick. It was very difficult for her to accept the fact that she had AIDS. She told her four children, who were "ashamed and frightened" (p. 38). The worst part for her is the total rejection by her mother. Having AIDS is shameful, and having almost anything else would be better. Laetitia's children are sick of hearing about her problems and will no longer help her (e.g., by bringing her food when she's too weak to get it herself). "One day local youths barged into her room, cursed her as a witch and a whore, and beat her. When she told the police, the youths returned, threatening to burn down the house" (p. 40).

*Scenario C:* Louis Chikoka, age 39, is a married truck driver with three children. Because work close to home is rarely available, it is common in Africa to have to work elsewhere and spend the majority of time away from home. When Louis is away from home for long periods, he has sex with other women. He knows this places him at great risk of contracting HIV, but he says he has needs and sees no other way to meet them. His life situation reflects a typical picture. The region is economically dependent on migrant laborers who often find themselves far from home, so having multiple sexual partners is common practice. Unfortunately, this frequently results in bringing the disease home to wives and girlfriends.

*Scenario D:* A tiny 3-year-old child whom we will arbitrarily call Adwowa lies dying of AIDS in the hospital. "Now her skin wrinkles around her body like an oversize suit, and her twig size bones can barely hold her vertical as nurses search for a vein to take blood. In the frail arms hooked up to transfusion tubes, her veins have collapsed.... She mews like a wounded animal" while the nurses struggle to raise a vein to obtain a minuscule sample of her blood (p. 44). Her mother, age 25, does not know the little girl has AIDS. She has heard of AIDS but knows little else about it. For example, she does not know that it can be contracted through sexual intercourse or passed on to an infant at birth. She doesn't even know if she or her husband has it. Adwowa's father works far away in a large city and can return home only a couple of times each year. He probably often seeks sexual solace from strangers.

*(27.7%). Recent data offer promising signs, with national HIV prevalence and/or incidence stabilizing or even declining in many countries in the region.*

*(KFF, 2015)*

The better news is that the epidemic appears to have peaked in the late 1990s, although it still remains a huge problem (AVERT, 2011; KFF, 2015).

Highlight 12.7 provides several scenarios describing what it might be like to have AIDS and live in sub-Saharan Africa.

HIV infection rates present a devastating problem. (This is true especially among women, who are significantly more likely to catch HIV through sexual intercourse [Macionis, 2013; Masland, 2000; UNAIDS, 2008].) Because of the stigma associated with AIDS, people cling to denial, often resulting in lack of treatment and death. The migrant worker lifestyle contributes to the commonplace acceptance of casual sex. Women are taught early on that men "rule the roost" and they should be obeyed sexually and in many other ways (Macionis, 2010). It's not uncommon for women who deny their partners sex or request that they use condoms to suffer severe beatings or even desertion. Men typically loathe condoms (Macionis, 2010). The following myths about condoms might prevail.

- Condoms inhibit erections and detract from pleasurable sensations.
- One is not a real man if he has to use a condom.

- When condoms fill up with semen, they spread HIV.
- Condoms manufactured by foreigners come to Africa already infected with HIV.

Focus on Critical Thinking 12.3 addresses issues and raises questions about what could be done to contend with the HIV problem in sub-Saharan Africa.

---

# FOCUS ON CRITICAL THINKING 12.3 — WHAT SHOULD BE DONE ABOUT HIV/AIDS IN SUB-SAHARAN AFRICA?

The following are suggested approaches to address the problem of HIV/AIDS in sub-Saharan Africa:

1. Launch serious and extensive preventive programs to educate people about HIV/AIDS and its transmission. The stigma associated with HIV/AIDS should be eliminated (AVERT, 2011; Cowley, 2000, p. 38).

   **EP 3b, 5c, 8a**

2. Publicize the potential consequences of unprotected casual sex with programs stressing safer sex (Cowley, 2000, p. 38). Some sub-Saharan African countries have carried out major prevention campaigns resulting in lower infection rates (AVERT, 2011). For instance, in Senegal political leaders initiated an intense campaign and significantly decreased the prevalence of HIV (AVERT, 2011). Senegal developed educational programming in addition to having "cut taxes on condoms and got[ten] religious leaders to participate in AIDS education" (Cowley, 2000; Lemonick, 2000, p. 39). Similarly, Uganda's prevention initiative decreased the prevalence of HIV among pregnant women (AVERT, 2011). Early on, the nation took steps to promote sex education;

   > [p]rimary schools and health centers tout the ABCs (abstinence, be faithful, and use condoms). The taboos [about discussing HIV] have eroded so much that personal ads in [one] ... steamy *Red Pepper* tabloid list HIV status along with age, height, and interests. Correspondingly, infection rates among the most vulnerable age groups dropped" considerably.

   *(Whitelaw, 2003, p. 19)*

South Africa, on the other hand, did little in terms of prevention, which led to "an unprecedented number of people living with HIV" (AVERT, 2011).

3. Empower women to have greater control over their sex lives. One option is the development of low-cost contraception over which they have more influence (Cowley, 2000).

4. Very importantly, have developed countries provide significant financial contributions and aid in the form of subsidized drug costs so that African nations can better afford to provide drug treatment. Everyone who needs antiretroviral drugs should have them; today only about 40% of Africans requiring treatment are receiving it (AVERT, 2011). "Millions are not even receiving treatment for opportunistic infections [e.g., bacterial diseases such as tuberculosis, fungal diseases, viral diseases, and HIV-associated cancers], which affect individuals whose immune systems have been weakened by HIV infection" (AVERT, 2011).

5. Develop a vaccine to prevent AIDS (Cowley, 2000).

## Critical Thinking Questions

- Which of the above suggestions do you think is (are) the most feasible to address the problem of HIV/AIDS in sub-Saharan Africa?
- Who might fund such a plan? How might a person go about getting such funding?
- What could you do as an individual do to address a problem such as this?

# Chapter Summary

The following summarizes this chapter's content as it relates to the learning objectives presented at the beginning of the chapter. Chapter content will help prepare students to:

**LO1 Identify major types of health problems.**

Health problems include those related to unhealthy lifestyles, physical injuries, environmental factors, poverty, and contagious diseases.

**LO2 Describe social work roles (in health-care provision).**

Social workers have been involved in preventive, primary, tertiary, restorative, and continuing care in health-care practice. Settings include hospitals, medical clinics, and diagnostic and treatment centers; public health departments and other health-care contexts; Veteran's Affairs hospitals; and managed care settings.

**LO3 Review the current status of health care in the United States.**

The Patient Protection and Affordable Care Act of 2010 (ACA) is summarized and discussed. Its intent is to provide health care to most Americans. Some of its pros and cons are examined.

Managed care is "the country's major approach to improving access, controlling cost, and ensuring quality of health care" (Dhooper, 2012, p. 281). It includes a broad range of health plans that "manage" and make decisions about patients' care. Problems in managed care include questions regarding the efficiency and effectiveness of capitation. Ethical dilemmas include the gate-keeping role of managed care organizations, potential issues with informed consent, and possible violations of confidentiality when patients seek treatment.

Problems plaguing health-care provision historically in the United States include variations in service provision involving race, gender, and socioeconomic status. People living in poverty, people with lower socioeconomic status, and people of color are at special risk of having poorer and unequal access to adequate health care. Escalating costs present another problem in health-care provision. The U.S. health-care system costs significantly more per capita than

the health-care system in any other industrialized nation.

**LO4 Engage in critical thinking (about health-care coverage, overgeneralizations regarding various racial and ethnic groups, and ways to address the HIV/AIDS problem in sub-Saharan Africa).**

Critical thinking questions were posed regarding the provision of national health insurance and the adoption of a liberal or conservative perspective. Other questions were raised concerning personal cultural values and avoiding overgeneralization about other cultures. Finally, questions were posed about how to address the HIV/AIDS problem in sub-Saharan Africa.

**LO5 Explore value discrepancies between cultural values (those of Asian and Pacific Islander [API] and health-care provision (in the United States).**

Five concepts directly related to API cultures that affect health-care provision include filial piety, collective versus individual decision making, emphasis on harmony versus conflict, nonverbal communication, and a sense of shame at asking for help. Potential conflicts between API cultures and the U.S. health-care system include informed consent, advance directives, decisions about nursing home placement, disclosure of terminal illness, and end-of-life decisions.

Suggestions include training health-care personnel to sensitize them to API cultural values, addressing end-of-life decisions with whole families instead of just individuals, assuming a family-centered decision-making model, establishing parallel services to traditional services that better meet the needs of API culture, and encouraging social workers to advocate for improved policies and practice strategies.

**LO6 Describe HIV and AIDS (including its essence, its treatment, empowerment for people living with AIDS, and social work roles).**

AIDS is caused by a retrovirus that attacks the immune system. People gradually become less resistant and more vulnerable to opportunistic diseases. Extremely low CD4 T-cell counts result in AIDS.

HIV is transmitted by the exchange of bodily fluids, especially by semen, blood, and vaginal secretions. Race and gender are variables involved in transmission. The most common test for HIV is the antibody screening test (immunoassay). Other tests include antibodies and antigen screening, rapid, follow-up diagnostic, RNA, and home screening tests. HIV/AIDS cannot be cured, but cocktail drugs (a mixture of different drugs) referred to as HAART (highly active antiretroviral therapy) have been used effectively to inhibit progression of the disease in many people.

Social workers can provide support and focus on strengths for people living with HIV/AIDS. They can provide counseling, crisis intervention, linkage with support systems, family counseling, support group referral, and advocacy.

## LO7 Examine AIDS as an international problem (particularly in sub-Saharan Africa).

In 2014, 1.2 million people died from AIDS around the globe, and there were an estimated 2 million new HIV infections. Currently, about 25 million people are HIV-positive in sub-Saharan Africa, the most severely affected global region. HIV infection is especially a problem for African women. Approaches to addressing the problem include providing education about HIV/AIDS, providing safe sex programming, empowering women to gain greater control over their lives, providing funding for treatment, and developing a cure.

## LOOKING AHEAD

Health care and mental health care are related. Each has important issues involving managed care, health-care access, and culturally competent service provision. Chapter 13 explores employment settings in mental health for social workers, as well as social work roles, policy issues, and cultural competence in mental health settings.

## COMPETENCY NOTES

The following identifies where Educational Policy (EP) competencies and their component behaviors are discussed in the chapter.

**EP 1 (Competency 1)—Demonstrate Ethical and Professional Behavior.** *(p. 387):* Professional social work roles in health care are discussed. *(p. 391):*

Social workers should engage in career-long learning about health care, as it involves an ever-changing array of conditions and issues. *(p. 405):* Professional social work roles involved in working with people living with HIV/AIDS are discussed.

**EP 1a Make ethical decisions by applying the standards of the NASW Code of Ethics, relevant laws and regulations, models for ethical decision-making, ethical conduct of research, and additional codes of ethics as appropriate to context.** *(p. 394):* Managed care is discussed and questions are raised concerning the extent to which such care complies with professional ethics.

**EP 1c Demonstrate professional demeanor in behavior; appearance; and oral, written, and electronic communication.** *(p. 397):* Behavior and communication respectful of cultural differences are part of professional demeanor. *(p. 399):* Professional social workers should demonstrate culturally sensitive communication skills when working with people from API cultures and assessing their needs and situations. *(p. 405):* Professional social workers should use the appropriate empowering terminology when referring to people living with HIV/AIDS.

**EP 2 (Competency 2)—Engage Diversity and Difference in Practice.** *(p. 392):* Unequal access to health care is a form of oppression. *(p. 395):* Class and race are dimensions of diversity. Social workers should recognize the extent to which society oppresses groups based on socioeconomic status, class and race with respect to health-care provision. *(p. 397):* Culture, ethnicity, and race are aspects of diversity. Social workers should recognize the extent to which the U.S. health-care system may marginalize or alienate people from API cultures.

**EP 2a Apply and communicate understanding of the importance of diversity and difference in shaping life experiences in practice at the micro, mezzo, and macro levels.** *(p. 397):* Social workers should recognize how cultural values and expectations shape life experiences.

**EP 3 (Competency 3)—Advance Human Rights and Social, Economic, and Environmental Justice.** *(p. 407):* Social workers should be knowledgeable about the global ramifications of HIV/AIDS in order to advance human rights.

**EP 3a Apply their understanding of social, economic, and environmental justice to advocate for human rights at the individual and system levels.** *(p. 391):* Social workers can apply their understanding of social and economic justice to advocate for improved health-care provision in the pursuit of social and economic justice. *(p. 396):* Practitioners can advocate for improved health-care provision in the managed care environment. *(p. 405):* Practitioners should advocate on the behalf of people living with HIV/AIDS to promote fair and equitable treatment.

**EP 3b Engage in practices that advance social, economic, and environmental justice.** *(p. 391):* Social workers should advocate for improved health-care provision in the pursuit of social and economic justice. *(p. 410):* Practices are recommended that would help people living with HIV/AIDS and advance social and economic justice on their behalf.

**EP 5 (Competency 5)—Engage in Policy Practice.**

**EP 5c Apply critical thinking to analyze, formulate, and advocate for policies that advance human rights and social, economic, and environmental justice.** *(p. 391):* Social workers should advocate for improved health-care provision in the pursuit of social and economic justice. *(p. 393):* Critical thinking questions promote thought about health-care costs and policy. *(p. 396):* Practitioners can apply critical thinking skills to analyze policies and advocate for improved health-care provision in the managed care environment. *(p. 402):* Social workers should advocate for policies that make the health-care system more culturally competent. *(p. 410):* Critical thinking questions invite thought about addressing the HIV/AIDS problems in sub-Saharan Africa through changes in policy and practice.

**EP 6 (Competency 6)—Engage with Individuals, Families, Groups, Organizations, and Communities.**

**EP 6b Use empathy, reflection, and interpersonal skills to effectively engage diverse clients and constituencies.** *(p. 388):* Social workers must use empathy and other interpersonal skills when helping clients who are dealing with

health issues. *(p. 409):* Case examples are presented to encourage empathy for people living with HIV/AIDS in sub-Saharan Africa.

**EP 7 (Competency 7)—Assess Individuals, Families, Groups, Organizations, and Communities.**

**EP 7a Collect and organize data, and apply critical thinking to interpret information from clients and constituencies.** *(p. 398):* Critical thinking questions encourage thought about cultural heritage, values, and acculturation, which practitioners must take into account during the assessment process.

**EP 7c Develop mutually agreed-on intervention goals and objectives based on the critical assessment of strengths, needs, and challenges within clients and constituencies.** *(pp. 405, 406):* Practitioners should assess and emphasize the strengths of people living with HIV/AIDS.

**EP 7d Select appropriate intervention strategies based on the assessment, research knowledge, and values and preferences of clients and constituencies.** *(p. 388):* Social workers should select the appropriate intervention strategies when working in health care. *(p. 397):* Practitioners should select culturally sensitive intervention strategies (as described in the following sections) when working with API peoples. *(p. 402):* Appropriate intervention strategies in health care for working with people from API cultures are discussed.

**EP 8 (Competency 8)—Intervene with Individuals, Families, Groups, Organizations, and Communities.**

**EP 8a Critically choose and implement interventions to achieve practice goals and enhance capacities of clients and constituencies.** *(p. 410):* Critical thinking questions invite thought about addressing the HIV/AIDS problems in sub-Saharan Africa through changes in policy and practice.

**EP 8c Use inter-professional collaboration as appropriate to achieve beneficial practice outcomes.** *(p. 396):* Social workers can collaborate with colleagues and clients to improve the managed care environment and encourage Medicaid recipients to provide input. *(p. 402):* Practitioners can collaborate with colleagues and clients to establish policies that make the health-care system more culturally competent.

**EP 8d Negotiate, mediate, and advocate with and on behalf of diverse clients and constituencies.** *(p. 391):* Social workers can advocate for improved health-care provision on their clients' behalf. *(p. 396):* Practitioners can advocate for improved health-care provision in the managed care environment. *(p. 402):* Social workers should advocate for policies that make the health-care system more culturally competent. *(p. 405):* Social workers should advocate on the behalf of people living with HIV/AIDS.

**EP 8e Facilitate effective transitions and endings that advance mutually agreed-on goals.** *(p. 388):* Social workers can help clients address end-of-life issues. *(p. 401):* Practitioners can assist with disclosure of terminal illness and end-of-life decisions for people from API cultures. *(p. 406):* Social workers can help people address and deal with the issue of their death.

# 13 Social Work and Services in Mental Health

© Gunter Nezhoda/Shutterstock.com

## Learning Objectives  This chapter will help prepare students to:

**LO 1** Examine the wide range of mental health settings in which social workers practice. **Mental Health, Mental Disorders, and Social Work Roles** (p. 417)

**LO 2** Identify the scope of psychiatric diagnoses for mental health problems. **Clients with Mental Health Problems** (p. 423)

**LO 3** Engage in critical thinking (about various issues related to mental health). **Focus on Critical Thinking 13.1** (p. 424)

**LO 4** Discuss social work roles in mental health settings. **What Social Workers Do in Mental Health** (p. 437)

**LO 5** Recognize some trends in evidence-based (mental health) practice. **Evidence-Based Practice in Mental Health** (p. 447)

**LO 6** Examine managed care within the mental health context. **Managed Care Policies and Programs in Mental Health** (p. 448)

**LO 7** Address cultural competence in mental health settings (including barriers to accessing services and improving cultural competence). **Cultural Competence in Mental Health Settings** (p. 451)

*Jennifer, age 18, is an extremely tall, thin young woman with olive skin and waist-length black hair. She is receiving psychotherapy for anorexia nervosa[1] and depression. She regularly found herself drinking a few shots of cheap whiskey prior to any social event she attended. Actually, she felt compelled to do so to avoid the inevitable panic attack she would abruptly experience. Each attack was characterized by extreme anxiety, dread, shortness of breath, sweaty palms, racing heart, and fears of going crazy. (Note that panic attacks had never been part of her diagnosis.) She always knew she'd get an attack at a party or a dance if she didn't come "prepared," but she never could predict exactly when it would happen. She was terrified of behaving "like a crazy woman" in front of everybody. She has even started to avoid social situations altogether if she can't figure out a way to drink discreetly first.[2]*

*Larry, a college sophomore, can't seem to get out of bed in the morning. He hasn't been to class in a week and a half. Nothing seems to matter to him anymore. Everything seems dark and murky. He feels his grades are terrible, his parents are disappointed in him, and people don't really like him. No one seems to care whether he lives or dies. Life is futile. What does anything matter? Larry is depressed.*

*Aquinnah, age 38, has murdered her 71-year-old mother. She responded to voices in her head commanding her to take the large kitchen knife and do so. Diagnosed with schizophrenia at age 18, she had a history of hearing voices and of getting into fights. She also compulsively collected hundreds of empty shampoo bottles and the shoelaces from discarded running shoes, which she kept in her mother's basement. Sometimes, when the voices told her to leave her mother's home, where she usually stayed, she would camp out behind dumpsters in parking lots of discount department stores. She was arrested for murder when found roaming around aimlessly in her mother's yard carrying the bloodied knife. At the time, she had her 11-year-old son with her; he was wearing girls' clothing and brilliantly colored makeup.*

*Roger, age 51, served two terms in Afghanistan. Since he left the military, "he has worked erratically in construction, a pattern that has contributed to marital problems. Roger reports having flashbacks of his war experiences, difficulty sleeping, and angry outbursts against others. Occasionally he has gotten into fistfights with men at work, and on a few occasions he has beaten his wife. He has been going to the VA [Veterans Affairs[3]] clinic on and off for 10 years, has been on medication,*

---

[1] *Anorexia nervosa*, mainly afflicting girls and young women, is a condition whereby a person refuses to maintain a normal minimal body weight and has an extreme dread of gaining weight.

[2] This vignette is loosely adapted from one described in Hayward and Collier (1996).

[3] The U.S. Department of Veterans' Affairs, formerly the Veterans' Administration, provides a wide range of services to veterans including health and mental health care, long-term care such as nursing homes, educational benefits, and housing (Becerra & Damron-Rodriquez, 1995).

*but has never been hospitalized. The mental health staff at the VA clinic suspect that he has minimal brain dysfunction, an organic condition, which is not war related, as well as posttraumatic stress disorder, which is war related. He has been turned down for disability"* (Sands, 1991, pp. 186–187).

*These vignettes illustrate various facets of emotional, psychological, and behavioral problems, also referred to as mental illness, a serious social problem. The first reflects a panic attack (a type of anxiety disorder), the second a case of depression, the third schizophrenia, and the fourth posttraumatic stress disorder. These represent the types of problems and issues social workers confront every day in mental health practice.*

*Note the following facts:*

- *"In 2013, there were an estimated 43.7 million adults aged 18 or older in the [United States who had a mental disorder] … in the past year. This represented 18.5 percent of all U.S. adults"* (National Institute of Mental Health [NIMH], 2014.
- *Only 39% of people having any mental illness and 61% of people experiencing a "serious mental disorder are receiving regular treatment"* (Macionis, 2013, p. 254).
- *Approximately 4.5%, or 1 in 22, people experience extreme forms of a mental disorder such as schizophrenia and bipolar (manic-depressive) disorder every year* (Kendall, 2013).

*A large percentage of social workers work in some aspect of the mental health field; of all mental health service providers, 60% are "clinically trained social workers"* (National Association of Social Workers [NASW], 2014a). *Of all mental health service providers, 10% are psychiatrists, 23% are psychologists, and 5% are psychiatric nurses* (NASW, 2014a). *The Encyclopedia of Social Work affirms that many social workers will indeed work in mental health contexts, but all social workers will come into contact with clients or clients' family members who are experiencing a mental disorder* (Greeno, 2008). *Therefore, significant time will be spent discussing what social workers do in mental health and where they do it.*

## Mental Health, Mental Disorders, and Social Work Roles  `LO 1`

The concept of mental health has many dimensions. **Mental health** is the state of relative psychological and emotional well-being in which an individual can make acceptably rational decisions, cope adequately with personal and external stresses, and maintain satisfactory adjustment to society.

A **mental disorder** is any of a wide range of psychological, emotional, or cognitive conditions that impair a person's ability to function effectively. Causes may be "biological, chemical, physiological, genetic, psychological, or social": mental disorders are "extremely variable in duration, severity, and prognosis" (Barker, 2014, p. 266). Primary symptoms of a mental disorder include extreme anxiety, disturbed thinking processes, perceptual distortions, extreme mood variations, and other difficulties in thinking (United States Department of Health and Human Services [USDHHS], 1999). Another common term for a mental disorder is **mental illness**. A later section of this chapter will describe some of the conditions clients face when they have a mental disorder.

## Employment Settings in Mental Health for Social Workers

Social workers practice in a broad range of settings and can assume many roles. Just as in other practice areas, advocacy for rights and services is a vital social work function here. Rising costs for mental health care and increasing numbers of people requiring treatment and resources will challenge social workers in the coming years. Mental health programs compete for limited funds just like other forms of social services. There is a constant struggle in the political environment to empower people by getting them the services they need.

Social workers are employed, along with professionals in other related fields, in a wide range of

mental health facilities. These include inpatient mental and psychiatric hospitals, psychiatric units in general hospitals, residential treatment centers for children and adolescents, outpatient treatment agencies, employee assistance programs, and community mental health centers. Highlight 13.1 addresses the differences between social workers with a BSW and those with an MSW.

## The Least Restrictive Setting on a Continuum of Care: Empowering Clients

A critical concept in mental health treatment is client treatment in the **least restrictive setting** possible. Earlier chapters defined this as the setting that allows the client maximum self-determination while providing the intensity of treatment needed to be effective. This involves the idea that clients should be empowered to have maximum control over their own lives while having access to the treatment level needed. The restrictiveness of the treatment setting is related to the concept of the **continuum of care**. The continuum of available services should provide a

---

## HIGHLIGHT 13.1 DIFFERENCES BETWEEN BSW AND MSW POSITIONS AND RESPONSIBILITIES

Both BSWs and MSWs can find employment in a wide range of mental health settings. Likewise, both can have field internships in mental health agencies. However, there are some differences in the types of jobs for which each is qualified. MSWs are considered more specialized than BSWs. The implication is that MSWs are competent to address more difficult psychological problems than BSWs and have the potential to assume greater responsibility. However, both can and do work in mental health settings.

Generalist social work practice can involve many facets of mental health. BSWs can provide both individual and group counseling to help clients make plans and solve problems. They can work with families, encouraging them to use their strengths to deal with issues. BSWs can also teach parents effective techniques for managing their children's behavior. BSWs often provide crisis intervention when clients face difficult or traumatic situations. They can link people in need to mental health resources within the community. They can also educate other professionals and community citizens about mental health issues.

A major difference between BSWs and MSWs is that providing psychotherapy is solely the domain of MSWs. **Psychotherapy** is a skilled treatment process whereby a therapist works with an individual, couple, family, or group to address a mental disorder or alleviate other problems the client(s) may be having in the social environment. Sometimes the term *therapy* is used, especially in reference to various psychotherapeutic approaches such as behavioral therapy, psychodynamic therapy, or cognitive therapy. The term **therapy**, however, can also refer to treatment of problems other than mental health and adjustment problems including physical difficulties. Examples are speech therapy, occupational therapy, and physical therapy.

Often, as Chapter 1 noted, higher-level supervisory and administrative positions require an MSW or other master's level degree. Such positions usually offer higher salaries. Finally, MSWs generally earn significantly more than BSWs, although years of experience enhance salaries for both groups.

range of treatment alternatives ranging from the least restrictive to the most. Chapter 9 discussed similar concepts with respect to substitute placements for children in out-of-home care.

One of the most restrictive settings is placement in a locked ward of a mental hospital. Clients placed here have minimal control over their lives and, theoretically, maximum access to treatment 24 hours a day. One of the least restrictive settings involves individuals receiving treatment in an outpatient facility for an hour or two each week while residing in their own homes and going about their regular daily activities.

One problem with the idea of minimal restrictiveness of setting is that adequate, effective services must be readily available in less restrictive parts of the continuum. For example, if a client released from an institution into the community requires some level of service, that service must be readily available to that client. The process of providing services and care for people within their own communities rather than in institutional settings is called **deinstitutionalization**.

Mental health settings that employ social workers include inpatient mental and psychiatric hospitals: residential treatment centers for children and adolescents; group homes; psychiatric units in general hospitals; outpatient treatment agencies; employee assistance programs; and community mental health centers, which provide a wide range of services.

## Inpatient Mental and Psychiatric Hospitals

*Inpatient treatment* facilities such as publicly funded state and county mental hospitals and private psychiatric clinics provide one employment setting for social workers. **Inpatient treatment** means that clients reside in the facility for some period. They are among the most restrictive treatment settings available. Depending on the problem, this period might be as short as days or as long as a lifetime. Medicare or Medicaid usually pays for treatment in public institutions. Private psychiatric facilities, which are usually quite expensive, most frequently are funded directly by clients or by their private insurance. Both types fulfill the functions of assessment, planning, provision of medications, and therapeutic treatment for various severe mental disorders.

Note that other long-term care facilities are also used when people with deteriorating or acute mental conditions can no longer remain in their own homes. Examples are nursing homes and foster care homes.

## Residential Treatment Centers for Children and Adolescents

An area in which child welfare and mental health overlap is **residential treatment centers (RTCs)** and group homes for children. An RTC is an agency that provides children who have serious emotional and behavioral problems with residential round-the-clock care, education (often with an emphasis on special education), interpersonal skills training, and individual, group, and sometimes family therapy. Although all RTCs, by definition, provide residential care, other aspects of their orientation and programming vary substantially. Treatment may involve any of a wide range of psychotherapeutic approaches (e.g., behavioral, cognitive, psychoanalytic). Some RTCs have a school right on the premises, and others use public schools. Some RTCs are located in rural settings; others are in urban metropolises. Some have only male residents, others have only females, and still others have both.

Residents spend most of their time with the residential staff (typically called something like child care workers or unit counselors) caring for them. Therefore, such staff can have a huge impact on the treatment process. Residents usually spend relatively little time with psychotherapists, who may be MSWs, psychiatrists, psychologists, or some combination of these.

Many settings emphasize behavioral programming and provide structured guidelines for how counselors should respond to various types of behavior on the part of residents. Techniques such as using positive reinforcement (e.g., praising), employing empathy, and giving feedback about behavior can be useful in chang-  **EP 6b** ing behavior for the better (Henderson & Thompson, 2011; Stein, 1995). **Positive reinforcement** is a procedure or consequence that increases the frequency of the behavior immediately preceding it. For example, a staff member might say to a resident, "Hey, Billy, you really did a nice job completing your chores this week. Way to go!" This is positive reinforcement if the result is that Billy continues doing his assigned chores on time. **Empathy** is the act of not only understanding how another person feels but also conveying to that person an awareness of how he or she feels. For example, a staff member might say to a client, "I can see how frustrated you are with your homework. I know how difficult it is for you." **Feedback** is the process of giving people information, positive or negative, about their performance or behavior.

Often RTCs use **token** or **point systems** in which tokens (i.e., symbolic objects such as poker chips or artificial coins that reflect units of value) or points on a chart are used in a coordinated system to control poor behavior, develop good behavior, and monitor progress. Appropriate and inappropriate behaviors are clearly defined, as are expectations and

consequences for various behaviors. Residents earn tokens or points for good behavior and lose them for bad conduct. Highlight 13.2 gives an example of how positive reinforcement (usually in the form of praise), empathy, and feedback are used by a staff member in an RTC (Stein, 1995, pp. 205–206).

## Group Homes

As Chapter 9 explained, group homes are considered less extreme on the continuum of care in terms of

---

**HIGHLIGHT 13.2** | **USING POSITIVE REINFORCEMENT, EMPATHY, AND FEEDBACK TO CHANGE BEHAVIOR**

*The scene:* Pete, age 12, is a resident of the Earl E. Bird Residential Treatment Center for Boys. He is quite unhappy. He needs to earn a certain number of points to go on a field trip to a big basketball game, which he *really* wants to do. But he lost points for poking another guy in the ear on Monday. Then, on Wednesday, Jethro, another kid in his unit, picked a fight with him. Although  **EP 6b** Pete ended up with a bloody nose, he gave Jethro a black eye, which cost him more points. He was so angry the entire week that he refused to make his bed, which resulted in still more points lost. By Thursday, it was impossible for Pete to earn enough points to go to the game. Furious, he stomps out of the unit and down the long driveway, contemplating running away. Rashaun, one of the residential staff on Pete's unit, catches up to Pete and starts to talk with him. (Note that in the following dialogue nonverbal behavior is indicated by regular roman type within brackets, and positive reinforcement [usually in the form of praise], empathy, and feedback are indicated by italic type within brackets.)

*Rashaun:* Pete, it's time to get back to the unit.
*Pete:* [Continues walking, trying to ignore Rashaun]
*Rashaun:* Pete, did you hear me?
*Pete:* F___ you, buzzard breath. I ain't goin' back and you can't make me!
*Rashaun:* You sound like you're upset about something [*expression of empathy*]. You'll only lose points if you don't get back [*feedback*].
*Pete:* Shove your f___ing points up your a___.
*Rashaun:* Come on. Let's walk over to the basketball court and talk. [Turns and walks toward the basketball court, which is empty right now]

*Pete:* [Pretends to ignore Rashaun at first, but eventually follows him, his eyes downcast]
*Rashaun:* It's been a bad week for you, hasn't it? [*empathy*]
*Pete:* Yeah ... [Said gloomily and without eye contact]
*Rashaun:* You haven't earned enough points to go to the game this weekend, have you?
*Pete:* Nope. Life's a b_____. I'll never get to go anywhere.
*Rashaun:* Well, you know, getting points for the game next weekend starts tomorrow [*feedback*]. How about starting fresh? You usually do a good job of keeping yourself together and getting enough points to go along [*praise as intended positive reinforcement*].
*Pete:* [Finally looking up] Maybe. But it's such a long time till then.
*Rashaun:* I know, it's really tough living up to all the rules around here [*empathy*]. But, come on now, you can do it. You need to start getting those points back so you can get to the game next weekend [*feedback*].
*Pete:* [Saying nothing, starts walking toward the unit, while Rashaun walks along with him]
*Rashaun:* I give you a lot of credit for getting yourself under control [*praise as intended positive reinforcement*]. I know it was hard for you [*empathy*]. I think you deserve 10 extra points for going back to the unit so quickly [*intended positive reinforcement*]. That should help you toward next week's goal so you can go to the game [*feedback*].
*Pete:* [Finally looking up at Rashaun and smiling just a little] OK, thanks.

restrictiveness of setting. Children and adolescents placed in group homes don't need the more extreme institutional placement in an RTC. However, group homes also vary dramatically in terms of restrictiveness and intensity. Some are run by married couples: others have staff available around the clock. Some provide intensive individual, group, and family psychotherapy; others provide little, if any, such treatment. Group homes are smaller than RTCs, usually limited by law to a maximum number of residents, such as eight.

The reasons children are placed in group homes also vary. The courts determine that they cannot remain in their own homes for reasons ranging from abusive situations to their own emotional and behavioral problems. Some simply need a protective environment with emotional support, consistent treatment, and exposure to positive role models. Others demonstrate extremely aggressive, deviant, or uncontrollable behavior and require a treatment setting almost as structured as an RTC, but smaller and more personal.

Why, then, are some children and adolescents placed in RTCs and others in group homes when their behavior is similar? Placement decisions involve complex issues. The value system of the person determining the placement (e.g., a judge or a social worker making recommendations to a judge), types of RTCs and group homes available, treatment methods used, openings within these settings, and cost can all contribute to decisions about where a young client is ultimately placed.

## Psychiatric Units in General Hospitals

Psychiatric units in general hospitals offer emergency psychiatric care on a temporary inpatient basis for people in crisis. They usually work closely with other, longer-term inpatient and outpatient facilities to provide care at whatever level on the continuum of care a client needs.

## Outpatient Treatment Agencies

Not all people, of course, need inpatient treatment. **Outpatient treatment** agencies and clinics provide individual, group, and family counseling for a wide range of mental health and substance abuse problems. Clients come in for their treatment and then leave when they're done.

Sometimes private practitioners, including social workers, psychologists, and psychiatrists, establish their own practice and serve their own clientele, working as individuals or with a small group of colleagues. Social workers who do this often call themselves **clinical social workers** (previously *psychiatric social workers*). This means that they provide psychotherapy to clients to address mental health issues and other life problems. Clinical social workers may also work for other types of mental health agencies.

A **family service association** is a type of outpatient treatment agency that offers various types of counseling, often in addition to child welfare services such as adoption and foster care. These agencies usually have multiple funding sources and are governed by a board of directors. Many are part of a national organization, such as Family Service America (FSA), Catholic Social Services, and Lutheran Social Services.

## Employee Assistance Programs

**Employee assistance programs (EAPs)** are services provided by organizations that focus on workers' mental health and on adjustment problems that interfere with their work performance. An underlying principle is that impaired worker performance due to factors such as absenteeism and stress costs companies money and that EAPs can significantly reduce such costs (Akabas, 2008; Gibelman, 2005). Problems addressed include substance abuse, family conflicts, financial problems, job stress, difficulties with day care for children or dependent parents, and other personal issues interfering with workers' psychological ability to do their jobs.

**Occupational social work** is the provision of mental health treatment by social workers in the workplace under the auspices of employers. Services can be either delivered by an internal office or purchased by employers from external contractors. EAPs have experienced "enormous" growth in recent years (NASW, 2009, p. 113). It is estimated that 63% of employees in organizations with 100 or more workers are served by EAPs (Akabas, 2008). Social workers comprise a substantial proportion of people providing EAP services (Akabas, 2008; NASW, 2009).

There is a vast range of services an EAP social worker can provide. Core services can include "assessment and referral" and "brief counseling" (NASW, 2009, p. 111). EAPs vary dramatically in terms of their scope (Akabas, 2008). For example, some are very limited in purpose and address a narrow range of identified problems such as substance abuse. Others target a wide range of difficulties including almost any personal issue. These may include grief counseling, stress and time management, marital problems, child care needs, financial issues, retirement planning, and crisis intervention. EAP social workers may provide individual or group counseling. For example, they might run a support group focused on some concern such as organizational downsizing to help employees cope with the organization's loss of staff (Gibelman, 2005). EAP social workers also may make referrals to more specialized community agencies to meet employees' specific needs. EAP services might also include consultation to management regarding supervision of employees, employee training (e.g., about sexual harassment), or assistance with administrative tasks such as rewriting an agency policy manual (Gibelman, 2005; NASW, 2009).

There are two issues that EAP social workers must carefully address (Akabas, 2008; Gibelman, 2005). First, they must be very careful about confidentiality. This might involve potential conflicts of interest because EAP social workers are employed by the organization and yet are there to help individual employees. The question involves the extent to which EAP social workers can ethically share information about employees with management. A breach of confidentiality could have serious effects on an employee such as losing a job or becoming victimized by discriminatory behavior (Gibelman, 2005).

This leads to the second issue, namely, where the EAP social worker's loyalty should lie. Is it with the organization or with the individual employees the social worker serves? EAP social workers should turn to the NASW *Code of Ethics* for guidance; it's critical for social workers to be honest with all involved, including management and employees, about their responsibilities and obligations (Akabas, 2008; Gibelman, 2005). It should be very clear regarding what an EAP social worker can and cannot reveal even before any problem develops.

## Community Mental Health Centers: A Macro Response to Individual Needs

**Community mental health centers** are versatile local organizations that provide a range of services, from mental health treatment to education about and prevention of mental illness. They fulfill a range of functions for which social workers may be employed. Ginsberg (2001, pp. 124–127) identifies and describes at least six functions community mental health centers perform:

1. *Case management:* This is the process of assessing clients' needs, linking clients to appropriate services, coordinating service provision, and monitoring its effectiveness. Whereas the broker role involves linking clients to resources, key concepts in the case manager role are coordinating and monitoring service provision. Kanter (1985) describes how case management can be used with clients having a serious mental illness:

   *[Such people] require a wide range of treatment and rehabilitation approaches that include medication, psychotherapy, family involvement, day treatment, crisis intervention, and brief and extended hospitalizations. Simultaneously, they often need a variety of social services that include housing, financial assistance, vocational training and placement, and medical care. Although obtaining needed services is not easy for "healthy persons,"[;] these ... [clients] have particular difficulty in locating and negotiating such assistance. (p. 78)*

   Case management is described more thoroughly in the discussion of what social workers do in the mental health context.

2. *Child and adolescent services:* These are aimed at enhancing the overall functioning of child and adolescent clients. Activities may include counseling, working with the schools on behalf of these young people, making referrals for services such as prescription drugs or family therapy, and involving clients in recreational activities.

3. *Information and education programs:* Staff including social workers educate community residents, family members of people with a mental disorder, and other professionals in the community about prevention, the problems involved, and the treatment of mental disorders.

4. *Long-term community care programs:* These serve people with mental illness on an ongoing basis. Often case managers help such people remain in the community by regularly visiting their homes, monitoring medication, and coordinating other needed services.

5. *Day treatment programs:* These provide daily activities for people with mental illness, including recreational pursuits such as games or crafts, health services, and educational programs.
6. *Alcohol and other drug treatment programs:* These provide treatment, including individual and group counseling. Often staff in such units work cooperatively with other inpatient facilities to give clients the type of care they need.

Highlight 13.3 addresses the fact that the titles of professionals working in community mental health settings can be confusing.

## Clients with Mental Health Problems    LO 2

Because of their significance to social work practice and to practitioners in the mental health field, a number of conditions affecting people's mental health will be described here. The most commonly used classification system for defining and diagnosing mental illness is the *Diagnostic and Statistical Manual of Mental Disorders* **EP 7b, 8b** (DSM-5) (APA, 2013), written by work groups composed of professional clinicians and published by the American Psychiatric Association.

The DSM-5 includes 22 major diagnostic categories and dozens of more specific diagnostic classifications. It describes each diagnosis in detail, providing a description of symptoms and diagnostic criteria to determine whether a person falls within that category.

Despite some serious concerns raised in Focus on Critical Thinking 13.1, the DSM-5 serves as the primary guideline for classifying various types of mental disorders. This, in turn, qualifies people to receive treatment paid for by the government (e.g., Medicaid or Medicare) or private health insurance. In other words, to be eligible for services and payment for these services, a person must first have the appropriate diagnosis. The DSM-5 includes not only mental disorders but also other conditions that may be the focus of clinical treatment. Note that psychiatrists usually must make the official diagnosis for clients to qualify for benefits.

To provide some insight into what mental illness is like, a number of conditions are arbitrarily chosen and briefly described here. These include neurocognitive disorders; schizophrenia and other psychotic disorders; depressive disorders; bipolar disorders; anxiety disorders; trauma- and other stressor-related disorders; dissociative disorders; sexual disorders; paraphilic disorders; eating disorders; disruptive, impulse control, and conduct disorders; obsessive–compulsive

and related disorders; and personality disorders (APA, 2013).

## Neurocognitive Disorders

A **neurocognitive disorder (NCD)** is a state in which people develop numerous cognitive problems due to some medical problem. The term **dementia** was used in the past. However, dementia implies a relationship with being an older adult. NCDs also refer to a variety of conditions affecting younger people. NCDs do not include conditions that were apparent at birth or very early in life. **Alzheimer's disease** is a common type of dementia of unknown origin, characterized by mental decline and usually occurring in late middle age.

*Case Example* Jose, age 59, has Alzheimer's disease, having been diagnosed five years ago. His wife Maria, age 56, first started noticing Jose gradually withdrawing from her and spending more time to himself. He began having more and more trouble accomplishing at first more complex and, later, simpler tasks. He had been a professional trumpet player. Now when he picks up his trumpet, he doesn't know what to do with it. Sometimes he bangs it against the

clothes dryer. Other times he picks up his razor and tries to make music with it. He constantly asks Maria questions. By the time she answers, he forgets what he asked and why. He has difficulty completing a simple task like drying the dishes because he forgets what he's doing even as he does it. He might put the dish down and walk away or else notice it in his hand and start washing it again.

While administering psychological testing to determine the extent of Jose's cognitive deterioration, a psychologist placed a pencil, a piece of paper, and fluorescent orange plastic scissors in front of him on a table. He then asked Jose to place the pen on the piece of paper. In response, Jose ignored the pen and paper, picking up the scissors and placing it back on the table upside down. His personality, what made Jose a special and unique individual, was gradually being drained from him. It was difficult for his family to cope.

## Schizophrenia and Other Psychotic Disorders

**Schizophrenia** is a severe mental disturbance characterized by delusions; hallucinations; confused, incoherent thinking and speech; bizarre behavior; flattened emotional responses; short, empty verbal responses that lack attentiveness; inability to participate in goal-directed activities; and often a noticeable disinterest in interpersonal interaction.

Schizophrenia is one of the most common forms of **psychosis**—any of a number of serious mental disorders characterized by disturbed, inappropriate behavior and loss of contact with reality. Psychosis is often contrasted with **neurosis**, a mental disorder characterized by "feelings of anxiety, obsessional thoughts, compulsive acts, and physical complaints without objective evidence of disease" that occur "in various degrees and patterns" (Nichols, 1999, p. 888). Psychosis is sometimes thought of as more severe than neurosis because psychotic people lose contact with reality. The key concepts involved in neurosis are anxiety and the behaviors resulting from its extreme forms.

*Case Example*  Frances, age 61, has been diagnosed with schizophrenia. She lives in a tiny 75-year-old house in a rural midwestern town 80 miles from the nearest city. Even in the heat of summer, she wears multiple layers of clothing to "keep the evil spirits away." She never turns her lights on at night because, she believes, hands reach out from the ceiling light fixtures and try to grab her. Although most of her neighbors shy away from her, she seeks them out whenever she sees them outdoors. A typical comment she makes to them is, "Sometimes Nicolas Cage appears and I take over his body and fight the spirits. But they can't tell who it is and sometimes we're the same. The dark makes the squash purple." Needless to say, this makes no sense. She also puts her garbage in small lunch bags, sometimes as many as 40, and lines them up in a perfect row along the curb for pickup. Frances periodically is hospitalized, in which event medication helps to curb her bizarre thought processes and behaviors. However, when she returns home she ceases taking her medication and her symptoms subsequently resume.

## Depressive Disorders

**Depressive disorders** (often referred to as depression in common conversation) are conditions characterized by extremely low spirits, unhappiness, lack of interest in daily activities, inability to experience pleasure, pessimism, significant weight loss not related to dieting (or significant weight gain), insomnia, extremely low energy levels, feelings of hopelessness and worthlessness, decreased capacity to focus and make decisions, and preoccupation with thoughts of suicide and death. It's depressing even reading that list of symptoms.

*Case Example*  Sharissa, age 31, is an example of a person suffering from a depressive disorder. She has been married for eight years to Jarell, age 34, who labors full-time as a welder in addition to working overtime whenever he can. Sharissa does not work outside the home. The couple has two sons, ages 3 and 5, both of whom have intellectual disabilities.

Sharissa consistently dwells on the negative aspects of her life, usually speaking to others in a high-pitched, whining tone. She complains that Jarell "never pays any attention" to her or the boys and doesn't "know the meaning of housework." When together, she criticizes him nonstop, to the point at which he simply "tunes her out." This only escalates her whining. In addition to complaining about Jarell, she grumbles about how difficult it is caring for the two boys with their special needs. She complains that all she does is work, and she gets no joy out of her life. She has no time for friends, and she and Jarell never go out anywhere together. Each night, she lies awake dwelling on all the supposedly horrible things that happened to her that day. She frequently says she is much too fat (although she is 5 feet 5 inches and weighs 125 pounds), but she has no time or money to go to a health club. She also claims that she is really "ugly" (although she is really quite attractive) and that she has a "shy, bad personality." A common lament is, "What is the point of living anymore when everything is so terrible?" Sharissa spews forth one negative statement after another whenever given the opportunity to talk to someone else, so it's difficult to get a word in edgewise. It's depressing and draining talking to Sharissa.

## Bipolar Disorders

**Bipolar disorders** (formerly referred to as *manic-depressive illness*) involve extreme mood swings and drastic changes in energy level and behavior. Although *mood* is a difficult word to define, most of us have a general idea of what it means. As with many other mental disorders, those concerning mood involve extremes beyond what people normally experience. Such extremes, involving intensity, duration, or fluctuation of mood, cause problems in a person's ability to function normally. With some bipolar disorders, people experience primarily **manic**

Vincent Oliver/The Image Bank/Getty Images

*Depression has negative effects on one's emotional state.*

episodes characterized by abnormally elevated levels of emotion, feelings of euphoria, a grandiose sense of self, excessive movement or talkativeness, extreme irritability, and poor judgment. With other bipolar disorders, people experience primarily periods of depression and at least one *manic* episode (i.e., being extremely irritable). Finally, bipolar disorders may involve mixed mood swings resulting in abrupt changes from manic to depressive episodes. Bipolar disorders reflect conditions that might be placed on a continuum somewhere between psychoses and depression (APA, 2013).

## Anxiety Disorders

**Anxiety disorders** are persistent or periodic states of extreme anxiety characterized by excessive fear, worry, apprehensiveness, dread of the future, and "related behavioral disturbances" (APA, 2013, p. 189). Physical symptoms include a rapid pulse, dizziness, perspiration, cold hands or feet, and rapid breathing

(National Mental Health Association [NMHA], 2008). Examples of anxiety disorders are phobias and panic disorders.

A **phobia** is extreme fear of "an object, activity, or situation" that is unrelenting and "far out of proportion to any potential danger posed" by the stimulus (APA, 2013, p. 827). Any exposure to what stimulates the fear results in avoidance of the stimulus or in intense discomfort. A **panic disorder** is characterized by "recurrent unexpected panic attacks" (APA, 2013, p. 209). **Panic attacks** are distinct episodes of extreme fear, intense anxiety, and excessive dread of the future. They are often accompanied by physical symptoms such as shortness of breath, sweaty palms, chest pains, racing heart, and fears of going crazy or dying. Unlike phobias, panic attacks are not associated with a specific stimulus, but rather happen "out of the blue" (APA, 2013, p. 826).

## Trauma- and Stressor-Related Disorders

**Trauma-** and **stressor-related disorders** are conditions involving the extreme emotional upset and behavioral reactions resulting after exposure to an extremely traumatic or stressful experience. The initiating stressor might be "[a]ny emotional, physical, social, economic, or other factor that disrupts the normal physiological, cognitive, emotional, or behavioral balance of an individual"; a traumatic stressor may be "[a]ny event (or events) that may cause or threaten death, serious injury, or sexual violence to an individual, a close family member, or a close friend" (APA, 2013, pp. 829–830). An example of a trauma- or stressor-related disorder is posttraumatic stress disorder.

**Posttraumatic stress disorder (PTSD)** is a condition in which a person continues to reexperience some traumatic event such as a bloody battle or a sexual assault. James and Gilliland (2013) explain that, regardless of the cause, the basis of PTSD "is maladaptive adjustment to a traumatic event. The disorder is both acute and chronic. In its chronic form it is insidious and may take months or years to appear. Its symptoms include, but are not limited to anxiety, depression, substance abuse, hypervigilance [excessive, heightened watchfulness], eating disorders, intrusive-repetitive thoughts, sleep disturbance, somatic [physical] problems, poor social relationships, suicidal ideation, and denial and affective numbing of the traumatic event" (p. 196).

James and Gilliland (2013) elaborate on how some people try to elude facing trauma through self-medication:

*Accompanying emotions of guilt, sadness, anger, and rage occur as the thoughts continue to intrude into awareness. To keep these disturbing thoughts out of awareness, the individual may resort to self-medication in the form of alcohol or drugs. Self-medication may temporarily relieve depressive, hostile, anxious, and fearful mood states ... , but what usually occurs is a vicious cycle that alternates between being anesthetized to reality by the narcotic and experiencing elevated intrusion of the trauma with every return to sobriety. The ultimate outcome is increased dependence on the addictive substance as a method of keeping the intrusive thoughts submerged. (p. 159)*

### War Veterans and Posttraumatic Stress Disorder (PTSD)

Just as in previous wars, veterans returning from Iraq, Afghanistan, and the Gulf War often experience PTSD (James & Gilliland, 20013; Kanel, 2015). Imagine seeing one of your best friends being blown up before your eyes. Or picture, because you were commanded to do so, mowing down a civilian who refuses to get out of your way with the convoy vehicle you're driving. That civilian may well be carrying deadly explosives that are much more likely to kill you and your fellow soldiers if that civilian has time to aim or detonate. What if that civilian is a child or a woman with a baby?

Many soldiers function and survive during deployment but begin to break down when they get home. Kanel (2015) explains:

*When soldiers are engaged in combat and see the trauma of war, some do experience acute stress disorder. They are often treated by doctors and given time to recuperate. However, the military trains soldiers to numb themselves to war trauma so that they may engage in warfare effectively. This allows them to deal with combat when it is happening. It is when they return home that many combat and support military personnel show signs of PTSD. The disorder has been delayed, almost by training. Once soldiers return home, many have difficulty adjusting to civilian life. They report being preoccupied with the troops that are still*

*fighting. They often feel guilty for leaving the other soldiers and think they should return to help fight. (p. 177)*

Variables increasing the risk of PTSD as veterans reintegrate into society include having experiences while deployed that involved dangerous military action, risk of exposure to deadly chemical weapons, and watching other soldiers being hurt or killed: other variables increasing PTSD risk include variables encountered upon return home, such as job loss, overwhelming financial obligations, feeling overloaded with new responsibilities, facing altered interpersonal relationships (as family members and others had adapted their behavior to cope with the veteran's absence), and disrupted everyday habits and regimens that had been established before deployment (Whealin, DeCarvalho, & Vega, 2008a).

At least four types of reactions are often experienced by returning veterans—reexperiencing, hyperarousal, avoidance, and emotional numbing):

*[Reexperiencing] includes "different ways that combat events may seem to repeat in our mind or body. Reexperiencing can include upsetting memories, thoughts, and images that come into your mind even when you are not trying to think about them, as well as dreams or nightmares about stressful events. The reminder—sometimes called triggers or cues—can be many different things. Following war, a trigger may occur when veterans see people who remind them of the enemy, when they are in places that are similar to the war zone, or when they hear sounds or smell odors that remind them of their deployment. Although reexperiencing often includes thoughts, memories, and images in the mind, it also causes reactions in the body. For example, a person might experience a physical stress reaction (heart beating faster, sweating more, muscles tensing up, etc.) when something reminds them of a severely stressful event....*

*[Hyperarousal is] the experience of being amped-up.... Arousal is just energy or activation in the body. We all need some level of arousal or we could not get up and move around. Hyperarousal just means more arousal than we need, or more than is healthy or makes sense. Some veterans may feel like they have to be on guard all the time. They may startle following sudden noises and they may feel "jacked up" or "amped" a lot of the time. Some may feel very anxious or panicky. Some veterans*

*find it hard to concentrate. They might be more irritable or angry than they used to. Also, veterans may have trouble falling asleep or staying asleep due to hyperarousal....*

*[**Avoidance**] refers to going out of our way not to think about or to stay away from something. Because the other reactions—reexperiencing and hyperarousal—feel bad, some veterans try to avoid reminders of their deployment or anything that might trigger these other stress reactions. If a veteran feels uncomfortable in a shopping mall, he or she might begin avoiding going to the mall.... Veterans might try to avoid thinking about the war zone, or talking to people about it. Some people start to keep to themselves or avoid watching TV or reading the news....*

*Related to avoidance, some people may experience emotional numbing [inability to feel or express emotions], or may feel depressed. This can include having a hard time relating to other people or having a hard time trusting others. Veterans with emotional numbing may feel fewer positive feelings, like happiness. Often after stressful events people have a harder time enjoying things they used to, such as hobbies or going out with other people. Sometimes veterans lose their interest in food or sex, or may not be able to function sexually.... After combat deployment, many people feel that they just don't have as much energy as they used to, or that their memory is not as good as it used to be."*

*(James & Gilliland, 2013; Whealin, DeCarvalho, & Vega, 2008b, pp. 19–20)*

Former Army National Guard Captain Jullian Goodrum's experiences upon returning from Iraq: "I was coming apart at the seams. There were the dreams, the edginess, the constant sense that I had something to fear—as if something or somebody that meant me harm was just around the corner. My mind was no longer my mind. I was going over a cliff" (Currey, 2007, p. 14).

Imagine what it would be like to be stationed in a place where almost anyone might be a suicide bomber or some other attacker who could kill you. Hypervigilance is required at all times for basic survival. You always carry a big weapon. Now envision returning home to Smalltown, USA. Think about what it might be like to switch gears suddenly from being in a war zone to being at home. How difficult might it be to make yourself stop worrying that the

checker at Pick 'n' Shop or the man standing at the stoplight waiting for the red light to change are potential martyrs ready to take you out with them?

Please keep in mind that "[m]ost service members do not develop PTSD. It is also important to remember that [a service member] ... can experience some PTSD symptoms without having a diagnosis of PTSD. PTSD cases often resolve on their own in the first three months, but even without a full diagnosis, if [a service member has] ... symptoms, [he or she] ... can benefit from counseling or therapy" (Philpott & Hill, 2009, p. 20).

*Treatment for Veterans with PTSD* PTSD is a complex condition that involves an "intricate interplay between traumatic events and the brain's physiological responses to the trauma. Contemporary treatment includes both group and individual intervention that is multimodal and considers psychological, biological, and social bases as equally important" (James & Gilliland, 2013, p. 196). Kanel (2015) indicates:

**EP 7d**

*The first phase of treatment with PTSD survivors and their families includes educating them about how people get PTSD and how it affects survivors and their loved ones, and other problems that are commonly associated with PTSD symptoms. It is helpful to inform people that PTSD is a medically recognized anxiety disorder that occurs in normal individuals under extremely stressful conditions. (p. 170)*

Treatment for PTSD then may involve a number of therapeutic approaches. These include: cognitive-behavioral therapy; medication; and individual, group, and family contexts for therapy (Kanel, 2015; VA, 2010; Whealin et al., 2008a). Note that here the focus is on social work therapists' work with veterans, although therapists from other disciplines, including psychologists, counselors, and psychiatrists also can provide therapy.

Cognitive-behavioral therapy involves commonly used and effective approaches that address changes in both thinking and behavior (James & Gilliland, 2013; Kanel, 2015; VA, 2010). One aspect of cognitive-behavioral therapy involves cognitive processing; "[t]his approach helps veterans learn about the relationship between thoughts, events and emotions and the negative beliefs held by veterans regarding their war zone experiences. The most useful aspect is that it helps veterans develop alternative interpretations about their thoughts which then influence their feelings" (Exum, Coll, & Weiss, 2011, p. 97). Thus, the social work therapist can help veterans understand how they think about their traumatic experiences and the psychological, emotional, and behavioral effects of these incidents. The intent is to help the veteran recognize how thinking patterns can trigger stress.

Another aspect of this therapy involves helping the veteran identify "extreme views" that are causing stress and replacing them with "a more reasonable perspective" that is more accurate and less upsetting (Armstrong, Best, & Domenici, 2006, p. 145). After war, a veteran's views can change because of vivid and disturbing experiences. Armstrong and his colleagues (2006, p. 145) provide an example. A veteran's views on "safety and trust" may change and become extreme, meaning "not rational, reasonable, or understandable." The veteran may think "I can't trust anybody anymore." A social worker or other therapist can help the veteran reevaluate this extreme perspective in terms of how true and rational it really is. Is there really no one anywhere that the veteran can trust? "Extreme views" like this "are sometimes called 'distorted thinking.' This type of thinking is not helpful because it can lead to further negative thoughts and feelings" such as "anxiety of depression."

A social work therapist can help the veteran identify distorted thinking, which often falls within the following areas:

- *Black-or-White Thinking:* Viewing your military experience in extremes and not seeing anything in between; seeing situations as either good or bad, black or white, all or none, perfect or imperfect. Example: "I completely failed all the men and women in my unit when I left Iraq."
- *Doomsday Thinking:* Viewing [the] ... future as hopeless from every angle. Thinking that bad outcomes are your destiny no matter what you do. Example: "I will never be able to relate to civilians after serving in war no matter how much I try."
- *Mind-Reading Thinking:* Thinking that other people have negative views about you or negative intentions toward you without any real reason or evidence to support this belief. Example:

"Everybody thinks I'm incompetent since I came home from the war."
- *If-Only Thinking:* Thinking about the past with regret and disappointment by wondering "If only I had ..." over and over again. Example: "If only I had waited five more minutes, the convoy wouldn't have been hit by an IED [improvised explosive device such as those terrorists might use]." (Armstrong et al., 2006, pp. 145–146)

After distorted thinking has been identified and targeted, the social work therapist can help the veteran restore more realistic thinking (Armstrong et al., 2006). For instance, the belief "I can't trust anybody anymore" can be replaced with "It's hard to trust people after going to war, but I do have a few friends I can rely on" (p. 146). This new perspective can be reinforced and repeated until it begins to replace the extreme, unrealistic view. It's also important for the social work therapist to reinforce any positive perspectives the veteran might have. For example, the fact that he or she is finally reunited with a significant other, family, and friends might be stressed. The perspective that "certain material things aren't as important anymore or that it's important to live each day fully" might also be emphasized (p. 146). An important goal is to identify and focus on the positive aspects of life and stop dwelling on the negative ones. Positive activities might include: caregiving for children, other family members, or sick friends; volunteering for a religious or social services organization; or even taking up a hobby, interest, or activity participated in prior to deployment.

Three other issues that might be addressed with veterans as they reintegrate into society after returning home—control, hypervigilance, and coping with civilians (Whealin et al., 2008a). A returning veteran, having had little control over his life or what he did in his wartime experience, may still feel out of *control.* However, a social work therapist may help such veterans think through and distinguish more realistically what they can control and what they can't. For example, they can't control military decisions about their deployment, other people's behavior, or the weather. However, they can control how they spend their time, who they spend it with, their communication with and behavior toward others, and their decisions about what to do in the future.

**Hypervigilance** means "being overly alert for possible dangers" (Whealin et al., 2008a, p. 98). "Over time … people in a war zone often get used to feeling threatened—in their environment or with other people—and they may continue to feel that way when they return home" (Whealin et al., 2008a, p. 98). However, hypervigilance is not constructive in a safe home environment. It may cause sleeplessness, stress, or anger. It may make others around the veteran tense and uncomfortable. A social work therapist can help veterans think through these feelings and evaluate the actual safety of any particular environment. Instead of avoiding places that make them anxious ("such as being in a crowd or going to the mall"), they can gradually make themselves enter such environments and use stress management techniques to help them cope (e.g., deep breathing exercises or progressive muscle relaxation) (Whealin et al., 2008a, p. 99). Thus, they can retrain their thinking and "adjust back to the fact" that they "are no longer in danger" (Whealin et al., 2008a, p. 99).

*Coping with civilians* can be another problem for returning veterans. People can make stupid, thoughtless, and offensive comments. Veterans may have experienced losses in terms of significant others or friends, or missed important events back home such as weddings or highlights in their children's lives. A social work therapist can help veterans prepare for the inevitable "culture shock" they experience as they try to reintegrate into civilian society (Whealin et al., 2008a, p. 99). They can work out decisions in advance regarding how to handle relationships and issues. A social work therapist can help veterans cope by thinking ahead about what problematic events they might encounter with civilians. Together, worker and veteran can discuss in advance how the veteran will handle the situations. For example, how might the veteran respond to a critical antiwar comment?

There are almost endless other approaches and techniques under the cognitive-behavioral therapy umbrella. For instance, other useful cognitive-behavioral techniques include "teaching clients how to engage in deep breathing and relaxation exercises, manage anger, prepare for future stress reactions, … and communicate and relate effectively with people" (Kanel, 2015, p. 170; Whealin et al., 2008a). It is beyond the scope of this text to go into a great deal of detail. The intent here is to give you a sample of what social workers can do.

Medications that are a type of antidepressant can help many veterans (VA, 2010). "Medication may

be necessary for some trauma survivors. It can reduce the anxiety, depression, and insomnia often experienced. It is useful for relieving symptoms so that the survivor is able to participate in psychological treatment" (Kanel, 2015, p. 170).

Highlight 13.4 addresses the contexts for treatment of veterans with PTSD within groups and families.

*Relevance for Social Workers*  Social workers don't have to work for the Department of Veterans Affairs in order to come into contact with returning veterans experiencing PTSD. Veterans or their family members may be involved in virtually any social work practice context. It is very important that, regardless of people's views about the war, veterans must not be abandoned. They must receive support and treatment or be referred to services where they can get what they need.

*Other Injuries*  Note that PTSD is only one of the many conditions faced by veterans returning from Afghanistan and other war-torn areas. A "signature injury" of the war is **traumatic brain injury (TBI)** where soldiers experience severe concussions such as those resulting from explosions; often TBI survivors "must relearn walking, speaking, and simple motor skills" (Armstrong et al., 2006; Currey, 2007, p. 15; Kanel, 2015).

Because of today's heavily armored vehicles and body armor, many soldiers survive experiences and injuries that would have killed them in the past; as a result, many veterans are living with lost limbs and severe burns. Social workers must prepare themselves to address any of these issues.

## Dissociative Disorders

**Dissociative disorders** involve "a disruption of … the normal integration of consciousness, memory, identity, emotion, perception, … and behavior" (APA, 2013, p. 291). An example of a dissociative disorder is **dissociative identity disorder** (formerly referred to as *multiple personality disorder*). This occurs when parts of a person's personality split off from the rest of that person's personality, resulting in at least two totally different identities existing within the same person.

I once had a student who confided in me that she had this disorder. She said that through therapy she was now down from several personalities to only two.

---

## HIGHLIGHT 13.4 — CONTEXTS FOR PTSD TREATMENT—VETERANS' GROUPS AND FAMILIES

A social work therapist can work with an individual veteran, with groups of veterans, or with the veteran and his or her family. Individual therapy can address any of the issues discussed earlier. Group therapy provides an alternative arena that allows veterans to talk about their trauma with others who understand because they've had similar experiences. It provides a forum where "[t]rauma survivors can share traumatic material within an atmosphere of safety, cohesion, and empathy provided by other survivors. By sharing their feelings of shame, fear, anger, and self-condemnation, survivors are enabled to resolve many issues related to their trauma" (Kanel, 2015, p. 170). Group therapy "can help ... build self-confidence and trust" in addition to providing a "focus on [one's] ... present life, rather than feeling overwhelmed by the past" (VA, 2010).

EP 7, 8

A social work therapist can also work with a veteran and his or her family to address whatever issues they are dealing with. Potential reasons for family involvement include the following:

> For veterans who get sent back home after being in a war zone, there may be some very mixed feelings about being reunited with their families and other loved ones. Most of them feel relieved to be getting into a safer living zone. Still, many veterans may also feel conflicted because they feel like the people they deployed with are the only ones who can understand them....

> [I]t is common for those returning from a war to get irritated more easily and to isolate from others due to feelings of discomfort. [We have already established that it] ... is possible that the veteran may experience numbing of affect, and he or she may find it hard to have feelings such as love, happiness, empathy, and sadness.

> Veterans may also be experiencing some underlying anger or resentment from the spouse or partner, as well as the children in the family, for leaving them....

> All of these issues can present some problems in communication between the veterans and their significant others.

> *(Whealin et al., 2008a, p. 105)*

A social work therapist can help the family articulate their feelings so that they can understand each other's emotions and address them. Family members should be encouraged to express honestly their "fears and concerns" and "to listen to others"; a therapist can help develop improved communication skills and establish positive, supportive relationships (VA, 2010). A therapist can help the family understand how the veteran feels about the war experience, his or her "PFSD symptoms and what triggers them," and the "important parts of treatment and recovery" (VA, 2010). "The major task for the service member is to accept the changes that have occurred in the family routine and family members during his or her absence and to reestablish his or her relationships with family members" (Exumetal., 2011, p. 110).

---

The one who was speaking to me at that moment was 35 years old; there was also Joey, age 7. She said Joey might come out at any time during class, so I should be prepared. I thought, "Prepared for what?" Luckily, Joey never did emerge in class.

Highlight 13.5 describes the world's most famous anonymous person with a multiple personality, who was finally identified right before she died.

### Sexual Disorders

A **sexual disorder**, also often referred to as a **sexual dysfunction**, is "a clinically significant disturbance in a person's ability to respond sexually or to experience sexual pleasure" (APA, 2013, p. 423). Examples are erectile disorders and orgasmic disorders.

An **erectile disorder** is a dysfunction where a male is unable to maintain an erection or have one at all, or he experiences a significant decrease in the rigidity or hardness of his erections. The disorder must occur on all or almost all encounters of sexual interaction and have been evident for at least six months. It may have always occurred throughout life or it may have begun to happen at some later time after sexual activity had already started. It may be "generalized," that is, occurring during all occasions of sexual interaction, or it may be "situational," occurring only under some circumstances (APA, 2013, p. 426). Erectile dysfunctions may have a physical basis (e.g., diabetes or some other ongoing serious medical condition) or have a psychological

# WHO WAS SYBIL? THE MOST FAMOUS CASE OF MULTIPLE PERSONALITIES

The condition of dissociative identity disorder gained the public's attention in 1973 when Flora Rheta Schreiber wrote her best-seller *Sybil*. The book concerned an anonymous woman identified as "Sybil" who suffered from having 16 different personalities as a result of severe childhood abuse. The book suggested that, with each major trauma Sybil experienced, a new personality split off from her initial identity.

Sybil has been identified as Shirley Ardell Mason.[4] (To avoid confusion, we will continue referring to Shirley as Sybil.) Sybil, a retired teacher and artist, died on February 26, 1998, in Lexington, Kentucky, only a few weeks after confessing that she was indeed the real Sybil. Before *Sybil*'s publication, only about 75 cases of dissociative identity disorder had been diagnosed (Miller & Kantrowitz, 1999).

It's very difficult to determine how many cases have been identified since then. Many mental health professionals are quite skeptical about the validity of the disorder, its relationship with other psychological problems, and the potential for people to fake the disorder (Nairne, 2011). One source indicates the condition characterizes .01% to 1% of the population (International Society for the Study of Trauma and Dissociation, 2011).

Many people who knew Sybil, as well as psychiatrists and others, have questioned whether she was diagnosed correctly. Sybil remained a patient of Cornelia Wilbur, the psychiatrist who provided the book's story, beginning in 1954 and continuing for 11 years, during which time she participated in more than 2,300 psychotherapy sessions. Sybil, described as "a very fragile and sensitive person," began treatment as an undergraduate at Mankato State Teacher's College after she "was questioned by an English teacher as to the originality of one of her poems"; this, in conjunction with financial pressures from home, caused Sybil to experience "anxiety attacks and even blackouts in the middle of class" (Romsdahl, 1997).

Sybil stayed in close contact with Wilbur in the years after her therapy. In 1991, when Wilbur developed Parkinson's disease, Sybil acted as her nurse and companion until Wilbur's death in 1992 (Miller & Kantrowitz, 1999).

Another psychiatrist who treated Sybil described her as "a brilliant hysteric" who was "highly hypnotizable" and subject to suggestion (Miller & Kantrowitz, 1999, p. 67). He indicated that Wilbur may well have helped create various characters during the therapeutic process, which involved frequent hypnosis and doses of sodium pentothal ("truth serum").

Sybil's parents were Mattie and Walter Mason, whom Miller and Kantrowitz (1999) describe as "strictly observant Seventh-Day Adventists" (p. 67). People from Sybil's hometown of Dodge Center, Minnesota, described Mattie, the supposed perpetrator of the abuse, as "bizarre" and having a "witchlike laugh" the few times she did see humor in things; some remember Mattie "as walking around after dark, looking in neighbors' windows" and at one time "apparently being diagnosed as schizophrenic" (Miller & Kantrowitz, 1999, p. 67). According to the book, alleged "tortures primarily featured enemas that she [Sybil] was forced to hold while her mother played piano concertos, but the sadistic parent also enjoyed pushing spoons and other items up her child's vagina, making Sybil watch sexual intercourse, and hoisting her up to hang helplessly from a pulley." Some neighbors report Mattie as being exceptionally strict with Sybil. However, no one seems to remember any physical or sexual abuse taking place, especially any resembling the horrors described in the book.

No one questions that Sybil had a serious mental illness, but the truth of her story and her diagnosis remains in doubt. In any case, Sybil never married or had children. During the last years of her life, apparently "happy," she primarily cared for her pets, gardened, and painted until arthritis prevented her from doing so (Miller & Kantrowitz, 1999, p. 68; Van Arsdale, 2002).

Among the 16 personalities attributed to Sybil in the book were the following (Van Arsdale, 2002):

- Peggy Lou, "an assertive, enthusiastic, and often angry pixie with a pug nose."
- Marcia, "a writer and painter" who was "extremely emotional" and had a British accent (Miller & Kantrowitz, 1999).
- Mike, a self-important, olive-skinned carpenter who hoped to get a woman pregnant (Miller & Kantrowitz, 1999).
- Sybil Ann, a pale, shy, fearful person with almost no energy.
- Mary, a heavyset, "thoughtful, contemplative, maternal, home-loving person."
- Vanessa, a tall, slim, attractive redhead.
- Ruthie, a toddler with an undeveloped and child-like personality.
- The Blonde, a playful, high-spirited, happy-go-lucky teenager.

[4]Facts presented here were retrieved from the following sources: Aestraea's Web (1998), Borch-Jacobsen (1997), Hewlett (1998), Quiet's Corner (2002a, 2002b), Romsdahl (1997), and Van Arsdale (2002).

origin; psychological factors may involve "fear of failure and performance anxiety" (Carroll, 2013b, p. 384).

A **female orgasmic disorder** is a dysfunction where a female has no or infrequent orgasms during sexual interaction. As with erectile disorders, to be diagnosed as a disorder the dysfunction must have occurred to at least six months, it may be "lifelong" or "acquired" at some point in life after sexual activity had begun, and it may be "generalized" or "situational" (APA, 2013, pp. 429–430). Female orgasmic disorders may a have physical or psychological basis, or they may result from a complex interaction of causes. Hyde and DeLamater (2014) reflect:

> *Laypersons may call it frigidity, but sex therapists reject this term because it has derogatory connotations and is imprecise.* **Frigidity** *may refer to a variety of conditions ranging from total lack of sexual arousal to arousal without orgasm. Therefore, the term* female orgasmic disorder *is preferred. (p. 431)*

## Paraphilic Disorders

A **paraphilia** is an extreme, persistent sexual interest and arousal "in response to unusual stimuli such as children or other nonconsenting persons (such as unsuspecting people whom one watches or to whom one exposes one's genitals), nonhuman objects (such as shoes, leather, rubber, or undergarments), or pain or humiliation" (Rathus, Nevid, & Fichner-Rathus, 2014, p. 507). "Literally meaning 'beyond usual or typical love,' this term stresses that such behaviors are usually not based on an affectionate or loving relationship but rather are expressions of behavior in which sexual arousal or response, or both, depends on some unusual, extraordinary, or even bizarre activity" (Crooks & Baur, 2014, p. 488).

"A **paraphilic disorder** is a paraphilia that is currently causing distress or impairment to the individual or a paraphilia whose satisfaction has entailed personal harm, or risk of harm, to others" (APA, 2013, pp. 685–686). Not all paraphilias are paraphilic disorders. "A man with a fetish [sexual fixation on an inanimate object or nongenital body part] for lingerie, for example, may find a partner who very much enjoys wearing it for him" (Carroll, 2013b, p. 439).

Paraphilic disorders include

> **voyeuristic disorder** *(spying on others in private activities),* **exhibitionistic disorder** *(exposing the genitals),* **frotteuristic disorder** *(touching or rubbing against a nonconsenting individual),* **sexual masochism disorder** *(undergoing humiliation, bondage, or suffering),* **sexual sadism disorder** *(inflicting humiliation, bondage, or suffering),* **pedophilic disorder** *(sexual focus on children),* **fetishistic disorder** *(using nonliving objects or having a highly specific focus on nongenital body parts), and* **transvestic disorder** *(engaging in sexually arousing cross-dressing) [emphasis added].*

> *(APA, 2013, p. 685)*

## Eating Disorders

An **eating disorder** is a dysfunction that involves extreme difficulties with eating behavior that results in "an altered consumption or absorption of food and that significantly impairs physical health" or interpersonal social functioning. Examples include anorexia nervosa and bulimia nervosa. Both of these conditions involve a fixation on food and how much (or little) one eats. Common psychological features include low self-esteem, extreme responsiveness to cultural expectations for thinness, the use of food as a means of coping with uncomfortable emotions, and rigid expectations for themselves (Mental Health America [MHA], 2011a). Most people with eating disorders are female; only an estimated 5% to 15% are male (MHA, 2011a) Anorexics and bulimics tend to have a distorted perception of their physical appearance. A young woman within a normal or low weight range might look into the mirror and "see" a fat person with a double chin and bulging stomach. People with either condition are obsessed with body image. Our culture places a high value on thinness and its clear-cut positive correlation with attractiveness. Two of the "Thin Commandments" include "If you aren't thin you aren't attractive" and "You can never be too thin" (Costin, 2008).

### Anorexia Nervosa

*Anorexia nervosa*, usually afflicting girls and young women, is a condition in which a person refuses to maintain a weight level significantly below normal and dreads gaining weight (APA, 2013). Essentially, the person starves herself because she never sees herself as "thin enough." An anorexic frequently will skip meals, develop rationales for why she doesn't want to eat, eat only extremely low-calorie foods, exercise "excessively and compulsively," view herself and others as having to live up to "rigid, perfectionist standards," experience hair loss, wear large or baggy clothes to disguise her low weight, and withdraw into herself, becoming socially isolated (MHA, 2011a). It is estimated that in Western countries this condition characterizes 0.3% to 0.5% of adolescent girls and young women and a smaller, but increasing proportion of boys and young men (Papalia & Feldman, 2012).

### Bulimia Nervosa

**Bulimia nervosa**, also primarily involving females, is characterized by experiencing a severe lack of control over eating behavior, binging (i.e., consuming huge amounts of food, often "junk food"), and using methods to get rid of calories (e.g., forcing oneself to vomit [purging], using laxatives or enemas, and undergoing extreme exercising). Several other factors characterize people suffering from bulimia nervosa (MHA, 2011a). First, like anorexics, they are obsessed with being thin. Second, bulimics experience poor impulse control that may affect decisions about money, relationships, and other aspects of life in addition to their consumption of food (MHA, 2011a). Third, bulimics tend to experience depression (Papalia & Feldman, 2012). However, it is unclear whether depression, along with its accompanying shame and loss of control, is a result of or a trigger for bulimia nervosa. Bulimia nervosa afflicts an estimated 1.1% to 4.2% of females in the United States and one-tenth as many males (MHA, 2011a).

*Bulimia's Pattern* A pattern typically characterizes people developing bulimia nervosa. First, a person concerned with being thin and attractive begins dieting. Second, dieting and the resulting deprivation become extremely difficult to maintain. Third, the craving for food results in overeating; this phase is usually initiated by some crisis or stress, and eating provides comfort that leads to contentment. Fourth, the person gains weight because of the overeating and so feels guilty, ashamed, and out of control. Fifth, the person discovers that weight can be somewhat controlled through methods such as purging, using laxatives or enemas, and exercising excessively.

Sixth, the binge/purge cycle becomes an established way of coping with life's stresses, and the person comes to depend upon it. Seventh, as guilt and shame continue to build, the person expends increasingly greater energy to conceal the binge/purge behavior from those around her (or him).

*Case Example* Elena, age 17, was an active high school junior—she was an attractive, popular cross-country runner and cheerleader. She also did some professional modeling on the side. Her cross-country coach and her modeling supervisor stressed the need for her to remain thin, and indicated that losing a few pounds couldn't hurt. (This demonstrates phase 1 of the bulimia nervosa pattern.)

Elena dieted to lose those few extra pounds and began to crave carbohydrates and sweets (phase 2). She had always adored Little Debbie snack cakes, doughnut holes, and potato chips. Finally, struggling to find time for cheerleading, running, modeling, and studying for exams, she broke down and ate two dozen snack cakes and two large bags of potato chips (phase 3). This happened more than once. A few days later, she discovered that she had gained a couple of pounds. She was ashamed of her gluttonous behavior and horrified at getting "fat" (phase 4). When she looked in the mirror, she saw every ounce of the added weight. She even thought she could see cellulite on her thighs that had never been there before.

Elena remembered hearing that girls could "get rid of" the food they've eaten by throwing up. She tried it after a binge (phase 5). She also discovered that laxatives and enemas helped. She continued to find comfort in binging and strove for control by purging, popping pills, and taking enemas. The binge/purge cycle was established (phase 6).

Elena continued to feel ashamed and guilty about her compulsive behavior. She expended great amounts of energy to hide it from her parents, siblings, and friends (phase 7). Usually she threw up in jars, which she hid in small brown paper bags in the back of her closet until she could get rid of them. She would also borrow her parents' car, tell them she was going out with friends, find a solitary place to park, and binge on junk food. The cycle continued.

### Treatment Approaches for Anorexia and Bulimia

Anorexia and bulimia are very difficult to treat because so many variables are involved including emotional needs, established behavioral patterns, and external social stresses. Papalia and Feldman (2012) explain:

> The immediate goal of treatment for anorexia is to get patients to eat and gain weight—goals that are often difficult to achieve given the strength of patients' beliefs about their bodies. One widely used treatment is a type of family therapy in which parents take control of their child's eating patterns. When the child begins to comply with parental directives, she (or he) may be given more age-appropriate autonomy (Wilson, Grilo, & Vitousek, 2007). **Cognitive behavioral therapy**, which seeks to change a distorted body image and rewards eating with such privileges as being allowed to get out of bed and leave the room, may be part of the treatment (Beumont, Russell, & Touyz, 1993; Wilson et al., 2007). [Cognitive behavioral therapy includes therapeutic approaches that "seek to change negative thoughts through gradual exposure, modeling, rewards, or talking to oneself" (Papalia & Feldman, 2012, p. 346)]. Patients who show signs of severe malnutrition, are resistant to treatment, or do not make progress on an outpatient basis may be admitted to a hospital, where they can be given 24-hour nursing. Once their weight is stabilized, patients may enter less intensive daytime care (McCallum & Bruton, 2003).
>
> Bulimia, too, may be treated with cognitive behavioral therapy (Wilson et al., 2007). Patients keep daily diaries of their eating patterns and are taught ways to avoid the temptation to binge. Individual, group, or family psychotherapy can help both anorexia and bulimia patients, usually after initial behavior therapy has brought symptoms under control. Because these patients are at risk for depression and suicide, antidepressant drugs may be combined with psychotherapy (McCallum & Bruton, 2003), but evidence of their long-term effectiveness on either anorexia or bulimia is lacking (Wilson et al., 2007). (pp. 366–367)

Medical attention is often necessary to treat any physical symptoms for people with an eating disorder resulting from nutritional deficits. For anorexics, "[b]esides interfering with reproductive functions, the condition is associated with low blood pressure, loss of bone density, and gastrointestinal problems. Anorexia nervosa is a very serious and chronic condition that needs immediate and prolonged treatment" (Nairne, 2014, p. 351). "Bulimia is also often associated with serious medical problems.... [R]epeated vomiting can damage the intestines, lead to nutritional problems, and even promote tooth decay.... Bulimia can be harder to diagnose than anorexia because the bingeing and purging usually occur in private" (Nairne, 2014, p. 351).

Treatment effectiveness varies (Papalia & Feldman, 2012). Approximately 10% of patients with anorexia eventually die. Of those remaining, "less than one-half make a full recovery and only one-third actually improve" (Papalia & Feldman, 2012, p. 367). About 20% continue to be plagued with the condition and suffer its severe consequences the remainder of their lives. People with bulimia have an improved recovery rate over anorexics of 30% to 50% for those who participated in cognitive behavioral therapy.

## Disruptive, Impulse-Control, and Conduct Disorders

**Disruptive**, **impulse-control**, and **conduct disorders** are "conditions involving problems in the self-control of emotions and behaviors" (APA, 2013, p. 461). These disorders involve behaviors that infringe upon other people's rights and can cause harm. These disorders may result in aggressive treatment including assaults, violence, hostility, belligerence, and property damage. Although anyone might display these behaviors, a diagnosis of one of these disorders involves extreme behavior. These disorders often entail the inability to constrain behavior and "negative emotionality" (APA, 2014, p. 462). Males are more likely than females to manifest a disruptive, impulse-control, or conduct disorder. Examples of these disorders include oppositional defiant disorder and Kleptomania.

**Oppositional defiant disorder** is exhibition of an extremely negative attitude and pattern of behavior including an "angry/irritable mood, argumentative/defiant behavior," and spitefulness (APA, 2013, p. 462). People with this diagnosis typically anger easily, readily lose their temper, fight with other people including those holding positions of authority, disobey instructions and rules, purposely irritate others, and refuse to take responsibility for bad behavior or personal errors. The disorder must be manifested for at least six months. It must be determined that behavior is significantly more extreme and unrelenting than what is socially acceptable for people without this disorder.

**Kleptomania** is a condition characterized by a compulsive desire to steal things, not for personal need or gain, but simply for the sake of stealing them. People with kleptomania typically enjoy the act of theft or experience relief that the deed is over. Of people apprehended for shoplifting, approximately 4% to 24% have this disorder (APA, 2014, p. 478).

## Obsessive–Compulsive and Related Disorders

**Obsessive–compulsive** *and related* **disorders** are dysfunctions "characterized by the presence of obsessions and/or compulsions. *Obsessions* are recurrent and persistent thoughts, urges, or images that are experienced as intrusive and unwanted, whereas *compulsions* are repetitive behaviors or mental acts that an individual feels driven to perform in response to an obsession or according to rules (made up in a person's head) that must be applied rigidly" (APA, 2013, p. 235). To apply this diagnosis, people must exhibit extreme forms of behavior that cause them psychological anguish and significantly and negatively affect their ability to perform daily activities. Examples of obsessive–compulsive and related disorders are obsessive–compulsive disorder, hoarding disorder, and trichotillomania.

**Obsessive–compulsive disorder** is a dysfunction where obsessions or compulsions or both exist. Obsessions include "persistent thoughts, urges, or images" that are disturbing and usually cause significant anguish and apprehension for the individual (APA, 2013, p. 235). People with this diagnosis often seek to stifle such obsessions by performing some act or becoming involved in some thought process (such as a compulsion). Compulsions then involve "[r]epetitive behaviors (e.g., hand washing, ordering, checking) or mental acts (e.g., praying counting, repeating words silently)" that the individual undertakes in order to decrease anxiety about the obsession (APA, 2013, p. 237). For example, a person might obsess that she left the water running after leaving the house and that the house will flood. She then might force herself to return to the house and compulsively check the faucets 25 times to make certain the water is turned off.

**Hoarding disorder** is a dysfunction where the individual feels compelled to save things, regardless of their value, and has extreme trouble getting rid of things. This diagnosis is applied when clutter accumulates to the extent of interfering with living space, safety, and ability to function.

**Trichotillomania** is the controlling impulse to pull out one's own hair, most frequently from "the scalp, eyebrows, and eyelids" to the extent that the loss is readily apparent to others (APA, 2013, p. 251). This diagnosis is used when the behavior causes "significant distress or impairment in social, occupation, or other important areas of functioning" (APA, 2013, p. 251).

## Personality Disorders

**Personality disorders** reflect long-term patterns of behavior, emotions, and views of self and the world that strikingly diverge from cultural expectations, cause considerable stress, and result in problematic social interactions. The following are the most common personality disorders and the persistent patterns characterizing each (APA, 2013, p. 645):

- **Paranoid:** Extreme lack of trust in and suspicions about others, in addition to expectations that others have evil motives and, essentially, "are out to get you."
- **Schizoid:** Disconnection from interpersonal relationships and an extremely limited ability to express emotions.
- **Schizotypal:** Social deficits characterized by difficulties forming close relationships and distorted views of appropriate behavior.
- **Antisocial:** Disrespect for and infringement on other people's rights.
- **Borderline:** Instability in interpersonal relationships, view of self, and emotional makeup, in addition to striking impulsivity.
- **Histrionic:** Excessive emotional expression and attention-seeking behavior.
- **Narcissistic:** Pompous and pretentious behavior, constant search for admiration, and inability to have and express empathy.
- **Avoidant:** The condition of being uncomfortable in social situations, "feelings of inadequacy," and oversensitivity to negative feedback.
- **Dependent:** Needy, "submissive and clinging" behavior resulting from the persistent and extreme "need to be taken care of" and to depend on others to make decisions for them.
- **Obsessive–compulsive:** Overly extreme concern with organization and neatness, perfectionism, and control.

One major study of American adults age 18 and older found a 9.1% prevalence rate for personality disorders according to DSM-IV-TR (Diagnostic and Statistical Manual of Mental Disorders-IV-Text Revision, American Psychiatric Association, 2000) criteria (National Institute of Mental Health [NIMH], 2007b). The study estimated rates of borderline personality rates at 1.4% and antisocial personality disorder at 0.6%. Of study respondents, 39% had received treatment within the past year an average of two times, usually from general medical providers instead of mental health therapists. The study also discovered that people with personality disorders often had more than one disorder at the same time.

# What Social Workers Do in Mental Health   LO 4

Generalist social workers can address mental illness at all three practice levels. At the micro level, social workers provide case management, counseling (e.g., crisis intervention or substance abuse counseling), and intensive psychotherapy for chronically (long-term) mentally ill people. At the mezzo level, they conduct group therapy and  **EP 1, 7, 8** provide various kinds of family treatment. Finally, at the macro level, they initiate changes in organizational and public policy to improve service provision to large groups of clients. Social workers may also assume administrative or supervisory responsibilities in agencies providing any level of service.

## Case Management in Micro Practice

We have established that case management is a micro-level method of service provision whereby a social worker coordinates ongoing multiple services for a client. Specific tasks include assessing client needs and strengths, linking clients to services, planning treatment strategies, monitoring the appropriateness and effectiveness of these services, and advocating for improved service provision when necessary. Earlier we established that coordination and monitoring of services are key concepts. Case management is the treatment of choice for clients with chronic mental illness who have many ongoing needs that can be met only through services from a range of sources. The idea is that somebody has to

take responsibility for making sure service provision makes sense and is effective.

Case managers may also provide direct services to clients that are related to the need for coordinated service provision. These include "crisis intervention (e.g., locating temporary housing for desperate, homeless people), supporting clients making difficult decisions, helping to modify clients' environments (e.g., arranging for transportation within the community), and helping clients overcome emotional reactions to their crisis situations" (Kirst-Ashman & Hull, 2015b, pp. 556–557). Case management is an important role for social workers in mental health at both the BSW and the MSW levels.

*Case Example*  Amos, a case manager at a community mental health center, provides an example of what a case manager does. One of his clients, Beth, age 28, has schizophrenia. When taking her medication, she can function in the community, living in an efficiency apartment. Amos conducted her original assessment and developed a plan with her. After helping  **EP 7a, 7c, 7d, 9c** link her to the appropriate resources, he now coordinates and monitors a number of services she receives. Amos regularly talks to Beth about how she's doing and what new goals she wants to set.

Amos keeps in touch with Beth's psychiatrist, making certain she keeps her appointments and continues taking her psychotropic medication. He also makes sure she keeps appointments with her general physician (she has diabetes). Amos helped her get a part-time job at Betty's Best Butter Burger Bistro, and he maintains contact with Betty, Beth's boss, to monitor Beth's performance at work.

Amos referred her to a support group at the community health center for people who have schizophrenia and are coping with independent life in the community. He periodically contacts the group's facilitator to monitor her progress and participation there.

Beth has a sister living within a couple of miles of her apartment who helps Beth with shopping and getting to the doctor. Amos checks with her regularly to make sure no problems are surfacing. Several times, Beth has stopped taking her medication when she felt she had recovered and didn't need it. Each time, she relapsed and was eventually found wandering half-naked through a park in her neighborhood. Once Amos advocated fervently on Beth's behalf when her benefits were mistakenly slashed. In summary, Amos watches over Beth, monitors the resources she receives, and helps her get new ones when she needs them.

## Micro Practice: Psychotherapy

Chapter 4 discussed the process of generalist social work practice that reflects the foundation of social work skills. Building on this foundation, there is an infinite array of specific approaches to social work intervention.

Specialized psychotherapy is often used to treat people with a mental disorder. The purpose of this book is not to teach you how to practice psycho-
therapy. But its intent is to introduce you to the range of interventions and perspectives that social work practice can involve. Because some MSWs enter the mental health field and become psychotherapists, the philosophies of a few psychotherapeu-
tic approaches, arbitrarily chosen, will be summarized briefly here. Two broad categories among the many specific theoretical approaches include humanistic theories and cognitive-behavioral theories. (Note that the terms *psychotherapy* and *therapy* are used interchangeably in this section as the discussion focuses only on mental health, not other types of therapy not involving mental health.)

**Humanistic theories** emphasize the importance of the individual's perception of reality and experience, a focus on strengths, and an optimistic approach to human character (Grogan & Richardson, 2008). Such theories emphasize "an individual's dignity and worth and capacity for self-realization through reason" (Mish, 2008, p. 604). "These approaches tend to focus on the 'here and now' and gently challenge clients to make new choices in their lives" (Neukrug, 2011, p. 143). The two humanistic theo-
ries discussed in subsequent sections include existen-
tial therapy and person-centered therapy.

Note that earlier in the chapter cognitive-
behavioral therapy was discussed in the context of treatment for veterans with PTSD. "Cognitive-
behavioral therapy [or cognitive behavioral therapy or cognitive behavior therapy, depending on the source] does *not* exist as a distinct therapeutic technique. The term 'cognitive-behavioral therapy (CBT)' is a very general term for a classification

EP 7b, 7d, 8, 8b, 9b

of therapies with similarities. There are several approaches to cognitive-behavioral therapy, including Rational Emotive Behavior Therapy, Rational Behavior Therapy, Rational Living Therapy, Cogni-
tive Therapy, and Dialectic Behavior Therapy" (National Association of Cognitive-Behavioral Therapy [NACBT], 2010, emphasis omitted). (It is beyond the scope of this text to explain every therapy.) All of these more specific approaches under the cognitive-behavioral umbrella are based on the idea that thinking and behavior are intimately intertwined. However, each therapy has differences in its philosophy and what it emphasizes. They all have in common the concept that changing thinking will ultimately affect behavior and emotion even though the surrounding circumstances don't change (e.g., other people and the general environment) (NACBT, 2010). Corey (2013) elaborates that all of the cognitive behavioral therapies:

> *are based on a structured psycho-educational model [stressing the importance of learning], emphasize the role of homework, place responsibil-
> ity on the client to assume an active role both dur-
> ing and outside of the therapy sessions, and draw from a variety of cognitive and behavioral strate-
> gies to bring about change….*
>
> *To a large degree, [cognitive behavior therapy] … is based on the assumption that a reorganization of one's self-statements will result in a corresponding reorganization of one's behavior. (p. 291)*

The two cognitive-behavioral therapies subse-
quently discussed here include behavior therapy, which, of course, emphasizes behavior, and cognitive therapy, which stresses changing thought processes.

### Existential Therapy

Sharf (2012) describes existential therapy:

> *Existential psychotherapy deals with important life themes. Rather than prescribing techniques and methods, existential psychotherapy is an attitudi-
> nal approach to issues of living. Themes include living and dying, freedom, responsibility to self and others, finding meaning in life, and dealing with a sense of meaninglessness. More than other therapies, existential psychotherapy examines indi-
> viduals' awareness of themselves and their ability to look beyond their immediate problems and*

*daily events to problems of human existence. Because individuals do not exist in isolation from others, developing honest and intimate relationships with others is a theme throughout existential therapy. (p. 161)*

In existential therapy, expanded self-awareness is the primary goal (Corey, 2013). Clients learn to alter their view of themselves and the world. They can discover alternatives they never would have considered in the past. Additionally, as Corey (2013) reflects:

- "They learn that in many ways they are keeping themselves prisoner by some of their past decisions, and they realize that they can make new decisions.
- They learn that although they cannot change certain events in their lives they can change the way they view and react to these events.
- They learn that they are not condemned to a future similar to the past, for they can learn from their past and thereby reshape their future....
- They are able to accept their limitations yet still feel worthwhile, for they understand that they do not need to be perfect to feel worthy." (p. 147)

### Person-Centered Therapy

According to Sharf (2012), "person-centered therapy ... developed by Carl Rogers, takes a positive view of individuals, believing that they tend to move toward becoming fully functioning. Rogers's work represents a way of being rather than a set of techniques for doing therapy" (p. 207). Corey (2013) continues:

*Rogers maintained that three therapist attributes create a growth-promoting climate in which individuals can move forward and become what they are capable of becoming: (1) **congruence** (genuineness or realness), (2) **unconditional positive regard** (acceptance and caring), and (3) **accurate empathic understanding** (an ability to deeply grasp the subjective world of another person). According to Rogers, if therapists communicate these attitudes, those being helped will become less defensive and more open to themselves and their world, and they will behave in prosocial and constructive ways. (p. 178)*

Sharf (2012) further explains:

*To become fully functioning, individuals must meet their need for positive regard from others and have positive regard for themselves. With these needs met, an individual can then experience an optimal level of psychological functioning....*

*Roger's view of what constitutes congruence and psychological maturity includes openness, creativity, and responsibility.... [A] fully functioning person is not defensive but open to new experiences without controlling them. This openness to congruent relationships with others and self allows an individual to handle new and old situations creatively. With this adaptability, individuals experience an inner freedom to make decisions and to be responsible for their own lives. As part of being fully functioning, they become aware of social responsibilities and the need for fully congruent relationships with others. Rather than being self-absorbed, such individuals have needs to communicate empathically. Their sense of what is right includes an understanding of the needs of others as well as themselves. (p. 213)*

During the process of person-centered therapy, clients work to become more psychologically congruent and self-actualized, that is, more conscious about how they really feel. During treatment "individuals come to understand how they have contributed to their own problems and may not blame others for them. Experiencing genuineness, acceptance, and empathy from the therapist leads to changes in how the individual relates to others" (Sharf, 2012, p. 221). Clients enhance their ability to get close to others and experience more natural and competent relationships.

### Behavior Therapy

Antony (2014) introduces behavior (or behavioral) therapy:

*Behavior therapy aims to change factors in the environment that influence an individual's behavior as well as the ways in which individuals respond to their environment. Behavior therapists define the term behavior broadly to include motor behaviors, physiological responses, emotions, and cognitions. (p. 193)*

Several concepts characterize behavior therapy (Antony, 2014). First, it concentrates on defining, observing, and changing specific behaviors. Second, behavior therapists assume an active role in changing behavior. Third, behavior therapy includes a wide range of techniques and approaches. Fourth, procedures and practices used in behavior therapy are based on a large body of empirical research.

A basic foundation of behavior therapy involves setting specific goals. Antony (2014) explains:

> Before therapy begins, the therapist and client set treatment goals. Goals should be both specific and measurable. For example, a client's goal "to stop hitting my children" is a more appropriate behavioral goal than "to become a better parent," which is both vague and difficult to quantify. Relatedly, goals should be anchored in particular behaviors or outcomes. For example, a client who wishes to be more "successful" at work must first identify exactly what it means to be successful (e.g., working more quickly, making fewer mistakes, receiving more positive feedback from supervisors, making more money). Goals should also be realistic and achievable. Finally, timelines should be set for achieving goals. (p. 209)

"Basic principles of behavior derived from classical conditioning, operant conditioning, and modeling directly affect the development of behavioral therapeutic approaches" (Sharf, 2012, p. 324). **Classical conditioning** is a view of understanding behavior that focuses on a stimulus and the response resulting from that stimulus. (A **stimulus** is a thing or happening perceived by a person that may subsequently influence that person's response or behavior.) **Operant conditioning** is a view of understanding behavior that focuses on how behavior is affected by its consequences. **Modeling** involves learning of behavior by observing someone else demonstrating that behavior.

Sharf (2012) reflects:

> One of the first methods used to help individuals was Wolpe's systematic desensitization procedure, a gradual process of introducing relaxation to reduce fear and anxiety. Other methods use intense and prolonged exposure to the feared stimulus and may use in vivo procedures, in which the client deals with anxiety in the natural environment. Virtual reality techniques simulate a natural environment. Modeling techniques using role-playing and other methods have been derived from observational learning. (p. 324)

## Cognitive Therapy

Cognitive therapy was originated by Aaron T. Beck as an outcome of his work with people affected by depression (Corey, 2013). It emphasizes that how people think and what they believe directly affect their actions, thoughts, and emotions. Corey (2009) continues:

> Cognitive therapy perceives psychological problems as stemming from commonplace processes such as faulty thinking, making incorrect inferences on the basis of inadequate or incorrect information, and failing to distinguish between fantasy and reality.... [It] is an insight-focused therapy that emphasizes recognizing and changing negative thoughts and maladaptive beliefs.... Cognitive therapy is based on the theoretical rationale that the way people feel and behave is determined by how they perceive and structure their experience. (pp. 287–288)

**Cognitive schemas** involve how clients "think about their world and their important beliefs and assumptions about people, events, and the environment" (Sharf, 2012, p. 375). Beck and Weishaar (2011) elaborate:

> Cognitive schemas contain people's perceptions of themselves and others and of their goals and expectations, memories, fantasies, and previous learning. These greatly influence, if not control, the processing of information.
>
> In various psychopathological conditions such as anxiety disorder, depressive disorders, mania, paranoid states, obsessive–compulsive neuroses, and others, a specific bias affects how the person incorporates new information. Thus, a depressed person has a negative bias, including a negative view of self, world, and future....
>
> Contributing to these shifts are certain specific attitudes or core beliefs that predispose people under the influence of certain life situations to interpret their experiences in a biased way. These are known as cognitive vulnerabilities. For example, a person who has the belief that any minor loss represents a major deprivation may react catastrophically to even the smallest loss. (p. 277)

**Cognitive distortion** occurs when a person experiences consistently flawed and inaccurate perceptions of reality (Beck & Weishaar, 2011; Sharf, 2012). One type of cognitive distortion involves "labeling and

## APPROACHES TO PSYCHOTHERAPY

What are your thoughts about the psychotherapeutic approaches just explained?
Which approaches correspond most

closely to your perception of people and how they function? Why? Which do you think might be most effective
and why?

**EP 7a, 8a**

mislabeling" (Corey, 2009, p. 289). Sharf (2012)
explains:

> *A negative view of oneself is created by self-*
> *labeling based on some errors or mistakes. A per-*
> *son who has had some awkward incidents with*
> *acquaintances might conclude, "I'm unpopular.*
> *I'm a loser" rather than "I felt awkward talking to*
> *Harriet." In labeling and mislabeling in this way,*
> *individuals can create an inaccurate sense of them-*
> *selves or their identity. (p. 342)*

The aim of cognitive therapy is to help clients identify their unproductive and negative thoughts (cognitions), evaluate their thought patterns (cognitive
schema), and alleviate inaccurate perceptions about
self, others, or circumstances (cognitive distortions).
For example, therapists using cognitive therapy can
help depressed clients evaluate their thinking and
eventually change their perceptions and behavior by
using the following process (Beck, Rush, Shaw, &
Emery, 1979; Beck & Weishaar, 2012). First, under
a psychotherapist's direction, clients identify and
monitor negative thoughts about themselves. Second,
clients examine their schema—that is, their typical
reactions to their negative thoughts. Third, clients
assess the extent to which such negative thoughts
are valid and realistic. To what extent have they
been exaggerating or even fabricating all the negative
things they've been thinking about themselves? To
what extent are they experiencing cognitive distortion? Fourth, clients begin to develop more realistic
ways of viewing themselves and the world. What are
their actual weaknesses, and, more important, what
are their genuine strengths? Fifth, clients develop
new beliefs and ways of thinking about themselves
that are more realistic and productive.

The following section portrays a case example in
which a psychotherapist who has an MSW practices
cognitive therapy with an adult male who has
depression. This does not imply that cognitive therapy is necessarily any better or worse than other
psychotherapeutic approaches. It merely represents
an example of one type of therapy applied to one
type of problem. Practitioners must evaluate or conduct research to find the evidence regarding what
psychotherapeutic approaches are most effective
with what mental disorders and other problems.

Focus on Critical Thinking 13.2 raises questions
concerning which of the therapeutic frameworks just
discussed you think might be most effective.

### Case Example: Cognitive Therapy for Depression

In the following case a therapist successfully uses cognitive therapy with Ed, a divorced 38-year-old male
(Geary, 1992). Ed was a soft-spoken,
composed man of medium height, with
a pale complexion and slightly receding
light brown hair. He came to Juana
Dance, a psychotherapist with an MSW,
for help with his depression. Ed had been   **EP 4c**
unemployed for over a year and, because he had
nowhere else to go, was living with his parents.

He described his childhood as stable, living with
both parents and two older brothers. He mentioned
that his family was neither very demonstrative in
showing affection nor very talkative with each other.
Ed did well in school and graduated from college with
a business degree. He married Anna, his college sweet-
heart, got a managerial job in sales, and had three
daughters.

Everything seemed to be going fine until he turned
30. Suddenly his world started to crumble. His
job was going nowhere—with no promotions or

significant raises in sight. Ed told Juana that Anna, bored with the marriage, "dumped" him for Hank, a singer in a country-western band. She ran off with Hank, taking Ed's three daughters and moving to another state 1,000 miles away. This devastated Ed.

Ed subsequently quit his job and started several new ones, trying to make something go right in his life. Failing miserably, he had been forced to accept his parents' invitation to live with them.

Ed was at an all-time low. He felt listless, useless, and inadequate. Whenever he talked about anything, self-degrading comments peppered his conversation. For example, he'd say things like "It seems as if I can't do anything right," "I don't have a future so I don't have much to live for," and "What a flop I turned out to be."

During the first several sessions, Juana spent time easing Ed into the therapeutic relationship and learning about his history and current status. Ed described his typical day as sitting around a lot, watching Home Shopping Network, and bothering his parents. He rarely went out and had virtually no social life. He broke off relationships with old friends, who he  **EP 7a, 7c, 7d** felt were getting sick of all his misery and whining. He told Juana that he felt like he was carrying a picket sign that read "I'm a useless, no good piece of crap." In better, happier days, he might have said that people generally treated him as if he'd just eaten a clove of garlic and forgotten his breath mints.

Juana administered test instruments that measured Ed's level of depression and the type and incidence of his negative self-statements. Results indicated moderate to severe depression and a significant frequency of negative thoughts about himself.

With Juana's help, Ed began identifying and monitoring his negative self-thoughts. Whenever he criticized himself, Juana would discuss with him the implications of what he said and what he really meant. Juana continued to explore with Ed his schema—how he automatically experienced self-critical thoughts and how they were directly related to feeling badly about himself. Periodically Juana administered the instruments measuring depression and incidence of negative self-statements to monitor progress.

Additionally, Juana assigned Ed graded homework assignments that he completed between sessions and subsequently discussed with her. *Graded assignments* refer to tasks of increasing difficulty and complexity that expand a client's repertoire of behavior. For example, at first Ed was to talk with a friend for 10 minutes each day to start opening his social world. Later he started attending a weekly support group for divorced men. Still later, he began a job search.

When reporting his progress, Ed continued to demean himself with comments like "Aw, that's nothin'" or "Anybody could do that." Juana praised his accomplishments and emphasized how so many small steps, taken together, eventually added up to real progress. She discussed with him the extent to which his perception of himself was realistic. Where was he being exceptionally and unfairly critical about himself? What strengths was he trying to ignore instead of giving himself realistic credit for solid accomplishments?

One way Ed began to demonstrate increased awareness of self-criticism was to verbalize more frequently how Juana would respond before she said it (Geary, 1992). In other words, he would give himself the same kind of feedback she had given him many times before. For example, he'd say, "I know what you're thinking—I should appreciate how I am improving. I guess it beats being poked in the eye with a sharp stick."

Juana initiated a treatment method during therapy called the "triple column technique" to help Ed recognize cognitive distortion concerning his self-concept (Burns, 1980, p. 60; Geary, 1992). In the first column he would identify his automatic negative self-thought (e.g., "I never do anything right"). In the second column he'd identify his cognitive distortion (e.g., "Of course, I do some things right, although certainly not everything"). In the third column he'd write logical, more realistic reactions to the automatic negative self-thought (e.g., "Although I sometimes feel that my progress is as lively as a turtle's, I know that I am gradually doing better").

Although Ed suffered several setbacks when he panicked when thinking about returning to work, he generally made steady progress. His activity level markedly increased, although he experienced a few ups and downs. His scores on the instruments measuring depression and incidence of negative self-statements also continued to improve.

Treatment began to focus on additional behavioral means Ed could use to validate his self-worth and improve how he thought about himself. Home-work assignments included talking to other people such as family members about his insights in therapy and seeking their perspective (Geary, 1992). He even contacted old friends he hadn't seen in years. What he found out was that a lot of people really cared about him. They appreciated him for being the pleasant, thoughtful, kind person with a good sense of humor that he was. This bolstered his self-confidence.

He got a dog, found a full-time job, and even started dating. Life still wasn't perfect, and dating was a lot harder than he remembered it in college. However, he was generally much happier and more self-confident, and emotionally stronger than he had been prior to therapy.

During his last session, Ed reverted to some imag-ery he had used during an earlier meeting, which can be a useful therapeutic technique (Geary, 1992). He indicated his new picket sign read, "I'm okay and proud of it." He said he was amazed at how much better other people responded to him now. He added that he responded to himself a lot better, too. He also told Juana that he felt he could look at himself, the world, and others more realistically now. Jokingly, he added, "And Hank really can't sing."

## The Use of Psychotropic Drugs to Treat Mental Disorders

We have established that psychotropic drugs are employed by psychiatrists and other physicians to alter thinking, mood, and behavior. Classes of psychotropic medication include antipsychotic, anti-depressant, mood-stabilizing, anti-anxiety, and psy-chostimulant (Francis, 2011; National Alliance on Mental Illness [NAMI], 2014). These are frequently used to treat various mental disorders, often very effectively. Their uses, in addition to examples of generic drugs in each category and their brand names (in parentheses), are given here (Francis, 2011; NAMI, 2014):

- **Antipsychotic drugs** are used to treat schizophre-nia. Examples are thioridazine (Mellaril) and chlorpromizine (Thorazine).
- **Antidepressant drugs** are employed in the treat-ment of major depression and anxiety disorders, particularly panic disorders. Examples are ami-triptyline (Elavil) and fluoxetine (Prozac).
- **Mood-stabilizing drugs** are used to treat bipolar disorder. An example is lithium (Lithobid).

- **Anti-anxiety drugs** are used to control anxiety dis-orders and insomnia. Examples are alprazolam (Xanax) and diazepam (Valium).
- **Psychostimulant drugs** are used to treat attention deficit hyperactivity disorder (ADHD). (ADHD is a syndrome of learning and behavioral prob-lems beginning in childhood that is characterized by a persistent pattern of inattention, excessive physical movement, and impulsivity that appear in at least two settings [including home, school, work, or social contexts].) An example is methyl-phenidate (Ritalin).

There has been significant controversy over the use of many psychotropic drugs. Are they used too frequently when other means of treatment would suffice? Are drugs prescribed too freely for children with ADHD? Why does the "dramatic increase" in their use "have some claiming that such use hides the 'true' origins of problems and leads to stunted growth and underuse of effective psychosocial inter-ventions"? Do some anti-depressants "change or modify personality" so that people are no longer really themselves?

These issues notwithstanding, psychotropic drugs have become a mainstay in mental health treatment. Thus it's critical for mental health professionals to review current research carefully and use such med-ications carefully.

Note that psychotropic drugs are not used for all disorders and that many other methods of treatment exist and are being developed. Focus on Critical Thinking 13.3 examines the use of electroconvulsive therapy.

## Mezzo Practice: Running Treatment Groups

As discussed in Chapter 5, *treatment groups* help individuals solve personal problems, change unwanted behaviors, cope with stress, and improve their quality of life. Types of treatment groups include therapy, sup-port, educational, growth, and socialization: here are some examples:

- *Therapy group:* A group of people diagnosed with schizophrenia who live in the community and meet at a local community health center.
- *Support group:* A group of adults caring for their parents who have Alzheimer's disease.
- *Educational group:* A group of parents learning about effective child management techniques.

## FOCUS ON CRITICAL THINKING 13.3

# ELECTROSHOCK THERAPY IS BACK[5]

What do you picture when you think about electroshock therapy (now referred to as **electroconvulsive therapy [ECT]**)? Is it a group of physicians and nurses gathered around a patient lying on a gurney with electrodes protruding from his head? Do you picture his body convulsing violently and then him drooling like an imbecile? Following treatment, might you perceive him as being docile and devoid of personality?

EP 9c

Electroconvulsive therapy (ECT) has been a controversial technique in modern psychiatry (Mental Health America [MHA], 2011b; National Mental Health Association [NMHA], 2008). It is used to treat mental health problems such as depression or schizophrenia, usually when drug therapies fail or patients are acutely suicidal (Mayo Clinic, 2015; NMHA, 2008). Apparently at least 100,000 Americans are treated with electroconvulsive therapy each year, although the actual number is hard to pinpoint because reporting is not formally required (MHA, 2011b; NMHA, 2008). The controversy focuses on the fact that for some it works wonderfully to temporarily control depressive and bipolar disorders. For others it represents a nightmare of memory loss, brain malfunction, and continued mood disorder. Cloud (2001) suggests that "it works a little bit like banging the side of a fuzzy TV—it just works, except when it doesn't" (p. 60).

So how does ECT work? No one really knows, except that it affects brain chemistry. Electrodes are placed on a patient's head, and an electrical burst powerful enough to light a 40-watt bulb is sent through the patient's brain usually for less than 60 seconds. Currently, prior to the procedure, patients are given a muscle relaxant and anesthesia to eliminate pain and prevent the violent flailing of limbs that caused broken bones in the past. During ECT, a mouth guard is inserted to protect the tongue and teeth, and an oxygen mask is put in place to sustain breathing. ECT usually involves 6–12 sessions administered two to three times per week. Theories about how ECT works focus on chemical interactions in the brain. It is thought that the electrical current either enhances the transmission of neurological impulses or releases hormones that influence (and thus improve) mood.

ECT technically dates back to the 16th century when torpedo fish (also known as electric rays), which transmit electrical impulses, were used to treat headaches.

During the 1930s, insulin and camphor were used to induce seizures and temporarily improve some mental health conditions. "In the Oscar-winning film *A Beautiful Mind,* math scholar John Nash undergoes such insulin shock treatment for schizophrenia" (Griner, 2002). In 1938 two Italians, Ugo Cerletti and Lucio Bini, were the first to actually use an electrical current to treat a schizophrenic man experiencing severe hallucinations.

Curtis Hartmann, age 47, a lawyer in Westfield, Massachusetts, who indicated that he had 100 treatments altogether, remains an avid advocate of ECT (Cloud, 2001). He stated it's the only treatment that had been consistently able to control his bipolar disorder for more than a decade. He felt infinitely better after a treatment, stating that "depression is like being a corpse with a pulse" (Cloud, 2001, p. 62).

Similarly, Diane (no last name) noted that "after numerous hospital visits over a two-year period, ECT treatments were presented as my last chance at controlling depression. Medications were unable to control the illness." Although she did experience some temporary memory loss, she concluded, "In retrospect, the ECT treatments allowed the depression to improve significantly to be treatable by medications alone" (Voices of Experience, 2002).

Opponents of the approach vehemently protest its use. For example, Liz McGillicuddy, "once a decorated Marine Lt. Colonel with several college degrees to her name," underwent ECT when suffering from severe depression ("The Horror," 2000). McGillicuddy claims that the "results were devastating." She subsequently couldn't remember her childhood or "anything" about her past; she also lost "her future" as she was "unable to form new memories" ("The Horror," 2000).

Juli Lawrence provides another example of a negative experience. Prior to her undergoing ECT, her attending physician told her family that "it was an absolute cure for depression." However, he did not caution her and her family about the potential side effects such as memory loss, "which can range from forgetting where you parked your car to forgetting that you own a car at all" (Cloud, 2001, p. 60). She attempted suicide a week later and subsequently claimed that she couldn't remember a thing from two years prior to the treatment to several months following it. Other people continue to voice complaints concerning memory loss and difficulties in thought processing (DailyStrength, 2012; NAMI, 2012).

*(continued)*

**FOCUS ON CRITICAL THINKING 13.3 (continued)**

Despite the debate over ECT, its use will likely continue. It does provide at least short-term relief for some people experiencing some types of severe mental disorders who don't respond to other treatment modalities (Mayo Clinic, 2015). But ECT is not a cure-all. Its effects are often only temporary and effects can vary radically from one recipient to the next. In any event, apparently ECT, for better or worse, is here.

## Critical Thinking Questions

What are your opinions about ECT? Do you think the advantages outweigh the disadvantages, or vice versa?

Would you ever consider ECT for yourself or for someone close to you? What are the reasons for your answer?

[5]Facts for this highlight are from "Electroshock Therapy Slowly Gains Greater Use" (2000); Familydoctor.org (2003); Griner (2002); Henderson (2002); Marcotty (1999); Mayo Foundation for Medical Education and Research (2010); Mental Health America (2011b); National Mental Health Association (2005, 2008); Paplos (2002); Sabbatini (2002); Sackheim, Devanand, and Nobler (2002); and U.S. Office of the Surgeon General (2001).

---

- *Growth group:* A group of gay men focusing on gay pride issues (Toseland & Rivas, 2012).
- *Socialization group:* A current events group at a nursing home that gets together to discuss their opinions.

## Mezzo Practice: Treating Families

Collins, Jordan, and Coleman (2013) state that the major purpose of social work with families is to help families "learn to function more competently while meeting the developmental and emotional needs of *all* members" (p. 2). They continue that "family social work embraces the following objectives:

1. Reinforce family strengths to get families ready for change (or intervention).
2. Create concrete changes in family functioning to sustain effective and satisfying daily routines independent of formal helpers.
3. Provide additional support following family therapy so families maintain effective family functioning.
4. Build relationships between families and their environmental supports to ensure that basic needs of members are being met....
5. Address the crisis needs of the family in a timely fashion so they can effectively address more long-standing issues" (p. 3).

Family counseling can involve virtually any aspect of family communication and dynamics. Chapter 9 discussed family preservation and social work with families at high risk of child maltreatment. Other issues for which families may need

treatment include members' inability to get along, parental inability to control children's behavior, divorce, stepfamily issues, or crises (e.g., a death in the family, an unwanted pregnancy, unemployment, a natural disaster).

At this point, are you considering a career in mental health? Highlight 13.6 poses some suggestions for helping you think about a possible career in mental health.

## Macro Practice and Policy Practice in Mental Health

Social workers practice in the mental health macro arena in at least three ways. First, they can advocate for positive change on behalf of large groups of clients. (The following section on managed care discusses some issues of concern and calls for advocacy to address these issues.) Second, social workers who function as managers and administrators in mental health agencies can strive to improve policies and service provision in collaboration with colleagues and clients. (A later section discusses the need to improve cultural competence in the mental health macro system.) Third, social workers can strive to develop innovative programs to meet mental health needs.

For example, Johnson, Noe, Collins, Strader, and Bucholtz (2000) describe a project in which members of local church communities were recruited "to implement and evaluate alcohol and other drug (AOD) abuse prevention

**EP 3a, 3b, 5c, 8c, 8d**

# HIGHLIGHT 13.6 — ARE YOU THINKING ABOUT WORKING IN THE MENTAL HEALTH FIELD?

If you're considering a social work major, choosing a field of practice is not necessarily easy. A number of issues, problem areas, or populations may sound interesting to you. There are at least eight suggestions for exploring the mental health field before you commit to a professional job and career (Kelly, 2002). Any of these suggestions can offer excellent opportunities for networking with mental health professionals. They may be effective ways of talking with practitioners about what they do and how they do it, in addition to finding out what jobs are available.

**EP 1, 1b**

1. Check out job possibilities and mental health issues through Mental Health America (MHA) at http://www.mentalhealthamerica.net/. The organization's "programs and initiatives fulfil" its "mission of promoting mental health, preventing mental disorders and achieving victory over mental illness through advocacy, education, research and services" (MHA, 2014).

2. Become a member of the U.S. Psychiatric Rehabilitation Association (USPRA) (formerly the International Association of Psychosocial Rehabilitation Services [IAPSRS]) at http://www.uspra.org/. This is "an organization of psycho-social rehabilitation agencies, practitioners, and interested organizations and individuals dedicated to promoting, supporting and strengthening community-oriented rehabilitation services and resources for persons with psychiatric disabilities" (USPRA, 2004).

3. Become a member of the National Association of Social Workers (NASW), an organization with chapters in all 50 states, Washington, D.C., Puerto Rico, the Virgin Islands, and Guam, that has 130,000 members (NASW, 2015) (http://www.naswdc.org/). NASW also provides an excellent resource for networking with social workers practicing in mental health. Members receive 10 issues annually of *NASW News,* containing updates on both issues and jobs in mental health and other social work fields of practice, in addition to the quarterly professional journal *Social Work.* "NASW membership connects you with cutting-edge ideas, current information, practice

expertise, and quality resources" (NASW, 2005). Numerous continuing education programs are offered in specific aspects of mental health and other areas in which social workers practice.

4. Volunteer at a local crisis intervention program. Such programs usually offer excellent training to prepare volunteers for answering crisis hotlines. This may offer experience in addressing a wide range of crises (for example, suicide threats, drug overdoses, loneliness, and depression). You never know what the next phone call may bring.

5. Work as a paraprofessional or volunteer in an inpatient mental health clinic or in other facilities with clients who are dealing with mental health issues. If inpatient hospitals are unavailable due to de-institutionalization, seek out opportunities "in community-based mental health centers, group homes for … [people with mental health issues], or day treatment programs" for people with chronic problems (Kelly, 2002, p. 5).

6. Work or volunteer at a homeless shelter. Although being homeless by no means indicates that a person has a mental disorder, many people who were living in inpatient facilities have been discharged into the community. Sometimes the community lacks funding and an adequate support network to sustain these people. The result may be that they stop taking their medication and suffer a significantly decreased ability to function—involving work, socializing with others, and maintaining a place to live. One result may be homelessness. Homeless shelters may let you learn about community resources and link people with supportive services and benefits so they can maintain themselves in the community.

7. "Attend open meetings of support groups related to mental health" (Kelly, 2002, p. 5). Groups may be available for people with specific types of disorders (for example, schizophrenia, anxiety disorders, or eating disorders) or for family members of people with disorders. Support groups can teach you about the mental health issues people must address and provide suggestions for how to cope. However, make sure the meetings are "open" (i.e., anyone who is interested may attend). Always honestly identify your purpose for being there.

*(continued)*

**HIGHLIGHT 13.6 (continued)**

8. Use continuing education opportunities to explore your interests. NASW is only one of the numerous organizations addressing mental health issues that provide chances to learn about specific mental health disorders and treatment approaches. The following are examples of continuing education topics from one brochure: "Eating Disorders"; "Sex Matters for Women"; "Master Your Panic"; "The Ethics of Professional Practice";  **EP 1**

"Anxiety and Depression"; "Child and Adolescent Counseling"; "Overcoming Binge Eating"; and "Anger Management" (Homestead Schools, 2004).

Note that after graduation your state might have certification or licensing requirements for a designated number of continuing education hours (CEHs) or units (CEUs). You can take these classes before you graduate, too, if there's an area in which you're exceptionally interested and are willing to pay the fee to attend.

---

programs" (p. 1). "Community advocate teams" were created, made up of significant church leaders, usually pastors (p. 7). These teams subsequently recruited families with children at high risk of AOD abuse. Families and children were then given "comprehensive training" consisting of 25 weeks of 2½-hour sessions along with case management services (pp. 10–11). Incentives were offered to keep families in the program, including "the provision of food for participants, day care assistance, family portraits, transportation provisions, social activities, and nominal payments for the research interviews" (p. 12). Evaluation research revealed that the program was "highly successful in White American rural and suburban church communities" although "only partially successful in urban African American church communities" (p. 21).

# Evidence-Based Practice in Mental Health    `LO 5`

Evidence-based practice in social work relies on the knowledge and established proof, the best evidence available, to determine what works. This, in turn, informs social workers how to proceed in planning and implementing interventions. At least five trends in mental health practice have been found to be evidence-based and effective (Solomon,  **EP 4c** 2008). They include comprehensive community support, family education and support, work encouragement and assistance, coordinated treatment for concurrent substance abuse issues, and educational and coping skill development groups. These should

be emphasized and pursued in future mental health program and practice skill development to increase effective treatment. Note that they involve various aspects of micro, mezzo, and macro practice.

## Comprehensive Community Support

Comprehensive community support and treatment involves establishing teams of professionals who are available in the community to work with people on a 24/7 basis. Development of such teams and involvement of people with mental illness in the community would require assertive and resourceful action. Intervention would involve find-  **EP 7d** ing and linking people who have psychiatric conditions with resources, providing treatment, and monitoring progress. This approach would focus on the 10–20% of people with mental illness who have the most relentless, extreme conditions that require continued monitoring (Solomon, 2008). Many of these people are currently homeless and adrift outside of support systems. Community teams would address whatever the clients' needs might involve, including securing housing, enrolling in vocational training, finding employment, getting and taking psychotropic medication, or establishing and monitoring support systems. The idea is to keep people with severe forms of mental illness actively involved in a productive life as part of the community.

## Family Education and Support

Family education and support targets the families of people with severe mental illness. Evidence proves that educating the family about mental illness and teaching family members problem-solving and coping skills have positive results for the person with the psychiatric disorder. Family members become better able to provide social support for the client to help him or her maintain a healthier existence in the community. Usually, a case manager oversees service provision and helps family members make certain the client takes prescribed medication.

## Work Encouragement and Assistance

Work encouragement and assistance involves ongoing provision of support to a client with a psychiatric disorder as he or she prepares for, seeks, obtains, and continues to work. This is another program that should provide ongoing support instead of limited treatment. Evidence indicates that this results in the enhanced ability of a person with a mental illness to maintain and support him- or herself in the community through employment.

## Coordinated Treatment for Concurrent Substance Abuse Issues

The current health-care environment emphasizes designated treatments for specific diagnoses. Therefore, in that context a person with a psychiatric disorder would receive a diagnosis and be treated by a professional according to the health-care organization's criteria. If that same person also was diagnosed with a sub-  **EP 3a, 8d** stance abuse disorder, in typical managed care environments, for example, that problem would be treated elsewhere by a different provider using the criteria established for that condition. Evidence concerning effective mental health practice indicates that this uncoordinated approach is not as effective as treatment of the two diagnoses together by the same provider. The multiple problems experienced by any individual are intertwined and interrelated. Therefore, to treat them as separate conditions is much less effective and really doesn't make much sense. Advocacy is needed to change the health-care provision system so that it will allow for and support treatments that are effective—namely, more coordinated, comprehensive approaches to mental illness and substance abuse.

## Educational and Coping Skill Development Groups

The fifth evidence-based best practice approach for people with mental health problems involves forming groups of clients. Goals are to help group members better understand their psychiatric conditions and develop methods to cope with them. Teaching people with psychiatric disorders how to manage their conditions and symptoms has been proven effective. Groups have the advantages of providing members with mutual support and the sharing of ideas about how to monitor medication and cope with situations related to the illness. The recommended protocol involves weekly sessions for a period of three to six months (Solomon, 2008). Family members and other members of a client's support system can also attend and learn. An alternative to group work is provision of education and the development of skills on an individual basis. Evidence has shown that this decreases relapses, increases adherence to medication schedules, and enhances the development and use of coping skills to control problematic behaviors.

At this point we have discussed various aspects of what social workers do in mental health and some of the approaches proven to be effective. Issues addressed next involve other dimensions of working in the mental health system. These include managed care, which is the context for service provision, and the importance of cultural competence when working with clients.

# Managed Care Policies and Programs in Mental Health LO 6

Most of the same issues apply to managed care in mental health as in other health-care settings, as discussed in Chapter 12. There **managed care** was defined as "a wide range of health plans and practices that depart from the traditional model of private health insurance provided by one's employer" (Kornblum & Julian, 2009, p. 61). It is "a healthcare system under which the insurer [the managed care organization] controls the person's health care, and health-care providers agree to accept a set fee per treatment or a flat rate per patient" (Chapin, 2014, pp. 1–22). An identified group or range of providers of health and mental health-care contracts with managed care agencies to provide health care at a negotiated rate. Two primary principles promoted by managed care involve retaining quality and access while controlling costs. In other words, care should be readily accessible and of high quality, and yet be as inexpensive as possible. This is a hard thing to accomplish. There is much pressure on physicians and clinicians to find the least expensive treatment modalities possible for any particular client in order to minimize costs. For example, because psychiatric hospitalization is very expensive, there is pressure to keep clients in that setting for as brief a time as possible. This pressure exists even when the client needs that kind of intensive treatment for a longer period. Less intensive settings, of course, include group homes and outpatient treatment facilities. Focus on Critical Thinking 13.4 questions the real intent of managed care.

## FOCUS ON CRITICAL THINKING 13.4

## WHAT IS THE REAL INTENT OF MANAGED CARE: CONTROL COSTS OR IMPROVE EFFECTIVENESS?

Mechanic, McAlpine, and Rochefort (2014) cite at least three concepts important in understanding the impact of managed care on mental health service provision: "capitation," "gatekeeping," and "utilization management" (pp. 193–195). **Capitation**, discussed in Chapter 12, is

**EP 3a, 5c**

a form of payment involving a fixed, predetermined payment per person for a specified range of services for a fixed period of time.... The capitation received by a provider organization is the same regardless of how many services the person actually uses or what they cost. Some provision can be made to adjust capitation to take account of differences in age, sex, illness history, or other characteristics, but the basic idea in any case is that such prospective payment induces providers to carefully consider how they use expensive resources. Use of too many expensive services can lead to financial losses, and efficient practices can result in higher earnings.

*(Mechanic et al., 2014, p. 193)*

A difference between mental health and other health care often involves the intensity of services needed (Dulmus & Roberts, 2008; Mechanic et al., 2014). With general health problems, managed care providers assume that patient claims will vary greatly in any one year, with some people getting very sick unpredictably. However, they also assume that most people will not get sick, so costs are spread out over a large number of people (Mechanic et al., 2014). Thus insurance premiums from the many who don't get that sick and their employers support health-care services for the few who do. People with mental illness, however, often require much

more intensive care over long periods, and sometimes forever. This can be very expensive for managed care organizations. Hence managed care programs usually distinguish between mental health and general health benefits, placing more stringent limitations on those available for mental health (Dulmus & Roberts, 2008; Mechanic et al., 2014).

Note that many people with mental illness don't have their own insurance, but receive benefits through government programs such as Medicare or Medicaid. "Both private insurers and government programs commonly contract with managed care companies to provide services for persons with behavioural disorders" and mental health issues (Mechanic et al., 2014, p. 199). The manner in which managed care programs address mental health issues varies widely. It's more difficult and expensive to treat people who have more severe, long-term disorders. Figuring out how to fund treatment for the mentally ill population with its intensive need for service is a complex process.

A second concept concerning managed care and mental health involves the **gatekeeping** function of a person's primary care physician. Gatekeeping is the process of monitoring and controlling access to services. Generally, patients in a managed care program pick their own doctor from a limited list. They then must go through this doctor to get referrals to any specialists they may need (e.g., psychotherapists, neurologists, ophthalmologists, proctologists). The main purpose of gatekeeping is to make certain patients see specialists only when necessary, essentially to cut down on costs. One problem is that a primary care physician may not be highly knowledgeable about a particular client's type of mental health problem—especially more severe, more chronic, or rarer disorders. Physicians may also be

*(continued)*

**FOCUS ON CRITICAL THINKING 13.4** *(continued)*

under pressure to make a number of referrals that fall within a targeted range, no more and no less, regardless of patients' real needs (Mechanic et al., 2014).

A third basic concept in managed care is **utilization management**, the requirement that certain medical and mental health services must be authorized ahead of time; otherwise the managed care organization won't pay for them. This involves a clinician or physician contacting the managed care organization and explaining the problem in sufficient detail to get permission for the service or procedure. A managed care representative, often a utilization reviewer or case manager, then reviews the documentation and, using a structured set of rules and steps, determines whether the symptoms and diagnosis warrant the requested procedure. There is potential to appeal decisions, but such appeals may "involve considerable time, effort, and hassle" (Mechanic et al., 2014, p. 195). In this process, clinicians have lost significant decision-making power regarding what should and can be done to help clients. Mechanic and his colleagues (2014) comment:

> Overall, the quality of utilization review is only as good as the quality of the criteria used and the experience and judgment of reviewers. Companies that offer these services have different operating procedures, as well as reviewers who may vary in training and experience. Companies also supervise reviewers in different ways. Some depend on carefully worked-out algorithms [meticulously defined step-by-step procedures for coming to decisions]; others depend to a greater extent on the professional judgements of staff. (p. 209)

Concerning the existence and effectiveness of managed care, Mechanic and his colleagues (2014) conclude:

> The complexity of organizational strategies, the many ways of combining them, and the different populations studied make it difficult to reach generalizable conclusions about managed care performance. Research is helpful in identifying particularly useful or damaging activities, and when findings are reasonably consistent across settings and populations, we can have more confidence in them. Most studies simply compare some form of managed care organization with some form of traditional care, measuring outcomes such as utilization, costs, rehospitalizations, and functional status [of patients]....
>
> The practice of managed mental health care is even less experienced and more uncertain than other areas [of managed health care].... To be sure, it is essential to be vigilant about underservice and other potential abuses. But it is also important to view managed care as an opportunity to define mental health needs more sharply, to develop broader and better integrated systems of mental health management, to define treatment norms in line with empirical evidence, and to develop performance indicators for tracking the provision of services. Managed care opens the door for training and using different types of mental health personnel, directing them to tasks badly neglected within a fragmented mental health sector. Managed care is here to stay for the foreseeable future. Simply railing against it has little point. The challenge is to evaluate and shape its constituent components so that the best possible outcomes for persons with mental illness and other disabilities may be achieved. (pp. 203, 213)

## Critical Thinking Questions

What do you think are the strengths and weaknesses of managed care in mental health? To what extent do you support or fail to support it? What are your reasons?

---

Social workers are responsible for advocating for their clients. Therefore, they should advocate on the behalf of people with mental illness. "Advocacy forms the root of this profession and is needed now more than ever to infuse social work values into insurance-dominated interests"; there are at least three specific suggestions

**EP 5c, 8d**

for pursuing this (Vandivort-Warren, 1998, p. 263). First, social workers can fight for more adequate funding for mental health services. Second, states should "be actively involved in evaluating the services provided under managed care rather than delegating quality concerns to managed care firms" (p. 264). The latter resembles asking you to decide what grade you deserve for this course. Third, social workers can advocate for services that go beyond mere "medical necessity" and help empower people to improve their psychosocial functioning and quality of life.

# Cultural Competence in Mental Health Settings

**LO 7**

**Cultural competence** has been defined as "mastery of a particular set of knowledge, skills, policies, and programs used by the social worker that address the cultural needs of individuals, families, groups, and communities" (Lum, 2005, p. 4). People of color underutilize the U.S. mental health system (Greeno, 2008; Leong, 2011; NIMH, 2007a, 2010; USDHHS, 1999). These groups include (1) African Americans, (2) Asians and Pacific Islanders [APIs], (3) Hispanics and Latinos, and (4) Native Americans, Alaskan Natives, and Hawaiian Natives.

**EP 2, 2a, 7b, 8b**

Several characteristics of these groups differentiate them to various degrees from the White mainstream (USDHHS, 1999). First, their cultural orientation in terms of values, traditions, and beliefs often conflicts with the existing mental health system. Second, for many reasons, these groups generally have lower income levels and higher levels of poverty. Third, their generally lower socioeconomic status (as measured by such variables as income, education, and occupation) is clearly related to mental illness.

## Barriers to Receiving Mental Health Services

Many people of color find the mental health system to be threatening, unresponsive, and noncompliant with many of their beliefs. Five barriers to these groups' access to services are lack of help-seeking behavior, mistrust, stigma, cost, and clinician bias (USDHHS, 1999).

### Lack of Help-Seeking Behavior

To receive services, people must acknowledge that a problem exists and seek help to address it. We have established that for various reasons people of color don't seek out and receive mental health services to the extent that White people do.

Yamashiro and Matsuoka (1997) explain some of the reasons people of Asian cultural heritage fail to utilize the mental health system adequately. They resemble some of the reasons Asian Americans may fail to seek formal services for other health problems, as discussed in Chapter 12. Reasons include an emphasis on collectivism and keeping problems within the family, communication differences based on cultural values and experience, and an association between mental illness, on the one hand, and physical and spiritual conditions, on the other.

As earlier chapters explained, the worldview of Asian Americans and Pacific Islanders (API) involves a greater sense of collective identity than dominant Euro-American culture, which stresses the importance of individualism. Dependence on the family, extended family, and cultural community are emphasized. The implication is that API people will first turn to their families and others in their cultural community to address problems, including mental health issues, before turning to strangers, whether professionals or not (Paniagua, 2014; Sandhu & Madathil, 2013). An Asian perspective views mental illness as shameful and something to be hidden versus something that can be helped or cured with appropriate treatment (Diller, 2015).

A second reason for underutilization of mental health services involves language. Not only might Asian American immigrants speak a different language or at least use a different language as their primary one, they also might use language differently in general. The Western world emphasizes the importance of people talking about emotions and feelings to improve how they feel. A clear connection between emotions and language is assumed. In Eastern psychology, no such clear connection exists (Kim & Park, 2013; Sandhu & Madathi, 2013). Paniagua (2014) explains:

> Asians often respond to the verbal communication of others by being quiet and passive. They may go to a great deal of effort to avoid offending others, sometimes answering all questions affirmatively to be polite even when they do not understand the questions, and they tend to avoid eye contact. (p. 122)

In Asian cultures "language may not accommodate all that individuals think and feel—especially for those who are not socialized to use language as a primary means for expressing feelings" (Yamashiro & Matsuoka, 1997, p. 463). Participating in some form of therapy that emphasizes talking about feelings and behavior may make no sense in the context of traditional Asian culture (Brammer, 2012).

A third reason Asian Americans and Pacific Islanders fail to seek mental health treatment involves their linkage of mental illness with physical and spiritual conditions (Brammer, 2012). Brammer (2012) explains that "mental illness is attributed to karma (either from the individual's present choices, past life, or family actions). Sometimes, the divine element becomes all-important, and mental health may be equated with spiritual unrest projected onto the individual from a vengeful spirit.... These spiritual elements will likely correspond to physical complaints, with the two working for or against each other. The worse a person's physical functioning, the more severe the affective symptoms may become" (pp. 158–159). This perspective may make treatment for mental illness as its own entity irrelevant.

Native American people also often fail to seek and receive formal mental health services for other reasons. First, like Asian Americans, they tend to address matters within the family and the tribe before turning to outside help (Paniagua, 2014). Second, Native Americans may avoid services because of a history of racist treatment and past bad experiences with the system (Garrett et al., 2013; Weaver, 2013). Some Native Americans who have had involvement with the mental health system note how biased it is concerning Western beliefs, which often clash with traditional cultural values.

### Mistrust

Mistrust is a second barrier to people of color receiving mental health treatment (Evans, 2013; Paniagua, 2014; USDHHS, 1999). For example, "considering the history of discrimination, psychological abuse, microaggressions [daily subtle and not so subtle reminders of being regarded in a different way because of racial or ethnic group membership], and continued racism in the United States, African Americans have a healthy distrust of European Americans, the government, and its institutions" (Diller, 2015; Evans, 2013, p. 145).

Central and South American immigrants and many from Southeast Asia who have experienced oppression and imprisonment, and have even had family members murdered in their countries of origin, fear involvement with any system, including that of mental health services (USDHHS, 1999). Illegal immigrants from Mexico also fear involvement because they dread being deported.

Native Americans have a long history of negative experiences with White mainstream culture. These include facing recurring attempts to squelch their traditional culture and absorb them into the mainstream: being denied U.S. citizenship until 1924; and not having a constitutional right to pursue traditional religious practices until the American Indian Religious Freedom Act of 1978 was passed (Herring, 1999).

### Stigma

A **stigma** is a smear of shame and reproach upon one's reputation. People of color often don't want to suffer the stigma of being labeled mentally ill (Kim & Park, 2013; USDHHS, 1999). African Americans generally make every effort to combat mental illness themselves, without having to rely on external formal resources (USDHHS, 1999). There is a strong tradition of shame regarding mental illness in many Asian American families; because of their collective identity, what one family member does also affects how other family members are viewed (Kim & Park, 2013). The mental illness of one family member makes the others feel ashamed, so it makes sense to keep it a secret instead of seeking help.

### Cost

Cost is yet another barrier to people of color using mental health services (Dulmus & Roberts, 2008; USDHHS, 1999). We have established that people of color generally have lower incomes than their White counterparts. Not only are they more unlikely than Whites to be covered by private health insurance, but even those who have such benefits underutilize services (USDHHS, 1999). As of this writing, it is unknown how the Affordable Care Act will affect this issue in the future.

### Clinician Bias

Clinician bias is the fifth barrier to people of color utilizing mental health services (Dulmus & Roberts, 2008; Paniagua, 2014; USDHHS, 1999). How the assessing clinician perceives a person's emotional state and behavioral symptoms directly relates to the diagnosis. Clinicians who are unfamiliar with the cultural customs of people having  **EP 1b, 2c** different beliefs, values, and behaviors may well misdiagnose the problem. Behaviors considered appropriate for other cultures might be considered quite inappropriate in Western eyes. For example,

> *Latino families seem to be more tolerant of unusual behavior, such as hearing voices or having delusions of grandeur, because of the way Latino cultures view religion.... In the Latino culture, people often talk to Jesus and the saints and feel close to spirits, so family members are not as concerned about a patient hearing voices as they are by disruptive or disrespectful behavior.*
>
> *(Schram & Mandell, 2000, pp. 176–177)*

Similarly, for Seneca Indians "such attributes as having visions and guiding one's life according to spirits may incorrectly appear to be symptoms of a serious mental disorder such as schizophrenia" when they are really expressions of traditional religious practices (Earle, 1999, p. 434).

Several studies report significant bias on the part of clinicians diagnosing African Americans for schizophrenia and depression; African Americans are much more likely than Whites to be diagnosed with schizophrenia and less likely to be diagnosed with depression (Evans, 2013; Paniagua, 2014; USDHHS, 1999).

Highlight 13.7 focuses on what can be done to improve mental health services to people of color.

## Macro Perspectives on Cultural Competence

From a macro perspective, not only do mental health agencies need to "employ individuals with multicultural counseling skills, but the agency itself needs to have a 'multicultural culture'" (Sue et al., 1998, p. 103). This involves establishing an organizational environment that celebrates diversity. Administrators should empower staff members by helping them develop and employ culturally competent skills. Agencies should be sensitive to the cultural perspectives of their clients and responsive to their needs.

Two important concepts concerning organizations are cultural competence and cultural proficiency. **Culturally competent mental health organizations** display "continuing self-assessment regarding culture, careful attention to the dynamics of difference, continuous expansion of cultural knowledge and resources, and a variety of adaptations to service models to better meet the

EP 4a, 4c, 5c, 8d

needs of culturally diverse populations" (Cross, Bazron, Dennis, & Isaacs, 1989, p. 17). Such agencies have a diverse staff reflecting a range of racial and cultural backgrounds. Administrators and staff have clear ideas about what cultural competence involves. Staff members have frequent opportunities to enhance their level of cultural competence. Any services delivered to specific cultural groups are viewed as a vital part of an agency's total package of programs.

**Culturally proficient agencies** strive to expand knowledge about cultural competence by "conducting research, developing new therapeutic approaches based on culture, and disseminating the results of demonstration projects" (Cross et al., 1989, p. 17). Few organizations ever reach this level of proficiency. Such organizations serve as dynamic models for creative program development focusing on cultural competence in other programs.

---

**HIGHLIGHT 13.7**   ## WHAT CAN BE DONE TO IMPROVE MENTAL HEALTH SERVICES TO PEOPLE OF COLOR?

An obvious suggestion for improving services for people of color involves all social workers continuously striving to enhance their own cultural competence. Developing guidelines to assist individual social workers in their practice is also helpful (Snowden, 2000). Lum (2003), for example, describes a cultural competence framework for social work that emphasizes four primary dimensions of competence. The first is *cultural awareness*—consciousness of one's own cultural values and

EP 1, 2b

"of ethnicity and racism and its impact on professional attitude, perception, and behavior" (p. 31). Second, *knowledge acquisition* is the process of gaining and organizing knowledge to critically think about ethnicity and to better understand its significance. Third, *skill development* involves learning effective ways to communicate with people of other cultures and applying culturally sensitive techniques to improve interventions. Finally, *inductive learning* is the creative quest for new information and the sharing of new ideas with others to enhance practice effectiveness.

# Chapter Summary

The following summarizes this chapter's content as it relates to the learning objectives presented at the beginning of the chapter. Chapter content will help prepare students to:

**LO1 Examine the wide range of mental health settings in which social workers practice.**

A large percentage of social workers practice in some aspect of the mental health field. A critical concept in mental health treatment is client treatment in the least restrictive setting possible. Mental health settings that employ social workers include inpatient mental and psychiatric hospitals, residential treatment centers for children and adolescents, group homes, psychiatric units in general hospitals, outpatient treatment agencies, employee assistance programs, and community mental health centers, which provide a wide range of services.

**LO2 Identify the scope of psychiatric diagnoses for mental health problems.**

Diagnoses for psychiatric disorders include neurocognitive disorders; schizophrenia and other psychotic disorders; depressive disorders; bipolar disorders; anxiety disorders; trauma- and other stressor-related disorders; dissociative disorders; sexual disorders; paraphilic disorders; eating disorders; disruptive, impulse control, and conduct disorders; obsessive–compulsive and related disorders; and personality disorders. Understanding of and practice with veterans who have posttraumatic stress disorder, one of the trauma- and stressor-related disorders, is explored.

**LO3 Engage in critical thinking (about various issues related to mental health).**

Critical thinking questions were posed regarding the extent to which the DSM-5's assessment and labeling system is fair and adequate. Questions were raised about the suitability of several approaches to psychotherapy, the advantages and disadvantages of electroconvulsive therapy, and the advantages, and disadvantages of managed care.

**LO4 Discuss social work roles in mental health settings.**

In micro practice social workers can be case managers. They can also provide counseling and crisis intervention, in addition to linking clients with needed resources and providing community education about mental health. MSWs can be psychotherapists. Four examples of therapeutic approaches—existential, person-centered, behavior, and cognitive therapies—are explained. In mezzo practice, social workers can run treatment groups and treat families. In macro practice, social workers can be advocates for change, function as managers and administrators who can improve policies and service provision, and develop innovative programs to meet mental health needs.

**LO5 Recognize some trends in evidence-based (mental health) practice.**

Trends in evidence-based practice include comprehensive community support, family education and support, work encouragement and assistance, coordinated treatment for concurrent substance abuse issues, and educational and coping skill development groups.

**LO6 Examine managed care within the mental health context.**

Most of the same issues apply to managed care in mental health as in other health-care settings. Three important concepts are capitation, gatekeeping, and utilization management. There is much pressure on physicians and clinicians to find the least expensive treatment modalities possible for any particular client to minimize cost. Often, this is not in the best interests of the client. It is therefore social workers' responsibility to advocate on their clients' behalf.

**LO7 Address cultural competence in mental health settings (including barriers to accessing services and improving cultural competence).**

Cultural competence, defined as "mastery of a particular set of knowledge, skills, policies, and programs used by the social worker that address the cultural needs of individuals, families, groups, and communities," is just as important in mental health as in other social work settings (Lum, 2005, p. 4). Barriers people of color often face in receiving mental health services include lack of help-seeking behavior, mistrust, stigma, cost, and clinician bias. Cultural competence can be enhanced by developing individual practitioners' skills. It can also be enhanced by culturally competent organizations that celebrate diversity and constantly strive to develop cultural competence throughout the agency.

## LOOKING AHEAD

Mental health issues and concerns overlap with many other areas of social work practice. For example, social workers frequently take part in the prevention and treatment of alcohol and other drug abuse. Chapter 14 explores some of the dynamics and treatment approaches involved in that area. Another example of overlap with mental health issues concerns social work in schools and with youths, addressed in Chapter 15. Such practice might focus on group work to address specific issues, the prevention of school violence, teenage sexual activity, pregnancy, and parenting issues.

## COMPETENCY NOTES

The following identifies where Educational Policy (EP) competencies and their component behaviors are discussed in the chapter.

**EP 1 (Competency 1)—Demonstrate Ethical and Professional Behavior.** *(p. 437):* Professional social work roles in mental health are identified including those of case manager, counselor, treatment group leader, and macro practitioner. *(p. 446):* Belonging to professional organizations such as the National Association of Social Workers is part of establishing a professional identity. *(p. 447):* Continuing education provides a means of career-long learning and is an important aspect of professional development. *(p. 453):* Developing cultural competence concerning mental health service provision is a lifelong process.

**EP 1b Use reflection and self-regulation to manage personal values and maintain professionalism in practice situations.** *(p. 446):* Choosing a career involves personal reflection regarding how to pursue the appropriate routes of professional development. *(p. 452):* Social workers should practice personal reflection and use self-regulation to address personal biases and provide culturally competent treatment.

**EP 2 (Competency 2)—Engage Diversity and Difference in Practice.** *(p. 451):* Social workers

should recognize how societal structures, policies, and barriers concerning mental health policies and services may oppress or alienate people from various cultures.

**EP 2a Apply and communicate understanding of the importance of diversity and difference in shaping life experiences in practice at the micro, mezzo, and macro levels.** *(p. 424):* The example given in this Highlight portrays how social class shapes life experiences. *(p. 451):* Social workers should recognize how cultural differences shape life experiences for people regarding their access to and use of mental health services.

**EP 2b Present themselves as learners and engage clients and constituencies as experts of their own experiences.** *(p. 453):* Social workers should view themselves as ongoing learners about cultural differences.

**EP 2c Apply self-awareness and self-regulation to manage the influence of personal biases and values in working with diverse clients and constituencies.** *(p. 452):* Social workers should strive for self-awareness and use self-regulation to address personal biases and provide culturally competent treatment.

**EP 3 (Competency 3)—Advance Human Rights and Social, Economic, and Environmental Justice.**

**EP 3a Apply their understanding of social, economic, and environmental justice to advocate for human rights at the individual and system levels.** *(p. 445):* Social workers should advocate for human rights in mental health. *(p. 448):* Practitioners should advocate for improved treatment policies as the right of people who have mental disorders. *(p. 449):* Social workers should advocate for managed care practices that respect human rights.

**EP 3b Engage in practices that advance social, economic, and environmental justice.** *(p. 445):* Social workers should engage in practices that advance social and economic justice in mental health service provision.

**EP 4 (Competency 4)—Engage in Practice-Informed Research and Research-Informed Practice.**

**EP 4a Use practice experience and theory to inform scientific inquiry and research.** *(p. 453):* Culturally competent mental health organizations should conduct research based on practice experience with clients.

**EP 4c Use and translate research evidence to inform and improve practice, policy, and service delivery.** *(p. 441):* Social workers should utilize research on the effectiveness of various therapeutic approaches with specific problems to inform and improve practice. *(p. 447):* Social workers should employ evidence-based interventions in their mental health practice. *(p. 453):* Social workers should utilize research on the effectiveness of culturally sensitive mental health treatment approaches to improve their practice.

**EP 5 (Competency 5)—Engage in Policy Practice.**

**EP 5c Apply critical thinking to analyze, formulate, and advocate for policies that advance human rights and social, economic, and environmental justice.** *(p. 445):* Social workers should analyze, formulate, and advocate for policies that address mental health issues and advance social well-being. *(p. 449):* Critical thinking questions are posed regarding the intent and effectiveness of managed care. *(p. 450):* Practitioners should analyze, formulate, and advocate for mental health policies that advance the human rights of people with mental disorders. *(p. 453):* Social workers and agencies should advocate for mental health policies that advance human rights, seek social and economic justice, and enhance people's well-being.

**EP 6 (Competency 6)—Engage with Individuals, Families, Groups, Organizations, and Communities.**

**EP 6b Use empathy, reflection, and interpersonal skills to effectively engage diverse clients and constituencies.** *(p. 419):* Using empathy and other interpersonal skills when working with clients in a residential treatment center is discussed. *(p. 420):* A case example illustrates the use of empathy and other interpersonal skills.

**EP 7 (Competency 7)—Assess Individuals, Families, Groups, Organizations, and Communities.**

*(p. 431):* Social workers conduct assessments of individuals, families, and groups in preparation for the treatment of PTSD. *(p. 437):* Social workers in mental health practice can conduct assessments and work with individuals, families, groups, organizations, and communities.

**EP 7a Collect and organize data, and apply critical thinking to interpret information from clients and constituencies.** *(p. 424):* Critical thinking questions address the potential shortcomings of the DSM-5 as an assessment tool. *(p. 437):* Case management includes collecting, organizing, and interpreting client data. *(p. 441):* Critical thinking questions encourage thought about the usefulness and relevance of the psychotherapeutic theories discussed here for assessment and practice. *(p. 442):* This case example demonstrates the importance of collecting, organizing, and interpreting client data.

**EP 7b Apply knowledge of human behavior and the social environment, person-in-environment, and other multidisciplinary theoretical frameworks in the analysis of assessment data from clients and constituencies.** *(p. 423):* Social workers and other mental health professions use the DSM-5 as a theoretical framework for assessing and understanding mental health problems. *(p. 438):* Theoretical frameworks are described that can guide the process of assessment in mental health treatment. *(p. 451):* Social workers should critique and apply knowledge about cultural differences to understand how people receive services and care in the mental health service provision environment.

**EP 7c Develop mutually agreed-on intervention goals and objectives based on the critical assessment of strengths, needs, and challenges within clients and constituencies.** *(p. 437):* Facets of case management include assessing client strengths and limitations. *(p. 442):* The social worker in the case example assesses the client's strengths and limitations.

**EP 7d Select appropriate intervention strategies based on the assessment, research knowledge, and values and preferences of clients and constituencies.** *(p. 428):* Appropriate intervention strategies are discussed for working with veterans who have PTSD. *(p. 437):* Case management involves selecting and coordinating appropriate intervention strategies. *(p. 438):* Social workers should select appropriate intervention strategies in micro, mezzo, and macro practice for mental health intervention. *(p. 442):* This case example demonstrates an appropriate intervention strategy using cognitive therapy with a person who has depression. *(p. 447):* This and subsequent sections discuss various macro approaches to intervention in mental health. Practitioners should use research evidence to select appropriate intervention strategies.

**EP 8 (Competency 8)—Intervene with Individuals, Families, Groups, Organizations, and Communities.** *(p. 431):* When providing treatment for PTSD, social workers intervene with individuals, families, and groups. *(p. 437):* Social workers in mental health practice can intervene with individuals, families, groups, organizations, and communities. *(p. 438):* This and subsequent sections address how social workers intervene with individuals, families, groups, organizations, and communities in mental health practice.

**EP 8a Critically choose and implement interventions to achieve practice goals and enhance capacities of clients and constituencies.** *(p. 441):* Critical thinking questions encourage thought about the usefulness and relevance of the psychotherapeutic theories discussed here for assessment and intervention.

**EP 8b Apply knowledge of human behavior and the social environment, person-in-environment, and other multidisciplinary theoretical frameworks in interventions with clients and constituencies.** *(p. 423):* Social workers and other mental health professions use the DSM-5 as a theoretical framework for assessing and understanding mental health problems in preparation for intervention. *(p. 438):* Theoretical frameworks are described that can guide the process of

intervention in mental health treatment. *(p. 451):* Social workers should critique and apply knowledge about cultural differences to understand how people receive services and care in the mental health service provision environment.

**EP 8c Use inter-professional collaboration as appropriate to achieve beneficial practice outcomes.** *(p. 445):* Practitioners can collaborate with colleagues and clients for effective mental health policy action.

**EP 8d Negotiate, mediate, and advocate with and on behalf of diverse clients and constituencies.** *(p. 445):* Social workers should advocate for policies that address mental health issues on the behalf of their clients. *(p. 448):* Practitioners should advocate for improved treatment policies on the behalf of people who have mental disorders. *(p. 450):* Practitioners should advocate on the behalf of people who have mental disorders. *(p. 453):* Social workers and agencies should advocate for effective mental health policies on their clients' behalf.

**EP 9 (Competency 9)—Evaluate Practice with Individuals, Families, Groups, Organizations, and Communities.**

**EP 9b Apply knowledge of human behavior and the social environment, person-in-environment, and other multidisciplinary theoretical frameworks in the evaluation of outcomes.** *(p. 438):* Theoretical frameworks are described that can guide the process of evaluation in mental health treatment.

**EP 9c Critically analyze, monitor, and evaluate intervention and program processes and outcomes.** *(p. 437):* A major aspect of case management entails ongoing analysis, monitoring, and evaluation of intervention processes and outcomes. *(p. 444):* Critical thinking questions are raised concerning the appropriateness and effectiveness of electroconvulsive therapy.

# 14 Social Work and Substance Use, Abuse, and Dependence

Janine Wiedel Photolibrary/Alamy

## Learning Objectives    This chapter will help prepare students to:

**LO 1** Define common terms used in the Alcohol and Other Drug Abuse (AODA) field. **Definitions in Alcohol and Other Drug Abuse (AODA)** (p. 462)

**LO 2** Describe the substances involved in abuse and dependence. **Alcohol and Other Substances Causing Abuse and Dependence** (p. 463)

**LO 3** Pose critical thinking questions (that address the dynamics of substance use disorders and compare treatment models). **Focus on Critical Thinking 14.1** (p. 465)

**LO 4** Identify methods of administering substances. **Methods of Ingesting Substances** (p. 466)

**LO 5** Explore common defense mechanisms used by people with substance use disorders. **Highlight 14.2** (p. 468)

**LO 6** Describe family relationships in families addressing substance abuse and dependence. **Alcohol and Other Drug Abuse and Dependence Affects Family Relationships** (p. 468)

**LO 7** Explain the treatment process for substance abuse and dependence. **The Treatment Process** (p. 469)

**LO 8** Identify community resources for people who abuse and are dependent on substances. **Resources for the Treatment of Substance Use Disorders** (p. 472)

**LO 9** Compare two treatment models for substance abusers. **Treatment Models** (p. 474)

*Jeremy has been using crystal meth for almost 10 years now. At first, he used it because it made him feel hyperenergized. Having been a shy, insecure teenager, meth changed his social life as it made him popular with other users. It made him feel heroic and important. Gradually, he found himself running out of money. Drugs are expensive when you use them a lot. At first, he couldn't pay the phone bill; then it was the rent. Then he lost his car. His wife left him and won't let him see his two kids at all anymore. The rest of his family is sick of him. Now he's homeless unless he can find somewhere to crash. He's barely got more than the clothes on his back. He's surviving by eating free meals for homeless people and transients at places like the Salvation Army's soup kitchen. He steals whatever he can to sell and rips people off whenever he has the chance because he has to buy his meth. His body is emaciated and his teeth are rotting. He doesn't think he's going to make it much longer.*

*Eva is a 42-year-old air traffic controller who likes to fly in her spare time. The problem is that she likes to fly without a plane. Eva's substance of choice is cocaine, which she freebases. Her mottoes since high school are "Party hearty" and "Life is too short to be sober." How she became an air traffic controller with this attitude and lifestyle choice remains a mystery. Somehow, she has been able to do her job and keep her drug use separate from her career.*

*Eva started to use illicit drugs when she was 14. Although her parents raised her with strong Mormon values in a small-town Utah home environment, Eva rebelled hard when she became a teenager. When her parents first discovered her drug use they threatened to ground her for life. Eva took off and moved in with a hippie cousin [who amazingly still existed as a "hippie"] in the big town, Salt Lake City (Barsky, 2006, p. 28).*

*Stephanie is a college junior who majors in education and loves to "party." She has been known to label herself a "party animal." She goes out drinking almost every night (after some studying, of course). She drank occasionally at parties during high school and even got drunk a dozen or two times. When she first got to college, she limited herself to going out and "getting plastered" only on Friday and Saturday nights. However, as time goes by, she's found herself wanting to go out every night.*

*She has fun, all right. But twice last month she found herself waking up in bed with some guy she didn't remember ever seeing before. Those guys were pretty "sleazy-looking," too. How embarrassing! Each time she surely got out of there in a hurry. She hopes she remembered to use condoms.*

*After all, she's doing okay in school. Sure, her grades have slumped a little bit. She's dropped from a B+ to a straight C average. But that's because the older she gets, the more difficult her courses get. For example, that stats course is pure misery. She often tells herself she's doing fine.*

*She's not crazy about the headaches she has most mornings. It takes her a while to get going. But she's only missed six or seven mornings of class since the semester started. She's doing okay. She surely isn't an alcoholic or anything like that.*

*The problem is that as she was driving from one bar to another the other night, a cop (who must've come out of the Twilight Zone because she surely didn't see him) busted her for drunk driving. Rats. What a bummer. What a fine. She also has to take a series of drug education courses, which surely is not fun either.*

*The preceding vignettes depict illustrations of people who use alcohol or other drugs. It is estimated that about 5% of the population around the globe is addicted to an illicit (illegal), mind-altering substance; however, 16% of the U.S. population over age 12 is addicted to alcohol, illicit drugs, or nicotine (Doweiko, 2015). This involves 40 million Americans, surpassing the 27 million with heart conditions, the 26 million with diabetes, and the 19 million with cancer (CASAColumbia, 2015). Clearly, alcohol and other drug use poses a big problem for many people and their families.*

EP 1, 7b,
8b

*Social workers need knowledge and understanding about substance abuse, also referred to as alcohol and other drug abuse (AODA) or alcohol and other drug (AOD) problems, for two basic reasons. First, social workers are "involved in the prevention and treatment of substance abuse work in a variety of settings, including health facilities, inpatient and outpatient substance abuse treatment centers, mental health centers, schools, and in the workplace.... [They are also] involved in many aspects of substance abuse treatment, including planning and program development, diagnosis and assessment, information and referral, counseling, and program evaluation" (Gibelman, 2005, pp. 243–244). Many social workers specialize in AODA treatment and provide AODA counseling to clients and their families.*

*A second reason for needing some background in AODA involves social workers' role as referral agents. Even if they don't work in such a specialized AODA setting, they will still probably have clients or family members of clients with alcohol and drug problems. Thus, they must be capable of making appropriate referrals to relevant occupational, health, employment, and social services in addition to helping clients navigate these complex systems.*

*Alcohol and other drug abuse is often masked by and interrelated to many other problems:*

> The addicted person may seek help in a medical setting, a crisis clinic, a mental health agency, a family service agency, or from a private practitioner or a public assistance agency. In the medical setting, the presenting problem may be pancreatitis, liver disease, traumatic injury, or broken bones. In the mental health setting, the person may present depression, suicidal feelings, self-destructive behavior, anxiety, psychotic symptoms, or problems associated with an organic brain syndrome. Each of these problems may be the result of alcoholism or drug addiction.
>
> *(Raskin & Daley, 1991, p. 25)*

*Thus, in almost any practice setting, a social worker may need to address AODA problems.*

# Definitions in Alcohol and Other Drug Abuse (AODA)  LO 1

Language commonly used in substance abuse intervention tends to revolve around the terms *alcohol, drug*, and *substance* (often referred to as *psychoactive substance*). In everyday usage the term **alcohol** refers to any type of fermented or distilled liquor containing alcohol, such as whiskey or beer. **Drug** refers to a wide range of materials that alter mood or consciousness when ingested, including amphetamines, cannabis, cocaine, and hallucinogens. **Substance** is commonly used to refer to mind-altering drugs, including alcohol (hence the term *alcohol and other substance abuse*). In the context of abuse described here, the terms *substance* and *drug* are often used interchangeably (Straussner & Isrolowitz, 2008). Several other terms that have been used in conjunction with alcohol, drugs, and substances are *tolerance, withdrawal, intoxication, alcoholism, alcoholic, dependence, addiction,* and *substance abuse.*

**Tolerance** is the need to use increased amounts of the substance to reach the same level of mood alteration initially achieved (Doweiko, 2015). **Withdrawal** is the array of symptoms that develop as a result of discontinued use of the substance or the compulsion to absorb the substance to avert these symptoms. Despite discontinued use, the user still craves the substance. Withdrawal symptoms may include severe abdominal pain, convulsions, anxiety attacks, depression, and uncontrollable trembling.

**Intoxication** is the development of a series of symptoms, often involving psychological or behavioral changes, directly related to intake of the substance and its influence on the central nervous system. Specific symptoms may include inability to think clearly, distorted perception, temporary euphoria, and impaired motor functioning.

**Alcoholism** is "a chronic disorder characterized by repeated excessive use of alcoholic beverages and decreased ability to function socially and vocationally" (Fetting, 2012; Nichols, 1999, p. 31). An **alcoholic** is a person who suffers from alcoholism. *Substance dependence* (or **addiction**) is reliance on the use of a substance to the extent that withdrawal occurs when the substance is not used; most now prefer the use of the word "dependence" to the term "addiction," which was commonly used in the past (Doweiko, 2015). **Substance abuse** is the use of a mind-altering substance with the resulting behavior having negative consequences or not being socially acceptable (Doweiko, 2015). Substance abuse does not necessarily involve physical dependence.

Professionals working with alcohol and other substance abusers may be referred to as *substance abuse, AODA,* or *chemical dependence counselors.* Practitioners counseling people who abuse or are dependent on alcohol may be called *alcoholism* or *alcohol abuse counselors.*

Note that people often have a substance of choice. That is, they prefer the type of mood alterations produced by one drug over that produced by another. For instance, one person may prefer beer over cocaine. Another person may feel just the opposite.

## Substance Use Disorder

The *Diagnostic and Statistical Manual of Mental Disorders* (DSM-5), published by the American Psychiatric Association (APA, 2013) was introduced and discussed in Chapter 13. It defines a **substance use disorder** as "a cluster of cognitive, behavioral, and physiological symptoms" resulting from continued use of a substance despite significant resulting difficulties and problematic issues (p. 483). The DSM-5 cites four categories of "pathological patterns of behaviors" concerning how the substance is used (p. 483). These groupings include "impaired control, social impairment, risky use, and pharmacological criteria" (emphasis omitted) (p. 483). These four categories include eleven criteria that characterize substance use disorders.

EP 7b, 8b

### Impaired Control

Criteria 1 through 4 involve impaired control or having difficulty managing the use of the drug. Criterion 1 concerns an individual's multiple failed attempts to decrease or halt use of the drug. Criterion 2 entails the individual spending significant amounts of time either trying to acquire the substance, using it, or recuperating from its negative consequences. Criterion 3 involves how an individual with a severe disorder may spend essentially all of his or her time in actions and pursuits concerning substance use. Finally, criterion 4 entails intense cravings for the substance. Such cravings are more likely to occur in contexts where the substance was used in the past.

### Social Impairment

Criteria 5 through 7 involve having difficulties in social contexts and relationships. Criterion 5 concerns inability to fulfill responsibilities "at work, school, or home" (p. 483). Criterion 6 entails experiencing problems in interpersonal relationships that are intensified by using the substance. Criterion 7 involves decreasing or stopping participation in activities involving social interaction that had been part of regular daily life in the past.

### Risky Use

Criteria 8 and 9 concern the individual's repeated use of the substance despite significant risk to the individual's well-being. Criterion 8 entails use of the substance in situations that may involve physical danger. For example, driving while under the influence of the substance is unsafe. Criterion 9 concerns persistent use of the substance despite experiencing acknowledged "physical or psychological" difficulties (p. 483).

### Pharmacological Issues

Criteria 10 and 11 concern pharmacological issues that involve physical consequences from substance use. Criteria 10 involves increased *tolerance* to the substance, which we have defined as the need to use increased amounts of the substance to reach the same level of mood alteration initially achieved. Criterion 11 entails the occurrence of *withdrawal*. We have defined withdrawal as the array of symptoms that develop as a result of discontinued use of the substance or the compulsion to absorb the substance to avert these symptoms.

## Alcohol and Other Substances Causing Abuse and Dependence

**LO 2**

A wide range of mind-altering substances can lead to abuse and dependence. These include central nervous system (CNS) stimulants, CNS depressants, and other mind-altering substances. After describing the specific drugs, we will discuss the ways in which they may be ingested.

**EP 7b, 8b**

## Types of Mind-Altering Substances

One way of dividing up mind-altering substances is to categorize them as CNS stimulants, CNS depressants, and other addictive substances (Dziegielewski, 2005; Johnson, 2004). The following explains how drugs work:

> *A psychoactive substance is any substance that directly affects the normal functioning of the central nervous system.* **Stimulants** *are psychoactive substances that boost the functioning of the central nervous system. Taking these substances usually causes excessive stimulation to the central nervous system that can result in medical problems such as increased heart rate, increased blood pressure, insomnia, decreased need for sleep, and decreased appetite....*
>
> *Amphetamines and their more potent amphetamine derivatives, methamphetamines (aka meth, ice, speed, and crank) and cocaine (aka freebase and crack) ... are often considered "top shelf" or "top of the line" stimulants. Although individuals addicted to these strong substances often experience dilated pupils and easily become angry and aggressive, reactions to use are unpredictable. Sometimes the individual may feel more confident, eager, and outgoing. At other times, particularly as the dosages increase, these feelings may change to paranoia, anxiety, an inability to experience pleasure (anhedonea), and confusion....*
>
> *Caffeine and nicotine ... are known as "bottom shelf" stimulants. Although these stimulants are considered weaker and less dangerous, [they may still have significant effects].... For example, repeated and excessive use of caffeine can lead to problems similar to those created by the stronger stimulants....*
>
> *Furthermore, use of tobacco, the source of nicotine, is responsible for more than 400,000 deaths in the United States each year (p. 53).... [Nicotine is] highly addictive.*
>
> (Dziegielewski, 2005, p. 105)

**Depressants** are

> *psychoactive substances that suppress, slow, or relax the central nervous system. The most commonly used major depressants are alcohol ... and the sedatives and hypnotics such as prescription painkillers. [Other examples of depressants are barbiturates, Xanax, Valium, and Quaaludes (NIDA, 2008).] Some of these substances, when used to the*

*advantage of the individual, can have great social or therapeutic value....*

*When depressants are misused or abused, the outcome can be disastrous.... Medical problems that often occur when the central nervous system becomes depressed range from mild sedation to breathing cessation to coma and possible death.*

*(Dziegielewski, 2005, p. 123)*

The club drugs GHB and Rohypnol (also known as "roofies") are depressants (NIDA, 2010). GHB (Xyrem) was approved in 2002 for treatment of a sleep disorder, but with severely restricted use; Rohypnol (flunitrazepam) is similar to sedatives such as Valium or Xanax, but is not legally approved for use in the United States (NIDA, 2010a). Both have been known as "date rape drugs" because they "can sedate and incapacitate unsuspecting victims, preventing them from resisting sexual assault" (NIDA. 2010a).

Other commonly used addictive drugs that don't fit into the stimulant or depressant categories include the following (NIDA, 2008):

- **Cannabinoids**, including hashish and marijuana, produce euphoria, slowed thinking, impaired coordination, confusion, and sometimes anxiety.
- **Dissociative anesthetics**, including ketamine (Special K) and PCP, can cause increased heart rate and blood pressure, slowed motor functioning, memory loss, and, potentially, nausea. PCP can cause aggression and depression.
- **Hallucinogens**, including LSD, mescaline (peyote), and psyilocybin (magic mushroom), result in unpredictably altered mental states, distorted perception, hallucinations, and, sometimes, flashbacks.
- **Opioids and morphine derivatives**, including heroin, morphine, and opium, cause euphoria, pain relief, drowsiness, and, potentially, coma and death.

Highlight 14.1 describes some newer drugs that have only more recently appeared on the substance use and abuse scene. Focus on Critical Thinking 14.1 raises some questions about why people use any of the wide range of drugs described here.

## HIGHLIGHT 14.1    NEW PSYCHOACTIVE SUBSTANCES

The National Institute on Drug Abuse (NIDA) has warned about a number of emerging new drugs that can be very dangerous (NIDA, 2015, n.d.). Many of these drugs use synthetic substances that are marketed legally, because they have not technically and legally been labeled as a potentially hazardous substance. Even when drugs are clearly identified as being illegal, cunning dealers often change the chemical formula slightly in order to market these drugs again. Sometimes, drugs are identified as one type of drug, but actually contain additional chemical substances that can have dangerous effects. Other times drugs are erroneously described as natural or herbal products, but really contain synthetic chemical additives. Drugs discussed include Molly, Spice, Krokodil, and bath salts. Any of these can be deadly.

**Molly**, also referred to as *MDMA* (based on an acronym for its chemical formula) or *Ecstasy*, is one of the so-called club drugs. It is a synthetic drug that has

characteristics resembling "both the stimulant amphetamine and the hallucinogen mescaline" (NIDA, 2013). Typically, it is consumed orally in "capsule or tablet form" (NIDA, 2013). It has hallucinogenic "psychedelic" properties, and produces mental stimulation, enhanced energy, euphoria, distorted thinking, and enhanced feelings of emotional intimacy. Negative effects can include confusion (both short- and long-term), depression, difficulty sleeping, memory loss, increased heart rate and blood pressure, nausea, and muscle cramping (NIDA, 2013). Many questions have been raised about the purity of any particular dose of Molly and what chemicals may have been added (Lallanilla, 2013; NIDA, 2013; Wait, 2015).

**Spice** or *synthetic marijuana* is also referred to by a range of other names "including *K2, fake weed, Yucatan Fire, Skunk,*" and a number of others (emphasis added) (NIDA, 2012a). It is marketed as a legal alternative to

*(continued)*

**HIGHLIGHT 14.1 (continued)**

marijuana that produces similar results. It usually contains "dried, shredded plant material" in addition to synthetic chemical additives, which produce the mind-altering results. Spice concoctions are frequently marketed as natural substances such as herbal mixtures, incense, or potpourris. Spice is often readily available in stores specializing in tobacco and other paraphernalia or gas stations, and over the Internet. Although some of the chemical additives have been deemed illegal, other "legal" (or, rather, "ununlegalized") chemicals are used, which can be hazardous. Spice is primarily consumed by smoking it. Effects include improved mood, feelings of being relaxed, and perceptual distortions (NIDA, 2012a). Negative effects can "include rapid heart rate, vomiting, agitation, confusion, and hallucinations" (NIDA, 2012a).

**Krokodil** is a homemade replacement for heroine that originated in rural Russia; it is prepared by combining codeine, an opioid, with common poisonous household chemicals such as "lighter fluid," "industrial cleaners" (NIDA, 2015), "paint thinner and gasoline" (Wait, 2015). It is consumed by injection with a hypodermic needle. Ingredients are readily available. It is easy to make and is much cheaper than heroine. Krokodil got its name because it results in areas of skin and tissue turning a grayish green and dying around injection sites. This results in tissue resembling a crocodile's skin. Gangrene sets in and sometimes flesh falls "off

the bone in chunks" (Shuster, 2013). Addicts often become "severely disfigured for life, suffering serious scarring, bone damage, amputated limbs, speech impediments, poor motor skills and varying degrees of brain damage" (Lallanilla, 2013).

**Bath salts** consist of an emerging category of drugs containing *synthetic cathinones*. Cathinone is a chemical substance derived from the khat plant, a shrub originating in East Africa and southern Arabia (NIDA, 2012b). Bath salts are stimulants producing effects resembling those of amphetamines. They usually come in the form of a powder that can be swallowed "orally, inhaled, or injected" (NIDA, 2012b). They are marketed in small bags that might be labeled "not for human consumption," "plant food," or "jewelry cleaner" under a range of brand names (McMillen, 2013; NIDA, 2012b). Effects upon consumption include euphoria and hyperactivity. Negative reactions can include increased heart rate and blood pressure, paranoia, and hallucinations (McMillen, 2013; NIDA, 2012b). Bath salts have been connected to a distressing nationwide "surge in visits to emergency" rooms. It is not possible to determine what specific synthetic chemical substances are contained in any given dose of bath salts. Although federal law banned some specific substances in 2012, makers of such substances are quite creative in developing new formulas that vary enough from banned substances to be marketed legally.

---

## FOCUS ON CRITICAL THINKING 14.1 — THE DYNAMICS OF SUBSTANCE USE AND ABUSE

**LO 3**

The use of alcohol and other drugs is running rampant. Many issues and questions are involved. Attention by government and policy-makers might focus on three strategies. These include prevention, treatment, and enforcement.

EP 5c, 7a

### Critical Thinking Questions

- What do you think are the reasons so many people use mind-altering substances—escape from a hectic, high-pressured reality, peer pressure, fun?

- Are you familiar with people who use alcohol and/or other drugs frequently? What do you think are their reasons for use?
- What, if anything, do you think should be done about substance abuse and dependence? New stricter laws and penalties? Prohibition? Legalization of currently illegal substances? Prevention through education?
- Where should public funding be focused—on prevention, treatment, or enforcement?

# Methods of Ingesting Substances

There are four major means of administering mind-altering substances: oral consumption, inhalation or smoking, injection, or ingestion via mucous membranes (Johnson, 2004). Except for alcohol, all drugs can be administered in more than one way. Sometimes, the means of ingestion can give you clues regarding the scope of the problem; for example, if a person "uses needles to inject cocaine, this can be a reliable indicator that he or she has, or is about to develop, serious problems" (Johnson, 2004, p. 33).

## Oral Ingestion

Oral consumption of a drug involves drinking or swallowing it. Such ingestion takes the most time because the stomach and intestine must absorb the drug into the bloodstream before it can affect the brain (Abadinsky, 2011). Subsequently, unlike other types of ingestion, user attributes may influence the drug's effects (Johnson, 2004). For example, if the drug is taken on a full stomach, it will take longer to produce effects than when consumed on an empty stomach.

## Inhalation or Smoking

Another common method of drug ingestion is inhalation or smoking. This is an efficient and fast means of getting an effect because the lungs are filled with tiny blood vessels that absorb the drug rapidly. The blood then quickly delivers the drug directly to the brain, which experiences its effects within a few seconds. "Most drugs of abuse can be smoked (cocaine, heroin, or marijuana) or inhaled (common household chemicals, gasoline, or model glue). The drug that is most commonly used in this manner is nicotine" (Johnson, 2004, p. 34).

## Injection

Another common means of drug ingestion involves injecting the drug directly into the bloodstream, usually via a vein (Johnson, 2004). This method also allows the substance to sidestep the digestive process and proceed directly to the brain, thereby producing nearly immediate, concentrated effects.

Johnson (2004) suggests that you can observe people's behavior to determine if they're injecting drugs. For example, people who wear long-sleeved shirts on a hot summer day "may be trying to hide needle tracks" (p. 34).

## Mucous Membranes

Johnson (2004) explains how drugs can be ingested using mucous membranes and how the method of ingestion provides clues concerning related physical problems:

> *Another route of administration is saturation of mucous membranes, allowing a drug to dissolve into the bloodstream....*
>
> *Most commonly known as "snorting," this route of administration is quicker than drinking/swallowing, but slower than either inhalation or injection. Users chop a drug into fine power and quickly inhale it into the nose. Powder cocaine is commonly used this way; however, most drugs can be snorted. Any drug that can be crushed into powder can be snorted. Many people choose to snort heroin instead of injecting it. People also use the mucous membranes in the eye (LSD), genital areas, and the rectum via suppositories.*
>
> *A client's chosen route of administration is important assessment information. Not only does it provide clues about the potential seriousness of the drug use, but also about medical issues that may require attention. For example, people who drink heavily often irritate the inside of the mouth, esophagus, and stomach lining. People who smoke or inhale drugs often develop lung infections, oral infections, or impaired breathing. IV drug users can develop a number of dangerous health problems, and those who regularly snort drugs can severely damage their nasal passages and sinuses. [Nosebleeds provide a clue concerning this practice.] (p. 35)*

# People Who Use Alcohol and Other Drugs

Historically, the concept of drug abuse and dependence was based on the medical model (i.e., it was considered a disease with the cure being abstinence). However, more current thought views drug abuse and dependence as a more complex problem that can be analyzed from a range of theoretical perspectives having their respective treatment approaches (Doweiko, 2015; Johnson, 2004; Perkinson, 2012; Velleman, 2011).

People who use, abuse, and become dependent on substances can't be categorized at fixed points on a substance use continuum. However, Doweiko (2015) explains that in "[i]n reality, substance use is considered a normal learned behavior that falls on a continuum ranging from abstinence through limited use to excessive use and dependence" (p. 10). Willenbring (2010) describes a continuum concerning alcohol use that has three categories. First, there are ordinary people who can drink normally and don't progress along a continuum so that alcohol intake becomes a problem. Second, some people are "at risk" of developing a substance use disorder because they're drinking more than is acceptable and their behavior may be becoming problematic. Third, there are people who meet the criteria for having a substance use disorder.

Doweiko (2015) explains that:

> *Substance use disorders are not static entities, but evolve over time. Movement up or down the spectrum is possible as the individual's substance use becomes more or less problematic….*
>
> *Admittedly this continuum is an artificial construct. There are few clear demarcations between one stage and the next, and it should not be assumed that a substance user will automatically move from one stage to the next. (pp. 10–11)*

However, Doweiko (2015) in addition to Lewis and her colleagues (2015) conclude that such a continuum can be useful in assessment and treatment of substance use disorders. It can provide a context for the social worker to view a client's history of substance use in addition to current patterns of such use.

Velleman (2011) suggests that a better term for alcohol abuse and dependence is an alcohol *problem*, defined as follows—"if someone's drinking causes problems with his or her health, finances, the law, work, friends or relationships, then that drinking is problematic; if it causes problems for husbands, wives, children, parents, bosses, or subordinates, then that drinking is problematic" (p. 5). The same would apply to the use of other substances. Therefore, perhaps, a better term for substance abuse and dependence would be a substance use *problem*.

Figure 14.1 reflects how people may fall anywhere on a continuum involving how much of the substance they ingest and how many problems it causes them. Of course, the legal issues involved in

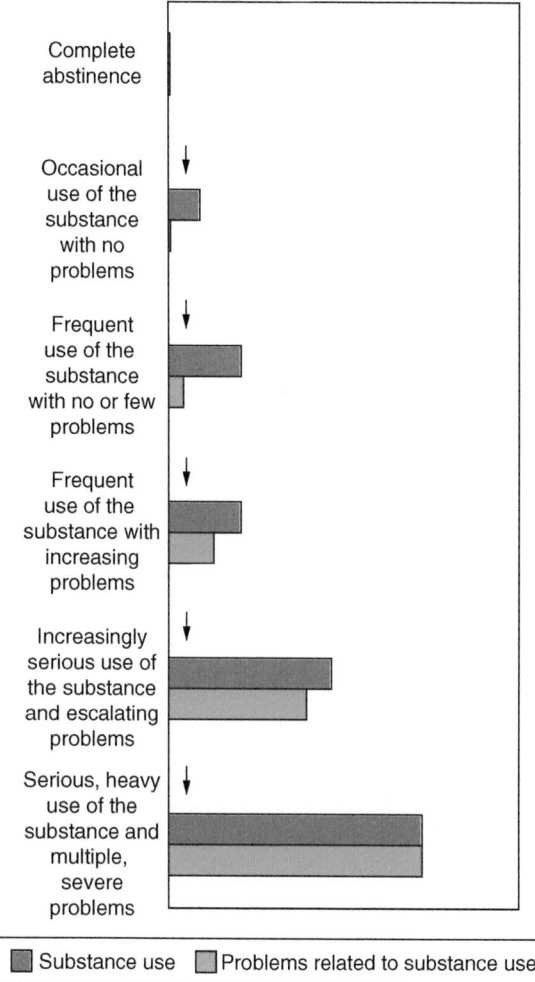

**FIG-14-1** The Continuum of Mind-Altering Substance Use and Resulting Problems

consuming illegal substances must also be considered and addressed.

Most people who use alcohol and other drugs do so on a social basis and consume socially acceptable amounts that do not result in drunkenness or total loss of control. Problems arise for people who lose control of their consumption and become increasingly dependent on the substance's effects. Each individual responds differently to alcohol and other substance dependence in terms of severity of physical and psychological effects and the length of time it takes to become dependent. Highlight 14.2 discusses common defense mechanisms employed by people who are substance dependent.

## HIGHLIGHT 14.2 COMMON DEFENSE MECHANISMS LO 5

People who abuse alcohol or other drugs typically adopt a series of defense mechanisms to protect themselves from having to deal with the problems caused by substance dependence. These include "minimization," "denial," and "rationalization" (Perkinson, 2012, p. 89). Each mechanism helps the person avoid taking responsibility for his or her behavior.

**Minimization** means assigning little importance to drug use or its consequences. The individual "distorts reality and makes it smaller than it actually is" (Perkinson, 2012, p. 89). The user will minimize the amount of the substance actually consumed by referring to it as being a smaller amount than it actually is. Minimization may also involve indicating that substance consumption actually had a lesser impact on behavior, a situation, or life in general than it actually did. Here the addicted person acknowledges that consumption is occurring but admits to very little and tries to make it unimportant. For example, an alcoholic might fill a 10-ounce glass halfway with whiskey instead of pouring it into a much smaller shot glass. This becomes "just one drink." Or an alcoholic might say, "I really don't drink that much," even though he drinks three six-packs of beer a night. Or, "I just have a snort or two of blow [cocaine] a day" when she really snorts up to a dozen times daily.

**Rationalization** involves making excuses for the problems caused by the dependence on the substance. For example, an alcoholic might say to herself, "I really

didn't flunk that exam because I had a hangover; the professor made the questions much harder than she said she would," or "It's been a rotten day. I deserve a drink or two," or, perhaps, "a couple of joints."

**Denial**, the most prevalent defense used by people who are substance dependent, involves insisting to oneself that nothing's wrong. There's no problem. Denial distorts reality so you just don't see the truth. An alcoholic who drinks a fifth of cheap vodka or 12 cans of beer a day might say to himself, "I don't really have to drink." Or a substance user might ignore his wife's complaints about spending money on booze or drugs or being verbally abusive to her when drunk or high. If you don't think about a problem, it doesn't exist: out of sight, out of mind.

Numerous social and relationship problems result from alcohol and other substance abuse. They include marital and family difficulties, disruptions in friendships, trouble in work and school performance, accidents when operating vehicles, and being arrested for crimes committed while under the influence.

Alcohol or another substance of choice (i.e., the preferred substance) becomes the abuser's "best friend." It is something the abuser can always depend on. The effects are pleasantly predictable, and the abuser can escape from life's stresses whenever he or she wants. People can disappoint or place pressure on you, but a drug always acts the same.

## Alcohol and Other Drug Abuse and Dependence Affects Family Relationships LO 6

AOD abuse and dependence are family system problems (Doweiko, 2015; Heanue & Lawton, 2012; Paylor, Measham, & Asher, 2012; Perkinson, 2012). That is, the problem affects the entire family; what happens to one family member affects all others.

People living in such families "live in a chaotic whirlwind" of stress and crisis (Perkinson, 2012, p. 215). Their lives focus on the abuser's substance-related behavior, whether it's coming home drunk or stoned, throwing up or hitting them, losing jobs and money, failing to carry through with any range of

responsibilities, breaking promises, or embarrassing them in front of friends and neighbors.

### Themes Characterizing Families of Substance Abusers

At least eight themes characterize the families of people who are substance dependent. First, the abuser's use of his or her substance of choice becomes the "most important thing in the family's life" (Johnson, 2004; Wegscheider, 1981, p. 81). Because the abuser's top goal is getting enough of the substance, other family members must structure their own behavior around this.

Second, family members strive to keep the family together even when conditions are deteriorating due to the abuser's behavior (Johnson, 2004;

Wegscheider, 1981). The unknown is scary. At least they know what the current conditions are, regardless of how bad.

Third, family members often act as **enablers** for the abuser's substance use (Perkinson, 2012; Wegscheider, 1981). Enablers assume increasing responsibility for maintaining family functioning and making excuses on the abuser's behalf (e.g., calling in sick for the abuser at work when the real problem is a terrible hangover). In essence, this role enables the dependent person to continue consuming the substance, yet assume less and less responsibility for the consequences of that behavior.

Fourth, "family members often feel tremendous guilt. They think that they are at fault. The addicted person keeps denying responsibility, and someone must be held accountable, so the family members often take the blame. The spouse might feel that everything would be okay if he or she could just be the right kind of husband or wife or could just do the right thing" (Perkinson, 2012, p. 215).

Fifth, family members often "do not know what they want. Their lives are centered around the addicted individual. They only know what the addict wants. That is the primary focus of attention. Most family members are trying to hold onto their sanity and to keep themselves, and the family, from going under" (Perkinson, 2012, p. 217).

Sixth, "family members feel worthless. They feel as though no one cares for how they feel or for what they want. They feel profoundly inadequate and unlovable. They feel rejected by others. They do not feel as though they have a fair chance in life, and somehow they feel as though this is fair—that it is their entire fault anyway. This would not be happening to them if they were better persons. This is all they deserve. This is the best they can get" (Perkinson, 2012, p. 217).

Seventh, family members don't trust others (Perkinson, 2012). They have been disappointed so many times by the dependent person's behavior that they can't afford to dream about things getting better. They avoid discussing the problem with others inside or outside the family. They don't want to rock the boat.

Eighth, family members "have poor communication skills. They learned a long time ago the credo of the addicted family: 'Don't talk, don't trust, and don't feel.' These individuals do not talk to their friends or other family members. They are cut off

from everyone. They feel afraid of open communication. If they talked openly, then the truth might come out and the family would be destroyed" (Perkinson, 2012, p. 218).

# The Treatment Process [LO 7]

There are numerous theoretical treatment approaches to chemical dependence. However, at least four features of treatment are important regardless of treatment approach or program. These include engagement, assessment, use of a multiple-system approach to individualized treatment, and development of a continuing care plan.

EP 6a, 6b, 7c

## Engagement

First, engagement with the social worker in a positive and supportive relationship is essential for successful treatment. Engagement is

*the process of building and maintaining a productive relationship with the client. It is the interaction between the client and clinician that results in both being motivated to work collaboratively to achieve mutually agreed upon goals.... It should be emphasized that engagement involves both the client and clinician. It is not the sole responsibility of the client to become engaged; it is also the responsibility of the clinician to motivate the client to become engaged.*

*It is important to remember that an engaged client is more than one who is punctual and attends all scheduled sessions. An engaged client is one who actively participates in both the selection of therapeutic goals and in each therapeutic activity. In other words, an engaged client is one who is invested in the entire treatment process.*

*(Boyle, 2000, p. 144)*

Perkinson (2012) makes additional suggestions for engaging a client with a substance use disorder. A good first impression is important. The social worker should be friendly and stress that he or she is on the client's side. It should be evident that the social worker is there to help clients, not to harm, criticize, or condemn them. Any questions clients have should be answered honestly and straightforwardly. The worker should begin cultivating the client's trust during the engagement period.

## Assessment

A second feature important in treatment involves a thorough assessment of the problem. Lewis and her colleagues (2015) explain:

**EP 7a, 7c**

*Assessment is the act of determining the nature and causes of a client's problem. During the early sessions of treatment, counselors [or social workers] gather data and increase their understanding of their clients. At the same time, clients can ask questions and clarify their role in counseling. At this point the counselor should fully address confidentiality and other expectations. (p. 82).*

Many structured assessment instruments are available to assess alcohol and other substance use. Lewis and her colleagues (2015) provide the example of the Comprehensive Drinker Profile (CDP) designed to assess alcohol use.[1] They indicate that "[i]t has been used and validated with both clinical and research populations, is appropriate for use with men and women in any type of treatment modality, and is culture-sensitive" (p. 85). It is devised to solicit information on the following topics:

**1.** *demographic information*
  *a. age and residence*
  *b. family status*
  *c. employment and income information*
  *d. educational history*
**2.** *drinking history*
  *a. development of the drinking problem*
  *b. present drinking pattern*
  *c. pattern history*
  *d. alcohol-related life history*
  *e. drinking settings*
  *f. associated behaviors*
  *g. beverage preferences*
  *h. relevant medical history*
**3.** *motivational information*
  *a. reasons for drinking*
  *b. effects of drinking*
  *c. other life problems*

*d. motivation for treatment*
*e. rating of type of drinker*

*(Lewis et al., 2015, pp. 85–86)*

The following describes an example of an assessment process for substance use:

*In the interview process, the counselor [or social worker] needs to ask the client what the client sees as the presenting problem. Although this answer may be different from the answer of the referral source (if the referral source is different from the client [for example, a spouse or an employer]) it may assist the counselor in determining the client's level of concern with his or her alcohol/drug use. In addition, gathering information about the client's family of origin, particularly around history of addiction, may be beneficial to the assessment process. Finally, knowledge of the client's living situation may underscore some environmental factors (e.g., roommate's usage) that are influencing client use and may be possible sources for relapse if it is determined that the client has an alcohol/drug problem. As to the chemical use history, a counselor should find out the date of the client's last use, drug of choice, drugs that have been used, prior treatments for abuse and addiction problems, and any consequences for using drugs (legal; family, significant others, friends; job, school, military; medical; financial; etc.).... The reported date of last use can provide the counselor with helpful baseline information for possible confrontation later in the interview. For example, the client may say he drinks only a couple of beers once a week on Fridays, yet he may say he had four mixed drinks on Tuesday....*

*When taking drug history information, the counselor should note the age of the client's first use and the age of last use for each drug reported. Then, for each drug, the counselor should examine the typical use pattern and the most recent typical use pattern (including how much, how often, use setting, and administration route). For example, a woman may have increased her marijuana usage to daily at the time of a divorce for about 2 years, even though she had been smoking marijuana once a week for 10 years, and in the past year (3 years since her divorce) she has smoked it only once a month. This provides an indication that she probably used the marijuana as a way to cope with the stress of her divorce.*

*(Miller, 2005, pp. 33–35)*

---

[1]The Comprehensive Drinker Profile was devised by G. Alan Marlatt and William R. Miller. It was initially published by Psychological Assessment Resources in 1984. Lewis et al. (2015) indicate that it "is in the public domain and can be freely used by all practitioners" (p. 85).

Highlight 14.3 provides some examples of questions that may be asked during an assessment interview.

## Multiple-System Approach to Individualized Treatment

A third feature involved in the treatment of substance dependence is that a multiple-system approach should be used. That is, an individualized treatment plan should be deep developed to address the "client's unique needs, issues, and strengths": the practitioner might

EP 6b, 7, 7d, 8

"provide individual, group, or family treatment, engage the client's local community if needed, and provide access to specialty services such as vocational, recreational, or spiritual counseling when appropriate" (Johnson, 2004, pp. 291–292; Lewis et al., 2015; Paylor et al., 2012).

The following comments on individualized and group treatment modalities:

*Individual counseling, although provided less frequently than group sessions in most agencies, provides an intimate and personal forum for self-disclosure. Often it is used as a preliminary introduction to and preparation for the group*

---

## HIGHLIGHT 14.3 POTENTIAL QUESTIONS DURING AN ASSESSMENT INTERVIEW

The following are potential questions to ask about a client during a substance abuse or dependence assessment. They focus on the following seven basic areas.

**EP 1c**

### Denial
- What is getting in the way of the client accepting that there is a drug/alcohol abuse problem?
- What are the client's mood and feelings? ...
- In what methods does the client engage to blame others concerning his/her problems? ...
- How is the client affecting the lives of others? ...

### Esteem
- How does the client view himself/herself?
- What is the client's self-image? ...
- What happens when the client experiences feelings of worthlessness? ...
- What are the client's best assets? ...

### Confusion
- What happens when the client recognizes that his/her life is out of control?
- What happens when the client loses self-control over his/her drinking/drugging?
- How often has the client experienced a loss of memory resulting from the abuse of drugs and/or alcohol? ...
- What experiences did the client have as a result of his/her first arrest and confinement [e.g., for drunk driving, disorderly conduct, injury]? ...

### Loss of Significant Resources
- What is the client's state of health?
- Does the client experience any difficulties in his/her sex life?
- Does the client have any difficulties in the workplace resulting from drug/alcohol abuse? ...
- What values does the client cherish the most? ...

### Acceptance ...
- Does the client admit to having a problem with drugs/alcohol?
- What caused the client to seek treatment? ...
- What, if any, plans does the client have for the future? ...
- What expectations does the client have about treatment? ...

### Resolution ...
- What level of commitment is the client willing to give?
- Does the client believe that there is any hope for him/her? ...
- How will the client live without the use of drugs and/or alcohol?
- What goals, if any, has the client established?

### Entry [into treatment] ...
- Who, if anyone, is supportive of the client?
- What plans has the client considered making in an effort to change his/her lifestyle?
- What problems does the client foresee?
- How will the client monitor himself/herself? (Taylor, 2005, pp. 41–43)

*setting. The skills of reflective listening [an inter-viewing technique where social workers or counse-lors translate what they think the client is feeling into words], making inquiries and giving feedback to encourage self-expression and exploration, re-framing [helping the client view a problem or issue with a different outlook or understand it in a differ-ent way] and restructuring the client's statements to provide new meaning or interpretations, summariz-ing key points, and affirming and supporting self-efficacy [a person's confidence in his or her ability to address issues and cope with problems] through the process can increase motivation toward problem solving and productive change....*

*[Regarding intervention with groups,] tradi-tional strategies in substance abuse groups often have had a confrontational focus for the purpose of targeting denial and rationalization processes.... This technique can be beneficial to some clients, but may have a detrimental effect on others, partic-ularly if their self-esteem is fragile and vulnerable in reaction to what may be overly harsh and ego-deflating tactics. Yet, the curative dimensions of groups can have a powerful effect on instilling hope, optimism, and increased motivation for indivi-duals struggling with addictive behaviors and their consequences. The recovery process is advanced through the group dynamics of sharing similar experiences and traumas, gaining constructive feed-back and support for problem solving and change, feeling that one is not alone with his or her dilem-mas, securing a sense of belonging and camaraderie, and the encouragement and inspiration to "make it" from others with longer-term sobriety (serving as role models).*

*(Burman, 2000, p. 209)*

We have established that family relationships and functioning are critically important parts of a substance-dependent person's life. Work with the abuser's family can be a major focus of treatment:

*According to the family system perspective, suc-cessful treatment of alcoholism [or other drug de-pendence] requires a multidimensional approach involving the abuser, his or her family, and the envi-ronment. The ... addicted individual is viewed as a human system that requires more than one interven-tion approach, often in combination. The family is viewed as a set of interconnected individuals acting*

*together to maintain a homeostatic balance. The basic premise of this model is to allow each member of the family to achieve a higher level of functioning and emotional security.... The view of the family as a system is essential to accomplishing the intended outcome. The ... addicted individual does not exist in a vacuum. Rather, he or she is a living, breathing, interacting element of his or her environment and the environment of his or her family. An exclusion-ary observation of the person, without consideration of these other factors, is impossible.*

*(Green, Dziegielewski, & Turnage, 2005, p. 141)*

Therefore, "family treatment interventions ... can elicit resilience and healing in family members" (Van Wormer & Davis, 2013, p. 508).

### Development of a Continuing Care Plan

The fourth feature involved in the treatment of sub-stance abuse and dependence is development of a continuing care plan after the primary treatment has ceased (Perkinson, 2012). This is critical to maintain progress and avoid relapse. Various resources are dis-cussed in a subsequent section.

**EP 9c**

One aspect of continuing care involves building a social network of "people or groups to call upon for support, guidance, and recreation" (Doweiko, 2015; Johnson, 2004, p. 292). These might include "12-step meetings, church groups, sober friends, family members, and other sources" (p. 292). Such a network helps them maintain control of their gains by providing "social and recreational outlets that replace key elements" in a lifestyle sustaining abuse or dependence (p. 292). The next section identifies a range of community resources that are available for peo-ple with substance use disorders and their families.

# Resources for the Treatment of Substance Use Disorders   **LO 8**

The following are some of the resources that are available for alcohol and other drug abusers (Doweiko, 2015; Johnson, 2004; Lewis et al., 2015):

1. **Detoxification** "is short-term treat-ment designed to oversee the client's safe withdrawal from the substance to which he or she is addicted"   **EP 7d**

(Lewis et al., 2015, p. 23). Clients may participate in an inpatient or outpatient program (both described here) overseen by medical personnel and professional counselors. The severity of withdrawal symptoms is one factor to consider when choosing the appropriate program.

2. **Outpatient treatment** is received by clients who participate in a program without staying overnight at a treatment facility. "The outpatient substance abuse rehabilitation program might best be defined as (a) a formal treatment program involving one or more professionals, (b) designed to help clients address their SUD [substance use disorder] and maintain a recovery program, (c) which will utilize a variety of treatment approaches (psycho-educational, family and marital therapies, individual and group therapy formats), which is (d) designed to do so on an outpatient basis" (Doweiko, 2015, pp. 429–430). This means that people who are drug dependent can remain in their own homes and still have

services available to them. Programs vary greatly regarding types of treatment involved and the extent of daily or weekly involvement. Outpatient programs have the advantage of providing "the client an opportunity to try out new behaviors in ordinary environments" (Lewis et al., 2015, p. 26).

3. **Inpatient treatment** offers "a more intensive focus on the individual's recovery … than outpatient treatment programs…. These programs thus usually work with the resistant client, suicidal or homicidal clients, or clients who are unable to abstain in the less restrictive outpatient treatment programs…. Most residential treatment programs have a strong 12-step [described in Highlight 14.5] group orientation, with clients being expected to attend multiple 12-step meetings during the week. Some programs utilize in-house 12-step programs while other programs utilize the resources of community based 12-step programs. Some residential programs carry out

*Many social workers specialize in AODA treatment and provide AODA counseling to clients and their families.*

all treatment activities in a group setting, whereas other programs allow for ancillary appointments with psychologists, social workers, dietary therapists, and others as indicated.... The client should meet with the case manager at least once a week, and usually more often than this as treatment issues are identified. Barriers to recovery are identified, including an assessment of the client's support system, client's level of motivation, and past treatment history" (Doweiko, 2015, p. 433). Thus, inpatient treatment provides a comprehensive, structured environment that maximizes control of the treatment process.

4. **Therapeutic communities** are residential programs where clients remain for one to three years, although some require only a six-month stay. Their intent is to immerse clients in an environment aimed at "a global change in lifestyle: abstinence from illicit substances, elimination of antisocial activity, development of employability, and prosocial attitudes" (Abadinsky, 2011; DeLeon, 1994, p. 392; Lewis et al., 2015).

5. **Halfway houses** are temporary residences to assist in the transition from an inpatient program to the real-life community. They provide support and supervision that is less extensive than that given on a 24-hour institutional basis. Emphasis is on gradually increasing each resident's ability to handle responsibility at his or her own pace.

6. **Pharmacological adjuncts** are prescribed medications that help addicts begin the recovery process. For example, Antabuse combats alcoholism as, when ingested, "drinking produces a severe physical reaction: nausea, flushing, and shortness of breath" (Van Wormer & Davis, 2013, p. 146). Such medication, of course, must be carefully monitored by medical staff.

7. **Self-help groups** are composed of "members who share the problem experienced by the other members of the group"; they are led by a group member who may be either a layperson or a professional, but who faces the same problem (Toseland & Rivas, 2012, p. 27). Group members voluntarily gather to provide mutual support and share information aimed at improving their lives. Specific programs include Alcoholics Anonymous (AA), Narcotics Anonymous (NA), and Cocaine Anonymous (CA). These groups

provide exceptionally relevant treatment approaches in view of their established success. Support from peers in the process of recovery is especially critical. Highlight 14.4 discusses AA.

# Treatment Models  **LO 9**

Two contrasting treatment models are briefly described here. One is based on the traditional abstinence approach to recovery, and the other is a strengths-based model focused on achieving greater control of substance consumption (which may not include total abstinence).

**EP 7b, 8b**

## A Four-Stage Recovery Model

One approach to substance dependence treatment maintains that dependence involves an entire lifestyle; therefore, to recover, one must abstain from consuming the substance entirely to establish a healthier, substance-free way of life. The following four steps are involved (Johnson, 2004, pp. 286–290):

*Stage 1—Abstinence:* During this stage, which can persist for as long as two years, clients strive to maintain sobriety. A major focus is on avoidance of mind-altering substances. In essence, "the individual learns to get through most days without experiencing or giving in to overwhelming cravings or urges to use" (p. 286). Relapses are common.

*Stage 2—Confrontation:* Lasting up to five years, this stage sees "clients begin confronting and changing the personal, family, and social issues that contributed to their chemically dependent lifestyle.... They learn how to conduct adult relationships, assume responsibility for their actions, and explore lifestyles that do not include drugs and the people associated with their chemically dependent past" (p. 287). Clients are often "obsessed" with their abstinence and recovery, confronting people and experiences in their past daily, often with shame and guilt about what happened. For example, a recovering client was with new friends who knew little about her past. She abruptly ran into old friends who unabashedly talked about the "good old days" when they got "really high" together and would do "wild and crazy things" like running through the city streets naked. The client felt extremely ashamed.

## HIGHLIGHT 14.4    ALCOHOLICS ANONYMOUS (AA)

Because of its prevalence, we will focus on AA here. This large nationwide group provides support, information, and guidance necessary for many recovering alcoholics to maintain their recovery process. The organization's success seems to rest on several principles. First, other people who "really understand" are available to give the recovering dependent person friendship and warmth. Each new member is given a "sponsor" who can be called for support at any time during the day or night. Whenever the dependent person feels depressed or tempted, he or she can always turn to the sponsor.

Additionally, AA provides the recovering alcoholic a new social group with whom to talk and enjoy activities. Old friends with established drinking patterns usually become difficult to associate with. The recovering alcoholic can no longer participate in the drinking activity, and social pressure is often applied to drink again. AA provides a respite from such pressure and the opportunity to meet new people.

AA also helps the recovering person to view alcoholism as a disease. This means that the alcoholic cannot cure himself or herself. He or she no longer needs to feel guilty about being an alcoholic. All that is required is to stop drinking.

The heart of AA involves 12 steps (Doweiko, 2015). AA doesn't mandate that people follow these steps, but strongly recommends following them in order to accomplish long-term recovery from drinking. AA maintains that individuals need "to draw upon the strength of the entire group in their battle to abstain from alcohol" (p. 516).

Doweiko (2015) continues:

The first 12 steps fall into three groups, the first of which includes steps 1–3.... First to confront the

social stigma associated with the addiction, second, accept that this disease does affect the individual, and third, admit that the individual is powerless over alcohol. Included in the first three steps is the act of surrendering and turning one's life over to a "Higher Power" of the individual's choice....

Steps 4–9 are a series of change-oriented procedures designed to help individuals (a) identify, (b) confront, and (c) ultimately overcome the personal character shortcomings that are thought to support the individual's addiction....

Finally, steps 10–12 challenge the individual to continue to build on the foundation established in earlier steps. Part of this process includes a continued search to identify additional personal shortcomings, which are then addressed by that person. (pp. 516–517)

AA thus encourages introspection. Members are encouraged to look deeply inside themselves and face whatever they see. They are urged to acknowledge the fact that they have flaws and will never be perfect. This perspective often helps people to stop fleeing from the pain of reality and hiding in alcohol or drugs. It helps them to redefine expectations for themselves and to gain control. Within the context of this honesty, people often can also acknowledge their strengths. They learn that they have some control over their own behavior and can accomplish things for themselves and for others.

Organizations are also available to provide support for other family members and to give them information and suggestions. For example, Al-Anon is an organization for the families of alcoholics, and Alateen is specifically for teenagers within these families.

---

*Stage 3—Growth:* Usually occurring after at least five years of abstinence, this phase reflects beginning a new lifestyle not involving substance use. New social support networks are established, and "daily life does not involve constant attention to maintaining abstinence and recovery" (p. 289).

*Stage 4—Transformation:* This stage marks a true change in life orientation from the former substance-using days. The client has established

"social networks and personal skills" to live and thrive. The mind-altering substance no longer has a place in this new existence (p. 289).

Note that although these stages are presented as if they occur in a "smooth and recognizable manner," in many (perhaps most) cases they don't (p. 290). People can move back and forth between stages, and sometimes relapses occur. A relapse "signals the need to discover which parts of the client's recovery foundation need work" (p. 290).

## The Strengths Perspective on Alcohol Abuse and Dependence Treatment

Practitioners "should find ways to recognize the strengths and abilities that clients bring with them to treatment and not just focus on their liabilities" McCollum & Trepper, 2001, p. 40). Identification of strengths provides clues to how clients can make positive changes occur.

Van Wormer and Davis (2013) propose a strengths-based approach to treating alcohol and other substance abuse and dependence based on *harm reduction,* a treatment approach emphasizing means "to reduce the harm to users" caused by the addiction (p. 34). They explain that the idea is

*to help people help themselves by moving from safer use, to managed use, to abstinence, if so desired. The labeling of clients, as is the custom in mental health circles ("He has an antisocial personality," "She is borderline") or in treatment circles ("He's*

*an alcoholic," "She has an eating disorder") is avoided; clients provide the definition of the situation as they see it. Clients who wish it are given advice on how to reduce the harm in drug use such as, "Don't drink on an empty stomach," or "Always make sure to use a clean needle." Most of the advice, however, is provided in a less direct fashion, such as, "Here are some options you might want to consider." Consistent with the strengths perspective, the counselor and client collaborate to consider a broad range of solutions to the client-defined problem; resources are gathered or located to meet the individual needs of the client. Above all, clients are viewed as amenable to change. (p. 34)*

Van Wormer and Davis (2013) state that a more traditional disease model espoused by AA and described previously may experience success with "extroverted, severely addicted, structure seeking" people (p. 34). However, a harm reduction approach

---

**HIGHLIGHT 14.5**

## A CASE EXAMPLE OF A PERSON WITH AN ALCOHOL USE PROBLEM IN TREATMENT: THE HARM REDUCTION APPROACH

Velleman (2011) describes his therapeutic work with a client named Steve who changed his goal from attaining abstinence to gaining greater control over his drinking without stopping it altogether:

**EP 7c, 7d**

Steve developed the goal that he wanted to abstain from drinking altogether. The two of us worked out a plan of action for the forthcoming week to enable him to do this, with the major thrust coming from Steve rather than from me: We identified possible at-risk situations, we clarified the strategies and tactics he was going to employ so as to successfully overcome these, and so on.

The next week, Steve returned saying he had failed: He had drunk four units of alcohol. He was out with one of his adult daughters, they went for a country walk, and ended up in a [tavern] ... for lunch. He had two [bottles of beer] ... with his meal, then continued with his walk, and had drunk nothing else throughout the week.

This information was used in a variety of ways. It added more material which was useful for exploration—Steve can successfully control his

intake under some circumstances, drinking four units did not precipitate a full-scale relapse, and so on. It also provided the possibility for reassessing the goal—perhaps some drinking, under controlled and monitored conditions, with certain people and in certain contexts might be a desired goal? This new material altered the plan of campaign for the next and subsequent weeks.

If abstinence was still the goal, new at-risk situations had been identified, and new strategies had to be developed to overcome them, that is, do not go for walks, ... or stop in a village with a cafe, ... [but do] get his daughter to buy the (non-alcoholic) drinks, or get her to hold the money, and so on.

Alternatively, if occasional controlled drinking was now the goal, the details of when, how much, with whom, where, and so on needed to be clarified; risky situations relating to these actions needed to be identified; and strategies to overcome them needed to be thought through—with, as always, the major thrust coming from Steve rather than me. (p. 48)

## COMPARING TREATMENT MODELS

We have talked about two very different approaches to treating a person who is abusing or dependent upon a mind-altering substance. The four-stage recovery model demands total abstinence, whereas the harm reduction approach allows greater flexibility in pursuing control over the substance.

**EP 8a**

### Critical Thinking Questions

- What are the strengths and weaknesses of each model?
- Which do you believe is more effective, and why?

provides more flexibility in terms of treatment planning and goals. It also stresses how clients have the strength to assume responsibility for changing their behavior. The emphasis is on what people can *do*, not the problems they have. This approach emphasizes "healing" instead of "punishment" (p. 35).

A key component of this approach is *"choice …* about goals of the helping relationship (harm reduction, including abstinence); informed choice about a variety of treatment contexts (same gender, group, individual, day treatment, outpatient, inpatient, mutual-help groups); and informed choice about treatment methods" (p. 406).

"Harm reduction strategies for alcohol [or other drug] misuse are based on the premise that alcohol [or other drug] use ranges across a continuum, starting with no consequences for use and ending with devastating consequences for use, with many states in between" (Van Wormer & Davis, 2013, p. 416). A client may choose to establish a state of controlled consumption (e.g., limiting the amount drunk or times when drinking occurs) instead of seeking total abstinence. A plan might entail drinking only during weekends or special occasions and then limiting it to some designated amount. Drinking less is not as harmful as heavy, continuous, uncontrolled drinking.

The practitioner does not force clients to place labels on themselves. Rather, the practitioner helps clients understand the costs of drinking and explore what options they have to gain greater control of their lives if that is what they desire. In essence, the practitioner focuses on the client's motivation to make positive changes.

Focus on Critical Thinking 14.2 urges you to compare the effectiveness of the two treatment models discussed here. Highlight 14.5 cites a case example where a practitioner works with a client who changes his goal from total abstinence to decreased use of alcohol.

## Chapter Summary

The following summarizes this chapter's content as it relates to the learning objectives presented at the beginning of the chapter. Chapter content will help prepare students to:

### LO1 Define common terms used in the Alcohol and Other Drug Abuse (AODA) field.

Language commonly used in substance abuse intervention tends to revolve around the terms alcohol, drug, and substance (often referred to as psychoactive substance). In everyday usage the term alcohol refers to any type of fermented or distilled liquor containing alcohol such as whiskey or beer. Drug refers to a wide range of materials that alter mood or consciousness when ingested, including amphetamines, cannabis, cocaine, and hallucinogens. Substance is commonly used to refer to mind-altering drugs, including alcohol (hence the term alcohol and other substance abuse). In the context of abuse described here, the terms substance and drug are often used interchangeably. AODA stands for Alcohol and Other Drug Abuse. Several other terms used in conjunction with alcohol, drugs, and substances are tolerance, withdrawal, intoxication, alcoholism, alcoholic, dependence, and addiction.

The Diagnostic and Statistical Manual (DSM-5) defines a substance use disorder based on 11 criteria in 4 categories. These categories include impaired control, social impairment, risky use, and pharmacological issues.

### LO2 Describe the substances involved in abuse and dependence.

Types of mind-altering substances include CNS stimulants, CNS depressants, and other addictive substances. "Stimulants are psychoactive substances that boost the functioning of the central nervous system"; "depressants are psychoactive substances that suppress, slow, or relax the central nervous system" (Dziegielewski, 2005, pp. 53, 123). Other substance categories include cannabinoids, dissociative anesthetics, hallucinogens, and opioids and morphine derivatives. Newer drugs more recently appearing on the substance use and abuse scene include Molly, Spice, Krokodil, and bath salts.

### LO3 Pose critical thinking questions (that address the dynamics of substance use disorders and compare treatment models).

Critical thinking questions are posed concerning the rationale for using and abusing substances. Other questions address the comparison of a traditional four-phase abstinence model of treatment with a treatment model focusing on strengths and the concept of least harm.

### LO4 Identify methods of administering substances.

Methods of substance administration include oral consumption, inhalation or smoking, injection, or ingestion via mucous membranes.

### LO5 Explore common defense mechanisms used by people with substance use disorders.

Common defense mechanisms employed by substance abusers include minimization, rationalization, and denial (Perkinson, 2012, p. 89).

### LO6 Describe family relationships in families addressing substance abuse and dependence.

Eight themes characterize the families of substance abusers that focus on the substance becoming the most important center of the family's life.

### LO7 Explain the treatment process for substance abuse and dependence.

The treatment process for substance abusers involves engagement; assessment; a multiple-system approach to individualized treatment including individual, group, and family treatment; and the importance of developing a continuing care plan.

### LO8 Identify community resources for people who abuse and are dependent on substances.

Community resources for substance abusers include detoxification, outpatient treatment, inpatient treatment, therapeutic communities, halfway houses, pharmacological adjuncts, and self-help groups. Alcoholics Anonymous (AA) provides an example of a self-help organization.

### LO9 Compare two treatment models for substance abusers.

Two contrasting treatment models are described. One is based on the traditional abstinence approach to recovery, and the other is a strengths-based model that emphasizes a least harm approach and focuses on achieving greater control of substance consumption (which may not include total abstinence).

## LOOKING AHEAD

This chapter addressed an important field of social work practice, alcohol and other drug abuse, that is often an issue for the client populations targeted in the next two chapters. Chapter 15 focuses on social work and services for youths and in the schools. Chapter 16 explores social work and services in the criminal justice system.

## COMPETENCY NOTES

The following identifies where Educational Policy (EP) competencies and their component behaviors are discussed in the chapter.

**EP 1 (Competency 1)—Demonstrate Ethical and Professional Behavior.** *(p. 461):* Professional social work roles with respect to AODA treatment are discussed.

**EP 1c Demonstrate professional demeanor in behavior; appearance; and oral, written,**

and electronic communication. *(p. 471):* Professional social workers should use effective communication techniques such as these questions when providing AODA treatment.

**EP 5 (Competency 5)—Engage in Policy Practice.**

**EP 5c Apply critical thinking to analyze, formulate, and advocate for policies that advance human rights and social, economic, and environmental justice.** *(p. 465):* Critical thinking questions are posed to encourage thinking about policies concerning AODA, and social and economic justice.

**EP 6 (Competency 6)—Engage with Individuals, Families, Groups, Organizations, and Communities.**

**EP 6a Apply knowledge of human behavior and the social environment, person-in-environment, and other multidisciplinary theoretical frameworks to engage with clients and constituencies.** *(p. 469):* Knowledge about AODA assessment and treatment and effective engagement with the client are both necessary for successful AODA intervention.

**EP 6b Use empathy, reflection, and interpersonal skills to effectively engage diverse clients and constituencies.** *(p. 469):* Practitioners use interpersonal skills during the engagement process in AODA treatment. *(p. 471):* Social workers should use interpersonal skills and carefully chosen techniques when providing AODA treatment.

**EP 7 (Competency 7)—Assess Individuals, Families, Groups, Organizations, and Communities.** *(p. 471):* Social workers' practice in AODA assessment and treatment may involve working with systems of all sizes, including families and groups.

**EP 7a Collect and organize data, and apply critical thinking to interpret information from clients and constituencies.** *(p. 465):* Critical thinking questions are posed to promote understanding of the dynamics of substance abuse and its treatment. *(p. 470):* Social workers must collect, organize, and interpret appropriate client data in order to prepare for AODA treatment provision.

**EP 7b Apply knowledge of human behavior and the social environment, person-in-environment, and other multidisciplinary theoretical frameworks in the analysis of assessment data from clients and constituencies.** *(p. 461):* Social workers require knowledge about AODA to understand how people involved function within their environments and conduct assessments. *(p. 462):* The DSM-5 provides a theoretical framework for AODA assessment to guide intervention. *(p. 463):* Social workers require knowledge about drugs, drug use, and drug abuse in order to understand the dynamics involved in AODA and conduct assessments. *(p. 474):* Two theoretical frameworks are described that can be used in the analysis of assessment data from clients in AODA intervention.

**EP 7c Develop mutually agreed-on intervention goals and objectives based on the critical assessment of strengths, needs, and challenges within clients and constituencies.** *(p. 469):* Collaboration with the client to establish mutually agreed-on goals is critical in AODA treatment. *(p. 470):* Practitioners should assess a client's strengths and limitations as part of AODA treatment. *(p. 476):* This case example demonstrates how the practitioner and client develop mutually agreed-on goals.

**EP 7d Select appropriate intervention strategies based on the assessment, research knowledge, and values and preferences of clients and constituencies.** *(p. 471):* Social workers should select appropriate intervention strategies when providing AODA treatment. *(p. 472):* Practitioners should select appropriate intervention strategies, potentially including one or more of the various AODA treatment approaches presented here. *(p. 476):* In this case example, the practitioner and client choose appropriate intervention strategies.

**EP 8 (Competency 8)—Intervene with Individuals, Families, Groups, Organizations, and Communities.** *(p. 471):* Social workers' practice in AODA treatment may involve working with systems of all sizes, including families and groups.

**EP 8a Critically choose and implement interventions to achieve practice goals and enhance capacities of clients and constituencies.** *(p. 477):* Critical thinking questions are raised to encourage the comparison and assessment of the two treatment models that have been discussed.

**EP 8b Apply knowledge of human behavior and the social environment, person-in-environment, and other multidisciplinary theoretical frameworks in interventions with clients and constituencies.** *(p. 461):* Social workers require knowledge about AODA to understand how people involved function within their environments in order to provide treatment and make appropriate referrals. *(p. 462):* The DSM-5 provides a theoretical framework for AODA assessment to guide intervention. *(p. 463):* Social workers require knowledge about drugs, drug use, and drug abuse in order

to understand the dynamics involved in AODA, conduct assessments, and provide treatment. *(p. 474):* Two theoretical frameworks are described that can be used in AODA intervention.

**EP 9 (Competency 9)—Evaluate Practice with Individuals, Families, Groups, Organizations, and Communities.**

**EP 9c Critically analyze, monitor, and evaluate intervention and program processes and outcomes.** *(p. 472):* The follow-up process provides one means of monitoring interventions in AODA treatment.

# 15 Social Work and Services for Youths and in the Schools

© Monkey Business Images/Shutterstock.com

## Learning Objectives   This chapter will help prepare students to:

**LO 1**  Describe school social work and school social work roles.   **School Social Work** (p. 482)

**LO 2**  Identify the types of groups school social workers run.   **Highlight 15.1** (p. 485)

**LO 3**  Propose ways to enhance multiculturalism and reduce racism in schools. **Highlight 15.2** (p. 489)

**LO 4**  Discuss issues faced by lesbian and gay youths (including the "coming-out" process). **Gay and Lesbian Youths: A Population at Risk** (p. 490)

**LO 5**  Identify and refute myths about lesbian and gay people.   **Highlight 15.3** (p. 493)

**LO 6**  Describe two community programs for youths (one that empowers Latino and Latina youths

through a community assets assessment and one that explores how an African American spiritual community empowers its youths). **Creative Empowerment for Youths Through Macro Practice** (p. 493)

**LO 7**  Discuss school violence and social workers' role in its prevention.   **School Violence** (p. 496)

**LO 8**  Examine teenage sexual activity, pregnancy, parenting issues, and social work roles. **Teenage Sexual Activity, Pregnancy, and Parenting Issues** (p. 502)

**LO 9**  Encourage critical thinking (about the reasons for teen pregnancy, what should be done about it, and the provision of sex education). **Focus on Critical Thinking 15.1** (p. 504)

Penny, a ninth-grader, tells Ms. Bijou, the school social worker, that Levina, her best friend, has been awfully moody lately. Levina has even said that she doesn't care much about living anymore, that every day gets gloomier, and that it just isn't worth it. Penny is worried that Levina might do something to hurt herself.

Jorge and Jeremy, both juniors in a multiracial high school, are concerned about the racial tensions and even fights in school. They're glad when Mr. Reinheich, the school social worker, announces that he's organizing some encounter discussion groups in which students can talk about racial issues, share things about their own cultures, and try to work out their conflicts.

Marinda, age 15, is terrified that she's pregnant. She hasn't had her period for almost two and a half months now. She hasn't told her boyfriend Teddy, age 16, the bad news yet, because she's afraid he'll break up with her. And she hasn't told her parents, either. What is she going to do?

*These examples reflect slices carved from adolescent life. Emotions run high, and a social crisis can erupt at any moment. Things are critically important right now—not tomorrow, next week, or next year.*

*Social work practitioners work with youths in a wide range of settings and fields of practice—school social work, corrections, mental health, child welfare, runaway shelters, and family planning clinics. This chapter will focus on three dimensions of social work with youths: (1) school social work, (2) macro programs servicing youths, and (3) teenage sexual activity, pregnancy, and parenting.*

## School Social Work    LO 1

School social work takes place in school settings, where practitioners work with students, families, other school personnel, and communities to provide the best education possible for today's youths. Constable (2009) explains:

> *The educational process is dynamic and wide ranging. Involving children, their families, and an institution called school, it is the context for school social work. School is no longer viewed as a building, or a collection of classrooms in which teachers and pupils work together. The school community, no longer simply bounded by geography, comprises all those who engage in the educational process.* (p. 23)

School social workers, then, strive to improve the overall functioning of students, teachers, school systems, and communities. They address any circumstances and relationships that hamper a student's ability to function and succeed in the educational environment. School social workers must be skilled and flexible because they assume a wide range of roles and usually must define their key functions within their own school setting (Constable, 2009). School social work involves not only providing clinical services such as counseling for students who have behavioral problems, are depressed, or are experiencing family difficulties. It also entails working with the multiple systems with which students are involved to strengthen them and make it easier for students to perform in the school environment.

EP 1

As students in colleges and universities, you know it takes substantial concentration, work, and stamina to succeed in a school environment. This is also true for students in earlier phases of the educational process. One of the first things to suffer when a child experiences social and emotional problems is school performance and attendance. Such children simply do not have the strength and endurance to expend the emotional energy required to cope with serious personal problems and still have enough energy left over to perform well in school. School becomes a lower priority.

School social workers, then, may become major players in helping such children, along with their families, teachers, school administration, and social service agencies within the community, develop a plan to empower them. The following case example illustrates how a school social worker collaborated with various systems in a child's environment to improve it and empower her.

*Case Example*  Minnie Minor, age 8, started having problems in school shortly after she entered third grade. She had transferred during the middle of the year when her family moved to the area. By that time the other third-graders had already formed friendships and cliques, so Minnie had a hard time fitting in. A shy, withdrawn child, she usually found herself on the fringes of  **EP 7a, 7c, 7d, 8d** class and recess activities. She also was having a hard time with her reading, spelling, and writing, in addition to having a terrible time concentrating on her lessons.

Minnie's teacher, Sybil Action, noticed these difficulties and referred Minnie to the school's multidisciplinary **Individualized Education Program (IEP)** team for evaluation and planning. (An IEP is a plan that "describes the goals the team [made up of various involved persons including relevant professionals] sets for a child during the school year, as well as any special support needed to help achieve them" (Nemours Foundation, 2011). In this case, part of the evaluation process involved the school social worker, Alan Aladdin, making a home visit and conducting a family assessment. Alan called Minnie's mother, Mary Minor, and requested permission to make a home visit, during which he gathered the following information.

Minnie had two siblings, Buffy and Brutus, both preschoolers, who also lived in the home. Minnie's father had abruptly left the family one year earlier and had not been heard from since. Mary appeared to be depressed: She expressed little emotion and emphasized how overwhelmed and alone she felt. She worked full time as a dental assistant and was having difficulty finding adequate day care for her preschool children.

At school, Alan met with Minnie, who seemed to lack self-confidence and made a number of derogatory remarks about herself. She also mentioned how she really missed her "Daddy" and wondered if he was OK. Sybil had told Alan that during their class art time, Minnie had drawn pictures of black daggers dripping red blood. Alan was concerned that Minnie was depressed.

Specialized testing revealed that Minnie had a mild learning disability, a disorder whereby a child has marked difficulty learning in some particular area (e.g., reading or working with numbers) while learning and functioning in other areas are normal or above average. Among other recommendations, the IEP team recommended unanimously that Minnie required special education. Although there was a special learning disabilities class at the school, it was currently jam-packed. Alan advocated with the school principal to open up another section of the class. The principal said that was not possible because of cost. However, the school was legally responsible for providing needed services. After doing his homework, Alan proposed that a special education teacher from another school would be willing to help. The school could purchase services from her for Minnie. Minnie could spend the rest of her school time with her regular third-grade class.

At a subsequent meeting with Mary, Alan discussed resources in the community that could potentially meet the family's needs. He suggested that Minnie become involved with recreational programming at a nearby community center and that she be signed up for the Big Sister program, which would pair Minnie with a young adult who would spend time regularly with her, provide support, and serve as a positive role model. Alan also helped Mary look into some day-care options for Buffy and Brutus. He suggested that Mary attend a Parents Without Partners meeting for companionship, support, and social activities.

Alan also recommended that Mary consider individual counseling for herself to address her feelings of being overwhelmed and isolated, and for Minnie to deal with personal issues, lack of self-confidence, feelings about her father, and social skills development. Although Mary was responsive to Alan's other suggestions, she was not at all interested in counseling. She maintained that she and Minnie were not "crazy" and so did not need it.

At school, Alan decided to provide Minnie with weekly counseling, which he had time to do with a select few students. Alan also urged Minnie to join a support group he ran for children of single parents. Minnie did so and began to develop a circle of friends she met there and in her learning disabilities class. As she became more outgoing, her relationships with children in her regular classes continued to improve.

Alan worked with Minnie's teacher Sybil to structure activities in the classroom so that Minnie could feel important and gain confidence. For example, at Alan's suggestion, Sybil gave Minnie the "special" responsibility of pinning up student artwork on the bulletin board and assigned Minnie to work in peer groups made up of children who were the most receptive to her.

This is not the end of Minnie's story. Alan, Minnie's teachers, and the Pupil Services team continued to monitor her progress and provide special services and attention. She persisted in making academic progress, developing social skills, and joining various social groups. As a sixth-grader, she was a socially and emotionally well-adjusted girl who could keep up with her classmates academically.

This case example illustrates how a school social worker can work with various individuals and aspects of systems to help students and their families get what they need. Alan worked with Minnie (providing individual and group counseling) and her family (linking her mother with needed services). He also provided consultation to Sybil and, in subsequent years, to other teachers to maximize Minnie's adjustment. He served as case manager to coordinate and oversee all aspects of service provision for Minnie. Additionally, he advocated with the school system's decision maker (i.e., the school principal) and helped to figure out a way to get Minnie the special education services she needed.

## School Social Work Roles

There are at least nine roles that school social workers may assume (Franklin, Harris, & Lagana-Riordan, 2010, pp. 294–304). These include

consultant, counselor, facilitator, educator, advocate, broker, case manager, community intervention collaborator, and "policy initiator and developer."

### Consultant

**EP 1**

First, a school social worker may be a **consultant**—a person with specialized knowledge and expertise to whom others turn for information, help, and advice. Consultation may entail providing information about behavior management techniques or emotional problems to teachers as Alan did in the case example involving Minnie, or helping a school administration develop a new program.

### Counselor

A second school social work role is that of **counselor**—a person who provides clinical intervention concerning social, emotional, or behavioral issues to individuals, families, groups, and communities. Clinical activities might include recognizing feelings, identifying issues and alternatives, offering information, and providing assistance to establish a plan of action. Problems that bring students to school social workers' attention may include behavioral difficulties in the classroom, controlled substance use and abuse, fighting and other acts of violence, truancy, and threats of suicide. In the earlier example, Alan counseled Minnie regarding her lack of self-confidence, depression, feelings about her father, and relationships with peers.

### Facilitator

A third role for school social workers is **facilitator**—a person who "suggests, guides, eases, or expedites the way for others" during a group experience (Kirst-Ashman & Hull, 2015b, p. 105). This role can involve groups of students, parents, teachers, administrators, and community leaders. Highlight 15.1 reviews 10 types of groups school social workers run.

### Educator

A fourth role for school social workers is that of **educator**—a person who gives information and teaches relevant skills. School social workers can offer workshops or training sessions for students, parents, teachers, administrators, and community leaders and residents. Such educational input might involve a wide range of topics. An example of education for students involves family life education and

| HIGHLIGHT **15.1** | FOCUS ON MEZZO PRACTICE: TYPES OF GROUPS SCHOOL SOCIAL WORKERS RUN |
|---|---|

**LO 2**

The following are among the advantages of using group work in a school setting:

- Groups enable children and adolescents to form bonds with peers and to discuss feelings and ideas openly.

**EP 7d**

- Groups enable children and adolescents to understand that their concerns are not unique and that there is nothing wrong with them.
- Groups allow participants to articulate personal feelings and obtain feedback from their peers.
- Groups with children and adolescents enable social workers to serve more young people [more quickly]....
- Groups often use play and art, which are a child's first language. (Bye & Alvarez, 2007, p. 158)

The following 10 types of groups are among the many groups that school social workers run (Pawlak, Wozniak, & McGowen, 1999, pp. 357–360) (emphasis omitted):

1. *"Groups for Parents of Students"*: School social workers may run such groups for any number of reasons, including dealing with children who have behavioral problems or eating disorders, helping parents who are recent immigrants cope with differences in language or customs, or discussing neighborhood issues such as crime.
2. *"Groups for Students Who Are Parents"*: Young single parents can face difficult issues including maintaining good health during pregnancy, balancing school and parenthood, caring for infants, and obtaining support from fathers.
3. *"Groups for Students Whose Families Are Experiencing Divorce"*: Divorce can have serious consequences for children's emotional well-being. Children might tackle many questions. (Was I to blame for my parents' breakup? How could Mom and Dad do this to me? What will happen to me now? Will I ever see Daddy [or Mommy] again? Why doesn't Dad [or Mom] talk to me much anymore? Will Daddy [or Mommy] like their new family better than me?) Groups for children of divorce can help them deal with a wide range of emotions including disappointment, anger, resentment, loss, remorse, guilt, vulnerability, and loneliness.

4. *"Groups for Students Dealing with Substance Abuse Issues"*: Such groups might deal with students' own or parental substance abuse, providing coping strategies in potentially abusive situations or peer support for abstinence. Groups can also be used to focus on substance abuse prevention (Franklin et al., 2010).
5. *"Groups for Students with Attention Deficit Hyperactivity Disorder"*: Recall that attention deficit hyperactivity disorder (ADHD) is a syndrome of learning and behavioral problems beginning in childhood that is characterized by a persistent pattern of inattention, excessive physical movement, and impulsivity that appears in at least two settings (including home, school, work, and social contexts). Such groups can focus on identifying and controlling emotions, improving and managing behavior, developing communication skills, managing conflict, enhancing self-esteem, and developing problem solving skills.
6. *"Groups for Trauma-Related Recovery"*: These groups can provide crisis intervention for students recovering from virtually any trauma, from a school bus accident, to a tornado in a small rural town, to a murderous assault by fellow students. Consider that there have been 44 shootings at K-12 (Kindergarten through twelfth grade) schools and colleges in 24 states since the December 2012 lethal assault at Sandy Hook Elementary School in Newtown, Connecticut (Strauss, 2014). The Sandy Hook massacre involved Adam Lanza who seized 3 guns, shot his mother Nancy Lanza, and then proceeded to the local elementary school; there he killed 20 students and 6 adults, after which he killed himself (CNN.com, 2015). Traumas can result in posttraumatic stress disorder (described in Chapter 13). Groups can help students confront their fears, deal with anxiety, and provide mutual support.
7. *"Groups for Students At Risk of Dropping Out"*: Groups for these students may address how to handle their personal or behavioral problems, confront their anger at "the system," improve study habits, deal with family problems, and plan positively for the future.
8. *"Groups Addressing Stress, Grief, and Loss Issues"*: These groups can focus on any type of

*(continued)*

**HIGHLIGHT 15.1 *(continued)***

grief or loss issues, including the death of a loved one, the closing of a manufacturing plant that was a town's primary employer, or a recent miscarriage. School social workers can also run stress management groups that might focus on stress related to family issues or academic pressures.

9. *"Groups Addressing Socialization and Peer Interaction Skills"*: Peer pressure in childhood and adolescence is awesome. Children want to fit in; they want to be popular; they want to feel important. These groups can address peer pressure issues, teach children more effective ways to communicate and interact with peers, and enhance self-confidence and self-esteem.

   LeCroy (2013) provides an example of an interpersonal skills building group for early adolescent girls. One of the group's goals involves assertiveness. Girls are taught "to act assertively

rather than passively or aggressively" (p. 617). First, assertiveness is explained and examples of passive, aggressive, and assertive behavior are provided. Then group members perform role plays where they can practice skills, which is followed by discussion and evaluation of each role play's effectiveness. An example of a practice situation is "You are in science class, and the boy you are partners with tells you that he wants to mix the chemicals and you can be the secretary. What do you do?" (p. 617).

10. *"Groups Addressing Racial and Cultural Issues"*: Such groups can address issues concerning stereotypes and prejudice, with students expressing their opinions and confronting inaccurate perceptions. Groups also can enhance cultural awareness, with students discussing their own cultural values and issues and educating each other to increase their appreciation of diversity.

information about sexuality (discussed later in the chapter). Other educational thrusts might include stress, time, or anger management; problem solving: and social skills. Workshops for parents

Rob Melnychuk/Getty Images

*Social workers counsel troubled young people.*

and teachers might cover such issues as parenting; behavior management; or improvement of listening, empathy, and other communication skills. Workshops for administrators or community leaders and residents might focus on current issues facing students or newly proposed school programs.

### Advocate

A fifth role assumed by school social workers is that of **advocate**—a person who steps forward, intervenes, represents, defends, supports, or recommends a course of action on behalf of one or more others. Advocacy can involve many facets. One aspect concerns advocating for humane, fair, and appropriate policies on the macro level. Bye and Alvarez (2007) emphasize:

*Effective child and family advocacy demands school social workers have considerable knowledge of educational legislation, Supreme Court decisions, and case law because they play a major role in defining practice. Additionally, it is of critical importance for school social workers to be informed about the following in*  **EP 3a, 8d** *order to be effective in their practice: knowledge of attendance and exceptional children policies and procedures, child abuse and neglect recognition and reporting, public health and public welfare* *statues, the rights of undocumented minors and pregnant and parenting teens, and policies regarding students facing suspension and expulsion. (p. 17)*

*Advocacy for Cultural Competence*  School social workers should advocate for culturally competent and responsive policies and services in schools (Caple & Salcido, 2009). Jansson (2014) reflects:

*The vast literature that has recently evolved on "Culturally sensitive practice" and "multidiversity" stresses the need to adapt programs to specific populations. This sensitivity must occur on two related levels. First, we need to examine the differences in specific social problems in different populations.... Second, services must be adapted to the culture and norms of specific ethnic and racial groups. (p. 234)*

EP 2, 2a

Kelly, Raines, Stone, and Frey (2010) cite the following seven facets about culturally competent practice in schools; when considering advocacy efforts, school social workers should:

- *recognize that certain protective factors have greater salience among certain groups (e.g., church attendance among African Americans)....*
- *recognize that different families have varying degrees of cultural assimilation and comfort levels with majority traditions....*
- *recognize intrafamily differences in acculturation so that children often adapt more quickly than their parents....*
- *note that there are considerable differences in the reasons for migration. Families that emigrate from their homelands voluntarily have a much easier time adjusting than those who are forced to emigrate....*
- *be alert to the possibility of trauma for families that have left their home countries because of political oppression....*
- *pay attention to the family's work status and economic stressors. Many former professionals lack credentials to practice in this country and are forced to assume low-paying jobs....*
- *[recognize that] schools should not assume that families are automatically literate in their native language. (pp. 49–50) [bullets added for emphasis]*

*Advocacy on the Behalf of Refugee and Immigrant Students*  Addressing issues of poverty, alienation, and need is more difficult for the children of immigrants than children of other citizens (Clarke, Kim, & Spencer, 2013). "Immigrant and refugee students are a disempowered group with many needs. Thus it is important for a school social worker to include in his or her management of  the case a strong advocacy tendency toward finding the services and resources to meet these needs" (Fong, Armour, Busch, Heffron, & McClendon, 2006, p. 806). The following is an example of a refugee family where the school social worker, also serving as case manager, can seek to provide relevant services:

EP 2

*The A family, consisting of two parents and three sons ages 14, 16, and 19, arrived in the United States in 2003 as political refugees from Eastern Europe. There the family was persecuted because of their ethnic identity; they fled their home during a war. After experiencing traumatic incidents of kidnapping and torture, they lived in bombed-out homes before taking refuge in a camp for dislocated persons.*

*The family has had several difficulties in adjusting to the school system in the United States. First, it had been years since the children attended school because of the conflict in their country of origin, and all arrived without documentation of grade level. The oldest son was encouraged to find work, and the younger children were placed in Grade 9. They were placed in ESL [English as a Second Language] classes, which were primarily in Spanish-English, despite the fact that neither child spoke Spanish or English upon arrival. Class scheduling presented additional problems. For example, the middle son, whose written name resembled a Hispanic name, was placed in Spanish 3. When the school counselor was contacted to discuss their situation, she suggested placing him in a flower-arranging course. It was difficult for the counselor to understand why neither scenario would be in the best interest of the student.*

*Absences and school suspension proved obstacles to this family, as they do with many refugee families. Refugees are often away from school for various reasons, such as initial medical checkups. Likewise, the A family children were often needed as interpreters during food stamp interviews, medical appointments, and immigration and documentation procedures. Not fully understanding the requirement of written parental permission, both students encountered difficulties with unexcused absences. Subsequently, Mrs. A missed parent-teacher conferences because of miscommunications and the language barrier. One child was also suspended for fighting with another student who insulted Mrs. A. The student explained that in his country of origin, these sorts of verbal attacks are incredibly hostile and provoking. The student did not understand why he was punished for defending his mother.*

*(Fong et al., 2006, pp. 806–807)*

A school social worker can engage in five steps concerning this case (Fong et al., 2006). The school social worker first should assess the situation and needs. The boys required an accurate appraisal of both grade level and language ability. Since they couldn't speak a word of Spanish, placement in Spanish-oriented ESL courses was totally inappropriate. The boys' perspective concerning their "strengths and interests" also required assessment to place them in classes that were relevant to them (Fong et al., 2006, p. 807). The social worker also should conduct a family assessment regarding its needs. The parents obviously had difficulties understanding the school system and its expectations, so they required information and clarification of these expectations.

The second step in handling this case involved identifying appropriate resources and services. An interpreter for their Eastern European language, instead of Spanish, was essential. The interpreter could assist the social worker in arranging for "assessments for the boys in the areas of language ability, strengths and vocational interests, and appropriate course selections" (Fong et al., 2006, p. 807). After assessing what the family required, the social worker should link the family with a refugee resettlement organization, if available, to determine what services the family could receive there. Connection with interpreters is especially important so that the family can conduct its daily business more effectively.

The third step the social worker should pursue involves establishing a thorough plan that addresses the broader picture for the boys and the family. For example, the boys happened to be exceptional soccer and basketball players and love to play. However, their poor grades made them ineligible for the teams. An IEP (Individualized Education Program)

that incorporates sports team involvement as an incentive to learn English and improve their grades could be appropriate.

Step four entails advocating for necessary services. "School social workers should lobby their principals to develop services for the growing immigrant and refugee student populations. Minimally, every educational institution should have on hand a list of relevant interpreters to be available to the school social workers" (Fong et al., 2006, p. 807).

Step five concerns continued advocacy and monitoring of the intervention process. The school social worker can advocate with the school administration in addition to medical and other service providers including refugee assistance agencies, so that the A family receives needed services. In addition to interpreters, organizations offering resettlement assistance to refugees can provide financial assistance, counseling, assistance with the migration process, and referrals to educational, vocational, and medical resources (Jewish Child and Family Services, n.d.). The social worker can also educate other school staff regarding the refugee experience and the obstacles such families encounter. Finally, the social worker can continue to help the family coordinate activities such as medical appointments, administration of medication, transportation arrangements, understanding involving language, and fulfillment of school-related expectations.

### Broker

A sixth role for school social workers is that of **broker**—a person who helps link clients with community resources and services. In Alan's case, he attempted to link Minnie and her mother with a therapist in an outside social services agency. Linkages or referrals might involve any type of resource (e.g., recreational programs, financial resources).

### Case Manager

Related to the role of broker is that of **case manager**—a person who coordinates services from a variety of sources. Alan also functioned as case manager in Minnie's case, coordinating services provided by Minnie's teachers, other school personnel, and outside resources.

### Community Intervention Collaborator

Another role assumed by school social workers is that of **community intervention collaborator**—a person who works with others in the community to initiate change or develop needed programs. Social workers can use their communication and organizational skills to educate and mobilize community groups. Potential goals include developing a shelter for runaways, crisis hot lines, bilingual education programs, or preschool day-care programs for student parents.

### Policy Initiator and Developer

The final role that school social workers might assume is that of **policy initiator and developer**—a person who works to "influence, initiate, and develop policy, which affects the social and emotional development of children and youth within the school and community.

EP 5c, 8c, 8d

Through participating in policymaking committees, writing grants, and as members of professional organizations, they are active in creating programs that benefit the education process" (Franklin et al., 2010, p. 304). An example is writing letters to or e-mailing legislators to support social welfare policies that benefit students and their families.

The importance of advocating for cultural competence in schools has already been introduced. Highlight 15.2 broadens the discussion of multiculturalism's importance in education. It suggests how social workers might enhance appreciation of cultural differences while assuming educator, advocate, community intervention collaborator, and policy initiator and developer roles.

---

## HIGHLIGHT 15.2 ENHANCING MULTICULTURALISM AND REDUCING RACISM IN THE SCHOOL ENVIRONMENT

LO 3

School populations are becoming more diverse. Now public schools are serving youths who are racially and culturally diverse. Many come from families that are economically disadvantaged. It is now important to broaden children's perspectives and appreciation of multiple cultures.

Multicultural education:

incorporates the study of racial and ethnic differences, as well as issues related to gender, age, socioeconomic status, and physical disabilities.... [Its aims] are to foster a sense of understanding and respect for differences, to overcome prejudice and discrimination and provide an understanding of the dynamics of racism, to replace historical and cultural misnomers [using wrong names] with accurate information, and to ensure that all students receive equitable benefits from the education system.

EP 2, 2a, 7d

*(Spencer, 1999, p. 155)*

Note that an "outgrowth" of the multicultural education movement is "global education" (Drum & Howard, 1989; Mapp, 2011; Spencer, 1999, p. 158). Spencer (1999) explains:

Global education deals with diversity at the global level and focuses on the interrelated

systems that affect the entire planet. The primary goal is to build understanding and respect for peoples and nations outside the United States. A global effort goes beyond the "Western-centric" curriculum pervasive in schools by providing an understanding of the dynamics of imperialism [nations extending their own power and authority over other nations and areas] and oppression and creating an awareness of the earth as an interrelated holistic system. (p. 158)

Social workers can pursue at least five approaches to enhancing the appreciation of multiculturalism and reducing racism in schools:

1. Initiate and encourage open discussions and dialogues among various ethnic, racial, and cultural groups. "Both small group counseling and classroom guidance units are excellent modalities for developing multicultural awareness. Small groups that are racially and culturally diverse give students the opportunity to share their heritage with the other members" (Sciarra, 2001, p. 721). Such interaction gives students a forum for discovering commonalities, appreciating differences, and working out conflicts.
2. Seek and adopt curricula that emphasize multiculturalism (and non-Western perspectives).

*(continued)*

**HIGHLIGHT 15.2 (continued)**

3. Empower children by focusing on and appreciating their racial, ethnic, and cultural identities, and by teaching them strategies to stop racism.
4. Give teachers and other school staff training and consultation regarding multiculturalism.
5. Involve parents in efforts to promote multiculturalism by encouraging their participation in and understanding of their children's education. Factors discouraging the parental involvement of people of color include value clashes with the mainstream culture, discrimination, poverty, and lack of culturally diverse service providers. Social workers can "work toward preventing and mediating cultural values conflicts and misunderstanding, taking measures to reduce feelings of

alienation, and assisting parents in overcoming socioeconomic hardships.... Ethnic minority parents benefit from community awareness workshops and parent training programs designed to familiarize them with school policies, procedures, and goals.... Sending letters to parents ... and making home visits ... are other tactics that have been recommended for keeping racial/ethnic minority parents informed about school activities and for promoting parental participation in those activities.... Other strategies for reducing alienation from the school system include genuinely showing an interest in how the parents feel about the educational system and working to empower parents." (Kiselica, Changizi, Cureton, & Gridley, 1995, pp. 521–522)

# Gay and Lesbian Youths: A Population at Risk  **LO 4**

Social workers must respond to the special issues and needs of all children with whom they work. This is the case for not only school social workers but any practitioners serving children and families. Just as social workers must attend to a child's cultural heritage and racial identity, so must they be competent to deal with the issues of an adolescent's sexual orientation.

 **EP 2, 2a**

Sexual orientation appears to be realized quite early in life. Hyde and DeLamater (2014) explain:

*Some experts believe that sexual orientation is determined by age 5 or 6 or even prenatally, whereas others say that it is determined by age 10 or 12. Scientists don't have exact answers to this question and without doubt it depends on the individual. (p. 331)*

Greenberg, Bruess, and Oswalt (2014) indicate:

*[G]ay adolescents face the same developmental challenges as their heterosexual counterparts, with the added burden of attempting to incorporate a stigmatized sexual identity with little support from school personnel. Teachers either avoid the topic of homosexuality or, when discussing it, frequently present it in a negative manner.*

*Ryan and Futterman (2001) pointed out that although the vast majority of lesbian and gay youth become well-adjusted adults who lead satisfying, productive lives, their additional developmental challenges require a range of coping skills and adaptation. Unfortunately, unlike most of their heterosexual peers, they have no built-in support system. They must learn to identify, explore, and ultimately integrate a positive adult identity despite persistent negative stereotypes of lesbian and gay people. They also must learn to protect themselves from ridicule, verbal and physical abuse, and exposure. The social and emotional isolation experienced by gay and lesbian youth is a unique stressor that increases risk for a range of health problems. (p. 380)*

Carroll (2013a) comments on what it's like growing up as a lesbian or gay person (This also can apply to bisexual and transgender people):

*Imagine that while all your friends were talking about the other sex, dating, and sex, you were experiencing a completely different set of emotions. Why, you wondered, can't I join in on these conversations? Why can't I feel the attractions that all my friends feel? Then, at some point in your early teens, you began to realize why you felt differently from your friends. All of a sudden you understood that all the models you had taken for granted your whole life did not apply to you. You began to look for other models that described your life and your feelings—and they simply were not there. In fact, in hundreds of subtle and not-so-subtle ways, society taught you that you were different—and possibly perverted, sinful, illegal, or disgusting. Now what are you supposed to do? Whom do you turn to? How can you possibly tell anyone your deep, painful secret? (p. 328)*

When LGBT youth experience problems typical during adolescence, they must deal not only with these problems but also with their own sexual identity and related issues. Individual and group counseling in which they are offered support and provided an arena to address feelings and discuss issues can help LGBT youths through this difficult period.

## Social Workers Can Assist in the Coming-Out Process

One such issue is **coming out**—the process of a person acknowledging that he or she is lesbian or gay. (People who are bisexual or transgender also may experience the coming-out process.) Becoming aware of one's identity as a gay or lesbian person takes time. It's not like a 250-watt light bulb suddenly being turned on in a pitch-dark room. Rather, it's a gradual, frequently difficult process in view of the homophobia[1] and stereotypes saturating our society.

**EP 7d, 8e**

Note that although we are discussing coming out in the context of adolescence, this process can occur during various stages of life (Alderson, 2013; Carroll, 2013a). We examine it here because of sexual orientation's significance beginning very early in life and extending across the life span.

Coming out involves both "coming out to oneself (recognizing one's sexual orientation) and coming out to others (declaring one's orientation to the world)" (Rathus, Nevid, & Fichner-Rathus, 2014, p. 285). After coming out to oneself, a person might come out to others in three ways: (1) getting to know other people within the gay and lesbian community, (2) sharing with family and friends that one is lesbian or gay, and (3) coming out of the closet—that is, openly and publicly acknowledging one's sexual orientation.

---

[1]We have established that *homophobia* is an irrational and obsessive fear and hatred of LGBT people.

### Coming Out to Oneself

Coming out to oneself is difficult because of the negativity associated with being gay. The logic might go something like this: "Society says gay and lesbian people are bad. I am gay. Therefore, I am bad."

Morrow (2006a) explains how social workers "can play a key role" in assisting adolescents and others as they work through the coming—out process:

*Social workers … can explore with clients the costs and benefits of coming out, and they can help clients make decisions about disclosure across a variety of social contexts. In addition, they can help clients gain necessary knowledge and interpersonal relationship skills that will facilitate their decisions and actions on disclosure. (p. 140)*

Practitioners must avoid minimizing or denying the young person's developing identity and sexual orientation. Rather, they can empower gay and lesbian adolescents by taking their expressed thoughts and feelings seriously and providing them with the information and support they need. The "fundamental approach" of professionals working with youths "who are questioning and exploring their sexual identity should be one of acceptance" (Hershberger & D'Augelli, 2000, p. 237).

### Coming Out to Others in the Lesbian and Gay Communities

*Another aspect of* the coming-out process involves the lesbian or gay adolescent seeking out other lesbian or gay people and learning about what it means to be gay. Social workers should strive to increase their own awareness, and that of their agency, regarding how to provide accessible services to gay and lesbian youths. Such services may include establishing peer support groups and recreational activities for lesbian and gay young people. Support groups can help to decrease isolation and encourage positive identity development. Integrating LGBT content into the curriculum and establishing anti-harassment policies are also helpful (Elze, 2013).

It is important for the person coming out to become knowledgeable about gay issues and concerns:

*Social workers can help clients brainstorm questions and concerns that they would likely encounter in coming out in various social contexts. Workers can assist clients in developing an accurate knowledge base of information to*

**EP 1b, 2b, 2c**

*address identified questions and concerns. Common issues of concern that might be raised by people unfamiliar with accurate information on GLBT issues can include the following: HIV/AIDS risk, sexual orientation versus sexual "preference" [people don't choose to be gay], misinformation and stereotypes regarding sexual perversion and child molestation, religious rhetoric commonly used to oppress gay and lesbian people, and the value of loving, committed GLBT relationships versus stereotypes of sexual promiscuity.*

(Morrow, 2006a, pp. 141–142)

### Coming Out to Family and Friends

In coming out, youths may take the risk of sharing this self-identity with people who are close to them. This is scary because they might be rejected purely on the basis of being gay or lesbian. Practitioners should help adolescents "proceed with caution" and "discuss the risks involved"; "unless youths are certain of support from family members who matter, they should not be encouraged to disclose" (Hershberger & D'Augelli, 2000, p. 239). A social worker "can help clients identify those who they expect will respond to their coming out in an accepting manner. Having at least one successful experience before disclosure to families can be a vital confidence builder for clients" (Morrow, 2006a, p. 142).

The next issues involve decisions about how and when the revelation should be made:

*Clients preparing for disclosure must select the method through which the news will be communicated. Typical options include person-to-person sharing, phone communication, letters, and e-mail correspondence. Workers can help clients explore these communication options....: Social workers can utilize role play and rehearsal exercises to help clients prepare their method of information delivery....*

*In some instances, a client may wish to make the disclosure to significant people (e.g., family members) in the presence of the social worker. If that is the case, the worker can serve as a facilitator of the process and as therapeutic support and intervention for both the client and the family members.*

(Morrow, 2006a, p. 143)

The specific timing of coming out should also be carefully considered; "[i]f at all possible, disclosure should be planned and deliberate—not reactive (e.g., in the midst of an argument). Ideally, coming out should be an act of care and relationship building ... rather than an act of argumentative confrontation" (Morrow, 2006a, p. 143).

Social workers should be prepared to address one other matter—the potential negative responses toward coming out (Greenberg et al., 2014; LaSala, 2010). A social worker can help prepare the adolescent in the event hostility or rejection occurs. The practitioner can teach the adolescent skills in how to react to and diminish hostility (LaSala, 2010). Rejection is not a pretty experience, but, if the adolescent considers the potential ahead of time, at least he or she won't be ambushed. She may be prepared with a response and, hopefully, coping skills. Role-playing such an event may be helpful in preparing for it.

Note that coming out can be a complicated issue for young people in substitute placements (e.g., foster family or group home care, discussed in Chapter 9). Young people are probably involved with a wide range of people in those environments. Whom should they tell? Whom can they trust?

### Coming Out to the World

Often a final step in coming out involves being open to the world about being gay or lesbian. This is also risky for a number of reasons, including the potential for victimization and violence simply because they are gay or lesbian (Greenberg et al., 2014; Hyde & DeLamater, 2014).

One college freshman attended a campus "Speak Out," in which students gathered to share their opinions about the topic of sexual orientation. She stood up and said, "Why not let people do what they want to, as long as they're not hurting anybody? It's really nobody else's business." Note that this was simply a neutral comment about minding one's own business, not a statement promoting different sexual orientations. Ironically, she was heterosexual. In the ensuing weeks, she was brutally attacked twice, but she was unable to identify her attackers. Additionally, four different times, she found notes under the windshield wiper blades on her car saying, "Die, dike! [sic] Go to hell!" Eventually the harassment stopped, although she remained terrified for a long time. Another sad aspect of the story is that the school chancellor refused to issue a statement saying that violence against gay and lesbian people would not be tolerated on campus. That was too controversial.

Social workers must also be aware of the increased risks for gay and lesbian youths of substance abuse and suicide (Goldman, 2008; Greenberg et al., 2014;

## HIGHLIGHT 15.3  MYTHS AND FACTS ABOUT LESBIAN AND GAY PEOPLE  LO 5

*Myth:* Lesbians and gay men are obviously homosexual based on how they look and dress.

*Fact:* You can't identify lesbian, gay, bisexual, or heterosexual people by physical appearance alone. "In reality, the gay population is as diverse as the heterosexual population not only in appearance, but also in social class, educational achievement, occupational status, race, ethnicity, and personality" (Greenberg et al., 2014; McCammon & Knox, 2007, p. 270).

EP 2

*Myth:* Gay men "are effeminate and weak," while lesbians are "masculine and physically strong" (Greenberg et al., 2014, p. 380).

*Fact:* "Sexual orientation has nothing to do with one's body type or style of movement, nor does body type dictate sexual orientation" (Greenberg et al., 2014, p. 380).

*Myth:* Gay men are child molesters.

*Fact:* The great majority of child molesters are heterosexual (Hyde & DeLamater, 2014; McCammon & Knox, 2007).

*Myth:* Lesbian and gay people really want to be the opposite gender.

*Fact:* Being lesbian or gay has nothing to do with wanting to be the opposite gender (Greenberg et al., 2014; Tully, 2001). Gender identity and sexual orientation are two totally distinct concepts.

**Gender identity** is a person's internal psychological self-concept of being either a male or a female.
**Sexual orientation** is sexual and romantic attraction to persons of one or both genders.

*Myth:* Lesbian and gay people in couples like to assume traditional gender role stereotypes.

*Fact:* Lesbian and gay people in couples have their own identities and personalities that have nothing to do with traditional gender role stereotypes (Berger & Kelly, 1995). Rathus, Nevid, and Fichner-Rathus (2011) explain: "Many gay people claim that labels of *masculine and feminine* only represent the 'straight community's' efforts to pigeon-hole them in terms that 'straights' can understand" (p. 303).

*Myth:* All LGBT people are promiscuous and incapable of sustaining long-term relationships.

*Fact:* Just like heterosexuals, some LGBT people have long-term relationships and some do not; just like heterosexuals, some have multiple partners and some do not (Crooks & Baur, 2014; Rathus et al., 2014).

*Myth:* Children growing up in LGBT families become psychologically damaged.

*Fact:* All indications are that children growing up in LGBT families do just as well as those raised in heterosexual families (Mallon, 2008; McCammon & Knox, 2007; Morrow, 2008).

---

Hyde & DeLamater, 2014). Because they feel different and out of place in a heterosexual world, gay and lesbian youths may isolate themselves. They may turn to substance abuse or suicide as a means of escaping what they may see as a hostile and impossible world.

Highlight 15.3 focuses on some of the myths and stereotypes about LGBT people that contribute to homophobia, discrimination, and potential emotional turmoil.

## Creative Empowerment for Youths Through Macro Practice  LO 6

A consistent theme throughout this book is how social workers address issues not only at the individual, family, and small-group level but also at the

macro level of organizations and communities. If a policy hurts clients, it is the social worker's responsibility to do something about it. If an absolutely necessary program for clients does not exist, it is also the worker's responsibility to initiate one to get clients the resources they need.

EP 8

Social workers must be flexible and creative. Sometimes they need to explore new ways to accomplish goals, new avenues to empower clients. This is despite the fact that thinking of new ways to help clients is probably not part of their formal job description. The two case examples presented in this section detail creative approaches to helping youths by using strengths and resources already existing in their communities. One involves conducting a community assets assessment, and the other mobilizing a spiritual community to help its youths in the academic realm. Both programs relate to education. The first was implemented through the schools because they provide relatively easy access to the at-risk Latino and Latina youths involved. The second concerns building on pre-existing resources to help African American students improve their computer skills. Although the two case examples involve the schools, such intervention is not necessarily limited to initiation by school social workers. Programs like this could be developed by any social workers working with youths.

### Empowering Latino and Latina Youths by Conducting a Community Assets Assessment[2]

We have emphasized the importance of using community strengths to empower communities. An example of how this might be done is a project conducted by New Bridges (*Nuevo Puente*), an agency established by a Center on Substance Abuse Prevention grant (Delgado, 1998). The grant targeted at-risk youths who were considered vulnerable to a variety of negative circumstances, including gang pressure, delinquency, emotional problems, substance abuse, and difficulties in school. New Bridges' purpose is to identify and recruit community resources for substance abuse prevention activities. Other facets of New Bridges include provision of "cultural and educational activities"; opportunities to learn about "the effect of substance abuse on individuals, families, and communities"; and training "to carry out school and community education on alcohol, tobacco, and other drugs" (Delgado, 1998, pp. 204–205).

### The Plan

New Bridges hired six girls and four boys to conduct a community strengths assessment of a 40-block urban community. The interviewers asked local business owners and operators about the type of business, the availability of contact people, the social services provided (if a social services agency), and their "willingness to collaborate with schools and agencies on community

**EP 4c**

projects" (Delgado, 1998, p. 205). Goals were to "provide youths with an appreciation of community strengths, raise school and human services agency awareness of community assets, and develop an assets directory" (Delgado, 1998, p. 205).

### Results and Recommendations

Results indicate that "the use of Latino adolescents in community asset assessments offers much promise" for social work (Delgado, 1998, p. 210). Although this assessment was conducted via a grant-created community agency, Delgado (1998) offers a number of suggestions for implementation of community assets assessments. This is accomplished mainly through the schools because they give easy access to youths, including those at risk.

First, school social workers can recruit youths to identify "potential student leaders, candidates for peer education programs, and possible projects involving natural support systems" (Delgado, 1998, p. 209). For example, the young people involved in the New Bridges project decided that they wanted to go on a trip and financed it by holding a car wash. They asked Latino and Latina businesses to contribute a small amount of money (e.g., a nickel or a quarter) for each car washed. In return, the youths listed the sponsors' names on a billboard to provide publicity for them. This is a good example of how community members can work together to enhance relationships among various facets (i.e., this group of young people and local businesses) to reach mutually positive goals (i.e., financial backing for the youths' trip and publicity for the businesses).

A second idea for using the community assets assessment is for schools to invite business owners from the community in to talk about how they started their businesses. In this way owners can provide positive role models for young people and sow some seeds related to career possibilities and goals.

A third idea is to use the information gathered in special school projects. Students might earn extra credit in a social studies course by investigating community strengths. They could record interviews with interested residents or community service representatives. They might then share these interviews with other students or even social service agencies to provide education about social issues and information about cultural strengths.

---

[2]From "Community Asset Assessments by Latino Youth" by M. Delgado. In P. L. Ewalt, E. M. Freeman, and D. L. Poole (Eds.), *Community Building: Renewal, Well-Being, and Shared Responsibility,* pp. 202–212. © 1998, National Association of Social Workers.

## Helping a Spiritual Community Empower Its African American Youths[3]

The following is an example of how social workers helped to empower African American youths by mobilizing a spiritual community in Utah. First, a study was conducted to identify the values and opinions of community members. Subsequently, a program was implemented that demonstrates how social workers can creatively work with a spiritual community to help meet the needs of its youths.

EP 7b

### The Study

An **ethnographic study**—that is, the scientific description of a culture—was conducted that targeted African American youths belonging to the First Baptist Church in Salt Lake City, Utah (Haight, 1998). The church was established more than a hundred years ago by "'a Baptist Prayer Band,' a group of African Americans who, excluded from worshipping in the White churches, met in one another's homes" (p. 215). "African American Utahns, like African Americans in other parts of the country, experience racial discrimination in employment, housing, education, and everyday social interactions" (Haight, 1998, p. 216). African Americans are a tiny minority in Utah. Additionally, most of the Utah population belongs to the Church of Jesus Christ of Latter-Day Saints, a tightly knit spiritual community that sponsors an array of social and cultural activities for its members.

Extensive interviews with First Baptist Church members revealed an environmental context for children that was "negligent at best and virulently racist at worst" (p. 216). Of special concern were the perceived "negative expectations" of White educators in the public school system (p. 216). First Baptist Church members felt that the church's spiritual community provided a safe, supportive environment in which children could learn about their cultural heritage. Emphasis was placed on "helping children understand the relevance of, and then apply, biblical concepts to their own lives" (p. 218). Additionally, children were strongly encouraged to participate in

ongoing learning activities and were expected to respond to a series of "call-and-response sequences. For example, when the teacher said that they would no longer be fishermen, but that they would be fishers of _____?, the class responded that they would be fishers of men" (p. 217). The nurturing spiritual community gave children an environment in which they could develop the resilience to cope with any rejection, isolation, or discrimination they experienced in the outside world. Church members also placed great importance on positive, supportive relationships between adults and children.

### The Intervention

Along with First Baptist Church leaders, social workers initiated and developed "an intervention, informed by knowledge generated through the ethnographic study, to support the development of children's resilience" (Haight, 1998, p. 219). This intervention strategy was the establishment of a "Computer Club" (p. 219). First Baptist Church members "both prioritized educational achievement and identified school as problematic for African American children" (p. 219). Furthermore, children's computer literacy was identified as "a specific area of need, and learning more about computers as an opportunity that children and families would embrace" (p. 219). Thus members viewed enhancing children's competence with computers as a valuable goal. Although the Computer Club's primary focus was educational computer games, student volunteers from a local university also participated with children in a range of activities, including field trips, parties, picnics, "several computer-generated art shows," African dance groups, and a gospel choir (p. 219). The activities enabled students and children to enjoy mutual experiences, share ideas, and develop positive relationships.

The workers portrayed in this example first explored the values and strengths of the community, and then worked with community members toward a mutually desirable goal. Haight (1998) concludes that

*the ability of social workers to develop knowledge of cultural beliefs and practices relevant both to African American communities in general and to the unique African American communities in which they are practicing is critical to the development of ethnic-sensitive social work interventions such as the Computer Club. (p. 220)*

[3]This study is from "'Gathering the Spirit' at First Baptist Church: Spirituality as a Protective Factor in the Lives of African American Children," by W. L. Haight, *Social Work, 43(3)*, 123–221. May 1998, National Association of Social Workers.

# School Violence

LO 7

*It was a phone call that will stay with Denver Police Officer John Lietz for the rest of his life. Shortly after 11 ... [on a] Tuesday morning, he picked up the line to hear the voice of Matthew Depew, the son of a fellow cop: Depew and 17 other Columbine High School students were trapped in a storage room off the school cafeteria,*  **EP 1** *hiding from kids with guns. Lietz himself had a daughter in the school, and he could hear bursts of gunfire in the background. Lietz told the kids to barricade the door with chairs and sacks of food, and to be ready to attack the gunmen if they got in. Several times Lietz heard the shooters trying to break into the room; they were so close that he could hear them reloading cartridges. At one point, as they pounded on the door, Depew calmly told Lietz that he was sure he was going to die. "Please tell my father I love him," he said.*

*(Mai, 1999, p. 25)*

Several hours later on April 20, 1999, 12 students, two gunmen, and a teacher at Columbine High in Littleton, Colorado, were dead; 21 more students were wounded (Mai, 1999). The shooters were high school students—Eric Harris, 18, and Dylan Klebold, 17. Isolated and filled with hatred, they shot themselves as part of the carnage. Harris allegedly explained his actions in an unnerving note: "Your children who have ridiculed me, who have chosen not to accept me, who have treated me like I am not worth their time are dead. THEY ARE (expletive) DEAD" (Williams, 1999, p. 18A). The two teens couldn't "manage their emotions. They feel rejected, enraged, jealous. They are kids who never learned how to solve problems. Combine that with easy access to guns, parents who may have too little time, as well as movies, video games, and music that toast violence, and the result can be lethal" (Cannon, Streisand, & McGraw, 1999, p. 19).

The tragedy in Colorado shook the nation and brought the issue of school violence to the forefront. Years later the Columbine incident remains a painful issue for those close to the ones who died (Markels, 2007). However, this was not an isolated incident. Consider the following:

- Luke Woodham, 16, who "first killed his mother, [and] then ... went to his high school and opened fire, killing three and wounding seven."

- Michael Carneal, 14, who "shot three students to death at an early-morning high school prayer meeting."
- Mitchell Johnson, 13, and Andrew Golden, 11, who "set off a fire alarm to draw their schoolmates outside and then started shooting, killing four students and a teacher."
- Kip Kinkel, 15, who "after killing his parents, ... shot 24 students at school. Two died. Wrestled to the ground, he yelled, 'Shoot me!'" (Begley, 1999, pp. 32–33).
- More recently, Seung-Hui Cho, 23, killed two people in a dorm room and then 30 more in four classrooms on the other side of the Virginia Tech campus on April 16, 2007; then he shot himself in the head (Potter, Schoetz, Esposito, & Thomas, 2007).

Violence among young people and in schools is amazingly common. The Centers for Disease Control and Prevention (CDC, 2015) surveyed students from grades 9 to 12 in a nationally representative sample. Findings indicated that 5.2% of students stated "they had carried a weapon (gun, knife, or club) on school property on one or more days in the 30 days before the survey." Another 7.1% indicated they would not go to school at least one day in the prior 30 days because they felt unsafe. Yet another "6.9% reported being threatened or injured with a weapon on school property" at least once in the past year. The study found that 8.1% of students said they had been in a physical fight at school in the past 12 months. Finally, "19.6% reported being bullied on school property and 14.8% reported being bullied electronically" during the past year.

The following reports on a violence assessment tool developed by Donald. A. Shulman, a crisis specialist at Crestwood Children's Center in Rochester, New Jersey, and explains the dynamics of youth violence:

*Children most likely to explode in violence are those who feel that nobody cares about them, who believe they have no support, and who feel truly alienated, according to Shulman. Therefore, what can be done to help potential perpetrators of violence and their possible victims? The answer, he states, is simple, inexpensive, and can be done by anyone, regardless of training or background. "When you, myself, or anyone—whether you are a social worker, teacher, or friend—look a child in the eye and say, 'You count. I care about you. You are important,' you can prevent a murder," Shulman offers. "It is when we feel meaningless and purposeless that we prey on others through violence."*

(Fiske, 2002a, p. 15)

Research indicates that the following are among risk factors that may predict youth violence:

- *Hyperactivity or attention deficits.*
- *Parent criminality.*
- *Poor family management practice.*
- *Low bonding to school [which is related to disinterest in school, truancy, and academic failure].*
- *Having delinquent friends.*
- *Gang membership.*

(Sciarra, 2004, p. 346)

Similarly, the following provide early warning signs for violence potential:

- *Social withdrawal.*
- *Excessive feelings of isolation and loneliness.*
- *Excessive feelings of rejection.*
- *Being a victim of violence.*
- *A feeling of being picked on or persecuted.*
- *Low interest in school and poor academic performance.*
- *Expressions of violence in writings and drawings.*
- *Uncontrolled anger.*
- *Patterns of impulsive and chronic hitting, intimidating, and bullying.*
- *A history of discipline problems.*
- *A history of violence and aggressive behaviors.*
- *Intolerance and prejudice.*
- *Drug and alcohol use.*
- *Gang membership.*
- *Inappropriate access to, possession of, and use of firearms.*
- *Serious threats of violence.*

(CDC, 2015b; Sciarra, 2004, p. 347)

On the other hand, the following are protective factors that decrease the risk of violence:

- *Intolerant attitude toward deviance*
- *High IQ*
- *High grade point average (as an indicator of high academic achievement)*
- *Positive social orientation....*
- *Religiosity....*

- *Connectedness to family or adults outside the family Ability to discuss problems with parents.*
- *Ability to discuss problems with parents.*
- *Perceived parental expectations about school performance are high.*
- *Frequent shared activities with parents.*
- *Consistent presence of parent during at least one of the following: when awakening, when arriving home from school, at evening mealtime or going to bed.*
- *Involvement in social activities....*
- *Commitment to school (an investment in school and in doing well at school)*
- *Close relationships with non-deviant peers....*
- *Involvement in prosocial activities.*

(CDC, 2015b)

## Bullying

Bullying is a dimension of violence that can occur in school settings. Consider the following scenarios:

- Billy, a fourth-grader, was bigger than most of the other kids in his class. He always went to the head of any line—for recess, the cafeteria, the school bus. If the other kids didn't step aside, he swatted them as hard as he could. Then they stepped aside, all right.
- Shelia, a seventh-grader, was pretty and popular. She couldn't stand Eva, who was withdrawn, had a big nose, and was overweight. She called Eva "Fatty" or "Miss Hippo" or worse whenever she had the chance.
- Dylan, a high school junior, loved to show off in front of his peers. He particularly liked to step in the way of smaller male students, especially those in special ed., and prevent them from using the restroom. He liked to watch them squirm. Twice a kid urinated right there in the hallway.

Then there are the victims of bullying. Sigelman and Rider (2015) provide an example:

*Phoebe Prince, a 15-year-old in Massachusetts who was believed to be moving in on other girls' boyfriends, was taunted mercilessly—jokes about an 'Irish slut' on Facebook (she had recently moved to the United States from Ireland), a humiliating accusation in the school cafeteria, kids cruising up next to her in a car as she walked home, throwing an empty soda can at her, and call her 'whore' (Bennett, 2010). Phoebe killed herself; some of her tormentors were charged with criminal offenses, pled guilty to reduced charges, and were placed on probation and required to do community service. (p. 424)*

Steinberg, Bornstein, Vandell, and Rook (2011) describe **bullying**:

*Bullying refers to aggression by an individual that is repeatedly directed toward particular peers (victims).... It may be physical (hitting, kicking, shoving, tripping), verbal (teasing, harassing, name-calling), or social (public humiliation or exclusion). Bullying differs from other forms of aggression in that it is characterized by specificity (bullies direct their acts to certain peers) and by an imbalance of power between the bully and the victim.... An older child bullies a younger one; a large child picks on a small, weaker one; a verbally assertive child torments a shy, quiet child. It is not bullying when equals have an occasional fight or disagreement. Bullies are more likely to use force unemotionally and outside of the flow of an ongoing conflict. (pp. 318–319)*

Although boys are more likely to bully, girls can also participate in such aggressive behavior (Dupper, 2013; Perren & Alsaker, 2006). Dupper (2013) comments on the incidence of bullying:

*Bullying at school has been on the rise since 2001 (DeVoe, Kaffenberger, & Chandler, 2005) and appears to be widespread in our public schools today. Estimates of bullying differ depending on whether it is measured on a daily, weekly, or monthly basis as well as the grade level where it occurs. According to recent national survey data ... a much higher percentage of middle schools (39%) reported bullying on a daily or weekly basis compared with high schools (20%) or elementary schools (20%) (Neiman, 2011).... Other studies have reported that 61% of girls and 60% of boys had been bullied one or more times a month (Nishioka, Coe, Burke, Hanita, & Sprague, 2011) and that 7% of students face bullying every day (Center for Mental Health in Schools at UCLA, 2011). (pp. 16–17).*

Therefore, it is a significant problem in children's social environment. Santrock (2012a) explains:

*Social contexts also influence bullying (Schwartz, Kelly, Duong, & Badaly, 2010). Recent research*

*indicates that 70 to 80 percent of victims and their bullies are in the same school classroom (Salmivalli & Peets, 2009). Classmates are often aware of bullying incidents and in many cases witness bullying. The larger social context of the peer group plays an important role in bullying (Salmivalli & Peets, 2009). In many cases, bullies torment victims to gain higher status in the peer group, and bullies need others to witness their power displays. (p. 343)*

Victims tend to fall into two categories (Newman & Newman, 2015; Rubin, Bukowski, & Parker, 2006). "The first are children who are shy, anxious, and socially withdrawn, which makes them easy prey. Often they do not have friends to protect them. But other victims are high in aggression themselves and engage in irritating behavior that elicits aggression. Other children see them as 'asking for it.'" (Steinberg et al., 2011, p. 319).

What results from bullying? Some research indicates that when bullies and bully-victims become adolescents, they are more likely to become depressed, think about committing suicide, and actually commit suicide (Brunstein Klomek, Marrocco, Kleinman, Schofeld, & Gould, 2007; Santrock, 2012a). Other research reveals that adolescents who had been either bullies or bully-victims "had more health problems (such as headaches, dizziness, sleep problems, and anxiety) than their counterparts who were not involved in bullying" (Santrock, 2012a, p. 363; Srabstein, McCarter, Shao, & Huang, 2006).

So what can be done about bullying? Santrock (2012a) suggests that school staff can implement the following approaches:

- "Get older peers to serve as monitors for bullying and intervene when they see it taking place.
- Develop school-wide rules and sanctions against bullying and post them throughout the school.
- Form friendship groups for [children and] adolescents who are regularly bullied by peers.
- Incorporate the message of the antibullying program into places of worship, school, and other community activities where [children and] adolescents are involved.
- Encourage parents to reinforce their [children's and] adolescent's positive behaviors and model appropriate interpersonal interactions.
- Identify bullies and victims early and use social-skills training [including teaching about empathy,

communication, and self-control] to improve their behavior.

● Encourage parents to contact the school's psychologist, counselor, or social worker and ask for help with their adolescent's bullying or victimization concerns." (p. 344)

Highlight 15.4 explores a dimension of bullying—cyberbullying.

---

## HIGHLIGHT 15.4    CYBERBULLYING

**Cyberbullying** is the use of communication technology (including cell phones, the Internet, and other newly developed technology) to intentionally "harm, harass, humiliate, threaten, or damage the reputation" of the targeted person through repeated hostile or disturbing communication (Dupper, 2013, p. 29). Cyberbullying can be conducted via "private (such as chat or text messaging), semi-public (such as posting a harassing message on an email list), or public communications (such as creating a website devoted to making fun of the victim)" (Schrock & Boyd, 2011, p. 374). Some of the ways cyberbullying occurs include when perpetrators:

EP 1d

● Pretend they are other people online to trick others
● Spread lies and rumors about victims
● Trick people into revealing personal information
● Send or forward mean text messages
● Post pictures of victims without their consent (National Crime Prevention Association [NCPA], 2011)

Dupper (2013) provides an example of cyberbullying:

Dean is a student at King Middle School who just tried out for the football team. As he comes off of the field after doing poorly on his throwing and running, he feels pretty discouraged. He can even hear the older players laughing at him, but he doesn't look up at them to see who they are. Certain he isn't going to make the team after such an awful tryout, Dean just wants to go home. After having dinner with his parents, Dean logs online to check his social network sites. To his horrific surprise, cell phone videos of Dean's embarrassing tryout have been uploaded and posted all over many students' social network sites. There are multiple comments making fun of Dean's performance by dozens of students. Just

when Dean thinks it can't get worse, he gets a text message from one of his friends asking if he knows about the pictures and videos being texted and sent via cell phone. Dean is sure by the next day that the whole school will [have] access to the video and picture proof of his bad tryout. He doesn't want to go to school to find out. (p. 12)

Almost half of American teenagers have experienced cyberbullying (NCPA, 2011). This behavior is difficult to control because it can take place in school or anywhere outside of school. "Often it is difficult to separate between violence that overflows from school grounds to after-school time and vice versa. The consequences of such victimization are felt at school, through mental health and academic problems and engagement in retaliatory violence" (Astor, Benbenishty, & Marachi, 2010, p. 146).

### Sexting

**Sexting**, referring to "sex texting," is becoming increasingly problematic (Rathus et al., 2014). One Texas study of high school students revealed "that 28% said they had transmitted a nude photo of themselves in a text message or an email (Temple, Paul, van den Berg, Le, McElhany, & Temple, 2012). Three in ten (31%) had requested a 'sext' message, and more than half (57%) had asked someone else to send them a sexual text or email. Girls who had engaged in sexting were significantly more like[ly] than those who had not to begin dating early and to engage in risky sexual behavior" (Rathus et al., 2014, p. 387).

The following is an example of sexting and its sad results:

Jessica Logan was 18 years old when she committed suicide. She had used her cell phone to snap and send nude photos of herself to her boyfriend. After they broke up, he forwarded the photos to other girls at their high school. The girls taunted Jessica mercilessly, calling her a whore

*(continued)*

**HIGHLIGHT 15.4 (continued)**

and a slut. Jessica told her depressing tale in a local TV interview, and two months later—finding no peace—she hanged herself in her bedroom.

*(Rathus et al., 2014, p. 387)*

Rathus and his colleagues (2014) make at least four suggestions concerning the use of caution when even considering texting:

1. "Don't believe that anything you post or send will remain private." It's really easy to share photos or information with whomever for whatever reason.
2. "Whatever you post or send may never go away." Something sent as an adolescent or a teen may haunt the adult years later.
3. "Don't give in to peer pressure to post or send something that makes you uncomfortable. Forty-seven percent of teens say that 'pressure from guys' is a reason that girls post and send sexually suggestive pictures and messages. Twenty-four percent of teens say boys also send and post sexually suggestive messages and images because of peer pressure."
4. "Consider the recipient's reaction before you press send." Some people may sext as a joke, but recipients may take it as a serious proposal for contact or sexual involvement. (Emphasis omitted) (p. 387)

## Suggestions for How School Systems Can Combat Cyberbullying

There are a number of recommendations regarding how school districts can combat all forms of cyberbullying. Strategies involve:

- *"Education of students, parents, and staff."* People should be educated regarding what cyberbullying is, what the warning signs are, and what the legal and school consequences entail. Students should be taught what is appropriate and what is inappropriate electronic communication. Parents and school staff should be taught prevention and intervention tactics.
- *"Acceptable use of the district's technological resources."* Policy regarding the use of technology and equipment should be clarified. Cyberbullying should be prohibited and its consequences clearly stated.

- *"Use of filters to block Internet sites."* Although this cannot block all potential cyberbullying, it can serve to curb it by blocking access to some social networking sites where cyberbullying easily occurs.
- *"Supervision and monitoring of students' online activity."* Students' online activity should be supervised. Staff doing such monitoring should be taught about the district's policy and what is considered the appropriate use of equipment.
- *"Mechanisms for reporting cyberbullying."* Students should be encouraged to report any incidents of cyberbullying. Because the victim often fears retaliation by the perpetrator, when possible, confidential or anonymous means of reporting should be established.
- *"Assessment of imminent threat."* The district should develop procedures for assessing the legitimacy of the threat and the potential for ensuing violence. Protection from harm should be a top priority.
- *"Investigation of reported incidents."* Procedures for other types of harassment should also be followed in incidents of cyberbullying. Students should be discouraged from responding to any cyberbullying that occurs and to save or print out any messages for evidence.
- *"Appropriate response to incidents of cyberbullying."* School disciplinary procedures should be followed. "Depending on the seriousness of the harassment, responses might include notifying the parents of both the victim and perpetrator, filing a complaint with the Internet service provider or social networking site to have the content removed and/or the student's user privileges revoked, using conflict resolution procedures, suspending or expelling the perpetrator, and/or contacting law enforcement if the behavior involves a possible crime. The student perpetrator and his or her parents should be informed of the potential consequences to which they may be subjected, including potential civil law liabilities. In addition, the [school system] ... should consider ways it can provide support to the victim through counselling or referral to mental health services." (California School Boards Association, 2010, pp. 3–5)

## What Social Workers Can Do

What can school social workers do to prevent school violence? "Violence prevention in schools is becoming a major focus of practice for school social workers"; "school social workers play an increasingly important role in shaping and implementing policy, interventions, and procedures that make U.S. schools safer" (Astor et al., 2010, p. 125). Regardless of how they proceed, school social workers must work closely with teachers, school administration, students, their families, and the community to effectively address school violence. Practitioners can assist "in the formulation of school policies and development of programs. Centrally involved in the school community, they are often the first to know about a problem. They have been trained to interpret the meanings of interpersonal behavior and to work with others to find respectful solutions. In so doing they draw on their skills of collaboration; consultation; individual, group, and family intervention; social skills education; crisis intervention; conflict resolution; and the development of mediation systems" (McDonald, Constable, & Moriarty, 2009, p. 729). Other specific suggestions practitioners might follow to prevent school violence include conducting needs assessments, establishing conflict resolution strategies and teams, and developing violence prevention programs.

### Needs Assessments

Social workers can work with teachers and school administrators to conduct **needs assessments**—systematic analyses of client problems and issues to determine clients' needs and develop problem-solving strategies. A needs assessment can be as easy as reviewing available data, or as complicated as conducting a multifaceted  **EP 4c** study over several years. Another way of gaining such information is through the use of **focus groups**, where members gather to discuss and explore designated subjects; such groups generate ideas, describe issues, and potentially propose recommendations to address problems (Toseland & Rivas, 2012). In the context of school violence, students representing various social factions might be selected for group membership and asked to describe their perceptions of student hostility and the potential for violence. Regardless of how a needs assessment is done, the important thing is to gain an understanding of the school climate and to identify potential hot spots where violence might be brewing.

### Conflict Resolution

Conflict resolution programs provide another means of addressing school violence (Woody, 2013). **Conflict resolution** is the process of resolving disputes to come to some sort of agreement or compromise between opposing parties. Students who are isolated or feel they just don't "fit in" are vulnerable to involvement in conflict. They may be victims of name calling, intimidation, unwarranted criticism, physical abuse, or other forms of bullying. Some students may experience low self-esteem, feelings of being treated unfairly, and extreme anger at school and life in general. Opposing groups of students may view another group as "the enemy" and seek out opportunities for conflict. Social workers can use conflict resolution skills to address these and other matters that encourage conflict.

"The actual process of conflict resolution has several components: (1) identification of the problem in specific language, (2) brainstorming possible solutions, (3) agreeing on a solution, and (4) confirming intent to make the resolution work" (McDonald et al., 2009, p. 739). Whereas the process of conflict resolution is usually the same, the way programs are implemented can differ. McDonald and her colleagues (2009) elaborate:

*Some school districts have instituted system-wide training in conflict resolution skills. Some have a formal program, such as specially trained teams of student-mediators or conflict resolvers. [**Mediators** are neutral referees or peacemakers who help resolve disputes between opposing parties.] These specially trained students are often identified as a team and have regular meetings. In schools that have such teams, there is likely to be a set policy regarding which types of problems are appropriate for referral to mediation. Other districts do some training with all students, but also train a [core group] ... of students who are available for more difficult situations. When emotions are running high, or when there seems to be an imbalance in power, the team would ensure that each party to the dispute is respectful to the other. Younger students may wear special vests on playgrounds and in lunchrooms or during special functions where students are not being closely supervised, to identify them as mediators. Some schools have students identified in each classroom as the designated conflict resolvers. They may hold dispute-resolution sessions in the classroom, ideally in an area* *somewhat removed from the rest of the class. In all cases, the school must have a way to oversee the referral process and mediation session so that conflict resolvers and mediators are at all times protected from serious problems or risks. (p. 739)*

### Violence Prevention Programs

Astor and his colleagues (2010) maintain that successful violence prevention programs must be organized endeavors with the following characteristics:

- "They raise the awareness and responsibility of students, teachers, and parents regarding the types of violence in their schools (e.g., sexual harassment, fighting, weapon use).
- They create clear guidelines and rules for the entire school [that reinforce appropriate positive behavior and stress penalties for aggressive behavior].
- They target the various social systems in the school and clearly communicate to the entire school community what procedures should be followed before, during, and after violent events.
- They focus on getting the school staff, students, and parents involved in the program.
- The interventions often fit easily into the normal flow and mission of the school setting.
- They utilize faculty, staff, and parents in the school setting in order to plan, implement, and sustain the program.
- They increase monitoring and supervision in nonclassroom areas.
- They are culturally sensitive, culturally competent, and immersed within the community/culture of the students." (p. 136)

Dupper (2013) provides an example of a violence prevention program:

*The Safe School Ambassadors Program (SSA) equips young people with nonviolent communication skills to speak up; intervene; and stop harassment, meanness and all forms of bullying. Students acquire skills they can use in the moment, with their friends, to defuse and deescalate potentially hurtful incidents. Key adults are trained to facilitate regular small-group meetings of Ambassadors, which sharpen their skills, sustain their commitment, and increase their reporting of dangerous activities like planned fights or weapons on*

*campus…. [SSA] is designed for students in the 4th–12th grades and has been implemented in 900 schools across 28 states and two Canadian provinces. The schools that have utilized the SSA program have seen results including decreased discipline referrals, suspensions, and expulsions; decreased tension and increased tolerance; increased flow of information to adults about potentially hurtful and violent acts; and improved school climate impacting attendance and academic performance. Detailed information … is available at: http://www.community-matters.org/safe-school-ambassadors. (pp. 78–79)*

# Teenage Sexual Activity, Pregnancy, and Parenting Issues  `LO 8`

Sexual activity and teenage pregnancy are important issues for young people today. Any social worker working with youths will likely address the decisions concerning and the consequences of early sexual activity. Social work settings overlap. Work with youths occurs in various settings and fields of practice, including school social work, corrections, mental health, child welfare, runaway shelters, and Planned Parenthood clinics.[4]

Of all births in the United States, 9.3% are to teenage mothers (ProQuest, 2013). There has been a decline in the pregnancy rate for this group over the past decades; births to teenage mothers in 1990 was 12.8% of all births. However, there still are about 750,000 such pregnancies annually (Crooks & Baur, 2014, p. 363; Guttmacher Institute, 2011). Papalia and Feldman (2012) elaborate:

*More than 4 in 10 adolescent girls in the United States have been pregnant at least once before age 20. More than half (51 percent) of pregnant teenagers in the United States have their babies…. Overall, 35 percent choose to abort. Fourteen percent of teen pregnancies end in miscarriage or stillbirth….*

*Although declines in teenage pregnancy and childbearing have occurred among all population groups,*

---

[4]Planned Parenthood is a national organization created in 1921 to promote research and disseminate information about contraception and family planning.

*birthrates have fallen most sharply among Black teenagers—by 46 percent. Still, Black and Hispanic girls are more likely to have babies than White, American Indian, or Asian American girls....*

*More than 90 percent of pregnant teenagers describe their pregnancies as unintended, and 50 percent of teen pregnancies occur within six months of sexual initiation. (p. 401)*

Santrock (2012b) reflects on the international picture:

*The United States continues to have one of the highest rates of adolescent pregnancy and child-bearing in the developed world, despite a considerable decline in the 1990s.... The U.S. adolescent pregnancy rate is eight times as high as in the Netherlands. This dramatic difference exists in spite of the fact that U.S. adolescents are no more sexually active than their counterparts in the Netherlands. (p. 397)*

Focus on Critical Thinking 15.1 raises questions regarding the reasons for the high rates of adolescent pregnancy in the United States.

## Reasons for Concern

What happens to these babies after birth? Teenage pregnancy is a serious social welfare concern for at least four reasons.

### Children Begetting Children

First, teen mothers are children themselves. Most babies born to single teens remain at home with their young mothers. "Among U.S. adolescents who do not abort their pregnancy, the vast majority—more than 90 percent—keep and raise the infant, whereas only 1 in 10 chooses to have the child adopted" (Steinberg et al., 2011, p. 344).

Keeping their babies places these young women in a situation very different from that of most of their peers. Adolescence and young adulthood are the usual times of life for finding a mate, obtaining an education, and making a career choice. The additional responsibility of motherhood places serious restrictions on the amount of freedom and time available for these activities. Additionally, such young women are often ill prepared for motherhood. They are usually in the midst of establishing their own identities and learning to care for themselves.

### Negative Physical Consequences

A second reason teenage pregnancy is a social welfare concern involves the likely negative physical consequences for mother and baby. Young mothers are more likely than more mature women to experience difficulties (Kail & Cavanaugh, 2013; Papalia & Feldman, 2012; Santrock, 2012b). Young mothers' problems include medical difficulties during the pregnancy and prolonged labor (Rathus, 2014). The infant is more likely to have a low birth weight, to be born prematurely, and to have neurological and developmental difficulties than infants born to adult mothers (Newman & Newman, 2015; Papalia & Feldman, 2012; Santrock, 2012b). Many of these problems are due to poor or nonexistent prenatal care and to poor nutrition.

### Long-Term Negative Effects for Mothers

Research indicates that negative effects on the young mother continue long after the baby's birth. Teenage mothers often drop out of school (Papalia & Feldman, 2012; Rathus, 2014; Santrock, 2012b). They are also more likely to be poor (Newman & Newman, 2015; Papalia & Feldman, 2012).

Very young mothers may not have had the opportunity to develop "the maturity, skills, and social support" to be effective parents (Papalia & Feldman, 2012, p. 402). The stress and responsibility of motherhood tend to take a heavy toll on teen mothers. Raising a child demands time, energy, and attention. Time taken to care for a baby must be subtracted from the time available for school and recreational activities.

All this sounds quite negative. Santrock (2012b) cautions that "not every adolescent female who bears a child lives a life of poverty and low achievement. Thus, although adolescent pregnancy is a high-risk circumstance, and adolescents who do not become pregnant generally fare better than those who do, some adolescent mothers do well in school and have positive outcomes" (p. 398). Adolescent motherhood puts adolescents at risk of hardship. It does not necessarily doom them to a bad life. "Several long-term studies find that, two decades after giving birth, most former adolescent mothers are not on welfare; many have finished high school and secured steady jobs; and they do not have large families" (Papalia & Feldman, 2012, p. 402). There is some evidence that "[c]omprehensive adolescent pregnancy

# THE PREGNANCY RATE FOR ADOLESCENTS IN THE UNITED STATES

**LO 9**

The teen pregnancy rate in the United States remains the highest in the developed world (Charlesworth, 2014; Larson, 2012; Roan, 2012). There are three possible reasons (Boonstra, 2002, pp. 9–10, cited in Santrock, 2007, pp. 464–465). First, in other countries, "*childbearing is considered an adult activity*" (Boonstra, 2002, pp. 9–10, cited in Santrock, 2007, p. 464). Adolescents are given clear messages that pregnancy is part of adulthood, not childhood. Employed, responsible adults are ready to assume caregiving responsibilities for children.

**EP 7a, 8a**

Second, adolescents in the United States don't receive

clear messages about sexual behavior. While adults in other countries strongly encourage teens to wait until they have established themselves before having children, they are generally more accepting than American adults of teens having sex. In France and Sweden, in particular, teen sexual expression is seen as normal and positive, but there is also widespread expectation that sexual intercourse will take place within committed relationships. (In fact, relationships among U.S. teens tend to be more sporadic and of shorter duration.) Equally strong is the expectation that young people who are having sex will take actions to protect themselves and their partners from pregnancy and sexually transmitted infections' which is much stronger in Europe than in the United States. 'In keeping with this view, schools in Great Britain, France, Sweden, and most of Canada' have sex education programs that provide more comprehensive information about prevention than U.S. schools. In addition, these countries use the media more often in 'government-sponsored campaigns for promoting responsible sexual behavior. (Boonstra, 2002, pp. 9–10, cited in Santrock, 2007, pp. 464–465; Crooks & Baur, 2014)

A third reason for the differences in teen pregnancy rates between the United States and other Western countries involves

*access to family planning services.* In countries that are more accepting of teenage sexual relationships, teenagers also have easier access to reproductive health services. In Canada, France, Great Britain, and Sweden, contraceptive services are integrated into other types of primary health care and are available free or at low cost for all teenagers. Generally, teens (in these countries) know where to obtain information and services and receive confidential and nonjudgmental care. In the United States, where attitudes about teenage sexual relationships are more conflicted, teens have a harder time obtaining contraceptive services. Many do not have health insurance or cannot get birth control as part of their basic health care.

*(Boonstra, 2002, pp. 9–10, cited in Santrock, 2007, pp. 464–465)*

## Critical Thinking Questions

- What do you think are the reasons why so many teenagers in the United States get pregnant? What are their motivating factors?
- Are U.S. teenagers getting the wrong messages about sexuality and pregnancy? If so, what are they? What messages should U.S. teenagers be getting?
- Should sexual expression by U.S. adolescents be more accepted? Why or why not? If so, how should society convey ideas about appropriate behavior?
- Should contraception be made more readily available to U.S. adolescents? Why or why not?

and home visitation programs" appear to contribute to adolescent mothers' improved life circumstances (Klein & AAP Committee on Adolescence, 2005; Papalia & Feldman, 2012, p. 402). Social workers can participate in such programs by providing pregnant adolescents with support, information, linkage with resources, and access to health care.

## Long-Term Negative Effects for Children

Studies also reveal negative effects on the children of teen pregnancies themselves. As the children of teenage mothers mature, they tend to have more difficulties in school (Rathus, 2014). Many of them "face a life of challenges that accompany poverty, including poor nutrition, violence in the local neighborhood, little schooling, and inadequate health care"; they also "grow up at high risk of becoming single parents themselves" (Macionis, 2013, p. 193).

What does all this mean for social workers? It means that children having children is a serious issue. Social work practitioners working with youths may need to provide these young people with information about contraception, sexually transmitted infections, and the responsibilities of parenthood. Social workers may also be in the position to help adolescents undertake a decision-making process whereby they make educated, responsible choices.

### Reasons Teens Get Pregnant

To determine what resources and services are needed, we must understand the dynamics behind a problem. Why does the problem exist? What are teenagers' needs? What can social services and social workers do to meet them?

Although female adolescents are more likely to use contraception than they've been in past decades, many fail to use it every time or in some situations. Consider the following facts (Guttmacher Institute, 2011):

- *Although only 13% of teens have ever had vaginal sex by age 15, sexual activity is common by the late teen years___ [Seventy percent have had sexual intercourse by age 19.]*
- *On average, young people have sex for the first time at about age 17, ... but they do not marry until their mid-20s___ [This long time frame increases the risk of pregnancy and sexually transmitted infections (STIs).]*
- *A sexually active teen who does not use a contraceptive has a 90% chance of becoming pregnant within a year....*
- *The majority of sexually experienced teens (79% of females and 87% of males) used contraceptives the first time they had sex....*
- *Contraceptive use at first premarital sex has been increasing. Fifty-six percent of women whose first premarital sex occurred before 1985 used a method, compared with 76% in 2000–2004 and 84% in 2005–2008....*
- *In 2006–2008, some 84% of female teens and 93% of male teens reported using contraceptives at last sex. These proportions represent a marked improvement since 1995, when only 71% of female teens and 82% of male teens*

*had reported using a method at last sex. However, the proportions were unchanged between 2002 and 2006–2008....*
- *Nearly one in five female teens at risk of unintended pregnancy (19%) were not using any contraceptive method at last intercourse.*

Teens who are not in stable relationships, have sexual intercourse only infrequently, have a significantly older partner, or begin having intercourse at an early age are less likely to use contraception (Crooks & Baur, 2014). Factors related to increased likelihood of contraceptive use include a close relationship with parents, including good communication channels, success in school, family values that stress responsible behavior, and having accurate information about contraception (Crooks & Baur, 2014).

### Failure to Use Birth Control

There are a number of reasons for imperfect contraceptive use. Adolescents often have a deep sense of privacy about sexual behavior and feel embarrassed discussing it with partners, friends, or parents (Crooks & Baur, 2014). Thus a young woman may feel extremely uncomfortable talking to a partner about such intimate issues as putting a condom on his penis or placing a diaphragm in her vagina.

Many adolescents may have inadequate knowledge about birth control methods and inadequate access to contraception (Crooks & Baur, 2014; Hyde & DeLamater, 2014). Other adolescents may adhere to myths about sex. For instance, many teens inaccurately believe that they are not old enough to conceive, that "the first time" doesn't count, that they must have intercourse much more frequently than they do in order to conceive, that it is perfectly safe to have sex during certain times of the month, and that withdrawal before ejaculation is an effective birth control method.

Focus on Critical Thinking 15.2 discusses conservative and liberal views concerning whose responsibility it is to provide young people with adequate sex education and information.

*Case Example* Once I gave a one-time sex education program (as an invited guest social work professor) to about 200 teenagers in which I responded to their questions, written anonymously. After the program, two teenagers sheepishly approached me. Apparently they had been too embarrassed to ask

# CONSERVATIVE AND LIBERAL VIEWS ON POLICY REGARDING THE PROVISION OF SEX EDUCATION

A *conservative* value orientation might emphasize that it is parents' responsibility to provide information about sex to their children and that schools should not interfere with parental prerogative. A *liberal* perspective, in contrast, might stress that children need information about sex regardless of who provides it. The important thing is that they get information so they can make responsible decisions.

**EP 8a**

## Critical Thinking Questions

- Should parents have primary responsibility for providing sex education to their children?
- Should schools ask parents permission to provide sex information to their children?
- In the event that parents refuse permission, should their children be denied information about sex?
- What type of content about sex should be provided to young people? Information about contraception? Moral values? Abortion?
- Do your answers to these questions reflect more of a conservative or a liberal perspective?

their questions even anonymously. The first young woman, age 16, said that she had had sex with her boyfriend and used vaginal foam as a contraceptive. Unfortunately, afterward she had noticed that the container had an expiration date of six months before. She asked if I thought that she would be all right, that she would not be pregnant. This was a difficult situation, and there was not much I could do. Even when they have not expired, spermicides (sperm killers) such as contraceptive foam used without other forms of contraception such as a condom have a failure rate as high as 28% (Hyde & DeLamater, 2014). I responded by encouraging the young woman to get a home pregnancy test or go to a Planned Parenthood clinic for one. Even if she chose the home test, I suggested going to Planned Parenthood anyway. In the event that she was pregnant, a counselor could help her make a decision about what to do. And if she was not pregnant, a counselor could assist her in determining what type of contraception would be most effective for her in the future. I made certain she knew the nearest Planned Parenthood clinic's location and that she had a means of getting there.

The second teen, a thin, gangly young woman with braces who looked like she was 12, hesitantly approached me. She bluntly asked, "If someone gives a guy oral sex and swallows it, can she get pregnant?" I had to keep myself from smiling and explained to her that someone could not get pregnant under those circumstances. I did caution her,

however, about the potential for contracting sexually transmitted infections, including HIV.

## Other Psychological Reasons

Other reasons for not using birth control involve psychologically wanting to have a baby. Strong, DeVault, Sayad, and Yarber (2005) comment, "The idea of having someone to love them exclusively and unconditionally is a strong incentive for some teenage girls" (pp. 402–403). In essence, they feel a baby will fulfill their own emotional needs. Unfortunately, they don't understand that it's supposed to be the other way around. The last person you should expect to meet all of your needs for nurturance is a helpless infant. Strong and his colleagues (2008) comment:

*Others see having a baby as a way to escape from an oppressive home environment. Both teen males and females may see parenthood as a way to enhance their status, to give them an aura of maturity, or to enhance their masculinity or femininity. Some believe a baby will cement a shaky relationship. (p. 180)*

There are yet other reasons teens may not use birth control. They might not want to bother with contraception. They might believe that sexual activity is more pleasurable without it. They may worry that their parents will find out. Finally, they may feel invulnerable to pregnancy, viewing it as something that happens only to other people.

## Social Work Roles

No consistent national policy exists for addressing teen pregnancies and parenting services; however, federal funding is available to develop programs through "block grants to states for direct services" (Mather & Lager, 2000, p. 204). Social workers may assume many roles and pursue various goals when providing services to adolescents concerning pregnancy and parenting. Goals include prevention of pregnancy, identification of pregnancy, counseling concerning alternatives, help during pregnancy, help for teenage fathers, and help after the pregnancy.

**EP 1**

### Prevention of Pregnancy

Primary prevention of pregnancy involves preventing the problem altogether, assuming that the pregnancy is a problem. Adolescents need both information and ready access to contraception so they can make responsible decisions.

**EP 4c, 7d, 8a**

Some people may wonder whether sex education programs in schools teach youths everything they need to know. The answer is, not necessarily. Program content and methods vary radically. They range from showing a couple of DVDs and handing out brochures to offering a comprehensive curriculum that uses a variety of teaching methods including DVDs, reading materials, lectures, discussion, and role plays.

In terms of the approach to sex education, Hyde and DeLamater (2014) remark:

> *Most efforts to provide sex education in schools have utilized one of two principal approaches: comprehensive sex education and abstinence-only programs. Comprehensive sex education treats abstinence as merely one option for youths in a curriculum that provides broad-based information about such topics as sexual maturation; contraception; abortion; strategies for effective decision making and for saying no to unwanted sex; STIs [sexually transmitted infections]; relationship issues; and sexual orientation. In abstinence-only programs, youths are instructed to abstain from sex until marriage, and discussions of contraception are either prohibited entirely or permitted only to emphasize the alleged shortcomings of birth control methods. (p. 370)*

Research strongly indicates that "comprehensive sex education programs that stress safer sex and provide accurate information about various contraceptive methods actually increase the use of birth control, reduce teenage pregnancies, reduce high-risk sexual behavior, do not hasten the onset of intercourse (and in some cases actually delay onset), do not increase the frequency of intercourse, and do not increase the number of an adolescent's sexual partners (in some cases they reduce partner number)" (Crooks & Baur, 2014, p. 370). Effective sex education programs:

- *focus on reducing risk-taking behavior....*
- *are based on theories of social learning....*
- *teach through experiential activities that personalize the messages....*
- *address media and other social influences that encourage sexual risk-taking behaviors....*
- *reinforce clear and appropriate values....*
- *enhance communication skills.*

*(Hyde & DeLamater, 2014, p. 540)*

Social workers working in social service agencies or schools may see the need to advocate for and develop sex education programs for adolescent clients. They may also provide information during counseling to individuals or groups. Highlight 15.5 offers some suggestions about how to provide straightforward information about sex.

Access to methods of birth control also is important in preventing pregnancy. Components that seem to increase adolescents' use of clinics include "free services, an absence of parental notification, convenient hours for students, walk-in service, a diversity of locations, and warm and caring staff" (Weatherley & Cartoof, 1988, p. 39).

### Identification of Pregnancy

It's important for social workers to help young clients identify a pregnancy as early as possible for two basic reasons. First, good nutrition, prenatal medical care, and avoidance of harmful substances are essential for healthy fetal development. A fetus is at greatest risk of harm early in the pregnancy. Second, adolescents have more options potentially available to them early in the pregnancy (e.g., a first-trimester abortion).

Social workers who work with teenagers should encourage them to confront and acknowledge the

| HIGHLIGHT 15.5 | PROVIDING STRAIGHTFORWARD INFORMATION ABOUT SEX |
|---|---|

Effectively conveying sensitive information about sexuality can be difficult. Social workers and other professionals in the position of supplying sexual information to teenagers (and adults, for that matter) ideally should do the following (Hyde & DeLamater, 2014):

1. *Have accurate information about sexuality.* To convey information about sex and answer explicit questions, accurate information is essential. Workers don't need a degree in sexology to convey such information. Rather, they can learn via taking courses, attending seminars, or reading sexuality textbooks. No one knows the answer to every question. Instead of being defensive about gaps in their knowledge, workers should feel comfortable enough to admit ignorance and simply look up the answer.

2. *Feel comfortable talking about sexuality.* Providing accurate information is only one part of teaching about sex. Teenagers should feel as comfortable as possible approaching a worker and asking questions. They should not fear that the worker will criticize them or make fun of them.

3. *Be a good listener.* No matter how much knowledge workers have or how warm and caring they are, if they don't connect with the teenager, they won't convey the information needed. Listening means striving to understand what the person making a statement or asking a question really means. What does she or he really want and need to know?

The following are actual questions asked anonymously by teenagers age 13–18. They are straightforward and may be considered vulgar by some. However, they reflect the serious need for specific, practical information concerning topics usually not addressed in school. They are cited as they were written, spelling errors and all (actually, these are some of the tamer questions asked).

As you read the questions, think about how you might answer them.

- What is the average age a woman has an organism?
- What happens if a girl is too tight?
- When a girl gives a guy "head" can she get any STDs?

- How big is the average penis?
- What are the girls erotic zones?
- Do women always bleed when the hymen is broken?
- What are the risks of having an abortion?
- How does it feel when you get devirginized?
- What can you do if your boyfriends is too big and it hurts every time you have sex?
- What can you do if the guy tries something and you say no but he keep going?
- Should you have sex if you're ashamed of your body?
- What is the percentage of boys that masturbate? Girls?
- When you're making love with a guy, does he honestly think of the emotional aspect or does he just want a piece?
- What is group sex?
- Why do males and females hide their feelings about each other?
- How can you have better orgasms?
- How do you know if you've had an orgasm? For female, what does it feel like inside?
- What is the next best contraceptive other than the pill for girls and guys?
- Can a man sperm and urine at the same time?

Note that professionals must be aware of the controversial nature of talk about sex. They must also be attuned to the attitudes and expectations of agencies, administrators, communities, and parents. This can pose a dilemma for workers. On the one hand, they may know what information teens require to make responsible decisions. On the other, they may face negative reactions by parents and others.[5]

[5]SIECUS (Sexuality Information and Education Council of the United States) is an excellent source of information concerning sex education programming, and how to work with agencies and communities to provide young people with information concerning sexuality. The New York office contact address is PO Box 5175, New York, NY 10185-5175. Phone: 212/819-9970. Fax: 212/819-9776. The Washington, DC, office is located at 1012 14th Street, NW, Washington, DC 20005. Phone: 202/265-2405. Fax: 202/462-2340. E-mail: http://www.siecus.org/

fact that pregnancy might result from sexual activities. As discussed previously, workers can give adolescents information about potential consequences of their behavior so they can make more responsible decisions. Workers can also help adolescents face the fact that they might be pregnant instead of ignoring the possibility as long as possible. Many pregnant teenagers adopt an "out of sight, out of mind" attitude: If they don't think about the pregnancy, it doesn't exist. Unfortunately, their options decrease as time goes on. Unless there's a miscarriage, pregnancy usually doesn't go away by itself.

### Counseling Concerning Alternatives

Once the pregnancy has been established as fact, decisions must be made. Social workers apply the basic approach of helping the adolescent identify her alternatives, and then evaluate the pros and cons of each.

**EP 7d**

Options include having an abortion, going through with the pregnancy and keeping the baby, or continuing with the pregnancy and giving the baby up for adoption.

For each individual, options will have different pros and cons. One individual may have strong religious beliefs that affect her decision; another will not have such convictions. States also have large variations regarding the legal circumstances under which abortions may be obtained. It's a social worker's job to help the client evaluate the situation from her unique perspective and make the choice that's best for her.

Mather and Lager (2000) also suggest that the father "needs to be given every opportunity to take part in this decision, if possible, and his legal rights need to be clearly laid out for him" (p. 205).

### Help During Pregnancy

Social workers can provide important help and support during pregnancy. It's easy for teenagers to become depressed and isolated during that time. Physical changes may have an impact, especially in view of the great emphasis placed on physical appearance, attractiveness, and popularity during adolescence. One junior high teacher once said that talking about the responsibility of pregnancy and teen parenthood had absolutely no effect on her students. However, the young women sat up with serious faces and widened eyes when told that once they

do have a baby, women often have stretch marks on their abdomens for the rest of their lives. To these young women, stretch marks were serious consequences.

Pregnant adolescents may also need help relating to friends and family members. This involves maintaining good communication with and receiving emotional support from others around them. Many times a social worker may need to do active outreach to the pregnant teen. Home visits may be especially useful. Counseling can be provided either individually or on a group basis.

Pregnant teens most often need counseling about good nutrition and the effects of lifestyle on the fetus. For instance, they need to be well informed about the results of alcohol and drug use during pregnancy. Teens also may need help in determining what to do about the pregnancy and making other plans involving living conditions, day care, education, and employment.

*The Importance of Prenatal Care*  Prenatal care is critically important for mothers and infants. Each year almost one million women in the United States go through pregnancy and have babies, but receive inadequate medical services and prenatal care (U.S. Department of Health and Human Services [HHS], n.d.). In a recent year, 17.2% of new mothers in 30 states indicated they couldn't get prenatal care as soon as they needed it; teenage mothers were the most likely to experience delayed receipt of care (29.8%) (USDHHS, 2013). Women who receive no prenatal care have babies "who are three times more likely to be born at low birth weight, and five times more likely to die" than their counterparts born to mothers receiving such care (USDHHS, n.d.). Barriers to receiving care include poverty, lack of transportation to receive care, and being unaware of the pregnancy (USDHHS, 2013). It makes senses that young women who are poor and relatively uneducated are likely to receive the poorest prenatal care.

Newman and Newman (2015) report:

*Comprehensive prenatal care programs can improve birth outcomes even in a high-risk population. This kind of coordination involves more than providing prenatal checkups and information about health care during pregnancy. It recognizes the complex challenges that face women in poverty, including violence, hazardous living conditions, poor quality services, and unstable or disruptive social relationships.... Effective interventions must include nonmedical support services, such as making sure the woman has access to food stamps [Supplemental Nutrition Assistance Program (SNAP)]; is part of the Women, Infants, and Children (WIC) food stamp program; has the transportation needed for prenatal and postnatal health care appointments; and receives housing assistance or job training as necessary. (p. 116)*

*Case Example*  Shared Beginnings, a Denver program, provides a good example of how various facets of a community came together to address the issue of at-risk young pregnant women and provide resources (Balsanek, 1998).[6] Initial consciousness-raising occurred through extensive media coverage of the problem, alerting the public to the fact that increasing numbers of poor, single, and young mothers were failing to seek or receive prenatal care. Although the program was spearheaded by a concerned volunteer philanthropist, it illustrates how social workers can start up a program to meet clients' needs. The initiator brought citizens, social services representatives, health-care personnel, and potential financial backers together to launch the project. Fund-raising efforts included a luncheon program supported by influential community members and solicitation of financial donations.

Participants involved in the project established five basic program goals. The first was to educate the community concerning the importance of prenatal health care and to alter attitudes on health care's behalf. The second goal was the initiation of a "Sharing Partners" program that sent volunteer paraprofessionals out into the community to educate residents about prenatal care and to encourage them to use services. The third goal was to establish an agency complete with director, administrative assistant, and volunteer coordinator to monitor progress. The fourth was the creation of a "Baby Store" located in a local hospital where "coupons could be redeemed for new baby care items to reinforce health care appointment attendance before the baby is born and immunizations after the baby is

born" (Balsanek, 1998, p. 414). The final goal was to integrate a research component to evaluate the program's effectiveness and provide suggestions for improvement. In summary, "Shared Beginnings represents a grassroots [developed and supported by citizens at lower levels of the power structure] approach to providing the community support that poor and at-risk families need to raise healthy children" (p. 418).

## Helping Adolescent Fathers

It's important not to forget that babies born to adolescent mothers also have fathers (Newman & Newman, 2015; Yarber & Sayad, 2013). Despite myths to the contrary, most teen fathers are significantly affected by their child's birth and are involved to various degrees in the child's early life (Yarber & Sayad, 2013).

Yarber and Sayad (2013) reflect:

*Adolescent fathers typically remain physically or psychologically involved throughout the pregnancy and for a least some time after the birth. It is usually difficult for teenage fathers to contribute much to the support of their children, although most express the intention of doing so during the pregnancy. Most have a lower income, less education, and more children than men who postpone having children until age 20 or older. They may feel overwhelmed by the responsibility and may doubt their ability to be good providers. Though many teenage fathers are the sons of absent fathers, most do want to learn to be fathers. Teen fathers are a seriously neglected group who face many hardships. Policies and interventions directed at reducing teen fatherhood will have to take into consideration the many factors that influence it and focus efforts throughout the life cycle. (pp. 180–181)*

An adolescent father may need help in expressing his feelings, defining his role, and contributing where he can in caring for his child. Additionally, adolescent fathers may need help and encouragement in pursuing educational and vocational goals.

## Helping Mothers After the Pregnancy

It's important to keep in mind the continuum of service that social workers may provide. The young mother's needs do not suddenly stop after the baby is born. The case is not automatically closed. There are at least three major areas where adolescent

---

[6]From "Addressing At-Risk Pregnant Women's Issues Through Community, Individual, and Corporate Grassroots Efforts," by J. Balsanek. In P. L. Ewalt, E. M. Freeman, and D. L. Poole (Eds.), *Community Building: Renewal, Well-Being, and Shared Responsibility*, pp. 411–419, 1998, National Association of Social Workers, Inc.

mothers may need ongoing help (Weatherley & Cartoof, 1988). First, they may need help in learning about positive parenting and child management skills. Second, adolescent mothers often need help in avoiding more pregnancies. Pregnancy is no guarantee that they have an ade-

**EP 8e**

quate knowledge of conception or of birth control methodology. Both information and ready access to contraception are necessary. Third, young mothers often need assistance in life planning. Issues include continuing their education, gaining employment, finding day care for their children, and determining where and how they will live.

# Chapter Summary

The following summarizes this chapter's content as it relates to the learning objectives presented at the beginning of the chapter. Chapter content will help prepare students to:

## LO1 Describe school social work and school social work roles.

School social workers strive to improve the overall functioning of students, teachers, school systems, and communities. Their roles include consultant, counselor, facilitator, educator, advocate, broker, case manager, community intervention collaborator, and policy initiator and developer. Advocacy for cultural competence and on the behalf of refugee and immigrant students is discussed.

## LO2 Identify the types of groups school social workers run.

Groups social workers run include groups for parents of students; for students who are parents; for students whose families are experiencing divorce; for students who are addressing substance abuse issues; for students with attention deficit hyperactivity disorder; for trauma-related recovery; for students at risk of dropping out; for students addressing stress, grief, and loss issues; for socialization and peer interaction skill development; and for addressing racial and cultural issues.

## LO3 Propose ways to enhance multiculturalism and reduce racism in schools.

Social workers can fight racism and encourage multiculturalism by leading open discussions, infusing such content in curricula, focusing on the appreciation of difference, providing school staff with multicultural training, and involving parents in efforts to promote multiculturalism.

## LO4 Discuss issues faced by lesbian and gay youths (including the "coming-out" process).

Same-gender sexual orientation may place additional social pressures on youths. Social workers can help lesbian and gay people explore their sexual identities and come out to others. Coming out involves both coming out to oneself and also to others including other people with the same sexual orientation, family and friends, and the world in general. Careful thought should be given to whom to trust and how to come out.

## LO5 Identify and refute myths about lesbian and gay people.

Untrue myths about lesbian and gay people are cited and refuted. They include several involving appearance, behavior, treatment of children, and relationships.

## LO6 Describe two community programs for youths (one that empowers Latino and Latina youths through a community assets assessment and one that explores how an African American spiritual community empowers its youths).

New Bridges targeted a group of Latino and Latina youths who were at risk and hired them to conduct a community assets assessment. Results included the identification of student leaders to sponsor community projects, the provision of invitations to local business leaders to come in to speak to students, and special school projects emphasizing community strengths.

An ethnographic study in Utah resulted in a church-sponsored support program for African American youth and the development of a computer literacy program.

## LO7 Discuss school violence and social workers' role in its prevention.

Violence has become a major problem in schools. The dynamics of school violence are discussed. To assist in the prevention of school violence, social workers can conduct needs assessments, provide conflict resolution, and develop violence prevention programs. Bullying and cyberbullying are also examined.

## LO8 Examine teenage sexual activity, pregnancy, parenting issues, and social work roles.

Of all births in the United States, 9.3% are to teenage mothers. More than half have their babies, 35% have abortions, and 14% have miscarriages. The U.S. pregnancy rate is significantly higher than that of other Western countries. Possible reasons include that society is not clearly conveying to teens that childbearing is an adult activity, they are not receiving clear messages about the normalcy of sexual behavior, and family planning information and contraception are not readily available. The importance of comprehensive sex education and the provision of straightforward information about sexuality is stressed.

## LO9 Encourage critical thinking (about the reasons for teen pregnancy, what should be done about it, and the provision of sex education).

Critical thinking questions were raised concerning the reasons for teen pregnancy and how the issue could be addressed. Other questions were raised concerning conservative and liberal views on policies regarding the provision of sex education and the programmatic content that should be included.

## LOOKING AHEAD

Chapter 16 explores the final field of social work practice in this book—social work and services in criminal justice. As with health care and mental health, there is some overlap between social work with youths and criminal justice—specifically, juvenile corrections and young people's involvement with gangs. Chapter 16 will introduce crime and criminal justice, describe social work roles, and explore primary criminal justice settings.

## COMPETENCY NOTES

The following identifies where Educational Policy (EP) competencies and their component behaviors are discussed in the chapter.

**EP 1 (Competency 1)—Demonstrate Ethical and Professional Behavior.** *(p. 482):* The wide range of professional roles assumed by social workers within school settings is introduced. *(p. 484):* Nine specific professional roles in school social work are identified and explained. *(p. 496):* A social worker's professional role in the prevention of school violence is discussed. *(p. 507):* The professional social work role with respect to the prevention of teen pregnancy is addressed.

**EP 1b Use reflection and self-regulation to manage personal values and maintain professionalism in practice situations.** *(p. 491):* Social workers should use self-reflection to manage personal values and maintain professionalism when working with LGBT people.

**EP 1d Use technology ethically and appropriately to facilitate practice outcomes.** *(p. 499):* Not only should professional social workers use technology ethically and appropriately, but they should also monitor students' use of technology so that it is ethical and appropriate.

**EP 2 (Competency 2)—Engage Diversity and Difference in Practice.** *(p. 487):* School social workers should recognize the extent to which societal structures in education may oppress and alienate people from diverse cultures. *(p. 487):* Immigration status is a dimension of diversity. *(p. 489):* School social workers should recognize the extent to which people from diverse cultures may be marginalized and alienated. *(p. 490):* School social workers should recognize the extent to which people with nonheterosexual orientations may be oppressed, marginalized, and alienated. *(p. 493):* Stereotypes and myths about LGBT people serve as forms of oppression and discrimination.

**EP 2a Apply and communicate understanding of the importance of diversity and difference in shaping life experiences in practice at the micro, mezzo, and macro levels.** *(p. 487):* Social workers should recognize how cultural differences shape life experiences in school settings.

*(p. 489):* Practitioners should recognize the extent to which cultural differences shape life experiences. *(p. 490):* School social workers should recognize that sexual orientation is important in shaping life experiences.

**EP 2b Present themselves as learners and engage clients and constituencies as experts of their own experiences.** *(p. 491):* Social workers should view themselves as learners about LGBT issues and engage lesbian and gay adolescents as informants.

**EP 2c Apply self-awareness and self-regulation to manage the influence of personal biases and values in working with diverse clients and constituencies.** *(p. 491):* Social workers should increase their own self-awareness about personal biases concerning LGBT people.

**EP 3 (Competency 3)—Advance Human Rights and Social, Economic, and Environmental Justice.**

**EP 3a Apply their understanding of social, economic, and environmental justice to advocate for human rights at the individual and system levels.** *(p. 486):* School social workers should advocate for human rights, and social and economic justice on the behalf of students.

**EP 4 (Competency 4)—Engage in Practice-Informed Research and Research-Informed Practice.**

**EP 4c Use and translate research evidence to inform and improve practice, policy, and service delivery.** *(p. 494):* The New Bridges program involved a community assets assessment that could be used to inform service delivery and practice. *(p. 501):* A needs assessment gathers information to inform practice. *(p. 507):* Research evidence should be used to inform and improve practice such as the provision of effective sex education.

**EP 5 (Competency 5)—Engage in Policy Practice.**

**EP 5c Apply critical thinking to analyze, formulate, and advocate for policies that advance human rights and social, economic, and environmental justice.** *(p. 489):* School social workers should strive to establish policies and programs that advance the social well-being of students and enhance the educational system.

**EP 7 (Competency 7)—Assess Individuals, Families, Groups, Organizations, and Communities.**

**EP 7a Collect and organize data, and apply critical thinking to interpret information from clients and constituencies.** *(p. 483):* This case example illustrates how school social workers collect, organize, and interpret client data. *(p. 504):* Critical thinking questions are posed regarding adolescent pregnancy and the dynamics involved.

**EP 7b Apply knowledge of human behavior and the social environment, person-in-environment, and other multidisciplinary theoretical frameworks in the analysis of assessment data from clients and constituencies.** *(p. 495):* An ethnographic study such as that employed here can be used to assess the person-in-environment context.

**EP 7c Develop mutually agreed-on intervention goals and objectives based on the critical assessment of strengths, needs, and challenges within clients and constituencies.** *(p. 483):* This case example reflects how a school social worker assesses individual and family strengths and limitations. It also demonstrates how the school social worker works with the mother to develop mutually agreed-on goals.

**EP 7d Select appropriate intervention strategies based on the assessment, research knowledge, and values and preferences of clients and constituencies.** *(p. 483):* This case example demonstrates how the school social worker selects appropriate intervention strategies. *(p. 485):* Examples of groups in school settings are explained, which a school social worker may select as appropriate intervention strategies. *(p. 489):* Appropriate intervention strategies for enhancing multiculturalism in schools are discussed. *(p. 491):* Appropriate intervention strategies are discussed for helping LGBT adolescents in the coming-out process. *(p. 507):* Assessment and implementation of interventions that prevent pregnancy (such as comprehensive sex education) are discussed. *(p. 509):* Social workers can help pregnant adolescents make decisions and select appropriate intervention strategies.

**EP 8 (Competency 8)—Intervene with Individuals, Families, Groups, Organizations, and Communities.** *(p. 493):* Social work intervention involves change and improvement at the organizational and community levels.

**EP 8a Critically choose and implement interventions to achieve practice goals and enhance capacities of clients and constituencies.** *(p. 504):* Critical thinking questions are posed regarding adolescent pregnancy, the dynamics involved, and how it should be addressed. *(p. 506):* Critical thinking questions are asked concerning conservative and liberal perspectives on sex education; such questions should help guide thought about effective intervention. *(p. 507):* Assessment and implementation of interventions that prevent pregnancy (such as comprehensive sex education) are discussed.

**EP 8c Use inter-professional collaboration as appropriate to achieve beneficial practice outcomes.** *(p. 489):* School social workers can collaborate with colleagues and clients to initiate and develop effective educational policies.

**EP 8d Negotiate, mediate, and advocate with and on behalf of diverse clients and constituencies.** *(p. 483):* This case example illustrates how a school social worker can advocate for clients. *(p. 486):* School social workers should advocate on the behalf of their students to improve conditions and services. *(p. 489):* School social workers should advocate for policies and programs on the behalf of students.

**EP 8e Facilitate effective transitions and endings that advance mutually agreed-on goals.** *(p. 491):* Social workers can help LGBT students make the transition of coming out. *(p. 511):* Social workers can help to facilitate adolescents' transition to motherhood.

# 16 Social Work and Services in the Criminal Justice System

A. Ramey/PhotoEdit

## Learning Objectives    This chapter will help prepare students to:

**LO 1** Review the criminal justice system (and define some of the key concepts involved). **Introducing Crime and Criminal Justice** (p. 516)

**LO 2** Examine who commits crime. **Who Commits Crimes? Race, Social Class, and Gender Issues** (p. 516)

**LO 3** Describe the types of crime. **Highlight 16.1** (p. 517)

**LO 4** Explore the incidence of crime. **Are Crime Rates Rising or Falling?** (p. 519)

**LO 5** Employ critical thinking skills (about the ethical dilemma of punishment versus empowerment,

and the issue of providing expensive health care for prisoners). **Focus on Critical Thinking 16.1** (p. 520)

**LO 6** Review the wide range of criminal justice settings in which social workers practice. **Criminal Justice Settings and Forensic Social Work** (p. 522)

**LO 7** Describe domestic violence (including its cycle, dynamics, and how to address the problem). **Domestic Violence Services** (p. 524)

**LO 8** Discuss youth gangs (including membership, types, prevention, and treatment). **Youth Gangs** (p. 528)

*Consider the following facts about crime and the criminal justice system:*

*At the end of 2013, approximately 1,574,700 people were jailed or imprisoned in federal or state correctional facilities; this reflected an increase of 4% in the number of persons admitted to such facilities compared to 2012 (Carson, 2014).*

*Every year 10 million serious crimes are committed in the United States; it's likely that every one of us will be victim of crime sometime in our lives (Macionis, 2013).*

*Although men are 14 times more likely than women to be imprisoned, the crime rate for women is increasing; "[w]omen experienced the largest increase in arrests (over a 30 percent increase) for larceny-theft, vagrancy, and driving under the influence" (Eitzen, Zinn, & Smith, 2014, p. 289).*

*African Americans, who represent about 13% of the population in the United States, commit and are arrested for 38.5% of all violent crimes and almost 29.3% of all property crimes (Mooney et al., 2015).*

*In the United States, a murder occurs every 36 minutes, a forcible rape every 6 minutes, a robbery every 90 seconds, a larceny-theft every 5 seconds, and a motor vehicle theft every 43 seconds (Macionis, 2013).*

*As these figures suggest, crime is a serious social problem in the United States. Social workers practice in a range of settings characterized by people who have committed or are accused of committing crimes.*

## Introducing Crime and Criminal Justice  **LO 1**

Social workers are among the many people who work in the **criminal justice system**—the complex, integrated system of programs, policies, laws, and agencies devoted to preventing and controlling crime. The system's functions include **adjudication** (passing legal judgment), **incarceration** (confining by putting in prison or jail), and **rehabilitation** (restoring to a state of productive, noncriminal functioning in society).

**Crime** is the commission of a harmful offense or act that is legally prohibited. **Criminals** include anyone whom the courts convict of a crime. **Law** is the body of formal principles and decisions established by government that determine what behavior is appropriate and allowed and what is not. Laws essentially guide social behavior. Highlight 16.1 describes the main types of crime committed in the United States.

## Who Commits Crimes? Race, Social Class, and Gender Issues  **LO 2**

Although people with virtually any characteristics can commit crimes, some people are simply more likely than others to do so. Crime is related to the variables of gender, age, race, and social class (Eitzen & Zinn, 2012; Mooney et al., 2015).

**EP 2, 2a**

### Gender and Crime

Although men make up about half the population, they are much more likely than women to commit crimes and these are much more likely to be violent crimes (Mooney et al., 2015). Taking all arrests into account, 73.8% are men including 80.1% for all violent crimes and 62.6% of all property crimes (Mooney et al., 2015). Women, however, are

# HIGHLIGHT 16.1    MAIN TYPES OF CRIME    LO 3

Crimes are either felonies or misdemeanors. **Felonies** are grave offenses punishable by at least a year in prison and possibly even death; **misdemeanors** are less severe offenses, with punishments ranging from incarceration of less than a year to monetary fines (Macionis, 2013). Two major categories of crime are violent crimes and property crimes. **Violent crime** (or crime against  **EP 7b, 8b** persons) is the act of using "force or the threat of force against others"; **property crime** (or crime against property) is "the taking of money or property from another without force, the threat of force, or the destruction of property" (emphasis omitted) (Kendall, 2013, pp. 195, 200). Note that the Uniform Crime Reporting (UCR) Program under the auspices of the Federal Bureau of Investigation (FBI) is the primary source of data on crimes committed in the United States.

Violent crimes include:

- *Murder:* The purposeful, unlawful killing of one person by another or a group of others.
- *Aggravated assault:* The act of attacking another person with the intent to inflict serious harm or kill that person.
- *Rape:* "Penetration, no matter how slight, of the vagina or anus with any body part or object, or oral penetration by a sex organ of another person, without the consent of the victim" (Uniform Crime Reporting Program, 2014). (Note that *statutory rape* is "[i]ntercourse with a person under the age of [legal] consent" (Crooks & Baur, 2014, p. G-7).
- *Robbery:* The act of stealing property in the hands of another person by using force or the threat of force. (Note that because of the force involved this is considered a violent crime even though it involves property.)

Property crimes include:

- *Larceny (simple theft):* The act of stealing property. Larceny includes "shoplifting, picking pockets, purse-snatching, taking property from a motor vehicle, and bicycle theft" (Macionis, 2013, p. 149).
- *Burglary:* The act of breaking into a house or other structure with the intent to steal.
- *Motor vehicle theft:* The act of "theft or attempted theft of a motor vehicle" (Kendall, 2013, p. 201).

- *Arson:* "Any willful or malicious burning or attempting to burn, with or without intent to defraud, a dwelling, house, public building, motor vehicle or aircraft, [or] personal property of another" Uniform Crime Report (UCR, 2011).

Other categories of crime involve those offenses not considered violent or property crimes. Examples include the following:

- *White-collar crime:* Offenses include crimes "committed by middle-class and upper-middle-class people in their business and social activities, (such as theft of company goods; embezzlement; bankruptcy fraud; swindles; tax evasion; forgery; theft of property by computer; passing bad checks; illicit copying of computer software, movies, and music; and fraudulent use of credit cards, automatic teller machines, and telephones)" (Eitzen et al., 2014, p. 294). Leon-Guerrero (2014) reports that "[o]ne of the most widespread forms of white-collar crime is Internet fraud and abuse, also known as **cybercrime**.... [C]rimes include identity theft, online credit card fraud schemes, theft of trade secrets, sales of counterfeit software, and computer intrusions (a hacker breaking into a system)" (p. 351).
- Identity theft is the illegal use of someone else's identifying or financial information for personal gain such as getting money or credit. Kornblum and Julian (2012) reflect: "The vast increase in the use of credit cards, in person or via the Internet, has resulted in an explosion in the crime of identity theft, which occurs when official identity cards and account numbers are copied or stolen and used for illegal purchases or other activities. Identity thieves use your personal information to impersonate you and either open new accounts with your background information or take existing accounts and spend as much money as they can in as short a time as possible before moving on to someone else's name and identifying information" (p. 153).
- *Corporate crime:* Illegal acts committed by large organizations to enhance profits. For example, consider the utility conglomerate Enron's fall into bankruptcy, one of the largest in U.S. history (CNN.com, 2001). Corporate leaders were

*(continued)*

accused of "fraudulent trading schemes" and devious "financial moves to hide debt and inflate profits that fueled Enron's downfall in 2001" (FindLaw Legal News and Commentary, 2005). The bankruptcy resulted in thousands of Enron "employees losing their life savings in 401(k) plans" linked with Enron stock (CNN.com, 2001). Another example involves Halliburton, one of the world's largest oilfield services providers. It had "been found guilty repeatedly of overcharging the government for fuel, services (food and housing of troops), and construction during and following the first and second Iraqi wars. More- over, contrary to federal laws prohibiting compa- nies from doing business with countries supporting terror—Iraq, Iran, and Libya—Halli- burton circumvented these restrictions by setting up subsidiaries in foreign countries (Herbert, 2003)" (Eitzen et al., 2014, p. 296).

- *Victimless (vice) crimes:* Illegal acts that technically have no victim or complainant (e.g., prostitution, selling illegal drugs, unlawful gambling). These are also referred to as "crimes against the moral

order" (Eitzen et al., 2014, p. 292) or "public-order crimes" (Kornblum & Julian, 2012, p. 149).

- *Organized (syndicated) crime:* Illegal acts com- mitted by an organized, hierarchical network of professional criminals working together to make money. Such crime organizations "tend to be large and diversified regional or national units. They may organize initially to carry on a particu- lar crime, such as drug trafficking, extortion, prostitution, or gambling. Later they may seek to control this activity in a given city or neighbor- hood, destroying or absorbing the competition. Eventually, they may expand into other types of crime, protecting their members from arrest through intimidation or bribery of public officials" (Eitzen & Zinn, 2012, p. 150).
- *Hate crime:* A "traditional offense like murder, arson, or vandalism with an added element of bias.... [It may involve] a criminal offense against a person or property motivated in whole or in part by an offender's bias against a race, religion, disability, ethnic origin or sexual orientation" (FBI, 2013b).

demonstrating an increased participation rate in some crimes "including larceny-theft (44 percent of arrests are of women), fraud (42 percent), embezzlement (51 percent), runaway youth (56 percent), and prosti- tution (69 percent). In addition, for all serious crimes, the gender gap is narrowing: From 2001 to 2010, the number of arrests of women increased by 10.5 percent, while arrests of men fell by 7 percent" (Macionis, 2013, p. 151).

Women are exposed to risk factors that can play a role in the increase in their criminal behavior. These factors include "substance abuse, mental illness," domestic violence, and the possibility of having been a victim of some type of abuse or crime in the past (National Criminal Justice Reference Service, n.d.).

## Age and Crime

Age is another factor related to crime. Younger peo- ple are more likely to commit crimes then older people (Eitzen et al., 20014; Mooney et al., 2015). Mooney and her colleagues (2015) explain:

*In 2012, 39.5 percent of all arrests in the United States were of people younger than age 25 (FBI, 2013a). Although those younger than age 25 made*

*up over half of all arrests in the United States for crimes such as robbery, burglary, vandalism, and arson, those younger than age 25 were significantly less likely to be arrested for white-color crimes such as embezzlement, fraud, forgery and counterfeiting. Those older than age 65 made up less than 1.0 per- cent of total arrests for the same year. (pp. 116–117)*

These high rates for young people may be attrib- uted to several possibilities. First, the penalties are not as severe for youths (Mooney et al., 2015). Second, young people often have trouble getting good jobs and adequate incomes. Third, police might "have their eye" on younger people more than older people as suspects, anticipating potential criminal activity.

## Race, Social Class, and Crime

Mooney and her colleagues (2015) report concerning the variables of race and social class, both also related to crime:

*Race is a factor in who gets arrested. Minorities are disproportionately represented in official statis- tics. [We have established that] ... although African Americans represent about 13% of the population, they account for 38.5% of all violent index offenses and 29.3% of all property index offenses.... They ... are six times more likely to be admitted to prison and, if admitted to prison for a violent crime, receive longer sentences than their [White] counterparts....*

*Nevertheless, it is inaccurate to conclude that race and crime are causally related. First, official statistics reflect the behaviors and policies of criminal justice actors. Thus the high rate of arrests, conviction, and incarceration of minorities may be a consequence of individual and institutional bias against minorities. For example, **racial profiling**—the practice of targeting suspects on the basis of race—may be responsible for their higher arrest rates. Proponents of the practice argue that because race, like gender, is a significant predictor of who commits crime, the practice should be allowed. Opponents hold that racial profiling is little more than discrimination, often based on stereotypes, and should therefore be abolished....*

*In a 2013 statement, President Obama acknowledged that he, as many other African American males, had been the victim of racial profiling.... Referring to the Trayvon Martin shooting, the President went on to say that "... the African American community is knowledgeable that there is a history of racial disparities in the application of our criminal laws, everything from the death penalty to enforcement of our drug laws" ... (Obama, 2013, p. 1). After the verdict, hundreds of protests occurred across the country with people carrying signs reading "Justice for Trayvon" and "Could I be the next?"...*

*Second, race and social class are closely related in that [non-Whites] are overrepresented in the lower classes. Because lower-class members lack legitimate means to acquire material goods, they may turn to instrumental, or economically motivated, crimes. In addition, although the "haves" typically earn social respect through their socioeconomic status, education achievement, and occupational role, the "have-nots" more often live in communities where respect is based on physical strength and violence. (pp. 117–119)*

Macionis (2013) proposes other rationales for racial differences:

*More police patrols are found in poor neighborhoods, which have a high African American population. Prejudice based on race and class can prompt people to suspect [Blacks] of criminal behavior simply on the basis of skin color.... Research suggests that such biases lead police to be quicker to arrest African Americans than [Whites]....*

*[An added] factor linking race and arrests involves family patterns. Seventy-three percent of [Black] children are born to single mothers, compared with twenty-nine percent of [White] children. Single mothers or fathers have less time to supervise children. The fact that single mothers typically earn less money adds to family pressures. For these reasons, children who grow up in poor families without fathers are at higher risk for criminality. (p. 152)*

Note that Asian Americans are less likely to be arrested for crimes; making up 3.7% of the population, they account for only 1.2% of arrests (Macionis, 2013). "This lower criminality is due to higher income levels and also a strong cultural emphasis on family, discipline, and honor, all of which tend to discourage criminal behavior" (Macionis, 2013, p. 152).

## Are Crime Rates Rising or Falling? `LO 4`

Crime rates are recorded in three basic ways: official statistics of crimes reported to police (e.g., the *Uniform Crime Reports*), surveys administered to population samples regarding victimization rates, and offenders' self-reports (Mooney et al., 2015).

According to the FBI Uniform Crime Reports, (FBI, 2013a), there was a 0.7% increase in the number of violent crimes from 2011 to 2012. Increases involved murder (+1.1%), aggravated assault (+1.1%), and forcible rape (+0.1%). The number of robberies decreased slightly (−0.1%). In terms of violent crime distribution in 2012, 62.6% were aggravated assaults, 29.2% were robberies, 6.9% were rapes, and 1.2% were murders. When looking at the 5- and 10-year trends in violent crime, the number of all violent crimes in 2012 decreased by 12.9% since 2008 and 12.2% since 2003.

The number of property crimes declined from 2011 to 2012 by 0.9% (FBI, 2013a). Burglaries decreased by 3.7%, larceny-thefts stayed the same, and motor vehicle thefts increased by 0.6%. Arson showed an increased occurrence of less than 0.1%. In terms of the type of property crime committed in

2012, 68.5% were larceny-theft, 23.4% were burglaries, and 8.0% were motor vehicle thefts. (The FBI does not report the number of arson incidents that occur because reporting practices vary so dramatically from one location to another.) The 10-year trend revealed that property crimes decreased by 14.1% between 2003 and 2012.

Macionis (2013) elaborates:

*Violent crimes, that is, crimes against persons, account for just 12 percent of all serious offenses; crimes against property account for the remaining 88 percent. Put differently, the crime rate for property offenses is about seven times higher than that for violent crimes against persons....*

*From 1960 until the early 1990s, the rate of violent crime rose quickly. After that, the trend turned downward. (The rate of property offenses also went up after 1960, with a downturn in the early 1980s and further decline through 2010.) What accounts for the drop in crime rates? Analysts point to a number of factors, including a strong economy during the 1990s (although rates have continued to drop during the recent economic downturn). In addition, the downward trend in crime reflects a drop in the use of crack cocaine, the hiring of more police, and tougher sentences for criminal convictions. (pp. 146–147)*

In any event, crime statistics may be misleading. For one thing, victimization surveys indicate that many crimes are not reported. Some surveys suggest less than half of serious crimes are actually reported to the police (Macionis, 2013). Why do victims fail to report crimes? People may believe that nothing can be done about the crime anyway or that the crime was too insignificant to report. They might also fear negative repercussions.

For example, Florence, age 78, was sideswiped by a young man as he was trying to pass her car. She had been driving along a familiar neighborhood road, being careful not to exceed the speed limit. The man, who looked to be about 20, stopped to see if she was all right but then jumped in his car and sped away. The accident was his fault. However, Florence's insurance agent suggested that filing a formal police report of the incident would almost certainly *not* result in the man's apprehension. But it *would* result in a significant increase in her own car insurance simply because the accident happened to a person of her age. Needless to say, Florence did not report the incident and paid for the repairs herself.

Focus on Critical Thinking 16.1 addresses a controversial issue concerning the purposes of imprisonment.

## FOCUS ON CRITICAL THINKING 16.1

## AN ETHICAL DILEMMA: PUNISHMENT VERSUS EMPOWERMENT

**LO 5**

### Disparity in Goals

A great debate rages regarding the purpose of imprisonment (or incarceration). Prisons exist to achieve four primary purposes (Kendall, 2013; Macionis, 2013). First, prisons punish people who commit crimes by denying them freedom for some designated period. Second, prisons discourage people who have committed crimes from committing them again and deter others from committing them in the first place—at least theoretically. Third, prisons protect potential victims from dangerous offenders by putting them behind bars. These first three goals basically focus on the rights of society. They might be clustered

EP 1b, 2, 2c, 3a, 3b, 5c, 8d

under the umbrella of **incapacitation**—namely, using various means to inhibit offenders from committing more crimes, thereby protecting other members of society.

The fourth goal, established much more recently in the 1940s and 1950s, involves inmate *rehabilitation* through programs involving therapy, education, and job training. The intent is to help criminals become productive members of society who do not commit crimes. The concept of *corrections* implies that people who break the law should be treated in ways that attempt to make them correct their inappropriate behavior and stop breaking the law. Rehabilitation ideally involves empowering offenders so they have viable alternatives to pursue other than a life of crime.

*(continued)*

**FOCUS ON CRITICAL THINKING 16.1 (continued)**

The wide disparity in goals poses a serious question for social workers: To what extent can offenders be empowered at the same time that they are incapacitated as a means of control and punishment? Prison life allows for few choices, and most prisoners definitely do not want to be there.

To make it worse, the public has increasingly supported stricter, more incapacitating policies. Tactics include longer mandatory sentences, less use of probation and parole, policies requiring lifetime imprisonment after committing three serious crimes (sometimes referred to as the *three strikes and you're out* approach), mandated sentences that reflect the seriousness of the crime, accelerated prison construction, and increased use of the death penalty (Karger & Stoesz, 2010, 2014).

Consider that:

[f]inding a compromise between what seems ethically appropriate and what is legally mandated can be a source of professional burnout. Feeling forced to make decisions and to take actions that cause internal conflict leads to feelings of helplessness and hopelessness and a belief that one is ineffective.

*(Kenyon, 1999, p. 162)*

## Issues and Potential Solutions

The following are examples of potential issues:

- Mandatory sentencing results in prisons accommodating more than double the number of prisoners for which they were built. Cells built to house two inmates now must house four. Prison conditions are almost unbearable.
- A prisoner made a mistake at age 19 and accidentally killed another teenager in a fight. The court sentenced him to several decades of time with no possibility of parole. Now, at age 21, he has expressed serious remorse for his crime and a willingness to shape up his life. A prison social worker sees great potential for rehabilitation. But what can be done when there is no hope of freedom for many years?
- A 25-year-old inmate has been sentenced to life imprisonment in a state requiring such punishment after the commission of three serious crimes—in his case, armed robberies. What kind of treatment and rehabilitation can help him?

To what extent does incapacitation as a means of control and punishment conflict with the basic social work values of self-determination and empowerment?

How can social workers who are empowerment oriented function in such a constricted and controlled setting? Should offenders be forced to participate in treatment activities against their will?

The following are five suggestions for working with offenders:

1. When possible, help offenders identify alternative behaviors to solve problems and address their needs. This is especially useful for inmates returning to their communities.
2. Advocate for inmates when prison conditions work against their best interests. In the community, social workers can advocate for prisoners' rights as they try to reintegrate themselves. For example, neighborhood residents might resent a former inmate living in their neighborhood. Or a parolee might be fired from her job when her employer finds out about her prison history.
3. Provide opportunities for individual and group treatment for inmates to work on personal issues (e.g., substance abuse treatment groups).
4. Seek positions in prison administration so as to improve prison policies concerning humane rehabilitation approaches.
5. Advocate in the macro arena for less punitive legislation that provides greater opportunity for rehabilitation. (Garvin & Tropman, 1998)

## Conservative Versus Liberal Value Orientations Toward Crime and Criminals: Critical Thinking Questions

- What are your personal values concerning the issues just described? To what extent do your values reflect a *conservative* perspective that emphasizes individuals' responsibility for their own behavior and that people who do bad things deserve to be punished?

**EP 5c, 7b, 8a, 8b**

- To what extent do you support a *liberal* approach that focuses on rehabilitating offenders and emphasizes the idea that people will thrive and do well when given enough support?
- To what extent should resources be used to build more prisons and keep offenders in prison longer? Or to what extent should resources be diverted to rehabilitation and the goal of reintegrating offenders into communities?

# Criminal Justice Settings and Forensic Social Work    LO 6

**Forensic social work** is "an area of social work practice in which social workers have direct involvement with the court system" (Patterson, 2012, p. 71). It involves social workers' practice and dealings with criminal and civil (concerning personal rights such as child custody) legal systems. Forensic social work tasks include conducting assessments regarding suspects' mental competence to understand their behavior and stand trial; making recommendations concerning child custody, divorce, and the placement of emotionally disturbed or delinquent juveniles; preparing for court presentations as expert witnesses; and advocating for welfare rights.

There are six broad criminal justice settings in which social workers can serve important functions (Ginsberg, 2001). These include adult correctional institutions, administrative planning centers, probation and parole services, victim assistance programs, domestic violence services, and juvenile corrections.

**EP 1**

## Adult Correctional Institutions

Social workers in adult correctional institutions perform at least five functions (Ginsberg, 2001). First, they can provide either individual or group counseling to inmates when needed or requested. Treatment might focus on such issues as anger management, preparation for release, and coping with substance abuse.

The second social work function involves helping prison administrators make determinations regarding job placement within the institution. Potential reasons that inmates seek prison jobs are to combat the boredom of prison life, to earn extra privileges, or to establish credit for good behavior thereby increasing the possibility of parole.

The third function for social workers in correctional facilities involves assisting prison personnel in determining how individual inmates are treated. Fourth, social workers can help develop and organize prison activities. Finally, practitioners can "assist in planning modifications in prison procedures" and advocate for improved conditions (Ginsberg, 2001, p. 148).

Focus on Critical Thinking 16.2 addresses the question of providing expensive health care for prison inmates.

## Administrative Planning Centers

As in other fields of practice, social workers can take on administrative and planning roles for correctional systems. These might involve planning new programs and procedures, developing more humane policies, and supervising lower-level administrators and other employees.

## Community-Based Corrections: Probation and Parole Services

The criminal justice system may give people who have been convicted of crimes alternatives to serving a full sentence of incarceration. Two primary options are probation and parole. These are considered *community-based*

**EP 8a**

*What provides greater hope—punishment or empowerment?*

mediaphotos/istockphoto.com

FOCUS **ON CRITICAL**
**THINKING 16.2**

# SHOULD PRISONERS GET EXPENSIVE HEALTH CARE?

The costs of keeping more people in prison longer are huge. The average annual cost for supervising a person on probation is more than $3,433 (La Vigne & Samuels, 2012). In prison the annual cost is approximately "$21,006 for minimum security, $25,378 for medium security, and $33,930 for high security" (La Vigne & Samuels, 2012, p. 2). However, note that spending varies widely from state to state (Leon-Guerrero, 2014).

Health care for aging and ill prisoners is also an expensive issue. Prisoners have the legal right to "adequate" health care (PEW Charitable Trusts, 2014). Spending on prison health care is up sharply in states; reasons include an aging prison population, the increasing incidence of serious "diseases, mental illness, and substance abuse" among prisoners entering prison already having these problems, and lack of adequate access to medical facilities and providers (PEW Charitable Trusts, 2014).

One estimate for the annual care of an older adult inmate is $70,000 (Kendall, 2010). Money spent on prison populations detracts from the total financial pool available for other benefits and services

**EP 1b, 8a**

including schools, police, the environment, and domestic security. A number of ethical questions can be raised: "Should a killer in a Minnesota prison have received a life-saving, $900,000 bone marrow transplant? Should a California robber have received a new heart" costing approximately $1 million? Both states provided these treatments because they determined it would be "cruel and unusual punishment" not to (Levine, 2002, p. 44).

## Critical Thinking Questions

- To what health-care standards should prisons adhere in providing treatment to prisoners?
- What is "adequate" health care?
- Should prisoners receive extremely expensive health-care treatment?
- How would you define "extremely expensive"?
- Should more time, money, and effort be expended to rehabilitate prisoners instead of imprisoning them so they will become responsible for their own health-care needs "on the outside"?

---

*corrections*—programs that supervise or monitor offenders' behavior while they reside in the community.

### Probation

**Probation** is the condition that occurs

> when a person is convicted [of a crime] but the judge determines that confinement is not warranted. Instead, that person is placed on probation and is allowed to live in society but under the court's supervision. Terms of probation often include psychological or chemical-dependence treatment and mandatory community service. People who receive probation are generally considered low risk, and the goal of probation officers is to involve them in community service and steer them away from criminal behavior. ( Morgan, 2000, pp. 142–143 )

Probation officers conduct assessments prior to when clients begin probation in order to provide recommendations to the court. They help clients

establish work and other living plans and subsequently see them regularly, overseeing their activities and often making home and work visits. Probation officers also link clients with needed resources.

To avoid incarceration, probationers must abide by whatever restrictions and terms the judge establishes. Typically these include obeying the law, getting and keeping a job, staying within a prescribed geographical location, avoiding relationships with other identified felons, and shunning firearms (Morgan, 2000). Individualized restrictions may also apply, such as getting substance abuse treatment or attending anger management groups.

### Parole

**Parole** is the early release of inmates from prison based on the "promise and likelihood of good behavior" (Morgan, 2000, p. 139). Parole officers must initially assess the amount of supervision necessary. Some parolees require extensive supervision to stay out of trouble; others require very little.

Parolees must abide by the general restrictions and requirements established by their parole officer. These include avoiding illegal activity, possession of firearms, involvement with identified felons, and use of alcohol or other drugs. They must also remain gainfully employed and attend regularly scheduled meetings with their parole officer.

Both probation and parole officer positions usually require a bachelor's degree in social work, psychology, criminal justice, or a related field in addition to "strong interpersonal skills" (Morgan, 2000, pp. 142, 144).

There are other community-based corrections programs in addition to probation and parole. For example, **victim and offender mediation programs** are face-to-face confrontations between victims and offenders in which an impartial third party serves as a mediator. The intent is to give victims an opportunity to confront offenders with the emotional and other consequences of their behavior, address emotional issues, and arrange compensation for losses. Similarly, **restitution programs** involve arranging cash reimbursement from offenders to victims (typically of property crimes) to compensate for losses.

## Victim/Witness Assistance Programs

Included under the victim assistance umbrella are both victim/witness assistance programs and crisis intervention programs. **Victim and witness assistance programs** include various facets intended to assist victims and witnesses in the stressful and potentially traumatic process of testifying in court against offenders, thereby enhancing their ability to testify effectively. Specific services include ongoing notification to witnesses of the case's legal status as it progresses through the courts; provision of separate, comfortable waiting rooms for witnesses; transportation to court; and support staff who accompany witnesses throughout the court process, helping them understand what's happening.

**Crisis intervention programs**, although not as common, provide wide-ranging services for crime victims, frequently within the first 24 hours after the crime occurs. Services can include crisis counseling, provision of transportation, assistance in making a legal complaint, linkage to needed resources such as support groups for survivors of violence, and temporary financial help. Agencies providing services include rape crisis centers and domestic

violence shelters. Jobs include counselor/advocate and administrator. Volunteers are also often used.

The FBI also administers specialized programs where social workers may be involved in service provision. Patterson (2012) explains:

*These programs include: the Terrorism Victim Assistance Unit, the Child Victim Identification Program (CVIP), the Forensic Child Interviewing Program, and the assignment of victim specialists who provide victim services to Native American victims of crime. Victim specialists provide resources and information to crime victims about local rape crisis centers, crime victims compensation programs, mental health and other services.... Additionally, the FBI implemented the Victim Assistance Rapid Deployment Team in 2004 to respond to the scene of mass disasters and violence.... Many of the victim specialists are primarily either licensed social workers or clinical social workers....[1] (p. 47)*

## Domestic Violence Services     `LO 7`

Domestic violence services and shelters for battered women have sprung up across the country. Often they have been initiated and are staffed and run by social workers. Women who have been battered by their male partners frequently need temporary shelter for themselves and their children, usually having nowhere else to go. Additional services include providing counseling and linking women with necessary resources. Battered women eventually need a permanent place to stay. They might require additional education or job training so they can support themselves and their families. They may need help finding employment and getting legal assistance.

Of course, females can batter their male partners, or one partner may batter the other of the same gender. However, as Shaw and Lee (2012) indicate:

*Although women are much less likely to be victims of violent crime overall, women are 5 to 8 times more likely [than men] to be victimized by an intimate partner. Intimate partner violence is primarily a crime against women and all races are equally vulnerable. In 2007, the Bureau of Justice reported that 96 percent of women experiencing nonfatal*

---

[1]For further information see the FBI Victim Assistance (n.d.) Website: http://www.fbi.gov/stats-services/victim_assistance

*partner violence were victimized by a male and about 85 percent of all victims were female. According to FBI statistics, every day about four women (approximately 1,400 a year) die in the United States as a result of domestic violence. Although about half a million reports of physical assault by intimates officially reach federal officials each year, it is estimated that 2 to 4 million women are battered each year; about one every 20 seconds or so. Women of all races and classes are battered, although rates are five times higher among families below poverty levels, and severe spouse abuse is twice as likely to be committed by unemployed men as by those working full time. These differences reflect economic vulnerability and lack of resources, as well as the ways these families have more contact with authorities like social services that increases opportunities for reporting. Women who are pregnant are especially at risk of violence. Approximately 17 percent of pregnant women report having been battered, and the results include miscarriages, stillbirths, and a two- to fourfold greater likelihood of bearing a low birth weight baby....*

*Women who are physically abused are also always emotionally abused because they experience emotional abuse by virtue of being physically terrorized.... Emotional abuse, however, does not always involve physical abuse. A man, for example, who constantly tells his partner that she is worthless, stupid, or ugly can emotionally abuse without being physically abusive. Sometimes the scars of emotional abuse take longer to heal than physical abuse and help explain why women might stay with abusive partners. (pp. 516–517)*

Therefore, Highlight 16.2 focuses on domestic violence as a women's issue.

## Juvenile Corrections

**Juvenile corrections** is the broad concept reflecting the many interventions for young people who are brought to the attention of police or the courts because of their behavior or alleged behavior. Juveniles—people under age 18—are generally treated differently than adults who commit crimes. **Juvenile delinquent offenses** are acts that are considered crimes if committed by adults. (Highlight 16.1 reviewed common crimes.) **Status offenses** are acts that are considered inappropriate when done by

juveniles but are not crimes if committed by adults. These include running away, being truant, being out of parental control, having sexual intercourse, and drinking alcohol. Considered together, juvenile delinquent and status offenses are regarded as **antisocial behaviors**—acts that are hostile, detrimental to others, and contrary to social expectations. **Juvenile courts** are those having jurisdiction over proceedings involving delinquent, dependent, or maltreated children and their parents or guardians.

We have already established that young people (particularly males of African American and, to a lesser extent, Hispanic heritage) are more likely than older people to commit crimes (Macionis, 2013; Mooney et al., 2015). Remember, however, that juveniles from virtually any racial, ethnic, and socioeconomic background can and do participate in antisocial behavior.

### A Special Perspective on Juveniles

Juveniles require a special perspective because they are minors whose parents (or guardians) are supposed to care for, supervise, and protect them. One ongoing question concerns the extent to which juveniles, on the one hand, and their parents, on the other, are responsible for juveniles' antisocial behavior. It is beyond the scope of this book to review all the potential causes of such behavior. However, the following are a few of the family, environmental, and individual factors that research suggests may contribute to violent behavior (Kail & Cavenaugh, 2013; McWhirter, McWhirter, McWhirter, & McWhirter, 2013; Sigelman & Rider, 2015).

**EP 7a**

- *Coercive Family Environments:* Sigelman and Rider (2015) explain the dynamics involved in coercive family environments:

*Highly antisocial children and adolescents often grow up in coercive family environments in which family members are locked in power struggles, each trying to control the others through negative, coercive tactics (Kiesner, Dishion, & Poulin, 2001; Patterson, 2008; Patterson, DeBaryshe, & Ramsey, 1989). Parents learn ... that they can stop their children's misbehavior, temporarily at least, by threatening, yelling, and hitting. Meanwhile, children learn ... that they can get their parents to lay off them by ignoring requests, whining, throwing*

## HIGHLIGHT 16.2

# THE CYCLE OF DOMESTIC VIOLENCE: EMPOWERING WOMEN AS SURVIVORS

The dynamics of domestic violence usually revolve around the male partner's need to control the victim. Over time, the perpetrator gradually cuts off his female partner from her family, friends, church, workplace, and other sources of support. He typically criticizes her on as many grounds as possible. Without support and validation from others, the victim often comes to believe what the perpetrator is saying—to see her-self as no good, stupid, and worthless, as a whore and a tramp. In some ways this process resembles brainwashing. Prior rational thinking is gradually erased and replaced with a barrage of criticism.

**EP 2, 7b, 8b**

### Phase 1: Buildup of Tension

The cycle of violence typically occurs in three phases. First, tension builds as the perpetrator becomes increasingly controlling, demanding, and annoyed with the victim. He might place impossible demands on her such as ordering her to have dinner ready at 5:30 sharp when he arrives home. Then he might show up at 7:00 and blame her for the food being cold and dried up. Or he might chastise her for making the wrong kind of food or not cooking it the way he likes it. He often plays a game with her, making demands and then changing them after she complies with his original instructions.

### Phase 2: The Explosion

The second phase in the cycle involves the explosion—the abusive incident in which he beats her to teach her a lesson. He then usually tells her it's all her fault. If she had cooked better or not yelled back or done what she was told, he wouldn't have *had* to hit her. She *made* him try to keep her in line.

### Phase 3: The Honeymoon

The third phase is the honeymoon period. The perpetrator has released his tension. The victim is frightened, hurt, emotionally beaten, downtrodden, and depressed.

She might be so damaged that she considers leaving him, but he will never allow her to do this. He makes up with her, says loving things, and perhaps brings her flowers or candy. He often tells her that he loves her and that he can't live without her. For that matter, he might also tell her that she could never survive without him. The pain is gone—temporarily—so she stays. And the cycle begins all over again.

### Reasons Women Stay

Women continue to stay with abusive partners for a number of reasons (Zastrow & Kirst-Ashman, 2016). These include economic dependence, lack of self-confidence, lack of power, fear of the abuser, guilt about what they did wrong or how they failed to nurture their relationship with the abuser, fear of isolation, fear for their children's safety, hope that things will somehow improve, and the fact they still feel they love their partners despite it all.

### Treatment Strategies

Social work treatment strategies involve empowering the victim and helping her survive. She changes from a victim to a survivor. Strategies include the following:

1. Offer support.
2. Identify and focus on her strengths.
3. Provide information regarding resources and services.
4. Assist her in identifying and evaluating the realistic alternatives available to her.
5. Help her establish a plan of action to ensure her safety.
6. Advocate on her behalf with legal, medical, and social services when necessary. (Zastrow & Kirst-Ashman, 2016)

**EP 7c, 7d, 8d, 8e**

The goal is to help the domestic violence survivor gain confidence and get back on her feet. It takes a brave and strong person to break the cycle of violence.

*full-blown temper tantrums, and otherwise being difficult. As both parents and children learn to rely on coercive tactics, parents increasingly lose control over their children's behavior until even the loudest lectures and hardest spankings have little effect and the child's conduct problems spiral out of control.*

*[Thus, coercive family environments are marked by conflict, in addition to harsh and inconsistent discipline.] It is easy to see how a child who has grown up in a coercive family environment might attribute hostile intent to other people and rely on aggressive tactics to resolve disputes.*

*Growing up in a coercive family environment sets in motion the next steps in the making of an antisocial adolescent.... The child, already aggressive and unpleasant to be around, ends up performing poorly in school and being rejected by other children. Having no better options, he becomes involved in a peer group made up of other low-achieving, antisocial, and unpopular youths, who positively reinforce one another's delinquency. There is much support [for the view] ... that ineffective parenting in childhood contributes to behavior problems, peer rejection, involvement with antisocial peers, and, in turn, antisocial behavior in adolescence. (pp. 422–423)*

- *Poverty and Economic Deprivation:* An environment marked by deprivation can contribute to the potential for delinquency (Kail & Cavanaugh, 2013). Children who live in poverty exhibit more violent and antisocial behavior than those who live in more prosperous surroundings (Williams, Conger, & Blozis, 2007). Poverty imposes stress on families that often must struggle just to survive and "often leads to the very parental behaviors that promote aggression—harsh discipline and lax monitoring (Tolan, Gorman-Smith, & Henry, 2003). In addition, violent crime is far more common in poverty-stricken neighborhoods. Older children and adolescents exposed to such violence are, as they get older, more likely to be aggressive and violent themselves (Binghenheimer, Brennan, & Earls, 2005)" (Kail & Cavanaugh, 2013, p. 338)

  Children whose families have a long history of continuous poverty are more apt to become "more antisocial" with time (Papalia & Feldman, pp. 413–414). In families that get out of poverty early on in a child's life, that child is no more likely to demonstrate subsequent problematic behavior than a child living in a family that never experienced poverty (Macmillan, McMorris, & Kruttschnitt, 2004; Papalia & Feldman, 2012).

- *Individual Factors:* Although personality variables do not directly produce a delinquent, they do increase the probability of delinquency. For example, having poor impulse control and an easily provoked temper can make delinquent behavior more likely (Sigelman & Rider, 2015; Smith & Darman, 2008). Kail and Cavanaugh (2013) explain:

*Adolescent boys often respond aggressively because they are not skilled at interpreting other people's intentions. Without a clear interpretation in mind, they respond aggressively by default. That is, aggressive boys far too often think, "I don't know what you're up to, and when in doubt, attack" (Crick & Dodge, 1994; Fontaine et al., 2009). Antisocial adolescents are often inclined to act impulsively, and they often are unable or unwilling to postpone pleasure (Fontaine, 2007). Seeing a fancy new CD player or a car, delinquent youth are tempted to steal it, simply so that they can have it right now. When others inadvertently get in their way, delinquent adolescents often respond without regard to the nature of the other person's acts or intentions. (p. 338)*

McWhirter and his colleagues (2013) note that levels of aggression often follow a pattern where "less serious problem behaviors precede more serious delinquency"; the authors continue that "disruptive and delinquent behavior generally progresses in an orderly, sequential fashion from authority conflict (e.g., defiance and disobedience), to covert actions (e.g., lying and stealing), to overt actions (e.g., fighting, delinquency, and violent behavior" (pp. 222–223).

As with adult offenders, the current trend in the juvenile justice system is an emphasis on punishment rather than treatment and rehabilitation for delinquent youth (Smith & Darman, 2008). One development involves passing laws that require more juvenile offenders who commit serious violent crimes to be treated as adults. Another concerns the imposition of stricter sentences on juvenile offenders who in the past might have been given a warning or probation.

We have established that social work values generally comply more directly with rehabilitation and treatment approaches than with punishment. The problem of juvenile delinquency can be tackled in many ways. None are accomplished easily and all require resources. Kail and Cavanaugh (2010) suggest the following tactics:

**EP 7d**

- "Delinquent adolescents can be taught more effective social skills and better methods of self control.
- Parents of delinquent youth can be taught the importance of supervising and monitoring their

children's behavior and the necessity for consistent discipline.

- Families of delinquents can learn to function more effectively as a unit, with special emphasis on better means of resolving conflict.
- Schools can develop programs that motivate delinquent youth to become invested in their school performance.
- Communities can improve economic conditions in neighborhoods where delinquency reigns." (p. 350)

An example of a preventive program is the Fast Track Project designed by the Conduct Problems Prevention Research Group (Fast Track Project, 2011). The study was conducted over a 10-year period and involved children in grades 1–10. It included training groups for parents regarding improved parent/school relations and behavior management, home visits to assist par-

**EP 7d, 9c**

ents in implementing skills, children's groups focusing on the development of social skills, tutoring, and encouraging the development of friendships within the classroom setting. The program "has proven effective in reducing antisocial behavior and preventing diagnoses of conduct disorder and related psychiatric disorders. The program worked best with those children who were at highest risk initially. It was very costly, however, suggesting the need to aim prevention programs more squarely at the children most in need of them" (Sigelman & Rider, 2015, p. 425).

Another suggestion for addressing the problem of antisocial behavior in young people involves stressing and developing strengths. The following "five Cs" are the goals:

- *Competence (academic, vocational, and so on)*
- *Confidence (self-esteem and self-efficacy)*
- *Character (moral development, respect for rules)*
- *Connections (bonds to family, friends, and institutions like schools and churches)*
- *Caring (empathy, prosocial behavior). (Emphasis added) (Sigelman & Rider, 2015, p. 425)*

## Overlaps Among Juvenile Corrections, Mental Health Services, and Child Welfare

Note that substantial overlap exists among juvenile corrections, mental health services, and, to some

extent, child welfare. Chapters 9 and 13 address issues concerning child welfare and mental health. Decisions about the needs and placement of each individual depend on a number of conditions. Statutes, policies, and agency practices may vary from state to state and from locality to locality. Available resources for placement also differ dramatically. Finally, juvenile court judges often have great discretion regarding the appropriate placement of juveniles.

## Youth Gangs LO 8

An additional concern related to violent behavior by youths involves escalating gang membership. It is estimated that more than 756,000 gang members belong to almost 29,400 gangs throughout the United States (Newman & Newman, 2015). Although most gang members are male, there are also female gangs and female adolescents who become members of mixed-gender gangs (Newman & Newman, 2015).

McWhirter and his colleagues (2013) provide a further overview of gang activity and composition:

**EP 7a**

*Youths in these gangs were responsible for a wide variety of offenses including street crime, drug trafficking, and witness intimidation, and they are highly likely to use firearms in an assault crime. Twenty percent of public schools in 2007–2008 reported gang activities at their school; 23% of students reported gangs at school with African American (38%) and Hispanic students (36%) reporting a larger number (Dinkes, Kemp, & Baum, 2009).*

*When one gang gains power and control in an area, rival gangs sometimes relocate to other areas of the city, even to other cities. Divisions of power and region are frequently related to ethnicity, although there is some evidence to suggest that a new type of hybrid gang is emerging. Hybrid gang culture is characterized by mixed racial and ethnic participation within a single gang and are driven by drug sale profits (Starbuck, Howell, & Lindquist, 2001). Economic opportunities (e.g., the availability of new markets for drug profits) may also play a part in a gang's decision to relocate or expand. Many neighborhoods untouched by organized violence now find themselves threatened by gang activity. The proliferation of youth gangs in recent decades is of concern, and of particular concern is the spread of homegrown youth gangs to rural communities (Howell, 2010). (p. 234)*

## Defining Youth Gangs

McWhirter and his colleagues (2013) arbitrarily define a **youth gang** as "a group consisting primarily of adolescents and young adults who interact frequently with one another, share a common identity expressed through a gang name and common symbols, claim control over a certain geographical area, and are deliberately involved in illegal activities" (p. 234).

Young people join gangs for a number of reasons—to gain self-esteem, respect, a feeling a belonging, security, support, protection, excitement, and financial benefits. Newman and Newman (2015) reflect on the reasons for joining a gang:

*The motives for joining a gang … do not differ much from the motives that adolescents have for joining any number of social groups and clubs. However, the focus of these gangs developed a delinquent emphasis and tradition that was passed from one generation of gang members to the next in a neighborhood. The ethical standards and values of these groups were often contrary to conventional values. In fact, actions that might bring a nondelinquent boy dishonor or shame—such as being arrested, appearing in juvenile court, or being sent to a correctional institution—would be viewed as a source of pride and distinction to a gang member. (p. 372)*

Highlight 16.3 offers a global perspective on gangs.

## Types of Gangs

Morales and his colleagues (2012, pp. 179–180) categorize juvenile gangs into four basic types. First. **criminal gangs** have as their "primary goal material gain through criminal activities" that include "theft of property from premises or persons, extortion, fencing, and obtaining and selling illegal substances such as drugs." Second, **conflict gangs** are extremely "turf oriented and will engage in violent battle with individuals or rival groups that invade their neighborhood or commit acts they consider insulting or degrading. Respect is highly valued or defended." **Retreatist gangs'** primary aim is to get "loaded" or "high" on various mind-altering substances and thereby withdraw from the stresses of real life. Retreatist gangs differ from criminal gangs despite the fact that they both may be involved in illegal drug activity. Retreatist gangs emphasize escape from reality, whereas criminal gangs focus on financial gain. **Cult/occult gangs** have appeared to emerge in more recent years. The term *cult* refers to devil worship or participation in evil practices, whereas the concept *occult* implies secretiveness or involvement in supernatural activities (Morales et al.,

---

**HIGHLIGHT 16.3** | INTERNATIONAL PERSPECTIVES: GANGS AROUND THE WORLD

Gangs as a group experience are a typically occurring pattern often characterizing the "adolescent subculture" that "represent an extreme manifestation of that age-typical emphasis on being together and belonging to something" (Hazen & Rodgers, 2014; Huff, 1993, p. 6). "Gangs are certainly not unique to the United States. In fact, most societies seem to have a term that corresponds, at least loosely, to our own term gang. Whether it is the *chimpira* of Japan, the *raggare* of Sweden, the Dutch *nozem,* the Italian *vitelloni,* the *stilyagi* of the USSR, the Yugoslavian *tapkaroschi,* or their counterparts in many other nations, there is usually some way of designating youth gangs." (Huff, 1993, p. 6)

Examples of youth gangs in the international arena include:

- Gangs in Germany and Great Britain formed because of "ongoing class rivalries and rising immigration problems, including rowdy and nationalist soccer hooligans and racist, violent skinheads."
- The "skollie gangs of South Africa, who provide protection, support, and economic survival for their members."
- Jamaican gangs who recruit from impoverished young people and that "commonly use violence and torture in their drug trafficking operations."
- Columbian gangs that "protect territory and carry out murders for drug cartels." (Encyclopedia of Children and Childhood in History and Society, 2008)

2012). Cult/occult gangs may focus their interests on hating some group such as gay people or non-Whites.

## Prevention and Intervention Involving Gangs

Young people often become gang members to meet personal needs and gain power. In a way, gang membership is a means for youths to empower themselves. Young people should be empowered in other ways so they don't have to turn to gangs for support, belongingness, financial gain, or social status.

**EP 7d**

Combating gangs can assume three primary thrusts: prevention, intervention, and suppression (Regulus, 1995; Williams & Van Dorn, 1999). *Prevention* involves providing enough resources and services to communities and individuals that young people don't need to seek out gang membership in the first place. Prevention requires communities to offer adequate social programs for reducing poverty, educating parents about children's needs and child management, enhancing policing resources, developing high-quality educational systems that respond to young people's needs, and diminishing accessibility to handguns (Williams & Van Dorn, 1999).

Prevention can also be geared to individual youths' needs. For example, the Peace Power program in New York City was developed by several social work graduate students in conjunction with some "local social service agencies and high schools." This empowerment approach emphasizes

> *four essential steps: recognizing contributions and successes [e.g., even simple things such as offering feedback notes recognizing specific positive actions on the part of young people]; acting with respect [e.g., initiating a "respect day" during which young people interview each other and share their own definitions of respect]; sharing power to build community [e.g., "working collectively and sharing responsibility"]; and making peace [e.g., teaching conflict resolution strategies]. (Vallianatos, 2001c, p. 3)*

Morales, Sheafor, and Scott (2012) comment on *intervention* with gangs in micro social work practice:

> *Many traditional forms of social work intervention are thought to be effective in helping individuals have their needs met in ways other than through participation in gangs. For example, the efforts of school social workers to engage teachers and parents in supporting a child's academic development helps the child find school more rewarding and satisfying. Hospital social workers are often among the first to interact with victims or family members of victims experiencing gang violence. They provide services involving acquisition of tangible resources, as well as counseling about the terrorizing event that helps to minimize psychological damage and lower the likelihood of escalating the situation into one of retaliatory violence. In mental health centers, residential treatment facilities, probation departments, and many other human services agencies, it is not uncommon for social workers to help gang members or the victims of gang violence address issues resulting from gang activities.*
>
> *What about the role of the family? [Many parents find it necessary to work even if they have children under age 6. This makes it hard to provide all the support and supervision children need. As a result, social programs are developed to provide alternative care.].... [F]amily counseling, family therapy, and other social work services to families can help to minimize family breakdown. Social programs such as Boys and Girls Clubs, Partners, and various recreation programs are examples of how social workers can assist youth in identifying with positive adult role models, as opposed to the role models represented by gang members. (p. 181)*

A *suppression* approach to gangs involves focusing on controlling them through law enforcement and prosecution. The focus, of course, is on punishment, not rehabilitation and treatment. Suppression generally involves "the local community, schools, public housing projects, or prison" (Spergel & Grossman, 1997, p. 457).

## A Case Example of a Macro Approach to Addressing Gangs: The Little Village Project

The Little Village Project in Chicago combines aspects of prevention, intervention, and suppression in a macro approach to dealing with gangs. It is founded on six major concepts (Morales et al., 2012; Spergel & Grossman, 1997, pp. 458–459):

1. *Community Mobilization.* To address the problems of gang conflict, violence, and illegal

behavior, a wide range of people in the community are mobilized to communicate with, work together with, and support each other (National Crime Prevention Council [NCPC], 2011). Those involved include "local residents and groups, youth agencies, police and probation officers, and former gang youths" (Spergel & Grossman, 1997, p. 458).

2. *Opportunities Provision.* This involves the idea that people need opportunities other than gang membership as means of preventing such involvement (NCPC, 2011). Opportunities can include "more and better jobs, special education programs, and training programs" (Spergel & Grossman, 1997, p. 458). Opportunities can also entail "recreation at safe locations," linkage of at-risk young people with community-based services, support for nonviolent neighborhood activities, and involvement of parents in actions aimed at preventing gang activities (NCPC, 2011).

3. *Social Intervention.* This essentially refers to "outreach to gang youths in the streets" (Morales et al., 2012, p. 182). Community youth workers can seek out gang members, get to know them, and help link them and other at-risk youths with "services and resources such as drug treatment, jobs, training, educational programs, and some recreation" (NCPC, 2011; Spergel & Grossman, 1997, p. 458). Youth workers can also help "gang youths avoid probation violations by getting them to report to their probation officers on time" and "avoid harassment from the police" (Spergel & Grossman, 1997, p. 462).

4. *Suppression.* "Suppression for purposes of gang control requires the application of a variety of informal as well as formal controls on the behavior of individual youths and the structure and process of their gangs. Not only supervision and surveillance, arrest, probation, and imprisonment, but also positive communication with youths, information sharing with other agency service and control providers, and joint decision making among agency and community group representatives are essential elements of social control" (Spergel & Grossman 1997, p. 458).

5. *Organizational Change and Development.* This emphasizes the need for social agencies, police, citizens, and others to work together to control crime. "Mutual trust, interdependence, and high levels of morale" need to be generated in a climate of collaboration (Spergel & Grossman, 1997, p. 459). For example, regular channels of communication can be established among residents involved in neighborhood organizations, police and probation administrators, staff in social service agencies, and job training program personnel (NCPC, 2011).

6. *Targeting.* Not all gang members are equally involved in the gang (Morales et al., 2012). Some hover at the fringes of gang involvement, either uncertain of what to do or not yet having gained the respect of other gang members. Other members experience various levels of intensity of criminal behavior (including homicide) and imprisonment. Targeting involves identifying the most deeply committed gang leaders as objects of attention.

# Chapter Summary

The following summarizes this chapter's content as it relates to the learning objectives presented at the beginning of the chapter. Chapter content will help prepare students to:

### LO1 Review the criminal justice system (and define some of the key concepts involved).

The criminal justice system is the complex, integrated system of programs, policies, laws, and agencies devoted to preventing and controlling crime. The system's functions include adjudication (passing legal judgment), incarceration (confining by putting in prison or jail), and rehabilitation (restoring to a state of productive, noncriminal functioning in society).

### LO2 Examine who commits crime.

Variables related to crime include gender, age, race, and social class. Men are much more likely to commit crimes, although the arrest rate for women is increasing. People younger than age 25 are the most likely to commit crimes and commit the most violent crimes. Crime is also related to race in that African

Americans have a much higher crime rate. However, the crime rate is also related to social class that involves poverty, increased police surveillance and potential racial profiling, and single-parent family structure. Asian Americans have a markedly lower crime rate than their representation in the population.

### LO3 Describe the types of crime.

Felonies are grave offenses punishable by at least a year in prison and possibly even death. Misdemeanors are less severe offenses, with punishments ranging from incarceration of less than a year to monetary fines. Categories of crime include violent, property, and offenses not fitting in these two categories. Such offenses involve white-collar, identity theft, corporate, victimless, organized, and hate crimes.

### LO4 Explore the incidence of crime.

The crime rate has experienced a decrease over the past decade. The crime rate appears to be related to the state of the economy, decreased crack cocaine use, a larger police force, and more severe sentences for criminals.

### LO5 Employ critical thinking skills (about the ethical dilemma of punishment versus empowerment, and the issue of providing expensive health care for prisoners).

Critical thinking questions were raised regarding conservative and liberal approaches to providing punishment versus empowerment to prisoners. Questions were also posed concerning the practice of providing prisoners with expensive health care.

### LO6 Review the wide range of criminal justice settings in which social workers practice.

Criminal justice settings include forensic social work, adult correctional institutions, administrative planning centers, community-based corrections involving probation and parole, victim assistance programs, domestic violence services, and juvenile corrections. Some settings reflect an overlap among juvenile corrections, mental health services, and child welfare.

### LO7 Describe domestic violence (including its cycle, dynamics, and how to address the problem).

The cycle involves buildup of tension, the explosion, and a honeymoon period. There are many reasons why women stay in abusive relationships. Treatment strategies emphasize providing support, emphasizing empowerment, and advocating for services.

### LO8 Discuss youth gangs (including membership, types, prevention, and treatment).

It is estimated that 29,400 gangs exist throughout the United States. Gangs provide members with a range of benefits including social support, respect, protection, excitement, and financial benefits. Gangs are an international phenomenon. Types of gangs include criminal, conflict, retreatist, and cult/occult. Prevention, intervention, and suppression are three means of combating gangs.

## LOOKING AHEAD

This book concludes by stressing the importance of critical thinking in evaluating social welfare policy issues in various fields of practice. It also encourages you to explore your personal values and ideas about your future career.

## COMPETENCY NOTES

The following identifies where Educational Policy (EP) competencies and their component behaviors are discussed in the chapter.

**EP 1 (Competency 1)—Demonstrate Ethical and Professional Behavior.** *(p. 522):* Social workers' professional role in forensic social work is discussed.

**EP 1a Make ethical decisions by applying the standards of the NASW Code of Ethics, relevant laws and regulations, models for ethical decision-making, ethical conduct of research, and additional codes of ethics as appropriate to context.** *(p. 535):* Examination of this case scenario requires the application of ethical principles. The Triple-A strategy to arrive at ethical decisions is employed.

**EP 1b Use reflection and self-regulation to manage personal values and maintain professionalism in practice situations.** *(p. 520):* Reflection about personal values concerning punishment versus empowerment allow practitioners to manage these values so that they don't interfere with professional values and ethics. *(p. 523):* Critical thinking questions encourage consideration of personal values concerning the provision of expensive health care to people in prison.

**EP 2 (Competency 2)—Engage Diversity and Difference in Practice.** *(p. 516):* The dimensions of diversity—race, culture, and class—operate to marginalize people and make it more likely that they turn to crime. *(p. 520):* The concept of punishment can be assessed to determine when it becomes oppressive. *(p. 526):* The dynamics involved in domestic violence oppress women.

**EP 2a Apply and communicate understanding of the importance of diversity and difference in shaping life experiences in practice at the micro, mezzo, and macro levels.** *(p. 516):* Social workers must recognize how race, class, and gender shape life experiences concerning participation in criminal behavior.

**EP 2c Apply self-awareness and self-regulation to manage the influence of personal biases and values in working with diverse clients and constituencies.** *(p. 520):* Practitioners must develop self-awareness regarding any prejudices and stereotypes they may harbor regarding people in prison.

**EP 3 (Competency 3)—Advance Human Rights and Social, Economic, and Environmental Justice.**

**EP 3a Apply their understanding of social, economic, and environmental justice to advocate for human rights at the individual and system levels.** *(p. 520):* Practitioners should advocate on the behalf of prisoners' human rights.

**EP 3b Engage in practices that advance social, economic, and environmental justice.** *(p. 520):* Social workers should engage in practices that advance social, economic, and environmental justice for prisoners.

**EP 5 (Competency 5)—Engage in Policy Practice.**

**EP 5c Apply critical thinking to analyze, formulate, and advocate for policies that advance human rights and social, economic, and environmental justice.** *(p. 520):* Social workers should advocate for policies and programs

that help prisoners in the rehabilitation process. *(p. 521):* Critical thinking questions are raised regarding the treatment of people in prison.

**EP 7 (Competency 7)—Assess Individuals, Families, Groups, Organizations, and Communities.**

**EP 7a Collect and organize data, and apply critical thinking to interpret information from clients and constituencies.** *(p. 525):* This section discusses the dynamics and variables related to delinquent behavior, which social workers must understand to effectively collect, organize, and interpret client data. *(p. 528):* The dynamics of gangs are discussed to prepare practitioners who work with gang members for the collection, organization, and interpretation of client data. *(p. 535):* Critical thinking questions are posed to help assess the case scenario in preparation for intervention planning.

**EP 7b Apply knowledge of human behavior and the social environment, person-in-environment, and other multidisciplinary theoretical frameworks in the analysis of assessment data from clients and constituencies.** *(p. 517):* Knowledge about types of crime is necessary when conducting assessments and working in the criminal justice system. *(p. 521):* Critical thinking questions encourage thought concerning the application of conservative and liberal conceptual frameworks to imprisonment and its purposes. *(p. 526):* The cycle of violence provides a useful theoretical framework for assessing domestic violence.

**EP 7c Develop mutually agreed-on intervention goals and objectives based on the critical assessment of strengths, needs, and challenges within clients and constituencies.** *(p. 526):* Practitioners can work with a domestic violence survivor to develop mutually agreed-on intervention goals based on what the survivor wants to do.

**EP 7d Select appropriate intervention strategies based on the assessment, research knowledge, and values and preferences of clients and constituencies.** *(p. 526):* Social workers should select the appropriate intervention strategies as suggested here when working with survivors of domestic violence. *(p. 527):* Potential appropriate intervention strategies for working with delinquent adolescents are described. *(p. 528):* An example of an intervention program aimed at improved parent/school relations and behavior management is provided. *(p. 530):* Intervention strategies for working with gang members at the macro and macro levels are discussed.

**EP 8 (Competency 8)—Intervene with Individuals, Families, Groups, Organizations, and Communities.**

**EP 8a Critically choose and implement interventions to achieve practice goals and enhance capacities of clients and constituencies.** *(p. 521):* Critical thinking questions are raised regarding the treatment of people in prison. *(p. 522):* Critical thinking questions encourage consideration concerning the provision of expensive health care to people in prison. *(p. 523):* Probation and parole provide intervention alternatives that may enhance clients' capacities.

**EP 8b Apply knowledge of human behavior and the social environment, person-in-environment, and other multidisciplinary theoretical frameworks in interventions with clients and constituencies.** *(p. 517):* Knowledge about types of crime is necessary when working in the criminal justice system. *(p. 521):* Critical thinking questions encourage thought concerning the application of conservative and liberal conceptual frameworks to imprisonment and its purposes. *(p. 526):* The cycle of violence provides a useful theoretical framework for intervention in situations involving domestic violence.

**EP 8d Negotiate, mediate, and advocate with and on behalf of diverse clients and constituencies.** *(p. 520):* Social workers should advocate for policies and programs that help prisoners in the rehabilitation process. *(p. 526):* Practitioners should advocate on the behalf of survivors of domestic violence.

**EP 8e Facilitate effective transitions and endings that advance mutually agreed-on goals.** *(p. 526):* Practitioners can work with a domestic violence survivor to facilitate her transition into life without the perpetrator.

**EP 9 (Competency 9)—Evaluate practice with individuals, families, groups, organizations, and communities.**

**EP 9c Critically analyze, monitor, and evaluate intervention and program processes and outcomes.** *(p. 528):* The program discussed was evaluated for its effectiveness and cost.

## CASE STUDY FOR CRITICAL THINKING

# A Client with a Serious Hereditary Disease

The case presented here represents an application of this entire section of the book on client populations and contexts (Chapters 9–16), not specifically on criminal justice. This case involves a hospital social worker talking with a client who just discovered she has a serious hereditary disease involving mental and physical deterioration and eventual death.[3] Subsequent questions are posed to promote critical thinking.

**EP 1a, 7a**[2]

**Case Study:** A hospital social worker is counseling Myla, age 24, a patient who has just been informed that she has a genetic marker for Huntington's chorea, a hereditary disease commencing in middle age that causes gradual deterioration of the brain and voluntary muscular movement. No cure currently exists for the disease. Myla greatly desires to have children, but they could all potentially be infected with the disease.

Myla states she does not want her husband, Richard, or her family to know about this. Myla fears that if Richard finds out he will refuse to have children with her and possibly leave her because he, too, desires children. Myla is reeling over the shocking news.

**Critical Thinking:** The first step in the critical thinking process involves *asking* questions about problems, needs, and issues. A number of basic ethical questions can be raised:

- What are the issues involving confidentiality in this case? Does Richard have the right to know that Myla has the disease and that their future children might also have it? Does he have the right to know that within the next 20 or 30 years Myla will likely begin experiencing serious mental and physical deterioration?
- "What is the best interest of the as-yet-unborn child?"
- "Who is the person or are the persons entitled to make such decisions?"
- "What are the religious implications for all concerned (if any) of playing God?"
- "Who speaks for the fetus?"
- "What are statistical relationships between a genetic marker and the actual occurrence of the genetic defect, and what bearing do they have on making a decision?"

---

[2]Competency Notes for this case study are located at the end of Chapter 16.

[3]This case study is based on one presented in Loewenberg, Dolgoff, and Harrington (2000, p. 218).

● "What is society's best interest in this situation?" (Loewenberg, Dolgoff, & Harrington, 2000, p. 218).

Additionally, what specific questions might be asked concerning Myla's responsibility to herself and others in addition to planning for the future? Consider the following:

● If Myla does not tell Richard, how will he react when he inevitably does find out about her condition? If she doesn't tell him beforehand, how will he feel toward her after having children who potentially harbor the disease?
● Might Myla consider the alternative of not having children or of adopting them?
● How can Myla plan her life over the next few decades to maximize her appreciation and enjoyment of it?
● How might she plan for the more distant future when she begins to experience symptoms of the disease?

Note that these latter questions are very solemn and would not be ones a social worker would pose to Myla flippantly. Rather, the practitioner would help Myla address them over time when she was emotionally ready. First Myla would have to work through her grief concerning the diagnosis and begin coping with her reality. Only then could she begin to make more objective decisions about and plans for her future.

The second step in critical thinking entails *assessing* the established facts and issues involved. What are the answers to the questions posed? Some require facts such as more information about Huntington's chorea. Others involve serious thinking about values and ethics.

The final step in critical thinking is the *assertion* of a concluding opinion. The social worker would assist Myla in *asking* questions about her situation and options and then in *assessing* her answers. The worker would also be forced to address the ethical questions posed and determine what was the right thing to do. For example, should Richard be told? There are no easy answers. If you were Myla, what would you do?

# EPILOGUE
## Your Values and Your Future
### APPLYING CRITICAL THINKING SKILLS

Fuse/Getty Images

This book has discussed a wide range of social welfare policy and programming issues. The emphasis has been on critical thinking about these issues using the Triple-A approach:

1. *Ask* questions.
2. *Assess* the established facts and issues involved.
3. *Assert* a concluding opinion.

At this point, what are your opinions and values concerning the following issues?

- What policies should the government adopt concerning the treatment of poor children and families?

- Can poverty be eliminated? If so, how? What policies and programs need to be developed? To what extent do you feel this is possible?
- What supportive and supplementary services best serve children and families? What are the most important concepts involved in developing policies and services?
- To what extent should society support older adults by providing services and benefits? What services and benefits are most critical? What new policies could improve their quality of life?
- To what extent should society promote self-determination on the part of people with disabilities by providing services and benefits? What policies could improve this population's quality of life? What important concepts are involved in policy development and service provision?
- What are the major issues involved in the provision of health care in the United States? What are the pros and cons of managed care? Should changes in health-care policy be pursued? If so, what changes? Who should pay for health care?
- What are the primary issues involved in mental health policy and service provision? What policy initiatives might be advanced to address these concerns?
- What are the principal issues and concerns in providing services to youths and in the schools? What methods of empowerment can be proposed?
- What are the main issues and concerns involved in criminal justice and service provision? To what extent does criminal justice policy reflect a punitive versus rehabilitative perspective? Can policy be improved, and if so, how?

Do these values and opinions tend to reflect a conservative or a liberal perspective? Do you tend to support a residual or an institutional orientation to service provision?

## The Importance of Values in Career Decision Making

This book has stressed the significance of professional values in social work practice. It has also emphasized the importance of social workers pursuing policy practice when advocacy is called for to improve social welfare policies and programming. It is important that professional values be acceptable to people who choose to become social workers. Of course, we all have personal opinions about an extensive range of topics. However, social workers' personal values must be in adequate compliance with professional values for individuals to be comfortable and productive professionals.

## Assessing Your Own Capabilities and Interests

The following sections encourage you to think about your personal capabilities, potential job preferences, and initial career goals. They are intended to give you some insight into whether social work might be the field for you.

## What Are Your Competencies?

Competencies involve your skills and abilities. In social work practice, *competencies* are measurable behaviors informed by knowledge, skills, and values that are identified and assessed as the foundation of social work practice (CSWE, 2015).

## BOX A  Assessing Your Capabilities

The following are areas that may reflect your professional knowledge, skills, and values. Place a check mark next to each item that you consider a strength:

_____ Assessment of individual, family, group, community, and organizational problems and functioning
_____ Communication
_____ Understanding people
_____ Problem solving
_____ Decision making
_____ Planning
_____ Organizing
_____ Recording
_____ Clear thinking
_____ Acceptance of responsibility
_____ Dependability
_____ Pacing efforts
_____ Coordination
_____ Case management
_____ Conducting meetings
_____ Use of critical thinking
_____ Application of ethical principles
_____ Understanding of diverse racial and ethnic groups
_____ Advocacy
_____ Creativity
_____ Initiating ideas
_____ Undertaking action

These concepts simply reflect the beginning of your capability assessment. The potential list is unlimited. These are merely intended to give you some initial ideas.

After giving your capabilities serious thought, write out several paragraphs summarizing and prioritizing your greatest strengths. This can help you articulate for yourself (and later for potential employers) the reasons you are or will be a capable professional.

---

What are you good at? What skills have you mastered that would enhance your performance in a professional social work setting? Think about the social work knowledge and values that you have acquired and the skills that you have mastered. Box A identifies some potential competencies.

## What Are Your Employment Goals?

This question concerns the context of employment. What aspects of work are important to you other than the type of social work skills you use or population you serve? In other words, what aspects of your working environment motivate you to perform and encourage you to like your job? Box B portrays a range of work dimensions that may be of varying importance to you. To what extent do you think that these would characterize a career as a social worker?

## BOX B  Employment Goals and Work Context

What aspects of the work environment are the most important to you? Prioritize the following:

_____ Salary
_____ Sick leave
_____ Hours of work
_____ Effective supervision
_____ Geographic location
_____ Potential for advancement
_____ Substantial discretion in decision making
_____ Vacation time
_____ Health-care benefits
_____ Not being "on call" during regular off-work hours
_____ In-service training opportunities
_____ Clear job description
_____ Opportunity to function independently
_____ Challenging environment
_____ Low stress levels
_____ Realistic record-keeping requirements
_____ Being rewarded for achievement
_____ Little travel
_____ Potential for new skill development
_____ Competent colleagues
_____ Good office
_____ Good relationships with colleagues
_____ Working as part of a team
_____ Potential for travel
_____ Respect from other staff members
_____ Clear rules and regulations
_____ Responsive administration
_____ Time flexibility

Is there anything else that would be motivating to you? If so, specify.

_____

_____

## What Are Your Job Preferences?

If you are considering a career in social work, what would the ideal job be? Think in terms of four areas: (1) the types of professional activities you would most like to pursue, (2) your preferred client population, (3) the problems you are interested in addressing, and (4) the type of agency setting in which you would like to work. The questions posed in Box C illustrate examples in each area.

Note that simple identification of your preferred job characteristics does not mean that you will get that exact job or even one very similar. The intent here is to help you seriously consider your own goals and career objectives. The better you know yourself, the more capable you will be of both presenting yourself to others (such as potential employers) and making decisions about what job to pursue and accept.

## BOX C  Job Preferences

1. What types of professional activities are you most interested in pursuing? Prioritize the following:

_____ Counseling
_____ Brokering resources
_____ Supervising volunteers
_____ Writing grants
_____ Running groups
_____ Management
_____ Community organizing
_____ Program evaluation
_____ Public relations
_____ Running meetings
_____ Budgeting
_____ Administrative activities in general
_____ Case management
_____ Supervising staff
_____ Lobbying
_____ Research
_____ Fund-raising
_____ Training staff
_____ Policy development
_____ Advocacy

What else? _____

_____ _____

_____ _____

2. Ideally, what client population would you prefer to work with? Prioritize the following:

_____ Children
_____ Young adults
_____ Older adults
_____ Women
_____ Intact families
_____ Teenagers
_____ Middle-aged adults
_____ Married couples
_____ Men
_____ Single parents
_____ Minority groups (If so, specify which) _____
_____ Other client populations (If so, specify which) _____

3. What problems and issues are you interested in addressing? Prioritize the following:

_____ Community development
_____ Alcohol and other drugs
_____ Child maltreatment
_____ Battered women
_____ Probation and parole
_____ Mental illness
_____ Family problems
_____ Crime in communities

(continued)

## BOX C   Job Preferences    *(Continued)*

_____ Teen pregnancy
_____ School problems (e.g., truancy, bullying)
_____ Financial resources acquisition
_____ Prison
_____ Couples conflict
_____ Unemployment
_____ Vocational rehabilitation
_____ Developmental disability
_____ Health
_____ Eating disorders
_____ Suicide prevention
_____ Physical challenges
_____ HIV/AIDS
_____ Homelessness
What else? _____
_____

4. In what type of agency setting would you prefer to work? Prioritize the following:

_____ Private or
_____ Public
_____ Large bureaucracy or
_____ Smaller agency
_____ County social services
_____ Institution
_____ Group home
_____ Primary social work setting
_____ Primary medical setting
_____ Primary educational setting
_____ Serving clients with a wide range of problems or
_____ Focusing on specialized problems
_____ Close, directive supervision or
_____ Supervision primarily on a consultation basis
_____ Hospital
_____ School
_____ Community organization
_____ Prison
_____ Family planning agency
_____ Mental health center or counseling agency
_____ Hospice
_____ Shelter (e.g., for homeless people or survivors of domestic violence)
_____ Other (Please explain): _____

## Looking Ahead

These exercises and this book only scratch the surface of what social work is all about. It's just the beginning if you're thinking about some area of social work as the career for you.

# References

Abadinsky, H. (2011). *Drug use and abuse: A comprehensive introduction* (7th ed.). Belmont, CA: Brooks/Cole.

Abdelkarim, R. Z. (2002, September October). American Muslims and 9/11: A community looks back … and to the future. *Washington Report on Middle East Affairs, 21*(1), 82–85. Retrieved July 9, 2004, from http://infotrac-college .thornsonlearning.com.

Abdul Rauf, F. (2004). *What's right with Islam: A new vision for Muslims and the West.* New York: Harper.

About.com. (2011). What are CD4 cells? Retrieved June 13, 2011, from http://aids.about.com/od/newlydiagnosed/qt/cd4 .htm.

Abramovitz, M. (1995). Aid to families with dependent children. In R. L. Edwards (Ed.), *Encyclopedia of social work* (19th ed., Vol. 1, pp. 183–194). Washington, DC: NASW Press.

Abramovitz, M. (1997). Temporary assistance to needy families. In R. L. Edwards (Ed.), *Encyclopedia of social work supplement* (pp. 311–330). Washington, DC: NASW Press.

Abramovitz, M. (2007). Ideological perspectives and conflicts. In J. Blau (Ed., with M. Abramovitz), *The dynamics of social welfare policy* (2nd ed., pp. 126–183). New York: Oxford.

Abramovitz, M. (2008). Political ideology and social welfare. In T. Mizrahi & L. E. Davis (Editors-in-Chief), *Encyclopedia of social work* (Vol. 3, pp. 368–374). Washington, DC: NASW Press.

Abramovitz, M. (2010). Ideological perspectives and conflicts. In J. Blau (Ed., with M. Abramovitz), *The dynamics of social welfare policy* (3rd ed., pp. 131–188). New York: Oxford.

Acs, G., & Lopres, P. (2007). Final report: TANF caseload composition and leavers synthesis report. Retrieved May 21, 2011, from http://www.urban.org/UploadedPDF/411553_ tanf_caseload.pdf.

ADA Amendments Act of 2008. (2008). P.L. 110–125. Retrieved from http://www.access-board.gov/about/laws/ada-amend-ments.htm.

ADA.gov. (2014). Americans with Disability Act of 1990 as amended. Retrieved from http://www.ada.gov/pubs/adasta-tute08.htm.

Administration on Aging (AOA). (2011). Profile of older Americans: 2011. Retrieved from http://www.aoa.gov/Aging_ Statistics/Profile/2011/docs/2011profile.pdf.

Administration on Aging (AOA). (2012). Profile of older Americans: 2011. Retrieved from http://www.aoa.gov/Aging_ Statistics/Profile/2012/docs/2012profile.pdf.

Administration for Children and Families (ACF). (2014). Temporary Assistance for Needy Families (TANF). U.S. Department of Health and Human Services. Retrieved from http:// www.acf.hhs.gov/programs/ofa/programs/tanf.

Administration for Children and Families (ACF). (n.d.). Family preservation services. Retrieved May 30, 2011, from http:// www.childwelfare.gov/supporting/preservation/.

Administration for Community Living (ACL). (2014). Administration on intellectual and developmental disabilities. Retrieved from http://www.acl.gov/programs/aidd/Programs/ PCPID/.

Administration for Community Living (ACL). (2015). Data and evaluations. Retrieved from http://www.acl.gov/Data_ Outcomes/Index.aspx.

Aestraea's Web. (1998). Was "Sybil" really a multiple personality? Retrieved April 27, 2002, from http://www.aestraeaweb .net/plural/sybilbogus.html.

Ahluwalia, M. K., & Zaman, N. K. (2010). Counseling Muslims and Sikhs in a post-9/11 world. In J. G. Ponterotto, J. M. Cases, L. A. Suzuki, & C. M. Alexander (Eds.), *Handbook of multicultural counseling* (3rd ed., pp. 467–478). Thousand Oaks, CA: Sage.

AIDS InfoNet.org. (2014). What is AIDS? Retrieved from http:// www.aidsinfonet.org/fact_sheets/view/101.

Ajrouch, K. J. (2008). Arab Americans. In T. Mizrahi & L. E. Davis (Editors-in-Chief), *Encyclopedia of social work* (Vol. 1, pp. 151–153). Washington, DC: NASW Press.

Akabas, S. H. (2008). Employee assistance programs. In T. Mizrahi & L. E. Davis (Editors-in-Chief), *Encyclopedia of social work* (Vol. 2, pp. 115–118). Washington, DC: NASW Press.

Alavi, K. (2001, October). At risk of prejudice: Teaching tolerance about Muslim Americans. *Social Education, 65*(6), 344–349. Retrieved July 13, 2004, from http://infotrac-college.thomson-learning.com/itw/infomark/145/808/51630275w5/22!ar_fmt.

Albrecht, G. (1992). *The disability business: Rehabilitation in America.* Newbury Park, CA: Sage.

Alderson, K. (2013). *Counseling LGBTI Clients.* Thousand Oaks, CA: Sage.

Alexander, S. (2004). Intervention with families. In C. R. Brittain & D. E. Hunt (Eds.), *Helping in child protective services: A competency-based casework handbook* (pp. 393–446). New York: Oxford.

Allen, J. A. (1995). African Americans: Caribbean. In R. L. Edwards (Ed.), *Encyclopedia of social work* (19th ed., Vol. 1, pp. 121–129). Washington, DC: NASW Press.

Alleman, N. F., & Holly, L. N. (2014). Accomplishing the four essential tasks for higher education access: The role of natural helping networks in rural Virginia. In T. L. Scales, C. L. Streeter, and H. S. Cooper (Eds.), *Rural social work: Building and sustaining community capacity* (2nd ed., pp. 59–73). Hoboken, NJ: Wiley.

543

Altshuler, S. J. (2007). Everything you never wanted to know about special education … and were afraid to ask (I.D.E.A.). *Journal of Social Work in Disability and Rehabilitation, 6*(112), 23–34.

American Association of Marriage and Family Therapists (AAMFT). (2014). Same-sex parents and their children. Retrieved from http://www.aamft.org/imis15/aamft/Content/Consumer_Updates/Same-sex_Parents_and_Their_Children.aspx.

American Experience. (2010). Jimmy Carter's post-presidency. Retrieved June 4, 2011, from http://www.pbs.org/wgbh/americanExperience/features/general-article/carter-post-presidency/.

American Psychiatric Association (APA). (2013). *Diagnostic and statistical manual of mental disorders: DSM-5* (5th ed.). Arlington, VA: Author.

American Psychological Association. (2000). *Diagnostic and statistical manual of mental disorders: Text Revision* (DSM-IV-TR). Washington, DC: Author.

American Psychological Association (APA). (2010). *Publication manual of the American psychological association* (6th ed.). Washington, DC: Author.

American Psychological Association (APA). (2014). Disability & socioeconomic status. Retrieved from http://www.apa.org/pi/ses/resources/publications/factsheet-disability.aspx.

Answers.USA.gov. (2014). Social Security: Maximum and minimum retirement benefits. Retrieved from http://answers.usa.gov/system/templates/selfservice/USAGov/#!portal/1012/article/4236/Social-Security-Maximum-and-Minimum-Retirement-Benefit.

Antony, M. M. (2014). Behavior therapy. In D. Wedding & R. J. Corsini (Eds.), *Current psychotherapies* (10th ed., pp. 193–229). Belmont, CA: Brooks/Cole.

Arc, The. (2011). Self-determination. Retrieved from http://www.thearc.org/page.aspx?pid=2359.

Arc, The. (2014). Home. Retrieved from http://www.thearc.org/.

Arc Milwaukee, The. (n.d., a). Employment programs. Milwaukee: Author.

Arc Milwaukee, The. (n.d., b). Figuring out funding. Milwaukee: Author.

ARC Milwaukee. The. (n.d., c). Services profile. Milwaukee, WI: Author.

Arc Racine County, The. (n.d.). Home. Retrieved from http://www.thearcofracine.org/.

Armstrong, K., Best, S., & Domenici, P. (2006). *Courage after fire.* Berkeley, CA: Ulysses Press.

Aronowitz, A. A. (2004). Victimization of trafficked persons and illegal migrants. *International Review of Victimology, 11,* 11–32.

Arredondo, P., et al. (1996). *Operationalization of the multicultural counseling competencies.* Washington, DC: Association for Multicultural Counseling and Development.

Asch, A. (1995). Visual impairment and blindness. In R. L. Edwards (Ed.), *Encyclopedia of social work* (19th ed., Vol. 3, pp. 2461–2468). Washington, DC: NASW Press.

Asch, A., & Mudrick, N. R. (2008). Blindness and visual impairment. In T. Mizrahi & L. E. Davis (Editors-in-Chief), *Encyclopedia of social work* (Vol. 1, pp. 206–214). Washington, DC: NASW Press.

Association of Baccalaureate Program Directors (BPD). (2008). Definition of generalist practice. Retrieved July 5, 2008, from http://www.bpdonline.org.

Association of Social Work Boards (ASWB). (2008). ASWB: Summer 2008. Retrieved July 6, 2008, from http://www.aswb.org/.

Association of Social Work Boards (ASWB). (2011). Association of social work boards. Retrieved May 6, 2011, from http://www.bls.gov/oco/ocos060.htm.

Association of Social Work Boards (ASWB). (2013). Home. Retrieved from http://www.aswb.org/.

Association of Social Work Boards (ASWB). (2014). Candidate handbook: ASWB social work licensing examinations. Retrieved from http://www.aswb.org/wp-content/uploads/2013/12/Candidate-Handbook.2014.pdf.

Astor, R. A., Benbenishty, R., & Marachi, R. (2010). Violence in schools. In P. Allen-Meares (Ed.), *Social work services in schools* (6th ed., pp. 125–156). Boston: Allyn & Bacon.

Atkins-Burnett, S. (2010). Children with disabilities. In P. Allen-Meares (Ed.), *Social work in schools* (6th ed., pp. 157–190). Boston: Allyn & Bacon.

AVERT. (2011). HIV and AIDS in Africa. Retrieved June 13, 2011, from http://www.avert.org/hiv-aids-africa.htm.

AVERT. (2014). HIV and AIDS in sub-Saharan Africa. Retrieved from http://www.avert.org/hiv-aids-sub-saharan-africa.htm.

Axinn, J., & Stern, M. J. (2008). *Social welfare: A history of the American response to need* (7th ed.). Boston: Allyn & Bacon.

Balgopal, P. R. (1995). Asian Americans overview. In R. L. Edwards (Ed.), *Encyclopedia of social work* (19th ed., Vol. 1, pp. 231–238). Washington, DC: NASW Press.

Balgopal, P. R. (2008). Asian Americans: Overview. In T. Mizrahi & L. E. Davis (Editors-in-Chief), *Encyclopedia of social work* (Vol. 1, pp. 153–160). Washington, DC: NASW Press.

Balsanek, J. (1998). Addressing at-risk pregnant women's issues through community, individual, and corporate grassroots efforts. In P. L. Ewalt, E. M. Freeman, & D. L. Poole (Eds.), *Community building: Renewal, well-being, and shared responsibility* (pp. 411–419). Washington, DC: NASW Press.

Barker, R. L. (1999). *Milestones.* Washington, DC: NASW Press.

Barker, R. L. (2003). *The social work dictionary* (5th ed.). Washington, DC: NASW Press.

Barker, R. L. (2014). *The social work dictionary* (6th ed.). Washington, DC: NASW Press.

Barnett, O. W., Miller-Perrin, C. L., & Perrin, R. D. (2011). *Family violence across the lifespan: An introduction* (3rd ed.). Thousand Oaks, CA: Sage.

Barsky, A. E. (2006). *Alcohol, other drugs, and addictions: A professional development manual for social workers and the human services.* Belmont, CA: Brooks/Cole.

Barth, R. P. (2008). Adoption. In T. Mizrahi & L. E. Davis (Editors-in-Chief), *Encyclopedia of social work* (Vol. 1, pp. 33–414). Washington, DC: NASW Press.

Bartlett, H. (1970). *The common base of social work practice.* New York: National Association of Social Workers.

Barusch, A. S. (2000). Social Security is not for babies: Trends and policies affecting older women in the United States. *Families in Society, 81*(6), 568–575.

Barusch, A. S. (2015). *Foundations of social policy: Social justice in human perspective* (5th ed.). Belmont, CA: Cengage Learning.

Baruth, L. G., & Manning, M. L. (1999). *Multicultural counseling and psychotherapy: A lifespan perspective* (2nd ed.). Upper Saddle River, NJ: Prentice-Hall.

Baruth, L. G., & Manning, M. L. (2007). *Multicultural counseling and psychotherapy: A lifespan perspective* (4th ed.). Upper Saddle River, NJ: Merrill.

Baskin, T. (2012). Age. In D. D. Choudhuri, A. L. Santiago-Rivera, & M. T. Garrett (Eds.), *Counseling & diversity* (pp. 153–178). Belmont, CA: Brooks/Cole.

Bearse, M. L. (2008). Native Americans: Practice interventions. In T. Mizrahi & L. E. Davis (Editors-in-Chief), *Encyclopedia of social work* (Vol. 3, pp. 299–308). Washington, DC: NASW Press.

Becerra, R. M., & Damron-Rodriguez, J. (1995). Veterans and veterans services. In R. L. Edwards (Ed.), *Encyclopedia of social work* (19th ed., Vol. 3, pp. 2431–2439). Washington, DC: NASW Press.

Beck, A. T., Rush, A. J., Shaw, B. F., & Emery, G. (1979). *Cognitive therapy of depression.* New York: Guilford Press.

Beck, A. T., & Weishaar, M. E. (2011). Cognitive therapy. In R. J. Corsini & D. Wedding (Eds.), *Current psychotherapies* (9th ed., pp. 276–309). Belmont, CA: Brooks/Cole.

Beckett, J. O., & Johnson, H. C. (1995). Human development. In R. L. Edwards (Ed.), *Encyclopedia of social work* (19th ed., Vol. 2, pp. 1385–1405). Washington, DC: NASW Press.

Begley, S. (1999, May 3). Why the young kill. *Newsweek,* 32–35.

Beless, D. W. (1995). Council on social work education. In R. L. Edwards (Ed.), *Encyclopedia of social work* (19th ed., Vol. 1, pp. 632–637). Washington, DC: NASW Press.

Bennett, B. (2006, April 23). Stolen away. Retrieved June 29, 2008, from http://www.time.com/time/printout/0, 8816, 1 186558, 00.html.

Bennett, J. (2010, October 11). From lockers to lockup. *Newsweek,* pp. 38–41.

Berg, I. K. (1994). *Family based services: A solution-focused approach.* New York: Norton.

Berg-Cross, L., Craig, K., & Wessel, T. (2001). Multiculturalism at historically black colleges and universities: A case study of Howard University. In J. G. Ponterotto, J. M. Casas, L. A. Suzuki, & C. M. Alexander (Eds.), *Handbook of multicultural counseling* (2nd ed., pp. 849–870). Thousand Oaks, CA: Sage.

Berger, R. M., & Kelly, J. J. (1995). Gay men overview. In R. L. Edwards (Ed.), *Encyclopedia of social work* (19th ed., Vol. 2, pp. 1064–1075). Washington, DC: NASW Press.

Berliner, L., & Elliott, D. M. (2002). Sexual abuse of children. In J. E. B. Myers, L. Berliner, J. Briere, C. T. Hendrix, C. Jenny, & T. A. Reid (Eds.), *The APSAC handbook on child maltreatment* (2nd ed., pp. 55–78). Thousand Oaks, CA: Sage.

Berry, M. (2005). Overview of family preservation. In G. P. Mallon & P. M. Hess (Eds.), *Child welfare for the 21st century: A handbook of practices, policies, and programs* (pp. 319–334). New York: Columbia.

Beumont, P. J. V., Russell, J. E., & Touyz, S. W. (1993). Treatment of anorexia nervosa. *Lancet, 341,* 1635–1640.

Bibus, A., & Link, R. J. (1999). Global approaches to learning social welfare policy. In C. S. Ramanathan & R. J. Link (Eds.), *All our futures: Principles and resources for social work practice in a global era.* Pacific Grove, CA: Brooks/Cole.

Biegel, D. E., Shore, B. K., & Gordon, E. (1984). *Building support networks for the elderly: Theory and application.* Thousand Oaks, CA: Sage.

Binghenheimer, J. B., Brennan, R. T., & Earls, F. J. (2005). Firearm violence exposure and serious violent behavior. *Science, 308,* 1323–1326.

Black, L. (1996). Families of African origin: An overview. In M. McGoldrick, J. Giordan, & J. K. Pearce (Eds.), *Ethnicity and family therapy* (2nd ed., pp. 57–65). New York: Guilford.

Blau, J., & Abramovitz, M. (2010). *The dynamics of social welfare policy* (3rd ed.). New York: Oxford.

Blau, J., & Abramovitz, M. (2014). *The dynamics of social welfare policy* (4th ed.). New York: Oxford.

Blundo, R. (2008). Men: Practice interventions. In T. Mizrahi & L. E. Davis (Editors-in-Chief), *Encyclopedia of social work* (Vol. 3, pp. 217–221). Washington, DC: NASW Press.

Blythe, B., & Reithoffer, A. (2000). Assessment and measurement issues in direct practice in social work. In P. Allen-Meares & C. Garvin (Eds.), *The handbook of social work practice* (pp. 551–564). Thousand Oaks, CA: Sage.

Boehm, W. W. (1959). *Objectives of the social work curriculum of the future.* New York: Council on Social Work Education.

Boonstra, H. (2002, February). Teen pregnancy: Trends and lessons learned. *The Guttmacher Report on Public Policy,* pp. 9–10.

Borch-Jacobsen, M. (1997, April 24). Sybil: The making of a disease? *New York Review of Books.* Retrieved April 28, 2002, from http://www.aestraeasweb.net/plural/spiegel.html.

Boyd-Franklin, N. (2003). *Black families in therapy: Understanding African American experience* (2nd ed.). New York: Guilford Press.

Boyle, C. (2000). Engagement: An ongoing process. In A. A. Abbott (Ed.), *Alcohol, tobacco, and other drugs: Challenging myths, assessing theories, individualizing interventions* (pp. 144–158). Washington, DC: NASW Press.

Brammer, R. (2012). *Diversity in counseling* (2nd ed.). Belmont, CA: Brooks/Cole.

Brandwein, R. A. (2008). Women: Overview. In T. Mizrahi & L. E. Davis (Editors-in-Chief), *Encyclopedia of social work* (Vol. 4, pp. 281–290). Washington, DC: NASW Press.

Braun, K. L., & Browne, C. V. (2000). Perceptions of dementia, caregiving, and help seeking among Asian and Pacific Islander Americans. In S. M. Keigher, A. E. Fortune, & S. L. Witkin (Eds.), *Aging and social work: The changing landscapes* (pp. 175–191). Washington, DC: NASW Press.

Braun, K. L., Mokuau, N., & Tsark, J. (1997). Cultural themes in health, illness, and rehabilitation for Native Hawaiians: Observations of rehabilitation staff and physicians. *Topics in Geriatric Rehabilitation, 12,* 19–37.

Brave Heart, M. Y. H., & Chase, J. (2005). Social work practice with First Nations Peoples. In D. Lum (Ed.), *Cultural competence, practice stages, and client systems: A case study approach* (pp. 32–58). Pacific Grove, CA: Brooks/Cole.

Breton, M., & Nosko, A. (1997). Group work with women who have experienced abuse. In G. L. Greif & P. H. Ephross (Eds.), *Group work with populations at risk* (pp. 134–146). New York: Oxford University Press.

Bricker-Jenkins, M., & Lockett, P. W. (1995). Women: Direct practice. In R. L. Edwards (Ed.), *Encyclopedia of social work*

(19th ed., Vol. 3, pp. 2529–2539). Washington, DC: NASW Press.

Brieland, D. (1995). Social work practice: History and evolution. In R. L. Edwards (Ed.), *Encyclopedia of social work* (19th ed., Vol. 3, pp. 2247–2258). Washington, DC: NASW Press.

Brill, S. (2013, March 4). Bitter pill. *Time Magazine, 181*(8), 16–55.

Brody, R. (2005). *Effectively managing human service organizations* (3rd ed.). Thousand Oaks, CA: Sage.

Brunstein Klomek, A., Marrocco, F., Kleinman, M., Schofeld, I. S., & Gould, M. S. (2007). Bullying, depression, and suicidality in adolescents. *Journal of the American Academy of Child and Adolescent Psychiatry, 46,* 40–49.

Buchan, V., Hull, G., Rogers, J., Rodenhiser, R., & Smith, M. (2004, November). BEAP use and outcome trend summary. Paper presented at the meeting of the Baccalaureate Association of (Social Work) Program Directors, Detroit, MI.

Bukatko, D., & Daehler, M. W. (2012). *Child development: A thematic approach* (6th ed.). Belmont, CA: Wadsworth.

Bureau of Indian Affairs. (2014). Frequently asked questions. Retrieved from http://www.bia.gov/FAQs/.

Bureau of Labor Statistics. (2014). *Occupational outlook handbook: Social workers.* Retrieved from http://www.bls.gov/ooh/community-and-social-service/social-workers.htm.

Burger, W. R., & Youkeles, M. (2000). *Human services in contemporary America* (5th ed.). Pacific Grove, CA: Brooks/Cole.

Burke, A. C. (2008). Alcohol and drug problems: Law enforcement and legal policy. In T. Mizrahi & L. E. Davis (Editors-in-Chief), *Encyclopedia of social work* (Vol. 1, pp. 131–136). Washington, DC: NASW Press.

Burman, S. (2000). Strategies for intervention with individuals. In A. A. Abbott (Ed.), *Alcohol, tobacco, and other drugs: Challenging myths, assessing theories, individualizing interventions* (pp. 204–246). Washington, DC: NASW Press.

Burn, S. M. (2005). *Women across cultures: A global perspective* (2nd ed.). New York: McGraw-Hill.

Butterfield, A. K. J., & Chisanga, B. (2008). Community development. In T. Mizrahi & L. E. Davis (Editors-in-Chief), *Encyclopedia of social work* (Vol. 1, pp. 375–381). Washington, DC: NASW Press.

Bye, L., & Alvarez, M. (2007). *School social work: Theory to practice.* Belmont, CA: Brooks/Cole.

California School Boards Association. (2010). Cyberbullying: Policy considerations for boards. Retrieved from http://www.csba.org/GovernanceAndPolicyResources/DistrictPolicyServices/~/media/CSBA/Files/GovernanceResources/PolicyNews_Briefs/SchoolSafety/2010_07_PolicyBrief_Cyberbullying.ashx.

Campos, A. P. (1995). Hispanics: Puerto Ricans. In R. L. Edwards (Ed.), *Encyclopedia of social work* (19th ed., Vol. 2, pp. 1245–1252). Washington, DC: NASW Press.

Canadian Association of Social Workers (CASW). (2014). CASW home. Retrieved from http://www.casw-acts.ca/.

Canby, W. (1981). *American Indian law in a nutshell.* St. Paul, MN: West.

Canda, E. R., & Furman, L. D. (2010). *Spiritual diversity in social work practice: The heart of helping* (2nd ed.). New York: Oxford.

Cannon, A., Streisand, B., & McGraw, D. (1999, May 3). Why? There were plenty of warnings, but no one stopped two twisted teens. *U.S. News & World Report,* 16–19.

Caple, F. S., & Salcido, R. M. (2009). A framework for cross-cultural practice in school settings. In C. R. Massat, R. Constable, S. McDonald, & J. P. Flynn (Eds.), *School social work: Practice, policy, and research* (7th ed., pp. 339–361). Chicago: Lyceum.

Carlton-LaNey, B., Edwards, R. L., & Reid, P. N. (1999). Small towns and rural communities: From romantic notions to harsh realities. In I. B. Carlton-LaNey, R. L. Edwards, & P. N. Reid (Eds.), *Preserving and strengthening small towns and rural communities* (pp. 5–12). Washington, DC: NASW Press.

Carroll, J. (2008). Retirement age expectations and realities. Retrieved July 17, 2008, from http://www.gallup.com/poll/16375/Retirement-Age-Expectations-Realities.aspx.

Carroll, J. L. (2013a). *Discovery series: Introduction to human sexuality.* Belmont, CA: Cengage Learning.

Carroll, J. L. (2013b). *Sexuality now: Embracing diversity* (4th ed.). Belmont, CA: Cengage Learning.

Carson, E. A. (2014). Prisoners in 2013. Retrieved from the Bureau of Justice Statistics website: http://www.bjs.gov/index.cfm?ty=pbdetail&iid=5109.

Carton, B. (1994, January 27). Growing up in a gay household. *Boston Globe,* 45.

CASAColumbia. (2015). What is addiction? Retrieved from http://www.casacolumbia.org/addiction?gclid=CPrpu9-nYwcMCFQmqaQod-GUA8g.

CBSNews.com. (2011, January 27). Social security on pace to be drained by 2037. Retrieved May 11, 2011, from http://www.cbsnews.com/stories/2011/0 l/26/politics/main7286861.shtml.

CDC Foundation. (2014). What is public health? Retrieved from http://www.cdcfoundation.org/content/what-public-health.

Center for Mental Health in Schools at UCLA. (2011). *Embedding bullying interventions into a comprehensive system of student and learning supports: A center policy & practice brief.* Los Angeles: Author.

Centers for Disease Control and Prevention (CDC). (2008b). Developmental disabilities: Topic home. Retrieved November 3, 2008, from http://www.cdc.gov/ncbddd/dd/.

Centers for Disease Control and Prevention (CDC). (2011b). Developmental disabilities: Topic home. Retrieved June 8, 2011, from http://www.cdc.gov/ncbddd/dd/default.htm.

Centers for Disease Control (CDC). (2013). Developmental disabilities. Retrieved from http://www.cdc.gov/ncbddd/developmentaldisabilities/index.html.

Centers for Disease Control (CDC). (2014). HIV/AIDS. Retrieved from http://www.cdc.gov/hiv/library/factsheets/index.html.

Centers for Disease Control (CDC). (2015a). Understanding school violence. Retrieved from http://www.cdc.gov/violence-prevention/pdf/school_violence_fact_sheet-a.pdf.

Centers for Disease Control (CDC). (2015b). Youth violence: Risk and protective factors. Retrieved from http://www.cdc.gov/violenceprevention/youthviolence/riskprotectivefactors.html.

Centers for Disease Control (CDC). (2015c). Key findings: Trends in the prevalence of developmental disabilities in U.S. Children, 1997–2008. Retrieved from http://www.cdc.gov/ncbddd/developmentaldisabilities/features/birthdefects-dd-keyfindings.html.

Centers for Medicare and Medicaid Services (CMS). (2011). Medicaid. Retrieved May 23, 2011, from https://www.cms.gov/home/medicaid.asp.

Centers for Medicare and Medicaid Services (CMS) (U.S. Department of Health & Human Services). (2014a, October 17). Medicaid & CHIP: August 2014 monthly applications, eligibility determinations and enrollment report. Retrieved from http://www.medicaid.gov/medicaid-chip-program-information/program-information/downloads/august-2014-enrollment-report.pdf.

Centers for Medicare and Medicaid Services (CMS) (U.S. Department of Health & Human Services). (2014b). *Medicare & you: 2015.* Baltimore, MD: Author.

Chadwick, D. L. (2002). Community organization of services to deal with and end child abuse. In J. E. B. Myers, L. Berliner, J. Briere, C. T. Hendrix, C. Jenny, & T. A. Reid (Eds.), *The APSAC handbook on child maltreatment* (2nd ed., pp. 509–523). Thousand Oaks, CA: Sage.

Chambers, D. E., & Wedel, K. R. (2005). *Social policy and social programs: A method for the practical public policy analyst* (4th ed.). Boston: Allyn & Bacon.

Chan, S., & Lee, E. (2004). Families with Asian roots. In E. W. Lynch & M. J. Hanson (Eds.), *Developing, cross-cultural competence: A guide for working with children and their families* (3rd ed., pp. 219–298). Baltimore, MD: Brookes.

Chapin, R. (2014). *Social policy for effective practice: A strengths approach* (3rd ed.). New York: Routledge.

Charlesworth, R. (2014). *Understanding child development* (9th ed.). Belmont, CA: Wadsworth.

Cherokee Messenger. (1995). Brief history of the trail of tears. Retrieved November 20, 2004, from http://www.powersource.com/cherokee/history.html.

Childress, S. (2006, March 6). Invasion of the body snatchers. *Newsweek,* 46.

Child Welfare Information Gateway. (2008). What is child abuse and neglect? Retrieved June 1, 2011, from http://www.childwelfare.gov/pubs/factsheets/whatiscan.cfm.

Child Welfare League of America (CWLA). (1994). *Kinship care: A natural bridge.* Washington, DC: Author.

Child Welfare League of America (CWLA). (2005). Position statement on residential services. Retrieved May 31, 2011, from http://www.cwla.org/programs/groupcare/rgcpositionstatement.pdf.

Child Welfare League of America (CWLA). (n.d.). *The history of White House conferences on children and youth.* Retrieved from http://www.cwla.org/advocacy/whitehouseconfhistory.pdf.

Christ, G. H., Sormanti, M., & Francoer, R. B. (2001). Chronic physical illness and disability. In A. Gitterman (Ed.), *Handbook of social work practice with vulnerable and resilient populations* (2nd ed., pp. 124–162). New York: Columbia University Press.

Clark, E. J. (2008). National association of social workers. In T. Mizrahi & L. E. Davis (Editors-in-Chief), *Encyclopedia of social work* (Vol. 3, pp. 292–295). Washington, DC: NASW Press.

Clarke, J. S., Kim, I., & Spencer, M. S. (2013). Engaging with culturally and racially diverse families. In C. Franklin, M. B. Harris, & P. Allen-Meares (Eds.), *The school services sourcebook* (2nd ed., pp. 765–774). New York: Oxford.

Cloud, J. (2001, Feb. 26). New sparks over electroshock. *Time,* 60–62.

Clute, M. A. (2008). Disability: Physical disabilities. In T. Mizrahi & L. E. Davis (Editors-in-Chief), *Encyclopedia of social work* (Vol. 2, pp. 49–55). Washington, DC: NASW Press.

CNN.com. (2001). The end of Enron? Retrieved February 5, 2005, from http://cnn.com/SPECIALS/2002/enron/.

CNN.com. (2015). Sandy Hook shooting: What happened? Retrieved from http://www.cnn.com/interactive/2012/12/us/sandy-hook-timeline/.

Cohen, N. A. (1992). The continuum of child welfare services. In N. A. Cohen (Ed.), *Child welfare: A multicultural approach* (pp. 39–83). Needham Heights, MA: Allyn & Bacon.

Coleman, J. W., & Kerbo, H. R. (2009). *Social problems* (10th ed.). New York: Vango.

Collins, D., Jordan, C., & Coleman, H. (2013). *An introduction to family social work* (4th ed.). Belmont, CA: Brooks/Cole.

Congress, E. P., & Gonzalez, M. J. (Eds.). (2013). *Multicultural perspectives in working with families* (3rd ed.). New York: Springer.

Congressional Research Institute for Social Work and Policy (CRISP). (2013). Social workers in Congress. Retrieved from http://crispinc.org/social-workers-in-congress/.

Congresswoman Susan Davis. (2014). About Susan. Retrieved from http://www.house.gov/susandavis/bio.shtml.

Connaway, R. S., & Gentry, M. E. (1988). *Social work practice.* Englewood Cliffs, NJ: Prentice-Hall.

Constable, R. (2009). The role of the school social worker. In C. R. Massat, R. Constable, S. McDonald, & J. P. Flynn (Eds.), *School social work: Practice, policy, and research* (7th ed., pp. 3–29). Chicago: Lyceum.

Cooper, C., Selwood, A., & Livingston, G. (2008). The prevalence of elder abuse and neglect: A systematic review. *Age and Ageing, 37,* 151–160.

Corcoran, K. (1997). Managed care: Implications for social work practice. In *Encyclopedia of social work 1997 supplement.* Washington, DC: NASW Press.

Corey, G. (2009). *Theory and practice of counseling and psychotherapy* (8th ed.). Belmont, CA: Brooks/Cole.

Corey, G. (2012). *Theory & practice of group counseling* (8th ed.). Belmont, CA: Brooks/Cole.

Corey, G. (2013). *Theory and practice of counseling and psychotherapy.* Belmont, CA: Cengage Learning.

Corey, G., Corey, M. S., Corey, C., & Callanan, P. (2015). *Issues and ethics in the helping professions* (9th ed.). Belmont, CA: Cengage Learning.

Corey, M. S., & Corey, G. (2011). *Becoming a helper* (6th ed.). Belmont, CA: Brooks/Cole.

Corey, M. S., Corey, G., & Corey, C. (2010). *Groups: Process and practice* (8th ed.). Belmont, CA: Brooks/Cole.

Corr, C. A., Nabe, C. M., & Corr, D. M. (2009). *Death & dying, life & living* (6th ed.). Belmont, CA: Wadsworth.

Costin, C. (2008). The thin commandments. Retrieved July 22, 2008, from http://www.edreferral.com/thin_commandments.htm.

Council on Social Work Education (CSWE). (2002). *Glossary to educational policy and accreditation standards developed by Commission of the Council on Social Work Education.* Alexandria, VA: Author.

Council on Social Work Education (CSWE). (2008). *Educational policy and accreditation standards.* Alexandria, VA: Author.

Council on Social Work Education (CSWE). (2014). CSWE. Retrieved from http://www.cswe.org/Home.aspx.

Council on Social Work Education (CSWE). (2015). *Educational policy and accreditation standards.* Alexandria, VA: Author.

Cournoyer, B. R. (2014). *The social work skills workbook* (7th ed.). Belmont, CA: Brooks/Cole.

Cowger, C. D. (1994). Assessing client strengths: Clinical assessment for client empowerment. *Social Work, 39*(3), 262–268.

Cowley, G. (2000, January 17). Fighting the disease: What can be done. *Newsweek, 38.*

Cox, C. B. (2005). Grandparents raising grandchildren from a multicultural perspective. In E. P. Congress & M. J. Gonzalez (Eds.), *Multicultural perspectives in working with families* (2nd ed., 128–141). New York: Springer.

Cox, E. O., & Parsons, R. J. (1994). *Empowerment-oriented social work practice with the elderly.* Pacific Grove, CA: Brooks/Cole.

Crick, N. R., & Dodge, K. A. (1994). A review and reformulation of social information-processing mechanisms in children's social adjustment. *Psychological Bulletin, 115,* 74–101.

Crooks, R., & Baur, K. (2014). *Our sexuality* (12th ed.). Belmont, CA: Wadsworth.

Cross, T. L., Bazron, B. J., Dennis, K. W., & Isaacs, M. R. (1989). *Toward a culturally competent system of care.* Washington, DC: Child and Adolescent Service System Program Technical Assistance Center.

Crosson-Tower, C. (2009). *Exploring child welfare: A practice perspective* (5th ed.). Boston: Allyn & Bacon.

Crosson-Tower, C. (2010). *Understanding child abuse and neglect* (8th ed.). Boston: Allyn & Bacon.

Crosson-Tower, C. (2013). *Exploring child welfare: A practice perspective* (6th ed.). Boston: Pearson.

Crosson-Tower, C. (2014). *Understanding child abuse and neglect* (8th ed.). Boston: Pearson.

Cummerton, J. M. (1986). A feminist perspective on research: What does it help us see? In N. Van Den Bergh & L. B. Cooper (Eds.), *Feminist visions for social work* (pp. 80–100). Washington, DC: NASW Press.

Cummins, L. K., Byers, K. V., & Pedrick, L. (2011). *Policy practice for social workers: New strategies for a new era.* Boston: Allyn & Bacon.

Curiel, H. (1995). Hispanics: Mexican Americans. In R. L. Edwards (Ed.), *Encyclopedia of social work* (19th ed., Vol. 2, pp. 1233–1244). Washington, DC: NASW Press.

Currey, R. (2007, July/August). PTSD in today's war veterans: The road to recovery. *Social Work Today,* 12–16.

Daft, R. L. (2012). *Management* (10th ed.). Mason, OH: Southwestern.

DailyStrength. (2012). Electroconvulsive therapy. Retrieved from http://www.dailystrength.org/treatments/Electroconvulsive_therapy.

Daley, M. R., & Avant, F. L. (2004). Rural social work: Reconceptualizing the framework for practice. In T. L. Scales & C. L. Streeter (Eds.), *Rural social work: Building and sustaining community assets* (pp. 34–41). Belmont, CA: Brooks/Cole.

Daley, M. R., & Avant, F. L. (2014). Down-home social work: A strength-based model for rural practice. In T. L. Scales, C. L. Streeter, and H. S. Cooper (Eds.), *Rural social work: Building and sustaining community capacity* (2nd ed., pp. 5–17). Hoboken, NJ: Wiley.

Daley, M. R., & Hickman, S. (2011). Dual relations and beyond: Understanding and addressing ethical challenges for rural social work. *Journal of Social Work Values & Ethics, 8*(1). Retrieved from http://www.socialworker.com/jswve.

Danner, D. (2010, May 27). ObamaCare vs. small business. *The Wall Street Journal.* Retrieved June 11, 2011, from http://online.wsj.com/article/SB1000142405274870411350457526480 2756326086.html.

Daro, D., & Donnelly, A. C. (2002). Child abuse prevention: Accomplishments and challenges. In J. E. B. Myers, L. Berliner, J. Briere, C. T. Hendrix, C. Jenny, & T. A. Reid (Eds.), *The APSAC handbook on child maltreatment* (2nd ed., pp. 431–448). Thousand Oaks, CA: Sage.

Davenport, J. A., & Davenport, J., III. (2008). Rural practice. In T. Mizrahi & L. E. Davis (Editors-in-Chief), *Encyclopedia of social work* (Vol. 3, pp. 536–541). Washington, DC: NASW Press.

Day, P. J. (2009). *A new history of social welfare* (6th ed.). Boston: Allyn & Bacon.

Day, P. J., & Schiele, J. (2013). *A new history of social welfare* (7th ed.). Boston: Pearson.

DeCesare, D. (1993, March). El Salvador: War, poverty and migration: A photo essay. *Fellowship, 59,* 3.

DeLeon, G. (1994). Therapeutic communities. In M. Galanter & H. D. Kleber (Eds.), *Textbook of substance abuse treatment.* Washington, DC: American Psychiatric Press.

Delgado, M. (1998). Community asset assessments by Latino youth. In P. L. Ewalt, E. M. Freeman, & D. L. Poole (Eds.), *Community building: Renewal, well-being, and shared responsibility* (pp. 202–212). Washington, DC: NASW Press.

Delgado, M., & Barton, K. (1999). Murals in Latino communities: Social indicators of community strengths. In P. L. Ewalt, E. M. Freeman, A. E. Fortune, D. L. Poole, & S. L. Witkin (Eds.), *Multicultural issues in social work: Practice and research* (pp. 229–244). Washington, DC: NASW Press.

Delgado, M., & Staples, L. (2008). *You-led community organizing: Theory and action.* New York: Oxford.

Delgado-Romero, E. A., Nevels, B. J., Capielo, C., Galvan, N., & Torres, V. (2013). Culturally alert counseling with Latino/Latina Americans. In McAuliffe, G., & Associates (Eds.), *Culturally alert counseling: A comprehensive introduction* (2nd ed., pp. 293–314). Thousand Oaks, CA: Sage.

Dembling, B. (1995). Colonial family care. *Psychiatric Services, 46*(2).

DePanfilis, D. (2011). Child protection system. In J. E. B. Myers (Ed.), *The APS AC handbook on child maltreatment* (3rd ed., pp. 39–52). Thousand Oaks, CA: Sage.

DePoy, E., & Gilson, S. F. (2004). *Rethinking disability: Principles for professional and social change.* Belmont, CA: Brooks/Cole.

Derezotes, D. S. (2006). *Spiritually oriented social work practice.* Boston: Allyn & Bacon.

Derochie, K. (2012, November 11). Can my spouse and children get benefits if I am approved for Social Security disability? Retrieved from http://www.disabilityadvisor.com/benefits-for-a-disabled-workers-family/.

de Silva, E. C. (2007, October). Slavery persists in modern day. *NASW News,* 3.

Devaney, B. (2007). WIC turns 35: Program effectiveness and future directions. Retrieved May 25, 2011, from http://www.earlychildhoodrc.org/events/presentations/devaney.pdf.

Developmental Disabilities Assistance and Bill of Rights Act of 1990. Pub. L. No. 101-496. (1990).

DeVoe, J. F., Kaffenberger, S., & Chandler, K. (2005). Student reports of bullying: Results from the 2001 school crime supplement to the National Crime Victimization Survey. Retrieved from the National Center for Education Statistics website: http://nces.ed.gov/pubs2005/2005310.pdf.

Devore, W. (2001). "Whence came these people?": An exploration of the values and ethics of African American individuals, families, and communities. In R. Fong & S. Furuto (Eds.), *Culturally competent practice: Skills, interventions, and evaluations* (pp. 33–46). Boston: Allyn & Bacon.

DeWeaver, K. L. (1995). Developmental disabilities: Definitions and policies. In R. L. Edwards (Ed.), *Encyclopedia of social work* (19th ed., Vol. 1, pp. 712–720). Washington, DC: NASW Press.

Dhooper, S. S. (2012). *Social work in health care: Its past and future* (2nd ed.). Thousand Oaks, CA: Sage.

Dhooper, S. S., & Moore, S. E. (2001). *Social work practice with culturally diverse people.* Thousand Oaks, CA: Sage.

Diament, M. (2010). Obama signs bill replacing "mental retardation" with "intellectual disability." Retrieved June 6, 2011, from http://www.disabilityscoop.com/2010/10/05/obama-signs-rosas-law/10547/.

Diller, J. V. (2015). *Cultural diversity: A primer for the human services* (5th ed.). Belmont, CA: Cengage Learning.

Dinkes, R., Kemp, J., & Baum, K. (2009). *Indicators of school crime and safety: 2009 (NCES 2010-012/NCJ 228478).* Washington, DC: National Center for Education Statistics, U.S. Department of Justice.

DiNitto, D. M. (2005). *Social welfare: Politics and public policy* (6th ed.). Boston: Allyn & Bacon.

DiNitto, D. M. (2011). *Social welfare: Politics and public policy* (7th ed.). Boston: Allyn & Bacon.

DiNitto, D. M., & Johnson, D. H. (2012). *Essentials of social welfare: Politics and public policy.* Boston: Pearson.

Dixon, R. (2009). Africa's bitter cycle of child slavery. Retrieved May 30, 2011, from http://articles.latimes.com/2009/jul/12/world/fg-ghana-slaveryl2.

Dobelstein, A. W. (2003). *Social welfare policy and analysis* (3rd ed.). Pacific Grove, CA: Brooks/Cole.

Dolgoff, R., & Feldstein, D. (2009). *Understanding social welfare: A search for social justice* (8th ed.). Boston: Allyn & Bacon.

Dolgoff, R., & Feldstein, D. (2013). *Understanding social welfare: A search for social justice* (9th ed.). Boston: Pearson.

Dolgoff, R., Harrington, D., & Loewenberg, F. M. (2012). *Ethical decisions for social work practice* (9th ed.). Belmont, CA: Brooks/Cole.

Dolgoff, R., Loewenberg, F. M., & Harrington, D. (2005). *Ethical decisions for social work practice* (7th ed.). Pacific Grove, CA: Brooks/Cole.

Doweiko, H. E. (2015). *Concepts of chemical dependency* (9th ed.). Belmont, CA: Cengage Learning.

Downs, S. W., Moore, E., & McFadden, E. J. (2009). *Child welfare and family services: Policies and practice* (8th ed.). Boston: Allyn & Bacon.

Drum, J., & Howard, G. (1989, January). Multicultural and global education: Seeking common ground (Summary). Paper presented at a conference cosponsored by Las Palomas de Taos, REACH Center for Multicultural and Global Education, and the Stanley Foundation, Taos, NM.

Dulmus, C. N., & Roberts, A. R. (2008). Mental illness: Adults. In T. Mizrahi & L. E. Davis (Editors-in-Chief), *Encyclopedia of social work* (Vol. 3, pp. 237–242). Washington, DC: NASW Press.

DuongTran, Q., & Matsuoka, J. K. (1995). Asian-Americans: Southeast Asians. In R. L. Edwards (Ed.), *Encyclopedia of social work* (19th ed., Vol. 1, pp. 249–255). Washington, DC: NASW Press.

Dupper, D. R. (2013). *School bullying: New perspectives on a growing problem.* New York: Oxford.

Dworkin, S. H. (2000). Individual therapy with lesbian, gay, and bisexual clients. In R. M. Perez, K. A. DeBord, & K. J. Bieschke (Eds.), *Handbook of counseling and psychotherapy with lesbian, gay, and bisexual clients* (pp. 157–181). Washington, DC: American Psychological Association.

Dziegielewski, S. F. (2005). *Understanding substance addictions: Assessment and intervention.* Chicago: Lyceum.

Earle, K. A. (1999). Cultural diversity and mental health: The Haudenosaunee of New York State. In P. L. Ewalt, E. M. Freeman, A. E. Fortune, D. L. Poole, & S. L. Witkin (Eds.), *Multicultural issues in social work: Practice and research* (pp. 423–438). Washington, DC: NASW Press.

Earth Charter Initiative. (2011). Earth Charter. Retrieved April 16, 2011, from http://www.earthcharterinaction.org/content/pages/Read-the-Charter.html#top.

Edwards, E. D., & Edwards, M. E. (2002). Social work practice with American Indians and Alaskan Natives. In A. T. Morales & B. W. Sheafor (Eds.), *The many faces of social work clients* (pp. 239–265). Boston: Allyn & Bacon.

Einbinder, S. D. (1995). Policy analysis. In R. L. Edwards (Ed.), *Encyclopedia of social work* (19th ed., Vol. 3, pp. 1849–1855). Washington, DC: NASW Press.

Eitzen, D. S., Zinn, M. B., & Smith, K. E. (2014). *Social problems* (13th ed.). Boston: Pearson.

Eitzen, D. S., & Zinn, M. B. (2012). Globalisation: An introduction. In D. S. Stanley Eitzen & M. B. Zinn (Eds.), *Globalization: The transformation of social worlds* (3rd ed., pp. 1–9). Belmont, CA: Cengage Learning.

Electroshock therapy slowly gains greater use in the treatment of mental illness. (2000, March April). *American Scientist.* Retrieved April 27, 2002, from http://www.signaI.org/news&events/ArchivesAmsci/0003summary.htm.

Elze, D. E. (2013). Working with lesbian, gay, bisexual, transgender, queer, and questioning students. In C. Franklin, M. B. Harris, & P. Allen-Meares (Eds.), *The school services sourcebook* (2nd ed., pp. 821–836). New York: Oxford.

Encyclopedia of Children and Childhood in History and Society. (2008). Youth gangs. Retrieved from http://www.faqs.org/childhood/Wh-Z-and-other-topics/Youth-Gangs.html.

Englekirk, A., & Marín, M. (n.d.). Hispanic business. Retrieved from http://www.everyculture.com/multi/Le-Pa/Mexican-Americans.html.

Epstein, L. (1981). Advocates on advocacy: An exploratory study. *Social work research and abstracts, 17*(2), 5–12.

Equal Employment Opportunity Commission, U.S. Department of Justice Civil Rights Division. (1997, May). *The Americans with Disabilities Act: Questions and answers.* Washington, DC: Author.

Erickson, M. F., & Egeland, B. (2011). Child neglect. In J. E. B. Myers (Ed.), *The APS AC handbook on child maltreatment* (3rd ed., pp. 103–124). Thousand Oaks, CA: Sage.

Evans, K. M. (2013). Culturally alert counseling with African Americans. In McAuliffe, G., & Associates (Eds.), *Culturally alert counseling: A comprehensive introduction* (2nd ed., pp. 125–155). Thousand Oaks, CA: Sage.

Everett, J. E. (2008). Foster care. In T. Mizrahi & L. E. Davis (Editors-in-Chief), *Encyclopedia of social work* (Vol. 2, pp. 223–236). Washington, DC: NASW Press.

Ewalt, P. L., Freeman, E. M., & Poole, D. L. (Eds.). (1998). *Community building: Renewal, well-being, and shared responsibility.* Washington, DC: NASW Press.

Ewalt, P. L., & Mokuau, N. (1996). Self-determination from a Pacific perspective. In P. L. Ewalt, M. Freeman, A. E. Fortune, D. L. Poole, & S. L. Witkin (Eds.), *Multicultural issues in social work: Practice and research* (pp. 225–268). Washington, DC: NASW Press.

Exum, H. A., Coll, J. E., & Weiss, E. L. (2011). *A civilian counselor's primer for counseling veterans* (2nd ed.). Deer Park, NY: Linus.

Families USA. (2011). Children's health: About CHIP. Retrieved May 23, 2011, from http://www.familiesusa.org/issues/childrens-health/about-chip/.

Familydoctor.org. (2003, March). Depression: Electroconvulsive therapy. Retrieved January 30, 2005, from http://familydoctor.org/058.sml?printMl.

Falk, G. (Congressional Research Service). (2014, September 19). The Temporary Assistance for Needy Families (TANF) block grant: Responses to frequently asked questions. Retrieved from http://fas.org/sgp/crs/misc/RL32760.pdf.

Falk, G. (2014, March 12). The Temporary Assistance to Needy Families (TANF) block grant: Responses to frequently asked questions. Retrieved from Congressional Research Service website: http://nationalaglawcenter.org/wp-content/uploads/assets/crs/RL32760.pdf.

Falk, G. (2015, July 9). The Temporary Assistance for Needy Families (TANF) block grant: Response to frequently asked questions. Retrieved from Congressional Research Service website: https://fas.org/sgp/crs/misc/RL32760.pdf.

Fang, B. (2001, September 3). On the trail of a killer. *U.S. News & World Report,* 22–26.

Fascoli, L. (1999). Developmentally appropriate play and turtle hunting. In E. Dau (Ed.), *Child's play: Revisiting play in early childhood* (pp. 53–59). Sydney, Australia: Maqclennan & Petty.

Fast Track Project. (2011). Fast track overview. Retrieved from http://www.fasttrackproject.org/overview.php.

Fatout, M., & Rose, S. R. (1995). *Task groups in the social services.* Thousand Oaks, CA: Sage.

Federal Bureau of Investigation (FBI). (2008). Human trafficking. Retrieved April 20, 2011, from http://www.fbi.gov/news/stories/2008/may/humantrafficking_050908.

Federal Bureau of Investigation (FBI). (2013a). Crime in the United States, 2012. *Annual Uniform Crime Report.* Washington, DC: U.S. Government Printing Office. Retrieved from http://www.fbi.gov/about-us/cjis/ucr/crime-in-the-u.s/2012/crime-in-the-u.s.-2012.

Federal Bureau of Investigation (FBI). (2013b). Hate crime—Overview. Retrieved from http://www.fbi.gov/about-us/investigate/civilrights/hate_crimes/overview.

Fellin, P. (1996). *Mental health and mental illness: Policies, programs, and services.* Itasca, IL: Peacock.

Fellin, P. (2001). *The community and the social worker* (3rd ed.). Itasca, IL: F. E. Peacock.

Fetting, M. (2012). *Perspectives on addiction: An integrative treatment model with clinical case studies.* Thousand Oaks, CA: Sage.

Figueira-McDonough, J. (2008). Women: Practice interventions. In T. Mizrahi & L. E. Davis (Editors-in-Chief), *Encyclopedia of social work* (Vol. 4, pp. 290–298). Washington, DC: NASW Press.

FindLaw Legal News and Commentary. (2005). Evidence shows longstanding Enron scams. Retrieved February 5, 2005, from http://news.findlaw.eom/ap_stories/f/1310/2-3-2005/20050203151127_17.html.

Fiske, H. (2002a, September 16). A youth violence assessment tool: Can we predict problems? *Social Work Today, 2*(23), 13–15.

Fiske, H. (2002b, November 11). Adolescent group therapy: Not just hearing, listening, too. *Social Work Today, 2*(23), 16–18.

Floyd, I., & Schott, L. (Center on Budget and Policy Priorities). (2013, October 21). TANF cash benefits continued to lose value in 2013. Retrieved from http://www.cbpp.org/cms/?fa=view&id=4034.

Folger, J. (2013, October 1). How to choose between bronze, silver, gold and platinum health insurance plans. Retrieved from Forbes website: http://www.forbes.com/sites/investopedia/2013/10/01/how-to-choose-between-bronze-silver-gold-and-platinum-health-insurance-plans/.

Fong, R. (2008). Asian Americans: Practice interventions. In T. Mizrahi & L. E. Davis (Editors-in-Chief), *Encyclopedia of social work* (Vol. 1, pp. 161–163). Washington, DC: NASW Press.

Fong, R., Armour, M., Busch, N., Heffron, L. C., & McClendon, A. (2006). Case management intervention with immigrant and refugee students and families. In C. Franklin, M. B. Harris, & P. Allen-Meares (Eds.), *The school services sourcebook: A guide for school-based professionals* (pp. 803–809). New York: Oxford.

Fontaine, R. G. (2007). On-line social decision making and antisocial behavior: Some essential but neglected issues. *Clinical Psychology Review, 28,* 17–35.

Fontaine, R. G., Yang, C., Dodge, K. A., Pettit, G. S., & Bates, J. E. (2009). Development of response evaluation and decision (RED) and antisocial behavior in childhood and adolescence. *Developmental Psychology, 45,* 447–459.

Food and Nutrition Board. (2002). *Dietary assessment in the WIC program.* Washington, DC: Institute of Medicine.

Food and Nutrition Service (FNS). (2009). About WIC: How WIC helps. Retrieved May 25, 2011, from http://www.fns.usda.gov/wic/aboutwic/howwichelps.htm.

Food and Nutrition Service (FNS). (2011). Nutrition assistance programs. Retrieved May 25, 2008, from http://www.fns.usda.gov/fns/.

Frame, M. W. (2003). *Integrating religion and spirituality into counseling: A comprehensive approach.* Pacific Grove, CA: Brooks/Cole.

Francis, E. (2011, December 2). Psychotropic drugs: What are they? Retrieved from ABC News website: http://abcnews.go.com/blogs/health/2011/12/02/what-you-need-to-know-about-psychotropic-drugs/.

Franklin, C, Harris, M. B., & Lagana-Riordan, C. (2010). The delivery of school social work services. In P. Allen-Meares (Ed.), *Social work services in schools* (6th ed., pp. 278–321). Boston: Allyn & Bacon.

Fred, S. (2004a, September). Human trafficking: Snaring the spirit. *NASW News, 4.*

Fred, S. (2004b, October 24). Social workers vie for federal office. *NASW News, 11.*

Freedman, R. I. (1995). Developmental disabilities: Direct practice. In R. L. Edwards (Ed.), *Encyclopedia of social work* (19th ed., Vol. 1, pp. 721–729). Washington, DC: NASW Press.

Freedom to Marry. (2014). The freedom to marry internationally. Retrieved from http://www.freedomtomarry.org/landscape/entry/c/international.

Freedom to Marry. (2015). The freedom to marry internationally. Retrieved from http://www.freedomtomarry.org/landscape/entry/c/international.

Friend, M. (2011). *Special education: Contemporary perspectives for school professionals* (3rd ed.). Boston: Pearson.

Gallup. (2015). Marriage. Retrieved from http://www.gallup.com/poll/117328/marriage.aspx.

Gamble, D. N., & Weil, M. (2008). Community: Practice interventions. In T. Mizrahi & L. E. Davis (Editors-in-Chief), *Encyclopedia of social work* (Vol. 1, pp. 355–368). Washington, DC: NASW Press.

Gambrill, E. (2000). The role of critical thinking in evidence-based social work. In P. Allen-Meares & C. Garvin (Eds.), *The handbook of social work direct practice* (pp. 43–64). Thousand Oaks, CA: Sage.

Gambrill, E. (2005). *Critical thinking in clinical practice: Improving the quality of judgments and decisions.* Hoboken, NJ: Wiley.

Gambrill, E., & Gibbs, L. (2009). *Critical thinking for helping professionals: A skills-based workbook* (3rd ed.). New York: Oxford.

Gans, H. J. (1971). The uses of poverty: The poor pay all. *Social Policy, 2,* 21–23.

Garcia, B. (2009). Theory and social work practice with immigrant populations. In F. Chang-Muy & E. P. Congress (Eds.), *Social work with immigrants and refugees: Legal issues, clinical skills, and advocacy* (pp. 79–101). New York: Springer.

Garrett, M. T., Garrett, J. T., Grayshield, L., Williams, Portman, T. A. A., Rivera, E. T., … Kawulich, B. (2013). Culturally alert counseling with Native Americans. In McAuliffe, G., & Associates (Eds.), *Culturally alert counseling: A comprehensive introduction* (2nd ed., pp. 185–222). Thousand Oaks, CA: Sage.

Garrett, M. T., & Pitchette, E. F. (2000). Red as an apple: Native American acculturation and counseling with or without reservation. *Journal of Counseling and Development, 78,* 3–13.

Garrett, M. T., & Portman, T. A. A. (2011). *Counseling & diversity: Counseling Native Americans.* Belmont, CA: Brooks/Cole.

Garvey, G., & Houde, G. (2009, July 26). Childhood sweethearts reconnect after 85 years. *Chicago Tribune.* Retrieved June 3, 2011, from http://articles.chicagotribune.com/2009-07-26/news/0907250224_1_sweethearts-family-friend-separate-ways.

Garvin, C. D., & Cox, F. M. (1995). A history of community organizing since the Civil War with special reference to oppressed communities. In J. Rothman, J. L. Erlich, & J. E. Tropman (Eds.), *Strategies of community intervention* (pp. 64–69). Itasca, IL: Peacock.

Garvin, C. D., & Tropman, J. E. (1998). *Social work in contemporary society* (2nd ed.). Boston: Allyn & Bacon.

Geary, B. B. (1992). Individual treatment of depression using cognitive therapy. In C. W. Lecroy (Ed.), *Case studies in social work practice.* Belmont, CA: Wadsworth.

George, J. (1997). Global graying. In M. C. Hokenstad & J. Midgley (Eds.), *Issues in international social work: Global challenges in a new century* (pp. 57–73). Washington, DC: NASW Press.

Gibbs, L., Gambrill, E., Blakemore, J., Begun, A., Keniston, A., Peden, B., & Lefcowitz, J. (1994). A measure of critical thinking about practice. Unpublished paper presented at the Fall Conference of the Wisconsin Council on Social Work Education, Stevens Point, WI.

Gibelman, M. (1995). *What social workers do.* Washington, DC: NASW Press.

Gibelman, M. (2005). *What social workers do* (2nd ed.). Washington, DC: NASW Press.

Gibelman, M., & Furman, R. (2008). *Navigating human service organizations* (2nd ed.). Chicago: Lyceum.

Gibelman, M., & Schervish, P. (1997). *Who we are: A second look.* Washington, DC: NASW Press.

Gilbert, M. J. (2008). Transgender people. In T. Mizrahi & L. E. Davis (Editors-in-Chief), *Encyclopedia of social work* (Vol. 4, pp. 238–241). Washington, DC: NASW Press.

Gilbert, N., & Terrell, P. (2013). *Dimensions of social welfare policy* (8th ed.). Boston: Pearson.

Gilson, S. F., Bricout, J. C., & Baskind, F. R. (1998). Listening to the voices of people with disabilities. *Families in Society: The Journal of Contemporary Human Services, 79*(2), 188–202.

Ginsberg, L. H. (2001). *Careers in social work* (2nd ed.). Boston: Allyn & Bacon.

Gisby, J., & Butler, G. (2012). Skills in safeguarding and supporting older people. In B. Hall & T. Scragg (Eds.), *Social work with older people* (pp. 201–220). New York: McGraw-Hill.

GlenMaye, L. (1998). Empowerment of women. In L. M. Gutierrez, R. J. Parsons, & E. O. Cox (Eds.), *Empowerment in social work practice: A sourcebook* (pp. 29–51). Pacific Grove, CA: Brooks/Cole.

Golden Ink. (1997). The trail of tears. Retrieved from http://ngeorgia.com/history/nghisttt.html.

Goldenberg, H., & Goldenberg, I. (2002). *Counseling today's families* (4th ed.). Pacific Grove, CA: Brooks/Cole.

Goldman, L. (2008). *Coming out, coming in: Nurturing the well-being and inclusion of gay youth in mainstream society.* New York: Routledge.

Goldstein, S. R., & Beebe, L. (1995). National Association of Social Workers. In R. L. Edwards (Editor-in-Chief), *Encyclopedia of social work* (19th ed., Vol. 1, pp. 1747–1764). Washington, DC: NASW Press.

Gomory, T. (1997). Mental health services. In M. Reisch & E. Gambrill (Eds.), *Social work in the 21st century* (pp. 163–174). Thousand Oaks, CA: Pine Forge.

Gonzalez, M. J., & Acevedo, G. (2013). Clinical practice with Hispanic individuals and families: An ecological perspective. In E. P. Congress & M. J. Gonzalez (Eds.), *Multicultural perspectives in social work practice with families* (3rd ed., pp. 141–156). New York: Springer.

Gonzalez, R. (2013). Puerto Rico's status debate continues as island marks 61 years as a commonwealth. Retrieved from http://www.huffingtonpost.com/2013/07/25/puerto-rico-status-debate_n_3651755.html.

Gotterer, R. (2001). The spiritual dimension in clinical social work practice: A client perspective. *Families in Society, 82*(20), 187–193.

GradSchools.com. (2014). Social work—Doctoral graduate programs. Retrieved from http://www.gradschools.com/search-programs/social-work-doctoral.

Graybeal, C. (2001). Strengths-based social work assessment: Transforming the dominant paradigm. *Families in Society, 82*(3), 233–242.

Green, C., Dziegielewski, S. F., & Turnage, B. F. (2005). Alcohol. In S. F. Dziegielewski (Ed.), *Understanding substance addictions: Assessment and treatment* (pp. 125–129). Chicago: Lyceum.

Green, J. W. (1999). *Cultural awareness in the human services: A multi-ethnic approach* (3rd ed.). Boston: Allyn & Bacon.

Greenberg, J. S., Bruess, C. E., & Oswalt, S. B. (2014). *Exploring the dimensions of human sexuality* (5th ed.). Burlington, MA: Jones & Bartlett.

Greene, R. R. (2000). *Social work with the aged and their families* (2nd ed.). New York: Aldine de Gruyter.

Greene, R. R. (2012). Human behavior theory: A resilience orientation. In R. R. Greene (Ed.), *Resiliency: An integrated approach to practice, policy, and research* (2nd ed., pp. 1–27). Washington, DC: NASW Press.

Greene, R. R., Cohen, H. G., Galambos, C. M., & Kropf, N. P. (2007). *Foundations of social work practice in the field of aging: A competency-based approach.* Washington, DC: NASW Press.

Greene, R. R., & Conrad, A. P. (2012). Resilience: Basic assumptions and terms. In R. R. Greene (Ed.), *Resiliency: An integrated approach to practice, policy, and research* (2nd ed., pp. 29–62). Washington, DC: NASW Press.

Greene, R. R., & Livingston, N. C. (2012). Resilience: A social construct. In R. R. Greene (Ed.), *Resiliency: An integrated approach to practice, policy, and research* (2nd ed., pp. 63–94). Washington, DC: NASW Press.

Greeno, C. G. (2008). Mental health: Overview. In T. Mizrahi & L. E. Davis (Editors-in-Chief), *Encyclopedia of social work* (Vol. 3, pp. 221–232). Washington, DC: NASW Press.

Griner, D. (2002, April 7). Electroshock therapy emerges from disrepute. *The Journal Gazette.* Retrieved April 27, 2002, from http://www.fortwayne.com/mld/journalgazette/3017094.htm.

Grogan, J., & Richardson, F. (2008). Humanistic therapies. In T. Mizrahi & L. E. Davis (Editors-in-Chief), *Encyclopedia of social work* (Vol. 2, pp. 395–398). Washington, DC: NASW Press.

Grotevant, H., & McRoy, R. G. (1998). *Openness in adoption: Exploring family connections.* Thousand Oaks, CA: Sage.

Guffey, M. E. (2008). *Business communication: Process and product* (6th ed.). Mason, OH: South-Western.

Guffey, M. E. (2010). *Essentials of business communication* (8th ed.). Mason, OH: South-Western.

Guffey, M. E., & Loewy, D. (2013). *Essentials of business communication* (9th ed.). Mason, OH: South-Western.

Gushue, G. V., & Sciarra, D. T. (1995). Culture and families: A multidimensional approach. In J. G. Ponterotto, J. M. Casas, L. A. Suzuki, & C. M. Alexander (Eds.), *Handbook of multicultural counseling* (2nd ed., pp. 586–606). Thousand Oaks, CA: Sage.

Gutierrez, L. M. (2001). Working with women of color: An empowerment perspective. In J. Rothman, J. L. Erlich, & J. E. Tropman (Eds.), *Strategies of community intervention* (6th ed., pp. 209–217). Itasca, IL: Peacock.

Gutierrez, L. M., & Lewis, E. A. (1998). A feminist perspective on organizing women of color. In F. G. Rivera & J. L. Erlich (Eds.), *Community organizing in a diverse society* (3rd ed., pp. 97–116). Needham Heights, MA: Allyn & Bacon.

Guttmacher Institute. (2011). Facts on American teens' sexual and reproductive health. Retrieved June 27, 2011, from http://www.guttmacher.org/pubs/FB-ATSRH.html.

Guzman, M. R., & Carrasco, N. (2011). *Counseling & diversity: Counseling Latino/a Americans.* Belmont, CA: Brooks/Cole.

Haberman, F. W. (Ed.). (1972). Jane Addams—Biography. In F. W. Haberman (Ed.), *Nobel lecture, peace 1926–1950.* Amsterdam: Elsevier. Retrieved June 14, 2005, from http://nobelprize.org/peace/laureates/1931/addams-bio.html.

Hagen, J. L., & Lawrence, C. K. (2008). Temporary assistance for needy families. In T. Mizrahi & L. E. Davis (Editors-in-Chief), *Encyclopedia of social work* (Vol. 4, pp. 225–229). Washington, DC: NASW Press.

Haight, W. L. (1998, May). "Gathering the spirit" at First Baptist Church: Spirituality as a protective factor in the lives of African American children. *Social Work, 43*(3), 123–221.

Hallahan, D. P., Kauffman, J. M., & Pullen, P. C. (2012). *Exceptional learners: An introduction to special education* (12th ed.). Boston: Pearson.

Halley, A. A., Kopp, J., & Austin, M. J. (1998). *Delivering human services: A learning approach to practice* (5th ed.). New York: Longman.

Haney, P. (1988, May-June). Comments on currents: Providing empowerment to persons with AIDS. *Social Work, 33*(3), 251–253.

Harjo, S. S. (1999). The American Indian experience. In H. P. McAdoo (Ed.), *Family ethnicity: Strength in diversity* (2nd ed., pp. 63–71). Thousand Oaks, CA: Sage.

Harkness, D. (2008). Consultation. In T. Mizrahi & L. E. Davis (Editors-in-Chief), *Encyclopedia of social work* (Vol. 3, pp. 295–299). Washington, DC: NASW Press.

Harrigan, M. P., & Farmer, R. L. (2000). The myths and facts about aging. In R. L. Schneider, N. P. Kropf, &

A. J. Kisor (Eds.), *Gerontological social work: Knowledge, service settings, and special populations* (2nd ed., pp. 26–64). Pacific Grove CA: Brooks/Cole.

Harris, J. J., & Pehrson, K. L. (2008). Military social work. In T. Mizrahi & L. E. Davis (Editors-in-Chief), *Encyclopedia of social work* (Vol. 1, pp. 420–423). Washington, DC: NASW Press.

Harris, M. B. (2008). Family life education. In T. Mizrahi & L. E. Davis (Editors-in-Chief), *Encyclopedia of social work* (Vol. 2, pp. 197–200). Washington, DC: NASW Press.

Hart, S. N., & Brassard, M. R. (1991, 2001). *Definition of psychological maltreatment.* Indianapolis: Office for the Study of the Psychological Rights of the Child, Indiana University School of Education.

Hart, S. N., Brassard, M. R., Davidson, H. A., Rivelis, E., Diaz, V., & Binggeli, N. J. (2011). Psychological maltreatment. In J. E. B. Myers (Ed.), *The APS AC handbook on child maltreatment* (3rd ed., pp. 125–144). Thousand Oaks, CA: Sage.

Hart, S. N., Brassard, M. R., & Karlson, H. C. (1996). Psychological maltreatment. In J. Briere, L. Berliner, J. A. Bulkley, C. Jenny, & T. Reid (Eds.), *The APSAC handbook on child maltreatment* (pp. 72–89). Thousand Oaks, CA: Sage.

Hartman, C. (1987). The housing part of the homeless problem. In Boston Foundation (Ed.), *Homelessness: Critical issues for policy and practice* (pp. 17–19). Boston: Boston Foundation.

Haynes, K. S., & Mickelson, J. S. (2003). *Affecting change: Social workers in the political arena* (5th ed.). Boston: Allyn & Bacon.

Haynes, K. S., & Mickelson, J. S. (2010). *Affecting change: Social workers in the political arena* (7th ed.). Boston: Pearson.

Hayward, C., & Collier, J. A. (1996). Anxiety disorders. In H. Steiner (Ed.), *Treating adolescents* (pp. 187–221). San Francisco: Jossey-Bass.

Hazen, J. M., & Rodgers, D. (2014). *Global gangs: Street violence across the world.* Minneapolis, MN: University of Minnesota Press.

Healthcare.gov. (2011). Strengthening Medicare. Retrieved May 19, 2011, from http://www.healthcare.gov/law/provisions/rebate/index.html.

Healthcare.gov. (n.d.). Mental health and substance abuse coverage. Retrieved from https://www.healthcare.gov/coverage/mental-health-substance-abuse-coverage/.

Healy, L. M. (2008). *International social work: Professional action in an independent world* (2nd ed.). New York: Oxford.

Heanue, K., & Lawton, C. (2012). *Working with substance users.* New York: McGraw-Hill.

Hellenbrand, S. (1987). Termination in direct practice. In A. Minahan (Ed.), *Encyclopedia of social work* (Vol. 2, pp. 765–770). Silver Spring, MD: NASW Press.

Hellriegel, D., Jackson, S. E., & Slocum, J. W., Jr. (2002). *Management: A competency-based approach* (9th ed.). Cincinnati, OH: South-Western.

Henderson, C. (2002). What is electroshock therapy? Retrieved April 27, 2002, from http://ky.essortment.com/whatiselectroc_riek.htm.

Henderson, D. A., & Thompson, C. L. (2011). *Counseling children* (8th ed.). Belmont, CA: Brooks/Cole.

Henslin, J. M. (2011). *Social problems: A down-to-earth approach* (10th ed.). Boston: Allyn & Bacon.

Hepworth, D. H., Rooney, R. H., Rooney, G. D., & Strom-Gottfried, K. (2013). *Direct social work practice: Theory and skills* (9th ed.). Belmont, CA: Cengage Learning.

Hepworth, D. H., Rooney, R. H., Rooney, G. D., Strom-Gottfried, K., & Larsen, J. (2010). *Direct social work practice: Theory and skills* (8th ed.). Belmont, CA: Brooks/Cole.

Herbert, B. (2003, May 22). Dancing with the devil. Retrieved October 22, 2008, from http://www.nytimes.com/2003/05/22/opinion/22HERB.html.

Hernandez, V. R. (2008). Generalist and advanced generalist practice. In T. Mizrahi & L. E. Davis (Editors-in-Chief), *Encyclopedia of social work* (Vol. 2, pp. 260–268). Washington, DC: NASW Press.

Herek, G. M., Gillis, R. J., & Cogan, J. (1997, May). Study offers "snapshot" of Sacramento area lesbian, gay and bisexual community. Retrieved from http://psychology.ucdavis.edu/rainbow/default.html.

Herring, R. D. (1999). *Counseling with Native American Indians and Alaska natives: Strategies for helping professionals.* Thousand Oaks, CA: Sage.

Hershberger, S. L., & D'Augelli, A. R. (2000). Issues in counseling lesbian, gay, and bisexual adolescents. In R. M. Perez, K. A. DeBord, & K. J. Bieschke (Eds.), *Handbook of counseling and psychotherapy with lesbian, gay, and bisexual clients* (pp. 225–247). Washington, DC: American Psychological Association.

Hewlett, J. (1998, December 23). Kentucky art teacher was "Sybil," scholar confirms. *Detroit Free Press.* Retrieved April 27, 2002, from http://www.asarian.org/~quiet/sybildfp.html.

Hillier, S. M., & Barrow, G. M. (2011). *Aging, the individual, and society.* Belmont, CA: Wadsworth.

Ho, M. K. (1987). *Family therapy with ethnic minorities.* Newbury Park, CA: Sage.

Ho, M. K. (1992). *Minority children and adolescents in therapy.* Thousand Oaks, CA: Sage.

Hoadley, J., Summer, L., Hargrave, E., Cubanski, J., & Newman, T. (2014). Medicare part D in its ninth year: The 2014 marketplace and key trends, 2005–2014. Retrieved from the Kaiser Family Foundation website: http://kff.org/medicare/report/medicare-part-d-in-its-ninth-year-the-2014-marketplace-and-key-trends-2006-2014/.

Hodge, D. R. (2008). Sexual trafficking in the United States: A domestic problem with transnational dimensions. *Social Work, 53*(2), 143–152.

Hodge, J. L., Struckmann, D. K., & Trost, L. D. (1975). *Cultural bases of racism and group oppression.* Berkeley, CA: Two Riders Press.

Hoefer, R. (2012). *Advocacy practice for social justice.* Chicago: Lyceum.

Hoffman, K. S. (2008). Social work education: Overview. In T. Mizrahi & L. E. Davis (Editors-in-Chief), *Encyclopedia of social work* (Vol. 4, pp. 107–114). Washington, DC: NASW Press.

Hokenstad, M. C., & Midgley, J. (1997). Realities of global interdependence: Challenges for social work in a new century. In M. B. Hokenstad & J. Midgley (Eds.), *Issues in international social work: Global challenges for a new century* (pp. 1–10). Washington, DC: NASW Press.

Holscher, D. (2012). Social justice. In L. M. Healy & R. J. Link (Eds.), *Handbook of international social work: Human rights, development, and the global perspective* (pp. 44–51). New York: Oxford.

Homan, M. S. (2011). *Promoting community change: Making it happen in the real world* (4th ed.). Belmont, CA: Brooks/Cole.

Homestead Schools, Inc. (2004, September). *Continuing education courses for social workers, counselors, and marriage family therapists.* Torrance, CA: Author.

Hooyman, N. R. (2008). Aging: Overview. In T. Mizrahi & L. E. Davis (Editors-in-Chief), *Encyclopedia of social work* (Vol. 4, pp. 144–156). Washington, DC: NASW Press.

Hooyman, N. R., & Kiyak, H. A. (1999). *Social gerontology: A multidisciplinaryperspective* (2nd ed.). Boston: Allyn & Bacon.

Hopps, J. G., & Lowe, T. B. (2008). Social work profession: Overview. In T. Mizrahi & L. E. Davis (Editors-in-Chief), *Encyclopedia of social work* (Vol. 1, pp. 88–96). Washington, DC: NASW Press.

Howell, J. C. (2010). Gang prevention: An overview of research and programs. Washington, DC: Office of Justice Programs, U.S. Department of Justice. Retrieved from https://www.ncjrs.gov/pdffiles1/ojjdp/231116.pdf.

Huber, R., Nelson, H. W., Netting, F. E., & Borders, K. W. (2008). *Elder advocacy: Essential knowledge & skills across settings.* Belmont, CA: Brooks/Cole.

Huff, C. R. (1993). Gangs in the United States. In A. P. Goldstein & C. R. Huff (Eds.), *The gang intervention handbook* (pp. 3–20). Champaign, IL: Research Press.

Hull, G. H. (2004, November 22). Personal communication.

Hyde, C. (2008). Feminist social work practice. In T. Mizrahi & L. E. Davis (Editors-in-Chief), *Encyclopedia of social work* (Vol. 2, pp. 216–221). Washington, DC: NASW Press.

Hyde, J. A., & Delamater, J. D. (2014). *Understanding human sexuality* (12th ed.). New York: McGraw-Hill.

Hyde, J. S., & Else-Quest, N. (2013). *Half the human experience: The psychology of women* (8th ed.). Belmont, CA: Cengage Learning.

International Association of Schools of Social Work (IASSW). (2014). IASSW home. Retrieved from http://www.iassw-aiets.org/.

International Federation of Social Workers (IFSW). (2014). IFSW home. Retrieved from http://ifsw.org/.

International Labor Organization (ILO). (2014). Forced labour, human trafficking, and slavery. Retrieved from http://www.ilo.org/global/topics/forced-labour/lang–en/index.htm.

International Society for the Study of Trauma and Dissociation. (2011). Frequently asked questions: Dissociation and dissociative disorders. Retrieved June 17, 2011, from http://www.isst-d.org/education/faq-dissociation.htm#prev.

Intersex Society of North America (ISNA). (2008a). How common is intersex? Retrieved from http://www.isna.org/faq/frequency.

Intersex Society of North America (ISNA). (2008b). What do doctors do now when they encounter a patient with intersex? Retrieved from http://www.isna.org/faq/standard_of_care.

Intersex Society of North America (ISNA). (2008c). What does ISNA recommend for children with intersex? Retrieved from http://www.isna.org/faq/patient-centered.

Ivey, A. E., Ivey, M. B., & Zalaquett, C. P. (2010). *Intentional interviewing and counseling* (7th ed.). Belmont, CA: Brooks/Cole.

Ivey, A. E., Ivey, M. B., & Zalaquett, C. P. (2012). *Essentials of intentional interviewing: Counseling in a multicultural world* (2nd ed.). Belmont, CA: Brooks/Cole.

Ivey, A. E., Ivey, M. B., & Zalaquett, C. P. (2014). *Intentional interviewing and counseling: Facilitating client development in a multicultural society* (8th ed.). Belmont, CA: Brooks/Cole.

Jacobs, E. E., Masson, R. L., & Harvil, L. H. (2009). *Group counseling: Strategies and skills* (6th ed.). Belmont, CA: Brooks/Cole.

James, R. K. (2008). *Crisis intervention strategies* (6th ed.). Belmont, CA: Brooks/Cole.

James, R. K., & Gilliland, B. E. (2013). *Crisis intervention strategies* (7th ed.). Belmont, CA: Brooks/Cole.

Jane Addams Hull House Museum. (1997, February). Biographical sketch of Jane Addams. Retrieved June 14, 2005, from http://www.uic.edu/jaddams/hull/ja_bio.html.

Jansson, B. S. (2011). *Becoming an effective policy advocate. From policy practice to social justice* (6th ed.). Belmont, CA: Brooks/Cole.

Jansson, B. S. (2012). *The reluctant welfare state: Engaging history to advance social work practice in contemporary society* (6th ed.). Belmont, CA: Brooks/Cole.

Jansson, B. S. (2014). *Becoming an effective policy advocate: From policy practice to social justice* (7th ed.). Belmont, CA: Brooks/Cole.

Jansson, B. S. (2015). *The reluctant welfare state: Engaging history to advance social work practice in contemporary society* (8th ed.). Belmont, CA: Cengage Learning.

Jewish Child and Family Services (n.d.). *Refugee resettlement services.* Retrieved June 24, 2011, from http://www.jcfs.org/p_program.cfm?cat=cs&id=6.

Jimenez, J., Pasztor, E. M., & Chambers, R. M., with Fujii, C. P. (2015). *Social policy & social change: Toward the creation of social and economic justice* (2nd ed.). Thousand Oaks, CA: Sage.

Johnson, J. L. (2004). *Fundamentals of substance abuse practice.* Belmont, CA: Brooks/Cole.

Johnson, K., Noe, T., Collins, D., Strader, T., & Bucholtz, G. (2000). Mobilizing church communities to prevent alcohol and other drug abuse: A model strategy and its evaluation. *Journal of Community Practice, 7*(2), 1–27.

Johnson, M. (2002, February 1). Fetuses may qualify for federal aid. *Milwaukee Journal Sentinel,* Al.

Johnson, M. A. (2005). *Hull House.* Retrieved May 9, 2011, from http://www.encyclopedia.chicagohistory.org/pages/615.html.

Jones, L. R. W. (1995). Unemployment compensation and workers' compensation. In R. L. Edwards (Ed.), *Encyclopedia of social work* (19th ed., Vol. 3, pp. 2413–2417). Washington, DC: NASW Press.

Kadushin, A., & Harkness, D. (2014). *Supervision in social work* (5th ed.). New York: Columbia.

Kadushin, A., & Martin, J. A. (1988). *Child welfare services* (4th ed.). New York: Macmillan.

Kail, R. V., & Cavanaugh, J. C. (2010). *Human development: A life-span view* (5th ed.). Belmont, CA: Wadsworth.

Kail, R. V., & Cavanaugh, J. C. (2013). *Human development: A life-span view* (6th ed.). Belmont, CA: Wadsworth.

Kaiser Family Foundation (KFF). (2009). The HIV/AIDS epidemic in sub-Saharan Africa. Retrieved June 13, 2011, from http://www.kff.org/hivaids/upload/7391-08.pdf.

Kaiser Family Foundation (KFF). (2011). Kaiser slides: Costs/insurance. Retrieved June 9, 2011, from http://facts.kff.org/results.aspx?view=slides&topic=3.

Kaiser Family Foundation (KFF). (2012a, May 1). Health care costs: A primer. Retrieved from http://kff.org/health-costs/issue-brief/health-care-costs-a-primer/.

Kaiser Family Foundation (KFF). (2012b). Total Medicaid spending. Retrieved from http://kff.org/medicaid/state-indicator/total-medicaid-spending/.

Kaiser Family Foundation (KFF). (2014a, December 1). The global HIV/AIDS epidemic. Retrieved from http://kff.org/global-health-policy/fact-sheet/the-global-hivaids-epidemic/.

Kaiser Family Foundation (KFF). (2014b, April 14). The HIV/AIDS epidemic in the United States. Retrieved from http://kff.org/hivaids/fact-sheet/the-hivaids-epidemic-in-the-united-states/.

Kaiser Family Foundation (KFF). (2014c). Medicare. Retrieved from http://kff.org/medicare/fact-sheet/medicare-at-a-glance-fact-sheet/.

Kaiser Family Foundation (KFF). (2015). HIV/AIDS. Retrieved from http://kff.org/topic/hivaids/?post_type=fact-sheet.

Kamya, H. A. (1999). African immigrants in the United States: The challenge for research and practice. In P. L. Ewalt, E. M. Freeman, A. E. Fortune, D. L. Poole, & S. L. Witkin (Eds.), *Multicultural issues in social work: Practice and research* (pp. 605–621). Washington, DC: NASW Press.

Kanel, K. (2012). *A guide to crisis intervention* (4th ed.). Belmont, CA: Brooks/Cole.

Kanel, K. (2015). *A guide to crisis intervention* (5th ed.). Belmont, CA: Cengage Learning.

Kanter, J. S. (1985). Case management of the young adult chronic patient: A clinical perspective. In J. S. Kanter (Ed.), *Clinical issues in treating the chronic mentally ill.* San Francisco: Jossey-Bass.

Karas, T. (2009, September 15). Teens give their elders some video gaming tips. *AARP: The Magazine.* Retrieved June 3, 2011, from http://www.highbeam.com/doc/lNl-129BFE62B 3E30908.html.

Karenga, M. (2000). Making the past meaningful: Kwanzaa and the concept of sankofa. In S. L. Abels (Ed.), *Spirituality in social work practice: Narratives for professional helping* (pp. 51–67). Denver, CO: Love.

Karger, H. J., & Stoesz, D. (2006). *American social welfare policy: A pluralist approach* (5th ed.). Boston: Allyn & Bacon.

Karger, H. J., & Stoesz, D. (2010). *American social welfare policy: A pluralist approach* (6th ed.). Boston: Allyn & Bacon.

Karger, H. J., & Stoesz, D. (2014). *American social welfare policy: A pluralist approach* (7th ed.). Boston: Pearson.

Kasee, C. R. (1995). Identity, recovery and religious imperialism: Native American women and the New Age. In J. Ochshorn & Cole (Eds.), *Women's spirituality, women's lives* (pp. 83–93). Binghamton, NY: Haworth.

Kaye, L. W. (2008). Aging: Practice interventions. In T. Mizrahi & L. E. Davis (Editors-in-Chief), *Encyclopedia of social work* (Vol. 1, pp. 96–100). Washington, DC: NASW Press.

Kelly, G. F. (2001). *Sexuality today: The human perspective* (7th ed.). Boston: McGraw-Hill.

Kelly, G. F. (2008). *Sexuality today* (9th ed.). Boston: McGraw-Hill.

Kelly, L. W. (2002, Summer). So you want to practice in mental health! *The New Social Worker,* 4–6.

Kelly, M. S., Raines, J. C., Stone, S., & Frey, A. (2010). *School social work: An evidence-informed framework for practice.* New York: Oxford.

Kemp, S. P., Bueke, R. K., Allen-Eckard, K., Becker, M. F., & Ackroyd, A. (2014). Family support services. In G. P. Mallon & P. M. Hess (Eds.), *Child welfare for the 21st century* (2nd ed., pp. 51–69). New York: Columbia.

Kendall, D. (2010). *Social problems in a diverse society* (5th ed.). Boston: Allyn & Bacon.

Kendall, D. (2013). *Social problems in a diverse society* (6th ed.). Boston: Pearson.

Kendall, D. (2015). *Sociology in our times* (10th ed.). Belmont, CA: Cengage Learning.

Kenyon, P. (1999). *What would you do? An ethical case workbook for human service professionals.* Pacific Grove, CA: Brooks/Cole.

Khinduka, S. K. (2008). Globalization. In T. Mizrahi & L. E. Davis (Editors-in-Chief), *Encyclopedia of social work* (Vol. 2, pp. 275–279). Washington, DC: NASW Press.

Kiesner, J., Dishion, T. J., & Poulin, F. (2001). A reinforcement model of conduct problems in children and adolescents: Advances in theory and intervention. In J. Hill & B. Maughan (Eds.), *Conduct disorders in childhood and adolescence.* New York: Cambridge University Press.

*King v. King,* 392 U.S. 309 (1968).

Kim, B. S. K. (2011). *Counseling & diversity: Counseling Asian Americans.* Belmont, CA: Cengage Learning.

Kim, B. S. K., & Park, Y. S. (2013). Culturally alert counseling with East and Southeast Asian Americans. In McAuliffe, G., & Associates (Eds.), *Culturally alert counseling: A comprehensive introduction* (2nd ed., pp. 157–183). Thousand Oaks, CA: Sage.

Kirk, G., & Okazawa-Rey, M. (2010). *Women's lives: Multicultural perspectives* (5th ed.). Boston: McGraw-Hill.

Kirk, G., & Okazawa-Rey, M. (2013). *Women's lives: Multicultural perspectives* (6th ed.). New York: McGraw-Hill.

Kirst-Ashman, K. K. (1992, Summer). Feminist values and social work: A model for educating nonfeminists. *Arete, 17*(1), 13–25.

Kirst-Ashman, K. K. (2011). *Human behavior in the macro social environment: An empowerment approach to understanding communities, organizations, and groups* (3rd ed.). Belmont, CA: Brooks/Cole.

Kirst-Ashman, K. K. (2014). *Human behavior in the macro social environment: An empowerment approach to understanding communities, organizations, and groups* (4th ed.). Belmont, CA: Brooks/Cole.

Kirst-Ashman, K. K., & Hull, G. H., Jr. (2012). *Understanding generalist practice* (6th ed.). Belmont, CA: Brooks/Cole.

Kirst-Ashman, K. K., & Hull, G. H., Jr. (2015a). *Generalist practice with organizations and communities* (7th ed.). Belmont, CA: Cengage Learning.

Kirst-Ashman, K. K., & Hull, G. H., Jr. (2015b). *Understanding generalist practice* (7th ed.). Belmont, CA: Cengage Learning.

Kiselica, M. S., Changizi, J. C., Cureton, V. L. L., & Gridley, B. E. (1995). Counseling children and adolescents in schools: Salient multicultural issues. In J. G. Ponterotto, J. M. Cases, L. A. Suzuki, & C. M. Alexander (Eds.), *Handbook of multicultural counseling* (pp. 516–532). Thousand Oaks, CA: Sage.

Kitano, H. H. L., & Maki, M. T. (1996). Continuity, change, and diversity: Counseling Asian Americans. In P. B. Pederson, J. G. Draguns, W. J. Lonner, & J. E. Trimble (Eds.), *Counseling across cultures* (4th ed., pp. 124–125). Thousand Oaks, CA: Sage.

Klein, J. D., & American Academy of Pediatrics (AAP) Committee on Adolescence. (2005). Adolescent pregnancy: Current trends and issues. *Pediatrics, 116,* 281–286.

Koch, G. (1979). Home-based support services: An alternative to residential placement for the developmentally disabled. In S. Maybanks & M. Bruce (Eds.), *Home-based services for children and families: Policy, practice, and research* (pp. 157–164). Springfield, IL: Thomas.

Kolb, P. J. (1999). A stage of migration approach to understanding nursing home placement in Latino families. *Journal of Multicultural Social Work, 7*(3/4), 95–112.

Kolb, T. (2007). The process of generalist practice. In V. Vogel & K. Kirst-Ashman (Eds.), *Careers in social work* (pp. 11–12). Belmont, CA: Brooks/Cole.

Kolko, D. J. (2002). Child physical abuse. In J. E. B. Myers, L. Berliner, J. Briere, C. T. Hendrix, C. Jenny, & T. A. Reid (Eds.), *The APSAC handbook on child maltreatment* (2nd ed., pp. 21–54). Thousand Oaks, CA: Sage.

Kopels, S. (1995). The Americans with Disabilities Act: A tool to combat poverty. *Journal of Social Work Education, 31*(3), 337–346.

Kornblum, W., & Julian, J. (2009). *Social problems* (13th ed.). Upper Saddle River, NJ: Prentice-Hall.

Kornblum, W., & Julian, J. (2012). *Social problems* (14th ed.). Boston: Pearson.

Kosberg, J. I., & Adams, J. I. (2008). Men: Overview. In T. Mizrahi & L. E. Davis (Editors-in-Chief), *Encyclopedia of social work* (Vol. 3, pp. 205–214). Washington, DC: NASW Press.

Kottman, T. (2001). *Play therapy: Basics and beyond.* Alexandria, VA: American Counseling Association.

Kozol, J. (1999). Savage inequalities. In J. M. Henslin (Ed.), *In down-to-earth sociology: Introductory readings* (10th ed., pp. 343–351). New York: Free Press.

KPMG Consulting. (2002). *Alberta's health gaining & seniors wellness strategic framework 2002–2012.* Edmonton, AB: Alberta Health and Wellness. Retrieved June 2, 2011, from http://www.gov.ab.ca/acn/images/2002/702/12861.pdf.

Kretzmann, J. P., & McKnight, J. L. (1993). *Building communities from the inside out: A path toward finding and mobilizing a community's assets.* Chicago: ACT Publications.

Kropf, N. P. (2000). Home health and community services. In R. L. Schneider, N. P. Kropf, & A. J. Kisor (Eds.), *Gerontological social work: Knowledge, service settings, and special populations* (pp. 167–190). Pacific Grove, CA: Brooks/Cole.

Kropf, N. P., & Hutchinson, E. D. (2000). Effective practice with elderly clients. In R. L. Schneider, N. P. Kropf, & A. J. Kisor (Eds.), *Gerontological social work: Knowledge, service settings, and special populations* (pp. 3–25). Pacific Grove, CA: Brooks/Cole.

Krout, J. (1994). Community size differences in senior center resources, programming, and participation. *Research on Aging, 16,* 440–462.

Kubler-Ross, E. (1969). *On death and dying.* New York: Macmillan.

Kurland, R., & Salmon, R. (1992). When problems seem overwhelming: Emphases in teaching, supervision, and consultation. *Social Work, 37*(3), 240–244.

Lallanilla, M. (2013, October 1). Krokodil, Molly and more: 5 wretched new street drugs. Retrieved from livescience website: http://www.livescience.com/40072-new-street-drugs-concern-officials.html.

Landon, P. S. (1995). Generalist and advanced generalist practice. In R. L. Edwards (Ed.), *Encyclopedia of social work* (19th ed., Vol. 2, pp. 1101–1108). Washington, DC: NASW Press.

Larson, R. (2012, April 18). Why is the teen birth rate in the U.S. so high and why does it matter? Retrieved from the Journalists' Resource website: http://journalistsresource.org/studies/society/public-health/teen-birth-rate-united-states-high-does-it-matter.

LaSala, M. C. (2010). *Coming out, coming home: Helping families adjust to a gay or lesbian child.* New York: Columbia.

La Vigne, N., & Samuels, J. (2012). The growth & increasing cost of the federal prison system: Drivers and potential solutions. Retrieved from the Urban Institute Justice Policy Center website: http://www.urban.org/uploadedpdf/412693-the-growth-and-increasing-cost-of-the-federal-prison-system.pdf.

The Leadership Conference. (2014). Tribal sovereignty. Retrieved from http://www.civilrights.org/indigenous/tribal-sovereignty/.

LeCroy, C. W. (2013). Designing and facilitating groups with children. In C. Franklin, M. B. Harris, & P. Allen-Meares (Eds.), *The school services sourcebook* (2nd ed., pp. 611–618). New York: Oxford University Press.

Lee, Y. S., Cheng, A. W., Ahmed, S. F., Shaw, N., J., & Hughes, I. A. (2007). Genital anomalies in Klinefelter's syndrome. *Hormonal Research, 68,* 150–153.

Leiby, J. (1987). History of social welfare. In A. Minahan (Ed.), *Encyclopedia of social work* (Vol. 1, pp. 755–777). Silver Spring, MD: National Association of Social Workers.

Leininger, M. M. (1990). Historic and epistemologic dimensions of care and caring with future directions. In J. Stevenson (Ed.), *American academy of nursing* (pp. 19–31). Kansas City, MO: American Nurses Association Press.

Leininger, M. M. (1992). *Cultural care diversity and universality: A theory of nursing* (Pub. No. 15-2401). New York: National League for Nursing Press.

Lemonick, M. D. (2000, July 24). Little hope, less help. *Time,* 38–39.

Lens, V. (2002). TANF: What went wrong and what to do next. *Social Work, 47*(3), 279–290.

Leong, F. T. (2011). Cross-cultural barriers to mental health services in the United States. Retrieved from the DANA Foundation website: http://dana.org/Cerebrum/2011/Cross-Cultural_Barriers_to_Mental_Health_Services_in_the_United_States/.

Leong, F. T. L., Lee, S-H., & Chang, D. (2008). Counseling Asian Americans. In P. B. Pedersen, J. G. Draguns, W. J. Lonner, & J. E. Trimble (Eds.), *Counseling across cultures* (6th ed., pp. 113–128). Thousand Oaks, CA: Sage.

Leon-Guerrero, A. (2014). *Social problems: Community, policy, and social action* (4th ed.). Thousand Oaks, CA: Sage.

LeVine, E. S., & Sallee, A. L. (1999). *Child welfare: Clinical theory and practice.* Dubuque, IA: Eddie Bowers.

Levine, S. (2002, August 5). Criminal care at a high price. *U.S. News & World Report,* 44–45.

Lewis, C. (2014, October 6). Meet Tanya Rhodes Smith—The new director of the Nancy A. Humphreys Institute for

Political Social Work. Retrieved from http://crispinc.org/2014/10/06/meet-tanya-rhodes-smith-the-new-director-of-the-nancy-a-humphreys-institute-for-political-social-work/.

Lewis, E. A., & Suarez, Z. E. (1995). Natural helping networks. In R. L. Edwards (Ed.), *Encyclopedia of social work* (19th ed., Vol. 2, pp. 1765–1772). Washington, DC: NASW Press.

Lewis, J. A., Dana, R. Q., & Blevins, G. A. (2015). *Substance abuse counseling* (5th ed.). Belmont, CA: Cengage Learning.

Lewis, J. A., Lewis, M. D., Packard, T., & Souflee, F., Jr. (2001). *Management of human service programs* (3rd ed.). Pacific Grove, CA: Brooks/Cole.

Lewis, R. G. (1995). American Indians. In R. L. Edwards (Ed.), *Encyclopedia of social work* (19th ed., Vol. 1, pp. 216–225). Washington, DC: NASW Press.

Library of Congress. (2004, May 14). *The treaty of Guadalupe Hidalgo.* Retrieved November 20, 2004, from http://www.loc.gov/eHibits/ghtreaty/.

Liederman, D. S. (1995). Child welfare overview. In R. L. Edwards (Ed.), *Encyclopedia of social work* (19th ed., Vol. 1, pp. 424–433). Washington, DC: NASW Press.

Lightfoot, E. (2009). Social policies for people with disabilities. In J. Midgley & M. Livermore (Eds.), *The handbook of social policy* (2nd ed., pp. 445–462). Thousand Oaks, CA: Sage.

Lin, A. M. P. (1995). Mental health overview. In R. L. Edwards (Ed.), *Encyclopedia of social work* (19th ed., Vol. 2, pp. 1705–1711). Washington, DC: NASW Press.

Lindberg, C. A. (Managing Ed.). (2007). *The Oxford college dictionary.* New York: Spark.

Link, R. J., Ramanathan, C. S., & Asamoah, Y. (1999). Understanding the human condition and human behavior in a global era. In C. S. Ramanathan & R. J. Link (Eds.), *All our futures: Principles and resources for social work practice in a global era* (pp. 30–51). Pacific Grove, CA: Brooks/Cole.

Locke, D. C. (1998). *Increasing multicultural understanding: A comprehensive model* (2nd ed.). Thousand Oaks, CA: Sage.

Loewenberg, F. M., Dolgoff, R., & Harrington, D. (2000). *Ethical decisions for social work practice* (6th ed.). Itasca, IL: Peacock.

Lohmann, N. (2005). Social work education for rural practice. In N. Lohmann & R. A. Lohmann (Eds.), *Rural social work practice* (pp. 293–311). New York: Columbia University Press.

Lohmann, R. A. (1997). Managed care: A review of recent research. In R. L. Edwards (Ed.), *Encyclopedia of social work: Supplement 1997* (19th ed., pp. 200–213). Washington, DC: NASW Press.

Longres, J. F. (1995). Biographies: Richmond, Mary Ellen (1861–1928). In R. L. Edwards (Ed.), *Encyclopedia of social work* (19th ed., Vol. 3, p. 2605). Washington, DC: NASW Press.

Longres, J. F. (2000). *Human behavior in the social environment* (3rd ed.). Itasca, IL: Peacock.

Longres, J. F., & Aisenberg, E. (2008). Latinos and Latinas: Overview. In T. Mizrahi & L. E. Davis (Editors-in-Chief), *Encyclopedia of social work* (Vol. 3, pp. 31–41). Washington, DC: NASW Press.

LongTermCare.gov. (2014). Find your path forward. Retrieved from http://longtermcare.gov/.

Lorber, J. (2010). Gender inequality: *Feminist theories and politics* (4th ed.). New York: Oxford.

Loue, W. (1998). Defining the immigrant. In S. Loue (Ed.), *Handbook of immigrant health* (pp. 19–36). New York: Plenum Press.

Lowe, G. R. (1995). Social development. In R. L. Edwards (Ed.), *Encyclopedia of social work* (19th ed., Vol. 3, pp. 2168–2173). Washington, DC: NASW Press.

Lowe, S. M., & Mascher, J. (2001). The role of sexual orientation in multicultural counseling: Integrating bodies of knowledge. In J. G. Ponterotto, J. M. Casas, L. A. Suzuki, & C. M. Alexander (Eds.), *Handbook of multicultural counseling* (2nd ed., pp. 755–778). Thousand Oaks, CA: Sage.

Lu, Y. E. (2008). Asian Americans: Chinese. In T. Mizrahi & L. E. Davis (Editors-in-Chief), *Encyclopedia of social work* (Vol. 1, pp. 164–166). Washington, DC: NASW Press.

Lum, D. (1995). Asian Americans: Chinese. In R. L. Edwards (Ed.), *Encyclopedia of social work* (19th ed., Vol. 1, pp. 238–241). Washington, DC: NASW Press.

Lum, D. (2003). *Culturally competent practice: A framework for understanding diverse groups and justice issues* (2nd ed.). Pacific Grove, CA: Brooks/Cole.

Lum, D. (2004). *Social work practice with people of color: A process-stage approach* (5th ed.). Belmont, CA: Brooks/Cole.

Lum, D. (2005). *Cultural competence, practice stages, and client systems: A case study approach.* Belmont, CA: Brooks/Cole.

Lum, D. (2007). *Culturally competent practice: A framework for understanding diverse groups and justice issues* (3rd ed.). Belmont, CA: Brooks/Cole.

Lum, D. (2011). *Culturally competent practice: A framework for understanding diverse groups and justice issues* (4th ed.). Belmont, CA: Brooks/Cole.

Macarov, D. (1995). *Social welfare structure and practice.* Thousand Oaks, CA: Sage.

Macionis, J. J. (2008). *Social problems* (3rd ed.). Upper Saddle River, NJ: Pearson.

Macionis, J. J. (2010). *Social problems* (4th ed.). Upper Saddle River, NJ: Pearson.

Macionis, J. J. (2013). *Social problems* (5th ed.). Boston: Pearson.

Mackelprang, R. (2008). Disability: Overview. In T. Mizrahi & L. E. Davis (Editors-in-Chief), *Encyclopedia of social work* (Vol. 2, pp. 36–43). Washington, DC: NASW Press.

Mackelprang, R. L. (2012). Disability. In M. Gray, J. Midgley, & S. A. Webb (Eds.), *The SAGE handbook of social work* (pp. 547–563). Thousand Oaks, CA: Sage.

Mackelprang, R., & Salsgiver, R. (1996). People with disabilities and social work: Historical and contemporary issues. *Social Work, 41*(1), 7–14.

Mackelprang, R., & Salsgiver, R. (1999). *Disability: A diversity model approach in human service practice.* Pacific Grove, CA: Brooks/Cole.

Mackelprang, R. W., & Salsgiver, R. O. (2009). *Disability: A diversity model approach in human service practice* (2nd ed.). Chicago: Lyceum.

Macmillan, R., McMorris, B. J., & Kruttschnitt, C. (2004). Linked lives: Stability and change in maternal circumstances and trajectories of antisocial behavior in children. *Child Development, 75,* 205–220.

Mai, M. (1999, May 3). Anatomy of a massacre. *Newsweek,* 25–31.

Major, E. (2000, Winter). Self-determination and the disabled adult. *The New Social Worker, 7*(1), 9–16.

Making music: The key to healthy aging. (2005, September 19). *The Norman Transcript.* Retrieved June 3, 2011, from http://normantranscript.com/features/x518929115/Making-music-The-key-to-healthy-aging.

Malai, R. (2014, July). Social work tackles human slavery issue: Sex trafficking of minors a growing concern. *NASW News, 59*(7), 8, 14.

Mallon, G. P. (2008). Gay parents and parenting. In T. Mizrahi & L. E. Davis (Editors-in-Chief), *Encyclopedia of social work* (Vol. 2, pp. 241–247). Washington, DC: NASW Press.

Maluccio, A. N. (1990). Family preservation: An overview. In A. L. Sallee & J. C. Lloyd (Eds.), *Family preservation: Papers from the institute for social work educators 1990.* Riverdale, IL: National Association for Family-Based Services.

Maluccio, A. N., Pine, B. A., & Tracy, E. M. (2002). *Social work practice with families and children.* New York: Columbia.

Manske, J. (2008). Veteran services. In T. Mizrahi & L. E. Davis (Editors-in-Chief), *Encyclopedia of social work* (Vol. 4, pp. 257–259). Washington, DC: NASW Press.

Mapp, S. (2008). *Human rights and social justice in a global perspective: An introduction to international social work.* New York: Oxford.

Mapp, S. C. (2011). *Global child welfare and well-being.* New York: Oxford.

March of Dimes. (2015). *Your premature baby.* Retrieved from http://www.marchofdimes.org/baby/low-birthweight.aspx.

Marcotty, J. (1999, November 11). Electroshock therapy revised. *Minnesota Star Tribune.* Retrieved April 27, 2002, from http://www.ect.org/news/revised.htm.

Markels, A. (2007, April 30). Recovery's long road. *U.S. News & World Report,* 54–55.

Marlatt, G. A., & Miller, W. R. (1984). The comprehensive drinker profile: Interview booklet. Retrieved from http://casaa.unm.edu/inst/CDP.pdf.

Marsella, A. J. (1998, June). Urbanization, mental health, and social deviancy. *American Psychologist, 55*(6), 624–634.

Marson, S. M. (1998). Major uses of the Internet for social workers: A brief report for new users. *Arete, 22*(2), 21–28.

Marsiglia, F. F., & Kulis, S. (2015). *Diversity, oppression & change.* Chicago: Lyceum.

Marson, S. M. (2000). Internet ethics for social workers. *The New Social Worker, 7*(3), 29–30.

Martin, T. K., Paglinawan, L. K., & Paglinawan, R. (2014). Pathways to healing the Native Hawaiian spirit through culturally competent practice. In H. F. O. Vakalahi & M. T. Godinet (Eds.), *Transnational Pacific Islander Americans and social work: Dancing to the beat of a different drum* (pp. 55–90). Washington, DC: NASW Press.

Martinez-Brawley, E. E. (1995). Community. In R. L. Edwards (Ed.), *Encyclopedia of social work* (19th ed., Vol. 1, pp. 539–548). Washington, DC: NASW Press.

Marx, J. D. (2004). *Social welfare: The American partnership.* Boston: Allyn & Bacon.

Mary, N. L. (1998). Social work and the support model of services for people with developmental disabilities. *Journal of Social Work Education, 34*(2), 247–260.

Mary, N. L. (2008). *Social work in a sustainable world.* Chicago: Lyceum.

Mary Ellen Wilson. (1874, April 22). *New York Times,* p. 8.

Maryland Manual On-line. (2014). Barbara A. Mikulski. Retrieved from http://msa.maryland.gov/msa/mdmanual/39fed/05ussen/html/msa02094.html.

Masland, T. (2000, July 17). Breaking the silence. *Newsweek,* 30–31.

Mather, J., Lager, P. B., & Harris, N. J. (2007). *Child welfare: Policies and best practices* (2nd ed.) Belmont, CA: Brooks/Cole.

Mather, J. H., & Lager, P. B. (2000). *Child welfare: A unifying model of practice.* Belmont, CA: Wadsworth.

Mather, M. (2015). *Fact sheet: The decline in U.S. fertility.* Retrieved from Population Reference Bureau (PBR) website: http://www.prb.org/publications/datasheets/2012/world-population-data-sheet/fact-sheet-us-population.aspx.

Mayo Clinic. (2015). Electroconvulsive shock therapy (ECT). Retrieved from Mayo Clinic website: http://www.mayoclinic.org/tests-procedures/electroconvulsive-therapy/basics/definition/prc-20014161.

Mayo Foundation for Medical Education and Research. (2010). Electroconvulsive therapy (ECT). Retrieved June 21, 2011, from http://www.mayoclinic.com/health/electroconvulsive-therapy/MY00129.

McAdoo, H. P. (2007). *Black families* (4th ed.). Thousand Oaks, CA: Sage.

McCammon, S., & Knox, D. (2007). *Choices in sexuality* (3rd ed.). Mason, OH: Thomson.

McCollum, E. E., & Trepper, T. S. (2001). *Family solutions for substance abuse.* Binghamton, NY: Haworth.

McCallum, K. E., & Bruton, J. R. (2003). The continuum of care in the treatment of eating disorders. *Primary Psychiatry, 10*(6), 48–54.

McCarthy, J. (2014). Same sex marriage support reaches new high at 55%. Retrieved from http://www.gallup.com/poll/169640/sex-marriage-support-reaches-new-high.aspx.

McCarty, M., Aussenberg, R. A., Falk, G., & Carpenter, D. H. (2013, September 17). Drug testing and crime-related restrictions in TANF, SNAP, and Housing Assistance. The Congressional Research Service. Retrieved from http://fas.org/sgp/crs/misc/R42394.pdf.

McDonald, S., Constable, R., & Moriarty, A. (2009). *Developing safe, responsive, and respectful school communities: Pathways to intervention.* In C. R. Massat, R. Constable, S. McDonald, & J. P. Flynn (Eds.), *School social work: Practice, policy, and research* (7th ed., pp. 728–752). Chicago: Lyceum.

McGeary, J. (2001, February 12). Death stalks a continent. *Time,* 36–45.

McInnis-Dittrich, K. (1994). *Integrating social welfare policy and social work practice.* Pacific Grove, CA: Brooks/Cole.

McInnis-Dittrich, K. (2014). *Social work with older adults* (4th ed.). Boston: Pearson.

McLaughlin, L. A., & Braun, K. L. (1999). Asian and Pacific Islander cultural values: Considerations for health care decision-making. In P. L. Ewalt, E. M. Freeman, A. E. Fortune, D. L. Poole, & S. L. Witkin (Eds.), *Multicultural issues in social work: Practice and research* (pp. 321–336). Washington, DC: NASW Press.

McMillen, M. (2013). "Bath salts" drug trend: Expert Q & A. Retrieved from the WebMD website: http://www.webmd.com/mental-health/addiction/features/bath-salts-drug-dangers.

McNutt, J. (2008). Social work practice: History and evolution. In T. Mizrahi & L. E. Davis (Editors-in-Chief), *Encyclopedia of social work* (Vol. 4, pp. 138–141). Washington, DC: NASW Press.

McRoy, R. G., & Lombe, M. (2011). Cultural competence with African Americans. In D. Lum, *Culturally competent practice* (4th ed., pp. 273–301). Belmont, CA: Brooks/Cole.

McWhirter, J. J., McWhirter, B. T., McWhirter, E. H., & McWhirter, R. J. (2013). *At risk youth: A comprehensive response for counselors, teachers, psychologists, and human service professionals* (5th ed.). Belmont, CA: Brooks/Cole.

Mechanic, D., McAlpine, D. D., & Rochefort, D. A. (2014). *Mental health and social policy: Beyond managed care* (6th ed.). Boston: Pearson.

Medicaid.gov. (2014). Children's Health Insurance Program (CHIP). Retrieved from http://www.medicaid.gov/medicaid-chip-program-information/by-topics/childrens-health-insurance-program-chip/childrens-health-insurance-program-chip.html.

MedicineNet.com. (2014). Definition of public health. Retrieved from http://www.medicinenet.com/script/main/art.asp?articlekey=5120.

Meenaghan, T. M., Kilty, K. M., & McNutt, J. G. (2004). *Social policy analysis and practice.* Chicago: Lyceum.

Meier, M. S. (1990). Politics, educations, and culture. In C. McWilliams (Ed.), *North from Mexico* (rev. ed., pp. 285–308). Westport, CT: Greenwood Press.

Menefee, D. (2000). What managers do and why they do it. In R. J. Patti (Ed.), *The handbook of social welfare management* (pp. 247–266). Thousand Oaks, CA: Sage.

Mental Health America (MHA). (2011a). Eating disorders. Retrieved June 17, 2011, from http://www.nmha.org/go/eating-disorders.

Mental Health America (MHA). (2011b). Electroconvulsive therapy (ECT). Retrieved June 21, 2011, from http://www.nmha.org/go/information/get-info/treatment/electroconvulsive-therapy-ect.

Mental Health America (MHA). (2014). Home. Retrieved from http://www.mentalhealthamerica.net/.

Mercer, S. O. (1996, March). Navajo elderly people in a reservation nursing home: Admission predictors and culture care practices. *Social Work, 41*(2), 181–189.

Meyer, D. R. (1995). Supplemental Security Income. In R. L. Edwards (Ed.), *Encyclopedia of social work* (19th ed., Vol. 3, pp. 2379–2385). Washington, DC: NASW Press.

Meyer, D. R. (2001, Spring). Income support for children in the United States. *Focus, 21*(3), 38–41.

Midgley, J. (1997). *Social welfare in global context.* Thousand Oaks, CA: Sage.

Midgley, J., & Livermore, M. (1997). The developmental perspective in social work: Educational implications for a new century. *Social Work, 33*(3), 573–585.

Miller, D. W. (2001, May 18). Programs in social work embrace the teaching of spirituality. *The Chronicle of Higher Education,* A12.

Miller, G. (2005). *Learning the language of addiction counseling* (2nd ed.). Hoboken, NJ: Wiley.

Miller, M., & Kantrowitz, B. (1999, January 25). Unmasking Sybil: A re-examination of the most famous psychiatric patient in history. *Newsweek,* 66–68.

Miller, R. L., Jr. (2008). Gay men: Overview. In T. Mizrahi & L. E. Davis (Editors-in-Chief), *Encyclopedia of social work* (Vol. 2, pp. 256–260). Washington, DC: NASW Press.

Miller-Perrin, C. L., & Perrin, R. C. (2013). *Child maltreatment: An introduction* (3rd ed.). Thousand Oaks, CA: Sage.

Mish, F. C. (Editor-in-Chief). (2008). *Merriam-Webster's collegiate dictionary* (11th ed.). Springfield, MA: Merriam-Webster, Inc.

Mitchell, E. P., & Mitchell, H. H. (1989). Black spirituality: The values in that ol'time religion. *Journal of the Interdenominational Theological Center, 17*(112), 98–109.

Mizrahi, T., & Davis, L. E. (Eds.). (2008). *Encyclopedia of social work.* New York: Oxford.

Mokuau, N. (1995). Pacific Islanders. In R. L. Edwards (Ed.), *Encyclopedia of social work* (19th ed., Vol. 3, pp. 1795–1801). Washington, DC: NASW Press.

Mokuau, N. (2008). Native Hawaiians and Pacific Islanders. In T. Mizrahi & L. E. Davis (Editors-in-Chief), *Encyclopedia of social work* (Vol. 3, pp. 308–310). Washington, DC: NASW Press.

Money, J. (1987). Sin, sickness, or status: Homosexual gender identify and psychoneuroendocrinology. *American Psychologist, 42,* 384–399.

Monzini, P. (2004). Trafficking in women and girls and the involvement of organized crime in Western and Central Europe. *International Review of Victimology, 11,* 73–88.

Mooney, L. A., Knox, D., & Schacht, C. (2009). *Understanding social problems* (6th ed.). Belmont, CA: Wadsworth.

Mooney, L. A., Knox, D., & Schacht, C. (2011). *Understanding social problems* (7th ed.). Belmont, CA: Wadsworth.

Mooney, L. A., Knox, D., & Schacht, C. (2015). *Understanding social problems* (9th ed.). Belmont, CA: Wadsworth.

Moore, S. E. (2008). African Americans: Practice interventions. In T. Mizrahi & L. E. Davis (Editors-in-Chief), *Encyclopedia of social work* (Vol. 1, pp. 81–85). Washington, DC: NASW Press.

Morales, A. T., Sheafor, B. W., & Scott, M. E. (2012). *Social work: A profession of many faces* (12th ed.). Boston: Allyn & Bacon.

Morales, J. (1995). Gay men: Parenting. In R. L. Edwards (Ed.), *Encyclopedia of social work* (19th ed., Vol. 2, pp. 1085–1095). Washington, DC: NASW Press.

Morgan, M. (2000). *Careers in criminology.* Los Angeles: RoBury Park.

Morris, R. (1987). Social welfare policy: Trends and issues. In A. Monahan (Ed.), *Encyclopedia of social work* (Vol. 2, pp. 664–681). Silver Spring, MD: NASW Press.

Morrow, D. F. (2006a). Coming out as a gay, lesbian, bisexual, and transgender. In D. F. Morrow & L. Messinger (Eds.), *Sexual orientation & gender expression in social work practice: Working with gay, lesbian, bisexual, & transgender people* (pp. 129–152). New York: Columbia.

Morrow, D. F. (2006b). Gay, lesbian, bisexual, and transgender adolescents. In D. F. Morrow & L. Messinger (Eds.), *Sexual orientation & gender expression in social work practice: Working with gay, lesbian, bisexual, & transgender people* (pp. 177–195). New York: Columbia.

Morrow, D. F. (2008). Lesbians: Practice interventions. In T. Mizrahi & L. E. Davis (Editors-in-Chief), *Encyclopedia of social work* (Vol. 3, pp. 79–87). Washington, DC: NASW Press.

Moxley, D. P. (1989). *The practice of case management.* Newbury Park, CA: Sage.

Mueller, R. S., III. (2002, July 15). American Muslims: All Americans pulling together (Robert S. Mueller III address). *Vital Speeches of the Day, 68*(19), 480–484. Retrieved from http://infotrac-college.thomsonlearning.com.

Murase, K. (1995). Asian Americans: Japanese. In R. L. Edwards (Ed.), *Encyclopedia of social work* (19th ed., Vol. 1, pp. 241–249). Washington, DC: NASW Press.

Murphy, B. C., & Dillon, C. (2011). *Interviewing in action in a multicultural world* (4th ed.). Belmont, CA: Brooks/Cole.

Murphy, K. C. (2004). Child development. In C. R. Brittain & D. E. Hunt (Eds.), *Helping in child protective services: A competency-based casework handbook* (pp. 249–306). Washington, DC: NASW Press.

Murphy, Y., Hunt, V., Zajicek, A. M., Norris, A. N., & Hamilton, L. (2009). *Incorporating intersectionality in social work practice, research, policy, and education.* Washington, DC: NASW Press.

Myers, J. E. B. (2002). Risk management for professionals working with maltreated children and adult survivors. In J. E. B. Myers, L. Berliner, J. Briere, C. T. Hendrix, C. Jenny, & T. A. Reid (Eds.), *The APSAC handbook on child maltreatment* (2nd ed., pp. 403–427). Thousand Oaks, CA: Sage.

Myers, R., & Granstaff, C. (2008). Political social work. In T. Mizrahi & L. E. Davis (Editors-in-Chief), *Encyclopedia of social work* (Vol. 3, pp. 383–387). Washington, DC: NASW Press.

Nackerud, L. (2008). Unemployment insurance. In T. Mizrahi & L. E. Davis (Editors-in-Chief), *Encyclopedia of social work* (Vol. 4, pp. 247–249). Washington, DC: NASW Press.

Nadir, A., & Dziegielewski, S. F. (2001). Islam. In M. Van Hook, B. Hugen, & M. Aguilar (Eds.), *Spirituality within religious traditions in social work practice* (pp. 146–166). Belmont, CA: Brooks/Cole.

Nairne, J. S. (2011). *Psychology* (5th ed.). Belmont, CA: Wadsworth.

Nairne, J. S. (2014). *Psychology* (6th ed.). Belmont, CA: Wadsworth.

Naleppa, M. J., & Reid, W. J. (2003). *Gerontological social work: A task-centered approach.* New York: Columbia.

NASW Center for Workforce Studies & Social Work Practice. (2011). *Social work salaries by gender: Occupational profile.* Retrieved from http://workforce.socialworkers.org/studies/profiles/Gender.pdf.

National Alliance to End Homelessness. (2014). About homelessness. Retrieved from http://www.endhomelessness.org/pages/about_homelessness.

National Alliance on Mental Illness (NAMI). (2012). Electroconvulsive therapy. Retrieved from http://www.nami.org/Template.cfm?Section=About_Treatments_and_Supports&Template=/ContentManagement/ContentDisplay.cfm&ContentID=142939.

National Alliance on Mental Illness (NAMI). (2014). Commonly prescribed pschotropic medications. Retrieved from http://www.nami.org/Template.cfm?Section=Policymakers_Toolkit&Template=/ContentManagement/HTMLDisplay.cfm&ContentID=18971.

National Association of Cognitive-Behavioral Therapy (NACBT). (2010). Cognitive-behavioral therapy. Retrieved June 18, 2011, from http://www.nacbt.org/whatiscbt.htm.

National Association of the Deaf (NAD). (2011). Community and culture—frequently asked questions. Retrieved June 8, 2011, from http://www.nad.org/issues/american-sign-language/community-and-culture-faq.

National Association of Social Workers (NASW). (1973). *Standards for social service manpower.* New York: Author.

National Association of Social Workers (NASW). (2005). The power of social work. Retrieved February 12, 2005, from http://www.socialworkers.org/.

National Association of Social Workers (NASW). (2008). *Code of ethics.* Washington, DC: Author.

National Association of Social Workers (NASW). (2009). *Social work speaks: National; Association of social workers policy statements 2009–2012* (8th ed.). Washington, DC: Author.

National Association of Social Workers. (2010). *Summary of key compensation findings: May 2010.* Retrieved from http://workforce.socialworkers.org/8-SalarySurvey.pdf.

National Association of Social Workers (NASW). (2012). *Social work speaks: National Association of Social Workers Policy Statement 2012–2014* (9th ed.). Washington, DC: NASW Press.

National Association of Social Workers (NASW). (2013). Social workers in Congress. Retrieved from https://www.socialworkers.org/pace/swcongress2013.pdf.

National Association of Social Workers (NASW). (2014a). Mental health. Retrieved from https://www.socialworkers.org/pressroom/features/issue/mental.asp.

National Association of Social Workers (NASW). (2014b). NASW credentialing center. Retrieved from http://www.naswdc.org/credentials/default.asp.

National Association of Social Workers (NASW). (2014c). PACE: Building political power for social workers. Retrieved from http://www.naswdc.org/pace/default.asp.

National Association of Social Workers (NASW). (2015a). Membership. Retrieved from http://www.naswdc.org/join.asp.

National Association of Social Workers (NASW). (2015b). *Social work speaks* (10th ed.). Washington, DC: NASW Press.

National Committee for the Prevention of Elder Abuse (NCPEA). (2008). *What services are available to stop abuse?* Retrieved from http://www.preventelderabuse.org/elderabuse/help/help2.html.

National Council on Aging (NCOA). (2014). Senior centers: Fact sheet. Retrieved from http://www.ncoa.org/press-room/fact-sheets/senior-centers-fact-sheet.html.

National Council on Aging (NCOA). (2015). Fact sheet: Senior Centers. Retrieved from https://www.ncoa.org/resources/fact-sheet-senior-centers/.

National Council on Family Relations (NCFR). (2014). What is family life education? Retrieved from https://www.ncfr.org/cfle-certification/what-family-life-education.

National Crime Prevention Association (NCPA). (2011). Cyberbullying. Retrieved June 26, 2011, from http://www.ncpc.org/cyberbullying.

National Crime Prevention Council (NCPC). (2011). Strategy: Gang prevention through community intervention with high-risk youth. Retrieved June 26, 2011, from http://www.ncpc.org/topics/violent-crime-and-personal-safety/strategies/strategy-gang-prevention-through-community-intervention-with-high-risk-youth.

National Criminal Justice Reference Service. (n.d.). In the spotlight: Women and girls in the criminal justice system. Retrieved from https://www.ncjrs.gov/spotlight/wgcjs/summary.html.

National Institute of Mental Health (NIMH). (2014). Any mental illness (AMI) among adults. Retrieved from http://www.nimh.nih.gov/health/statistics/prevalence/any-mental-illness-ami-among-adults.shtml.

National Institute of Mental Health (NIMH). (n.d.). Mental health. Retrieved from http://www.nimh.nih.gov/health/topics/index.shtml.

National Institute of Mental Health (NIMH). (n.d.). Statistics home. Retrieved from http://www.nimh.nih.gov/health/statistics/index.shtml.

National Institute of Mental Health (NIMH). (2007a). African Americans, Black Caribbeans, and Whites differ in depression risk and treatment. Retrieved June 21, 2011, from http://www.nimh.nih.gov/science-news/2007/african-americans-black-caribbeans-and-whites-differ-in-depression-risk-treatment.shtml.

National Institute of Mental Health (NIMH). (2007b). National survey tracks prevalence of personality disorders in U.S. population. Retrieved June 18, 2011, from http://www.nimh.nih.gov/science-news/2007/national-survey-tracks-prevalence-of-personality-disorders-in-us-population.shtml.

National Institute of Mental Health (NIMH). (2010). Just over half of Americans diagnosed with major depression receive care. Retrieved June 21, 2011, from http://www.nimh.nih.gov/science-news/2010/just-over-half-of-americans-diagnosed-with-major-depression-receive-care.shtml.

National Institute on Aging. (2009). A good night's sleep. Retrieved June 3, 2011, from http://www.nia.nih.gov/healfhinformation/publications/sleep.htm.

National Institute on Drug Abuse (NIDA). (2008). Prescription drug abuse chart. Retrieved November 12, 2008, from http://www.drugabuse.gov/DrugPages/PrescripDrugsChart.html.

National Institute on Drug Abuse (NIDA). (2010). NIDA Info-Facts: Club drugs (GHB, Ketamine, and Rohypnol. Retrieved June 22, 2011, from http://www.drugabuse.gov/infofacts/clubdrugs.html.

National Institute on Drug Abuse (NIDA). (2012a). DrugFacts: Spice ("Synthetic marijuana"). Retrieved from http://www.drugabuse.gov/publications/drugfacts/spice-synthetic-marijuana.

National Institute on Drug Abuse (NIDA). (2012b). DrugFacts: Synthetic cathinones ("bath salts"). Retrieved from http://www.drugabuse.gov/publications/drugfacts/synthetic-cathinones-bath-salts.

National Institute on Drug Abuse (NIDA). (2013). DrugFacts: MDMA (Ecstasy or Molly). Retrieved from http://www.drugabuse.gov/publications/drugfacts/spice-synthetic-marijuana.

National Institute on Drug Abuse (NIDA). (2015). Emerging trends. Retrieved from http://www.drugabuse.gov/drugs-abuse/emerging-trends.

National Institute on Drug Abuse (NIDA). (n.d.). Drugs of abuse. Retrieved from http://www.drugabuse.gov/drugs-abuse.

National Mental Health Association. (2005). Electroconvulsive therapy (ECT). Retrieved January 30, 2005, from http://www.nmha.org/infoctr/factsheets/ect.cfm.

National Mental Health Association (NMHA). (2008). Mental health America. Retrieved July 22, 2008, from http://www.nmha.org.

National Program Office on Self-Determination (NPOSD). (1998). *The Robert Wood Johnson Foundation initiative in self-determination for persons with developmental disabilities* [online]. Princeton, NJ: The Robert Wood Johnson Foundation. Retrieved from http://www.selfdetermination.org.

National Resource Center (NRC). (2010). On TANF & transportation. Retrieved May 19, 2010, from http://nrccapitolclips.blogspot.com/2010/06/on-tanf-transportation.html.

Negroni-Rodriguez, L. K., & Morales, J. (2001). Individual and family assessment skills with Latino/Hispanic Americans. In R. Fong & S. Furuto (Eds.), *Culturally competent practice: Skills, interventions, and evaluations* (pp. 132–146). Boston: Allyn & Bacon.

Neiman, S. (2011). *Crime, violence, discipline, and safety in U.S. public schools: Findings from the School Survey on Crime and Safety: 2009–10.* (NCES 2011-320). U.S. Department of Education, National Center for Education Statistics. Washington, DC: U.S. Government Printing Office.

Nemours Foundation. (2011). Individualized education programs (IEPs). Retrieved June 24, 2011, from http://kidshealth.org/parent/growfh/learning/iep.html.

Neukrug, E. S. (2011). *Counseling theory and practice.* Belmont, CA: Brooks/Cole.

Neukrug, E. (2013). *Theory, practice, and trends in human services: An introduction* (5th ed.). Belmont, CA: Cengage Learning.

Newman, B. M., & Newman, P. R. (2015). *Development through life: A psychosocial approach* (12th ed.). Belmont, CA: Cengage Learning.

Newman, C. (2000, August 10). Older, healthier and wealthier. *Washington Post,* A3.

Nichols, R., & Braun, K. L. (1996). *Death and dying in five Asian and Pacific Islander cultures: A preliminary study.* Honolulu: University of Hawaii, School of Public Health, Center on Aging.

Nichols, W. R. (Ed.). (1999). *Random House Webster's college dictionary* (2nd ed.). New York: Random House.

NIHSenior Health.gov. (2015). Long-term care. Retrieved from http://nihseniorhealth.gov/longtermcare/facilitybasedservices/01.html.

Nishioka, V., Coe, M., Burke, A., Hanita, M., & Sprague, J. (2011). *Student-reported overt and relational aggression and victimization in grades 3–8.* (Issues and Answers Report, REL 2011-No. 114). Washington, DC: U.S. Department of Education, Institute of Education Sciences, National Center for Education Evaluation and Regional Assistance, Regional Educational Laboratory Northwest.

Nittle, N. K. (2011). *The national urban league: An overview.* Retrieved May 10, 2011, from http://racerelations.about.com/od/organizations/a/NationalUrbanLeagueOverview.htm.

NOLO. (2014). Workers' compensation benefits faqs. Retrieved from http://www.nolo.com/legal-encyclopedia/your-right-to-workers-comp-benefits-faq-29093.html.

Norman, E. (2000). Introduction: The strengths perspective and resiliency enhancement—A natural partnership. In E. Norman (Ed.), *Resiliency enhancement: Putting the strengths perspective into social work practice* (pp. 1–16). New York: Columbia.

Obama, B. (2013). Statement to the press corps: Remarks about Trayvon Martin. Retrieved from http://www.onbeingablack-lawyer.com/wordpress/president-obamas-remarks-to-white-house-press-corp-on-trayvon-martin-the-zimmerman-verdict.

Obamacare Facts. (2014). ObamaCare subsidies. Retrieved from http://obamacarefacts.com/obamacare-subsidies/.

*O'Connor v. Donaldson,* 422 U.S. 563 (1975).

Office of Family Assistance. (2009). *Fact sheet.* Washington, DC: Author. Retrieved August 25, 2011, from www.acf.hhs.gov/opa/fact_sheets/tanf_factsheet.html.

Office of the Surgeon General. (2001). Youth violence: A report of the surgeon general. Retrieved February 6, 2005, from http://www.surgeongeneral.gov/library/youthviolence/.

Official Kwanzaa Web Site. (2013). Kwanzaa. Retrieved from http://www.officialkwanzaawebsite.org/index.shtml.

Okazawa-Rey, M. (1998). Empowering poor communities of color: A self-help model. In L. M. Gutierrez, R. J. Parsons, & E. O. Cox (Eds.), *Empowerment in social work practice: A sourcebook.* Pacific Grove, CA: Brooks/Cole.

O'Neill, J. V. (1999, September). Social work turns back to the spiritual. *NASW News, 3.*

O'Neill, J. V. (2003, February). Private sector employs most members. *NASW News, 8.*

Orshansky, M. (1965). Measuring poverty. In *The social welfare forum: Proceedings of the 92nd annual forum of the national conference on social welfare.* New York: Columbia University Press.

Ortman, J. M., Velkoff, V. A., & Hogan, H. (2014, May). *An aging nation: The older population in the United States: Population estimates and projections.* Retrieved from the U.S. Census Bureau wesite: https://www.census.gov/prod/2014pubs/p25-1140.pdf.

Pace, P. R. (2010, June). Salary survey released. *NASW News, 55*(6), 8.

Pace, P. R. (2011, January). CSWE meeting addresses profession's sustainability. *NASW News, 10.*

Pace, P. R. (2014, July). Committee focuses on social justice for women. *NASW News, 59*(7), 11.

Page, R. M. (2014). Conservative governments and the welfare state since 1945. In H. Bochel & G. Daly (Eds.), *Social policy* (3rd ed.). New York: Routledge.

Paniagua, F. A. (2005). *Assessing and treating culturally diverse clients: A practical guide* (3rd ed.). Thousand Oaks, CA: Sage.

Paniagua, F. A. (2014). *Assessing and treating culturally diverse clients: A practical guide* (4th ed.). Thousand Oaks, CA: Sage.

Papalia, D. E., & Feldman, R. D., with Martorell, G. (2012). *Experience human development* (12th ed.). New York: McGraw-Hill.

Papalia, D. E., Olds, S. W., & Feldman, R. D. (2009). *Human development* (11th ed.). Boston: McGraw-Hill.

Paplos, D. (2002). *About ECT—Electroconvulsive therapy.* Retrieved April 27, 2002, from http://www.medhelp.org/lib/ect.htm.

Parents Anonymous. (2014). Home. Retrieved from http://parentsanonymous.org/.

Parke, R. D. (2004). Development in the family. *Annual Review of Psychology, 55,* 365–399.

*Parrish v. Civil Service Commission,* 66 Cal.2d 260 (1967).

Parsons, R. D. (2001). *The ethics of professional practice.* Boston: Allyn & Bacon.

Patchner, L. S., & DeWeaver, K. L. (2008). Disability: Neuro-cognitive disabilities. In T. Mizrahi & L. E. Davis (Editors-in-Chief), *Encyclopedia of social work* (Vol. 2, pp. 43–49). Washington, DC: NASW Press.

Patterson, C. J. (2014). Lesbian and gay parenting. (American Psychological Association). Retrieved from http://www.apa.org/pi/lgbt/resources/parenting.aspx.

Patterson, G. R. (2008). A comparison of models for interstate wars and for individual violence. *Perspectives on Psychological Science, 3,* 203–223.

Patterson, G. R., DeBaryshe, B. D., & Ramsey, E. (1989). A developmental perspective on antisocial behavior. *American Psychologist, 44,* 329–335.

Patterson, G. T. (2012). *Social work practice in the criminal justice system.* New York: Routledge.

Patterson, L. E., & Welfel, E. R. (2000). *The counseling process* (5th ed.). Pacific Grove, CA: Brooks/Cole.

Pavetti, L., Finch, I., & Schott, L. (Center for Budget and Policy Priorities). (2013, March 1). TANF emerging from the downturn a weaker safety net. Retrieved from http://www.cbpp.org/files/3-1-13tanf.pdf.

Pawlak, E. J., Wozniak, D., & McGowen, M. (1999). Perspectives on groups for school social workers. In R. Constable, S. McDonald, & J. P. Flynn (Eds.), *School social work: Practice, policy, and research perspectives* (4th ed., pp. 356–375). Chicago: Lyceum.

Paylor, I., Measham, I. P., & Asher, H. (2012). *Social work and drug use.* New York: McGraw-Hill.

Payne, M. (2012). *Citizen social work with older people.* Chicago: Lyceum.

Pecora, P. J., Whittaker, J. K., Maluccio, A. N., Barth, R. P., DePanfilis, D., with Plotnick, R. D. (2010). *The child welfare challenge: Policy, practice, and research* (3rd ed.). New Brunswick, NJ: Transaction.

Perkinson, R. R. (2012). *Chemical dependency counseling: A practical guide* (4th ed.). Thousand Oaks, CA: Sage.

Perren, S., & Alsaker, F. D. (2006). Social behavior and peer relationships of victims, bullyvictims, and bullies in kindergarten. *Journal of Child Psychology and psychiatry, 47*(1), 45–57.

Petr, C. G. (2004). *Social work with children and their families: Pragmatic foundations* (2nd ed.). Washington, DC: NASW Press.

Petrocelli, A. M. (2012). *Prejudice to pride: Moving from homophobia to acceptance.* Washington, DC: NASW Press.

PEW Charitable Trusts. (2014). Managing prison health care spending. Retrieved from http://www.pewtrusts.org/en/research-and-analysis/reports/2014/05/15/managing-prison-health-care-spending.

Phillips, N. K., & Straussner, S. L. (2002). *Urban social work: An introduction to policy and practice in cities.* Boston: Allyn & Bacon.

Philpott, D., & Hill, J. (2009). *The wounded warrior handbook: A resource guide for returning veterans.* Lanham, MD: Government Institutes.

Piccola, T. D., & Tracy, E. M. (2008). Family preservation and home-based services. In T. Mizrahi & L. E. Davis (Editors-in-Chief), *Encyclopedia of social work* (Vol. 2, pp. 200–206). Washington, DC: NASW Press.

Pickett, J. P. (Ed.). (2002). *The American Heritage college dictionary* (4th ed.). Boston: Houghton Mifflin.

Pietsch, J. H., & Braun, K. L. (2000). Autonomy, advance directives, and the patient self-determination act. In K. L. Braun, J. H. Pietsch, & P. L. Blanchette (Eds.), *Cultural issues in end-of-life decision making* (pp. 37–54). Thousand Oaks, CA: Sage.

Pincus, A., & Minahan, A. (1973). *Social work practice: Model and method.* Itasca, IL: Peacock.

Plassman, B. L. Langa, K. M., Fisher, G. G., Heeringa, S. G., Weir, D. R., Ofstedal, M. B., ... Wallace, R. B. (2007). Prevalence of dementia in the United States: The aging, demographics, and memory study. *Neuroepidemiology, 29,* 125–132.

Pollard, W. L. (1995). Civil rights. In R. L. Edwards (Ed.), *Encyclopedia of social work* (19th ed., Vol. 1, pp. 740–751). Washington, DC: NASW Press.

Popple, P. R. (1995). The social work profession: History. In R. L. Edwards (Ed.), *Encyclopedia of social work* (19th ed., Vol. 3, pp. 2282–2292). Washington, DC: NASW Press.

Popple, P. R., & Leighninger, L. (2002). *Social work, social welfare, and American society* (5th ed.). Boston: Allyn & Bacon.

Popple, P. R., & Leighninger, L. (2005). *Social work, social welfare, and American society* (6th ed.). Boston: Allyn & Bacon.

Popple, P. R., & Leighninger, L. (2011). *The policy-based profession: An introduction to social welfare policy analysis for social workers* (5th ed.). Boston: Allyn & Bacon.

Popple, P. R., & Leighninger, L. (2015). *The policy-based profession: An introduction to social welfare policy analysis for social workers* (6th ed.). Boston: Pearson.

Porter, E., & Walsh, M. (2005, February 9). Retirement turns into a rest stop as benefits dwindle. *New York Times.* Retrieved November 3, 2008, from http://www.nytimes.com/2005/02/09/business/09retire.html?_r=l&scp=l&sq=\retirement%20turns%20into%20a%20rest%20stop&st=cse&oref=slogin.

Potocky, M. (2008). Immigrants and refugees. In T. Mizrahi & L. E. Davis (Editors-in-Chief), *Encyclopedia of social work* (Vol. 2, pp. 441–445). Washington, DC: NASW Press.

Potocky-Tripodi, M. (2002). *Best practices for social work with refugees & immigrants.* New York: Columbia.

Potter, N., Schoetz, D., Esposito, R., & Thomas, P. (2007, April 17). Killer's note: "You caused me to do this." Retrieved June 26, 2011, from http://abcnews.go.com/US/story?id=3048108&page=1.

Practitioners surveyed: Incomes increase. (2003, February). *NASW News,* pp. 1, 8.

Proch, K., & Taber, M. A. (1987). Alienated adolescents in foster care. *Social Work Research & Abstracts, 23*(2), 9–13.

ProQuest. (2014). *ProQuest statistical abstract of the United States 2014.* Lanham, MD: Bernan.

Quadagno, J. (2005). *Aging and the life course.* Boston: McGraw-Hill.

Quam, J. K. (1995). Biographies: Addams, Jane (1860–1935). In R. L. Edwards (Ed.), *Encyclopedia of social work* (19th ed., Vol. 3, pp. 2571–2572). Washington, DC: NASW Press.

Queiro-Tajalli, I., & Campbell, C. (2012). Resilience and violence at the macro level. In R. R. Greene (Ed.), *Resiliency: An integrated approach to practice, policy, and research* (2nd ed., pp. 183–201). Washington, DC: NASW Press.

Quiet's Corner. (2002a). Shirley Ardell Mason's (Sybil's) obituary. Retrieved April 27, 2002, from http://www.asarian.org/-quiet/sybilobit.html.

Quiet's Corner. (2002b). *Where multiple personal(ity) bodies are considered normal.* Retrieved April 27, 2002, from http://www.pooh.asarian.org/~quiet/.

Race, P. R. (2008, January). Evidence-based practice moves ahead. *NASW News,* 4.

Ragg, D. M. (2006). *Building family practice skills: Methods, strategies, and tools.* Belmont, CA: Brooks/Cole.

Rank, M. R. (2008). Poverty. In T. Mizrahi & L. E. Davis (Editors-in-Chief), *Encyclopedia of social work* (Vol. 3, pp. 387–395). Washington, DC: NASW Press.

Rasheed, M. N., & Rasheed, J. M. (2008). Family: Practice interventions. In T. Mizrahi & L. E. Davis (Editors-in-Chief), *Encyclopedia of social work* (Vol. 2, pp. 182–191). Washington, DC: NASW Press.

Raskin, M. S., & Daley, D. C. (1991). Assessment of addiction problems. In M. S. Raskin & D. C. Daley (Eds.), *Treating the chemically dependent and their families* (pp. 22–56). Newbury Park, CA: Sage.

Rathus, S. A. (2014). *Childhood & adolescence: Voyages in development* (5th ed.). Belmont, CA: Wadsworth.

Rathus, S. A., Nevid, J. S., & Fichner-Rathus, L. (2011). *Human sexuality in a world of diversity* (8th ed.). Boston: Allyn & Bacon.

Rathus, S. A., Nevid, J. S., & Fichner-Rathus, L. (2014). *Human sexuality in a world of diversity* (9th ed.). Boston: Pearson.

Rautkis, M. E., & Koeske, G. R. (1994). Maintaining social work morale: When supportive supervision is not enough. *Administration in Social Work, 18*(1), 39–60.

Reamer, F. G. (1998). *Ethical standards in social work.* Washington, DC: NASW Press.

Reamer, F. G. (2001). *Tangled relationships: Managing boundary issues in the human services.* New York: Columbia.

Reamer, F. G. (2006). *Ethical standards in social work: A review of the NASW Code of Ethics* (2nd ed.). Washington, DC: NASW Press.

Reese, D. J. (2013). *Hospice social work.* New York: Columbia.

Regulus, T. A. (1995). Gang violence. In R. L. Edwards (Ed.), *Encyclopedia of social work* (19th ed., Vol. 2, pp. 1045–1055). Washington, DC: NASW Press.

Reid, P. M. (1995). Social welfare history. In R. L. Edwards (Ed.), *Encyclopedia of social work* (19th ed., Vol. 3, pp. 2206–2225). Washington, DC: NASW Press.

Reinhardt, U. E. (2008, November 21). Why does U.S. health care cost so much? (Part II: Indefensible administrative costs). Retrieved June 10, 2011, from http://economix.blogs.nytimes.com/2008/11/21/why-does-us-healfh-care-cost-so-much-part-ii-indefensible-administrative-costs/.

Renz-Beaulaurier, R. (1998). Empowering people with disabilities: The role of choice. In L. M. Gutierrez, R. J. Parsons, & E. O. Cox (Eds.), *Empowerment in social work practice: A sourcebook* (pp. 73–84). Pacific Grove, CA: Brooks/Cole.

Renzetti, C. M., Curran, D. J., & Maier, S. L. (2012). *Women, men, and society* (6th ed.). Boston: Pearson.

Resnick, H. (1980a). Effecting internal change in human service organizations. In H. Resnick & R. J. Patti (Eds.), *Change from within: Humanizing social welfare organizations* (pp. 187–199). Philadelphia: Temple University Press.

Resnick, H. (1980b). Tasks in changing the organization from within. In H. Resnick & R. J. Patti (Eds.), *Change from within: Humanizing social welfare organizations* (pp. 200–216). Philadelphia: Temple University Press.

Richmond, L. J., & Guindon, M. H. (2013). Culturally alert counseling with European Americans. In McAuliffe, G., & Associates (Eds.), *Culturally alert counseling: A comprehensive introduction* (2nd ed., pp. 231–262). Thousand Oaks, CA: Sage.

Riley, D. P. (1995). Family life education. In R. L. Edwards (Ed.), *Encyclopedia of social work* (19th ed., Vol. 2, pp. 960–965). Washington, DC: NASW Press.

Rizzo, V. M., & Seidman, J. (2009). Section 2: A framework for health promotion in aging. Gero-Ed Center *Health Resource Review.* Retrieved June 2, 2011, from http://www.cswe.org/CentersInitiatives/GeroEdCenter/Programs/MAC/Reviews/Health.aspx.

Roan, S. (2012, January 19). U.S. teen pregnancy rate remains highest in developed world. Retrieved from the *Los Angeles Times* website: http://articles.latimes.com/2012/jan/19/news/la-heb-teen-pregnancy-20120119.

Robinson, S., & Palus, N. (2001, April 30). An awful human trade. *Time,* 40–41.

Robison, W., & Reeser, L. C. (2000). *Ethical decision making in social work.* Boston: Allyn & Bacon.

Rocha, C. J. (2007). *Essentials of social work policy practice.* Hoboken, NJ: Wiley.

Rochefort, D. A. (1993). *From poor houses to homelessness: Policy analysis and mental health care.* Westport, CT: Auburn House.

Romsdahl, I. (1997, April 27). Sybil: Multiple personalities manufactured. Retrieved April 27, 2002, from http://www.mankato.msus.edu/dept/reporter/reparchive/04_27_97/news3.html.

Rosenthal, M. S. (2013). *Human sexuality: From cells to society.* Belmont, CA: Cengage Learning.

Rothman, J. (2001). Approaches to community intervention. In J. Rothman, J. L. Erlich, & J. E. Tropman (Eds.), *Strategies of community intervention* (6th ed., pp. 27–64). Pacific Grove, CA: Brooks/Cole.

Rothman, J. (2007). Multi modes of intervention at the macro level. *Journal of Community Practice, 15*(4), 11–40.

Rothman, J. C. (2003). *Social work practice across disability.* Boston: Allyn & Bacon.

Royse, D. (2011). *Research methods in social work* (6th ed.). Belmont, CA: Brooks/Cole.

Rubin, K. H., Bukowski, W., & Parker, J. G. (2006). Peer interactions, relationships, and groups. In W. Damon & R. M. Lerner (Series Eds.), & N. Eisenberg (Vol. Ed.), *Handbook of child psychology: Vol. 3. Social, emotional, and personality development* (6th ed., pp. 571–645). New York: Wiley.

Rubin, A., & Babbie, E. R. (2014). *Research methods for social work* (8th ed.). Belmont, CA: Brooks/Cole.

Runyon, M. D., & Urquiza, A. J. (2011). Child physical abuse. In J. E. B. Myers (Ed.), *The APSAC handbook on child maltreatment* (3rd ed., pp. 195–212). Thousand Oaks, CA: Sage.

Ryan, C., & Futterman, D. (2001). Social and developmental challenges for lesbian, gay, and bisexual youth. *SIECUS Report, 29*(4), 5–18.

Rycus, J. S., Hughes R. C., & Ginther, N. (1988). *Separation and placement in child protective services: A training curriculum.* Washington, DC: Child Welfare League of America.

Sabbatini, R. M. E. (2002). The history of shock therapy in psychiatry. Retrieved April 28, 2002, from http://www.epub.org.br/cm/n04/historia/shock_i/htm.

Sackheim, H. A., Devanand, D. P., & Nobler, M. S. (2002). Electroconvulsive therapy. Retrieved April 28, 2002, from http://www.acrip.org/g4/GN401000108/CH106.html.

Sahlins, J. (2010). *Social work practice in nursing homes: Creativity, leadership, and program development.* Chicago: Lyceum.

Saleebey, D. (2006a). Introduction: Power in the people. In D. Saleebey (Ed.), *The strengths perspective in social work practice* (4th ed., pp. 77–92). Boston: Allyn & Bacon.

Saleebey, D. (2006b). The strengths approach to practice. In D. Saleebey (Ed.), *The strengths perspective in social work practice* (4th ed., pp. 1–24). Boston: Allyn & Bacon.

Saleebey, D. (2013). Introduction: Power in the people. In D. Saleebey (Ed.), *The strengths perspective in social work practice* (pp. 1–24). Boston: Pearson.

Salmivalli, C., & Peets, K. (2009). Bullies, victims, and bully-victim relationships in middle childhood and adolescence. In K. H. Rubin, W. M. Bukowski, & B. Laursen (Eds.), *Handbook of peer interactions, relationships, and groups.* New York: Guilford.

Sanchez, J. P. (n.d.). The American Park Service and American latino heritage. Retrieved from http://www.nps.gov/nr/travel/american_latino_heritage/National_Park_Service_and_American_Latino_Heritage_Entire_Essay.html#top.

Sandhu, D. S., & Madathil, J. (2013). Culturally alert counseling with South Asian Americans. In McAuliffe, G., & Associates (Eds.), *Culturally alert counseling: A comprehensive introduction* (2nd ed., pp. 315–344). Thousand Oaks, CA: Sage.

Sands, R. G. (1991). *Clinical social work practice in community mental health.* New York: Macmillan.

Santiago-Rivera, A. L., Arredondo, P., & Gallardo-Cooper, M. (2002). *Counseling Latinos and la familia: A practical guide.* Thousand Oaks, CA: Sage.

Santrock, J. W. (2007). *A topical approach to life-span development* (3rd ed.). Boston: McGraw-Hill.

Santrock, J. W. (2009). *Child development* (12th ed.). Boston: McGraw-Hill.

Santrock, J. W. (2012a). *Adolescence* (14th ed.). New York: McGraw-Hill.

Santrock, J. W. (2012b). *A topical approach to life-span development* (6th ed.). New York: McGraw-Hill.

Scarr, S. (1998). American child care today. *American Psychologist, 53*(2), 95–108.

Schaefer, R. T. (2011). *Racial and ethnic groups* (12th ed.). Upper Saddle River, NJ: Prentice-Hall.

Schott, L., & Pavetti, L. (Center on Budget and Policy Priorities). (2011, October 3). Many states cutting TANF benefits harshly despite high unemployment and unprecedented need. Retrieved from http://www.cbpp.org/cms/?fa=view&id=3498.

Schram, B., & Mandell, B. R. (2000). *An introduction to human services* (4th ed.). Boston: Allyn & Bacon.

Schrock, A., & Boyd, D. (2011). Problematic youth interaction online: Solicitation, harassment, and cyberbullying (pp. 368–396). In K. B. Wright & L. M. Webb (Eds.), *Computer-mediated communication in personal relationships.* New York: Peter Lang.

Schwartz, D., Kelly, B. M., Duong, M., & Badaly, D. (2010). Contextual perspective on intervention and prevention efforts for bully-victim problems. In E. M. Vernberg & B. K. Biggs (Eds.), *Preventing and treating bullying and victimization.* New York: Oxford.

Schwartz, W. (1961). The social worker in the group. In W. Schwartz (Ed.), *New perspectives on services to groups: Theory, organization, practice* (pp. 104–111). New York: National Association of Social Workers.

Sciarra, D. T. (2001). School counseling in a multicultural society. In J. G. Ponterotto, J. M. Casas, L. A. Suzuki, & C. M. Alexander (Eds.), *Handbook of multicultural counseling* (2nd ed., pp. 701–728). Thousand Oaks, CA: Sage.

Sciarra, D. T. (2004). *School counseling: Foundations and contemporary issues.* Belmont, CA: Brooks/Cole.

Scruton, R. (2013). Postmodern Tories. *Prospect,* March, pp. 34–36.

Seeman, T. E., & Adler, N. (1998, Spring). Older Americans: Who will they be? *National Forum,* 22–25.

Segal, E., & Brzuzy, S. (1998). *Social welfare, policy, programs, and practice.* Itasca, IL: Peacock.

Segal, E. A. (2010). *Social welfare policy and social programs: A values perspective* (2nd ed.). Belmont, CA: Brooks/Cole.

Segal, E. A. (2013). *Social welfare policy and social programs: A values perspective* (3rd ed.). Belmont, CA: Brooks/Cole.

Segal, E. A., Gerdes, K. E., & Steiner, S. (2004). *Social work: An introduction to the profession.* Belmont, CA: Brooks/Cole.

Segal, S. P. (2008). Deinstitutionalization. In T. Mizrahi & L. E. Davis (Eds.), *Encyclopedia of social work* (20th ed., pp. 10–20). Washington, DC: NASW Press.

Segal, U. A. (2010). United States: The changing face of the United States of America. In U. A. Segal, D. Elliott, & N. S. Mayadas (Eds.), *Immigration worldwide: Policies, practices, and trends* (pp. 29–46). New York: Oxford.

Shapiro, J. P. (1995, September 11). Who cares how high her IQ really is? *U.S. News & World Report,* 59.

*Shapiro v. Thompson,* 364 U.S. 618 (1969).

Sharf, R. S. (2012). *Theories of psychotherapy and counseling* (5th Ed.). Belmont, CA: Brooks/Cole.

Shaw, S. M., & Lee, J. (2012). *Women's voices, feminist visions: Classic and contemporary readings* (5th ed.). New York: McGraw-Hill.

Sheafor, B. W., & Horejsi, C. R. (2008). *Techniques and guidelines for social work practice* (8th ed.). Boston: Allyn & Bacon.

Sheafor, B. W., & Horejsi, C. R. (2012). *Techniques and guidelines for social work practice* (9th ed.). Boston: Allyn & Bacon.

Sheler, J. L. (2001, October 29). Muslim in America. *U.S. News & World Report,* pp. 50–52.

Sheridan, M. A., & White, B. J. (2008). Deafness and hardness of hearing. In T. Mizrahi & L. E. Davis (Editors-in-Chief), *Encyclopedia of social work* (Vol. 2, pp. 1–10). Washington, DC: NASW Press.

Shlonsky, A., & Gambrill, E. D. (2005). Risk assessment in child welfare. In G. P. Mallon & P. M. Hess (Eds.), *Child welfare for the 21st century: A handbook of practices, policies, and programs* (pp. 302–318). New York: Columbia.

Shore, S. (2003). My life with Asperger syndrome. In R. W. Du Charme & T. P. Gullotta (Eds.), *Asperger syndrome: A guide for professionals and* families (pp. 189–209). New York: Kluwer Academic/Plenum.

Shuster, S. (2013, December 5). The world's deadliest drug: Inside a krokodil cookhouse. Retrieved from the *Time* website: http://time.com/3398086/the-worlds-deadliest-drug-inside-a-krokodil-cookhouse/.

Sigelman, C. K., & Rider, E. A. (2015). *Life-span human development* (8th ed.). Belmont, CA: Cengage Learning.

Simmons, C. A., & Rycraft, J. R. (2010). Ethical challenges of military social workers serving in a combat zone. *Social Work,* 55(1), 9–18.

Siporin, M. (1975). *Introduction to social work practice.* New York: Macmillan.

Slattery, J. M. (2004). *Counseling diverse clients: Bringing context into therapy.* Pacific Grove, CA: Brooks/Cole.

Smith, C., & Darman, J. (2008). Juvenile delinquency. In T. Mizrahi & L. E. Davis (Editors-in-Chief), *Encyclopedia of social work* (Vol. 3, pp. 9–12). Washington, DC: NASW Press.

Smith, D. (2009, June 28). Frances Woofenden started skiing when she was 50. *Palm Beach Post.* Retrieved June 3, 2011, from http://www.theledger.com/article/20090628/news/906285058.

Smith, D. D., & Tyler, N. C. (2010). *Introduction to special education: Making a difference* (7th ed.). Upper Saddle River, NJ: Merrill.

Smith, R. F. (1995). Settlements and neighborhood centers. In R. L. Edwards (Ed.), *Encyclopedia of social work* (19th ed., Vol. 3, pp. 2129–2135). Washington, DC: NASW Press.

Smith, S. L., & Howard, J. A. (1999). *Promoting successful adoptions: Practice with troubled families.* Thousand Oaks, CA: Sage.

Smolowe, J. (1995, July 31). Noble aims, mixed results. *Time,* 54–55.

Snowden, L. R. (2000). The new world of practice in physical and mental health: Comorbidity, cultural competence, and managed care. In P. Allen-Meares & C. Garvin (Eds.), *The handbook of social work direct practice* (pp. 437–450). Thousand Oaks, CA: Sage.

Social Security Administration (SSA). (2010). Annual statistical supplement. Retrieved May 17, 2011, from http://www.ssa.gov/policy/docs/statcomps/supplement/.

Social Security Administration (SSA). (2014a). 2015 Social Security changes. Retrieved from http://www.ssa.gov/news/press/factsheets/colafacts2015.html.

Social Security Administration (SSA). (2014b). Compilation of the Social Security laws: Mandatory Work Requirements. Retrieved from http://www.ssa.gov/OP_Home/ssact/title04/0407.htm.

Social Security Administration (SSA). (2014c). Disability planner. Retrieved from http://www.ssa.gov/dibplan/dqualify7.htm.

Social Security Administration (SSA). (2014d). Social Security basic facts. Retrieved from http://www.ssa.gov/news/press/basicfact.html.

Social Security Administration (SSA). (2014e). Understanding Supplemental Security Income SSI home page: 2014 edition. Retrieved from http://www.ssa.gov/ssi/text-understanding-ssi.htm.

Social Security Administration (SSA). (2015). SSI federal payment amounts for 2015. Retrieved from http://www.ssa.gov/oact/cola/SSI.html.

Social Work License Map. (2014). Social work salaries. Retrieved from http://socialworklicensemap.com/social-worker-salary/.

SocialWorkLicensure.org. (2014). What is the ASWB licensing exam? Retrieved from http://www.socialworklicensure.org/articles/aswb-exam.html.

Soifer, S. (2002). Principles and practices of community economic development. In A. R. Roberts & G. J. Greene (Eds.), *Social workers' desk reference* (pp. 557–562). New York: Oxford University Press.

Solomon, B. B. (2002). Social work practice with African Americans. In A. T. Morales & B. W. Sheafor (Eds.), *The many faces of social work clients* (pp. 295–315). Boston: Allyn & Bacon.

Solomon, P. (2008). Mental illness: Practice interventions. In T. Mizrahi & L. E. Davis (Editors-in-Chief), *Encyclopedia of social work* (Vol. 3, pp. 232–237). Washington, DC: NASW Press.

Spencer, M. S. (1999). Reducing racism in schools: Moving beyond the rhetoric. In P. L. Ewalt, E. M. Freeman, A. E. Fortune, D. L. Poole, & S. L. Witkin (Eds.), *Multicultural issues in social work: Practice and research* (pp. 151–163). Washington, DC: NASW Press.

Spergel, I. A., & Grossman, S. F. (1997). The Little Village Project: A community approach to the gang problem. *Social Work, 42*(5), 456–470.

Spragins, E. E. (1998, September 28). Does managed care work? *Newsweek,* 61–66.

Squires, D. A. (2012, May). Explaining high health care spending in the United States: An international comparison of supply, utilization, prices, and quality. *Issues in International Health Policy.* Retrieved from the Commonwealth Fund website: www.commonwealthfund.org.

Srabstein, J. C., McCarter, R. J., Shao, C., & Huang, Z. J. (2006). Morbidities associated with bullying behaviors in adolescents: School based study of American adolescents. *International Journal of Adolescent Medicine and Health, 18,* 587–596.

Stahlman, S. D., & Kisor, A. J. (2000). Nursing homes. In R. L. Schneider, N. P. Kropf, & A. J. Kisor (Eds.), *Gerontological social work: Knowledge, service settings, and special populations* (2nd ed., pp. 225–254). Pacific Grove, CA: Brooks/Cole.

Staples, L. H. (2004). In C. D. Garvin, L. M. Gutierrez, & M. J. Galinsky (Eds.), *Handbook of social work with groups* (pp. 344–359). New York: Guilford.

Starbuck, D., Howell, J. C., & Lindquist, D. (2001, December). Hybrid and other modern gangs. *Bulletin of the Office of Juvenile Justice and Delinquency Prevention.* Washington, DC: U.S. Department of Justice, Office of Justice Programs.

Stein, J. A. (1995). *Residential treatment of adolescents & children: Issues, principles, and techniques.* Chicago: Nelson-Hall.

Steinberg, L., Bornstein, M. H., Vandell, D. L., & Rook, K. S. (2011). *Lifespan development: Infancy through adulthood.* Belmont, CA: Wadsworth.

Stern, M. J. (2015). *Engaging social welfare: An introduction to policy analysis.* Boston: Pearson.

Stern, M. J., & Axinn, J. (2012). *Social welfare: A history of the American response to need.* Boston: Pearson.

Stoesen, L. (2007, September). Putting the profession in public office. *NASW News,* 4.

Strauss, V. (2014, February 13). At least 44 school shootings since Newtown—New analysis. Retrieved from http://www.washingtonpost.com/blogs/answer-sheet/wp/2014/02/13/at-least-44-school-shootings-since-newtown-new-analysis/.

Straussner, S. L. A., & Isralowitz, R. (2008). Alcohol and drug problems: Overview. In T. Mizrahi & L. E. Davis (Editors-in-Chief), *Encyclopedia of social work* (Vol. 1, pp. 121–130). Washington, DC: NASW Press.

Strom-Gottfried, K. (2007). *Straight talk about professional ethics.* Chicago: Lyceum.

Strong, B., DeVault, C., Sayad, B. W., & Yarber, W. L. (2005). *Human sexuality: Diversity in contemporary America* (5th ed.). Boston: McGraw-Hill.

Stroup, H. (1986). *Social welfare pioneers.* Chicago: Nelson-Hall.

Stuart, P. H. (2008). Social welfare: History. In T. Mizrahi & L. E. Davis (Editors-in-Chief), *Encyclopedia of social work* (Vol. 4, pp. 156–164). Washington, DC: NASW Press.

Sue, D. W. (1992). The challenge of multiculturalism: The road less traveled. *American Counselor, 7*(1), 6–15.

Sue, D. W. (2006). *Multicultural social work practice.* Hoboken, NJ: Wiley.

Sue, D. W., Carter, R. T., Casas, J. M., Fouad, N. A., Ivey, A. E., Jensen, M., LaFromboise, T., Manese, J. E., Ponterotto, J. G., & Vazquez-Nutall, E. (1998). *Multicultural counseling competencies: Individual and organizational development.* Thousand Oaks, CA: Sage.

Sue, D. W., & Sue, D. (2008). *Counseling the culturally diverse—Theory and practice* (5th ed.). Hoboken, NJ: Wiley.

Sullivan, W. P. (2008). Disability: Psychiatric disabilities. In T. Mizrahi & L. E. Davis (Editors-in-Chief), *Encyclopedia of social work* (Vol. 2, pp. 55–60). Washington, DC: NASW Press.

Survey data show earnings increased. (2004, October). *NASW News,* pp. 1, 8.

Syme, G. (2003). *Dual relationships in counseling & psychotherapy.* Thousand Oaks, CA: Sage.

Taylor, P. (2005). *Diagnosis & treatment of substance-related disorders: The DECLARE model.* Boston: Pearson.

Taylor-Brown, S. (1995). HIV/AIDS: Direct practice. In R. L. Edwards (Ed.), *Encyclopedia of social work* (19th ed., Vol. 2, pp. 1291–1305). Washington, DC: NASW Press.

Temple, J. R., Paul, J. A., van den Berg, P., Le, V. D., McElhany, A., & Temple, B. W. (2012). Teen sexting and its association with sexual behaviors. *Archives of Pediatric & Adolescent Medicine, 166*(9), 828–833.

Terrell, P. (2008). Workers' compensation. In T. Mizrahi & L. E. Davis (Editors-in-Chief), *Encyclopedia of social work* (Vol. 4, pp. 304–306). Washington, DC: NASW Press.

The horror of electroshock therapy. (2000, March 1). *Extra: Daily News.* Retrieved April 27, 2002, from http://extratv.warnerbros.com.cmp/spotlight/2000/03_01b.htm.

Tice, C. J. (2005). Celebrating rural communities: A strengths assessment. In L. H. Ginsberg (Ed.), *Social work in rural communities* (4th ed., pp. 95–108). Alexandria, VA: CSWE Press.

Tice, C. J., & Perkins, K. (2002). *The faces of social policy: A strengths perspective.* Pacific Grove, CA: Brooks/Cole.

Tolan, P. H., Gorman-Smith, D., & Henry, D. B. (2003). The developmental ecology of urban males' youth violence. *Developmental Psychology, 39,* 274–291.

Torres-Gil, F. M., & Puccinelli, M. A. (1995). Aging: Public policy issues and trends. In R. L. Edwards (Ed.), *Encyclopedia of social work* (19th ed., Vol. 1, pp. 159–164). Washington, DC: NASW Press.

Toseland, R. W. (1995). Aging: Direct practice. In R. L. Edwards (Eds.), *Encyclopedia of social work* (19th ed., Vol. 1, pp. 153–159). Washington, DC: NASW Press.

Toseland, R. W., & Horton, H. (2008). Group work. In T. Mizrahi & L. E. Davis (Editors-in-Chief), *Encyclopedia of social work* (Vol. 2, pp. 298–308). Washington, DC: NASW Press.

Toseland, R. W., & Rivas, R. F. (2012). *An introduction to group work practice* (7th ed.). Boston: Allyn & Bacon.

Tower, K. D. (1994, March). Consumer-centered social work practice: Restoring client self-determination. *Social Work, 39*(2), 191–196.

Tracy, E. M. (1995). Family preservation and home-based services. In R. L. Edwards (Ed.), *Encyclopedia of social work* (19th ed., Vol. 2, pp. 973–983). Washington, DC: NASW Press.

Tracy, E. M. (2002). Working with and strengthening social networks. In A. R. Roberts & G. J. Greene (Eds.), *Social workers' desk reference* (pp. 402–405). Washington, DC: NASW Press.

Tracy, E. M., Haapala, D. A., Kinney, J. M., & Pecora, P. J. (1991). Intensive family preservation services: A strategic response to families in crisis. In E. M. Tracy, D. A. Haapala, J. M. Kinney, & P. J. Pecora (Eds.), *Intensive family preservation services.' An instructional sourcebook*. Cleveland, OH: Case Western Reserve University.

Trattner, W. I. (1999). *From poor law to welfare state: A history of social welfare in America* (6th ed.). New York: Free Press.

Treguer, A. (1992). The Chicanos—Muralists with a message. *UNESCO Courier, 45*, 22–24.

Tripodi, T., & Lalayants, M. (2008). Research: Overview. In T. Mizrahi & L. E. Davis (Editors-in-Chief), *Encyclopedia of social work* (Vol. 3, pp. 512–520). Washington, DC: NASW Press.

Tully, C. T. (2000). *Lesbians, gays, and the empowerment perspective*. New York: Columbia University Press.

Tully, C. T. (2001). Gay and lesbian persons. In A. Gitterman (Ed.), *Handbook of social work practice with vulnerable and resilient populations* (2nd ed., pp. 582–627). New York: Columbia University Press.

UNAIDS. (2008). AIDS epidemic update. Retrieved from http:// www.unaids.org.

United Nations (UN). (1948). Universal Declaration of Human Rights. Retrieved June 28, 2008, from http://www.un.org/ Overview/rights.html.

Uniform Crime Report (UCR). (2011). Arson. Retrieved from http://www.fbi.gov/about-us/cjis/ucr/crime-in-the-u.s/2010/ crime-in-the-u.s.-2010/property-crime/arsonmain.pdf.

Uniform Crime Reporting (UCR) Program. (2014). Reporting rape in 2013. Retrieved from http://www.fbi.gov/about-us/cjis/ ucr/recent-program-updates/reporting-rape-in-2013-revised.

University of Nebraska Omaha. (2015). *UNO study: Fertility rate gap between races, ethnicities is shrinking*. Retrieved from University of Nebraska website: http://www.unomaha.edu/ news/2015/01/fertility.php.

U.S. Census Bureau. (2009). *Statistical abstract of the United States: 2010*. (129th ed.). Washington, DC: Author.

U.S. Census Bureau. (2010). *Statistical abstract of the United States: 2011* (130th ed.). Washington, DC: Author.

U.S. Census Bureau. (2011). *Statistical abstract of the United States: 2012*. Washington, DC: Author.

U.S. Census Bureau. (2014). Aging boomers will increase dependency ration, Census Bureau predicts. Retrieved from https:// www.census.gov/newsroom/releases/archives/aging_population/cb10-72.html.

U.S. Department of Agriculture. (2013). Guide to long-term care insurance. Retrieved from http://publications.usa.gov/ USAPubs.php?PubID=5879/.

U.S. Department of Health and Human Services (USDHHS). (1999). *Mental health: A report of the Surgeon General—Executive summary*. Rockville, MD: Author. Retrived from http://www.nimh.nih.gov.

U.S. Department of Health and Human Services (USDHHS). (2010). Fiscal year 2010 budget in brief. Retrieved May 23, 2011, from http://dhhs.gov/asfr/ob/docbudget/2010budgetinbriefm.html.

U.S. Department of Health and Human Services (USDHHS). (2013). Child Health USA 2013. Rockville, MD: U.S. Department of Health and Human Services, Health Resources and Services Administration, Maternal and Child Health Bureau. Retrieved from http://mchb.hrsa.gov/chusa13/ health-services-utilization/p/barriers-to-prenatal-care.html.

U.S. Department of Health and Human Services (USDHHS). (2014). About the law. Retrieved from http://www.hhs.gov/ healthcare/rights/index.html.

U.S. Department of Health and Human Services (USDHHS). (n.d.). Prenatal services. Rockville, MD: U.S. Department of Health and Human Services, Health Resources and Services Administration, Maternal and Child Health Bureau. Retrieved from http://mchb.hrsa.gov/programs/womeninfants/ prenatal.html.

U.S. Department of Housing and Urban Development. (2011). Federal definition of homelessness. Retrieved August 25, 2011, from http://portal.hud.gov/hudportal/HUD?src=/topics/ homelessness/definition.

U.S. Department of Housing and Urban Development (HUD). (2104). Public housing programs. Retrieved from http:// portal.hud.gov/hudportal/HUD?src=/program_offices/public_ indian_housing/programs/ph/programs.

U.S. Department of Justice, Civil Rights Division. (2011). ADA requirements: Effective date/compliance date. Retrieved from http://www.ada.gov/revised_effective_dates-2010.htm.

U.S. Department of Justice, Civil Rights Division. (2014). Americans with Disabilities Act and revised ADA regulations implementing Title II and Title III. Retrieved November 30, 2014, from http://www.ada.gov/2010_regs.htm.

U.S. Department of Labor, Bureau of Labor Statistics. (2014). *Occupational outlook handbook: Social workers*. Retrieved from http://www.bls.gov/ooh/community-and-social-service/ social-workers.htm.

U.S. Department of Veterans Affairs (VA). (2010). Treatment for PTSD. Retrieved June 16, 2011, from http://www.ptsd .va.gov/public/pages/treatment-ptsd.asp.

U.S. Department of Veterans Affairs (VA). (2011a). *About VHA*. Retrieved May 5, 2011, from http://www.va.gov/health/ aboutVHA.asp.

U.S. Department of Veterans Affairs (VA). (2011b). Cognitive processing therapy. Retrieved June 16, 2011, from http:// www.ptsd.va.gov/public/pages/cognitive_processing_therapy .asp.

U.S. Department of Veterans Affairs (VA). (2011c). VA home. Retrieved June 9, 2011, from http://www.va.gov/.

U.S. Department of Veterans Affairs (VA). (2011d). VA social work. Retrieved June 9, 2011, from http://www.socialwork.va.gov/index.asp.

U.S. Department of Veterans Affairs (VA). (2014a). About VHA. Retrieved from http://www.va.gov/health/aboutVHA.asp.

U.S. Department of Veterans Affairs (VA). (2014b). PTSD: National Center for PTSD. Retrieved from http://www.ptsd.va.gov/index.asp.

U.S. Department of Veterans' Affairs (VA). (2014c). Social work. Retrieved from http://www.socialwork.va.gov/index.asp.

U.S. Department of Veterans Affairs (VA). (2014d). VA home. Retrieved from http://www.va.gov/.

U.S. Environmental Protection Agency (EPA). (2015). *Environmental justice.* Retrieved from http://www.epa.gov/environmentaljustice/.

U.S. National Archives & Records Administration. (n.d.). The Treaty of Guadalupe Hidalgo. Retrieved from http://www.archives.gov/digital_classroom/lessons/treaty_of_guadalupe_hidalgo/treaty_of_guadalupe_hidalgo.html.

U.S. Office of the Surgeon General. (2001). Report on mental health: Adults and mental health treatment of mood disorders. Retrieved April 28, 2002, from http://www.loren.bennett.org/osgtreat.htm.

U.S. Psychiatric Rehabilitation Association (USPRA). (2004). Who we are. Retrieved February 12, 2005, from http://www.iapsrs.org/.

Vakalahi, H. F. O., & Godinet, M. T. (2014). Considerations for social work practice with Pacific Islander Americans. In Vakalahi, H. F. O., & Godinet, M. T. (Eds.), *Transnational Pacific Islander Americans and social work: Dancing to the beat of a different drum* (pp. 139–152). Washington, DC: NASW Press.

Vallianatos, C. (2001a). Managed care is faulted. *NASW News, 46*(1), 7.

Vallianatos, C. (2001b). Profession extolled on Hill. *NASW News, 46*(5), 1.

Vallianatos, C. (2001c, July). Programs keep the peace among teens. *NASW News,* p. 3.

Van Arsdale, S. (2002, January 8). Sybil: Famous multiple-personality case was stranger in our midst. *Ace Weekly.* Retrieved from http://www.aceweekly.com/Backissues_ACE-Weekly/010802/cover_story010802.html.

Van Den Bergh, N., & Cooper, L. B. (1986). *Feminist visions for social work.* Washington, DC: NASW Press.

Vandiver, V. L. (2008). Managed care. In T. Mizrahi & L. E. Davis (Editors-in-Chief), *Encyclopedia of social work* (Vol. 3, pp. 144–148). Washington, DC: NASW Press.

Vandivort-Warren, R. (1998). How social workers can manage managed care. In G. Schamess & A. Lightburn (Eds.), *Human managed care?* (pp. 255–267). Washington, DC: NASW Press.

Van Wormer, K., & Davis, D. R. (2013). *Addiction treatment: A strengths perspective* (3rd ed.). Belmont, CA: Cengage Learning.

Velleman, R. (2011). *Counselling for alcohol problems* (3rd ed.). Thousand Oaks, CA: Sage.

Voices of Experience. (2002). *Electroshock therapy: Firstperson stories from our community.* Retrieved April 27, 2002, from http://bipolar.about.com/library/uc/uc-shockl.htm.

Wait, M. (2015). Recreational new drugs: 3 new threats to worry about. Retrieved from WebbMD: http://www.webmd.com/parenting/features/recreational-drugs-threats_.

Walsh, J. A. (1990). From clinician to supervisor: Essential ingredients for training. *Families in Society, 71*(2), 82–87.

Watkins, J. M., & Holmes, J. (2008). Council on Social Work Education. In T. Mizrahi & L. E. Davis (Editors-in-Chief), *Encyclopedia of social work* (Vol. 1, pp. 457–460). Washington, DC: NASW Press.

Watkins, M. L. (2002). Listening to girls: A study in resilience. In R. R. Greene (Ed.), *Resiliency: An integrated approach to practice, policy, and research* (pp. 115–131). Washington, DC: NASW Press.

Watkins, S. A. (1990). The Mary Ellen myth: Correcting child welfare history. *Social Work, 35*(6), 500–503.

Watkins, T. R. (2004). Natural helping networks: Assets for rural communities. In T. L. Scales & C. L. Streeter (Eds.), *Rural social work: Building and sustaining community assets* (pp. 65–76). Belmont, CA: Brooks/Cole.

Weatherley, R. A., & Cartoof, V. G. (1988). Helping single adolescent parents. In C. Chilman, E. Nunnally, & F. Cox (Eds.), *Variant family forms.* Newbury Park, CA: Sage.

Weaver, H. N. (2003). Cultural competence with First Nations Peoples. In D. Lum (Ed.), *Culturally competent practice: A framework for understanding diverse groups and justice issues* (2nd ed., pp. 197–216). Pacific Grove, CA: Brooks/Cole.

Weaver, H. N. (2005). *Explorations in cultural competence: Journeys to the four directions.* Pacific Grove, CA: Brooks/Cole.

Weaver, H. N. (2007). Cultural competence with First Nations Peoples. In D. Lum (Ed.), *Culturally competent practice: A framework for understanding diverse groups and justice issues* (3rd ed., pp. 254–275). Belmont, CA: Brooks/Cole.

Weaver, H. N. (2008). Native Americans: Overview. In T. Mizrahi & L. E. Davis (Editors-in-Chief), *Encyclopedia of social work* (Vol. 3, pp. 295–299). Washington, DC: NASW Press.

Weaver, H. N. (2011). Cultural competence with First Nations Peoples. In D. Lum (Ed.), *Culturally competent practice: A framework for understanding diverse groups and justice issues* (4th ed., pp. 223–247). Pacific Grove, CA: Brooks/Cole.

Weaver, H. N. (2013). Assisting Native American families: Striving for well-being in the seventh generation. In E. P. Congress & M. J. Gonzalez (Eds.), *Multicultural perspectives in social work practice with families* (3rd ed., pp. 171–184). New York: Springer.

Webster.edu. (2005). Mary Ellen Richmond. Retrieved June 14, 2005, from http://www.webster.edu/~woolflm/richmond.html.

Wegscheider, S. (1981). *Another chance: Hope and health for the alcoholic family.* Palo Alto, CA: Science Behavior Books.

Weiner, T. (2001, January 5). Terrific news in Mexico City: Air is sometimes breathable. *The New York Times.* Retrieved from http://www.nytimes.com/2001/01/05/world/05MEI.html.

Wells, S. J. (2008). Child abuse and neglect. In T. Mizrahi & L. E. Davis (Editors-in-Chief), *Encyclopedia of social work* (Vol. 1, pp. 236–240). Washington, DC: NASW Press.

West-Olatunji, C. A., & Conwill, W. (2011). *Counseling & diversity: Counseling African Americans.* Belmont, CA: Brooks/Cole.

Whealin, J. M., DeCarvalho, L. R., & Vega, E. M. (2008a). *Clinician's guide to treating stress after war.* Hoboken, NJ: John Wiley.

Whealin, J. M., DeCarvalho, L. R., & Vega, E. M. (2008b). *Strategies for managing stress after war: Veteran's workbook and guide to wellness.* Hoboken, NJ: John Wiley.

Wheeler, J., Newring, K., & Draper, C. (2008). Transvestic fetishism: Psychopathology and theory. In D. Laws & W. O'Donohue (Eds.), *Sexual deviance: Theory, assessment and treatment* (2nd ed., pp. 272–285). New York: Guilford Press.

White House. (2005a). 4. Modernize and reform Social Security. Retrieved January 8, 2005, from http://www.whitehouse.gov/news/usbudget/blueprint/bud04.html.

White House. (2005b). 5. Modernize and reform Medicare. Retrieved January 8, 2005, from http://www.whitehouse.gov/news/usbudget/blueprint/bud04.html.

WhiteHouse.gov. (2011a). Foreign policy. Retrieved May 12, 2011, from http://www.whitehouse.gov/issues/foreign-policy.

WhiteHouse.gov. (2011b). Health care reform in action. Retrieved May 11, 2011, from http://www.whitehouse.gov/healthreform.

White House, The. (2014, September 10). Fact sheet: Strategy to counter the Islamic State of Syria and the Levant (ISIL). Retrieved from http://www.whitehouse.gov/the-press-office/2014/09/10/fact-sheet-strategy-counter-islamic-state-iraq-and-levant-isil.

Whitelaw, K. (2003, July 21). In death's shadow. *U.S. News & World Report,* 17–20.

Whiteman, V. L. (2001). *Social Security: What every human services professional should know.* Boston: Allyn & Bacon.

Willenbring, M. L. (2010). The past and future of research on treatment of alcohol dependence. *Alcohol Research & Health, 33*(1), 55–63.

Williams, J. B. W. (2008). Diagnostic and statistical manual of mental disorders. In T. Mizrahi & L. E. Davis (Editors-in-Chief), *Encyclopedia of social work* (Vol. 2, pp. 26–31). Washington, DC: NASW Press.

Williams, J. H., & Van Dorn, R. A. (1999). Delinquency, gangs, and youth violence. In J. M. Jenson & M. O. Howard (Eds.), *Youth violence: Current research and recent practice innovations* (pp. 199–225). Washington, DC: NASW Press.

Williams, M. (1999, April 25). Diary reveals school attack "timeline." *Milwaukee Journal Sentinel,* 1A, 18A.

Williams, S. T., Conger, K. J., & Blozis, S. A. (2007). The development of interpersonal aggression during adolescence: The importance of parents, siblings, and family economics. *Child Development, 78,* 1526–1542.

Wilson, G. T., Grilo, C. M., & Vitousek, K. M. (2007, April). Psychological treatment of eating disorders. *American Psychologist, 62*(3), 199–216.

Wimberly, E. P. (1991). *African American pastoral care.* Nashville: Abingdon Press.

Winkelman, M. (1999). *Ethnic sensitivity in social work practice.* Dubuque, IA: Eddie Bowers.

Winton, M. A., & Mara, B. A. (2001). *Child abuse and neglect: Multidisciplinary approaches.* Boston: Allyn & Bacon.

Wirth, L. (1945). The problem of minority groups. In R. Linton (Ed.), *The science of man in the world crisis* (pp. 347–372). New York: Columbia University Press.

Women in History. (2005). Jane Addams biography. Lakewood Public Library. Retrieved June 14, 2005, from http://www.lkwdpl.org/wihohio/adda-jan.htm.

Wong, I. (2008). Homelessness. In T. Mizrahi & L. E. Davis (Editors-in-Chief), *Encyclopedia of social work* (Vol. 2, pp. 377–383). Washington, DC: NASW Press.

Woodward, K. L., & Johnson, P. (1995, December 11). The advent of Kwanzaa: Will success spoil an African-American fest? *Newsweek,* 88.

Woody, D. J. (2013). Effective peer conflict resolution. In C. Franklin, M. B. Harris, & P. Allen-Meares (Eds.), *The school services sourcebook* (2nd ed., pp. 481–489). New York: Oxford.

World Health Organization (WHO). (2002). *Active ageing: A policy framework.* Geneva, Switzerland: Author. Retrieved June 3, 2011, from http://whqlibdoc.who.int/hq/2002/who_nmh_nph_02.8.pdf.

World Health Organization (WHO). (2014a). Frequently asked questions. Retrieved from http://www.who.int/suggestions/faq/en/.

World Health Organization (WHO). (2014b). Public health. Retrieved from http://www.who.int/trade/glossary/story076/en/.

*Wyatt v. Stickney,* 324 F. Supp 781 (1971).

Yamashiro, G., & Matsuoka, J. K. (1997). Help-seeking among Asian and Pacific Americans: A multiperspective analysis. *Social Work, 42*(2), 176–186.

Yarber, W. L., & Sayad, B. W. (2013). *Human sexuality: Diversity in contemporary America* (8th ed.). New York: McGraw-Hill.

Yeo, G., & Hikoyeda, N. (2000). Cultural issues in end-of-life decision making among Asians and Pacific Islanders in the United States. In K. L. Braun, J. H. Pietsch, & P. L. Blanchette (Eds.), *Cultural issues in end-of-life decision making* (pp. 101–125). Thousand Oaks, CA: Sage.

Yessian, M. R., & Broskowski, A. (1983). Generalists in human service systems: Their problems and prospects. In R. M. Kramer & H. Specht (Eds.), *Readings in community organization practice* (pp. 180–197). Englewood Cliffs, NJ: Prentice-Hall.

Zastrow, C. H., & Kirst-Ashman, K. K. (2013). *Understanding human behavior and the social environment* (9th ed.). Belmont, CA: Brooks/Cole.

Zastrow, C. H., & Kirst-Ashman, K. K. (2016). *Understanding human behavior and the social environment* (10th ed.). Belmont, CA: Cengage Learning.

Zhang, W. (2010). Use with care—Culturally incorrect attending can be rude. In A. E. Ivey, M. B. Ivey, & C. P. Zalaquett (Eds.), *Intentional interviewing & counseling* (7th ed., p. 76). Belmont, CA: Brooks/Cole.

Zuniga, M. E. (1995). Aging: Social work practice. In R. L. Edwards (Ed.), *Encyclopedia of social work* (19th ed., Vol. 1, pp. 173–183). Washington, DC: NASW Press.

# Name Index

# Subject Index

Health care (*Continued*)
ethical dilemmas, 394–395, 396
insurance, 255
international perspectives, 397–401
living will, 348
macro practice in, 390–391, 396
managed care settings, 390. *See also*
    Managed care
for men, 94
    national health insurance, 392, 411
and older adults, 333
Patient Protection and Affordable Care
    Act (2010), 208–209, 216
and poverty, 254–255
poverty, social class, race and, 395–397
prisoners and expensive, 523
problems, 387, 395–397, 411
public, 389
reform, 208
social work roles in, 165, 168,
    387–391, 411
in the U.S. today, 391–396
value dimensions in API cultures
    relating to, 397–401
veteran's affairs hospitals, 389–390
Health Insurance for the Aged Act (1965),
    261, 269
Health Maintenance Organizations
    (HMOs). *See* Managed care
Health and welfare services, 257
Hearing impaired. *See* Deaf
Help, shame of asking for, 399
Help lines, 377
Help-seeking behavior, 451–452
Helping hands icon, 6
Helping networks, 143
Hereditary disease, 535–536
Hermaphrodite, 90
Heroin, 464, 465
Heterosexual, 95
Highly active antiretroviral therapy
    (HAART), 405
Hispanics, 76–79, 104. *See also* Chicano/
    Chicana; Latino/Latina
barriers to mental health, 451–453
common language cultural values, 77–78
extended families, 77, 78
gangs, 528
gender role divisions, 77, 78–79
Muslims, 101
older adults, 77, 328
population, 74, 75
and poverty, 246, 248, 331
primary groups, 74
spirituality/religion, 77, 78
terms, 74, 76
History, social work and social welfare,
    13, 179, 181–209, 215–216, 237
child welfare, 288
public assistance, 263–264
Histrionic disorder, 436
HIV. *See* AIDS
Hoarding disorder, 436

Hogan, 350
Holy People, 350
Home access test, 403
Home-based services, 338–339, 352.
    *See also* Family preservation
    services; Older adults
Home visits, 253
Homeland Security Agency, 205
Homeless Assistance Act, 256
Homelessness, 256–257, 272
Homeless shelter, 446
Homework, 148
Homophobia, 96–97, 336–337, 491n1
Homosexual, 95. *See also* Gay and
    Lesbian; Sexual orientation
Hospice, 46, 165, 261, 339–340, 348
Hospital
    inpatient mental and psychiatric, 419
    psychiatric units in, 421
    social work, 341–342, 388–389, 535
Housing Assistance, 259, 271
Housing bubble, 207
Housing, low-income, 229, 255
Housing and Urban Development (HUD)
    Act (1968), 200, 271
Hull House, 188–189, 212
Human capital, 252
Human dignity, 60
Human diversity, 66–102
    African Americans, 77, 82–84
    age, 72, 97
    American Indians/Native Americans/
        First Nations Peoples, 77, 79–82
    Asian Americans, 77, 84–86
    assessment, 127, 130
    class, 72, 88
    competency, 24
    culture and cultural competence, 72, 74,
        75–76
    definition of, 24, 102
    differential treatment, 66–68
    dimensions of, 72, 103
    disability, 72, 98
    and families, 285, 287
    feminism, 92–94
    gender, gender identity, and gender
        expressions, 72, 89–95
    Hispanics, 74, 76–79
    and individual differences, 346
    intersectionality, 73
    Islam and Muslims, 99–102
    marital status, 72, 97
    men's issues, 94–95
    national origin and immigration status,
        72, 86–88
    and older adults, 343–351
    people of color, 72
    political ideology, 72, 88
    race and ethnicity, 72, 73–74
    religion and spirituality, 72, 98–99
    sexual orientation, 72, 95–97
    tribal sovereign status, 72
    urban social work, 146

Human rights
    areas of, 55
    child slave trade, 292
    competency, 24
    definition of, 24, 55, 62
    empowerment of victims, 57
    global, 55–58
    human trafficking, 55–58, 62, 292
    NASW policy on, 57
    organ harvesting, 56
Human services agency. *See* Agency;
    Social agency
Human trafficking, 55–58, 62, 292
Humanistic theories, 438–439
Huntington's chorea, 535
Hybrid gangs, 528
Hypervigilance, 428, 429–430
Hyperarousal, 427–428

Ice, 463
Identities, 95
Identity and conduct, 119, 135
Identity, quest for, 316
Identity theft, 517
If only thinking, 429
Illegal immigrants, 86
Immigrants, 86
Immigrants' Protective League, 189
Immigration Act (1924), 193, 213
Immigration status, 72, 86–88, 104, 186
    advocacy for students, 487–488
Impaired control, 462–463
Implementation, in the planned-change
    process, 131, 132–133
    of policy, 227
Impotent poor, 180
Impulse control disorders, 435–436
Incapacitation, 520
Incarceration, 516
Incest, 290–291, 318
Income, 248
    median, 246
Income maintenance programs, 229, 258
Income test. *See* Means test
Independent adoptions, 313, 317
Independent living services, 313,
    319, 377
Indian Child Welfare Act (1978), 204,
    213, 216
Indian General Allotment Act (1887), 191
Indian Removal Act (1830), 184, 215
Indian Reorganization Act (1934), 191
Indian Muslims, 101
Individual pathology, 368
Individual versus collective decision-
    making, 398
Individual program planning, 369
Individuals with Disabilities Education
    Improvement Act, 374, 382
Individuals, social work with, 26–27, 114,
    145–148. *See also* Micro practice
Individualization, 370